T0122334

Lecture Notes in Computer Science   13695

More information about this series at https://link.springer.com/bookseries/558

Shai Avidan · Gabriel Brostow ·
Moustapha Cissé · Giovanni Maria Farinella ·
Tal Hassner (Eds.)

Computer Vision – ECCV 2022

17th European Conference
Tel Aviv, Israel, October 23–27, 2022
Proceedings, Part XXXV

 Springer

Editors
Shai Avidan
Tel Aviv University
Tel Aviv, Israel

Gabriel Brostow (iD)
University College London
London, UK

Moustapha Cissé
Google AI
Accra, Ghana

Giovanni Maria Farinella (iD)
University of Catania
Catania, Italy

Tal Hassner (iD)
Facebook (United States)
Menlo Park, CA, USA

ISSN 0302-9743   ISSN 1611-3349 (electronic)
Lecture Notes in Computer Science
ISBN 978-3-031-19832-8   ISBN 978-3-031-19833-5 (eBook)
https://doi.org/10.1007/978-3-031-19833-5

This Springer imprint is published by the registered company Springer Nature Switzerland AG
The registered company address is: Gewerbestrasse 11, 6330 Cham, Switzerland

Foreword

Organizing the European Conference on Computer Vision (ECCV 2022) in Tel-Aviv during a global pandemic was no easy feat. The uncertainty level was extremely high, and decisions had to be postponed to the last minute. Still, we managed to plan things just in time for ECCV 2022 to be held in person. Participation in physical events is crucial to stimulating collaborations and nurturing the culture of the Computer Vision community.

There were many people who worked hard to ensure attendees enjoyed the best science at the 16th edition of ECCV. We are grateful to the Program Chairs Gabriel Brostow and Tal Hassner, who went above and beyond to ensure the ECCV reviewing process ran smoothly. The scientific program includes dozens of workshops and tutorials in addition to the main conference and we would like to thank Leonid Karlinsky and Tomer Michaeli for their hard work. Finally, special thanks to the web chairs Lorenzo Baraldi and Kosta Derpanis, who put in extra hours to transfer information fast and efficiently to the ECCV community.

We would like to express gratitude to our generous sponsors and the Industry Chairs, Dimosthenis Karatzas and Chen Sagiv, who oversaw industry relations and proposed new ways for academia-industry collaboration and technology transfer. It's great to see so much industrial interest in what we're doing!

Authors' draft versions of the papers appeared online with open access on both the Computer Vision Foundation (CVF) and the European Computer Vision Association (ECVA) websites as with previous ECCVs. Springer, the publisher of the proceedings, has arranged for archival publication. The final version of the papers is hosted by SpringerLink, with active references and supplementary materials. It benefits all potential readers that we offer both a free and citeable version for all researchers, as well as an authoritative, citeable version for SpringerLink readers. Our thanks go to Ronan Nugent from Springer, who helped us negotiate this agreement. Last but not least, we wish to thank Eric Mortensen, our publication chair, whose expertise made the process smooth.

October 2022

Rita Cucchiara
Jiří Matas
Amnon Shashua
Lihi Zelnik-Manor

Preface

Welcome to the proceedings of the European Conference on Computer Vision (ECCV 2022). This was a hybrid edition of ECCV as we made our way out of the COVID-19 pandemic. The conference received 5804 valid paper submissions, compared to 5150 submissions to ECCV 2020 (a 12.7% increase) and 2439 in ECCV 2018. 1645 submissions were accepted for publication (28%) and, of those, 157 (2.7% overall) as orals.

846 of the submissions were desk-rejected for various reasons. Many of them because they revealed author identity, thus violating the double-blind policy. This violation came in many forms: some had author names with the title, others added acknowledgments to specific grants, yet others had links to their github account where their name was visible. Tampering with the LaTeX template was another reason for automatic desk rejection.

ECCV 2022 used the traditional CMT system to manage the entire double-blind reviewing process. Authors did not know the names of the reviewers and vice versa. Each paper received at least 3 reviews (except 6 papers that received only 2 reviews), totalling more than 15,000 reviews.

Handling the review process at this scale was a significant challenge. To ensure that each submission received as fair and high-quality reviews as possible, we recruited more than 4719 reviewers (in the end, 4719 reviewers did at least one review). Similarly we recruited more than 276 area chairs (eventually, only 276 area chairs handled a batch of papers). The area chairs were selected based on their technical expertise and reputation, largely among people who served as area chairs in previous top computer vision and machine learning conferences (ECCV, ICCV, CVPR, NeurIPS, etc.).

Reviewers were similarly invited from previous conferences, and also from the pool of authors. We also encouraged experienced area chairs to suggest additional chairs and reviewers in the initial phase of recruiting. The median reviewer load was five papers per reviewer, while the average load was about four papers, because of the emergency reviewers. The area chair load was 35 papers, on average.

Conflicts of interest between authors, area chairs, and reviewers were handled largely automatically by the CMT platform, with some manual help from the Program Chairs. Reviewers were allowed to describe themselves as senior reviewer (load of 8 papers to review) or junior reviewers (load of 4 papers). Papers were matched to area chairs based on a subject-area affinity score computed in CMT and an affinity score computed by the Toronto Paper Matching System (TPMS). TPMS is based on the paper's full text. An area chair handling each submission would bid for preferred expert reviewers, and we balanced load and prevented conflicts.

The assignment of submissions to area chairs was relatively smooth, as was the assignment of submissions to reviewers. A small percentage of reviewers were not happy with their assignments in terms of subjects and self-reported expertise. This is an area for improvement, although it's interesting that many of these cases were reviewers hand-picked by AC's. We made a later round of reviewer recruiting, targeted at the list of authors of papers submitted to the conference, and had an excellent response which helped provide enough emergency reviewers. In the end, all but six papers received at least 3 reviews.

The challenges of the reviewing process are in line with past experiences at ECCV 2020. As the community grows, and the number of submissions increases, it becomes ever more challenging to recruit enough reviewers and ensure a high enough quality of reviews. Enlisting authors by default as reviewers might be one step to address this challenge.

Authors were given a week to rebut the initial reviews, and address reviewers' concerns. Each rebuttal was limited to a single pdf page with a fixed template.

The Area Chairs then led discussions with the reviewers on the merits of each submission. The goal was to reach consensus, but, ultimately, it was up to the Area Chair to make a decision. The decision was then discussed with a buddy Area Chair to make sure decisions were fair and informative. The entire process was conducted virtually with no in-person meetings taking place.

The Program Chairs were informed in cases where the Area Chairs overturned a decisive consensus reached by the reviewers, and pushed for the meta-reviews to contain details that explained the reasoning for such decisions. Obviously these were the most contentious cases, where reviewer inexperience was the most common reported factor.

Once the list of accepted papers was finalized and released, we went through the laborious process of plagiarism (including self-plagiarism) detection. A total of 4 accepted papers were rejected because of that.

Finally, we would like to thank our Technical Program Chair, Pavel Lifshits, who did tremendous work behind the scenes, and we thank the tireless CMT team.

October 2022

Gabriel Brostow
Giovanni Maria Farinella
Moustapha Cissé
Shai Avidan
Tal Hassner

Organization

General Chairs

Rita Cucchiara	University of Modena and Reggio Emilia, Italy
Jiří Matas	Czech Technical University in Prague, Czech Republic
Amnon Shashua	Hebrew University of Jerusalem, Israel
Lihi Zelnik-Manor	Technion – Israel Institute of Technology, Israel

Program Chairs

Shai Avidan	Tel-Aviv University, Israel
Gabriel Brostow	University College London, UK
Moustapha Cissé	Google AI, Ghana
Giovanni Maria Farinella	University of Catania, Italy
Tal Hassner	Facebook AI, USA

Program Technical Chair

Pavel Lifshits	Technion – Israel Institute of Technology, Israel

Workshops Chairs

Leonid Karlinsky	IBM Research, Israel
Tomer Michaeli	Technion – Israel Institute of Technology, Israel
Ko Nishino	Kyoto University, Japan

Tutorial Chairs

Thomas Pock	Graz University of Technology, Austria
Natalia Neverova	Facebook AI Research, UK

Demo Chair

Bohyung Han	Seoul National University, Korea

Social and Student Activities Chairs

Tatiana Tommasi   Italian Institute of Technology, Italy
Sagie Benaim   University of Copenhagen, Denmark

Diversity and Inclusion Chairs

Xi Yin   Facebook AI Research, USA
Bryan Russell   Adobe, USA

Communications Chairs

Lorenzo Baraldi   University of Modena and Reggio Emilia, Italy
Kosta Derpanis   York University & Samsung AI Centre Toronto,
                                     Canada

Industrial Liaison Chairs

Dimosthenis Karatzas   Universitat Autònoma de Barcelona, Spain
Chen Sagiv   SagivTech, Israel

Finance Chair

Gerard Medioni   University of Southern California & Amazon,
                                     USA

Publication Chair

Eric Mortensen   MiCROTEC, USA

Area Chairs

Lourdes Agapito   University College London, UK
Zeynep Akata   University of Tübingen, Germany
Naveed Akhtar   University of Western Australia, Australia
Karteek Alahari   Inria Grenoble Rhône-Alpes, France
Alexandre Alahi   École polytechnique fédérale de Lausanne,
                                     Switzerland
Pablo Arbelaez   Universidad de Los Andes, Columbia
Antonis A. Argyros   University of Crete & Foundation for Research
                                     and Technology-Hellas, Crete
Yuki M. Asano   University of Amsterdam, The Netherlands
Kalle Åström   Lund University, Sweden
Hadar Averbuch-Elor   Cornell University, USA

Matthijs Douze	Facebook AI Research, USA
Mohamed Elhoseiny	King Abdullah University of Science and Technology, Saudi Arabia
Sergio Escalera	University of Barcelona, Spain
Yi Fang	New York University, USA
Ryan Farrell	Brigham Young University, USA
Alireza Fathi	Google, USA
Christoph Feichtenhofer	Facebook AI Research, USA
Basura Fernando	Agency for Science, Technology and Research (A*STAR), Singapore
Vittorio Ferrari	Google Research, Switzerland
Andrew W. Fitzgibbon	Graphcore, UK
David J. Fleet	University of Toronto, Canada
David Forsyth	University of Illinois at Urbana-Champaign, USA
David Fouhey	University of Michigan, USA
Katerina Fragkiadaki	Carnegie Mellon University, USA
Friedrich Fraundorfer	Graz University of Technology, Austria
Oren Freifeld	Ben-Gurion University, Israel
Thomas Funkhouser	Google Research & Princeton University, USA
Yasutaka Furukawa	Simon Fraser University, Canada
Fabio Galasso	Sapienza University of Rome, Italy
Jürgen Gall	University of Bonn, Germany
Chuang Gan	Massachusetts Institute of Technology, USA
Zhe Gan	Microsoft, USA
Animesh Garg	University of Toronto, Vector Institute, Nvidia, Canada
Efstratios Gavves	University of Amsterdam, The Netherlands
Peter Gehler	Amazon, Germany
Theo Gevers	University of Amsterdam, The Netherlands
Bernard Ghanem	King Abdullah University of Science and Technology, Saudi Arabia
Ross B. Girshick	Facebook AI Research, USA
Georgia Gkioxari	Facebook AI Research, USA
Albert Gordo	Facebook, USA
Stephen Gould	Australian National University, Australia
Venu Madhav Govindu	Indian Institute of Science, India
Kristen Grauman	Facebook AI Research & UT Austin, USA
Abhinav Gupta	Carnegie Mellon University & Facebook AI Research, USA
Mohit Gupta	University of Wisconsin-Madison, USA
Hu Han	Institute of Computing Technology, Chinese Academy of Sciences, China

Ivan Laptev	Inria Paris, France
Laura Leal-Taixé	Technical University of Munich, Germany
Erik Learned-Miller	University of Massachusetts, Amherst, USA
Gim Hee Lee	National University of Singapore, Singapore
Seungyong Lee	Pohang University of Science and Technology, Korea
Zhen Lei	Institute of Automation, Chinese Academy of Sciences, China
Bastian Leibe	RWTH Aachen University, Germany
Hongdong Li	Australian National University, Australia
Fuxin Li	Oregon State University, USA
Bo Li	University of Illinois at Urbana-Champaign, USA
Yin Li	University of Wisconsin-Madison, USA
Ser-Nam Lim	Meta AI Research, USA
Joseph Lim	University of Southern California, USA
Stephen Lin	Microsoft Research Asia, China
Dahua Lin	The Chinese University of Hong Kong, Hong Kong, China
Si Liu	Beihang University, China
Xiaoming Liu	Michigan State University, USA
Ce Liu	Microsoft, USA
Zicheng Liu	Microsoft, USA
Yanxi Liu	Pennsylvania State University, USA
Feng Liu	Portland State University, USA
Yebin Liu	Tsinghua University, China
Chen Change Loy	Nanyang Technological University, Singapore
Huchuan Lu	Dalian University of Technology, China
Cewu Lu	Shanghai Jiao Tong University, China
Oisin Mac Aodha	University of Edinburgh, UK
Dhruv Mahajan	Facebook, USA
Subhransu Maji	University of Massachusetts, Amherst, USA
Atsuto Maki	KTH Royal Institute of Technology, Sweden
Arun Mallya	NVIDIA, USA
R. Manmatha	Amazon, USA
Iacopo Masi	Sapienza University of Rome, Italy
Dimitris N. Metaxas	Rutgers University, USA
Ajmal Mian	University of Western Australia, Australia
Christian Micheloni	University of Udine, Italy
Krystian Mikolajczyk	Imperial College London, UK
Anurag Mittal	Indian Institute of Technology, Madras, India
Philippos Mordohai	Stevens Institute of Technology, USA
Greg Mori	Simon Fraser University & Borealis AI, Canada

Mathieu Salzmann	École polytechnique fédérale de Lausanne, Switzerland
Dimitris Samaras	Stony Brook University, USA
Aswin Sankaranarayanan	Carnegie Mellon University, USA
Imari Sato	National Institute of Informatics, Japan
Yoichi Sato	University of Tokyo, Japan
Shin'ichi Satoh	National Institute of Informatics, Japan
Walter Scheirer	University of Notre Dame, USA
Bernt Schiele	Max Planck Institute for Informatics, Germany
Konrad Schindler	ETH Zurich, Switzerland
Cordelia Schmid	Inria & Google, France
Alexander Schwing	University of Illinois at Urbana-Champaign, USA
Nicu Sebe	University of Trento, Italy
Greg Shakhnarovich	Toyota Technological Institute at Chicago, USA
Eli Shechtman	Adobe Research, USA
Humphrey Shi	University of Oregon & University of Illinois at Urbana-Champaign & Picsart AI Research, USA
Jianbo Shi	University of Pennsylvania, USA
Roy Shilkrot	Massachusetts Institute of Technology, USA
Mike Zheng Shou	National University of Singapore, Singapore
Kaleem Siddiqi	McGill University, Canada
Richa Singh	Indian Institute of Technology Jodhpur, India
Greg Slabaugh	Queen Mary University of London, UK
Cees Snoek	University of Amsterdam, The Netherlands
Yale Song	Facebook AI Research, USA
Yi-Zhe Song	University of Surrey, UK
Bjorn Stenger	Rakuten Institute of Technology
Abby Stylianou	Saint Louis University, USA
Akihiro Sugimoto	National Institute of Informatics, Japan
Chen Sun	Brown University, USA
Deqing Sun	Google, USA
Kalyan Sunkavalli	Adobe Research, USA
Ying Tai	Tencent YouTu Lab, China
Ayellet Tal	Technion – Israel Institute of Technology, Israel
Ping Tan	Simon Fraser University, Canada
Siyu Tang	ETH Zurich, Switzerland
Chi-Keung Tang	Hong Kong University of Science and Technology, Hong Kong, China
Radu Timofte	University of Würzburg, Germany & ETH Zurich, Switzerland
Federico Tombari	Google, Switzerland & Technical University of Munich, Germany

Todd Zickler   Harvard University, USA
Wangmeng Zuo   Harbin Institute of Technology, China

Technical Program Committee

Davide Abati
Soroush Abbasi
  Koohpayegani
Amos L. Abbott
Rameen Abdal
Rabab Abdelfattah
Sahar Abdelnabi
Hassan Abu Alhaija
Abulikemu Abuduweili
Ron Abutbul
Hanno Ackermann
Aikaterini Adam
Kamil Adamczewski
Ehsan Adeli
Vida Adeli
Donald Adjeroh
Arman Afrasiyabi
Akshay Agarwal
Sameer Agarwal
Abhinav Agarwalla
Vaibhav Aggarwal
Sara Aghajanzadeh
Susmit Agrawal
Antonio Agudo
Touqeer Ahmad
Sk Miraj Ahmed
Chaitanya Ahuja
Nilesh A. Ahuja
Abhishek Aich
Shubhra Aich
Noam Aigerman
Arash Akbarinia
Peri Akiva
Derya Akkaynak
Emre Aksan
Arjun R. Akula
Yuval Alaluf
Stephan Alaniz
Paul Albert
Cenek Albl

Filippo Aleotti
Konstantinos P.
  Alexandridis
Motasem Alfarra
Mohsen Ali
Thiemo Alldieck
Hadi Alzayer
Liang An
Shan An
Yi An
Zhulin An
Dongsheng An
Jie An
Xiang An
Saket Anand
Cosmin Ancuti
Juan Andrade-Cetto
Alexander Andreopoulos
Bjoern Andres
Jerone T. A. Andrews
Shivangi Aneja
Anelia Angelova
Dragomir Anguelov
Rushil Anirudh
Oron Anschel
Rao Muhammad Anwer
Djamila Aouada
Evlampios Apostolidis
Srikar Appalaraju
Nikita Araslanov
Andre Araujo
Eric Arazo
Dawit Mureja Argaw
Anurag Arnab
Aditya Arora
Chetan Arora
Sunpreet S. Arora
Alexey Artemov
Muhammad Asad
Kumar Ashutosh

Sinem Aslan
Vishal Asnani
Mahmoud Assran
Amir Atapour-Abarghouei
Nikos Athanasiou
Ali Athar
ShahRukh Athar
Sara Atito
Souhaib Attaiki
Matan Atzmon
Mathieu Aubry
Nicolas Audebert
Tristan T.
  Aumentado-Armstrong
Melinos Averkiou
Yannis Avrithis
Stephane Ayache
Mehmet Aygün
Seyed Mehdi
  Ayyoubzadeh
Hossein Azizpour
George Azzopardi
Mallikarjun B. R.
Yunhao Ba
Abhishek Badki
Seung-Hwan Bae
Seung-Hwan Baek
Seungryul Baek
Piyush Nitin Bagad
Shai Bagon
Gaetan Bahl
Shikhar Bahl
Sherwin Bahmani
Haoran Bai
Lei Bai
Jiawang Bai
Haoyue Bai
Jinbin Bai
Xiang Bai
Xuyang Bai

Yang Bai
Yuanchao Bai
Ziqian Bai
Sungyong Baik
Kevin Bailly
Max Bain
Federico Baldassarre
Wele Gedara Chaminda
  Bandara
Biplab Banerjee
Pratyay Banerjee
Sandipan Banerjee
Jihwan Bang
Antyanta Bangunharcana
Aayush Bansal
Ankan Bansal
Siddhant Bansal
Wentao Bao
Zhipeng Bao
Amir Bar
Manel Baradad Jurjo
Lorenzo Baraldi
Danny Barash
Daniel Barath
Connelly Barnes
Ioan Andrei Bârsan
Steven Basart
Dina Bashkirova
Chaim Baskin
Peyman Bateni
Anil Batra
Sebastiano Battiato
Ardhendu Behera
Harkirat Behl
Jens Behley
Vasileios Belagiannis
Boulbaba Ben Amor
Emanuel Ben Baruch
Abdessamad Ben Hamza
Gil Ben-Artzi
Assia Benbihi
Fabian Benitez-Quiroz
Guy Ben-Yosef
Philipp Benz
Alexander W. Bergman

Urs Bergmann
Jesus Bermudez-Cameo
Stefano Berretti
Gedas Bertasius
Zachary Bessinger
Petra Bevandić
Matthew Beveridge
Lucas Beyer
Yash Bhalgat
Suvaansh Bhambri
Samarth Bharadwaj
Gaurav Bharaj
Aparna Bharati
Bharat Lal Bhatnagar
Uttaran Bhattacharya
Apratim Bhattacharyya
Brojeshwar Bhowmick
Ankan Kumar Bhunia
Ayan Kumar Bhunia
Qi Bi
Sai Bi
Michael Bi Mi
Gui-Bin Bian
Jia-Wang Bian
Shaojun Bian
Pia Bideau
Mario Bijelic
Hakan Bilen
Guillaume-Alexandre
  Bilodeau
Alexander Binder
Tolga Birdal
Vighnesh N. Birodkar
Sandika Biswas
Andreas Blattmann
Janusz Bobulski
Giuseppe Boccignone
Vishnu Boddeti
Navaneeth Bodla
Moritz Böhle
Aleksei Bokhovkin
Sam Bond-Taylor
Vivek Boominathan
Shubhankar Borse
Mark Boss

Andrea Bottino
Adnane Boukhayma
Fadi Boutros
Nicolas C. Boutry
Richard S. Bowen
Ivaylo Boyadzhiev
Aidan Boyd
Yuri Boykov
Aljaz Bozic
Behzad Bozorgtabar
Eric Brachmann
Samarth Brahmbhatt
Gustav Bredell
Francois Bremond
Joel Brogan
Andrew Brown
Thomas Brox
Marcus A. Brubaker
Robert-Jan Bruintjes
Yuqi Bu
Anders G. Buch
Himanshu Buckchash
Mateusz Buda
Ignas Budvytis
José M. Buenaposada
Marcel C. Bühler
Tu Bui
Adrian Bulat
Hannah Bull
Evgeny Burnaev
Andrei Bursuc
Benjamin Busam
Sergey N. Buzykanov
Wonmin Byeon
Fabian Caba
Martin Cadik
Guanyu Cai
Minjie Cai
Qing Cai
Zhongang Cai
Qi Cai
Yancheng Cai
Shen Cai
Han Cai
Jiarui Cai

Bowen Cai
Mu Cai
Qin Cai
Ruojin Cai
Weidong Cai
Weiwei Cai
Yi Cai
Yujun Cai
Zhiping Cai
Akin Caliskan
Lilian Calvet
Baris Can Cam
Necati Cihan Camgoz
Tommaso Campari
Dylan Campbell
Ziang Cao
Ang Cao
Xu Cao
Zhiwen Cao
Shengcao Cao
Song Cao
Weipeng Cao
Xiangyong Cao
Xiaochun Cao
Yue Cao
Yunhao Cao
Zhangjie Cao
Jiale Cao
Yang Cao
Jiajiong Cao
Jie Cao
Jinkun Cao
Lele Cao
Yulong Cao
Zhiguo Cao
Chen Cao
Razvan Caramalau
Marlène Careil
Gustavo Carneiro
Joao Carreira
Dan Casas
Paola Cascante-Bonilla
Angela Castillo
Francisco M. Castro
Pedro Castro

Luca Cavalli
George J. Cazenavette
Oya Celiktutan
Hakan Cevikalp
Sri Harsha C. H.
Sungmin Cha
Geonho Cha
Menglei Chai
Lucy Chai
Yuning Chai
Zenghao Chai
Anirban Chakraborty
Deep Chakraborty
Rudrasis Chakraborty
Souradeep Chakraborty
Kelvin C. K. Chan
Chee Seng Chan
Paramanand Chandramouli
Arjun Chandrasekaran
Kenneth Chaney
Dongliang Chang
Huiwen Chang
Peng Chang
Xiaojun Chang
Jia-Ren Chang
Hyung Jin Chang
Hyun Sung Chang
Ju Yong Chang
Li-Jen Chang
Qi Chang
Wei-Yi Chang
Yi Chang
Nadine Chang
Hanqing Chao
Pradyumna Chari
Dibyadip Chatterjee
Chiranjoy Chattopadhyay
Siddhartha Chaudhuri
Zhengping Che
Gal Chechik
Lianggangxu Chen
Qi Alfred Chen
Brian Chen
Bor-Chun Chen
Bo-Hao Chen

Bohong Chen
Bin Chen
Ziliang Chen
Cheng Chen
Chen Chen
Chaofeng Chen
Xi Chen
Haoyu Chen
Xuanhong Chen
Wei Chen
Qiang Chen
Shi Chen
Xianyu Chen
Chang Chen
Changhuai Chen
Hao Chen
Jie Chen
Jianbo Chen
Jingjing Chen
Jun Chen
Kejiang Chen
Mingcai Chen
Nenglun Chen
Qifeng Chen
Ruoyu Chen
Shu-Yu Chen
Weidong Chen
Weijie Chen
Weikai Chen
Xiang Chen
Xiuyi Chen
Xingyu Chen
Yaofo Chen
Yueting Chen
Yu Chen
Yunjin Chen
Yuntao Chen
Yun Chen
Zhenfang Chen
Zhuangzhuang Chen
Chu-Song Chen
Xiangyu Chen
Zhuo Chen
Chaoqi Chen
Shizhe Chen

Xiaotong Chen
Xiaozhi Chen
Dian Chen
Defang Chen
Dingfan Chen
Ding-Jie Chen
Ee Heng Chen
Tao Chen
Yixin Chen
Wei-Ting Chen
Lin Chen
Guang Chen
Guangyi Chen
Guanying Chen
Guangyao Chen
Hwann-Tzong Chen
Junwen Chen
Jiacheng Chen
Jianxu Chen
Hui Chen
Kai Chen
Kan Chen
Kevin Chen
Kuan-Wen Chen
Weihua Chen
Zhang Chen
Liang-Chieh Chen
Lele Chen
Liang Chen
Fanglin Chen
Zehui Chen
Minghui Chen
Minghao Chen
Xiaokang Chen
Qian Chen
Jun-Cheng Chen
Qi Chen
Qingcai Chen
Richard J. Chen
Runnan Chen
Rui Chen
Shuo Chen
Sentao Chen
Shaoyu Chen
Shixing Chen

Shuai Chen
Shuya Chen
Sizhe Chen
Simin Chen
Shaoxiang Chen
Zitian Chen
Tianlong Chen
Tianshui Chen
Min-Hung Chen
Xiangning Chen
Xin Chen
Xinghao Chen
Xuejin Chen
Xu Chen
Xuxi Chen
Yunlu Chen
Yanbei Chen
Yuxiao Chen
Yun-Chun Chen
Yi-Ting Chen
Yi-Wen Chen
Yinbo Chen
Yiran Chen
Yuanhong Chen
Yubei Chen
Yuefeng Chen
Yuhua Chen
Yukang Chen
Zerui Chen
Zhaoyu Chen
Zhen Chen
Zhenyu Chen
Zhi Chen
Zhiwei Chen
Zhixiang Chen
Long Chen
Bowen Cheng
Jun Cheng
Yi Cheng
Jingchun Cheng
Lechao Cheng
Xi Cheng
Yuan Cheng
Ho Kei Cheng
Kevin Ho Man Cheng

Jiacheng Cheng
Kelvin B. Cheng
Li Cheng
Mengjun Cheng
Zhen Cheng
Qingrong Cheng
Tianheng Cheng
Harry Cheng
Yihua Cheng
Yu Cheng
Ziheng Cheng
Soon Yau Cheong
Anoop Cherian
Manuela Chessa
Zhixiang Chi
Naoki Chiba
Julian Chibane
Kashyap Chitta
Tai-Yin Chiu
Hsu-kuang Chiu
Wei-Chen Chiu
Sungmin Cho
Donghyeon Cho
Hyeon Cho
Yooshin Cho
Gyusang Cho
Jang Hyun Cho
Seungju Cho
Nam Ik Cho
Sunghyun Cho
Hanbyel Cho
Jaesung Choe
Jooyoung Choi
Chiho Choi
Changwoon Choi
Jongwon Choi
Myungsub Choi
Dooseop Choi
Jonghyun Choi
Jinwoo Choi
Jun Won Choi
Min-Kook Choi
Hongsuk Choi
Janghoon Choi
Yoon-Ho Choi

Yukyung Choi
Jaegul Choo
Ayush Chopra
Siddharth Choudhary
Subhabrata Choudhury
Vasileios Choutas
Ka-Ho Chow
Pinaki Nath Chowdhury
Sammy Christen
Anders Christensen
Grigorios Chrysos
Hang Chu
Wen-Hsuan Chu
Peng Chu
Qi Chu
Ruihang Chu
Wei-Ta Chu
Yung-Yu Chuang
Sanghyuk Chun
Se Young Chun
Antonio Cinà
Ramazan Gokberk Cinbis
Javier Civera
Albert Clapés
Ronald Clark
Brian S. Clipp
Felipe Codevilla
Daniel Coelho de Castro
Niv Cohen
Forrester Cole
Maxwell D. Collins
Robert T. Collins
Marc Comino Trinidad
Runmin Cong
Wenyan Cong
Maxime Cordy
Marcella Cornia
Enric Corona
Huseyin Coskun
Luca Cosmo
Dragos Costea
Davide Cozzolino
Arun C. S. Kumar
Aiyu Cui
Qiongjie Cui

Quan Cui
Shuhao Cui
Yiming Cui
Ying Cui
Zijun Cui
Jiali Cui
Jiequan Cui
Yawen Cui
Zhen Cui
Zhaopeng Cui
Jack Culpepper
Xiaodong Cun
Ross Cutler
Adam Czajka
Ali Dabouei
Konstantinos M. Dafnis
Manuel Dahnert
Tao Dai
Yuchao Dai
Bo Dai
Mengyu Dai
Hang Dai
Haixing Dai
Peng Dai
Pingyang Dai
Qi Dai
Qiyu Dai
Yutong Dai
Naser Damer
Zhiyuan Dang
Mohamed Daoudi
Ayan Das
Abir Das
Debasmit Das
Deepayan Das
Partha Das
Sagnik Das
Soumi Das
Srijan Das
Swagatam Das
Avijit Dasgupta
Jim Davis
Adrian K. Davison
Homa Davoudi
Laura Daza

Matthias De Lange
Shalini De Mello
Marco De Nadai
Christophe De
    Vleeschouwer
Alp Dener
Boyang Deng
Congyue Deng
Bailin Deng
Yong Deng
Ye Deng
Zhuo Deng
Zhijie Deng
Xiaoming Deng
Jiankang Deng
Jinhong Deng
Jingjing Deng
Liang-Jian Deng
Siqi Deng
Xiang Deng
Xueqing Deng
Zhongying Deng
Karan Desai
Jean-Emmanuel Deschaud
Aniket Anand Deshmukh
Neel Dey
Helisa Dhamo
Prithviraj Dhar
Amaya Dharmasiri
Yan Di
Xing Di
Ousmane A. Dia
Haiwen Diao
Xiaolei Diao
Gonçalo José Dias Pais
Abdallah Dib
Anastasios Dimou
Changxing Ding
Henghui Ding
Guodong Ding
Yaqing Ding
Shuangrui Ding
Yuhang Ding
Yikang Ding
Shouhong Ding

Haisong Ding
Hui Ding
Jiahao Ding
Jian Ding
Jian-Jiun Ding
Shuxiao Ding
Tianyu Ding
Wenhao Ding
Yuqi Ding
Yi Ding
Yuzhen Ding
Zhengming Ding
Tan Minh Dinh
Vu Dinh
Christos Diou
Mandar Dixit
Bao Gia Doan
Khoa D. Doan
Dzung Anh Doan
Debi Prosad Dogra
Nehal Doiphode
Chengdong Dong
Bowen Dong
Zhenxing Dong
Hang Dong
Xiaoyi Dong
Haoye Dong
Jiangxin Dong
Shichao Dong
Xuan Dong
Zhen Dong
Shuting Dong
Jing Dong
Li Dong
Ming Dong
Nanqing Dong
Qiulei Dong
Runpei Dong
Siyan Dong
Tian Dong
Wei Dong
Xiaomeng Dong
Xin Dong
Xingbo Dong
Yuan Dong

Samuel Dooley
Gianfranco Doretto
Michael Dorkenwald
Keval Doshi
Zhaopeng Dou
Xiaotian Dou
Hazel Doughty
Ahmad Droby
Iddo Drori
Jie Du
Yong Du
Dawei Du
Dong Du
Ruoyi Du
Yuntao Du
Xuefeng Du
Yilun Du
Yuming Du
Radhika Dua
Haodong Duan
Jiafei Duan
Kaiwen Duan
Peiqi Duan
Ye Duan
Haoran Duan
Jiali Duan
Amanda Duarte
Abhimanyu Dubey
Shiv Ram Dubey
Florian Dubost
Lukasz Dudziak
Shivam Duggal
Justin M. Dulay
Matteo Dunnhofer
Chi Nhan Duong
Thibaut Durand
Mihai Dusmanu
Ujjal Kr Dutta
Debidatta Dwibedi
Isht Dwivedi
Sai Kumar Dwivedi
Takeharu Eda
Mark Edmonds
Alexei A. Efros
Thibaud Ehret

Max Ehrlich
Mahsa Ehsanpour
Iván Eichhardt
Farshad Einabadi
Marvin Eisenberger
Hazim Kemal Ekenel
Mohamed El Banani
Ismail Elezi
Moshe Eliasof
Alaa El-Nouby
Ian Endres
Francis Engelmann
Deniz Engin
Chanho Eom
Dave Epstein
Maria C. Escobar
Victor A. Escorcia
Carlos Esteves
Sungmin Eum
Bernard J. E. Evans
Ivan Evtimov
Fevziye Irem Eyiokur
  Yaman
Matteo Fabbri
Sébastien Fabbro
Gabriele Facciolo
Masud Fahim
Bin Fan
Hehe Fan
Deng-Ping Fan
Aoxiang Fan
Chen-Chen Fan
Qi Fan
Zhaoxin Fan
Haoqi Fan
Heng Fan
Hongyi Fan
Linxi Fan
Baojie Fan
Jiayuan Fan
Lei Fan
Quanfu Fan
Yonghui Fan
Yingruo Fan
Zhiwen Fan

Zicong Fan
Sean Fanello
Jiansheng Fang
Chaowei Fang
Yuming Fang
Jianwu Fang
Jin Fang
Qi Fang
Shancheng Fang
Tian Fang
Xianyong Fang
Gongfan Fang
Zhen Fang
Hui Fang
Jiemin Fang
Le Fang
Pengfei Fang
Xiaolin Fang
Yuxin Fang
Zhaoyuan Fang
Ammarah Farooq
Azade Farshad
Zhengcong Fei
Michael Felsberg
Wei Feng
Chen Feng
Fan Feng
Andrew Feng
Xin Feng
Zheyun Feng
Ruicheng Feng
Mingtao Feng
Qianyu Feng
Shangbin Feng
Chun-Mei Feng
Zunlei Feng
Zhiyong Feng
Martin Fergie
Mustansar Fiaz
Marco Fiorucci
Michael Firman
Hamed Firooz
Volker Fischer
Corneliu O. Florea
Georgios Floros

Wolfgang Foerstner
Gianni Franchi
Jean-Sebastien Franco
Simone Frintrop
Anna Fruehstueck
Changhong Fu
Chaoyou Fu
Cheng-Yang Fu
Chi-Wing Fu
Deqing Fu
Huan Fu
Jun Fu
Kexue Fu
Ying Fu
Jianlong Fu
Jingjing Fu
Qichen Fu
Tsu-Jui Fu
Xueyang Fu
Yang Fu
Yanwei Fu
Yonggan Fu
Wolfgang Fuhl
Yasuhisa Fujii
Kent Fujiwara
Marco Fumero
Takuya Funatomi
Isabel Funke
Dario Fuoli
Antonino Furnari
Matheus A. Gadelha
Akshay Gadi Patil
Adrian Galdran
Guillermo Gallego
Silvano Galliani
Orazio Gallo
Leonardo Galteri
Matteo Gamba
Yiming Gan
Sujoy Ganguly
Harald Ganster
Boyan Gao
Changxin Gao
Daiheng Gao
Difei Gao

Chen Gao
Fei Gao
Lin Gao
Wei Gao
Yiming Gao
Junyu Gao
Guangyu Ryan Gao
Haichang Gao
Hongchang Gao
Jialin Gao
Jin Gao
Jun Gao
Katelyn Gao
Mingchen Gao
Mingfei Gao
Pan Gao
Shangqian Gao
Shanghua Gao
Xitong Gao
Yunhe Gao
Zhanning Gao
Elena Garces
Nuno Cruz Garcia
Noa Garcia
Guillermo
    Garcia-Hernando
Isha Garg
Rahul Garg
Sourav Garg
Quentin Garrido
Stefano Gasperini
Kent Gauen
Chandan Gautam
Shivam Gautam
Paul Gay
Chunjiang Ge
Shiming Ge
Wenhang Ge
Yanhao Ge
Zheng Ge
Songwei Ge
Weifeng Ge
Yixiao Ge
Yuying Ge
Shijie Geng

Zhengyang Geng
Kyle A. Genova
Georgios Georgakis
Markos Georgopoulos
Marcel Geppert
Shabnam Ghadar
Mina Ghadimi Atigh
Deepti Ghadiyaram
Maani Ghaffari Jadidi
Sedigh Ghamari
Zahra Gharaee
Michaël Gharbi
Golnaz Ghiasi
Reza Ghoddoosian
Soumya Suvra Ghosal
Adhiraj Ghosh
Arthita Ghosh
Pallabi Ghosh
Soumyadeep Ghosh
Andrew Gilbert
Igor Gilitschenski
Jhony H. Giraldo
Andreu Girbau Xalabarder
Rohit Girdhar
Sharath Girish
Xavier Giro-i-Nieto
Raja Giryes
Thomas Gittings
Nikolaos Gkanatsios
Ioannis Gkioulekas
Abhiram
   Gnanasambandam
Aurele T. Gnanha
Clement L. J. C. Godard
Arushi Goel
Vidit Goel
Shubham Goel
Zan Gojcic
Aaron K. Gokaslan
Tejas Gokhale
S. Alireza Golestaneh
Thiago L. Gomes
Nuno Goncalves
Boqing Gong
Chen Gong

Yuanhao Gong
Guoqiang Gong
Jingyu Gong
Rui Gong
Yu Gong
Mingming Gong
Neil Zhenqiang Gong
Xun Gong
Yunye Gong
Yihong Gong
Cristina I. González
Nithin Gopalakrishnan
   Nair
Gaurav Goswami
Jianping Gou
Shreyank N. Gowda
Ankit Goyal
Helmut Grabner
Patrick L. Grady
Ben Graham
Eric Granger
Douglas R. Gray
Matej Grcić
David Griffiths
Jinjin Gu
Yun Gu
Shuyang Gu
Jianyang Gu
Fuqiang Gu
Jiatao Gu
Jindong Gu
Jiaqi Gu
Jinwei Gu
Jiaxin Gu
Geonmo Gu
Xiao Gu
Xinqian Gu
Xiuye Gu
Yuming Gu
Zhangxuan Gu
Dayan Guan
Junfeng Guan
Qingji Guan
Tianrui Guan
Shanyan Guan

Denis A. Gudovskiy
Ricardo Guerrero
Pierre-Louis Guhur
Jie Gui
Liangyan Gui
Liangke Gui
Benoit Guillard
Erhan Gundogdu
Manuel Günther
Jingcai Guo
Yuanfang Guo
Junfeng Guo
Chenqi Guo
Dan Guo
Hongji Guo
Jia Guo
Jie Guo
Minghao Guo
Shi Guo
Yanhui Guo
Yangyang Guo
Yuan-Chen Guo
Yilu Guo
Yiluan Guo
Yong Guo
Guangyu Guo
Haiyun Guo
Jinyang Guo
Jianyuan Guo
Pengsheng Guo
Pengfei Guo
Shuxuan Guo
Song Guo
Tianyu Guo
Qing Guo
Qiushan Guo
Wen Guo
Xiefan Guo
Xiaohu Guo
Xiaoqing Guo
Yufei Guo
Yuhui Guo
Yuliang Guo
Yunhui Guo
Yanwen Guo

Akshita Gupta

Ankush Gupta

Kamal Gupta

Kartik Gupta

Ritwik Gupta

Rohit Gupta

Siddharth Gururani

Fredrik K. Gustafsson

Abner Guzman Rivera

Vladimir Guzov

Matthew A. Gwilliam

Jung-Woo Ha

Marc Habermann

Isma Hadji

Christian Haene

Martin Hahner

Levente Hajder

Alexandros Haliassos

Emanuela Haller

Bumsub Ham

Abdullah J. Hamdi

Shreyas Hampali

Dongyoon Han

Chunrui Han

Dong-Jun Han

Dong-Sig Han

Guangxing Han

Zhizhong Han

Ruize Han

Jiaming Han

Jin Han

Ligong Han

Xian-Hua Han

Xiaoguang Han

Yizeng Han

Zhi Han

Zhenjun Han

Zhongyi Han

Jungong Han

Junlin Han

Kai Han

Kun Han

Sungwon Han

Songfang Han

Wei Han

Xiao Han

Xintong Han

Xinzhe Han

Yahong Han

Yan Han

Zongbo Han

Nicolai Hani

Rana Hanocka

Niklas Hanselmann

Nicklas A. Hansen

Hong Hanyu

Fusheng Hao

Yanbin Hao

Shijie Hao

Udith Haputhanthri

Mehrtash Harandi

Josh Harguess

Adam Harley

David M. Hart

Atsushi Hashimoto

Ali Hassani

Mohammed Hassanin

Yana Hasson

Joakim Bruslund Haurum

Bo He

Kun He

Chen He

Xin He

Fazhi He

Gaoqi He

Hao He

Haoyu He

Jiangpeng He

Hongliang He

Qian He

Xiangteng He

Xuming He

Yannan He

Yuhang He

Yang He

Xiangyu He

Nanjun He

Pan He

Sen He

Shengfeng He

Songtao He

Tao He

Tong He

Wei He

Xuehai He

Xiaoxiao He

Ying He

Yisheng He

Ziwen He

Peter Hedman

Felix Heide

Yacov Hel-Or

Paul Henderson

Philipp Henzler

Byeongho Heo

Jae-Pil Heo

Miran Heo

Sachini A. Herath

Stephane Herbin

Pedro Hermosilla Casajus

Monica Hernandez

Charles Herrmann

Roei Herzig

Mauricio Hess-Flores

Carlos Hinojosa

Tobias Hinz

Tsubasa Hirakawa

Chih-Hui Ho

Lam Si Tung Ho

Jennifer Hobbs

Derek Hoiem

Yannick Hold-Geoffroy

Aleksander Holynski

Cheeun Hong

Fa-Ting Hong

Hanbin Hong

Guan Zhe Hong

Danfeng Hong

Lanqing Hong

Xiaopeng Hong

Xin Hong

Jie Hong

Seungbum Hong

Cheng-Yao Hong

Seunghoon Hong

Yi Hong
Yuan Hong
Yuchen Hong
Anthony Hoogs
Maxwell C. Horton
Kazuhiro Hotta
Qibin Hou
Tingbo Hou
Junhui Hou
Ji Hou
Qiqi Hou
Rui Hou
Ruibing Hou
Zhi Hou
Henry Howard-Jenkins
Lukas Hoyer
Wei-Lin Hsiao
Chiou-Ting Hsu
Anthony Hu
Brian Hu
Yusong Hu
Hexiang Hu
Haoji Hu
Di Hu
Hengtong Hu
Haigen Hu
Lianyu Hu
Hanzhe Hu
Jie Hu
Junlin Hu
Shizhe Hu
Jian Hu
Zhiming Hu
Juhua Hu
Peng Hu
Ping Hu
Ronghang Hu
MengShun Hu
Tao Hu
Vincent Tao Hu
Xiaoling Hu
Xinting Hu
Xiaolin Hu
Xuefeng Hu
Xiaowei Hu

Yang Hu
Yueyu Hu
Zeyu Hu
Zhongyun Hu
Binh-Son Hua
Guoliang Hua
Yi Hua
Linzhi Huang
Qiusheng Huang
Bo Huang
Chen Huang
Hsin-Ping Huang
Ye Huang
Shuangping Huang
Zeng Huang
Buzhen Huang
Cong Huang
Heng Huang
Hao Huang
Qidong Huang
Huaibo Huang
Chaoqin Huang
Feihu Huang
Jiahui Huang
Jingjia Huang
Kun Huang
Lei Huang
Sheng Huang
Shuaiyi Huang
Siyu Huang
Xiaoshui Huang
Xiaoyang Huang
Yan Huang
Yihao Huang
Ying Huang
Ziling Huang
Xiaoke Huang
Yifei Huang
Haiyang Huang
Zhewei Huang
Jin Huang
Haibin Huang
Jiaxing Huang
Junjie Huang
Keli Huang

Lang Huang
Lin Huang
Luojie Huang
Mingzhen Huang
Shijia Huang
Shengyu Huang
Siyuan Huang
He Huang
Xiuyu Huang
Lianghua Huang
Yue Huang
Yaping Huang
Yuge Huang
Zehao Huang
Zeyi Huang
Zhiqi Huang
Zhongzhan Huang
Zilong Huang
Ziyuan Huang
Tianrui Hui
Zhuo Hui
Le Hui
Jing Huo
Junhwa Hur
Shehzeen S. Hussain
Chuong Minh Huynh
Seunghyun Hwang
Jaehui Hwang
Jyh-Jing Hwang
Sukjun Hwang
Soonmin Hwang
Wonjun Hwang
Rakib Hyder
Sangeek Hyun
Sarah Ibrahimi
Tomoki Ichikawa
Yerlan Idelbayev
A. S. M. Iftekhar
Masaaki Iiyama
Satoshi Ikehata
Sunghoon Im
Atul N. Ingle
Eldar Insafutdinov
Yani A. Ioannou
Radu Tudor Ionescu

Umar Iqbal
Go Irie
Muhammad Zubair Irshad
Ahmet Iscen
Berivan Isik
Ashraful Islam
Md Amirul Islam
Syed Islam
Mariko Isogawa
Vamsi Krishna K. Ithapu
Boris Ivanovic
Darshan Iyer
Sarah Jabbour
Ayush Jain
Nishant Jain
Samyak Jain
Vidit Jain
Vineet Jain
Priyank Jaini
Tomas Jakab
Mohammad A. A. K.
  Jalwana
Muhammad Abdullah
  Jamal
Hadi Jamali-Rad
Stuart James
Varun Jampani
Young Kyun Jang
YeongJun Jang
Yunseok Jang
Ronnachai Jaroensri
Bhavan Jasani
Krishna Murthy
  Jatavallabhula
Mojan Javaheripi
Syed A. Javed
Guillaume Jeanneret
Pranav Jeevan
Herve Jegou
Rohit Jena
Tomas Jenicek
Porter Jenkins
Simon Jenni
Hae-Gon Jeon
Sangryul Jeon

Boseung Jeong
Yoonwoo Jeong
Seong-Gyun Jeong
Jisoo Jeong
Allan D. Jepson
Ankit Jha
Sumit K. Jha
I-Hong Jhuo
Ge-Peng Ji
Chaonan Ji
Deyi Ji
Jingwei Ji
Wei Ji
Zhong Ji
Jiayi Ji
Pengliang Ji
Hui Ji
Mingi Ji
Xiaopeng Ji
Yuzhu Ji
Baoxiong Jia
Songhao Jia
Dan Jia
Shan Jia
Xiaojun Jia
Xiuyi Jia
Xu Jia
Menglin Jia
Wenqi Jia
Boyuan Jiang
Wenhao Jiang
Huaizu Jiang
Hanwen Jiang
Haiyong Jiang
Hao Jiang
Huajie Jiang
Huiqin Jiang
Haojun Jiang
Haobo Jiang
Junjun Jiang
Xingyu Jiang
Yangbangyan Jiang
Yu Jiang
Jianmin Jiang
Jiaxi Jiang

Jing Jiang
Kui Jiang
Li Jiang
Liming Jiang
Chiyu Jiang
Meirui Jiang
Chen Jiang
Peng Jiang
Tai-Xiang Jiang
Wen Jiang
Xinyang Jiang
Yifan Jiang
Yuming Jiang
Yingying Jiang
Zeren Jiang
ZhengKai Jiang
Zhenyu Jiang
Shuming Jiao
Jianbo Jiao
Licheng Jiao
Dongkwon Jin
Yeying Jin
Cheng Jin
Linyi Jin
Qing Jin
Taisong Jin
Xiao Jin
Xin Jin
Sheng Jin
Kyong Hwan Jin
Ruibing Jin
SouYoung Jin
Yueming Jin
Chenchen Jing
Longlong Jing
Taotao Jing
Yongcheng Jing
Younghyun Jo
Joakim Johnander
Jeff Johnson
Michael J. Jones
R. Kenny Jones
Rico Jonschkowski
Ameya Joshi
Sunghun Joung

Felix Juefei-Xu
Claudio R. Jung
Steffen Jung
Hari Chandana K.
Rahul Vigneswaran K.
Prajwal K. R.
Abhishek Kadian
Jhony Kaesemodel Pontes
Kumara Kahatapitiya
Anmol Kalia
Sinan Kalkan
Tarun Kalluri
Jaewon Kam
Sandesh Kamath
Meina Kan
Menelaos Kanakis
Takuhiro Kaneko
Di Kang
Guoliang Kang
Hao Kang
Jaeyeon Kang
Kyoungkook Kang
Li-Wei Kang
MinGuk Kang
Suk-Ju Kang
Zhao Kang
Yash Mukund Kant
Yueying Kao
Aupendu Kar
Konstantinos Karantzalos
Sezer Karaoglu
Navid Kardan
Sanjay Kariyappa
Leonid Karlinsky
Animesh Karnewar
Shyamgopal Karthik
Hirak J. Kashyap
Marc A. Kastner
Hirokatsu Kataoka
Angelos Katharopoulos
Hiroharu Kato
Kai Katsumata
Manuel Kaufmann
Chaitanya Kaul
Prakhar Kaushik

Yuki Kawana
Lei Ke
Lipeng Ke
Tsung-Wei Ke
Wei Ke
Petr Kellnhofer
Aniruddha Kembhavi
John Kender
Corentin Kervadec
Leonid Keselman
Daniel Keysers
Nima Khademi Kalantari
Taras Khakhulin
Samir Khaki
Muhammad Haris Khan
Qadeer Khan
Salman Khan
Subash Khanal
Vaishnavi M. Khindkar
Rawal Khirodkar
Saeed Khorram
Pirazh Khorramshahi
Kourosh Khoshelham
Ansh Khurana
Benjamin Kiefer
Jae Myung Kim
Junho Kim
Boah Kim
Hyeonseong Kim
Dong-Jin Kim
Dongwan Kim
Donghyun Kim
Doyeon Kim
Yonghyun Kim
Hyung-Il Kim
Hyunwoo Kim
Hyeongwoo Kim
Hyo Jin Kim
Hyunwoo J. Kim
Taehoon Kim
Jaeha Kim
Jiwon Kim
Jung Uk Kim
Kangyeol Kim
Eunji Kim

Daeha Kim
Dongwon Kim
Kunhee Kim
Kyungmin Kim
Junsik Kim
Min H. Kim
Namil Kim
Kookhoi Kim
Sanghyun Kim
Seongyeop Kim
Seungryong Kim
Saehoon Kim
Euyoung Kim
Guisik Kim
Sungyeon Kim
Sunnie S. Y. Kim
Taehun Kim
Tae Oh Kim
Won Hwa Kim
Seungwook Kim
YoungBin Kim
Youngeun Kim
Akisato Kimura
Furkan Osman Kınlı
Zsolt Kira
Hedvig Kjellström
Florian Kleber
Jan P. Klopp
Florian Kluger
Laurent Kneip
Byungsoo Ko
Muhammed Kocabas
A. Sophia Koepke
Kevin Koeser
Nick Kolkin
Nikos Kolotouros
Wai-Kin Adams Kong
Deying Kong
Caihua Kong
Youyong Kong
Shuyu Kong
Shu Kong
Tao Kong
Yajing Kong
Yu Kong

Zishang Kong
Theodora Kontogianni
Anton S. Konushin
Julian F. P. Kooij
Bruno Korbar
Giorgos Kordopatis-Zilos
Jari Korhonen
Adam Kortylewski
Denis Korzhenkov
Divya Kothandaraman
Suraj Kothawade
Iuliia Kotseruba
Satwik Kottur
Shashank Kotyan
Alexandros Kouris
Petros Koutras
Anna Kreshuk
Ranjay Krishna
Dilip Krishnan
Andrey Kuehlkamp
Hilde Kuehne
Jason Kuen
David Kügler
Arjan Kuijper
Anna Kukleva
Sumith Kulal
Viveka Kulharia
Akshay R. Kulkarni
Nilesh Kulkarni
Dominik Kulon
Abhinav Kumar
Akash Kumar
Suryansh Kumar
B. V. K. Vijaya Kumar
Pulkit Kumar
Ratnesh Kumar
Sateesh Kumar
Satish Kumar
Vijay Kumar B. G.
Nupur Kumari
Sudhakar Kumawat
Jogendra Nath Kundu
Hsien-Kai Kuo
Meng-Yu Jennifer Kuo
Vinod Kumar Kurmi

Yusuke Kurose
Keerthy Kusumam
Alina Kuznetsova
Henry Kvinge
Ho Man Kwan
Hyeokjun Kweon
Heeseung Kwon
Gihyun Kwon
Myung-Joon Kwon
Taesung Kwon
YoungJoong Kwon
Christos Kyrkou
Jorma Laaksonen
Yann Labbe
Zorah Laehner
Florent Lafarge
Hamid Laga
Manuel Lagunas
Shenqi Lai
Jian-Huang Lai
Zihang Lai
Mohamed I. Lakhal
Mohit Lamba
Meng Lan
Loic Landrieu
Zhiqiang Lang
Natalie Lang
Dong Lao
Yizhen Lao
Yingjie Lao
Issam Hadj Laradji
Gustav Larsson
Viktor Larsson
Zakaria Laskar
Stéphane Lathuilière
Chun Pong Lau
Rynson W. H. Lau
Hei Law
Justin Lazarow
Verica Lazova
Eric-Tuan Le
Hieu Le
Trung-Nghia Le
Mathias Lechner
Byeong-Uk Lee

Chen-Yu Lee
Che-Rung Lee
Chul Lee
Hong Joo Lee
Dongsoo Lee
Jiyoung Lee
Eugene Eu Tzuan Lee
Daeun Lee
Saehyung Lee
Jewook Lee
Hyungtae Lee
Hyunmin Lee
Jungbeom Lee
Joon-Young Lee
Jong-Seok Lee
Joonseok Lee
Junha Lee
Kibok Lee
Byung-Kwan Lee
Jangwon Lee
Jinho Lee
Jongmin Lee
Seunghyun Lee
Sohyun Lee
Minsik Lee
Dogyoon Lee
Seungmin Lee
Min Jun Lee
Sangho Lee
Sangmin Lee
Seungeun Lee
Seon-Ho Lee
Sungmin Lee
Sungho Lee
Sangyoun Lee
Vincent C. S. S. Lee
Jaeseong Lee
Yong Jae Lee
Chenyang Lei
Chenyi Lei
Jiahui Lei
Xinyu Lei
Yinjie Lei
Jiaxu Leng
Luziwei Leng

Jan E. Lenssen
Vincent Lepetit
Thomas Leung
María Leyva-Vallina
Xin Li
Yikang Li
Baoxin Li
Bin Li
Bing Li
Bowen Li
Changlin Li
Chao Li
Chongyi Li
Guanyue Li
Shuai Li
Jin Li
Dingquan Li
Dongxu Li
Yiting Li
Gang Li
Dian Li
Guohao Li
Haoang Li
Haoliang Li
Haoran Li
Hengduo Li
Huafeng Li
Xiaoming Li
Hanao Li
Hongwei Li
Ziqiang Li
Jisheng Li
Jiacheng Li
Jia Li
Jiachen Li
Jiahao Li
Jianwei Li
Jiazhi Li
Jie Li
Jing Li
Jingjing Li
Jingtao Li
Jun Li
Junxuan Li
Kai Li

Kailin Li
Kenneth Li
Kun Li
Kunpeng Li
Aoxue Li
Chenglong Li
Chenglin Li
Changsheng Li
Zhichao Li
Qiang Li
Yanyu Li
Zuoyue Li
Xiang Li
Xuelong Li
Fangda Li
Ailin Li
Liang Li
Chun-Guang Li
Daiqing Li
Dong Li
Guanbin Li
Guorong Li
Haifeng Li
Jianan Li
Jianing Li
Jiaxin Li
Ke Li
Lei Li
Lincheng Li
Liulei Li
Lujun Li
Linjie Li
Lin Li
Pengyu Li
Ping Li
Qiufu Li
Qingyong Li
Rui Li
Siyuan Li
Wei Li
Wenbin Li
Xiangyang Li
Xinyu Li
Xiujun Li
Xiu Li

Xu Li
Ya-Li Li
Yao Li
Yongjie Li
Yijun Li
Yiming Li
Yuezun Li
Yu Li
Yunheng Li
Yuqi Li
Zhe Li
Zeming Li
Zhen Li
Zhengqin Li
Zhimin Li
Jiefeng Li
Jinpeng Li
Chengze Li
Jianwu Li
Lerenhan Li
Shan Li
Suichan Li
Xiangtai Li
Yanjie Li
Yandong Li
Zhuoling Li
Zhenqiang Li
Manyi Li
Maosen Li
Ji Li
Minjun Li
Mingrui Li
Mengtian Li
Junyi Li
Nianyi Li
Bo Li
Xiao Li
Peihua Li
Peike Li
Peizhao Li
Peiliang Li
Qi Li
Ren Li
Runze Li
Shile Li

Sheng Li
Shigang Li
Shiyu Li
Shuang Li
Shasha Li
Shichao Li
Tianye Li
Yuexiang Li
Wei-Hong Li
Wanhua Li
Weihao Li
Weiming Li
Weixin Li
Wenbo Li
Wenshuo Li
Weijian Li
Yunan Li
Xirong Li
Xianhang Li
Xiaoyu Li
Xueqian Li
Xuanlin Li
Xianzhi Li
Yunqiang Li
Yanjing Li
Yansheng Li
Yawei Li
Yi Li
Yong Li
Yong-Lu Li
Yuhang Li
Yu-Jhe Li
Yuxi Li
Yunsheng Li
Yanwei Li
Zechao Li
Zejian Li
Zeju Li
Zekun Li
Zhaowen Li
Zheng Li
Zhenyu Li
Zhiheng Li
Zhi Li
Zhong Li

Zhuowei Li
Zhuowan Li
Zhuohang Li
Zizhang Li
Chen Li
Yuan-Fang Li
Dongze Lian
Xiaochen Lian
Zhouhui Lian
Long Lian
Qing Lian
Jin Lianbao
Jinxiu S. Liang
Dingkang Liang
Jiahao Liang
Jianming Liang
Jingyun Liang
Kevin J. Liang
Kaizhao Liang
Chen Liang
Jie Liang
Senwei Liang
Ding Liang
Jiajun Liang
Jian Liang
Kongming Liang
Siyuan Liang
Yuanzhi Liang
Zhengfa Liang
Mingfu Liang
Xiaodan Liang
Xuefeng Liang
Yuxuan Liang
Kang Liao
Liang Liao
Hong-Yuan Mark Liao
Wentong Liao
Haofu Liao
Yue Liao
Minghui Liao
Shengcai Liao
Ting-Hsuan Liao
Xin Liao
Yinghong Liao
Teck Yian Lim

Che-Tsung Lin
Chung-Ching Lin
Chen-Hsuan Lin
Cheng Lin
Chuming Lin
Chunyu Lin
Dahua Lin
Wei Lin
Zheng Lin
Huaijia Lin
Jason Lin
Jierui Lin
Jiaying Lin
Jie Lin
Kai-En Lin
Kevin Lin
Guangfeng Lin
Jiehong Lin
Feng Lin
Hang Lin
Kwan-Yee Lin
Ke Lin
Luojun Lin
Qinghong Lin
Xiangbo Lin
Yi Lin
Zudi Lin
Shijie Lin
Yiqun Lin
Tzu-Heng Lin
Ming Lin
Shaohui Lin
SongNan Lin
Ji Lin
Tsung-Yu Lin
Xudong Lin
Yancong Lin
Yen-Chen Lin
Yiming Lin
Yuewei Lin
Zhiqiu Lin
Zinan Lin
Zhe Lin
David B. Lindell
Zhixin Ling

Zhan Ling
Alexander Liniger
Venice Erin B. Liong
Joey Litalien
Or Litany
Roee Litman
Ron Litman
Jim Little
Dor Litvak
Shaoteng Liu
Shuaicheng Liu
Andrew Liu
Xian Liu
Shaohui Liu
Bei Liu
Bo Liu
Yong Liu
Ming Liu
Yanbin Liu
Chenxi Liu
Daqi Liu
Di Liu
Difan Liu
Dong Liu
Dongfang Liu
Daizong Liu
Xiao Liu
Fangyi Liu
Fengbei Liu
Fenglin Liu
Bin Liu
Yuang Liu
Ao Liu
Hong Liu
Hongfu Liu
Huidong Liu
Ziyi Liu
Feng Liu
Hao Liu
Jie Liu
Jialun Liu
Jiang Liu
Jing Liu
Jingya Liu
Jiaming Liu

Jun Liu
Juncheng Liu
Jiawei Liu
Hongyu Liu
Chuanbin Liu
Haotian Liu
Lingqiao Liu
Chang Liu
Han Liu
Liu Liu
Min Liu
Yingqi Liu
Aishan Liu
Bingyu Liu
Benlin Liu
Boxiao Liu
Chenchen Liu
Chuanjian Liu
Daqing Liu
Huan Liu
Haozhe Liu
Jiaheng Liu
Wei Liu
Jingzhou Liu
Jiyuan Liu
Lingbo Liu
Nian Liu
Peiye Liu
Qiankun Liu
Shenglan Liu
Shilong Liu
Wen Liu
Wenyu Liu
Weifeng Liu
Wu Liu
Xiaolong Liu
Yang Liu
Yanwei Liu
Yingcheng Liu
Yongfei Liu
Yihao Liu
Yu Liu
Yunze Liu
Ze Liu
Zhenhua Liu

Zhenguang Liu
Lin Liu
Lihao Liu
Pengju Liu
Xinhai Liu
Yunfei Liu
Meng Liu
Minghua Liu
Mingyuan Liu
Miao Liu
Peirong Liu
Ping Liu
Qingjie Liu
Ruoshi Liu
Risheng Liu
Songtao Liu
Xing Liu
Shikun Liu
Shuming Liu
Sheng Liu
Songhua Liu
Tongliang Liu
Weibo Liu
Weide Liu
Weizhe Liu
Wenxi Liu
Weiyang Liu
Xin Liu
Xiaobin Liu
Xudong Liu
Xiaoyi Liu
Xihui Liu
Xinchen Liu
Xingtong Liu
Xinpeng Liu
Xinyu Liu
Xianpeng Liu
Xu Liu
Xingyu Liu
Yongtuo Liu
Yahui Liu
Yangxin Liu
Yaoyao Liu
Yaojie Liu
Yuliang Liu

Yongcheng Liu
Yuan Liu
Yufan Liu
Yu-Lun Liu
Yun Liu
Yunfan Liu
Yuanzhong Liu
Zhuoran Liu
Zhen Liu
Zheng Liu
Zhijian Liu
Zhisong Liu
Ziquan Liu
Ziyu Liu
Zhihua Liu
Zechun Liu
Zhaoyang Liu
Zhengzhe Liu
Stephan Liwicki
Shao-Yuan Lo
Sylvain Lobry
Suhas Lohit
Vishnu Suresh Lokhande
Vincenzo Lomonaco
Chengjiang Long
Guodong Long
Fuchen Long
Shangbang Long
Yang Long
Zijun Long
Vasco Lopes
Antonio M. Lopez
Roberto Javier
  Lopez-Sastre
Tobias Lorenz
Javier Lorenzo-Navarro
Yujing Lou
Qian Lou
Xiankai Lu
Changsheng Lu
Huimin Lu
Yongxi Lu
Hao Lu
Hong Lu
Jiasen Lu

Juwei Lu
Fan Lu
Guangming Lu
Jiwen Lu
Shun Lu
Tao Lu
Xiaonan Lu
Yang Lu
Yao Lu
Yongchun Lu
Zhiwu Lu
Cheng Lu
Liying Lu
Guo Lu
Xuequan Lu
Yanye Lu
Yantao Lu
Yuhang Lu
Fujun Luan
Jonathon Luiten
Jovita Lukasik
Alan Lukezic
Jonathan Samuel Lumentut
Mayank Lunayach
Ao Luo
Canjie Luo
Chong Luo
Xu Luo
Grace Luo
Jun Luo
Katie Z. Luo
Tao Luo
Cheng Luo
Fangzhou Luo
Gen Luo
Lei Luo
Sihui Luo
Weixin Luo
Yan Luo
Xiaoyan Luo
Yong Luo
Yadan Luo
Hao Luo
Ruotian Luo
Mi Luo

Tiange Luo
Wenjie Luo
Wenhan Luo
Xiao Luo
Zhiming Luo
Zhipeng Luo
Zhengyi Luo
Diogo C. Luvizon
Zhaoyang Lv
Gengyu Lyu
Lingjuan Lyu
Jun Lyu
Yuanyuan Lyu
Youwei Lyu
Yueming Lyu
Bingpeng Ma
Chao Ma
Chongyang Ma
Congbo Ma
Chih-Yao Ma
Fan Ma
Lin Ma
Haoyu Ma
Hengbo Ma
Jianqi Ma
Jiawei Ma
Jiayi Ma
Kede Ma
Kai Ma
Lingni Ma
Lei Ma
Xu Ma
Ning Ma
Benteng Ma
Cheng Ma
Andy J. Ma
Long Ma
Zhanyu Ma
Zhiheng Ma
Qianli Ma
Shiqiang Ma
Sizhuo Ma
Shiqing Ma
Xiaolong Ma
Xinzhu Ma

Gautam B. Machiraju
Spandan Madan
Mathew Magimai-Doss
Luca Magri
Behrooz Mahasseni
Upal Mahbub
Siddharth Mahendran
Paridhi Maheshwari
Rishabh Maheshwary
Mohammed Mahmoud
Shishira R. R. Maiya
Sylwia Majchrowska
Arjun Majumdar
Puspita Majumdar
Orchid Majumder
Sagnik Majumder
Ilya Makarov
Farkhod F.
  Makhmudkhujaev
Yasushi Makihara
Ankur Mali
Mateusz Malinowski
Utkarsh Mall
Srikanth Malla
Clement Mallet
Dimitrios Mallis
Yunze Man
Dipu Manandhar
Massimiliano Mancini
Murari Mandal
Raunak Manekar
Karttikeya Mangalam
Puneet Mangla
Fabian Manhardt
Sivabalan Manivasagam
Fahim Mannan
Chengzhi Mao
Hanzi Mao
Jiayuan Mao
Junhua Mao
Zhiyuan Mao
Jiageng Mao
Yunyao Mao
Zhendong Mao
Alberto Marchisio

Diego Marcos
Riccardo Marin
Aram Markosyan
Renaud Marlet
Ricardo Marques
Miquel Martí i Rabadán
Diego Martin Arroyo
Niki Martinel
Brais Martinez
Julieta Martinez
Marc Masana
Tomohiro Mashita
Timothée Masquelier
Minesh Mathew
Tetsu Matsukawa
Marwan Mattar
Bruce A. Maxwell
Christoph Mayer
Mantas Mazeika
Pratik Mazumder
Scott McCloskey
Steven McDonagh
Ishit Mehta
Jie Mei
Kangfu Mei
Jieru Mei
Xiaoguang Mei
Givi Meishvili
Luke Melas-Kyriazi
Iaroslav Melekhov
Andres Mendez-Vazquez
Heydi Mendez-Vazquez
Matias Mendieta
Ricardo A. Mendoza-León
Chenlin Meng
Depu Meng
Rang Meng
Zibo Meng
Qingjie Meng
Qier Meng
Yanda Meng
Zihang Meng
Thomas Mensink
Fabian Mentzer
Christopher Metzler

Gregory P. Meyer
Vasileios Mezaris
Liang Mi
Lu Mi
Bo Miao
Changtao Miao
Zichen Miao
Qiguang Miao
Xin Miao
Zhongqi Miao
Frank Michel
Simone Milani
Ben Mildenhall
Roy V. Miles
Juhong Min
Kyle Min
Hyun-Seok Min
Weiqing Min
Yuecong Min
Zhixiang Min
Qi Ming
David Minnen
Aymen Mir
Deepak Mishra
Anand Mishra
Shlok K. Mishra
Niluthpol Mithun
Gaurav Mittal
Trisha Mittal
Daisuke Miyazaki
Kaichun Mo
Hong Mo
Zhipeng Mo
Davide Modolo
Abduallah A. Mohamed
Mohamed Afham
Mohamed Aflal
Ron Mokady
Pavlo Molchanov
Davide Moltisanti
Liliane Momeni
Gianluca Monaci
Pascal Monasse
Ajoy Mondal
Tom Monnier

Aron Monszpart
Gyeongsik Moon
Suhong Moon
Taesup Moon
Sean Moran
Daniel Moreira
Pietro Morerio
Alexandre Morgand
Lia Morra
Ali Mosleh
Inbar Mosseri
Sayed Mohammad
  Mostafavi Isfahani
Saman Motamed
Ramy A. Mounir
Fangzhou Mu
Jiteng Mu
Norman Mu
Yasuhiro Mukaigawa
Ryan Mukherjee
Tanmoy Mukherjee
Yusuke Mukuta
Ravi Teja Mullapudi
Lea Müller
Matthias Müller
Martin Mundt
Nils Murrugarra-Llerena
Damien Muselet
Armin Mustafa
Muhammad Ferjad Naeem
Sauradip Nag
Hajime Nagahara
Pravin Nagar
Rajendra Nagar
Naveen Shankar Nagaraja
Varun Nagaraja
Tushar Nagarajan
Seungjun Nah
Gaku Nakano
Yuta Nakashima
Giljoo Nam
Seonghyeon Nam
Liangliang Nan
Yuesong Nan
Yeshwanth Napolean

Dinesh Reddy
  Narapureddy
Medhini Narasimhan
Supreeth
  Narasimhaswamy
Sriram Narayanan
Erickson R. Nascimento
Varun Nasery
K. L. Navaneet
Pablo Navarrete Michelini
Shant Navasardyan
Shah Nawaz
Nihal Nayak
Farhood Negin
Lukáš Neumann
Alejandro Newell
Evonne Ng
Kam Woh Ng
Tony Ng
Anh Nguyen
Tuan Anh Nguyen
Cuong Cao Nguyen
Ngoc Cuong Nguyen
Thanh Nguyen
Khoi Nguyen
Phi Le Nguyen
Phong Ha Nguyen
Tam Nguyen
Truong Nguyen
Anh Tuan Nguyen
Rang Nguyen
Thao Thi Phuong Nguyen
Van Nguyen Nguyen
Zhen-Liang Ni
Yao Ni
Shijie Nie
Xuecheng Nie
Yongwei Nie
Weizhi Nie
Ying Nie
Yinyu Nie
Kshitij N. Nikhal
Simon Niklaus
Xuefei Ning
Jifeng Ning

Yotam Nitzan
Di Niu
Shuaicheng Niu
Li Niu
Wei Niu
Yulei Niu
Zhenxing Niu
Albert No
Shohei Nobuhara
Nicoletta Noceti
Junhyug Noh
Sotiris Nousias
Slawomir Nowaczyk
Ewa M. Nowara
Valsamis Ntouskos
Gilberto Ochoa-Ruiz
Ferda Ofli
Jihyong Oh
Sangyun Oh
Youngtaek Oh
Hiroki Ohashi
Takahiro Okabe
Kemal Oksuz
Fumio Okura
Daniel Olmeda Reino
Matthew Olson
Carl Olsson
Roy Or-El
Alessandro Ortis
Guillermo Ortiz-Jimenez
Magnus Oskarsson
Ahmed A. A. Osman
Martin R. Oswald
Mayu Otani
Naima Otberdout
Cheng Ouyang
Jiahong Ouyang
Wanli Ouyang
Andrew Owens
Poojan B. Oza
Mete Ozay
A. Cengiz Oztireli
Gautam Pai
Tomas Pajdla
Umapada Pal

Simone Palazzo
Luca Palmieri
Bowen Pan
Hao Pan
Lili Pan
Tai-Yu Pan
Liang Pan
Chengwei Pan
Yingwei Pan
Xuran Pan
Jinshan Pan
Xinyu Pan
Liyuan Pan
Xingang Pan
Xingjia Pan
Zhihong Pan
Zizheng Pan
Priyadarshini Panda
Rameswar Panda
Rohit Pandey
Kaiyue Pang
Bo Pang
Guansong Pang
Jiangmiao Pang
Meng Pang
Tianyu Pang
Ziqi Pang
Omiros Pantazis
Andreas Panteli
Maja Pantic
Marina Paolanti
Joao P. Papa
Samuele Papa
Mike Papadakis
Dim P. Papadopoulos
George Papandreou
Constantin Pape
Toufiq Parag
Chethan Parameshwara
Shaifali Parashar
Alejandro Pardo
Rishubh Parihar
Sarah Parisot
JaeYoo Park
Gyeong-Moon Park

Hyojin Park
Hyoungseob Park
Jongchan Park
Jae Sung Park
Kiru Park
Chunghyun Park
Kwanyong Park
Sunghyun Park
Sungrae Park
Seongsik Park
Sanghyun Park
Sungjune Park
Taesung Park
Gaurav Parmar
Paritosh Parmar
Alvaro Parra
Despoina Paschalidou
Or Patashnik
Shivansh Patel
Pushpak Pati
Prashant W. Patil
Vaishakh Patil
Suvam Patra
Jay Patravali
Badri Narayana Patro
Angshuman Paul
Sudipta Paul
Rémi Pautrat
Nick E. Pears
Adithya Pediredla
Wenjie Pei
Shmuel Peleg
Latha Pemula
Bo Peng
Houwen Peng
Yue Peng
Liangzu Peng
Baoyun Peng
Jun Peng
Pai Peng
Sida Peng
Xi Peng
Yuxin Peng
Songyou Peng
Wei Peng

Weiqi Peng
Wen-Hsiao Peng
Pramuditha Perera
Juan C. Perez
Eduardo Pérez Pellitero
Juan-Manuel Perez-Rua
Federico Pernici
Marco Pesavento
Stavros Petridis
Ilya A. Petrov
Vladan Petrovic
Mathis Petrovich
Suzanne Petryk
Hieu Pham
Quang Pham
Khoi Pham
Tung Pham
Huy Phan
Stephen Phillips
Cheng Perng Phoo
David Picard
Marco Piccirilli
Georg Pichler
A. J. Piergiovanni
Vipin Pillai
Silvia L. Pintea
Giovanni Pintore
Robinson Piramuthu
Fiora Pirri
Theodoros Pissas
Fabio Pizzati
Benjamin Planche
Bryan Plummer
Matteo Poggi
Ashwini Pokle
Georgy E. Ponimatkin
Adrian Popescu
Stefan Popov
Nikola Popović
Ronald Poppe
Angelo Porrello
Michael Potter
Charalambos Poullis
Hadi Pouransari
Omid Poursaeed

Shraman Pramanick
Mantini Pranav
Dilip K. Prasad
Meghshyam Prasad
B. H. Pawan Prasad
Shitala Prasad
Prateek Prasanna
Ekta Prashnani
Derek S. Prijatelj
Luke Y. Prince
Véronique Prinet
Victor Adrian Prisacariu
James Pritts
Thomas Probst
Sergey Prokudin
Rita Pucci
Chi-Man Pun
Matthew Purri
Haozhi Qi
Lu Qi
Lei Qi
Xianbiao Qi
Yonggang Qi
Yuankai Qi
Siyuan Qi
Guocheng Qian
Hangwei Qian
Qi Qian
Deheng Qian
Shengsheng Qian
Wen Qian
Rui Qian
Yiming Qian
Shengju Qian
Shengyi Qian
Xuelin Qian
Zhenxing Qian
Nan Qiao
Xiaotian Qiao
Jing Qin
Can Qin
Siyang Qin
Hongwei Qin
Jie Qin
Minghai Qin

Yipeng Qin
Yongqiang Qin
Wenda Qin
Xuebin Qin
Yuzhe Qin
Yao Qin
Zhenyue Qin
Zhiwu Qing
Heqian Qiu
Jiayan Qiu
Jielin Qiu
Yue Qiu
Jiaxiong Qiu
Zhongxi Qiu
Shi Qiu
Zhaofan Qiu
Zhongnan Qu
Yanyun Qu
Kha Gia Quach
Yuhui Quan
Ruijie Quan
Mike Rabbat
Rahul Shekhar Rade
Filip Radenovic
Gorjan Radevski
Bogdan Raducanu
Francesco Ragusa
Shafin Rahman
Md Mahfuzur Rahman
    Siddiquee
Hossein Rahmani
Kiran Raja
Sivaramakrishnan
    Rajaraman
Jathushan Rajasegaran
Adnan Siraj Rakin
Michaël Ramamonjisoa
Chirag A. Raman
Shanmuganathan Raman
Vignesh Ramanathan
Vasili Ramanishka
Vikram V. Ramaswamy
Merey Ramazanova
Jason Rambach
Sai Saketh Rambhatla

Clément Rambour
Ashwin Ramesh Babu
Adín Ramírez Rivera
Arianna Rampini
Haoxi Ran
Aakanksha Rana
Aayush Jung Bahadur
    Rana
Kanchana N. Ranasinghe
Aneesh Rangnekar
Samrudhdhi B. Rangrej
Harsh Rangwani
Viresh Ranjan
Anyi Rao
Yongming Rao
Carolina Raposo
Michalis Raptis
Amir Rasouli
Vivek Rathod
Adepu Ravi Sankar
Avinash Ravichandran
Bharadwaj Ravichandran
Dripta S. Raychaudhuri
Adria Recasens
Simon Reiß
Davis Rempe
Daxuan Ren
Jiawei Ren
Jimmy Ren
Sucheng Ren
Dayong Ren
Zhile Ren
Dongwei Ren
Qibing Ren
Pengfei Ren
Zhenwen Ren
Xuqian Ren
Yixuan Ren
Zhongzheng Ren
Ambareesh Revanur
Hamed Rezazadegan
    Tavakoli
Rafael S. Rezende
Wonjong Rhee
Alexander Richard

Christian Richardt
Stephan R. Richter
Benjamin Riggan
Dominik Rivoir
Mamshad Nayeem Rizve
Joshua D. Robinson
Joseph Robinson
Chris Rockwell
Ranga Rodrigo
Andres C. Rodriguez
Carlos Rodriguez-Pardo
Marcus Rohrbach
Gemma Roig
Yu Rong
David A. Ross
Mohammad Rostami
Edward Rosten
Karsten Roth
Anirban Roy
Debaditya Roy
Shuvendu Roy
Ahana Roy Choudhury
Aruni Roy Chowdhury
Denys Rozumnyi
Shulan Ruan
Wenjie Ruan
Patrick Ruhkamp
Danila Rukhovich
Anian Ruoss
Chris Russell
Dan Ruta
Dawid Damian Rymarczyk
DongHun Ryu
Hyeonggon Ryu
Kwonyoung Ryu
Balasubramanian S.
Alexandre Sablayrolles
Mohammad Sabokrou
Arka Sadhu
Aniruddha Saha
Oindrila Saha
Pritish Sahu
Aneeshan Sain
Nirat Saini
Saurabh Saini

Takeshi Saitoh
Christos Sakaridis
Fumihiko Sakaue
Dimitrios Sakkos
Ken Sakurada
Parikshit V. Sakurikar
Rohit Saluja
Nermin Samet
Leo Sampaio Ferraz
      Ribeiro
Jorge Sanchez
Enrique Sanchez
Shengtian Sang
Anush Sankaran
Soubhik Sanyal
Nikolaos Sarafianos
Vishwanath Saragadam
István Sárándi
Saquib Sarfraz
Mert Bulent Sariyildiz
Anindya Sarkar
Pritam Sarkar
Paul-Edouard Sarlin
Hiroshi Sasaki
Takami Sato
Torsten Sattler
Ravi Kumar Satzoda
Axel Sauer
Stefano Savian
Artem Savkin
Manolis Savva
Gerald Schaefer
Simone Schaub-Meyer
Yoni Schirris
Samuel Schulter
Katja Schwarz
Jesse Scott
Sinisa Segvic
Constantin Marc Seibold
Lorenzo Seidenari
Matan Sela
Fadime Sener
Paul Hongsuck Seo
Kwanggyoon Seo
Hongje Seong

Dario Serez
Francesco Setti
Bryan Seybold
Mohamad Shahbazi
Shima Shahfar
Xinxin Shan
Caifeng Shan
Dandan Shan
Shawn Shan
Wei Shang
Jinghuan Shang
Jiaxiang Shang
Lei Shang
Sukrit Shankar
Ken Shao
Rui Shao
Jie Shao
Mingwen Shao
Aashish Sharma
Gaurav Sharma
Vivek Sharma
Abhishek Sharma
Yoli Shavit
Shashank Shekhar
Sumit Shekhar
Zhijie Shen
Fengyi Shen
Furao Shen
Jialie Shen
Jingjing Shen
Ziyi Shen
Linlin Shen
Guangyu Shen
Biluo Shen
Falong Shen
Jiajun Shen
Qiu Shen
Qiuhong Shen
Shuai Shen
Wang Shen
Yiqing Shen
Yunhang Shen
Siqi Shen
Bin Shen
Tianwei Shen

Xi Shen
Yilin Shen
Yuming Shen
Yucong Shen
Zhiqiang Shen
Lu Sheng
Yichen Sheng
Shivanand Venkanna
   Sheshappanavar
Shelly Sheynin
Baifeng Shi
Ruoxi Shi
Botian Shi
Hailin Shi
Jia Shi
Jing Shi
Shaoshuai Shi
Baoguang Shi
Boxin Shi
Hengcan Shi
Tianyang Shi
Xiaodan Shi
Yongjie Shi
Zhensheng Shi
Yinghuan Shi
Weiqi Shi
Wu Shi
Xuepeng Shi
Xiaoshuang Shi
Yujiao Shi
Zenglin Shi
Zhenmei Shi
Takashi Shibata
Meng-Li Shih
Yichang Shih
Hyunjung Shim
Dongseok Shim
Soshi Shimada
Inkyu Shin
Jinwoo Shin
Seungjoo Shin
Seungjae Shin
Koichi Shinoda
Suprosanna Shit

Palaiahnakote
   Shivakumara
Eli Shlizerman
Gaurav Shrivastava
Xiao Shu
Xiangbo Shu
Xiujun Shu
Yang Shu
Tianmin Shu
Jun Shu
Zhixin Shu
Bing Shuai
Maria Shugrina
Ivan Shugurov
Satya Narayan Shukla
Pranjay Shyam
Jianlou Si
Yawar Siddiqui
Alberto Signoroni
Pedro Silva
Jae-Young Sim
Oriane Siméoni
Martin Simon
Andrea Simonelli
Abhishek Singh
Ashish Singh
Dinesh Singh
Gurkirt Singh
Krishna Kumar Singh
Mannat Singh
Pravendra Singh
Rajat Vikram Singh
Utkarsh Singhal
Dipika Singhania
Vasu Singla
Harsh Sinha
Sudipta Sinha
Josef Sivic
Elena Sizikova
Geri Skenderi
Ivan Skorokhodov
Dmitriy Smirnov
Cameron Y. Smith
James S. Smith
Patrick Snape

Mattia Soldan
Hyeongseok Son
Sanghyun Son
Chuanbiao Song
Chen Song
Chunfeng Song
Dan Song
Dongjin Song
Hwanjun Song
Guoxian Song
Jiaming Song
Jie Song
Liangchen Song
Ran Song
Luchuan Song
Xibin Song
Li Song
Fenglong Song
Guoli Song
Guanglu Song
Zhenbo Song
Lin Song
Xinhang Song
Yang Song
Yibing Song
Rajiv Soundararajan
Hossein Souri
Cristovao Sousa
Riccardo Spezialetti
Leonidas Spinoulas
Michael W. Spratling
Deepak Sridhar
Srinath Sridhar
Gaurang Sriramanan
Vinkle Kumar Srivastav
Themos Stafylakis
Serban Stan
Anastasis Stathopoulos
Markus Steinberger
Jan Steinbrener
Sinisa Stekovic
Alexandros Stergiou
Gleb Sterkin
Rainer Stiefelhagen
Pierre Stock

Ombretta Strafforello
Julian Straub
Yannick Strümpler
Joerg Stueckler
Hang Su
Weijie Su
Jong-Chyi Su
Bing Su
Haisheng Su
Jinming Su
Yiyang Su
Yukun Su
Yuxin Su
Zhuo Su
Zhaoqi Su
Xiu Su
Yu-Chuan Su
Zhixun Su
Arulkumar Subramaniam
Akshayvarun Subramanya
A. Subramanyam
Swathikiran Sudhakaran
Yusuke Sugano
Masanori Suganuma
Yumin Suh
Yang Sui
Baochen Sun
Cheng Sun
Long Sun
Guolei Sun
Haoliang Sun
Haomiao Sun
He Sun
Hanqing Sun
Hao Sun
Lichao Sun
Jiachen Sun
Jiaming Sun
Jian Sun
Jin Sun
Jennifer J. Sun
Tiancheng Sun
Libo Sun
Peize Sun
Qianru Sun

Shanlin Sun
Yu Sun
Zhun Sun
Che Sun
Lin Sun
Tao Sun
Yiyou Sun
Chunyi Sun
Chong Sun
Weiwei Sun
Weixuan Sun
Xiuyu Sun
Yanan Sun
Zeren Sun
Zhaodong Sun
Zhiqing Sun
Minhyuk Sung
Jinli Suo
Simon Suo
Abhijit Suprem
Anshuman Suri
Saksham Suri
Joshua M. Susskind
Roman Suvorov
Gurumurthy Swaminathan
Robin Swanson
Paul Swoboda
Tabish A. Syed
Richard Szeliski
Fariborz Taherkhani
Yu-Wing Tai
Keita Takahashi
Walter Talbott
Gary Tam
Masato Tamura
Feitong Tan
Fuwen Tan
Shuhan Tan
Andong Tan
Bin Tan
Cheng Tan
Jianchao Tan
Lei Tan
Mingxing Tan
Xin Tan

Zichang Tan
Zhentao Tan
Kenichiro Tanaka
Masayuki Tanaka
Yushun Tang
Hao Tang
Jingqun Tang
Jinhui Tang
Kaihua Tang
Luming Tang
Lv Tang
Sheyang Tang
Shitao Tang
Siliang Tang
Shixiang Tang
Yansong Tang
Keke Tang
Chang Tang
Chenwei Tang
Jie Tang
Junshu Tang
Ming Tang
Peng Tang
Xu Tang
Yao Tang
Chen Tang
Fan Tang
Haoran Tang
Shengeng Tang
Yehui Tang
Zhipeng Tang
Ugo Tanielian
Chaofan Tao
Jiale Tao
Junli Tao
Renshuai Tao
An Tao
Guanhong Tao
Zhiqiang Tao
Makarand Tapaswi
Jean-Philippe G. Tarel
Juan J. Tarrio
Enzo Tartaglione
Keisuke Tateno
Zachary Teed

Ajinkya B. Tejankar
Bugra Tekin
Purva Tendulkar
Damien Teney
Minggui Teng
Chris Tensmeyer
Andrew Beng Jin Teoh
Philipp Terhörst
Kartik Thakral
Nupur Thakur
Kevin Thandiackal
Spyridon Thermos
Diego Thomas
William Thong
Yuesong Tian
Guanzhong Tian
Lin Tian
Shiqi Tian
Kai Tian
Meng Tian
Tai-Peng Tian
Zhuotao Tian
Shangxuan Tian
Tian Tian
Yapeng Tian
Yu Tian
Yuxin Tian
Leslie Ching Ow Tiong
Praveen Tirupattur
Garvita Tiwari
George Toderici
Antoine Toisoul
Aysim Toker
Tatiana Tommasi
Zhan Tong
Alessio Tonioni
Alessandro Torcinovich
Fabio Tosi
Matteo Toso
Hugo Touvron
Quan Hung Tran
Son Tran
Hung Tran
Ngoc-Trung Tran
Vinh Tran

Phong Tran
Giovanni Trappolini
Edith Tretschk
Subarna Tripathi
Shubhendu Trivedi
Eduard Trulls
Prune Truong
Thanh-Dat Truong
Tomasz Trzcinski
Sam Tsai
Yi-Hsuan Tsai
Ethan Tseng
Yu-Chee Tseng
Shahar Tsiper
Stavros Tsogkas
Shikui Tu
Zhigang Tu
Zhengzhong Tu
Richard Tucker
Sergey Tulyakov
Cigdem Turan
Daniyar Turmukhambetov
Victor G. Turrisi da Costa
Bartlomiej Twardowski
Christopher D. Twigg
Radim Tylecek
Mostofa Rafid Uddin
Md. Zasim Uddin
Kohei Uehara
Nicolas Ugrinovic
Youngjung Uh
Norimichi Ukita
Anwaar Ulhaq
Devesh Upadhyay
Paul Upchurch
Yoshitaka Ushiku
Yuzuko Utsumi
Mikaela Angelina Uy
Mohit Vaishnav
Pratik Vaishnavi
Jeya Maria Jose Valanarasu
Matias A. Valdenegro Toro
Diego Valsesia
Wouter Van Gansbeke
Nanne van Noord

Simon Vandenhende
Farshid Varno
Cristina Vasconcelos
Francisco Vasconcelos
Alex Vasilescu
Subeesh Vasu
Arun Balajee Vasudevan
Kanav Vats
Vaibhav S. Vavilala
Sagar Vaze
Javier Vazquez-Corral
Andrea Vedaldi
Olga Veksler
Andreas Velten
Sai H. Vemprala
Raviteja Vemulapalli
Shashanka
    Venkataramanan
Dor Verbin
Luisa Verdoliva
Manisha Verma
Yashaswi Verma
Constantin Vertan
Eli Verwimp
Deepak Vijaykeerthy
Pablo Villanueva
Ruben Villegas
Markus Vincze
Vibhav Vineet
Minh P. Vo
Huy V. Vo
Duc Minh Vo
Tomas Vojir
Igor Vozniak
Nicholas Vretos
Vibashan VS
Tuan-Anh Vu
Thang Vu
Mårten Wadenbäck
Neal Wadhwa
Aaron T. Walsman
Steven Walton
Jin Wan
Alvin Wan
Jia Wan

Jun Wan
Xiaoyue Wan
Fang Wan
Guowei Wan
Renjie Wan
Zhiqiang Wan
Ziyu Wan
Bastian Wandt
Dongdong Wang
Limin Wang
Haiyang Wang
Xiaobing Wang
Angtian Wang
Angelina Wang
Bing Wang
Bo Wang
Boyu Wang
Binghui Wang
Chen Wang
Chien-Yi Wang
Congli Wang
Qi Wang
Chengrui Wang
Rui Wang
Yiqun Wang
Cong Wang
Wenjing Wang
Dongkai Wang
Di Wang
Xiaogang Wang
Kai Wang
Zhizhong Wang
Fangjinhua Wang
Feng Wang
Hang Wang
Gaoang Wang
Guoqing Wang
Guangcong Wang
Guangzhi Wang
Hanqing Wang
Hao Wang
Haohan Wang
Haoran Wang
Hong Wang
Haotao Wang

Hu Wang
Huan Wang
Hua Wang
Hui-Po Wang
Hengli Wang
Hanyu Wang
Hongxing Wang
Jingwen Wang
Jialiang Wang
Jian Wang
Jianyi Wang
Jiashun Wang
Jiahao Wang
Tsun-Hsuan Wang
Xiaoqian Wang
Jinqiao Wang
Jun Wang
Jianzong Wang
Kaihong Wang
Ke Wang
Lei Wang
Lingjing Wang
Linnan Wang
Lin Wang
Liansheng Wang
Mengjiao Wang
Manning Wang
Nannan Wang
Peihao Wang
Jiayun Wang
Pu Wang
Qiang Wang
Qiufeng Wang
Qilong Wang
Qiangchang Wang
Qin Wang
Qing Wang
Ruocheng Wang
Ruibin Wang
Ruisheng Wang
Ruizhe Wang
Runqi Wang
Runzhong Wang
Wenxuan Wang
Sen Wang

Shangfei Wang
Shaofei Wang
Shijie Wang
Shiqi Wang
Zhibo Wang
Song Wang
Xinjiang Wang
Tai Wang
Tao Wang
Teng Wang
Xiang Wang
Tianren Wang
Tiantian Wang
Tianyi Wang
Fengjiao Wang
Wei Wang
Miaohui Wang
Suchen Wang
Siyue Wang
Yaoming Wang
Xiao Wang
Ze Wang
Biao Wang
Chaofei Wang
Dong Wang
Gu Wang
Guangrun Wang
Guangming Wang
Guo-Hua Wang
Haoqing Wang
Hesheng Wang
Huafeng Wang
Jinghua Wang
Jingdong Wang
Jingjing Wang
Jingya Wang
Jingkang Wang
Jiakai Wang
Junke Wang
Kuo Wang
Lichen Wang
Lizhi Wang
Longguang Wang
Mang Wang
Mei Wang

Min Wang
Peng-Shuai Wang
Run Wang
Shaoru Wang
Shuhui Wang
Tan Wang
Tiancai Wang
Tianqi Wang
Wenhai Wang
Wenzhe Wang
Xiaobo Wang
Xiudong Wang
Xu Wang
Yajie Wang
Yan Wang
Yuan-Gen Wang
Yingqian Wang
Yizhi Wang
Yulin Wang
Yu Wang
Yujie Wang
Yunhe Wang
Yuxi Wang
Yaowei Wang
Yiwei Wang
Zezheng Wang
Hongzhi Wang
Zhiqiang Wang
Ziteng Wang
Ziwei Wang
Zheng Wang
Zhenyu Wang
Binglu Wang
Zhongdao Wang
Ce Wang
Weining Wang
Weiyao Wang
Wenbin Wang
Wenguan Wang
Guangting Wang
Haolin Wang
Haiyan Wang
Huiyu Wang
Naiyan Wang
Jingbo Wang

Jinpeng Wang
Jiaqi Wang
Liyuan Wang
Lizhen Wang
Ning Wang
Wenqian Wang
Sheng-Yu Wang
Weimin Wang
Xiaohan Wang
Yifan Wang
Yi Wang
Yongtao Wang
Yizhou Wang
Zhuo Wang
Zhe Wang
Xudong Wang
Xiaofang Wang
Xinggang Wang
Xiaosen Wang
Xiaosong Wang
Xiaoyang Wang
Lijun Wang
Xinlong Wang
Xuan Wang
Xue Wang
Yangang Wang
Yaohui Wang
Yu-Chiang Frank Wang
Yida Wang
Yilin Wang
Yi Ru Wang
Yali Wang
Yinglong Wang
Yufu Wang
Yujiang Wang
Yuwang Wang
Yuting Wang
Yang Wang
Yu-Xiong Wang
Yixu Wang
Ziqi Wang
Zhicheng Wang
Zeyu Wang
Zhaowen Wang
Zhenyi Wang

Zhenzhi Wang
Zhijie Wang
Zhiyong Wang
Zhongling Wang
Zhuowei Wang
Zian Wang
Zifu Wang
Zihao Wang
Zirui Wang
Ziyan Wang
Wenxiao Wang
Zhen Wang
Zhepeng Wang
Zi Wang
Zihao W. Wang
Steven L. Waslander
Olivia Watkins
Daniel Watson
Silvan Weder
Dongyoon Wee
Dongming Wei
Tianyi Wei
Jia Wei
Dong Wei
Fangyun Wei
Longhui Wei
Mingqiang Wei
Xinyue Wei
Chen Wei
Donglai Wei
Pengxu Wei
Xing Wei
Xiu-Shen Wei
Wenqi Wei
Guoqiang Wei
Wei Wei
XingKui Wei
Xian Wei
Xingxing Wei
Yake Wei
Yuxiang Wei
Yi Wei
Luca Weihs
Michael Weinmann
Martin Weinmann

Congcong Wen
Chuan Wen
Jie Wen
Sijia Wen
Song Wen
Chao Wen
Xiang Wen
Zeyi Wen
Xin Wen
Yilin Wen
Yijia Weng
Shuchen Weng
Junwu Weng
Wenming Weng
Renliang Weng
Zhenyu Weng
Xinshuo Weng
Nicholas J. Westlake
Gordon Wetzstein
Lena M. Widin Klasén
Rick Wildes
Bryan M. Williams
Williem Williem
Ole Winther
Scott Wisdom
Alex Wong
Chau-Wai Wong
Kwan-Yee K. Wong
Yongkang Wong
Scott Workman
Marcel Worring
Michael Wray
Safwan Wshah
Xiang Wu
Aming Wu
Chongruo Wu
Cho-Ying Wu
Chunpeng Wu
Chenyan Wu
Ziyi Wu
Fuxiang Wu
Gang Wu
Haiping Wu
Huisi Wu
Jane Wu

Jialian Wu
Jing Wu
Jinjian Wu
Jianlong Wu
Xian Wu
Lifang Wu
Lifan Wu
Minye Wu
Qianyi Wu
Rongliang Wu
Rui Wu
Shiqian Wu
Shuzhe Wu
Shangzhe Wu
Tsung-Han Wu
Tz-Ying Wu
Ting-Wei Wu
Jiannan Wu
Zhiliang Wu
Yu Wu
Chenyun Wu
Dayan Wu
Dongxian Wu
Fei Wu
Hefeng Wu
Jianxin Wu
Weibin Wu
Wenxuan Wu
Wenhao Wu
Xiao Wu
Yicheng Wu
Yuanwei Wu
Yu-Huan Wu
Zhenxin Wu
Zhenyu Wu
Wei Wu
Peng Wu
Xiaohe Wu
Xindi Wu
Xinxing Wu
Xinyi Wu
Xingjiao Wu
Xiongwei Wu
Yangzheng Wu
Yanzhao Wu

Yawen Wu
Yong Wu
Yi Wu
Ying Nian Wu
Zhenyao Wu
Zhonghua Wu
Zongze Wu
Zuxuan Wu
Stefanie Wuhrer
Teng Xi
Jianing Xi
Fei Xia
Haifeng Xia
Menghan Xia
Yuanqing Xia
Zhihua Xia
Xiaobo Xia
Weihao Xia
Shihong Xia
Yan Xia
Yong Xia
Zhaoyang Xia
Zhihao Xia
Chuhua Xian
Yongqin Xian
Wangmeng Xiang
Fanbo Xiang
Tiange Xiang
Tao Xiang
Liuyu Xiang
Xiaoyu Xiang
Zhiyu Xiang
Aoran Xiao
Chunxia Xiao
Fanyi Xiao
Jimin Xiao
Jun Xiao
Taihong Xiao
Anqi Xiao
Junfei Xiao
Jing Xiao
Liang Xiao
Yang Xiao
Yuting Xiao
Yijun Xiao

Yao Xiao
Zeyu Xiao
Zhisheng Xiao
Zihao Xiao
Binhui Xie
Christopher Xie
Haozhe Xie
Jin Xie
Guo-Sen Xie
Hongtao Xie
Ming-Kun Xie
Tingting Xie
Chaohao Xie
Weicheng Xie
Xudong Xie
Jiyang Xie
Xiaohua Xie
Yuan Xie
Zhenyu Xie
Ning Xie
Xianghui Xie
Xiufeng Xie
You Xie
Yutong Xie
Fuyong Xing
Yifan Xing
Zhen Xing
Yuanjun Xiong
Jinhui Xiong
Weihua Xiong
Hongkai Xiong
Zhitong Xiong
Yuanhao Xiong
Yunyang Xiong
Yuwen Xiong
Zhiwei Xiong
Yuliang Xiu
An Xu
Chang Xu
Chenliang Xu
Chengming Xu
Chenshu Xu
Xiang Xu
Huijuan Xu
Zhe Xu

Jie Xu
Jingyi Xu
Jiarui Xu
Yinghao Xu
Kele Xu
Ke Xu
Li Xu
Linchuan Xu
Linning Xu
Mengde Xu
Mengmeng Frost Xu
Min Xu
Mingye Xu
Jun Xu
Ning Xu
Peng Xu
Runsheng Xu
Sheng Xu
Wenqiang Xu
Xiaogang Xu
Renzhe Xu
Kaidi Xu
Yi Xu
Chi Xu
Qiuling Xu
Baobei Xu
Feng Xu
Haohang Xu
Haofei Xu
Lan Xu
Mingze Xu
Songcen Xu
Weipeng Xu
Wenjia Xu
Wenju Xu
Xiangyu Xu
Xin Xu
Yinshuang Xu
Yixing Xu
Yuting Xu
Yanyu Xu
Zhenbo Xu
Zhiliang Xu
Zhiyuan Xu
Xiaohao Xu

Yanwu Xu
Yan Xu
Yiran Xu
Yifan Xu
Yufei Xu
Yong Xu
Zichuan Xu
Zenglin Xu
Zexiang Xu
Zhan Xu
Zheng Xu
Zhiwei Xu
Ziyue Xu
Shiyu Xuan
Hanyu Xuan
Fei Xue
Jianru Xue
Mingfu Xue
Qinghan Xue
Tianfan Xue
Chao Xue
Chuhui Xue
Nan Xue
Zhou Xue
Xiangyang Xue
Yuan Xue
Abhay Yadav
Ravindra Yadav
Kota Yamaguchi
Toshihiko Yamasaki
Kohei Yamashita
Chaochao Yan
Feng Yan
Kun Yan
Qingsen Yan
Qixin Yan
Rui Yan
Siming Yan
Xinchen Yan
Yaping Yan
Bin Yan
Qingan Yan
Shen Yan
Shipeng Yan
Xu Yan

Yan Yan
Yichao Yan
Zhaoyi Yan
Zike Yan
Zhiqiang Yan
Hongliang Yan
Zizheng Yan
Jiewen Yang
Anqi Joyce Yang
Shan Yang
Anqi Yang
Antoine Yang
Bo Yang
Baoyao Yang
Chenhongyi Yang
Dingkang Yang
De-Nian Yang
Dong Yang
David Yang
Fan Yang
Fengyu Yang
Fengting Yang
Fei Yang
Gengshan Yang
Heng Yang
Han Yang
Huan Yang
Yibo Yang
Jiancheng Yang
Jihan Yang
Jiawei Yang
Jiayu Yang
Jie Yang
Jinfa Yang
Jingkang Yang
Jinyu Yang
Cheng-Fu Yang
Ji Yang
Jianyu Yang
Kailun Yang
Tian Yang
Luyu Yang
Liang Yang
Li Yang
Michael Ying Yang

Yang Yang
Muli Yang
Le Yang
Qiushi Yang
Ren Yang
Ruihan Yang
Shuang Yang
Siyuan Yang
Su Yang
Shiqi Yang
Taojiannan Yang
Tianyu Yang
Lei Yang
Wanzhao Yang
Shuai Yang
William Yang
Wei Yang
Xiaofeng Yang
Xiaoshan Yang
Xin Yang
Xuan Yang
Xu Yang
Xingyi Yang
Xitong Yang
Jing Yang
Yanchao Yang
Wenming Yang
Yujiu Yang
Herb Yang
Jianfei Yang
Jinhui Yang
Chuanguang Yang
Guanglei Yang
Haitao Yang
Kewei Yang
Linlin Yang
Lijin Yang
Longrong Yang
Meng Yang
MingKun Yang
Sibei Yang
Shicai Yang
Tong Yang
Wen Yang
Xi Yang

Xiaolong Yang
Xue Yang
Yubin Yang
Ze Yang
Ziyi Yang
Yi Yang
Linjie Yang
Yuzhe Yang
Yiding Yang
Zhenpei Yang
Zhaohui Yang
Zhengyuan Yang
Zhibo Yang
Zongxin Yang
Hantao Yao
Mingde Yao
Rui Yao
Taiping Yao
Ting Yao
Cong Yao
Qingsong Yao
Quanming Yao
Xu Yao
Yuan Yao
Yao Yao
Yazhou Yao
Jiawen Yao
Shunyu Yao
Pew-Thian Yap
Sudhir Yarram
Rajeev Yasarla
Peng Ye
Botao Ye
Mao Ye
Fei Ye
Hanrong Ye
Jingwen Ye
Jinwei Ye
Jiarong Ye
Mang Ye
Meng Ye
Qi Ye
Qian Ye
Qixiang Ye
Junjie Ye

Sheng Ye
Nanyang Ye
Yufei Ye
Xiaoqing Ye
Ruolin Ye
Yousef Yeganeh
Chun-Hsiao Yeh
Raymond A. Yeh
Yu-Ying Yeh
Kai Yi
Chang Yi
Renjiao Yi
Xinping Yi
Peng Yi
Alper Yilmaz
Junho Yim
Hui Yin
Bangjie Yin
Jia-Li Yin
Miao Yin
Wenzhe Yin
Xuwang Yin
Ming Yin
Yu Yin
Aoxiong Yin
Kangxue Yin
Tianwei Yin
Wei Yin
Xianghua Ying
Rio Yokota
Tatsuya Yokota
Naoto Yokoya
Ryo Yonetani
Ki Yoon Yoo
Jinsu Yoo
Sunjae Yoon
Jae Shin Yoon
Jihun Yoon
Sung-Hoon Yoon
Ryota Yoshihashi
Yusuke Yoshiyasu
Chenyu You
Haoran You
Haoxuan You
Yang You

Quanzeng You
Tackgeun You
Kaichao You
Shan You
Xinge You
Yurong You
Baosheng Yu
Bei Yu
Haichao Yu
Hao Yu
Chaohui Yu
Fisher Yu
Jin-Gang Yu
Jiyang Yu
Jason J. Yu
Jiashuo Yu
Hong-Xing Yu
Lei Yu
Mulin Yu
Ning Yu
Peilin Yu
Qi Yu
Qian Yu
Rui Yu
Shuzhi Yu
Gang Yu
Tan Yu
Weijiang Yu
Xin Yu
Bingyao Yu
Ye Yu
Hanchao Yu
Yingchen Yu
Tao Yu
Xiaotian Yu
Qing Yu
Houjian Yu
Changqian Yu
Jing Yu
Jun Yu
Shujian Yu
Xiang Yu
Zhaofei Yu
Zhenbo Yu
Yinfeng Yu

Zhuoran Yu
Zitong Yu
Bo Yuan
Jiangbo Yuan
Liangzhe Yuan
Weihao Yuan
Jianbo Yuan
Xiaoyun Yuan
Ye Yuan
Li Yuan
Geng Yuan
Jialin Yuan
Maoxun Yuan
Peng Yuan
Xin Yuan
Yuan Yuan
Yuhui Yuan
Yixuan Yuan
Zheng Yuan
Mehmet Kerim Yücel
Kaiyu Yue
Haixiao Yue
Heeseung Yun
Sangdoo Yun
Tian Yun
Mahmut Yurt
Ekim Yurtsever
Ahmet Yüzügüler
Edouard Yvinec
Eloi Zablocki
Christopher Zach
Muhammad Zaigham
    Zaheer
Pierluigi Zama Ramirez
Yuhang Zang
Pietro Zanuttigh
Alexey Zaytsev
Bernhard Zeisl
Haitian Zeng
Pengpeng Zeng
Jiabei Zeng
Runhao Zeng
Wei Zeng
Yawen Zeng
Yi Zeng

Yiming Zeng

Tieyong Zeng

Huanqiang Zeng

Dan Zeng

Yu Zeng

Wei Zhai

Yuanhao Zhai

Fangneng Zhan

Kun Zhan

Xiong Zhang

Jingdong Zhang

Jiangning Zhang

Zhilu Zhang

Gengwei Zhang

Dongsu Zhang

Hui Zhang

Binjie Zhang

Bo Zhang

Tianhao Zhang

Cecilia Zhang

Jing Zhang

Chaoning Zhang

Chenxu Zhang

Chi Zhang

Chris Zhang

Yabin Zhang

Zhao Zhang

Rufeng Zhang

Chaoyi Zhang

Zheng Zhang

Da Zhang

Yi Zhang

Edward Zhang

Xin Zhang

Feifei Zhang

Feilong Zhang

Yuqi Zhang

GuiXuan Zhang

Hanlin Zhang

Hanwang Zhang

Hanzhen Zhang

Haotian Zhang

He Zhang

Haokui Zhang

Hongyuan Zhang

Hengrui Zhang

Hongming Zhang

Mingfang Zhang

Jianpeng Zhang

Jiaming Zhang

Jichao Zhang

Jie Zhang

Jingfeng Zhang

Jingyi Zhang

Jinnian Zhang

David Junhao Zhang

Junjie Zhang

Junzhe Zhang

Jiawan Zhang

Jingyang Zhang

Kai Zhang

Lei Zhang

Lihua Zhang

Lu Zhang

Miao Zhang

Minjia Zhang

Mingjin Zhang

Qi Zhang

Qian Zhang

Qilong Zhang

Qiming Zhang

Qiang Zhang

Richard Zhang

Ruimao Zhang

Ruisi Zhang

Ruixin Zhang

Runze Zhang

Qilin Zhang

Shan Zhang

Shanshan Zhang

Xi Sheryl Zhang

Song-Hai Zhang

Chongyang Zhang

Kaihao Zhang

Songyang Zhang

Shu Zhang

Siwei Zhang

Shujian Zhang

Tianyun Zhang

Tong Zhang

Tao Zhang

Wenwei Zhang

Wenqiang Zhang

Wen Zhang

Xiaolin Zhang

Xingchen Zhang

Xingxuan Zhang

Xiuming Zhang

Xiaoshuai Zhang

Xuanmeng Zhang

Xuanyang Zhang

Xucong Zhang

Xingxing Zhang

Xikun Zhang

Xiaohan Zhang

Yahui Zhang

Yunhua Zhang

Yan Zhang

Yanghao Zhang

Yifei Zhang

Yifan Zhang

Yi-Fan Zhang

Yihao Zhang

Yingliang Zhang

Youshan Zhang

Yulun Zhang

Yushu Zhang

Yixiao Zhang

Yide Zhang

Zhongwen Zhang

Bowen Zhang

Chen-Lin Zhang

Zehua Zhang

Zekun Zhang

Zeyu Zhang

Xiaowei Zhang

Yifeng Zhang

Cheng Zhang

Hongguang Zhang

Yuexi Zhang

Fa Zhang

Guofeng Zhang

Hao Zhang

Haofeng Zhang

Hongwen Zhang

Hua Zhang
Jiaxin Zhang
Zhenyu Zhang
Jian Zhang
Jianfeng Zhang
Jiao Zhang
Jiakai Zhang
Lefei Zhang
Le Zhang
Mi Zhang
Min Zhang
Ning Zhang
Pan Zhang
Pu Zhang
Qing Zhang
Renrui Zhang
Shifeng Zhang
Shuo Zhang
Shaoxiong Zhang
Weizhong Zhang
Xi Zhang
Xiaomei Zhang
Xinyu Zhang
Yin Zhang
Zicheng Zhang
Zihao Zhang
Ziqi Zhang
Zhaoxiang Zhang
Zhen Zhang
Zhipeng Zhang
Zhixing Zhang
Zhizheng Zhang
Jiawei Zhang
Zhong Zhang
Pingping Zhang
Yixin Zhang
Kui Zhang
Lingzhi Zhang
Huaiwen Zhang
Quanshi Zhang
Zhoutong Zhang
Yuhang Zhang
Yuting Zhang
Zhang Zhang
Ziming Zhang

Zhizhong Zhang
Qilong Zhangli
Bingyin Zhao
Bin Zhao
Chenglong Zhao
Lei Zhao
Feng Zhao
Gangming Zhao
Haiyan Zhao
Hao Zhao
Handong Zhao
Hengshuang Zhao
Yinan Zhao
Jiaojiao Zhao
Jiaqi Zhao
Jing Zhao
Kaili Zhao
Haojie Zhao
Yucheng Zhao
Longjiao Zhao
Long Zhao
Qingsong Zhao
Qingyu Zhao
Rui Zhao
Rui-Wei Zhao
Sicheng Zhao
Shuang Zhao
Siyan Zhao
Zelin Zhao
Shiyu Zhao
Wang Zhao
Tiesong Zhao
Qian Zhao
Wangbo Zhao
Xi-Le Zhao
Xu Zhao
Yajie Zhao
Yang Zhao
Ying Zhao
Yin Zhao
Yizhou Zhao
Yunhan Zhao
Yuyang Zhao
Yue Zhao
Yuzhi Zhao

Bowen Zhao
Pu Zhao
Bingchen Zhao
Borui Zhao
Fuqiang Zhao
Hanbin Zhao
Jian Zhao
Mingyang Zhao
Na Zhao
Rongchang Zhao
Ruiqi Zhao
Shuai Zhao
Wenda Zhao
Wenliang Zhao
Xiangyun Zhao
Yifan Zhao
Yaping Zhao
Zhou Zhao
He Zhao
Jie Zhao
Xibin Zhao
Xiaoqi Zhao
Zhengyu Zhao
Jin Zhe
Chuanxia Zheng
Huan Zheng
Hao Zheng
Jia Zheng
Jian-Qing Zheng
Shuai Zheng
Meng Zheng
Mingkai Zheng
Qian Zheng
Qi Zheng
Wu Zheng
Yinqiang Zheng
Yufeng Zheng
Yutong Zheng
Yalin Zheng
Yu Zheng
Feng Zheng
Zhaoheng Zheng
Haitian Zheng
Kang Zheng
Bolun Zheng

Haiyong Zheng
Mingwu Zheng
Sipeng Zheng
Tu Zheng
Wenzhao Zheng
Xiawu Zheng
Yinglin Zheng
Zhuo Zheng
Zilong Zheng
Kecheng Zheng
Zerong Zheng
Shuaifeng Zhi
Tiancheng Zhi
Jia-Xing Zhong
Yiwu Zhong
Fangwei Zhong
Zhihang Zhong
Yaoyao Zhong
Yiran Zhong
Zhun Zhong
Zichun Zhong
Bo Zhou
Boyao Zhou
Brady Zhou
Mo Zhou
Chunluan Zhou
Dingfu Zhou
Fan Zhou
Jingkai Zhou
Honglu Zhou
Jiaming Zhou
Jiahuan Zhou
Jun Zhou
Kaiyang Zhou
Keyang Zhou
Kuangqi Zhou
Lei Zhou
Lihua Zhou
Man Zhou
Mingyi Zhou
Mingyuan Zhou
Ning Zhou
Peng Zhou
Penghao Zhou
Qianyi Zhou

Shuigeng Zhou
Shangchen Zhou
Huayi Zhou
Zhize Zhou
Sanping Zhou
Qin Zhou
Tao Zhou
Wenbo Zhou
Xiangdong Zhou
Xiao-Yun Zhou
Xiao Zhou
Yang Zhou
Yipin Zhou
Zhenyu Zhou
Hao Zhou
Chu Zhou
Daquan Zhou
Da-Wei Zhou
Hang Zhou
Kang Zhou
Qianyu Zhou
Sheng Zhou
Wenhui Zhou
Xingyi Zhou
Yan-Jie Zhou
Yiyi Zhou
Yu Zhou
Yuan Zhou
Yuqian Zhou
Yuxuan Zhou
Zixiang Zhou
Wengang Zhou
Shuchang Zhou
Tianfei Zhou
Yichao Zhou
Alex Zhu
Chenchen Zhu
Deyao Zhu
Xiatian Zhu
Guibo Zhu
Haidong Zhu
Hao Zhu
Hongzi Zhu
Rui Zhu
Jing Zhu

Jianke Zhu
Junchen Zhu
Lei Zhu
Lingyu Zhu
Luyang Zhu
Menglong Zhu
Peihao Zhu
Hui Zhu
Xiaofeng Zhu
Tyler (Lixuan) Zhu
Wentao Zhu
Xiangyu Zhu
Xinqi Zhu
Xinxin Zhu
Xinliang Zhu
Yangguang Zhu
Yichen Zhu
Yixin Zhu
Yanjun Zhu
Yousong Zhu
Yuhao Zhu
Ye Zhu
Feng Zhu
Zhen Zhu
Fangrui Zhu
Jinjing Zhu
Linchao Zhu
Pengfei Zhu
Sijie Zhu
Xiaobin Zhu
Xiaoguang Zhu
Zezhou Zhu
Zhenyao Zhu
Kai Zhu
Pengkai Zhu
Bingbing Zhuang
Chengyuan Zhuang
Liansheng Zhuang
Peiye Zhuang
Yixin Zhuang
Yihong Zhuang
Junbao Zhuo
Andrea Ziani
Bartosz Zieliński
Primo Zingaretti

Nikolaos Zioulis
Andrew Zisserman
Yael Ziv
Liu Ziyin
Xingxing Zou
Danping Zou
Qi Zou

Shihao Zou
Xueyan Zou
Yang Zou
Yuliang Zou
Zihang Zou
Chuhang Zou
Dongqing Zou

Xu Zou
Zhiming Zou
Maria A. Zuluaga
Xinxin Zuo
Zhiwen Zuo
Reyer Zwiggelaar

Contents – Part XXXV

Efficient One-Stage Video Object Detection by Exploiting Temporal Consistency

Guanxiong Sun[1,2]($\boxtimes$)(iD), Yang Hua[1](iD), Guosheng Hu[2](iD), and Neil Robertson[1](iD)

[1] EEECS/ECIT, Queen's University Belfast, Belfast, UK
{gsun02,y.hua,n.robertson}@qub.ac.uk
[2] Oosto, Belfast, UK

Abstract. Recently, one-stage detectors have achieved competitive accuracy and faster speed compared with traditional two-stage detectors on image data. However, in the field of video object detection (VOD), most existing VOD methods are still based on two-stage detectors. Moreover, directly adapting existing VOD methods to one-stage detectors introduces unaffordable computational costs. In this paper, we first analyse the computational bottlenecks of using one-stage detectors for VOD. Based on the analysis, we present a simple yet efficient framework to address the computational bottlenecks and achieve efficient one-stage VOD by exploiting the temporal consistency in video frames. Specifically, our method consists of a location prior network to filter out background regions and a size prior network to skip unnecessary computations on low-level feature maps for specific frames. We test our method on various modern one-stage detectors and conduct extensive experiments on the ImageNet VID dataset. Excellent experimental results demonstrate the superior effectiveness, efficiency, and compatibility of our method. The code is available at https://github.com/guanxiongsun/EOVOD.

1 Introduction

Recently, in the field of object detection on still image data, great attention has been paid to one-stage detectors [7,17,26,31,38,39], as they have shown many stunning advantages compared to traditional two-stage detectors [3,9,11,27]. For example, one-stage detectors are more efficient, straightforward, and well aligned with other fully convolutional tasks, e.g., semantic segmentation, facilitating these tasks to share ideas and tricks. Given these advantages, many researchers work in different directions to further improve the accuracy of one-stage detectors, such as label assignment [6,37], feature alignment [4,22], loss design [18,20,35], and multilevel feature aggregation [8,19,21]. Until now, compared with two-stage detectors, one-stage detectors can achieve very competitive accuracy with faster run-time speed.

Supplementary Information The online version contains supplementary material available at https://doi.org/10.1007/978-3-031-19833-5_1.

However, the field of video object detection (VOD) has been dominated by two-stage detectors [1,5,30,33,41,42] for many years and very little research has been investigated to transfer the merits of one-stage detectors from still images to videos [34]. This phenomenon contradicts empirical intuitions that one-stage detectors are more suitable for VOD task, which requires faster speed. To investigate the underlying reasons for this phenomenon, we conduct a comprehensive quantitative analysis (detailed in Sect. 3) and share the following facts: (1) The SOTA VOD methods apply attention-based feature aggregation to achieve promising speed-and-accuracy trade-offs; (2) In two-stage SOTA VOD methods, the computational cost is reasonable since the attention module take a small number of proposals as inputs, e.g., 300 proposals; (3) Directly adapting existing VOD methods to one-stage detectors introduces unacceptably high computations, due to the drastically increased number of inputs for attention modules, for example, 13k pixels in FCOS [31]; (4) For one-stage detectors on images or videos, the detection heads on low-level features take 80% computations.

On the basis of the aforementioned analysis, we propose two modules to achieve an efficient one-stage video object detector by fully taking advantage of the temporal consistency of video data. Here, the temporal consistency denotes the fact that objects change gradually in terms of *locations* and *sizes* in a sequence of consecutive frames. Inspired by this, we propose two novel modules, the location prior network (LPN) and the size prior network (SPN). Specifically, first, detected bounding boxes in the previous frame can guide the model to find regions where objects may appear in the current frame. Our LPN utilises this location prior knowledge to filter out background regions and thus reduces the computational cost. Second, objects keep in similar *sizes* within a short time. Another fact is that one-stage detectors divide objects into different levels of feature maps, and each level is responsible for detecting objects in a specific size range. Given the object sizes in the current frame, the proposed SPN enables our method to skip unnecessary computations on unrelated feature levels in several following frames.

In summary, our main contributions are:

- To our best knowledge, we are the first to investigate the obstacles to the development of one-stage VOD and conclude two bottlenecks causing high computations: very high-dimensional input for attention modules and unnecessary computations on low-level feature levels.
- We propose a simple yet effective framework to achieve efficient one-stage object detection. Specifically, a location prior network (LPN) filters out background regions and a size prior network (SPN) to skip computations on unnecessary feature levels. Note that our method can easily be incorporated into various one-stage detectors.
- Extensive experiments are conducted on ImageNet VID datasets with various one-stage detectors, i.e., FCOS [31], CenterNet [38] and YOLOX [7]. The results demonstrate that our method achieves superior speed-accuracy trade-offs and promising compatibility.

2   Related Work

One-Stage Detectors. One-stage detectors can be classified into two categories. Firstly, key point based methods that predict pre-defined key points of objects to generate bounding boxes. For example, CornerNet [17] treats a bounding box as a pair of top-left corner and bottom-right corner and detects objects by grouping predicted corner pairs. ExtremeNet [39] predicts four extreme points (i.e., top-most, left-most, bottom-most, and right-most) and one center point to produce bounding boxes. CenterNet [38] detects the center point of an object bounding box. It predicts heat maps of center points and several regression values (i.e., center offset and size of the bounding box) to generate bounding boxes. In this paper, we use CenterNet as a representative of key point based one-stage detectors.

Another category of one-stage detectors is the center-based method, which regards the center pixels of an object as positives, and then predicts the distances from positives to bounding box boundaries. YOLO series [24–26] are the most well-known center-based one-stage detector. Recently, YOLOX [7] presents many empirical improvements to YOLO series, forming a new high-performance detector. DenseBox [14] utilises a filled circle located in the center of an object and predicts four distances from each location inside the circle to the boundaries of the object bounding box. FCOS [31] regards all locations inside an object as positives and introduces a centerness branch to measure distances between positives to the center point of the object. The centerness branch can effectively reduce false positives in the inference stage. In this paper, we use FCOS and YOLOX as representatives of center-based one-stage detectors.

Video Object Detection (VOD). VOD methods explore using temporal information within a video to improve the performance and the speed of single-frame detectors. Existing VOD methods can be divided into two categories: box-level methods and feature-level methods. Box-level methods try to refine the detection results using temporal associations of predicted bounding boxes. These methods are performed in a post-processing manner. For example, TPN [15] and TCNN [16] use LSTM and tracking to model temporal associations between detected bounding boxes. SeqNMS [10] extends NMS to the time domain and greatly reduces false positives. CHP [34] proposes a heat map propagation method for CenterNet [38], which makes detection results temporally smooth. In contrast, feature-level methods are investigated to improve the accuracy of video object detection by feature enhancement and can be trained end-to-end. FGFA [41], MANET [32] and THP [40] utilise optical flow to propagate and aggregate feature maps. SELSA [33], MEGA [1], LRTR [29] and RDN [5] enhance the instance features (proposals) of the current frame by reasoning the relationships between objects within a video via attention mechanisms.

3   Analysis of the Computational Bottlenecks in Attention-based One-stage VOD

The key reason why recent video object detection (VOD) methods [1,5,29,33] achieve state-of-the-art performance is the utilisation of attention mechanisms.

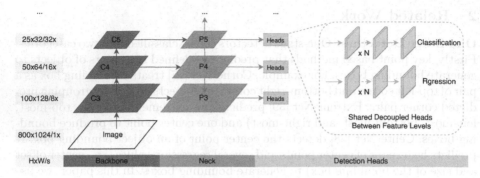

Fig. 1. General architecture of modern one-stage detectors, where H, W, and s are the height, width, and stride (down-sampling ratio) of feature maps, respectively. C3, C4 and C5 denote the output feature maps of the backbone. P3, P4, P5, etc. denote the feature levels in the neck, e.g., FPN. The decoupled detection heads, which usually contain a classification branch and a regression branch, are shared through all feature levels. *Best viewed in colour.* (Color figure online)

However, these methods are based on two-stage detectors. We first apply attention-based VOD methods directly to one-stage detectors and demonstrate the high computational cost in this naive adaptation. Then, we conduct an elaborate analysis to locate the reasons for this high cost.

3.1   Preliminary Knowledge

Before we dive into a detailed analysis, we introduce some preliminary knowledge and define the necessary terms.

General Architecture of Modern One-Stage Detectors. Modern one-stage detectors [7,20,26,31,38] are designed with different modules and settings, but they share a general architecture. The general architecture can be summarised as three parts: backbone, neck, and detection head. Specifically, backbone networks extract feature maps from input images, for example, ResNet-50/101 [12], DarkNet-53 [24], and HGNet [23]. Then, the feature maps $\{C\}$ are forwarded into the neck module, such as FPN [19] and PAN [21], to conduct multi-level feature aggregation. At last, the detection heads are performed on all feature levels $\{P\}$ to generate detections. A detailed general architecture is shown in Fig. 1, where s denotes the stride or down-sampling ratio of a feature level to the input image.

Complexity of the Attention Module. We introduce the complexity of the attention module because it is the key of designing an efficient one-stage VOD method. Given a query set $\mathbf{Q} = \{q_i\} \in \mathbb{R}^{N_q \times C}$ and a key set $\mathbf{K} = \{k_i\} \in \mathbb{R}^{N_k \times C}$, an attention module enhances each query q_i by measuring relation features as the weighted sum of all the keys in K. Here, N and C denote the number and the dimension of query or key elements, respectively. For simplicity, we use one-head attention for demonstration. Specifically, the enhanced feature of q_i is:

$$A(q_i, K) = q_i + \sum_j w_{ij} \cdot (W \cdot k_j), \tag{1}$$

where W denotes a linear transformation matrix, and w_{ij} is an element in the correlation matrix computed based on the similarity of all q-k pairs. Since the number of key elements N_k is usually equal or linearly related to the number of query elements N_q, and the complexity of an attention module is $O(N_q^2 \times C)$, the computational cost of the attention module is very sensitive to N_q.

3.2 Naive Adaptation of Attention-Based One-Stage VOD

In SOTA VOD methods, attention modules are introduced in the second stage of two-stage detectors [3,27], where object proposals are treated as query elements. Specifically, the proposals of the current frame are considered as the query Q and proposals from reference frames are regarded as the key K for the attention module. Then, Q is enhanced with K by attention modules as Eq. (1). Since one-stage detectors generate proposals, a naive adaptation from SOTA methods to one-stage VOD is to conduct attention-based feature aggregation on the feature maps of one-stage detectors. Although the idea is straightforward, problems arise because of the difference between the number of proposals and the number of pixels on feature maps. For example, the number of proposals is quite small, e.g., 300 in FasterRCNN [27], while the number of pixels in one-stage detectors is usually thousands, e.g., ~13K in FCOS [31]. This naive adaption highly increases the computational cost of the attention module.

We design several models to quantitatively demonstrate the increased computational cost problem of the naive adaptation method. Specifically, we use SELSA [33] as the baseline for its simplicity and promising performance. The analysis and conclusions in this subsection are suitable for other attention-based VOD methods because they have similar computation costs to SELSA. Following SELSA, the key set K is generated by randomly sampling n_r reference frames in the current video. The naive adaption is to treat all pixels on the feature maps as the query or key elements. For every time step, Q and K consist of pixels on feature maps of the current frame and the randomly sampled reference frames, respectively.

In the next two subsections, we analyse the experimental results and conclude two bottlenecks for the computational issue.

3.3 Bottleneck 1: Drastically Increased N_q

In Table 1, we show the computational cost of the SELSA baseline and naive adaptions with three one-stage detectors, denoted as $FCOS^A$, $CenterNet^A$, and $YOLOX^A$. Although most SOTA VOD methods use more than 10 reference

Table 1. Comparisons of N_q and computational costs between SELSA and directly applying attention mechanisms on one-stage detectors, FCOS, CenterNet, and YOLOX.

Method	Input Size	Strides $\{s\}$	N_q	GPU Mem	FPS
SELSA	(600, 1000)	{16}	300	1.8 GB	18.5
FCOS[A]	(600, 1000)	{8,16,32,64,128}	12,958	21.9 GB	4.6
CenterNet[A]	(512, 512)	{4}	16,384	31.2 GB	4.3
YoloX[A]	(640, 640)	{8, 16, 32}	8,400	16.7 GB	8.9

frames during inference, we only test with 2 reference frames because we suffer from GPU out-of-memory errors on Tesla V100 (32GB) GPU if more than 2 reference frames are used for naive one-stage adaption models. For example, in SELSA [33], $N_q = 300$ is the number of proposals of the current frame. Differently, in the naive one-stage adaption model, N_q is related to the size of the input image. For FCOS[A], we follow the protocols in SOTA VOD methods [1,5,33] to resize the input image to a shorter side being 600 and a longer side less or equal to 1000, and thus N_q is ~13K. For CenterNet[A] [38] and YOLOX[A] [7], following the original papers, the input images are resized to 512 × 512 and 640 × 640, and thus N_q are ~16.4K and 8.4K, respectively. Compared with SELSA, N_q of naive adaption models drastically increases nearly 50 times. As analysed in Sect. 3.1, the computational complexity of attention modules is quadratic to N_q. As a result, the GPU memory usage and the run-time speed of attention-based one-stage detectors are much larger and slower than SELSA, which makes them impossible to work in real-world applications.

To overcome this problem, one straightforward solution is to reduce the N_q for one-stage detectors. In two-stage detectors, RPN predicts proposals around the object regions to remove the background regions and thus produce a small number of proposals. However, RPN is removed in one-stage detectors, leading to a heavy computational cost. Here, we ask a question: can we utilise temporal information in videos to filter out background regions in a frame and reduce N_q? This question leads us to design the location prior network which uses the detection results of the previous frame to find possible foreground regions on the current frame.

3.4   Bottleneck 2: Detection Heads on Low Feature Levels

To further boost the speed and perform an efficient one-stage video object detector, we dissect the run time consumption in each part of the one-stage detector. We use FCOS as a representative for the demonstration. As shown in Table 2, the backbone and the neck module can run relatively fast. Nearly 80% of the running time is spent on the detection head. Then, we dissect the runtime consumption in the detection head according to feature levels. Specifically, around 65% of the running time is spent on the first feature level in the detection heads.

Table 2. Runtime dissection of a one-stage detector.

Part		Specification	Runtime (ms)	Ratio%
Backbone		R-50	7.7	18.0
Neck		FPN	0.5	1.2
Head	Level 1	$s = 8$	27.7	64.9
	Level 2	$s = 16$	3.9	9.1
	Level 3	$s = 32$	1.4	3.3
	Level 4	$s = 64$	0.8	1.9
	Level 5	$s = 128$	0.7	1.6
All		–	42.7	100.0

The reason for this computational bottleneck is that the feature maps in low levels have very high resolutions. Therefore, the decoding process, i.e., generating detections for every location, is very time-consuming. The high-resolution feature maps are demonstrated to be useful for detecting small objects [19,21,31] and they inevitably consume huge computational costs.

However, it is possible to reduce the computational bottleneck on low-level feature maps by utilising the size prior knowledge of videos. Specifically, since the size of objects in consecutive frames changes gradually, we can skip the detection head on low-level feature maps for several frames if there is not any small object in the previous frame. Inspired by this observation, we design the size prior network and achieve a very fast one-stage VOD.

4   Methodology

We introduce two modules, the location prior network (LPN) and the size prior network (SPN), to address the two computational bottlenecks, respectively. In this section, we illustrate the details in the LPN and SPN and FCOS [31] as a representative one-stage detector for demonstration.

4.1   Location Prior Network

As analysed in Sect. 3.3, reducing N_q is the key of performing an efficient one-stage video object detection with attention-based multi-frame aggregation. We propose a location prior network (LPN) to select foreground regions in the current frame to conduct partial feature aggregation. The LPN has two steps: First, the foreground region selection guided by the detected bounding boxes from the previous frame; Second, the partial feature aggregation to enhance the selected foreground pixels using attention modules.

We follow the open-source implementation[1] of SELSA [33] and use 14 random selected reference frames. The comparisons between conducting feature aggregation with and without LPN are shown in Fig. 2.

---
[1] https://github.com/open-mmlab/mmtracking

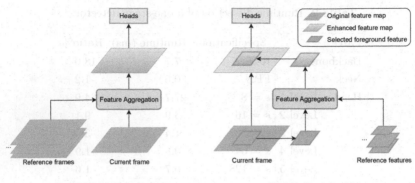

Fig. 2. (a) shows the process of directly conducting attention-based feature aggregation, where the purple rounded rectangle denotes the attention module. In (a), the input of the attention module is all pixels on the current frame and reference frames. (b) shows the pipeline of using location prior network for feature aggregation, where the red bounding box denotes the propagated bounding boxes from the previous frame. In (b), the input of the attention is foreground pixels on the current frame and the reference frames. *Best viewed in colour.* (Color figure online)

Foreground Region Selection. Given detected bounding boxes of the previous frame, pixels within validated bounding boxes $\{D^v\}$ are regarded as foreground pixels for partial feature aggregation. Here, validated bounding boxes $\{D^v\}$ denote the detected boxes whose classification scores are greater than 0.5. If there is not a validated bounding box, the partial feature aggregation is skipped. Specifically, we project boxes in $\{D^v\}$ to each feature level by dividing the stride s of the level, e.g., 4 and 8. Then, we generate a binary mask $M \in \mathbb{R}^{1 \times H \times W}$ of foreground regions for every level. The value of the mask at a location (x, y) is assigned as 1, if (x, y) falls into any validated bounding boxes. Otherwise, it is set to 0. In addition, before generating M, boxes in $\{D^v\}$ are resized with an adjustment ratio r to control the computational overhead.

Partial Feature Aggregation. Given the binary mask M, the pixel of location (x, y) is regarded as a foreground pixel if $M(x, y) = 1$. Then, foreground pixels are enhanced with features from reference frames $\mathbf{F}^r$ via attention modules. At last, the enhanced pixels are used to replace the pixels of the feature maps F in the same location. Specifically, the enhanced feature maps $\hat{F}$ are computed as follows:

$$\hat{F}(x,y) = \begin{cases} \mathbf{A}[F(x,y), \mathbf{F}^r] & \text{if } M(x,y) = 1, \\ F(x,y) & \text{else,} \end{cases} \qquad (2)$$

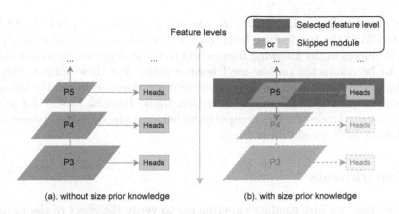

Fig. 3. (a) shows a normal detection process on multi-level feature maps where all levels of feature maps are passed to detection heads. (b) shows the detection process guided by the size prior network. The pink box denotes the feature level which the bounding boxes of the previous frame are generated from. In the current frame, computations on feature levels not in the pink box are skipped, denoted with the transparent boxes and dotted lines. *Best viewed in colour.* (Color figure online)

where $\mathbf{A}(\cdot, \cdot)$ is defined as in Eq. (1) and (x, y) enumerates all locations on the feature maps. Finally, the new feature maps of the current frame are used for detection heads to predict bounding boxes.

Training and Inference. At the training stage, we adopt the strategy of temporal dropout used in [41] to randomly select two support frames within the same video of the current frame I_t. Then the ground truth boxes are used to generate the foreground mask and select query and key pixels. The whole network is optimised with the detection losses computed on the current frame in an end-to-end manner. During the inference stage, at a time step, the foreground mask of the current frame I_t is propagated from the detection results of the previous frame I_{t-1}. The key set consists of the pixels within detected bounding boxes on the reference frames.

4.2 Size Prior Network

The second computational bottleneck for efficient one-stage detection is due to the computations on low-level feature maps. We introduce the size prior network (SPN) to skip computations on low-level feature maps in unnecessary frames. Specifically, after the detection process of a frame at time step t, SPN selects validated bounding boxes $\{D_t^v\}$. Here, the validated boxes are obtained in the same way as mentioned in our LPN Sect. 4.1 (classification score > 0.5). For the next T time steps, the detection heads are conducted only on the feature levels that boxes in $\{D_t^v\}$ are generated from.

For example, in a video frame I_t, the validated bounding boxes $\{D_t^v\}$ are generated from the top feature level, e.g., P5, which indicates there might not be small objects in the following frames and thus the detection process is unnecessary to be conducted on low-level feature maps. For these frames, skipping the huge computations on low-level feature maps does not affect the detection accuracy. In practice, we set the detection frame interval $T = 7$ for a good speed-accuracy trade-off. The comparisons between the detection process with and without SPN are shown in Fig. 3.

5   Experiments

In this section, we first conduct experiments to verify the effect of the proposed location prior network (LPN) and size prior network (SPN). We use three modern one-stage detectors as the base detector, i.e., FCOS [31], CenterNet [38], and YOLOX [7], which also demonstrate the good compatibility of our method. At last, we compare our method with SOTA video object detection methods.

5.1   Experimental Setting

Dataset. We evaluate our method on the ImageNet VID [28] dataset which contains 3,862 training and 555 validation videos. We follow previous approaches [1,33,41,42] and train our model on the overlapped 30 classes of ImageNet VID and DET set. Specifically, we sample 15 frames from each video in VID dataset and at most 2,000 images per class from DET dataset as our training set.

Backbone and Detection Architecture. For the backbone models, we use ResNet-101 [12] in FCOS and CenterNet, and DarkNet-53 [7] in YOLOX. For the neck architectures, FPN [19] and PAN [21] are used for FCOS and YOLOX, respectively. For CenterNet, following the same structure as in the original paper, the neck is built with 3 de-convolutional layers with 256, 128, and 64 channels, respectively. One 3×3 deformable convolutional layer is added before each deconvolution with channels 256, 128, and 64, respectively. In FCOS and YOLOX, shared detection heads are performed on all levels of feature maps to generate the detections. Specifically, there are two separate branches inside the detection head. Each branch contains four 3×3 convolution layers with 256 channels and one 3×3 convolution layer for predicting regression and classification result maps. In CenterNet, the detection head is built with a 3×3 convolutional layer with 64 channels followed by a 1×1 convolution with corresponding channels (e.g., number of classes) to generate detection outputs.

Training and Inference Details. We train all models on 4 T V100 GPUs. For FCOS, images are resized to a shorter side of 600 pixels and the longer side less than or equal to 1000 pixels. With batch size equal to 4, we train the network for 3 epochs using the SGD optimizer (momentum: 0.9, weight decay: 0.0001).

Table 3. Effect of the LPN on different one-stage detectors.

Method	LPN	AP	AP50	AP75	APs	APm	APl	FPS
FCOS [31]		49.8	73.3	54.6	10.1	22.4	56.1	25.1
FCOS [31]	✓	54.1	79.8	59.5	10.5	28.3	60.1	20.4
CenterNet [38]		49.3	73.4	55.4	10.2	16.3	56.5	40.9
CenterNet [38]	✓	53.4	79.8	58.5	10.3	21.9	59.5	35.5
YoloX-M [7]		49.4	69.4	55.4	11.1	25.0	55.4	39.7
YoloX-M [7]	✓	53.3	75.1	58.1	11.6	30.2	58.9	35.8

The learning rate is 10^{-3} for the first 2 epochs and 10^{-4} for the last epoch. For CenterNet, we follow [34] to resize the input images to 512 × 512. Random flip and random scaling from 0.6 to 1.4 are used as data augmentation and SGD is used as the optimizer. We train the network with a batch size of 32 and a learning rate of 10^{-4} for 50 epochs followed by a learning rate of 10^{-5} for 30 epochs. For YOLOX, we follow [7] to resize the input images to 640 × 640 and use additional data augmentations, including MixUp [36], Mosaic, RadomCrop, etc. We train the network with batch size 32 using the SGD optimizer. The initial learning rate is set to 10^{-3} with a cosine learning rate schedule for 80 epochs. In the inference phase, we resize the input image in the same way as in the training phase and reserve the top 100 confident detections per frame.

5.2 Effect of the Location Prior Network (LPN)

We first adapt LPN to three modern one-stage detectors to verify its effectiveness. Then, we conduct experiments using different bounding box adjustment ratios r in LPN to find an optimal speed-accuracy trade-off.

LPN on Various One-Stage Detectors. To study how the proposed location prior network (LPN) influences the overall performance, we integrate LPN on three one-stage detectors and show the results in Table 3. LPN can improve the performance of all three detectors. Specifically, single-frame FCOS achieves 49.8% of AP. By utilising LPN to conduct multi-frame feature aggregation, the performance of FCOS+LPN is significantly improved by 4.3% to 54.1% of AP. Similarly, we can observe improvements in experiments of using LPN on more lightweight detectors, i.e., CenterNet and YOLOX-M. CenterNet+LPN and YOLOX-M+LPN boost their baseline performance from 49.3/49.4% of AP to 53.4/53.0% of AP, respectively. These experimental results demonstrate the effectiveness and compatibility of the LPN.

Effect of the Box Adjustment Ratios r. We show the experimental results on FCOS to study the effect of employing different bounding box adjustment ratios r. A smaller r results in fewer selected foreground pixels to be enhanced and thus leads to a faster speed. In contrast, a larger r selects more pixels to

Table 4. Effect of the bounding box adjustment ratios r in LPN.

r	AP	AP50	AP75	APs	APm	APl	FPS
0.5	53.6	78.5	57.9	9.6	27.0	58.5	21.4
0.8	54.1	79.8	59.5	10.5	28.3	60.1	20.4
1.0	54.2	80.0	59.7	10.5	28.5	60.2	19.1
1.2	54.2	80.0	59.8	10.6	28.4	60.2	17.5
1.5	54.2	79.9	59.9	10.9	28.4	60.2	14.7

Table 5. Effect of the SPN on different one-stage detectors.

Method	LPN	SPN	AP	AP50	AP75	APs	APm	APl	FPS
FCOS	✓		54.1	79.8	59.5	10.5	28.3	60.1	20.4
FCOS	✓	✓	53.8	76.9	58.9	9.8	27.3	59.5	26.9
YoloX-S	✓		53.3	75.1	58.1	11.6	30.2	58.9	35.8
YoloX-S	✓	✓	52.7	74.5	56.7	11.2	28.9	57.7	50.5

be enhanced but causes a slower speed. In our experiments, we vary r from 0.5 to 1.5. Our LPN achieves the optimal speed-accuracy trade-off when $r = 0.8$, i.e., 54.1% AP and 20.4 FPS. Once the adjustment ratio is larger than 0.8, the performance is less affected by the change in the adjustment ratios, but the run time keeps increasing. In our experiments, we set r as 0.8 by default.

5.3   Effect of the Size Prior Network (SPN)

Similar to the experimental design in Sect. 5.2, we conduct experiments by adding the size prior network (SPN) to two modern one-stage detectors to verify its effectiveness and compatibility. We use FCOS [31] and YOLOX [7] as representatives because they work with multi-level feature maps. Then, we conduct experiments using different frame intervals in SPN to find an optimal setting.

SPN on Various One-Stage Detectors. The location prior network (LPN) is designed to improve the accuracy of one-stage video object detection by conducting efficient multi-frame feature aggregation. While the size prior network (SPN) mainly focuses on improving the run-time speed by skipping the unnecessary computations in specific feature levels. Specifically, by introducing SPN, the run-time speed of FCOS+LPN and YOLOX+LPN are improved from 20.4/35.8 FPS to 26.9/50.5 FPS, respectively. At the same time, the accuracy is still at a comparable level with 53.8/52.7% of AP. As illustrated in Sect. 3.4, most computations of one-stage detectors happen on feature maps of low levels. Therefore, the run time saved by using SPN is mainly because of the computations saved in video frames where no small objects appear. To further understand the speed improvement, we list the portion of skipped frames and the portion of frames according to different object sizes in the supplementary material.

Table 6. Effect of temporal frame interval T in SPN.

T	AP	AP50	AP75	APs	APm	APl	FPS
0	54.1	79.8	59.5	10.5	28.3	60.1	20.4
7	53.8	76.9	58.9	9.8	27.3	59.5	26.9
14	53.0	75.4	56.6	9.6	26.9	58.7	28.4
21	51.9	73.8	55.7	9.2	25.4	56.9	29.0
28	48.5	73.3	54.0	8.9	24.6	55.4	29.5

Effect of the Temporal Frame Interval T. To explore the effect of temporal frame interval T in SPN, we show the performance of introducing SPN on FCOS+LPN under various T settings from 0 to 28 in Table 6. During inference, we first conduct a full detection on all feature levels of the current frame and then we use SPN to skip computations on some feature levels for T following frames. In the extreme case of $T = 0$, full detections are conducted on all frames. With $T = 7$, full detections happen in every 8 frames and partial detections happen in the 7 interval frames. In this setting, the run-time speed is significantly improved from 25.1 FPS to 40 FPS with the performance slightly decreased by 0.2% to 53.9% AP. By increasing the temporal interval T to larger numbers, the run-time speed continuously increases, however, the performance also degrades at the same time. In practice, we set the temporal interval $T = 7$ to obtain a good speed-accuracy trade-off.

5.4   Comparisons with SOTA Methods

We compare our method with SOTA VOD methods, and the results are shown in Table 7. As most SOTA methods are neither report with the run-time speed nor test on the same device, we re-implement recent SOTA methods and test them on our device for fair comparisons. The methods with * denote our re-implementation versions. In addition, most SOTA methods are based on the two-stage detector, FasterRCNN, while we propose an efficient one-stage VOD method.

All results are reported with the same backbone R-101 except the YOLOX whose backbone is DarkNet-53. Overall, our method achieves a better speed-accuracy trade-off. In particular, our method with FCOS achieves 54.1% of AP at 20.4 FPS, which makes 0.7% accuracy improvement and nearly 3× speed improvement over the best competitor RDN. As expected, our method can achieve very good efficiency. Compared with the only existing one-stage VOD method, CHP, our method with CenterNet makes a 3.1% improvement of AP50. Considering the run-time speed, we adapt LPN and SPN on the YOLOX-M detector. Our method, YOLOX-M+LPN+SPN, runs very fast at 50.5 FPS on V100 GPU, much faster than other existing VOD methods. Moreover, the YOLOX-M+LPN+SPN model achieves good performance with 52.7% of AP, which is comparable to the SOTA method SELSA in our implementation. These

Table 7. Comparisons with SOTA video object detection methods.

Method	Base Detector	AP	AP50	AP75	APs	APm	APl	FPS	Device
RDN [5]	FasterRCNN	–	81.8	–	–	–	–	10.6	V100
SELSA [33]	FasterRCNN	–	80.3	–	–	–	–	–	–
LRTR [29]	FasterRCNN	–	81.0	–	–	–	–	10	Titan Xp
MEGA [1]	FasterRCNN	–	82.9	–	–	–	–	8.7	2080ti
TFB [2]	FasterRCNN	–	83.8	–	–	–	–	4.9	2080ti
MAMBA [30]	FasterRCNN	–	**84.6**	–	–	–	–	9.1	Titan RTX
TransVOD [13]	Deform. DETR	–	81.9	–	–	–	–	–	–
CHP [34]	CenterNet	–	76.7	–	–	–	–	37	–
FasterRCNN* [27]	–	49.7	75.6	55.9	7.4	23.7	56.0	22.5	V100
FCOS* [31]	–	49.8	73.3	54.6	10.1	22.4	56.1	25.1	V100
CenterNet* [38]	–	49.3	73.4	55.4	10.2	16.3	56.5	40.9	V100
YoloX-M* [7]	–	49.4	69.4	55.4	11.1	25.0	55.4	39.7	V100
RDN* [5]	FasterRCNN	53.4	81.2	**60.1**	8.5	27.4	59.6	7.1	V100
SELSA* [33]	FasterRCNN	52.6	81.6	57.9	9.3	28.6	58.4	6.4	V100
MEGA* [1]	FasterRCNN	53.2	82.4	59.2	9.1	29.4	59.1	5.3	V100
Ours(+LPN)	FCOS	**54.1**	79.8	59.5	10.5	28.3	**60.1**	20.4	V100
Ours(+LPN)	CenterNet	53.4	79.8	58.5	10.3	21.9	59.5	35.5	V100
Ours(+LPN)	YOLOX-M	53.3	75.1	58.1	**11.6**	**30.2**	58.9	35.8	V100
Ours(+LPN+SPN)	YOLOX-M	52.7	74.5	56.7	11.2	28.9	57.7	**50.5**	V100

results highlight the advantages of our method in terms of accuracy and speed. It is worth noting that, in our implementation, the two-stage FasterRCNN and the one-stage FCOS, CenterNet, and YOLOX achieve 49.7/49.8/49.3/49.4% of AP, respectively. The comparable performance of these base detectors demonstrates that the superior performance of our method is solely gained from the modules we proposed instead of the replacement of base detectors.

6 Conclusion

By comprehensive analysis, we indicate the computational cost is the underlying obstacle to achieving efficient one-stage video object detection. To address the computational bottlenecks, we propose a simple yet effective framework that can be incorporated into various one-stage detectors. Specifically, our method consists of two novel modules: (1) The location prior network that selects the foreground regions of the current frame using the detection results of the previous frame; (2) The size prior network to skip unnecessary computations on the low-level feature maps when there is not any small object appears. Extensive experiments are conducted, and excellent experimental results demonstrate the superior effectiveness, efficiency, and compatibility of our method.

References

1. Chen, Y., Cao, Y., Hu, H., Wang, L.: Memory enhanced global-local aggregation for video object detection. In: CVPR (2020)
2. Cui, Y., Yan, L., Cao, Z., Liu, D.: TF-blender: temporal feature blender for video object detection. In: ICCV (2021)
3. Dai, J., Li, Y., He, K., Sun, J.: R-FCN: object detection via region-based fully convolutional networks. In: NeurIPS (2016)
4. Dai, X., et al.: Dynamic head: unifying object detection heads with attentions. In: CVPR (2021)
5. Deng, J., Pan, Y., Yao, T., Zhou, W., Li, H., Mei, T.: Relation distillation networks for video object detection. In: ICCV (2019)
6. Ge, Z., Liu, S., Li, Z., Yoshie, O., Sun, J.: Ota: optimal transport assignment for object detection. In: CVPR (2021)
7. Ge, Z., Liu, S., Wang, F., Li, Z., Sun, J.: Yolox: exceeding yolo series in 2021. arXiv preprint arXiv:2107.08430 (2021)
8. Ghiasi, G., Lin, T.Y., Le, Q.V.: NAS-FPN: learning scalable feature pyramid architecture for object detection. In: CVPR (2019)
9. Girshick, R.: Fast R-CNN. In: ICCV (2015)
10. Han, W., et al.: SEQ-NMS for video object detection. arXiv preprint arXiv:1602.08465 (2016)
11. He, K., Gkioxari, G., Dollár, P., Girshick, R.: Mask R-CNN. In: ICCV (2017)
12. He, K., Zhang, X., Ren, S., Sun, J.: Deep residual learning for image recognition. In: CVPR (2016)
13. He, L., et al.: End-to-end video object detection with spatial-temporal transformers. In: ACMMM (2021)
14. Huang, L., Yang, Y., Deng, Y., Yu, Y.: Densebox: unifying landmark localization with end to end object detection. arXiv preprint arXiv:1509.04874 (2015)
15. Kang, K., et al.: Object detection in videos with tubelet proposal networks. In: CVPR (2017)
16. Kang, K., et al.: T-CNN: Tubelets with convolutional neural networks for object detection from videos. IEEE Trans. Circuits Syst. Video Technol. **28**(10), 2896–2907 (2017)
17. Law, H., Deng, J.: CornerNet: detecting objects as paired keypoints. In: Ferrari, V., Hebert, M., Sminchisescu, C., Weiss, Y. (eds.) Computer Vision – ECCV 2018. LNCS, vol. 11218, pp. 765–781. Springer, Cham (2018). https://doi.org/10.1007/978-3-030-01264-9_45
18. Li, X., et al.: Generalized focal loss: learning qualified and distributed bounding boxes for dense object detection. In: NeurIPS (2020)
19. Lin, T.Y., Dollár, P., Girshick, R., He, K., Hariharan, B., Belongie, S.: Feature pyramid networks for object detection. In: CVPR (2017)
20. Lin, T.Y., Goyal, P., Girshick, R., He, K., Dollár, P.: Focal loss for dense object detection. In: ICCV (2017)
21. Liu, S., Qi, L., Qin, H., Shi, J., Jia, J.: Path aggregation network for instance segmentation. In: CVPR (2018)
22. Lu, X., Li, Q., Li, B., Yan, J.: MimicDet: bridging the gap between one-stage and two-stage object detection. In: Vedaldi, A., Bischof, H., Brox, T., Frahm, J.-M. (eds.) ECCV 2020. LNCS, vol. 12359, pp. 541–557. Springer, Cham (2020). https://doi.org/10.1007/978-3-030-58568-6_32

23. Newell, A., Yang, K., Deng, J.: Stacked hourglass networks for human pose estimation. In: Leibe, B., Matas, J., Sebe, N., Welling, M. (eds.) ECCV 2016. LNCS, vol. 9912, pp. 483–499. Springer, Cham (2016). https://doi.org/10.1007/978-3-319-46484-8_29

24. Redmon, J., Divvala, S., Girshick, R., Farhadi, A.: You only look once: Unified, real-time object detection. In: CVPR (2016)

25. Redmon, J., Farhadi, A.: Yolo9000: better, faster, stronger. In: CVPR (2017)

26. Redmon, J., Farhadi, A.: Yolov3: an incremental improvement. arXiv preprint arXiv:1804.02767 (2018)

27. Ren, S., He, K., Girshick, R., Sun, J.: Faster R-CNN: towards real-time object detection with region proposal networks. In: NeurIPS (2015)

28. Russakovsky, O., et al.: Imagenet large scale visual recognition challenge. IJCV **115**(3), 211–252 (2015)

29. Shvets, M., Liu, W., Berg, A.C.: Leveraging long-range temporal relationships between proposals for video object detection. In: ICCV (2019)

30. Sun, G., Hua, Y., Hu, G., Robertson, N.: Mamba: multi-level aggregation via memory bank for video object detection. In: AAAI (2021)

31. Tian, Z., Shen, C., Chen, H., He, T.: FCOS: fully convolutional one-stage object detection. arXiv preprint arXiv:1904.01355 (2019)

32. Wang, S., Zhou, Y., Yan, J., Deng, Z.: Fully motion-aware network for video object detection. In: Ferrari, V., Hebert, M., Sminchisescu, C., Weiss, Y. (eds.) ECCV 2018. LNCS, vol. 11217, pp. 557–573. Springer, Cham (2018). https://doi.org/10.1007/978-3-030-01261-8_33

33. Wu, H., Chen, Y., Wang, N., Zhang, Z.: Sequence level semantics aggregation for video object detection. In: ICCV (2019)

34. Xu, Z., Hrustic, E., Vivet, D.: CenterNet heatmap propagation for real-time video object detection. In: Vedaldi, A., Bischof, H., Brox, T., Frahm, J.-M. (eds.) ECCV 2020. LNCS, vol. 12370, pp. 220–234. Springer, Cham (2020). https://doi.org/10.1007/978-3-030-58595-2_14

35. Zhang, H., Wang, Y., Dayoub, F., Sunderhauf, N.: Varifocalnet: an IOU-aware dense object detector. In: CVPR (2021)

36. Zhang, H., Cisse, M., Dauphin, Y.N., Lopez-Paz, D.: Mixup: beyond empirical risk minimization. In: ICLR (2018)

37. Zhang, S., Chi, C., Yao, Y., Lei, Z., Li, S.Z.: Bridging the gap between anchor-based and anchor-free detection via adaptive training sample selection. In: CVPR (2020)

38. Zhou, X., Wang, D., Krähenbühl, P.: Objects as points. arXiv preprint arXiv:1904.07850 (2019)

39. Zhou, X., Zhuo, J., Krähenbühl, P.: Bottom-up object detection by grouping extreme and center points. In: CVPR (2019)

40. Zhu, X., Dai, J., Zhu, X., Wei, Y., Yuan, L.: Towards high performance video object detection for mobiles. arXiv preprint arXiv:1804.05830 (2018)

41. Zhu, X., Wang, Y., Dai, J., Yuan, L., Wei, Y.: Flow-guided feature aggregation for video object detection. In: ICCV (2017)

42. Zhu, X., Xiong, Y., Dai, J., Yuan, L., Wei, Y.: Deep feature flow for video recognition. In: CVPR (2017)

Leveraging Action Affinity
and Continuity for Semi-supervised
Temporal Action Segmentation

Guodong Ding⑩ and Angela Yao$^{(\boxtimes)}$⑩

National University of Singapore, Singapore, Singapore
{dinggd,ayao}@comp.nus.edu.sg

Abstract. We present a semi-supervised learning approach to the temporal action segmentation task. The goal of the task is to temporally detect and segment actions in long, untrimmed procedural videos, where only a small set of videos are densely labelled, and a large collection of videos are unlabelled. To this end, we propose two novel loss functions for the unlabelled data: an action affinity loss and an action continuity loss. The action affinity loss guides the unlabelled samples learning by imposing the action priors induced from the labelled set. Action continuity loss enforces the temporal continuity of actions, which also provides frame-wise classification supervision. In addition, we propose an Adaptive Boundary Smoothing (ABS) approach to build coarser action boundaries for more robust and reliable learning. The proposed loss functions and ABS were evaluated on three benchmarks. Results show that they significantly improved action segmentation performance with a low amount (5% and 10%) of labelled data and achieved comparable results to full supervision with 50% labelled data. Furthermore, ABS succeeded in boosting performance when integrated into fully-supervised learning.

1 Introduction

Temporal action segmentation aims to segment long, untrimmed procedural video sequences into multiple actions and assign semantic labels for each frame. This task requires the arduous collection of frame-wise labelling for minutes-long videos. Previous works have reduced the annotation effort via weaker supervision in the form of transcripts [15], action sets [10], and timestamp labels [21]. With each method, annotators are still required to watch or scrub through each video in the training set to provide labels for *every* training video. Different from the previous methods, we work under a semi-supervised setting where frame-wise annotations are provided for only a small portion (5% and 10%) of the videos in the training set, while the remaining videos are unlabelled. This setting greatly reduces the annotation efforts.

Semi-supervised learning has been studied extensively in image-based vision tasks such as image classification [23], object detection [33], semantic segmentation [11], *etc.* Two popular semi-supervised learning techniques are consistency regularization [25,31] and pseudo-labelling [18]. Consistency regularization

© The Author(s), under exclusive license to Springer Nature Switzerland AG 2022
S. Avidan et al. (Eds.): ECCV 2022, LNCS 13695, pp. 17–32, 2022.
https://doi.org/10.1007/978-3-031-19833-5_2

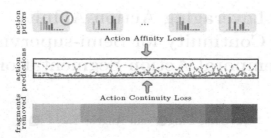

Fig. 1. Overview of our two complementary loss functions. The Action Affinity loss imposes the best matched (denoted by a check mark) prior of action compositions and distributions from the labelled data. The Action Continuity Loss removes the fragments of action labels.

assumes that realistic augmentations on the input data will not change the output distribution. Psuedo-labelling generates labels for unlabelled data before training. These techniques are not suitable for video-based tasks for several reasons. Firstly, it is non-trivial to perform realistic data augmentation operations required by consistency regularization methods as the prevailing practice in temporal action segmentation is to use pre-computed feature vectors as input. Furthermore, directly extending naïve pseudo-labelling on videos may result in confirmation bias [1], *i.e.*, overfitting to incorrect pseudo-labels.

Constructing conceivable supervision for unlabelled data in temporal action segmentation task raises questions such as *"What action compositions are likely to occur?"*, *"What is a reasonable temporal proportion for each action to take?"* and *"What kind of constraints should the action labels follow?"* We propose to tackle these questions by leveraging two unique observations we made on procedural videos: 1) **Action Affinity**, procedural videos performing a specific activity (*e.g.*, 'making_coffee') comprise correlated action units (*e.g.*, 'take_cup', 'pour_coffee', 'pour_milk', and 'stir_coffee') and there exist pairs of videos that have resembling temporal portions for action unit pairs; 2) **Action Continuity**, action labels stay locally constant and action labels only transit at true boundaries. The former is an observation on relations between video instances, while the latter is a video-wise trait. In this work, we propose two novel unsupervised loss functions, action affinity loss and action continuity loss, each leveraging one of these observations. An overview of our losses is depicted in Fig. 1.

As opposed to previous work [21], which uses sparse per-segment labelled frames for *every* video, we use datasets that consist of a small set of densely labelled videos and a large set of unlabelled videos. Dense labels do more than just provide frame-level action labels in the video. They can also be used to establish prior information about the action compositions and distributions. We thus define for a labelled video a high-level representation – its action frequency, *i.e.*, the temporal proportion of actions. For unlabelled video without action information, we adopt a soft version based on the network predictions. Action frequency naturally indicates the relative action lengths as it is normalised by video lengths. The fact that it does not constrain the action ordering allows for flexibility as some actions do not necessarily follow a rigid sequence. Considering the action frequency of labelled videos as action priors, we exploit the action affinities between labelled and unlabelled video samples in a heuristic way and integrate them in the action affinity loss function for model training.

Fragmentation or over-segmentation is a common problem in action segmentation [13], which is exacerbated in a semi-supervised setting when networks train and overfit on few labelled samples. To mitigate this, we first propose an action sequence extraction scheme that better captures the underlying action ordering. These sequentially sub-sampled actions are later compared against the original network predictions with dynamic time warping [24] to estimate our action continuity loss. We show that the action continuity loss can take the same form as the classification cross-entropy loss with a proper distance function adopted in dynamic time warping. Although our loss function also aims to maintain the temporal continuity of actions, it differs from the commonly used agnostic smoothing loss of [8]. Ours enforces a specific action ordering while providing frame-wise action supervision.

To add robustness to the action boundaries found by dynamic time warping for the unlabelled videos, we propose a soft transitional boundary. Specifically, we smooth the rigid boundaries so that frames around the boundaries have a mixed probability of belonging to both consecutive action classes. This was previously explored in a weakly-supervised setting [6], albeit in a highly rigid form. In our work, we vary the number of boundary frames depending on the action duration and use a sigmoid function for mixing.

In summary, this paper offers four key contributions:

1. By investigating the correlation of actions between labelled and unlabelled procedural videos, we propose an action affinity loss to integrate action priors for semi-supervised learning.
2. Building on the continuity property of procedural actions, we propose an action continuity loss to enforce action ordering constraints and provide classification supervision for unlabelled data.
3. For more robust and reliable learning, we propose a general adaptive boundary smoothing (ABS) technique that generates smoothed coarse action probabilities for boundary frames. Our ABS improves segmentation performance in both semi- and fully-supervised settings.
4. Experimental results show that our proposed approach improves the segmentation performance by a large margin with a small amount of labelled data (5% and 10%) and achieve comparable performance to the fully-supervised setting with 50% of labelled data.

2   Related Work

2.1   Temporal Action Segmentation

Temporal action segmentation in videos has been explored with various levels of supervision. **Fully-supervised** approaches require the long videos in the training set to be densely annotated. The input and label pairs are fed into a Temporal Convolution Network (TCN) to learn a mapping to frame-wise action labels [8,17,19,28]. **Weakly-supervised** methods use action lists [15] or action sets [22] to learn the alignment between actions and frames. Specifically, D3TW [2] proposed a differentiable dynamic time warping loss with continuous relaxation to discriminatively learn the best alignment when multiple action lists were provided. Compared to their work, we do not use any action list supervision, and we utilise DTW as an optimisation tool for making the best assignment that meets the ordering constraints. A more recent weakly-supervised work [21] learns to segment actions via a small percentage of action timestamps. Although weak supervision reduces the effort in frame-wise action labelling, it is still necessary to provide supervision for *every* video. **Unsupervised** approaches address action segmentation by combining clustering methods with temporal models (*e.g.*, Hidden Markov Model) [16,20,27]. While some work simply perform clustering on the input features which do not involve any learning and achieve very competitive results [7,26]. Since no semantic labels are provided during learning, performances are evaluated based on the best Hungarian matching scores. One recent work ICC [29] proposed a contrastive learning approach for unsupervised learning of frame-wise features. The learned representations are then adapted to a semi-supervised setting by learning a post-hoc linear classifier. The classifier incorporates the unlabelled data with naïve pseudo-labels, which weakens the overall contribution to the semi-supervised learning area.

2.2   Semi-supervised Learning

Existing dominant approaches to image-based semi-supervised learning include consistency regularization [25,31] and pseudo-labelling [18]. Consistency regularization methods, such as Temporal Ensembling [25] and Mean-teacher [31], aim to learn the prediction consistency in different epochs or models with augmented inputs. Applying augmentations analogous to the image domain such as flipping, rotation, and transformation to videos for action segmentation is non-trivial as the inputs are pre-computed feature vectors.

Pseudo-labelling methods generate labels for unlabelled data to guide learning [18]. To generate pseudo-labels, [5] leverages the sample similarity in the feature space to assign soft labels, whereas [12] implements a graph-based label propagation framework. Some researchers [4,32] have attempted to apply semi-supervised learning to video tasks by adapting image-based techniques to take video input. However, little has been done to evaluate the effectiveness of semi-supervised learning in temporal action segmentation. To address this research gap, we propose two novel loss functions designed based on the observation of two unique properties of procedural task videos.

3   Method

3.1   Preliminaries

We denote a labelled sample video sequence of temporal length T as $\{(x^t, y^t)\}_{t=1}^T$, where x^t is the video frame feature indexed at time t and y^t is its semantic action label. In a semi-supervised scenario, a labelled set $\mathcal{D}_L = \{(x_i, y_i)\}_{i=1}^N$ of N labelled videos and an unlabelled set $\mathcal{D}_U = \{(x_j)\}_{j=1}^M$ of M videos are given, where $M \gg N$. For every video in the small labelled set $\mathcal{D}_L$, each frame has a label from one of K classes, i.e., $y_i^t \in \{1, 2, \ldots, K\}$. The complete training set is denoted by $\mathcal{D} = \mathcal{D}_L + \mathcal{D}_U$.

To learn a semi-supervised action segmentation model $\mathcal{M}$ parameterised by θ, we use the labelled and unlabelled videos with the following objective:

$$\min_\theta \sum_{(x,y) \in \mathcal{D}_L} \mathcal{L}^L(x, y; \theta) + \alpha \sum_{(x) \in \mathcal{D}_U} \mathcal{L}^U(x; \theta) + \beta \sum_{(x) \in \mathcal{D}} \mathcal{R}^D(x; \theta), \tag{1}$$

where $\mathcal{L}^L$ denotes a supervised loss (Sect. 3.2), $\mathcal{L}^U$ denotes an unsupervised loss, and $\mathcal{R}^D$ is some regularization loss (Sect. 3.2), weighted by hyperparameters $\alpha, \beta \in \mathbb{R}_{>0}$. In the above objective, formulating the unsupervised loss $\mathcal{L}_u$ is vital for effective semi-supervised learning. In this work, we designed two novel loss functions for unlabelled data, i.e. action affinity loss (Sect. 3.3) and action continuity loss (Sect. 3.4), each attending to one characteristic we observed in procedural videos.

3.2 Supervised Temporal Action Segmentation

Existing supervised approaches [8,17,28] take sequences of video frames as input and predict frame-wise action labels as a classification task. For the labelled data, we follow the same scheme to train the segmentation model $\mathcal{M}$ that estimates frame-wise action probabilities $p^t(k) = \mathcal{M}(x^t)$ with the classification loss formulated as:

$$\mathcal{L}_{cls}^L = \frac{1}{T} \sum_t -\log(p^t(y^t)) \tag{2}$$

where $p^t \in \mathbb{R}^K$ is the estimated action class probability for frame x^t. It is also common to apply a smoothing loss with threshold τ to encourage smooth transitions between frames:

$$\mathcal{L}_{sm} = \frac{1}{TK} \sum_{t,k} \tilde{\Delta}_{t,k}^2, \quad \tilde{\Delta}_{t,k} = \begin{cases} \Delta_{t,k} & : \Delta_{t,k} \leq \tau \\ \tau & : \text{otherwise} \end{cases}, \tag{3}$$

$$\Delta_{t,k} = \left| \log p^t(k) - \log p^{t-1}(k) \right|. \tag{4}$$

We follow [8] and set τ to 4.

3.3 Action Affinity

Videos performing the same (procedural) activity will share the same or a similar set of composing actions. We assume we can find similar videos that match and share resembling temporal proportions. With this motivation in mind, we define for a labelled video i a video-level representation based on the action frequency:

$$q_i(k) = \frac{1}{T_i} \sum_t \mathbb{1}(y_i^t == k); \quad k \in [1, \ldots, K] \tag{5}$$

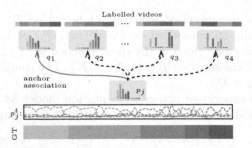

Fig. 2. Action affinity loss overview. Action frequencies q, p are first built for both labelled and unlabelled videos. The action affinity loss associates (red arrow) for p_j its nearest anchor q_1 in labelled set and then imposes the action prior from q_1 on p_j to supervise the learning. Our affinity loss allows variations of action ordering (green and purple segments in GT and q_1). (Color figure online)

For an unlabelled video j, we define a soft action frequency based on the network prediction outputs:

$$p_j(k) = \frac{1}{T_j} \sum_t^{T_j} p_j^t(k); \quad k \in [1, \ldots, K]. \tag{6}$$

Unless explicitly stated otherwise, we denote q, indexed by i, for labelled videos and p with index j for unlabelled videos.

Anchor Association. We want to provide action-level supervision for unlabelled videos by finding their most similar peers from the labelled set. Given some distance function $d(\cdot)$, we refer to a labelled video i as an anchor a_j for a unlabelled video j if their action frequencies are the closest amongst the entire labelled set, *i.e.*

$$a_j = q_{i^*}, \quad i^* = \arg\min_i d(q_i, p_j) \tag{7}$$

Affinity Loss. Formally, we use the Kullback-Leibler (KL) divergence as the distance criterion and define our action affinity loss as the affinity between the best matched pairs (p_j, a_j), which is also the minimum distance between p over the entire labelled set:

$$\mathcal{L}_{\text{aff}} = \sum_k a_j(k) \log \left(\frac{a_j(k)}{p_j(k)} \right) = \min_i \sum_k q_i(k) \log \left(\frac{q_i(k)}{p_j(k)} \right) \tag{8}$$

Minimising the above action affinity loss imposes pair-wise action frequency prior from the labelled set; it guides network outputs to have similar action composition to labelled videos, which is especially important when using unlabelled sequences for training. Figure 2 depicts our affinity loss. Empirically, this loss combined with a frame-wise entropy loss outperforms pseudo-labels (see. Sect. 4.4).

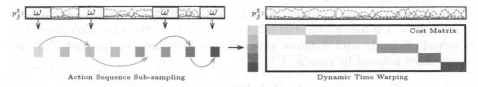

Fig. 3. Action continuity loss overview. Given network predictions for an unlabeled video p_j, a sliding window sub-sampling is first performed to obtain an action sequence (order indicated by coloured arrows); the sequence is later compared against p_j to construct a cost matrix. The action continuity loss is the average cost along the optimal assignment path (coloured segments in the cost matrix) found via dynamic time warping. (Color figure online)

3.4   Action Continuity

A simple way to generate pseudo-labels $\hat{y}$ for unlabelled video sequences is to use the class label with the maximum probability, which can be used to supervise the learning of unlabelled data with the classification loss:

$$\mathcal{L}_{\text{pse}} = -\frac{1}{T}\sum_t \log(p^t(\hat{y}^t)), \text{ where } \hat{y}^t = \arg\max_k p^t(k). \tag{9}$$

However, such naïve pseudo-labels directly inferred from network outputs tend to be temporally over-fragmented [13]. This breaks the temporal continuity of actions, *i.e.*, label changes should occur only at (true) action boundaries. To this end, we propose an action continuity loss to impose such action transition constraints. For an unlabelled video, this loss takes as input its frame-wise predictions, sub-samples in time and then estimates the learning objective via dynamic time warping as illustrated in Fig. 3.

Action Sequence Sub-sampling. We first generate action candidates which have maximum average class probability within a sliding window of stride ω,

$$o = \arg\max_k \frac{1}{\omega}\sum_{t=t'}^{t'+\omega} p^t(k), \tag{10}$$

where t' is the previous temporal window location. Subsequently, we yield an ordered sequence with $\lceil\frac{T}{\omega}\rceil$ elements denoted as $\mathcal{O} = \{o^l\}_{l=1}^{\lceil\frac{T}{\omega}\rceil}$. This sequence can be further reduced in length by removing the adjacent action repetitions, *i.e.*, $o^l = o^{l+1}$, to a length of L.

Dynamic Time Warping. Given an unlabelled video with its frame-wise action probabilities p_j of length T and its inferred action sequence $\mathcal{O}$ of length L as described above, a cost matrix of alignment $\Delta = \{d(l,t)\} \in \mathbb{R}^{L\times T}$ can be constructed with some distance function $d(\cdot,\cdot)$. Using dynamic time warping, we find the best possible alignment Y^* defined by the following objective:

$$Y^* = \arg\min_Y \langle Y, \Delta\rangle \tag{11}$$

where $\langle \cdot, \cdot \rangle$ is the inner product and $Y \subset \{0,1\}^{L \times T}$ is a binary assignment matrix. $Y_{tl} = 1$ if frame t has the label o^l and $Y_{tl} = 0$ otherwise. Equation (11) is solved efficiently with dynamic programming. The label assignment $\tilde{y}^t$ for p^t can be then inferred by parsing Y^*:

$$\tilde{y}^t = \sum_l o^l \mathbb{1}(Y_{lt}^* == 1) \tag{12}$$

Continuity Loss. An intuitive way of forming the continuity loss is to take the optimal objective of dynamic time warping and minimise it:

$$\mathcal{L}_{\text{cont}} = \langle Y^*, \Delta \rangle \tag{13}$$

We achieve this by choosing a specific distance function d. With a slight abuse of notation, we denote the categorical label o (Eq. (10)) as its one-hot embedding when written as $o(k)$ and designate the distance function as the KL divergence:

$$d(l,t) = KL(o^l \| p^t) = \sum_k o^l(k) \log \left(\frac{o^l(k)}{p^t(k)} \right). \tag{14}$$

If we replace the o^l with the final assignment $\tilde{y}^t$ for p^t in Eq. (14), the cost for p^t in the optimal Y^* would become the negative log-likelihood $-\log(p^t(\tilde{y}^t))$. Averaging the cost over the entire video sequence leads to our final action continuity loss formulation:

$$\mathcal{L}_{\text{cont}} = \frac{1}{T} \min_Y \langle Y, \Delta \rangle = \frac{1}{T} \sum_t -\log(p^t(\tilde{y}^t)). \tag{15}$$

We note that with the KL divergence distance function, this continuity loss is consistent with the frame-wise classification loss enforcing the network predictions to approximate $\tilde{y}$, which is temporally continuous.

Adopting Eq. (2) for labelled data ($\mathcal{L}^L$), Eq. (8) and Eq. (15) for the unlabelled data ($\mathcal{L}^U$), and Eq. (3) for the regularization ($\mathcal{R}^D$), we can rewrite Eq. (1) as our semi-supervised learning objective with the following form:

$$\mathcal{L} = \mathcal{L}_{\text{cls}}^L + \alpha \mathcal{L}_{\text{aff}}^U + \beta \mathcal{L}_{\text{cont}}^U + \gamma \mathcal{L}_{\text{sm}}^D \tag{16}$$

where α, β, γ are trade-off parameters balancing the terms. The smoothing loss L_{sm}^D is imposed on the full set of data.

3.5   Adaptive Boundary Smoothing (ABS)

In our semi-supervised setting, the action boundaries of an unlabelled video inferred from the best possible assignment Y^* or $\tilde{y}$ may still be inaccurate. As such, we propose an adaptive boundary smoothing (ABS) technique to provide softer action boundary supervision for more robust and reliable learning. Boundary smoothing was initially proposed in [6] and has been explored in the

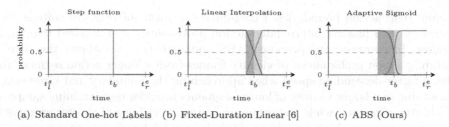

(a) Standard One-hot Labels   (b) Fixed-Duration Linear [6]   (c) ABS (Ours)

Fig. 4. Probability assignment approaches around the action boundary as a function of time. Let t_b denote the estimated boundary between the left action in $[t_l^s, t_b)$ and the right action $[t_b, t_r^e)$. The blue and red shaded segments denote the boundary vicinities V_l and V_r. (a) The standard one-hot labels adopt a step function and assign hard action labels for all the frames. (b) The fixed-duration linear approach [6] mixes the action probabilities linearly with a fixed slope around the boundary. (c) ABS (Ours) uses a sigmoid function with a decay proportional to the action duration. (Color figure online)

weakly-supervised setting to improve the segmentation performance. Unlike [6], which uses a fixed linear-interpolation scheme for smoothing, we use an adaptive scheme based on the estimated action duration. This allows us to elastically mix action probabilities for frames within the vicinity of the boundary.

Duration Aware Boundary Vicinity. Given left and right action segments $(\mathcal{S}_l : [t_l^s, t_l^e, y_l], \mathcal{S}_r : [t_r^s, t_r^e, y_r])$ consecutive in time, let t^s, t^e denote the starting and ending timestamps of the action and $y \in [1, \ldots, K]$ the corresponding semantic label. The action boundary in between can be denoted as $t_b = t_r^s = t_l^e + 1$. With a vicinity parameter $v \in [0, 0.5]$, we define the boundary vicinities or ranges V_l and V_r for the left and right actions respectively:

$$V_l = [t_b - (t_b - t_l^s) * v, t_b), \quad \text{and} \quad V_r = [t_b, t_b + (t_r^e - t_b) * v). \tag{17}$$

Adaptive Sigmoid. Within each action boundary vicinity V, we utilize an adaptive sigmoid function to assign mixed probabilities. For a frame within the left boundary vicinity, *i.e.*, $t \in V_l$, its smoothed probabilities for two action classes (y_l, y_r) are written as:

$$y^t(y_l) = \frac{1}{1 + e^{-\frac{\epsilon}{|V_l|}(t - t_b)}}, \quad \text{and} \quad y^t(y_r) = 1 - y^t(y_l) \tag{18}$$

where ϵ is a predefined parameter which is set to 5 to ensure that the furthest frame to the boundary in a vicinity set has close to 1 probability for the action label of the segment it belongs to. $|V|$ denotes the temporal length of V. Probability assignment for V_r is identical to Eq. (18) but with y_r and y_l changed.

ABS can be efficiently incorporated in our approach by replacing the one-hot action probability within each boundary vicinity from $\tilde{y}$ (Eq. (12)) with the above mixed probabilities. With $v = 0$, our ABS degenerates into the one-hot setting. Figure 4 compares three types of action probability assignments around the action boundaries. One-hot labels (Fig. 4a) are standard in practice and assume rigid action boundaries. Fixed-duration linear [6] (Fig. 4b) softens the boundary with linearly interpolated action probabilities in a fix-sized temporal window. In contrast, our proposed ABS approach (Fig. 4c) allows the corresponding action probabilities of vicinity frames from a longer action segment to have a faster-descending speed when approaching the boundary and vice-versa. Smoothing in a larger vicinity of longer segments provides more training samples for shorter segments, while smoothing in a smaller vicinity of shorter segments helps preserve more high confident middle frames for learning.

4   Experiments

4.1   Datasets, Protocols and Evaluation

Datasets. We conducted our experiments on the three benchmark datasets. **Breakfast Actions** [14] comprises in total 1712 videos performing ten different activities with 48 actions. On average, each video contains six action instances. **50Salads** [30] has 50 videos with 17 action classes. **GTEA** [9] contains 28 videos of seven kitchen activities composing 11 different actions.

Protocols. We used the standard train-test splits for each dataset; we randomly selected 5%, 10% of the training set as the labelled set $\mathcal{D}_L$ and regarded the remaining training videos as the unlabelled set $\mathcal{D}_U$. The labelled set was ensured to contain at least one segment instance of each action. For 50Salads and GTEA, 3 and 5 videos were sampled in place of 5% and 10% of labelled data as the datasets are relatively small.

Evaluation. We adopted the same evaluation metrics as fully-supervised action segmentation and reported frame-wise accuracy (Acc), segmental edit score (Edit), and segmental F1 score with varying overlap thresholds 10%, 25%, and 50%. For all datasets, we randomly sampled five labelled subsets from the original training data. We cross-validated over the standard splits and reported the average over the splits across the five runs.

4.2   Implementation Details

We use the multi-stage temporal convolutional network (MS-TCN) [8] as the backbone segmentation model $\mathcal{M}$. Our model was first warmed up with only labelled data for 30 epochs, and then unlabelled data was incorporated for another 20 epochs. The initial learning rate was set as $5e^{-4}$. We used the Adam optimiser, with weights settings of $\alpha = 0.1$, $\beta = 0.01$, and $\gamma = 0.15$, as per [8]. The action sequence sub-sampling stride ω was set to 20. We set the vicinity parameter $v = 0.05$ for all three datasets.

4.3   Effectiveness

Table 1 reports the improvements of our method compared with the supervised baseline (*Base*) and naïve pseudo-labelling approach (*Pseudo*) on three benchmarks. *Base* is trained with only labelled data while *Pseudo* assigns pseudo-labels

Table 1. Performance of our proposed approach on three benchmark datasets

$\%D_L$	Method	Breakfast					50Salads					GTEA				
		F1@{10, 25, 50}			Edit	Acc	F1@{10, 25, 50}			Edit	Acc	F1@{10, 25, 50}			Edit	Acc
5	Base	36.7	28.4	19.5	37.5	28.2	26.8	19.7	11.5	26.1	28.1	29.9	25.8	14.8	31.0	37.2
	Pseudo	40.2	28.5	20.1	41.3	20.9	22.6	17.0	12.1	22.0	24.0	48.4	42.3	30.2	45.4	48.1
	Ours	44.5	35.3	26.5	45.9	38.1	37.4	32.3	25.5	32.9	52.3	59.8	53.6	39.0	55.7	55.8
	Gain	7.8	6.9	7.0	8.4	9.9	10.6	12.6	14.0	6.8	24.2	29.9	27.8	24.2	24.7	18.6
10	Base	46.8	41.1	29.2	50.9	37.1	27.6	24.3	16.0	27.4	32.0	38.1	29.6	15.3	39.6	41.1
	Pseudo	49.3	44.8	33.9	49.7	40.2	36.2	32.4	24.5	33.5	41.1	65.5	60.7	45.8	59.9	57.9
	Ours	56.9	51.3	39.0	57.7	49.5	47.3	42.7	31.8	43.6	58.0	71.5	66.0	52.9	67.2	62.6
	Gain	10.1	10.2	9.8	6.8	12.4	19.7	18.4	15.8	16.2	26.0	33.4	36.4	37.6	27.6	21.5

Table 2. Comparison of frame accuracy boost between different dataset variances

	labelled	50Salads	GTEA	Breakfast
var	–	$8e^{-4}$	$3e^{-3}$	$6e^{-3}$
Gain	5%	24.2	18.6	9.9
Gain	10%	26.0	21.5	12.4

Table 3. Effect of activity labels on Breakfast (5%)

	F1@{10,25,50}			Edit	Acc
w/o activity	44.5	35.3	26.5	45.9	38.1
w/ activity	56.6	49.3	35.8	59.4	56.6
Gain	**12.1**	**14.0**	**9.3**	**13.5**	**18.5**

and trains with $\mathcal{L}_{\text{pse}}$ (Eq. (9)). In both the 5% and 10% settings, our model consistently outperformed the *Base* model by a large margin. Specifically, on the 50Salads dataset, the accuracy of our model increased by 26% (from 32.0% $\rightarrow$ 58.0%). The overall increase in performance across datasets was greater when more labelled data (5%$\rightarrow$10%) was provided. It is noteworthy that on 50Salads with 5% labelled data, the segmentation performances for *Pseudo* are lower than the *Base* by around 3%, which shows that the model overfitted to inaccurate pseudo-labels, likely due to confirmation bias. On the contrary, our proposed approach can still significantly boost the accuracy performance by a large gain of 24.2%. This verifies the effectiveness of the valuable action affinity prior information inferred from the rarely few labelled video samples.

Affinity Association. Amongst all three datasets in Table 1, the increase in Acc performance was the greatest on 50Salads and the least on Breakfast. We speculate that this is related to how accurate the affinity association (Eq. (7)) is in finding the anchor videos from the labelled set. We validated this by calculating the total variance amongst the full set $\mathcal{D}$. The total variance is defined as the trace of the action frequency covariance matrix $\mathcal{C} \in \mathbb{R}^{K \times K}$ normalized by the number of actions, *i.e.*, $var = \text{tr}(\mathcal{C})/K$. The lower the variance, the more likely our affinity loss provided accurate supervision. The extreme case where the full set of videos share the identical action composition and frequency ($var = 0$) guarantees that the supervision by affinity loss is always accurate and precise. Table 2 verifies that datasets with smaller variances had higher accuracy gains. Breakfast has the largest variance because it has 10 activities with slightly overlapping composing actions. By extension, its dispersed action frequency representations would cause the variance for a single action to be high.

We also evaluated our approach on the Breakfast dataset with video-level activity labels provided for all videos and reported the results in Table. 3. In this setting, we only searched for anchors from labelled videos with the same activity label. As we can see, when activity labels were given, the performance had a striking improvement of 18.5% in accuracy. This is because these high-level labels excluded the incorrect anchor associations across two different activities. Such improvement validates our affinity observation in the same activity videos.

4.4   Ablation Studies

Loss Functions and ABS. Table 4 reports the ablation study results on different variants of loss functions and ABS. The first row is the baseline model trained with only labelled data and $\mathcal{L}_{\text{cls}}$. Results for naïve pseudo-labelling loss $\mathcal{L}_{\text{pse}}$ (Eq. (9)) in the second row show a mild increase in F1 scores and accuracy compared to the baseline. While more unlabelled data was accessible for learning, using them in the form of pseudo-labels brought little advantage. On the other hand, our proposed action affinity loss $\mathcal{L}_{\text{aff}}$ (third row) surpassed the pseudo-labelling counterpart by a margin of around 2% on all metrics. We imposed an extra frame-wise entropy loss formulated as $-\sum_k p_i^t(k) \log p_i^t(k)$ in this variant, which forced the network to produce confident frame-wise predictions as the affinity loss does not provide frame-level supervision. The combination of action affinity and naïve pseudo-labelling (fourth row) further enhanced the performance. Such improvements show that our affinity loss $\mathcal{L}_{\text{aff}}$ can improve the quality of pseudo-labels, which we will evaluate in the following text. Our model combining $\mathcal{L}_{\text{aff}}$ and $\mathcal{L}_{\text{cont}}$ achieved better performance than all the above variants. Lastly, as indicated by the last row, the integration of our proposed ABS further boosted the segmentation performance on Breakfast.

Table 4. Loss function ablation study on Breakfast (10%)

$\mathcal{L}_{\text{cls}}$	$\mathcal{L}_{\text{pse}}$	$\mathcal{L}_{\text{aff}}$	$\mathcal{L}_{\text{cont}}$	ABS	F1@{10, 25, 50}			Edit	Acc
✓					47.9	40.6	28.6	51.8	36.8
✓	✓				49.3	44.8	33.9	49.7	40.2
✓		✓			52.0	46.5	34.3	53.4	44.0
✓	✓	✓			54.1	46.7	34.9	54.1	47.8
✓		✓	✓		53.8	50.1	37.6	56.6	49.2
✓		✓	✓	✓	**56.9**	**51.3**	**39.0**	**57.7**	**49.5**

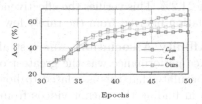

Fig. 5. Pseudo-label accuracy against training epochs on GTEA (10%).

Pseudo-labels. We studied the quality of estimated action classes on the unlabelled data $\mathcal{D}_U$. Fig. 5 shows a plot of the pseudo-label accuracy between training epochs. In the first epoch that unlabelled data was incorporated for training, all variants achieved the same accuracy, but the scores diverged as the training progressed. Imposing $\mathcal{L}_{\text{aff}}$ led to better accuracy compared to $\mathcal{L}_{\text{pse}}$, while our full loss formulation predicted the most accurate pseudo-labels for unlabelled data.

Table 5. Sub-sampling stride ω on Breakfast (10%)

ω	10	15	20	25	30	60
Acc	48.5	48.8	**49.5**	49.0	47.9	45.6

Table 6. Effect of α, β on GTEA (10%)

β	α			
	1	0.1	0.01	0.001
1	57.0	59.3	58.7	54.5
0.1	58.9	60.3	61.5	57.9
0.01	59.2	**62.6**	61.9	58.0
0.001	58.3	61.4	60.5	57.3

Table 7. Effectiveness of ABS for fully-supervised action segmentation

	Breakfast			50Salads			GTEA		
	F1@{10,25,50}	Edit	Acc	F1@{10,25,50}	Edit	Acc	F1@{10,25,50}	Edit	Acc
Base	63.2 57.7 45.6	65.5	65.1	66.8 63.7 55.2	59.8	78.2	84.9 82.4 67.6	79.7	76.6
+ABS	71.3 65.9 52.2	71.8	68.9	72.5 70.1 61.8	66.8	79.8	87.6 85.4 71.7	82.8	77.4
Gain	**8.1 8.2 6.6**	**6.3**	**3.8**	**5.7 6.4 6.6**	**7.0**	**1.6**	**2.7 3.0 4.1**	**3.1**	**0.8**

Sub-sampling Stride ω. Table 5 shows the accuracy changes with respect to the sub-sampling stride ω in Eq. (10) on Breakfast with 10% labelled data. The frame accuracy fluctuates around 49% with small strides, but when the stride becomes too large, e.g., $\omega = 60$, the performance dropped by a margin of 3.9% as some actions are likely to be fully skipped during sub-sampling. The best accuracy of 49.5% was achieved when $\omega = 20$.

Loss Hyperparameters. The effect of hyperparameters is presented in Table 6. A very small weight on our affinity loss ($\alpha = 0.001$) led to the lowest performance, as indicated by the last column. Increasing α boosted the performance, which shows that the action priors from affinity loss is vital. The comparison between the rows indicates that a large weight for the action continuity loss, e.g., $\beta = 1$, caused the model to overfit to the inaccurate pseudo-labels and produced inferior results since it also provided frame-wise pseudo-supervision. The overall best performance arrived at 62.6% with $\alpha = 0.1, \beta = 0.01$.

Vicinity Parameter v. Table 8 compares ABS against One-hot and Fixed-duration linear [6]. ASB with $v = 0.05$ enhanced the segmentation results by 1-2% compared to the baseline One-hot ($v = 0$). Fixed-duration linear [6] was also helpful, but the performance gain was only marginal. Setting $v = 0.1$ doubles the vicinity, which experienced a performance drop compared to $v = 0.05$; this likely indicates that the smoothing range is too large.

ABS for Supervised Learning. Given that ABS is a general smoothing technique, we further integrated ABS with the fully-supervised setting and report the results in Table 7. A consistent increase in segmentation performance compared to the baseline was observed across all three datasets. Also, the relatively large improvements were made in segmental metrics (F1 and Edit scores).

Table 8. Comparison of vicinity v on Breakfast (10%)

Method	F1@{10,25,50}			Edit	Acc
One-hot($v = 0$)	53.8	50.1	37.6	56.6	49.2
Fixed-duration [6]	54.7	50.5	38.1	56.9	49.1
$v = 0.05$	**56.9**	**51.3**	**39.0**	**57.7**	**49.5**
$v = 0.1$	55.1	50.9	37.9	57.0	48.9

Table 9. Accuracy performance comparison with approaches under various supervisions, * denotes test data used for training

	Method	Breakfast	50salads	GTEA
Full	MSTCN [8]	65.1	78.2	76.6
	SSTDA [3]*	**70.2**	**83.2**	79.8
	Ours (100%)*	69.3	82.5	**80.4**
Weak	Timestamp [21]	64.1	75.6	66.4
	SSTDA [3] (65%)*	65.8	80.7	75.7
Semi	Ours (5%)	38.1	52.3	55.8
	Ours (10%)	49.5	58.0	62.6
	Ours (50%)	**63.9**	**78.8**	**77.9**

4.5 Comparison to State-of-the-Art Approaches

We list in Table 9 relevant state-of-the-art approaches adopting MS-TCN [8] or its variants as the backbone for a fair comparison. We did not include ICC [29] as their approach cannot work with the MS-TCN architecture. For the "Full" comparison, we followed SSTDA [3] and applied our semi-supervised method to 100% labelled data. We used the test data as the unlabelled set and achieved comparable performance. The frame accuracy of Timestamp [21], which uses per-segment supervision for all video samples, is close to fully-supervised MS-TCN [8] except on GTEA. With 50% labelled data, our approach managed to achieve comparable or better performance compared to Timestamp [21], MS-TCN [8] as well as SSTDA [3] using a larger percentage (65%) of labelled data.

5 Conclusion

Procedural videos performing the same tasks exhibit affinity in action composition and continuity in action duration. Based on these unique characteristics, we proposed two novel loss functions for the semi-supervised temporal action segmentation task. The action affinity loss harnessed the action priors from the labelled set to supervise the unlabelled data. The action continuity loss function sub-sampled action sequence to enforce the temporal continuity of actions and provided frame-wise supervision. Furthermore, we proposed an adaptive boundary smoothing technique for more robust action boundaries. Our approach significantly improves the segmentation performance with a very small amount (5% and 10%) of labelled data and reaches comparable performance to the full supervision methods with 50% labelled videos.

Acknowledgements. This research is supported by the National Research Foundation, Singapore under its NRF Fellowship for AI (NRF-NRFFAI1–2019–0001). Any opinions, findings and conclusions or recommendations expressed in this material are those of the author(s) and do not reflect the views of National Research Foundation, Singapore.

References

1. Arazo, E., Ortego, D., Albert, P., O'Connor, N.E., McGuinness, K.: Pseudo-labeling and confirmation bias in deep semi-supervised learning. In: IJCNN, pp. 1–8. IEEE (2020)
2. Chang, C.Y., Huang, D.A., Sui, Y., Fei-Fei, L., Niebles, J.C.: D3TW: discriminative differentiable dynamic time warping for weakly supervised action alignment and segmentation. In: CVPR, pp. 3546–3555 (2019)
3. Chen, M.H., Li, B., Bao, Y., AlRegib, G., Kira, Z.: Action segmentation with joint self-supervised temporal domain adaptation. In: CVPR, pp. 9454–9463 (2020)
4. Cho, S., Lee, H., Kim, M., Jang, S., Lee, S.: Pixel-level bijective matching for video object segmentation. In: WACV, pp. 129–138 (2022)
5. Ding, G., Zhang, S., Khan, S., Tang, Z., Zhang, J., Porikli, F.: Feature affinity-based pseudo labeling for semi-supervised person re-identification. TMM **21**(11), 2891–2902 (2019)
6. Ding, L., Xu, C.: Weakly-supervised action segmentation with iterative soft boundary assignment. In: CVPR, pp. 6508–6516 (2018)
7. Du, Z., Wang, X., Zhou, G., Wang, Q.: Fast and unsupervised action boundary detection for action segmentation. In: Proceedings of the IEEE/CVF Conference on Computer Vision and Pattern Recognition, pp. 3323–3332 (2022)
8. Farha, Y.A., Gall, J.: MS-TCN: multi-stage temporal convolutional network for action segmentation. In: CVPR, pp. 3575–3584 (2019)
9. Fathi, A., Ren, X., Rehg, J.M.: Learning to recognize objects in egocentric activities. In: CVPR (2011)
10. Fayyaz, M., Gall, J.: SCT: set constrained temporal transformer for set supervised action segmentation. In: CVPR, pp. 501–510 (2020)
11. He, R., Yang, J., Qi, X.: Re-distributing biased pseudo labels for semi-supervised semantic segmentation: a baseline investigation. In: ICCV, pp. 6930–6940 (2021)
12. Iscen, A., Tolias, G., Avrithis, Y., Chum, O.: Label propagation for deep semi-supervised learning. In: CVPR, pp. 5070–5079 (2019)
13. Ishikawa, Y., Kasai, S., Aoki, Y., Kataoka, H.: Alleviating over-segmentation errors by detecting action boundaries. In: WACV, pp. 2322–2331 (2021)
14. Kuehne, H., Arslan, A., Serre, T.: The language of actions: Recovering the syntax and semantics of goal-directed human activities. In: CVPR (2014)
15. Kuehne, H., Richard, A., Gall, J.: Weakly supervised learning of actions from transcripts. CVIU **163**, 78–89 (2017)
16. Kukleva, A., Kuehne, H., Sener, F., Gall, J.: Unsupervised learning of action classes with continuous temporal embedding. In: CVPR, pp. 12066–12074 (2019)
17. Lea, C., Flynn, M.D., Vidal, R., Reiter, A., Hager, G.D.: Temporal convolutional networks for action segmentation and detection. In: CVPR, pp. 156–165 (2017)
18. Lee, D.H., et al.: Pseudo-label: the simple and efficient semi-supervised learning method for deep neural networks. In: Workshop on Challenges in Representation Learning, vol. 3, p. 896. ICML (2013)
19. Lei, P., Todorovic, S.: Temporal deformable residual networks for action segmentation in videos. In: CVPR, pp. 6742–6751 (2018)
20. Li, J., Todorovic, S.: Action shuffle alternating learning for unsupervised action segmentation. In: CVPR, pp. 12628–12636 (2021)
21. Li, Z., Abu Farha, Y., Gall, J.: Temporal action segmentation from timestamp supervision. In: CVPR, pp. 8365–8374 (2021)

22. Richard, A., Kuehne, H., Gall, J.: Action sets: weakly supervised action segmentation without ordering constraints. In: CVPR, pp. 5987–5996 (2018)
23. Rizve, M.N., Duarte, K., Rawat, Y.S., Shah, M.: In defense of pseudo-labeling: an uncertainty-aware pseudo-label selection framework for semi-supervised learning. arXiv preprint arXiv:2101.06329 (2021)
24. Sakoe, H., Chiba, S.: Dynamic programming algorithm optimization for spoken word recognition. IEEE Trans. Acoust. Speech Sig. Process. **26**(1), 43–49 (1978)
25. Samuli, L., Timo, A.: Temporal ensembling for semi-supervised learning. In: ICLR, vol. 4, p. 6 (2017)
26. Sarfraz, S., Murray, N., Sharma, V., Diba, A., Van Gool, L., Stiefelhagen, R.: Temporally-weighted hierarchical clustering for unsupervised action segmentation. In: Proceedings of the IEEE/CVF Conference on Computer Vision and Pattern Recognition, pp. 11225–11234 (2021)
27. Sener, F., Yao, A.: Unsupervised learning and segmentation of complex activities from video. In: CVPR, pp. 8368–8376 (2018)
28. Singhania, D., Rahaman, R., Yao, A.: Coarse to fine multi-resolution temporal convolutional network. arXiv preprint arXiv:2105.10859 (2021)
29. Singhania, D., Rahaman, R., Yao, A.: Iterative contrast-classify for semi-supervised temporal action segmentation. arXiv preprint arXiv:2112.01402 (2021)
30. Stein, S., McKenna, S.J.: Combining embedded accelerometers with computer vision for recognizing food preparation activities. In: ACM International Joint Conference on Pervasive and Ubiquitous Computing, pp. 729–738. ACM (2013)
31. Tarvainen, A., Valpola, H.: Mean teachers are better role models: weight-averaged consistency targets improve semi-supervised deep learning results. In: NeurIPS, pp. 1195–1204 (2017)
32. Wang, X., Zhang, S., Qing, Z., Shao, Y., Gao, C., Sang, N.: Self-supervised learning for semi-supervised temporal action proposal. In: CVPR, pp. 1905–1914 (2021)
33. Wang, Z., Li, Y., Guo, Y., Fang, L., Wang, S.: Data-uncertainty guided multi-phase learning for semi-supervised object detection. In: CVPR, pp. 4568–4577 (2021)

Spotting Temporally Precise, Fine-Grained Events in Video

James Hong[1(✉)], Haotian Zhang[1], Michaël Gharbi[2], Matthew Fisher[2], and Kayvon Fatahalian[1]

[1] Stanford University, Stanford, USA
james.hong@cs.stanford.edu
[2] Adobe Research, San Francisco, USA

Abstract. We introduce the task of spotting temporally precise, fine-grained events in video (detecting the precise moment in time events occur). Precise spotting requires models to reason globally about the full-time scale of actions and locally to identify subtle frame-to-frame appearance and motion differences that identify events during these actions. Surprisingly, we find that top performing solutions to prior video understanding tasks such as action detection and segmentation do not simultaneously meet both requirements. In response, we propose E2E-Spot, a compact, end-to-end model that performs well on the precise spotting task and can be trained quickly on a single GPU. We demonstrate that E2E-Spot significantly outperforms recent baselines adapted from the video action detection, segmentation, and spotting literature to the precise spotting task. Finally, we contribute new annotations and splits to several fine-grained sports action datasets to make these datasets suitable for future work on precise spotting.

Keywords: Temporally precise spotting · Video understanding

1 Introduction

Detecting the precise moment in time events occur in a video (temporally precise event 'spotting') is an important video analysis task that stands to be essential to many future advanced video analytics and video editing [66] applications. However, despite significant progress in fine-grained video understanding [12,29, 44,58], temporal action detection (TAD) [5,11,28,47,62], and temporal action segmentation (TAS) [20,30,52], precise event spotting has rarely been studied by the video understanding community.

We address this gap by focusing on the challenge of precisely spotting events in sports video. We study sports video because of the quantity of data available and the high temporal accuracy needed to analyze human performances. For

Supplementary Information The online version contains supplementary material available at https://doi.org/10.1007/978-3-031-19833-5_3.

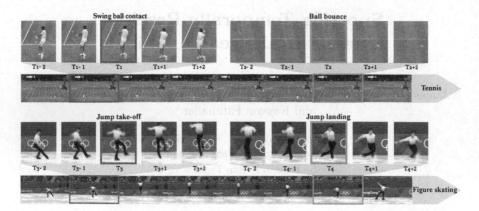

Fig. 1. We perform temporally precise spotting of events in video, where success requires detecting the occurrence of an event within a single or small tolerance of frames. Examples of precise events: in *tennis*, the moment a player contacts the ball during a swing (red) or when a ball bounces on the court (blue); in *figure skating*, the moment of take-off (red) and landing (blue) during a jump. (Color figure online)

example, we wish to determine the frame in which a tennis player hits the ball, the frame a ball bounces on the court, or the moment a figure skater starts or lands a jump. Figure 1 shows examples from these sports and illustrates why precise spotting is challenging. The goal is to identify the precise frame when an event occurs, but adjacent frames are extremely similar visually; looking at one or two frames alone, it can be difficult even for a human to judge when a racket makes contact with a ball or when a figure skater lands a jump. However, inspection of longer sequences of frames makes the task significantly more tractable since the observer knows when to expect the event of interest in the context of a longer action (e.g., the swing of the racket, the preparation for a jump, or a ball's trajectory). Therefore, we hypothesize that precise spotting requires models that can (1) represent subtle appearance and motion clues, and also (2) make decisions using information spread over long temporal contexts.

Surprisingly, we have found that the large body of literature on video understanding lacks solutions that meet these two requirements in the regime of temporally precise spotting. For example, action recognition (classification) models are not designed to operate efficiently on large temporal windows and struggle to learn in the heavily class-imbalanced setting created by precise spotting of rare events. Sequence models from segmentation and detection extract patterns over longer timescales, but training these complex models end-to-end has led to optimization challenges. This has resulted in many solutions that operate in two phases, relying on pre-trained (or modestly fine-tuned) input features that are not particularly specialized to capture the subtle (and often highly domain-specific) visual details needed to spot events with temporal precision.

We propose a simpler alternative (E2E-Spot) to satisfy our hypothesized requirements. The key to training a sequence model end-to-end over a wide temporal context is an efficient per-frame feature extractor that can process hundreds of contiguous frames without exceeding platform memory. We demonstrate how to combine existing modules from the video processing literature to accomplish this goal without introducing new, bespoke architectures.

Despite its simplicity, E2E-Spot significantly outperforms prior baselines, which opt for a two-phase approach, as well as naive end-to-end learning approaches on precise spotting. Moreover, E2E-Spot is computationally efficient at inference time and can complete the full end-to-end spotting task in less time than just the feature extraction phase of many prior methods [2,6].

This paper makes three main contributions:

1. The novel task of temporally precise spotting of fine-grained events. We introduce frame-accurate labels for two existing fine-grained sports action datasets: Tennis [66] and Figure Skating [25]. We also adapt the temporal annotations from FineGym [44] and FineDiving [60] to show the generality of the precise spotting task.
2. E2E-Spot, a from-the-ground-up, end-to-end learning approach to precise spotting that combines well-established architectural components [8,43,53] and can be trained quickly on a single GPU.
3. Analysis of spotting performance. E2E-Spot outperforms strong baselines (Sect. 5) on precise temporal spotting (by 4–11 mAP, spotting within 1 frame). E2E-Spot is also competitive on coarser spotting tasks (within 1–5 s), achieving second place in the 2022 SoccerNet Action Spotting challenge [13,14] (within 1.1 avg-mAP) and a lift of 14.8–16.5 avg-mAP over prior work.

Our code and data are publicly available.

2   Related Work

Action Spotting. Previous work on spotting [13] focuses on *coarse* action spotting, where a detection is deemed correct if it occurs within some time-window around the true event, with a loose error tolerance (1–5 or 5–60 s, equating to 10–100 s of frames). On the Tennis [66] and Figure Skating [25] datasets described in Sect. 4, a spotting error larger than 1–2 frames is essentially equivalent to missing the event altogether (e.g., a ball impact's on the ground; Fig. 1). For demanding applications that require precise temporal annotations, we argue the relevant task is *precise* event spotting, where detection thresholds are much more stringent tolerances (1–5 frames; as little as 33 ms in 25–30 FPS video). We use a similar metric to coarse action spotting: mean Average Precision (mAP @ δ) but with a short temporal tolerance δ.

Temporal Action Detection (TAD) and Segmentation (TAS) localize *intervals*, often spanning several seconds and containing an 'action'. Depending on the dataset, these can be atomic actions such as "standing up" [47] or broad activities such as "billiards" [28]. For such action definitions, it is often unclear what would be considered a temporally precise event to spot.

The success criteria for TAD and TAS also differ from that of precise spotting. TAD [5,11,28,47,62] is evaluated on interval-based metrics such as mAP @ temporal Intersection-over-Union (IoU) or at sub-sampled time points, neither of which enforce frame accuracy on the action boundaries. Down-sampling in time (up to 16×) is a common preprocessing step [3,36,37,45,61,65]. TAS [20,30,52] also optimizes interval-based metrics such as F1 @ temporal overlap. Frame-level metrics for TAS reward accuracy on densely labeled, intra-segment frames; in contrast, event frames in our spotting datasets are sparse. Spatial-temporal detection benchmarks [31,33] differ from standard TAD, TAS, and precise spotting by combining both spatial and temporal IoU [33].

Recent approaches for TAD [10,36,37,55,61,64] and TAS [1,7,19,27,49,63] often proceed in two stages: (1) feature extraction then (2) head learning for the end task. Fixed, pre-trained features from video classification on Kinetics-400 are often used for the first stage [2,6,59], and state-of-the-art TAD methods with these features [39,65,68] often perform comparably to if not better than recent end-to-end learning approaches [34,38]. Indirect fine-tuning using classification in the target domain is sometimes performed to improve feature encoding [2, 45]. Early end-to-end approaches encode video as non-overlapping segments [3] (e.g., 16 frames) or downsample in time [46,48], producing features that are too temporally coarse to be effective for spotting frame-accurate events.

Like TAD and TAS, precise spotting is a temporal localization task performed on untrimmed video. As is the case, many models for TAD and TAS can be adapted for precise spotting. We use MS-TCN [19], GCN [61], GRU [8], and ASFormer [63] as baselines, and we test these models with different features [2,6,18] in Sect. 5. However, we find that relying on fixed or indirectly fine-tuned features as input for these models is a critical limitation. Our experiments show that (1) E2E-Spot is a strong baseline for precise spotting and (2) more complex architectures do not necessarily provide additional benefit when feature learning is end-to-end. Finally, we note the long history of CNN-RNN architectures in TAD/TAS [3,4,16,48,62]; E2E-Spot is a simple design from this family, motivated by our requirements for frame-dense processing and end-to-end learning, and implemented using a modern CNN for spatial-temporal feature encoding.

Video Classification predicts one label for an entire video, as opposed to per-frame labels for spotting. This leads to two key differences: (1) sparsely sampling frames [21,59] is effective, whereas precise spotting requires dense sampling; (2) to obtain a video-level prediction, popular architectures for classification typically perform global space-time pooling [57] or temporal consensus [35,59, 69]. E2E-Spot shows that omitting temporal pooling[1] and training end-to-end yields an efficient pipeline for precise, per-frame spotting.

E2E-Spot incorporates ideas from popular video classification models for spatial-temporal feature extraction. TSM [35] introduced the temporal shift operation, which converts a 2D CNN into a spatial-temporal feature extractor by mixing channels between time steps. GSM [53] learns the shift. We find the combination of RegNet-Y [43] and GSM [53] to be effective and suggest these building blocks as a starting point for future spotting research.

---

[1] Omission of temporal pooling is similar to concurrent work, E2E-TAD [38].

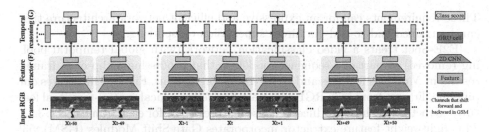

Fig. 2. Overview of E2E-Spot. RGB video frames are first input to a local spatial-temporal feature extractor F (a RegNet-Y [43] with GSM [53]) to produce a feature for each frame that captures subtle differences and motion across neighboring frames (red dotted box). The feature sequence is then processed by a sequence model G, which builds a long-scale temporal context (blue dotted box; one direction drawn) and outputs a class prediction for every frame. (Color figure online)

Sports Activity Datasets are a fertile testing ground for video action recognition and understanding [13,24–26,32,33,44,60,66]. We evaluate using temporal annotations from several recent datasets [13,25,44,60,66]. These datasets are fine-grained, meaning that all event and class labels relate to a single activity (i.e., a single sport), as compared to coarse-grained datasets [5,28], where classes comprise a broad mix of generic activities. Supporting fine-grained concepts and labels is an important requirement of many practical, real-world applications.

3   E2E-Spot: An End-to-End Model for Precise Spotting

We define the precise temporal event spotting task as follows: given a video with N frames $\mathbf{x}_1, \ldots, \mathbf{x}_N$ and a set of K event classes $\mathbf{c}_1, \ldots, \mathbf{c}_K$, the goal is to predict the (sparse) set of frame indices when an event occurs, as well as the event's class $(t, \hat{\mathbf{y}}_t) \in \mathbb{N} \times \{\mathbf{c}_1, \ldots, \mathbf{c}_K\}$. A prediction is deemed correct if its timestamp falls within δ frames of a labeled ground-truth event and it has the correct class label. In precise spotting, the temporal tolerance δ is small—i.e., a few frames only. We assume that the frame rate of the video is sufficiently high to capture the precise event and that frame rates are similar across videos.

We identified several key design requirements for a model to perform well on the temporally precise spotting task:

1. Task-specific **local spatial-temporal features** that capture subtle visual differences and motion across neighboring frames.
2. A **long-term temporal reasoning** mechanism, which provides a long temporal window to spot short, rare events. For instance, it is difficult to identify the precise time a figure skater enters a jump from a handful of frames. But spotting becomes much less ambiguous given the wider context of the acceleration (before) and landing (after the jump) (see Fig. 1). These contexts can occur over many seconds and frames.
3. **Dense frame prediction** at the temporal granularity of a single frame.

These requirements call for an expressive and efficient network architecture that can be trained end-to-end via direct supervision on spotting.

E2E-Spot treats a video classification network (with global temporal pooling removed) as part of a sequence model, so that processing a clip of N frames results in N output features and N per-frame predictions. Figure 2 illustrates our pipeline. Frames from each RGB video are first fed to a local spatial-temporal feature extractor F, which produces a dense feature vector for each frame (Sect. 3.1). This lightweight feature extractor incorporates Gate Shift Modules (GSM) [53] into a generic 2D convolutional neural network (CNN) [43]. The feature sequence is then further processed by a sequence model G, which builds a long-scale temporal context and outputs a class prediction for every frame, including a 'background' class to indicate when no event was detected (Sect. 3.2).

3.1   Local Spatial-Temporal Feature Extractor, F

The first stage of our pipeline extracts spatial-temporal features for each frame. We strive to keep the feature extractor as lightweight as possible, but found that a simple 2D CNN that processes frames independently [9,22,56,59] is often insufficient for precise spotting (see Sect. 5.2). This is because a 2D CNN does not capture the spatially-local temporal correlations between frames. In videos that are densely sampled (24–30 FPS), this temporal signal is critical to learn features that can robustly differentiate otherwise very similar frames: for instance, the speed and travel direction of a tennis ball, when each frame likely exhibits motion blur. To obtain more expressive, motion-sensitive features we implement F as a 2D CNN with Gate Shift Modules (GSM) [53]. We choose RegNet-Y [43], a recent and compact CNN, as the 2D backbone.

Our feature extractor is similar to models for video classification [35,53,59], but with two key differences: (1) it samples frames *densely* and (2) it uses no final temporal consensus/pooling because our goal is to obtain one output per frame, rather than one for the whole video or multi-frame segment.

Efficiency Compared to Other Per-frame Feature Extractors. A common alternative for per-frame feature extraction [2,19] is to stride a video classification model densely—i.e., by using a model which takes M frames as input and produces a single feature and by running it on the M frame neighborhood of every frame. The overhead of processing each frame multiple times in overlapping windows makes end-to-end feature learning or fine-tuning difficult for tasks like spotting that require dense processing of frames. In contrast, our approach processes each frame once and can be trained as part of an end-to-end pipeline with much longer sequences (100 s of frames), even on a single GPU (see Table 1).

3.2   Long-term Temporal Reasoning Module, G

To gather long-term temporal information, we use a 1-layer bidirectional Gated Recurrent Unit (GRU [8]) network G, which processes the dense per-frame features produced by F. We set the hidden dimension of G to match that of F.

Table 1. E2E-Spot efficiency and throughput. We compare the model complexity, the maximum batch size for *end-to-end training on 100 frame clips* (at 224×224), and per-frame inference time on a Nvidia A5000 GPU with 24GB of VRAM [42]. E2E-Spot is significantly faster at inferring features than striding a video classification model and allows for practical end-to-end trained spotting.

Architecture	Params (M)	Max batch size	Inference time (ms)
E2E-Spot: RegNet-Y 200MF w/ GSM + GRU	(2.8 + 1.7)	18	0.3
E2E-Spot: RegNet-Y 800MF w/ GSM + GRU	(5.5 + 7.1)	8	0.6
Comparison to other feature extractors: (* := exceeds GPU memory)			
RegNet-Y 200MF w/ GSM (7 frames per window)	2.8	2	1.6
RegNet-Y 200MF w/ GSM (15 frames per window)	2.8	1	3.2
I3D (21 frames; used by [19])	12.3	*	8.5
R(2+1)D-34 [57] (12 frames, 128×128; used by [2])	63.7	*	11.0
ResNet-152 (1 frame only; used by [9,22,56])	60.2	2	1.8
Feature combination (for SoccerNet-v2) [70]	>200	–	–

Finally, we apply a fully connected layer and softmax on the GRU outputs to make a per-frame $K+1$ way prediction (including 1 'no-event' background class).

We found that a single-layer GRU suffices and that more complex sequence models such as MS-TCN [19] or a deeper GRU do not necessarily improve accuracy (see Sect. 5.2). We hypothesize that as a result of end-to-end training, the features produced by F capture subtle temporal cues that are specific to a given activity's and task's requirements. This shifts the burden of representations to F so that G only needs to propagate the temporal context.

3.3 Per-frame Cross-Entropy Loss

For a N-frame clip, we output a sequence of N class scores—i.e. a $(K + 1)$-dimensional vector $\hat{\mathbf{y}}_t$ for each frame t, accounting for the background class:

$$(\hat{\mathbf{y}}_1, \ldots, \hat{\mathbf{y}}_N) = G \circ F(\mathbf{x}_1, \ldots, \mathbf{x}_N). \tag{1}$$

Each frame has a ground-truth label $\mathbf{y}_t \in \{\mathbf{c}_1, \ldots, \mathbf{c}_K\} \cup \{\mathbf{c}_{background}\}$ encoded as a one-hot vector. We optimize per-frame classification with cross-entropy loss:

$$l(\mathbf{x}_1, \ldots, \mathbf{x}_N) = \sum_{t=1}^{N} \mathrm{CE}(\hat{\mathbf{y}}_t, \mathbf{y}_t) \tag{2}$$

3.4 Implementation Details

We conduct experiments with two versions of F utilizing RegNet-Y 200MF and 800MF (MF refers to MFLOPs [43]). These CNN backbones are initialized with pre-trained weights from ImageNet-1K [15]. Details of the complexity and throughput of these models is given in Table 1.

We train E2E-Spot on 100-frame-long clips sampled randomly and use standard data-augmentations (e.g., crop, jitter, and mixup [67]). Frames are resized to 224 pixels in height and cropped to 224 × 224 unless otherwise stated (see supplement Sect. A). We optimize using AdamW [41] and LR annealing [40]. To mitigate imbalance arising from the rarity of precise events (<3% of frames), we boost the loss weight of the foreground classes (5×) relative to the background.

At test time, we disable data-augmentation and overlap clips by 50%, averaging the per-frame predictions. To convert per-frame class scores into a set of spotting predictions, we rank all of the frames by their predicted score for each class. We follow standard procedure from coarse spotting [13] and other detection tasks [23] by reporting our results with non-maximum suppression (NMS). Empirically, we found NMS's efficacy to vary by model and dataset (see Table 2). Refer to supplement Sect. A for more implementation details.

4   Datasets

We evaluate precise spotting on four fine-grained sports video datasets with frame-level labels: Tennis [66], Figure Skating [25], FineDiving [60], and FineGym [44]. For full details about these datasets, please refer to supplement Sect. D.

Tennis is an extension of the dataset from Vid2Player [66]. It consists of 3,345 video clips from 28 tennis matches (each clip is a 'point'), with video frame rates of either 25 or 30 FPS. The dataset has 33,791 frame-accurate events divided into six classes: "player serve ball contact," "regular swing ball contact," and "ball bounce" (each divided by near- and far-court). Video from 19 matches are used for training and validation, while 9 matches are held out for testing.

Figure Skating [25] consists of 11 videos (all 25 FPS) containing 371 short program performances from the Winter Olympics (2010–2018) and World Championships (2017–2019). We refine the original labels by manually (re-)annotating the take-off and landing frames of jumps and flying spins, resulting in 3,674 event annotations across four classes. We consider two splits for evaluation:

- *Competition split* (FS-Comp): holds out all videos from the 2018 season for testing [25]. This split tests generalization to new videos (e.g., the next Olympics), despite domain-shift such as a new background in a new venue.
- *Performance split* (FS-Perf): stratifies each competition across train/val/test. This split tests a model's ability to learn precise temporal events (by different skaters) without the background bias of the previous split.

FineDiving [60] contains 3,000 diving clips with temporal segment annotations. We spot the step transition frames for four classes, which include transitions into somersaults (pike and tuck), twists, and entry.

FineGym [44] contains 5,374 gymnastics performances, each treated as an untrimmed video. It has 32 spotting classes, derived from a hierarchy of action categories (e.g., balance beam dismounts; floor exercise turns). The original annotations denote the start and end of actions; we treat these boundaries as events—for instance, "balance beam dismount start" and "balance beam dismount end". We ignore the original splits, which are designed for action recognition and have overlap in videos, and we propose a 3:1:1 split between train/val/test. To reduce the variation in the frame rates of the source videos (which are 25–60 FPS), we resample all 50 and 60 FPS videos to 25 and 30 FPS, respectively.

Upon inspecting the FineGym labels for frame accuracy, we found the annotations for action start frames to be more visually consistent than those for end frames. For example, unlike in the Figure Skating dataset, the end frame is often several frames after the frame of landing for a jump. Thus, we also report results for a subset, FineGym-Start, which contains only start-of-action events.

5   Evaluation

In Sect. 5.1, we demonstrate that the quality of per-frame feature representations extracted from the video has the greatest impact on results, rather than the choice of head architecture, and that end-to-end learning with E2E-Spot outperforms methods using pre-trained or indirectly fine-tuned features. In Sect. 5.2 and Sect. 5.3 we analyze the effect of temporal context, the importance of temporal modeling, and additional variations of E2E-Spot. In Sect. 5.4 we report results on SoccerNet-v2, a temporally coarser spotting task.

Evaluation Metric. We measure Average Precision within a tolerance of δ frames (AP @ δ). AP is computed for each event class, and mAP is the mean across classes. We focus on tight tolerances such as $\delta = 1$ and $\delta = 2$. Precise temporal events are rare as a percentage of frames (0.2–2.9%), so metrics such as frame-level accuracy are not meaningful for precise spotting.

Baselines. We evaluate E2E-Spot against recent baselines from TAS, TAD, and coarse spotting that we adapted to the precise spotting task. These methods are not trained end-to-end; they adopt a two-phase separation between feature extraction and head training (i.e., downstream model) for the end-task. We form our baselines by pairing a *feature extraction strategy* with a *spotting head*. The latter is trained on extracted features to perform precise spotting, using the per-frame loss from Eq. 2. See supplement Sect. B for implementation details.

The baselines use the following head architectures: MS-TCN [19], GRU [8], ASFormer [63] from TAS; GCN [61] from TAD; and NetVLAD++ [22] and transformer [70] from action spotting. MS-TCN, GRU, and ASFormer performed best in our experiments, so we relegate results from the remaining architectures to supplement Sect. C.1. We further attempt to boost the performance of these baselines using additional losses from the spotting literature, such as CALF [9] and label dilation[2], and by post-processing using non-maximum suppression (within ± 1 frames). We report results from the best configuration of each baseline.

We pair each head architecture with pre-extracted input features, grouped into three broad categories:

1. *Pre-trained features* from video classification on Kinetics-400 [29], which are often used without any fine-tuning for TAD and TAS. Like Farha et al. [19],

---

[2] Label dilation is defined as naive propagation to $[-1, +1]$ frames to mitigate sparsity.

42   J. Hong et al.

Table 2. Spotting performance (mAP @ δ frames). The top results in each category and each column are underlined. SOTA is **bold**. We report best results under the following: † indicates NMS; * indicates CALF [9] or dilation. (e) E2E-Spot, trained with RGB only, generally outperforms the non-pose baselines and is competitive with the pose baselines on Figure Skating. E2E-Spot can further be improved with a larger 800MF CNN and a 2-stream ensemble with flow.

Feature	Model	Tennis		FS-Comp		FS-Perf		FineDiving		FG-Full		FG-Start	
		$\delta=1$	2	1	2	1	2	1	2	1	2	1	2
(a) Pre-trained features (from Kinetics-400)													
I3D [6]	MS-TCN	62.7	†*75.4	60.8	†*79.5	*69.0	†*89.3	–	–	–	–	–	–
(RGB & flow)	GRU	†*45.7	†*70.5	*41.8	†*69.8	*52.5	†*77.5	–	–	–	–	–	–
	ASFormer	*58.1	†*76.5	*61.2	†*82.4	69.0	†*89.7	–	–	–	–	–	–
MViT-B [18]	MS-TCN	67.0	†*80.1	*57.4	†*79.9	*64.8	†*84.3	*59.3	†*78.3	†31.0	†*48.6	†41.7	†*64.8
(RGB)	GRU	64.8	†*80.8	45.6	†*73.1	56.8	†*79.1	57.3	76.7	†*28.5	†*48.6	†*39.1	†*62.2
	ASFormer	*63.9	†79.9	55.8	†*81.8	*56.5	†*81.7	*38.5	†*67.4	†*25.3	†*42.9	†*32.5	†*55.3
(b) Fine-tuned features													
TSP [2]	MS-TCN	*90.9	†*95.1	72.4	†*87.8	*76.8	*89.9	*57.7	†76.0	†40.5	†58.5	†53.9	†*73.5
(RGB)	GRU	89.5	†*96.0	*68.4	†*88.3	75.5	†*90.6	*57.0	†78.2	†*38.7	†*58.8	†*53.2	†*74.2
	ASFormer	89.8	†*95.5	77.7	†94.1	80.2	†94.5	*51.3	†*77.4	†38.8	†57.6	†51.1	†*72.9
$(K+1)$-VC	MS-TCN	91.1	†*95.1	66.5	†77.2	*77.2	†*89.9	63.2	†*83.5	†40.9	†*58.2	†53.2	†*73.8
(RGB)	GRU	†*91.5	†*96.2	†*61.7	†*78.9	†*76.8	†*89.4	*61.8	†82.6	†41.1	†57.9	†54.3	†*73.6
	ASFormer	92.1	†*96.2	†*67.6	†*79.8	77.1	†*89.8	*58.9	†*83.5	†40.0	†*56.9	†*53.6	†*72.9
(c) Hand-engineered tracking & pose features (top scores shown; see supplement Sect. C for GRU and ASFormer)													
2D-VPD [25]	MS-TCN	–	–	**83.5**	†*96.2	*85.2	†*96.4	–	–	–	–	–	–
(d) VC-Spot: video classification baseline using RGB													
RegNet-Y 200MF w/ GSM		†92.4	†96.0	†61.8	†75.5	†56.2	†75.3	†62.4	†85.6	†18.7	†28.6	†25.9	†38.3
(e) E2E-Spot													
Default: 200MF (RGB)		96.1	†97.7	†*81.0	†*93.5	†*85.1	†*95.7	**68.4**	†85.3	†47.9	†65.2	†61.0	†78.4
Best: 800MF (2-stream)		†**96.9**	†**98.1**	†*83.4	†*94.9	†*83.3	†*96.0	66.4	†84.8	†51.8	†68.5	†65.3	†81.6

we extract per-frame I3D features by densely striding a 21-frame window around each frame. To test the impact of better pre-trained models, we also extract features with MViT-B [18], a state-of-the-art model from 2021.

2. *Fine-tuned features* using TSP [2] and $(K+1)$-way clip classification[3]. These features come from a classifier trained to predict whether a small window (e.g., 12 frames) contains an event, and they have the benefit of being adapted to the target video domain (e.g., tennis, skating, gymnastics).

3. *Pose features* (VPD) for the Figure Skating dataset only, which utilize a hand-engineered pipeline for subject tracking and fine-tuning [25]. *These features utilize domain-knowledge and are costly to develop for new datasets*, which may include phenomena not captured by pose (e.g., ball bounce in tennis). In activities such as figure skating, defined heavily by human motion, VPD features serve as a ceiling for E2E-Spot, which is domain agnostic.

Finally, we add a naive, end-to-end learned baseline that adapts video classification directly to the spotting task (VC-Spot). VC-Spot is given a 15-frame clip and tasked to predict whether the middle frame is a precise event. This baseline is to show that precise spotting is a distinct task from video classification.

---

[3] For direct comparison, $(K+1)$-VC uses the same RegNet-Y 200MF w/ GSM CNN backbone as E2E-Spot. See supplement Sect. B for details.

Table 3. Ablation and analysis experiments (mAP @ $\delta = 1$). We compare to E2E-Spot defaults in the top row (RegNet-Y 200MF w/ GSM and GRU). (a) Varying clip lengths show that temporal context from longer clips is generally helpful. (b) Removing temporal information in the feature extractor F (GSM) and in the stateful predictions G (GRU) generally reduces mAP. (c) Reducing input resolution from 224 to 112 pixels reduces mAP. (d) More complex models for G than the 1-layer GRU do not significantly improve mAP. (e) Enlarging F to 800MF and/or adding flow can improve mAP slightly on some datasets.

Experiment	Tennis		FS-Comp		FS-Perf		FineDiving		FineGym-Full	
	mAP	Δ	mAP	Δ	mAP	Δ	mAP	Δ	mAP	Δ
E2E-Spot default: clip length = 100	96.1		†81.0		†85.1		68.4		†47.4	
(a) clip length = 8	†95.8	−0.3	†73.7	−7.3	†74.7	−10.4	†67.3	−1.1	†32.3	−15.1
clip length = 16	†96.2	+0.1	†74.4	−6.6	†80.1	−5.0	†64.8	−3.6	†40.8	−6.6
clip length = 25	†96.2	+0.1	†74.5	−6.5	†80.6	−4.5	†67.2	−1.2	†43.9	−3.5
clip length = 50	†96.4	+0.3	†76.9	−4.1	†82.3	−2.8	65.0	−3.4	†46.6	−0.8
clip length = 250	96.4	+0.3	†81.3	+0.3	†85.6	+0.5	68.9	+0.5	†48.5	+1.1
clip length = 500	95.9	−0.2	†78.9	−2.1	†87.5	+2.4	–	–	†48.1	+0.7
(b) w/o GRU	†95.7	−0.4	†74.3	−6.7	†77.9	−7.2	64.1	−4.3	†32.9	−14.5
w/ TSM [35] instead of GSM	96.1	+0.0	†78.6	−2.4	†83.3	−1.8	†65.3	−3.1	†48.1	+0.7
w/o GSM	†94.1	−2.0	†75.5	−5.5	†85.6	+0.4	68.9	+0.5	†44.2	−3.2
w/o GSM & GRU	†60.1	−36.0	†26.9	−54.1	†41.1	−44.0	†47.0	−21.4	†22.1	−25.3
(c) w/ 112 px resolution (height)	†88.5	−7.6	†75.4	−5.6	†80.9	−4.2	†64.9	−3.5	†45.3	−2.6
(d) w/ MS-TCN	95.7	−0.4	†77.6	−3.4	†84.7	−0.4	67.0	−1.4	†44.1	−3.3
w/ ASFormer	95.7	−0.4	†68.4	−12.6	†75.4	−9.7	70.4	+2.0	†36.8	−10.6
w/ Deeper GRU	96.5	+0.4	†80.2	−0.8	†83.5	−1.6	67.2	−1.2	†46.4	−1.0
w/ GRU* (see supplement)	96.2	+0.1	†78.1	−2.9	†86.0	+0.9	67.4	−1.0	†47.9	+0.5
(e) 200MF (Flow)	†58.2	−37.9	†72.4	−8.6	†76.6	−8.5	†60.7	−7.7	†44.4	−3.0
200MF (RGB + flow; 2-stream)	†96.3	+0.2	†82.2	+1.2	†85.1	+0.0	†70.1	+1.7	†49.0	+1.6
800MF (RGB)	96.8	+0.7	†84.0	+3.0	†83.6	−1.5	64.6	−3.8	†50.1	+2.7
800MF (Flow)	†59.2	−36.9	†74.9	−6.1	†74.2	−10.9	†59.8	−8.6	†46.9	−0.5
800MF (RGB + flow; 2-stream)	†96.9	+0.8	†83.4	+2.4	†83.3	−1.8	†66.4	−2.0	†51.8	+4.4

5.1 Spotting Performance

We present two variations of E2E-Spot in the main results: (1) a default configuration with a RegNet-Y [43] 200MF CNN backbone and RGB input only, and (2) a configuration using RegNet-Y 800MF with RGB and flow input.

E2E-Spot with a 200MF CNN and RGB inputs consistently outperforms all non-pose baselines, while being comparable to the pose ones. The benefits of E2E-Spot are most striking at the most stringent tolerance, $\delta = 1$ frame (Table 2e). We summarize the key takeaways of our evaluation below.

Pre-trained features generalize poorly when no fine-tuning is used, regardless of the head architecture: between 9.1–29.1 worse than E2E-Spot in mAP at $\delta = 1$ (Table 2a). *Fine-tuning yields a significant improvement* over pre-trained features: between 3.9–25.1 mAP at $\delta = 1$ (Table 2b), indicating a large domain gap between Kinetics and the fine-grained spotting datasets. However, *E2E-Spot further outperforms the two-phase approaches with fine-tuned features* by 3.3–6.8

mAP, showing that indirect fine-tuning strategies for temporal localization tasks should be compared against directly supervised, end-to-end learned baselines. Finally, the wide variation in baseline performance (by sport) highlights the importance of evaluating new tasks, such as precise spotting, and their methods on a visually and semantically diverse set of activities and datasets.

VC-Spot performs poorly compared to E2E-Spot (Table 2d), especially on Figure Skating and FineGym, which require temporal understanding at longer timescales (e.g., several seconds) compared to Tennis and FineDiving.

E2E-Spot achieves similar results to pose features (2D-VPD [25]) on Figure Skating, within 0.1–2.5 mAP at $\delta = 1$. This is encouraging because E2E-Spot assumes no domain knowledge and is a more generally applicable approach.

Table 2e also shows E2E-Spot's *best configuration*, using the larger 800MF CNN and both RGB and flow [54]. Neither of these enhancements (e.g., a larger CNN or flow) require domain knowledge, but can provide a small boost to the final performance over our 200MF defaults (0.8 mAP on Tennis and 3.9–4.3 mAP on FineGym). Details for other E2E-Spot configurations are presented in Sect. 5.3.

5.2   Ablations of E2E-Spot

We analyze the requirements of precise spotting with respect to temporal context and network architecture. Refer to supplement Sect. C for additional ablations.

Sensitivity to Clip Length. As a sequence model, E2E-Spot can benefit from and make stateful predictions over a long temporal context (e.g., 100 s of frames). A long clip length allows for greater temporal context for each prediction, but linearly increases memory utilization per batch. We consider the number of frames needed for peak accuracy and train E2E-Spot with different clip lengths. Table 3a shows that different activities require different amounts of temporal context; the fast-paced events in Tennis can be successfully detected even when context is only 8–16 frames. In contrast, Figure Skating and FineGym show a clear drop in performance when clip length is reduced from 100 frames. Even longer clip lengths may be desirable (e.g., 250 frames), though with diminishing returns.

Value of Temporal Information in the Per-frame Features. E2E-Spot incorporates temporal information both in the 2D CNN backbone F (with GSM) and after global spatial-pooling in G (with GRU). We show the criticality of both of these components in Table 3b at $\delta = 1$. With neither GSM nor the GRU, the spotting task becomes a single-image classification problem; as expected, the results are poor (at least -21 mAP). The best results are achieved with both GSM and the GRU, except on FS-Perf and FineDiving, where results with and without GSM are similar. Replacing GSM with TSM [35] (fixed shift) ranges from comparable to worse, showing GSM to be a reasonable starting default.

Spatial Resolution. Lowering spatial resolution [34,38] can speed up end-to-end learning and inference but degrades mAP on precise spotting (Table 3c), where the subjects may, at times, occupy only a small portion of the frame.

Table 4. Average-mAP @ t for tolerances in seconds. SOTA in **bold**. We show the top results from the CVPR 2021 and 2022 SoccerNet Action Spotting challenges. ‡ indicates challenge results—trained on the train, validation, and test splits. Shown and unshown refer to whether actions are visible; E2E-Spot is better at detecting the former, but Soares et al. [50] is superior at the latter.

Average-mAP @ tolerances	Test split		Challenge split		
	Tight (1–5 s)	Loose (5–60 s)	Tight (1–5 s)	Shown	Unshown
RMS-Net [56]	28.83	63.49	27.69	–	–
NetVLAD++ [22]	–	–	43.99	–	–
Zhou et al. [70] (2021 challenge; 1st)	47.05	73.77	49.56	54.42	45.42
‡Soares et al. [50] (2022 challenge; 1st)	–	–	‡**67.81**	‡72.84	‡**60.17**
E2E-Spot 200MF	61.19	73.25	63.28	70.41	45.98
E2E-Spot 800MF	61.82	74.05	66.01	72.76	51.65
‡E2E-Spot 800MF (2022 challenge; 2nd)	–	–	‡66.73	‡**74.84**	‡53.21

5.3 Additional Variations of E2E-Spot

More Complex Architectures, G. Prior TAD and TAS works catalog a rich history of head architectures (see related; Sect. 2) operating on pre-extracted features. We examine whether these architectures can directly benefit from end-to-end learning with E2E-Spot by replacing the 1-layer GRU. Table 3d shows that improvement is not guaranteed; MS-TCN, ASFormer, and deeper GRUs neither consistently nor significantly outperform a single layer GRU. This suggests that *end-to-end learned spatial-temporal features can already capture much of the logic previously handled by the downstream architecture.*

Enhancements to Feature Extractor, F. We explore two basic enhancements to F that do not require new assumptions or domain knowledge: a larger CNN backbone (such as RegNet-Y 800MF) and optical flow [54] input. Table 3e shows that these enhancements can yield modest improvements (up to 4.4 mAP on FineGym). Flow, by itself, is worse than RGB but can improve results when ensembled with RGB. Larger models show promise on some datasets, but the improvements are not as significant as the lift from end-to-end learning.

5.4 Results on the SoccerNet Action Spotting Challenge

E2E-Spot also generalizes to temporally coarse spotting tasks, such as SoccerNet-v2 [13], which studies 17 action classes in 550 matches—split across train/val/test/challenge sets. As in prior work [9,22,56], we extract frames at 2 FPS and evaluate using average-mAP across tolerances, defined as $\pm\delta/2$ second ranges around events. In Table 4, we compare E2E-Spot to the best results from the CVPR 2021 (lenient tolerances of 5–60 s) and CVPR 2022 (less coarse, 1–5 s tolerances) SoccerNet Action Spotting challenges [14].

E2E-Spot, with the 200MF CNN, matches the top prior method from the 2021 competition [70] in the 5–60 s setting while outperforming it by 13.7–14.1 avg-mAP points in the less coarse, 1–5 s setting. Increasing the CNN to 800MF improves avg-mAP slightly (by 0.4–2.7 avg-mAP). E2E-Spot places second in the (concurrent) 2022 competition (within 1.1 avg-mAP), after Soares et al. [50], due to the latter's strong performance on unshown actions (not visible in the frame). Soares et al. [50,51] and Zhou et al. [70] are two-phase approaches, combining pre-extracted features from multiple (5 to 6) heterogeneous, fine-tuned feature extractors and proposing downstream architectures and losses on those features. In contrast, E2E-Spot shows that direct, end-to-end training of a simple and compact model can be a surprisingly strong baseline.

6   Discussion and Future Work

In this paper, we have presented a from-the-ground-up study of end-to-end feature learning for spotting in the temporally stringent setting.

E2E-Spot is a simple baseline that obtains competitive or state-of-the-art performance on temporally precise (and coarser) spotting tasks, outperforming conventional approaches derived from related work on TAD and TAS (Sect. 2). The secondary benefits we obtain from end-to-end learning are a simplified analysis pipeline, trained in a single phase under direct supervision, and the ability to use smaller, simpler models, without sacrificing accuracy on the frame-accurate task. Methodological enhancements such as improved architectures (e.g., based on ViT [17]) for feature extraction, training methodologies, head architectures, and losses that benefit from end-to-end learning are interesting research directions. We hope that E2E-Spot serves as a principled baseline for this future work.

Video understanding encapsulates a broad body of tasks, of which spotting frame-accurate events is a single example. We consider it future work to analyze other tasks and their datasets, and we anticipate situations where end-to-end learning alone may be insufficient: e.g., when reliable priors such as pose are readily available, or when training data is limited or exhibits domain-shift in the pixel domain. Learning to spot accurately with few or weak labels will accelerate the curation new datasets for more advanced, downstream video analysis tasks.

7   Conclusion

We have introduced temporally precise spotting in video, supported by four fine-grained sports datasets. Many recent advances in TAD, TAS, and spotting trend towards increasingly complex models and processing pipelines, which generalize poorly for this strict, but practical setting. E2E-Spot shows that a few key design principles—task-specialized spatial-temporal features, reasoning over sufficient temporal context, and efficient end-to-end learning—can go a long way for improving accuracy and simplifying solutions.

Acknowledgements. This work is supported by the National Science Foundation (NSF) under III-1908727, Intel Corporation, and Adobe Research. We also thank the anonymous reviewers for their comments and feedback.

References

1. Ahn, H., Lee, D.: Refining action segmentation with hierarchical video representations. In: Proceedings of the IEEE/CVF International Conference on Computer Vision (ICCV), pp. 16302–16310, October 2021
2. Alwassel, H., Giancola, S., Ghanem, B.: TSP: temporally-sensitive pretraining of video encoders for localization tasks. In: Proceedings of the IEEE/CVF International Conference on Computer Vision (ICCV) Workshops, pp. 3173–3183, October 2021
3. Buch, S., Escorcia, V., Ghanem, B., Niebles, J.C.: End-to-end, single-stream temporal action detection in untrimmed videos. In: Proceedings of the British Machine Vision Conference (BMVC), September 2017
4. Buch, S., Escorcia, V., Shen, C., Ghanem, B., Carlos Niebles, J.: SST: single-stream temporal action proposals. In: Proceedings of the IEEE Conference on Computer Vision and Pattern Recognition (CVPR), July 2017
5. Caba Heilbron, F., Escorcia, V., Ghanem, B., Carlos Niebles, J.: ActivityNet: a large-scale video benchmark for human activity understanding. In: Proceedings of the IEEE Conference on Computer Vision and Pattern Recognition (CVPR), June 2015
6. Carreira, J., Zisserman, A.: Quo Vadis, action recognition? A new model and the Kinetics dataset. In: Proceedings of the IEEE Conference on Computer Vision and Pattern Recognition (CVPR), July 2017
7. Chen, M.H., Li, B., Bao, Y., AlRegib, G.: Action segmentation with mixed temporal domain adaptation. In: Proceedings of the IEEE/CVF Winter Conference on Applications of Computer Vision (WACV), March 2020
8. Chung, J., Gulcehre, C., Cho, K., Bengio, Y.: Empirical evaluation of gated recurrent neural networks on sequence modeling. In: Proceedings of NIPS Deep Learning and Representation Learning Workshop (2014)
9. Cioppa, A., et al.: A context-aware loss function for action spotting in soccer videos. In: IEEE/CVF Conference on Computer Vision and Pattern Recognition (CVPR), June 2020
10. Dai, R., Das, S., Minciullo, L., Garattoni, L., Francesca, G., Bremond, F.: PDAN: pyramid dilated attention network for action detection. In: Proceedings of the IEEE/CVF Winter Conference on Applications of Computer Vision (WACV), pp. 2970–2979, January 2021
11. Dai, R., et al.: Toyota smarthome untrimmed: real-world untrimmed videos for activity detection (2020). arXiv:2010.14982
12. Damen, D., et al.: Scaling egocentric vision: the EPIC-kitchens dataset. In: Ferrari, V., Hebert, M., Sminchisescu, C., Weiss, Y. (eds.) ECCV 2018. LNCS, vol. 11208, pp. 753–771. Springer, Cham (2018). https://doi.org/10.1007/978-3-030-01225-0_44
13. Deliege, A., et al.: SoccerNet-v2: a dataset and benchmarks for holistic understanding of broadcast soccer videos. In: Proceedings of the IEEE/CVF Conference on Computer Vision and Pattern Recognition (CVPR) Workshops, pp. 4508–4519, June 2021
14. Deliège, A., et al.: SoccerNet - action spotting (2022). https://github.com/SoccerNet/sn-spotting
15. Deng, J., Dong, W., Socher, R., Li, L.J., Li, K., Fei-Fei, L.: ImageNet: a large-scale hierarchical image database. In: Proceedings of the IEEE/CVF Conference on Computer Vision and Pattern Recognition (CVPR), June 2009

16. Ding, L., Xu, C.: TricorNet: a hybrid temporal convolutional and recurrent network for video action segmentation (2017). arXiv:1705.07818
17. Dosovitskiy, A., et al.: An image is worth 16x16 words: transformers for image recognition at scale. In: International Conference on Learning Representations (ICLR) (2021)
18. Fan, H., et al.: Multiscale vision transformers. In: Proceedings of the IEEE/CVF International Conference on Computer Vision (ICCV), pp. 6824–6835, October 2021
19. Farha, Y.A., Gall, J.: MS-TCN: multi-stage temporal convolutional network for action segmentation. In: Proceedings of the IEEE/CVF Conference on Computer Vision and Pattern Recognition (CVPR), June 2019
20. Fathi, A., Ren, X., Rehg, J.M.: Learning to recognize objects in egocentric activities. In: Proceedings of the IEEE/CVF Conference on Computer Vision and Pattern Recognition (CVPR), June 2011
21. Feichtenhofer, C., Fan, H., Malik, J., He, K.: SlowFast networks for video recognition. In: Proceedings of the IEEE/CVF International Conference on Computer Vision (ICCV), October 2019
22. Giancola, S., Ghanem, B.: Temporally-aware feature pooling for action spotting in soccer broadcasts. In: Proceedings of the IEEE/CVF Conference on Computer Vision and Pattern Recognition (CVPR) Workshops, pp. 4490–4499, June 2021
23. Girshick, R., Donahue, J., Darrell, T., Malik, J.: Rich feature hierarchies for accurate object detection and semantic segmentation. In: Proceedings of the IEEE Conference on Computer Vision and Pattern Recognition (CVPR), June 2014
24. Hao, Y., Zhang, H., Ngo, C.W., Liu, Q., Hu, X.: Compact bilinear augmented query structured attention for sport highlights classification. In: Proceedings of the 28th ACM International Conference on Multimedia, pp. 628–636. Association for Computing Machinery, New York (2020)
25. Hong, J., Fisher, M., Gharbi, M., Fatahalian, K.: Video pose distillation for few-shot, fine-grained sports action recognition. In: Proceedings of the IEEE/CVF International Conference on Computer Vision (ICCV), pp. 9254–9263, October 2021
26. Ibrahim, M.S., Muralidharan, S., Deng, Z., Vahdat, A., Mori, G.: A hierarchical deep temporal model for group activity recognition. In: Proceedings of the IEEE Conference on Computer Vision and Pattern Recognition (CVPR), June 2016
27. Ishikawa, Y., Kasai, S., Aoki, Y., Kataoka, H.: Alleviating over-segmentation errors by detecting action boundaries. In: Proceedings of the IEEE/CVF Winter Conference on Applications of Computer Vision (WACV), pp. 2322–2331, January 2021
28. Jiang, Y.G., et al.: THUMOS challenge: action recognition with a large number of classes (2014)
29. Kay, W., et al.: The Kinetics human action video dataset (2017). arXiv:1705.06950
30. Kuehne, H., Arslan, A., Serre, T.: The language of actions: recovering the syntax and semantics of goal-directed human activities. In: Proceedings of the IEEE Conference on Computer Vision and Pattern Recognition (CVPR), June 2014
31. Li, A., Thotakuri, M., Ross, D.A., Carreira, J., Vostrikov, A., Zisserman, A.: The AVA-kinetics localized human actions video dataset (2020). arXiv:2005.00214
32. Li, Y., Li, Y., Vasconcelos, N.: RESOUND: towards action recognition without representation bias. In: Ferrari, V., Hebert, M., Sminchisescu, C., Weiss, Y. (eds.) ECCV 2018. LNCS, vol. 11210, pp. 520–535. Springer, Cham (2018). https://doi.org/10.1007/978-3-030-01231-1_32

33. Li, Y., Chen, L., He, R., Wang, Z., Wu, G., Wang, L.: MultiSports: a multi-person video dataset of spatio-temporally localized sports actions. In: Proceedings of the IEEE/CVF International Conference on Computer Vision (ICCV), pp. 13536–13545, October 2021

34. Lin, C., et al.: Learning salient boundary feature for anchor-free temporal action localization. In: Proceedings of the IEEE/CVF Conference on Computer Vision and Pattern Recognition (CVPR). pp. 3320–3329, June 2021

35. Lin, J., Gan, C., Han, S.: TSM: temporal shift module for efficient video understanding. In: Proceedings of the IEEE/CVF International Conference on Computer Vision (ICCV), October 2019

36. Lin, T., Liu, X., Li, X., Ding, E., Wen, S.: BMN: boundary-matching network for temporal action proposal generation. In: Proceedings of the IEEE/CVF International Conference on Computer Vision (ICCV), October 2019

37. Lin, T., Zhao, X., Su, H., Wang, C., Yang, M.: BSN: boundary sensitive network for temporal action proposal generation. In: Ferrari, V., Hebert, M., Sminchisescu, C., Weiss, Y. (eds.) ECCV 2018. LNCS, vol. 11208, pp. 3–21. Springer, Cham (2018). https://doi.org/10.1007/978-3-030-01225-0_1

38. Liu, X., Bai, S., Bai, X.: An empirical study of end-to-end temporal action detection. In: Proceedings of the IEEE/CVF Conference on Computer Vision and Pattern Recognition (CVPR), pp. 20010–20019, June 2022

39. Liu, X., Hu, Y., Bai, S., Ding, F., Bai, X., Torr, P.H.S.: Multi-shot temporal event localization: a benchmark. In: Proceedings of the IEEE/CVF Conference on Computer Vision and Pattern Recognition (CVPR), pp. 12596–12606, June 2021

40. Loshchilov, I., Hutter, F.: SGDR: stochastic gradient descent with warm restarts. In: Proceedings of the International Conference on Learning Representations (ICLR) (2017)

41. Loshchilov, I., Hutter, F.: Decoupled weight decay regularization. In: Proceedings of the International Conference on Learning Representations (ICLR) (2019)

42. Nvidia: Nvidia RTX A5000 data sheet (2021)

43. Radosavovic, I., Kosaraju, R.P., Girshick, R., He, K., Dollar, P.: Designing network design spaces. In: Proceedings of the IEEE/CVF Conference on Computer Vision and Pattern Recognition (CVPR), June 2020

44. Shao, D., Zhao, Y., Dai, B., Lin, D.: FineGym: a hierarchical video dataset for fine-grained action understanding. In: Proceedings of the IEEE/CVF Conference on Computer Vision and Pattern Recognition (CVPR), June 2020

45. Sigurdsson, G., Choi, J.: Charades challenge (2017)

46. Sigurdsson, G.A., Divvala, S., Farhadi, A., Gupta, A.: Asynchronous temporal fields for action recognition. In: Proceedings of the IEEE Conference on Computer Vision and Pattern Recognition (CVPR), July 2017

47. Sigurdsson, G.A., Varol, G., Wang, X., Farhadi, A., Laptev, I., Gupta, A.: Hollywood in homes: crowdsourcing data collection for activity understanding. In: Leibe, B., Matas, J., Sebe, N., Welling, M. (eds.) ECCV 2016. LNCS, vol. 9905, pp. 510–526. Springer, Cham (2016). https://doi.org/10.1007/978-3-319-46448-0_31

48. Singh, B., Marks, T.K., Jones, M., Tuzel, O., Shao, M.: A multi-stream bidirectional recurrent neural network for fine-grained action detection. In: Proceedings of the IEEE Conference on Computer Vision and Pattern Recognition (CVPR), June 2016

49. Singhania, D., Rahaman, R., Yao, A.: Coarse to fine multi-resolution temporal convolutional network (2021). arXiv:2105.10859

50. Soares, J.V.B., Shah, A.: Action spotting using dense detection anchors revisited: submission to the SoccerNet Challenge 2022 (2022). arXiv:2206.07846

51. Soares, J.V.B., Shah, A., Biswas, T.: Temporally precise action spotting in soccer videos using dense detection anchors (2022). arXiv:2205.10450

52. Stein, S., McKenna, S.J.: Combining embedded accelerometers with computer vision for recognizing food preparation activities. In: Proceedings of ACM International Joint Conference on Pervasive and Ubiquitous Computing (UbiComp), pp. 729–738. Association for Computing Machinery, New York (2013)

53. Sudhakaran, S., Escalera, S., Lanz, O.: Gate-shift networks for video action recognition. In: Proceedings of the IEEE/CVF Conference on Computer Vision and Pattern Recognition (CVPR), June 2020

54. Teed, Z., Deng, J.: RAFT: recurrent all-pairs field transforms for optical flow. In: Vedaldi, A., Bischof, H., Brox, T., Frahm, J.-M. (eds.) ECCV 2020. LNCS, vol. 12347, pp. 402–419. Springer, Cham (2020). https://doi.org/10.1007/978-3-030-58536-5_24

55. Tirupattur, P., Duarte, K., Rawat, Y.S., Shah, M.: Modeling multi-label action dependencies for temporal action localization. In: Proceedings of the IEEE/CVF Conference on Computer Vision and Pattern Recognition (CVPR), pp. 1460–1470, June 2021

56. Tomei, M., Baraldi, L., Calderara, S., Bronzin, S., Cucchiara, R.: RMS-Net: regression and masking for soccer event spotting. In: 2020 25th International Conference on Pattern Recognition (ICPR), pp. 7699–7706. IEEE Computer Society, Los Alamitos, January 2021

57. Tran, D., Wang, H., Torresani, L., Ray, J., LeCun, Y., Paluri, M.: A closer look at spatiotemporal convolutions for action recognition. In: Proceedings of the IEEE Conference on Computer Vision and Pattern Recognition (CVPR), June 2018

58. TwentyBN: The 20BN-something-something dataset v2

59. Wang, L., et al.: Temporal segment networks: towards good practices for deep action recognition. In: Leibe, B., Matas, J., Sebe, N., Welling, M. (eds.) ECCV 2016. LNCS, vol. 9912, pp. 20–36. Springer, Cham (2016). https://doi.org/10.1007/978-3-319-46484-8_2

60. Xu, J., Rao, Y., Yu, X., Chen, G., Zhou, J., Lu, J.: FineDiving: a fine-grained dataset for procedure-aware action quality assessment. In: Proceedings of the IEEE/CVF Conference on Computer Vision and Pattern Recognition (CVPR), pp. 2949–2958, June 2022

61. Xu, M., Zhao, C., Rojas, D.S., Thabet, A., Ghanem, B.: G-TAD: sub-graph localization for temporal action detection. In: Proceedings of the IEEE/CVF Conference on Computer Vision and Pattern Recognition (CVPR), June 2020

62. Yeung, S., Russakovsky, O., Jin, N., Andriluka, M., Mori, G., Fei-Fei, L.: Every moment counts: dense detailed labeling of actions in complex videos. Int. J. Comput. Vision 126(2–4), 375–389 (2018)

63. Yi, F., Wen, H., Jiang, T.: ASFormer: transformer for action segmentation. In: Proceedings of the British Machine Vision Conference (BMVC), November 2021

64. Zeng, R., et al.: Graph convolutional networks for temporal action localization. In: Proceedings of the IEEE/CVF International Conference on Computer Vision (ICCV), October 2019

65. Zhang, C., Wu, J., Li, Y.: ActionFormer: localizing moments of actions with transformers (2022). arXiv:2202.07925

66. Zhang, H., Sciutto, C., Agrawala, M., Fatahalian, K.: Vid2Player: controllable video sprites that behave and appear like professional tennis players. ACM Trans. Graph. 40(3) (2021)

67. Zhang, H., Cisse, M., Dauphin, Y.N., Lopez-Paz, D.: mixup: Beyond empirical risk minimization. In: Proceedings of the International Conference on Learning Representations (ICLR) (2018)
68. Zhao, C., Thabet, A.K., Ghanem, B.: Video self-stitching graph network for temporal action localization. In: Proceedings of the IEEE/CVF International Conference on Computer Vision (ICCV), pp. 13658–13667, October 2021
69. Zhou, B., Andonian, A., Oliva, A., Torralba, A.: Temporal relational reasoning in videos. In: Ferrari, V., Hebert, M., Sminchisescu, C., Weiss, Y. (eds.) ECCV 2018. LNCS, vol. 11205, pp. 831–846. Springer, Cham (2018). https://doi.org/10.1007/978-3-030-01246-5_49
70. Zhou, X., Kang, L., Cheng, Z., He, B., Xin, J.: Feature combination meets attention: Baidu soccer embeddings and transformer based temporal detection (2021). arXiv:2106.14447

Unified Fully and Timestamp Supervised Temporal Action Segmentation via Sequence to Sequence Translation

Nadine Behrmann[1], S. Alireza Golestaneh[1(✉)], Zico Kolter[1], Jürgen Gall[2], and Mehdi Noroozi[1]

[1] Bosch Center for Artificial Intelligence, Pittsburgh, USA
isalirezag@gmail.com
[2] University of Bonn, Bonn, Germany

Abstract. This paper introduces a unified framework for video action segmentation via sequence to sequence (seq2seq) translation in a fully and timestamp supervised setup. In contrast to current state-of-the-art frame-level prediction methods, we view action segmentation as a seq2seq translation task, *i.e.*, mapping a sequence of video frames to a sequence of action segments. Our proposed method involves a series of modifications and auxiliary loss functions on the standard Transformer seq2seq translation model to cope with long input sequences opposed to short output sequences and relatively few videos. We incorporate an auxiliary supervision signal for the encoder via a frame-wise loss and propose a separate alignment decoder for an implicit duration prediction. Finally, we extend our framework to the timestamp supervised setting via our proposed constrained k-medoids algorithm to generate pseudo-segmentations. Our proposed framework performs consistently on both fully and timestamp supervised settings, outperforming or competing state-of-the-art on several datasets.

Keywords: Video understanding · Action segmentation · Timestamp supervised learning · Transformers · Auto-regressive learning

1 Introduction

The ability to analyze, comprehend, and segment video content at a temporal level is crucial for many computer vision, video understanding, robotics, and surveillance applications. Recent state-of-the-art methods for action segmentation mainly formalize the task as a frame-wise classification problem; that is, the objective is to assign an

---

N. Behrmann and S. A. Golestaneh—Equal contribution. JG has been supported by the Deutsche Forschungsgemeinschaft (DFG, German Research Foundation) GA1927/4–2 (FOR 2535 Anticipating Human Behavior), MKW NRW iBehave, and the ERC Consolidator Grant FORHUE (101044724).

Supplementary Information The online version contains supplementary material available at https://doi.org/10.1007/978-3-031-19833-5_4.

S. Avidan et al. (Eds.): ECCV 2022, LNCS 13695, pp. 52–68, 2022.
https://doi.org/10.1007/978-3-031-19833-5_4

action label to each frame, based upon the full sequence of video frames. We illustrate this general approach in Fig. 1 (a). However, this formulation suffers several drawbacks, such as over-segmentation when trained on relatively small datasets (which typically need to consist of expensive frame-level annotations).

In this work, we propose an alternative approach to the action segmentation task. Our approach involves a transformer-based seq2seq architecture that aims to map from the video frames directly to a *higher-level sequence* of action segments, *i.e.,* a sequence of action label/duration pairs that describes the full predicted segmentation.

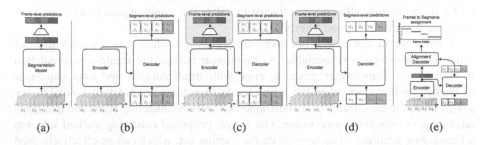

(a)   (b)   (c)   (d)   (e)

Fig. 1. Using Transformers for Action Segmentation. Instead of frame-level predictions, which are prone to over-segmentation (a), we propose a seq2seq transformer model for segment-level predictions (b). To provide more direct feedback to the encoder we apply a frame-wise loss (c); the resulting features enhance the decoder predictions. However, duration prediction still suffers, so we focus on transcript prediction (d) and use a separate alignment decoder to fuse encoder and decoder features to arrive at an implicit form of duration prediction (e).

The basic structure of our model follows traditional Transformer-based seq2seq models: the encoder branch takes as input a sequence of video frames and maps them to a set of features with the same length; the decoder branch then takes these features as input and generates a predicted sequence of high-level action segments in an auto-regressive manner. This approach, illustrated in Fig. 1 (b), is a natural fit for action segmentation because it allows the decoder to directly output sequences in the higher-level description space. The main advantage over the frame-level prediction is that it is less prone to over-segmentation.

However, this seemingly natural approach does not immediately perform well on the action segmentation task by itself. In contrast to language translation, action segmentation typically involves long input sequences of very similar frames opposed to short output sequences of action segments. This difference together with the relatively small amount of training videos, makes it challenging for the encoder and decoder to keep track of the full information flow that is necessary to predict the high-level segmentation alone. For this reason, we incorporate several modifications and additional loss terms into our system, which together make this approach compete with or improve upon the state-of-the-art.

First, to provide more immediate feedback to the encoder, we employ a frame-wise loss that linearly classifies each frame with the corresponding action label given the encoder features, Fig. 1 (c). As a result, the encoder performs frame-wise classification with high localization performance, *i.e.,* high frame-wise accuracy, but low discrimination performance, *i.e.,* over-segmentation with low Edit distance to the ground truth. Nonetheless, its features provide the decoder an informative signal to predict the sequence of actions more accurately. This immediate auxiliary supervision signal allows the decoder to learn more discriminative features for different actions. While the frame-wise loss improves the transcript prediction, the decoder still suffers from low localization performance for duration prediction. As the next step, we fuse the decoder predictions with the encoder, for which we propose two solutions. First, we propose to fuse the discriminative features of the decoder with the encoder features via a cross-attention mechanism in an alignment decoder, Fig. 1 (d, e). Second, the high performance of our decoder on predicting transcripts and the high performance of our encoder on localizing actions allows us to effectively utilize the common post-processing algorithm such as FIFA [33] and Viterbi [21,30].

Finally, we further extend our proposed framework when only a weaker form of timestamp supervision is available. As mentioned before, the frame-wise prediction is vital in our Transformer model to cope with small datasets and long sequences of frames. In this case, when the frame-level annotations are not fully available, we assign a label to each frame by a constrained k-medoids clustering algorithm that takes advantage of timestamp supervision. Our simple proposed clustering method achieves a frame-wise accuracy of up to 81% on the training set, which can be effectively used to train our seq2seq model. We further show that the clustering method can also be used in combination with frame-wise prediction methods such as ASFormer [42].

We evaluate our model on three challenging action segmentation benchmarks: 50Salads [35], GTEA [12], and Breakfast [19]. While our method achieves competitive frame-wise accuracies compared to the state-of-the-art, our method substantially outperforms other approaches in predicting the action sequence of a video, which is measured by the Edit distance. By using Viterbi [21,30] or FIFA [33] as post-processing, our approach also achieves state-of-the-art results in terms of segmental F1 scores. To the best of our knowledge, this work is the first that utilizes Transformers in an autoregressive manner for action segmentation and is applicable to both the fully and timestamp supervised setup.

2   Related Work

Fully Supervised Action Segmentation. Early approaches for action segmentation are based on sliding window and non-maximum suppression [18,31]. Other traditional approaches use hidden Markov Models (HMM) for high-level temporal modeling [20,36]. [28] use a language and length model to model the probability of action sequences and convert the frame-wise probabilities into action segments using dynamic programming.

More recent approaches are based on temporal convolutions: [22] propose temporal convolutional networks (TCN) with temporal pooling to capture long-range dependencies within the video. However, such temporal pooling operations struggle to maintain fine-grained temporal information. Therefore, [1,25] use multi-stage TCNs, which maintain a high temporal resolution, with a smoothing loss and refinement modules. These methods solve the action segmentation task by predicting an action class for each frame, which is prone to over-segmentation and requires refinement modules and smoothing or expensive inference algorithms. [17] address this issue by adding a boundary regression branch to detect action boundaries, which are used during inference to refine the segmentation. [16] propose a graph-based temporal reasoning module that can be built on top of existing methods to refine predicted segmentations.

Weakly Supervised Action Segmentation. To avoid the costly frame-wise annotations, many methods have been proposed that rely on a weaker form of supervision [5,9,24,29,34], such as transcript supervision [5]: Here, only the ordered sequence of actions in the video are given. [15] extend the connectionist temporal classification framework, originally introduced for speech recognition, to videos to efficiently evaluate all possible frame-to-action alignments. [10] propose an iterative soft boundary assignment strategy to generate frame-wise pseudo-labels from transcripts. [30] generate frame-wise pseudo-labels with the Viterbi algorithm. [24] extend this work by adding a loss that discriminates between valid and invalid segmentations. [34] use a two-branch neural network with a frame classification branch and a segment generation branch and enforce the two representations to be consistent via a mutual consistency loss. Similar to our method, their segment generation branch also predicts the transcript in an auto-regressive manner and achieves high Edit scores, validating our aspiration for segment-level predictions. While transcript supervision reduces the annotation cost significantly, the performance suffers. As an alternative, timestamp supervision [26] has been proposed, where for each action segment a single frame is annotated. The annotation cost for such timestamps is comparable to transcript annotations [26] but provides stronger supervision as it gives information about the rough location of the segments.

Transformers. Transformers [38] originally emerged in the field of natural language processing, and solely rely on the attention mechanism to capture contextual information from the entire sequence. Recently, Transformers have also seen wide adoption in vision-related tasks, *e.g.*, image classification [11], segmentation [40,43] and action classification [2,4]. Current standard Transformer-based models are unable to process very long sequences [3,8,27,37,44]. One reason for this is the self-attention operation, which scales quadratically with the sequence length. [3] showed that using sliding window attention can reduce the time and memory complexity of the Transformer while preserving the performance. Recently, ASFormer [42] leveraged multi-stage TCNs [1] and transformer-based models for action segmentation. For each dilated temporal convolutional layer of MS-TCN, an additional self-attention block with instance normalization is added. The first stage is the encoder while the later stages are the decoders, which take the concatenated features of the encoder and the features at the end of the previous stage as input. While we use a similar encoder as ASFormer [42], our decoder is very different. While ASFormer and MS-TCN perform frame-level prediction as illustrated in Fig. 1 (a), our decoder predicts the action segments in an autoregressive manner as illustrated in Fig. 1 (d, e).

3   Method

In this section, we introduce our Unified Video Action Segmentation model via Transformers (*UVAST*). The goal of action segmentation is to temporally segment long, untrimmed videos and classify each of the obtained segments. Current state-of-the-art methods are based on *frame-level* predictions – they assign an action label to each individual frame – which are prone to *over-segmentation*: The video is not accurately segmented into clean, continuous segments, but fragmented into many shorter pieces of alternating action classes. We challenge this view of frame-level predictions and propose a novel approach that directly predicts the segments. By focusing on *segment-level* predictions – an alternative but equivalent representation of segmentations – our method overcomes the deep-rooted over-segmentation problem of frame-level predictions.

3.1 Transformer for Auto-Regressive Segment Prediction

In this work, we view action segmentation from a sequence-to-sequence (seq2seq) perspective: mapping a sequence of video frames to a sequence of action segments, *e.g.,* as pairs of action label and segment duration. The Transformer model [38] has emerged as a particularly powerful tool for seq2seq tasks and may seem like the natural fit. The vanilla Transformer model consists of an encoder module that captures long-range dependencies within the input sequence and a decoder module that translates the input sequence to the desired output sequence in an auto-regressive manner. In contrast to language translation tasks, action segmentation faces a strong mismatch between input and output sequence lengths, *i.e.,* inputs are long and untrimmed videos with various sequence lengths, while outputs are relatively short sequences of action segments. Therefore, we incorporate several modifications to address these issues, which we will go over in more detail in the following.

Notation. Given an input sequence of T frame-wise features x_t, for frame $t \in \{1, \ldots, T\}$, our goal is to temporally segment and classify the T frames. The ground-truth labels of a segmentation can be represented in two equivalent forms: 1) a sequence of frame-wise action labels $\hat{y}_t \in C$ for frame t, where C is the set of action classes, 2) a sequence of segment-wise annotations, which consists of ground-truth segment action classes $\hat{a}_i \in C$ (also known as *transcript*), and segment durations $\hat{u}_i \in \mathbb{R}_+$ for each segment $i \in \{1, \ldots, N\}$.

Transformer Encoder. Our input sequence $X \in \mathbb{R}^{T \times d}$ consists of T frame-wise features x_t, where d denotes the feature dimension. We embed them using a linear layer and then feed them to the Transformer encoder, which consists of several layers and allows the model to capture long-range dependencies within the video via the self-attention mechanism. The output of the encoder, $E \in \mathbb{R}^{T \times d'}$, is a sequence of frame-wise features e_t, which will be used in the cross-attention module of the decoder. To provide direct feedback to the encoder, we apply a linear layer to obtain frame-level predictions for e_t. This enables the encoder to accurately localize the action classes within the video and provides more informative features to the decoder. In practice, we use a modified version of the encoder proposed in [42], which locally restricts the self-attention mechanism and uses dilated convolutions (see supplemental material for more details).

Transformer Decoder. Given a sequence of frame-wise features $E \in \mathbb{R}^{T \times d'}$, we use a Transformer decoder to auto-regressively predict the transcript, *i.e.,* the action labels of the segments. Starting with a *start-of-sequence (sos)* token, we feed the sequence of segments $S \in \mathbb{R}^{N \times d'}$ – embedded using learnable class tokens and positional encoding – up until segment i to the decoder. Via the cross-attention between the current sequence of segments and frame-wise features, the decoder determines the next segment $i + 1$ in the video. In principle, the decoder could predict the segment duration as well (Fig. 1 (c)), however, in practice we found that the decoder's duration prediction suffers from low localization performance, see Table 4. While it is sufficient to pick out a single or few frames in the cross-attention mechanism for predicting the correct action class of a segment, the duration prediction is more difficult since it requires to assign frames to a segment and count them. Since the number of segments is much smaller than the number of frames, the cross-attention mechanism tends to assign only a subset of the frames to the correct segment. To address this issue, we propose a separate decoder module, which fuses the discriminative decoder features with the highly localized encoder features to obtain a more accurate duration prediction, which we describe in Sect. 3.3.

3.2 Training Objective

Although our ultimate goal is segment-level predictions, we provide feedback to both the encoder and decoder model to make the best use of the labels. To that end, we apply a frame-wise cross-entropy loss on the frame-level predictions of the encoder:

$$\mathcal{L}_{\text{frame}} = -\frac{1}{T} \sum_{t=1}^{T} \log(y_{t,\hat{c}}), \tag{1}$$

where $y_{t,c}$ denotes the predicted probability of label c at time t, and $\hat{c}$ denotes the ground-truth label of frame t. Analogously, we apply a segment-wise cross-entropy loss on the segment-level predictions of the decoder:

$$\mathcal{L}_{\text{segment}} = -\frac{1}{N} \sum_{i=1}^{N} \log(a_{i,\hat{c}}), \tag{2}$$

where $a_{i,c}$ denotes the predicted probability of label c at segment i, and $\hat{c}$ denotes the ground-truth label of segment i.

Regularization via Grouping. To regularize the encoder and decoder predictions, we additionally apply *group-wise* cross-entropy losses. To that end, we group the frames and segments by ground-truth labels $L = \{c \in \mathcal{C} | c \in \{\hat{a}_1, \ldots, \hat{a}_n\}\}$ that occur in the video: $T_c = \{t \in \{1, \ldots, T\} | \hat{y}_t = c\}$ are the indices of frames with class c, and $N_c = \{i \in \{1, \ldots, N\} | \hat{a}_i = c\}$ the indices of segments with class c. We apply a cross-entropy loss to the averaged prediction of each group:

$$\mathcal{L}_{\text{g-frame}} = -\frac{1}{|L|} \sum_{c \in L} \log(\frac{1}{|T_c|} \sum_{t \in T_c} y_{t,c}) \tag{3}$$

$$\mathcal{L}_{\text{g-segment}} = -\frac{1}{|L|} \sum_{c \in L} \log(\frac{1}{|N_c|} \sum_{i \in N_c} a_{i,c}) \tag{4}$$

3.3 Cross-Attention Loss

We utilize a loss through a cross-attention mechanism between the encoder and decoder features to allow further interactions between them. Let us assume that T video frames and corresponding N actions in the encoder and decoder are represented by their features $E \in \mathbb{R}^{T \times d'}$ and $D \in \mathbb{R}^{N \times d'}$, respectively. The cross-attention loss involves obtaining a cross-attention matrix $M = \texttt{softmax}(\frac{ED^T}{\tau' \sqrt{d'}})$, where τ' is a stability temperature, and each row of M includes a probability vector that assigns each encoder feature (frame) to decoder features (actions). We then use M in the following cross-entropy loss function:

$$\mathcal{L}_{CA}(M) = -\frac{1}{T} \sum_t \log(M_{t,\hat{n}}), \qquad (5)$$

where $\hat{n}$ is the ground-truth segment index to which frame t belongs. We use this loss in our transcript decoder (main decoder) and alignment decoder in the following.

Cross-Attention Loss for the Transcript Decoder. The cross-attention loss, when applied to the transcript decoder, provides more intermediate feedback to the decoder about the action location in the input sequence, see Fig. 4. We found this loss function especially effective on smaller datasets such as 50Salads (see Table 5). Our main objective for the encoder and the transcript decoder is:

$$\mathcal{L} = \mathcal{L}_{\text{frame}} + \mathcal{L}_{\text{segment}} + \mathcal{L}_{\text{g-frame}} + \mathcal{L}_{\text{g-segment}} + \mathcal{L}_{CA}(M), \qquad (6)$$

Cross-Attention Loss for the Alignment Decoder. While the transcript decoder generates the sequence of actions in a video, it does not predict the duration of each action. Although it is possible to predict the duration as well, as illustrated in Fig. 1 (c), the transcript decoder still struggles to localize actions through direct duration prediction as shown in Table 4. One reason for this could be the high mismatch between input and output sequence length and the relatively small number of training videos. While picking up a single segment frame is sufficient to predict the action class, the duration prediction effectively requires counting the number of frames in the segment, resulting in a more challenging task. Therefore, we design an alternative alignment decoder for predicting segment durations implicitly.

A high Edit score of our decoder indicates that it has already learned discriminative features of the actions. The motivation for our alignment decoder is to align the encoder features to the highly discriminative features of the decoder, which can be further used for the duration prediction (see Fig 1 (e)). In essence, our proposed alignment decoder is a one-to-many mapping from the decoder features to the encoder features. The alignment decoder takes the encoder and decoder features $E \in \mathbb{R}^{T \times d'}$ and $D \in \mathbb{R}^{N \times d'}$ with positional encoding as input and generates the aligned features $A \in \mathbb{R}^{T \times d'}$. Since the alignment decoder aims to explore the dependencies between the encoder features and the decoder features, we employ a cross-attention mechanism in its architecture similar to the transcript decoder. To this end, we compute an assignment matrix $\overline{M} \in \mathbb{R}^{T \times N}$ via cross-attention between the alignment decoder features (A) and positional encoded features of the transcript decoder (D) by $\overline{M} = \texttt{softmax}(\frac{AD^T}{\tau})$ with a small value of τ. Note that with a small value of τ each row of $\overline{M}$ will be close to a one-hot-encoding indicating the segment index the frame is assigned to. The positional encoding for D resolves ambiguities if the same action occurs at several locations in the video.

In contrast to the decoder from the previous section, the alignment decoder is not auto-regressive since the full sequences of frame-wise and segment-wise features are already available from the previous encoder and decoder. During inference, we compute the segment durations by taking the sum over the assignments:

$$u_i = \sum_t \overline{M}_{t,i}, \tag{7}$$

where $i \in \{1, ..., n\}$ and $\overline{M}_{t,i}$ denotes whether frame t is assigned to segment i. We found that training the alignment decoder using only the loss for $\overline{M}$ (7) in a separate stage on top of the frozen encoder and decoder features results in a more robust model that suffers less from overfitting.

Algorithm 1: Constrained K-medoids to generate temporally continuous clusters.

1 **Input:** T features x_t, timestamps $[t_1, ..., t_n]$
2 **Init:** $m_i = x_{t_i}$ # initialize medoids
3 **repeat**
4    $D_{i,j} = \text{dist}(m_i, x_j)$ # pairwise costs
5    $b_0 = 0; b_n = T$ # compute boundaries
6   **for** $i = 1, ..., n - 1$ **do**
7       $\mid$ $b_i = \text{argmin}_l(\sum_{j=t_i}^{l} D_{i,j} + \sum_{j=l+1}^{t_{i+1}} D_{i+1,j})$
8   **end**
9   **for** $i = 1, ..., n$ **do**
10      $\mid$ $t_i = \text{argmin}_l(\sum_{j=b_{i-1}+1}^{b_i} \text{dist}(x_l, x_j))$
11      $\mid$ $m_i = x_{t_i}$ # new medoids
12   **end**
13 **until** *until convergence*;
14 **return** $l_i = b_i - b_{i-1}$

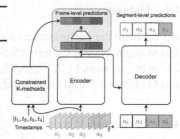

Fig. 2. Constrained K-medoids. Given frame-wise features and timestamps, k-medoids generates a pseudo-segmentation that guides the encoder during the training instead of ground truth frame-level labels in a fully supervised setup.

3.4 Timestamp Supervision

In this section, we show how our proposed framework can be extended to the timestamp supervised setting. In this setting, we are given a single annotated frame for each segment in the video, *i.e.,* frame annotations are reduced dramatically, and ground-truth segment durations are no longer available for all frames. As we extensively discussed before, our proposed framework relies on the frame-level supervisory signal on top of the encoder. However, it turns out that a noisy frame-level annotation provides a solid signal to the encoder. To obtain such frame-level annotations, we propose a constrained k-medoids algorithm that propagates the timestamp supervision to all frames.

A typical k-medoids algorithm starts with random data points as the cluster centers. It iteratively updates the cluster centers chosen from the data points and the assignments based on their similarity to the cluster center. Having access to the timestamp supervision, we can use them as initialization and cluster the input features. However, in a standard k-medoids algorithm, a temporally continuous set of clusters are not taken for granted. We call our method constrained k-medoids because we force the clusters to be temporally continuous. This can be simply achieved by modifying the assignment step of the k-medoids algorithm. Instead of assigning pseudo-labels to each frame, we find the temporal boundaries of each cluster. In the assignment step, we update the boundaries such that the accumulative distance of each cluster to the current center is minimized. Algorithm 1 summarizes the steps of our clustering method. In principle, we can apply k-medoids using the frame-wise input features x_t, the encoder features e_t, or a combination of both. In practice, we found that using input features alone gives surprisingly accurate segmentations, see Table 3 or supplemental material for more analyses.

4 Experiments

4.1 Datasets

We evaluate the performance of our proposed model extensively on three challenging action segmentation datasets (50Salads [35], GTEA [12], and Breakfast [19]). We follow previous work [1,7,17,25,41,42] and perform 4-fold cross-validation on Breakfast and GTEA and 5-fold cross-validation on 50Salads.

4.2 Evaluation Metrics

For evaluation, following previous works, we report the frame-wise accuracy (Acc), segmental edit score (Edit), and the segmental F1 score at overlapping thresholds 10%, 25%, and 50%, denoted by F1@$\{10, 25, 50\}$ [22]. The overlapping threshold is determined based on the intersection over union (IoU) ratio. Although frame-wise accuracy is the most commonly used metric for action segmentation, it does not portray a thorough picture of the performance of action segmentation models. A major disadvantage of frame-wise accuracy is that long action classes have a higher impact than short action classes and dominate the results. Furthermore, over-segmentation errors have a relatively low impact on Acc, which is particularly problematic for applications such as video summarization. On the other hand, Edit and F1 scores establish more comprehensive measures of the quality of the segmentations [22]; Edit measures the quality of the predicted transcript of the segmentation, while F1 scores penalize over-segmentation and are also insensitive to the duration of the action classes. Our proposed method performs particularly well on the Edit, and F1 scores on all datasets and in fully and timestamp supervised setups, achieving state-of-the-art results in most cases.

4.3 Implementation Details and Training

We follow the standard training strategy from existing algorithms [1,17,25,32,42] and train our main network (Sect. 3.1) end-to-end with batch size of 1. We train our model for at most 800 epochs using Adam optimizer with learning rate 0.0005 and the loss (6). In the cross-attention loss, Eq. (7), we set $\tau = 1$ during training to ensure training stability, and $\tau = 0.0001$ during inference. As input for our model, we use the same I3D [6] features that were used in many previous works. For the encoder, we used a modified version of the encoder proposed in [42]. For the decoder, we use a standard decoder architecture [38], with two layers and single head attention. Due to a strong imbalance in the segment durations, we propose a *split-segment* approach for improved training: longer action segments are split up into several shorter ones so that segment durations are more uniformly distributed; for details and ablations, see supplemental material. During the inference, we do not use any split-segment and use the entire video.

For the alignment decoder (Sect. 3.3), we use a single layer, single head decoder. To train this model, we use similar hyper-parameters and optimizers while freezing the encoder-decoder model from Sect. 3.1 and only train the alignment decoder with our cross-attention loss. For positional encoding, we use the standard sinusoidal positional encoding [38]. Furthermore, we use random dropping of the features as an augmentation method, where we randomly drop $\sim 1\%$ of the features in the sequence.

Table 1. Fully supervised results on all three datasets. Best and second best results are shown in bold and underlined, respectively. With the assistance of Viterbi/FIFA our method outperforms state-of-the-art in terms of Edit and F1 scores on all datasets.

		Breakfast					50Salads					GTEA				
		F1@{10,25,50}			Edit	Acc	F1@{10,25,50}			Edit	Acc	F1@{10,25,50}			Edit	Acc
TDRN [23]		–	–	–	–	–	72.9	68.5	57.2	66.0	68.1	79.2	74.4	62.7	74.1	70.1
SSA-GAN [13]		–	–	–	–	–	74.9	71.7	67.0	69.8	73.3	80.6	79.1	74.2	76.0	74.4
MuCon [34]		73.2	66.1	48.4	76.3	62.8	–	–	–	–	–	–	–	–	–	–
DTGRM [39]		68.7	61.9	46.6	68.9	68.3	79.1	75.9	66.1	72.0	80.0	87.3	85.5	72.3	80.7	77.5
Gao *et al.* [14]		74.9	69.0	55.2	73.3	70.7	80.3	78.0	69.8	73.4	82.2	89.9	87.3	75.8	84.6	78.5
MS-TCN++ [25]		64.1	58.6	45.9	65.6	67.6	80.7	78.5	70.1	74.3	83.7	88.8	85.7	76.0	83.5	80.1
BCN [41]		68.7	65.5	55.0	66.2	70.4	82.3	81.3	74.0	74.3	84.4	88.5	87.1	77.3	84.4	79.8
SSTDA [7]		75.0	69.1	55.2	73.7	70.2	83.0	81.5	73.8	75.8	83.2	90.0	89.1	78.0	86.2	79.8
Singhania *et al.* [32]		70.1	66.6	56.2	68.2	**73.5**	76.6	73.0	62.5	69.2	80.1	90.5	88.5	77.1	87.3	**80.3**
ASRF [17]		74.3	68.9	56.1	72.4	67.6	84.9	83.5	77.3	79.3	84.5	89.4	87.8	79.8	83.7	77.3
ASFormer [42]		76.0	70.6	57.4	75.0	**73.5**	85.1	83.4	76.0	79.6	85.6	90.1	88.8	79.2	84.6	79.7
UVAST (Ours)	w/o duration	–	–	–	76.9	–	–	–	–	83.9	–	–	–	–	**92.1**	–
	+ alignment decoder	76.7	70.0	56.6	77.2	68.2	86.2	81.2	70.4	83.9	79.5	77.1	69.7	54.2	90.5	62.2
	+ Viterbi	75.9	70.0	57.2	76.5	66.0	**89.1**	**87.6**	**81.7**	83.9	**87.4**	**92.7**	**91.3**	**81.0**	**92.1**	80.2
	+ FIFA	**76.9**	**71.5**	**58.0**	77.1	69.7	88.9	87.0	78.5	83.9	84.5	82.9	79.4	64.7	90.5	69.8

4.4 Performance Evaluation

Here, we provide the overall performance comparison of our proposed method, *UVAST*, on three challenging action segmentation datasets with different levels of supervision. We demonstrate the effectiveness of our proposed method for both the fully supervised and timestamp supervised setup and achieve competitive results on both settings.

We provide the results of our proposed model for four scenarios: Transcript prediction of our encoder-decoder architecture (referred to as "w/o duration") and three different approaches to obtain durations for the segments, namely alignment decoder from Sect. 3.3 ("+ alignment decoder"), Viterbi ("+ Viterbi"), and FIFA [33] ("+ FIFA"). We only report the Edit score for "w/o duration", as it does not provide segment durations. A significant advantage of our method is that a predicted transcript is readily available and can be used in these inference algorithms instead of the previous methods, which need to iterate over the training transcripts. Furthermore, we can optionally use the predicted duration of the alignment decoder to initialize the segment lengths in FIFA.

Fully Supervised Comparison. Table 1 shows the performance of our method in the fully supervised setting compared with state-of-the-art methods. At the bottom of Table 1 we provide the results of our proposed model for the four scenarios explained above. *UVAST* achieves significantly better Edit score on transcript prediction ("w/o duration") than all other existing methods on all three datasets, which demonstrates the effectiveness of our model to capture and summarize the actions occurring in the video. In the last three rows of Table 1, we use three different approaches to compute the duration of the segments. Combining *UVAST* with the alignment decoder from Sect. 3.3 achieves competitive results. However, it is important to note that Transformers are very data-hungry and training them on small datasets can be challenging. We observe that *UVAST* with alignment decoder outperforms other methods in terms of Edit score. While the F1 scores are comparable to the state-of-the-art on the Breakfast dataset, the small size of the GTEA dataset hinders the training of the alignment decoder.

Table 2. Timestamp supervision results on all three datasets. UVAST, ASFormer [42], and MSTCN [1] are trained via our constrained k-medoids pseudo-labels. Best result shown in bold. *UVAST* outperforms SOTA on all datasets and metrics except for Acc on Breakfast. The performance in terms of Edit distance is significant, and is comparable to the fully supervised setup.

	Breakfast					50Salads					GTEA				
	F1@{10,25,50}			Edit	Acc	F1@{10,25,50}			Edit	Acc	F1@{10,25,50}			Edit	Acc
Li et al. [26]	70.5	63.6	47.4	69.9	**64.1**	73.9	70.9	60.1	66.8	75.6	78.9	73.0	55.4	72.3	66.4
MS-TCN [1]	56.1	50.0	36.8	61.7	62.5	74.4	70.4	57.7	66.8	72.8	82.8	80.3	63.5	79.5	67.7
MS-TCN [1] + Viterbi	43.3	37.2	25.6	43.5	35.9	74.0	70.0	55.5	68.2	72.8	82.6	79.7	61.6	81.0	68.1
ASFormer [42]	70.9	62.9	44.0	71.6	61.3	76.6	72.1	59.6	70.0	76.9	**87.2**	83.1	67.5	83.0	68.8
ASFormer [42] + Viterbi	71.3	63.1	44.3	71.1	60.7	76.3	72.1	59.4	68.8	**77.0**	87.1	83.1	**68.2**	83.0	69.1
UVAST (Ours) + alignment decoder	**72.0**	64.1	**48.6**	**74.3**	60.2	75.7	70.6	58.2	78.4	67.8	70.8	63.5	49.2	88.2	55.3
+ Viterbi	71.3	63.3	48.3	74.1	60.7	**83.0**	**79.6**	**65.9**	78.2	**77.0**	**87.2**	**83.7**	66.0	**89.3**	**70.5**
+ FIFA	**72.0**	**64.2**	47.6	74.1	60.3	80.2	74.9	61.6	**78.6**	72.5	80.7	75.2	57.4	88.7	66.0

Moreover, with frame-wise predictions and transcript prediction available, our method conveniently allows applying inference algorithms at test time, such as FIFA and Viterbi, without the need to expensively iterate over the training transcripts. Combining our method with Viterbi outperforms the existing methods on GTEA and 50Salads in terms of Edit and F1 scores, and achieves competitive results on Breakfast. We also provide the results of *UVAST* with FIFA, where we initialize the duration with the predicted duration. It achieves strong performance on Breakfast and 50Salads. Note that although FIFA is a fast approximation of Viterbi, it achieves better results on the Breakfast dataset. This is due to the fact that the objective function that is minimized by FIFA/Viterbi does not optimize the evaluation metrics directly, *i.e.,* the global optimum of the Viterbi objective function does not guarantee the global optimum of the evaluation metrics. This observation is consistent with the results reported in [33].

The comparison to ASFormer [42] is also interesting. While ASFormer performs like most other approaches frame-level prediction, Fig. 1 (a), *UVAST* predicts the action segments in an autoregressive manner, Fig. 1 (d,e). As expected, ASFormer achieves in general a better frame-wise accuracy while *UVAST* achieves a better Edit score. Since ASFormer uses a smoothing loss and multiple refinement stages to address over-segmentation similar to MS-TCN [1, 25], it has $\sim$ 1.3M learnable parameters, whereas our proposed model has $\sim$ 1.1M parameters. Our approach with Viterbi achieves similar F1 scores on the Breakfast dataset, but higher F1 scores on the other datasets.

Overall, we find that our method achieves strong performance in terms of Edit and F1 scores, while Acc is compared to the state-of-the-art lower on Breakfast. Note that Acc is dominated by long segments and less sensitive to over-segmentation errors. Lower Acc and higher Edit/F1 scores indicate that *UVAST* localizes action boundaries, which are difficult to annotate precisely, less accurately. It is therefore an interesting research direction to improve the segment boundaries, *e.g.,* by using an additional refinement like ASFormer.

Timestamp Supervision Comparison. We use our proposed constrained k-medoids to generate pseudo-segmentation using the frame-wise input features and ground truth timestamps. The output consists of continuous segments, which can be identified with the transcript to yield a pseudo-segmentation. While this approach can be applied both to the input features and encoder features in principle, we find that using the input features already gives a surprisingly good performance; we report Acc and F1 scores in Table 3 averaged over all splits. Note that this is not a temporal segmentation method as it requires timestamp supervision as input. We use the resulting pseudo-segmentation as the auxiliary signal to our encoder during the training where we have access to the timestamp supervision.

In Table 2, we compare our proposed timestamp model with the recently proposed method [26] on the three action segmentation datasets. To the best of our knowledge, [26] is the first work that proposed and applied timestamp supervision for the temporal action segmentation task. Although other weakly supervised methods exist, they are based on *transcript* supervision, a weaker form of supervision; therefore, we additionally train MS-TCN [1] and ASFormer [42] with our constrained k-medoids. To get more thorough and fair comparisons, we further show their performance when combined with the Viterbi algorithm during inference.

Table 2 shows that: I) our method largely outperforms the other methods by achieving the best performance on 13 out of 15 metrics. Analogously to the fully supervised case, we observe the strong performance of our alignment decoder in terms of Edit and F1 scores on Breakfast; with FIFA and Viterbi, we outperform the method of [26] on 50Salads and GTEA. Notably, *UVAST* achieves significantly higher performance in terms of Edit distance, which is comparable to the fully supervised setup. II) ASFormer and MSTCN perform reasonably well in the timestamp supervision setup when trained on the pseudo-labels of our constrained k-medoids algorithm, which demonstrates one more time the effectiveness of our proposed constrained k-medoids algorithm. III) ASFormer and MSTCN do not benefit from the Viterbi algorithm in this case. This is due to the relatively lower Edit distance of these methods. Namely, Viterbi hurts MSTCN on Breakfast as it achieves significantly lower Edit distance compared to ours.

4.5 Qualitative Evaluation

We show qualitative results of two videos from the Breakfast dataset in the fully supervised and timestamp supervised setting in Fig. 3. We visualize the ground truth segmentations (first row) as well as the predicted segmentations of our encoder (second row) and decoder with alignment decoder, FIFA or Viterbi for duration prediction (last three rows). The encoder predictions demonstrate well the common problem of oversegmentation with frame-level predictions; the segment-level predictions of our decoder on the other hand yield coherent action segments.

4.6 Ablations Studies

Duration Prediction. As discussed in Sect. 1, the vanilla Transformer model, Fig. 1 (b), does not generalize to the action segmentation task, see Table 4. We train this model using $\mathcal{L}_{segment}$ and MSE between predicted and ground truth durations, which are scaled to $[0, 1]$ by dividing by the total number of frames T. Our first modification involves applying a frame-wise loss to the encoder features, which drastically improves the results. However, this explicit duration prediction still struggles to accurately localize the segments. Predicting duration implicitly via our alignment decoder instead, Fig. 1 (d)+(e), on the other hand improves the localization, increasing Acc and F1.

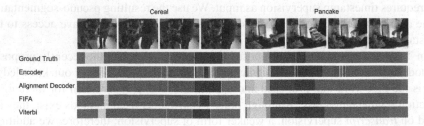

Fig. 3. Qualitative results. We show ground truth and predicted segmentation of fully supervised (left) and timestamp supervised (right) *UVAST* of two videos from the Breakfast dataset.

Table 3. Constrained K-medoids results. We evaluate the pseudo-segmentations of our constrained k-medoids algorithm, Alg. 1, given the frame-wise input features and ground truth timestamps.

	F1@{10,25,50}			Acc
Breakfast	95.5	87.5	70.0	76.9
50Salads	97.5	90.4	75.6	81.3
GTEA	99.8	97.7	83.0	75.3

Table 4. Explicit duration prediction on Breakfast split 1. We show the results of different steps described in Sect. 1 from explicit duration prediction via the vanilla Transformer to implicit duration prediction with our alignment decoder.

	F1@{10,25,50}			Edit	Acc
Vanilla Transformer, Fig. 1 (b)	48.1	42.3	26.7	52.9	35.0
+ Frame-wise Loss, Fig. 1 (c)	70.7	63.5	44.4	73.9	59.1
+ Alignment Decoder, Fig. 1 (d)+(e)	73.5	68.3	54.3	75.2	67.7

Impact of the Loss Terms. In Table 5 we investigate the impact of the different loss terms (Sect. 3.2) on split 1 of Breakfast and 50Salads. In the first row of Table 5, we evaluate the encoder when trained only using the frame-wise loss, *i.e.*, following the frame-wise prediction design as previous works. As expected, solely relying on the frame-wise loss leads to over-segmentation and poor performance. The rest of Table 5 shows the performance of our proposed model when using both encoder and decoder as explained in Sects. 3.1 and 3.2, and reflect the key idea of our method to directly predict the segments. While the most basic version using the segment-wise loss (2) improves over frame-wise predictions, we observe that using both the frame-wise (1) and segment-wise (2) loss term increases the performance drastically. Moreover, we observe that adding the cross-attention loss (5) further improves the results, demonstrating its effectiveness for longer sequences with many action segments, such as 50Salads. While adding the group-wise loss terms (3) and (4) individually improves the performance moderately, the real benefit is revealed when combining them all together.

To shed more light on the contribution of our cross-attention loss we visualize its impact in Fig. 4. Given the ground truth segmentation, Fig. 4 (a), of a video, Fig. 4 (b) shows our expected target activations (output of softmax) of the decoder's cross-attention map; we hypothesize that activations should be higher in areas that belong

Table 5. Loss terms. Contribution of different loss terms on Breakfast and 50Salads (split 1).

	Breakfast				50Salads			
	F1@{10,25,50}			Edit	F1@{10,25,50}			Edit
$\mathcal{L}_{\text{frame}}$	8.9	7.7	5.9	14.1	13.5	12.8	10.8	11.4
$\mathcal{L}_{\text{segment}}$	49.5	39.7	22.9	55.6	20.1	16.3	8.6	29.2
$\mathcal{L}_{\text{frame}}+\mathcal{L}_{\text{segment}}$	71.8	66.3	52.6	73.4	55.0	52.4	37.5	45.3
$\mathcal{L}_{\text{frame}}+\mathcal{L}_{\text{segment}}+\mathcal{L}_{\text{CA}}$	73.8	67.0	54.8	74.5	74.2	71.0	58.4	65.5
$\mathcal{L}_{\text{frame}}+\mathcal{L}_{\text{segment}}+\mathcal{L}_{\text{g-frame}}$	73.3	65.8	52.8	73.6	56.6	53.4	40.2	44.0
$\mathcal{L}_{\text{frame}}+\mathcal{L}_{\text{segment}}+\mathcal{L}_{\text{g-segment}}$	72.8	64.3	53.7	73.2	59.1	56.1	42.8	51.6
$\mathcal{L}_{\text{frame}}+\mathcal{L}_{\text{segment}}+\mathcal{L}_{\text{g-frame}}+\mathcal{L}_{\text{g-segment}}$	73.5	67.9	55.0	73.1	57.0	54.5	40.4	42.4
$\mathcal{L}_{\text{frame}}+\mathcal{L}_{\text{segment}}+\mathcal{L}_{\text{g-frame}}+\mathcal{L}_{\text{g-segment}}+\mathcal{L}_{\text{CA}}$	75.1	68.9	54.9	76.1	73.6	71.5	55.3	78.4

to the corresponding segment. Figure 4 (c) shows the output of the cross-attention when using our cross-attention loss. We observe that this loss indeed guides the cross-attention to have higher activations in the regions that belong to the related segment for an action. Figure 4 (d) shows that lack of our cross-attention loss causes the attention map to be noisy; it's unclear which region is used for the segment classification.

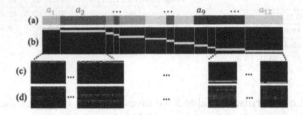

Fig. 4. Impact of the Cross-Attention Loss for the Transcript Decoder. (a) A ground truth example of a video with 13150 frames and 12 segments from the 50Salads dataset. (b) The target cross-attention map after softmax with dimension 12×13150. (c) and (d) show the zoomed-in segments of the cross-attention map of the decoder when using the cross-attention loss (top) or not using it (bottom). In (b-d) brighter color means higher values of the activations.

5   Conclusion

We presented *UVAST*, a new unified design for fully and timestamp supervised temporal action segmentation via Transformers in a seq2seq style. While the segment-level predictions of our model effectively address the over-segmentation problem, this new design entails a new challenge: predicting the duration of segments explicitly does not work out of the box. Therefore, we proposed three different approaches to alleviate this problem, enabling our model to achieve competitive performance on all three datasets.

References

1. Abu Farha, Y., Gall, J.: MS-TCN: multi-stage temporal convolutional network for action segmentation. In: CVPR (2019)
2. Arnab, A., Dehghani, M., Heigold, G., Sun, C., Lučić, M., Schmid, C.: ViViT: a video vision transformer. In: ICCV (2021)
3. Beltagy, I., Peters, M.E., Cohan, A.: Longformer: the long-document transformer. arXiv preprint arXiv:2004.05150 (2020)
4. Bertasius, G., Wang, H., Torresani, L.: Is space-time attention all you need for video understanding? In: ICML (2021)
5. Bojanowski, P., et al.: Weakly supervised action labeling in videos under ordering constraints. In: Fleet, D., Pajdla, T., Schiele, B., Tuytelaars, T. (eds.) ECCV 2014. LNCS, vol. 8693, pp. 628–643. Springer, Cham (2014). https://doi.org/10.1007/978-3-319-10602-1_41
6. Carreira, J., Zisserman, A.: Quo vadis, action recognition? CVPR, a new model and the kinetics dataset (2017)

7. Chen, M.H., Li, B., Bao, Y., AlRegib, G., Kira, Z.: Action segmentation with joint self-supervised temporal domain adaptation. In: CVPR (2020)
8. Dai, Z., Yang, Z., Yang, Y., Carbonell, J., Le, Q.V., Salakhutdinov, R.: Transformer-xl: attentive language models beyond a fixed-length context. arXiv preprint arXiv:1901.02860 (2019)
9. Ding, L., Xu, C.: Weakly-supervised action segmentation with iterative soft boundary assignment. In: CVPR (2018)
10. Ding, L., Xu, C.: Weakly-supervised action segmentation with iterative soft boundary assignment. In: CVPR (2018)
11. Dosovitskiy, A., et al.: An image is worth 16x16 words: transformers for image recognition at scale. In: ICLR (2021)
12. Fathi, A., Ren, X., Rehg, J.M.: Learning to recognize objects in egocentric activities. In: CVPR (2011)
13. Gammulle, H., Denman, S., Sridharan, S., Fookes, C.: Fine-grained action segmentation using the semi-supervised action GAN. Pattern Recogn. **98**, 107039 (2020)
14. Gao, S.H., Han, Q., Li, Z.Y., Peng, P., Wang, L., Cheng, M.M.: Global2local: efficient structure search for video action segmentation. In: CVPR (2021)
15. Huang, D.-A., Fei-Fei, L., Niebles, J.C.: Connectionist temporal modeling for weakly supervised action labeling. In: Leibe, B., Matas, J., Sebe, N., Welling, M. (eds.) ECCV 2016. LNCS, vol. 9908, pp. 137–153. Springer, Cham (2016). https://doi.org/10.1007/978-3-319-46493-0_9
16. Huang, Y., Sugano, Y., Sato, Y.: Improving action segmentation via graph-based temporal reasoning. In: CVPR (2020)
17. Ishikawa, Y., Kasai, S., Aoki, Y., Kataoka, H.: Alleviating over-segmentation errors by detecting action boundaries. In: WACV (2021)
18. Karaman, S., Seidenari, L., Bimbo, A.D.: Fast saliency based pooling of fisher encoded dense trajectories. In: ECCV Workshops (2014)
19. Kuehne, H., Arslan, A., Serre, T.: The language of actions: recovering the syntax and semantics of goal-directed human activities. In: CVPR (2014)
20. Kuehne, H., Gall, J., Serre, T.: An end-to-end generative framework for video segmentation and recognition. In: WACV (2016)
21. Kuehne, H., Richard, A., Gall, J.: A hybrid RNN-HMM approach for weakly supervised temporal action segmentation. IEEE Trans. Pattern Anal. Mach. Intell. **42**(4), 765–779 (2020)
22. Lea, C., Flynn, M.D., Vidal, R., Reiter, A., Hager, G.D.: Temporal convolutional networks for action segmentation and detection. In: CVPR (2017)
23. Lei, P., Todorovic, S.: Temporal deformable residual networks for action segmentation in videos. In: CVPR (2018)
24. Li, J., Lei, P., Todorovic, S.: Weakly supervised energy-based learning for action segmentation. In: ICCV (2019)
25. Li, S.J., Abu Farha, Y., Liu, Y., Cheng, M.M., Gall, J.: MS-TCN++: multi-stage temporal convolutional network for action segmentation. In: TPAMI (2020)
26. Li, Z., Abu Farha, Y., Gall, J.: Temporal action segmentation from timestamp supervision. In: CVPR (2021)
27. Nawrot, P., et al.: Hierarchical transformers are more efficient language models. arXiv preprint arXiv:2110.13711 (2021)
28. Richard, A., Gall, J.: Temporal action detection using a statistical language model. In: CVPR (2016)
29. Richard, A., Kuehne, H., Gall, J.: Action sets: weakly supervised action segmentation without ordering constraints. In: CVPR (2018)
30. Richard, A., Kuehne, H., Iqbal, A., Gall, J.: NeuralNetwork-Viterbi: a framework for weakly supervised video learning. In: CVPR (2018)

31. Rohrbach, M., Amin, S., Andriluka, M., Schiele, B.: A database for fine grained activity detection of cooking activities. In: CVPR (2012)
32. Singhania, D., Rahaman, R., Yao, A.: Coarse to fine multi-resolution temporal convolutional network. arXiv preprint arXiv:2105.10859 (2021)
33. Souri, Y., Abu Farha, Y., Despinoy, F., Francesca, G., Gall, J.: FIFA: fast inference approximation for action segmentation. In: GCPR (2021)
34. Souri, Y., Fayyaz, M., Minciullo, L., Francesca, G., Gall, J.: Fast weakly supervised action segmentation using mutual consistency. In: TPAMI (2021)
35. Stein, S., McKenna, S.J.: Combining embedded accelerometers with computer vision for recognizing food preparation activities. In: Proceedings of the 2013 ACM International Joint Conference on Pervasive and Ubiquitous Computing (2013)
36. Tang, K., Fei-Fei, L., Koller, D.: Learning latent temporal structure for complex event detection. In: CVPR (2012)
37. Tay, Y., et al.: Long range arena : a benchmark for efficient transformers. In: ICLR (2021)
38. Vaswani, A., et al.: Attention is all you need. In: NeurIPS (2017)
39. Wang, D., Hu, D., Li, X., Dou, D.: Temporal relational modeling with self-supervision for action segmentation. arXiv preprint arXiv:2012.07508 (2020)
40. Wang, H., Zhu, Y., Adam, H., Yuille, A., Chen, L.C.: MaX-DeepLab: end-to-end panoptic segmentation with mask transformers. In: CVPR (2021)
41. Wang, Z., Gao, Z., Wang, L., Li, Z., Wu, G.: Boundary-aware cascade networks for temporal action segmentation. In: Vedaldi, A., Bischof, H., Brox, T., Frahm, J.-M. (eds.) ECCV 2020. LNCS, vol. 12370, pp. 34–51. Springer, Cham (2020). https://doi.org/10.1007/978-3-030-58595-2_3
42. Yi, F., Wen, H., Jiang, T.: ASFormer: Transformer for action segmentation. In: BMVC (2021)
43. Zheng, S., et al.: Rethinking semantic segmentation from a sequence-to-sequence perspective with transformers. In: CVPR (2021)
44. Zhu, C., et al.: Long-short transformer: efficient transformers for language and vision. In: NeurIPS (2021)

Efficient Video Transformers
with Spatial-Temporal Token Selection

Junke Wang[1,2], Xitong Yang[3], Hengduo Li[3], Li Liu[4],
Zuxuan Wu[1,2(✉)], and Yu-Gang Jiang[1,2]

[1] Shanghai Key Lab of Intelligent Information Processing, School of CS,
Fudan University, Shanghai, China
zxwu@fudan.edu.cn
[2] Shanghai Collaborative Innovation Center on Intelligent Visual Computing,
Shanghai, China
[3] University of Maryland, College Park, USA
[4] BirenTech Research, Shanghai, China

Abstract. Video transformers have achieved impressive results on major video recognition benchmarks, which however suffer from high computational cost. In this paper, we present STTS, a token selection framework that dynamically selects a few informative tokens in both temporal and spatial dimensions conditioned on input video samples. Specifically, we formulate token selection as a ranking problem, which estimates the importance of each token through a lightweight scorer network and only those with top scores will be used for downstream evaluation. In the temporal dimension, we keep the frames that are most relevant to the action categories, while in the spatial dimension, we identify the most discriminative region in feature maps without affecting the spatial context used in a hierarchical way in most video transformers. Since the decision of token selection is non-differentiable, we employ a perturbed-maximum based differentiable Top-K operator for end-to-end training. We mainly conduct extensive experiments on Kinetics-400 with a recently introduced video transformer backbone, MViT. Our framework achieves similar results while requiring 20% less computation. We also demonstrate our approach is generic for different transformer architectures and video datasets. Code is available at https://github.com/wangjk666/STTS.

Keywords: Transformer · Efficient action recognition

1 Introduction

The exponential growth of online videos has stimulated the research on video recognition, which classifies video content into actions and events for applications like content-based retrieval [12,70] and recommendation [10,25,33,43]. At the core of video recognition is spatial-temporal modeling, which aims to learn how humans and objects move and interact with one another over time. Recently,

---

J. Wang and X. Yang—Equal contributions.

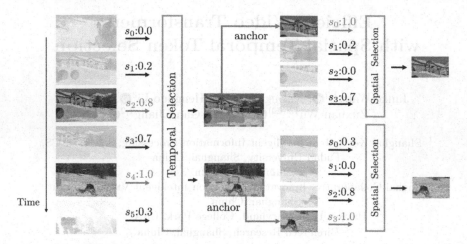

Fig. 1. A conceptual overview of our approach. We introduce a token selection method to improve the inference efficiency of video transformers by formulating token selection as a ranking problem. We use a lightweight scorer network to assign an importance score for each token, and only those with Top-K scores will be kept for computation. In the temporal dimension, we select the most informative frames, while in the spatial dimension, we preserve the most discriminative region with pre-defined anchors.

vision transformers [6,13] have attracted increasing attention due to their strong track record for capturing long-range dependencies in natural language processing (NLP) tasks [11,54]. While achieving superior performance on major benchmarks, video transformers [3,14,39,57] are however computationally expensive. The problem stems from the fact that the number of input tokens grows linearly with respect to the number of frames in a clip, which further incurs a quadratic cost for computing self-attention. As a result, video transformers are oftentimes too compute-intensive to be deployed in resource-constrained scenarios.

While there are extensive studies on efficient video recognition for CNNs [16, 17,32,35,51,53,59,60,65,76], limited effort has been made for transformer-based video architectures. Unlike standard CNNs, transformers operate on image patches, which are then tokenized to a sequence of embeddings. The relationships among patches are modeled with stacked self-attention layers. In the image domain, a few very recent approaches have attempted to reduce the computational cost of transformers by learning to drop redundant tokens [46,49], as transformers are shown to be resilient to patch drop behaviors [44].

Directly generalizing such an idea from image transformers to video transformers, while appealing, is non-trivial. Tokens in videos usually take the form of 3D cubes, and the tokenization layer in video transformers typically flattens all cubes into a sequence of 3D vectors. As a result, simply learning what to keep in the sequence with sampling based approaches [46,49] inevitably produces a set of *discontinuous* tokens in space and time, thus destroying the structural information in videos. This also conflicts with the recent design of video transformers, which processes 3D tokens in a hierarchical manner preserving both spatial and temporal context [14,39]. Instead, we argue that the selection of spatial-temporal tokens in video transformers should be processed in a *sequential* manner—attending to salient frames over the entire time horizon first, and then diving into those frames to look for the most important spatial region[1].

In this paper, we introduce Spatial-Temporal Token Selection (STTS), a lightweight and plug-and-play module that learns to allocate computational resources spatially and temporally in video transformers. In particular, STTS consists of a temporal token selection network and a spatial token selection network, collaborating with each other to use as few tokens as possible. Each selection network is a multi-layer perceptron (MLP) that predicts the importance score of each token and can be attached to any location of a transformer model. Conditioned on these scores, we choose a few tokens with higher scores for downstream processing. More specifically, given a sequence of input tokens, STTS first selects a few important frames over the entire time horizon. Then for each frame, we split the token sequences into anchors with regular shapes, and select only one anchor which contributes most to video recognition. However, it is worth pointing out that selecting tokens with top scores is not differentiable and thus poses challenges for training. To mitigate this issue, we resort to a recently proposed differentiable Top-K selection algorithm [4] to make selection end-to-end trainable using the perturbed maximum method. This also allows us to explicitly control how many tokens are used.

We conduct extensive experiments on two large-scale video datasets Kinetics-400 [28] and Something-Something-v2 [21] using MViT [14] and VideoSwin [39] as backbones, to illustrate the effectiveness of our method. The experimental results demonstrate that STTS can effectively improve the efficiency at the cost of only a slight loss of accuracy. In particular, by keeping only 50% of the input tokens, STTS reduces the computational cost measured in giga floating-point operations (GFLOPs) by more than 33% with a drop of accuracy within 0.7% on Kinetics-400 by using MViT [14] as backbone. When more computational resources are allocated, STTS achieves a similar performance as the original model but saves more than 20% of the computation.

2 Related Work

Vision Transformers. The great success of Transformer models [54] in NLP has inspired the shift of backbone architectures from CNNs to transformers in the computer vision community [13,24,52,71]. Vision transformers have demonstrated the capability to achieve state-of-the-art results in image domain, spanning a wide range of tasks like image classification [71], object detection [75], semantic segmentation [73], *etc.*, with large-scale pre-training data.

---

[1] Here the notion of "frame" can be either a single frame or multiple frames within a clip in the original video, depending on whether clip-based video models with 3D convolutions are used.

Recently, a series of approaches [2,3,14,19,39,50,61] explored the use of vision transformers in the video domain. TimeSformer [3] adapts the standard transformer architecture to videos by concatenating the patches from different frames in the time dimension. MViT [14] uses a hierarchical transformer architecture, which progressively expands the channel dimension and reduce the spatial resolution to extract the multiscale visual features for video recognition. VideoSwin [39] extends the window-based local self-attention [38] to video modeling by incorporating the inductive bias of locality. These approaches typically split the input video into spatial-temporal tokens to learn temporal relationships. While offering decent results, video transformers are computationally expensive. This motivates us to explore spatial and temporal redundancies in videos for efficient video recognition.

Efficient Video Recognition. Over the past few years, there are extensive studies on video recognition investigating the use of convolutional neural networks [17,18,22,67] and transformer models [3,14,39]. However, these models are usually computationally expensive, which spurs the development of efficient video recognition methods [5,40,56,64,65,69,74,76] to speed up the inference time of video recognition. Several studies [16,17,31,62,76] explore designing lightweight models for video recognition by compressing 3D CNNs. Despite the significant memory footprint savings, they still need to attend to every temporal clip of the input video, thus bringing no gains in the computational complexity reduction. A few recent approaches [5,32,63,65], on the other hand, propose to select the most salient temporal clips to input to backbone models for resource-efficient video recognition. Unlike these approaches that focus on the acceleration of CNN-based video recognition models, to the best of our knowledge, we are the first to explore efficient recognition for video transformers. It is also worth pointing out that STTS is orthogonal and complementary to recent approaches on designing efficient vision transformers [30,58].

Differentiable Token Selection. The decision of token selection is discrete, making it unsuitable for end-to-end training. To overcome this limitation, one solution is to resort Gumbel-Softmax trick [26] to decide whether each token should be pruned [46,49]. This however cannot explicitly control the number of preserved tokens during training, thus conflicting with the common hierarchical design of video transformers [14,34,39]. Another way is to formulate the token selection as a ranking problem, in which the optimal-transport based methods [9,66] can be employed to match an auxiliary probability measure supported on increasing values. In this paper, we follow [8] to apply a perturbed maximum method, which is verified by [8] to outperform Sinkhorn operator [66].

3   Spatial-Temporal Token Selection

In this section, we begin with a brief review of video transformers (Sect. 3.1). Then we describe our token selection module that adaptively chooses a few

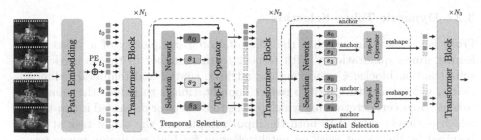

Fig. 2. Overview of the proposed STTS. The temporal token selection networks and spatial token selection networks can be inserted between the transformer blocks to perform token selection in the temporal and spatial dimension, respectively. N_1, N_2, N_3 could be 0.

important tokens, and introduce an important technique, the perturbed maximum method, for end-to-end optimization of the model (Sect. 3.2). Finally, we elaborate how to instantiate the token selection modules in both temporal and spatial dimensions (Sect. 3.3). The overall framework is illustrated in Fig. 2.

3.1 Review of Video Transformers

Given a video $\mathcal{V} \in \mathbb{R}^{T \times H \times W \times 3}$ consisting of T RGB frames with the size of $H \times W$, video transformers typically adopt one of the two possible methods to map the video frames to a sequence of patch embeddings. The first is to tokenize 2D patches within each frame independently with 2D convolutions and concatenate all the tokens together along the time dimension [3], while the other is to directly extract 3D tubes from the input videos and use 3D convolutions to linearly project them into 3D embeddings [14,39]. In both cases, the number of tokens is proportional to the temporal length and spatial resolution of the input video. We denote the resulting spatial-temporal patch embeddings as $\mathbf{x} \in \mathbb{R}^{M \times N \times C}$, where M and N denote the length of the token sequence in time and space dimensions respectively, and C is the embedding dimension. Positional encodings are added to $\mathbf{x}$ to inject location information [3,14,39].

In order to model the appearance and motion cues in videos, the patch embeddings $\mathbf{x}$ are fed to a stack of transformer blocks which compute the spatial and temporal self-attention jointly [14,39] or separately [2,3]. The self-attention is generally formulated as:

$$Attention(\mathbf{Q}, \mathbf{K}, \mathbf{V}) = \texttt{softmax}(\frac{\mathbf{Q}\mathbf{K}^{\mathrm{T}}}{\sqrt{C}})\mathbf{V}, \tag{1}$$

where $\mathbf{Q}$, $\mathbf{K}$, $\mathbf{V}$ denote the query, key, and value embeddings based on $\mathbf{x}$, respectively, and $\texttt{softmax}$ denotes the normalization function.

3.2   Dynamic Token Selection

From Eq. 1, we can see that the computational complexity of a video transformer grows quadratically with respect to the number of tokens used in the
self-attention blocks. Considering the intrinsic spatial and temporal redundancies in videos, a nature way to reduce computation is to reduce the number of
tokens. However, determining which tokens to be kept or discarded is non-trivial,
which is closely related to both the input sample and the target task at hand.
Inspired by the recent work on patch selection for high-resolution image recognition [8], we formulate the token selection as a ranking problem—importance
scores of input tokens are first estimated using a lightweight scorer network and
the top K scoring tokens are then selected for downstream processing. Below we
introduce these two steps in details and present how to apply them to spatial
and temporal token selection, respectively.

Scorer Network. Given a sequence of input tokens $\mathbf{q} \in \mathbb{R}^{L \times C}$, the goal of the
scorer network is to generate an input-conditioned importance score for each
token. Here, L denotes the flattened sequence length and C is the embedding
dimension. We adopt a standard two-layer fully connected (FC) network to generate such scores. In particular, the input tokens are first mapped to a *local
representation* $\mathbf{f}^l$ via a linear projection:

$$\mathbf{f}^l = \text{FC}\,(\mathbf{q};\,\boldsymbol{\theta}_1) \in \mathbb{R}^{L \times C'}, \tag{2}$$

where $\boldsymbol{\theta}_1$ denotes the network weights and we use $C' = C/2$ to save computation.
To leverage the contextual information of the whole sequence, we average $\mathbf{f}^l$ to
get a *global representation* $\mathbf{f}^g$ and concatenate it with each local representation
along the channel dimension: $\mathbf{f_i} = \left[\mathbf{f}_i^l, \mathbf{f}^g\right] \in \mathbb{R}^{2C'} (1 \le i \le L)$. The concatenated
features are then fed to a second FC layer to generate the importance scores:

$$\mathbf{s}' = \text{FC}\,(\mathbf{f};\,\boldsymbol{\theta}_2) \in \mathbb{R}^{L \times 1},$$
$$\mathbf{s} = \frac{\mathbf{s}' - \min(\mathbf{s}')}{\max(\mathbf{s}') - \min(\mathbf{s}')}, \tag{3}$$

where $\boldsymbol{\theta}_2$ is the network weights and $\mathbf{s} \in \mathbb{R}^L$ is the score vector of all tokens
normalized with the min-max normalization [8]. It is worth mentioning that the
additional computational overhead brought by the scorer network is negligible
compared to the computation cost saved by pruning the uninformative tokens,
as shown in Sect. 4.2.

Differentiable Top-K Selection. Given the importance scores $\mathbf{s}$ generated
from the scorer network, we select the K highest scores and extract the corresponding tokens. We denote this process as a Top-K operator which returns the
indices of the K largest entries:

$$\mathbf{y} = \text{Top-K}(\mathbf{s}) \in \mathbb{N}^K. \tag{4}$$

We assume that the indices are sorted to preserve the order of the *input sequence*. To implement token selection using matrix multiplication, we convert $\mathbf{y}$ into a stack of K one-hot L-dimensional vectors $\mathbf{Y} = [I_{y_1}, I_{y_2}, ..., I_{y_K}] \in \{0,1\}^{L \times K}$. As a result, tokens with top K scores can be extracted as $\mathbf{q}' = \mathbf{Y}^T \mathbf{q}$. Note that this operation is non-differentiable because both Top-K and one-hot operations are non-differentiable.

To learn the parameters of the scorer network using an end-to-end training without introducing any auxiliary losses, we resort to the perturbed maximum method [4, 8] to construct a differentiable Top-K operator. In particular, selecting Top-K tokens is equivalent to solving a linear program of the following form:

$$\arg\max_{\mathbf{Y} \in \mathcal{C}} \langle \mathbf{Y}, \mathbf{s1}^T \rangle, \tag{5}$$

where $\mathbf{s1}^T$ is the score vector $\mathbf{s}$ replicated K times, and $\mathcal{C}$ is the convex polytope constrain set defined as:

$$\mathcal{C} = \left\{ \mathbf{Y} \in \mathbb{R}^{N \times K} : \mathbf{Y}_{n,k} \geq 0, \mathbf{1}^T \mathbf{Y} = 1, \mathbf{Y1} \leq 1, \right.$$
$$\left. \sum_{i \in [N]} i \mathbf{Y}_{i,k} < \sum_{j \in [N]} j \mathbf{Y}_{j,k'}, \forall k < k' \right\}. \tag{6}$$

We follow [4] to perform forward and backward operations to solve Eq. 5.

 – **Forward:** A smoothed version of the Top-K operation in Eq. 5 could be implemented by taking the expectation with respect to random perturbations:

$$\mathbf{Y}_\sigma = \mathbb{E}_Z \left[\arg\max_{\mathbf{Y} \in \mathcal{C}} \langle \mathbf{Y}, \mathbf{s1}^T + \sigma \mathbf{Z} \rangle \right], \tag{7}$$

where $\mathbf{Z}$ is a random noise vector sampled from the uniform Gaussian distribution and σ is a hyper-parameter controlling the noise variance. In practice, we run the Top-K algorithm for n (which is set to 500 in all our experiments) times, and compute the expectation of n independent samples.

 – **Backward:** Following [1], the Jacobian of the above forward pass can be calculated as:

$$J_\mathbf{s} \mathbf{Y} = \mathbb{E}_Z \left[\arg\max_{\mathbf{Y} \in \mathcal{C}} \langle \mathbf{Y}, \mathbf{s1}^T + \sigma \mathbf{Z} \rangle \mathbf{Z}^T / \sigma \right]. \tag{8}$$

The equation above has been simplified in the special case where $\mathbf{Z}$ follows a normal distribution. With this, we can back-propagate through the Top-K operation.

We train the backbone models together with the token selection networks using the cross-entropy loss in an end-to-end fashion. During inference, we leverage hard Top-K (implemented as torch.topk in Pytorch [47]) to further boost the efficiency. We follow [8], where only a single Top-K operation will be performed (instead of n perturbed repetitions) and token selection is implemented with slicing the tensor. However, applying hard Top-K during inference results in a train-test gap. To bridge this, we linearly decay σ to zero during training. Note that when $\sigma = 0$, the differentiable Top-K operation is equivalent to hard Top-K and the gradients flowing into the scorer network vanish.

3.3   Instantiations in Space and Time

Considering the distinct structure of appearance and motion cues in videos, we perform token selection *separately* in space and time—attending to salient frames first and then diving into those frames to look for the most important spatial region. Similar idea has been explored in prior work for decoupling 3D convolutional kernels [53], spatio-temporal non-local blocks [23] and self-attention [3].

Temporal Selection. Given the input tokens $x \in \mathbb{R}^{M \times N \times C}$, the goal of temporal selection is to select K of the M frames and discard the rest. We first average-pool x along the spatial dimension to get a sequence of frame-based tokens $x^t \in \mathbb{R}^{M \times C}$, which is then fed to the scorer network and the Top-K operator (Sect. 3.2) to generate the indicator matrix of the frames with top K highest scores: $Y^t \in \mathbb{R}^{M \times K}$. Finally, we reshape the input x to $\overline{x} \in \mathbb{R}^{M \times (N \times C)}$ and extract the selected K frames using the indicator matrix:

$$\overline{z} = {Y^t}^T \overline{x} \in \mathbb{R}^{K \times (N \times C)}. \tag{9}$$

The selected tokens are reshaped to $z \in \mathbb{R}^{K \times N \times C}$ for downstream processing.

Spatial Selection. In contrast to temporal selection, spatial selection is performed on each frame separately, and we aim to select K of the N tokens for each frame. More specifically, we first feed the tokens of the mth frame $x_m \in \mathbb{R}^{N \times C}$ to the scorer network to generate the importance scores $s_m \in \mathbb{R}^N$. We omit the subscript m for brevity since the same operations are applied to all frames. To obtain the top K spatial tokens, a naive approach is to apply the Top-K operator (Sect. 3.2) directly to the token-based scores s. However, this design inevitably breaks the spatial structure of the input tokens, which is especially inappropriate for spatial selection in video transformers. First, recent top-performing video transformers [14,38] involve a hierarchical architecture which gradually decreases the spatial resolutions in multiple stages. The discontinuous dropping behavior of tokens is detrimental to local operations like convolutions and pooling for spatial down-sampling. Second, the misalignment of spatial tokens along the temporal dimension makes the temporal modeling [3] much more challenging, if not impossible. We provide empirical evidence in Table 6 to support our claim.

Instead of performing token-based selection, we introduce a novel anchor-based design for spatial selection. After obtaining the importance scores $s \in \mathbb{R}^N$ for each frame, we first reshape it to a 2D score map $s^s \in \mathbb{R}^{\sqrt{N} \times \sqrt{N}}$ and split the map into a grid of overlapping anchors $\widetilde{s}^s \in \mathbb{R}^{G \times K}$ with anchor size K, where $G = (\frac{\sqrt{N} - \sqrt{K}}{\alpha} + 1)^2$ is the number of anchors and α is the stride. Visual examples of the anchors can be found in Fig. 1 and 4. After that, we aggregate the scores within each anchor via average pooling to obtain the anchor-based scores $s^a \in \mathbb{R}^G$. The original Top-K selection is now cast to a Top-1 selection problem, and we again leverage the Top-K operator (with $K = 1$) in Sect. 3.2 to obtain the indicator matrix and finally extract the anchor with the highest score.

4 Experiments

In this section, we evaluate the effectiveness of STTS by conducting extensive experiments on two large-scale video recognition datasets using two recent video transformer backbones. We introduce the experimental setup in Sect. 4.1, present main results in Sect. 4.2, and conduct ablation studies to validate the impact of different components in Sect. 4.3.

4.1 Experimental Setup

Dataset and Backbone. We mainly use MViT-B16 [14], a state-of-the-art video transformer, as the base model and evaluate the effectiveness of STTS on Kinetics-400 [28]. To demonstrate that our approach is generic for different transformer architectures and datasets, we also experiment with the Video Swin Transformer [39] on both Kinetics-400 and Something-Something-V2 (SSV2) [21]. Specifically, Kinetics-400 consists of 240k training videos and 20k validation videos belonging to 400 action categories. SSV2 is a temporally-sensitive dataset, containing 220,847 videos covering 174 action classes.

We represent different variants of STTS by B-T$_R^L$-S$_R^L$, where B indicates the backbone network, T and S represent the token selection performed along the temporal and spatial dimension, respectively. L and R denote the position where the token selection modules are inserted and the corresponding ratios of selected tokens. For example, MViT-B16-T$_{0.4}^0$-S$_{0.6}^4$ indicates performing temporal token selection before the 0th self-attention block with a selection ratio of 0.4, and spatial token selection before the 4th block with a ratio of 0.6, using MViT-B16 as the base model.

Evaluation Metrics. To measure the classification performance, we report the top-1 accuracy on the validation set. We measure the computational cost with FLOPs (floating-point operations), which is a hardware-independent metric.

Implementation Details. In our experiments, we finetune the pre-trained video transformers with our STTS modules. Parameters in the STTS modules are randomly initialized. We set σ in Eq. 7 to 0.1. The learning rate of the backbone layers is set to be 0.01× of the one in the STTS modules.

To train the MViT models on Kinetics-400, we follow [14] to sample a clip of 16 frames with a temporal stride of 4 and a spatial size of 224×224. The model is trained with AdamW [42] for 20 epochs with the first 3 epochs for linear warm-up [20]. The initial learning rate is set to $1e^{-4}$ for the dynamic token selection module and $1e^{-6}$ for the backbone network, with a mini-batch size of 16. The cosine learning rate schedule [41] is adopted. For the implementation of Video Swin Transformer, we sample a clip of 32 frames from each full-length video using a temporal stride of 2 and spatial size of 224×224. We set the learning rate of selection networks to $3e^{-4}$, and use 0.01× learning rate for the backbone model. The batch-size is set to 64. When training on Kinetics-400, we employ an AdamW optimizer [29] for 10 epochs using a cosine decay learning rate scheduler

Table 1. Comparisons of different token selection methods on K400 using the MViT-B16 as backbone.

Configs	Rand.	Atten.	GS	STTS
-$T_{0.5}^0$	75.5	N/A	75.8	**77.3**
-$T_{0.3}^4$	74.6	76.2	74.7	**77.3**
-$S_{0.5}^0$	75.6	N/A	N/A	**76.2**
-$S_{0.3}^4$	73.6	75.6	N/A	**76.8**
-$T_{0.8}^0$-$S_{0.7}^0$	75.7	N/A	N/A	**76.4**
-$T_{0.6}^0$-$S_{0.9}^4$	76.4	N/A	N/A	**77.5**

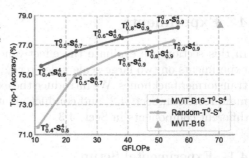

Fig. 3. Computational cost *vs.* recognition accuracy on Kinetics-400.

and 0.8 epochs of linear warm-up. When training on Something-Something-V2, we adopt the AdamW optimizer for longer training of 20 epochs with 0.8 epochs of linear warm-up. For inference, we apply the same testing strategies as the original backbone models for fair comparison.

4.2 Main Results

Effectiveness of STTS. We first compare STTS with some common token selection baselines: (1) Random (*Rand.*), which randomly samples K tokens without considering their visual content; (2) Attention (*Atten.*), which selects the tokens with the top K highest attention scores with the class token[2]; (3) Gumbel-Softmax (*GS*), which uses a Gumbel-softmax trick [26] for token selection. Note that *GS* cannot be applied to spatial token selection due to the existence of spatial downsampling in recent video transformers. Please refer to the supplementary material for more details.

We summarize the results for temporal-only, spatial-only and joint token selection in Table 1. The unfeasible baseline settings are filled with N/A. It can be observed that STTS achieves the best accuracy compared to all baseline methods under a similar computational budget. In particular, STTS outperforms *GS* by a large margin, although they share the same design of the scorer network (Sect. 3.2), indicating the effectiveness of our differentiable Top-K operator for dynamic token selection.

We further compare our STTS with the *Rand.* baseline under different computational budgets. As shown in Fig. 3, STTS consistently achieves superior results, especially for the settings with high reduction rate in computation. For example, MViT-B16-$T_{0.4}^0$-$S_{0.6}^4$ outperforms *Rand.* by 5.7% when using similar 12 GFLOPs. This verifies that informative tokens can be well preserved through our dynamic token selection modules. It can also be observed that the computational overhead of our token selection module is negligible—actually, the parameters and FLOPs of the scorer network are only 1.0% and 0.7% of those in the original MViT-B16 backbone.

---

[2] Note that Attention-K cannot be applied if class tokens are not used (*e.g.*, VideoSwin) or self-attention is not yet computed (*e.g.*, 0th block of the model).

Table 2. Results of STTS and comparisons with state-of-the-art methods on Kinetics-400.

Model	Pretrain	TFLOPs	Top-1
X3D-L [16]	–	0.74	77.5
TimeSformer [3]	IN-21K	0.59	78.0
MViT-B16 [14]	–	0.35	78.4
MViT-B16-$T_{0.8}^0$-$S_{0.9}^4$	–	0.24	77.9
MViT-B16-$T_{0.9}^0$-$S_{0.9}^4$	–	0.28	78.1
SlowFast 8×8 [17]	–	3.18	77.9
CorrNet-101 [55]	–	6.72	79.2
ViT-B-VTN [45]	IN-21K	4.22	78.6
TimeSformer-HR [3]	IN-21K	5.11	79.7
Mformer-HR [48]	IN-21K	28.76	81.1
VideoSwin-B [39]	IN-21K	3.38	82.7
VideoSwin-B-$T_{0.6}^0$	IN-21K	2.17	81.4
VideoSwin-B-$T_{0.8}^0$	IN-21K	3.02	81.9

Table 3. Results of STTS and comparisons with state-of-the-art methods on Something-Something-V2.

Model	Pretrain	TFLOPs	Top-1
TSM [37]	K400	0.37	63.3
STM [27]	IN-1K	2.00	64.2
TEA [36]	IN-1K	2.10	65.1
blVNet [15]	IN-1K	3.86	65.2
SlowFast 8×8 [17]	K400	0.32	63.1
TimeSformer-HR [3]	IN-21K	5.11	62.5
ViViT-L [2]	K400	47.90	65.4
MViT-B16 [14]	K400	0.51	67.1
Mformer-HR [48]	K400	2.88	67.1
VideoSwin-B [39]	K400	0.96	69.6
VideoSwin-B-$T_{0.6}^0$	K400	0.57	68.1
VideoSwin-B-$T_{0.7}^0$	K400	0.71	68.7

Comparison with the State of the Art. In Table 2, we compare STTS with state-of-the-art video recognition models on Kinetics-400 [7], including both CNN-based and Transformer-based models. To demonstrate that our approach can be generalized to different transformer architectures, we use both MViT [14] and VideoSwin [39] as the base models. We report the overall computational cost at inference—the cost for a single view × the number of views in space and time, given in Tera-FLOPs (TFLOPs). For clear comparison, we separate the models into two groups and compare STTS with those with comparable TFLOPs. Note that the default settings of our STTS are MViT-T^0-S^4 and VideoSwin-B-T^0 as they achieve the most competitive results according to the ablation study, and we will explore other options in Sect. 4.3. Furthermore, we only perform temporal selection for VideoSwin-B, since window shuffling operations are complicated [72] in the Swin transformer, which makes the spatial selection particularly challenging. It has been recently shown that the shifting operation might not be necessary in modern architectures [68].

We observe that models equipped with our STTS exhibit favorable complexity/accuracy trade-offs at the two complexity levels. Notably, our MViT-B16-$T_{0.9}^0$-$S_{0.9}^4$ achieves comparable results with the recent TimeSformer [3] while requiring only 47% of the computational cost. Similarly, our VideoSwin-B-$T_{0.6}^0$ outperforms the recent video transformers (e.g., TimeSformer-HR [3], Mformer-HR [48]) while saving more than 50% in computation. It is also worth mentioning that for both two base models, our STTS is capable of saving at least 10% of the computational cost with less than 1% accuracy drop.

We also conduct experiments on Something-Something-V2 [21] in Table 3. Given that the pretrained models on MViT [14] are not available on SSV2, we only evaluate STTS using the VideoSwin Transformer as backbone. We observe that STTS outperforms recent transformer models by a large margin with much

Table 4. Ablation on token selection at different locations.

Config	GFLOPs	Top-1
MViT-B16	70.5	78.4
$-S_{0.6}^0$	31.2 ($\downarrow$55.7%)	76.2
$-S_{0.3}^4$	35.2 ($\downarrow$50.1%)	76.8
$-T_{0.6}^0$	41.3 ($\downarrow$41.4%)	77.5
$-T_{0.3}^4$	37.5 ($\downarrow$46.8%)	77.3
$-T_{0.8}^0-S_{0.7}^0$	36.0 ($\downarrow$48.9%)	76.4
$-T_{0.6}^0-S_{0.9}^4$	38.1 ($\downarrow$46.0%)	**77.5**

Table 5. Multi-step token selection on Kinetics-400 using MViT as the base model. The savings in GFLOPs are all around 50%.

Temporal		Spatial		GFLOPs	Top-1
Location	Ratio	Location	Ratio		
0, 4	0.9, 0.7	0, 4	0.9, 0.7	35.8 ($\downarrow$49.2%)	76.4
4, 8	0.6, 0.4	4, 8	0.7, 0.7	36.0 ($\downarrow$48.9%)	76.5
0, 4, 8	0.9, 0.9, 0.7	0, 4, 8	0.9, 0.9, 0.8	36.6 ($\downarrow$48.1%)	76.6
0	0.6	4	0.9	37.5 ($\downarrow$46.8%)	**77.5**

less computational cost. For example, VideoSwin-B-$T_{0.6}^0$ achieves an accuracy of 68.1%, 2.7%/1.0% higher than ViViT-L [2]/Mformer-HR [48]. We would like to point out that action recognition on SSV2 relies heavily on temporal information, and we believe that the competitive results of our VideoSwin-B-$T_{0.7}^0$ again verifies the effectiveness of our STTS modules in selecting salient temporal tokens.

4.3 Discussion

Token Selection at Different Locations/Multiple Steps. The flexibility of our STTS module implies that different choices of token selection configuration are available in order to achieve a similar computational reduction rate. For example, in order to reduce the computation of MViT-B16 by approximately 50%, one can either apply (1) a spatial-only/temporal-only token selection at early stages with a higher selection ratio (*e.g.*, $-S_{0.6}^0/-T_{0.6}^0$); (2) a spatial-only/temporal-only token selection at later stages with a lower selection ratio (*e.g.*, $-S_{0.3}^4/-T_{0.3}^4$); or (3) a joint token selection (*e.g.*, $-T_{0.6}^0-S_{0.9}^4$), optionally in a multi-step manner (Table 5). We provide an in-depth analysis of these choices in this section, taking MViT-B16 as an example and evaluating on Kinetics-400. We report the inference cost for a single view.

Table 4 shows the performance of STTS when token selection is performed at different locations. For all the settings, *the ratios of selected tokens are adjusted to ensure the overall computational cost is reduced by approximately 50%*. We observe that temporal selection exceeds the spatial selection by a large margin, which demonstrates that temporal redundancy is more significant than spatial redundancy in videos. In addition, joint token selection (with temporal token selection at the early layer and spatial token selection at the deep layer, *i.e.*, $-T_{0.6}^0-S_{0.9}^4$) achieves the best result. We also perform the token selection in a multi-step manner, *i.e.*, performing multiple token selections at different layers of a transformer network with a higher selection ratio for each of them. The results in Table 5 shows that although sharing a similar computational cost, multi-step

Table 6. Impact of anchor-based spatial selection.

Config	Anchor	Score	Top-1
$Rand.$-$S^0_{0.5}$	✗	–	16.7
	✓	–	75.6
MViT-B16-$S^0_{0.5}$	✗	T	57.6
	✓	A	75.4
	✓	T	**76.2**

Table 7. Comparison of the inference time.

Config	GFLOPs	Throughput (video/s)
MViT-B16	70.5	79.3
-$T^0_{0.9}$-$S^4_{0.9}$	56.4	96.5
-$T^0_{0.8}$-$S^4_{0.9}$	47.2	112.9
-$T^0_{0.6}$-$S^0_{0.9}$	38.1	129.7

Table 8. Impact of σ values.

Config	σ	Top-1
Rand	–	75.5
-$T^0_{0.5}$	0.05	77.2
-$T^0_{0.5}$	0.1	**77.3**
-$T^0_{0.5}$	0.2	77.1

selection produces inferior results than the single-step selection. We hypothesize that the multi-step selection leads to frequent changes of the spatio-temporal structures of the videos and is more difficult to train.

Impact of Anchor-Based Spatial Selection. To verify the effectiveness of our anchor-based spatial selection described in Sect. 3.3, we compare different spatial selection strategies in Table 6. Specifically, ✓ in the second column indicates using the anchor-based spatial selection while ✗ indicates using the token-based selection. T and A in the third column denote taking token-level features or anchor-level features (average-pooled features within each anchor) as input for computing the importance scores, respectively.

We observe that the naive token-based spatial selection results in a remarkable performance drop (76.2% → 57.6%). It is clear that such a spatial selection strategy breaks the spatial structure of the original backbone model and therefore the $Rand.$ baseline performs particularly poorly (16.7%) without finetuning model parameters. We also observe that taking anchor-level features as input for scorer network performs worse than our default setting.

Inference Time. To verify that our method effectively reduces the computational overhead, we measure the inference time of STTS and MViT-B16 on a single 8 RTX 3090 GPU server. The comparison results are reported in Table 7, which illustrate that STTS indeed reduces the inference time in practice.

Impact of σ. To investigate the influence of σ in Eq. 7, we train MViT-B16-$T^0_{0.5}$ using different σ values and report the comparison results in Table 8. We can see that STTS is insensitive to the choice of hyper-parameters, and it consistently outperforms the $Rand.$ baseline. Unless otherwise mentioned, we set $\sigma = 0.1$ in our experiment since it achieves slightly better performance than other settings.

Qualitative Results. We visualize the temporal-only, spatial-only, and joint token selection results in Fig. 4, where the masked frames and regions are discarded by STTS. We observe that our STTS can not only effectively identify the most informative frames in a video clip, but also locate the discriminative regions inside each frame. With such token pruning in temporal and spatial

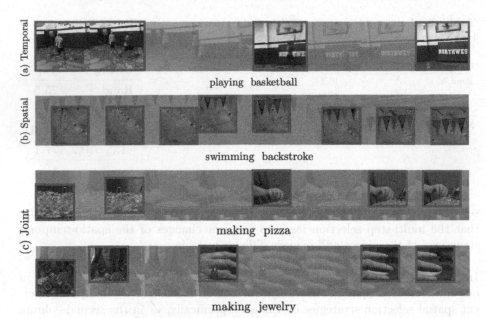

(a) Temporal

playing basketball

(b) Spatial

swimming backstroke

(c) Joint

making pizza

making jewelry

Fig. 4. Visualization of the temporal, spatial, and joint token selection results by our STTS, where the masked frames/regions are pruned and only the tokens inside the bounding box will be fed to the subsequent video transformers.

dimensions, only the tokens that are important for correctly recognizing the actions are retained and fed into the subsequent video transformers, resulting in a saved computational cost with minimal drop of classification accuracy.

5 Conclusion

In this paper, we introduced STTS, a dynamic spatio-temporal token selection framework, to reduce both temporal and spatial redundancies of video transformers for efficient video recognition. We formulated the token selection as a ranking problem, where the importance of different tokens was predicted by a lightweight selection network and only those with Top-K scores will be preserved for subsequent processing. In the temporal dimension, we selected a subset of frames with the highest relevance to the action category, while in the spatial dimension, we retained the most discriminative region within each frame to preserve the structural information of the input frame. To enable the end-to-end training of the backbone model together with the token selection module, we leveraged a perturbed-maximum based differentiable Top-K operator. Extensive experiments on several video recognition benchmarks validated our STTS could achieve competitive efficiency-accuracy trade-offs.

Acknowledgement. Y.-G. Jiang was sponsored in part by "Shuguang Program" supported by Shanghai Education Development Foundation and Shanghai Municipal Education Commission (No. 20SG01). Z. Wu was supported by NSFC under Grant No. 62102092.

References

1. Abernethy, J., Lee, C., Tewari, A.: Perturbation techniques in online learning and optimization. Perturbations, Optimization, and Statistics (2016)
2. Arnab, A., Dehghani, M., Heigold, G., Sun, C., Lučić, M., Schmid, C.: ViViT: a video vision transformer. In: ICCV (2021)
3. Bertasius, G., Wang, H., Torresani, L.: Is space-time attention all you need for video understanding? In: ICML (2021)
4. Berthet, Q., Blondel, M., Teboul, O., Cuturi, M., Vert, J.P., Bach, F.: Learning with differentiable perturbed optimizers. arXiv preprint arXiv:2002.08676 (2020)
5. Bhardwaj, S., Srinivasan, M., Khapra, M.M.: Efficient video classification using fewer frames. In: CVPR (2019)
6. Carion, N., Massa, F., Synnaeve, G., Usunier, N., Kirillov, A., Zagoruyko, S.: End-to-end object detection with transformers. In: Vedaldi, A., Bischof, H., Brox, T., Frahm, J.-M. (eds.) ECCV 2020. LNCS, vol. 12346, pp. 213–229. Springer, Cham (2020). https://doi.org/10.1007/978-3-030-58452-8_13
7. Carreira, J., Zisserman, A.: Quo Vadis, action recognition? A new model and the kinetics dataset. In: CVPR (2017)
8. Cordonnier, J.B., et al.: Differentiable patch selection for image recognition. In: CVPR (2021)
9. Cuturi, M., Teboul, O., Vert, J.P.: Differentiable ranking and sorting using optimal transport. In: NeurIPS (2019)
10. Davidson, J., et al.: The YouTube video recommendation system. In: RS (2010)
11. Devlin, J., Chang, M.W., Lee, K., Toutanova, K.: BERT: pre-training of deep bidirectional transformers for language understanding. arXiv preprint arXiv:1810.04805 (2018)
12. Dong, J., et al.: Dual encoding for zero-example video retrieval. In: CVPR (2019)
13. Dosovitskiy, A., et al.: An image is worth 16x16 words: transformers for image recognition at scale. In: ICLR (2021)
14. Fan, H., et al.: Multiscale vision transformers. In: ICCV (2021)
15. Fan, Q., Chen, C.F.R., Kuehne, H., Pistoia, M., Cox, D.: More is less: learning efficient video representations by temporal aggregation modules. In: NeurIPS (2019)
16. Feichtenhofer, C.: X3D: expanding architectures for efficient video recognition. In: CVPR (2020)
17. Feichtenhofer, C., Fan, H., Malik, J., He, K.: SlowFast networks for video recognition. In: ICCV (2019)
18. Feichtenhofer, C., Pinz, A., Zisserman, A.: Convolutional two-stream network fusion for video action recognition. In: CVPR (2016)
19. Gabeur, V., Sun, C., Alahari, K., Schmid, C.: Multi-modal transformer for video retrieval. In: Vedaldi, A., Bischof, H., Brox, T., Frahm, J.-M. (eds.) ECCV 2020. LNCS, vol. 12349, pp. 214–229. Springer, Cham (2020). https://doi.org/10.1007/978-3-030-58548-8_13
20. Goyal, P., et al.: Accurate, large minibatch SGD: training ImageNet in 1 hour. arXiv preprint arXiv:1706.02677 (2017)

21. Goyal, R., et al.: The "something something" video database for learning and evaluating visual common sense. In: ICCV (2017)
22. Hara, K., Kataoka, H., Satoh, Y.: Can spatiotemporal 3d CNNs retrace the history of 2d CNNs and ImageNet? In: CVPR (2018)
23. He, B., Yang, X., Wu, Z., Chen, H., Lim, S.N., Shrivastava, A.: GTA: global temporal attention for video action understanding. In: BMVC (2021)
24. Heo, B., Yun, S., Han, D., Chun, S., Choe, J., Oh, S.J.: Rethinking spatial dimensions of vision transformers. arXiv preprint arXiv:2103.16302 (2021)
25. Huang, Y., Cui, B., Jiang, J., Hong, K., Zhang, W., Xie, Y.: Real-time video recommendation exploration. In: ICMD (2016)
26. Jang, E., Gu, S., Poole, B.: Categorical reparameterization with Gumbel-softmax. arXiv preprint arXiv:1611.01144 (2016)
27. Jiang, B., Wang, M., Gan, W., Wu, W., Yan, J.: STM: spatiotemporal and motion encoding for action recognition. In: ICCV (2019)
28. Kay, W., et al.: The kinetics human action video dataset. arXiv preprint arXiv:1705.06950 (2017)
29. Kingma, D.P., Ba, J.: Adam: a method for stochastic optimization. arXiv preprint arXiv:1412.6980 (2014)
30. Kitaev, N., Kaiser, L., Levskaya, A.: Reformer: the efficient transformer. In: ICLR (2020)
31. Kondratyuk, D., et al.: MoviNets: mobile video networks for efficient video recognition. In: CVPR (2021)
32. Korbar, B., Tran, D., Torresani, L.: SCSampler: sampling salient clips from video for efficient action recognition. In: ICCV (2019)
33. Lee, J., Abu-El-Haija, S.: Large-scale content-only video recommendation. In: ICCVW (2017)
34. Li, K., et al.: UniFormer: unified transformer for efficient spatial-temporal representation learning. In: ICLR (2022)
35. Li, T., Liu, J., Zhang, W., Ni, Y., Wang, W., Li, Z.: UAV-human: a large benchmark for human behavior understanding with unmanned aerial vehicles. In: CVPR (2021)
36. Li, Y., Ji, B., Shi, X., Zhang, J., Kang, B., Wang, L.: TEA: temporal excitation and aggregation for action recognition. In: CVPR (2020)
37. Lin, J., Gan, C., Han, S.: TSM: temporal shift module for efficient video understanding. In: ICCV (2019)
38. Liu, Z., et al.: Swin transformer: hierarchical vision transformer using shifted windows. In: ICCV (2021)
39. Liu, Z., et al.: Video swin transformer. arXiv preprint arXiv:2106.13230 (2021)
40. Liu, Z., et al.: TEINet: towards an efficient architecture for video recognition. In: AAAI (2020)
41. Loshchilov, I., Hutter, F.: SGDR: stochastic gradient descent with warm restarts. arXiv preprint arXiv:1608.03983 (2016)
42. Loshchilov, I., Hutter, F.: Fixing weight decay regularization in adam (2018)
43. Mei, T., Yang, B., Hua, X.S., Li, S.: Contextual video recommendation by multimodal relevance and user feedback. TOIS 29, 1–24 (2011)
44. Naseer, M., Ranasinghe, K., Khan, S., Hayat, M., Khan, F., Yang, M.H.: Intriguing properties of vision transformers. In: NeurIPS (2021)
45. Neimark, D., Bar, O., Zohar, M., Asselmann, D.: Video transformer network. arXiv preprint arXiv:2102.00719 (2021)

46. Pan, B., Panda, R., Jiang, Y., Wang, Z., Feris, R., Oliva, A.: IA-RED[2]: Interpretability-aware redundancy reduction for vision transformers. In: NeurIPS (2021)
47. Paszke, A., et al.: PyTorch: an imperative style, high-performance deep learning library. In: NeurIPS (2019)
48. Patrick, M., et al.: Keeping your eye on the ball: trajectory attention in video transformers. In: NeurIPS (2021)
49. Rao, Y., Zhao, W., Liu, B., Lu, J., Zhou, J., Hsieh, C.J.: DynamicViT: efficient vision transformers with dynamic token sparsification. In: NeurIPS (2021)
50. Ryoo, M.S., Piergiovanni, A., Arnab, A., Dehghani, M., Angelova, A.: Token-Learner: adaptive space-time tokenization for videos. In: NeurIPS (2021)
51. Sun, Z., Ke, Q., Rahmani, H., Bennamoun, M., Wang, G., Liu, J.: Human action recognition from various data modalities: a review. IEEE TPAMI, 1–20 (2022)
52. Touvron, H., Cord, M., Douze, M., Massa, F., Sablayrolles, A., Jégou, H.: Training data-efficient image transformers & distillation through attention. In: ICML (2021)
53. Tran, D., Wang, H., Torresani, L., Ray, J., LeCun, Y., Paluri, M.: A closer look at spatiotemporal convolutions for action recognition. In: CVPR (2018)
54. Vaswani, A., et al.: Attention is all you need. In: NeurIPS (2017)
55. Wang, H., Tran, D., Torresani, L., Feiszli, M.: Video modeling with correlation networks. In: CVPR (2020)
56. Wang, L., Tong, Z., Ji, B., Wu, G.: TDN: temporal difference networks for efficient action recognition. In: CVPR (2021)
57. Wang, R., et al.: BEVT: BERT pretraining of video transformers. In: CVPR (2022)
58. Wang, S., Li, B.Z., Khabsa, M., Fang, H., Ma, H.: Linformer: self-attention with linear complexity. arXiv preprint arXiv:2006.04768 (2020)
59. Wang, Y., Chen, Z., Jiang, H., Song, S., Han, Y., Huang, G.: Adaptive focus for efficient video recognition. In: ICCV (2021)
60. Wang, Y., et al.: AdaFocus V2: end-to-end training of spatial dynamic networks for video recognition. In: CVPR (2022)
61. Wang, Y., et al.: End-to-end video instance segmentation with transformers. In: CVPR (2021)
62. Wu, C.Y., Zaheer, M., Hu, H., Manmatha, R., Smola, A.J., Krähenbühl, P.: Compressed video action recognition. In: CVPR (2018)
63. Wu, Z., Li, H., Xiong, C., Jiang, Y.G., Davis, L.S.: A dynamic frame selection framework for fast video recognition. IEEE TPAMI **44**, 1699–1711 (2022)
64. Wu, Z., Li, H., Zheng, Y., Xiong, C., Jiang, Y., Davis, L.S.: A coarse-to-fine framework for resource efficient video recognition. In: IJCV (2021)
65. Wu, Z., Xiong, C., Ma, C.Y., Socher, R., Davis, L.S.: AdaFrame: adaptive frame selection for fast video recognition. In: CVPR (2019)
66. Xie, Y., et al.: Differentiable top-k with optimal transport. In: NeurIPS (2020)
67. Xu, L., Huang, H., Liu, J.: SUTD-TrafficQA: a question answering benchmark and an efficient network for video reasoning over traffic events. In: CVPR (2021)
68. Yang, J., et al.: Focal self-attention for local-global interactions in vision transformers. In: NeurIPS (2021)
69. Yeung, S., Russakovsky, O., Mori, G., Fei-Fei, L.: End-to-end learning of action detection from frame glimpses in videos. In: CVPR (2016)
70. Yuan, L., et al.: Central similarity quantization for efficient image and video retrieval. In: CVPR (2020)

71. Zhang, D., Zhang, H., Tang, J., Wang, M., Hua, X., Sun, Q.: Feature pyramid transformer. In: Vedaldi, A., Bischof, H., Brox, T., Frahm, J.-M. (eds.) ECCV 2020. LNCS, vol. 12373, pp. 323–339. Springer, Cham (2020). https://doi.org/10.1007/978-3-030-58604-1_20

72. Zhang, Z., Zhang, H., Zhao, L., Chen, T., Pfister, T.: Aggregating nested transformers. In: AAAI (2022)

73. Zheng, S., et al.: Rethinking semantic segmentation from a sequence-to-sequence perspective with transformers. In: CVPR (2021)

74. Zheng, Y.D., Liu, Z., Lu, T., Wang, L.: Dynamic sampling networks for efficient action recognition in videos. TIP **29**, 7970–7983 (2020)

75. Zhu, X., Su, W., Lu, L., Li, B., Wang, X., Dai, J.: Deformable DETR: deformable transformers for end-to-end object detection. In: ICLR (2021)

76. Zolfaghari, M., Singh, K., Brox, T.: ECO: efficient convolutional network for online video understanding. In: Ferrari, V., Hebert, M., Sminchisescu, C., Weiss, Y. (eds.) ECCV 2018. LNCS, vol. 11206, pp. 713–730. Springer, Cham (2018). https://doi.org/10.1007/978-3-030-01216-8_43

Long Movie Clip Classification
with State-Space Video Models

Md Mohaiminul Islam$^{(\boxtimes)}$ and Gedas Bertasius

UNC Chapel Hill, Chapel Hill, USA
mmiemon@cs.unc.edu

Abstract. Most modern video recognition models are designed to operate on short video clips (e.g., 5–10 s in length). Thus, it is challenging
to apply such models to long movie understanding tasks, which typically require sophisticated long-range temporal reasoning. The recently
introduced video transformers partially address this issue by using long-
range temporal self-attention. However, due to the quadratic cost of self-
attention, such models are often costly and impractical to use. Instead,
we propose ViS4mer, an efficient long-range video model that combines
the strengths of self-attention and the recently introduced structured
state-space sequence (S4) layer. Our model uses a standard Transformer
encoder for short-range spatiotemporal feature extraction, and a multi-
scale temporal S4 decoder for subsequent long-range temporal reasoning. By progressively reducing the spatiotemporal feature resolution and
channel dimension at each decoder layer, ViS4mer learns complex long-
range spatiotemporal dependencies in a video. Furthermore, ViS4mer is
2.63× faster and requires 8× less GPU memory than the corresponding
pure self-attention-based model. Additionally, ViS4mer achieves state-of-
the-art results in 6 out of 9 long-form movie video classification tasks on
the Long Video Understanding (LVU) benchmark. Furthermore, we show
that our approach successfully generalizes to other domains, achieving
competitive results on the Breakfast and the COIN procedural activity datasets. The code is publicly available (https://github.com/md-
mohaiminul/ViS4mer).

1 Introduction

Suppose we ask someone to describe the relationship between the characters
from the 'Interstellar' movie illustrated in Fig. 1. It might be difficult for them
to do so just by looking at a short video clip of several seconds. However, this is
a much easier task if a person watches the whole movie. Thus, in this work, we
pose the question of whether we can develop a computer vision model that can
leverage long-range temporal cues to answer complex questions such as 'What
is the genre of the movie?', 'What is the relationship among the characters?',
'Who is the director of the movie?', etc.

Supplementary Information The online version contains supplementary material
available at https://doi.org/10.1007/978-3-031-19833-5_6.

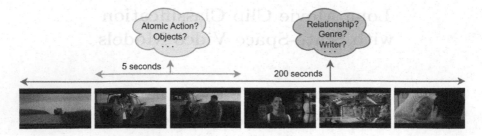

Fig. 1. Most traditional video models are designed for local prediction tasks (e.g., atomic action recognition, object detection, etc.) in short video clips (e.g., 5 s in length). In contrast, we aim to understand complex video understanding tasks in long movie videos (e.g., 200 s long), such as classifying the relationships among movie characters, predicting the writer of the story, categorizing the genre of the movie, etc.

The majority of modern video recognition models [2,5,8,14–16,25,36,39,43, 48] are unfortunately not equipped to solve these tasks as they are designed for short-range videos (e.g., 5–10 s in duration). Furthermore, extending these models to the long-range video setting by stacking more input video frames is impractical due to excessive computational cost and GPU memory consumption.

Recently, several Transformer models [5,53] have been shown to perform well on long-range video understanding tasks. However, due to the quadratic cost of standard self-attention, these models are either very computationally costly [5], or they have to operate on pre-extracted CNN features [53], which discard fine-grained spatiotemporal information, thus, limiting the expressivity of the final video model. The latter characteristic is particularly important for long-range movie clip analysis, since fine-grained spatiotemporal cues may be indicative of the relationships between different movie characters, the genre of a movie, etc.

To address the efficiency-related issues of standard self-attention, recent work in Natural Language Processing (NLP) has proposed a structured state-space sequence model (S4) [19] for long-range sequence analysis. Unlike self-attention, the S4 layer has linear memory and computation cost with respect to the input length. As a result, it can handle much longer input sequences.

Combining the strengths of the self-attention and the S4 layer, we propose ViS4mer, a long-range **Vi**deo classification model composed of a standard transformer encoder and a multi-scale temporal **S4** decoder. The transformer encoder is used for spatial short-range video feature extraction whereas the S4 decoder performs long-range temporal reasoning, which is necessary for complex movie clip classification tasks. We build our temporal S4 decoder using a multi-scale architecture progressively reducing the number of tokens and the channel dimension with every layer. This allows our model to learn hierarchical spatiotemporal video representation while also reducing the computational cost associated with operating on a large number of video tokens.

We validate ViS4mer on the recently introduced Long Video Understanding (LVU) benchmark [53], which consists of nine diverse movie understanding tasks.

We show that ViS4mer outperforms previous approaches in 6 out of 9 long-range video classification tasks. Moreover, compared to its self-attention counterpart, ViS4mer is 2.63× faster and requires 8× less GPU memory. Lastly, ViS4mer generalizes to other domains, achieving competitive results on the Breakfast [30] and COIN [45] long-range procedural activity datasets.

2 Related Work

Modeling Long Sequences. Long sequence modeling is a fundamental task in Natural Language Processing (NLP). Previously, Bahdanau *et al.* [3] proposed a recurrent attention scheme for machine translation. Improving upon this work, Vaswani *at el.* [49] introduced a self-attention operation for the same machine translation task. Subsequently, a plethora of transformer-based architectures has been proposed for various NLP tasks [6,10,12,34,41,55]. However, one major drawback of the transformer architecture is the quadratic complexity of standard self-attention. Various efficient self-attention schemes have been proposed for reducing the computation cost when modeling long sequences [9,26,29,56]. Most relevant to our work, is the method of Gu *at el.* [17,19,20] that proposes an efficient structured state-space sequence (S4) layer for long sequence modeling. Inspired by this work, in this paper, we design a video architecture that incorporates the ideas from [19,20] for long-range movie understanding tasks.

Video Recognition. Most existing video recognition methods are built using 2D and 3D Convolutional Neural Networks [8,15,16,25,31,40,43,48,52,58,60]. Due to the local nature of 2D and 3D convolutions, most of these models typically operate on short video clips of a few seconds. Inspired by the success of Transformer models in natural language processing (NLP), recently the transformer-based models have been successfully used for video recognition tasks [2,5,14,36,39]. However, due to the quadratic cost of the self-attention operation, these models are very computationally costly and, thus, only applied to short-range video segments. Our work aims to address this issue by proposing a novel efficient ViS4mer model for long movie clip understanding tasks.

Understanding Long-Form Movie Videos. Movie understanding is a popular area of video understanding with many prior methods designed for movie-based tasks. Tapaswi *et al.* [47] introduce a movie question answering dataset. Bain *et al.* [4] and Zellers *at al.* [57] propose text-to-video retrieval and question answering benchmarks. However, these multi-modal benchmarks are often biased towards the language domain and are not ideal for evaluating video-only models. Several prior works introduced movie understanding datasets [22,50,54], which are not publicly accessible for copyright issues. Recently, Wu *et al.* [53] introduced a Long-form Video Understanding (LVU) benchmark that uses publicly available MovieClips [1]. The proposed LVU benchmark contains nine diverse tasks covering a wide range of aspects of long-form video understanding, which makes it suitable for evaluating our work as well. The current state-of-the-art Object Transformer method [53] applied on this benchmark, uses a Transformer architecture, and a variety of external modules (e.g., short-term video feature

Table 1. Theoretical runtime and memory requirement of state-space and self-attention operations w.r.t sequence length (L), batch size (B), and hidden dimension (H). Tildes denote log factors [19]. The runtime and memory cost of the state-space layer is linear w.r.t the input sequence length as opposed to the quadratic cost of self-attention.

	Self-attention	State-space
Parameters	H^2	H^2
Memory	$B(L^2 + HL)$	BLH
Training	$B(L^2H + LH^2)$	$BH(\tilde{H} + \tilde{L}) + B\tilde{L}H$
Inference	$L^2H + LH^2$	H^2

extractor [16,51], object detection, and tracking modules [21,32,42], and self-supervised pretraining) Instead, in this work, we propose ViS4mer, a simple and efficient long-range video recognition model.

3   Background: Structured State-Space Sequence Model

Before describing our method, we first review some background information on Structured State-Spaces Sequence layers [19], which is one of the key components of our ViS4mer architecture. We start from the fundamental State-Space Model (SSM), which is defined by the simple Eq. (1). It maps a 1-dimensional input signal $u(t)$ to an N-dimensional latent space $x(t)$, then projects the hidden state $x(t)$ to a 1-dimensional output signal $y(t)$.

$$x'(t) = Ax(t) + Bu(t)$$
$$y(t) = Cx(t) + Du(t)$$
(1)

Here, A, B, C, and D are parameters learned using gradient descent. Unfortunately, the standard implementation of SSM can be very costly because computing the hidden state requires L successive multiplications with the matrix A. This results in $O(N^2L)$ operations and $O(NL)$ space for state dimension N and sequence length L. Moreover, this operation suffers from the vanishing/exploding gradients problem. To address this issue, the recent work [19] leverages HiPPO theory [18], which requires the A matrix to be defined as:

$$A_{nk} = \begin{cases} (2n+1)^{1/2}(2k+1)1/2 & \text{if } n > k \\ n+1 & \text{if } n = k \\ 0 & \text{if } n < k \end{cases}$$
(2)

This provides theoretical guarantees allowing SSMs to capture long-range dependences in the sequential data. Building on this work, the method in [19] develops a structured state-space sequence (S4) layer, which significantly reduces the computation cost of a basic SSM.

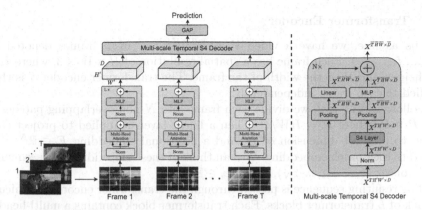

Fig. 2. Overview of the ViS4mer model. First, we split the video frames into fixed-size patches and use a short-range transformer encoder to extract contextual patch-level features for each video frame. Next, we feed the resulting spatiotemporal patch tokens from the whole video to a novel multi-scale temporal S4 decoder for modeling long-range temporal interactions in movie clips. Each S4 decoder block reduces the spatiotemporal resolution and the channel dimension using a Pooling and an MLP layer for learning multi-scale features. Afterward, the outputs from the S4 decoder are aggregated using global average pooling (GAP), and fed into the classification layer for the final downstream task prediction.

In Table 1, we compare the theoretical time and space complexity of the self-attention and structured state-space sequence layers. We observe that self-attention has quadratic complexity w.r.t input sequence length L for training time, inference time, and memory requirement. In contrast, the state-space operation has linear time and space dependency w.r.t the input sequence length L. We refer the reader to the original paper [19] for further details.

4 The ViS4mer Model

Our goal is to design a model for long-range movie clip analysis. To this end, we propose ViS4mer, a long-range video recognition model comprised of a transformer encoder and a multi-scale temporal S4 decoder. Following Vision Transformer [13], we first divide input video frames into smaller patches. We then apply a standard transformer encoder to extract fine-grained patch-level features from each video frame. Afterward, we use our proposed multi-scale temporal S4 decoder for long-range temporal reasoning over the patch-level features. Since the decoder has access to fine-grained spatiotemporal video patch information, it can effectively recognize the complex global properties of a long-range video. In Fig. 2, we illustrate the overall architecture of our proposed ViS4mer model. Below, we also discuss each of these components in more detail.

4.1 Transformer Encoder

Let us assume, we have a video $V \in \mathbb{R}^{T \times H \times W \times 3}$ of T frames denoted by $(f_1, ..., f_i, ..., f_T)$. Each frame has a spatial resolution of $H \times W \times 3$, where H is the height, and W is the width of the frame. The transformer encoder $\mathscr{E}$ is then applied to each frame independently.

Following ViT [13], we divide each frame into N non-overlapping patches of size $P \times P$, where $N = HW/P$. Then a linear layer is applied to project each patch to a latent dimension of D, and a positional embedding $E \in \mathbb{R}^{N \times D}$ is added to each patch embedding. We can think of these embeddings as a sequence of N tokens $(z_1, ..., z_i, ..., z_N)$, where $z_i \in \mathbb{R}^D$.

The resulting sequence is passed through the transformer encoder $\mathscr{E}$ which is a stack of L transformer blocks. Each transformer block contains a multi-headed attention (MHA) and a multi-layer perceptron (MLP) block. Layer normalization (LN) is applied before each block, and a skip connection layer is added after each block. These operations can be expressed as:

$$z' = \text{MHA}(\text{LN}(z_{in})) + z_{in}$$
$$z_{out} = \text{MLP}(\text{LN}(z')) + z' \tag{3}$$

The spatiotemporal token outputs of the transformer encoder can then be denoted as $(h_1, ..., h_i, ..., h_T)$, where $h_i = \mathscr{E}(f_i) \in \mathbb{R}^{H' \times W' \times D}$, $H' = H/P$, $W' = W/P$. All of these outputs are stacked into a single matrix $X \in \mathbb{R}^{T \times H' \times W' \times D}$.

4.2 Multi-scale Temporal S4 Decoder

Next, we describe our framework for modeling complex long-range temporal dependencies among the spatiotemporal tokens produced by the transformer encoder. One obvious choice is to use another transformer model to process such a sequence of tokens. However, this can be challenging due to (i) a large number of spatiotemporal tokens and (ii) the quadratic complexity of the self-attention operation. To illustrate this point, we note that processing a video of 60 frames of 224×224 spatial resolution using a patch size of 16×16 yields a total of $14 \times 14 \times 60 = 11,760$ output tokens. Using a standard self-attention operator on such a large number of tokens requires ∼138 million pairwise comparisons which is extremely costly. Another solution would be to only consider CLS token outputs for each frame. However, doing so removes fine-grained spatiotemporal information, thus, degrading the performance of long-range movie understanding tasks (as shown in our experimental evaluation).

To overcome this challenge we design a temporal multi-scale S4 decoder architecture for complex long-range reasoning. Instead of using self-attention, our decoder model utilizes the recently introduced S4 layer (described in Sect. 3). Since the S4 layer has a linear computation and memory dependency with respect to the sequence length, this significantly reduces the computational cost of processing such long sequences.

To effectively adapt the S4 layer to the visual domain, we design a multi-scale S4 decoder architecture. Our temporal multi-scale S4 decoder consists of multiple blocks where each block operates on different spatial resolution and channel dimensions. Starting from a high spatial resolution and high channel dimension, the proposed model gradually decreases spatiotemporal resolution and channel dimension at each block. Our multi-scale architecture is inspired by several successful multi-scale models in the visual domain such as Feature Pyramid Networks [32], and Swin transformer [35]. Because of this multi-scale strategy, different blocks can effectively learn features at different scales, which helps the model to learn complex spatiotemporal dependencies over long videos. Furthermore, operating on shorter input sequences of smaller channel dimensions in the deeper blocks helps us to reduce overfitting on a relatively small LVU benchmark. Overall, as will be shown in our experimental section, in addition to producing better performance, our multi-scale strategy further reduces the computational cost and GPU memory requirements.

Figure 2 (right) shows the architecture of the multi-scale temporal S4 decoder. The decoder network $\mathscr{D}$ consists of N blocks, which are defined below:

$$
\begin{aligned}
x_{s4} &= \text{S4}(\text{LN}(x_{in})) \\
x_{mlp} &= \text{MLP}(\text{Pooling}(x_{s4})) \\
x_{skip} &= \text{Linear}(\text{Pooling}(x_{in})) \\
x_{out} &= x_{mlp} + x_{skip}
\end{aligned}
\tag{4}
$$

S4 Layer. We flatten the input tensor X to a sequence of L vectors $x_{in} = (x_1, ..., x_i, ..., x_L)$, where $L = T \times H' \times W'$, and $x_i \in \mathbb{R}^D$. We then pass this sequence to the S4 layer, which outputs the feature tensor $x_{s4} \in \mathbb{R}^{L \times D}$.

Spatiotemporal Resolution Reduction. We reduce the space-time resolution of our input tensor by a factor of $s_T \times s_H \times s_W$ using a max-pooling layer where $s_T \times s_H \times s_W$ is the stride along each axis of the input tensor. The resulting tensor has dimensionality of $\overline{T} \times \overline{H} \times \overline{W}$. This allows our model to learn multi-scale spatiotemporal representations while also reducing the computational cost of operating on long sequences.

Channel Reduction. After the pooling layer, we apply an MLP, which reduces the channel dimension of the input tensor. In addition to decreasing the computational cost, this also reduces overfitting on the LVU benchmark.

Skip Connections. We use skip connections from the input tensor to the final output of a decoder block. Due to the mismatch of feature dimensionalities, we apply an additional pooling layer to the input tensor. Furthermore, to handle the channel dimension mismatch, we use an additional linear layer.

4.3 Loss Functions

Following [53], we use a cross-entropy loss for the classification tasks, and the mean squared error (MSE) for the regressions tasks.

$$L_{ce}(\mathcal{F}_{\mathcal{C}}(\theta)) = -\frac{1}{B}\sum_{i=1}^{B}\sum_{j=1}^{K} y_j^i \log(\mathcal{F}_{\mathcal{C}}(\theta; x^i)_j) \qquad (5)$$

$$L_{mse}(\mathcal{F}_{\mathcal{R}}(\theta)) = -\frac{1}{B}\sum_{i=1}^{B}(y^i - \mathcal{F}_{\mathcal{R}}(\theta; x^i))^2 \qquad (6)$$

Here, $\mathcal{F}_{\mathcal{C}}(\theta)$ and $\mathcal{F}_{\mathcal{R}}(\theta)$ are our classification and regression models respectively, B is the batch size, K is the number of classes (for the classification task), y is the label, x is the input, and θ are the learnable model parameters.

4.4 Implementation Details

We resize each video frame to the spatial resolution of 224×224 and use a patch size of 16×16. For the transformer encoder, we use a 24-block transformer with hidden dimension 1024 pretrained on ImageNet [11]. For our multi-scale temporal S4 decoder, we use a 3-block architecture. Each block has a pooling layer with a kernel of $1 \times 2 \times 2$, stride of $1 \times 2 \times 2$, and padding of $1 \times 1 \times 1$. As discussed above, each block also has an MLP layer, which reduces the feature dimension by a factor of $2\times$. For all of our experiments, we use Adam optimizer [28] with a learning rate of 10^{-3}, and with a weight decay of 0.01. We train our models using NVIDIA RTX A6000 GPU with a batch size of 16.

5 Experiments

We evaluate ViS4mer on the recently proposed Long-form Video Understanding (LVU) benchmark [53] which contains nine diverse tasks related to long-form movie understanding. Moreover, we also perform thorough ablation studies (i) comparing our S4-based model to an equivalent self-attention baseline, (ii) studying the efficiency of ViS4mer, (iii) comparing our method with other efficient attention schemes, (iv) analyzing the design choices of our model, (v) validating the robustness to different short-range encoders, and (vi) lastly investigating our model's long-range modeling capability. Additionally, to demonstrate the generalization of our approach, we also validate ViS4mer on two long-range procedural activity datasets, COIN [45,46] and Breakfast [30].

5.1 Main Results on the LVU Benchmark

The long-form video understanding benchmark (LVU) [53] is constructed using the publicly available MovieClip dataset [1], which contains ~30K videos from ~3K movies. Each video is typically one to three minutes long. The benchmark contains nine tasks covering a wide range of long-form video understanding tasks. These 9 tasks fall into three main categories: (i) **content understanding**, which consists of (*'relationship'*, *'speaking style'*, *'scene/place'*) prediction, (ii) **metadata prediction**, which includes (*'director'*, *'genre'*, *'writer'*, *and 'movie*

Table 2. Comparison to prior works on the LVU dataset. Compared to previous long-range video models (VideoBERT, and Object Transformer), ViS4mer achieves significantly better accuracy in most tasks. Furthermore, ViS4mer also outperforms our implemented Long Sequence Transformer baseline, which uses the same design as our model, except for the S4 layers, which are replaced with the self-attention layers.

	Sequence model	Content (↑)			Metadata (↑)				User (↓)	
		Relation	Speak	Scene	Director	Genre	Writer	Year	Like	Views
SlowFast+NL [16,51]	Non-local	52.40	35.80	54.70	44.90	53.00	36.30	**52.50**	0.38	3.77
VideoBERT [44]	Self-attention	52.80	37.90	54.90	47.30	51.90	38.50	36.10	0.32	4.46
Obj. Transformer [53]	Self-attention	53.10	39.40	56.90	51.20	54.60	34.50	39.10	**0.23**	**3.55**
Long Seq. Transformer	Self-attention	52.38	37.31	62.79	56.07	52.70	42.26	39.16	0.31	3.83
ViS4mer	State-space	**57.14**	**40.79**	**67.44**	**62.61**	**54.71**	**48.8**	44.75	0.26	3.63

release year') classification, and (iii) **user engagement**, which requires predicting (*'YouTube like ratio', and 'YouTube popularity'*).

The content understanding and the metadata prediction tasks are evaluated using the standard top-1 accuracy metric, whereas the user engagement prediction tasks are evaluated using mean-squared error (MSE). Following [53], we use standard splits and train our model using video clips of 60 s.

We compare our proposed ViS4mer model with the previous methods validated on this benchmark. In particular, we use the same baselines as in [53]. Additionally, we implement our own Long Sequence Transformer (**LST**) baseline, which follows exactly the same design as our ViS4mer model except for the S4 layers, which are replaced with standard self-attention layers.

We present our results in Table 2 where we show that ViS4mer achieves state-of-the-art performance in most tasks. Specifically, ViS4mer outperforms both long-range video models (VideoBERT, and Object Transformer) in the content understanding and metadata prediction tasks by a significant margin and achieves comparable performance in the user engagement tasks. Furthermore, we also demonstrate that ViS4mer outperforms our Long Sequence Transformer baseline, which suggests the superiority of S4 layers over the standard self-attention layers for these tasks.

5.2 Ablation Studies

Detailed Comparison with Self-attention. Since most previous methods predominantly use self-attention for long sequence video modeling, we compare our state-space (i.e., S4) based design with the equivalent self-attention-based approaches. For these comparisons, we use the same Long Sequence Transformer baseline (described in the previous subsection), which replaces all state-space layers of the ViS4mer model with the self-attention layers.

Specifically, we compare the performance of ViS4mer and Long Sequence Transformer by varying the number of input tokens for both models. We use video clips of 60 s and a frame per second rate of 1. We vary the number of input tokens to 60, 1500, 2940, and 11760 by applying spatial max-pooling with a varying stride individually on each frame before feeding the tokens into the

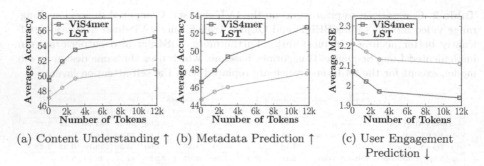

(a) Content Understanding ↑   (b) Metadata Prediction ↑   (c) User Engagement
                                                               Prediction ↓

Fig. 3. We compare the performance of our ViS4mer and Long Sequence Transformer (LST) as a function of the number of input tokens on **(a)** the content understanding (using top-1 acc.), **(b)** the metadata prediction (using top-1 acc.), and **(c)** the user engagement prediction (using MSE) tasks. ViS4mer performs better for all number of tokens in all tasks.

model. Note that the 60 token baseline corresponds to a model that operates only on the frame-level CLS tokens.

We present our results for this study in Fig. 3, where we plot (a) the average accuracy of three content understanding tasks, (b) the average accuracy of four metadata prediction tasks, and (c) the average MSE of two user engagement prediction tasks as a function of the number of input tokens. Based on these results, we observe that increasing the number of input tokens increases the performance of both ViS4mer and Long Sequence Transformer. We also note that ViS4mer achieves better performance than LST in all cases, which suggests that the state-space layers are superior to self-attention layers in this setting. Furthermore, our results indicate that the performance gap between the two methods increases as we increase the number of tokens. This observation suggests that the proposed ViS4mer architecture is more effective at incorporating information from very long video sequences.

Computational Cost Analysis. Additionally, in Table 3, we investigate the GPU memory requirements (in GB) and the training speed (sample/second) of ViS4mer and Long Sequence Transformer while varying the number of input tokens in the same way as was done in our previous analysis. These results indicate that in addition to being more accurate, ViS4mer is also significantly more memory-efficient and faster in all settings. It is worth mentioning, that when increasing the number of tokens to a large number (11, 760) the memory requirement of the self-attention-based model grows very rapidly, requiring 41.38 GB of GPU memory. In contrast, ViS4mer is much more memory-efficient, requiring only 5.15 GB of GPU memory. Moreover, based on these results, we observe that ViS4mer is 2.63× faster compared to Long Sequence Transformer when operating on sequences consisting of 11, 760 spatiotemporal tokens.

Comparison with Other Efficient Attention Schemes. We also compare our method with other efficient self-attention schemes (e.g., Performer [9] and

Table 3. The GPU memory requirements (in GB) and the training speed (sample/seconds) of our state-space-based ViS4mer and the self-attention-based Long Sequence Transformer (LST). We compare both of these approaches while varying the number of input tokens. As we increase the number of tokens, the GPU memory and computation requirement of self-attention grows more rapidly for the LST baseline than for ViS4mer. Overall, ViS4mer requires 8× less GPU memory and is 2.63× times faster than the self-attention baseline while operating on very long video sequences (i.e., 11,760 spatiotemporal tokens).

# of tokens	Samples/s (↑)		GPU memory (GB)(↓)	
	ViS4mer	LST	ViS4mer	LST
60	**12.46**	8.85	**2.23**	2.45
1,500	**8.27**	6.31	**3.61**	3.99
2,940	**6.25**	4.47	**3.67**	5.43
11,760	**4.95**	1.88	**5.15**	41.38

Table 4. Comparison with other efficient attention schemes. ViS4mer outperforms Performer [9] and Orthoformer [39] on the LVU benchmark while requiring similar memory and computation cost.

	Content (↑)			Metadata (↑)				User (↓)		Sam./s (↑)	Mem (↓)
	Relation	Speak	Scene	Director	Genre	Writer	Year	Like	Views		
Self-attention	52.38	37.31	62.79	56.07	52.70	42.26	39.16	0.31	3.83	1.88	41.38
Performer	50.00	38.80	60.46	58.87	49.45	48.21	41.25	0.31	3.93	4.67	5.93
Orthoformer	50.00	39.30	66.27	55.14	**55.79**	47.02	43.35	0.29	3.86	4.85	5.56
State-space	**57.14**	**40.79**	**67.44**	**62.61**	54.71	**48.8**	**44.75**	**0.26**	3.63	4.95	5.15

Table 5. Ablation on the ViS4mer architecture design. We observe that both (i) multi-scale feature learning (enabled by pooling) and (ii) progressive channel dimension reduction are critical for the best performance on the LVU benchmark. ViS4mer achieves substantially better performance compared to the vanilla S4 model while being 1.41× faster and requiring 2.2× less GPU memory.

Pooling	Scaling	Content (↑)	Metadata (↑)	User (↓)	Samples/s (↑)	Memory (GB)(↓)
✗	✗	49.53	49.26	2.30	2.25	7.27
✓	✗	48.96	49.77	2.10	3.98	5.96
✗	✓	52.25	48.79	2.09	4.12	5.95
✓	✓	**55.12**	**52.72**	**1.94**	4.95	5.15

Orthoformer [39]) that do not require quadratic complexity with respect to the input length. We construct such models by replacing the state-space layers of the ViS4mer with the corresponding efficient self-attention layers and keeping all other settings the same as for our model. Table 4 shows the results of these comparisons. We can observe that ViS4mer achieves the best performance in most LVU benchmark tasks while requiring similar memory and computation cost as other efficient attention schemes (e.g., Performer and Orthoformer).

Table 6. Short-range encoder ablation. ViS4mer outperforms Object Transformer in 6 out of the 9 tasks while using the same short-range model (SlowFast [16]). Moreover, we observe that using ViT as our short-range encoder produced the best results in 6 out of 9 LVU benchmark tasks.

Model	Encoder	Content (↑)			Metadata (↑)				User (↓)	
		Relation	Speak	Scene	Director	Genre	Writer	Year	Like	Views
Obj. Trans. [53]	SlowFast [16]	53.10	39.40	56.90	51.20	54.60	34.50	39.10	**0.23**	**3.55**
	ViT [13]	54.76	33.17	52.94	47.66	52.74	36.30	37.76	0.30	3.68
ViS4mer	SlowFast [16]	**59.52**	40.29	60.46	53.27	52.74	42.85	39.86	0.27	3.70
	ConvNeXt [37]	**59.52**	38.30	62.79	57.00	54.40	45.83	42.65	0.30	3.74
	Swin [35]	54.76	37.31	61.62	56.07	49.45	47.61	39.86	0.31	3.56
	ViT [13]	57.14	**40.79**	**67.44**	**62.61**	**54.71**	**48.8**	**44.75**	0.26	3.63

ViS4mer Architecture Analysis. In Table 5, we analyze the significance of (i) multi-scale feature learning, which is enabled by the pooling layers, and (ii) the channel dimensionality reduction, which improves efficiency and reduces overfitting. These results indicate that both of these architecture design choices contribute not only to better performance on the LVU benchmark but also to the higher efficiency of ViS4mer. Specifically, compared to the vanilla S4 model, our final ViS4mer achieves 5.5%, and 3.5% better performance on the content understanding and metadata prediction tasks respectively, and 0.36 lower MSE on the user engagement tasks. Furthermore, ViS4mer has 2.2× faster run-time and 1.41× smaller GPU memory usage than the vanilla S4 model.

Short-range Encoder Ablation. To validate the robustness of our model, we also conduct experiments with different short-range encoder models. Specifically, we experiment with four popular short-range models, which includes both CNN and Transformer-based encoders: (i) SlowFast [16], which was used by the previous Object Transformer method [53], (ii) ConvNeXt [37], (iii) Swin Transformer [35], and (iv) ViT [13]. We report our results of this analysis in Table 6. Based on these results, we first note that ViS4mer outperforms Object Transformer in 6 tasks while using SlowFast [16], and 9 tasks while using ViT [13]. Furthermore, we observe that using ViT as our short-range encoder leads to the best performance in 6 out of 9 LVU benchmark tasks.

Temporal Extent Ablation. Additionally, we compare the long-range temporal reasoning abilities of our state-space-based ViS4mer and an equivalent self-attention-based Long Sequence Transformer. In particular, we train both of these models using video inputs spanning 1, 20, 40, and 60 s. In Fig. 4, we illustrate our results on three LVU tasks (*i.e.*, Writer prediction, Year prediction, and Speaking style prediction). Our results suggest that while the self-attention-based approach performs better when applied on clips that span short temporal extent (*i.e.*, 1 s in duration), the state-space model achieves much better performance when video inputs span long temporal extents (i.e., 40 s and more). These results suggest that compared to self-attention, the state-space layers enable more effective long-range temporal reasoning.

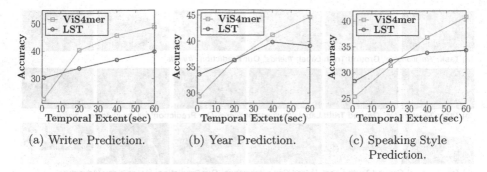

(a) Writer Prediction.   (b) Year Prediction.   (c) Speaking Style Prediction.

Fig. 4. Performance on the **(a)** Writer Prediction, **(b)** Year Prediction, and **(c)** Speaking Style Prediction tasks as a function of the input video duration. Based on these results, we observe that the Long Sequence Transformer (LST) performs better on very short clips. However, ViS4mer excels on much longer clips indicating its effectiveness at modeling long video sequences.

Table 7. Evaluation on two long-range procedural activity classification datasets, *i.e.*, COIN [45,46], and Breakfast [30]. ViS4mer achieves comparable performance as the best performing, Distant Supervision [33] framework, while using significantly less pretraining data. This indicates ViS4mer's ability to generalize to other domains.

(a) Long-range procedural activity classification on the Breakfast [30] dataset

Model	Pretraining dataset	Pretraining samples	Accuracy (↑)
VideoGraph [24]	Kinetics-400	306K	69.50
Timeception [23]	Kinetics-400	306K	71.30
GHRM [59]	Kinetics-400	306K	75.50
Distant Supervision [33]	HowTo100M	**136M**	**89.90**
ViS4mer	Kinetics-600	495K	<u>88.17</u>

(b) Long-range procedural activity classification on the COIN [45] dataset

Model	Pretraining dataset	Pretraining samples	Accuracy (↑)
TSN [46]	Kinetics-400	306K	73.40
Distant Supervision [33]	HowTo100M	**136M**	**90.00**
ViS4mer	Kinetics-600	495K	<u>88.41</u>

5.3 Evaluation on Other Datasets

Lastly, to evaluate ViS4mer's ability to generalize to other domains, we conduct experiments on two long-range procedural activity classification datasets: Breakfast [30] and COIN [45,46]. The Breakfast dataset contains 1,712 videos of 10 complex cooking activities. The average duration of the videos is 2.32 min. The COIN dataset consists of 11,827 videos capturing 180 diverse procedural tasks. The average length of a video is 2.36 min.

Given the long duration of the videos in both datasets, we believe that these datasets are well suited to test our model's ability for long-range activity under-

(a) **Task**: *'Relationship'*, **Ground Truth Label**: *'friends'*, **Our Prediction**: *'friends'*

(b) **Task**: *'Relationship'*, **Ground Truth Label**: *'boyfriend-girlfriend'*, **Our Prediction**: *'ex_boyfriend-ex_girlfriend'*

(c) **Task**: *'Genre'*, **Ground Truth Label**: *'Action/Crime/Adventure'*, **Our Prediction**: *'Action/Crime/Adventure'*

(d) **Task**: *'Genre'*, **Ground Truth Label**: *'Comedy'*, **Our Prediction**: *'Romance'*

Fig. 5. Our qualitative results on the LVU dataset. ViS4mer can effectively identify **(a)** the relationship among the characters and **(c)** the genre of the movie. Furthermore, the complex examples shown in the rows **(b) (d)** illustrate the difficulties of long-range movie understanding tasks.

standing. For all of our experiments, we use standard splits [24, 46] and measure performance in terms of activity classification accuracy.

We report our results on these two datasets in Table 7. Based on these results, we observe that ViS4mer outperforms previous approaches pretrained on Kinetics [7, 27]. Moreover, ViS4mer achieves competitive performance as the state-of-the-art Distant Supervision method [33], which uses several orders of magnitude more pretraining data (i.e., HowTo100M [38]). Thus, we believe that these results provide sufficient evidence of ViS4mer's generalization ability.

5.4   Qualitative Results

In Fig. 5, we also illustrate some qualitative results on the LVU dataset. In particular, we demonstrate several instances of the correct and incorrect predictions of our ViS4mer model on the relationship and genre prediction tasks. These results indicate that our method can effectively identify the relationships among the characters (Fig. 5(a)) and the genre of the movie (Fig. 5(c)). Furthermore, these qualitative examples highlight some movie instances which are difficult to classify even for a human (Figs. 5(b), (d)), thus, illustrating the challenging nature of long-range movie understanding tasks.

6   Conclusion

Combining the strength of self-attention and structured state-space sequence models, we introduce ViS4mer, an efficient framework for long-range movie video classification. Our method (i) is conceptually simple, (ii) achieves state-of-the-art results on several complex movie understanding tasks, (iii) has low memory requirement and computation cost, and (iv) successfully generalizes to other domains such as procedural activity classification. In the future, we plan to extend our work to other long-range video understanding tasks such as video summarization, question answering, and video grounding.

References

1. Movieclips. https://www.movieclips.com/
2. Arnab, A., Dehghani, M., Heigold, G., Sun, C., Lučić, M., Schmid, C.: ViViT: a video vision transformer. arXiv preprint arXiv:2103.15691 (2021)
3. Bahdanau, D., Cho, K., et al.: Neural machine translation by jointly learning to align and translate. arxiv preprint arxiv: 1409.0473 (2014)
4. Bain, M., Nagrani, A., Brown, A., Zisserman, A.: Condensed movies: story based retrieval with contextual embeddings. In: Ishikawa, H., Liu, C.-L., Pajdla, T., Shi, J. (eds.) ACCV 2020. LNCS, vol. 12626, pp. 460–479. Springer, Cham (2021). https://doi.org/10.1007/978-3-030-69541-5_28
5. Bertasius, G., Wang, H., Torresani, L.: Is space-time attention all you need for video understanding? In: Proceedings of the International Conference on Machine Learning (ICML), July 2021
6. Brown, T., et al.: Language models are few-shot learners. Adv. Neural. Inf. Process. Syst. **33**, 1877–1901 (2020)
7. Carreira, J., Noland, E., Banki-Horvath, A., Hillier, C., Zisserman, A.: A short note about kinetics-600. arXiv preprint arXiv:1808.01340 (2018)
8. Carreira, J., Zisserman, A.: Quo Vadis, action recognition? A new model and the kinetics dataset. In: proceedings of the IEEE Conference on Computer Vision and Pattern Recognition, pp. 6299–6308 (2017)
9. Choromanski, K., et al.: Rethinking attention with performers. arXiv preprint arXiv:2009.14794 (2020)
10. Dai, Z., Yang, Z., Yang, Y., Carbonell, J., Le, Q.V., Salakhutdinov, R.: Transformer-XL: attentive language models beyond a fixed-length context. arXiv preprint arXiv:1901.02860 (2019)
11. Deng, J., Dong, W., Socher, R., Li, L.J., Li, K., Fei-Fei, L.: ImageNet: a large-scale hierarchical image database. In: 2009 IEEE Conference on Computer Vision and Pattern Recognition, pp. 248–255. IEEE (2009)
12. Devlin, J., Chang, M.W., Lee, K., Toutanova, K.: BERT: pre-training of deep bidirectional transformers for language understanding. arXiv preprint arXiv:1810.04805 (2018)
13. Dosovitskiy, A., et al.: An image is worth 16x16 words: transformers for image recognition at scale. arXiv preprint arXiv:2010.11929 (2020)
14. Fan, H., et al.: Multiscale vision transformers. arXiv preprint arXiv:2104.11227 (2021)
15. Feichtenhofer, C.: X3D: expanding architectures for efficient video recognition. In: Proceedings of the IEEE/CVF Conference on Computer Vision and Pattern Recognition, pp. 203–213 (2020)
16. Feichtenhofer, C., Fan, H., Malik, J., He, K.: SlowFast networks for video recognition. In: Proceedings of the IEEE/CVF International Conference on Computer Vision, pp. 6202–6211 (2019)

17. Goel, K., Gu, A., Donahue, C., Ré, C.: It's raw! Audio generation with state-space models. arXiv preprint arXiv:2202.09729 (2022)
18. Gu, A., Dao, T., Ermon, S., Rudra, A., Ré, C.: HiPPO: recurrent memory with optimal polynomial projections. Adv. Neural. Inf. Process. Syst. **33**, 1474–1487 (2020)
19. Gu, A., Goel, K., Ré, C.: Efficiently modeling long sequences with structured state spaces. arXiv preprint arXiv:2111.00396 (2021)
20. Gu, A., et al.: Combining recurrent, convolutional, and continuous-time models with linear state space layers. In: Thirty-Fifth Conference on Neural Information Processing Systems (2021)
21. He, K., Gkioxari, G., Dollár, P., Girshick, R.: Mask R-CNN. In: Proceedings of the IEEE International Conference on Computer Vision, pp. 2961–2969 (2017)
22. Huang, Q., Xiong, Yu., Rao, A., Wang, J., Lin, D.: MovieNet: a holistic dataset for movie understanding. In: Vedaldi, A., Bischof, H., Brox, T., Frahm, J.-M. (eds.) ECCV 2020. LNCS, vol. 12349, pp. 709–727. Springer, Cham (2020). https://doi.org/10.1007/978-3-030-58548-8_41
23. Hussein, N., Gavves, E., Smeulders, A.W.: Timeception for complex action recognition. In: Proceedings of the IEEE/CVF Conference on Computer Vision and Pattern Recognition, pp. 254–263 (2019)
24. Hussein, N., Gavves, E., Smeulders, A.W.: VideoGraph: recognizing minutes-long human activities in videos. arXiv preprint arXiv:1905.05143 (2019)
25. Karpathy, A., Toderici, G., Shetty, S., Leung, T., Sukthankar, R., Fei-Fei, L.: Large-scale video classification with convolutional neural networks. In: Proceedings of the IEEE conference on Computer Vision and Pattern Recognition, pp. 1725–1732 (2014)
26. Katharopoulos, A., Vyas, A., Pappas, N., Fleuret, F.: Transformers are RNNs: fast autoregressive transformers with linear attention. In: International Conference on Machine Learning, pp. 5156–5165. PMLR (2020)
27. Kay, W., et al.: The kinetics human action video dataset. arXiv preprint arXiv:1705.06950 (2017)
28. Kingma, D.P., Ba, J.: Adam: a method for stochastic optimization. arXiv preprint arXiv:1412.6980 (2014)
29. Kitaev, N., Kaiser, L., Levskaya, A.: Reformer: the efficient transformer. arXiv preprint arXiv:2001.04451 (2020)
30. Kuehne, H., Arslan, A., Serre, T.: The language of actions: recovering the syntax and semantics of goal-directed human activities. In: Proceedings of the IEEE Conference on Computer Vision and Pattern Recognition, pp. 780–787 (2014)
31. Li, X., Wang, Y., Zhou, Z., Qiao, Y.: SmallBigNet: integrating core and contextual views for video classification. In: Proceedings of the IEEE/CVF Conference on Computer Vision and Pattern Recognition, pp. 1092–1101 (2020)
32. Lin, T.Y., Dollár, P., Girshick, R., He, K., Hariharan, B., Belongie, S.: Feature pyramid networks for object detection. In: Proceedings of the IEEE Conference on Computer Vision and Pattern Recognition, pp. 2117–2125 (2017)
33. Lin, X., Petroni, F., Bertasius, G., Rohrbach, M., Chang, S.F., Torresani, L.: Learning to recognize procedural activities with distant supervision. arXiv preprint arXiv:2201.10990 (2022)
34. Liu, Y., et al.: RoBERTa: a robustly optimized BERT pretraining approach. arXiv preprint arXiv:1907.11692 (2019)
35. Liu, Z., et al.: Swin transformer: hierarchical vision transformer using shifted windows. In: Proceedings of the IEEE/CVF International Conference on Computer Vision, pp. 10012–10022 (2021)

36. Liu, Z., et al.: Video swin transformer. arXiv preprint arXiv:2106.13230 (2021)
37. Liu, Z., Mao, H., Wu, C.Y., Feichtenhofer, C., Darrell, T., Xie, S.: A convnet for the 2020s. arXiv preprint arXiv:2201.03545 (2022)
38. Miech, A., Zhukov, D., Alayrac, J.B., Tapaswi, M., Laptev, I., Sivic, J.: Howto100m: learning a text-video embedding by watching hundred million narrated video clips. In: Proceedings of the IEEE/CVF International Conference on Computer Vision, pp. 2630–2640 (2019)
39. Patrick, M., et al.: Keeping your eye on the ball: trajectory attention in video transformers. arXiv preprint arXiv:2106.05392 (2021)
40. Peng, Y., Zhao, Y., Zhang, J.: Two-stream collaborative learning with spatial-temporal attention for video classification. IEEE Trans. Circuits Syst. Video Technol. **29**(3), 773–786 (2018)
41. Raffel, C., et al.: Exploring the limits of transfer learning with a unified text-to-text transformer. arXiv preprint arXiv:1910.10683 (2019)
42. Ren, S., He, K., Girshick, R., Sun, J.: Faster R-CNN: towards real-time object detection with region proposal networks. In: Advances in Neural Information Processing Systems, vol. 28 (2015)
43. Simonyan, K., Zisserman, A.: Two-stream convolutional networks for action recognition in videos. arXiv preprint arXiv:1406.2199 (2014)
44. Sun, C., Myers, A., Vondrick, C., Murphy, K., Schmid, C.: VideoBERT: a joint model for video and language representation learning. In: Proceedings of the IEEE/CVF International Conference on Computer Vision, pp. 7464–7473 (2019)
45. Tang, Y., et al.: Coin: a large-scale dataset for comprehensive instructional video analysis. In: Proceedings of the IEEE/CVF Conference on Computer Vision and Pattern Recognition, pp. 1207–1216 (2019)
46. Tang, Y., Lu, J., Zhou, J.: Comprehensive instructional video analysis: the coin dataset and performance evaluation. IEEE Trans. Pattern Anal. Mach. Intell. **43**(9), 3138–3153 (2020)
47. Tapaswi, M., Zhu, Y., Stiefelhagen, R., Torralba, A., Urtasun, R., Fidler, S.: MovieQA: understanding stories in movies through question-answering. In: Proceedings of the IEEE Conference on Computer Vision and Pattern Recognition, pp. 4631–4640 (2016)
48. Tran, D., Wang, H., Torresani, L., Feiszli, M.: Video classification with channel-separated convolutional networks. In: Proceedings of the IEEE/CVF International Conference on Computer Vision, pp. 5552–5561 (2019)
49. Vaswani, A., et al.: Attention is all you need. In: Advances in Neural Information Processing Systems, vol. 30 (2017)
50. Vicol, P., Tapaswi, M., Castrejon, L., Fidler, S.: MovieGraphs: towards understanding human-centric situations from videos. In: Proceedings of the IEEE Conference on Computer Vision and Pattern Recognition, pp. 8581–8590 (2018)
51. Wang, X., Girshick, R., Gupta, A., He, K.: Non-local neural networks. In: Proceedings of the IEEE Conference on Computer Vision and Pattern Recognition, pp. 7794–7803 (2018)
52. Wu, C.Y., Girshick, R., He, K., Feichtenhofer, C., Krahenbuhl, P.: A multigrid method for efficiently training video models. In: Proceedings of the IEEE/CVF Conference on Computer Vision and Pattern Recognition, pp. 153–162 (2020)
53. Wu, C.Y., Krahenbuhl, P.: Towards long-form video understanding. In: Proceedings of the IEEE/CVF Conference on Computer Vision and Pattern Recognition, pp. 1884–1894 (2021)

54. Xiong, Y., Huang, Q., Guo, L., Zhou, H., Zhou, B., Lin, D.: A graph-based framework to bridge movies and synopses. In: Proceedings of the IEEE/CVF International Conference on Computer Vision, pp. 4592–4601 (2019)
55. Yang, Z., Dai, Z., Yang, Y., Carbonell, J., Salakhutdinov, R.R., Le, Q.V.: XLNet: generalized autoregressive pretraining for language understanding. In: Advances in Neural Information Processing Systems, vol. 32 (2019)
56. Zaheer, M., et al.: Big bird: transformers for longer sequences. Adv. Neural. Inf. Process. Syst. **33**, 17283–17297 (2020)
57. Zellers, R., Bisk, Y., Farhadi, A., Choi, Y.: From recognition to cognition: visual commonsense reasoning. In: Proceedings of the IEEE/CVF Conference on Computer Vision and Pattern Recognition, pp. 6720–6731 (2019)
58. Zhou, B., Andonian, A., Oliva, A., Torralba, A.: Temporal relational reasoning in videos. In: Ferrari, V., Hebert, M., Sminchisescu, C., Weiss, Y. (eds.) ECCV 2018. LNCS, vol. 11205, pp. 831–846. Springer, Cham (2018). https://doi.org/10.1007/978-3-030-01246-5_49
59. Zhou, J., Lin, K.Y., Li, H., Zheng, W.S.: Graph-based high-order relation modeling for long-term action recognition. In: Proceedings of the IEEE/CVF Conference on Computer Vision and Pattern Recognition, pp. 8984–8993 (2021)
60. Zolfaghari, M., Singh, K., Brox, T.: ECO: efficient convolutional network for online video understanding. In: Ferrari, V., Hebert, M., Sminchisescu, C., Weiss, Y. (eds.) ECCV 2018. LNCS, vol. 11206, pp. 713–730. Springer, Cham (2018). https://doi.org/10.1007/978-3-030-01216-8_43

Prompting Visual-Language Models
for Efficient Video Understanding

Chen Ju[1], Tengda Han[2], Kunhao Zheng[1], Ya Zhang[1]($\boxtimes$), and Weidi Xie[1,2]($\boxtimes$)

[1] Cooperative Medianet Innovation Center, Shanghai Jiao Tong University,
Shanghai, China
{ju_chen,dyekuu,ya_zhang,weidi}@sjtu.edu.cn,
[2] Visual Geometry Group, University of Oxford, Oxford, England
htd@robots.ox.ac.uk
https://ju-chen.github.io/efficient-prompt

Abstract. Image-based visual-language (I-VL) pre-training has shown
great success for learning joint visual-textual representations from large-
scale web data, revealing remarkable ability for "zero-shot" generalisation. This paper presents a simple but strong baseline to efficiently
adapt the pre-trained I-VL model for video understanding tasks, with
minimal training. Specifically, we propose to optimise a few random vectors, termed as "continuous prompt vectors", that convert video-related
tasks into the same format as the pre-training objectives. In addition, to
bridge the gap between static images and videos, temporal information
is encoded with lightweight Transformers stacking on top of frame-wise
visual features. Experimentally, we conduct extensive ablation studies
to analyse the critical components. On ten public benchmarks of action
recognition, action localisation, and text-video retrieval, across closed-
set, few-shot, and zero-shot scenarios, we achieve competitive or state-of-
the-art performance to existing methods, despite optimising significantly
fewer parameters. Due to space limitation, we refer the readers to the
arXiv version at https://arxiv.org/abs/2112.04478.

1 Introduction

While the research in computer vision has mainly focused on tackling particular
tasks, the grand goal towards human-level perception has always been to learn
general-purpose visual representation, that can solve various problems with *minimal tunings*. Towards such a goal, recent work for training image-based visual-
language (**I-VL**) models has shown promising progress. For example, CLIP [60]
and ALIGN [30] learn the joint representation for image and text with simple
noise contrastive learning, greatly benefiting from the rich information in text
descriptions, *e.g.* actions, objects, human-object interactions, and object-object
relationships. As a result, these pre-trained I-VL models have demonstrated

Supplementary Information The online version contains supplementary material
available at https://doi.org/10.1007/978-3-031-19833-5_7.

remarkable "zero-shot" generalisation for various image classification tasks. Crucially, the data used to train these powerful I-VL models can simply be crawled from the Internet at scale, without any laborious manual annotation. It is therefore reasonable to believe, with the growing computation, larger datasets will be collected, and more powerful models will be trained in the near future.

Given this promise, one question naturally arises: *how can we best exploit the ability in the powerful I-VL models, and effectively adapt it to solve novel vision tasks of interest?* One possible solution would be to finetune the image encoder end-to-end on the downstream tasks, however, since each task needs to finetune and save its own set of parameters, we end up developing hundreds of models for hundreds of individual tasks. Even more problematic, discarding the text encoder loses the model's ability for "zero-shot" generalisation, thus the resultant model can only work for a fixed set of pre-determined categories. Alternatively, as shown in CLIP [60], given properly designed "prompts", the model is able to work on a variety of downstream tasks including "zero-shot", with classifiers being dynamically generated by the text encoder, from category names or other free-form texts. The prompts here are handcrafted close templates to facilitate classifier generation, so that novel tasks can be formulated in the same format as pre-training objectives, effectively closing the gap between pre-training and downstream tasks. One remaining issue is, such handcrafted prompts require extensive expert knowledge and labor, limiting the use for efficient adaptation.

In this paper, we continue the vein of prompt-based learning [39,40], with the goal of exploring a comprehensive and strong baseline to adapt I-VL models for *efficient* video understanding. We here focus on the resource-hungry video tasks, for three reasons: 1) From the *data* perspective, comparing to image-text pairs, video-text pairs are harder to collect, and may suffer from misalignment issues [25]; 2) Solving video tasks demands more computational power. Given the same budget, training on image-text pairs enables the model to learn more *diversity*, making it more cost-effective to understand video with I-VL models; 3) Videos are composed of frame sequences, establishing temporal dependencies on powerful image-based models is a natural choice.

Specifically, we consider a simple idea by prepending/appending a sequence of random vectors, termed as "continuous prompt vectors", to the textual input. These prompt vectors consist entirely of free parameters that do not correspond to any real concrete words, and the subsequent layers of the text encoder will attend these vectors, as if they were a sequence of "virtual tokens" to generate the corresponding classifier or embedding. During training, we freeze the weights of the I-VL text encoder, and the gradients are back-propagated to optimise these learnable prompt vectors. Consequently, a single copy of the visual backbone is able to perform various video tasks, with the minimal number of trainable parameters for each task. To further exploit the video temporal information, we also append *lightweight* Transformers on top of frame-wise visual representation. As a result, the various video tasks can be formulated under the same umbrella, *i.e.* to maximise the similarity matching between visual and textual embeddings, with texts being action category names or fine-grained descriptions.

To summarise, building on scalable and powerful I-VL models, we first propose a simple baseline for *efficient* and *lightweight* video understanding, by learning task-specific prompt vectors, which facilitates possible future research in action recognition, action localisation, and text retrieval; We extensively evaluate on ten public benchmarks, across closed-set, few-shot, and zero-shot scenarios, thoroughly dissect critical components; Lastly, despite training only a few free parameters, *i.e.* several prompt vectors and two Transformer layers, in the closed-set scenario, we achieve competitive or state-of-the-art performance to existing methods. In the few-shot and zero-shot scenarios, we significantly outperform all previous methods on seven popular benchmarks, sometimes by over 10% gains.

2   Related Work

Joint Visual-Textual Learning. In the literature, [57] has explored the connection between images and words using paired text documents, and [17,75] proposed to jointly learn image-text embeddings with the category name annotations. Recently, CLIP [60], ALIGN [30] and FILIP [81] have further scaled up the training with large-scale web data. Using simple noise contrastive learning, it is shown that powerful visual representation can be learnt from paired image-caption. In video domains, similar idea has also been explored for representation learning [52] and video retrieval [1,38,53]. In this paper, we establish baselines on steering the pre-trained CLIP model to video understanding tasks, the same technique should be applicable to other I-VL models as well.

Prompting refers to designing proper "instructions" that the pre-trained language model can understand, and generate desired outputs, using a few examples as demonstrations. Given properly handcrafted prompt templates, GPT-3 [6] has shown strong few-shot or zero-shot generalisations. However, such handcrafted templates require extensive expert knowledge, limiting the flexibility. Later work proposes to automate prompt engineering by searching discrete prompts [22,33,62,63], and continuous prompts [39,40]. This work considers to search continuous prompts for steering I-VL models to tackle various video tasks.

Video Action Recognition. Effective architecture research has gone through rapid developments, from two-stream networks [16,66,71] to more recent single stream RGB networks [3,10,14,15,70,76]. With the help of abundant data [9], recognition accuracy has been steadily improved. In addition, data-efficient learning has been explored: few-shot and zero-shot action recognition. Specifically, few-shot recognition makes only a few training samples available from each action category. [91–93] proposed compound memory networks to match and rank videos; [8,13,59] used GANs, dynamic time warping, and CrossTransformer to synthesize or align examples for novel categories. While zero-shot recognition requires to generalise towards action categories that are unseen during training. One typical idea lies in learning a common representation space shared by seen and unseen categories, such as attributes space [19,29,47], semantic space [5,20,28,41], synthesizing features [54], using objects to create common space [51].

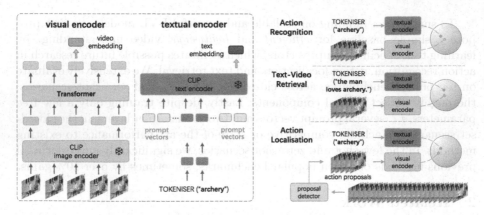

Fig. 1. Framework Overview. We prepend/append several learnable prompt vectors to the CLIP text encoder to generate action classifiers or embeddings; adopt a lightweight Transformer on top of the CLIP image encoder for temporal modeling. During training, both the image and text encoders are kept *frozen*. By optimising task-specific prompt vectors and temporal Transformer, we efficiently adapt CLIP to various video understanding tasks: action recognition, retrieval, and localisation, across closed-set, few-shot, and zero-shot scenarios.

Video Action Localisation aims to detect and classify actions in untrimmed long videos. In general, there are two popular detection paradigms: the two-stage paradigm [11, 34, 44, 46, 65, 69, 73, 77, 88] first localises class-agnostic action proposals, which covers correct segments with high recall, then classifies and refines each proposal. The one-stage paradigm [7, 35, 45, 58, 82, 84] combines localisation and classification, *i.e.* densely classifies each frame into actions or background.

Concurrent Work. Several recent papers [21, 31, 86, 89, 90] also explore prompt learning for efficient transfer from pre-trained CLIP to downstream image tasks. In the video domains, [50, 72] propose to end-to-end finetune CLIP on individual video tasks, *e.g.* action recognition and retrieval. In contrast, we favor efficient adaptation from image to video, present the first yet simple approach on prompt learning, to establish strong and wide baselines for video understanding.

3   Method

Our goal is to efficiently steer a pre-trained **I**mage-based **V**isual-**L**anguage model (**I-VL**) to tackle novel downstream tasks, which we term as model adaptation. Here, we consider resource-hungry video understanding, *i.e.* action recognition, action localisation, and text-video retrieval. To be self-contained, in Sect. 3.1, we briefly review the pre-training and inference of I-VL models; in Sect. 3.2, we describe the proposed prompt learning and temporal modeling.

3.1   Image-Based Visual-Language Model

Pre-training. Given N (image, text) pairs in one batch, the feature embeddings for image and text are computed with two individual encoders, and a dense cosine similarity matrix is calculated between all N possible (image, text) pairs. The training objective is to jointly optimise the image and text encoders, by maximizing the similarity between N correct pairs of (image, text) associations, while minimizing the similarity for $N \times (N-1)$ incorrect pairs by a symmetrical cross-entropy over the dense matrix, *i.e.* noise contrastive learning.

Note that, both encoders contain a **tokeniser** for converting image patches or language words to vectors. In particular, the input images are divided into patches and flattened into vectors, also called "visual tokens"; while the input texts are converted into vectors ("textual tokens") by a trainable look-up table.

Inference. Once trained, the I-VL model can be deployed for image classification tasks on open vocabulary (zero-shot generalisation), with the corresponding visual classifiers being generated from the text encoder Φ_{text}, which resembles the idea of hypernetwork [24]. For example, to classify an image as cat or dog, the classifiers (c_{cat} and c_{dog}) can be generated as:

$$c_{cat} = \Phi_{text}(\text{TOKENISER}(\text{"this is a photo of } [\underline{cat}]\text{"}))$$
$$c_{dog} = \Phi_{text}(\text{TOKENISER}(\text{"this is a photo of } [\underline{dog}]\text{"}))$$

and "this is a photo of [·]" is a handcrafted prompt template, which has shown to be effective for image classification [60].

Discussion. Despite the tremendous success on "zero-shot" image classification, the I-VL model has also shown to be sensitive to the handcrafted prompt template, clearly posing limitations on its efficient adaptation for novel downstream tasks, where the expert knowledge might be difficult to condense or unavailable. Therefore, we consider to automate such prompt design procedures, exploring efficient approaches to adapt the pre-trained image-based visual-language model for novel downstream tasks, with minimal training.

3.2   Prompting CLIP for Video Understanding

In general, we believe that prompt learning on I-VL models will shine in video tasks, for two main reasons: 1) Video tasks are resource-hungry. From the *data* perspective, video-text pairs are harder to collect than image-text pairs. From the computation perspective, given the same budget, training on image-text pairs enables the model to learn more *diversity*. Thus, it is more cost-effective to train large-scale I-VL models, and prompt them for efficient video understanding. 2) Videos are composed of frame sequences, establishing temporal dependencies on powerful image-based models is a natural and economical choice (Fig. 1).

Next, we start by formulating the problem scenario and notations; then introduce the idea for efficient model adaptation through prompt learning; lastly, we augment the I-VL image encoder via temporal modeling, disambiguating the actions that require temporal reasoning. Among the I-VL models, CLIP [60] is the publicly available milestone, we hence base this research on it, but the same technique should be applicable to other I-VL models as well.

Problem Scenario. Given a video dataset that consists of training and validation sets, $\mathcal{D} = \{\mathcal{D}_{\text{train}}, \mathcal{D}_{\text{val}}\}$, e.g. $\mathcal{D}_{\text{train}} = \{(\mathcal{V}_1, y_1), \ldots, (\mathcal{V}_n, y_n)\}$. The video $\mathcal{V}_i \in \mathbb{R}^{T \times H \times W \times 3}$ can range from seconds (recognition and retrieval), to minutes long (localisation). Respectively, y_i either refers to *one* of the $\mathcal{C}_{\text{train}}$ action labels in the text format for recognition, e.g. y_i = 'archery'; or *dense* action category labels of T timestamps for localisation, e.g. $y_i \in \mathbb{R}^{T \times \mathcal{C}_{\text{train}}}$; or fine-grained text descriptions for retrieval, e.g. y_i = 'fry the onion in a pan'.

In the closed-set scenario, the action categories for training and evaluation are the same, *i.e.* $\mathcal{C}_{\text{train}} = \mathcal{C}_{\text{val}}$; while in the zero-shot case, the action categories for training and evaluation are disjoint, *i.e.* $\mathcal{C}_{\text{train}} \cap \mathcal{C}_{\text{val}} = \emptyset$.

Model Adaptation by Learning Prompts. The goal here is to steer pre-trained CLIP to perform various video tasks with minimal training. In specific, we strive for efficient model adaptation by prepending/appending a sequence of continuous random vectors ("prompt vectors") with the textual tokens. While training, both the image and text encoders of CLIP are kept *frozen*, and the gradients will flow through the text encoder to only update the prompt vectors. Ultimately, these learnable vectors end up constructing "virtual" prompt templates that can be understood by the text encoder, and to generate desired classifiers or query embeddings, as detailed below.

(a) Action Recognition considers to classify the video clip or snippet into one of action categories. To generate the action classifier, we construct the "virtual" prompt template via feeding the tokenised category name into the pre-trained text encoder Φ_{text}, for instance:

$$c_{\text{archery}} = \Phi_{\text{text}}(a_1, \ldots, \text{TOKENISER}(\underline{\text{``archery''}}), \ldots, a_k)$$
$$c_{\text{bowling}} = \Phi_{\text{text}}(a_1, \ldots, \text{TOKENISER}(\underline{\text{``bowling''}}), \ldots, a_k)$$

where $a_i \in \mathbb{R}^D$ denotes the i-th prompt vector, consisting of several learnable parameters, and D is the vector dimension. c_{archery} refers to the generated classifier for the action of "archery". Note that, the prompt vectors $\{a_i\}$ are shared for all action categories, thus they are only task-specific.

(b) Action Localisation considers to localise and classify actions in untrimmed long videos. Here, we adopt the two-stage paradigm [11,87] to first detect potential class-agnostic action proposals (detailed in Sect. 4.1), and followed by performing action classification on these detected proposals.

(c) Text-Video Retrieval considers to jointly learn visual and textual embeddings that pair the video and its corresponding textual description. In contrast to action recognition, where a video snippet is coarsely labeled by an action category, the text description in video retrieval contains more fine-grained details, usually a sentence. We here similarly TOKENISE the entire sentence, and feed the tokenised results to the text encoder with learnable prompt vectors, to generate the *query embedding* for each sentence.

(d) Summary. Generally speaking, learning prompts for model adaptation offers the following benefits: 1) As both classification and retrieval can be tackled with one framework, with classifiers or query embeddings generated from text, either category names or free-form descriptions, all tasks can utilise *one* shared backbone, yet achieve competitive performance (Sect. 4); 2) Adapting to novel tasks only requires to optimise several prompt vectors, facilitating the few-shot problem (Table 3); 3) It enables to make better use of abundant training data, and further generalise beyond the closed-set categories (Table 4 and 6).

Temporal Modeling. As for pre-training, CLIP has thoroughly relied on the (image, text) pairs, posing clear pros on cons. On the one hand, the training data can be easily crawled from the web, which enables to learn much richer contents under a given compute constraint. However, on the other hand, it ignores the temporal component of the visual scene, and struggles to recognise the dynamic events, *e.g.* push or pull, open or close. In this section, we bridge this image-to-video gap with a simple and lightweight temporal modeling module.

To be specific, we upgrade the CLIP image encoder Φ_{image} into a video one Φ_{video}, by attaching a Transformer Encoder on top of frame-wise features from the frozen image encoder:

$$v_i = \Phi_{\text{video}}(\mathcal{V}_i) = \Phi_{\text{TEMP}}(\{\Phi_{\text{image}}(I_{i1}), \ldots, \Phi_{\text{image}}(I_{iT})\})$$

where Φ_{TEMP} refers to temporal modeling module, which is a multi-layer Transformer Encoder, consisting of Multi-head Self-attention, Layer Norm, and MLPs. To indicate the temporal order, we also add learnable temporal positional encoding onto image features. $v_i \in \mathbb{R}^{T \times D}$ is dense feature embeddings of T frames.

Training Loss. Given a batch of (video, text) training pairs, the visual stream ends up with dense frame-wise feature embeddings (v_i); while for the textual stream, depending on the considered downstream tasks, it ends up with a set of action classifiers ($c_i \in \mathcal{C}_{\text{action}}$) or textual query embeddings ($c_i \in \mathcal{C}_{\text{query}}$).

For action recognition and text-video retrieval, we further compute the video-snippet-level feature by taking the mean pooling of the dense features:

$$\overline{v}_i = \Phi_{\text{POOL}}(v_i) \in \mathbb{R}^{1 \times D} \tag{1}$$

For action localisation, we take the mean pooling of the dense features within each detected action proposal, to obtain the proposal-level feature. And for simplicity, we also denote this proposal-level feature as $\overline{v}_i$.

During training, we jointly optimise the textual prompt vectors and temporal Transformer, such that the video snippet (proposal) features and its paired

Table 1. Ablation study for closed-set action recognition. Baseline-I denotes the "zero-shot" CLIP inference with the handcrafted prompt template ("a photo of [·]."). Baseline-II is the standard practice for training linear probe on the CLIP image encoder. TFM is the number of temporal Transformer layers.

Model	Prompt	Temporal	K-400			K-700		
			TOP1	TOP5	AVG	TOP1	TOP5	AVG
Baseline-I [60]	Hand-craft	✗	–	–	–	–	–	52.4
Baseline-II [60]	✗	✗	–	–	–	–	–	66.1
A0	2+X+2	✗	65.4	88.7	77.1	56.3	81.9	69.1
A1	4+X+4	✗	66.1	89.0	77.6	56.6	82.4	69.5
A2	8+X+8	✗	67.9	90.0	79.0	57.4	83.0	70.2
A3	16+X+16	✗	68.8	90.1	79.5	57.8	83.1	70.5
A4	16+X+16	1-TFM	75.8	92.9	84.4	64.2	87.3	75.8
A5	16+X+16	2-TFM	76.6	93.3	85.0	64.7	88.5	76.6
A6	16+X+16	3-TFM	76.9	93.5	85.2	64.8	88.4	76.6
A7	16+X+16	4-TFM	76.8	93.5	85.2	64.9	87.9	76.4

classifier or textual query embedding emit the highest similarity score among others. This is achieved with a simple NCE loss:

$$\mathcal{L} = -\sum_i \left(\log \frac{\exp(\overline{v}_i \cdot c_i / \tau)}{\sum_j \exp(\overline{v}_i \cdot c_j / \tau)} \right) \tag{2}$$

Note that, both $\overline{v}_i$ and c_j have been L2-normalised here, and τ refers to the temperature hyper-parameter for scaling. In this way, various video tasks are formulated under the same umbrella, we therefore effectively close the optimisation objective gap between CLIP pre-training and video understanding.

4   Experiments

We experiment 3 fundamental video tasks, across 10 standard datasets. In Sect. 4.2, we conduct ablation studies on action recognition. In Sect. 4.3 and 4.4, we further benchmark on action localisation and text retrieval.

4.1   Implementation Details

The image and text encoders are adopted from pre-trained CLIP (ViT-B/16). Prompt vectors and temporal Transformer are both initialized with $\mathcal{N}(0, 0.01)$. All video frames are pre-processed to 224×224 spatial resolution, the maximum number of textual tokens is 77, vector dimension $D = 512$ and τ is set to 0.07.

For action recognition, all the videos are decoded to 30 fps, and each video is sampled 16 frames with a random frame gap (gap $\in \{1, 2, 3, 4, 5, 6, 10, 15\}$) [71].

Table 2. Comparison on closed-set action recognition. On all datasets, our model performs comparably to existing methods, training far fewer parameters.

Method	HMDB-51		UCF-101		K-400		K-700	
	TOP1	TOP5	TOP1	TOP5	TOP1	TOP5	TOP1	TOP5
I3D [10]	74.3	–	95.1	–	71.6	90.0	58.7	81.7
S3D-G [76]	75.9	–	96.8	–	74.7	93.4	–	–
R(2+1)D [70]	74.5	–	96.8	–	72.0	90.0	–	–
TSM [43]	–	–	–	–	74.7	–	–	–
R3D-50 [26]	66.0	–	92.0	–	–	–	54.7	–
NL-I3D [74]	66.0	–	–	–	76.5	92.6	–	–
X3D-XXL [14]	–	–	–	–	80.4	94.6	–	–
TimeSformer-L [3]	–	–	–	–	80.7	94.7	–	–
Ours (A5)	66.4	92.1	93.6	99.0	76.6	93.3	64.7	88.5

The temporal positional encodings consist of each frame's index and the frame sampling gap (video playing speed). For video retrieval, we utilise the 16-frame input with a random frame gap (gap $\in \{10, 15, 30\}$). The model is optimised using AdamW [49] with a learning rate of 10^{-4}, and a batch size of 64 videos.

For action localisation, we follow the two-stage paradigm: class-agnostic proposal detection and proposal classification. To obtain high-quality action proposals, we first divide the entire video into equal-frame segments; then use the CLIP image encoder with one Transformer layer to extract frame-wise embeddings; finally feed these embeddings to the off-the-shelf proposal detectors [42,80]. Note that, our method is flexible to the choice of proposal detectors, and we do not innovate on such candidate proposal procedures. To generate proposal classifiers, we adopt the same implementation as for action recognition.

4.2 Action Recognition

Datasets and Metrics. HMDB-51 [37] contains 7k videos of 51 categories. Its standard split is 3570 training videos, and 1530 testing videos. **UCF-101** [67] contains 13k videos spanning 101 categories. The standard split is 9537 training videos and 3783 testing videos. **Kinetics-400** [36] (K-400) covers around 230k 10-second video clips sourced from YouTube. **Kinetics-700** [9] (K-700) is simply an extension of K-400, with around 650k video clips. For evaluation metrics, we report the standard TOP1 and TOP5 accuracy, and the average of the two.

Closed-set Action Recognition is the common scenario, where the model is trained and evaluated on videos from the same categories, i.e. $\mathcal{C}_{train} = \mathcal{C}_{val}$. For comprehensive comparisons, we here adopt the standard splits of four datasets.
• *Ablation Studies* are conducted on two largest benchmarks. Table 1 presents the results for prompt learning and temporal modeling. The prompt here follows the

Table 3. Comparison on few-shot action recognition. Baseline-I refers to the "zero-shot" CLIP inference with handcrafted prompts. $\mathcal{C}_{ALL}$ refers to the case where the method is evaluated on all action categories of the corresponding dataset, rather than only 5-way classification, *e.g.* 400 categories for K-400.

Method	K-shot	N-way	Prompt	Temporal	UCF-101	HMDB-51	K-400
CMN [91]	5	5	–	–	–	–	78.9
TARN [4]	5	5	–	–	–	–	78.5
ARN [85]	5	5	–	–	83.1	60.6	82.4
TRX [59]	5	5	–	–	96.1	75.6	85.9
Baseline-I [60]	–	5	Hand-craft	✗	91.9	68.9	95.1
Ours	5	5	✓	✗	**98.3**	**85.3**	**96.4**
	5	5	✓	✓	97.8	84.9	96.0
Baseline-I [60]	–	$\mathcal{C}_{ALL}$	Hand-craft	✗	64.7	40.1	54.2
Ours	5	$\mathcal{C}_{ALL}$	✓	✗	77.6	56.0	57.1
	5	$\mathcal{C}_{ALL}$	✓	✓	**79.5**	**56.6**	**58.5**

format of $[a_1, .., a_k, X, a_{k+1}, .., a_{2k}]$. Note that, although we prepend and append the equal number of prompt vectors, the optimisation can perfectly learn to ignore any of these vectors, thus, we do not ablate other prompt formats.

As the baselines, we compare with the official results reported in the original CLIP [60]. Specifically, Baseline-I refers to the "zero-shot" inference with handcrafted prompt templates ("a photo of [·]."), and Baseline-II denotes the standard practice for training linear classifiers on top of the pre-trained CLIP image encoder with the considered downstream datasets.

Generally speaking, training more text prompt vectors brings consistent improvements on both TOP1 and TOP5 accuracy; In addition, adding temporal modeling also brings immediate benefits, with average gains of 4.9% and 5.3% on K-400 and K-700. However, it gives diminishing returns as more Transformer layers are added. Overall, all the results suggest that, both the prompt learning and temporal modeling are essential. While comparing with Baseline-I, the A3 model demonstrates a performance boost of 18.1%, clearly showing the benefits of learning prompt vectors over handcrafted ones. Moreover, even with fewer trainable parameters (only 16K), the A3 model also surpasses Baseline-II, with 4.4% gains, showing the superiority of prompting adaptation.

For all the following action recognition experiments, we inherit the best practice from the ablation studies, *i.e.* prepend/append 16 prompt vectors to category names, and only use two Transformer layers (5M parameters) for temporal modeling, for its best trade-off on performance and computational cost.

• *Comparison to SOTA*. Table 2 compares our method with existing state-of-the-art approaches on four popular action recognition benchmarks. Overall, on all datasets, our model performs comparably with the competitors, although we only need to train *far fewer* parameters (around 5M), *i.e.* two Transformer layers and several prompt vectors, advocating efficient model adaptation.

Table 4. Ablation study for zero-shot action recognition on K-700. The model is trained on 400 action categories and evaluated on the other 300 disjoint categories. Baseline-I refers to the results from the CLIP zero-shot evaluation.

Model	Prompt	Temporal	TOP1	TOP5	AVG
Baseline-I [60]	Hand-craft	✗	52.4	77.3	64.9
B0	4+X+4	✗	57.4	83.3	70.4
B1	8+X+8	✗	57.7	82.6	70.2
B2	16+X+16	✗	**58.4**	82.6	70.5
B3	32+X+32	✗	57.5	**84.6**	**71.1**
B4	16+X+16	1-TFM	47.9	76.8	62.4
B5	16+X+16	2-TFM	45.5	75.4	60.5
B6	16+X+16	3-TFM	45.6	75.2	60.4

Few-Shot Action Recognition aims to classify videos with only a few training samples, in this section, we benchmark on two different settings. The first part follows the previous literature [8,59,85], that is, evaluates the standard K-shot, N-way classification; while the second one considers a more challenging setting that classifies all categories with K-shot support samples. As baselines, in both settings, we use the "zero-shot" CLIP inference with handcrafted templates.

• 5-*Shot*-5-*Way Setting.* For fair comparisons, this setting adopts the publicly accessible few-shot splits. Specifically, for HMDB-51 and UCF-101, we follow [85] to collect 10 and 21 testing action categories respectively; while for K-400, we follow [59,91] to collect 24 testing categories, each containing 100 videos. During training, we sample 5 categories (ways) from the above data, with 5 videos (shots) from each category, and utilise the remaining data for evaluation. To ensure the statistical significance, we conduct 200 trials with random samplings.

Table 3 presents the average TOP1 accuracy for three datasets. Our method (with/without temporal modeling) outperforms all previous methods by a large margin, around 10% on HMDB-51 and K-400, showing the superiority.

• 5-*Shot*-C-*Way Setting.* Here, we further consider a more challenging scenario: scaling the problem up to classifying all action categories in the dataset with only 5 training samples per category, for example, $\mathcal{C}_{\text{ALL}} = 400$ for K-400, $\mathcal{C}_{\text{ALL}} = 101$ for UCF-101. Specifically, on each dataset, we sample 5 videos (shots) from the training set for each category, to form the few-shot support set, and then measure performance on the corresponding standard testing set.

For this experiment setting, we conduct 10 random sampling rounds, and also record the average TOP1 accuracy in Table 3. Comparing to the 5-way classification, the $\mathcal{C}$-way setting is clearly more challenging, our model (with/without temporal modeling) still shows promising results. While comparing to the Baseline-I, our performance gains on both UCF-101 and HMDB-51 are around 15%.

Zero-Shot Action Recognition refers to the novel scenario, where videos for training and validation are from different action categories, *i.e.* $\mathcal{C}_{\text{train}} \cap \mathcal{C}_{\text{val}} = \emptyset$.

Table 5. Comparison on closed-set action localisation. Baseline-III adopts the same first-stage proposal detector as our method, but uses the original CLIP with handcrafted prompts as the second-stage proposal classifier. AVG is the average mAP in [0.3:0.1:0.7] on THUMOS14, and [0.5:0.05:0.95] on ActivityNet1.3.

Method	Date	Modality	THUMOS14						ActivityNet1.3			
			0.3	0.4	0.5	0.6	0.7	AVG	0.5	0.75	0.95	AVG
CDC [64]	2017	RGB+Flow	40.1	29.4	23.3	13.1	7.9	22.8	45.3	26.0	0.2	23.8
TALNET [11]	2018	RGB+Flow	53.2	48.5	42.8	33.8	20.8	39.8	38.2	18.3	1.3	20.2
DBS [23]	2019	RGB+Flow	50.6	43.1	34.3	24.4	14.7	33.4	–	–	–	–
A2NET [80]	2020	RGB+Flow	58.6	54.1	45.5	32.5	17.2	41.6	43.6	28.7	3.7	27.8
GTAD [79]	2020	RGB+Flow	66.4	60.4	51.6	37.6	22.9	47.8	50.4	34.6	9.0	34.1
BSN++ [68]	2021	RGB+Flow	59.9	49.5	41.3	31.9	22.8	41.1	51.3	**35.7**	8.3	**34.9**
AFSD [42]	2021	RGB+Flow	**67.3**	**62.4**	**55.5**	**43.7**	**31.1**	**52.0**	52.4	35.3	6.5	34.4
TALNET [11]	2018	RGB	42.6	–	31.9	–	14.2	–	–	–	–	–
A2NET [80]	2020	RGB	45.0	40.5	31.3	19.9	10.0	29.3	39.6	25.7	2.8	24.8
Baseline-III	2022	RGB	36.3	31.9	25.4	17.8	10.4	24.3	28.2	18.3	3.7	18.2
Ours	2022	RGB	**50.8**	**44.1**	**35.8**	**25.7**	**15.7**	**34.5**	**44.0**	**27.0**	**5.1**	**27.3**

Specifically, we split K-700 into two parts, with $C_{train} = 400$ categories for training, and the remaining $C_{val} = 300$ categories for evaluation.

As a baseline, we evaluate the CLIP with handcrafted prompt templates. As reported in Table 4, our model achieves 6.0% gains on TOP1 accuracy over the Baseline-I, showing the effectiveness of prompt learning for zero-shot recognition. Interestingly, the number of learnable prompt vectors does not make a difference, and adding temporal modeling diminishes the performance gain. We conjecture this is because the additional Transformer layer could specialise on the training set, thus harming the generalisation towards unseen action categories.

Conclusion and Discussion. Among all recognition benchmarks, we have demonstrated the effectiveness of prompt learning and temporal modeling. For closed-set recognition, even without temporal modeling, learnable prompts clearly surpass the handcrafted ones, and linear probe settings. While comparing to state-of-the-art methods, despite training *far fewer* parameters, our model still shows competitive performance. For few-shot recognition, model adaptation by prompt learning really shines, outperforming all previous methods significantly. Lastly, for zero-shot recognition, textual prompts enable to make better use of abundant training data, and further improve the generalisation beyond the seen categories.

4.3   Action Localisation

Datasets and Metrics. THUMOS14 [32] covers 413 untrimmed sports videos from 20 action categories, with an average of 15 instances per video. The standard split is 200 training videos and 213 validation videos. **ActivityNet1.3** [27] has around 20k untrimmed videos of 200 action categories. The standard split is

Table 6. Results of zero-shot action localisation. Baseline-III uses the same proposal detector as our method, but adopts the original CLIP with handcrafted prompts as the proposal classifier. Our model is trained on 75% (or 50%) action categories and tested on the remaining 25% (or 50%) action categories.

Method	Train $v.s$ Test	THUMOS14						ActivityNet1.3			
		0.3	0.4	0.5	0.6	0.7	AVG	0.5	0.75	0.95	AVG
Baseline-III	75% $v.s$ 25%	33.0	25.5	18.3	11.6	5.7	18.8	35.6	20.4	2.1	20.2
Ours	75% $v.s$ 25%	**39.7**	**31.6**	**23.0**	**14.9**	**7.5**	**23.3**	**37.6**	**22.9**	**3.8**	**23.1**
Baseline-III	50% $v.s$ 50%	27.2	21.3	15.3	9.7	4.8	15.7	28.0	16.4	1.2	16.0
Ours	50% $v.s$ 50%	**37.2**	**29.6**	**21.6**	**14.0**	**7.2**	**21.9**	**32.0**	**19.3**	**2.9**	**19.6**

$10,024$ training videos and $4,926$ validation videos. We evaluate with the mean Average Precision (mAP) at various IoU thresholds. For THUMOS14, the IoU set is $[0.3 : 0.1 : 0.7]$; as for ActivityNet1.3, the IoU set is $[0.5 : 0.05 : 0.95]$.

Closed-Set Action Localisation is the commonly adopted setting, where the model is trained and tested on videos of the same categories, $i.e.$ $\mathcal{C}_{train} = \mathcal{C}_{val}$. For fair comparisons, we use the standard dataset splits as in the literature.

Table 5 reports the results. As a baseline, we adopt the same first-stage proposal detector, but utilise the original CLIP with handcrafted prompts ("this is an action of $[\cdot]$") for the second-stage proposal classifier. On both datasets, our model significantly outperforms the Baseline-III. While comparing to other existing methods that use pre-trained RGB stream, our method also demonstrates superior performance, with around 5.2% and 2.5% gains on average mAP.

Zero-Shot Action Localisation refers to the novel scenario, where the action categories for training and testing are disjoint. As we are not aware of any existing benchmarks on this challenging scenario, we initiate two evaluation settings: one is to train with 75% categories and test on the left 25% categories; the other is to train with 50% categories and test on the left 50% categories. To ensure statistical significance, we conduct 10 random samplings for data splits.

Table 6 shows the average performance. As proposals are class-agnostic, the key of two-stage localisation is the proposal classifier. For comparisons, we also implement the baseline, which uses the same proposal detector as our model, but classifies action proposals using original CLIP with handcrafted prompts. In both settings, our model shows superior performance than the Baseline-III. However, when comparing with closed-set, the zero-shot performance drops dramatically. Note that, such drop now comes from two sources: one is the recall drop from the first-stage class-agnostic proposals, and the other comes from the second-stage classification errors. See the supplementary materials for complete ablations.

Table 7. Results of text-video retrieval. E2E denotes if the model has been trained end-to-end. Baseline-IV denotes the original CLIP model with text query naïvely encoded, *i.e.* without using any prompt. As these methods are pre-trained on different datasets with variable sizes, it is unlikely to make fair comparisons.

Method	E2E	MSRVTT(9K)		LSMDC		DiDeMo		SMIT	
		R@1	R@5	R@1	R@5	R@1	R@5	R@1	R@5
CE [48]	✗	21.7	51.8	12.4	28.5	16.1	41.1	–	–
MMT [18]	✗	24.6	54.0	13.2	29.2	–	–	–	–
TT-CE+ [12]	✗	29.6	61.6	**17.2**	**36.5**	21.6	48.6	–	–
Baseline-IV	✗	31.2	53.7	11.3	22.7	28.8	54.6	39.3	62.8
Ours	✗	**36.7**	**64.6**	13.4	29.5	**36.1**	**64.8**	**66.6**	**87.8**
Frozen [2]	✓	31.0	59.5	15.0	30.8	34.6	65.0	–	–
CLIP4Clip [50]	✓	44.5	71.4	22.6	41.0	43.4	70.2	–	–

4.4 Text-Video Retrieval

Datasets and Metrics. MSRVTT [78] contains $10,000$ videos and $200,000$ captions. We train on "Training-9K" split [18], and test on "test 1k-A" [83] of $1,000$ clip-text pairs. **LSMDC** [61] contains $118,081$ videos of 2 to 30 seconds. We train on $7,408$ validation videos, and evaluate on another $1,000$ videos. **DiDeMo** [1] contains $10,464$ videos annotated with $40,543$ sentences. **SMIT** [55] contains more than 500k videos randomly chosen from M-MiT training set [56], and 10k validation videos. We evaluate with the average recall at K (R@K).

Results. Table 7 presents text-retrieval results on four benchmarks. Note that, we here only employ 8 learnable prompt vectors, *i.e.* [4+X+4]. This is because the pre-trained CLIP text encoder takes limited number of textual tokens up to 77, whereas the retrieval query can be long. For the cases where the tokenised text query is longer than the maximum supported length of CLIP, we simply truncate the sequence to fit our specified pattern, as such cases are few in practice.

While comparing with the Baseline-IV that denotes the results from the original CLIP with naïvely-encoded text queries, our proposed prompt learning and temporal modeling demonstrate clear benefits on all three benchmarks. Comparing with the existing approaches that are specifically targeting on text-video retrieval, our proposed method can still perform competitively, although it only requires to optimise several prompt vectors, along with two Transformer layers. Note that, as these methods are usually pre-trained on different datasets with variable sizes, this is by no means to make fair comparisons.

5   Conclusion

Building on CLIP, this paper constructs wide and strong baselines for efficient video understanding, with the simple idea of learning lightweight prompt vectors and temporal Transformer. We evaluate on 10 popular benchmarks from: action recognition, action localisation, and text-video retrieval. Thorough comparisons and ablations are conducted to analyse the critical components. In the closed-set scenario, despite training only a few free parameters, we achieve competitive performance to the modern state-of-the-art methods. In few-shot and zero-shot scenarios, we significantly outperform existing methods on 7 public benchmarks.

Acknowledgement. This work is supported by the National Key Research and Development Program of China (No. 2020YFB1406801), 111 plan (No. BP0719010), STCSM (No. 18DZ2270700), State Key Laboratory of UHD Video and Audio Production and Presentation, the UK EPSRC Programme Grant Visual AI (EP/T028572/1), and a Google-DeepMind Scholarship.

References

1. Anne Hendricks, L., Wang, O., Shechtman, E., Sivic, J., Darrell, T., Russell, B.: Localizing moments in video with natural language. In: Proceedings of the International Conference on Computer Vision (2017)
2. Bain, M., Nagrani, A., Varol, G., Zisserman, A.: Frozen in time: a joint video and image encoder for end-to-end retrieval. Proceedings of the International Conference on Computer Vision (2021)
3. Bertasius, G., Wang, H., Torresani, L.: Is space-time attention all you need for video understanding? In: Proceedings of the International Conference on Machine Learning (2021)
4. Bishay, M., Zoumpourlis, G., Patras, I.: TARN: temporal attentive relation network for few-shot and zero-shot action recognition. In: Proceedings of the British Machine Vision Conference (2019)
5. Brattoli, B., Tighe, J., Zhdanov, F., Perona, P., Chalupka, K.: Rethinking zero-shot video classification: end-to-end training for realistic applications. In: Proceedings of the IEEE Conference on Computer Vision and Pattern Recognition (2020)
6. Brown, T., et al.: Language models are few-shot learners. In: Advances in Neural Information Processing Systems (2020)
7. Buch, S., Escorcia, V., Ghanem, B., Fei-Fei, L., Niebles, J.C.: End-to-end, single-stream temporal action detection in untrimmed videos. In: Proceedings of the British Machine Vision Conference (2019)
8. Cao, K., Ji, J., Cao, Z., Chang, C.Y., Niebles, J.C.: Few-shot video classification via temporal alignment. In: Proceedings of the IEEE Conference on Computer Vision and Pattern Recognition (2020)
9. Carreira, J., Noland, E., Hillier, C., Zisserman, A.: A short note on the kinetics-700 human action dataset. arXiv preprint arXiv:1907.06987 (2019)
10. Carreira, J., Zisserman, A.: Quo Vadis, action recognition? A new model and the kinetics dataset. In: Proceedings of the IEEE Conference on Computer Vision and Pattern Recognition (2017)
11. Chao, Y.W., Vijayanarasimhan, S., Seybold, B., Ross, D.A., Deng, J., Sukthankar, R.: Rethinking the faster R-CNN architecture for temporal action localisation. In: Proceedings of the IEEE Conference on Computer Vision and Pattern Recognition (2018)

12. Croitoru, I., et al.: TeachText: crossmodal generalized distillation for text-video retrieval. In: Proceedings of the International Conference on Computer Vision (2021)
13. Dwivedi, S.K., Gupta, V., Mitra, R., Ahmed, S., Jain, A.: ProtoGAN: towards few shot learning for action recognition. In: Proceedings of the IEEE Conference on Computer Vision and Pattern Recognition (2019)
14. Feichtenhofer, C.: X3D: expanding architectures for efficient video recognition. In: Proceedings of the IEEE Conference on Computer Vision and Pattern Recognition (2020)
15. Feichtenhofer, C., Fan, H., Malik, J., He, K.: SlowFast networks for video recognition. In: Proceedings of the International Conference on Computer Vision (2019)
16. Feichtenhofer, C., Pinz, A., Zisserman, A.: Convolutional two-stream network fusion for video action recognition. In: Proceedings of the IEEE Conference on Computer Vision and Pattern Recognition (2016)
17. Frome, A., et al.: Devise: a deep visual-semantic embedding model. In: Advances in Neural Information Processing Systems (2013)
18. Gabeur, V., Sun, C., Alahari, K., Schmid, C.: Multi-modal transformer for video retrieval. In: Vedaldi, A., Bischof, H., Brox, T., Frahm, J.-M. (eds.) ECCV 2020. LNCS, vol. 12349, pp. 214–229. Springer, Cham (2020). https://doi.org/10.1007/978-3-030-58548-8_13
19. Gan, C., Yang, T., Gongi, B.: Learning attributes equals multi-source domain generalization. In: Proceedings of the IEEE Conference on Computer Vision and Pattern Recognition (2016)
20. Gan, C., Yang, Y., Zhu, L., Zhao, D., Zhuang, Y.: Recognizing an action using its name: a knowledge-based approach. Int. J. Comput. Vision **120**, 61–77 (2016)
21. Gao, P., et al.: Clip-adapter: better vision-language models with feature adapters. arXiv preprint arXiv:2110.04544 (2021)
22. Gao, T., Fisch, A., Chen, D.: Making pre-trained language models better few-shot learners. In: Association for Computational Linguistics (2021)
23. Gao, Z., Wang, L., Zhang, Q., Niu, Z., Zheng, N., Hua, G.: Video imprint segmentation for temporal action detection in untrimmed videos. In: Proceedings of the AAAI Conference on Artificial Intelligence (2019)
24. Ha, D., Dai, A., Le, Q.: Hypernetworks. In: Proceedings of the International Conference on Learning Representations (2016)
25. Han, T., Xie, W., Zisserman, A.: Temporal alignment network for long-term video. In: Proceedings of the IEEE Conference on Computer Vision and Pattern Recognition (2022)
26. Hara, K., Kataoka, H., Satoh, Y.: Can spatiotemporal 3d CNNs retrace the history of 2d CNNs and ImageNet? In: Proceedings of the IEEE Conference on Computer Vision and Pattern Recognition (2018)
27. Heilbron, F.C., Escorcia, V., Ghanem, B., Niebles, J.C.: ActivityNet: a large-scale video benchmark for human activity understanding. In: Proceedings of the IEEE Conference on Computer Vision and Pattern Recognition (2015)
28. Jain, M., Van Gemert, J.C., Mensink, T., Snoek, C.G.: Objects2action: classifying and localizing actions without any video example. In: Proceedings of the International Conference on Computer Vision (2015)
29. Jain, M., Van Gemert, J.C., Snoek, C.G.: What do 15,000 object categories tell us about classifying and localizing actions? In: Proceedings of the IEEE Conference on Computer Vision and Pattern Recognition (2015)

30. Jia, C., et al.: Scaling up visual and vision-language representation learning with noisy text supervision. In: Proceedings of the International Conference on Machine Learning (2021)
31. Jia, M., et al.: Visual prompt tuning. arXiv preprint arXiv:2203.12119 (2022)
32. Jiang, Y.G., et al.: THUMOS challenge: action recognition with a large number of classes (2014). https://crcv.ucf.edu/THUMOS14/
33. Jiang, Z., Xu, F.F., Araki, J., Neubig, G.: How can we know what language models know? Trans. Assoc. Comput. Linguist. **8**, 423–438 (2020)
34. Ju, C., Zhao, P., Chen, S., Zhang, Y., Wang, Y., Tian, Q.: Divide and conquer for single-frame temporal action localization. In: Proceedings of the International Conference on Computer Vision (2021)
35. Ju, C., Zhao, P., Chen, S., Zhang, Y., Zhang, X., Tian, Q.: Adaptive mutual supervision for weakly-supervised temporal action localization. arXiv preprint arXiv:2104.02357 (2021)
36. Kay, W., et al.: The kinetics human action video dataset. arXiv preprint arXiv:1705.06950 (2017)
37. Kuehne, H., Jhuang, H., Garrote, E., Poggio, T., Serre, T.: HMDB: a large video database for human motion recognition. In: Proceedings of the International Conference on Computer Vision (2011)
38. Lei, J., et al.: Less is more: ClipBERT for video-and-language learning via sparse sampling. In: Proceedings of the IEEE Conference on Computer Vision and Pattern Recognition (2021)
39. Lester, B., Al-Rfou, R., Constant, N.: The power of scale for parameter-efficient prompt tuning. In: Proceedings of the Conference on Empirical Methods in Natural Language Processing (2021)
40. Li, X.L., Liang, P.: Prefix-tuning: optimizing continuous prompts for generation. In: Association for Computational Linguistics (2021)
41. Li, Y., hung Hu, S., Li, B.: Recognizing unseen actions in a domain-adapted embedding space. In: IEEE International Conference on Image Processing (2016)
42. Lin, C., et al.: Learning salient boundary feature for anchor-free temporal action localization. In: Proceedings of the IEEE Conference on Computer Vision and Pattern Recognition (2021)
43. Lin, J., Gan, C., Han, S.: TSM: temporal shift module for efficient video understanding. In: Proceedings of the International Conference on Computer Vision (2019)
44. Lin, T., Liu, X., Li, X., Ding, E., Wen, S.: BMN: boundary-matching network for temporal action proposal generation. In: Proceedings of the International Conference on Computer Vision (2019)
45. Lin, T., Zhao, X., Shou, Z.: Single shot temporal action detection. In: Proceedings of the ACM International Conference on Multimedia (2017)
46. Lin, T., Zhao, X., Su, H., Wang, C., Yang, M.: BSN: boundary sensitive network for temporal action proposal generation. In: Ferrari, V., Hebert, M., Sminchisescu, C., Weiss, Y. (eds.) ECCV 2018. LNCS, vol. 11208, pp. 3–21. Springer, Cham (2018). https://doi.org/10.1007/978-3-030-01225-0_1
47. Liu, J., Kuipers, B., Savarese, S.: Recognizing human actions by attributes. In: Proceedings of the IEEE Conference on Computer Vision and Pattern Recognition (2011)
48. Liu, Y., Albanie, S., Nagrani, A., Zisserman, A.: Use what you have: video retrieval using representations from collaborative experts. In: Proceedings of the British Machine Vision Conference (2019)

49. Loshchilov, I., Hutter, F.: Decoupled weight decay regularization. In: Proceedings of the International Conference on Learning Representations (2019)

50. Luo, H., et al.: CLIP4Clip: an empirical study of clip for end to end video clip retrieval. arXiv preprint arXiv:2104.08860 (2021)

51. Mettes, P., Thong, W., Snoek, C.G.M.: Object priors for classifying and localizing unseen actions. Int. J. Comput. Vision **129**, 1954–1971 (2021)

52. Miech, A., Alayrac, J.B., Smaira, L., Laptev, I., Sivic, J., Zisserman, A.: End-to-end learning of visual representations from uncurated instructional videos. In: Proceedings of the IEEE Conference on Computer Vision and Pattern Recognition (2020)

53. Miech, A., Laptev, I., Sivic, J.: Learning a text-video embedding from incomplete and heterogeneous data. arXiv preprint arXiv:1804.02516 (2018)

54. Mishra, A., Pandey, A., Murthy, H.A.: Zero-shot learning for action recognition using synthesized features. Neurocomputing **390**, 117–130 (2020)

55. Monfort, M., et al.: Spoken moments: learning joint audio-visual representations from video descriptions. In: Proceedings of the IEEE Conference on Computer Vision and Pattern Recognition (2021)

56. Monfort, M., et al.: Multi-moments in time: Learning and interpreting models for multi-action video understanding. IEEE Trans. Pattern Anal. Mach. Intell., 1 (2021)

57. Mori, Y., Takahashi, H., Oka, R.: Image-to-word transformation based on dividing and vector quantizing images with words. In: First International Workshop on Multimedia Intelligent Storage and Retrieval Management (ACM Multimedia Conference) (1999)

58. Nawhal, M., Mori, G.: Activity graph transformer for temporal action localization. arXiv preprint arXiv:2101.08540 (2021)

59. Perrett, T., Masullo, A., Burghardt, T., Mirmehdi, M., Damen, D.: Temporal relational cross transformers for few-shot action recognition. In: Proceedings of the IEEE Conference on Computer Vision and Pattern Recognition (2021)

60. Radford, A., et al.: Learning transferable visual models from natural language supervision. In: Proceedings of the International Conference on Machine Learning (2021)

61. Rohrbach, A., et al.: Movie description. Int. J. Comput. Vision **123**, 94–120 (2017)

62. Schick, T., Schütze, H.: Exploiting cloze questions for few shot text classification and natural language inference. In: Proceedings of the Conference of the European Chapter of the Association for Computational Linguistics (2021)

63. Shin, T., Razeghi, Y., IV, R.L.L., Wallace, E., Singh, S.: AutoPrompt: eliciting knowledge from language models with automatically generated prompts. In: Proceedings of the Conference on Empirical Methods in Natural Language Processing (2020)

64. Shou, Z., Chan, J., Zareian, A., Miyazawa, K., Chang, S.F.: CDC: convolutional-de-convolutional networks for precise temporal action localization in untrimmed videos. In: Proceedings of the IEEE Conference on Computer Vision and Pattern Recognition (2017)

65. Shou, Z., Wang, D., Chang, S.F.: Temporal action localization in untrimmed videos via multi-stage CNNs. In: Proceedings of the IEEE Conference on Computer Vision and Pattern Recognition (2016)

66. Simonyan, K., Zisserman, A.: Two-stream convolutional networks for action recognition in videos. In: Advances in Neural Information Processing Systems (2014)

67. Soomro, K., Zamir, A.R., Shah, M.: UCF101: a dataset of 101 human actions classes from videos in the wild. arXiv preprint arXiv:1212.0402 (2012)

68. Su, H., Gan, W., Wu, W., Qiao, Y., Yan, J.: BSN++: complementary boundary regressor with scale-balanced relation modeling for temporal action proposal generation. In: Proceedings of the AAAI Conference on Artificial Intelligence (2021)

69. Tan, J., Tang, J., Wang, L., Wu, G.: Relaxed transformer decoders for direct action proposal generation. In: Proceedings of the International Conference on Computer Vision (2021)

70. Tran, D., Wang, H., Torresani, L., Ray, J., LeCun, Y., Paluri, M.: A closer look at spatiotemporal convolutions for action recognition. In: Proceedings of the IEEE Conference on Computer Vision and Pattern Recognition (2018)

71. Wang, L., et al.: Temporal segment networks: towards good practices for deep action recognition. In: Leibe, B., Matas, J., Sebe, N., Welling, M. (eds.) ECCV 2016. LNCS, vol. 9912, pp. 20–36. Springer, Cham (2016). https://doi.org/10.1007/978-3-319-46484-8_2

72. Wang, M., Xing, J., Liu, Y.: ActionCLIP: a new paradigm for video action recognition. arXiv preprint arXiv:2109.08472 (2021)

73. Wang, Q., Zhang, Y., Zheng, Y., Pan, P.: RCL: recurrent continuous localization for temporal action detection. In: Proceedings of the IEEE Conference on Computer Vision and Pattern Recognition (2022)

74. Wang, X., Girshick, R., Gupta, A., He, K.: Non-local neural networks. In: Proceedings of the IEEE Conference on Computer Vision and Pattern Recognition (2018)

75. Weston, J., Bengio, S., Usunier, N.: WSABIE: scaling up to large vocabulary image annotation. In: Proceedings of the International Joint Conference on Artificial Intelligence (2011)

76. Xie, S., Sun, C., Huang, J., Tu, Z., Murphy, K.: Rethinking spatiotemporal feature learning: speed-accuracy trade-offs in video classification. In: Ferrari, V., Hebert, M., Sminchisescu, C., Weiss, Y. (eds.) ECCV 2018. LNCS, vol. 11219, pp. 318–335. Springer, Cham (2018). https://doi.org/10.1007/978-3-030-01267-0_19

77. Xu, H., Das, A., Saenko, K.: R-C3D: region convolutional 3d network for temporal activity detection. In: Proceedings of the International Conference on Computer Vision (2017)

78. Xu, J., Mei, T., Yao, T., Rui, Y.: MSR-VTT: a large video description dataset for bridging video and language. In: Proceedings of the IEEE Conference on Computer Vision and Pattern Recognition (2016)

79. Xu, M., Zhao, C., Rojas, D.S., Thabet, A., Ghanem, B.: G-TAD: sub-graph localization for temporal action detection. In: Proceedings of the IEEE Conference on Computer Vision and Pattern Recognition (2020)

80. Yang, L., Peng, H., Zhang, D., Fu, J., Han, J.: Revisiting anchor mechanisms for temporal action localization. IEEE Trans. Image Process. **29**, 8535–8548 (2020)

81. Yao, L., et al.: FILIP: fine-grained interactive language-image pre-training. In: Proceedings of the International Conference on Learning Representations (2022)

82. Yeung, S., Russakovsky, O., Mori, G., Fei-Fei, L.: End-to-end learning of action detection from frame glimpses in videos. In: Proceedings of the IEEE Conference on Computer Vision and Pattern Recognition (2016)

83. Yu, Y., Kim, J., Kim, G.: A joint sequence fusion model for video question answering and retrieval. In: Ferrari, V., Hebert, M., Sminchisescu, C., Weiss, Y. (eds.) ECCV 2018. LNCS, vol. 11211, pp. 487–503. Springer, Cham (2018). https://doi.org/10.1007/978-3-030-01234-2_29

84. Zhang, C., Wu, J., Li, Y.: ActionFormer: localizing moments of actions with transformers. arXiv preprint arXiv:2202.07925 (2022)

85. Zhang, H., Zhang, L., Qi, X., Li, H., Torr, P.H.S., Koniusz, P.: Few-shot action recognition with permutation-invariant attention. In: Vedaldi, A., Bischof, H., Brox, T., Frahm, J.-M. (eds.) ECCV 2020. LNCS, vol. 12350, pp. 525–542. Springer, Cham (2020). https://doi.org/10.1007/978-3-030-58558-7_31

86. Zhang, R., et al.: Tip-adapter: training-free clip-adapter for better vision-language modeling. arXiv preprint arXiv:2111.03930 (2021)

87. Zhao, P., Xie, L., Ju, C., Zhang, Y., Wang, Y., Tian, Q.: Bottom-up temporal action localization with mutual regularization. In: Vedaldi, A., Bischof, H., Brox, T., Frahm, J.-M. (eds.) ECCV 2020. LNCS, vol. 12353, pp. 539–555. Springer, Cham (2020). https://doi.org/10.1007/978-3-030-58598-3_32

88. Zhao, Y., Xiong, Y., Wang, L., Wu, Z., Tang, X., Lin, D.: Temporal action detection with structured segment networks. In: Proceedings of the International Conference on Computer Vision (2017)

89. Zhou, K., Yang, J., Loy, C.C., Liu, Z.: Learning to prompt for vision-language models. arXiv preprint arXiv:2109.01134 (2021)

90. Zhou, K., Yang, J., Loy, C.C., Liu, Z.: Conditional prompt learning for vision-language models. In: Proceedings of the IEEE Conference on Computer Vision and Pattern Recognition (2022)

91. Zhu, L., Yang, Y.: Compound memory networks for few-shot video classification. In: Ferrari, V., Hebert, M., Sminchisescu, C., Weiss, Y. (eds.) ECCV 2018. LNCS, vol. 11211, pp. 782–797. Springer, Cham (2018). https://doi.org/10.1007/978-3-030-01234-2_46

92. Zhu, L., Yang, Y.: Label independent memory for semi-supervised few-shot video classification. IEEE Trans. Pattern Anal. Mach. Intell. 44, 273–285 (2020)

93. Zhu, X., Toisoul, A., Perez-Rua, J.M., Zhang, L., Martinez, B., Xiang, T.: Few-shot action recognition with prototype-centered attentive learning. In: Proceedings of the British Machine Vision Conference (2021)

Asymmetric Relation Consistency Reasoning for Video Relation Grounding

Huan Li, Ping Wei$^{(\boxtimes)}$, Jiapeng Li, Zeyu Ma, Jiahui Shang, and Nanning Zheng

Xi'an Jiaotong University, Xi'an, China
pingwei@xjtu.edu.cn

Abstract. Video relation grounding has attracted growing attention in the fields of video understanding and multimodal learning. While the past years have witnessed remarkable progress in this issue, the difficulties of multi-instance and complex temporal reasoning make it still a challenging task. In this paper, we propose a novel Asymmetric Relation Consistency (ARC) reasoning model to solve the video relation grounding problem. To overcome the multi-instance confusion problem, an asymmetric relation reasoning method and a novel relation consistency loss are proposed to ensure the consistency of the relationships across multiple instances. In order to precisely localize the relation instance in temporal context, a transformer-based relation reasoning module is proposed. Our model is trained in a weakly-supervised manner. The proposed method was tested on the challenging video relation dataset. Experiments manifest that the performance of our method outperforms the state-of-the-art methods by a large margin. Extensive ablation studies also prove the effectiveness and strength of the proposed method.

Keywords: Video relation grounding · Asymmetric relation consistency · Weakly-supervised

1 Introduction

Video relation grounding (VRG) plays a crucial role in cross-modal understanding of visual scene and natural language, which has been attracting increasing attention for its significance in applications such as video caption [29] and visual question answering [12]. Given an untrimmed video and a 3-tuple query relation description $\langle subject, predicate, object \rangle$, the task is to return the spatial and temporal ranges of the *subject* and *object* in the relation connected by *predicate* [34], as shown in Fig. 1(a). Usually the spatial and temporal ranges are represented as a temporal sequence of bounding boxes containing the entities [34], e.g. the blue box sequence of *subject* : *person* and the brown box sequence of *object* : *bicycle* connected by *predicate* : *ride* in Fig. 1(a).

Video relation grounding is a challenging problem for two reasons. First, VRG needs to localize fine-grained spatial and temporal locations of the *subject* and the *object* in a weakly-supervised manner, which means in training only video-level labels are provided, but without the spatial or temporal locations. Second,

S. Avidan et al. (Eds.): ECCV 2022, LNCS 13695, pp. 125–141, 2022.
https://doi.org/10.1007/978-3-031-19833-5_8

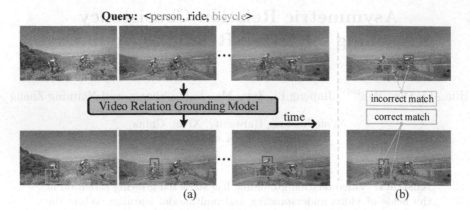

Fig. 1. Illustration of video relation grounding (VRG). (a) The VRG task requires the model to return one of the relation instance in both spatial and temporal domains. (b) Multi-instance confusion in video relation grounding.

compared with the other related video grounding tasks [4,24,31,37] which focus on the localization of temporal intervals or a single target object, VRG is defined to jointly localize a pair of object entities in both spatial and temporal domains.

The well-established VRG model [34] formulates this task as a hierarchical spatio-temporal region graph and achieved state-of-the-art results. However the *multi-instance confusion* remains to be an unsolved problem which greatly impedes the performance improvement. As shown in Fig. 1(b), the video frame contains two instances of the relation ⟨*person, ride, bicycle*⟩. In a specific frame of the video, the grounding system may output the *subject* box engaged in one relation instance but the *object* box in another instance, which forms incorrect match pair. One of the major reasons is that the *subject* and the *object* are assumed to be symmetric or conditionally independent for relation reasoning. In this way, the semantic dependency and the spatial relationships between them would not be taken into consideration. Consequently the *subject* box and the *object* box may separately appear in different instances of the relation.

In this paper, we contend that the *subject* and the *object* are asymmetric in relation reasoning and propose a novel Asymmetric Relation Consistency (ARC) model to ground relations in videos. Different from the symmetric reasoning approaches [10,34], our model first localizes the *subject* box in each frame, and then the *object* box is searched for conditioned on the localized *subject* box. In turn, the *subject* box is sought again conditioned on the found *object* box. Intuitively, these two query results of *subject* should follow the same distribution. To model this consistency, we design a new relation consistent loss. Furthermore, to learn more precise relation semantic representation and mitigate the impact of data biases, we further propose a transformer-based [5] relation-aware reasoning module which utilizes the relation phrase of context to search for the most relevant relation duration. Similar to vRGV [34], our model is trained in a weakly-supervised manner which means only the video-level labels are available but without the fine-grained spatio-temporal annotations.

The proposed method was tested on the challenging relation dataset ImageNet-VidVRD [22]. Experimental results manifest that our model outperforms the SOTA methods by a large margin. Extensive ablation studies also prove the effectiveness of the model.

This paper makes three contributions. Firstly, it proposes a novel asymmetric relation consistency reasoning method and designs novel loss functions for video relation grounding. Secondly, it presents a transformer-based baseline and a transformer-based relation-aware module to reason about the relationship between relation phrases and video features. Finally, the performance of the proposed method outperforms the state-of-the-art methods by a large margin.

2 Related Work

Since videos are not simple sets of separate object trajectories, modeling the interactions between two different object instances in videos enables us to deeply understand scenes and videos. Visual relation has been studied for a long time and made significant progress in recent years [6,9,11,14–17,26,30,33,35,36]. Many studies paid attention to video relation detection [13,19,22,25,27], which aims to spatio-temporally detect all the relation instances from untrimmed videos [22]. The work [22] proposes a segment-based method, where the segment-level relation class is obtained by a classifier and the final relation instance is obtained by a greedy relational association algorithm. Shang et al. [21] proposed a iterative inference method that effectively enhances the performance of visual video relation detection. Recently, a transformer-based method [7] is proposed to solve video relation detection task, where the relation instances are detected by set prediction. Unlike the relation detection task, Xiao et al. [34] proposed a more challenging task named visual relation grounding in videos, where the subject and object trajectories are localized by adopting a symmetric method with parameter-shared modules. Although this solution has achieved impress results, it overlooks the conditionally dependence between the subject and the object. In this paper, we propose an asymmetric relation reasoning method to further solve the video relation grounding problem.

The studies related to our method are vRGV [34] and SSAS [10]. The main differences are three-fold. First, these two studies adopt symmetric modes to localize subject and object with parameter-shared modules, while our model employs an asymmetric scheme. Second, the previous approaches model the relationship between subject and object by using implicit attention shifting. Instead, our model explicitly utilizes the conditional pattern. Third, vRGV takes the graph module and message passing to compute attention distribution, and SSAS uses convolution and iterative inference. Our model designs two new localizers based on transformers [5] to reason about the attention distribution.

Video grounding [4,24,37] aims to localize the temporal intervals of the targets in an untrimmed video by referring to the given sentence query. It provides backbones for some more high-level tasks such as video caption. Considering the fact that fine-grained annotation of video is time-consuming, some studies have focused on weakly-supervised video grounding [3,31,32] that means the frame-level annotations are unavailable during training. The work [23] proposes a multi-instance learning based method, where the contextual similarity is considered to model the similarity between two frames and a visual clustering loss is proposed to learn visual features. AsyNCE-CMT [3] proposes a novel AsyNCE loss and uses a cross modal transformer block to advance the weakly-supervised video grounding task. However, these existing methods are not suitable for the video relation grounding task. The video relation grounding is required to seek a pair of objects of the relation instances and their temporal ranges. Modeling the dependency between the two object entities and the temporal continuity are key problems for video relation grounding.

3   Method

3.1   Formulation

We follow the work vRGV [34] to define the problem of video relation grounding (VRG). A video V of n frames is represented as a sequence of region proposals $V = (B_1, ..., B_n)$, where B_i is the set of regions in the ith frame. In each frame, m regions are proposed without labels or scores as $B_i = \{B_{i,j} \mid j = 1, ..., m\}$, where $B_{i,j}$ represents the jth region in the ith frame. A relation R is defined as a 3-tuple $R = \langle subject, predicate, object \rangle$, which usually means the $subject$ is doing some actions described by $predicate$ towards or with the $object$, such as $R = \langle person, ride, bicycle \rangle$. Relations in videos are not only dependent on features in each frame but also temporal information over a video segment span.

Given a video V of n frames and a relation $R = \langle subject, predicate, object \rangle$, video relation grounding aims to spatially and temporally localize the $subject$ and the $object$ connected by $predicate$ in the video. With the region proposal representation of V, VRG is represented as to predict a $subject$ box sequence $S = (S_k, ..., S_l)$ and an $object$ box sequence $O = (O_k, ..., O_l)$, where $k, l \in [1, n]$ and $k < l$. S_i and O_i ($i \in [k, l]$) are the $subject$ box and the $object$ box in the ith frame, respectively, which come from the region proposal set B_i.

Following vRGV [34], VRG task is formulated as to solve the maximization problem:

$$(S^*, O^*) = \arg\max_{S,O} P(S, O | V, R) P(R | S, O, V). \tag{1}$$

The term $P(S, O | V, R)$ describes the joint posterior probability of the $subject$ box sequence and the $object$ box sequence. $P(R | S, O, V)$ characterizes the reconstruction of relation R given S, O and V. The final optimal output (S^*, O^*) is achieved by jointly maximizing the posterior and reconstruction terms. The above VRG definition and Eq. (1) follows the work [34]. One subtle difference is that the predicted $subject$ box or the $object$ box in our work represent the bounding box of the proposed region, not the region itself with the content.

Asymmetry in Relation. The previous method [34] hypothesize that the variable S and O are conditionally independent given V and R, i.e., $P(S, O|V, R) = P(S|V, R) * P(O|V, R)$. Thus the *subject* and the *object* are symmetric in the relation reasoning and the model uses a parameter-shared structure to localize the S and O respectively. However, this hypothesis overlooks two problems in VRG. First, in multi-instance scenarios, the co-occurrence of multiple $\langle subject, predicate, object \rangle$ instances may confuse the grounding system. For example, the system may return a *subject* sequence S in one relation instance but an *object* sequence O in another relation instance. Second, seeking the *subject* sequence and the *object* sequence separately ignores the semantic dependency and spatial relationships between the *subject* and *object*.

We contend that the *subject* and the *object* are asymmetric in relation reasoning and propose a novel Asymmetric Relation Consistency (ARC) model to resolve the above issues. In our model, grounding S and O are conditionally dependent given V and R. Correspondingly, our model first grounds the *subject* box in each frame according to the *subject* word embedding, and then the *object* box is searched for conditioned on the *subject* box. In turn, the *subject* box is sought again conditioned on the *object* box. Intuitively, the two query results of the *subject* should follow the same distribution, which is expressed with a novel asymmetric relation consistent loss. Since this strategy considers the semantic and spatial dependencies of the *subject* and the *object*, the multi-instance confusion can be alleviated and therefore the performance is improved.

3.2 Architecture Overview

Figure 2 shows the overall architecture of the proposed method. It adopts a spatio-temporal detached way to conduct video relation grounding. First, we use the backbone network to extract region proposals and visual features from video frames and relation phrases. Second, the proposed asymmetric relation consistency reasoning module is utilized to localize the spatial position of the *subject* and *object* in each frame. Then the proposed relation-aware temporal reasoning module is utilized to compute the temporal boundaries of the given relation. Finally, the relation reconstruction module reconstructs the given relation based on the grounded results. The details of each part are described as follows.

3.3 Backbone Network

As shown in Fig. 2, given a video with n frames, we first use a pretrained Faster R-CNN [20] to generate m region proposals for each frame and extract the corresponding ROI-aligned regional features with ResNet [8]. Let $x_i \in \mathbb{R}^{m \times d}$ be the features of m regions in the ith frame, where each row of x_i represents the features extracted from a region and d is the feature dimension. The spatial feature of each region is a 1×5 vector $\left[\frac{x_{min}}{W}, \frac{y_{min}}{H}, \frac{x_{max}}{W}, \frac{y_{max}}{H}, \frac{area}{W*H}\right]$, where W, H are the width and height of the frame, respectively. $(x_{min}, y_{min}, x_{max}, y_{max})$ is the bounding box position and $area$ is the area of the box. The spatial features of all the regions in the ith frame form a $m \times 5$ matrix.

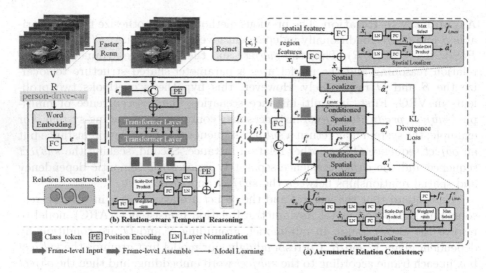

Fig. 2. The overall architecture of the proposed method.

A liner layer is used to transform the region features x_i into features of dimension $m \times D$. We learn the position embedding by mapping the $m \times 5$ spatial feature matrix into features of dimension $m \times D$. We then add the position embedding features to the transformed region features as input region features $\hat{x}_i \in \mathbb{R}^{m \times D}$. Similar to vRGV [34], for each word in the relation phrase, we use Glove [18] to extract 300-dimensional word embeddings. Then we transform the word embedding into the same dimension with the input region features. It is represented as $e \in \mathbb{R}^{l \times D}$, where l represents the length of the relation phrase.

3.4   Asymmetric Relation Consistency Reasoning

The asymmetric relation consistency reasoning module is designed to localize the spatial boxes of *subject* and *object* in each frame. As discussed in Sect. 3.1, grounding the subject and object boxes symmetrically ignores the spatial and semantic dependence between the subject and object, which may result in poor performance in the multi-instance scenes, as shown in Fig. 1(b). To overcome this limitation, our model adopts an asymmetric reasoning scheme. Inspired by conditional dependency intuitively, reasoning about the object box based on the subject box is convenient for reducing the search space, thereby avoiding confusion of multi-instance, and vice versa. As shown in Fig. 2(a), the asymmetric relation reasoning module contains two key components: spatial localizer and conditioned spatial localizer. The asymmetric reasoning process is composed of four steps: localizing *subject*, localizing *object* based on *subject*, re-localizing *subject* based on *object*, and consistency evaluation.

Step 1: Localizing *Subject*. Given the input region features $\hat{x}_i$ and relation phrase features e, the task in this step is to localize the *subject* box with the spatial localizer. In this case, we only use the *subject* word embedding feature e_s. Our spatial localizer is built based on the self-attention structure [5,28], as shown in Fig. 2(a).

We first normalize e_s and $\hat{x}_i$ by a layer normalization layer, then following a fully-connected layer to map the normalized features into $\bar{e}_s$ and $\bar{x}_i$, respectively. Then the *subject* attention is computed by a cross attention [28] operation:

$$\hat{\alpha}_{i,j}^s = \frac{\exp(\beta_i^j)}{\sum_{j=1}^m \exp(\beta_i^j)}, \beta_i = \frac{\bar{e}_s(\bar{x}_i)^T}{\sqrt{d_k}}, \tag{2}$$

where $\frac{1}{\sqrt{d_k}}$ is a scaling factor. $\hat{\alpha}_i^s = \{\hat{\alpha}_{i,j}^s\}_{j=1}^m$ is the subject-aware attention distribution, which reflects the score of each region proposal in the ith frame. Based on the score, we select the most relevant region box as the current *subject* box and output the corresponding region feature $\hat{f}_{i,max}^s$.

Step 2: Localizing *Object* Based on *Subject*. In this step, we use the proposed conditioned spatial localizer, an shown in Fig. 2(a), to localize the *object* box based on the localized *subject* box in Step 1. Concretely, we first concatenate $\hat{f}_{i,max}^s$ and the word embedding of *object* e_o, and input it into a fully-connected layer with relu activation function and a layer normalization layer. The input region features $\hat{x}_i$ are also normalized as $\tilde{x}_i$ by a layer normalization layer, then following a fully-connected layer to map the normalized features $\tilde{x}_i$ into $\dot{x}_i$. Following the similar process implemented in the spatial localizer, we can obtain the object-aware attention distribution $\alpha_i^o = \{\alpha_{i,j}^o\}_{j=1}^m$ and the feature $f_{i,max}^o$ of the most relevant region of *object*. The object-aware frame feature is computed as:

$$f_i^o = g(\sum_{j=1}^m \alpha_{i,j}^o \tilde{x}_{i,j}), \tag{3}$$

where $\tilde{x}_{i,j}$ is the jth row of $\tilde{x}_i$, i.e. the normalized feature of the jth box. g is a fully-connected layer.

Step 3: Re-localizing *Subject* Based on *Object*. With the feature $f_{i,max}^o$ obtained in Step 2, we re-calculate the attention weight of the region proposals for *subject*. The $f_{i,max}^o$ and e_s are input into the same conditioned spatial localizer to regenerate the region proposal attention weight and output $\alpha_i^s = \{\alpha_{i,j}^s\}_{j=1}^m$ and compute the subject-aware frame feature f_i^s. This regenerating operation implies that the most relevant bounding box of *subject* is searched for based on the most relevant box of *object*.

Step 4: Consistency Evaluation. Intuitively, we also expect the most relevant box of *object* is searched for based on the most relevant box of *subject*. Unfortunately, one video may contain multiple relation instances, which results in smooth attention weight distribution for adjusting to multiple instances in Step 1. In this case, the most relevant box of *subject* selected in Step 1 may be inaccurate, which further causes difficulty for localizing *object* in Step 2. To overcome this problem, we expect the most relevant box selected in Step 1 is the

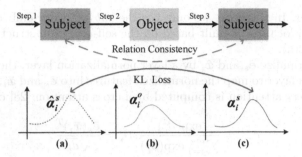

Fig. 3. Illustration of the asymmetric relation consistency. (a) Attention distribution of *subject* computed in Step 1. (b) Attention distribution of *object*. (c) Attention distribution of *subject* obtained in Step 3.

same as the box selected in Step 3. Thus, we can drive the attention distributions in Step 1 and Step 3 to follow the same distribution. As shown in Fig. 3. Specifically, we adopt the Kullback-Leibler divergence to optimize the learning process. Based on KL divergence, we propose a relation consistent loss function as follows:

$$\mathcal{L}_{arc} = \frac{1}{n} \sum_{i=1}^{n} D_{KL}(\boldsymbol{\alpha}_i^s \parallel \hat{\boldsymbol{\alpha}}_i^s), \tag{4}$$

where n is the frame number. $\boldsymbol{\alpha}_i^s$ is the attention distribution of *subject* computed in Step 3 and $\hat{\boldsymbol{\alpha}}_i^s$ is the one in Step 1. Since the grounding process employs an asymmetric and redistribution pattern, inspired by CycleGAN [38], we name this scheme as Asymmetric Relation Consistency (ARC).

Given the subject-aware frame feature $\boldsymbol{f}_i^s$ and object-aware frame feature $\boldsymbol{f}_i^o$, we concatenate these two features and then use a fully connected layer to get a final frame-level feature $\boldsymbol{f}_i$ for each frame. Thus the frame-level feature of the video can be donated as: $\boldsymbol{f} = \{\boldsymbol{f}_i\} \in \mathbb{R}^{n \times D}$.

3.5   Relation-Aware Temporal Reasoning

In the asymmetric relation reasoning process, a latent hypothesis is that all the frames contain the given relation instance. However, it is inapplicable in the VRG task since it requires not only localizing the spatial positions but also the temporal boundaries. In this section, based on the frame-level features extracted by the asymmetric relation consistency reasoning module, we propose a transformer-based relation-aware temporal reasoning (RTR) method for precisely localizing the temporal boundaries.

Since transformer [1,5] possesses the ability to extract global context information of long sequences, we use transformer to learn the relation semantics. We take the given relation as a phrase: *subject-predicate-object*. As shown in Fig. 2(b), our RTR module receives the frame-level feature and word embeddings of relation phrases as inputs. For learning global relation semantics, an extra learnable class token e_c is inserted into the word embedding sequence. Following the work [5], we add the fixed positional encoding into the word embedding sequence. Then the word embedding sequence is input into L successive transformer layers to learn relation representations. The relation representations are learned and meanwhile the relation of *subject* and *object* is reasoned implicitly. By multi-layer passing, the updated class token $\bar{e}_c$ is used for temporal reasoning.

For temporal reasoning, we first supplement the frame-level feature with the fixed positional encoding and then normalize it with a normalization layer, where the normalized result is denoted as $\bar{f}$. We use a fully-connected layer to map the updated class token $\bar{e}_c$ and the normalized feature $\bar{f}$ into $\hat{e}_c$ and $\hat{f}$, respectively. Finally, the temporal attention distribution is computed as,

$$\tau_i = \frac{\exp(\sigma_i)}{\sum_{i=1}^{n} \exp(\sigma_i)}, \sigma = \frac{\hat{e}_c(\hat{f})^T}{\sqrt{d_k}}. \tag{5}$$

$\tau = \{\tau_i\}_{i=1}^{n}$ is the frame-level attention distribution. The final video-level feature z about the given relation $\langle subject, predicate, object \rangle$ is represented as,

$$z = h(\sum_{i=1}^{n} \tau_i \bar{f}_i), \tag{6}$$

where h is a fully-connected layer.

3.6   Train and Inference

Following [34], we train our model using phrase reconstruction of the given relation in a weakly-supervised way. The reconstruction loss is represented as:

$$\mathcal{L}_{res} = -\sum_{t=1}^{l} \log(P(R_t \mid R_{0:t-1}, z)), \tag{7}$$

where l is the number of words in the relation phrase and R_t represents each word in the phrase. The total loss is described as:

$$\mathcal{L} = \mathcal{L}_{res} + \lambda \mathcal{L}_{arc}. \tag{8}$$

$\mathcal{L}_{arc}$ is the relation consistency loss defined in Eq. (4). λ is a hyper-parameter.

In inference, we employ the similar method used in vRGV [34] to obtain the *subject* box sequence S and the *object* sequence O. We first generate candidate segments set for each video in temporal dimension based on the learned temporal frame-level distribution τ by setting a threshold η. For each candidate segment, we then use the Viterbi algorithm to search for an optimal path for the *subject* box sequence S and the *object* sequence O, respectively. The linking cost of the successive frames is defined as:

$$c(B_{i,p}, B_{i+1,q}) = \alpha_{i,p} + \alpha_{i+1,q} + \theta \cdot IoU(B_{i,p}, B_{i+1,q}), \tag{9}$$

where $B_{i,p}$ represent the pth region in ith frame. $\boldsymbol{\alpha}_i$ is the subject-aware attention distribution $\boldsymbol{\alpha}_i^s = \{\alpha_{i,j}^s\}_{j=1}^m$ or the object-aware attention distribution $\boldsymbol{\alpha}_i^o = \{\alpha_{i,j}^o\}_{j=1}^m$. For example, to obtain the *subject* box sequence S, $\boldsymbol{\alpha}_i^s$ is used to compute the linking cost. θ is a hyper-parameter and IoU is the intersection over union. We average linking cost of the searched *subject* box sequence S and *object* sequence O as the segment score, and then we select the segment with the maximal score as the relation grounding result.

4   Experiments

4.1   Settings

Implementation Details. Our model is built on the basic transformer configuration [5]. Following vRGV [34], each video is sampled $n = 120$ frames and the number of proposals for each frame is set to 40. The region features are extracted from the pretrained Faster R-CNN [20] with the backbone ResNet101 [8]. The region features and spatial features along with the word embeddings are transformed into the same dimension $D = 512$. All the experiments are conducted on 8 NVIDIA 3090 GPUs and The batch size is set to 32 for each GPU. We use the Pytorch toolbox with FP16 training. The model is trained with Adam optimizer with basic learning rate 1e−4.

Dataset and Evaluation Criteria. We test our model on the challenging ImageNet-VidVRD video relation dataset [22]. It consists of 1000 videos, 35 object classes, 132 predicate classes, and over 30,000 relation instances.

Our model is evaluated and compared with the previous studies using accuracy (Acc). Given a video V and the corresponding relation 3-tuple R, a result is a true positive if the tIoUs (temporal intersection over union) of *subject* box sequence S and *object* box sequence O with one of the ground-truth instance are both larger than 0.5. The tIoU is computed under three different spatial intersection over union (sIoU) thresholds (0.3, 0.5 and 0.7). Following vRGV [34], we report the whole relation accuracy (Acc_R), the subject accuracy (Acc_S) and the object accuracy (Acc_O), respectively.

4.2   Result Comparison and Analysis

Table 1 shows the experiment result comparisons on different spatial overlap thresholds. We compare our model with some previous methods: T-Rank [2], Co-occur [10], and vRGV [34], where the results of T-Rank [2] and Co-occur [10] were reported in [34]. We also report the results obtained by selecting the regions with the maximal attention scores without using IoU in inference (marked with *). We also compare our model with the baseline method which is designed based on the basic transformers. From Table 1, we can find our ARC model performs better than the baseline model under all threshold settings. And it is obvious that the ARC model outperforms all the existing methods. Specifically, compared to the

Table 1. Video relation grounding comparison on different spatial overlap thresholds (Acc %). * means not using IoU in inference).

Models	sIOU = 0.3			sIOU = 0.5			sIOU = 0.7			Average		
	Acc_S	Acc_O	Acc_R	Acc_S	Acc_O	Acc_R	Acc_S	Acc_O	Acc_R	Acc_S	Acc_O	Acc_R
T-Rank V1 [2]	33.55	27.52	17.25	22.61	12.79	4.49	6.31	3.30	0.76	20.27	10.68	3.99
T-Rank V2 [2]	34.35	21.71	15.06	23.00	9.18	3.82	7.06	2.09	0.50	20.83	7.35	3.16
Co-occur* [10]	27.84	25.62	18.44	23.50	20.40	13.81	17.02	14.93	7.29	22.99	19.33	12.80
Co-occur [10]	31.31	30.65	21.79	28.02	27.69	18.86	21.99	21.64	13.16	25.90	25.23	16.48
vRGV* [34]	37.61	37.75	27.54	32.17	32.32	21.43	21.34	21.02	10.62	31.64	30.92	20.54
vRGV [34]	42.31	41.31	29.95	37.11	37.52	24.77	29.71	29.72	17.09	36.77	36.30	24.58
Our baseline*	40.94	38.76	29.13	35.18	33.69	23.77	27.03	25.46	13.94	34.08	32.75	22.97
Our baseline	41.41	38.86	29.84	36.75	35.14	24.78	29.66	27.78	15.43	35.58	34.60	24.38
ARC*	41.60	40.61	30.23	37.13	36.78	26.09	28.65	29.41	17.56	34.96	34.72	23.75
ARC	**45.66**	**44.01**	**32.53**	**40.99**	**40.41**	**27.83**	**33.24**	**33.39**	**20.44**	**39.66**	**39.20**	**26.42**

Table 2. Video relation grounding comparison on different temporal overlap thresholds (Acc %).

Models	tIOU = 0.3			tIOU = 0.5			tIOU = 0.7		
	Acc_S	Acc_O	Acc_R	Acc_S	Acc_O	Acc_R	Acc_S	Acc_O	Acc_R
T-Rank V1 [2]	36.51	28.67	15.05	20.27	10.68	3.99	6.15	2.67	0.55
T-Rank V2 [2]	36.99	20.70	12.81	20.83	7.35	3.16	6.19	1.30	0.21
Co-occur [10]	35.30	35.50	23.23	25.90	25.23	16.48	16.81	15.04	8.94
vRGV [34]	49.97	48.98	33.16	36.77	36.30	24.58	24.27	22.11	13.69
Our baseline*	49.05	46.43	33.75	34.08	32.75	22.97	22.05	19.62	10.94
Our baseline	49.72	47.83	34.27	35.58	34.60	24.38	24.53	21.58	12.08
ARC*	49.61	49.43	35.68	34.96	34.72	23.75	24.14	25.25	14.46
ARC	**52.74**	**52.41**	**35.61**	**39.66**	**39.20**	**26.42**	**28.68**	**28.68**	**17.67**

SOTA method vRGV, our method gets 45.66%, 44.01%, and 32.53% performance for Acc_S, Acc_O, and Acc_R, respectively under the threshold $sIoU = 0.3$, while the SOTA method vRGV achieves 42.31% Acc_S, 41.31% Acc_O, and 29.95% Acc_R, respectively. Under the threshold $sIoU = 0.5$, our model achieves 27.83% Acc_R, 40.99% Acc_S and 40.41% Acc_O, respectively, and outperforms vRGV by a large margin. Under the setting of $sIoU = 0.7$, the performance of our ARC still has a significant improvement. These results illustrate the effectiveness of the proposed model.

To make a deeper comparison, we compare the results obtained without using IoU as the linking cost in inference. In this case, the model is required to possess the capacity of modeling temporal continuity for localizing the relation instance. In Table 1, the performance of our model still exceeds the SOTA method vRGV. We also compare our method with the previous models on different temporal overlap thresholds shown in Table 2, where our method outperform all previous models under all settings. These results prove that our model has the ability to capture the relation temporal continuity.

Table 3. Ablation study results on ImageNet-VidVRD dataset (Acc %).

Models	sIOU = 0.3			sIOU = 0.5			sIOU = 0.7			Average		
	Acc_S	Acc_O	Acc_R	Acc_S	Acc_O	Acc_R	Acc_S	Acc_O	Acc_R	Acc_S	Acc_O	Acc_R
w/o ARC	43.03	42.19	31.99	38.70	37.89	27.08	30.18	29.59	16.13	37.08	36.43	24.86
w/o RC Loss	42.75	41.76	30.88	37.20	38.43	25.48	29.53	31.13	16.67	35.99	36.85	23.61
w/o RTR	43.86	43.97	33.03	38.04	38.42	26.25	30.34	29.32	17.39	36.59	36.58	23.86
ARC	**45.66**	**44.01**	**32.53**	**40.99**	**40.41**	**27.83**	**33.24**	**33.39**	**20.44**	**39.66**	**39.20**	**26.42**

4.3 Ablation Study

Effect of Asymmetric Relation Consistency. In this section, we validate the effect of the asymmetric consistency reasoning and compare it with the symmetric method. Table 3 shows the ablation comparison results, where 'w/o' means 'without'. w/o ARC represents the model without the asymmetric reasoning and it achieves 16.13 %Acc_R under $sIoU = 0.7$ setting and 24.86 %Acc_R under *Average* setting, while our model ARC surpasses it by a large margin. This phenomenon manifests the asymmetric consistency reasoning can significantly improve the performance and plays an important role in relation grounding. As discussed in Sect. 3.1, the proposed asymmetric reasoning method can mitigate the multi-instance confusion problem and learn the semantic dependency between *subject* and *object*, and thus the performance is improved.

Influence of Relation Consistent Loss. The second row in Table 3 shows the results of asymmetric relation reasoning without relation consistency KL loss. We can find that removing the consistency supervision significantly impairs the performance of the system, where the model get a 23.61% Acc_R in *Average* setting and the ability of the model nearly degenerates into the baseline level. Without the consistency loss, the model can hardly select the most relevant box for *subject* with the spatial localizer in Step 1, and further results in a false region for *object* in Step 2, which leads to the performance decline.

We visualize the attention distributions learned in Step 1 and Step 3. As shown in Fig. 4, in order to validate the ability to cope with the multi-instance cases, we implement the comparison on multi-instance videos. The first row shows the model without using the relation consistent loss (w/o RC Loss) while the second row shows the results from our ARC. When the relation consistent loss was removed, the attention distribution $\hat{\alpha}^s$ learned in Step 1 becomes quite smooth, thus the most relevant region for *subject* is difficult to be selected. This difficulty will influences the localizing process of Step 2, thereby indirectly making the Step 3 be caught in a dilemma. On the contrary, training the model with KL loss makes the attention distribution univocal and pushes $\hat{\alpha}^s$ and α^s follow the similar distribution, which reduces the difficulty for relation grounding and thereby enhances the performance.

Effect of Relation-Aware Temporal Reasoning. Our ARC uses the proposed transformer-based relation-aware representation module (RTR). We compare ARC with the method without using the relation-aware temporal reasoning (w/o RTR), which merges the *subject* embedding and *object* embedding as query

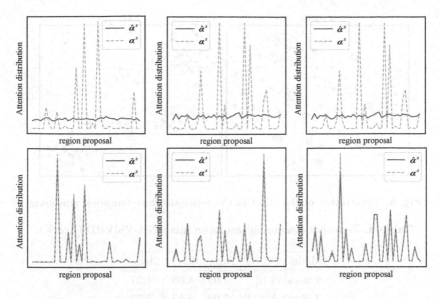

Fig. 4. Illustration of the effect of the relation consistent loss.

to localize the given relation. ARC outperforms w/o RTR by a large margin, which adequately demonstrates the validity of the proposed RTR module.

As shown in Fig. 5, we visualize video-level feature z that is used to reconstruct the given relation. All features are extracted from the relations with the same subject *person* and object *bicycle* but maybe different predicates. In Fig. 5, the same color represents the relations with same subject, object and predicate. The figure shows that the model without RTR module (w/o RTR) is apt to regard the relation with different predicates as the same relations. As shown in the red circles, the different relations closely intertwine and are inseparable. We attribute this phenomenon to data biases. For example, the video only consists of one person and one bicycle, thus the model without RTR module will neglect the predicate and directly localize the person and bicycle to get a plausible result. However this scheme may result in performance degradation in complex scenes with multiple relation instances. While our model (ARC) can effectively separate different relations and mitigate the influence of data biases, thereby improving the performance.

4.4 Zero-Shot Evaluation

Due to the diversity of relations, many new relation triplets do not appear in the training set. Thus, the ability to handle the zero-shot problem is vitally important in video relation grounding. For zero-shot evaluation, we compare our model with some previous models. Table 4 shows the comparison results, where our model still outperforms the existing methods. In this case, the SOTA method vRGV achieves 10.27 % Acc_R, while our model gets 11.19% Acc_R. These

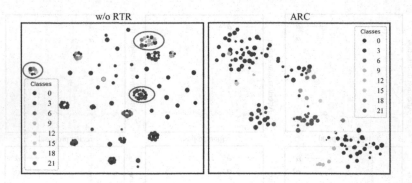

Fig. 5. Illustration of the effect of the relation-aware temporal reasoning.

Table 4. Zero-shot evaluation results on ImageNet-VidVRD (Acc %).

Model	Acc_S	Acc_O	Acc_R
T-Rank V1 [2]	4.05	4.08	1.37
T-Rank V2 [2]	7.09	4.13	1.37
Co-occur [10]	11.60	10.99	7.38
vRGV [34]	18.94	17.23	10.27
Our model	17.34	**19.01**	**11.19**

results verify the generalization capability and the power of our model to solve the zero-shot problem in video relation grounding task.

5   Conclusion

This paper addresses the challenging problem of weakly-supervised video relation grounding. The existing methods adopted symmetric reasoning schemes without considering the dependency between the subject and the object. We propose a novel asymmetric relation reasoning method with a relation consistency loss to overcome this weakness. A transformer-based relation-aware relation reasoning module is proposed to learn a better relation representation. The extensive experiments proved the effectiveness of the proposed method. The future work will focus on exploring the asymmetry mechanism in other grounding tasks.

Acknowledgement. This research was supported by the grants Key Research and Development Program of China (No. 2018AAA0102501), and National Natural Science Foundation of China (No. 61876149, No. 62088102).

References

1. Carion, N., Massa, F., Synnaeve, G., Usunier, N., Kirillov, A., Zagoruyko, S.: End-to-end object detection with transformers. In: Vedaldi, A., Bischof, H., Brox, T., Frahm, J.-M. (eds.) ECCV 2020. LNCS, vol. 12346, pp. 213–229. Springer, Cham (2020). https://doi.org/10.1007/978-3-030-58452-8_13
2. Chen, Z., Ma, L., Luo, W., Wong, K.Y.K.: Weakly-supervised spatio-temporally grounding natural sentence in video. In: The Annual Meeting of the Association for Computational Linguistics (2019)
3. Da, C., Zhang, Y., Zheng, Y., Pan, P., Xu, Y., Pan, C.: Asynce: disentangling false-positives for weakly-supervised video grounding. In: ACM International Conference on Multimedia (2021)
4. Ding, X., et al.: Support-set based cross-supervision for video grounding. In: IEEE CVPR (2021)
5. Dosovitskiy, A., et al.: An image is worth 16×16 words: Transformers for image recognition at scale. In: International Conference on Learning Representations (2021)
6. Gao, C., Xu, J., Zou, Y., Huang, J.-B.: DRG: dual relation graph for human-object interaction detection. In: Vedaldi, A., Bischof, H., Brox, T., Frahm, J.-M. (eds.) ECCV 2020. LNCS, vol. 12357, pp. 696–712. Springer, Cham (2020). https://doi.org/10.1007/978-3-030-58610-2_41
7. Gao, K., Chen, L., Huang, Y., Xiao, J.: Video relation detection via tracklet based visual transformer. In: ACM International Conference on Multimedia (2021)
8. He, K., Zhang, X., Ren, S., Sun, J.: Deep residual learning for image recognition. In: IEEE Conference on Computer Vision and Pattern Recognition (2016)
9. Kim, B., Lee, J., Kang, J., Kim, E.S., Kim, H.J.: Hotr: end-to-end human-object interaction detection with transformers. In: IEEE CVPR (2021)
10. Krishna, R., Chami, I., Bernstein, M., Fei-Fei, L.: Referring relationships. In: IEEE Conference on Computer Vision and Pattern Recognition (2018)
11. Li, J., Wei, P., Zhang, Y., Zheng, N.: A slow-i-fast-p architecture for compressed video action recognition. In: ACM International Conference on Multimedia (2020)
12. Li, Q., Tao, Q., Joty, S., Cai, J., Luo, J.: VQA-E: explaining, elaborating, and enhancing your answers for visual questions. In: Ferrari, V., Hebert, M., Sminchisescu, C., Weiss, Y. (eds.) ECCV 2018. LNCS, vol. 11211, pp. 570–586. Springer, Cham (2018). https://doi.org/10.1007/978-3-030-01234-2_34
13. Li, Y., Yang, X., Shang, X., Chua, T.S.: Interventional video relation detection. In: ACM International Conference on Multimedia (2021)
14. Liao, Y., Liu, S., Wang, F., Chen, Y., Qian, C., Feng, J.: Ppdm: parallel point detection and matching for real-time human-object interaction detection. In: IEEE CVPR (2020)
15. Lu, C., Krishna, R., Bernstein, M., Fei-Fei, L.: Visual relationship detection with language priors. In: Leibe, B., Matas, J., Sebe, N., Welling, M. (eds.) ECCV 2016. LNCS, vol. 9905, pp. 852–869. Springer, Cham (2016). https://doi.org/10.1007/978-3-319-46448-0_51
16. Ma, Z., Wei, P., Li, H., Zheng, N.: Hoig: end-to-end human-object interactions grounding with transformers. In: IEEE International Conference on Multimedia and Expo (2022)
17. Mi, L., Chen, Z.: Hierarchical graph attention network for visual relationship detection. In: IEEE/CVF Conference on Computer Vision and Pattern Recognition (2020)

18. Pennington, J., Socher, R., Manning, C.D.: Glove: global vectors for word representation. In: Conference on Empirical Methods in Natural Language Processing (2014)
19. Qian, X., Zhuang, Y., Li, Y., Xiao, S., Pu, S., Xiao, J.: Video relation detection with spatio-temporal graph. In: ACM International Conference on Multimedia (2019)
20. Ren, S., He, K., Girshick, R., Sun, J.: Faster r-cnn: towards real-time object detection with region proposal networks. Advances in Neural Information Processing Systems (2015)
21. Shang, X., Li, Y., Xiao, J., Ji, W., Chua, T.S.: Video visual relation detection via iterative inference. In: ACM International Conference on Multimedia (2021)
22. Shang, X., Ren, T., Guo, J., Zhang, H., Chua, T.S.: Video visual relation detection. In: ACM International Conference on Multimedia (2017)
23. Shi, J., Xu, J., Gong, B., Xu, C.: Not all frames are equal: Weakly-supervised video grounding with contextual similarity and visual clustering losses. In: IEEE CVPR (2019)
24. Soldan, M., Xu, M., Qu, S., Tegner, J., Ghanem, B.: Vlg-net: video-language graph matching network for video grounding. In: IEEE/CVF International Conference on Computer Vision (2021)
25. Sun, X., Ren, T., Zi, Y., Wu, G.: Video visual relation detection via multi-modal feature fusion. In: ACM International Conference on Multimedia (2019)
26. Tamura, M., Ohashi, H., Yoshinaga, T.: Qpic: query-based pairwise human-object interaction detection with image-wide contextual information. In: IEEE CVPR (2021)
27. Tsai, Y.H.H., Divvala, S., Morency, L.P., Salakhutdinov, R., Farhadi, A.: Video relationship reasoning using gated spatio-temporal energy graph. In: IEEE/CVF Conference on Computer Vision and Pattern Recognition (2019)
28. Vaswani, A., et al.: Attention is all you need. In: NIPS (2017)
29. Venugopalan, S., Rohrbach, M., Donahue, J., Mooney, R., Darrell, T., Saenko, K.: Sequence to sequence - video to text. In: IEEE International Conference on Computer Vision (2015)
30. Wang, T., Yang, T., Danelljan, M., Khan, F.S., Zhang, X., Sun, J.: Learning human-object interaction detection using interaction points. In: IEEE CVPR (2020)
31. Wang, W., Gao, J., Xu, C.: Weakly-supervised video object grounding via stable context learning. In: ACM International Conference on Multimedia (2021)
32. Wang, Y., Zhou, W., Li, H.: Fine-grained semantic alignment network for weakly supervised temporal language grounding. In: Findings of the Association for Computational Linguistics (2021)
33. Wei, P., Zhao, Y., Zheng, N., Zhu, S.C.: Modeling 4d human-object interactions for joint event segmentation, recognition, and object localization. In: IEEE Trans. Pattern Anal. Mach. Intell., 1165–1179 (2017)
34. Xiao, J., Shang, X., Yang, X., Tang, S., Chua, T.-S.: Visual relation grounding in videos. In: Vedaldi, A., Bischof, H., Brox, T., Frahm, J.-M. (eds.) ECCV 2020. LNCS, vol. 12351, pp. 447–464. Springer, Cham (2020). https://doi.org/10.1007/978-3-030-58539-6_27
35. Yu, R., Li, A., Morariu, V.I., Davis, L.S.: Visual relationship detection with internal and external linguistic knowledge distillation. In: IEEE International Conference on Computer Vision (2017)
36. Zhan, Y., Yu, J., Yu, T., Tao, D.: On exploring undetermined relationships for visual relationship detection. In: IEEE/CVF Conference on Computer Vision and Pattern Recognition (2019)

37. Zhao, Y., Zhao, Z., Zhang, Z., Lin, Z.: Cascaded prediction network via segment tree for temporal video grounding. In: IEEE CVPR (2021)
38. Zhu, J.Y., Park, T., Isola, P., Efros, A.A.: Unpaired image-to-image translation using cycle-consistent adversarial networks. In: IEEE International Conference on Computer Vision (2017)

Self-supervised Social Relation Representation for Human Group Detection

Jiacheng Li[1], Ruize Han[1]([⊠]), Haomin Yan[1], Zekun Qian[1], Wei Feng[1], and Song Wang[2]

[1] Intelligence and Computing College, Tianjin University, Tianjin, China
{threeswords,han_ruize,yan_hm,clarkqian,wfeng}@tju.edu.cn
[2] University of South Carolina, Columbia, USA
songwang@cec.sc.edu

Abstract. Human group detection, which splits crowd of people into groups, is an important step for video-based human social activity analysis. The core of human group detection is the human social relation representation and division. In this paper, we propose a new two-stage multi-head framework for human group detection. In the first stage, we propose a human behavior simulator head to learn the social relation feature embedding, which is self-supervised trained by leveraging the socially grounded multi-person behavior relationship. In the second stage, based on the social relation embedding, we develop a self-attention inspired network for human group detection. Remarkable performance on two state-of-the-art large-scale benchmarks, i.e., PANDA and JRDB-Group, verifies the effectiveness of the proposed framework. Benefiting from the self-supervised social relation embedding, our method can provide promising results with very few (labeled) training data. We have released the source code to the public.

Keywords: Group detection · Self-supervised learning · Video analysis

1 Introduction

Scenes with a crowd are very common in the real world, e.g., outdoor parades and social gatherings [20,21]. Such scenes lead to many important video-surveillance tasks, such as human counting, pedestrian tracking [13,18,19], and group activity recognition [45]. These tasks involve crowd analysis either locally for individuals or more globally for the whole crowd. With the use of wide-view cameras in surveillance, we can now collect videos to cover a large-scale crowd composed of

J. Li and R. Han—Equal contribution.

Supplementary Information The online version contains supplementary material available at https://doi.org/10.1007/978-3-031-19833-5_9.

multiple groups of people with high resolution. In this case, we usually need to first identify all these groups [27] before conducting further human activity analysis. This leads to the important task of (video-based) human group detection, which tries to divide the crowd into multiple non-overlapped human groups.

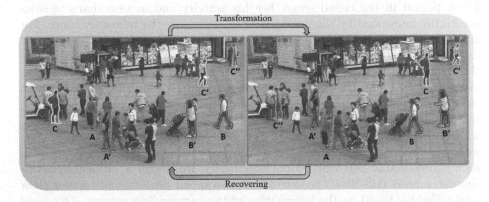

Fig. 1. A conceptual illustration of the rationale of our insight. We swap some people in the scene and try to discover the unreasonable states in the transformed scene (right) by implicitly learning the human social relations. Specifically, in the left image, we swap person A with A', B with B' and C, C', C'' with C', C'', C, respectively, resulting in the right image. Such swapped results in the right contain persons with abnormal behaviors. To recover the above augmentation, the method needs to understand the reasonable state of the person in the crowd considering itself and its surrounding people, which can be used for the social relation representation.

The human group detection task is very challenging since groups can be formed in complicated ways [22, 34], whose characteristic is more complex than the pedestrians acting alone or the crowds as a whole. Previous works for group detection mainly leverage the features extracted from either the pedestrian trajectories [29] or local spatial structure [6], followed by a similarity measurement and clustering analysis, e.g., the weighted graph model [4], potentially infinite mixture model [15] and correlation clustering [34]. In a recent work of PANDA [39], a new video benchmark that uses gigapixel-level cameras for capturing a supersized scene with hundreds of people was developed, together with an official baseline method that combines the global trajectory and local interaction information for group detection.

However, the above methods commonly have two weaknesses. First, the features used in most of the previous group detection methods are pre-defined, many are actually hand-crafted features, including temporal trajectories and spatial distances [6, 30, 34, 41]. Second, previous works based on machine learning are usually fully supervised and require large-scale annotations [39, 41]. Nevertheless, the human group detection labels in a dense crowd are very laborious and costly to annotate manually.

To address these problems, in this paper, we study spontaneous learning of human relation embedding features for human group detection. This is inspired by the sociological interpretation of group – two or more people interacting to reach a common goal and perceiving a shared membership, based on both physical identity (spatial proximity) and social identity (intra-group rules) [37]. For a person in the crowd scene, her/his activity and motion characteristics are highly influenced by the nearby people, especially the interactive ones. For example, as shown in Fig. 1, we swap the spatial positions of some people (left and right images are the ones before and after the swapping). We can easily find that the 'transformed' people in the right image show unreasonable behaviors, e.g., in the right of Fig. 1, the strange pose (A, B'), dangerous moving direction with close distance to something (A', B). Such visual unreasonability, in the human sense, is dependent on the human-human interactive behavior and social relation, which are very important for human group detection. Inspired by this rationale, we try to develop a method to automatically learn human social relations through such unreasonable behaviors. More specifically, we design a rational-behavior simulator head (BS-Head) to discover the swapped persons and recover their original states based on the information of the surrounding persons. This head is used as a self-supervised training head to learn the human social relation embedding. After that, we use the embedding feature produced by BS-Head to train another self-attention-based group prediction network for human group detection. The main contributions in this work are:

- We propose a two-branch group detection framework, which contains a shared relation embedding module and two heads for two-stage training. It is effective for social group detection problems in large-scale crowds.
- We develop a self-supervised relation embedding training strategy, which models the socially grounded human social relations in the crowd scene as the pretext task. The self-supervised representation can benefit the network training using only very few (labeled) data.
- Experiment results on two newly proposed large-scale benchmarks, i.e., PANDA and JRDB-Group, verify the effectiveness of the proposed method. The proposed method achieves significant group detection performance improvement compared to the state-of-the-art baselines – $20.7 \rightarrow 53.2\%$ and $31.4\% \rightarrow 56.9\%$ in F_1 score on PANDA and JRDB-Group, respectively. We release the source code to the public at https://github.com/Jiaoma/SHGD.

2   Related Work

Human Group Detection. Human group detection is an essential task in computer vision, which, however, has not been widely studied recently. Early human group detection methods can be divided into three categories, including group-based methods, individual-group methods, and individual-based methods. In group-based methods, no individual information is considered [11,33]. The individual-group methods try to integrate the information of human trajectories instead of separately using each one [3,28]. The individual-based methods consider individual subjects, leading to many models, such as predicting the social group relations by using the weighted graph [4], potentially infinite mixture model [15] and correlation clustering [34], etc. Recently, Shao et al. [32] employed the goal directions instead of traditional positions and velocities to find group members. More recently, instead of focusing only on the position-aware group detection, PANDA [39] proposes to integrate the dynamic human inter-actions for human group detection. As mentioned earlier, these methods either use pre-defined, usually hand-crafted, features [6,30,34,41] or require large-scale annotated data [39,41] for training.

Human Relation Discovery. A key problem for the group detection task is the discovery of human relations, especially social relationship [16,23], e.g., friends and colleagues, via various human attributes, e.g., age, job, etc. Other relations include the human-object interaction (HOI) [46,47], human-human interaction (HHI) [26,45], and gaze communication [10], etc. For HOI or HHI, relations are usually specific and mostly determined by the involved subjects/objects, e.g., a scene with a human and a bike is more likely to be detected as 'ride bike'. Differently, our task explores the relations without the above specific prior knowledge, e.g., the social relationships among people in the crowd.

Human Relation Modeling in the Multi-person Scene. Group-wise human relation is also collaboratively or implicitly used in many other related tasks, and human group detection is often accompanied by pedestrian trajectory prediction [12,30,41]. The method in [30] tries to jointly achieve the pedestrian trajectory prediction and group membership estimation using a Conditional Ran-dom Field (CRF) model. Similarly, an SVM-based method is proposed in [41] to handle the estimations of pedestrian trajectory and social (group) relation-ships. A GAN pipeline is proposed in [32] that learns informative latent features for joint pedestrian trajectory forecasting and group detection. Social-GAN [17] proposes to predict the socially-accepted motion trajectories in crowded scenes by considering human social relations. Multi-human relations have also been considered in group activity recognition (GAR) [2,14,31,40,42,43]. For exam-ple, ARG [40] proposes to build a flexible and efficient actor relation graph to simultaneously capture the appearance and position relation between actors. The method in [31] considers multiple cliques with different scales of the locality to account for the diversity of the actors' relations in group activities. The above methods all take the human relation modeling or detection as an auxiliary task but do not divide the crowd into groups that is our focus in this paper.

3   Proposed Method

3.1   Overview

We first give an overview of the proposed method. Given a video clip recording a crowded multi-person scene, we denote N as the maximum number of people (referred to as subject in this paper) within T frames[1], e.g., 10 frames, where N

---

[1] If a subject is missing in a frame, we fill it with blank (all-zero feature vector).

could be very large, e.g., over 1,000 in PANDA dataset. We first extract a feature encoding vector $\mathbf{v}_i^t \in \mathbb{R}^{C_v}$ for the i-th subject in t-th frame, where C_v is the number of feature dimensions. The encoding vector can be represented by both the human skeleton joints and spatial location. We model all the the subjects in the scene as an undirected graph $\mathcal{G} = <\mathbf{V}, \mathbf{R}>$, in which $\mathbf{V} \in \mathbb{R}^{T \times N \times C_v}$ denotes the set for all $\mathbf{v}_i^t$, and $\mathbf{R} \in \mathbb{R}^{T \times N^2}$ encodes the *group relation* $r_{i,j}^t$ between subject i and subject j at frame t. It is in the range of $[0, 1]$, where 1 means the subject j and subject i belong to the same group. The relation matrix $\mathbf{R}$ can be used to divide the crowd of people into groups by label propagation methods [44].

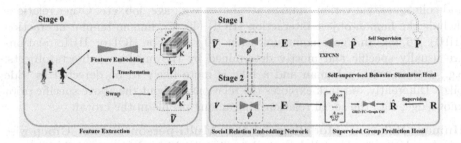

Fig. 2. An illustration of the overall framework of our method, which is composed of an offline feature extraction module and a social relation embedding module for feature construction, followed by two heads, i.e., the behavior simulator head (BS-Head) and the group prediction head. The overall network is trained in two stages. In stage 1, we train the relation embedding network with the BS-Head in a self-supervised manner. In stage 2, based on the relation embedding features obtained by stage 1, we train our network with the group prediction head for generating the group detection results.

To obtain such relation matrix $\mathbf{R}$, many deep learning methods [35,36] generally first encode the features $\mathbf{V}$ into a group relation embedding space and then predict $\mathbf{R}$ using a relation modeling algorithm, like the graph neural networks (GNN). In this paper, we aim at developing an effective group relation embedding method in a self-supervised manner, and then use such embedding $\mathbf{E}$ to predict the relation matrix $\mathbf{R}$. The pipeline of the proposed method could be summarized as two stages: 1) We first train a real-world surrounding-subject-aware *human behavior simulator* in a self-supervised manner, which is to spontaneously learn the natural human behavior within a group and embed the features into a relation embedding space. 2) Based on the relation embedding, we then learn a group prediction sub-network, which is trained for discovering the human-human group relations among multiple persons. This stage can only use a small number of labeled data to train. The architecture of the whole network is shown in Fig. 2. It consists of two prediction heads that share the same feature extraction and social relation embedding network. The whole network uses the human detection bounding boxes of the N persons each frame in T frames as input for feature construction, as discussed in Sect. 3.2. It has two kinds of outputs produced by its two heads separately in the two-stage training, as presented in Sect. 3.3 and Sect. 3.4, respectively.

3.2 Feature Construction Module

Social Relation Embedding Network. The original feature $\mathbf{V} \in \mathbb{R}^{T \times N \times C_v}$ is constructed by concatenating both the 2D skeleton joints $\mathbf{K} \in \mathbb{R}^{T \times N \times C_k}$ and the positional feature $\mathbf{P} \in \mathbb{R}^{T \times N \times C_p}$ of all N subjects at frame t.

The social relation embedding network uses $\mathbf{V}$ as input and outputs a social relation embedding feature $\mathbf{E}$, i.e.,

$$\mathbf{E} = \phi(\mathbf{V}) \in \mathbb{R}^{T \times N \times C_e}. \tag{1}$$

Specifically, first, for the skeleton feature $\mathbf{K}$, we adopt the Shift-GCN [5] alike network to extract the temporal action features from the human skeleton joint. Also, for the positional feature $\mathbf{P}$, we concatenate it with the skeleton feature $\mathbf{K}$ and utilize the architecture in spatial-temporal graph convolutional network (ST-GCNN) [25] to model the spatial and temporal information.

3.3 Self-supervised Behavior Simulator Head

In this section, we present the rationale and process to train the social relation embedding network in a self-supervised manner with the proposed rational-behavior simulator head (BS-Head). Specifically, we aim to establish a human behavior simulator to model the *reasonable behavior* of the humans in a crowd with the constraint of its social relation/rules/etiquette with other people, e.g., the greeting from surrounding people and the relative position distribution to the others. Our basic assumption is that every person should behave logically and not do unreasonable things like talking to nobody, stepping over others, totally ignoring others' greetings, etc. This way, we assume that a person with its surrounding subjects can be modeled by an implicit distribution D. Specifically, given a person c and its neighbors (with closer distance), we have

$$H_c \triangleq (\mathbf{V}_c, \mathbf{V}_n) \sim D, n \in \mathcal{N}_c, \tag{2}$$

where $\mathbf{V}_c$ is the extracted feature of the center subject c, and $\mathbf{V}_n$ with $n \in \mathcal{N}_c$ denotes the features of the neighboring subjects, which are identified by the spatial distance (in the image) to c within a threshold. We define H_c as the *neighbor feature cluster* by pairing the center subject and surrounding subjects.

To learn such distribution, we propose a self-supervised learning method. Our basic idea is that if the state (e.g., spatial position, human behavior) of a center subject is artificially changed, the states of its surrounding subjects can synergistically guide the center subject to be recovered to its original state. This way, as shown in Fig. 3, we first destroy the state of the feature block $\mathbf{V}$ and vary it by spatial-temporal transformation, i.e., swapping its position with another

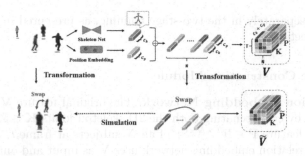

Fig. 3. An illustration of the feature transformation.

one, as shown in Fig. 1. We can perform the swapping directly in the feature space, to get $\tilde{\mathbf{V}}$ as

$$\tilde{\mathbf{V}} = \chi(\mathbf{V}) \in \mathbb{R}^{N \times C_v}, \tag{3}$$

where χ denotes the transformation operation.

The transformed feature $\tilde{\mathbf{V}}$ and its surrounding subjects are then fed to the BS-Head, which tries to recover the original feature $\mathbf{V}$. This way, with the BS-Head, the training process of the first-stage network can be implemented as

$$\hat{\mathbf{V}} = \text{BSHead}(\phi(\tilde{\mathbf{V}})) \to \mathbf{V}, \tag{4}$$

where BSHead denotes the rational-behavior simulator head. It tries to generate a recovered feature $\hat{\mathbf{V}}$ tending to approximate the original feature $\mathbf{V}$. Here ϕ denotes the social relation embedding network as discussed in Sect. 3.2. For the behavior simulator head (BS-Head), we adopt the structure in the graph convolution neural network TXP-CNN [25].

Discussion. As shown in the left of Fig. 4, the transformed feature $\tilde{\mathbf{V}} \in \mathbb{R}^{T \times N \times C_v}$ is constructed by the skeleton feature $\mathbf{K}$ and the positional feature $\tilde{\mathbf{P}}$, where the transformation operation χ is only applied to the positional feature $\mathbf{P}$, i.e., we simulate to exchange the position of a subject with another while maintaining its skeleton (representing the action and pose of a human). This may make the subject with original behavior in the swapped position look unreasonable with its (new) neighbors (see subjects A and B' in the right of Fig. 1). Also, the BSHead actually only outputs the recovered positional feature $\hat{\mathbf{P}}$ (not including the skeleton feature), which is self-supervised by that from the original feature block $\mathbf{P}$, as shown in Fig. 2.

3.4   Supervised Group Prediction Head

The above behavior simulator head is mainly used for training the social relation embedding network ϕ in a self-supervised manner, which, however, can not provide the group detection results. We propose the group detection head, as shown in Fig. 5, which consists of a stacked attention module (Stack-Att), a GRU, and a linear layer to predict the human relation matrix, which will be

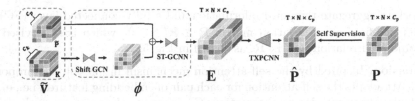

Fig. 4. An illustration of the self-supervised behavior simulator head, which trains the relation embedding network with the BS-Head in a self-supervised manner.

post-processed by a label propagation method [44] to generate the predicted human group results.

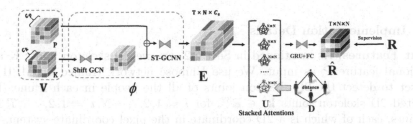

Fig. 5. An illustration of the second stage of our method, based on the relation embedding features obtained by the first stage, which trains the network with the group prediction head for generating the final group detection results.

This head takes the original feature block $\mathbf{V}$ as input, which is first fed into the embedding network ϕ (trained by the first stage) to get social relation embedding $\mathbf{E} \in \mathbb{R}^{T \times N \times C_e}$. We then apply a stacked attention modules (Stack-Att), which uses M (a pre-set parameter) independent attention module operating separately as

$$\text{att}^m(\mathbf{e}_i, \mathbf{e}_j) = \frac{\theta(\mathbf{e}_i)^T \theta(\mathbf{e}_j)}{\sqrt{L}} \in \mathbb{R}, \quad m = 1, 2, \cdots, M, \quad (5)$$

where $\mathbf{e}_i \in \mathbb{R}^{C_e}$ denotes an element of $\mathbf{E}$, and $\theta(\mathbf{e}_i) = \mathbf{W}_\theta \mathbf{e}_i + \mathbf{b}_\theta$ is the learnable linear transformations, L denotes the vector length of $\theta(\mathbf{e}_i)$. For each frame containing N subjects, we generate $N \times N$ pairs of elements (i, j). For all $T \times N \times N$ element pairs (i, j) in T frames, we get the pair-wise relation map $\mathbf{A}^m \in \mathbb{R}^{T \times N \times N}$ with the value $A^m_{(i,j)} = \text{att}^m(\mathbf{e}_i, \mathbf{e}_j)$, calculated by the attention module. Then we stack all the relation map from M attention modules for all T frames to be a *stacked attention block* $\mathbf{U} \in \mathbb{R}^{T \times N \times N \times M}$ as a multi-channel relation feature block. Besides, considering the camera view in this problem is often very wide, and the persons with far distance couldn't be in one group, we also stack a distance matrix $\mathbf{D} \in \mathbb{R}^{T \times N \times N \times 1}$ on $\mathbf{U}$ to get the final relation block $\mathbf{U}_D \in \mathbb{R}^{T \times N \times N \times (M+1)}$. This block is then fed to a single layer GRU temporal network to aggregate temporal information and a fully-connected layer (FC) to predict the final group relation matrix $\hat{\mathbf{R}} \in \mathbb{R}^{T \times N \times N}$, which is supervised by the annotated relation matrix $\mathbf{R}$, as shown in Fig. 5.

Discussion. Inspired by the self-attention mechanism in [38,40], the proposed Stack-Att adopts the self-attention for each pair of embedding features, i.e., $\mathbf{e}_i, \mathbf{e}_j$ to calculate their relation representation. Compared to the previous methods for relation (edge) feature representation, e.g., directly concatenating the embedding features, the proposed strategy is more memory-efficient, which can handle the challenge of a large number of people in the crowd scene. Besides, the self-attention mechanism can better represent the relation between two embedding features. Our method is also different from [38,40], which only produce 1-channel edge attention matrix. We apply it M times independently and stack them as a multi-channel edge feature block.

3.5   Implementation Details

Input Features. As mentioned in Sect. 3.2, we use 2D skeleton joints $\mathbf{K}$ and positional feature $\mathbf{P}$ as input. We use Unipose network trained on MPII [1] dataset to detect the 2D skeleton joints of all the people in each frame. The detected 2D skeleton joints $\mathbf{k}_i^t \in \mathbb{R}^{32}$, for $i = 1, 2, \cdots, N, t = 1, 2, \cdots, T$ has 16 joints, each of which is a 2D coordinate in the pixel coordinate system. We also use the positional encoding method [38] to project the 2D position of each subject's center to the 32-dimension space as the positional feature $\mathbf{P}$.

Two-Stage Training. In the first stage, we use the self-supervised training strategy as discussed in Sect. 3.3 to train the whole network using the relation-behavior simulator head, which outputs $\hat{\mathbf{P}}$ and we use MSE as loss criterion to enforce $\hat{\mathbf{P}}$ be close to $\mathbf{P}$. In the first training stage, we apply the swap operation to the training data. For the PANDA dataset, we first randomly select 10% persons in the scene and shuffle their positions as the swap operation. For JRDB dataset, since some frames only contain less than 10 persons, the selection ratio is 20%. Besides, to make the recovering of swap not equal to copying one's origin position, we add small random noises following the uniform distribution on the swapped positions.

In the second stage, we use the trained social relation embedding network ϕ (in the first stage) with only the group prediction head to predict the group relation matrix $\hat{\mathbf{R}}$, which is enforced to be close to the ground-truth $\mathbf{R}$. Here we flatten the group relation matrix and use the cosine similarity loss as a criterion during training. This stage of training is a supervised training process, but it mainly updates the parameters of the group prediction head. This stage also fine-tunes the parameters of the social relation embedding network ϕ, which could further boost the performance of the whole framework on the group detection task. With the first stage self-supervised training for ϕ, the second stage can use few labeled data for training, which is also verified in the experiments.

We use stochastic gradient descent with Adam optimizer to optimize the parameters. The training of stage 1 takes 200 epochs with the learning rate of

1×10^{-4}. And the training of stage 2 takes 100 epochs with the learning rate of 7×10^{-3}. The proposed method is implemented based on the PyTorch framework.

Network Inference. Given the input features $\mathbf{V}$, the inference stage only goes through the group prediction head and outputs the group relation matrix $\hat{\mathbf{R}} \in \mathbb{R}^{T \times N \times N}$. Then we use the label propagation method [44] to split N persons of each frame into non-overlapped groups, where the number of groups is automatically estimated by the algorithm. The groups only containing one person are dropped.

4   Experiments

4.1   Datasets and Metrics

- *PANDA benchmark.* We first choose the state-of-the-art dataset PANDA [39] for group detection evaluation. It is a multi-human video dataset covering real-world street scenes with a very wide field-of-view (1 km^2 area) and a very dense crowd in the scene, e.g., $4k$ subjects in one frame. For the group detection task, it provides 9 long-term videos in different scenes. The training set has 8 videos while the testing set has 1 video, as specified in the benchmark. The average number of frames and bounding boxes per video in the training set is $2,713$ and $1,070.4k$, respectively, while the number of frames and bounding boxes in the testing set is $3,500$ and $335.2k$, respectively. The average number of the human group per video is 144.6 and 75 in the training and testing video sets, respectively. The PANDA dataset provides human tracking for the group detection task and their baseline methods with evaluation metrics for comparison.
- *JRDB-Group benchmark.* We also include a new benchmark, i.e., JRDB-Group [8], for performance evaluation. JRDB-Group is built based on the JRDB dataset [24], which is captured by a panoramic camera equipped on a robot walking around in the crowded outdoor/indoor multi-person scenes. JRDB-Group provides the human social group annotation, and we use 20 training and 7 testing videos in JRDB-Group in our experiment. Following the setting in JRDB-Group, we evaluate the group detection task on the key frames, which are also sampled every 15 frames, generating $1,419$ training and 404 testing samples.

Following the metrics in PANDA benchmark [39], we use the classical Half metrics [6] including precision, recall, and F$_1$ scores with group member $IoU > 0.5$ for group detection evaluation.

4.2   Results

Comparison Methods. We find that most group detection methods are obsolete without available source code. We try our best to include more related methods with necessary modifications for comparison.

- *Dis.Mat* + [44]: We first consider a straightforward method in which we calculate the distance among all subjects in the crowd and apply the label propagation algorithm [44] used in our inference stage to get the group division.
- *GNN w GRU*: We apply a graph neural network (GNN) with the features in our method as the node feature to model the group relations among the subjects, in which we also apply a GRU model to integrate the temporal information.
- *ARG* is a state-of-the-art method [40] for human group activity recognition. ARG trains an Inception-v3 network to extract the appearance features and uses GNN to model the mutual relations among the subjects in the crowd. We use the affinity matrix in GNN as the relation matrix for group membership division.
- *Global-to-local* [39] is the baseline method proposed in PANDA [39], which applies a global-to-local zoom in framework to validate the incremental effectiveness of local visual clues to global trajectories. More specifically, human entities and their relationships are represented as a graph. Then a global-to-local strategy is applied, and the video interaction scores among subjects are estimated by a spatial-temporal ConvNet. The edges in the graph are merged using label propagation, and the cliques remaining in the graph are the group detection results.
- *Joint* and *JRDB-Group* are the baselines in JRDB-Group benchmark [8]. *Joint* [7] proposes to integrate the human group detection task into the group activity recognition problem. Based on it, *JRDB-Group* adds the human spatial features and number of group constraints as losses for the group detection task.

We compare the group detection results of the proposed method and other comparison methods. Table 1 shows the comparative results on the PANDA benchmark. We can see that all the comparison methods, including the state-of-the-art baseline method Global-to-local reported in the PANDA benchmark and its variants, generate unsatisfactory results. The comparison method with the best performance, i.e., *ARG*, generates an F_1 score of 25.4%. The proposed method significantly improves the group detection performance and provides a promising result with an F_1 score of 53.2%. We can see similar results on JRDB-Group as shown in Table 2, in which we can see that the comparison methods can generate relatively better results than in PANDA. We also surprisingly find that the simple baseline methods, i.e., the 'distance matrix + [44]' and the 'GNN + GRU', provide not bad performance. This is because the number of pedestrians and crowd density in JRDB-Group is lower than those in PANDA. The proposed method provides the best performance on JRDB-Group, which also outperforms the comparison methods by a large margin.

4.3 Ablation Study

To verify the effectiveness of our method, we conduct the ablation study as below.

Table 1. Comparative group detection results on PANDA (%).

Method	Precision	Recall	F1
Dis.Mat + [44]	42.9	12.0	18.8
GNN w GRU	41.9	17.3	24.5
ARG [40]	34.9	20.0	25.4
Group-to-local [39]	23.7	12.0	16.0
Group-to-local w Random [39]	24.4	13.3	17.2
Group-to-local w Uncertainty [39]	29.3	16.0	20.7
Ours	**55.9**	**50.7**	**53.2**

Table 2. Comparative group detection results on JRDB-Group (%).

Method	Precision	Recall	F1
Dis.Mat + [44]	57.3	23.5	33.4
GNN w GRU	43.4	28.6	34.5
ARG [40]	32.5	38.4	35.2
Joint [7]	30.0	28.4	29.1
JRDB-Group [9]	39.0	37.9	38.4
Ours	**57.7**	**56.2**	**56.9**

- **Ours w/o self-sup. 1st-train.** denotes removing the self-supervised representation training in the first stage in our method, and we directly train the whole network (including the representation embedding module and the group forming module) using the training dataset.
- **Ours w/o self-rep. fine-tune.** denotes removing the representation's fine-tuning in our method, and we fix the parameters in the representation embedding module obtained by the self-supervised first-stage training and only train the group prediction head with the training dataset.

As shown in Table 3, we can first see that the proposed network with direct one-stage training can provide acceptable performance at both datasets, which outperforms the baseline methods significantly with F_1 scores of 44.5% on PANDA and 48.8% on JRDB-Group, respectively. Compared with the full two-stage training version of our method, we can also see that the self-supervised representation in the first-stage training is very effective, which further improves the F_1 score to 53.2% on PANDA and 56.9% on JRDB-Group, respectively. Besides, we find that representation networko fine-tuning with the training dataset is also useful in our method.

Table 3. Ablation study results on PANDA and JRDB-Group datasets (%).

Method	PANDA			JRDB-Group		
	Precision	Recall	F1	Precision	Recall	F1
w/o (self-sup.) 1st-train	48.4	41.3	44.6	49.8	47.8	48.8
w/o (self-rep.) fine-tune.	58.6	45.3	51.1	50.3	48.1	49.2
Ours	55.9	50.7	53.2	57.7	56.2	56.9

4.4   In-depth Analysis

Label annotations for the human group detection in a large-scale scene are laborious. Therefore, we propose the self-supervised relation representation, and further investigate the its performance using different amounts of training data.

As shown in Table 4, we can first see that the proposed method without the self-supervised first-stage training provides a poor performance with the reduction of training data. Specifically on the PANDA dataset, using very few training data, i.e., 10% of all, the group detection F_1 score is only 27.6%, which is much inferior to that using all training data. For the method with the self-supervised first-stage training but without fine-tuning, although performance drops, the results using 10% training data are acceptable with the F_1 score of 37% and 43.8% on PANDA and JRDB-Group, respectively. Similarly, the full version of our method provides very promising results with only 10% training data on two benchmarks. We can see that, on PANDA benchmark with 10% training

Table 4. Performance analysis using different amount of training data on PANDA and JRDB-Group datasets (%).

Method	Data	PANDA			JRDB-Group		
		Precision	Recall	F1	Precision	Recall	F1
Ours w/o 1st-train	10% Train.	37.7	30.7	33.8	40.5	22.7	29.1
	30% Train.	41.9	34.7	38.0	39.1	46.0	42.2
	50% Train.	49.1	37.3	42.2	37.5	48.8	42.4
	100% Train.	48.4	41.3	44.6	49.8	47.8	48.8
Ours w/o fine-tune.	10% Train.	61.7	38.7	47.5	38.4	50.9	43.8
	30% Train.	54.1	44.0	48.5	51.6	44.0	47.5
	50% Train.	54.8	45.3	49.6	49.1	45.5	47.3
	100% Train.	58.6	45.3	51.1	50.3	48.1	49.2
Ours	10% Train.	43.5	36.0	39.4	42.2	46.4	44.2
	30% Train.	46.9	40.0	43.2	52.9	42.8	47.3
	50% Train.	55.1	50.7	52.8	53.9	42.4	47.4
	100% Train.	55.9	50.7	53.2	57.7	56.2	56.9

data, the full version 'Ours' produces 40.9% F_1 score, significantly outperforming the version without first-stage training (27.6% F_1 score). It is even higher than the version without first-stage training using 50% labeled training data (39.8% F_1 score). Similar results can be seen on the JRDB-Group benchmark. This demonstrates the effectiveness of the proposed self-supervised first-stage training strategy, which can reduce the dependence of the deep network on large-scale annotated training data. We can also see that 'Ours w/o fine-tune.' produces promising results when using a small amount of training data, e.g., 10% and 30%. This is because this setting without training the first-stage representation network significantly reduces the network parameters to be learned.

We further provide the group detection results using two new metrics. The commonly-used Half metric [6] takes a fixed threshold of 0.5 of group IOU for evaluating the group detection accuracy. In some cases, the threshold of 0.5 is a little loose, and a single threshold may bring in bias. This way, we vary the group IOU threshold of 0.5 in the classical Half metric to larger values until 1 and then calculate the corresponding group detection performance. We plot the curve using the abscissa axis as the threshold, and the vertical axis is the F_1 score under each threshold. Then we compute the AUC (Area Under The Curve) score as the metric for evaluation.

As a harsher metric, we also calculate the matrix IOU of the predicted group relation matrix $\hat{\mathbf{R}}$ and the ground-truth $\mathbf{R}_{gt}$ by $IOU^{GM} = \frac{\sum AND(\hat{\mathbf{R}}, \mathbf{R}_{gt})}{\sum OR(\hat{\mathbf{R}}, \mathbf{R}_{gt})}$, where AND and OR denotes the logical operations functions, and $\sum$ denotes the summation over all values. The group relation metric encodes the group relations between each pair of subjects, and the metric IOU^{GM} evaluates the pair-wise group relation accuracy among all subjects.

Table 5. Comparative group detection results using IOU-AUC and IOU^{GM} (%).

	PANDA		JRDB-Group	
	IOU-AUC	IOU^{GM}	IOU-AUC	IOU^{GM}
Dis.Mat + [44]	17.0	5.9	14.1	12.9
GNN w GRU	16.3	6.5	21.7	20.1
ARG [40]	19.3	6.4	21.6	19.3
Joint [7]	–	–	20.4	16.6
JRDB-Group [9]	–	–	26.3	20.6
Ours	41.2	31.2	42.5	32.5

We show the results using the new metrics in Table 5. Note that, on the PANDA dataset, we do not conduct the experiments using the methods of Joint and JRDB-Group, since their deep CNN features can not be applied to the scene with thousands of people in the PANDA dataset. We can not provide the evaluation of new metrics for the baseline methods in PANDA, i.e., 'Group-to-local', because it did not provide the source code and raw results. From Table 5 we can first see that our method shows remarkable performance compared to the other methods. Specifically, on the JRDB dataset under the metrics of IOU-AUC and IOU^{GM}, the simple baseline method using the distance metric based method can not provide comparable or better results than other methods like that in Table 2. We can also see that the performance under IOU^{GM} is generally low. This also leaves space for the development of more effective algorithms.

5   Conclusion

In this paper, we have proposed a new framework for social group detection in large-scale multi-person scenes. We developed a double-head two-stage network for the human relation representation and group detection, in which we designed a self-supervised first-stage training strategy for relation representation. We evaluated the proposed method on two state-of-the-art benchmarks, i.e., PANDA and JRDB-Group. The proposed method outperforms all the comparison methods by a very large margin. We also verified the effectiveness of the self-supervised representation training strategy by using very few (labeled) training data.

Acknowledgment. This work was supported in part by the National Natural Science Foundation of China under Grants U1803264, 62072334, and the Tianjin Research Innovation Project for Postgraduate Students under Grant 2021YJSB174.

References

1. Andriluka, M., Pishchulin, L., Gehler, P., Schiele, B.: 2D human pose estimation: new benchmark and state of the art analysis. In: IEEE Conference on Computer Vision and Pattern Recognition (2014)
2. Bagautdinov, T., Alahi, A., Fleuret, F., Fua, P., Savarese, S.: Social scene understanding: end-to-end multi-person action localization and collective activity recognition. In: IEEE Conference on Computer Vision and Pattern Recognition (2017)
3. Bazzani, L., Cristani, M., Murino, V.: Decentralized particle filter for joint individual-group tracking. In: IEEE Conference on Computer Vision and Pattern Recognition (2012)
4. Chang, M.C., Krahnstoever, N., Ge, W.: Probabilistic group-level motion analysis and scenario recognition. In: IEEE International Conference on Computer Vision (2011)
5. Cheng, K., Zhang, Y., He, X., Chen, W., Cheng, J., Lu, H.: Skeleton-based action recognition with shift graph convolutional network. In: IEEE/CVF Conference on Computer Vision and Pattern Recognition (2020)
6. Choi, W., Chao, Y.W., Pantofaru, C., Savarese, S.: Discovering groups of people in images. In: European Conference on Computer Vision (2014). https://doi.org/10.1007/978-3-319-10593-2_28

7. Ehsanpour, M., Abedin, A., Saleh, F., Shi, J., Reid, I., Rezatofighi, H.: Joint learning of social groups, individuals action and sub-group activities in videos. In: European Conference on Computer Vision (2020)
8. Ehsanpour, M., Saleh, F., Savarese, S., Reid, I., Rezatofighi, H.: JRDB-Act: a large-scale multi-modal dataset for spatio-temporal action, social group and activity detection. arXiv Preprint arXiv:2106.08827 (2021)
9. Ehsanpour, M., Saleh, F.S., Savarese, S., Reid, I.D., Rezatofighi, H.: JRDB-Act: a large-scale dataset for spatio-temporal action, social group and activity detection (2021)
10. Fan, L., Wang, W., Huang, S., Tang, X., Zhu, S.C.: Understanding human gaze communication by spatio-temporal graph reasoning. In: IEEE/CVF International Conference on Computer Vision (2019)
11. Feldmann, M., Fränken, D., Koch, W.: Tracking of extended objects and group targets using random matrices. IEEE Trans. Signal Process. 59(4), 1409–1420 (2010)
12. Fernando, T., Denman, S., Sridharan, S., Fookes, C.: GD-GAN: generative adversarial networks for trajectory prediction and group detection in crowds. In: Jawahar, C.V., Li, H., Mori, G., Schindler, K. (eds.) ACCV 2018. LNCS, vol. 11361, pp. 314–330. Springer, Cham (2019). https://doi.org/10.1007/978-3-030-20887-5_20
13. Gan, Y., Han, R., Yin, L., Feng, W., Wang, S.: Self-supervised multi-view multi-human association and tracking. In: ACM International Conference on Multimedia (2021)
14. Gavrilyuk, K., Sanford, R., Javan, M., Snoek, C.G.: Actor-transformers for group activity recognition. In: IEEE/CVF Conference on Computer Vision and Pattern Recognition (2020)
15. Ge, W., Collins, R.T., Ruback, R.B.: Vision-based analysis of small groups in pedestrian crowds. IEEE Trans. Patt. Anal. Mach. Intell. 34(5), 1003–1016 (2012)
16. Goel, A., Ma, K.T., Tan, C.: An end-to-end network for generating social relationship graphs. In: Proceedings of the IEEE/CVF Conference on Computer Vision and Pattern Recognition (2019)
17. Gupta, A., Johnson, J., Fei-Fei, L., Savarese, S., Alahi, A.: Social GAN: socially acceptable trajectories with generative adversarial networks. In: IEEE Conference on Computer Vision and Pattern Recognition (2018)
18. Han, R., Feng, W., Zhang, Y., Zhao, J., Wang, S.: Multiple human association and tracking from egocentric and complementary top views. IEEE TPAMI (2021). https://doi.org/10.1109/TPAMI.2021.3070562
19. Han, R., et al.: Complementary-view multiple human tracking. In: AAAI Conference on Artificial Intelligence (2020)
20. Han, R., Gan, Y., Li, J., Wang, F., Feng, W., Wang, S.: Connecting the complementary-view videos: joint camera identification and subject association. In: IEEE/CVF Conference on Computer Vision and Pattern Recognition (2022)
21. Han, R., Wang, Y., Yan, H., Feng, W., Wang, S.: Multi-view multi-human association with deep assignment network. IEEE TIP 31, 1830–1840 (2022)
22. Lerner, A., Chrysanthou, Y., Lischinski, D.: Crowds by example. In: Computer Graphics Forum (2007)
23. Li, W., Duan, Y., Lu, J., Feng, J., Zhou, J.: Graph-based social relation reasoning. In: Vedaldi, A., Bischof, H., Brox, T., Frahm, J.-M. (eds.) ECCV 2020. LNCS, vol. 12360, pp. 18–34. Springer, Cham (2020). https://doi.org/10.1007/978-3-030-58555-6_2
24. Martín-Martín, R., et al.: JRDB: a dataset and benchmark of egocentric robot visual perception of humans in built environments. IEEE Trans. Patt. Anal. Mach. Intell. (2021)

25. Mohamed, A., Qian, K., Elhoseiny, M., Claudel, C.: Social-STGCNN: a social spatio-temporal graph convolutional neural network for human trajectory prediction. In: IEEE/CVF Conference on Computer Vision and Pattern Recognition (2020)

26. Monfort, M., et al.: Moments in time dataset: one million videos for event understanding. IEEE Trans. Pattern Anal. Mach. Intell. **42**(2), 502–508 (2019)

27. Moussaïd, M., Perozo, N., Garnier, S., Helbing, D., Theraulaz, G.: The walking behaviour of pedestrian social groups and its impact on crowd dynamics. PloS One **5**(4), e10047 (2010)

28. Pang, S.K., Li, J., Godsill, S.J.: Detection and tracking of coordinated groups. IEEE Trans. Aerosp. Electron. Syst. **47**(1), 472–502 (2011)

29. Pellegrini, S., Ess, A., Schindler, K., Van Gool, L.: You'll never walk alone: modeling social behavior for multi-target tracking. In: IEEE International Conference on Computer Vision (2009)

30. Pellegrini, S., Ess, A., Van Gool, L.: Improving data association by joint modeling of pedestrian trajectories and groupings. In: European Conference on Computer Vision (2010)

31. Pramono, R.R.A., Chen, Y.T., Fang, W.H.: Empowering relational network by self-attention augmented conditional random fields for group activity recognition. In: Vedaldi, A., Bischof, H., Brox, T., Frahm, J.-M. (eds.) ECCV 2020. LNCS, vol. 12346, pp. 71–90. Springer, Cham (2020). https://doi.org/10.1007/978-3-030-58452-8_5

32. Shao, J., Dong, N., Zhao, Q.: A real-time algorithm for small group detection in medium density crowds. Patt. Recognit. Image Anal. **28**(2), 282–287 (2018)

33. Shao, J., Loy, C.C., Wang, X.: Scene-independent group profiling in crowd. In: IEEE Conference on Computer Vision and Pattern Recognition (2014)

34. Solera, F., Calderara, S., Cucchiara, R.: Socially constrained structural learning for groups detection in crowd. IEEE Trans. Pattern Anal. Mach. Intell. **38**(5), 995–1008 (2015)

35. Swofford, M., et al.: Improving social awareness through DANTE: deep affinity network for clustering conversational interactants. ACM Hum.-Comput. Interact. **4**(CSCW1), 1–23 (2020)

36. Thompson, S., Gupta, A., Gupta, A.W., Chen, A., Vázquez, M.: Conversational group detection with graph neural networks. In: International Conference on Multimodal Interaction (2021)

37. Turner, J.C.: Towards a cognitive redefinition of the social group. In: Research Colloquium on Social Identity of the European Laboratory of Social Psychology. Psychology Press (2010)

38. Vaswani, A., et al.: Attention is all you need. In: Advances in Neural Information Processing Systems (2017)

39. Wang, X., et al.: PANDA: a gigapixel-level human-centric video dataset. In: IEEE/CVF Conference on Computer Vision and Pattern Recognition (2020)

40. Wu, J., Wang, L., Wang, L., Guo, J., Wu, G.: Learning actor relation graphs for group activity recognition. In: IEEE/CVF Conference on Computer Vision and Pattern Recognition (2019)

41. Yamaguchi, K., Berg, A.C., Ortiz, L.E., Berg, T.L.: Who are you with and where are you going? In: IEEE Conference on Computer Vision and Pattern Recognition (2011)

42. Yan, R., Xie, L., Tang, J., Shu, X., Tian, Q.: Social adaptive module for weakly-supervised group activity recognition. In: Vedaldi, A., Bischof, H., Brox, T., Frahm,

J.-M. (eds.) ECCV 2020. LNCS, vol. 12353, pp. 208–224. Springer, Cham (2020). https://doi.org/10.1007/978-3-030-58598-3_13

43. Yuan, H., Ni, D.: Learning visual context for group activity recognition. In: AAAI Conference on Artificial Intelligence (2021)

44. Zhan, X., Liu, Z., Yan, J., Lin, D., Loy, C.C.: Consensus-driven propagation in massive unlabeled data for face recognition. In: European Conference on Computer Vision (2018)

45. Zhao, J., Han, R., Gan, Y., Wan, L., Feng, W., Wang, S.: Human identification and interaction detection in cross-view multi-person videos with wearable cameras. In: ACM International Conference on Multimedia (2020)

46. Zhou, T., Wang, W., Qi, S., Ling, H., Shen, J.: Cascaded human-object interaction recognition. In: IEEE/CVF Conference on Computer Vision and Pattern Recognition (2020)

47. Zou, C., et al.: End-to-end human object interaction detection with HOI transformer. In: IEEE/CVF Conference on Computer Vision and Pattern Recognition (2021)

K-centered Patch Sampling for Efficient Video Recognition

Seong Hyeon Park[1][✉], Jihoon Tack[1], Byeongho Heo[2], Jung-Woo Ha[2],
and Jinwoo Shin[1]

[1] Korea Advanced Institute of Science and Technology (KAIST),
Daejeon, South Korea
{seonghyp,jihoontack,jinwoos}@kaist.ac.kr
[2] NAVER AI LAB, Paris, France
{bh.heo,jungwoo.ha}@navercorp.com

Abstract. For decades, it has been a common practice to choose a sub-set of video frames for reducing the computational burden of a video understanding model. In this paper, we argue that this popular heuristic might be sub-optimal under recent transformer-based models. Specifically, inspired by that transformers are built upon patches of video frames, we propose to sample patches rather than frames using the greedy K-center search, *i.e.*, the farthest patch to what has been chosen so far is sampled iteratively. We then show that a transformer trained with the selected video patches can outperform its baseline trained with the video frames sampled in the traditional way. Furthermore, by adding a certain spatiotemporal structuredness condition, the proposed K-centered patch sampling can be even applied to the recent sophisticated video transformers, boosting their performance further. We demonstrate the superiority of our method on Something–Something and Kinetics datasets.

Keywords: Patch sampling · Video transformers · Efficient video recognition · K-center search · Farthest point sampling

1 Introduction

Video recognition, *i.e.*, recognizing events in a sequence of image frames, in real-world scenarios is an important yet challenging problem in computer vision [21]. Typically, the challenges originate from the dimensional complexity due to spatiotemporal characteristics of video data, *i.e.*, one has to design a model to handle both spatial information and temporal extent simultaneously. In this respect, transformer-based architectures [45] have recently shown remarkable performance for video recognition tasks [1,35], following their success in both spatial [3] and temporal [2,37] domains; they map each video frame to non-overlapping image patches and model the temporal sequence of frames as a sequence of patches.

Supplementary Information The online version contains supplementary material available at https://doi.org/10.1007/978-3-031-19833-5_10.

Table 1. Effects of sampling methods. We experiment with a simple extension of a DeiT-base (an image transformer) [43] to videos. We report Top-1 and Top-5 classification accuracies (%) on Something-Something v2 dataset. The bold denotes the best results. Values in parenthesis are relative improvements compared to the Random Frame sampling scheme.

Sampling methods	Top-1	Top-5
Random frame	58.95 (–)	85.03 (–)
Random patch	61.64 ($\triangle$4.56%)	86.32 ($\triangle$1.52%)
K-centered (ours)	**64.31**($\triangle$9.09%)	**90.38**($\triangle$6.29%)

(a) K-centered sampling   (b) Frame-based sampling

Fig. 1. Our proposed K-centered sampling and the frame-based sampling methods demonstrated in a Something-Something v2 video clip. The highlighted region denotes the sampled parts. As depicted, our method finds diverse and important patches from all frames, while the frame-based sampling ignores most of the frames. Note that the number of sampled patches are equal in (a) and (b).

Video transformers are, however, notorious for their high computing demand and CO_2 footprint [39], mainly due to the quadratic computational complexity (with respect to the number of patches) of the self-attention mechanism [45]. To address the issue, video transformers simply choose a subset of video frames to process and reduce the range of the self-attention to secure feasible computation costs, *e.g.*, dividing the spatiotemporal self-attention [3] or using local temporal self-attention [4]. Our motivation here is that the common heuristics of partially sampling frames from a long video [14,51], which we refer to as the frame-based sampling methods, can be improved or replaced.

Before the video transformers emerge, the frame-based sampling has been an inevitable design choice for prior convolutional architectures that require a regularly-structured input (*e.g.*, complete frames). However, it may not be an optimal choice with respect to representing the entire video information succinctly; the frame-based sampling might ignore an entire important frame and even contain redundant features, *e.g.*, backgrounds, with high probability [46,52]. In particular, the rationality of using this sampling strategy in video transformers is more questionable since transformers handle videos as patches (not frames); hence, they do not require such regular structures of the frame to be sampled.

Contribution. In this paper, we indeed argue that the popular frame-based sampling can be a sub-optimal choice for transformer-based models under several video recognition benchmarks. For example, we found that even randomly

sampling patches outperforms the frame-based sampling under a simple extension of a vision transformer [43] for video (see Table 1 for the details).

Motivated by this finding, we propose a simple yet effective patch-based
sampling strategy suitable for recent transformer-based video recognition models. To be specific, our scheme utilizes the greedy K-center search [16,19], where
patches farthest from each other in the geometric distance[1] are selected iteratively. Intuitively, such a strategy forces models to sample diverse yet discriminative patches from the video. Hence, models are expected to learn more informative spatiotemporal features. As in Fig. 1, our sampling scheme selects patches
that contain objects and humans, while frame-based sampling contains many
redundant background parts. By utilizing our scheme in a vision transformer
[43], we show that it outperforms both the frame-based sampling and the uniform random sampling, as reported in Table 1.

We further show that the proposed K-centered patch sampling strategy is
even applicable to sophisticated transformers variants [3,4,35] on video domain
that assumes a regular spatiotemporal structure in input patches. To this end,
we extend our scheme to control the level of structuredness in the sampling by
enforcing a constraint on how the sample patches are distributed in spatiotemporal regions of a given video. As a result, our method is compatible not only
with a plain vision transformer architecture but the sophisticated variants of
video transformers; one can achieve performance improvements purely due to
the replacement of their frame-based sampling method with our patch-based
sampling scheme.

We demonstrate the efficacy of our method through evaluations on video
recognition datasets, including Kinetics 200 & 400 [22,49] and Something-
Something v2 (SSv2) [18] datasets. Overall, our scheme consistently improves
the action classification accuracy compared to the frame-based sampling across
various transformer architectures ranging from a simple vision transformer to
recent video transformers, *e.g.*, it improves the top-1 classification accuracy by
(relatively) up to 4.80% (71.42% → 74.85%) and 2.13% (62.50% → 63.83%) for
Kinetics-400 and SSv2, respectively.

The importance of how to manipulate video data for building efficient video
understanding models has been largely dismissed in the literature. Along with
recent developments of video transformer architectures, we show that the conventional frame sampling method can underperform a new simple patch-based
sampling scheme. We believe that our work would inspire many new future
intriguing directions for the important problem. Our code is available at https://
github.com/kami93/kcenter_video.

2   Related Works

Convolution-Based Video Recognition. Recent works approach video
recognition tasks as a temporal extension of image classification. To this end,

---

[1] Denotes a vector distance between patches; not a distance between patch's coordinates in the video.

most of the prior works suggested a temporal extension of convolutional neural networks (CNNs) based on the remarkable success of CNNs in modeling spatial distributions, *e.g.*, 2D CNNs with an additional network for temporal dimension [10,40] and 3D CNNs for joint spatiotemporal modeling [5,15,44]. However, despite the great success of CNNs in video recognition, recent works found vision transformer-based models outperform their CNN counterparts [1]. Upon this success of transformer-based video models, we develop a new patch-based sampling method for an efficient video transformer.

Transformer-Based Video Recognition. The transformer-based architecture has recently gained interest for modeling both spatial [25,43] and temporal distributions [9,50]. Following this line of research, recent works considered the temporal extension of vision transformer (ViT) [11] for an effective spatiotemporal understanding of videos [12,23,26,34,35]. However, due to the computational burden of the self-attention mechanism [45] of the transformer, only recently, some proposed efficient self-attention methods to overcome this issue [3,4]. In this paper, we tackle this problem in a different yet orthogonal direction by suggesting a new efficient patch sampling strategy from the video.

Efficient Video Recognition. Due to the high dimensional nature of video datasets, various works have focused on developing efficient video recognition frameworks, *e.g.*, architectural design [13,31], frame quantization [41], and resolution control [30]. Among various approaches, frame-based sampling, *e.g.*, randomly sampling frames from a long video, is one the most commonly used scheme for efficient learning [5,21,44]. In this regard, more advanced frame-based sampling methods have been proposed, *e.g.*, Wu *et al.* [48] sample relevant frames with reinforcement learning, and Gowda *et al.* [17] consider the relationship between the selected frames when sampling. Nevertheless, these sampling methods were mainly built upon convolution-based architectures. In this paper, we propose a sampling strategy that is specialized for video transformers.

Efficient Token Pooling. Recent works found that vision transformers often rely on a small portion of patches, *i.e.*, also referred to as tokens, when classifying the objects [33,38]. Motivated by this, there were several attempts to drop or aggregate redundant tokens at the internal feature space for efficient training [6,24,28,29]. Concurrent to our work, Wang *et al.* [47] proposed a token selection scheme for video transformers by pooling informative tokens in both spatial and temporal dimensions. While it is maybe seemingly similar to our work, we remark that our work does not access any internal representation of transformers. Therefore, it is orthogonal to the prior token pooling works.

3   *K*-centered Patch Sampling

In this section, we compare the frame-based and the patch-based sampling approaches and explain how the latter can be applied to video data (Sect. 3.1). Then, we describe our proposed *K*-center search for more enhancing patch-based sampling of a video (Sect. 3.2). Finally, we introduce an extension of our method for controlling the amount of the structural characteristics in a set of patch-based samples of a video, which is required and exploited by sophisticated video transformer architectures (Sect. 3.3).

As for the notations, we use plain lower-case letters to denote vectors (e.g., $x \in \mathbb{R}^D$), boldface lower-case letters for multi-dimensional matrices (e.g., $\boldsymbol{x} \in \mathbb{R}^{N \times D}$ and $\boldsymbol{y} \in \mathbb{R}^{N \times M \times D}$), and other letters are scalars unless otherwise defined (e.g., an upper-case letter $X \in \mathbb{R}$). Letters with subscripts are used to denote the ith element given an ordered finite set (e.g., $x_i \in \mathbb{R}^D$ given $\{x_1, ..., x_N\} \equiv \boldsymbol{x} \in \mathbb{R}^{N \times D}$).

3.1   Patch-Based Sampling

Consider a video clip $\boldsymbol{v} \in \mathbb{R}^{T \times H \times W \times C}$, where T is the frame length, $H \times W$ is the spatial resolution, and C is the number of channels (e.g., for RGB, $C = 3$) for the video. The frame-based sampling has been a common standard in video recognition models, which maps $\boldsymbol{v}$ to a matrix of sample frames $\boldsymbol{f} \in \mathbb{R}^{F \times H \times W \times C}$, by indexing the frame indices (i.e., the time dimension) so that the frame length to be used for recognition is reduced to $F < T$. The frame-based sampling has served as a core component to curtail the computational burden in video recognition tasks, specifically well mingling with video convolutional neural networks (CNNs).

Meanwhile, the emergence of transformer models in image recognition tasks [11,20,25,43] has also brought a paradigm shift in video models [1,3,4,35], where a video should be viewed as a set of patch vectors instead of the long-established $H \times W$ grid view. These patch vectors, each of which serves an elementary input entity in vision transformers, are derived by rearranging an image (or equivalently a video frame) $\boldsymbol{i} \in \mathbb{R}^{H \times W \times C}$ into a patch matrix $\boldsymbol{p} \in \mathbb{R}^{(H \cdot W / P^2) \times D}$, where $D = P^2 \cdot C$ and P is a patch's edge length as initially proposed by ViT [11]. It is straightforward to prolong this concept for videos by simply prepending an additional time dimension and considering a rearrange mapping $\boldsymbol{v} \in \mathbb{R}^{T \times H \times W \times C} \mapsto \boldsymbol{p} \in \mathbb{R}^{(T \cdot H \cdot W / P^2) \times D}$. In this way, the video is presented as a matrix with its rows composed of patch vectors (without forcing explicit multidimensional structure present in the indices; i.e., the indices are flattened). Note that the rearrange operation does not materialize a new data matrix nor require any extra FLOPs, as it just produces an alternate view of the same data.

Nevertheless, the previous art for video transformers is mostly built upon the traditional frame-based scheme for sampling[2]: $\mathbb{R}^{T \times (H \cdot W / P^2)} \mapsto \mathbb{R}^{F \times (H \cdot W / P^2)} \mapsto \mathbb{R}^{(F \cdot H \cdot W / P^2)}$. Instead, we argue that, for the transformers, directly sampling on the patches—$\mathbb{R}^{(T \cdot H \cdot W / P^2)} \mapsto \mathbb{R}^K$—can be more effective, and we refer to this alternate sampling scheme as the patch-based sampling. Likewise the frame-based sampling, there can also be many instances of patch-based sampling, including the grid-sampling, random sampling, and our proposed K-centered sampling that we describe in the following subsection.

---

[2] We omit the last dimension D for simplicity.

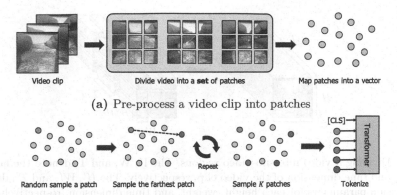

(a) Pre-process a video clip into patches

(b) Select *K*-centered patches with greedy farthest point sampling

Fig. 2. Concept figure of our *K*-centered patch sampling for video transformers. Our method first (a) pre-processes a video clip into a set of patches and maps each patch into a vector with a fixed position encoding. Then (b) sample *K* patches by running the greedy farthest point sampling algorithm. Note that we utilize a learnable positional embedding when training the video transformers.

3.2 Greedy *K*-center Search

Given a video represented by a set of patch vectors $p \equiv \{p_1, ..., p_N\} \in \mathbb{R}^{N \times D}$, we propose to employ the greedy *K*-center searching [16,19], also known as the farthest point sampling (FPS) [36] algorithm, for sampling *K* patches $p' \equiv \{p'_1, p'_2, ..., p'_K\} \in \mathbb{R}^{K \times D}$. It basically chooses a subset of patches iteratively, in a way that p'_k is the farthest vector in geometric distance (*e.g.*, Euclidean norm $\|\cdot\|$ of the difference) with respect to previously sampled patches, as described by (1):

$$p'_k = \operatorname*{argmax}_{p_i \in p \setminus \{p'_1, ..., p'_{k-1}\}} \min_{p'_j \in \{p'_1, ..., p'_{k-1}\}} \|p_i - p'_j\|. \tag{1}$$

The complexity of the greedy *K*-center searching is $\mathcal{O}(KN)$, and it has long been considered one of the valid options for sampling from a set, known to have better coverage over the original set compared to random sampling methods [16,19,36].

The motivation for choosing greedy *K*-center search, however, is not limited to its computational efficiency or the excellence in the coverage but includes its generality and flexibility in designing sampling attributes. For example, while sampling algorithms such as random sampling or grid sampling determine the sampling indices solely based on the coordinate of patches in videos, we might want to consider the other attributes, such as the RGB feature of patches.

Since the greedy *K*-center search is built upon comparing mutual distances between vectors, adding extra attributes can simply be done by concatenating any attributes to the vectors. In other words, we can build *K*-center considering

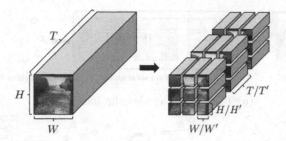

Fig. 3. Dividing a video into sub-video regions. The H, W, and T, denote the height, weight, and time dimension of the video clip, respectively. The H', W', and T', denote the division parameters for each height, weight, and time dimension, respectively.

spatial and temporal distance by concatenating spatiotemporal coordinates to the RGB color vectors.

Concerning the scale, without loss of generality, we normalize the range of the patch's values (*e.g.*, the RGB values) to $\left[0, D^{-\frac{1}{4}}\right]$. Then, we encode the spatiotemporal coordinate of a patch v_i, $T_i \in [1, T]$, $H_i \in [1, H]$ and $W_i \in [1, W]$ to a normalized positional encoding $\left(\frac{T_i-1}{T-1}, \frac{H_i-1}{\sqrt{2}(H-1)}, \frac{W_i-1}{\sqrt{2}(W-1)}\right)$ to concatenate it with the patch vector prior to performing the K-center search based on color shape, spatial and temporal distance. In addition, we introduce the coefficients ω_s and ω_t, which give priority between colors, temporal distance, and spatial distance upon searching:

$$\tilde{p}_i = \left(p_i; \left(\frac{\omega_t\,(T_i-1)}{T-1}, \frac{\omega_s\,(H_i-1)}{\sqrt{2}(H-1)}, \frac{\omega_s\,(W_i-1)}{\sqrt{2}(W-1)}\right)\right). \tag{2}$$

By adjusting ω_s and ω_t in (2), one can customize how the samples are chosen given a vector. Some examples are depicted in Fig. 6.

3.3   Structure-Aware K-Center Search

Although the greedy K-center search is directly applicable to general vision transformer models, we may further consider an extension of our method toward video transformers.

In general, video transformers are composed of sophisticated attention mechanisms that leverage the structured shape in frame-based inputs (*i.e.*, inputs with $T \times H \times W$ shape). Since patch-based sampling methods inherently break this structure by rearranging a video into a 1-dimensional sequence of vectors, it is often non-trivial for them to sample patches without losing a certain structure demanded by video transformers.

To preserve the structural information for video transformers, we design an extension of our method coined *structure-aware* K-centered sampling, which controls the amount of structuredness by defining a video with a set of spatiotemporal chunks as shown in Fig. 3, which enforces the same numbers of patches to be sampled for every chunk.

To be specific, we introduce the division parameters T', H' and W' to our method and consider the set of sub-tensor regions of an input video $v \equiv \{\bar{v}_1, ..., \bar{v}_S\}$ where $\bar{v}_s \in \mathbb{R}^{\frac{T}{T'} \times \frac{H}{H'} \times \frac{W}{W'} \times C}$. Then, throughout the iterations for K-centered sampling, we track the number of patches sampled at each region and constrain them to be equal in all regions.

As a consequence, the resultant sample patches from the structure-aware K-centered sampling can have a certain amount of spatiotemporal structuredness controlled by the division parameters T', H' and W'. Intuitively, the higher we set the values for the division parameters, the more structuredness in the sample patches would be preserved by the sampler. We employ this extension to enable our method to be compatible with recent video transformer architectures.

Finally, we also consider another way to bring out extra structuredness in inputs by combining patch sampling with frame sampling, which we refer to as hybrid sampling. Specifically, we grid-sample some frames from a video, and then we conduct patch sampling from the remaining frames. It is just the same as patch sampling on a video with fewer frames. We find empirically that hybrid sampling is sometimes useful to further boost the model performance in a practical scenario.

4 Experiments

We verify the effectiveness of our technique on video action classification datasets. First, the performance gain achieved by our K-centered patch-based sampling compared to the frame-based sampling is investigated. To do so, we compare the classification accuracies of various transformers, varying from a naïve extension of ViT [11] (an image transformer) tweaked for video processing to recent sophisticated video transformers [3,4,35] trained with the two sampling methods in different datasets. Our results exhibit that incorporating our K-centered sampling into these transformer models generally provides performance gains without architectural modification. Finally, we perform various analyses to understand the effect of our patch-based sampling in video recognition.

4.1 Experimental Setups

Datasets. We evaluate the performance of our proposed models on two sets of video classification benchmarks:

- **Kinetics 400 and 200** [22,49]. Kinetics-400 consists of 10-second videos sampled at 25 frame-per-second from YouTube, categorized into 400 action classes. For the ablation study, we evaluate on Kinetics-200 dataset, which is a subset with 200 classes randomly sampled from the full Kinetics-400 dataset. As Kinetics is a dynamic dataset (videos may be removed from YouTube), we note our training and validation dataset sizes are approximately 240,000 and 20,000, respectively, for Kinetics-400, and 80,000 and 5,000, respectively, for Kinetics-200.

– **Something–Something v2 (SSv2)** [18]. SSv2 contains 220,847 videos, with 168,913 in the training set, 24,777 in the validation set, and 27,157 in the test set. The dataset consists of 174 labels and the video duration range from 2 to 6 s. In contrast to the other video datasets, the objects and backgrounds are consistent across different action classes. Hence, the model requires understanding temporal motion to generalize on SSv2 dataset.

Network Architectures. We compare the video classification performance of the patch-based sampled transformer (our method) with frame-based baselines comprising various recent video transformer models [3, 4, 11, 35]. For each model, we consider several different choices of the number of the input frames considered by models (or, equivalently, the number of patches for our model). For fair comparisons, we use the ImageNet-1k [8] pre-trained ViT-Base model[3] when initializing all video transformers. The details of each architecture are as:

– **ViT** [11]. ViT learns the spatial relationship of the patches with a learnable position encoding which is added during the tokenization step. To extend ViT to video recognition, we additionally consider temporal positional embedding when tokenizing the patches.
– **TimeSformer** [3]. TimeSformer adapts the ViT to video by proposing a divided space-time attention mechanism to learn the temporal feature in an efficient manner. We use the base TimeSformer architecture, which requires 8 frames as an input, *i.e.*, equivalent to 1,568 patches.
– **Motionformer** [35]. Motionformer extends the ViT with a newly proposed trajectory attention which implicitly aggregates the motion path of the object. We utilize the base Motionformer model, which processes 1,568 tokens.
– **XViT** [4]. XViT proposes local temporal attention and a space-time mixing scheme to reduce the computational burden of the full self-attention mechanism. We use the XViT model with 16 frames input for SSv2 dataset and 8 frames input for Kinetics dataset.

Training Details. For all experiments, we follow most training details of Patrick *et al.* [35]—especially dataset augmentation methods—for training all baselines and our method. Concretely, we use the AdamW optimizer [27] with a weight decay of 0.05, label smoothing [42] with a smoothing constant of 0.2, and mixed precision training [32]. For the data augmentation, we utilize random frame selection, random size jittering, and random crop for all datasets. For SSv2, we additionally utilize RandAugment [7] with a severity magnitude of 20 and one augmentation operation per video clip; note that we apply the same augmentation per video clip. Unless otherwise specified, we set both the spatial and temporal search coefficients of K-centered patch sampling, *i.e.*, ω_s, ω_t, to 1.0.

---

[3] We utilize the original ViT-B weights to ensure the fair comparison, unlike Table 1 that utilizes DeiT-base.

Table 2. Comparison of our K-centered sampling and frame-based sampling methods in Kinetics-400 (K400) and Something-Something v2 (SSv2) datasets. We report Top-1 and Top-5 action classification accuracies (%) on validation sets of the datasets. Computational budgets for forwarding a video sample are equal between the same model. For a fair comparison, we unify all models to use the same ImageNet-1k pre-training and evaluation protocols. The bold denotes the best result.

Model	Sampling	K400		SSv2	
		Top-1	Top-5	Top-1	Top-5
ViT [11]	Frame-based	74.80	91.65	62.50	88.06
	K-centered (ours)	**75.65**	**92.04**	**63.83**	**88.89**
TimeSformer [3]	Frame-based	77.95	**93.29**	63.76	88.53
	K-centered (ours)	**77.98**	93.09	**63.81**	**88.59**
Motionformer [35]	Frame-based	71.42	88.62	61.79	86.82
	K-centered (ours)	**74.85**	**91.27**	**62.15**	**87.19**
XViT [4]	Frame-based	72.73	90.25	62.40	87.82
	K-centered (ours)	**73.05**	**90.48**	**62.78**	**88.27**

Inference Details. For inference, we follow the previous benchmark standard of 3 × 1 ensemble testing [3]. To be specific, we sample a fixed-length clip from the video and then crop 3 different spatial views (top-left, center, bottom-right) from the clip. The final prediction is made by averaging the scores for all crops. We fix the same inference video pre-processing for all baselines and our method for a fair comparison.

4.2 Main Results

Comparison with Frame-Based Sampling. We consider comparing our K-centered sampling with conventional frame-based sampling strategy. To this end, we adapt our scheme to various video transformer models. As shown in Table 2, our K-centered sampling consistently outperforms the frame-based sampling on Kinetics-400 and SSv2 datasets. For instance, for Motionformer on Kinetics-400 dataset, our sampling improves the Top-1 action classification accuracy by 4.8% relatively (71.42% → 74.85%). Moreover, our sampling uniformly improves the accuracy for all models in the SSv2 dataset (e.g., relative 2.86% Top-1 accuracy gain on ViT), where it especially requires a high level of temporal understanding. This indicates that our sampling scheme contains more temporal dynamics information than conventional frame-based sampling. In video models that are highly optimized under the frame-based inputs (e.g., TimeSformer [3] assumes a fixed number of patches in space and time axes), the gain from our method could diminish. We believe developing new architectures optimized for K-centered patch-based sampling would be interesting future work.

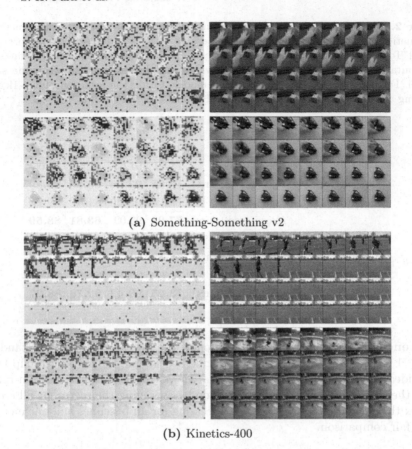

(a) Something-Something v2

(b) Kinetics-400

Fig. 4. Visualization examples of our K-centered patch sampling on Something-Something v2 and Kinetics-400 dataset. The highlighted region in the left video denotes the sampled patches, and the right video indicates the original video.

Visualization of Sampled Patches. Figure 4 visualizes the patches sampled by our strategy. One can observe that our sampling tends to focus on the target objects while less frequently sampling the redundant patches, *e.g.*, backgrounds. For instance, most of the sampled patches in the first example of Kinetics include the moving human rather than the repeating background patches with similar colors. This supports the result that our methods show effectiveness for datasets with complex temporal dynamics.

4.3 Ablation Study

Since our study is the first introduction of patch sampling in video transformers, we intend to provide various analyses to facilitate future video transformer research using patch sampling. We demonstrate the effects of using color chan-

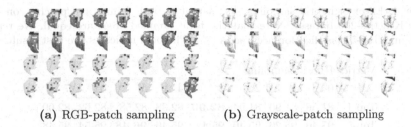

(a) RGB-patch sampling   (b) Grayscale-patch sampling

Fig. 5. Visualization of sampled patches by K-centered sampling on (a) RGB patches and (b) Grayscale patches in a Kinetics video clip. The highlighted region denotes the sampled parts.

Table 3. Comparison of our K-centered sampling with RGB patches and Grayscale patches in Kinetics-200 dataset. We report Top-1 and Top-5 classification accuracies (%). Note that Grayscale patches are used only for determining patch indices, and the actual inputs are normal RGB patches.

Model	Channel	Top-1	Top-5
ViT [11]	RGB	82.90	95.42
	Grayscale	81.94	95.58
TimeSformer [3]	RGB	84.24	96.10
	Grayscale	83.60	96.00

nels for K-centered sampling and of sampling hyperparameters—hybrid sampling and distance coefficients.

Effect of Color Channels in Sampling Distance. We notice that the color information is important for the patch sampling as it directly changes the distance of the patches. To investigate the effect of the color information, we consider sampling the patch index with a Grayscale video when measuring distances between patches[4]. As shown in Table 3, the patch selection with RGB videos shows better performance compare to the patch sampling with Grayscale videos. Also, in Fig. 5, we visualize the sampled patches from each configuration.

Effect of the Hybrid Sampling. Depending on the choice of models and datasets, sometimes, the full patch-based sampling leads to sub-optimal results. For the Kinetics dataset, specifically, the full patch-based sampling underperforms the frame-based sampling. In this respect, we consider taking advantage of both patch and frame sampling; we introduce the hybrid sampling-X, where X denotes the number of complete frames involved in the sampled patches. Table 4 depicts the number of hybrid sampling and their corresponding performances measured in Kinetics-200 dataset. We find that for ViT, hybrid sampling leads

---

[4] Grayscale is only used for sampling, *i.e.*, we use RGB patches for network input.

Table 4. Effect of hybrid sampling, *i.e.*, sampling both frames and patches, on ViT under Kinetics-200 dataset. Note that the total sampled areas are equal. We report Top-1 and Top-5 classification accuracies (%). The bold indicates the best result.

Metric	Hybrid sampling							
	0	1	2	3	4	5	6	7
Top-1	81.56	81.90	81.94	**82.90**	82.38	82.58	82.62	82.00
Top-5	95.40	95.26	95.40	95.42	95.46	**96.48**	95.54	95.48

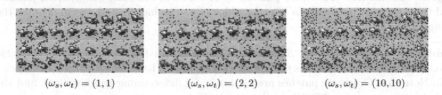

$(\omega_s, \omega_t) = (1,1)$ $(\omega_s, \omega_t) = (2,2)$ $(\omega_s, \omega_t) = (10,10)$

Fig. 6. Visualization of our K-centered patch sampling under different distance coefficients ω_s and ω_t upon search. The highlighted region in the video denotes the sampled patches, and the numbers of sampled patches are equal. Higher coefficients force models to sample patches with large spatiotemporal diversity.

to meaningful performance improvements, *i.e.*, 81.56% to 82.90% improvement in Top-1 accuracy when 3 frames were used in the hybrid sampling. Intriguingly, patch-based sampling only was enough for Motionformer, *i.e.*, the best performance is observed when no hybrid frames are used.

Effect of Spatiotemporal Distance Coefficients. We also investigate the effect of spatiotemporal distance coefficients ω_s, ω_t for the K-centered patch sampling. As shown in Fig. 6, samples under higher search coefficients tend to be more diversely distributed in spatiotemporal regions of video. We empirically test some selections for w_s and w_t for our experiments as done similarly to Table 5 and report the best performance among them.

Effect of the Test-Time Sampling. We also demonstrate the effect of test-time sampling by dropping some proportion of patches or dropping patches and swapping the sampling methods used in test time (*e.g.*, training with K-centered sampling, then testing with frame-based sampling). As shown in Table 6, models trained with our K-centered sampling strategy generally outperform models trained with the frame-based sampling, up to dropping 75% of the input patches, when tested with the identical sampling method to the training time. Interestingly, in cases where dropping an extremely high portion of patches, applying the frame-based sampling at *test time* can be useful to avoid sudden performance drop observed around dropping 87.5% of input patches. This is because watching a complete frame, albeit static, can give more useful information for recognizing a video when the number of input patches is scarce.

Table 5. Effect of distance coefficients ω_s, ω_t in the patch sampling. We report Top-1 and Top-5 classification accuracies (%) on ViT trained with Kinetics-200 dataset. The bold indicates the best result.

Metric	Sampling coefficients				
	$\omega_s = 1$ $\omega_t = 1$	$\omega_s = 1$ $\omega_t = 2$	$\omega_s = 2$ $\omega_t = 1$	$\omega_s = 2$ $\omega_t = 2$	$\omega_s = 10$ $\omega_t = 10$
Top-1	**82.90**	82.00	82.38	81.72	81.56
Top-5	95.42	**95.74**	95.43	95.26	95.16

Table 6. Effect of test-time sampling on ViT trained with Kinetics-200 dataset. We report the Top-1 classification accuracy (%) by (a) controlling the sampling method and (b) reducing the number of frames (or patches) at test time. The bold indicates the best result. For K-centered samples, we drop those patches sampled in the latest search iterations. For frame-based samples, we drop *frames* (if possible), *i.e.*, dropping $12.5 \times n\%$ indicates dropping $n = 1, 2, \ldots, 7$ frames given the original 8-frame input (for the extreme cases of 93.8 % and 96.9 % drops, we sample the half, and the quarter portion of a frame, respectively).

Train sampling	Test sampling	Proportion of droped patches at inference (%)								
		12.5	25.0	37.5	50.0	62.5	75.0	87.5	93.8	96.9
Frame-based	Frame-based	80.20	78.82	77.44	75.64	73.47	69.97	**63.45**	35.85	14.44
	K-centered (ours)	76.38	75.08	73.33	70.41	66.81	59.09	40.39	21.16	9.3
K-centered (ours)	Frame-based	77.56	76.32	75.20	73.99	71.83	67.97	62.79	**37.89**	**15.46**
	K-centered (ours)	**81.32**	**80.92**	**80.16**	**79.28**	**77.16**	**72.89**	57.43	32.65	12.88

5   Conclusion

In this paper, we address a fundamental issue in video recognition models by arguing that the conventional frame-based sampling approach is sub-optimal for recent transformer-based models processing a sequence of video patches. We propose a new patch-based sampling scheme, coined the greedy K-center search, outperforming the conventional one. We believe our work would guide new future directions for building efficient video understanding models.

Acknowledgement. This work was mainly supported by Institute of Information & communications Technology Planning & Evaluation (IITP) grant funded by the Korea government (MSIT) (No. 2021-0-02068, Artificial Intelligence Innovation Hub; No. 2019-0-00075, Artificial Intelligence Graduate School Program (KAIST)). This work was partly supported by KAIST-NAVER Hypercreative AI Center.

References

1. Arnab, A., Dehghani, M., Heigold, G., Sun, C., Lučić, M., Schmid, C.: VIVIT: a video vision transformer. In: IEEE International Conference on Computer Vision (2021)
2. Baevski, A., Zhou, H., Mohamed, A., Auli, M.: wav2vec 2.0: a framework for self-supervised learning of speech representations. In: Advances in Neural Information Processing Systems (2020)
3. Bertasius, G., Wang, H., Torresani, L.: Is space-time attention all you need for video understanding? In: International Conference on Machine Learning (2021)
4. Bulat, A., Perez-Rua, J.M., Sudhakaran, S., Martinez, B., Tzimiropoulos, G.: Space-time mixing attention for video transformer. In: Advances in Neural Information Processing Systems (2021)
5. Carreira, J., Zisserman, A.: Quo vadis, action recognition? A new model and the kinetics dataset. In: IEEE Conference on Computer Vision and Pattern Recognition (2017)
6. Chen, B., et al.: PSViT: better vision transformer via token pooling and attention sharing. arXiv preprint arXiv:2108.03428 (2021)
7. Cubuk, E.D., Zoph, B., Shlens, J., Le, Q.V.: RandAugment: practical automated data augmentation with a reduced search space. In: Advances in Neural Information Processing Systems (2020)
8. Deng, J., Dong, W., Socher, R., Li, L.J., Li, K., Fei-Fei, L.: ImageNet: a large-scale hierarchical image database. In: IEEE Conference on Computer Vision and Pattern Recognition (2009)
9. Devlin, J., Chang, M.W., Lee, K., Toutanova, K.: BERT: pre-training of deep bidirectional transformers for language understanding. In: Annual Conference of the North American Chapter of the Association for Computational Linguistics (2019)
10. Donahue, J., et al.: Long-term recurrent convolutional networks for visual recognition and description. In: IEEE Conference on Computer Vision and Pattern Recognition (2015)
11. Dosovitskiy, A., et al.: An image is worth 16 × 16 words: transformers for image recognition at scale. In: International Conference on Learning Representations (2021)
12. Fan, H., et al.: Multiscale vision transformers. In: IEEE International Conference on Computer Vision (2021)
13. Feichtenhofer, C.: X3D: expanding architectures for efficient video recognition. In: IEEE Conference on Computer Vision and Pattern Recognition (2020)
14. Feichtenhofer, C., Fan, H., Malik, J., He, K.: SlowFast networks for video recognition. In: IEEE International Conference on Computer Vision (2019)
15. Feichtenhofer, C., Pinz, A., Wildes, R.P.: Spatiotemporal residual networks for video action recognition. In: Advances in Neural Information Processing Systems (2016)
16. Gonzalez, T.F.: Clustering to minimize the maximum intercluster distance. Theoret. Comput. Sci. **38**, 293–306 (1985)
17. Gowda, S.N., Rohrbach, M., Sevilla-Lara, L.: Smart frame selection for action recognition. In: AAAI Conference on Artificial Intelligence (2021)
18. Goyal, R., et al.: The "something something" video database for learning and evaluating visual common sense. In: IEEE International Conference on Computer Vision (2017)

19. Har-Peled, S.: Geometric approximation algorithms. No. 173, American Mathematical Soc. (2011)
20. Heo, B., Yun, S., Han, D., Chun, S., Choe, J., Oh, S.J.: Rethinking spatial dimensions of vision transformers. In: IEEE International Conference on Computer Vision (2021)
21. Karpathy, A., Toderici, G., Shetty, S., Leung, T., Sukthankar, R., Fei-Fei, L.: Large-scale video classification with convolutional neural networks. In: IEEE Conference on Computer Vision and Pattern Recognition (2014)
22. Kay, W., et al.: The kinetics human action video dataset (2017)
23. Li, K., et al.: Uniformer: unified transformer for efficient spatiotemporal representation learning. arXiv preprint arXiv:2201.04676 (2022)
24. Liang, Y., Ge, C., Tong, Z., Song, Y., Wang, J., Xie, P.: Not all patches are what you need: expediting vision transformers via token reorganizations. In: International Conference on Learning Representations (2022)
25. Liu, Z., et al.: Swin transformer: hierarchical vision transformer using shifted windows. In: IEEE International Conference on Computer Vision (2021)
26. Liu, Z., et al.: Video swin transformer. arXiv preprint arXiv:2106.13230 (2021)
27. Loshchilov, I., Hutter, F.: Decoupled weight decay regularization. In: International Conference on Learning Representations (2019)
28. Marin, D., Chang, J.H.R., Ranjan, A., Prabhu, A., Rastegari, M., Tuzel, O.: Token pooling in vision transformers. arXiv preprint arXiv:2110.03860 (2021)
29. Meng, L., et al.: AdaViT: adaptive vision transformers for efficient image recognition. arXiv preprint arXiv:2111.15668 (2021)
30. Meng, Y., et al.: AR-Net: adaptive frame resolution for efficient action recognition. In: European Conference on Computer Vision (2020)
31. Meng, Y., et al.: AdaFuse: adaptive temporal fusion network for efficient action recognition. In: International Conference on Learning Representations (2021)
32. Micikevicius, P., et al.: Mixed precision training. In: International Conference on Learning Representations (2018)
33. Naseer, M., Ranasinghe, K., Khan, S., Hayat, M., Khan, F.S., Yang, M.H.: Intriguing properties of vision transformers. In: Advances in Neural Information Processing Systems (2021)
34. Neimark, D., Bar, O., Zohar, M., Asselmann, D.: Video transformer network. arXiv preprint arXiv:2102.00719 (2021)
35. Patrick, M., et al.: Keeping your eye on the ball: trajectory attention in video transformers. In: Advances in Neural Information Processing Systems (2021)
36. Qi, C.R., Yi, L., Su, H., Guibas, L.J.: PointNet++: deep hierarchical feature learning on point sets in a metric space. In: Advances in Neural Information Processing Systems (2017)
37. Radford, A., Narasimhan, K., Salimans, T., Sutskever, I.: Improving language understanding by generative pre-training (2018)
38. Rao, Y., Zhao, W., Liu, B., Lu, J., Zhou, J., Hsieh, C.J.: DynamicViT: efficient vision transformers with dynamic token sparsification. In: Advances in Neural Information Processing Systems (2021)
39. Schwartz, R., Dodge, J., Smith, N.A., Etzioni, O.: Green AI. arXiv preprint arXiv:1907.10597 (2019)
40. Simonyan, K., Zisserman, A.: Two-stream convolutional networks for action recognition in videos. In: Advances in Neural Information Processing Systems (2014)
41. Sun, X., Panda, R., Chen, C.F., Oliva, A., Feris, R., Saenko, K.: Dynamic network quantization for efficient video inference. In: IEEE International Conference on Computer Vision (2021)

42. Szegedy, C., Vanhoucke, V., Ioffe, S., Shlens, J., Wojna, Z.: Rethinking the inception architecture for computer vision. In: IEEE Conference on Computer Vision and Pattern Recognition (2016)

43. Touvron, H., Cord, M., Douze, M., Massa, F., Sablayrolles, A., Jegou, H.: Training data-efficient image transformers & distillation through attention. In: International Conference on Machine Learning (2021)

44. Tran, D., Bourdev, L., Fergus, R., Torresani, L., Paluri, M.: Learning spatiotemporal features with 3D convolutional networks. In: IEEE International Conference on Computer Vision (2015)

45. Vaswani, A., et al.: Attention is all you need. In: Advances in Neural Information Processing Systems (2017)

46. Wang, J., et al.: Removing the background by adding the background: Towards background robust self-supervised video representation learning. In: Proceedings of the IEEE/CVF Conference on Computer Vision and Pattern Recognition, pp. 11804–11813 (2021)

47. Wang, J., Yang, X., Li, H., Wu, Z., Jiang, Y.G.: Efficient video transformers with spatial-temporal token selection. arXiv preprint arXiv:2111.11591 (2021)

48. Wu, Z., Xiong, C., Ma, C.Y., Socher, R., Davis, L.S.: AdaFrame: adaptive frame selection for fast video recognition. In: IEEE Conference on Computer Vision and Pattern Recognition (2019)

49. Xie, S., Sun, C., Huang, J., Tu, Z., Murphy, K.: Rethinking spatiotemporal feature learning: speed-accuracy trade-offs in video classification. In: Proceedings of the European Conference on Computer Vision (ECCV), pp. 305–321 (2018)

50. Yan, W., Zhang, Y., Abbeel, P., Srinivas, A.: VideoGPT: video generation using VQ-VAE and transformers. arXiv preprint arXiv:2104.10157 (2021)

51. Yeung, S., Russakovsky, O., Mori, G., Fei-Fei, L.: End-to-end learning of action detection from frame glimpses in videos. In: IEEE Conference on Computer Vision and Pattern Recognition (2016)

52. Zhi, Y., Tong, Z., Wang, L., Wu, G.: MGSampler: an explainable sampling strategy for video action recognition. In: Proceedings of the IEEE/CVF International Conference on Computer Vision, pp. 1513–1522 (2021)

A Deep Moving-Camera Background Model

Guy Erez[✉][iD], Ron Shapira Weber[iD], and Oren Freifeld[iD]

Ben-Gurion University of the Negev, Be'er Sheva, Israel
{ergu,ronsha}@post.bgu.ac.il, orenfr@cs.bgu.ac.il

Abstract. In video analysis, background models have many applications such as background/foreground separation, change detection, anomaly detection, tracking, and more. However, while learning such a model in a video captured by a static camera is a fairly-solved task, in the case of a Moving-camera Background Model (MCBM), the success has been far more modest due to algorithmic and scalability challenges that arise due to the camera motion. Thus, existing MCBMs are limited in their scope and their supported camera-motion types. These hurdles also impeded the employment, in this unsupervised task, of end-to-end solutions based on deep learning (DL). Moreover, existing MCBMs usually model the background either on the domain of a typically-large panoramic image or in an online fashion. Unfortunately, the former creates several problems, including poor scalability, while the latter prevents the recognition and leveraging of cases where the camera revisits previously-seen parts of the scene. This paper proposes a new method, called DeepMCBM, that eliminates all the aforementioned issues and achieves state-of-the-art results. Concretely, first we identify the difficulties associated with joint alignment of video frames in general and in a DL setting in particular. Next, we propose a new strategy for joint alignment that lets us use a spatial transformer net with neither a regularization nor any form of specialized (and non-differentiable) initialization. Coupled with an autoencoder conditioned on unwarped robust central moments (obtained from the joint alignment), this yields an end-to-end regularization-free MCBM that supports a broad range of camera motions and scales gracefully. We demonstrate DeepMCBM's utility on a variety of videos, including ones beyond the scope of other methods. Our code is available at https://github.com/BGU-CS-VIL/DeepMCBM.

Keywords: Unsupervised · Background model · Background subtraction · Moving camera · Joint alignment · Regularization-free · Deep learning · Video analysis

1 Introduction

The unsupervised video-analysis task this paper focuses on is learning a background model in a video captured by a moving camera. In the simpler case

Supplementary Information The online version contains supplementary material available at https://doi.org/10.1007/978-3-031-19833-5_11.

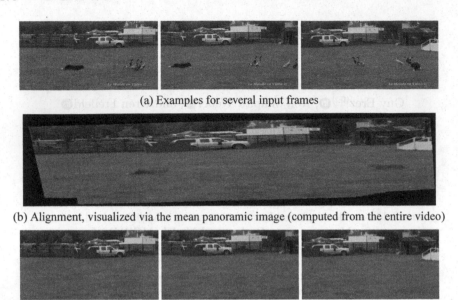

(a) Examples for several input frames

(b) Alignment, visualized via the mean panoramic image (computed from the entire video)

(c) Background estimation using the Conditional Autoencoder

Fig. 1. Typical results of the proposed module. Note that despite the fact that the dog spent long times being static in two locations (as is evident by the corresponding ghosting effects in (b)) the model succeeded in eliminating it from the background.

where the camera is static, such models have been used successfully in many computer-vision applications such as background/foreground separation, change or anomaly detection, and tracking. Static-camera solutions, however, cannot be easily extended to the moving-camera case since we do not know, a-priori, how the video frames should be aligned to each other. Thus, most of the tools traditionally used in background models become less applicable; *e.g.*, methods based on learning a low-dimensional subspace via Robust Principal Component Analysis (RPCA) assume that the frames are aligned to each other.

Seemingly, there is a straightforward solution: "simply" align the frames to each other to reduce the problem back to the static-camera case, and then build a static-camera background model based on the aligned frames. However, this is more complicated than it might seem. First, the alignment problem itself is often difficult. For example, methods based on creating a panoramic image by sequentially aligning each pair of consecutive frames suffer from drift errors. Moreover, such methods cannot exploit the information conveyed in situations where the camera revisits (possibly from a different viewpoint) a previously-seen region in the scene. This, among other considerations, motivates solutions based on Joint Alignment (JA) of the frames. However, even in this formulation the problem is often still hard to solve, partially due to reasons we analyze later in Sect. 4. Second, and regardless of how the alignment is done, there is the issue of scalability which pertains to not only the alignment problem itself but also the subsequent learning of the background model: when the accumulative motion of the camera throughout the video is substantial, the domain of the panoramic image can be huge so background models learned in that domain must scale gracefully. Furthermore, in such cases, when a frame is warped (*i.e.*, aligned) towards the panorama, it captures only a small portion of the latter. This means that *most* of the data in the panoramic version of the warped images is missing. This is problematic in our context since existing solutions for subspace learning in the presence of missing data usually struggle in such cases. Therefore, the missing-data issue, together with the scalability requirement, considerably complicates the task. Due to the above reasons, the success in the case of a **Moving-camera Background Model (MCBM)** is lagging far behind its static-camera counterpart. Moreover, the difficulties above have also largely prevented the use of Deep Learning (DL) for this task. This is unfortunate not only because the idea of harnessing the power of DL is attractive but also since it hinders the usage of MCBMs within larger end-to-end pipelines.

With this in mind, the goal of this paper is to provide an effective and scalable DL-based MCBM. To that aim, we start by identifying more precisely what makes JA of video frames challenging: first in the general case and then in the more specific DL context. Next, we design a new JA strategy based on a regularization-free Spatial Transformer Net (STN) and a JA loss involving a memory aspect. Our method requires no auxiliary tools (such as the brittle and non-differentiable initialization used in [10]) that would prohibit its usage within end-to-end pipelines. We also propose a new deep module for learning a background model. The model, based on a Conditional Autoencoder (CAE) and the output of the JA module, is learned in the small domain of the input frames instead of the much-larger panoramic domain. This eliminates scalability issues and targets the goal of estimating the background more directly. Importantly, this module too can be used within end-to-end pipelines. Figure 1 demonstrates the type of results obtained by the proposed modules. Taken together, the proposed two modules give rise to a new and highly-effective MCBM method, coined **DeepMCBM**, which supports a broad range of camera motions and scales gracefully. We demonstrate DeepMCBM's utility on a variety of videos, including ones beyond the scope of competing methods.

Our key contributions are: 1) a DL module, for jointly aligning video frames, that relies on an STN-based optimization and a new training strategy that requires neither regularization nor initialization; 2) a DL background-modeling module that leverages the JA via a CAE conditioned on unwarped robust central moments derived from the JA; 3) together, these two modules form an end-to-end unsupervised MCBM that achieves SOTA results, that scales gracefully, and that supports a wide range of camera motions.

2   Related Work

STN [26] is a DL module that learns and applies a parameterized input-dependent spatial transformation. Given a parameterized transformation family and an input image f, the STN's output consists of a parameter vector θ and a warped image obtained by warping f using T^{θ} (a transformation parameterized by θ). During training, the differentiation of a loss propagates through the STN. In practice, however, and despite their elegance, potential strength, and usage in numerous papers, STNs are often hard to train. Part of our solution addresses exactly such a case, where we take an STN-based optimization problem that was thought to be too difficult [10] and show how it can, in fact, be solved easily, without resorting to a regularization or a sophisticated limiting initialization.

Static-Camera Background Models. Early methods were pixelwise (*e.g.*, [41]) but later the focus has shifted to subspace estimation using Robust Principal Component Analysis and its variants (*e.g.*, [7,20,44,50]). While those models usually do not scale well, there also exist scalable RPCA models (*e.g.*, [8,21]).

Image Alignment. In [13,34], pairwise homographies are estimated between consecutive frames while [27] uses a multi-layer homography. An adaptive panoramic image is built in [32,47] while [43] relies on the assumption that a PTZ camera is used. Most of the works above make stringent assumptions about the camera motion and estimate transformations between pairs of images, sometimes even sequentially. This approach, however, can lead to accumulative errors and/or significant distortions. To avoid such issues, AutoStitch [6] employs bundle adjustment. However, publicly-available implementations of AutoStitch scale poorly with the number of images (*e.g.*, cannot handle more than a few hundreds of frames). This is unlike the proposed approach which scales gracefully. Alignment methods relying on depth or expensive 3D information/reconstruction include [29,30,35,46]. Unlike those works, and similarly to, *e.g.*, [10], the JA approach in this paper is purely 2D-based.

MCBMs. Online RPCA methods (*e.g.*, [3,19,22]) were extended to the case of camera jitter [23] as well as more significant motions [18]. DECOLOR [49] is another MCBM, based on motion detection, that is restricted to small motions. IncPCP-PTI [9] targets a PTZ-camera setting by updating a low-dimensional subspace with the help of an estimated rigid motion between consecutive frames. Several MCBMs are built by first aligning the frames to each other, and then, in the usually-large domain of the obtained panoramic image, learning a background model from the warped images using a static-camera background model that can handle missing data (since each warped image covers only a portion of the panoramic domain). A prime example for such methods is PRPCA [34]. Also of note are methods targeting **moving-object detection in a moving camera**; *e.g.*, [4,39,48]. These works, however, cannot detect changes unrelated to motion and also do not scale well.

STN-Based JA. As we explain in Sect. 4, STN-based JA poses several difficulties. On that note, the closest work to ours is JA-POLS [10] which handles some of the difficulties via the usage of a non-differentiable and non-robust initialization, together with a fairly-restrictive regularization. While JA-POLS is effective in cases where it is applicable, it is limited in the camera-motion types it supports and is not an end-to-end solution. We will return to JA-POLS in more detail later on.

Learning Background Models in the Panoramic Domain. Once alignment is obtained, in principle a background model can be learned. However, panoramic-size models (*e.g.*, [34]) do not scale while using an ensemble of Partially-overlapping Local Subspaces (POLS) [10] is cumbersome and also suffers from the fact the number of models grows with the size of the panorama. Either way, the existing methods do not offer an end-to-end solution that can be used easily within DL pipelines.

3   Preliminaries: Joint Alignment (JA)

Let $(f^n)_{n=1}^N$ be the frames of the input video and assume the size of each frame is $h \times w$ pixels. Let C be the number of input channels; *e.g.*, $C = 3$ for RGB images (the case considered in this paper). Let $\Omega \subset \mathbb{R}^2$ denote the rectangular $h \times w$ common domain of each f^n, and let θ_n denote the (latent) parameter vector of the spatial transformation associated with the sought-after alignment of $f^n : \Omega \to \mathbb{R}^C$. The transformation itself, denoted by T^{θ_n}, is viewed as an $\mathbb{R}^2 \to \mathbb{R}^2$ map (not just $\Omega \to \mathbb{R}^2$). The value of $d = \dim(\theta_n)$ depends on the transformation family; *e.g.*, in the affine case, $d = 6$. The warped version of Ω is $\Omega^n \triangleq T^{\theta_n}(\Omega) \triangleq \{x : \exists x' \in \Omega \text{ s.t. } T^{\theta_n}(x') = x\} \subset \mathbb{R}^2$. Mathematically, we define the warped image as $g^n : \Omega^n \to \mathbb{R}^C$ using the equality

$$g^n(T^{\theta_n}(x')) = f^n(x') \quad \forall x' \in \Omega. \tag{1}$$

However, due to technical reasons related to image warping [42], it is more convenient and customary to define g^n via the inverse transformation of T^{θ_n}:

$$g^n_x \triangleq g^n(x) = f^n((T^{\theta_n})^{-1}(x)) \quad \forall x \in \Omega^n. \tag{2}$$

Note that g^n depends on θ_n and f^n. Let H and W be the height and width, respectively, of a rectangle, denoted by $\Omega_{\text{scene}} \subset \mathbb{R}^2$, that is large enough to contain $\bigcup_n \Omega^n$. We now define a mask that will be useful for reasons to become clear shortly. Let M^Ω be a single-channel $h \times w$ image whose domain is Ω and whose values are all equal to 1. Let $M^n : \Omega_{\text{scene}} \mapsto [0,1]$ be a non-binary $H \times W$ mask obtained by image warping of M^Ω, according to T^{θ_n}, using zero padding and a bilinear interpolation kernel. That is, for any integral location x in Ω_{scene}, the value of M^n at x, denoted by M^n_x, is given by

$$M^n_x = \widetilde{M^\Omega}_{x'} \qquad x' = T^{-\theta_n}(x) \in \mathbb{R}^2 \tag{3}$$

where $\widetilde{M^\Omega}_{x'}$ is interpolated from the values of M^Ω at the 4 integral locations nearest to x' where whenever any of those integral locations falls outside Ω the value of M^Ω at that location is taken to be zero. Thus, $M^n_x = 0$ if all those 4 locations are outside Ω, $M^n_x = 1$ it they all fall inside it, and $0 < M^n_x < 1$ otherwise. Let $g^n_{x,c}$ denote the value of g^n_x at channel c. We will refer to $p_{x,c} \triangleq (g^n_{x,c})_{n=1}^N$ where $c \in \{1, \dots, C\}$ as the C pixel stacks at location x. Similarly, we define the mask stack at location x as $m_x \triangleq (M^n_x)_{n=1}^N$. Note that $p_{x,c}$ and m_x

(a) A typical problem: if Ω_{scene} is not very large, the process is prone to a poor *global* minimum.

(b) A typical problem: drastic spatial changes in μ (note also that the end result is quite blurry).

Fig. 2. Typical problems in JA. Rightmost images are post-convergence results.

depend on $(\boldsymbol{\theta}_n)_{n=1}^N$. A **joint-alignment loss**, to be minimized w.r.t.$(\boldsymbol{\theta}_n)_{n=1}^N$, may be formulated in terms of

$$\mathcal{L}_{JA} = \text{func}(((p_{\boldsymbol{x},c})_{c=1}^C, m_{\boldsymbol{x}})_{\boldsymbol{x} \in \Omega_{\text{scene}}}). \tag{4}$$

For example, in the early works on *congealing* (*e.g.*, [24,25,31,33]) that loss was based on entropy minimization. Later, other researchers [11,12] showed the benefits of a loss based on least squares. A robust variant (used in [10]) of the latter is

$$\mathcal{L}_{JA} = \frac{1}{N} \sum_{n=1}^N \frac{1}{C} \sum_{c=1}^C \frac{\sum_{\boldsymbol{x} \in \Omega_{\text{scene}}} M_{\boldsymbol{x}}^n \rho_{\text{JA}}(g_{\boldsymbol{x},c}^n - \mu_{\boldsymbol{x},c})}{\sum_{\boldsymbol{x} \in \Omega_{\text{scene}}} M_{\boldsymbol{x}}^n} \tag{5}$$

where $\mu_{\boldsymbol{x},c} = \frac{\sum_{n=1}^N M_{\boldsymbol{x}}^n g_{\boldsymbol{x}}^n}{\sum_{n=1}^N M_{\boldsymbol{x}}^n}$ and ρ_{JA} is a differentiable robust error function [5].

Let μ be the mean of the warped images; *i.e.*, the value of μ at location $\boldsymbol{x}$ and channel c is $\mu_{\boldsymbol{x},c}$. Note that μ may be viewed as the "moving target" to which the frames should be aligned. It "moves", during the optimization, in the following sense. As the alignment of the frames keeps changing, μ changes too since it is computed using the (weighted) average of the warped images. Assuming that the parameterization $\boldsymbol{\theta}_n \to T^{\theta_n}$ is differentiable and that the transformation family is sufficiently well-behaved (as is the case, *e.g.*, with the affine group or, more generally, spaces of diffeomorphisms [15,16,28,38,40]), the loss in Eq. (5) is differentiable. Thus, if $\boldsymbol{\theta}_n$ is predicted using an STN (so, in particular, $\boldsymbol{\theta}_n$ is a differentiable function of f^n, the STN's input), the loss can, at least in principle, be minimized using standard DL training.

4   Identifying Key Challenges in Solving Joint-Alignment Problems

Below we discuss three issues that might arise when solving JA problems: **1)** poor *global* minima; **2)** the need of regularization; **3)** the need of a good initialization.

Usually when trying to minimize a loss, reaching a global minimum is hard or even impossible, and if this feat happens to be achieved, it is deemed to be the ultimate success. Sadly, global minima of $\mathcal{L}_{\mathrm{JA}}$, while being (very) easy to achieve, reflect, in fact, an ultimate failure; $e.g.$, the non-negative $\mathcal{L}_{\mathrm{JA}}$ can attain its global minimum ($i.e.$, zero) when all the frames are shrunk to an infinitesimally-small point. A similar phenomenon occurs if all the frames are warped outside Ω_{scene} ($e.g.$, see Fig. 2a) or if the frames are warped such that there will be no pairwise overlap between them.

A popular solution in such cases is adding some type of regularization over $(\boldsymbol{\theta}_n)_{n=1}^N$. However, while various forms of regularization have been suggested, each of them imposes a certain bias; $e.g.$, the regularization term in [31] favors symmetric distributions while the one in [10] pushes the (affine) transformations towards the Special Euclidean group, denoted by SE(2). The implied assumptions in both these cases are limiting. Likewise, penalizing the size of the transformations ($e.g.$, by penalizing some norm of $\boldsymbol{\theta}_n$) is problematic when the accumulative motion of the camera is large, while regularization favoring temporal smoothness is not always compatible with real camera motions. Another issue is the need of hyperparameter tuning for the weight of the regularization term. Moreover, finding a combination of a regularization type and a weight that will work well for a sufficiently-large variety of videos is difficult.

JA is usually a difficult non-convex problem. Thus, a good initialization can be useful; $e.g.$, in JA-POLS [10] an STN-based JA module had to rely on an initialization based on SE-Sync [37]. The latter provides a useful globally-optimal solution to a different-but-related problem: the estimation of $absolute$ transformations that are consistent as possible with noisy measurements of pairwise $relative$ transformations between pairs of frames, where both the latent absolute transformations and the observed relative ones are in SE(2). With that initialization, the STN needs to solve an easier problem and does so over the more expressive Affine group. There are, however, several problems with the JA approach in [10] (we will later also discuss problems related to the background-modeling approach in [10]). First, pre-processing and heuristics are needed for extracting the relative transformations. Second, in cases where some of the true latent absolute transformations are far from SE(2) ($e.g.$: when the video contains a significant accumulative variation in the distance between the camera and the scene; when the camera zoom is changing; when there is a strong perspective effect; $etc.$.), the initialization breaks and this leads in turn to JA-POLS' failure. Moreover, SE-Sync is neither robust nor differentiable w.r.t. the input frames. As there is no easy way to differentiate SE-Sync w.r.t. the input frames, the STN-based JA module in JA-POLS cannot be used in an end-to-end DL pipeline.

4.1   An Additional Challenge with Joint Alignment When Using Batches

Typically, due to the data size and as it is almost always the case in DL, the optimization is done batch by batch where each batch consists of a subset (selected at random) of the frames from the entire video. A single epoch then represents a full pass over the entire data, and the frames are reshuffled between epochs. This typically-necessary batch-by-batch processing creates an optimization difficulty which might appear to be minor but is, in fact, far more critical than it may seem (we will revisit this point in Sect. 5.1). The issue is that the mean image μ (from Eq. (5)) is a function of the entire video, not just the frames in the current batch. A seemingly-obvious solution is to hold μ fixed during each epoch – so it does not affect the computation of the loss' gradient – and then, at the end of each epoch, recompute μ. However, a problem that arises with that approach is that the difference between the alignment targets (that is, the previous μ and the recomputed one) in each pair of consecutive epochs might be large, making the optimization difficult since the optimal transformations for one target might be quite far from those that are optimal for the next target. For an illustration, see Fig. 2b. A different approach, used in [10], picks the target μ to be the mean of only the (warped) frames in the current batch. Besides the fact that this is somewhat inconsistent with the cost-function formulation, that approach too can cause significant changes in the targets between consecutive batches. The jumping-target problem complicates the optimization more than one may expect. This is especially an issue at the beginning of the process when the frames are completely misaligned. For example, in retrospect, this is partly why JA-POLS [10] had to rely on the SE-Sync-based initialization scheme: as shown in [10], except in the simple case where the accumulative camera motion is small, without that initialization JA-POLS usually fails.

5   The Proposed Method: DeepMCBM

The proposed modules of joint alignment (using an STN) and background modeling (using a CAE) are presented in Sect. 5.1 and Sect. 5.2, respectively. Together, they form the proposed method, DeepMCBM. The goal of the STN straining is 1) to jointly align the video frames, implicitly forming a panoramic image, and 2) to learn how to warp an input frame towards that panoramic image. The goal of the CAE training is to learn the variability in the differences between the panoramic image and the input frames, while taking the warping into account but ignoring the foreground objects. The conditioning is done using the robust version of the panoramic pixelwise mean and variance.

Algorithm 1: Training an STN for Joint Alignment

Input: N_{epochs}, N_{batches}, $\rho(\cdot)$, data_loader
Data: $(f^n)_{n=1}^N$
Output: A trained STN for Joint Alignment

1 Initialize accumulators $\mathcal{G} \in \mathbb{R}^{H \times W \times C}$ and $\mathcal{M} \in \mathbb{R}^{H \times W}$ // see text
2 **for** $e \in \{1, \ldots, N_{\text{epochs}}\}$ **do**
3   **for** $i \in \{1, \ldots, N_{\text{batches}}\}$ **do**
4          $(f^b)_{b \in B} \leftarrow$ data_loader   // Load batch: $B \subset \{1, \ldots, N\}$
5          $(\theta_b, g^b)_{b \in B} \leftarrow \text{STN}((f^b)_{b \in B})$ // Note that $g^b = f^b \circ T^{\theta_b}$
6          $(M^b)_{b \in B} \leftarrow (M^\Omega \circ T^{\theta_b})_{b \in B}$ // Warp masks
7          $\mathcal{G}, \mathcal{M}, \mathcal{L}_{\text{batch}} \leftarrow$ Algorithm 2($\mathcal{G}, \mathcal{M}, (g^b)_{b \in B}, (M^b)_{b \in B}$) // Update $\mathcal{G}$ and $\mathcal{M}$; measure $\mathcal{L}_{\text{batch}}$ (*i.e.*, the batch loss)
8   Perform an optimization step to minimize the $\mathcal{L}_{\text{batch}}$ loss.
9          $(\mathcal{G}, \mathcal{M}) \leftarrow (\lambda \mathcal{G}, \lambda \mathcal{M})$ // Keep the history, but downweight it

---

5.1 A Regularization-Free Strategy for Joint Alignment

Having identified, in Sect. 4.1, that the jumps in the values of μ cause a major difficulty in the STN-based optimization of $\mathcal{L}_{\text{JA}}$ (Eq. (5)), we design a simple but surprisingly-effective optimization strategy, summarized in Algorithm 1 (which, in turn, uses Algorithm 2 as its subroutine). During the training epochs, instead of computing μ using only the current batch (as was done in [10]), or instead of recomputing μ from scratch each epoch, we construct our μ from the warped frames in the current batch while also taking into account, albeit with a lower weight, all the warped frames from the previous epochs as well as the previous batches in the current epoch. The proposed algorithm uses accumulators, denoted by $\mathcal{G}$ and $\mathcal{M}$. The former is used to accumulate weighted sums of the values of the pixels in the warped frames while the latter serves a similar purpose with the values of the pixels in the warped masks. Concretely, let e denote the index of the current epoch and let e' denote the index of some previous epoch. When evaluating the loss in a batch during epoch e, the contribution of the results from epoch e' becomes smaller and smaller as the "time" difference, $e - e'$, grows. This is done in line 9 in Algorithm 1 by multiplying the accumulators of the warped frames and the warped masks by a positive factor λ where $\lambda < 1$ (we use $\lambda = 0.9$).

As shown in Fig. 3, the resulting targets (*i.e.*, the μ sequence formed during the optimization) change smoothly between epochs. Importantly, this behaviour has a profound and fourfold positive effect: **1. No complicated initialization is needed.** As the optimization becomes much easier, the initial transformations are simply taken to be the identity. **2. Regularization-free JA.** No form of regularization on $(\theta_n)_{n=1}^N$ is needed; *e.g.*, there is no need to worry about the poor global minima from Sect. 4. Since the optimization is gradient-based and since each epoch lingers in the "history" of the process for many epochs before its effective weight decays to zero (due to the repeating multiplications by $\lambda \in (0, 1)$), such undesired cases are eliminated altogether. For instance, as the stack

Algorithm 2: Update $(\mu, \mathcal{G}, \mathcal{M})$ and measure the loss on the batch

Input: $\mathcal{G}, \mathcal{M}, (g^b)_{b \in B}, (M^b)_{b \in B}$
Output: $\mathcal{G}, \mathcal{M}, \mathcal{L}_{\text{batch}}$

1 $\mathcal{G} \leftarrow \mathcal{G} + \sum_{b=1}^{B} g^b$ // update warped-image accumulator
2 $\mathcal{M} \leftarrow \mathcal{M} + \sum_{b=1}^{B} M^b$ // update warped-mask accumulator
3 $\mu \leftarrow \mathbf{0}_{H \times W \times C}$
4 **for** $x \in \{x : x \in \Omega_{\text{scene}} \text{ and } \mathcal{M}_x \geq 0\}$ **do in parallel**
5   **for** $c \in \{1, \dots, C\}$ **do in parallel**
6          $\mu_{x,c} \leftarrow \frac{\mathcal{G}_{x,c}}{\mathcal{M}_x}$
7 $\mathcal{L}_{\text{batch}} \leftarrow \frac{1}{B} \sum_{b=1}^{B} \frac{1}{C} \sum_{c=1}^{C} \left[\left(\sum_{x \in \Omega_{\text{scene}}} M_x^b \rho(g_{x,c}^b - \mu_{x,c}) \right) / \left(\sum_{x \in \Omega_{\text{scene}}} M_x^b \right) \right]$

(a) Compared with Figure 2a, the process is more stable and successful. Also, even when μ nears the border of Ω_{scene}, it never goes outside it.

(b) Compared with Figure 2b, the drastic jumps are eliminated. Also, with the proposed term the results are less affected by the specified size of Ω_{scene}.

Fig. 3. Results analogous to those in Fig. 2 except they were obtained with the proposed memory-based approach. Rightmost images are post-convergence results.

of the original frames overlaid over each other (from the first epoch) contributes to the computation of μ, either shrinking the frames to a point or moving them outside Ω_{scene} will incur a loss. Our regularization-free JA is in sharp contrast to many algorithms including classical works (*e.g.*, [31]) and more recent ones (*e.g.*, [10]). **3. Higher expressiveness.** The formulation lets us increase the expressiveness of the transformation family as needed. For example, JA-POLS is so crucially dependent on its SE-Sync initialization and SE-based regularization, that the affine transformations it predicts are nearly in SE(2) themselves. In contrast, our method can not only predict more general transformations in the Affine group but also use broader transformation families. In our experiments we demonstrate this using the group of homographies but one may also try richer STNs such as those based on diffemorphisms [1,14,40]. **4. Our JA module can be used in end-to-end pipelines.** This is unlike not only non-DL methods but also JA-POLS [10] whose non-differentiable initialization prevents its JA module from being used in an end-to-end manner. The technical details of the training process appear in our **Supplemental Material (Supmat)**.

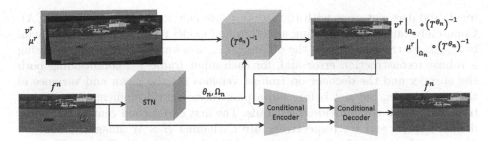

Fig. 4. The background-modeling module. After the STN module was trained using Algorithm 1, the robust panoramic moments, μ^r and v^r, are computed. A CAE is trained for a robust reconstruction task, using the transformation parameters, $(\theta_n)_{n=1}^N$, estimated by the (frozen) STN. The CAE's output is $\widehat{f^n}$, the estimated background associated with f^n and the conditioning is done by (un)warping μ^r and v^r towards each input training image, f^n. During test time the process is similar, except that the transformation being used is the one predicted by the STN.

5.2 Background Modeling in Ω (not Ω_{scene}) via a Conditional Autoencoder

Upon the training of the STN, the frames become jointly aligned. In principle, at this point all that is left to do is to learn a background model using either non-DL methods (*e.g.*, based on either pixelwise mixture models or RPCA methods; see Sect. 2) or deep ones (such as using a robust loss when training an autoencoder for reconstruction). However, there are several problems with this approach. First, it does not scale well: if the accumulating motion of the camera throughout the video is large, the panoramic image (of the entire scene covered throughout the video) can be huge. Moreover, in such a case even scalable RPCA methods will have to face an additional problem: since the domain of each warped image captures only a small region inside the domain of the panoramic image, it means that *most* of the pixels will represent missing data. Thus, one would need an RPCA method which can not only scale well but also succeed in situations where more than, say, 90%–95% of the data is missing. Also important is the following. Recall that given an input image, our goal is to estimate a background image, of the same size, that corresponds to that image. Thus, why should we even bother with trying to learn a panoramic-size background model? In [10], the discussion above motivated the learning of multiple local RPCA models and then, for estimating the background of a given image, only a subset of those models whose domains overlapped with the frame of interest were used. That solution, however, means that the number of models to be learned grows with the size of the panoramic image. Moreover, its non-DL formulation was another reason why JA-POLS was not an end-to-end method.

Here we propose a better alternative, whose pipeline is summarized in Fig. 4: use a CAE to learn a background model whose domain is small. This has two advantages: 1) It does not compromise the end-to-end nature of the method. 2) We need to learn only a single model (unlike in [10]) and its domain is small, fixed, and does not grow with the size of panoramic image (unlike in PRPCA). Concretely, rather than learning a background model (or models) whose domain is Ω_{scene}, we train a CAE on the original (*i.e.*, non-warped) input frames, using a robust reconstruction error and, for each input frame f^n, conditioning both the encoder and the decoder on (robust versions of) the mean and variance of the pixel stacks, but not before unwarping those central moments from Ω_{scene} towards f^n. We now provide the details. The first and second central moments, denoted by μ^r and v^r, respectively, are C-channel $H \times W$ images defined on Ω_{scence} and computed robustly using trimmed averaging as follows. Fix $x \in \Omega_{\text{scene}}$, let $N_x = |\{n : M_x^n > 0\}|$, and let $(g_{x,c}^{(1)}, \ldots, g_{x,c}^{(N_x)})$ be the order statistics of $p_{x,c}$. The values of μ^r and v^r at x in channel c are computed, respectively, by

$$\mu_{x,c}^r = \frac{1}{(1-2\alpha)N_x} \sum_{i=\alpha N_x}^{(1-\alpha)N_x} g_{x,c}^{(i)} \quad v_{x,c}^r = \frac{1}{(1-2\alpha)N_x} \sum_{i=\alpha N_x}^{(1-\alpha)N_x} (g_{x,c}^{(i)} - \mu_{x,c}^r)^2 . \quad (6)$$

Such trimmed averaging is a standard technique for computing robust moments [21]. The trimming parameter, α, was empirically set to $\alpha = 0.3$ as it provided a good balance between sample size and robustness. That said, the results when using any other value in the wide range between 20% and almost 50% were similar. Next, when f^n is fed into the CAE, the encoder and the decoder are conditioned by

$$\mu^n \triangleq \left(\mu^r|_{\Omega_n}\right) \circ (T^{\theta_n})^{-1} \text{ and } v^n \triangleq \left(v^r|_{\Omega_n}\right) \circ (T^{\theta_n})^{-1} \quad (7)$$

which are $h \times w$ images (with C channels) defined on Ω and are nothing more than the portion of μ^r and v^r that is relevant for f^n. Using a code whose length was only 4, the CAE was trained with the following loss:

$$\mathcal{L}_{AE} = \sum_{n=1}^N \sum_{c=1}^C \sum_{x' \in \Omega} \rho_{\text{recon}}(f_{x',c}^n - \widehat{f}_{x',c}^n) \quad (8)$$

$$\widehat{f}^n = \text{Decoder}(\text{Encoder}(f^n; \mu^n, v^n); \mu^n, v^n) \quad (9)$$

where $\widehat{f}^n$ is the output of the CAE and ρ_{recon} is a differentiable robust error function. We remark that, by design, the fact that μ^n and v^n are of the same dimensions as the input, f^n, also means it is easy to implement the conditioning via a convolutional layer. For more details about the CAE (whose architecture is based on the AE from [2]) as well as other training details, see our **Supmat**. Finally, ρ_{recon} should usually be more robust than ρ_{JA}. The reason is that while in JA the influence of foreground objects is relatively small, in the CAE-based reconstruction it is important, in every pixel, to eliminate the outliers (*i.e.*, the foreground pixels) as much as possible. Thus, we use the smoothed ℓ_1 loss (which is closely-related to Huber's function [5]) for ρ_{JA} and the Geman-McClure error function [17] for ρ_{recon}. See **Supmat** for details.

6   Results

We experimented with 4 variants of the proposed DeepMCBM: 1. **Basic/Aff**: This version uses only the STN-based JA module, without the CAE. It estimates the background by simply unwarping the robust mean towards the input image. The transformations used in the STN belong to the Affine group (the invertibility of the transformations was guaranteed via the matrix exponential; see **Supmat**). 2. **CAE/Aff**: This version too uses the Affine STN but also uses the CAE module (for estimating the background). 3. **Basic/Hom** and 4. **CAE/Hom**: Similar to Basic/Aff and CAE/Aff, respectively, except that homographies are used instead of affine transformations. We compared those 4 variants with several methods: PRPCA [34]; JA-POLS [10]; PanGAEA [18]; DECOLOR [49]; PCP_PTI [9]; PRAC [19]. The 13 videos that we tested on are ones typically used for evaluation of methods in this area and are taken from well-known datasets [36,45]. Those movies cover camera motions in a variety of types, sizes, speed, zoom changes, *etc.*. It should be noted that, due to their scalability limitaitons, PRPCA and PanGAEA could not run on the **ContinuousPan** video as the covered scene in the latter was too large. JA-POLS failed running on **zoomInZoomOut** (the significant zoom changes broke its key assumption). Figure 5 contains a visual comparison, on select example videos, of DeepMCBM (in its CAE/Hom variant), PRPCA, JA-POLS, and PanGAEA. Results of the other (and less successful) methods (DECOLOR; PCP_PTI; PRAC), as well as more visual results (including videos) are in the **Supmat**.

Given an estimate of the background, subtracting it from the original frame yields a difference that can serve to determine foreground/background separation. To quantify the results in a threshold-independent way, for each method and each video we computed the Receiver Operating Characteristic (ROC) curve (using the ground truth) and its Area Under the Curve (AUC). The ROC curves are included in **Supmat**. We emphasize that our method is unsupervised and the ground truth information was used only for evaluation. Table 1, summarizing the AUC results, shows that DeepMCBM, especially with its CAE variants, is, overall, the leading method. In cases where DeepMCBM is not the first it is typically the runner-up. Moreover, unlike some competitors, DeepMCBM was applicable in all cases considered. The visual examples also illustrate how the CAE helps achieving a better estimate of the background than that one obtained by merely using the unwarped μ^r. We remark that our fixed code size, 4, is so small since: 1) the goal is not a typical reconstruction but to filter out foreground objects; 2) our AE is conditional so it is unsurprising a small size suffices. We could have made the code size video-dependent and thus improve results even further, but felt that a fixed size is simpler and makes a comparison with other methods fairer.

Predicting Background for Previously-Unseen Misaligned Frames. In the comparison above, we focused on background/foreground estimation in the input videos on which the competing models (ours included) were learned. However, like JA-POLS, but unlike all the other methods, our method can predict the background in frames that were not included in the learning (more accurately, some of the competing methods can predict the background in the next constitutive frame, but they are unable to do so for misaligned frames in general such as those that are not consecutive). Due to space limits, we demonstrate that capability of DeepMCBM in the **Supmat**.

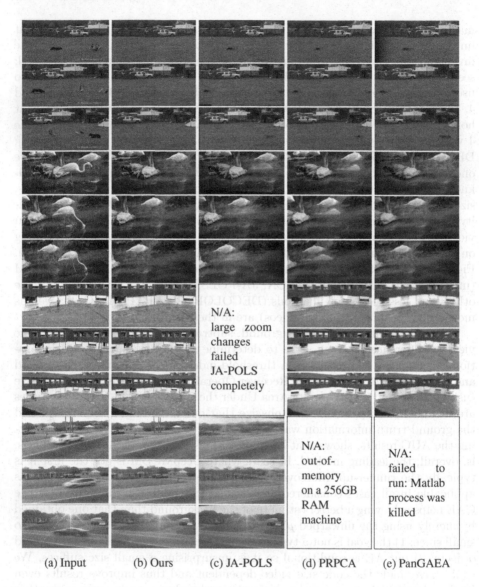

(a) Input   (b) Ours   (c) JA-POLS   (d) PRPCA   (e) PanGAEA

Fig. 5. Visual Comparison: Select Results. Note the ghosting artifacts and/or distortion in the other methods' results. **Please zoom in to better appreciate the results.**

Ablation Study. As Table 1 shows, the AE usually improves performance. In particular, its role is especially important when a foreground object spends a long portion of time in a static position (*e.g.*, the dog in the dog-gooses or the flamingo). In such cases, the robust mean alone still tends to capture some "ghosting" artifacts (as usually do all the competing methods) while the CAE helps correctly identifying that object as belonging to the foreground. The impor-

Table 1. AUC scores for each method on each sequence.

| Sequence | DeepMCBM (Ours) | | | | [34] | [18] | [9] | [10] | [19] | [49] |
	Basic/Aff	CAE/Aff	Basic/Hom	CAE/Hom						
bmx-trees	.898	.896	.916	.908	.894	.786	.837	**.930**	.664	.737
boxing-fisheye	.924	.893	.927	.898	**.935**	.932	.728	.892	.627	.763
breakdance-flare	.931	.933	.953	.963	.960	**.972**	.740	.897	.806	.667
continuousPan	.897	**.940**	.895	.938	N/A	N/A	.846	.449	.656	.760
dog-gooses	.954	**.984**	.955	**.984**	.942	.917	.721	.947	.747	.886
flamingo	.962	**.980**	.961	**.980**	.891	.957	.638	.947	.560	.656
horsejump-high	.932	.942	.932	.943	**.958**	.908	.783	.914	.713	.892
sidewalk	.886	.908	.889	.932	.812	.702	.635	.851	.780	**.935**
stroller	.877	.885	.740	.756	.762	**.904**	.594	.807	.613	.721
stunt	.963	**.979**	.961	.978	.959	.954	.899	.930	.711	.781
swing	.880	.877	.887	.897	**.942**	.879	.805	.874	.722	.812
tennis	.960	.961	.959	**.963**	.943	.929	.831	.932	.787	.852
zoomInZoomOut	.981	**.994**	.981	**.994**	.979	.958	.720	N/A	.885	.957

tance of the memory-based approach was also demonstrated in Fig. 2 and Fig. 3. In particular, the JA failures in Fig. 2 imply that no subsequent background model could be built there, making a quantitative comparison (between using the memory term and not using it) a moot point. Finally, note that a basic (*i.e.*, unconditional AE) that knows nothing about the alignment has no chance here as it can only either simply reconstruct the entire frames (*i.e.*, with the undesired foreground objects) or fail in the reconstruction. Thus, when simply dropping the conditioning from our CAE, the resulting AE fails badly in background modeling; *e.g.*, its AUC for the Tennis video is 0.701 while DeepMCBM's AUC score is 0.963.

7   Conclusion

The proposed DeepMCBM is an end-to-end DL solution for modeling background in a video from a moving camera. It supports a wide range of camera-motion types and sizes, scales gracefully, and achieves SOTA results. While we experimented with either affine transformations or homographies, DeepMCBM also supports more expressive transformations. The proposed regularization-free STN-based JA strategy may find usage in other applications, thereby the potential impact of this work may be broader than MCBMs. One limitation of our work is that, since DL involved, the training is slower in comparison to some competitors (JA-POLS excluded). However, we believe the SOTA results together with the other benefits DeepMCBM brings (end-to-end; scalability; the ability to predict background for previously-unseen misaligned frames; *etc.*.) justifies it. The main failure case of the method is when foreground objects are large and much closer to the camera than the background is.

Acknowledgement. This work was supported in part by the Lynn and William Frankel Center at BGU CS and by Israel Science Foundation Personal Grant #360/21. G.E. was also funded by the VATAT National excellence scholarship for female Master's students in Hi-Tech-related fields.

References

1. Balakrishnan, G., Zhao, A., Sabuncu, M.R., Guttag, J., Dalca, A.V.: An unsupervised learning model for deformable medical image registration. In: CVPR (2018)
2. Ballé, J., Laparra, V., Simoncelli, E.P.: End-to-end optimized image compression. In: ICLR (2017)
3. Balzano, L., Nowak, R., Recht, B.: Online identification and tracking of subspaces from highly incomplete information. In: Allerton (2010)
4. Berger, M., Seversky, L.M.: Subspace tracking under dynamic dimensionality for online background subtraction. In: CVPR (2014)
5. Black, M.J., Rangarajan, A.: On the unification of line processes, outlier rejection, and robust statistics with applications in early vision. IJCV (1996). https://doi. org/10.1007/BF00131148
6. Brown, M., Lowe, D.G.: Automatic panoramic image stitching using invariant features. In: IJCV (2007). https://doi.org/10.1007/s11263-006-0002-3
7. Candès, E.J., Li, X., Ma, Y., Wright, J.: Robust principal component analysis? JACM (2011)
8. Chakraborty, R., Hauberg, S., Vemuri, B.C.: Intrinsic Grassmann averages for online linear and robust subspace learning. In: CVPR (2017)
9. Chau, G., Rodríguez, P.: Panning and jitter invariant incremental principal component pursuit for video background modeling. In: ICCV (2017)
10. Chelly, I., Winter, V., Litvak, D., Rosen, D., Freifeld, O.: JA-POLS: a moving-camera background model via joint alignment and partially-overlapping local subspaces. In: CVPR (2020)
11. Cox, M., Sridharan, S., Lucey, S., Cohn, J.: Least squares congealing for unsupervised alignment of images. In: CVPR (2008)
12. Cox, M., Sridharan, S., Lucey, S., Cohn, J.: Least-squares congealing for large numbers of images. In: ICCV (2009)
13. Cuevas, C., Mohedano, R., García, N.: Statistical moving object detection for mobile devices with camera. In: ICCE (2015)
14. Dalca, A., Rakic, M., Guttag, J., Sabuncu, M.: Learning conditional deformable templates with convolutional networks. In: NeurIPS (2019)
15. Freifeld, O., Hauberg, S., Batmanghelich, K., Fisher III, J.W.: Highly-expressive spaces of well-behaved transformations: keeping it simple. In: ICCV (2015)
16. Freifeld, O., Hauberg, S., Batmanghelich, K., Fisher III, J.W.: Transformations based on continuous piecewise-affine velocity fields. IEEE TPAMI (2017)
17. Geman, S., McClure, D.E.: Statistical methods for tomographic image reconstruction. In: BISI (1987)
18. Gilman, K., Balzano, L.: Panoramic video separation with online Grassmannian robust subspace estimation. In: ICCV Workshops (2019)
19. Guo, H., Qiu, C., Vaswani, N.: Practical reprocs for separating sparse and low-dimensional signal sequences from their sum-part 1. In: ICASSP (2014)
20. Guyon, C., Bouwmans, T., Zahzah, E.H.: Foreground detection via robust low rank matrix decomposition including spatio-temporal constraint. In: ACCV (2012). https://doi.org/10.1007/978-3-642-37410-4_28

21. Hauberg, S., Feragen, A., Black, M.J.: Grassmann averages for scalable robust PCA. In: CVPR (2014)
22. He, J., Balzano, L., Szlam, A.: Incremental gradient on the Grassmannian for online foreground and background separation in subsampled video. In: CVPR (2012)
23. He, J., Zhang, D., Balzano, L., Tao, T.: Iterative Grassmannian optimization for robust image alignment. Image Vis. Comput. **32**, 800–813 (2014)
24. Huang, G., Mattar, M., Lee, H., Learned-Miller, E.G.: Learning to align from scratch. In: NIPS (2012)
25. Huang, G.B., Jain, V., Learned-Miller, E.: Unsupervised joint alignment of complex images. In: ICCV (2007)
26. Jaderberg, M., Simonyan, K., Zisserman, A., et al.: Spatial transformer networks. In: NeurIPS (2015)
27. Jin, Y., Tao, L., Di, H., Rao, N.I., Xu, G.: Background modeling from a free-moving camera by multi-layer homography algorithm. In: ICIP (2008)
28. Kaufman, I., Weber, R.S., Freifeld, O.: Cyclic diffeomorphic transformer nets for contour alignment. In: ICIP (2021)
29. Kendall, A., Grimes, M., Cipolla, R.: PoseNet: a convolutional network for real-time 6-DOF camera relocalization. In: ICCV (2015)
30. Klein, G., Murray, D.: Parallel tracking and mapping for small AR workspaces. In: International Symposium on Mixed and Augmented Reality (2007)
31. Learned-Miller, E.G.: Data driven image models through continuous joint alignment. IEEE TPAMI (2006)
32. Meneghetti, G., Danelljan, M., Felsberg, M., Nordberg, K.: Image alignment for panorama stitching in sparsely structured environments. In: Scandinavian Conference on Image Analysis (2015). https://doi.org/10.1007/978-3-319-19665-7_36
33. Miller, E.G., Matsakis, N.E., Viola, P.A.: Learning from one example through shared densities on transforms. In: CVPR (2000)
34. Moore, B.E., Gao, C., Nadakuditi, R.R.: Panoramic robust PCA for foreground-background separation on noisy, free-motion camera video. IEEE Trans. Comput. Imaging **5**, 195–211 (2019)
35. Newcombe, R.A., Lovegrove, S.J., Davison, A.J.: DTAM: dense tracking and mapping in real-time. In: ICCV (2011)
36. Pont-Tuset, J., Perazzi, F., Caelles, S., Arbeláez, P., Sorkine-Hornung, A., Van Gool, L.: The 2017 DAVIS challenge on video object segmentation. arXiv preprint arXiv:1704.00675 (2017)
37. Rosen, D.M., Carlone, L., Bandeira, A.S., Leonard, J.J.: SE-Sync: a certifiably correct algorithm for synchronization over the special Euclidean group. Int. J. Robot. Res. **38**, 95–125 (2019)
38. Weber, R.S., Eyal, M., Detlefsen, N.S., Shriki, O., Freifeld, O.: Diffeomorphic temporal alignment nets. In: NeurIPS (2019)
39. Sheikh, Y., Javed, O., Kanade, T.: Background subtraction for freely moving cameras. In: ICCV (2009)
40. Detlefsen, N.S., Freifeld, O., Hauberg, S.: Deep diffeomorphic transformer networks. In: CVPR (2018)
41. Stauffer, C., Grimson, W.E.L.: Adaptive background mixture models for real-time tracking. In: CVPR (1999)
42. Szeliski, R.: Computer vision: algorithms and applications. Springer Science & Business Media (2010). https://doi.org/10.1007/978-1-84882-935-0
43. Thurnhofer-Hemsi, K., López-Rubio, E., Domínguez, E., Luque-Baena, R.M., Molina-Cabello, M.A.: Panoramic background modeling for PTZ cameras with competitive learning neural networks. In: IJCNN (2017)

44. De la Torre, F., Black, M.J.: Robust principal component analysis for computer vision. In: ICCV (2001)
45. Wang, Y., Jodoin, P.M., Porikli, F., Konrad, J., Benezeth, Y., Ishwar, P.: CDnet 2014: an expanded change detection benchmark dataset. In: CVPR Workshop (2014)
46. Wu, C.: Towards linear-time incremental structure from motion. In: International Conference on 3D Vision (2013)
47. Xue, K., Liu, Y., Chen, J., Li, Q.: Panoramic background model for PTZ camera. In: International Congress on Image and Signal Processing (2010)
48. Yalcin, H., Hebert, M., Collins, R., Black, M.J.: A flow-based approach to vehicle detection and background mosaicking in airborne video. In: CVPR (2005)
49. Zhou, X., Yang, C., Yu, W.: Moving object detection by detecting contiguous outliers in the low-rank representation. TPAMI (2012)
50. Zhou, Z., Li, X., Wright, J., Candes, E., Ma, Y.: Stable principal component pursuit. In: ISIT (2010)

GraphVid: It only Takes a Few Nodes to Understand a Video

Eitan Kosman$^{(\boxtimes)}$ ⓘ and Dotan Di Castro

Bosch Center of AI, Haifa, Israel
{Eitan.Kosman,Dotan.DiCastro}@bosch.com

Abstract. We propose a concise representation of videos that encode perceptually meaningful features into graphs. With this representation, we aim to leverage the large amount of redundancies in videos and save computations. First, we construct superpixel-based graph representations of videos by considering superpixels as graph nodes and create spatial and temporal connections between adjacent superpixels. Then, we leverage Graph Convolutional Networks to process this representation and predict the desired output. As a result, we are able to train models with much fewer parameters, which translates into short training periods and a reduction in computation resource requirements. A comprehensive experimental study on the publicly available datasets Kinetics-400 and Charades shows that the proposed method is highly cost-effective and uses limited commodity hardware during training and inference. **It reduces the computational requirements 10-fold** while achieving results that are comparable to state-of-the-art methods. We believe that the proposed approach is a promising direction that could open the door to solving video understanding more efficiently and enable more resource limited users to thrive in this research field.

1 Introduction

The field of video understanding has gained prominence thanks to the rising popularity of videos, which has become the most common form of data on the web. On each new uploaded video, a variety of tasks can be performed, such as tagging [18], human action recognition [37], anomaly detection [46], etc. New video-processing algorithms are continuously being developed to automatically organize the web through the flawless accomplishment of the aforementioned tasks.

Nowadays, Deep Neural Networks are the de-facto standard for video understanding [35]. However, with every addition of a new element to the training set (that is, a full training video), more resources are required in order to satisfy the enormous computational needs. On the one hand, the exponential increment in the amount of data raises concerns regarding our ability to handle it in the future. On the other hand, it has also spurred an highly creative research field aimed at finding ways to mitigate this burden.

Among the first-generation of video processing methods were ones geared toward adopting 2D convolution neural networks (CNNs), due to their computational efficiency [43]. Others decomposed 3D convolutions [14,56] into simpler

S. Avidan et al. (Eds.): ECCV 2022, LNCS 13695, pp. 195–212, 2022.
https://doi.org/10.1007/978-3-031-19833-5_12

operators, or split a complex neural network into an ensemble of lightweight networks [9]. However, video understanding has greatly evolved since then, with the current state-of-the-art methods featuring costly attention mechanisms [3,4,6,15,20,30,31]. Beyond accuracy, a prominent advantage of the latest generation of methods is that they process raw data, that is, video frames that do not undergo any advanced pre-processing. Meanwhile, pursuing new video representations and incorporating pre-computed features to accelerate training is a promising direction that requires more extensive research.

(a) Original image   (b) Mean superpixels

Fig. 1. A visual comparison between a pixel and a mean-superpixel representation. On the left, the original image is presented. On the right, we present the image formed by generating superpixel regions using SLIC and filling each region with its mean color. (Color figure online)

Prior to the renaissance of deep learning [29], much research was done on visual feature generation. Two prominent visual feature generation methods are superpixels[1] and optic-flow[2]. These techniques' ability to encode perceptually meaningful features has greatly contributed to the success of computer vision algorithms. Superpixels provide a convenient, compact representation of images that can be very useful for computationally demanding problems, while optic-flow provides hints about motion. We rely on these methods to construct a novel representation of videos that encodes sufficient information for video understanding: 1) adjacent pixels are grouped together in the form of superpixels, and 2) temporal relations and proximities are expressed via graph connectivity. The example depicted in Fig. 1 provides an intuition for the sufficiency of superpixel representation for scene understanding. It contains the superpixel regions obtained via SLIC [2], with each region filled with the mean color. One can clearly discern a person playing a guitar in both images. A different way of depicting the relations between superpixels is a graph with nodes representing superpixels [5,11,33]. Such a representation has the advantage of being invariant to rotations and flips, which obviates the need for further augmentations. We here demon-

---

[1] Superpixel techniques segment an image into regions by considering similarity measures, defined using perceptual features.

[2] Optic-flow is the pattern of the apparent motion of an object(s) in the image between two consecutive frames due to the movement of the object or the camera.

strate how this representation can reduce the computational requirements for processing videos.

Recent years have seen a surge in the utilization of Graph Neural Networks (GNNs) [26] in tasks that involve images [5,11,33], audio [12,61] and other data forms [1,54,55]. In this paper, we propose *GraphVid*, a concise graph representation of videos that enables video processing via GNNs. *GraphVid* constructs a graph representation of videos that is subsequently processed via a GCN to predict a target. We intend to exploit the power of graphs for efficient video processing. To the best of our knowledge, we are the first to utilize a graph-based representation of videos for efficiency. *GraphVid* dramatically reduces the memory footprint of a model, enabling large batch-sizes that translate to better generalization. Moreover, it utilizes models with an order-of-magnitude fewer parameters than the current state-of-the-art models while preserving the predictive power. **In summary, our contributions are:**

1. We present *GraphVid* - a simple and intuitive, yet sufficient representation of video clips. This simplicity is crucial for delivering efficiency.
2. We propose a dedicated GNN for processing the proposed representation. The proposed architecture is compared with conventional GNN models in order to demonstrate the importance of each component of *GraphVid*.
3. We present 4 types of new augmentations that are directly applied to the video-graph representation. A thorough ablation study of their configurations is preformed in order to demonstrate the contribution of each.
4. We perform a thorough experimental study, and show that *GraphVid* greatly outperforms previous methods in terms of efficiency - first and foremost, the paper utilizes GNNs for efficient video understanding. We show that it successfully reduces computations while preserving much of the performance of state-of-the-art approaches that utilize computationally demanding models.

2   Related Work

2.1   Deep Learning for Video Understanding

CNNs have found numerous applications in video processing [32,49,59]. These include LSTM-based networks that perform per-frame encoding [44,50,59] and the extension of 2D convolutions to the temporal dimension, *e.g.*, 3D CNNs such as C3D [48], R2D [43] and R(2+1)D [49].

The success of the Transformer model [51] has led to the development of attention-based models for vision tasks, via self-attention modules that were used to model spatial dependencies in images. NLNet [53] was the first to employ self-attention in a CNN. With this novel attention mechanism, NLNet is possible to model long-range dependencies between pixels. The next model to be developed was GCNet [7], which simplified the NL-module, thanks to its need for fewer parameters and computations, while preserving its performance. A more prominent transition from CNNs to Transformers began with Vision Transformer (ViT) [13], which prompted research aimed at improving its effectiveness on small datasets, such as Deit [47]. Later, vision-transformers were adapted for video tasks [4,6,15,30,31,34], now crowned as the current state-of-the-art that top the leader-boards of this field.

The usage of graph representation in video understanding sparsely took place in the work of Wang [54]. They used pre-trained Resnet variants [22] for generating object bounding boxes of interest on each frame. These bounding boxes are later used for the construction of a spatio-temporal graph that describes how objects change through time, and perform classification on top of the spatio-temporal graph with graph convolutional neural networks [26]. However, we note that the usage of a large backbone for generating object bounding boxes is harmful for performance. We intend to alleviate this by proposing a lighter graph representation. In combination of a dedicated GNN architecture, our representation greatly outperforms [54] in all metrics.

2.2   Superpixel Representation of Visual Data

Superpixels are groups of perceptually similar pixels that can be used to create visually meaningful entities while heavily reducing the number of primitives for subsequent processing steps [45]. The efficiency of the obtained representation has led to the development of many superpixel-generation algorithms for images [45]. This approach was adapted for volumetric data via the construction of supervoxels [36], which are the trivial extension to depth. These methods were adjusted for use in videos [57] by treating the temporal dimension as depth. However, this results in degraded performance, as inherent assumptions regarding neighboring points in the 3D space do not apply to videos with non-negligible motion. Recent approaches especially designed to deal with videos consider the temporal dimensions for generating superpixels that are coherent in time. Xu et al. [58] proposed a hierarchical graph-based segmentation method. This was followed by the work of Chang et al. [8], who suggested that Temporal Superpixels (TSPs) can serve as a representation of videos using temporal superpixels by modeling the flow between frames with a bilateral Gaussian process.

2.3   Graph Convolutional Neural Networks

Introduced in [26], Graph Convolutional Networks (GCNs) have been widely adopted for graph-related tasks [28,60]. The basic GCN uses aggregators, such as average and summation, to obtain a node representation given its neighbors. This basic form was rapidly extended to more complex architectures with more sophisticated aggregators. For instance, Graph Attention Networks [52] use dot-product-based attention to calculate weights for edges. Relational GCNs [41] add to this framework by also considering multiple edge types, namely, relations (such as temporal and spatial relations), and the aggregating information from each relation via separate weights in a single layer. Recently, GCNs have been adopted for tasks involving audio [12,61] and images [5,11,33]. Following the success of graph models to efficiently perform image-based tasks, we are eager to demonstrate our extension of the image-graph representation to videos.

3   *GraphVid* - A Video-Graph Representation

In this section, we introduce the methodology of *GraphVid*. First, we present our method for video-graph representation generation, depicted in Fig. 2 and described in Algorithm 1. Then, we present our training methodology that utilizes this representation. Finally, we discuss the benefits of *GraphVid* and propose several augmentations.

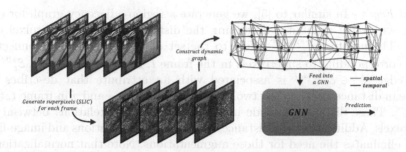

Fig. 2. The flow of *GraphVid*. Given a video clip, we generate superpixels using SLIC for each frame. The superpixels are used to construct a region-adjacency graph of a frame, with superpixels as nodes. Then, the graph sequence is connected via temporal proximities to construct a dynamic graph, which is later fed into a GNN for prediction.

3.1   Overview

In our framework, we deal with video clips that are sequences of T video frames $v \in \mathbb{R}^{T \times C \times H \times W}$. The goal is to transform v into a graph that is sufficiently informative for further processing. To achieve this, we use SLIC [2] to generate S segmented regions, called *superpixels*, over each frame. We denote each segmented region as $R_{t,i}$, where $t \in [T]$ represents the temporal frame index, and $i \in [S]$ the superpixel-segmented region index. The following is a description of how we utilize the superpixels to construct our video-graph representation.

Graph Elements - We define the undirected graph $\mathcal{G}$ as a 3-tuple $\mathcal{G} = (\mathcal{V}, \mathcal{E}, \mathcal{R})$, where $\mathcal{V} = \{R_{t,i} | t \in [T], i \in [S]\}$ is the set of nodes representing the segmented regions, $\mathcal{E}$ is the set of labeled edges (to be defined hereunder) and $\mathcal{R} = \{spatial, temporal\}$ is a set of relations as defined in [41]. Each node $R_{t,i}$ is associated with an attribute $R_{t,i}.c \in \mathbb{R}^3$ representing the mean RGB color in that segmented region. Additionally, we refer to $R_{t,i}.y$ and $R_{t,i}.x$ as the coordinates of the superpixel's centroid, which we use to compute the distances between superpixels. These distances, which will later serve as the edge attributes of the graph, are computed by

$$d_{i,j}^{t_q \to t_p} = \sqrt{\left(\frac{R_{t_q,i}.y - R_{t_p,j}.y}{H}\right)^2 + \left(\frac{R_{t_q,i}.x - R_{t_p,j}.x}{W}\right)^2}. \qquad (1)$$

Here, $t_q, t_p \in [T]$ denote frame indices, and $i, j \in [S]$ denote superpixel indices generated for the corresponding frames. The set of edges $\mathcal{E}$ is composed of: **1)** intra-frame edges (denoted $\mathcal{E}^{spatial}$) - edges between nodes corresponding to superpixels in the same frame. We refer to these as *spatial edges*. **2)** inter-frame edges (denoted $\mathcal{E}^{temporal}$) - edges between nodes corresponding to superpixels in two sequential frames. We refer to edges as *temporal edges*. Finally, the full set of edges is $\mathcal{E} = \mathcal{E}^{spatial} \cup \mathcal{E}^{temporal}$. Following is a description of how we construct both components.

Spatial Edges - In similar to [5], we generate a region-adjacency graph for each frame, with edge attributes describing the distances between superpixel centroids. The notation $\mathcal{E}_t^{spatial}$ refers to the set of the spatial-edges connecting nodes corresponding to superpixels in the frame t, and $\mathcal{E}^{spatial} = \bigcup_{t=1}^{T} \mathcal{E}_t^{spatial}$. Each edge $e_{i,j}^t \in \mathcal{E}^{spatial}$ is associated with an attribute that describes the euclidean distance between the two superpixel centroids i and j in frame t, that is, $d_{i,j}^{t \to t}$. These distances provide information about the relations between the superpixels. Additionally, the distances are invariant to rotations and image-flips, which eliminates the need for those augmentations. Note that normalization of the superpixels' centroid coordinates is required in order to obscure information regarding the resolution of frames, which is irrelevant for many tasks, such as action classification. In Fig. 3, we demonstrate the procedure of spatial edge generation for a cropped image that results in a partial graph of the whole image. Each superpixel is associated with a node, which is connected via edges to other adjacent nodes (with the distances between the superpixels' centroids serving as edge attributes).

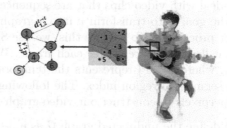

Fig. 3. Spatial edge generation. First, superpixels are generated. Each superpixel is represented as a node, which is connected via its edges to other such nodes within a frame. Each node is assigned the mean color of the respective segmented region, and each edge is assigned the distances between the superpixel centroids connected by that edge. (Color figure online)

Temporal Edges - In modeling the temporal relations, we aim to connect nodes that tend to describe the same objects in subsequent frames. To do so, we rely on the assumption that in subsequent frames, such superpixels are attributed similar colors and the same spatial proximity. To achieve this, for each superpixel $R_{t,i}$, we construct a neighborhood $\mathcal{N}_{t,i}$ that contains superpixels from its subsequent frame whose centroids have a proximity of at most $d_{proximity} \in (0, 1]$ with respect to the euclidean distance. Then, we find the superpixel with the most similar color in this neighborhood. As a result, the tth frame is associated with the set of edges $\mathcal{E}_{t \to t+1}^{temporal}$ that model temporal relations with its subsequent frame, formally:

$$\mathcal{N}_{t,i} = \{R_{t+1,j} | d_{i,j}^{t \to t+1} < d_{proximity}\}, \tag{2}$$

$$neighbor(R_{t,i}) = \underset{R_{t+1,j} \in \mathcal{N}_{t,i}}{argmin} |R_{t,i}.c - R_{t+1,j}.c|_2, \tag{3}$$

$$\mathcal{E}_{t \to t+1}^{temporal} = \{(R_{t,i}, temporal, neighbor(R_{t,i}) | i \in [S]\}. \tag{4}$$

Equipped with these definitions, we define the set of temporal edges connecting nodes corresponding to superpixels in frame t to superpixels in frame $t+1$ as the union of the temporal edge sets generated for all the frames: $\mathcal{E}^{temporal} = \bigcup_{t=1}^{T-1} \mathcal{E}_{t \to t+1}^{temporal}$.

Algorithm 1. Graph Generation

Input: $v \in \mathbb{R}^{T \times C \times H \times W}$ ▷ The input video clip
Parameters: $S \in \mathbb{N}$ ▷ Number of superpixels per frame
               $d_{proximity} \in (0,1]$ ▷ Diameter of neighborhoods
Output: $\mathcal{G} = (\mathcal{V}, \mathcal{E}, \mathcal{R})$ ▷ A video-graph
$\mathcal{V}, \mathcal{V}_{last}, \mathcal{E}^{spatial}, \mathcal{E}^{temporal} \leftarrow \emptyset, \emptyset, \emptyset, \emptyset$
for $t \in [T]$ **do**
    $SP \leftarrow SLIC(v[t], S)$
    $\mathcal{V} \leftarrow \mathcal{V} \cup SP$
    $\mathcal{E}^{spatial} \leftarrow \mathcal{E}^{spatial} \cup regionAdjacetEdges(SP)$
    $\mathcal{E}_{t-1 \to t}^{temporal} \leftarrow \emptyset$
    for $R_{t-1,i} \in \mathcal{V}_{last}$ **do**
        $\mathcal{N}_{t-1,i} \leftarrow \{R_{t,j} | d_{i,j}^{t-1 \to t} < d_{proximity}\}$
        $nn_{t-1,i} \leftarrow argmin_{R_{t,j} \in \mathcal{N}_{t,i}} |R_{t,i}.c - R_{t,j}.c|_2)$
        $\mathcal{E}_{t-1 \to t}^{temporal} \leftarrow \mathcal{E}_{t-1 \to t}^{temporal} \cup \{(R_{t-1,i}, temporal, nn_{t-1,i})\}$
    end for
    $\mathcal{E}^{temporal} \leftarrow \mathcal{E}^{temporal} \cup \mathcal{E}_{t-1 \to t}^{temporal}$
    $\mathcal{V}_{last} \leftarrow SP$
end for
return $\mathcal{G} = (\mathcal{V}, \mathcal{E} = \mathcal{E}^{spatial} \cup \mathcal{E}^{temporal}, \mathcal{R} = \{spatial, tempo\})$

3.2   Model Architecture

In order to model both the spatial and temporal relations between superpixels, our model primarily relies on the Neural Relational Model [41], which is an extension of GCNs [26] to large-scale relational data. In a Neural Relational Model, the propagation model for calculating the forward-pass update of a node, denoted by v_i, is defined as

$$h_i^{(l+1)} = \sigma \left(\sum_{r \in \mathcal{R}} \sum_{j \in \mathcal{N}_i^r} \frac{1}{c_{i,r}} W_r^{(l)} h_j^{(l)} + W_0^{(l)} h_i^{(l)} \right), \tag{5}$$

where $\mathcal{N}_i^r$ denotes the set of neighbor indices of node i under relation $r \in \mathcal{R}$ (not to be confused with the notation $\mathcal{N}_{t,i}$ from Eq. 2). $c_{i,r}$ is a problem-specific normalization constant that can either be learned or chosen in advance (such as $c_{i,r} = |\mathcal{N}_i^r|$). To incorporate edge features, we adapt the approach proposed in [10], that concatenates node and edge attributes as a layer's input, yielding the following:

$$h_i^{(l+1)} = \sigma \left(\sum_{r \in \mathcal{R}} \sum_{j \in \mathcal{N}_i^r} \frac{1}{c_{i,r}} W_r^{(l)} [h_j^{(l)}, e_{i,j}] + W_0^{(l)} h_i^{(l)} \right), \tag{6}$$

where $e_{i,j}$ is the feature of the edge connecting nodes v_i, v_j.

3.3   Augmentations

We introduce a few possible augmentations that we found useful for training our model as they improved the generalization.

Additive Gaussian Edge Noise (AGEN) - Edge attributes represent distances between superpixel centroids. The coordinates of those centroids may vary due to different superpixel shapes with different centers of mass. To compensate for this, we add a certain amount of noise to each edge attribute. Given a hyper-parameter σ_{edge}, for each edge attribute $e_{u,v}$ and for each training iteration, we sample a normally distributed variable $z_{u,v} \sim N(0, \sigma_{edge})$ that is added to the edge attribute.

Additive Gaussian Node Noise (AGNN) - Node attributes represent the colors of regions in each frame. Similar to edge attributes, the mean color of each segmented region may vary due to different superpixel shapes. To compensate for this, we add a certain amount of noise to each node attribute. Given a hyper-parameter σ_{node}, for each node attribute $v.c$ of dimension d_c and for each training iteration, we sample a normally distributed variable $z_v \sim N_{d_c}(0, \sigma_{node} \cdot I_{d_c})$ that is added to the node attribute.

Random Removal of Spatial Edges (RRSE) - This augmentation tends to mimic the regularization effect introduced in DropEdge [39]. Moreover, since the removal of edges leads to fewer message-passings in a GCN, this also accelerates the training and inference. To perform this, we choose a probability $p_{edge} \in [0,1]$. Then, each edge e is preserved with a probability of p_{edge}.

Random Removal of Superpixels (RRS) - SLIC [2] is sensitive to its initialization. Consequently, each video clip may have several graph representations during different training iterations and inference. This can be mitigated by removing a certain amount of superpixels. The outcome is fewer nodes in the corresponding representative graph, as well as fewer edges. Similar to RRSE, we choose a probability $p_{node} \in [0,1]$ so that each superpixel is preserved with a probability of p_{node}.

3.4 Benefits of *GraphVid*

Invariance - The absence of coordinates leads to invariance in the spatial dimension. It is evident that such a representation is invariant to rotations and flips since the relations between different parts of the image are solely characterized by distances. This, in turn, obviates the need to perform such augmentations during training.

Efficiency - We argue that our graph-based representation is more efficient than raw frames. To illustrate this, let T, C, H and W be the dimensions of a clip; that is, the number of frames, number of channels, height and width of a frame, respectively. Correspondingly, the raw representation requires $T \cdot C \cdot H \cdot W$. To calculate the size of the graph-video, let S be the number of superpixels in a frame. By construction, there are at most $4 \cdot S$ edges in each frame because SLIC constraints each to have 4 neighbors. Each edge contains 3 values, corresponding to the distance on the grid, source and target nodes. Additionally, there are, at most, S edges between every temporal step. This results in $3 \cdot (4 \cdot S + (T - 1) \cdot S) + C \cdot T \cdot S$ parameters in total. Typically, the second requires much fewer parameters because we choose S so that $S \ll H \cdot W$.

Prior Knowledge Incorporation - Optical-flow and over-segmentation are encoded within the graph-video representation using the inter-frame and intra-frame edges. This incorporates strong prior knowledge within the resultant representation. For example, optical-flow dramatically improved the accuracy in the two-stream methodology that was proposed in [43]. Additionally, over-segmentation using superpixels has been found useful as input features for machine learning models due to the limited loss of important details, accompanied by a dramatic reduction in the expended time by means of reducing the number of elements of the input [5,11,21].

4 Experiments

We validated *GraphVid* on 2 human-action-classification benchmarks. The goal of human action classification is to determine the human-involved action that occurs within a video. The objectives of this empirical study were twofold:

- Analyze the impact of the various parameters on the accuracy of the model.
- As we first and foremost target efficiency, we sought to examine the resources' consumption of *GraphVid* in terms of Floating Point Operations (FLOPs). We followed the conventional protocol [16], which uses single-clip FLOPs as a basic unit of computational cost. We show that we are able to achieve a significant improvement in efficiency over previous methods while preserving state-of-the-art performance.

4.1 Setup

Datasets - We use two common datasets for action classification: *Kinetics-400 (K400)* [23] and *Charades* [42]. Kinetics-400 [23] is a large-scale video dataset released in 2017 that contains 400 classes, with each category consisting of more than 400 videos. It originally had, in total, around 240K, 19K, and 38K videos for training, validation and testing subsets, respectively. Kinetics is gradually shrinking over time due to videos being taken offline, making it difficult to compare against less recent works. We used a dataset containing 208K, 17K and 33K videos for training, validation and test respectively. We report on the most recently available videos. Each video lasts approximately 10 s. The Charades dataset [42] is composed of 9,848 videos of daily indoor activities, each of an average length of 30 s. In total, the dataset contains 66,500 temporal annotations for 157 action classes. In the standard split, there are 7,986 training videos and 1,863 validation videos, sampled at 12 frames per second. We follow prior arts by reporting the Top-1 and Top-5 recognition accuracy for Kinetics-400 and mean average precision (mAP) for Charades.

Network Architecture and Training - We use GNN variants and feed each of them with our video-graphs. Specifically, we consider Graph Convolutional Networks [26] (GCNs), Graph Attention Networks [52] (GATs) and Relational Graph Convolutional Networks [41] (RGCNs). The general architecture of our backbones is depicted in Fig. 4. It consists of 2 fully-connected (FC) layers with exponential linear unit (ELU) activations that project the node features into a $256D$ feature space. Then come 4 layers of the corresponding GNN layer (either GCN, GAT or RGCN along with an edge feature concatenation from Eq. 6) with a hidden size of 512 with ELU activations, followed by global mean pooling, dropout with a probability of 0.2 and a linear layer whose output is the predicted logits. For the GAT layers, we use 4 attention heads in each layer, and average the attention heads' results to obtain the desired hidden layer size. For the RGCN layers, we specify 2 relations, which correspond to the spatial and temporal relations, as described in Sect. 3. We use the Adam [25] with a constant learning rate of $1e-3$ for optimization. While choosing this architecture, the core idea was to keep the architecture simple and shallow, while changing the interaction module to better model the relations between parts of the clip. We divide the videos into clips using a sliding window of 20 frames, using a stride of 2 between consecutive frames and a stride of 10 between clips. In all the experiments, we used a fixed batch size of 200.

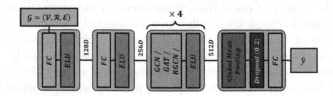

Fig. 4. The general graph neural network architecture we use in our experiments.

Inference - At the test phase, we use the same sliding window methodology as in the training. We follow the common practice of processing multiple views of a long video and average per-view logits to obtain the final results. The views are drawn uniformly across the temporal dimension of the video, without spatial cropping. The number of views is determined by the validation dataset.

Implementation Details - All experiments were run on a Ubuntu 18.04 machine with Intel i9-10920X, 93GB RAM and 2 GeForce RTX 3090 GPUs. Our implementation of *GraphVid* is in Python3. To generate superpixels, we use *fast-slic* [24] with the AVX2 instruction set. To train the graph neural models, we use Pytorch-Geometric [19]. We use a fixed seed for SLIC and cache the generated graphs during the first training epochs in order to further reduce the computations. We also store the edge indexes as int16 instead of int64 in order to reduce the memory footprint. Eventually, the memory footprints of the cached datasets is comparable to those of the original ones.

4.2   Ablation Study

We conduct an in-depth study on Kinetics-400 to analyze the performance gain contributed by incorporating the different components of *GraphVid*.

Graph Neural Network Variants and Number of Superpixels per Frame - We assess the performance of different GNN variants: GCN [26] is trained without edge relations (*i.e.* temporal and spatial edges are treated via the same weights). GAT [52] is trained by employing the attention mechanism for neighborhood aggregation without edge relations. RGCN [41] is trained with edge relations, as described in Sect. 3.2.

The results of the action classification on K-400 are shown in Fig. 5. In this series, the number of views is fixed at 8, which is the number of views that was found to be most effective for the validation set. For all variants, increasing the number of superpixels per frame (S) contributes to the accuracy. We notice a significant improvement in accuracy for the lower range of the number of superpixels, while the accuracy begins to saturate for $S \geq 650$. Increasing further the number of superpixels leads to bigger inputs, which require more computations. As our goal is to maximize the efficiency, we do not experiment with larger inputs in this section. We further present in Table 1 the models' specifications for 800 superpixels, which is the best-performing configuration in this series of

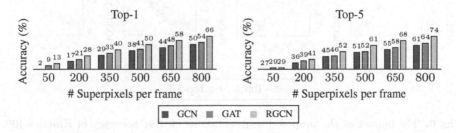

Fig. 5. The effect of varying the number of superpixels on test accuracy on K-400.

experiments. Unsurprisingly, the GCN variant requires the least amount of computations. Meanwhile, the RGCN variant requires fewer computations than GAT and achieves a higher level of accuracy. We conclude that it is beneficial to incorporate edge relations when wishing to encode temporal and spatial relations in videos, and that those features are not easily learned by heavy computational models, such as GAT.

Table 1. Comparison of model specifications for various architectures. We report the Top-1 and Top-5 accuracy on Kinetics-400.

Model	Top-1	Top-5	FLOPs ($\cdot 10^9$)	Params ($\cdot 10^6$)
GCN	50.1	61.6	28	2.08
GAT	54.7	64.5	56	3.93
RGCN	66.2	74.1	42	2.99

Augmentations - We assessed the impact of augmentations on the performance and their ability to alleviate over-fitting. For this purpose, we chose the best configuration obtained from the previous experiments, that is, RGCN with 800 superpixels per frame, and trained it while adding one augmentation at a time. The results of this series are depicted in Fig. 7. Each graph shows the level of accuracy reached by training the model with one of the parameters that control the augmentation (Fig. 7).

We begin with the analysis of the AGEN and AGNN, both relate to the addition of Gaussian noise to the graph components, with the corresponding parameters controlling the standard deviations. Their impact is unnoticeable as these parameters head towards 0, since lower values reflect the scenarios in which little or no augmentations are applied. Slightly increasing the parameter brings about a gradual improvement in the accuracy, until a turning point is reached, after which the level of accuracy declines until it reaches $\sim \frac{1}{400}$, which resembles a random classifier. The decrease in accuracy stems from the noise obscuring the

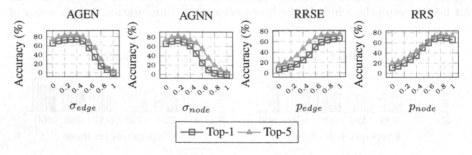

Fig. 6. The impact of the proposed augmentations on test accuracy of Kinetics-400: Additive Gaussian edge noise (AGEN). Additive Gaussian node noise (AGNN). Random removal of spatial edges (RRSE). Random removal of superpixels (RRS).

original signal, allegedly forcing the classifier to classify ungeneralizable noise. For RRSE and RRS, the random removal of spatial edges harms the accuracy of the model. This finding leads us to conclude that spatial edges encode meaningful information about relations between the entities. Moreover, slightly removing the nodes contributes to the level of accuracy, reaching a peak at $p_{node} \approx 0.8$. To conclude, we present the values that lead to the best Top-1 accuracy score in Table 2.

Table 2. Augmentation parameters and their optimized values.

Param	σ_{edge}	σ_{node}	p_{edge}	p_{node}
Value	0.4	0.2	1	0.8
Top-1	74.5	73	66	70
Top-5	85	83	74	76

4.3 Comparison to the State-of-the-Art

Kinetics-400 - We present the K-400 results for our RGCN variant in Table 3 and Fig. 7a, along with comparisons to previous arts, including convolutional-based and transformer-based methods. Our results are denoted RGCN-d, where d represents the number of superpixels. Additionally, we use the set of augmentations with the parameters from Table 2. First, when the RGCN-800 model is trained with the full set of augmentations (denoted Full-Aug), it achieves a significantly higher Top-1 accuracy than when it is trained without any augmentation (denoted No-Aug) or when each augmentation is applied individually. These results demonstrate the effectiveness of our model and that our augmentations can alleviate overfitting and improve the generalization over the test set.

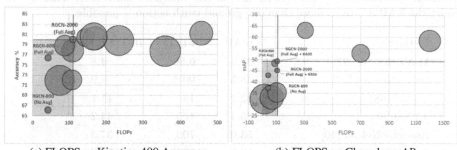

(a) FLOPS vs Kinetics-400 Accuracy   (b) FLOPS vs Charades mAP

Fig. 7. Model FLOPs vs. performance - Green bubbles indicates *GraphVid* variants, radius indicates the number of parameters. To avoid overloading, identities of the other models are omitted. For both datasets, RGCN-2000 with the full set of augmentations is on par with the state-of-the-art, while greatly reducing model size and FLOPs. (Color figure online)

Second, all our RGCNs require orders-of-magnitude fewer computations than the previous arts, as well as more than ×10 fewer parameters.

Table 3. Comparisons to state-of-the-art on the K-400 dataset. We report the Top-1 and Top-5 accuracies. The top section of the table depicts convolution-based models, The middle section depicts transformer-based models, and the bottom section depicts ours.

Method	Top-1	Top-5	Views	FLOPs ($\cdot 10^9$)	Param ($\cdot 10^6$)
SlowFast R101+N [17]	79.8	93.9	30	234	59.9
X3D-XXL R101+N [16]	80.4	94.6	30	144	20.3
MViT-B, 32×3 [15]	80.2	94.4	5	170	36.6
TimeSformer-L [6]	80.7	94.7	3	2380	121.4
ViT-B-VTN [34]	78.6	93.7	1	4218	11.04
ViViT-L/16x2 [4]	80.6	94.7	12	1446	310.8
Swin-S [31]	80.6	94.5	12	166	49.8
RGCN-800 (No/Full Aug)	66.2/76.4	74.1/91.1	8	**42**	**2.57**
RGCN-2000 (Full Aug)	80.0	94.3	8	**110**	**2.57**

Charades - We train RGCN variants with 800 and 2000 superpixels with the set of augmentations found in Table 2. We also follow prior arts [15,17] by pre-training on K-400 followed by replacing the last FC layer and fine-tuning on Charades. Table 4 and Fig. 7b show that when our RGCN model is trained with 2000 superpixels, its mAP score is comparable to the current state-of-the-art, but this score is reached with orders-of-magnitude fewer computations and using considerably fewer parameters.

Table 4. Comparisons to state-of-the-art on the Charades multi-label dataset. We report the mAP scores as more than one ground truth action is possible.

Method	mAP	FLOPs ($\cdot 10^9$)	Params ($\cdot 10^6$)
MoVieNet-A2 [27]	32.5	6.59	4.8
MoVieNet-A4 [27]	48.5	90.4	4.9
TVN-1 [38]	32.2	13	11.1
TVN-4 [38]	35.4	106	44.2
AssembleNet-50 [40]	53.0	700	37.3
AssembleNet-101 [40]	58.6	1200	53.3
SlowFast 16 × 8 R101 [17]	45.2	7020	59.9
RGCN-800 (No Aug/Full Aug)	37.4/43.1	**42**	**2.57**
RGCN-2000 (Full Aug/+K400)	45.3/49.4	**110**	**2.57**

4.4 Video-Graph Generation Run-Time

The transition into a video-graph representation requires the consideration
of the time needed for generating
it. In Fig. 8, we measured the average time needed using our setup,
which include the whole pipeline: **1.**
Superpixels calculation, and **2.** Graph
structure generation, that is, creating
edges between adjacent super-pixels
and features calculation as described
in Sect. 3. Interestingly, the first step
is relatively short compared to the
second. Apparently, the optimized
fast-slic [24] performs well, while the
search for adjacent superpixels is time
consuming. This opens the possibilities of further optimization.

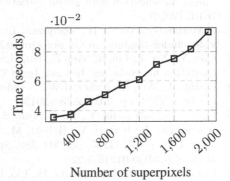

Fig. 8. Time of generation depending on
the number of superpixels.

5 Conclusions and Future Work

In this paper, we present *GraphVid*, a graph video representations that enable
video-processing via graph neural networks. Furthermore, we propose a relational graph convolutional model that suits this representation. Our experimental study demonstrates this model's efficiency in performing video-related tasks
while achieving comparable performance to the current state-of-the-art. An interesting avenue for future work is to explore new graph representations of videos,
including learnable methods. Additionally, we consider the development of new
dedicated graph neural models for processing the unique and dynamic structure
of the video-graph as an interesting research direction. Finally, unified models for
image and video understanding that disregard temporal edges could be explored
in order to take advantage of the amount of data in both worlds.

References

1. Abadal, S., Jain, A., Guirado, R., López-Alonso, J., Alarcón, E.: Computing graph
   neural networks: a survey from algorithms to accelerators. ACM Computi. Surv.
   (CSUR) **54**(9), 1–38 (2021)
2. Achanta, R., Shaji, A., Smith, K., Lucchi, A., Fua, P., Süsstrunk, S.: Slic superpixels. Technical report (2010)
3. Akbari, H., et al.: Vatt: transformers for multimodal self-supervised learning from
   raw video, audio and text. arXiv preprint arXiv:2104.11178 (2021)
4. Arnab, A., Dehghani, M., Heigold, G., Sun, C., Lučić, M., Schmid, C.: ViViT: a
   video vision transformer. arXiv preprint arXiv:2103.15691 (2021)

5. Avelar, P.H., Tavares, A.R., da Silveira, T.L., Jung, C.R., Lamb, L.C.: Superpixel image classification with graph attention networks. In: SIBGRAPI, pp. 203–209. IEEE (2020)
6. Bertasius, G., Wang, H., Torresani, L.: Is space-time attention all you need for video understanding? arXiv preprint arXiv:2102.05095 (2021)
7. Cao, Y., Xu, J., Lin, S., Wei, F., Hu, H.: GCNet: non-local networks meet squeeze-excitation networks and beyond. In: ICCV Workshops, pp. 0–0 (2019)
8. Chang, J., Wei, D., Fisher, J.W.: A video representation using temporal superpixels. In: CVPR, pp. 2051–2058 (2013)
9. Chen, Y., Kalantidis, Y., Li, J., Yan, S., Feng, J.: Multi-fiber networks for video recognition. In: Ferrari, V., Hebert, M., Sminchisescu, C., Weiss, Y. (eds.) ECCV 2018. LNCS, vol. 11205, pp. 364–380. Springer, Cham (2018). https://doi.org/10.1007/978-3-030-01246-5_22
10. Corso, G., Cavalleri, L., Beaini, D., Liò, P., Veličković, P.: Principal neighbourhood aggregation for graph nets. arXiv preprint arXiv:2004.05718 (2020)
11. Dadsetan, S., Pichler, D., Wilson, D., Hovakimyan, N., Hobbs, J.: Superpixels and graph convolutional neural networks for efficient detection of nutrient deficiency stress from aerial imagery. In: CVPR, pp. 2950–2959 (2021)
12. Dokania, S., Singh, V.: Graph representation learning for audio & music genre classification. arXiv preprint arXiv:1910.11117 (2019)
13. Dosovitskiy, A., et al.: An image is worth 16x16 words: transformers for image recognition at scale. arXiv preprint arXiv:2010.11929 (2020)
14. Du Tran, H.W., Torresani, L., Ray, J., Lecun, Y., Paluri, M.: A closer look at spatiotemporal convolutions for action recognition (2017)
15. Fan, H., et al.: Multiscale vision transformers. arXiv preprint arXiv:2104.11227 (2021)
16. Feichtenhofer, C.: X3D: expanding architectures for efficient video recognition. In: CVPR, pp. 203–213 (2020)
17. Feichtenhofer, C., Fan, H., Malik, J., He, K.: Slowfast networks for video recognition. In: ICCV, pp. 6202–6211 (2019)
18. Fernández, D., et al.: ViTs: video tagging system from massive web multimedia collections. In: ICCV Workshops, pp. 337–346 (2017)
19. Fey, M., Lenssen, J.E.: Fast graph representation learning with PyTorch geometric. arXiv preprint arXiv:1903.02428 (2019)
20. Girdhar, R., Carreira, J., Doersch, C., Zisserman, A.: Video action transformer network. In: CVPR, pp. 244–253 (2019)
21. Gonzalo-Martin, C., Garcia-Pedrero, A., Lillo-Saavedra, M., Menasalvas, E.: Deep learning for superpixel-based classification of remote sensing images, September 2016. https://proceedings.utwente.nl/401/
22. He, K., Zhang, X., Ren, S., Sun, J.: Deep residual learning for image recognition. In: Proceedings of the IEEE Conference on Computer Vision and Pattern Recognition, pp. 770–778 (2016)
23. Kay, W., et al.: The kinetics human action video dataset. arXiv preprint arXiv:1705.06950 (2017)
24. Kim, A.: fast-slic (2019). https://github.com/Algy/fast-slic
25. Kingma, D.P., Ba, J.: Adam: a method for stochastic optimization. arXiv preprint arXiv:1412.6980 (2014)
26. Kipf, T.N., Welling, M.: Semi-supervised classification with graph convolutional networks. arXiv preprint arXiv:1609.02907 (2016)
27. Kondratyuk, D., et al.: MoviNets: mobile video networks for efficient video recognition. In: CVPR, pp. 16020–16030 (2021)

28. Kumar, A., Singh, S.S., Singh, K., Biswas, B.: Link prediction techniques, applications, and performance: a survey. Physica A: Stat. Mech. Appl. **553**, 124289 (2020)
29. LeCun, Y., Bengio, Y., Hinton, G.: Deep learning. Nature **521**(7553), 436–444 (2015)
30. Li, X., et al.: ViDTR: video transformer without convolutions. arXiv preprint arXiv:2104.11746 (2021)
31. Liu, Z., et al.: Video swin transformer. arXiv preprint arXiv:2106.13230 (2021)
32. Mittal, S., et al.: A survey of accelerator architectures for 3D convolution neural networks. J. Syst. Archit. 102041 (2021)
33. Monti, F., Boscaini, D., Masci, J., Rodola, E., Svoboda, J., Bronstein, M.M.: Geometric deep learning on graphs and manifolds using mixture model CNNs. In: CVPR, pp. 5115–5124 (2017)
34. Neimark, D., Bar, O., Zohar, M., Asselmann, D.: Video transformer network. arXiv preprint arXiv:2102.00719 (2021)
35. Oprea, S., et al.: A review on deep learning techniques for video prediction. IEEE Trans. Pattern Anal. Mach. Intell. (2020)
36. Papon, J., Abramov, A., Schoeler, M., Worgotter, F.: Voxel cloud connectivity segmentation-supervoxels for point clouds. In: CVPR, pp. 2027–2034 (2013)
37. Pareek, P., Thakkar, A.: A survey on video-based human action recognition: recent updates, datasets, challenges, and applications. Artif. Intell. Rev. **54**(3), 2259–2322 (2021)
38. Piergiovanni, A., Angelova, A., Ryoo, M.S.: Tiny video networks. Appl. AI Lett. e38 (2019)
39. Rong, Y., Huang, W., Xu, T., Huang, J.: DropEdge: towards deep graph convolutional networks on node classification. arXiv preprint arXiv:1907.10903 (2019)
40. Ryoo, M.S., Piergiovanni, A., Tan, M., Angelova, A.: AssembleNet: searching for multi-stream neural connectivity in video architectures. arXiv preprint arXiv:1905.13209 (2019)
41. Schlichtkrull, M., Kipf, T.N., Bloem, P., van den Berg, R., Titov, I., Welling, M.: Modeling relational data with graph convolutional networks. In: Gangemi, A., et al. (eds.) ESWC 2018. LNCS, vol. 10843, pp. 593–607. Springer, Cham (2018). https://doi.org/10.1007/978-3-319-93417-4_38
42. Sigurdsson, G.A., Varol, G., Wang, X., Farhadi, A., Laptev, I., Gupta, A.: Hollywood in homes: crowdsourcing data collection for activity understanding. In: Leibe, B., Matas, J., Sebe, N., Welling, M. (eds.) ECCV 2016. LNCS, vol. 9905, pp. 510–526. Springer, Cham (2016). https://doi.org/10.1007/978-3-319-46448-0_31
43. Simonyan, K., Zisserman, A.: Two-stream convolutional networks for action recognition in videos. arXiv preprint arXiv:1406.2199 (2014)
44. Srivastava, N., Mansimov, E., Salakhudinov, R.: Unsupervised learning of video representations using LSTMs. In: ICML, pp. 843–852. PMLR (2015)
45. Stutz, D., Hermans, A., Leibe, B.: Superpixels: an evaluation of the state-of-the-art. Comput. Vis. Image Underst. **166**, 1–27 (2018)
46. Suarez, J.J.P., Naval Jr., P.C.: A survey on deep learning techniques for video anomaly detection. arXiv preprint arXiv:2009.14146 (2020)
47. Touvron, H., Cord, M., Douze, M., Massa, F., Sablayrolles, A., Jégou, H.: Training data-efficient image transformers & distillation through attention. In: ICML, pp. 10347–10357. PMLR (2021)
48. Tran, D., Bourdev, L., Fergus, R., Torresani, L., Paluri, M.: Learning spatiotemporal features with 3D convolutional networks. In: ICCV, pp. 4489–4497 (2015)

49. Tran, D., Wang, H., Torresani, L., Ray, J., LeCun, Y., Paluri, M.: A closer look at spatiotemporal convolutions for action recognition. In: CVPR, pp. 6450–6459 (2018)

50. Ullah, A., Ahmad, J., Muhammad, K., Sajjad, M., Baik, S.W.: Action recognition in video sequences using deep bi-directional LSTM with CNN features. IEEE Access **6**, 1155–1166 (2017)

51. Vaswani, A., et al.: Attention is all you need. In: Advances in Neural Information Processing Systems, pp. 5998–6008 (2017)

52. Veličković, P., Cucurull, G., Casanova, A., Romero, A., Lio, P., Bengio, Y.: Graph attention networks. arXiv preprint arXiv:1710.10903 (2017)

53. Wang, X., Girshick, R., Gupta, A., He, K.: Non-local neural networks. In: CVPR, pp. 7794–7803 (2018)

54. Wang, X., Gupta, A.: Videos as space-time region graphs. In: Ferrari, V., Hebert, M., Sminchisescu, C., Weiss, Y. (eds.) ECCV 2018. LNCS, vol. 11209, pp. 413–431. Springer, Cham (2018). https://doi.org/10.1007/978-3-030-01228-1_25

55. Xie, R., Liu, Z., Jia, J., Luan, H., Sun, M.: Representation learning of knowledge graphs with entity descriptions. In: Proceedings of the AAAI Conference on Artificial Intelligence, vol. 30 (2016)

56. Xie, S., Sun, C., Huang, J., Tu, Z., Murphy, K.: Rethinking spatiotemporal feature learning: speed-accuracy trade-offs in video classification. In: Ferrari, V., Hebert, M., Sminchisescu, C., Weiss, Y. (eds.) ECCV 2018. LNCS, vol. 11219, pp. 318–335. Springer, Cham (2018). https://doi.org/10.1007/978-3-030-01267-0_19

57. Xu, C., Corso, J.J.: Evaluation of super-voxel methods for early video processing. In: 2012 IEEE Conference on Computer Vision and Pattern Recognition, pp. 1202–1209 (2012). https://doi.org/10.1109/CVPR.2012.6247802

58. Xu, C., Xiong, C., Corso, J.J.: Streaming hierarchical video segmentation. In: Fitzgibbon, A., Lazebnik, S., Perona, P., Sato, Y., Schmid, C. (eds.) ECCV 2012. LNCS, vol. 7577, pp. 626–639. Springer, Heidelberg (2012). https://doi.org/10.1007/978-3-642-33783-3_45

59. Yue-Hei Ng, J., Hausknecht, M., Vijayanarasimhan, S., Vinyals, O., Monga, R., Toderici, G.: Beyond short snippets: deep networks for video classification. In: CVPR, pp. 4694–4702 (2015)

60. Zhang, D., Yin, J., Zhu, X., Zhang, C.: Network representation learning: a survey. IEEE Trans. Big Data **6**(1), 3–28 (2018)

61. Zhang, S., Qin, Y., Sun, K., Lin, Y.: Few-shot audio classification with attentional graph neural networks. In: INTERSPEECH, pp. 3649–3653 (2019)

Delta Distillation for Efficient Video Processing

Amirhossein Habibian[1]([✉]), Haitam Ben Yahia[1], Davide Abati[1],
Efstratios Gavves[2], and Fatih Porikli[1]

[1] Qualcomm AI Research, California, USA
{ahabibia,hyahia,dabati,fporikli}@qti.qualcomm.com
[2] University of Amsterdam, Amsterdam, Netherlands
egavves@uva.nl

Abstract. This paper aims to accelerate video stream processing, such as object detection and semantic segmentation, by leveraging the temporal redundancies that exist between video frames. Instead of propagating and warping features using motion alignment, such as optical flow, we propose a novel knowledge distillation schema coined as Delta Distillation. In our proposal, the student learns the variations in the teacher's intermediate features over time. We demonstrate that these temporal variations can be effectively distilled due to the temporal redundancies within video frames. During inference, both teacher and student cooperate for providing predictions: the former by providing initial representations extracted only on the key-frame, and the latter by iteratively estimating and applying deltas for the successive frames. Moreover, we consider various design choices to learn optimal student architectures including an end-to-end learnable architecture search. By extensive experiments on a wide range of architectures, including the most efficient ones, we demonstrate that delta distillation sets a new state of the art in terms of accuracy vs. efficiency trade-off for semantic segmentation and object detection in videos. Finally, we show that, as a by-product, delta distillation improves the temporal consistency of the teacher model.

1 Introduction

The goal of this paper is to accelerate the processing of video streams, such as object detection and semantic segmentation. Despite the great progress in the development of efficient architectures [2,15,23,42,44,50], highly accurate models are still too expensive to process video frames in real-time. This aspect hinders the deployment of accurate models on constrained settings, *i.e.* mobile devices.

To this end, recent works apply accurate yet expensive models only on a subset of frames, referred to as key-frames, and process the remaining ones using

---

Qualcomm AI Research is an initiative of Qualcomm Technologies, Inc.

Supplementary Information The online version contains supplementary material available at https://doi.org/10.1007/978-3-031-19833-5_13.

S. Avidan et al. (Eds.): ECCV 2022, LNCS 13695, pp. 213–229, 2022.
https://doi.org/10.1007/978-3-031-19833-5_13

Fig. 1. Feature distillation vs. Delta distillation. Instead of distilling features z computed with an expensive layer f, we distill to a cheap student g their changes across frames, Δz. Due to temporal correlation in videos, transitions between frames are smooth and deltas are smaller (as visible) thus easier to distill.

a lighter architecture [18, 24–26, 54, 56]. The representations from the light model are then aggregated with the key-frame representations from the expensive model in a recurrent structure: this step is typically performed at a deep layer, in order to leverage the representation power of the expensive model. Due to the misalignment between the current frame and key-frame, this strategy proves to be effective only when explicit motion alignment is carried out, typically by means of optical flow warping [18, 54, 56]. For this reason, feature aggregation is a viable solution under the assumption that the overhead for extracting motion vectors is lower than in computations within the bypassed feature extraction. Although this condition is easy to meet for expensive backbones such as ResNet-101, it has become less reasonable with the development of efficient models such as EfficientDet [42] or HRNet [44].

This paper introduces a novel approach to leverage the redundancies in a video to speed up the inference. Our proposal does not rely on explicit motion alignment and is applicable to any architecture, including the most efficient ones, $i.e.$EfficientDet-D0 [42], HRNet [44] and the very recent DDRNet [13]. Our approach, coined as Delta Distillation, is based on knowledge distillation [7,12], a popular technique to accelerate an expensive *teacher* network by distilling it into a lightweight *student*. Given an expensive teacher processing only key-frames, for every block of layers, we instantiate a cheap student counterpart, that is fed with a pair of frames and regresses their corresponding difference (delta) in teacher activations. During training, the teacher provides target deltas, and the regression error of the student is minimized by an ℓ_2 objective. During inference, the teacher provides the representations for the key-frame, and the student iteratively updates them by adding predicted deltas in the following frames. Due to the dense interplay between the teacher and student, happening at every block of the network, delta distillation effectively aggregates the features across frames without any explicit motion alignment.

Delta distillation has major differences to the common knowledge distillation setting, where the student learns to regress the teacher features as in Fig. 1 (left). Instead of *distilling the features*, delta distillation aims for *distilling the temporal changes in the features* as illustrated in Fig. 1 (right). Intuitively, instead of learning the feature space embedding of their teacher, the delta distillation students learn the manifolds generated by transitions between samples, which we assume to be smooth in the case of correlated video frames. We therefore hypothesize - and verify experimentally - that delta distillation, as compared to feature distillation, allows for learning much cheaper student functions for comparable performance. Moreover, in contrast to the common knowledge distillation that relies solely on the student network to process all the test samples, delta distillation leverages both teacher and student during the inference. This trait enables delta distillation to enjoy having more parameters (coming from both models) without increasing the computational cost, as each test sample is processed by either the teacher or student network.

We summarize our contributions as follows: *i)* We propose delta distillation, a novel approach to accelerate video inference without any explicit motion compensation involved. *ii)* We elaborate various design choices to learn optimal student architectures including an end-to-end learnable architecture search. *iii)* We conduct extensive experiments on two different tasks and a wide range of models, including the most efficient architectures. Our analysis demonstrates that delta distillation sets a new state of the art in terms of accuracy vs. efficiency trade-off for semantic segmentation and object detection in videos. *iv)* We show that, as a by-product, delta distillation improves the temporal consistency of the teacher model, even though it is not explicitly optimized to do so.

2   Related Work

Efficiency in Deep Learning. Improving efficiency of neural networks is an active research area studied from multiple directions, comprising: quantization, to represent weights and activations with a low bit precision [9,16,20,31], pruning, to discard unimportant or redundant channels [6,11,23], neural architecture search, to find network designs with good accuracy vs. efficiency trade-offs [2,30], and low rank kernel decompositions [11,50]. However, for models operating on videos, redundancy among consecutive frames represents the most essential leverage to improve efficiency. In recent years, several works investigated in this direction, and they represent the closest efforts to our proposal. To avoid extracting expensive representations at every frame, feature aggregation using optical flow was explored [18,54,56]. Nevertheless, the application of such an approach on modern efficient architectures has become harder, as it requires careful model design and a proper cost balance between the feature extraction and motion alignment. Other works aim at building powerful representations over time, by aggregating features extracted by efficient models on past frames [14,24–26]. These recurrent methods, however, prove more effective whenever explicit motion alignment operations are carried out [14], which incur an extra computational cost. Finally, sparse computation models limit the feature extraction to sparse spatial locations that change over time, *e.g.* at a pixel [10] or at patch level [1]. However, this strategy is not robust to highly dynamic scenes, where most pixels change. Additionally, the theoretical compute gains do not always translate to latency improvement due to the inefficiency of sparse operations in most platforms.

Knowledge Distillation. Another well established direction to accelerate deep neural networks is knowledge distillation [12], where an efficient student network is optimized to match the output of an expansive teacher network or model ensemble. This approach was then extended by performing such an optimization within network stages, effectively distilling intermediate functions rather than the output only [36]. After these seminal works, efforts have been spent towards online distillation methods, dropping the asynchronous training regimes of teacher and students in favor of a single optimization procedure. For instance, in [51] multiple networks learn collaboratively without any teacher, and more recent works formalize the latter as ensemble of multiple students [8,21,47]. However, all these approaches do not specifically target video use-cases, and therefore transfer knowledge between models without explicitly distilling any temporal dynamic. Differently, the proposed delta distillation directly operates on temporal changes of features and, as demonstrated by experiments, allows for much cheaper student models for comparable quality.

Furthermore, some recent works adapt the general framework to specific recognition tasks, for instance by selecting specific spatial locations for teacher-student distillation in for anchor-based object detection [5,45]. We hereby remark that our approach is task-agnostic and can be applied to any video task.

3   Delta Distillation

We start with a teacher $\mathcal{F}$ as a *spatial* network generating accurate representations for a given downstream task, *e.g.*HRNet [44] or FasterRCNN [34]. Our goal is to distill this model into a more efficient *spatio-temporal* equivalent. We first break $\mathcal{F}$ down into a composition of L parametric blocks, as:

$$\mathcal{F} = f^L \circ \cdots \circ f^2 \circ f^1.$$

We describe delta distillation for a single block, however highlighting that we carry out the procedure in all blocks within a given network. The l-th block f^l takes the form:

$$z^l = f^l_{\theta_l}(x^l),$$

where x^l and z^l denote the input and output of the block respectively, and θ_l describes its learnable parameters. To simplify the notation, we will omit the block index l as we focus on a single block ($z = f_\theta(x)$), and will reintroduce it in Sect. 3.3, where we define the overall network.

Feature Distillation. Feature distillation [36] treats every block f_θ as a teacher block, providing target feature maps to supervise a student block g_ϕ, parametrized by ϕ, typically designed to be much cheaper. For instance, a distillation objective optimizes the expected ℓ_2 norm of the error between f_θ and g_ϕ:

$$\mathcal{L}_d(x; \phi) = \mathbb{E}_x \left[\| f_\theta(x) - g_\phi(x) \|_2 \right]. \tag{1}$$

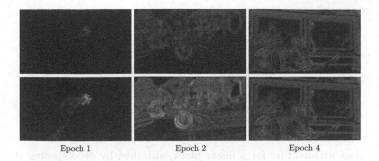

Epoch 1   Epoch 2   Epoch 4

Fig. 2. The student deltas $\Delta\tilde{\mathbf{z}}_t$ (top) vs. teacher deltas $\Delta\mathbf{z}_t$ (bottom). Thorough train-ing the student learns to approximate the deltas from its teacher.

Delta Distillation. Given a sequence of inputs $\mathbf{x}_t$, the output of a block f_θ at a time-step t can be written as:

$$\mathbf{z}_t = \mathbf{z}_{t-1} + \Delta\mathbf{z}_t,$$

where $\Delta\mathbf{z}_t$ represents how the output of the teacher changes over time. Consid-ering the correlation between the consecutive samples in a video, we hypothesize that $\Delta\mathbf{z}_t$, being a transition function in the feature manifold, has a lower rank compared to the mapping f_θ. For example, in the extreme case of identical frames, $\Delta\mathbf{z}_t$ will be of rank 0. We argue that $\Delta\mathbf{z}_t$ can be distilled more effec-tively than $\mathbf{z}_t$ by a student with the same number of parameters, as verified by our experiments. In delta distillation, the student approximates the deltas given the current and previous frames as:

$$\Delta\tilde{\mathbf{z}}_t \approx g_\phi(\mathbf{x}_t, \mathbf{x}_{t-1}).$$

This idea represents the core of our proposal that shifts the perspective from distilling the function, in Eq. 1, to distilling its temporal changes as:

$$\mathcal{L}_{dd}(\mathbf{x}_t, \mathbf{x}_{t-1}; \phi) = \mathbb{E}_{\mathbf{x}_t, \mathbf{z}_t} \left[\| \Delta\mathbf{z}_t - g_\phi(\mathbf{x}_t, \mathbf{x}_{t-1})\|_2\right]. \tag{2}$$

By optimizing this objective, the student deltas $\Delta\tilde{\mathbf{z}}_t$ converge to the teacher deltas $\Delta\mathbf{z}_t$ as shown in Fig. 2.

3.1 Student Architectures

As in any distillation approach, delta distillation admits diverse architectural choices [7], in terms of $i)$ granularity at which it should operate, $e.g.$distilling single convolutions vs distilling residual blocks or branches and $ii)$ possible archi-tectures for the student block. In our implementation, we consider the following:

Linear blocks that define the teachers and students at every convolution. In this case, we only feed the student with the input residual $\Delta\mathbf{x}_t = \mathbf{x}_t - \mathbf{x}_{t-1}$:

$$g_\phi(\mathbf{x}_t, \mathbf{x}_{t-1}) = g_\phi^{conv}(\Delta\mathbf{x}_t).$$

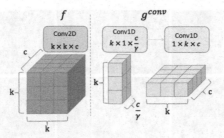

Fig. 3. Student architecture for a linear block, obtained by decomposing the teacher kernel as a sequence of two 1D kernels with $\gamma\times$ less number of intermediate channels. For simplicity, we only visualize the output channels.

This choice is motivated by the Taylor approximation of f_θ where, if the function f_θ is linear, only the first order term is non-zero, and the derivative $\nabla f_\theta(\mathbf{x}_{t-1})$ is a constant:

$$\Delta\mathbf{z}_t = \nabla f_\theta(\mathbf{x}_{t-1})\Delta\mathbf{x}_t + \frac{1}{2}\nabla^2 f_\theta(\mathbf{x}_{t-1})\Delta\mathbf{x}_t^2 + \dots \qquad (3)$$

As the student architecture, we rely on a spatial kernel factorization as depicted in Fig. 3. Similar to the spatial SVD [17], we decompose each 2D kernel as a sequence of two 1D kernels while reducing the number of intermediate channels by a compression factor γ.

Non-linear blocks that define the teachers and students at a coarser granularity as a sequence of residual blocks. In this case, according to the Taylor approximation in Eq. 3, we parameterize the student as a function of both the previous input $\mathbf{x}_{t-1}$ and input residual $\Delta\mathbf{x}_t$ concatenated along the channel dimension:

$$g_\phi(\mathbf{x}_t, \mathbf{x}_{t-1}) = g_\phi^{block}(\mathbf{x}_{t-1}, \Delta\mathbf{x}_t).$$

As the student architecture, we envision two strategies: *i) channel reduction*, where the student mirrors the teacher but with fewer channels: we add two pointwise convolution to the block as first and last layer to shrink and expand the channels respectively by a fixed factor. *ii) spatial reduction*, where the student resembles the teacher but operates on a smaller resolution: we add a strided pointwise convolution and a pixel shuffle up-sampling to the beginning and the end of each block, respectively.

3.2   Student Architecture Search

Different layers within a network may be compressible to different extents. We empirically found that there might exist a few critical layers[1] that are not amenable to distillation: if compressed, they hinder the model performance. Therefore, instead of committing to the same student architecture for all the

---

[1] As an example, transition layers in HRNets [44].

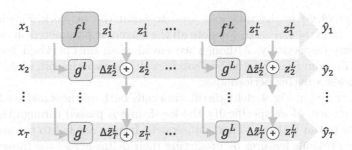

Fig. 4. Delta distillation at inference. The teacher computes the features for the key-frame, while the student updates the features by predicting deltas over time.

blocks, we introduce two candidates: *i)* non-compressed architecture, identical to the teacher, preferred for hard-to-compress blocks. *ii)* compressed architecture using the techniques introduced above for linear and non-linear blocks.

To find optimal student architectures, we introduce a learnable parameter $\psi \in \mathbb{R}^2$ per block, that is learned jointly with the student parameters. During training, architectures are sampled from a categorical distribution q_ψ over the two candidate models, obtained by feeding ψ to a softmax layer. We rely on the Gumbel-softmax [19, 28] reparametrization to estimate gradients. To encourage the search algorithm to opt for the compressed architecture, we introduce a sparsity regularization objective as:

$$\mathcal{L}_s(;\psi) = \mathbb{E}_{g_\phi \sim q_\psi}\left[\text{FLOPs}(g_\phi)\right], \tag{4}$$

where FLOPs is the complexity of the sampled architecture g_ϕ in terms of the number of floating point operations. This loss encourages the model to select the more efficient student architecture as much as possible. If not regularized, ψ would converge to the trivial solution of selecting the non-compressed architecture as it has a higher capacity and a better distillation performance.

3.3 Training and Inference

Given a trained teacher network $\mathcal{F}$, comprising the teacher blocks, and a training set of labeled clips with T frames $\{(\mathbf{x}_{1:T}, \mathbf{y}_{1:T})\}$, we train the delta distillation by optimizing the following objective:

$$\mathbb{E}_{\mathbf{x}_{1:T}, \mathbf{y}_{1:T}}\left[\frac{1}{T}\sum_{t=1}^{T}\left(\mathcal{L}_t + \alpha \sum_{l=1}^{L}\mathcal{L}_{dd}^l + \beta \sum_{l=1}^{L}\mathcal{L}_s^l\right)\right] \tag{5}$$

where $\mathcal{L}_{dd}^l$ and $\mathcal{L}_s^l$ denote the delta distillation and the sparsity regularization losses, computed for the l-th block, as defined in Eqs. 2 and 4 respectively. The hyper-parameters α and β balance the contribution of the losses to learn a model yielding the best accuracy vs. efficiency trade-off.

$\mathcal{L}_t(\mathbf{x}_t, \mathbf{y}_t; \Theta, \Phi)$ is the task loss used to train the network $\mathcal{F}$, where $\Theta = \{\theta_1 \ldots \theta_L\}$ and $\Phi = \{\phi_1 \ldots \phi_L\}$ denote all the learnable parameters in the teacher and student, respectively. Although we envision an unsupervised training, by excluding $\mathcal{L}_t$ from the objective, we conduct all our experiments while including $\mathcal{L}_t$ as it yields a better performance.

As illustrated in Fig. 4, delta distillation calls both teachers and students during the inference. More specifically, the key-frame is passed through the teacher to compute initial features. Then, subsequent frames are fed to the students to update the previous features by predicting their deltas across the frames. This is different from typical knowledge distillation settings, such as feature distillation, where the teacher is only used during training and not during inference. Pseudo code for training and inference is provided in the supplementary material.

3.4   Temporal Consistency

Another aspect of increasing importance for video streaming tasks is temporal consistency of model responses [22,27,33]. Indeed, flickering predictions can make decision-making difficult in critical scenarios. Although our main motivation is to improve the model efficiency, we argue that delta distillation can also improve the temporal consistency in predictions (as verified experimentally in Sec. 4.2). As an explanation, we argue that delta distillation converts the *spatial* teacher network to a *spatio-temporal* model, as it propagates states from one timestep to the next, and explicit temporal dynamics improve the overall temporal stability, as also noted in several prior works [33,40]. Moreover, in delta distillation, the students have a regularization effect on the teacher. More specifically, the teacher should generate smooth and low-rank features so as to be learnable by a student with a limited number of parameters. This penalizes the teacher from generating hard to distill deltas, *e.g.* from representations that are inconsistent over time.

4   Experiments

We evaluate delta distillation on two video tasks: object detection and semantic segmentation, in Sects. 4.1 and 4.2, respectively. Several ablation studies are reported in Sect. 4.3. Further analysis are provided in the supplementary material.

4.1   Object Detection

Dataset and Metrics. We experiment with Imagenet VID [37], which contains 3862, 555, and 937 annotated snippets for training, validation, and test, respectively. All frames come with bounding boxes belonging to 30 target categories. Following the standard protocol [3,54–56], we augment the training snippets with still images from ImageNet DET sampled at 1 : 1 ratio, and report results on the validation set. We rely on mean Average Precision (mAP) with an IoU

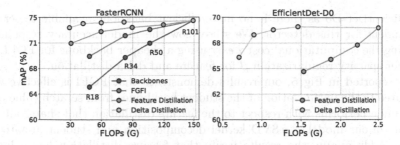

Fig. 5. Comparisons to knowledge distillations on ImageNet VID. Delta distillation outperforms the alternatives. The gap is higher for EfficientDet-D0 that is already highly optimized so is more challenging to be accelerated further.

threshold of 0.5 as the accuracy metric. To be hardware-agnostic, we report the efficiency of models in terms of number of floating point operations (FLOPs[2]).

Training Details. We conduct our experiments using a single-stage and a two-stage object detector, namely EfficientDet-D0 [42] and Faster-RCNN [34] with a ResNet-101 backbone. We first train the teacher networks $\mathcal{F}$ using a SGD optimizer with a learning rate of 0.01 for 7 epochs. The learning rate is reduced by a factor of 10 at epochs 2 and 5. Clips are resized to have a longer side of $512\,px$ and $600\text{--}1000\,px$ for EfficientDet and Faster-RCNN, respectively. We train the models on four GPUs using a batch size of 16 and 4 for the EfficientDet and Faster-RCNN, respectively. Starting from the trained teacher network and randomly initialized students, we optimize the training objective, Eq. 5, setting α and β to 1000 and 10 for Faster-RCNN, and to 100 and 10 for EfficientDet. We report the experiments for distilling at every linear block though similar conclusions hold for distilling non-linear blocks as a stack of multiple layers. We use a compression ratio $\gamma = 16$, as illustrated in Fig. 3, to define the student architectures.

Evaluation Details. Following [56], we split each video into sequences of equal length $T = 10$. The first frame in a sequence (key-frame) is processed by the teacher while other frames are processed by the student networks. We report mAP and FLOPs averaged over all frames in the sequence. In the supplement, we report detailed analysis teacher and student cost, illustrating per-frame FLOPS as well as their capacity in terms of parameters.

Comparison to Knowledge Distillations. We evaluate our key hypothesis, namely that $\Delta\mathbf{z}_t$ can be distilled more effectively than $\mathbf{z}_t$, by training students using two different distillation objectives: feature vs. delta distillation as defined in Eqs. 1 and 2. Additionally, we compare to Fine Grained Feature Imitation (FGFI) [45], as a knowledge distillation devised for object detection that distills the features around the object anchor locations from a ResNet-101 backbone using a lighter student backbone (R50, R34, and R18). We omit applying FGFI

---

[2] FLOPs denotes number of multiply-adds.

on EfficientDet-D0 as there is no more efficient backbone available to serve as the student for this detector. We study how the model accuracy responds to reducing the computational cost *i.e.*by using a cheaper backbone for FGFI, and a higher sparsity regularization β for feature and delta distillation.

As reported in Fig. 5, our results demonstrate that FGFI is effective when compared to the optimization of the student backbones from scratch (blue plot), yet it underperforms with respect to the feature distillation that shares all components of our model, *e.g.*SVD kernel decomposition and student architecture search. Additionally, the results verify that feature distillation has a limited effectiveness in reducing the model complexity especially for a highly optimized architecture such as EfficientDet-D0. However, by leveraging temporal redundancy, delta distillation reduces the compute cost by 2× with a negligible drop in the accuracy. For EfficientDet-D0, it reduces the GFLOPs from 2.5 to 1.14 with a negligible mAP drop, from 69.0 to 68.8.

Comparison to State of the Art. We compare to the state of the art video object detectors that leverage temporal redundancies to speed up the inference, as categorized into: *i)* feature warping, *i.e.*DFF [56] and Mobile-DFF [54], that bypass feature computation by warping the previous features using optical flow. *ii)* feature aggregation, *i.e.*TAFM [25], that instead of extracting expensive features at every frame, it relies on an aggregation of cheaper features over time. *iii)* feature sparsification, *i.e.*PatchWork [1] and Skip-Conv [10], that restrict the feature

Table 1. Comparisons with efficient video object detectors on ImageNet VID, for some light (top) and heavy (bottom) networks. Delta distillation achieves the lowest FLOPs while being more accurate than others.

Model	FLOPs (G)	mAP
TAFM [25]	1.18	64.1
PatchWork [1]	0.97	57.4
Skip-Conv [10]	0.78	62.9
PatchNet [29]	0.73	58.9
Mobile-DFF [54]	0.71	62.8
EfficientDet-D0 [42]	2.50	69.0
+ **Delta Distillation**	0.71	66.1
DFF [56]	34.9	72.5
PatchNet [29]	34.2	73.1
Faster-RCNN [34]	149.1	74.5
+ **Delta Distillation**	29.2	73.5

computation only to a sparse set of regions or pixels that change significantly across frames. *vi)* detection by tracking, *i.e.*PatchNet [29], that interleaves running an expensive detector with cheap object trackers. As reported in Table 1, we divide object detectors into two groups: light detectors (top) developed for mobile devices, using MobileNet-v2 [38] and EfficientNet [41] backbones, and expensive detectors (bottom), using ResNet-101 backbone.

Our results show that delta distillation achieves the lowest FLOPs while being more accurate than both the light and expensive detectors. Moreover, despite the differences between FasterRCNN-R101 and EfficientDet-D0 in terms of architectures and computational bottlenecks, delta distillation consistently reduces their FLOPs without any architectural adaption, *i.e.*from 2.5 to 0.71 and from 149.1 to 29.2 respectively. This is not the case for feature warping methods, that require a careful architecture design to find a right cost and accuracy balance between feature extractor and optical flow model.

4.2 Semantic Segmentation

Dataset and Metrics. We conduct experiments on the Cityscapes dataset [4] that is partitioned into 2975, 500 and 1525 snippets as training, validation, and test splits respectively. We rely on the standard training split to train and report results on the validation set. The dataset provides pixel-level annotations into 19 classes for one frame per snippet. We extract the remaining per-frame pseudo-annotations, which are required to train video models, by applying an off the shelf segmentation network [43] on unannotated frames in the training set. We evaluate the accuracy using mean intersection-over-union (mIoU). As a mean to compare computational cost, we rely again on FLOPs also reporting latency measurements in the supplementary materials.

Training Details. We conduct experiments using two state-of-the-art segmentation model: HRNet [44] and DDRNet [13]. We follow the same training protocol as in [13,44]: models are initialized with ImageNet weights and trained using a SGD optimizer with a learning rate of 0.01, that is reduced using a polynomial decay policy with a power of 0.9. Training runs for 484 epochs using a batch size of 12 on four GPUs and SyncBN. The models are trained on random crops of 512×1024 and tested on 1024 × 2048. For DDR-Net [13], we use online hard example mining [39] as in [13]. Starting from the trained teacher and randomly initialized students, we optimize Eq. 5, using α and β set to 1 and 0.5 respectively. We rely on linear blocks with a compression ratio γ of 4 and 8 for DDR-Nets and HRNet, as illustrated in Fig. 3, to define the student architectures.

Table 2. Comparison with efficient image (top) and video (middle) based models on Cityscapes validation set.

Model	FLOPs (G)	mIoU
FANet-34 [15]	65.0	76.3
BiseNet-v1-18 [49]	55.3	74.8
FANet-18 [15]	49.0	75.0
LedNet [46]	45.8	71.5
ICNet [52]	28.2	67.7
FasterSeg [2]	28.2	73.1
ERFNet [35]	27.7	70.0
SwiftNet-18 [32]	26.0	70.2
BiseNet-v2 [48]	21.1	73.4
TDNet-PSPNet [14]	541.0	79.9
DFF [56]	109.3	69.2
TDNet-BiseNet [14]	101.3	76.4
Skip-Conv [10]	29.0	75.5
DDRNet-39 [13]	282.0	79.5
+ **Delta Distillation**	140.0	79.9
DDRNet-23 [13]	143.7	78.7
+ **Delta Distillation**	71.8	78.9
HRNet-w18-small [44]	77.9	76.1
+ **Delta Distillation**	34.1	75.7
DDRNet-23-slim [13]	36.6	76.1
+ **Delta Distillation**	**17.9**	76.2

Evaluation Details. Each video is split into sequences of equal length T. We fix the sequence length $T = 3$ as it yields the best trade-off between accuracy vs. efficiency though the model is relatively robust to longer sequences as reported in Fig. 6. Since the videos in Cityscapes have temporally sparse annotation, we

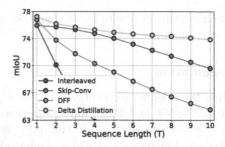

Fig. 6. Robustness to temporal variations. By increasing the distance to the key-frame, delta distillation retains better performances of prior methods.

repeat evaluations by opting each annotated frame in all possible positions within the sequence and report the averaged mIoU following [14]. Similarly we report FLOPs averaged over all frames in the sequence counting for the both teacher and student costs.

Comparison to State of the Art. We first assess the effect of delta distillation on different segmentation backbones with varying computational cost: HRNet-W18-small, DDRNet-23-slim, DDRNet-23, and DDRNet-39. As reported in Tab. 2 (bottom), delta distillation consistently reduces computational cost by a factor of ∼2× for all the backbones, with no or small drop in accuracy.

Table 2 compares delta distillation with efficient image[3] (top) and video (middle) based semantic segmentation models. The results show that delta distillation outperforms all the image-based models while being at the same time more efficient. Compared to BiseNet-v2 [48], the most efficient frame-based model, delta distillation achieves a mIoU of 76.2 vs. 73.4, with a lower cost of 17.9 vs 21.1 GFLOPs. Moreover, delta distillation achieves a more favorable accuracy vs. efficiency trade-off compared to the other video-based models. For instance, at the same mIoU of 79.9, delta distillation is 3.8× more efficient (541 vs 140 GFLOPs) than a TDNet [14] with PSPNet backbone. Finally, the delta distilled DDRNet-23-slim model significantly outperforms DFF [56] and Skip-conv [10], both in terms of accuracy and efficiency. Per-class analysis, reported in the supp. material, highlights that accuracies are retained on both static and dynamic classes.

Robustness to Temporal Variations. We evaluate the impact of sequence length (T) on the performance of delta distillation as reported in Fig. 6. The longer the sequence is, the less frequently features are refreshed by running the teacher model. This drops the accuracy as the student model has a limited capacity compared to the teacher. However, as highlighted in the results, the performance drop is smaller for delta distillation, especially on longer sequences, compared to competing methods. As a lower bound, we include an interleaved baseline that copies the predictions from the key-frame to consecutive frames. These findings verify the effectiveness of delta distillation in handling long range temporal variations.

---

[3] We limit our comparisons to efficient models with less than 100 GFLOPs.

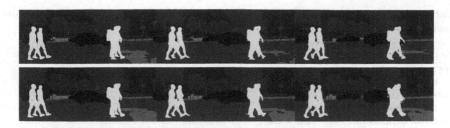

Fig. 7. Example predictions on Cityscapes, with DDRNet23 on top and DDRNet23 + Delta Distillation below. The latter shows more consistency over the baseline model. More examples are reported in the supplementary material.

Choice of Backbone. In Table 2 we evaluate video-based models using the backbones originally used by authors *i.e.*ResNet-101 for DFF and ResNet-50 for TDNet-PSPNet. Since these backbones are too expensive to run in real-time we rely on more efficient backbones, *e.g.*DDRNet, that are arguably more challenging to be further accelerated. As a further analysis, we implement several video-based models using DDRNet-23-slim backbone as reported in Fig 6. The figure confirms the superiority of delta distillation as compared to alternative video efficiency models all using the same backbone.

Temporal Consistency. As motivated in Sect. 3.4, we evaluate the effectiveness of delta distillation at improving the temporal consistency (TC) on the validation set. We follow the TC metric introduced in [27]: in a nutshell, it computes the average IoU among model predictions across successive frames, after motion compensation by optical flow warping. Our results, presented in Table 3, suggests several insights: First, the training procedure of delta distillation effectively regularizes the teacher model towards more temporally consistent predictions, even when run on different frames independently (T), as testified by the improvement of 1.8 points with respect to the baseline. Furthermore, by using the inference procedure comprising of both teacher and student (T+S), the TC metric further improves. Finally, we compare to the temporal consistency reported by ETC [27] which explicitly includes a temporal consistency loss in the optimization. Figure 7 shows qualitative results of DDRNet23 both with and without delta distillation.

4.3 Ablation Studies

Student Architecture. We analyze the effect of different choices of architecture, following the designs described in Sect. 3.1. In Table 4, we show the results of training *Linear* vs *Non-Linear* blocks as well as the *channel* vs *spatial* reduction. First, we note that delta distillation, regardless of architectural choice, has lower GFLOPs than the base Image Model. This trait is desirable, as it suggests the computational savings are not bound to a unique student architecture. However, we do see some notable differences within architecture differences

Table 3. Temporal consistency (TC) measured on Cityscapes.

Model	TC	Δ TC
PSPNET18 [53]	83.3	-
+ ETC [27]	84.6	+1.3
DDRNet23 [13]	82.6	-
+ **Delta Distillation** (T)	84.4	+1.8
+ **Delta Distillation** (T+S)	**85.2**	**+2.6**

Table 4. Ablation on student architecture designs.

Student architecture	FLOPs (G)	mIoU
DDRNet23	143.7	78.7
+ Linear	71.8	78.9
+ Non-Linear (spatial)	110.3	78.4
+ Non-linear (channel)	84.3	79.0
+ Non-linear (channel + spatial)	96.13	78.7

themselves. By comparing both *Linear* and *Non-Linear - Channel*, we appreciate that the former enjoys a slightly smaller computational footprint (71.8 vs 84.3 GFLOPs) with similar mIoU. We hypothesize this difference could be due to the fact that linear functions are easier to distill. Finally, when we compare the *channel* and *spatial* variants, we observe the latter architecture performs slightly worse.

Student Architecture Search.
We study how the architecture search, (Sect. 3.1), selects the student architectures. For this purpose, we observe the effect of gradually increasing the sparsity coefficient, β from Eq. 5. We report the proportion of compressed blocks for DDRNet23-slim grouped by its four main stages: stem convolutions at the entry, low and high-resolution branches to process the input in parallel, and a pyramid pooling module (PPM) at the

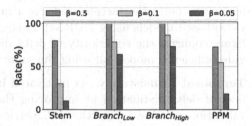

Fig. 8. Ablation on student architecture search. We report the proportion of the compressed layers per stage.

end to fuse feature maps across resolutions. We normalize the number of the compressed blocks per stage and report it as the compression rate in Fig. 8. We note that a higher β indeed translates to a higher proportion of compressed blocks across all stages. Moreover, as we reduce β, the search algorithm opts for selecting less compressed blocks in the stem. We hypothesize that since all the layers follow the stem, this layer represents a single point of failure: at this stage, a non effective distillation might hinder the whole model's performance. We observe a similar pattern for the PPM stage, likely due to its closeness to the output, thus having a bigger impact on the performance.

5   Conclusion

We proposed delta distillation, a novel method for efficient video processing exploiting the temporal redundancy of frames. Our proposal optimizes the regression, by means of cheap student models, of temporal variations in feature maps computed by an expensive teacher network. During inference, the teacher provides the initial representations for the first frame; such feature maps are then iteratively refined for the next frames by adding deltas estimated by students, the latter operating at a low computational cost. We show through extensive experiments that delta distillation outperforms feature distillation for comparable student architectures, and delivers state-of-the-art results for efficient video segmentation and object detection.

References

1. Chai, Y.: Patchwork: a patch-wise attention network for efficient object detection and segmentation in video streams. In: ICCV (2019)
2. Chen, W., Gong, X., Liu, X., Zhang, Q., Li, Y., Wang, Z.: FasterSeg: searching for faster real-time semantic segmentation. In: ICLR (2020)
3. Chen, Y., Cao, Y., Hu, H., Wang, L.: Memory enhanced global-local aggregation for video object detection. In: CVPR (2020)
4. Cordts, M., et al.: The cityscapes dataset for semantic urban scene understanding. In: CVPR (2016)
5. Dai, X., et al.: General instance distillation for object detection. In: CVPR (2021)
6. Denil, M., Shakibi, B., Dinh, L., Ranzato, M., de Freitas, N.: Predicting parameters in deep learning. In: NeurIPS (2013)
7. Gou, J., Yu, B., Maybank, S.J., Tao, D.: Knowledge distillation: a survey. In: IJCV (2021)
8. Guo, Q., et al.: Online knowledge distillation via collaborative learning. In: CVPR (2020)
9. Gupta, S., Agrawal, A., Gopalakrishnan, K., Narayanan, P.: Deep learning with limited numerical precision. In: ICML (2015)
10. Habibian, A., Abati, D., Cohen, T.S., Bejnordi, B.E.: Skip-convolutions for efficient video processing. In: CVPR (2021)
11. He, Y., Zhang, X., Sun, J.: Channel pruning for accelerating very deep neural networks. In: ICCV (2017)
12. Hinton, G., Vinyals, O., Dean, J.: Distilling the knowledge in a neural network. arXiv preprint arXiv:1503.02531 (2015)
13. Hong, Y., Pan, H., Sun, W., Jia, Y., et al.: Deep dual-resolution networks for real-time and accurate semantic segmentation of road scenes. arXiv preprint arXiv:2101.06085 (2021)
14. Hu, P., Caba, F., Wang, O., Lin, Z., Sclaroff, S., Perazzi, F.: Temporally distributed networks for fast video semantic segmentation. In: CVPR (2020)
15. Hu, P., et al.: Real-time semantic segmentation with fast attention. In: ICRA (2020)
16. Jacob, B., et al.: Quantization and training of neural networks for efficient integer-arithmetic-only inference. In: CVPR (2018)
17. Jaderberg, M., Vedaldi, A., Zisserman, A.: Speeding up convolutional neural networks with low rank expansions. In: BMVC (2014)
18. Jain, S., Wang, X., Gonzalez, J.E.: Accel: a corrective fusion network for efficient semantic segmentation on video. In: CVPR (2019)
19. Jang, E., Gu, S., Poole, B.: Categorical reparameterization with gumbel-softmax. In: ICLR (2017)

20. Krishnamoorthi, R.: Quantizing deep convolutional networks for efficient inference: a whitepaper. arXiv preprint arXiv:1806.08342 (2018)
21. Lan, X., Zhu, X., Gong, S., et al.: Knowledge distillation by on-the-fly native ensemble. In: NeurIPS (2018)
22. Lei, C., Xing, Y., Chen, Q.: Blind video temporal consistency via deep video prior. In: NeurIPS (2020)
23. Li, H., Kadav, A., Durdanovic, I., Samet, H., Graf, H.P.: Pruning filters for efficient convnets. arXiv preprint arXiv:1608.08710 (2017)
24. Li, Y., Shi, J., Lin, D.: Low-latency video semantic segmentation. In: CVPR (2018)
25. Liu, M., Zhu, M.: Mobile video object detection with temporally-aware feature maps. In: CVPR (2018)
26. Liu, M., Zhu, M., White, M., Li, Y., Kalenichenko, D.: Looking fast and slow: memory-guided mobile video object detection. arXiv preprint arXiv:1903.10172 (2019)
27. Liu, Y., Shen, C., Yu, C., Wang, J.: Efficient semantic video segmentation with per-frame inference. In: Vedaldi, A., Bischof, H., Brox, T., Frahm, J.-M. (eds.) ECCV 2020. LNCS, vol. 12355, pp. 352–368. Springer, Cham (2020). https://doi.org/10.1007/978-3-030-58607-2_21
28. Maddison, C.J., Mnih, A., Teh, Y.W.: The concrete distribution: a continuous relaxation of discrete random variables. In: ICLR (2017)
29. Mao, H., Zhu, S., Han, S., Dally, W.J.: PatchNet-short-range template matching for efficient video processing. arXiv preprint arXiv:2103.07371 (2021)
30. Moons, B., et al.: Distilling optimal neural networks: rapid search in diverse spaces. In: ICCV (2021)
31. Nagel, M., van Baalen, M., Blankevoort, T., Welling, M.: Data-free quantization through weight equalization and bias correction. In: ICCV (2019)
32. Orsic, M., Kreso, I., Bevandic, P., Segvic, S.: In defense of pre-trained imagenet architectures for real-time semantic segmentation of road-driving images. In: CVPR (2019)
33. Rebol, M., Knöbelreiter, P.: Frame-to-frame consistent semantic segmentation. In: Joint Austrian Computer Vision And Robotics Workshop (ACVRW) (2020)
34. Ren, S., He, K., Girshick, R., Sun, J.: Faster R-CNN: towards real-time object detection with region proposal networks. In: NeurIPS (2015)
35. Romera, E., Alvarez, J.M., Bergasa, L.M., Arroyo, R.: ERFNet: efficient residual factorized convnet for real-time semantic segmentation. IEEE Trans. Intell. Transp. Syst. (2017)
36. Romero, A., Ballas, N., Kahou, S.E., Chassang, A., Gatta, C., Bengio, Y.: FitNets: hints for thin deep nets. In: ICLR (2015)
37. Russakovsky, O., et al.: ImageNet large scale visual recognition challenge. In: IJCV (2015)
38. Sandler, M., Howard, A., Zhu, M., Zhmoginov, A., Chen, L.C.: MobileNetv 2: inverted residuals and linear bottlenecks. In: CVPR (2018)
39. Shrivastava, A., Gupta, A., Girshick, R.: Training region-based object detectors with online hard example mining. In: CVPR (2016)
40. Sibechi, R., Booij, O., Baka, N., Bloem, P.: Exploiting temporality for semi-supervised video segmentation. In: ICCV Workshops (2019)
41. Tan, M., Le, Q.: EfficientNet: rethinking model scaling for convolutional neural networks. In: ICML (2019)
42. Tan, M., Pang, R., Le, Q.V.: EfficientDET: scalable and efficient object detection. In: CVPR (2020)

43. Tao, A., Sapra, K., Catanzaro, B.: Hierarchical multi-scale attention for semantic segmentation. arXiv preprint arXiv:2005.10821 (2020)
44. Wang, J., et al.: Deep high-resolution representation learning for visual recognition. TPAMI (2019)
45. Wang, T., Yuan, L., Zhang, X., Feng, J.: Distilling object detectors with fine-grained feature imitation. In: CVPR (2019)
46. Wang, Y., et al.: LedNet: a lightweight encoder-decoder network for real-time semantic segmentation. In: ICIP (2019)
47. Wu, G., Gong, S.: Peer collaborative learning for online knowledge distillation. In: AAAI (2021)
48. Yu, C., Gao, C., Wang, J., Yu, G., Shen, C., Sang, N.: BiseNet v2: bilateral network with guided aggregation for real-time semantic segmentation. In: IJCV (2021)
49. Yu, C., Wang, J., Peng, C., Gao, C., Yu, G., Sang, N.: BiSeNet: bilateral segmentation network for real-time semantic segmentation. In: Ferrari, V., Hebert, M., Sminchisescu, C., Weiss, Y. (eds.) ECCV 2018. LNCS, vol. 11217, pp. 334–349. Springer, Cham (2018). https://doi.org/10.1007/978-3-030-01261-8_20
50. Zhang, X., Zou, J., He, K., Sun, J.: Accelerating very deep convolutional networks for classification and detection. TPAMI (2016)
51. Zhang, Y., Xiang, T., Hospedales, T.M., Lu, H.: Deep mutual learning. In: CVPR (2018)
52. Zhao, H., Qi, X., Shen, X., Shi, J., Jia, J.: ICNet for real-time semantic segmentation on high-resolution images. In: Ferrari, V., Hebert, M., Sminchisescu, C., Weiss, Y. (eds.) ECCV 2018. LNCS, vol. 11207, pp. 418–434. Springer, Cham (2018). https://doi.org/10.1007/978-3-030-01219-9_25
53. Zhao, H., Shi, J., Qi, X., Wang, X., Jia, J.: Pyramid scene parsing network. In: CVPR (2017)
54. Zhu, X., Dai, J., Zhu, X., Wei, Y., Yuan, L.: Towards high performance video object detection for mobiles. arXiv preprint arXiv:1804.05830 (2018)
55. Zhu, X., Wang, Y., Dai, J., Yuan, L., Wei, Y.: Flow-guided feature aggregation for video object detection. In: ICCV (2017)
56. Zhu, X., Xiong, Y., Dai, J., Yuan, L., Wei, Y.: Deep feature flow for video recognition. In: CVPR (2017)

MorphMLP: An Efficient MLP-Like Backbone for Spatial-Temporal Representation Learning

David Junhao Zhang[1], Kunchang Li[3,4], Yali Wang[3], Yunpeng Chen[2],
Shashwat Chandra[1], Yu Qiao[3,5], Luoqi Liu[2], and Mike Zheng Shou[1(✉)]

[1] National University of Singapore, Singapore, Singapore
mike.zheng.shou@gmail.com
[2] Meitu Inc., Xiamen, China
[3] ShenZhen Key Lab of Computer Vision and Pattern Recognition,
SIAT-SenseTime Joint Lab, Shenzhen Institutes of Advanced Technology,
Chinese Academy of Sciences, Shenzhen, China
[4] University of Chinese Academy of Sciences, Beijing, China
[5] Shanghai AI Laboratory, Shanghai, China

Abstract. Recently, MLP-Like networks have been revived for image recognition. However, whether it is possible to build a generic MLP-Like architecture on video domain has not been explored, due to complex spatial-temporal modeling with large computation burden. To fill this gap, we present an efficient self-attention free backbone, namely MorphMLP, which flexibly leverages the concise Fully-Connected (FC) layer for video representation learning. Specifically, a MorphMLP block consists of two key layers in sequence, i.e., MorphFC$_s$ and MorphFC$_t$, for spatial and temporal modeling respectively. MorphFC$_s$ can effectively capture core semantics in each frame, by progressive token interaction along both height and width dimensions. Alternatively, MorphFC$_t$ can adaptively learn long-term dependency over frames, by temporal token aggregation on each spatial location. With such multi-dimension and multi-scale factorization, our MorphMLP block can achieve a great accuracy-computation balance. Finally, we evaluate our MorphMLP on a number of popular video benchmarks. Compared with the recent state-of-the-art models, MorphMLP significantly reduces computation but with better accuracy, e.g., MorphMLP-S only uses 50% GFLOPs of VideoSwin-T but achieves 0.9% top-1 improvement on Kinetics400, under ImageNet1K pretraining. MorphMLP-B only uses 43% GFLOPs of MViT-B but achieves 2.4% top-1 improvement on SSV2, even though MorphMLP-B is pretrained on ImageNet1K while MViT-B is pretrained on Kinetics400. Moreover, our method adapted to the image domain outperforms previous SOTA MLP-Like architectures. Code is available at https://github.com/MTLab/MorphMLP.

Keywords: MLP · Video classification · Representation learning

---

D. J. Zhang, K. Li and Y. Wang—Contribute equally.
D. J. Zhang—Work is done during internship at Meitu, Inc.

1   Introduction

Since the seminal work of Vision Transformer (ViT) [13], attention-based architectures have shown the great power in a variety of computer vision tasks, ranging from image domain [12,39,64,72] to video domain [3,40,44,45,74]. However, recent studies have demonstrated that, self-attention maybe not critical and it can be replaced by simple Multiple Layer Perceptron (MLP) [54]. Following this line, a number of MLP-Like architectures have been developed on image-domain tasks with promising results [7,23,38,54,55,71].

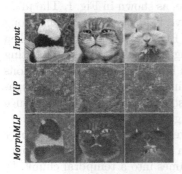

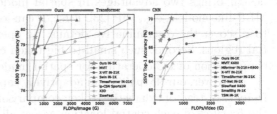

Fig. 1. Visualization of spatial feature in 3rd layer.

Fig. 2. Our MorphMLP vs. other SOTA Transformers and CNNs for video classification. Left: Kinetics400 [6]; Right: SthV2 [20].

A natural question is that, is it possible to design a generic MLP-Like architecture for video domain? Unfortunately, it has not been explored in the literature, to our best knowledge. Motivated by this fact, we analyze the main challenges of using MLP on spatial-temporal representation learning. **First**, from the *spatial* perspective, we find that the current MLP-Like models lack progressive understanding of semantic details. This is mainly because that, they often operate MLP globally on all the tokens in the space, while ignoring hierarchical learning of visual representation. For illustration, we visualize the feature map of the well-known MLP-like model (i.e., ViP [23]) in Fig. 1. Clearly, it suffers from difficulty in capturing key details, even in the shallow layer. Hence, how to discover semantics in each frame is important for designing spatial operation of MLP-like video backbone. **Second**, from the *temporal* perspective, the critical challenge is to learn long-range dependencies over frames. As shown in Fig. 2, the current video-based transformers can leverage self-attention to achieve this goal, but with huge computation cost. Hence, how to efficiently replace self-attention for long-range aggregation is important for designing temporal operation of MLP-like video backbone.

To tackles these challenges, we propose an effective and efficient MLP-like architecture, namely MorphMLP, for video representation learning. Specifically, it consists of two key layers, i.e., MorphFC$_s$ and MorphFC$_t$, which leverage the concise FC operations on spatial and temporal modeling respectively. Our MorphFC$_s$

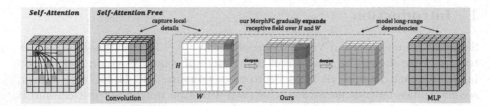

Fig. 3. Overview of progressive token construction in MorphMLP.

can effectively capture core semantics in the space, as shown in Fig. 1. The main reason is that, we gradually expand the receptive field of visual tokens along both height and width dimensions as shown in Fig. 3. Such progressive token design brings two advantages in spatial modeling, compared with the existing MLP-like models, e.g., ViP [23]. First, it can learn hierarchical token interactions to discover the discriminative details, by operating FC from small to big spatial regions. Second, such small-to-big token construction can effectively reduce computation of FC operation for spatial modeling.

Moreover, our $\texttt{MorphFC}_t$ can adaptively capture long-range dependencies over frames. Instead of exhausting token comparison in self-attention, we concatenate the features of each spatial location across all frames into a temporal chunk. In this way, each temporal chunk can be processed efficiently by FC, which adaptively aggregates token relations in the chunk to model temporal dependencies. Finally, we build up a MorphMLP block by arranging $\texttt{MorphFC}_s$ and $\texttt{MorphFC}_t$ in sequence, and stack these blocks into our generic MorphMLP backbone for video modeling. On one hand, such hierarchical manner can enlarge the cooperative power of $\texttt{MorphFC}_s$ and $\texttt{MorphFC}_t$ to learn complex spatial-temporal interactions in videos. On the other hand, such multi-scale and multi-dimension factorization allows our MorphMLP to achieve a preferable balance between accuracy and efficiency.

To our best knowledge, we are the first to build efficient MLP-Like architecture for video domain. Compared with the recent state-of-the-art video models, MorphMLP significantly reduces computation but with better accuracy.

We further apply our architecture to an image classification task on ImageNet-1K [11] and a semantic segmentation task on ADE20K [75], by simply removing the temporal dimension of the video. Our method adapted to the image domain achieves competitive results compared to previous SOTA MLP-Like architectures.

2   Related Work

Self-Attention Based Backbones. Vision Transformer (ViT) [13] firstly applies Transformer architecture to a sequence of image tokens. It utilizes multi-head self-attention to capture long-range dependencies, thus achieving surprising results on image classification. Following works [12,39,50,64,67,72] make a series of breakthroughs to achieve state-of-art performance on several image tasks, i.e., semantic segmentation [28,68] and object detection [5,76]. In video domain, a couple of woks [3,15,40,45,70,74] explore space-time self-attention to model spatial-temporal relation and achieve state-of-the-art performance. It seems that self-attention based architectures have been gradually dominating the computer vision community.

In this paper, we aim to explore a simple yet effective self-attention free architecture, which builds upon the FC layer to extract features. Our comparisons show that MorphMLP can achieve competitive results compared with Transformers not only in images but also in videos without self-attention layers.

CNN Based Backbones. CNNs [24,25,32,33,46,48,69] have dominated vision tasks in the past few years. In image domain, beginning with AlexNet [30], more effective and deeper networks, VGG [49], GoogleNet [51], ResNet [22], DenseNet [26] and EfficientNet [52] are proposed and achieve great success in computer vision. In the video domain, several works [6,18,58,60] explore how to utilize convolution to learn effective spatial-temporal representation. However, the typical spatial and temporal convolution are so local that they struggle to capture long-range information well even if stacked deeper. A series of works propose efficient modules (e.g., Non-local [65], Double Attention [8]) to enhance local features via integrating long-range relation. The improvement of these methods can not be achieved without the supplement of self-attention layers.

In contrast, we propose the MorphMLP, which is self-attention free but not limited to capture local structure. The FC filter of MorphFC operates from small to big spatial regions. Meanwhile, the MorphFC$_t$ can capture long-term temporal information.

MLP-Like Based Backbones. Recent works [38,54,55,71] try to replace self-attention layer with FC layer to explore the necessity of self-attention in Transformer architecture. But they suffer from dense parameters and computation. [21,23,53] apply FC layer along horizontal, vertical, and channel directions, respectively, in order to reduce the number of parameters and computation cost. However, the parameters of FC layer are still determined by the input resolution, so it is hard to handle different image scales. CycleMLP [7] addresses such problem with padding, but it only focuses on global information, ignoring local inductive bias. Meanwhile, the ability of MLP-Like architecture for video modeling has not been explored.

On the contrary, our MorphMLP can cope with diverse scales via splitting the sequence of tokens into chunks. Furthermore, it is able to effectively capture local to global information by gradually expanding chunk length. More importantly, we are the first to build MLP-Like architecture on videos to explore its generalization ability as a new paradigm of versatile backbone.

3   Method

In this section, we present our MorphMLP. We first introduce the two critical components of MorphMLP, MorphFC$_s$ and MorphFC$_t$. Then, we illustrate how to build efficient spatial-temporal MorphMLP block. Finally, the overall spatial-temporal network architecture and its adaption to image domain are provided.

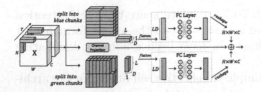
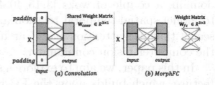

Fig. 4. MorphFC$_s$ on the spatial dimension. Note that chunk length L hierarchically expands as network goes deeper. (Color figure online)

Fig. 5. Comparison with the typical convolution.

3.1   MorphFC for Spatial Modeling

As discussed above, mining core semantics is critical to video recognition. Typical CNN and previous MLP-Like architectures only focus on either local or global information modeling thus they fail to do that. To tackle this challenge, we propose a novel MorphFC$_s$ layer that can hierarchical expand the receptive field of FC and make it operate from small to big regions. Our MorphFC$_s$ processes each frame of video independently in horizontal and vertical pathways. We take the horizontal one (blue chunks in Fig. 4) for example.

Specifically, given one frame of input videos $\mathbf{X} \in \mathbb{R}^{HW \times C}$ that has been projected into a sequence of tokens, we first split $\mathbf{X}$ along horizontal direction. We set chunk length to L and thus obtain $\mathbf{X}_i \in \mathbb{R}^{L \times C}$, where $i \in \{1, ..., HW/L\}$. Furthermore, to reduce computation cost, we also split each $\mathbf{X}_i$ into multiple groups along channel dimension, where each group has D channels. Thus we get split chunks, and each single chunk is $\mathbf{X}_i^k \in \mathbb{R}^{LD}$, where $k \in \{1, ..., C/D\}$. Next, we flatten each chunk into 1D vector and apply a FC weight matrix $\mathbf{W} \in \mathbb{R}^{LD \times LD}$ to transform each chunk, yielding

$$\mathbf{Y}_i^k = \mathbf{X}_i^k \mathbf{W}. \tag{1}$$

After feature transformation, we reshape all chunks $\mathbf{Y}_i^k$ back to the original dimension $\mathbf{Y} \in \mathbb{R}^{H \times W \times C}$. The vertical way (green chunks in Fig. 4) does likewise except splitting the sequence of tokens along vertical direction. To make communication among groups along channel dimension, we also apply a FC layer to process each token individually. Finally, we get the output by element-wise summing horizontal, vertical, and channel features together. The chunks length L hierarchically increases as the network deepens, thereby enabling the FC filter to discover more core semantics progressively from small to big spatial region.

Difference Between our MorphFC$_s$ and Convolution. (i) Typical convolution utilizes fixed small kernel size (e.g., 3×3), which only aggregates local context. On the contrary, the chunks lengths in MorphFC$_s$ hierarchically increase as the network deepens, which can model short-to-long range information progressively. **(ii)** Convolution uses sliding windows to obtain overlapping tokens, which requires cumbersome operations, including unfold, reshape and fold. In contrast, we simply reshape the feature map to obtain our chunks with non-overlapping tokens. **(iii)**

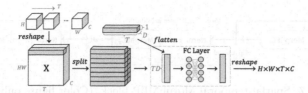

Fig. 6. MorphFC$_t$ on the temporal dimension.

As shown in Fig. 5, given a 1×3 input, to get the 1×3 output, the convolution kernel of 1×3 window size needs to slide three times, and each 1×1 output is generated by the shared weight matrix $\mathbf{W}_{conv} \in \mathbb{R}^{3 \times 1}$. In contrast, FC layer applies weight matrix $\mathbf{W}_{fc} \in \mathbb{R}^{3 \times 3}$ to the input yielding 1×3 output. Each 1×1 output is equivalent to being generated by non-shared weight matrix $\mathbf{W} \in \mathbb{R}^{3 \times 1}$, which brings more flexible spatial encoding than convolution.

Comparisons with ViP [24]. Our design is related to the well-known ViP designed for image domain, which also leverages the multi-branch features in spatial modeling. Hence, we further discuss the differences. **(i)** The FC filters of whole ViP network have the fixed size and receptive field, thus they only capture global information. On the contrary, our FC filters are morphable, as shown in Fig. 3. In shallow layers, they have small size to model local structure, while in deeper layers, they gradually change to large size to model long-range information. Hence, ours can discover more detailed semantics by progressively operating FC from small to big spatial region. **(ii)** As shown in Fig. 8, at the network level, ours have hierarchical downsampling after each stage but ViP does not. **(iii)** As ViP paper said, ViP is hard to transfer to downstream tasks i.e. segmentation with spatial resolution 2048×512, since its filter size is always equal to the height/weight of features. But it is easy for ours, because the filter size is equal to pre-defined chunk size in the pre-training.

3.2 MorphFC$_t$ on Temporal Modeling

In addition to the horizontal and vertical pathways in MorphFC$_s$, we introduce another temporal pathway MorphFC$_t$. It aims at capturing long-term temporal information using the simple FC layer with low computation cost. Specifically, as shown in Fig. 6, given an input video clip tokens $\mathbf{X} \in \mathbb{R}^{H \times W \times T \times C}$, we first split X into a couple of groups along channel dimension (D channels in each group) to reduce computation cost and get $\mathbf{X}^k \in \mathbb{R}^{H \times W \times T \times D}$, where $k \in \{1, ..., C/D\}$. For each spatial position s, we concatenate features across all frames into a chunk $\mathbf{X}_s^k \in \mathbb{R}^{TD}$, where $s \in \{1, ..., HW\}$. Then we apply a FC matrix $\mathbf{W} \in \mathbb{R}^{TD \times TD}$, to transform temporal features and get

$$\mathbf{Y}_s^k = \mathbf{X}_s^k \mathbf{W}. \tag{2}$$

Finally, we reshape all chunks $\mathbf{Y}_s^k \in \mathbb{R}^{TD}$ back to original tokens dimension and output $\mathbf{Y} \in \mathbb{R}^{H \times W \times T \times C}$. In this way, the FC filter can simply aggregate token relations along time dimension in the chunk to model temporal dependencies.

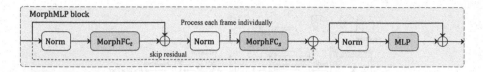

Fig. 7. Spatial-temporal MorphMLP block. (Color figure online)

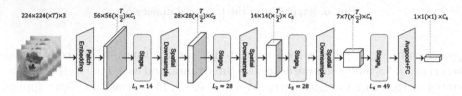

Fig. 8. Architecture of our MorphMLP L means chuck length.

Spatial-Temporal MorphMLP Block. Based on the MorphFC$_s$ and MorphFC$_t$, we propose a factorized spatial-temporal MorphMLP block in the video domain for efficient video representation learning. As shown in Fig. 7, our MorphMLP block contains MorphFC$_t$, MorphFC$_s$ and MLP [61] modules in a sequential order. On one hand, it is difficult for joint spatial-temporal optimization [3]. On the other hand, factorizing spatial and temporal modeling is able to reduce the computation cost significantly. Therefore, we place temporal and spatial MorphFC$_s$ layers in the sequential style. The LN [2] layer is applied before each module, and the standard residual connections are used after MorphFC$_t$ and MLP module. Instead of applying a standard residual connection [22] after MorphFC$_s$, we add a skip residual connection (red line) between the original input and output features from MorphFC$_s$ layer. We found that such a connection can make training more stable.

3.3 Network Architecture

For video recognition, as shown in Fig. 8, we hierarchically stack spatial-temporal MorphMLP blocks to build up our network. Given an video sequence $\mathbf{X} \in \mathbb{R}^{H \times W \times T \times 3}$, taking $H = W = 224$ for example, our MorphMLP backbone first performs patch embedding on the video clip and gets a sequence of tokens with dimension $56 \times 56 \times T/2 \times C_1$. Then, we have four sequential stages and each of them contains a couple of MorphMLP blocks. The feature size remains unchanged as passing through layers inside the same stage. At the end of each stage excluding the last one, we expand the channel dimension and downsample the spatial resolution of features by ratio 2.

Note that we set chunk lengths of MorphFC$_s$ to be 14, 28, 28, 49 for stage 1–4, respectively. Horizontal/vertical chunks with lengths 14, 28, 28, 49 of stage 1–4 can cover quarter, one, two, all rows/columns of feature maps of stage 1–4, respectively. In shallow layers, our network can learn detailed representation from the local spatial context in small chunk length, e.g., length 14 for

$56 \times 56 \times C_1$ feature map. In deep layers, our network can capture long-range information from the global semantic context in considerable chunk length, e.g., length 49 for $7 \times 7 \times C_4$ feature map. With downsampling the spatial resolution and expanding chunk length as the network goes deeper, our MorphMLP is capable of discovering more core semantics progressively by operating the FC filter from small to big spatial regions.

We provide two model variants for the video recognition depending on the number of MorphMLP blocks in four stages: $\{3, 4, 9, 3\}$ for MorphMLP-Small(S) and $\{4, 6, 15, 4\}$ for MorphMLP-Base(B). The numbers of channels of four stages are $\{112, 224, 392, 784\}$. Additionally, for image-domain architecture, we simply exclude the temporal dimension and drop MorphFC$_t$ in the MorphMLP block. In addition to small and base settings, we provide two extra model variants for image domain, depending on the number of MorphMLP blocks in four stages, i.e., $\{3, 4, 7, 3\}$ for MorphMLP-Tiny(T) and $\{4, 8, 18, 6\}$ for MorphMLP-Large(L).

4   Experiment

In this section, we first examine the performance of MorphMLP and evaluate its spatiotemporal effectiveness on Kinetics-400 [6], and Something-Something V1&V2 [20] datasets. For fair comparisons and due to GPU resources limitation, we only report MorphMLP-S and B for video classification. Then we verify the effectiveness of its adaption to image domain, including ImageNet-1K [11] image classification and ADE20K [75] semantic segmentation.

4.1   Video Classification on Kinetics-400

Settings. Kinetics-400 [6] is a large-scale scene-related video benchmark. It contains around 240K training videos and about 20K validation videos in 400 classes. Our code heavily relies on PySlowFast [14] repository and the training recipe mainly follows MViT [15]. We directly load the parameters of MorphFC$_s$ pre-trained on ImageNet and randomly initialize the parameters of MorphFC$_t$ in the video domain. We adopt a dense sampling strategy [65] and AdamW optimizer to train the whole network. The warm-up epoch, total epoch, batch size, base learning rate, and weight decay are 10, 60, 64, 2e−4, and 0.05 respectively. We utilize the stochastic depth rates 0.1 and 0.3 for MorphMLP-S and B.

Results. As shown in Table 1, our method achieves outstanding performance with fewer computation costs. Compared with CNN models such as Slow-Fast [18], our MorphMLP requires 8× fewer GFLOPS but achieves 1.9% accuracy improvement (80.8% vs. 78.9%). With only ImageNet-1K pre-training, our method surpasses most of the self-attention based Transformer backbones with larger dataset pre-training. For example, compared with ViViT-L [1] pre-trained on ImageNet-21K, our MorphMLP obtains better performance with 20× fewer computations. When our model is scaled larger, the accuracy increases as well. Since the computation cost is relatively low, our method still has great potential for better performance. It demonstrates that our MorphMLP is a strong MLP-Like backbone for video recognition.

Table 1. Comparisons with the state-of-the-art on Kinetics-400 [6]. Our MorphMLP achieves outstanding results with much fewer computation costs. For example, compared with VideoSwin-T, our MorphMLP-S only requires 2× fewer GFLOPs but gets 0.9% accuracy improvement (79.7% *vs.* 78.8%).

Method	Pretrain	#Frame	GFLOPs	K400	
				Top-1	Top-5
Self-Attention free – CNN					
SlowFast R101 [18]	–	(16+64) × 3 × 10	6390	78.9	93.5
CorrNet-101 [62]	–	32 × 3 × 10	6720	79.2	–
ip-CSN [59]	Sports1M	32 × 3 × 10	3264	79.2	93.8
X3D-XL [17]	–	16 × 3 × 10	1452	79.1	93.9
SmallBig$_{EN}$ [34]	IN-1K	(8+32) × 3 × 4	5700	78.7	93.7
TDN$_{EN}$ [63]	IN-1K	(8+16) × 3 × 10	5940	79.4	94.4
CT-Net$_{EN}$ [31]	IN-1K	(16+16) × 3 × 4	2641	79.8	94.2
Self-Attention based – Transformer					
Timesformer-L [3]	IN-21K	96 × 3 × 1	7140	80.7	94.7
VidTr-L [74]	IN-21K	32 × 3 × 10	11760	79.1	93.9
ViViT-L [1]	IN-21K	16 × 3 × 4	17357	80.6	94.7
X-ViT [4]	IN-21K	16 × 3 × 1	850	80.2	94.7
Mformer [45]	IN-21K	32 × 3 × 10	11085	80.2	94.8
Mformer-L [45]	IN-21K	32 × 3 × 10	35550	80.2	94.8
MViT-B, 16 × 4 [15]	–	16 × 1 × 5	355	78.4	93.5
MViT-B, 32 × 3 [15]	–	32 × 1 × 5	850	80.2	94.4
VideoSwin-T [40]	IN-1K	32 × 3 × 4	1056	78.8	93.6
VideoSwin-B [40]	IN-1K	32 × 3 × 4	3384	80.6	94.6
Self-Attention free – MLP-Like					
MorphMLP-S	IN-1K	16 × 1 × 4	268	78.7	93.8
MorphMLP-S	IN-1K	32 × 1 × 4	532	79.7	94.2
MorphMLP-B	IN-1K	16 × 1 × 4	392	79.5	94.4
MorphMLP-B	IN-1K	32 × 1 × 4	788	**80.8**	**94.9**

4.2   Video Classification on Something-Something

Settings. Something-Something [20] is another large-scale dataset, in which the temporal relationship modeling is critical for action understanding. It includes two versions, i.e., V1 and V2, both of which contain plentiful videos over 174 categories. We adopt the same training setting as used for Kinetics-400, except that a random horizontal flip is not applied. We utilize the sparse sampling strategy. The warm-up epoch, total epoch, batch size, base learning rate, and weight decay are 5, 50, 64, 4e−4, and 0.05, respectively. We set the stochastic depth rates to be 0.3 and 0.6 for Morph-S and B respectively.

Results. The comparison results on Something V2&V1 are shown in Table 2 and Table 3 respectively. For SSV2, CNN architectures perform worse than Transformer architectures since they are limited to capturing local spatial and temporal information and struggle to model long-term dependencies. Transformer architectures can achieve better results, but they heavily rely on large-scale dataset pre-training which requires high computation. Compared with CT-Net [31], our MorphMLP can reduce 2.5× computation but achieves 1.2% accuracy gain. Compared with the-state-of-art method MViT [15], which is pre-trained on large video dataset Kinetics-600, our MorphMLP only pre-trained on ImageNet-1K can

Table 2. Comparisons with the SOTA on SSV2 [20]. Our MorphMLP outperforms previous sota Transformers and CNNs with IN-1K pretraining only.

Method	Pretrain	#Frame	GFLOPs	SSV2	
				Top-1	Top-5
Self-Attention free – CNN					
SlowFast R50 [18]	K400	(8+32) × 3 × 1	197	61.7	46.6
TSM [37]	K400	16 × 3 × 2	374	63.4	88.5
STM [27]	IN-1K	16 × 3 × 10	1995	64.2	89.8
bLVNet [16]	IN-1K	32 × 3 × 10	3870	65.2	90.3
TEA [35]	IN-1K	16 × 3 × 10	2100	65.1	–
CT-Net [31]	IN-1K	16 × 3 × 2	450	65.9	90.1
Self-Attention based – Transformer					
Timesformer [3]	IN-21K	16 × 3 × 1	5109	62.5	–
VidTr-L [74]	IN-21K+K400	32 × 3 × 10	10530	60.2	–
ViViT-L [1]	IN-21K+K400	16 × 3 × 4	11892	65.4	89.8
X-ViT [4]	IN-21K	32 × 3 × 1	1269	65.4	90.7
Mformer [45]	IN-21K+K400	16 × 3 × 1	1110	66.5	90.1
Mformer-L [45]	IN-21K+K400	32 × 3 × 1	3555	68.1	91.2
MViT-B, 16 × 4 [15]	K400	16 × 3 × 1	510	67.1	90.8
MViT-B, 32 × 3 [15]	K400	32 × 3 × 1	1365	67.7	90.9
MViT-B-24, 32 × 3 [15]	K600	32 × 3 × 1	708	68.7	91.5
Self-Attention free – MLP-like					
MorphMLP-S	IN-1K	16 × 3 × 1	201	67.1	90.9
MorphMLP-S	IN-1K	32 × 3 × 1	405	68.3	91.3
MorphMLP-B	IN-1K	16 × 3 × 1	294	67.6	91.3
MorphMLP-B	IN-1K	32 × 3 × 1	591	**70.1**	**92.8**

Table 3. Comparisons with the state-of-the-art on Something-Something V1 [20].

Method	Pretrain	#Frame	GFLOPs	SSV1	
				Top-1	Top-5
I3D [66]	IN-1K+K400	32 × 3 × 2	918	41.6	72.2
NLI3D [66]	IN-1K+K400	32 × 3 × 2	1008	44.4	76.0
NLI3D+GCN [66]	IN-1K+K400	32 × 3 × 2	1818	46.1	76.8
TSM [37]	IN-1K+K400	16 × 1 × 1	65	47.2	77.1
SmallBig [34]	IN-1K	16 × 1 × 1	105	49.3	79.5
TEINet [41]	IN-1K	16 × 3 × 10	1980	51.0	–
TEA [35]	IN-1K	16 × 3 × 10	2100	52.3	81.9
CT-NET [31]	IN-1K	16 × 3 × 2	447	53.4	81.7
MorphMLP-S	IN-1K	16 × 1 × 1	67	50.6	78.0
MorphMLP-S	IN-1K	16 × 3 × 1	201	53.9	81.3
MorphMLP-B	IN-1K	16 × 3 × 1	294	55.5	82.4
MorphMLP-B	IN-1K	32 × 3 × 1	591	**57.4**	**84.5**

obtain better performance (70.1% *vs.* 68.7%) with smaller GFLOPS (591G *vs.* 708G). For SSV1, our MorphMLP also achieves outstanding results.

The superior results of our method on this dataset can be attributed to our unique progressively core semantics discovering manner and efficient spatial-temporal block design in MorpMLP. Table 6 and 7 can also demonstrate our point. Note that even if we do not add any complicated and unique temporal attention operation, our simple method can achieve such great performance. This indicates that our model can serve as a strong backbone for further improvement.

Table 4. ImageNet-1K results. As shown in (a), our method achieves the best performance among SOTA MLP-Like architectures. From (b), we can see that our MorphMLP also achieves the comparable results with SOTA self-attention based and hybrid models even with small computation.

(a) Comparisons with MLP-Like models

Model	Param	FLOPs	Top-1
Mixer-B/16 [54]	59M	12.7G	76.4
Mixer-B/16† [54]	59M	12.7G	77.3
ResMLP-S12 [55]	15M	3.0G	76.6
ResMLP-S24 [55]	30M	6.0G	79.4
ResMLP-B24 [55]	116M	23.0G	81.0
gMLP-Ti [38]	6M	1.4G	72.3
gMLP-S [38]	20M	4.5G	79.6
gMLP-B [38]	73M	15.8G	81.6
S^2-MLP-wide [71]	71M	14.0G	80.0
S^2-MLP-deep [71]	51M	10.5G	80.7
ViP-Small/7 [23]	25M	6.9G	81.5
ViP-Medium/7 [23]	55M	16.3G	82.7
ViP-Large/7 [23]	88M	24.4G	83.2
AS-MLP-T [36]	28M	4.4G	81.3
AS-MLP-S [36]	50M	8.5G	83.1
AS-MLP-B [36]	88M	15.2G	83.3
CycleMLP-B2 [7]	27M	3.9G	81.6
CycleMLP-B3 [7]	38M	6.9G	82.6
CycleMLP-B4 [7]	52M	10.1G	83.0
CycleMLP-B5 [7]	76M	12.3G	83.1
MorphMLP-T	23M	3.9G	81.6
MorphMLP-S	38M	6.9G	82.6
MorphMLP-B	58M	10.2G	83.2
MorphMLP-L	76M	12.5G	**83.4**

(b) Comparisons with SOTA models

Model	Family	Scale	Param	FLOPs	Top-1
ResNet50 [22]	CNN	224^2	26M	4.1G	79.2
DeiT-S [56]	Trans	224^2	22M	4.6G	79.8
ResNest50 [73]	CNN	224	28M	4.3G	80.6
T2T-ViT-14 [72]	Trans	224^2	22M	4.8G	81.5
PVT-S [64]	Trans	224^2	25M	3.8G	79.8
Swin-T [39]	Trans	224^2	29M	4.5G	81.3
GFNet-H-S [47]	FFT	224^2	32M	4.5G	81.5
BoT-S1-50 [50]	Hybrid	224^2	21M	4.3G	79.1
CoAtNet-0 [10]	Hybrid	224^2	23M	4.2G	81.6
MorphMLP-T	MLP	224^2	23M	3.9G	**81.6**
ResNet101 [22]	CNN	224^2	45M	7.9G	79.8
ResNest101 [73]	CNN	224^2	48M	8.0G	82.0
RegNetY-8G [46]	CNN	224^2	39M	8.0G	81.7
T2T-ViT-19 [72]	Tran	224^2	39M	8.5G	81.9
PVT-M [64]	Trans	224^2	44M	6.7G	81.2
BoT-S1-59 [50]	Hybrid	224^2	34M	7.3G	81.7
CoAtNet-1 [10]	Hybrid	224^2	42M	8.4G	**83.3**
MorphMLP-S	MLP	224^2	38M	6.9G	82.6
ViT-B/16 [56]	Trans	384^2	86M	55.4G	77.9
DeiT-B [56]	Trans	224^2	86M	17.5G	81.8
DeiT-B [56]	Trans	384^2	86M	55.4G	83.1
T2T-ViT-24 [72]	Tran	224^2	64M	13.8G	82.3
Swin-B [39]	Trans	224^2	88M	15.4G	83.4
CaiT-S36 [57]	Trans	224^2	68M	13.9G	83.3
MorphMLP-L	MLP	224^2	76M	12.5G	**83.4**

4.3 Image Classification on ImageNet-1K

Settings. We train our models from scratch on the ImageNet-1K dataset [11], which consists of 1.2M training images and 50K validation images from 1,000 categories. Our code is implemented based on DeiT [56] repository, and we follow the same training strategy proposed in DeiT [56], including strong data augmentation and regularization. Stochastic depth rates are set to be 0.1, 0.1, 0.2, 0.3 for our 4 model variants. We adopt AdamW [42] optimizer with cosine learning rate schedule [43] for 300 epochs, while the first 20 epochs are used for linear warm-up [19]. The total batch size, weight decay, and initial learning rate are set to 1024, 5×10^{-2} and 0.01 respectively.

Results. As shown in Table 4a, our MorphMLP outperforms the state-of-the-art MLP-Like architectures. Compared with ViP-S [23], our method can get much higher accuracy (82.6% *vs.* 81.5%) with similar GFLOPS (7.0G *vs.* 6.9G). This

Table 5. Semantic segmentation with Semantic FPN [29] on ADE20K [75] val.

Method	Arch	#Param.(M)	mIoU
ResNet50 [22]	CNN	28.5	36.7
PVT-S [64]	Trans	28.2	39.8
Swin-T [39]	Trans	31.9	41.5
GFNet-H-T [47]	FFN	26.6	41.0
CycleMLP-B2 [7]	MLP-Like	30.6	42.4
MorphMLP-T	MLP-Like	26.4	**43.0**
ResNet101 [22]	CNN	47.5	38.8
ResNeXt101-32×4d [69]	CNN	47.1	39.7
PVT-M [64]	Trans	48.0	41.6
GFNet-H-S [47]	FFN	47.5	42.5
CycleMLP-B3 [7]	MLP-Like	42.1	44.5
MorphMLP-S	MLP-Like	41.0	**44.7**
PVT-L [64]	Trans	65.1	42.1
Swin-S [39]	Trans	53.2	45.2
CycleMLP-B4 [7]	MLP-Like	55.6	45.1
MorphMLP-B	MLP-Like	59.3	**45.9**

demonstrates the effectiveness of our progressively short-to-long range pattern. In Table 4b, our MorphMLP can achieve competitive results with popular self-attention based models. Compared with other tiny models, e.g., Swin-T [39], our method can achieve better results (81.6% *vs.* 81.3%) with fewer parameters and GFLOPS (23M *vs.* 29M, 3.9G *vs.* 4.5G). As for larger settings, our method can achieve comparable result to Swin-B [39] with fewer GFLOPS.

4.4   Semantic Segmentation on ADE20K

Settings. We conduct semantic segmentation experiments on ADE20K [75], which consists of 20K training images and 2K validation images over 150 semantic categories. Our code is based on mmsegmentation [9] and we follow the experiment setting used in PVT [64]. We simply apply Semantic FPN [29] for fair comparisons, and all the backbones are pre-trained on ImageNet-1K. We adopt AdamW [42] optimizer with cosine learning rate schedule [43], while the initial learning rate is 1e−4. The input images are randomly resized and cropped to 512×512 for training, and the shorter sides of images are set to 512 while testing.

Results. The results on ADE20k dataset are shown in Table 5. Our MorphMLP outperforms ResNet [46] and PVT [64] significantly. Compared with Swin-T, our MorphMLP-T can achieve better mIoU with fewer parameters (26.4M *vs.* 31.9M).

Table 6. Impact of chunk length.

Stage 1	Stage 2	Stage 3	Stage 4	SSV1 Top-1	ImageNet Top-1	ADE20K mIoU
56	28	14	7	48.6	79.1	41.6
3	3	3	3	48.0	78.2	41.0
7	7	7	7	48.4	79.0	41.9
14	14	14	14	48.7	79.0	42.0
14	28	28	7	49.2	79.3	42.0
28	28	28	49	49.1	79.4	42.3
14	28	28	49	50.6	79.6	42.6

Table 7. Detail designs of spatial-temporal MorphMLP block.

Method	Order	Standard residual	Skip residual	SSV1 Top-1
Parallel	T‖S	✔		49.2
Sequential	T+S	✔		49.8
	S+T	✔		50.2
	T+S		✔	50.6
	S+T		✔	31.7

4.5 Ablation Study

For Tables 6, 8, and 9, we train all the models based on MorphMLP-T for 100 epochs on ImageNet. To explore the variants of our spatial-temporal design, we adopt MorphMLP-S as the backbone on SSV1.

Impact of Chunk Length. In the MorphMLP, we expand the chunk length gradually. The spatial resolutions of feature maps of Stages 1–4 are 56, 28, 14, 7, respectively. For the horizontal/vertical directions, chunk lengths 14, 28, 28, 49 in Stages1-4 can cover quarter, one, two and all rows/columns of the tokens, respectively, which can discover core semantics progressively by operating the FC filter from small to big spatial region.

As shown in Table 6, there are some alternative ways to set chunk length. The first line represents that MorphFC_s in each stage covers one row of image/video tokens, which only models global information. The second, third and fourth line utilize the small chunk length, which only captures local structure. The results show that our progressively expanding pattern can perform better than the solely local or global pattern. The reason is that, in the shallow layer, the original texture and shape information of the image/videos is relatively intact. Therefore, it is critical to capture detailed structures in the early stage. The features in the deep layers cover more semantic information, thus long-range relation modeling is significant. **Note** that the improvement brought by expanding chunk lengths on video is larger than image because such pattern is conducive to discovering more fine-grained semantics for many tiny movement actions.

It is also worth noting that since chunk sizes are equal to H, W of features in each stage if input is 224×224, 1st row is no 'Morph' (progressively discovering core semantics), but with hierarchical downsampling only. Last row is our final model (w/ both 'Morph' and same downsampling as the 1st row). Comparisons show benefits are from MorphFC design instead of hierarchical downsampling.

Detail Designs of Spatial-Temporal MorphMLP Block. We explore some alternative designs for our spatial-temporal MorphMLP block in the Table 7. To begin with, in addition to applying MorphFC_t and MorphFC_s in a sequential way, we can add the features from MorphFC_t and MorphFC_s in parallel. As shown in Table 7, the parallel way performs worse than the sequential way. We argue that it is more difficult for joint spatial and temporal optimization. Moreover, we explore different spatial-temporal orders and residual connections. Standard

Table 8. Spatial design of MorphMLP.

Operation	#Param. (M)	FLOPs (G)	Throughput (images/s)	ImageNet Top-1
3 × 3 Conv	34.5	6.2	676	77.3
7 × 7 Conv	113	20.6	532	77.7
Group Conv	23.4	4.0	620	79.0
MorphFC$_s$	23.4	4.0	734	**79.6**

Table 9. Different operations.

Dimension	Style	Weight sum	SSV1 Top-1	ImageNet Top-1
H+W+C	Transformer	✔	50.6	**79.6**
H+W	Transformer	✔	49.4	78.5
H+W+C	CNN	✔	47.2	77.2
H+W+C	Transformer	✘	50.2	79.3

Table 10. Temporal design.

Operation	#Param.(M)	FLOPs(G)	SSV1
3 × 1 × 1 Conv	46.0	62.7	47.9
5 × 1 × 1 Conv	52.5	72.9	48.6
MorphFC$_t$	47.0	66.4	**50.6**

Table 11. Training cost.

Video model	TFLOPs	K400	Training	Cost
SlowFast	1.11	71.0	30 epoch	444 h
Timesformer	0.59	75.8	30 epoch	416 h
Morph-S	0.27	77.0	30 epoch	408 h

residual refers to applying a residual connection after each module in MorphMLP block of Fig. 7. Skip residual means that a connection is applied between input features of MorphMLP block and output features of the MorphFC$_s$ (red line in Fig. 7). The results show that sequential temporal and spatial order with skip residual connection is the optimal setting.

Comparisons with Convolution. To compared with spatial convolution, we replace the MorphFC$_s$ layer with typical 3 × 3 and 7 × 7 convolution on image domain. As shown in Table 8, our MorphFC$_s$ can outperform typical convolution by a large margin. This demonstrates that typical convolution is difficult to capture long-range information, which is crucial to the recognition problem. Furthermore, we adopt two 1D group convolutions along the horizontal and vertical direction, whose kernel sizes are exactly the same as our chunk lengths in each stage. The results show that our method is much better than group conv in terms of speed and accuracy. This indicates the effectiveness of our MorphFC$_s$.

Moreover, we do comparisons between MorphFC$_t$ and typical temporal convolutions, i.e., 3 × 1 × 1 and 5 × 1 × 1. As shown in Table 10, our MorphFC$_t$ outperforms typical temporal convolutions greatly. This is because that typical convolutions only focus on local temporal information aggregation. On the contrary, our MorphFC$_t$ is able to capture long-term temporal dependencies.

Importance of Different Operations. We explore the importance of different operations in Table 9. First, we evaluate the necessity of FC layers from three directions. It shows that each direction plays an important role. Second, we replace the 3 × 3 convolution with our MorphFC$_s$ layer in ResNet [22]/R(2+1)D [60] and the result shows that Transformer structure is more suitable for our MorphFC than the bottleneck block of CNN. Third, following the ViP [23], we utilize a weighted sum after three directions FC layers. Results show that weighted sum can bring a slight improvement (0.3%).

Training Speed. As shown in Table 11, considering speed and accuracy trade-off, our approach is more efficient for training with other SOTA video methods.

5 Conclusion

In this paper, we propose a self-attention free, MLP-Like backbone for video representation learning, named MorphMLP. MorphMLP is capable of progressively discovering core semantics and capturing long-term temporal information. To our best knowledge, we are the first to apply MLP-Like architecture in the video domain. The experiments demonstrate that such self-attention free models can be as strong as and even outperform self-attention based architectures.

Acknowledgements. This project is supported by the National Research Foundation, Singapore under its NRFF Award NRF-NRFF13-2021-0008, and Mike Zheng Shou's Start-Up Grant from NUS. David Junhao Zhang is supported by NUS IDS-ISEP scholarship.

References

1. Arnab, A., Dehghani, M., Heigold, G., Sun, C., Lučić, M., Schmid, C.: ViViT: a video vision transformer. In: Proceedings of the IEEE/CVF International Conference on Computer Vision (2021)
2. Ba, J., Kiros, J.R., Hinton, G.E.: Layer normalization. arXiv abs/1607.06450 (2016)
3. Bertasius, G., Wang, H., Torresani, L.: Is space-time attention all you need for video understanding? In: Proceedings of the International Conference on Machine Learning (ICML) (2021)
4. Bulat, A., Perez-Rua, J.M., Sudhakaran, S., Martinez, B., Tzimiropoulos, G.: Space-time mixing attention for video transformer. In: Advances in Neural Information Processing Systems (2021)
5. Carion, N., Massa, F., Synnaeve, G., Usunier, N., Kirillov, A., Zagoruyko, S.: End-to-end object detection with transformers. In: Vedaldi, A., Bischof, H., Brox, T., Frahm, J.-M. (eds.) ECCV 2020. LNCS, vol. 12346, pp. 213–229. Springer, Cham (2020). https://doi.org/10.1007/978-3-030-58452-8_13
6. Carreira, J., Zisserman, A.: Quo Vadis, action recognition? A new model and the kinetics dataset. In: 2017 IEEE Conference on Computer Vision and Pattern Recognition (CVPR) (2017)
7. Chen, S., Xie, E., GE, C., Chen, R., Liang, D., Luo, P.: CycleMLP: a MLP-like architecture for dense prediction. In: International Conference on Learning Representations (2022)
8. Chen, Y., Kalantidis, Y., Li, J., Yan, S., Feng, J.: A^2-nets: double attention networks. In: Advances in Neural Information Processing Systems (2018)
9. Contributors, M.: MMSegmentation: Openmmlab semantic segmentation toolbox and benchmark (2020). www.github.com/open-mmlab/mmsegmentation
10. Dai, Z., Liu, H., Le, Q.V., Tan, M.: CoatNet: marrying convolution and attention for all data sizes. In: Advances in Neural Information Processing Systems (2021)

11. Deng, J., Dong, W., Socher, R., Li, L.J., Li, K., Fei-Fei, L.: ImageNet: a large-scale hierarchical image database. In: 2009 IEEE Conference on Computer Vision and Pattern Recognition (2009)

12. Dong, X., et al.: CSWin transformer: a general vision transformer backbone with cross-shaped windows. arXiv abs/2107.00652 (2021)

13. Dosovitskiy, A., et al.: An image is worth 16x16 words: transformers for image recognition at scale. In: International Conference on Learning Representations (2021)

14. Fan, H., Li, Y., Xiong, B., Lo, W.Y., Feichtenhofer, C.: Pyslowfast (2020). www.github.com/facebookresearch/slowfast

15. Fan, H., Xiong, B., Mangalam, K., Li, Y., Yan, Z., Malik, J., Feichtenhofer, C.: Multiscale vision transformers. In: Proceedings of the IEEE/CVF International Conference on Computer Vision (2021)

16. Fan, Q., Chen, C.F.R., Kuehne, H., Pistoia, M., Cox, D.: More is less: learning efficient video representations by temporal aggregation modules. In: Advances in Neural Information Processing Systems (2019)

17. Feichtenhofer, C.: X3D: expanding architectures for efficient video recognition. In: 2020 IEEE/CVF Conference on Computer Vision and Pattern Recognition (CVPR) (2020)

18. Feichtenhofer, C., Fan, H., Malik, J., He, K.: Slowfast networks for video recognition. In: 2019 IEEE/CVF International Conference on Computer Vision (ICCV) (2019)

19. Goyal, P., et al.: Accurate, large minibatch SGD: training imagenet in 1 hour. arXiv abs/1706.02677 (2017)

20. Goyal, R., et al.: The "something something" video database for learning and evaluating visual common sense. In: 2017 IEEE International Conference on Computer Vision (ICCV) (2017)

21. Guo, J., et al.: Hire-MLP: vision MLP via hierarchical rearrangement. arXiv preprint arXiv:2108.13341 (2021)

22. He, K., Zhang, X., Ren, S., Sun, J.: Deep residual learning for image recognition. In: 2016 IEEE Conference on Computer Vision and Pattern Recognition (CVPR) (2016)

23. Hou, Q., Jiang, Z., Yuan, L., Cheng, M.M., Yan, S., Feng, J.: Vision permutator: a permutable MLP-like architecture for visual recognition. IEEE Trans. Pattern Anal. Mach. Intell. (2022)

24. Howard, A.G., et al.: MobileNets: efficient convolutional neural networks for mobile vision applications. arXiv abs/1704.04861 (2017)

25. Hu, J., Shen, L., Albanie, S., Sun, G., Wu, E.: Squeeze-and-excitation networks. IEEE Trans. Pattern Anal. Mach. Intell. (2020)

26. Huang, G., Liu, Z., Weinberger, K.Q.: Densely connected convolutional networks. In: 2017 IEEE Conference on Computer Vision and Pattern Recognition (CVPR) (2017)

27. Jiang, B., Wang, M., Gan, W., Wu, W., Yan, J.: STM: spatiotemporal and motion encoding for action recognition. In: 2019 IEEE International Conference on Computer Vision (ICCV) (2019)

28. Jin, Y., Han, D.K., Ko, H.: TRSEG: transformer for semantic segmentation. Pattern Recogn. Lett. (2021)

29. Kirillov, A., Girshick, R., He, K., Dollár, P.: Panoptic feature pyramid networks. In: Proceedings of the IEEE/CVF Conference on Computer Vision and Pattern Recognition (2019)

30. Krizhevsky, A., Sutskever, I., Hinton, G.E.: Imagenet classification with deep convolutional neural networks. In: Advances in Neural Information Processing Systems (2012)
31. Li, K., Li, X., Wang, Y., Wang, J., Qiao, Y.: CT-Net: channel tensorization network for video classification. In: International Conference on Learning Representations (2021)
32. Li, T., Ke, Q., Rahmani, H., Ho, R.E., Ding, H., Liu, J.: Else-net: elastic semantic network for continual action recognition from skeleton data. In: Proceedings of the IEEE/CVF International Conference on Computer Vision (2021)
33. Li, T., Liu, J., Zhang, W., Duan, L.: HARD-Net: hardness-AwaRe discrimination network for 3D early activity prediction. In: Vedaldi, A., Bischof, H., Brox, T., Frahm, J.-M. (eds.) ECCV 2020. LNCS, vol. 12356, pp. 420–436. Springer, Cham (2020). https://doi.org/10.1007/978-3-030-58621-8_25
34. Li, X., Wang, Y., Zhou, Z., Qiao, Y.: SmallBigNet: integrating core and contextual views for video classification. In: 2020 IEEE Conference on Computer Vision and Pattern Recognition (CVPR) (2020)
35. Li, Y., Ji, B., Shi, X., Zhang, J., Kang, B., Wang, L.: Tea: temporal excitation and aggregation for action recognition. In: Proceedings of the IEEE/CVF Conference on Computer Vision and Pattern Recognition (2020)
36. Lian, D., Yu, Z., Sun, X., Gao, S.: AS-MLP: an axial shifted MLP architecture for vision. In: International Conference on Learning Representations (2022)
37. Lin, J., Gan, C., Han, S.: TSM: temporal shift module for efficient video understanding. In: 2019 IEEE International Conference on Computer Vision (ICCV) (2019)
38. Liu, H., Dai, Z., So, D., Le, Q.: Pay attention to MLPs. In: Advances in Neural Information Processing Systems (2021)
39. Liu, Z., et al.: Swin transformer: hierarchical vision transformer using shifted windows. In: Proceedings of the IEEE/CVF International Conference on Computer Vision (2021)
40. Liu, Z., et al.: Video swin transformer. arXiv abs/2106.13230 (2021)
41. Liu, Z., et al.: TeiNet: towards an efficient architecture for video recognition. In: Proceedings of the AAAI Conference on Artificial Intelligence (2020)
42. Loshchilov, I., Hutter, F.: Fixing weight decay regularization in Adam. arXiv abs/1711.05101 (2017)
43. Loshchilov, I., Hutter, F.: SGDR: stochastic gradient descent with warm restarts. In: International Conference on Learning Representations (2017)
44. Neimark, D., Bar, O., Zohar, M., Asselmann, D.: Video transformer network. In: Proceedings of the IEEE/CVF International Conference on Computer Vision (2021)
45. Patrick, M., et al: Keeping your eye on the ball: trajectory attention in video transformers. In: Advances in Neural Information Processing Systems (2021)
46. Radosavovic, I., Kosaraju, R.P., Girshick, R.B., He, K., Dollár, P.: Designing network design spaces. In: 2020 IEEE/CVF Conference on Computer Vision and Pattern Recognition (CVPR) (2020)
47. Rao, Y., Zhao, W., Zhu, Z., Lu, J., Zhou, J.: Global filter networks for image classification. In: Advances in Neural Information Processing Systems (2021)
48. Sandler, M., Howard, A., Zhu, M., Zhmoginov, A., Chen, L.C.: MobileNetv 2: inverted residuals and linear bottlenecks. In: Proceedings of the IEEE Conference on Computer Vision and Pattern Recognition (2018)
49. Simonyan, K., Zisserman, A.: Very deep convolutional networks for large-scale image recognition. arXiv preprint arXiv:1409.1556 (2014)

50. Srinivas, A., Lin, T.Y., Parmar, N., Shlens, J., Abbeel, P., Vaswani, A.: Bottleneck transformers for visual recognition. In: Proceedings of the IEEE/CVF Conference on Computer Vision and Pattern Recognition (2021)

51. Szegedy, C., et al.: Going deeper with convolutions. In: Proceedings of the IEEE Conference on Computer Vision and Pattern Recognition (2015)

52. Tan, M., Le, Q.V.: EfficientNet: rethinking model scaling for convolutional neural networks. In: International Conference on Machine Learning (2019)

53. Tang, C., Zhao, Y., Wang, G., Luo, C., Xie, W., Zeng, W.: Sparse MLP for image recognition: is self-attention really necessary? arXiv preprint arXiv:2109.05422 (2021)

54. Tolstikhin, I., et al.: MLP-mixer: an all-MLP architecture for vision. In: Beygelzimer, A., Dauphin, Y., Liang, P., Vaughan, J.W. (eds.) Advances in Neural Information Processing Systems (2021)

55. Touvron, H., et al.: ResMLP: feedforward networks for image classification with data-efficient training. arXiv abs/2105.03404 (2021)

56. Touvron, H., Cord, M., Douze, M., Massa, F., Sablayrolles, A., J'egou, H.: Training data-efficient image transformers & distillation through attention. In: ICML (2021)

57. Touvron, H., Cord, M., Sablayrolles, A., Synnaeve, G., J'egou, H.: Going deeper with image transformers. In: Proceedings of the IEEE/CVF International Conference on Computer Vision (2021)

58. Tran, D., Bourdev, L.D., Fergus, R., Torresani, L., Paluri, M.: Learning spatiotemporal features with 3D convolutional networks. In: 2015 IEEE International Conference on Computer Vision (ICCV) (2015)

59. Tran, D., Wang, H., Torresani, L., Feiszli, M.: Video classification with channel-separated convolutional networks. In: 2019 IEEE/CVF International Conference on Computer Vision (ICCV) (2019)

60. Tran, D., Xiu Wang, H., Torresani, L., Ray, J., LeCun, Y., Paluri, M.: A closer look at spatiotemporal convolutions for action recognition. In: 2018 IEEE Conference on Computer Vision and Pattern Recognition (CVPR) (2018)

61. Vaswani, A., et al.: Attention is all you need. In: Advances in Neural Information Processing Systems (2017)

62. Wang, H., Tran, D., Torresani, L., Feiszli, M.: Video modeling with correlation networks. In: 2020 IEEE/CVF Conference on Computer Vision and Pattern Recognition (CVPR) (2020)

63. Wang, L., Tong, Z., Ji, B., Wu, G.: TDN: temporal difference networks for efficient action recognition. In: Proceedings of the IEEE/CVF Conference on Computer Vision and Pattern Recognition (2021)

64. Wang, W., et al.: Pyramid vision transformer: a versatile backbone for dense prediction without convolutions. In: Proceedings of the IEEE/CVF International Conference on Computer Vision (2021)

65. Wang, X., Girshick, R.B., Gupta, A., He, K.: Non-local neural networks. In: 2018 IEEE/CVF Conference on Computer Vision and Pattern Recognition (2018)

66. Wang, X., Gupta, A.: Videos as space-time region graphs. In: Ferrari, V., Hebert, M., Sminchisescu, C., Weiss, Y. (eds.) ECCV 2018. LNCS, vol. 11209, pp. 413–431. Springer, Cham (2018). https://doi.org/10.1007/978-3-030-01228-1_25

67. Wu, B., et al.: Visual transformers: token-based image representation and processing for computer vision. arXiv abs/2006.03677 (2020)

68. Xie, E., Wang, W., Yu, Z., Anandkumar, A., Alvarez, J.M., Luo, P.: SegFormer: simple and efficient design for semantic segmentation with transformers. In: Advances in Neural Information Processing Systems (2021)

69. Xie, S., Girshick, R.B., Dollár, P., Tu, Z., He, K.: Aggregated residual transformations for deep neural networks. In: 2017 IEEE Conference on Computer Vision and Pattern Recognition (CVPR) (2017)
70. Yang, J., et al.: Focal self-attention for local-global interactions in vision transformers. In: Advances in Neural Information Processing Systems (2021)
71. Yu, T., Li, X., Cai, Y., Sun, M., Li, P.: S2-MLP: spatial-shift MLP architecture for vision. In: Proceedings of the IEEE/CVF Winter Conference on Applications of Computer Vision (2022)
72. Yuan, L., et al.: Tokens-to-token ViT: training vision transformers from scratch on imagenet. arXiv abs/2101.11986 (2021)
73. Zhang, H., et al.: ResNest: split-attention networks. arXiv preprint arXiv:2004.08955 (2020)
74. Zhang, Y., et al.: VidTR: video transformer without convolutions. In: Proceedings of the IEEE/CVF International Conference on Computer Vision (2021)
75. Zhou, B., et al.: Semantic understanding of scenes through the ade20k dataset. Int. J. Comput. Vision (2019)
76. Zhu, X., Su, W., Lu, L., Li, B., Wang, X., Dai, J.: Deformable DETR: deformable transformers for end-to-end object detection. In: International Conference on Learning Representations (2021)

COMPOSER: Compositional Reasoning of Group Activity in Videos with Keypoint-Only Modality

Honglu Zhou[1]([⊠]), Asim Kadav[2], Aviv Shamsian[3], Shijie Geng[1], Farley Lai[2], Long Zhao[4], Ting Liu[4], Mubbasir Kapadia[1], and Hans Peter Graf[2]

[1] Department of Computer Science, Rutgers University, Piscataway, NJ, USA
{hz289,sg1309,mk1353}@cs.rutgers.edu
[2] NEC Laboratories America, Inc., San Jose, CA, USA
{asim,farleylai,hpg}@nec-labs.com
[3] Bar-Ilan University, Ramat Gan, Israel
aviv.shamsian@biu.ac.il
[4] Google Research, Los Angeles, CA, USA
{longzh,liuti}@google.com

Abstract. Group Activity Recognition detects the activity collectively performed by a group of actors, which requires compositional reasoning of actors and objects. We approach the task by modeling the video as tokens that represent the multi-scale semantic concepts in the video. We propose COMPOSER, a Multiscale Transformer based architecture that performs attention-based *reasoning* over tokens at each scale and learns group activity *compositionally*. In addition, prior works suffer from scene biases with privacy and ethical concerns. We only use the keypoint modality which reduces scene biases and prevents acquiring detailed visual data that may contain private or biased information of users. We improve the multiscale representations in COMPOSER by clustering the intermediate scale representations, while maintaining consistent cluster assignments between scales. Finally, we use techniques such as auxiliary prediction and data augmentations tailored to the keypoint signals to aid model training. We demonstrate the model's strength and interpretability on two widely-used datasets (Volleyball and Collective Activity). COMPOSER achieves up to +5.4% improvement with just the keypoint modality (Code is available at https://github.com/hongluzhou/composer.).

Keywords: Keypoint-only group activity recognition ·
Compositionality · Multiscale representations · Transformer · Video
understanding

H. Zhou—Work done as a NEC Labs intern.

Supplementary Information The online version contains supplementary material available at https://doi.org/10.1007/978-3-031-19833-5_15.

1   Introduction

Group Activity Recognition (GAR) detects the activity collectively performed by a group of actors in a short video clip [11,48]. GAR has widespread societal implications in a variety of domains including security, surveillance, kinesiology, sports analysis, robot-human interaction, and rehabilitation [15,16,38,55].

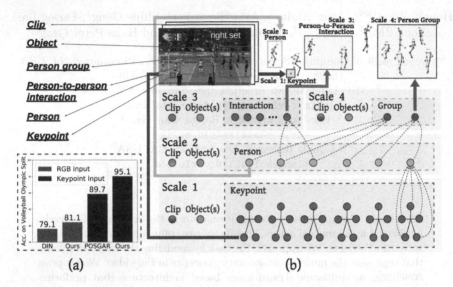

Fig. 1. (a) **The keypoint-only setup generalizes better for GAR.** The Volleyball Olympic split [44] ensures videos having vastly different scene background between training and testing, which can examine GAR model's scene generalization ability. RGB-based methods severely suffer from scene biases and have poor model generalizability. (b) **Main idea.** We propose COMPOSER that uses keypoint only modality for GAR by modeling a video as *tokens* that represent the multiscale semantic concepts in the video, which include *keypoint*, *person*, person-to-person *interaction*, person *group*, *object* if present, and the *clip*. Four scales are formed by grouping actor-related tokens according to their semantic hierarchy. Representations of tokens in coarser scales are learned and aggregated from tokens of the finer scales. COMPOSER (Fig. 3) facilitates compositional reasoning of group activity in videos

The task requires addressing two challenges. First, GAR requires a *compositional understanding* of the scene [2]. Because of the crowded scene, it is challenging to learn meaningful representations for GAR over the entire scene [48]. Since group activity often consists of sub-group(s) of actors and scene objects, the final action label depends on a compositional understanding of these entities [48,54]. Second, GAR benefits from *relational reasoning* over scene elements to understand the relative importance of entities and their interactions [19,52]. For example, in a volleyball game, persons around the ball performing the jumping action are more important than others standing in the scene.

Existing work has proposed to jointly learn the group activity with individual actions [4,5,22,23,39,40] or person sub-groups [15,29,33] for a compositional understanding of the group activity. Meanwhile, graph [19,22,47,55] and transformer [16,29] based models have been proposed for relational reasoning over scene entities. However, these methods do not sufficiently make use of the multiscale scene elements in the GAR task by modeling over entities at either one semantic scale (e.g., person [16,19,47,55]) or two scales (person and person group [15,29,33], or keypoint and person [37]). More importantly, explicit multiscale modeling is neglected, lacking consistent compositional representations for the group action tasks. Furthermore, majority of the prior GAR methods rely on the RGB modality (see Table 3), which causes the model more likely to have privacy and ethical issues when deployed in real-world applications [18]. Last but not least, the RGB input hinders the model's robustness to changes in background, lighting conditions or textures, and often results in poor model generalizability due to scene biases (see Fig. 1 (a)) [10,42].

In this paper, we present COMPOSER that addresses *compositional learning* of entities in the video and *relational reasoning* about these entities. Inspired by how humans are particularly adept at representing objects in different granularities meanwhile reasoning their interactions to turn sensory signals into a high-level knowledge [21,28], we approach GAR by modeling a video as tokens that represent the multi-scale semantic concepts in the video (Fig. 1 (b)). Compared to the aforementioned prior works, we consider more fine-grained scene entities that are grouped into *four* scales. By combining the scales together with Multiscale Transformer (Fig. 4), COMPOSER provides attention-based reasoning over tokens at each scale, which makes the higher-level understanding of the group activity possible. Moreover, COMPOSER uses only the keypoint modality. Using only the 2D (or 3D) keypoints as input, our method can prevent the sensor camera from acquiring detailed visual data that may contain private or biased information of users[1]. Keypoints also allow the model to focus on the action-specific cues, and help the model be more invariant to the scene biases. COMPOSER generalizes much better to testing data with different scene backgrounds (see the Volleyball Olympic split results in Table 1).

COMPOSER learns *consistent* multiscale representations which boost the performance for GAR (Fig. 2). This is achieved by contrastive clustering assignments of clips. Intuitively, a model can recognize the group activity using representations of entities at just one particular scale. Hence, we consider representations of the clip token learned across scales as representations of different *views* of the clip. Such perspective allows us to cluster clip representations learned at all scales while enforcing consistency between cluster assignments produced from different scales of the *same* clip. In order to enforce this consistency, we follow [7] and use a *swapped* prediction mechanism where we predict the cluster assignment of a scale from the representation of another scale. However, distinct from related works [3,7,9], which use information from multiple augmentations or modalities for self-supervised learning from unlabelled images or videos, we use information from multiple scales for the task of group activity recognition. Contrasting clustering assignments enhance our intermediate representations and the overall

---

[1] Even for the keypoint extraction backbone which our method is agnostic to, there are existing works [18] that perform privacy-preserving keypoint estimation.

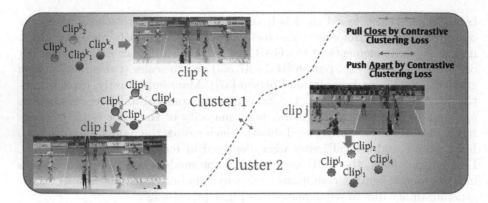

Fig. 2. Embedding space learned by COMPOSER. COMPOSER exploits a contrastive clustering objective (Sect. 3.3) to learn *consistent* multiscale representations for GAR. This is achieved by clustering clip representations learned at all scales. The clustering objective encourages an "agreement" between scales on the high-level knowledge learned ('Pull Close' representations of the same clip). Contrastive learning is performed on the clusters, which also helps the model to discriminate between clips with different semantic characteristics ('Pull Close' representations of the semantically-similar clips and 'Push Apart' those that are semantically-different). In the illustration, we use subscript to denote the scale and use superscript to indicate different clips

performance. Finally, we use techniques such as auxiliary prediction at each scale and data augmentation methods such as *Actor Dropout* to aid training.

Our contributions are three-fold:

1. We present COMPOSER for compositional reasoning of group activity in videos. COMPOSER can distill and convey high-level semantic knowledge from the elementary elements of the human-centered videos. We learn contrastive clustering assignment to improve the multiscale representations. By maintaining a consistent cluster assignment across the multiple scales of the *same* clip, an agreement between scales on the high-level knowledge learned can be promoted to optimize the representations across scales.
2. We use only the keypoint modality that allows COMPOSER to address the privacy and ethical concerns and to be robust to changes in background, with auxiliary prediction and data augmentation methods tailored to learning group activity from the keypoint modality.
3. We demonstrate the model's strength and interpretability on two commonly-used datasets (Volleyball and Collective Activity) and COMPOSER achieves up to +5.4% improvement using just the keypoint modality.

2   Related Work

Much of the recent research on GAR explores how to capture the actor relations [4,19,22,38,47]. Several works tackle this problem from a graph-based perspective [22,31,51,52]. Some utilize attention modeling [31,39,49,54] including

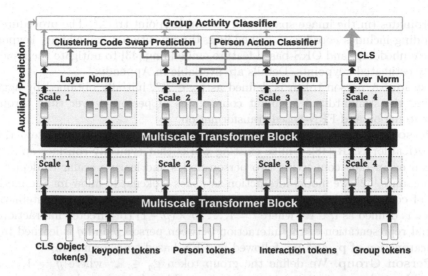

Fig. 3. COMPOSER. Given tokens that represent the multiscale semantic concepts (Fig. 1) in the human-centered video, COMPOSER jointly learns group activity, individual actions and contrastive clustering assignments of clips. Auxiliary predictions are enforced to aid training (Sect. 3.5)

using Transformers [16,29]. Existing works have primarily used RGB- and/or optical-flow-based features with RoIAlign [17] to represent actors [5,39,47,51]. A few recent works replace or augment these features with keypoints/poses of the actors [16,37,44,54]. In this paper, we use only the light-weight coordinate-based keypoint representation. We propose a Multiscale Transformer block to hierarchically reason about entities at different semantic scales and we aid learning group activities by improving the musicale representations. Please see an in-depth discussion on related works in Appendix G.

3 Methodology

We present COMPOSER (Fig. 3), a novel Multiscale Transformer based architecture for GAR. In Sect. 3.1, we describe the multi-scale semantic tokens representing a video with group activities. We introduce COMPOSER and especially its reasoning module Multiscale Transformer in Sect. 3.2. We describe data augmentations in Sect. 3.4 and the exact formulation of auxiliary prediction in Sect. 3.5.

3.1 Tokenizing a Video as Hierarchical Semantic Entities

We model a video as semantic tokens that allow our method easily adaptable to understanding any videos with multi-actor multi-object interactions [32].
• **Person Keypoint.** We define a person keypoint token, $\mathbf{k}_p^j \in \mathbb{R}^d$ that represents a keypoint joint j ($j = 1, \ldots, j'$) of person p ($p = 1, \ldots, p'$) in all timestamps, where j' is the number of joint types and p' is the number of actors. The initial d-dimensional person keypoint token is learned by encoding the numerical

coordinates (in the image space) of a certain keypoint track[2]. The procedure of encoding includes coordinate embedding, time positional embedding, keypoint type embedding, and OKS-based feature embedding [43] to mitigate the issue of noisy estimated keypoints. Details are available in Appendix.

• **Person.** A person token is defined as $\mathbf{p}_p \in \mathbb{R}^d$, initially obtained by aggregating the standardized keypoint coordinates of person p over time through concatenation and FFN-based transformation.

• **Person-to-Person Interaction.** Modeling the person-to-person interactions is critical for GAR [48]. Unlike existing works that typically consider an interaction as an *edge* connecting two person nodes and learn a scalar to depict its importance [52], we model interaction as *nodes* (tokens) to allow for the modeling of complex higher-order interactions [32]. The person-to-person interaction token is defined as $\mathbf{i}_i \in \mathbb{R}^d$ where $i = 1, \ldots, p' \times (p'-1)$ (bi-directed interactions). Initial representation of the interaction between person p and q is learned from concatenation of $\mathbf{p}_p$ and $\mathbf{p}_q$, followed by FFN-based transformation.

• **Person Group.** We define the group token $\mathbf{g}_g \in \mathbb{R}^d$ where $g = 1, \ldots, g'$ for videos where sub-groups are often separable. g' denotes the num. of subgroups in the video. Given the person-to-group mapping which can be obtained through various mechanisms (e.g., heuristics [37], k-means [29], etc. [15,26].), representation of a group is an aggregate over representations of persons in the group similarly through concatenation and FFN.

• **Clip.** The special [CLS] token ($\in \mathbb{R}^d$) is a learnable embedding vector and is considered as the clip representation. CLS stands for classification and is often used in Transformers to "summarize" the task-related representative information from all tokens in the input sequence [14].

• **Object.** Scene objects can play a crucial role in videos where human(s) interact with object(s). E.g., in a volleyball game where one person is spiking and multiple nearby actors are all jumping with arms up, it can be difficult to tell which person is the key person with information of just the person keypoints due to their similar poses. The ball keypoints can help to distinguish the key person. Object keypoints can be used to represent an object in the scene with similar benefits of person keypoints (e.g., to boost model robustness [24]). Object keypoint detection [6,30] benefits downstream tasks such as human action recognition [20], object detection [24,53], tracking [34], etc. [27]. Thus, we use object keypoints to represent each object for GAR. We denote object token $\mathbf{e}_e \in \mathbb{R}^d$ where $e = 1, \ldots, e'$ and e' is the maximal number of objects a video might have. Similar to person tokens, the initial object tokens are learned from aggregating the coordinate-represented object keypoints.

3.2 Multiscale Transformer

Multiscale Transformer takes a sequence of multiple-scale tokens as input, and refines representations of these tokens. Specifically, tokens of the four scales are:

---

[2] We use track-based representations [16,29,44,56] to represent each token.

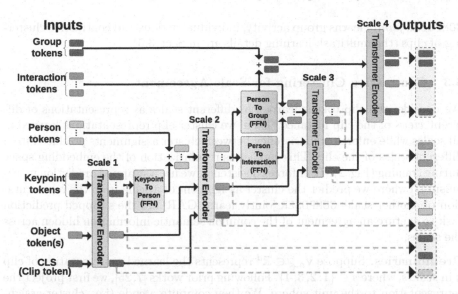

Fig. 4. Multiscale Transformer performs relational reasoning with four Transformer Encoders to operate self-attention on tokens of each scale, while stringing tokens of the four scales together with FFNs and Skip Connections to learn hierarchical representations that make a high-level understanding of group activity possible

$$
\begin{aligned}
&\text{Scale 1:} \quad \left\{ [\text{CLS}], \mathbf{e}_1, \cdots, \mathbf{e}_{e'}, \mathbf{k}_1^1, \cdots, \mathbf{k}_{p'}^{j'} \right\}, \\
&\text{Scale 2:} \quad \left\{ [\text{CLS}], \mathbf{e}_1, \cdots, \mathbf{e}_{e'}, \mathbf{p}_1, \cdots, \mathbf{p}_{p'} \right\}, \\
&\text{Scale 3:} \quad \left\{ [\text{CLS}], \mathbf{e}_1, \cdots, \mathbf{e}_{e'}, \mathbf{i}_1, \cdots, \mathbf{i}_{p' \times (p'-1)} \right\}, \\
&\text{Scale 4:} \quad \left\{ [\text{CLS}], \mathbf{e}_1, \cdots, \mathbf{e}_{e'}, \mathbf{g}_1, \cdots, \mathbf{g}_{g'} \right\}.
\end{aligned}
\tag{1}
$$

We utilize a Transformer encoder [45] at each scale to perform relational reasoning of tokens in that scale. We review details of Transformer in the Appendix.

Hierarchical representations of tokens are maintained in an elaborately designed Multiscale Transformer block (Fig. 4). In the Multiscale Transformer block, operations in the four scales are the same (but with different parameters) to maintain simplicity. Specifically, given a sequence of tokens of scale s (Eq. 1), Transformer encoder outputs refined representations of these tokens. Then, concatenation and FFN are used to aggregate refined representations of *actor-related* tokens, in order to form representations of actor-related tokens in the subsequent coarser scale $s+1$. Such learned representations are summed with their initial representations (input to the Multiscale Transformer) (i.e. Skip Connection). The resulting actor-related tokens, as well as scale s updated [CLS] token and object token(s) form the input sequence of the Transformer encoder in the scale $s+1$ (see wiring in Fig. 4).

COMPOSER uses the initial representations of the multi-scale semantic tokens (Sect. 3.1) as input, and utilizes multiple blocks of Multiscale Transformer to perform relational reasoning over these tokens. With refined token representations,

COMPOSER *jointly* learns group activity, individual actions and contrastive clustering of clips (the multitask-learning details are in Sect. 3.5).

3.3   Contrastive Clustering for Scale Agreement

We consider the clip tokens learned at different scales as representations of different *views* of the clip instance. Then, we cluster clip representations learned in all scales while enforcing consistency between cluster assignments produced from different scales of the clip. This can act as regularization of the embedding space during training (Fig. 2). To enforce consistency, we use a swapped prediction mechanism [7] where we predict the cluster assignment of a scale from the representation of another scale. COMPOSER jointly learns GAR and the swapped prediction task to capture an agreement of the common semantic information hidden across the scales.

Preliminaries. Suppose $\mathbf{v}_{n,s} \in \mathbb{R}^d$ represents the learned representation of clip n in scale s, where $s \in \{1, 2, 3, 4\}$. Following prior works [7,25], we first project the representation to the unit sphere. We then compute a code (i.e., cluster assignment) $\mathbf{q}_{n,s} \in \mathbb{R}^K$ by mapping $\mathbf{v}_{n,s}$ to a set of K *trainable* prototype vectors, $\{\mathbf{c}_1, \ldots, \mathbf{c}_K\}$. We denote by $C \in \mathbb{R}^{K \times d}$ the matrix whose rows are the $\mathbf{c}_1, \ldots, \mathbf{c}_K$.

Swapped Prediction. Suppose s and w denote 2 different scales from the four representation scales. The swapped prediction problem aims to predict the code $\mathbf{q}_{n,s}$ from $\mathbf{v}_{n,w}$, and $\mathbf{q}_{n,w}$ from $\mathbf{v}_{n,s}$, with the following loss function:

$$\mathcal{L}_{\text{swap}}(\mathbf{v}_{n,w}, \mathbf{v}_{n,s}) = \ell(\mathbf{v}_{n,w}, \mathbf{q}_{n,s}) + \ell(\mathbf{v}_{n,s}, \mathbf{q}_{n,w}) \tag{2}$$

where $\ell(\mathbf{v}_{n,w}, \mathbf{q}_{n,s})$ measures the fit between $\mathbf{v}_{n,w}$ and $\mathbf{q}_{n,s}$. $\ell(\mathbf{v}_{n,w}, \mathbf{q}_{n,s})$ is the cross entropy loss between $\mathbf{q}_{n,s}$ and the probability obtained by taking a softmax of the dot products of $\mathbf{v}_{n,w}$ and prototypes in C:

$$\ell(\mathbf{v}_{n,w}, \mathbf{q}_{n,s}) = -\sum_{k=1}^{K} \mathbf{q}_{n,s}^{(k)} \log \frac{\exp\left(\frac{1}{\tau}\mathbf{v}_{n,w}\mathbf{c}_k^{\top}\right)}{\sum_{k'=1}^{K} \exp\left(\frac{1}{\tau}\mathbf{v}_{n,w}\mathbf{c}_{k'}^{\top}\right)} \tag{3}$$

where τ is a temperature parameter. The total loss of the swapped prediction problem is taking Eq. (2) computed over all pairs of scales and all N clips,

$$\mathcal{L}_{\text{cluster}} = \frac{1}{N} \sum_{n=1}^{N} \left(\sum_{w,s \in \{1,2,3,4\} \& w \neq s} \mathcal{L}_{\text{swap}}(\mathbf{v}_{n,w}, \mathbf{v}_{n,s}) \right) \tag{4}$$

Online Clustering. This step produces the cluster assignments using the learned prototypes C and the learned clip representations *only within a batch*, $V \in \mathbb{R}^{B \times d}$ where B denotes the batch size. We perform the clustering in an online fashion for faster training and use the method proposed in [7]. Specifically, online clustering yields the codes $Q \in \mathbb{R}^{B \times K}$. We compute codes Q such that all examples in a batch are equally partitioned by the prototypes (which prevents the trivial solution where every clip has the same code). Q is opti-mized to maximize the similarity between the learned clip representations and the prototypes,

$$\max_{Q \in \mathcal{Q}} \operatorname{Tr}\left(QCV^\top\right) + \varepsilon H(Q), \tag{5}$$

$$\mathcal{Q} = \left\{ Q \in \mathbb{R}_+^{B \times K} \mid 1_B Q = \frac{1}{K} 1_K, Q 1_K^\top = \frac{1}{B} 1_B^\top \right\}$$

where the trace Tr is the sum of the elements on the main diagonal, H is the entropy function, and ε is a parameter that controls the smoothness of the map-ping. $1_K \in \mathbb{R}^K$ and $1_B \in \mathbb{R}^B$ are a vector of ones to enforce the equipartition constraint. The continuous solution Q^* of Eq. (5) is computed with the iterative Sinkhorn-Knopp algorithm [7,13].

3.4 Data Augmentation for Keypoint Modality

We use the following data augmentations to aid training and improve general-ization ability of the model learned from the *keypoint* modality.

Actor Dropout is performed by removing a random actor in a random frame, inspired by [35] that masks agents with probabilities to predict agent behaviors for autonomous driving. We remove actors by replacing the representation of the actor with a zero vector.

Horizontal Flip is often used by existing GAR methods [37,44,56], which is performed on the video frame level. This augmentation causes the pose of each person and positions of (left and right) sub-groups flipped horizontally. We add a small random perturbation on each flipped keypoint.

Horizontal Move means we horizontally move all keypoints in the clip by a certain number of pixel locations, which is randomly determined per video and bounded by a pre-defined number (i.e., 10). Similarly, afterwards a small random perturbation is applied on each keypoint.

Vertical Move is done similar to the Horizontal Move, except we move the keypoints in the vertical direction.

Novel practices like Actor Dropout, Horizontal/Vertical Move and random perturbations help the model to perform GAR from noisy estimated keypoints.

3.5 Auxiliary Prediction and Multitask Learning

We take the learned representation of the clip at *each* scale of *each* Multiscale Transformer block, and perform *auxiliary group activity predictions* (Fig. 3). Specifically, each of the clip representations learned at each scale of each block is sent as input to the group activity classifier to produce one GAR result. In addition, person representation from the last Multiscale Transformer block is the input to a person action classifier. Meanwhile, the loss of the swapped prediction problem is computed given the learned representations of the clip of all 4 scales from the last Multiscale Transformer block. The total loss is:

$$\mathcal{L}_{\text{total}} = \sum_{m=1}^{M-1} \mathcal{L}_{\text{groupAux}} + \lambda\left(\mathcal{L}_{\text{groupLast}} + \mathcal{L}_{\text{person}} + \mathcal{L}_{\text{cluster}}\right) \qquad (6)$$

where $\mathcal{L}_{\text{groupAux}}$ represents the loss from Auxiliary Prediction incurred by clip representations at different scales and early blocks of the Multiscale Transformer, $\mathcal{L}_{\text{groupLast}}$ is from the last Multiscale Transformer block, $\mathcal{L}_{\text{person}}$ is the person action classification loss, and $\mathcal{L}_{\text{cluster}}$ is the contrastive clustering loss (Eq. 4). m denotes the index of the Multiscale Transformer block, M is the total number of the Multiscale Transformer blocks, and λ is a hyper-parameter that weights the importance of predictions from the last block. For metric evaluation, we use the clip token from the last scale in the last Multiscale Transformer as input to the group activity classifier.

4   Experimental Evaluation

4.1   Dataset

The Volleyball dataset [23] (VD) comprises 4, 830 clips from 55 videos. The group activity labels include 8 activities: 4 main activities (*set*, *spike*, *pass*, *winpoint*) which are divided into two subgroups, *left* and *right*. Each player can perform one of the 9 actions: *blocking*, *digging*, *falling*, *jumping*, *moving*, *setting*, *spiking*, *standing* and *waiting*. The dataset has a default '**Original**' split in which train/test videos were randomly splitted (39 train and 16 test videos). A skewed '**Olympic**' split [44] was later released in which train/test videos are splitted according to the match venues: 29 train videos are from the same 2012 London Olympics venue, while the rest 26 test videos are from numerous venues, and thus largely differs from the train videos w.r.t. the scene background.

The Collective Activity Dataset. [12] (CAD) is a dataset with 44 real-life videos [48]. The group activity labels are *crossing*, *waiting*, *queueing*, *walking* and *talking* (person action labels have an additional 'N/A' class). We follow prior works to merge the class *crossing* and *walking* into *moving* [46,50,51,55], and use the same train-test split [39,47,55] and actor tracklets [5,55]. Please refer to Appendix for implementation details on both datasets.

4.2   Comparison with State-of-the-Arts

Scene Generalization for Keypoint-only Setup. To support the keypoint-only setup for GAR, we first compare the generalization capability of models using either RGB or the keypoint modality. In Table 1, I3D and VGG-16 are two commonly-used image backbone by prior RGB-based GAR methods; the rest are all GAR models (all use VGG-16 as the backbone).

Table 1. Test accuracy on VD **under different train/test splits.** Yellow shaded rows highlight the methods use RGB input, and blue for keypoint

Model	VD Acc. (%) ↑	
	Olympic	Original
I3D [8]	73.9	84.6
VGG-16 [41]	76.4	91.6
PCTDM [50]	75.2	91.7
SACRF [38]	71.1	91.8
AT [16]	76.9	93.0
ARG [47]	77.8	93.3
TCE-STBiP [54]	78.5	93.5
DIN [55]	79.1	93.6
POGARS [44]	89.7	93.2
COMPOSER (ours)	95.1	93.7
Improvement	+5.4%	+0.1%

Note: Keypoint-based methods do NOT use ball keypoint in this table in order to have a rigorous comparison because RGB-based methods are unaware of such info.

Table 2. Comparisons with state-of-the-art (SOTA) methods that leverage **only keypoint information** on the **VD Original split.** COMPOSER outperforms existing methods and achieves a new highest record (+0.7% improvement)

Model	Keypoint		Acc.
	Actor	Object	
Zappardino *et al.* [56]	✓		91.0
GIRN [37]	✓		88.4
	✓	✓	92.2
AT [16]	✓		92.3
	✓	✓	92.8
POGARS [44]	✓		93.2
	✓	✓	93.9
COMPOSER (ours)	✓		93.7
	✓	✓	**94.6**

On VD Olympic split, the best prior RGB-based method is DIN [55] in Table 1. We substitute DIN with a COMPOSER variant[3] (Sect. 1) that also consumes RGB input instead of keypoint, and the result is 81.1% which is 2% higher than DIN, suggesting the stronger reasoning strength of COMPOSER, but the accuracy is still low due to the RGB signals. POGARS [44] uses the keypoint modality and has an accuracy of 89.7%, higher than all RGB-based methods. COMPOSER with the keypoint-only modality obtains 95.1% accuracy and *significantly outperforms* prior methods, yielding +5.4% improvement. These results imply that the keypoint-only setup can reduce scene biases, and generalize better than approaches relying on the RGB modality to testing data with different visual characteristics from training.

We also report the results of these methods that we obtained on VD Original split in Table 1. From this side-by-side comparison, the difference between the Olympic and Original split is vivid. Current GAR methods have quite saturated performances on the Original split of VD and the results are all very high (more evidence later). Therefore, we recommend readers using the more challenging VD Olympic split for future research on GAR. Note that the COMPOSER that outperforms prior methods in Table 1 is only an ablated version of ours in that not using the object token(s). In addition, GroupFormer [29] is currently the best-performing method (Table 4 in Appendix) and its RGB-only variant has the result of 94.1% accuracy on VD Original split. However, GroupFormer uses additional scene features with the Inception-v3 backbone.

---

[3] This COMPOSER variant consumes RGB-based ROI-aligned person features as input, and thus only models 3 scales: person, interaction, and the group scale.

Table 3. Comparisons with SOTA methods that use **a single or multiple modalities** on the original split of VD and CAD. "Flow" denotes optical flow input, and "Scene" denotes features of the entire frames. Fewer modalities indicates a stronger capability of the model itself (*fewer checks are better*). The top 3 performance scores are highlighted as: First, *Second**, *Third*. COMPOSER outperforms the latest GAR methods that use a single modality (+0.7% improvement on VD and +2.8% improvement on CAD), and performs favorably compared with methods that exploit multiple expensive modalities

Model	Modality				Dataset	
	Keypoint	RGB	Flow	Scene	VD	CAD
HDTM [23]		✓			81.9	81.5
CERN [40]		✓			83.3	87.2
stagNet [39]		✓			89.3	89.1
RCRG [22]		✓			89.5	N/A
SSU [5]		✓			90.6	N/A
PRL [19]		✓			91.4	N/A
ARG [47]		✓			92.5	91.0
HiGCIN [51]		✓			91.5	93.4
DIN [55]		✓			93.6	N/A
Zappardino *et al.* [56]	✓				91.0	N/A
GIRN [37]	✓				92.2	N/A
AT [16]	✓				92.3	N/A
POGARS [44]	✓				93.9	N/A
CRM [4]		✓	✓		93.0	85.8
AT [16]		✓	✓		93.0	92.8
Ehsanpour *et al.* [15]		✓		✓	93.1	89.4
GIRN [37]	✓	✓	✓		94.0	N/A
TCE+STBiP [54]	✓	✓		✓	*94.7*	N/A
SACRF [38]	✓	✓	✓	✓	95.0*	*95.2*
GroupFormer [29]	✓	✓	✓	✓	95.7	96.3
COMPOSER (ours)	✓				94.6	96.2*

* Note: The best results of each method that were reported by the method authors are listed in the table in order to be compared with ours most rigidly. 'N/A' stands for 'not available'. Yellow shaded rows highlight that the methods use just the RGB-based input, whereas blue for just keypoint.

Comparisons of Methods Using Keypoint-only Modality In Table 2, we compare COMPOSER with more GAR methods that use only the keypoint modality on VD Original split following conventions. COMPOSER achieves a new SOTA 94.6% accuracy with **+0.7%** improvement.

Among these methods, Zappardino et al. [56] use CNNs to learn group activity in Volleyball games, given sequence of person keypoint coordinates, their temporal differences, and keypoint differences from each actor to the pivot-actor that is selected by the model. The model does not model human-object interactions. AT [16] does not consider human-object interactions either, but because AT is also a Transformer-based model like ours, we can easily improve it by

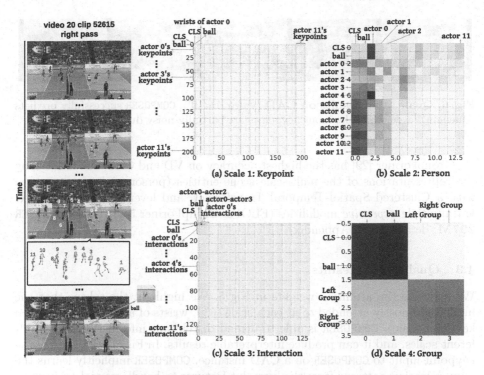

Fig. 5. Qualitative results of COMPOSER **on VD** – showcasing attention matrices of an instance in the "**right pass**" class (key actor is actor 0)

feeding our object tokens as additional inputs to AT. Moreoever, GIRN [37] and POGARS [44] are designed to leverage ball trajectory for learning group activity in videos of Volleyball games. As shown in Table 2, the object keypoint information can greatly boost the performance by providing additional context. GIRN models interactions between joints within an actor and across actors, as well as joint-object interactions. POGARS uses 1D CNNs to learn spatiotemporal dynamics of actors. AT, GIRN, and POGARS all use dot-product-based attention mechanisms similar to ours, however, they fail to fully model the hierarchical entities in the video (e.g., they all only use attention to learn person-wise importance, and at most consider two scales: keypoint and person), and more importantly, they lack explicit strategy to improve the multiscale representations in order to aid the compositional reasoning of group activity recognition.

Comparisons of Methods Using Other Modalities We compare results of COMPOSER with the best reported results of SOTA methods that use a single or multiple modalities in Table 3 on both VD and CAD. COMPOSER still achieves competitive performance – outperforming methods that use only RGB signals, obtaining +0.7% improvement on VD and +2.8% improvement on CAD if compared with methods that use a single modality (RGB or keypoint), and performing favorably compared with methods that exploit multiple expensive input modalities.

Fig. 6. Qualitative results on CAD (video ID '10'). COMPOSER successfully predicts 'Queueing' even when the input keypoints are partially noisy due to occlusion

GroupFormer [29] has the highest accuracy on VD and CAD due to learning the representations of the multiscale scene entities (person and person group) with a Clustered Spatial-Temporal Transformer, and leveraging scene context and multiple *expensive* modalities (FLOPs: GroupFormer **595M** v.s. COMPOSER **297M**; details are in Appendix).

4.3 Qualitative Results

We visualize the attention weights in Fig. 5. We highlight the tokens that the model has mostly attended to at each scale (e.g., wrists of actor 0 at the person keypoint scale). COMPOSER is able to attend to relevant information across different scales, and it can produce interpretable results. In Fig. 6, we visualize the keypoint input to COMPOSER on a CAD instance. COMPOSER implicitly learns the human motion patterns from the keypoint features to handle partial occlusions.

Please check Appendix for more analyses including ablation studies, confusion matrices, parameter sensitivity analyses w.r.t. the number of scales and the number of prototypes, more qualitative results including failure cases, etc.

5 Conclusion

We propose COMPOSER that uses a Multiscale Transformer to learn compositional reasoning at different scales for group activity recognition. We also improve the intermediate representations using contrastive clustering, auxiliary prediction, and data augmentation techniques. We demonstrate the model's strength and interpretability on two widely-used datasets (Volleyball and Collective Activity). COMPOSER achieves up to +5.4% improvement with just the keypoint modality.

One limitation is that videos with severe occlusions remain challenging for COMPOSER like other existing methods, due to errors from detecting keypoints. Adopting 3D keypoints or stronger backbones that estimate keypoints directly from the video [1,36] can help to address the issue. Possible future directions include 1) expanding our methods to more complex scenarios, such as crowd understanding that may require modeling additional hierarchical scales; and 2) exploring effective multimodal fusion methods in order to use additional modalities like RGB but without suffering from scene biases, since RGB can be beneficial for activities that involve significant interaction with the background scene.

Acknowledgments. The research was supported in part by NSF awards: IIS-1703883, IIS-1955404, IIS-1955365, RETTL-2119265, and EAGER-2122119. This material is based upon work supported by the U.S. Department of Homeland Security under Grant Award Number 22STESE00001 01 01. Disclaimer: The views and conclusions contained in this document are those of the authors and should not be interpreted as necessarily representing the official policies, either expressed or implied, of the U.S. Department of Homeland Security.

References

1. Mediapipe pose: Ml solution for high-fidelity body pose tracking from rgb video frames. www.google.github.io/mediapipe/solutions/pose.html
2. Abkenar, A.B., Loke, S.W., Zaslavsky, A., Rahayu, W.: Groupsense: recognizing and understanding group physical activities using multi-device embedded sensing. ACM Trans. Embedded Comput. Syst. (TECS) **17**(6), 1–26 (2019)
3. Asano, Y.M., Patrick, M., Rupprecht, C., Vedaldi, A.: Labelling unlabelled videos from scratch with multi-modal self-supervision. arXiv preprint arXiv:2006.13662 (2020)
4. Azar, S.M., Atigh, M.G., Nickabadi, A., Alahi, A.: Convolutional relational machine for group activity recognition. In: Proceedings of the IEEE/CVF Conference on Computer Vision and Pattern Recognition, pp. 7892–7901 (2019)
5. Bagautdinov, T., Alahi, A., Fleuret, F., Fua, P., Savarese, S.: Social scene understanding: End-to-end multi-person action localization and collective activity recognition. In: Proceedings of the IEEE Conference on Computer Vision and Pattern Recognition, pp. 4315–4324 (2017)
6. Blomqvist, K., Chung, J.J., Ott, L., Siegwart, R.: Semi-automatic 3d object keypoint annotation and detection for the masses. arXiv preprint arXiv:2201.07665 (2022)
7. Caron, M., Misra, I., Mairal, J., Goyal, P., Bojanowski, P., Joulin, A.: Unsupervised learning of visual features by contrasting cluster assignments. In: Thirty-fourth Conference on Neural Information Processing Systems (NeurIPS) (2020)
8. Carreira, J., Zisserman, A.: Quo vadis, action recognition? a new model and the kinetics dataset. In: proceedings of the IEEE Conference on Computer Vision and Pattern Recognition, pp. 6299–6308 (2017)
9. Chen, B., et al.: Multimodal clustering networks for self-supervised learning from unlabeled videos. arXiv preprint arXiv:2104.12671 (2021)
10. Choi, J., Gao, C., Messou, J.C., Huang, J.B.: Why can't i dance in a mall? learning to mitigate scene bias in action recognition. In: Proceedings of the 33rd International Conference on Neural Information Processing Systems, pp. 853–865 (2019)
11. Choi, W., Savarese, S.: Understanding collective activities of people from videos. IEEE Trans. Pattern Anal. Mach. Intell. **36**(6), 1242–1257 (2013)
12. Choi, W., Shahid, K., Savarese, S.: What are they doing?: Collective activity classification using spatio-temporal relationship among people. In: 2009 IEEE 12th international conference on computer vision workshops, ICCV Workshops, pp. 1282–1289. IEEE (2009)
13. Cuturi, M.: Sinkhorn distances: Lightspeed computation of optimal transport. Adv. Neural. Inf. Process. Syst. **26**, 2292–2300 (2013)
14. Devlin, J., Chang, M.W., Lee, K., Toutanova, K.: Bert: Pre-training of deep bidirectional transformers for language understanding. arXiv preprint arXiv:1810.04805 (2018)

15. Ehsanpour, M., Abedin, A., Saleh, F., Shi, J., Reid, I., Rezatofighi, H.: Joint learning of social groups, individuals action and sub-group activities in videos. In: Vedaldi, A., Bischof, H., Brox, T., Frahm, J.-M. (eds.) ECCV 2020. LNCS, vol. 12354, pp. 177–195. Springer, Cham (2020). https://doi.org/10.1007/978-3-030-58545-7_11

16. Gavrilyuk, K., Sanford, R., Javan, M., Snoek, C.G.: Actor-transformers for group activity recognition. In: Proceedings of the IEEE/CVF Conference on Computer Vision and Pattern Recognition, pp. 839–848 (2020)

17. He, K., Gkioxari, G., Dollár, P., Girshick, R.: Mask r-cnn. In: Proceedings of the IEEE International Conference on Computer Vision, pp. 2961–2969 (2017)

18. Hinojosa, C., Niebles, J.C., Arguello, H.: Learning privacy-preserving optics for human pose estimation. In: Proceedings of the IEEE/CVF International Conference on Computer Vision, pp. 2573–2582 (2021)

19. Hu, G., Cui, B., He, Y., Yu, S.: Progressive relation learning for group activity recognition. In: Proceedings of the IEEE/CVF Conference on Computer Vision and Pattern Recognition, pp. 980–989 (2020)

20. Huang, Y., Kadav, A., Lai, F., Patel, D., Graf, H.P.: Learning higher-order object interactions for keypoint-based video understanding (2021)

21. Hudson, D., Manning, C.D.: Learning by abstraction: The neural state machine. Adv. Neural. Inf. Process. Syst. **32**, 5903–5916 (2019)

22. Ibrahim, M.S., Mori, G.: Hierarchical relational networks for group activity recognition and retrieval. In: Ferrari, V., Hebert, M., Sminchisescu, C., Weiss, Y. (eds.) ECCV 2018. LNCS, vol. 11207, pp. 742–758. Springer, Cham (2018). https://doi.org/10.1007/978-3-030-01219-9_44

23. Ibrahim, M.S., Muralidharan, S., Deng, Z., Vahdat, A., Mori, G.: A hierarchical deep temporal model for group activity recognition. In: Proceedings of the IEEE Conference on Computer Vision and Pattern Recognition, pp. 1971–1980 (2016)

24. Jaiswal, A., Singh, S., Wu, Y., Natarajan, P., Natarajan, P.: Keypoints-aware object detection. In: NeurIPS 2020 Workshop on Pre-registration in Machine Learning, pp. 62–72. PMLR (2021)

25. Khosla, P., et al.: Supervised contrastive learning. arXiv preprint arXiv:2004.11362 (2020)

26. Koshkina, M., Pidaparthy, H., Elder, J.H.: Contrastive learning for sports video: Unsupervised player classification. In: Proceedings of the IEEE/CVF Conference on Computer Vision and Pattern Recognition, pp. 4528–4536 (2021)

27. Kulkarni, T.D., et al.: Unsupervised learning of object keypoints for perception and control. In: Advances in Neural Information Processing Systems, vol. 32 (2019)

28. Lake, B.M., Ullman, T.D., Tenenbaum, J.B., Gershman, S.J.: Building machines that learn and think like people. Behav. Brain Sci. **40**, e253 (2017)

29. Li, S., Cao, Q., Liu, L., Yang, K., Liu, S., Hou, J., Yi, S.: Groupformer: Group activity recognition with clustered spatial-temporal transformer. In: Proceedings of the IEEE/CVF International Conference on Computer Vision, pp. 13668–13677 (2021)

30. Lu, C., Koniusz, P.: Few-shot keypoint detection with uncertainty learning for unseen species. arXiv preprint arXiv:2112.06183 (2021)

31. Lu, L., Lu, Y., Yu, R., Di, H., Zhang, L., Wang, S.: Gaim: Graph attention interaction model for collective activity recognition. IEEE Trans. Multimedia **22**(2), 524–539 (2019)

32. Luo, Z., et al.: Moma: Multi-object multi-actor activity parsing. In: Advances in Neural Information Processing Systems, vol. 34 (2021)

33. Nakatani, C., Sendo, K., Ukita, N.: Group activity recognition using joint learning of individual action recognition and people grouping. In: 2021 17th International Conference on Machine Vision and Applications (MVA), pp. 1–5. IEEE (2021)

34. Nebehay, G., Pflugfelder, R.: Consensus-based matching and tracking of keypoints for object tracking. In: IEEE Winter Conference on Applications of Computer Vision, pp. 862–869. IEEE (2014)

35. Ngiam, J., et al.: Scene transformer: A unified architecture for predicting multiple agent trajectories. arXiv preprint arXiv:2106.08417 (2021)

36. Pavllo, D., Feichtenhofer, C., Grangier, D., Auli, M.: 3d human pose estimation in video with temporal convolutions and semi-supervised training. In: Proceedings of the IEEE/CVF Conference on Computer Vision and Pattern Recognition, pp. 7753–7762 (2019)

37. Perez, M., Liu, J., Kot, A.C.: Skeleton-based relational reasoning for group activity analysis. Pattern Recogn. **122**, 108360 (2021)

38. Pramono, R.R.A., Chen, Y.T., Fang, W.H.: Empowering relational network by self-attention augmented conditional random fields for group activity recognition. In: Vedaldi, A., Bischof, H., Brox, T., Frahm, J.-M. (eds.) ECCV 2020. LNCS, vol. 12346, pp. 71–90. Springer, Cham (2020). https://doi.org/10.1007/978-3-030-58452-8_5

39. Qi, M., Qin, J., Li, A., Wang, Y., Luo, J., Van Gool, L.: stagNet: An attentive semantic rnn for group activity recognition. In: Ferrari, V., Hebert, M., Sminchisescu, C., Weiss, Y. (eds.) ECCV 2018. LNCS, vol. 11214, pp. 104–120. Springer, Cham (2018). https://doi.org/10.1007/978-3-030-01249-6_7

40. Shu, T., Todorovic, S., Zhu, S.C.: Cern: confidence-energy recurrent network for group activity recognition. In: Proceedings of the IEEE Conference on Computer Vision and Pattern Recognition, pp. 5523–5531 (2017)

41. Simonyan, K., Zisserman, A.: Very deep convolutional networks for large-scale image recognition. arXiv preprint arXiv:1409.1556 (2014)

42. Singh, K.K., Mahajan, D., Grauman, K., Lee, Y.J., Feiszli, M., Ghadiyaram, D.: Don't judge an object by its context: Learning to overcome contextual bias. In: Proceedings of the IEEE/CVF Conference on Computer Vision and Pattern Recognition, pp. 11070–11078 (2020)

43. Snower, M., Kadav, A., Lai, F., Graf, H.P.: 15 keypoints is all you need. In: Proceedings of the IEEE/CVF Conference on Computer Vision and Pattern Recognition, pp. 6738–6748 (2020)

44. Thilakarathne, H., Nibali, A., He, Z., Morgan, S.: Pose is all you need: The pose only group activity recognition system (pogars). arXiv preprint arXiv:2108.04186 (2021)

45. Vaswani, A., et al.: Attention is all you need. In: Advances in Neural Information Processing Systems, pp. 5998–6008 (2017)

46. Wang, M., Ni, B., Yang, X.: Recurrent modeling of interaction context for collective activity recognition. In: Proceedings of the IEEE Conference on Computer Vision and Pattern Recognition, pp. 3048–3056 (2017)

47. Wu, J., Wang, L., Wang, L., Guo, J., Wu, G.: Learning actor relation graphs for group activity recognition. In: Proceedings of the IEEE/CVF Conference on Computer Vision and Pattern Recognition, pp. 9964–9974 (2019)

48. Wu, L.F., Wang, Q., Jian, M., Qiao, Y., Zhao, B.X.: A comprehensive review of group activity recognition in videos. Int. J. Autom. Comput. **18**, 1–17 (2021)

49. Xu, D., Fu, H., Wu, L., Jian, M., Wang, D., Liu, X.: Group activity recognition by using effective multiple modality relation representation with temporal-spatial attention. IEEE Access **8**, 65689–65698 (2020)

50. Yan, R., Tang, J., Shu, X., Li, Z., Tian, Q.: Participation-contributed temporal dynamic model for group activity recognition. In: Proceedings of the 26th ACM international conference on Multimedia, pp. 1292–1300 (2018)
51. Yan, R., Xie, L., Tang, J., Shu, X., Tian, Q.: Higcin: hierarchical graph-based cross inference network for group activity recognition. IEEE Transactions on Pattern Analysis and Machine Intelligence (2020)
52. Yan, R., Xie, L., Tang, J., Shu, X., Tian, Q.: Social adaptive module for weakly-supervised group activity recognition. In: Vedaldi, A., Bischof, H., Brox, T., Frahm, J.-M. (eds.) ECCV 2020. LNCS, vol. 12353, pp. 208–224. Springer, Cham (2020). https://doi.org/10.1007/978-3-030-58598-3_13
53. Yang, Z., Liu, S., Hu, H., Wang, L., Lin, S.: Reppoints: Point set representation for object detection. In: Proceedings of the IEEE/CVF International Conference on Computer Vision, pp. 9657–9666 (2019)
54. Yuan, H., Ni, D.: Learning visual context for group activity recognition. In: Proceedings of the AAAI Conference on Artificial Intelligence, vol. 35, pp. 3261–3269 (2021)
55. Yuan, H., Ni, D., Wang, M.: Spatio-temporal dynamic inference network for group activity recognition. In: Proceedings of the IEEE/CVF International Conference on Computer Vision, pp. 7476–7485 (2021)
56. Zappardino, F., Uricchio, T., Seidenari, L., Del Bimbo, A.: Learning group activities from skeletons without individual action labels. In: 2020 25th International Conference on Pattern Recognition (ICPR), pp. 10412–10417. IEEE (2021)

E-NeRV: Expedite Neural Video Representation with Disentangled Spatial-Temporal Context

Zizhang Li, Mengmeng Wang, Huaijin Pi, Kechun Xu, Jianbiao Mei, and Yong Liu[✉]

Zhejiang University, Hangzhou, China
{zzli,mengmengwang,hjpi,kcxu,jianbiaomei}@zju.edu.cn,
yongliu@iipc.zju.edu.cn

Abstract. Recently, the image-wise implicit neural representation of videos, NeRV, has gained popularity for its promising results and swift speed compared to regular pixel-wise implicit representations. However, the redundant parameters within the network structure can cause a large model size when scaling up for desirable performance. The key reason of this phenomenon is the coupled formulation of NeRV, which outputs the spatial and temporal information of video frames directly from the frame index input. In this paper, we propose E-NeRV, which dramatically expedites NeRV by decomposing the image-wise implicit neural representation into separate spatial and temporal context. Under the guidance of this new formulation, our model greatly reduces the redundant model parameters, while retaining the representation ability. We experimentally find that our method can improve the performance to a large extent with fewer parameters, resulting in a more than 8× faster speed on convergence. Code is available at https://github.com/kyleleey/E-NeRV.

Keywords: Implicit representation · Neural video representation · Spatial-temporal disentanglement

1 Introduction

Implicit neural representation (INR) have become popular in recent days. It presents a new manner to represent continuous signals as $f_\theta : \mathbb{R}^m \to \mathbb{R}^n$, which encodes the signal property as a function that maps the m-dimensional input (e.g. coordinates) to desired n-dimensional output (e.g. RGB values, occupancy, density), and the function is parameterized by deep neural networks with weight θ. Unlike regular grid-wise representations, the compact

---

Z. Li and M. Wang—Equal contributions.

Supplementary Information The online version contains supplementary material available at https://doi.org/10.1007/978-3-031-19833-5_16.

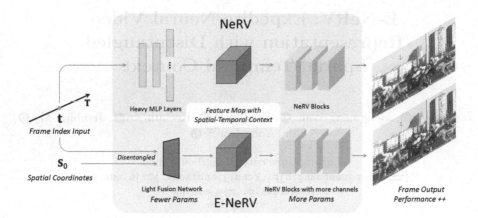

Fig. 1. Main motivation of our proposed method. We can greatly reduce the size of the parameters by introducing disentangled spatial-temporal representations with a light network, while maintaining the majority of performance. Furthermore, we distribute the saved parameters to increase channel dimensions in convolution blocks, resulting in an E-NeRV model with similar or fewer parameters but much better performance.

INRs are proved to be suitable for complex scenes [30] and arbitrary scale sampling [6], as well as in lots of 3D tasks [24,30,34,37] and image representations [6,27,40,43,57,59,64]. Despite the prevalence of INRs, few works have studied the compatible INR for video signals.

Video has been treated as an additional supplement of the image in past INR works [27,43]. They usually take the 3-dimensional spatial-temporal coordinate (x, y, t) as input and output RGB values. Most of the following works [41,63] focusing on video INRs adopt this configuration. However, the training and inference speed of this type of video INR will increase by the order of the third power when processing the video sequences with large resolution and numerous frames. In contrast, a recently proposed method, NeRV [2], reformulates the INR of video signals as $f_\theta : \mathbb{R} \rightarrow \mathbb{R}^{3 \times H \times W}$. Based on the concept that video is a tile of images, NeRV presents an image-wise video INR different from other pixel-wise video INRs. With the frame index in the time axis as input, NeRV directly outputs the desired frame image. The training and inference speed is proved to be much faster than previous methods [43,47] experimentally in [2]. And NeRV combines the success of convolution architecture and GAN's network design for its NeRV Blocks, which endows the ability to reconstruct frames of large resolution with high fidelity. By changing the channel dimensions in NeRV Blocks, we can obtain a series of NeRV models with different sizes (NeRV models with more parameters will naturally perform better). However, as the channel dimensions increase, the model size will increase rapidly. This drawback mainly comes from the architecture of NeRV model, which brings lots of unnecessary and redundant parameters (2× larger model size when channel dimensions increase 25%). We ascribe it to the design motivation of NeRV: NeRV considers the spatial and temporal information that lies in each frame image in a hybrid manner and is directly generated from one particular temporal frame index, which results in the heavy model and sub-optimal performance.

Inspired by the video GAN researches [14,50,62] that decompose the content and motion information, we propose the image-wise video INR that explicitly disentangles the spatial-temporal context and fuses them for final prediction, and refactor the original NeRV's network accordingly. Based on this motivation (illustrated in Fig. 1), we can effectively lower the parameter size of the baseline model (from 12M to 5M) while maintaining the majority of performance. We further introduce the temporal embeddings in convolutional blocks to facilitate the representation ability. Besides, we spot the redundant design lying in the NeRV Block and upgrade it. We name our method E-NeRV since it *Expedites* the original NeRV from a disentangled perspective for video implicit representation. We systematically investigate multiple design choices and compare our method with the baseline NeRV model. Our contributions are summarized as follows:

- We identify the redundant structures in the image-wise video INR NeRV, which is its major limitation when scaling up for better performance, and attribute this disadvantage to its hybrid formulation.
- We propose E-NeRV, a novel image-wise video INR with disentangled spatial-temporal context.
- We demonstrate our method can consistently outperform the NeRV baseline in convergence speed (8×) and performance with fewer parameters. Moreover, the superior performance is consistent among different video INR's downstream applications.

2   Related Work

2.1   Implicit Neural Representation

Recently, Implicit Neural Representation (INR) has gained much popularity for its strong power in modeling a variety of signals. It parameterizes a specific signal by a function that outputs desired properties of the provided coordinate-like input and employs deep neural networks (usually Multi-Layer Perceptron, MLP) to approximate the function. Thus the signal is implicitly encoded in network's parameters. For instance, the images [6,27,43] can be defined as RGB values of each pixel location, and 3D objects or scenes can be represented as occupancy [29,38], signed distance [35] or radiance field [30] of each 3D point. INRs are primarily popular in 3D vision tasks like reconstruction [19,22,33,36, 39,52,56] and novel-view synthesis [1,30,45,60,61].

Implicit Representations of Videos have not been thoroughly studied in this trend. Regular video implicit representations often take the spatial and temporal index of a pixel, i.e. $(x, y, t) \in \mathbf{R}^3$, as input and output the RGB values of the certain pixel in the certain frame. This simple definition suits short video clips with small image sizes, like $7 \times 224 \times 224$ in [27,43].[41] further estimates optical flow for continuous video representation. But this setting is no longer suitable for videos containing hundreds of frames with image resolution at large scale, which requires a long time to optimize and inference [2] because of the increasing number of frames and pixels. In addition, the paradigm proposed in [27] for contextual embeddings also can not support the videos with a large amount of frames. Another line of research of video INRs focuses on generative adversarial networks (GAN) [9]. Instead of generating videos from latent code directly, DiGAN [62] generates parameters of video INRs from context and motion latent code. StyleGAN-V [44] further utilizes convolutional operators for large-scale image synthesis. However, in this work we focus on fitting INR to the particular video instead of generating diverse contents in GAN-based methods.

Recently proposed NeRV [2] employs an image-wise implicit representation for videos instead of pixel-wise representations before. By combining the implicit representation with advances in convolution for image synthesis, NeRV achieves promising results with less time in training and inference. Following NeRV, our E-NeRV further improves the architecture via a disentangled formulation for a superior performance and fast convergence.

2.2   Optimization of INRs

Despite the success of INRs' expression ability, they naturally cost a long time to optimize for considerable performance. Many methods have been proposed to alleviate this problem and also acquire a better representation ability.

From the perspective of function characteristics, researches can be divided into studying an optimal encoding method and applying network regularization. Given that INRs tend to learn better mapping functions with a higher dimensional network input, many following works focus on a better encoding approach. Radial basis function (RBF) [7] utilizes the weighted sums of embedded RBF encodings. Positional encoding (PE) proposed in Fourier Feature Networks (FFN) [47] employs a set of Fourier functions to project inputs into high dimensions, and follow-up works [13,21] adopt a coarse-to-fine strategy on frequency for better convergence. Different from using existing functions, SPE [53] uses learnable spline functions and the latest instant-ngp [31] constructs a trainable hash map for shared embedding space. As for the regularization, many consistency constraints [8,16,32] regarding the 3D property have been studied in view synthesis. [46] regularize the in-domain initialization by a meta-learning approach. The distribution-based [40] and Lipschitz-based [23] regularizations can be applied on MLP regarding the smoothness prior for better convergence and generalization.

From the network architecture perspective, some recent works aim to accelerate the training and/or inference of 3D INRs with delicately designed architecture regarding the 3D sparsity. A common approach is to store the feature of MLP inside a pre-defined voxel space [23], point cloud [58] or octree structure [60], thus reducing the numbers of point query in both training and inference. To a greater range, SIREN [43] replaces the commonly used RELU activations in existing MLPs with sinusoidal activation functions and shows the solid fitting ability to complex signals. ACORN [26] and CoordX [20] aim at reducing the number of queries to coordinate-based models with different approaches: ACORN [26] adopts a hierarchical way to decompose the multi-scale coordinates while CoordX [20] designs a split MLP architecture to leverage the locality between input coordinate points. The following MINER [42] improves ACORN via a cross-scale similarity prior.

Our work expedites NeRV from an architecture perspective as we observe the existing unnecessary and redundant structures. By introducing our disentangled formulation, we demonstrate that the resulting model with much fewer parameters can keep the majority of performance or even exceed the NeRV baseline. When scaling up to the same size with baseline NeRV model, our E-NeRV shows greater performance and faster convergence speed.

3   Preliminaries

NeRV [2], as an image-wise representation, represents the video as a mapping function $f_\theta : \mathbb{R} \to \mathbb{R}^{3 \times H \times W}$ parameterized by the network weight θ. Given a video with $\mathbf{T}$ frames $\mathbf{V} = \{\mathbf{v_t}\}_{t=1}^{\mathbf{T}}$, the input is a scalar frame index value which is normalized to $\mathbf{t} \in [0, 1]$, and the output is the whole corresponding frame image $\mathbf{v_t} \in \mathbb{R}^{3 \times H \times W}$. By taking a closer look at its architecture, the formulation can be split into two parts:

$$\mathbf{f_t} = \text{RESHAPE}\left(F\left(\gamma\left(\mathbf{t}\right)\right)\right) \in \mathbb{R}^{C \times h \times w},$$
$$\mathbf{v_t} = G\left(\mathbf{f_t}\right). \tag{1}$$

The $\gamma\left(\mathbf{t}\right)$ means the regular frequency positional encoding proposed in [30]:

$$\gamma\left(\mathbf{t}\right) = (\sin(b^0 \pi \mathbf{t}), \cos(b^0 \pi \mathbf{t}), \dots, \sin(b^{l-1} \pi \mathbf{t}), \cos(b^{l-1} \pi \mathbf{t})), \tag{2}$$

where b and l are hyper-parameters. The function F stands for the MLP while the function G stands for the convolutional generator. To be more specific, it contains a sequence of NeRV Blocks with convolution and pixel-shuffle layers for the up-sample and image generation purpose. The network first maps the positional encoding of input frame index to a 1-$\mathbf{d}$ feature vector and then reshapes the vector to a 2-$\mathbf{d}$ feature map $\mathbf{f_t} \in \mathbb{R}^{C \times h \times w}$, where $(h, w) = (9, 16)$ in NeRV's setting. The following convolution and pixel-shuffle operation gradually transform the feature map to the original image size. And the 1×1 convolution with sigmoid generates the desired three channels of normalized RGB values.

The success of NeRV comes from several reasons. It employs an image-wise representation, which avoids per-pixel training and inference. The quantitative comparison in [2] shows great training and inference speed improvement compared to pixel-wise representations. The NeRV Block containing convolution and pixel-shuffle is suitable for image generation and leads to about 40 PSNR of final performance, superior to other video implicit neural representations.

A series of models with different sizes and performances are provided in [2]. A larger model can obtain better performance, and the way to scale up the model size is to increase the channel dimensions within the NeRV Blocks. However, this paradigm remains drawbacks. First is the last layer of MLP. To generate a feature vector that can be reshaped to feature map of size $C \times h \times w$ ($\sim 10^5$), the last layer of MLP can be extensive, and some naive solutions will cause a large

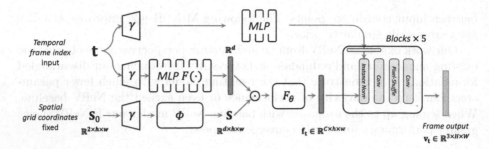

Fig. 2. Architecture of proposed E-NeRV. Our spatial-temporal feature map f_t is generated from disentangled spatial and input temporal contexts with fewer parameters (Sect. 4.1). The temporal information is also introduced to the convolution stages as a normalization procedure (Sect. 4.1) for better performance. In addition, we redesign the NeRV Blocks to further remove the redundant structures (Sect. 4.2).

performance drop (details in Sect. 5.4). Then, the convolution kernel can also be vast because of the following large-scale factor pixel-shuffle layer. NeRV considers the image-wise video implicit representation as an index-to-image formulation, while we consider it as a generation process with disentangled formulation, and the frame index only represents the temporal context. In Sect. 4, we elaborate our attempt to upgrade the redundant structure with spatial-temporal disentanglement, and we quantitatively and qualitatively show the significant performance and convergence speed of our method in Sect. 5.

4   Methodology

The overall architecture of the proposed E-NeRV is illustrated in Fig. 2. This section will introduce our approach towards the redundant parameters and structures. More specifically, in Sect. 4.1 we state how to disentangle spatial and temporal representation and the resulting formulation and architecture. And in Sect. 4.2 we elaborate on our upgraded design of NeRV block.

4.1   Disentangled Image-Wise Video INR

The first redundant part in NeRV emerges at the last layer of MLP. For instance, the NeRV-L model with 12.5M parameters, almost 70% of its size comes from the last MLP layer, which outputs $f_t \in \mathbb{R}^{112 \times 9 \times 16}$. Although the height and width of the feature map are relatively small, it requires large channel numbers to guarantee the final performance. In experiments (Sect. 5.4), we show some trivial modifications that may ease the large size of parameters, but lead to a dramatic performance drop compared to ours. We claim that this structure needs to exist because NeRV generates frame feature map f_t directly and only from the input t, which means to derive the spatial and temporal information *together* from the temporal input.

As an alternative, we propose to disentangle the spatial-temporal information, and let temporal input become a feature vector to manipulate over the
spatial space. In detail, we reformulate the generation of $\mathbf{f_t}$ as follows:

$$\mathbf{f_t} = F_\theta(F(\gamma(\mathbf{t})) \odot \mathbf{S}). \tag{3}$$

Here F still stands for an MLP network, but with a much less parameter
size because the output of F in our method is only a d-dimensional vector,
where $d \ll C \times h \times w$. We decompose the spatial-temporal information into the
temporal one encoded in $F(\gamma(\mathbf{t}))$, and the spatial one encoded in the spatial
context embeddings $\mathbf{S} \in \mathbb{R}^{d \times h \times w}$. Then a lightweight network F_θ is employed to
fuse the separated spatial and temporal information into the spatial-temporal
embeddings.

Since $\mathbf{S}$ is expected to contain the spatial context, we initialize it using the
normalized grid coordinates. Accordingly we get the initialized spatial context
$\mathbf{S_0} \in \mathbb{R}^{2 \times h \times w}$. First, we encode the $\mathbf{S_0}$ into $\hat{\mathbf{S}}_0$ using similar frequency positional
encoding $\gamma(\cdot)$ in Eq. 2. Then, we adopt a small transformer [49] with single-
head self-attention and residual connection here to encourage the feature fusion
among spatial locations to get the spatial context $\mathbf{S}$:

$$\begin{aligned}
\mathbf{S} = \Phi(\hat{\mathbf{S}}_0) &= \texttt{softmax}(\mathbf{q}^T\mathbf{k})\mathbf{v} + \hat{\mathbf{S}}_0 \\
&= \texttt{softmax}(f_q(\hat{\mathbf{S}}_0)^T f_k(\hat{\mathbf{S}}_0))f_v(\hat{\mathbf{S}}_0) + \hat{\mathbf{S}}_0.
\end{aligned} \tag{4}$$

where f_* stands for different projection networks to project input feature map's
channel dimension to desired dimension d_t. $\mathbf{q}, \mathbf{k}, \mathbf{v}$ denote for the query, key and
value of the transformer. Now the $\mathbf{S}$ can be considered as embeddings containing
the desired spatial context. And when representing different videos, the learnable parameters in Φ are different. In other words, we parameterize the spatial
information in a video in the weights of Φ.

Next, after the disentangled procedure, we need to fuse the temporal vector
$F(\gamma(\mathbf{t})) \in \mathbb{R}^d$ with the spatial context $\mathbf{S} \in \mathbb{R}^{d \times h \times w}$ to obtain the spatial-temporal
information. First, we element-wise multiply the temporal vector with each fea-
ture vector from all the locations in $\mathbf{S}$. Then, we utilize F_θ to further fuse the features together. F_θ here can be any operations as long as it can encourage spatial
and channel feature fusion. We employ a tiny multi-head attention transformer
network similar to Φ for its ability of long-range modeling and feature fusion. In
experiments, we further compare this choice with other alternatives (Sect. 5.4).

Besides, we observe that temporal information in NeRV is only related to the
feature map at the beginning of function G in Eq. 1. Therefore, we further fuse
temporal context to each NeRV Blocks in G to make sufficient and thorough use
of the temporal embedding. In experiments we find this design can further boost
the performance. In detail, we take inspiration from the design of GAN [15],
and consider the temporal context as a concept of style vector. Unlike using
element-wise multiplication to get coarse spatial-temporal feature map, here the
temporal information only plays a role of distribution shift. As illustrated in the
upper part of Fig. 2, we adopt a tiny MLP ($\sim 0.2M$) to generate temporal feature
$\mathbf{l_t} \in \mathbb{R}^{d_0}$. Then for the i-th block ($i = 1, \ldots, 5$), a linear layer M_i generates per-
channel mean μ_i and standard deviation σ_i accordingly. We denote the input

feature map for the i-th block as $\mathbf{f}_t^i$. This newly generated distribution shifts the feature map as an instance normalization with temporal context:

$$IN(\mathbf{f}_t^i) = \sigma_i \left(\frac{\mathbf{f}_t^i - \mu(\mathbf{f}_t^i)}{\sigma(\mathbf{f}_t^i)} \right) + \mu_i \tag{5}$$

where $\mu(\mathbf{f}_t^i)$ and $\sigma(\mathbf{f}_t^i)$ are computed across spatial dimensions. This operation is conducted at the beginning of each block to let the temporal information guide the generation of the corresponding frame.

4.2 Upgraded NeRV Block

As stated in Sect. 3, another redundant structure lies in NeRV block. Because the convolution needs to generate enough channels for further pixel-shuffle operation, if the input feature map's channel dimension is C_1, desired output dimension is C_2, the up-sample scale factor is s and kernel size is 3×3, regardless of the bias, the size of trainable weight is $C_1 \times C_2 \times s \times s \times 3 \times 3$. When scale factor s is large, for example, $s = 5$ in the first NeRV block, the size can be enormous (up to 65% of the overall model) if we scale up the input and output channel dimension for better performance.

In order to tackle this problem, we modify the NeRV block with a subtle design: we replace the convolution kernel with two consecutive convolution kernels with small channels. Then we place the pixel-shuffle operation in the middle and introduce an intermediate dimension C_0. By using $\texttt{conv}(\cdot, \cdot)$ to denote convolution kernel with corresponding input and output channel dimensions, our new architecture can be formulated as:

$$\texttt{conv}(C_1, C_0 \times s \times s) \rightarrow \texttt{pixel-shuffle}(s) \rightarrow \texttt{conv}(C_0, C_2), \tag{6}$$

and the parameters in this new formula are: $3 \times 3 \times C_0 \times (C_1 \times s \times s + C_2)$.

In practice, we set $C_0 = \min(C_1, C_2)/4$. If $C_1 \leq C_2$, the ratio of the parameters size is $(C_1/4C_2 + 1/4s^2) \approx C_1/4C_2 \leq 1/4$. We find replacing the first NeRV Block with this design can bring largely simplified size while maintaining most of the performance (see Sect. 5.2). The reason is that the scale factor of the first block equals 5 and thus results in an oversize model. The following blocks with factor equaling 2 will not benefit much from this modification, so in our final setting, we replace the first NeRV block with our upgraded version.

5   Experiments

5.1   Datasets and Implementation Details

We conduct quantitative and qualitative comparison experiments on 8 different video sequences collected from scikit-video and UVG [28] datasets, similar to experiment settings in [2]. Each video sequence contains about 150 frames and with a resolution of 1280×720.

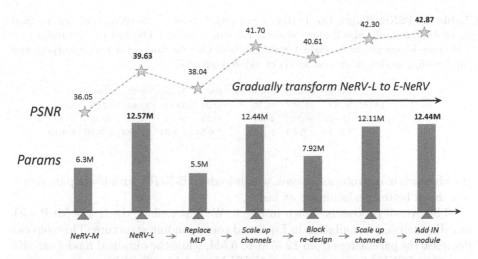

Fig. 3. Process of gradually transforming original 12.57M NeRV-L with 39.63 PSNR to our E-NeRV with slightly fewer parameters but much better performance. PSNR results are tested on "Bunny" video. Please see Sect. 5.2 for detailed descriptions.

We set up-scale factors $5, 2, 2, 2, 2$ for each block of our model to reconstruct a 1280×720 image from the feature map of size 16×9. We follow the training schedule of the original NeRV implementation for a fair comparison. We train the model using Adam optimizer [17]. Each model is trained for 300 epochs on each video sequence unless specified, with the batchsize of 1.

We adopt NeRV-L with 12.57M parameters as our baseline. For the part in our model that is orthogonal to our modification, we follow the same settings as in NeRV, like activation choice. We set $d = d_t = 256$ for spatial and temporal feature fusion, $d_0 = 128$ for temporal instance normalization. We set all the positional encoding layers in our model identical to NeRV's positional encoding formulated in Eq. 2, and we use $b = 1.25$ and $l = 80$ if not otherwise denoted. For training objective, we use the same combination of L1 and SSIM loss as [2]:

$$L = \frac{1}{T} \sum_{t=1}^{T} \alpha ||\mathbf{v}_t - \hat{\mathbf{v}}_t||_1 + (1 - \alpha)(1 - \texttt{SSIM}(\mathbf{v}_t, \hat{\mathbf{v}}_t)). \qquad (7)$$

The α is set to 0.7, T stands for the total number of frames, $\mathbf{v}_t$ denotes the reconstructed frame image while $\hat{\mathbf{v}}_t$ denotes its corresponding ground truth. Please refer to the supplementary material for more implementation details, experiments, results and visualizations.

5.2   Process of Removing Redundant Part and Scaling Up

In this section, we show how to replace the redundant structures and parameters with our proposed methods, and gradually distribute the saved parameters to

Table 1. PSNR (larger the better) comparison between NeRV-L and our method given similar model size under the same training schedule. The last row indicates performance improvement brought by our method. Our method consistently outperforms the baseline model on diverse kinds of video sequences.

		Bunny	Beauty	Bosphorus	Bee	Jockey	SetGo	Shake	Yacht
NeRV-L	12.57M	39.63	36.06	37.35	41.23	38.14	31.86	37.22	32.45
Ours	12.49M	42.87	36.72	40.06	41.74	39.35	34.68	39.32	35.58
		↑ **3.24**	↑ **0.66**	↑ **2.71**	↑ **0.51**	↑ **1.21**	↑ **2.82**	↑ **2.10**	↑ **3.13**

the channels in convolution stages, which leads to E-NeRV with fewer parameters but much better performance at last.

The overall process is shown in Fig. 3. We first replace the heavy MLP with our disentangled formulation in Eq. 3 and corresponding structure. This step can decrease the parameters from 12.57M to 5.5M, while the obtained model can still get 38.04 PSNR. As a comparison, NeRV-M model in [2] with more parameters can only reach a much worse performance of 36.05 PSNR. Then we first scale up the channels in convolution blocks for a model with a size similar to NeRV-L, and the model after scaling can get 41.70 PSNR.

After the first scaling, another redundant structure emerges: the NeRV Block with up-scale factor 5 and large channel dimension can be overwhelming, so we replace it with our new design. As shown in Fig. 3, the resulting model reduces 37% parameters. It is notable that the obtained model already has less parameters (7.92M *vs.* 12.57M) but better performance (40.61M *vs.* 39.63M) compared to origination NeRV-L. Then we scale up channels again and add temporal instance normalization branch at last for our proposed E-NeRV.

5.3   Main Results

We provide a comparison of our method and NeRV in Table 1. We refer to [2] for further comparison to pixel-wise video INRs such as SIREN [43] and FFN [30], which demonstrates that NeRV surpasses these methods in both performance and speed. Although our proposed E-NeRV has similar speed and parameters, it consistently performs better than the NeRV on different video sequences.

Because the design of our proposed E-NeRV does not employ any kinds of data prior, we claim this improvement exists when using E-NeRV to represent any video sequences. Notably, our method can bring larger promotion for the videos with more dynamic contents in Table 1, for example, the "Bunny" and "Yacht" videos. We assume this is because our disentangled implicit representation can better model the spatial and temporal variations for the videos with more dynamic contents.

Since training the INRs to fit a video sequence is an over-fitting process, longer schedule naturally leads to better performance. In other words, if the proposed method's performance surpasses another method with the same schedule, it guarantees a better performance and faster convergence speed simultaneously. In Fig. 4, we provide a comparison between our method and NeRV on "Bunny"

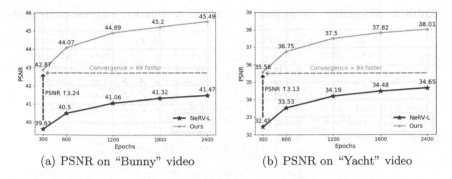

(a) PSNR on "Bunny" video   (b) PSNR on "Yacht" video

Fig. 4. PSNR *vs.* Epochs. Comparison of NeRV-L and our method on "Bunny" and "Yacht" videos. Our method's performance within 300 epochs is better than NeRV's at 2400 epochs, which shows better performance and faster convergence.

and "Yacht" videos with different training schedules. Our method's performance at 300 epochs exceeds the baseline's with a large margin. It also surpasses the baseline's performance at 2400 epochs, as 8× faster on convergence. Actually, our method's performances at 300 epochs beat the baseline's at 2400 epochs on all the diverse videos. We provide the detailed results in supplementary.

5.4   Comparison with Alternatives

We compare our method with four alternative approaches attempting to remove the redundant parameters or conduct fusion of F_θ in Eq. 3:

NeRV-C_S. Since the last layer of MLP with an output size of $C \times h \times w$ causes overwhelming parameters, we add an intermediate channel dimension C_S which is lower than C. The MLP outputs feature map at size $C_S \times h \times w$, and a following 1×1 convolution will increase the channel dimension to C as original setting before the NeRV Blocks.

NeRV-Split. Inspired by split architecture in [20], we redesign the MLP structure and let it output the tensor with size $C \times (h + w)$, then split it into two parts with size $C \times h$ and $C \times w$ respectively. A tensor product is conducted to generate the desired $C \times h \times w$ feature map $\mathbf{f_t}$ accordingly.

E-NeRV-MLP. Since the function F_θ is responsible for feature fusion of spatial and temporal context, any fusion operation is applicable. We replace our original setting, a small transformer block with attention mechanism, with two successive MLPs on spatial channels ($h \times w$) and feature channels (C).

E-NeRV-Conv. We use 3×3 convolution block to replace the transformer block. The convolution block fuses the features within a window region and scans over the entire feature map in a sliding window manner.

The results are shown in Table 2. For fair comparison on how to lower the size of the parameter, we establish two versions of our method: we remove the part

Table 2. Alternative comparison

	Size	PSNR ↑	MS-SSIM ↑
NeRV-C_S	5.8M	33.72	0.9562
Ours-1†	5.8M	35.91	0.9738
NeRV-Split	7.2M	35.78	0.9724
Ours-2†	7.2M	36.74	0.9782
E-NeRV-MLP	12M	38.54	0.9861
E-NeRV-Conv	12.5M	38.67	0.9865
E-NeRV	12.5M	38.79	0.9866

Table 3. Ablation study on components

	$\varPhi$	F_θ	IN	PSNR ↑	MS-SSIM ↑
NeRV-L	–	–	–	36.74	0.9802
Variant 1	✗	✗	✗	37.89	0.9837
Variant 2	✓	✗	✗	38.09	0.9843
Variant 3	✓	✓	✗	38.45	0.9855
E-NeRV	✓	✓	✓	38.79	0.9866

of the structure to introduce the temporal context in convolution blocks stage as described in 4.1 since it can further boost the performance, and decrease the convolution's channel dimensions to make the resulting models' parameter sizes identical to the sizes of two alternatives. It can be seen that our method surpasses these alternatives given similar parameters settings.

As for the alternatives for feature fusion in F_θ, transformer can bring incremental performance growth compared with MLP or Conv. However, all three models can beat NeRV-L with a large margin. The disentangled representation and structure itself can significantly lower the size, so that we can distribute the saved parameters to the convolution for much better performance. With the rapid growth of vision transformer research [10], any other more complicated structures, like the combination of transformer and convolution, are also welcomed and may further raise the performance. We claim that on some videos with almost still content, like "Beauty" and "Bee", the differences between each alternative are slight compared to the improvement on more dynamic videos. Since metrics are averaged over all videos, the difference between alternatives may also seem incremental in Table 2, but the partial ordering relation is the same over 8 videos.

5.5 Ablation Studies

In this section, we study the effects of three novel components of our proposed method: the spatial fusion function $\varPhi$ at the beginning of the network, the spatial and temporal fusion F_θ and the temporal instance normalization method to introduce temporal context in each convolution blocks. The ablation experiments are executed on all the video sequences and obtained metrics are averaged.

As shown in Table 3, E-NeRV obtains better performance as gradually adding these modules, and this increasing property exists on all the experiment video sequences. It is notable that the "Variant 1", without the fusion and temporal context in convolution stages, can still outperform baseline on both metrics among different video sequences. To be more specific, simply using the proposed disentanglement formulation to reduce the redundant parameters and distributing them to the following convolution blocks, the obtained model with similar parameters can already surpass the NeRV-L. We claim this further proves the effectiveness of our disentanglement motivation to some extent.

Table 4. Denoising(**left**) and compression(**right**) results comparison of our method and NeRV.

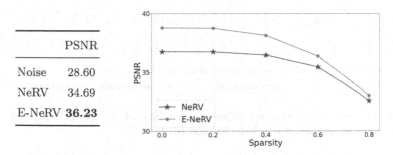

	PSNR
Noise	28.60
NeRV	34.69
E-NeRV	**36.23**

5.6 Downstream Application Results

In addition to the representation ability, we also compare the E-NeRV's performance to NeRV's on different downstream tasks for video INR, including video denoising and compression. The results are shown in Table 4.

Both experiments follow the NeRV's pipeline and we further conduct an ablation on different prune ratios for compression. The PSNR metrics are average among all the video sequences. In denoising results the "Noise" refers to noisy frames before any denoising. Here we only compare to NeRV since they beat other filter-based and learning-based methods in their paper. The denoising results of E-NeRV also prove the advantage of our disentangled spatial representation, which serves as a spatial prior in video denoising.

For the compression experiments, the performances of both methods drop as increasing the compression ratio (Sparsity in the figure), but E-NeRV remains better performance at all different compression ratios. The results also show that the compression ability of frame-wise video INR, i.e. the pipeline of pruning the network weight as compressing the video sequence, remains intact for the proposed E-NeRV. The detailed overall results can be found in the supplementary.

5.7 Temporal Frequency Analysis

The frequency of Fourier feature mapping can greatly influence the INR's representation ability [47]. A minor frequency may lead to smoothness among input and suitable for interpolation but also degrade INR's fitting on training points.

In this section, we study the effect of different frequency in our disentangled representation. We devide the video at a ratio of 3 : 1 into seen and unseen frames, and adjust the frequency which is 1.25 in our general setting. The results are provided in Fig. 5.

Starting from NeRV's interpolation (39.3/28.58) at frequency 1.25, we can see that since NeRV consider spatial and temporal in a coupled manner, lowering the frequency can boost the interpolation but also cause a performance drop on seen frames (Fig. 5 (a)). On the contrary, our disentangled representation allows

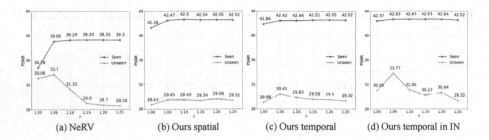

Fig. 5. Frequency variation for different encodings of: (a) NeRV's input **t**, (b) our spatial map S_0, (c) input **t** in E-NeRV and (d) **t** for IN.

manipulating frequency in three encodings: spatial grid coordinates, temporal input **t** and **t** used in temporal IN. In detail, adjusting the frequency in IN module from 1.25 to 1.05 leads to the optimal interpolation while perserving the performance on training points (Fig. 5 (d)), which can be considered as another advantage from our disentangle structure. More dataset partition details, interpolation results and visualization are available in supplementary.

6   Conclusion

In this paper we present E-NeRV, an image-wise video implicit representation with disentangled spatial and temporal context. Following previous image-wise video INR [2], our method retains its advantages on training and inference speed compared to pixel-wise video INRs [27,43,47], but boosts the performance and convergence speed with a large margin. We quantitatively show that our proposed disentanglement structures together with other modifications can greatly reduce the original unnecessary and redundant parameters. By reallocating the saved parameters, our method with fewer parameters can perform much better, with an 8× faster convergence speed. We experimentally analyze the function of each component in our method on diverse video sequences.

Finally, we remark our method can be further improved by applying a more effective and sophisticated feature fusion method for our disentangled representations. In future work, we plan to apply our image-wise video INR to other downstream tasks like optical flow estimation and video super-resolution.

Acknowledgments. We thank all authors and reviewers for the contributions. This work is supported by a Grant from the National Natural Science Foundation of China (No. U21A20484).

References

1. Barron, J.T., Mildenhall, B., Tancik, M., Hedman, P., Martin-Brualla, R., Srinivasan, P.P.: Mip-nerf: A multiscale representation for anti-aliasing neural radiance fields. In: Proceedings of the IEEE/CVF International Conference on Computer Vision, pp. 5855–5864 (2021)

2. Chen, H., He, B., Wang, H., Ren, Y., Lim, S.N., Shrivastava, A.: Nerv: Neural representations for videos. In: Advances in Neural Information Processing Systems, vol. 34 (2021)
3. Chen, T., Kornblith, S., Norouzi, M., Hinton, G.: A simple framework for contrastive learning of visual representations. In: International Conference on Machine Learning, pp. 1597–1607. PMLR (2020)
4. Chen, X., et al.: Context autoencoder for self-supervised representation learning. arXiv preprint arXiv:2202.03026 (2022)
5. Chen, X., He, K.: Exploring simple siamese representation learning. In: Proceedings of the IEEE/CVF Conference on Computer Vision and Pattern Recognition, pp. 15750–15758 (2021)
6. Chen, Y., Liu, S., Wang, X.: Learning continuous image representation with local implicit image function. In: Proceedings of the IEEE/CVF Conference on Computer Vision and Pattern Recognition, pp. 8628–8638 (2021)
7. Dash, C.S.K., Behera, A.K., Dehuri, S., Cho, S.B.: Radial basis function neural networks: a topical state-of-the-art survey. Open Comput. Sci. **6**(1), 33–63 (2016)
8. Deng, K., Liu, A., Zhu, J.Y., Ramanan, D.: Depth-supervised nerf: Fewer views and faster training for free. arXiv preprint arXiv:2107.02791 (2021)
9. Goodfellow, I., et al.: Generative adversarial nets. In: Advances in Neural Information Processing Systems, vol. 27 (2014)
10. Han, K., et al.: A survey on vision transformer. arXiv preprint arXiv:2012.12556 (2020)
11. He, K., Chen, X., Xie, S., Li, Y., Dollár, P., Girshick, R.: Masked autoencoders are scalable vision learners. In: Proceedings of the IEEE/CVF Conference on Computer Vision and Pattern Recognition, pp. 16000–16009 (2022)
12. He, K., Fan, H., Wu, Y., Xie, S., Girshick, R.: Momentum contrast for unsupervised visual representation learning. In: Proceedings of the IEEE/CVF Conference on Computer Vision and Pattern Recognition, pp. 9729–9738 (2020)
13. Hertz, A., Perel, O., Giryes, R., Sorkine-Hornung, O., Cohen-Or, D.: Sape: Spatially-adaptive progressive encoding for neural optimization. In: Advances in Neural Information Processing Systems, vol. 34 (2021)
14. Hsieh, J.T., Liu, B., Huang, D.A., Fei-Fei, L.F., Niebles, J.C.: Learning to decompose and disentangle representations for video prediction. In: Advances in Neural Information Processing Systems, vol. 31 (2018)
15. Huang, X., Belongie, S.: Arbitrary style transfer in real-time with adaptive instance normalization. In: Proceedings of the IEEE International Conference on Computer Vision, pp. 1501–1510 (2017)
16. Jain, A., Tancik, M., Abbeel, P.: Putting nerf on a diet: Semantically consistent few-shot view synthesis. In: Proceedings of the IEEE/CVF International Conference on Computer Vision, pp. 5885–5894 (2021)
17. Kingma, D.P., Ba, J.: Adam: A method for stochastic optimization. arXiv preprint arXiv:1412.6980 (2014)
18. Lai, Z., Liu, S., Efros, A.A., Wang, X.: Video autoencoder: self-supervised disentanglement of static 3d structure and motion. In: Proceedings of the IEEE/CVF International Conference on Computer Vision, pp. 9730–9740 (2021)
19. Li, Z., Niklaus, S., Snavely, N., Wang, O.: Neural scene flow fields for space-time view synthesis of dynamic scenes. In: Proceedings of the IEEE/CVF Conference on Computer Vision and Pattern Recognition, pp. 6498–6508 (2021)
20. Liang, R., Sun, H., Vijaykumar, N.: Coordx: Accelerating implicit neural representation with a split mlp architecture. arXiv preprint arXiv:2201.12425 (2022)

21. Lin, C.H., Ma, W.C., Torralba, A., Lucey, S.: Barf: Bundle-adjusting neural radiance fields. In: Proceedings of the IEEE/CVF International Conference on Computer Vision, pp. 5741–5751 (2021)

22. Littwin, G., Wolf, L.: Deep meta functionals for shape representation. In: Proceedings of the IEEE/CVF International Conference on Computer Vision, pp. 1824–1833 (2019)

23. Liu, H.T.D., Williams, F., Jacobson, A., Fidler, S., Litany, O.: Learning smooth neural functions via lipschitz regularization. arXiv preprint arXiv:2202.08345 (2022)

24. Liu, L., Gu, J., Zaw Lin, K., Chua, T.S., Theobalt, C.: Neural sparse voxel fields. Adv. Neural. Inf. Process. Syst. **33**, 15651–15663 (2020)

25. Liu, Y., Wang, K., Liu, L., Lan, H., Lin, L.: Tcgl: Temporal contrastive graph for self-supervised video representation learning. IEEE Trans. Image Proces. **31**, 1978–1993 (2022)

26. Martel, J.N., Lindell, D.B., Lin, C.Z., Chan, E.R., Monteiro, M., Wetzstein, G.: Acorn: Adaptive coordinate networks for neural scene representation. arXiv preprint arXiv:2105.02788 (2021)

27. Mehta, I., Gharbi, M., Barnes, C., Shechtman, E., Ramamoorthi, R., Chandraker, M.: Modulated periodic activations for generalizable local functional representations. In: Proceedings of the IEEE/CVF International Conference on Computer Vision, pp. 14214–14223 (2021)

28. Mercat, A., Viitanen, M., Vanne, J.: Uvg dataset: 50/120fps 4k sequences for video codec analysis and development. In: Proceedings of the 11th ACM Multimedia Systems Conference, pp. 297–302 (2020)

29. Mescheder, L., Oechsle, M., Niemeyer, M., Nowozin, S., Geiger, A.: Occupancy networks: Learning 3d reconstruction in function space. In: Proceedings of the IEEE/CVF Conference on Computer Vision and Pattern Recognition, pp. 4460–4470 (2019)

30. Mildenhall, B., Srinivasan, P.P., Tancik, M., Barron, J.T., Ramamoorthi, R., Ng, R.: NeRF: Representing scenes as neural radiance fields for view synthesis. In: Vedaldi, A., Bischof, H., Brox, T., Frahm, J.-M. (eds.) ECCV 2020. LNCS, vol. 12346, pp. 405–421. Springer, Cham (2020). https://doi.org/10.1007/978-3-030-58452-8_24

31. Müller, T., Evans, A., Schied, C., Keller, A.: Instant neural graphics primitives with a multiresolution hash encoding. arXiv preprint arXiv:2201.05989 (2022)

32. Niemeyer, M., Barron, J.T., Mildenhall, B., Sajjadi, M.S., Geiger, A., Radwan, N.: Regnerf: Regularizing neural radiance fields for view synthesis from sparse inputs. arXiv preprint arXiv:2112.00724 (2021)

33. Niemeyer, M., Mescheder, L., Oechsle, M., Geiger, A.: Differentiable volumetric rendering: Learning implicit 3d representations without 3d supervision. In: Proceedings of the IEEE/CVF Conference on Computer Vision and Pattern Recognition, pp. 3504–3515 (2020)

34. Oechsle, M., Peng, S., Geiger, A.: Unisurf: Unifying neural implicit surfaces and radiance fields for multi-view reconstruction. In: Proceedings of the IEEE/CVF International Conference on Computer Vision, pp. 5589–5599 (2021)

35. Park, J.J., Florence, P., Straub, J., Newcombe, R., Lovegrove, S.: Deepsdf: Learning continuous signed distance functions for shape representation. In: Proceedings of the IEEE/CVF Conference on Computer Vision and Pattern Recognition, pp. 165–174 (2019)

36. Park, K., et al.: Nerfies: Deformable neural radiance fields. In: Proceedings of the IEEE/CVF International Conference on Computer Vision, pp. 5865–5874 (2021)

37. Peng, S., et al.: Neural body: Implicit neural representations with structured latent codes for novel view synthesis of dynamic humans. In: Proceedings of the IEEE/CVF Conference on Computer Vision and Pattern Recognition, pp. 9054–9063 (2021)

38. Peng, S., Niemeyer, M., Mescheder, L., Pollefeys, M., Geiger, A.: Convolutional occupancy networks. In: Vedaldi, A., Bischof, H., Brox, T., Frahm, J.-M. (eds.) ECCV 2020. LNCS, vol. 12348, pp. 523–540. Springer, Cham (2020). https://doi.org/10.1007/978-3-030-58580-8_31

39. Pumarola, A., Corona, E., Pons-Moll, G., Moreno-Noguer, F.: D-nerf: Neural radiance fields for dynamic scenes. In: Proceedings of the IEEE/CVF Conference on Computer Vision and Pattern Recognition, pp. 10318–10327 (2021)

40. Ramasinghe, S., MacDonald, L., Lucey, S.: On regularizing coordinate-mlps. arXiv preprint arXiv:2202.00790 (2022)

41. Rho, D., Cho, J., Ko, J.H., Park, E.: Neural residual flow fields for efficient video representations. arXiv preprint arXiv:2201.04329 (2022)

42. Saragadam, V., Tan, J., Balakrishnan, G., Baraniuk, R.G., Veeraraghavan, A.: Miner: Multiscale implicit neural representations. arXiv preprint arXiv:2202.03532 (2022)

43. Sitzmann, V., Martel, J., Bergman, A., Lindell, D., Wetzstein, G.: Implicit neural representations with periodic activation functions. Adv. Neural. Inf. Process. Syst. **33**, 7462–7473 (2020)

44. Skorokhodov, I., Tulyakov, S., Elhoseiny, M.: Stylegan-v: A continuous video generator with the price, image quality and perks of stylegan2. arXiv preprint arXiv:2112.14683 (2021)

45. Tancik, M., et al.: Block-nerf: Scalable large scene neural view synthesis. arXiv preprint arXiv:2202.05263 (2022)

46. Tancik, M., et al.: Learned initializations for optimizing coordinate-based neural representations. In: Proceedings of the IEEE/CVF Conference on Computer Vision and Pattern Recognition, pp. 2846–2855 (2021)

47. Tancik, M., et al.: Fourier features let networks learn high frequency functions in low dimensional domains. Adv. Neural. Inf. Process. Syst. **33**, 7537–7547 (2020)

48. Tong, Z., Song, Y., Wang, J., Wang, L.: Videomae: Masked autoencoders are data-efficient learners for self-supervised video pre-training. arXiv preprint arXiv:2203.12602 (2022)

49. Vaswani, A., et al.: Attention is all you need. In: Advances in Neural Information Processing Systems, vol. 30 (2017)

50. Villegas, R., Yang, J., Hong, S., Lin, X., Lee, H.: Decomposing motion and content for natural video sequence prediction. arXiv preprint arXiv:1706.08033 (2017)

51. Wang, G., Wang, K., Wang, G., Torr, P.H., Lin, L.: Solving inefficiency of self-supervised representation learning. In: Proceedings of the IEEE/CVF International Conference on Computer Vision, pp. 9505–9515 (2021)

52. Wang, P., Liu, L., Liu, Y., Theobalt, C., Komura, T., Wang, W.: Neus: Learning neural implicit surfaces by volume rendering for multi-view reconstruction. arXiv preprint arXiv:2106.10689 (2021)

53. Wang, P.S., Liu, Y., Yang, Y.Q., Tong, X.: Spline positional encoding for learning 3d implicit signed distance fields. arXiv preprint arXiv:2106.01553 (2021)

54. Wang, X., Gupta, A.: Unsupervised learning of visual representations using videos. In: Proceedings of the IEEE International Conference on Computer Vision, pp. 2794–2802 (2015)

55. Wu, Z., Xiong, Y., Yu, S.X., Lin, D.: Unsupervised feature learning via non-parametric instance discrimination. In: Proceedings of the IEEE Conference on Computer Vision and Pattern Recognition, pp. 3733–3742 (2018)
56. Xian, W., Huang, J.B., Kopf, J., Kim, C.: Space-time neural irradiance fields for free-viewpoint video. In: Proceedings of the IEEE/CVF Conference on Computer Vision and Pattern Recognition, pp. 9421–9431 (2021)
57. Xie, Y., et al.: Neural fields in visual computing and beyond. arXiv preprint arXiv:2111.11426 (2021)
58. Xu, Q., et al.: Point-nerf: Point-based neural radiance fields. arXiv preprint arXiv:2201.08845 (2022)
59. Xu, X., Wang, Z., Shi, H.: Ultrasr: Spatial encoding is a missing key for implicit image function-based arbitrary-scale super-resolution. arXiv preprint arXiv:2103.12716 (2021)
60. Yu, A., Li, R., Tancik, M., Li, H., Ng, R., Kanazawa, A.: Plenoctrees for real-time rendering of neural radiance fields. In: Proceedings of the IEEE/CVF International Conference on Computer Vision, pp. 5752–5761 (2021)
61. Yu, A., Ye, V., Tancik, M., Kanazawa, A.: pixelnerf: Neural radiance fields from one or few images. In: Proceedings of the IEEE/CVF Conference on Computer Vision and Pattern Recognition, pp. 4578–4587 (2021)
62. Yu, S., et al.: Generating videos with dynamics-aware implicit generative adversarial networks. In: International Conference on Learning Representations (2021)
63. Zhang, Y., van Rozendaal, T., Brehmer, J., Nagel, M., Cohen, T.: Implicit neural video compression. arXiv preprint arXiv:2112.11312 (2021)
64. Zhuang, Y.: Filtering in implicit neural networks. arXiv preprint arXiv:2201.13013 (2022)

TDViT: Temporal Dilated Video Transformer for Dense Video Tasks

Guanxiong Sun[1,2](✉) , Yang Hua[1] , Guosheng Hu[2] , and Neil Robertson[1]

[1] EEECS/ECIT, Queen's University Belfast, Northern Ireland, UK
{gsun02,y.hua,n.robertson}@qub.ac.uk
[2] Oosto, Belfast, UK

Abstract. Deep video models, for example, 3D CNNs or video transformers, have achieved promising performance on sparse video tasks, i.e., predicting one result per video. However, challenges arise when adapting existing deep video models to dense video tasks, i.e., predicting one result per frame. Specifically, these models are expensive for deployment, less effective when handling redundant frames and difficult to capture long-range temporal correlations. To overcome these issues, we propose a Temporal Dilated Video Transformer (TDViT) that consists of carefully-designed temporal dilated transformer blocks (TDTB). TDTB can efficiently extract spatiotemporal representations and effectively alleviate the negative effect of temporal redundancy. Furthermore, by using hierarchical TDTBs, our approach obtains an exponentially expanded temporal receptive field and therefore can model long-range dynamics. Extensive experiments are conducted on two different dense video benchmarks, i.e., ImageNet VID for video object detection and YouTube VIS for video instance segmentation. Excellent experimental results demonstrate the superior efficiency, effectiveness, and compatibility of our method. The code is available at https://github.com/guanxiongsun/TDViT.

1 Introduction

In the past decade, 2D convolutional neural network (CNN) based architectures [22,38–41,52] have dominated various computer vision tasks for still image understanding, e.g., image classification, object detection and semantic segmentation. Given the excellent performance on still images, 2D CNNs are adapted to video understanding by extending the 2D convolutional layer through the temporal axis, i.e., 3D CNNs [9,34,43]. Recently, the computer vision community has seen a model shift from conventional CNNs to vision transformers [27,46]. This trend began with the pioneering approach, ViT [27], which leverages Transformers [46] to understand an image as a sequence of non-overlapping patches. Some follow-up approaches focus on improving ViT in different aspects, such as finer feature representations [20,32,47], better token generations [51,57], more

---

Supplementary Information The online version contains supplementary material available at https://doi.org/10.1007/978-3-031-19833-5_17.

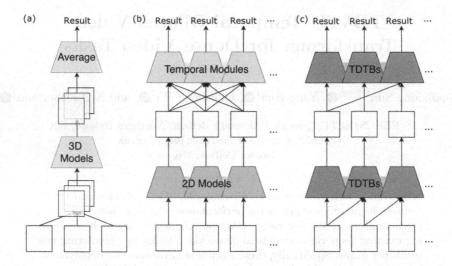

Fig. 1. Architecture (a) is widely used in sparse video tasks. 3D models, e.g., 3D CNNs, take multiple frames as input and generate one output by averaging the spatiotemporal representations. Architecture (b) is used for dense video tasks. Considering the computational cost, 2D models are used to extract features of independent frames, and then temporal modules, e.g., correlation filters, are leveraged to model spatiotemporal correspondences. Our TDViT (c) is designed for dense video tasks, which can efficiently and effectively extract spatiotemporal representations using temporal dilated transformer blocks (TDTB). *Best viewed in colour.* (Color figure online)

efficient training processes [42], etc. Not surprisingly, the great success of transformers on still-image tasks also leads to investigation of the use of transformers for video tasks [2,5,33].

Most video models (3D CNNs [9,17,43] or video transformers [5,14,33]) are designed for *sparse* video tasks, e.g., video classification [1,25,44] and action recognition [9,16,18], whose goal is to predict one label for one given video. These models utilise 3D operations, e.g., 3D convolutional layers or spatiotemporal self-attentions, to learn a spatiotemporal representation for a video. The architecture of sparse video models is shown in Fig. 1(a). Differently, *dense* video tasks aim to predict one result per frame, e.g., video object detection [10,37] and video instance segmentation [6,54]. However, problems arise when integrating video models into dense video tasks. Specifically, these models are (1) computationally intensive, resulting in high deployment costs; (2) unable to extract relevant information from redundant frames; and (3) challenging to capture long-range temporal correlations. In practise, therefore, state-of-the-art approaches for dense video tasks are still built in a hybrid manner: extracting spatial features using 2D models and adding temporal modules [13,46] to generate spatiotemporal representations. The architecture of sparse models is shown in Fig. 1(b).

In this paper, we propose a Temporal Dilated Video Transformer (TDViT) whose overall architecture is shown in Fig. 1(c). Inspired by visual transformers [27,32,42] which are naturally suitable for sequence modelling, we exploit transformers to extract spatiotemporal features. Unlike most video models that are based on self-attention transformers, we present a novel temporal dilated transformer block (TDTB) with two distinct designs. Firstly, a memory structure that stores features of previous frames is introduced to each TDTB. During inference, the query tokens are derived from the current frame for each time step, whereas the key and value tokens are sampled from the memory structure. In this way, TDTB can extract multi-frame spatiotemporal features with a single-frame overhead. Secondly, a temporal dilation factor is proposed to control the temporal frequency of feature sampling by skipping neighbouring frames. Therefore, TDTB can alleviate the negative effects of video redundancy. Furthermore, by employing hierarchical TDTBs in stages, TDViT acquires an exponentially expanded temporal receptive field. Here, the temporal receptive field represents the number of video frames considered when extracting spatiotemporal features. As a result, TDViT can effectively capture long-range temporal correlations and achieve higher accuracy.

To better demonstrate the differences between our TDViT and other visual models, we categorise existing visual models based on their architectures and their target tasks. For example, ResNets [22,52] and Inceptions [39,40] are CNN-based models designed for image tasks. VSwin [33] and TSFMR [5] are transformer-based models designed for sparse video tasks. Our approach is also a transformer based model but designed for dense video tasks. The details and categorisation of existing video models are presented in Table 1.

To sum up, our contributions are listed as follows:

- Unlike the existing hybrid solutions (2D image models equipped with temporal modules [13,46]) for dense video tasks, we propose a neat and compact architecture, Temporal Dilated Video Transformers (TDViT), for spatiotemporal representation learning.
- We design a novel temporal dilated transformer block (TDTB) that can efficiently extract spatiotemporal representations and alleviate the negative effect of video redundancy by cooperating with a memory structure and temporal dilated feature sampling process. Furthermore, by employing hierarchical TDTBs, our approach can effectively capture long-range temporal correlations.
- We conduct extensive experiments on two datasets for different dense video tasks, i.e., ImageNet VID for video object detection and YouTube VIS for video instance segmentation. Excellent experimental results demonstrate the superior effectiveness, efficiency, and compatibility of our method. Given these advantages, we believe that our TDViT can serve as a general-purpose backbone for various dense video tasks.

Table 1. Categorization of visual models based on their architectures and their target tasks. For dense video tasks, most SOTA methods use 2D models as their backbone and leverage temporal modules, e.g., attention [46] or correlation filter [13] to get spatiotemporal representations. To the best of our knowledge, our approach is the first end-to-end backbone designed for dense video tasks.

Arch	2D models	3D sparse models	3D dense models
CNN	ResNet [22,52] Inception [39,40] EffNet [41]	R3D [45] I3D [9] SFNet [17]	2D models + Temporal modules [13,46]
Transformer	ViT [27] DeiT [42] Swin [32]	Non-local [48] TimeSformer [5] VSwin [33]	TDViT (Ours)

2   Related Work

2.1   Video Models for Sparse Video Tasks

For video modelling, 3D CNNs are investigated in pioneering approaches [9,34,43]. These methods extend 2D CNNs through the temporal axis, but the performance is limited by their small temporal receptive fields. To address this, multi-head attentions [46] are introduced to fuse spatiotemporal representations. For example, NLNet [48] adopts self-attentions to model pixel-level dependency globally. GCNet [7] presents a lightweight global context block and achieves good performance with less computation. DNL [56] captures better visual clues using disentangled NL blocks.

2.2   Dense Video Tasks

Dense video tasks aim to output one prediction per frame. For video object detection, DFF [60], FGFA [59] and THP [58] use optical flow to propagate or aggregate feature maps of neighbour frames. Recent methods, SELSA [50], RDN [12] and MEGA [10], perform proposal-level aggregation by modelling relationships between objects using attention mechanisms [46]. For video instance segmentation, MaskTrack R-CNN [54] extends instance segmentation from image domain to video domain. MaskProp [4] uses mask propagation to obtain smoother results. StemSeg [3] treats the video clip as 3D spatial-temporal volume and segments instances by clustering methods. TransVOD [23] and VisTR [49] adapt DETR [8] for VOD and VIS tasks, respectively, in a query-based end-to-end fashion. These methods are built in a hybrid manner, extracting features with 2D models and relying on additional temporal modules. In contrast, our TDViT is a neat and compact model that is built with unified TDTBs.

2.3   Vision Transformers

Our approach is inspired by the recent trend of attention based vision transformers. Among these methods, ViT [27] is the first to use consecutive transformers to replace the CNN backbones. It reshapes an image into a sequence of

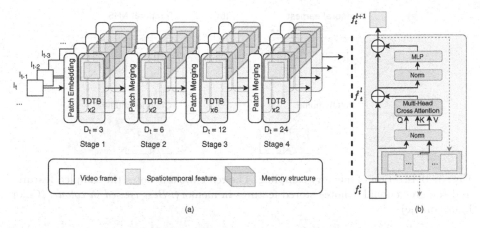

(a)

(b)

Fig. 2. (a) Overview. TDViT contains four stages which consist of several temporal dilated transformer blocks (TDTB). A memory structure (purple cuboids) is introduced into the TDTB, which stores features of previous frames (yellow rectangles) and enables our approach to dynamically establish temporal connections. The temporal dilation factor D_t is used to control the memory sampling process and reduce the video redundancy. (b) Details of a TDTB. For every time step, the query tokens are from the current frame I_t but the key and value tokens are derived from memory sampling. Finally, the memory structure saves the output features and deletes the oldest features. *Best viewed in colour.* (Color figure online)

non-overlapping flattened 2D patches and achieves a good speed-accuracy trade-off for image classification. Many recent papers improve the performance of ViT in different aspects. For example, Deit [42] addresses the issue that ViT requires a large amount of data by knowledge distillation. TiT [20] and PVT [47] generate multi-scale feature maps to capture finer visual clues. T2T [57] uses a small transformer network to generate better token representations. The most related work to ours is the Swin [32], which uses local attention to gradually reduce the resolution of feature maps and achieves impressive performance in various vision tasks. These methods demonstrate that transformers do well in modelling spatial dependencies. Inspired by these methods, we dive deeper into the essence of transformers and find that they are naturally suitable for modelling the correlations of sequence data.

3   Method

3.1   Overall Architecture

An overview of our TDViT is presented in Fig. 2(a). Our approach consists of four stages. Each stage is obtained by stacking several temporal dilated transformer blocks (TDTB). Each TDTB has a memory structure to store and sample features of previous frames. TDViT takes a frame I_t of one video $\{I_\tau\}_{\tau=1}^{T}$ as input, where T is the length of the video and t denotes the current time step. The previous frames of the video can be denoted as $\{I_\tau\}_{\tau=1}^{t-1}$. By modelling the spatiotemporal correlations between I_t and $\{I_\tau\}_{\tau=1}^{t-1}$, TDViT can output more accurate predictions for every frame.

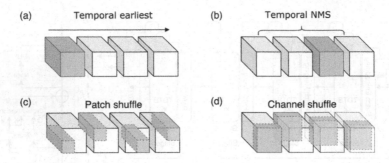

Fig. 3. Illustration of memory sampling. The red cuboid denotes the sampled features and the grey cuboid denotes stored features in memory. *Best viewed in colour.* (Color figure online)

3.2   Temporal Dilated Transformer Block

Inspired by the dilated convolutions which introduce spatial skip steps for feature aggregation, we propose the temporal dilated transformer block to construct skip connections in the temporal dimension. Specifically, unlike existing self-attention based transformer modules, the temporal dilated transformer block (TDTB) has two novel designs: (1) a memory structure $\mathcal{M}$ to explicitly store previous features; (2) a temporal dilation factor D_t to control the stride of temporal connections. The input of a TDTB is the features of the current frame, which can be in different forms, such as feature maps with arbitrary sizes or proposal features. Given $D_t=d$, the l-th TDTB samples features from $\{I\tau\}_{t-d}^{t}$ as reference features f^R. Then I_t is enhanced with f^R using multi-head cross attention (MCA). Specifically, the tokens for query Q, key K and value V are obtained by normalising features of the current frame f_t^l and reference features f^R, respectively. A 2-layer MLP with GELU non-linearity is applied to the MCA's output features $\hat{f}_t^l$. Two LayerNorm LN layers are applied before MCA and MLP, respectively. The output feature f_t^{l+1} is obtained by applying residual connections after MCA and MLP layers. Formally,

$$
\begin{aligned}
f^R &= Sampling(\mathcal{M}, D_t), \\
\hat{f}_t^l &= MCA(LN(f_t^l), LN(f^R)) + f_t^l, \\
f_t^{l+1} &= MLP(LN(\hat{f}_t^l)) + \hat{f}_t^l,
\end{aligned}
\tag{1}
$$

where $Sampling(\cdot, \cdot)$ denotes the sampling process guided by D_t. An illustration of TDTB is shown in Fig. 2 (b).

Memory Sampling and Feature Reuse. The memory structure $\mathcal{M}$ is updated at every time step by replacing the oldest frame with f_t^{l+1}. Given a temporal dilation D_t, we design different strategies to sample reference features f^R. The temporal *earliest* strategy selects the oldest feature map in the memory. The temporal NMS selects the feature map that has the maximum L2 norm.

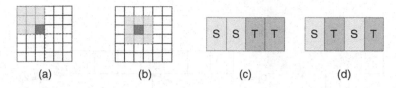

Fig. 4. (a) Window and (b) correlation based local attentions. The blue rectangle denotes one query token, the red dotted rectangle denotes the range of participated key tokens. (c) Split and (d) factorised spatiotemporal schemes. The blue and red boxes denote space-only self-attention and TDTB, respectively. *Best viewed in colour.* (Color figure online)

The *patch*-wise shuffle strategy first splits the feature maps into four windows, i.e., top left, top right, bottom left, and bottom right. Then, it randomly selects four time steps from four groups, respectively, and combines them as the reference feature map. Similarly, the *channel*-wise shuffle strategy split the feature maps into C groups according to channels, where C is the number of channels. Among these strategies, the first two are feature-level operations, while the last two are more fine-grained group-wise operations. The differences between these strategies are shown in Fig. 3.

Once we obtain the sample features f^R, we reuse the feature for D_t time steps and then sample new f^R from the updated memory. Instead of computing query, key, and value tokens for every frame, TDTB only extracts query tokens from the current frame and reuses f^R to obtain key and value tokens. As a result, TDViT achieves a slightly faster speed compared to its 2D counterpart, the Swin [32].

Efficient Local Attentions. The most well-known transformers are built with multi-head self-attention (MSA) modules in which one query token attends to all key tokens globally. We exploit local attentions because they have lower computational costs. In addition, local attentions are very suitable for dense video tasks since the movement of an object is continuous and should be inside a local region for a short time. Specifically, we introduce two different local attentions. Firstly, following the protocol of [32], we adapt the window-based local attention (Fig. 4(a)), where key tokens are from reference frames within the same window of the query token. Secondly, inspired by [13,19,24], we design a local attention based on correlation (Fig. 4(b)), where key tokens are from reference frames within a neighbour region of the query token.

3.3   Spatiotemporal Attention Schemes

We investigate different spatiotemporal attention schemes, i.e., the order of the space block and the temporal block (TDTB) in a stage. Inspired by [5,33], we design two spatiotemporal schemes: split and factorised schemes. The split scheme adds several temporal blocks (TDTB) after consecutive space blocks (Fig. 4(c)), while the factorised scheme adds one TDTB after each space block as shown in Fig. 4(d).

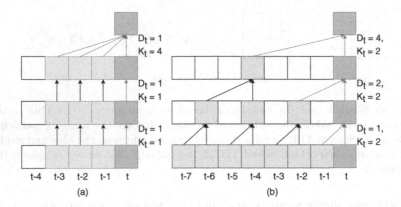

Fig. 5. Illustration of how hierarchical TDTBs increase the temporal receptive field. (a) and (b) show the framework of RDN [12] and our TDViT, respectively. The red and blue rectangles denote the current frame and frames within the temporal receptive field, respectively. *Best viewed in colour.* (Color figure online)

3.4   Temporal Receptive Field of Hierarchical TDTB

One TDTB with temporal dilation D_t can aggregate temporal information from time step $t - D_t$ to t. We use TDTBs in multiple hierarchical stages to obtain an exponentially expanded temporal receptive field. For a better demonstration, we introduce the temporal kernel size K_t which denotes the number of frames considered in an aggregation process. For example, an aggregation process with $K_t = 2$ and $D_t = 4$ aggregates 2 frames whose temporal distance is 4. Using K_t and D_t, we can describe the process of TDViT and other SOTA methods for VOD from a unified perspective. Figure 5(a) shows a simplified version of RDN [12] where $D_t = \{1, 1, 1\}$ and $K_t = \{1, 1, 4\}$ from bottom to top. For RDN, temporal aggregation only happens in the detection head after the backbone feature extraction. TDViT hierarchically fuses temporal features onto the current frame. Figure 5(b) shows a simplified version of TDViT, where $D_t = \{1, 2, 4\}$ and $K_t = \{2, 2, 2\}$. With similar complexity, i.e., the times of feature aggregation shown as the number of red connections in Fig. 5, the temporal receptive fields of RDN and TDViT are 4 and 8, respectively.

3.5   Architecture and Variants

Following the design principles of Swin [32], we build three basic variants of our models, called TDViT-T (tiny), TDViT-S (small) and TDViT-B (base), whose sizes and computational complexities are similar to Swin-T, Swin-S and Swin-B. The query dimension of each transformer head is 32, and the expansion layer of each MLP is 4. Two hyperparameters are introduced to describe each variant: C denotes dimensions of the linear embedding in the first stage and L denotes the number of transformers in each stage. The *basic* variants are represented as TDViT-T: $C = 96$, $L = (2,2,6,2)$; TDViT-S: $C = 96$, $L = (2,2,18,2)$; TDViT-B:

$C = 128$, $L = (2,2,18,2)$. By adding two additional TDTBs at the end of stage 3, we further obtain the *advanced* variants which can be represented as TDViT-T$^+$: $C = 96$, $L = (2,2,8,2)$; TDViT-S$^+$: $C = 96$, $L = (2,2,20,2)$; TDViT-B$^+$: $C = 128$, $L = (2,2,20,2)$.

4   Experiments

To verify the generality of our TDViT, we conduct experiments on two datasets, i.e., ImageNet VID [36] for video object detection (VOD) and YouTube VIS [54] for video instance segmentation (VIS). Firstly, we compare TDViT with other backbones. Then, we adapt TDViT to SOTA VOD and VIS methods to evaluate its compatibility. Finally, we conduct ablation studies on different designs, as mentioned in the Section 3. We report detailed evaluation results in the COCO [30] format. Specifically, we use the average precision (AP^{box}) metric which computes the average precision over ten IoU thresholds [0.5: 0.05: 0.95] for all categories. Meanwhile, we report other important metrics, e.g., AP$^{box}_{50}$ and AP$^{box}_{75}$ are calculated at IoU thresholds of 0.50 and 0.75 [15], and AP$^{box}_S$, AP$^{box}_M$, AP$^{box}_L$ are calculated on different object scales, i.e., small, medium and large. All training and testing are performed on Tesla V100 GPUs.

Video Object Detection Setup. The ImageNetVID dataset [36] contains 3,862 training and 555 validation videos. Following previous approaches [37,50, 59], we add overlapped 30 classes of the ImageNet DET dataset into the training set. Specifically, we sample 15 frames from each video in the VID training set and at most 2,000 images per class from the DET training set. We employ an AdamW [26] optimizer for 3 epochs in total, with an initial learning rate of 10^{-3} and 10^{-4} after the *2nd* epoch, using a weight decay of 0.05. We follow the augmentation and regularisation strategies of Swin [32]. Given the key frame I_k, we randomly sample four frames from $\{I_\tau\}_{k-D_t}^{k+D_t}$ to approximately form the memory of TDTBs in four stages, respectively. During training, detection losses are only computed for the key frame I_k.

Video Instance Segmentation Setup. We also evaluate TDViT for video instance segmentation on YouTube VIS 2019 dataset [54] and report the validation results as [3,6]. There are 3,471 training videos and 507 validation videos. For training and testing, the original images are resized to 640×360. The metrics are computed on masks, denoted as AP^{mask} and AP$^{mask}_{75}$, etc.

4.1   Video Object Detection

We first compare TDViT with other backbones using single-frame FasterRCNN [35] as the base detector. Then, we integrate TDViT with the SELSA [50] video object detection (VOD) method and compare it with other SOTA VOD methods.

Table 2. Comparisons with other widely used backbones for video object detection.

Backbone	Arch	AP^{box}	AP^{box}_{50}	AP^{box}_{75}	AP^{box}_{S}	AP^{box}_{M}	AP^{box}_{L}	# Param	FPS
R-50 [22]	CNN	44.3	72.5	47.2	6.3	19.7	49.3	44.4 M	23.0
R-101 [22]		48.5	75.5	53.1	7.6	23.1	53.7	63.4 M	19.5
Swin-T [32]	ViT	47.1	77.2	51.5	9.5	23.2	52.4	47.8 M	22.8
Swin-S [32]		52.6	82.4	59.3	10.0	26.5	58.6	69.1 M	16.7
Swin-B [32]		53.2	82.7	60.4	9.1	27.7	59.0	107.1 M	12.8
TDViT-T	ViT	49.1	78.5	52.7	8.0	25.6	53.1	47.8 M	23.9
TDViT-T$^+$		50.9	79.9	55.7	9.1	26.9	57.2	51.3 M	21.9
TDViT-S		55.4	84.1	63.4	10.3	29.3	61.2	69.1 M	16.8
TDViT-S$^+$		55.7	84.1	63.2	10.5	30.4	61.4	72.7 M	16.2
TDViT-B		56.0	84.4	64.1	10.7	28.0	62.3	107.1 M	12.9
TDViT-B$^+$		56.1	84.7	64.2	10.0	29.9	61.8	113.5 M	12.2

Comparisons with Other Backbones. We compare TDViT with various widely used backbones, e.g., R-50 and R-101 as baselines. We also introduce a transformer-based backbone, Swin [32] as the baseline for fair comparisons. Detailed evaluation results are tested with the single-frame FasterRCNN [35] as shown in Table 2. All TDViT variants greatly surpass other architectures with comparable model sizes, i.e., number of parameters denoted as #Param. For *basic* variants, TDViT-T achieves 49.1% of AP^{box}, outperforming R-50/Swin-T (44.3/47.1%) by +4.8/2.0% of AP^{box}, respectively. TDViT-S/B achieves 55.4/ 56.0% of AP^{box}, outperforming Swin-S/B (52.6/53.2%) by +2.8% and TDViT-S outperforms R-101 (48.5%) by +6.9% of AP^{box}. Using the *advanced* variants, i.e., TDViT-T$^+$/S$^+$/B$^+$, the performance is improved to 50.9/55.7/56.1% of AP^{box}_{50}, respectively. To compare the run-time speed, we test all models on the same device, and the detailed results (FPS) are listed in the last column of Table 2. TDViT achieves better speed-accuracy trade-offs, and the speed-accuracy curve is shown in Fig. S1 in the supplementary material.

Comparisons with SOTA. SOTA VOD methods use multi-frame proposal aggregation to learn the relationships of objects in a video and achieve promising performance. We use SELSA [50] as our baseline for simplicity. In our re-implementation of SELSA, we introduce the distillation strategy proposed in RDN [12] where the top 75 out of total 300 proposals on the reference frames are selected for conducting aggregation. We follow previous methods [10,12,37,59] and use Average Precision with IoU threshold 0.5 (AP^{box}_{50}) as the default evaluation metric. Following the protocol in [59], we use motion IoU ($mIoU$) to split the dataset into three groups: slow ($mIoU < 0.7$), medium ($0.7 < mIoU < 0.9$) and fast ($mIoU > 0.9$), and report AP^{box}_{50} on three subsets, respectively. As shown in Table 3, our reimplemented SELSA with R-101 [22] achieves 81.5% of AP^{box}_{50} at 14.5 FPS. Then, we replace the R-101 backbone with our TDViT-T, and the performance is improved by 2.4% to 83.9% of AP^{box}_{50} at 16.2 FPS. We further intro-

Table 3. Comparisons with SOTA video object detection methods.

Methods	Backbone	AP_{50}^{box}	Slow	Medium	Fast	FPS	Hardware
FGFA [59]	R-101	76.3	83.5	75.8	57.6	1.2	K40
PSLA [19]	R-101+DCN	80.0	–	–	–	26.0	Titan V
CHP [53]	R-101	76.7	–	–	–	37.0	–
TransVOD [23]	R-101	81.9	–	–	–	–	–
SELSA [50]	R-101	80.3	86.9	78.9	61.4	–	–
RDN [12]	R-101	81.8	89.0	80.0	59.5	10.6	Tesla V100
MEGA [10]	R-101	82.9	89.4	81.6	62.7	8.7	2080 Ti
TFBlender [11]	R-101	83.8	–	–	–	4.9	2080 Ti
MAMBA [37]	R-101	84.6	–	–	–	9.1	Titan RTX
SELSA*	R-101	81.5	87.8	79.9	65.4	14.5	Tesla V100
SELSA+Ours	TDViT-T	83.9	88.6	83.8	67.7	16.2	Tesla V100
SELSA+Ours	TDViT-T$^+$	84.5	88.9	84.3	69.4	15.7	Tesla V100

Table 4. Comparisons with other backbones for video instance segmentation.

Backbone	Arch	AP^{mask}	AP_{50}^{mask}	AP_{75}^{mask}	AP_S^{mask}	AP_M^{mask}	AP_L^{mask}	#Param	FPS
R-50 [22]	CNN	30.3	50.0	32.1	11.8	30.5	40.6	58.1 M	18.0
R-101 [22]		32.9	52.3	35.6	9.8	33.0	44.1	77.1 M	17.2
Swin-T [32]	ViT	33.7	57.1	35.1	12.8	33.5	44.2	61.5 M	18.6
Swin-S [32]		36.8	60.9	40.1	16.0	37.3	48.8	82.8 M	14.3
TDViT-T	ViT	35.4	59.6	38.6	13.6	36.9	46.4	61.5 M	18.6
TDViT-T$^+$		36.1	60.2	39.9	14.0	37.5	48.1	65.0 M	18.0
TDViT-S		37.7	61.9	40.5	16.9	37.9	49.6	82.8 M	14.3
TDViT-S$^+$		38.2	62.5	41.6	17.6	38.1	51.2	86.3 M	13.9

duce the advanced variant TDViT$^+$, and our method achieves 84.5% of AP_{50}^{box} at 15.7 FPS. Compared to other SOTA methods, our method achieves a better speed-accuracy trade-off. For example, MAMBA [37] and TFBlender+MEGA [11] achieve 84.6% and 83.8% of AP_{50}^{box}, respectively, but they run at relatively slow speeds, 9.1 and 4.9 FPS.

4.2 Video Instance Segmentation

Similar to the experiment designs in video object detection, we first compare TDViT with other backbones using MaskTrack R-CNN [54] as the base sgementor. Then, we compare the performance with other SOTA video instance segmentation methods.

Table 5. Comparisons of our approach with SOTA methods for video instance segmentation.

Methods	Backbone	AP^{mask}	AP^{mask}_{50}	AP^{mask}_{75}	FPS	Hardware
Stem-Seg [3]	R-50	30.6	50.7	33.5	12.1	Titan RTX
SipMask [6]	R-50	33.7	54.1	35.8	28.0	Titan RTX
SG-Net [31]	R-50	34.8	56.1	36.8	22.9	Titan RTX
TFBlender [11]	R-50	35.7	57.1	37.6	21.3	Titan RTX
CrossVis [55]	R-50	36.3	56.8	38.9	–	–
VisTR [49]	R-50	36.2	59.8	36.9	30.0	Tesla V100
MaskTrack R-CNN* [54]	R-50	30.3	50.0	32.1	18.0	Tesla V100
MaskTrack R-CNN+Ours	TDViT-T	35.4	59.6	38.6	18.6	Tesla V100
MaskTrack R-CNN+Ours	TDViT-T$^+$	36.1	60.2	39.9	18.0	Tesla V100

Comparisons with Other Backbones. We compare our TDViT-T with other backbones with similar model sizes, i.e., number of parameters (#Param) in Table 4. The pre-trained Mask R-CNN [21] model on the COCO [30] dataset is used to initialise the network. We first report results using R-50 and R-101 backbones. Then, we replace the backbone with a stronger Swin model [32]. Compared with using R-50/101, the performance of using Swin-T/S is improved by 3.4/3.9% to 33.7/36.8% of AP^{mask}, respectively. Then, we replace the backbone with TDViT. Compared to Swin-T/S, the performance of TDViT-T/S is improved by 1.7/0.9% to 35.4/37.7% of AP^{mask}, respectively. By introducing the advanced variants, TDViT-T$^+$/S$^+$, the performance is further improved to 36.1/38.2% of AP^{mask}. We also test the run-time speed of these backbones. As shown in Table 4, our method can achieve better speed-accuracy trade-offs.

Comparisons with SOTA. We compare our method with SOTA video instance segmentation methods and report detailed results in Table 5. We use MaskTrack R-CNN [54] as the base segmentor and use * to denote our reimplemented version. Using R-50 as the backbone, MaskTrack R-CNN * achieves 30.3% AP^{mask} at 18.0, which is the baseline. By replacing the backbone with TDViT-T/T$^+$, the performance is improved to 35.4/36.1% of AP^{mask} and runs at 18.6/18.0 FPS, respectively. The performance and speed are comparable to recent SOTA methods, e.g., VisTR [49] and CrossVis [55].

4.3 Ablation Study

Spatiotemporal Attention Schemes. We conduct experiments on the split and factorised schemes. Detailed orders of space-only blocks and temporal blocks (TDTB) inside the stage 3 are listed in Table 6. Other stages contain 2 blocks, and we use one space-only block followed by one TDTB. More details of spatiotemporal schemes on different variants are shown in the supplementary material. The split scheme has 0.5% higher AP^{box}_{50} than the factorised scheme, and

Table 6. Effect of different spatiotemporal attention schemes.

Scheme	Backbone	Stage 3		AP_{50}^{box}
		Details	Depth	
Space-only	Swin-T	[s]*6	6	77.2
Factorised scheme	TDViT-T	[s, t]*3	6	78.0
Split scheme	TDViT-T	s*3, t*3	6	**78.5**
Split scheme	TDViT-T$^+$	s*3, t*5	8	**79.9**

Table 7. Effect of different temporal dilations. The four numbers denote the temporal dilations in four stages, respectively.

$\{D_t\}$	AP_{50}^{box}	AP_{75}^{box}	AP_{S}^{box}	AP_{M}^{box}	AP_{L}^{box}
(1,2,4,8)	77.2	51.5	8.6	23.2	52.4
(2,4,8,16)	77.9	52.0	8.6	23.4	53.0
(3,6,12,24)	78.1	52.1	**8.7**	23.8	52.2
(4,8,16,32)	**78.5**	**52.7**	8.0	**25.6**	53.1
(5,10,20,40)	78.4	52.5	8.5	24.9	**53.4**

thus we use the split scheme by default. With a increased number of TDTBs, e.g., from 6 to 8, TDViT-T$^+$ achieves better performance with 79.9% of AP_{50}^{box}.

Temporal Dilations. Larger temporal dilations enable TDViT to fuse temporal information over a longer time span. However, larger temporal dilations increase the difficulty of learning the spatiotemporal correspondences. In this part, we conduct experiments to find a good trade-off between the large temporal receptive field and the learning difficulty. We gradually increase the temporal dilations from the lower stage to the higher stage. The specific number of temporal dilations and the corresponding results are listed in Table 7. Temporal dilations of four stages are denoted as $\{D_t\}$. Performance improves when we increase the temporal dilations. In our experiments, with temporal dilations $\{D_t\} = \{4, 8, 16, 32\}$, our method achieves the optimal performance 78.5% of AP_{50}^{box} and we use this setting by default. The performance improvement is saturated when we further increase the temporal dilations. For example, with $\{D_t\} = \{5, 10, 20, 40\}$, the performance drops by 0.1% of AP_{50}^{box}.

Memory Sampling Strategies. In the TDTB, a good sampling strategy should be able to generate informative features from the memory structure. For example, given the temporal dilation $D_t = 16$, the sampled features should well represent 16 neighbour frames. We design different sampling strategies and conduct experiments to find a better solution. Their differences are illustrated in §3.2 and Fig. 3. The detailed results are shown in Table 8. Among these strategies,

Table 8. Comparisons between different sampling strategies.

	AP_{50}^{box}	AP_{75}^{box}	AP_S^{box}	AP_M^{box}	AP_L^{box}	FPS
Temporal earliest	78.5	52.7	8.0	25.6	53.1	**23.9**
Temporal NMS	78.5	52.6	8.3	**25.7**	53.0	19.9
Channel shuffle	77.7	51.4	8.4	25.1	52.1	20.2
Patch shuffle	**78.8**	**53.0**	**8.5**	**25.7**	**53.3**	19.7

Table 9. Comparisons of local attentions according to region sizes.

Size	Window	Correlation	AP_{50}^{box}	FPS
7×7		✓	**78.8**	18.4
7×7	✓		78.5	23.9
5×5	✓		77.6	**25.2**
9×9	✓		78.1	22.1

patch shuffle achieves the best performance 78.8% of AP_{50}^{box} because the sampled features have good diversities. However, considering the run-time speed, we use the temporal earliest strategy by default, which achieves a comparable accuracy with 78.5% of AP_{50}^{box} but a much faster speed at 23.9 FPS.

Efficient Local Attention. Local attention is important for TDViT to achieve a good speed-accuracy trade-off. We conduct experiments on different local attentions. Firstly, the window based local attention, which is used in Swin [32]. The feature maps are split into non-overlapping windows and then attentions are computed within each window locally. Secondly, the correlation based local attention, which is used in PSLA [19], optical flow [13] and tracking methods [28,29]. Given one query token, local attentions are computed within a small region around the query location. The differences between these two designs are illustrated in §3.2 and Fig. 4. We also test with different local region sizes. The detailed settings and results are presented in Table 9. By default, we use the window based attention with size 7×7 for a good speed-accuracy trade-off.

5 Conclusion

We present a Temporal Dilated Video Transformer (TDViT) for dense video tasks. The key component in TDViT is the temporal dilated transformer block (TDTB), which can obtain accurate multi-frame spatiotemporal representations with a single-frame computational cost and effectively sample useful information from redundant frames. Moreover, by using hierarchical TDTBs, our approach can capture long-range temporal correlations, further improving accuracy. TDViT achieves excellent speed-accuracy trade-offs on the ImageNet VID and

YouTube VIS datasets and is compatible with different frameworks. The simplicity and strong performance suggest that TDViT can potentially serve as a general-purpose backbone for various dense video tasks.

References

1. Abu-El-Haija, S., et al.: Youtube-8m: A large-scale video classification benchmark. arXiv preprint arXiv:1609.08675 (2016)
2. Arnab, A., Dehghani, M., Heigold, G., Sun, C., Lučić, M., Schmid, C.: Vivit: A video vision transformer. In: ICCV (2021)
3. Athar, A., Mahadevan, S., Ošep, A., Leal-Taixé, L., Leibe, B.: STEm-Seg: Spatio-temporal embeddings for instance segmentation in videos. In: Vedaldi, A., Bischof, H., Brox, T., Frahm, J.-M. (eds.) ECCV 2020. LNCS, vol. 12356, pp. 158–177. Springer, Cham (2020). https://doi.org/10.1007/978-3-030-58621-8_10
4. Bertasius, G., Torresani, L.: Classifying, segmenting, and tracking object instances in video with mask propagation. In: CVPR (2020)
5. Bertasius, G., Wang, H., Torresani, L.: Is space-time attention all you need for video understanding? In: ICML (2021)
6. Cao, J., Anwer, R.M., Cholakkal, H., Khan, F.S., Pang, Y., Shao, L.: SipMask: Spatial information preservation for fast image and video instance segmentation. In: Vedaldi, A., Bischof, H., Brox, T., Frahm, J.-M. (eds.) ECCV 2020. LNCS, vol. 12359, pp. 1–18. Springer, Cham (2020). https://doi.org/10.1007/978-3-030-58568-6_1
7. Cao, Y., Xu, J., Lin, S.C.F., Wei, F., Hu, H.: Gcnet: Non-local networks meet squeeze-excitation networks and beyond. In: ICCVW (2019)
8. Carion, N., Massa, F., Synnaeve, G., Usunier, N., Kirillov, A., Zagoruyko, S.: End-to-end object detection with transformers. In: Vedaldi, A., Bischof, H., Brox, T., Frahm, J.-M. (eds.) ECCV 2020. LNCS, vol. 12346, pp. 213–229. Springer, Cham (2020). https://doi.org/10.1007/978-3-030-58452-8_13
9. Carreira, J., Zisserman, A.: Quo vadis, action recognition? a new model and the kinetics dataset. In: CVPR (2017)
10. Chen, Y., Cao, Y., Hu, H., Wang, L.: Memory enhanced global-local aggregation for video object detection. In: CVPR (2020)
11. Cui, Y., Yan, L., Cao, Z., Liu, D.: Tf-blender: Temporal feature blender for video object detection. In: ICCV (2021)
12. Deng, J., Pan, Y., Yao, T., Zhou, W., Li, H., Mei, T.: Relation distillation networks for video object detection. In: ICCV (2019)
13. Dosovitskiy, A., et al.: Flownet: Learning optical flow with convolutional networks. In: ICCV (2015)
14. Duan, H., Zhao, Y., Xiong, Y., Liu, W., Lin, D.: Omni-sourced webly-supervised learning for video recognition. In: Vedaldi, A., Bischof, H., Brox, T., Frahm, J.-M. (eds.) ECCV 2020. LNCS, vol. 12360, pp. 670–688. Springer, Cham (2020). https://doi.org/10.1007/978-3-030-58555-6_40
15. Everingham, M., Gool, L.V., Williams, C.K.I., Winn, J.M., Zisserman, A.: The pascal visual object classes (voc) challenge. IJCV 88, 303–338 (2009)
16. Heilbron, F.C., Victor Escorcia, B.G., Niebles, J.C.: Activitynet: A large-scale video benchmark for human activity understanding. In: CVPR (2015)
17. Feichtenhofer, C., Fan, H., Malik, J., He, K.: Slowfast networks for video recognition. In: ICCV (2019)

18. Goyal, R., et al.: The "something something" video database for learning and evaluating visual common sense. In: ICCV (2017)
19. Guo, C., et al.: Progressive sparse local attention for video object detection. In: ICCV (2019)
20. Han, K., Xiao, A., Wu, E., Guo, J., Xu, C., Wang, Y.: Transformer in transformer. In: NeurIPS (2021)
21. He, K., Gkioxari, G., Dollár, P., Girshick, R.: Mask r-cnn. In: ICCV (2017)
22. He, K., Zhang, X., Ren, S., Sun, J.: Deep residual learning for image recognition. In: CVPR (2016)
23. He, L., et al.: End-to-end video object detection with spatial-temporal transformers. In: ACMMM (2021)
24. Ilg, E., Mayer, N., Saikia, T., Keuper, M., Dosovitskiy, A., Brox, T.: Flownet 2.0: Evolution of optical flow estimation with deep networks. In: CVPR (2017)
25. Karpathy, A., Toderici, G., Shetty, S., Leung, T., Sukthankar, R., Fei-Fei, L.: Large-scale video classification with convolutional neural networks. In: CVPR (2014)
26. Kingma, D.P., Ba, J.: Adam: A method for stochastic optimization. arXiv preprint arXiv:1412.6980 (2014)
27. Kolesnikov, A., et al.: An image is worth 16×16 words: Transformers for image recognition at scale. In: ICLR (2021)
28. Li, B., Wu, W., Wang, Q., Zhang, F., Xing, J., Yan, J.: Siamrpn++: Evolution of siamese visual tracking with very deep networks. In: CVPR (2019)
29. Li, B., Yan, J., Wu, W., Zhu, Z., Hu, X.: High performance visual tracking with siamese region proposal network. In: CVPR (2018)
30. Lin, T.-Y., et al.: Microsoft COCO: Common objects in context. In: Fleet, D., Pajdla, T., Schiele, B., Tuytelaars, T. (eds.) ECCV 2014. LNCS, vol. 8693, pp. 740–755. Springer, Cham (2014). https://doi.org/10.1007/978-3-319-10602-1_48
31. Liu, D., Cui, Y., Tan, W., Chen, Y.: Sg-net: Spatial granularity network for one-stage video instance segmentation. In: CVPR (2021)
32. Liu, Z., et al.: Swin transformer: Hierarchical vision transformer using shifted windows. In: ICCV (2021)
33. Liu, Z., et al.: Video swin transformer. arXiv preprint arXiv:2106.13230 (2021)
34. Qiu, Z., Yao, T., Mei, T.: Learning spatio-temporal representation with pseudo-3d residual networks. In: ICCV (2017)
35. Ren, S., He, K., Girshick, R., Sun, J.: Faster r-cnn: Towards real-time object detection with region proposal networks. In: NeurIPS (2015)
36. Russakovsky, O., et al.: Imagenet large scale visual recognition challenge. IJCV 115(3), 211–252 (2015)
37. Sun, G., Hua, Y., Hu, G., Robertson, N.: Mamba: Multi-level aggregation via memory bank for video object detection. In: AAAI (2021)
38. Szegedy, C., Ioffe, S., Vanhoucke, V., Alemi, A.A.: Inception-v4, inception-resnet and the impact of residual connections on learning. In: AAAI (2017)
39. Szegedy, C., et al.: Going deeper with convolutions. In: CVPR (2015)
40. Szegedy, C., Vanhoucke, V., Ioffe, S., Shlens, J., Wojna, Z.: Rethinking the inception architecture for computer vision. In: CVPR (2016)
41. Tan, M., Le, Q.: Efficientnet: Rethinking model scaling for convolutional neural networks. In: ICML (2019)
42. Touvron, H., Cord, M., Douze, M., Massa, F., Sablayrolles, A., Jégou, H.: Training data-efficient image transformers & distillation through attention. In: ICML (2021)
43. Tran, D., Bourdev, L., Fergus, R., Torresani, L., Paluri, M.: Learning spatiotemporal features with 3d convolutional networks. In: ICCV (2015)

44. Tran, D., Wang, H., Torresani, L., Feiszli, M.: Video classification with channel-separated convolutional networks. In: ICCV (2019)
45. Tran, D., Wang, H., Torresani, L., Ray, J., LeCun, Y., Paluri, M.: A closer look at spatiotemporal convolutions for action recognition. In: CVPR (2018)
46. Vaswani, A., et al.: Attention is all you need. In: NeurIPS (2017)
47. Wang, W., et al.: Pyramid vision transformer: A versatile backbone for dense prediction without convolutions. arXiv preprint arXiv:2102.12122 (2021)
48. Wang, X., Girshick, R., Gupta, A., He, K.: Non-local neural networks. In: CVPR (2018)
49. Wang, Y., et al.: End-to-end video instance segmentation with transformers. In: CVPR (2021)
50. Wu, H., Chen, Y., Wang, N., Zhang, Z.: Sequence level semantics aggregation for video object detection. In: ICCV (2019)
51. Wu, H., et al.: Cvt: Introducing convolutions to vision transformers. In: ICCV (2021)
52. Xie, S., Girshick, R., Dollár, P., Tu, Z., He, K.: Aggregated residual transformations for deep neural networks. In: CVPR (2017)
53. Xu, Z., Hrustic, E., Vivet, D.: CenterNet heatmap propagation for real-time video object detection. In: Vedaldi, A., Bischof, H., Brox, T., Frahm, J.-M. (eds.) ECCV 2020. LNCS, vol. 12370, pp. 220–234. Springer, Cham (2020). https://doi.org/10.1007/978-3-030-58595-2_14
54. Yang, L., Fan, Y., Xu, N.: Video instance segmentation. In: ICCV (2019)
55. Yang, S., et al.: Crossover learning for fast online video instance segmentation. In: ICCV (2021)
56. Yin, M., et al.: Disentangled non-local neural networks. In: Vedaldi, A., Bischof, H., Brox, T., Frahm, J.-M. (eds.) ECCV 2020. LNCS, vol. 12360, pp. 191–207. Springer, Cham (2020). https://doi.org/10.1007/978-3-030-58555-6_12
57. Yuan, L., et al.: Tokens-to-token vit: Training vision transformers from scratch on imagenet. In: ICCV (2021)
58. Zhu, X., Dai, J., Yuan, L., Wei, Y.: Towards high performance video object detection. In: CVPR (2018)
59. Zhu, X., Wang, Y., Dai, J., Yuan, L., Wei, Y.: Flow-guided feature aggregation for video object detection. In: ICCV (2017)
60. Zhu, X., Xiong, Y., Dai, J., Yuan, L., Wei, Y.: Deep feature flow for video recognition. In: CVPR (2017)

Semi-supervised Learning of Optical Flow by Flow Supervisor

Woobin Im, Sebin Lee, and Sung-Eui Yoon[(✉)]

Korea Advanced Institute of Science and Technology (KAIST), Daejeon, South Korea
{iwbn,seb.lee,sungeui}@kaist.ac.kr

Abstract. A training pipeline for optical flow CNNs consists of a pre-training stage on a synthetic dataset followed by a fine tuning stage on a target dataset. However, obtaining ground truth flows from a target video requires a tremendous effort. This paper proposes a practical fine tuning method to adapt a pretrained model to a target dataset without ground truth flows, which has not been explored extensively. Specifically, we propose a flow supervisor for self-supervision, which consists of parameter separation and a student output connection. This design is aimed at stable convergence and better accuracy over conventional self-supervision methods which are unstable on the fine tuning task. Experimental results show the effectiveness of our method compared to different self-supervision methods for semi-supervised learning. In addition, we achieve meaningful improvements over state-of-the-art optical flow models on Sintel and KITTI benchmarks by exploiting additional unlabeled datasets. Code is available at https://github.com/iwbn/flow-supervisor.

1 Introduction

Optical flow describes the pixel-level displacement in two images, and is a fundamental step for various motion understanding tasks in computer vision. Recently, supervised deep learning methods have shown remarkable performance in terms of overcoming challenges – such as motion blur, change of brightness and color, deformation, and occlusion – and predicting more accurate flows. The key to success is end-to-end learning from large-scale data. For optical flow learning, large-scale datasets have been released [4,7,14] and deep architectures have been advanced [7,32,34].

Building a good optical flow model on a target dataset is critical; most training data are synthetic, and it requires tremendous effort to label random video frames by pixel-wise dense correspondences. Thus, to obtain a good model on a target dataset, synthetic training set generation [24,31] and GAN-based adaptation [20,36] have been studied. In addition, unsupervised loss functions [25,30] – used without ground truth – have been proposed. However, generating a synthetic dataset for a target domain is often computationally expensive or confined

---

Supplementary Information The online version contains supplementary material available at https://doi.org/10.1007/978-3-031-19833-5_18.

S. Avidan et al. (Eds.): ECCV 2022, LNCS 13695, pp. 302–318, 2022.
https://doi.org/10.1007/978-3-031-19833-5_18

to a specific domain. Moreover, unsupervised losses do not reach the state-of-the-arts, compared to supervised methods. Therefore, there have been needs for a simpler, general, and high-performance method to build a better model on a target dataset.

In this paper, we propose a fine tuning strategy for semi-supervised optical flow learning, which helps to build a better model on unlabeled or partly-labeled target datasets. Figure 1 demonstrates the concept of our approach. Our method is a fine tuning method, where the pre-trained network is adapted to the unlabeled target data. In the fine tuning stage, we use a labeled dataset with an unlabeled target dataset, further reducing errors on the target dataset.

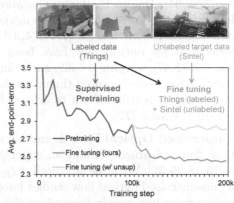

Fig. 1. End-point-error on Sintel. Our method is used to adapt a pretrained model to a target domain without a target domain label; it is designed to overcome an unstable convergence and low accuracy in traditional methods. For instance, our method outperforms the unsupervised loss (Eq. 2) in fine tuning, which makes our method favorably better

To build our method, we investigate unsupervised and self-supervised approaches, where a network learns optical flow by unlabeled samples. However, the existing unsupervised loss does not show better performance in the fine tuning stage (Fig. 1). Moreover, self-supervision methods tend to show highly unstable behavior or lower performance in the fine tuning stage. To address the issue, we propose our flow supervisor with two strategies: the parameter separation and passing student outputs, which are effective for higher performance and stable semi-supervised learning. As shown in Fig. 1, our fine tuning method clearly reduces the error of the pretrained model, even without a label of the target dataset.

To summarize, we propose a semi-supervised fine tuning strategy to improve an optical flow network on a target dataset, which has not been explored extensively. Our strategy is distinguished by the flow supervisor module, designed with the parameter separation and passing student outputs. We show the effectiveness of our method by comparing it with alternative self-supervision methods, and confirm that our approach stabilizes the learning process and results in better accuracy. In addition, we test our method on Sintel and KITTI benchmarks and achieve meaningful improvements over the state-of-the-arts by exploiting additional unlabeled data.

2   Related Work

Supervised Optical Flow has been studied with the development of datasets for optical flow learning [7,14,31] and the advances of deep network architectures [7,32,34]. Due to the high annotation cost and label ambiguity in a raw video, synthetic datasets have been made, where optical flow fields are generated together with images [7,14,24,31]. Along with the datasets, network architectures for optical flow have been significantly improved by the cost-volume [7,32,37], warping [14,32], and refinement scheme [13,34]. Although generalization has been improved thanks to the synthetic datasets and the network architectures, it is still difficult to achieve better performance while being blind to a target domain [27].

Unsupervised Optical Flow is another stream of optical flow research, where optical flow is learned without an expensive labeling or label generation process [15,18,25,30]. With the advanced deep architectures from supervised optical flow, unsupervised optical flow studies have focused on designing loss functions. Previous work has mainly focused on the fully unsupervised setting, while we explore semi-supervised optical flow where labeled data is accessible in addition to unlabeled target domain data.

Semi-supervised Optical Flow has been studied to utilize unlabeled target domain data with existing labeled synthetic data [20]. The experimental setting – similar to unsupervised domain adaptation [9] – is designed since it is relatively easier to exploit synthetic training datasets than annotating images of a target dataset. A simple baseline method for a target domain would be using a traditional unsupervised loss [25] and supervised learning, which, unfortunately, has shown inferior performance than the supervision-only training [20,27] (Table 1). Thus, reducing the domain gap [20] and stabilizing unsupervised loss gradients [27] have been proposed.

In this work, we introduce the flow supervisor, which consists of the separate parameters and the student output connection. We found our design scheme is superior to the baseline designs in terms of training stability and performance in the semi-supervised setting.

Knowledge Distillation and Self-supervision in neural networks are proposed to train a network under the guidance of a teacher network [12,29] or itself [6,10]. Interestingly, the technique can build a better student network even when the same network architecture is used for both student and teacher, i.e., self-distillation [12,29]. In the optical flow field, knowledge distillation and self-supervision have been studied actively in the context of unsupervised optical flow [21,22,30]. Generally, these methods can be interpreted as learning using privileged information [35], in that a student usually sees a limited view, e.g., cropped images, while a teacher is given a privileged view, e.g., full images. In this work, we investigate the effectiveness of self-supervision in terms of semi-supervised optical flow, which has not been explored in previous work. In addition, we found that the traditional self-supervision method for optical flow [30] tends to make a loss diverge in the semi-supervised setting.

Thus, we propose a novel self-supervision method to ameliorate the unstable convergence; we found that the parameter separation of a teacher model and passing student output are the key components to make the training stable. By applying our method, a network can successfully exploit the unlabeled target data in the semi-supervised setting. In addition, we show that our method can address the lack of a target labeled dataset, e.g., 200 labeled pairs for KITTI, by the ability to utilize unlabeled samples.

3   Approach

3.1   Preliminaries on Deep Optical Flow

Deep optical flow estimation is defined with an optical flow estimator $f_\theta(\mathbf{x}_1, \mathbf{x}_2)$, which predicts optical flow $\hat{\mathbf{y}} \in \mathbb{R}^{H \times W \times 2}$ from two images $\mathbf{x}_1, \mathbf{x}_2 \in \mathbb{R}^{H \times W \times C}$, where H is height, W is width, and C is channel.

In supervised learning, we train f_θ by minimizing the supervised loss:

$$\mathcal{L}_{\text{sup}}(\theta) = \mathbb{E}_{(\mathbf{x}_1, \mathbf{x}_2, \mathbf{y}) \sim p_s}[\ell_{\text{sup}}(f_\theta(\mathbf{x}_1, \mathbf{x}_2), \mathbf{y})], \tag{1}$$

where p_s is the labeled data distribution, $\mathbf{y}$ is the ground truth optical flow, and ℓ_{sup} is L_1, L_2 [32] or the generalized Charbonnier loss [25].

On the other hand, an unsupervised method defines a loss function with a differentiable target function $\ell_{\text{unsup}}(\cdot)$ which can be computed without a ground truth $\mathbf{y}$, resulting in the unsupervised loss:

$$\mathcal{L}_{\text{unsup}}(\theta) = \mathbb{E}_{(\mathbf{x}_1, \mathbf{x}_2) \sim p_u}[\ell_{\text{unsup}}(f_\theta(\mathbf{x}_1, \mathbf{x}_2), \mathbf{x}_1, \mathbf{x}_2)], \tag{2}$$

where p_u is an unlabeled data distribution. Most commonly, ℓ_{unsup} is defined with the photometric loss $\ell_{\text{photo}} = \rho(\text{warp}(\mathbf{x}_2, \hat{\mathbf{y}}) - \mathbf{x}_1)$ where ρ is the Charbonnier loss [25] and warp($\cdot$) is the differentiable backward warping operation [16].

3.2   Problem Definition and Background

We train our model on labeled data and unlabeled data, which is similar to experimental settings that appear in [20,27]. For instance, FlyingThings3D (rendered scene) and KITTI (driving scene) can be considered as labeled and unlabeled datasets, respectively. We aim to build a high-performance model on a target domain, with only a labeled synthetic dataset and an unlabeled target dataset. This is a practical scenario since a synthetic dataset is relatively inexpensive and publicly available, whereas specific target domain data is rarely annotated.

We focus on designing a self-supervision method with a stable convergence and better accuracy, since it is not trivial to adopt unsupervised losses and self-supervision for semi-supervised learning. First, unsupervised loss functions often lead a network to a worse local minimum when it is naively fine tuned from supervised (pretrained) weights. Second, traditional self-supervision strategies for semi-supervised learning do not converge well. Thus, we propose a simple and effective practice for semi-supervised learning, where we utilize synthetic datasets for better performance on a target dataset. By our strategy, a network can successfully exploit the unlabeled target data for better fine tuning performance. Detailed method is discussed in the next section.

3.3   Flow Supervisor

Our design for semi-supervised optical flow learning is based on self-supervised learning where a student network learns from a pseudo-label predicted by a teacher network. This concept has been explored in the optical flow field in terms of unsupervised learning, which is not directly applicable in the semi-supervised case due to unstable convergence.

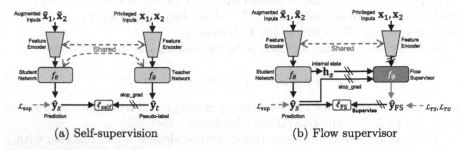

(a) Self-supervision   (b) Flow supervisor

Fig. 2. (a) Self-supervision for optical flow is configured with a teacher network which is given privileged images as an input, i.e., full images before cropping. **(b) Flow supervisor** reviews the student flow $\hat{\mathbf{y}}_s$ and outputs the pseudo-label $\hat{\mathbf{y}}_{FS}$ to supervise the student without ground truth flows. We use the separate flow supervisor with parameter ϕ, which improves the stability and accuracy

Thus, we introduce two distinctive design schemes compared to the existing self-supervision techniques for optical flow, depicted in Fig. 2. First, we introduce a supervisor parameter ϕ, distinguished from the student parameter θ, which learns to supervise the student network. Second, we add a connection from the student network to the supervisor network, which enables the supervisor network to learn conditional knowledge, i.e., $P(\mathbf{y}|\hat{\mathbf{y}}_s)$, instead of predicting from scratch.

We define the student network f_θ and the flow supervisor network f_ϕ, as shown in Fig. 2b. The student network f_θ includes a feature encoder and a flow decoder; for simplicity, we abstract the feature encoder and decoder parameters with θ. The flow decoder has the internal feature $\mathbf{h}_s$, and outputs the predicted flow $\hat{\mathbf{y}}_s$. The student network is the optical flow network used for inference, whereas the supervisor network is only used for training; this results in no additional computational cost for the testing time. In training time, we use the flow supervisor (FS) loss function $\mathcal{L}_{FS}$ to supervise the student flow $\hat{\mathbf{y}}_s$ with the teacher flow $\hat{\mathbf{y}}_{FS}$:

$$\mathcal{L}_{FS}(\theta) = \mathbb{E}_{d_s \sim p_s, d_u \sim p_u}[\ell_{sup}(d_s) + \alpha\ell_{FS}(d_u)], \tag{3}$$

where $\ell_{FS}(\cdot) = \rho(\hat{\mathbf{y}}_{FS} - \hat{\mathbf{y}}_s)$, α is a hyper-parameter weight and (d_s, d_u) are sampled data from (p_s, p_u). We use loss function $\mathcal{L}_{FS}$ for the student network to learn from both labeled and unlabeled data.

Separate Parameters. We empirically observed that the plain self-supervision (Fig. 2a) leads to divergence in semi-supervised optical flow learning. This undesirable behavior is also observed in siamese self-supervised learning, where preventing undesirable equilibria is important [6,10]. As our solution, we have the separate module, i.e., the flow supervisor to prevent the unstable learning behavior. Our flow supervisor is related to the predictor module in self-supervised learning work [6], which also prevents the unstable training. We also compare our design with the mean-teacher [10,33] with exponential moving average (EMA), and a fixed teacher [39] in Fig. 3, since these designs have been widely adopted in semi-supervised learning.

Passing Student Outputs. We design our supervisor model to have input nodes for student outputs. Thus, the teacher output flow is conditioned by the student output. Specifically, our teacher model includes a residual function $\Delta f_\phi(\cdot)$, such that $f_\phi(\mathbf{x}, \hat{\mathbf{y}}_s, \mathbf{h}_s) = \Delta f_\phi(\cdot) + \hat{\mathbf{y}}_s$. We realize this concept with the residual flow decoder in the RAFT [34] architecture.

In residual learning, it has been believed and shown that learning a residual function $\Delta f(\mathbf{x}) = f(\mathbf{x}) - \mathbf{x}$, instead of the original function $f(\mathbf{x})$, is better for deeper inference [11] or domain discrepancy modeling [23]. With residual teacher function Δf_ϕ, the flow supervisor loss is reformulated as:

$$\ell_{FS} = \rho(\hat{\mathbf{y}}_{FS} - \hat{\mathbf{y}}_s) = \rho(f_\phi(\hat{\mathbf{y}}_s) - \hat{\mathbf{y}}_s) = \rho(\Delta f_\phi(\hat{\mathbf{y}}_s)). \tag{4}$$

Relation of $f_\phi(\cdot)$ to a Meta Learner. Meta-learning [1,8] defines how to learn by learning an update rule $\Delta\theta^t$ within the parameter update $\theta^{t+1} \leftarrow \theta^t + \Delta\theta^t$. The residual function $\Delta f_\phi(\dots, \hat{\mathbf{y}}_s)$ is regarded as a meta learner predicting update rule $\Delta\theta^t$, conditioned by student predictions. Assuming ρ is the square function, learning by $\mathcal{L}_{FS}$ is equivalent to using the update rule $\Delta\theta^t = -2\frac{\partial \hat{\mathbf{y}}_s}{\partial \theta^t}^T \cdot \Delta f_\phi(\hat{\mathbf{y}}_s)$; where ϕ is the parameter of our flow supervisor. That is, the learning rule is learned by the supervisor parameter ϕ to supervise the student parameter θ.

3.4 Supervision

Learning supervisor parameters ϕ is important for supervising the student network. Basically, the supervisor learns to maximize the likelihood, e.g., $\log P(\mathbf{y} - \hat{\mathbf{y}}_s | \mathbf{x}_1, \mathbf{x}_2, \hat{\mathbf{y}}_s, \phi)$, where the student output $\hat{\mathbf{y}}_s$ is inferred from an augmented input $\tilde{\mathbf{x}}_1, \tilde{\mathbf{x}}_2$. First, it is natural to give the conditional knowledge from the labeled data p_s. For this purpose, we minimize $\mathcal{L}_{TS}$ – which stands for supervised teacher loss – to train the supervisor:

$$\mathcal{L}_{TS}(\phi) = \mathbb{E}_{(\mathbf{x}_1, \mathbf{x}_2, \mathbf{y}) \sim p_s}[\ell_{sup}(f_\phi(\mathbf{x}_1, \mathbf{x}_2, f_\theta(\tilde{\mathbf{x}}_1, \tilde{\mathbf{x}}_2)), \mathbf{y})]. \tag{5}$$

In addition to using the labeled data, we found that if a labeled dataset and an unlabeled dataset are distant, e.g., Things ↔ KITTI, using the unsupervised loss is especially effective. The unsupervised teacher loss $\mathcal{L}_{TU}$ on unlabeled data p_u is defined by:

$$\mathcal{L}_{TU}(\phi) = \mathbb{E}_{(\mathbf{x}_1, \mathbf{x}_2) \sim p_u}[\ell_{unsup}(f_\phi(\mathbf{x}_1, \mathbf{x}_2, \hat{\mathbf{y}}_s), \mathbf{x}_1, \mathbf{x}_2)]. \tag{6}$$

In the pretraining stage, we train the student model from scratch using the supervised loss $\mathcal{L}_{sup}$, resulting in a pretrained weight θ. In the fine tuning stage, we initialize ϕ with θ and jointly optimize θ and ϕ on labeled and unlabeled datasets. Formally, we use stochastic gradient descent to minimize

$$\mathcal{L}(\theta, \phi) = \mathcal{L}_{FS}(\theta) + \lambda_{TS}\mathcal{L}_{TS}(\phi) + \lambda_{TU}\mathcal{L}_{TU}(\phi), \tag{7}$$

with hyper-parameter loss weights λ_{TS} and λ_{TU}.

4   Experiments

4.1   Experimental Setup

Pretraining. Our pretraining stage follows the original RAFT [34]. We pretrain our student network with FlyingChairs [7] and FlyingThings3D [14] with random cropping, scaling, color jittering, and block erasing. The pretraining scheme includes 100k steps for FlyingChairs and additional 100k steps for FlyingThings3D, with the same learning rate schedule of RAFT, on which we base our network. For the supervised loss (Eq. 1), we use L_1 loss.

Flow Supervisor. The flow supervisor is implemented with the GRU update module of RAFT, which performs an iterative refinement process with the output flow of the previous step. At the start of the semi-supervised training phase, we initialize the supervisor model with the pretrained weights of the GRU update module. To match the student prediction from cropped inputs to the supervisor module with full resolution, i.e., privileged, we pad the student predictions with zero. In a training and testing phase, we use 12 iterations for both the student and supervisor GRUs.

Semi-supervised Dataset. To compare semi-supervised learning performance on Sintel [4] and KITTI [26], we follow the protocol [18], which utilizes the unlabeled portion, i.e., testing set, of each dataset for training; the difference is that we use a labeled dataset, e.g., FlyingThings3D, into training. Specifically, we use the unlabeled portion of Sintel for fine tuning on Sintel and unlabeled KITTI multiview dataset for fine tuning on KITTI; then the labeled splits are used for evaluation.

Optimization. We initialize our student and supervisor models with the pretrained weights, then minimize the joint loss (Eq. 7) for 100k steps. We use $\alpha = 1.0$, $\lambda_{TS} = 1.0$ and $\lambda_{TU} = 0$ by default and $\lambda_{TU} = 0.01$ for the Things + KITTI setting, unless otherwise stated. Detailed optimization settings and hyper-parameters are provided in the supplementary material and the code.

4.2   Empirical Study

Comparison to Semi-Supervised Baselines. In Table 1 and Fig. 3, we perform an empirical study, comparing ours with several baselines for semi-supervised learning. In the experiments, we use FlyingThings3D as the labeled data p_s and each target dataset as the unlabeled data p_u.

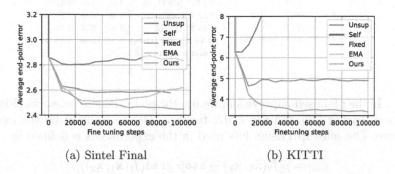

(a) Sintel Final   (b) KITTI

Fig. 3. Plots comparing finetuning stage. We use FlyingThings3D as labeled data, and each target dataset as an unlabled data. The EPEs are measured on unseen portion of data

Unsupervised Loss. An unsupervised loss is designed to learn optical flow without labels. Exploring the unsupervised loss is a good start for the research since we could expect a meaningful supervision signal from unlabeled images.

In the second row of Table 1, we report results by the unsupervised loss. We use the loss function in Eq. 2, which includes the census transform, full-image warping, smoothness prior, and occlusion handling as used in the prior work [30]. Unfortunately, the unsupervised loss function does not give a meaningful supervision signal

Table 1. Comparison to semi-supervised baselines. Semi-supervised baselines and ours are compared, as well as the supervised loss only (Sup) result. We use widely-used metrics in optical flow: end-point error (EPE) and ratio of erroneous pixels (Fl)

Method	Sintel		KITTI	
	Clean	Final	EPE	Fl-all (%)
Sup	1.46	2.80	5.79	18.79
Sup + Unsup	1.47	2.73	9.21	16.95
Sup + Self	diverged		diverged	
Sup + EMA	1.40	2.63	diverged	
Sup + Fixed	1.32	2.58	4.91	15.92
Sup + FS (Ours)	**1.30**	**2.46**	**3.35**	**11.12**

when jointly used with the supervised loss, resulting in a degenerated EPE on KITTI (5.79 → 9.21). Interestingly, applying the identical loss to our supervisor, i.e., $\mathcal{L}_{TU}$, results in a better EPE on KITTI (5.79 → 3.35), see also Table 3.

Self- and Teacher-Supervision. We summarize the results of the self-supervision and teacher-based methods in Table 1 and Fig. 3. The baseline models include the plain self-supervision (Self), the fixed teacher (Fixed), and the EMA teacher

Table 2. Comparison to optical flow approaches. We report a percentage of improvement over each baseline in the parentheses. We mark used datasets: FlyingChairs (C), FlyingThings (T), unlabeled KITTI (K), and AutoFlow (A) [31]

(a) Comparsion to SemiFlowGAN [20]

Data	Method	KITTI	
		EPE	Fl-all (%)
C	SFGAN [20]	17.19	40.82
C+K	SFGAN [20]	16.02 (−6.8%)	38.77 (−5.0%)
C+T	RAFT	5.79	18.79
T+K	RAFT + FS	**3.35 (−42.1%)**	**11.12 (−40.8%)**

(b) Comparsion to AutoFlow [31]

Method	Sintel		KITTI	
	Clean	Final	EPE	Fl-all (%)
RAFT† (C+T) [31]	1.68	2.80	5.92	–
RAFT (C+T)	1.46	2.80	5.79	18.79
RAFT† (A) [31]	1.95	2.57	4.23	–
RAFT + FS (Ours)	**1.30**	**2.46**	**3.35**	**11.12**

† model implemented by [31]

(EMA). In the plain self-supervision, we use the plain siamese networks (Fig. 2a). The fixed teacher [39] and the EMA teacher [33] are inspired by the existing literature. The self-supervision loss used in the experiments is defined by:

$$\ell_{\text{self}} = \rho[f_\theta(\tilde{\mathbf{x}}_1, \tilde{\mathbf{x}}_2) - \texttt{stop\_grad}(f_t(\mathbf{x}_1, \mathbf{x}_2))], \tag{8}$$

where f_t is the teacher network of each baseline: $t = \theta$ for plain self-supervision, $t = \text{EMA}(\theta)$ for mean teacher, and $t = \theta_{\text{pretrained}}$ for fixed teacher. The plain self-supervision (Self) quickly diverges during the early fine tuning step for both Sintel and KITTI. In the EMA teacher (EMA) results, more stable convergence is observed for Sintel, not KITTI. We speculate that this unstable convergence is caused by the domain gap between the unlabeled data and the labeled data; there exists a wider domain difference between FlyingThings3D (p_s) and KITTI (p_u) than the difference between FlyingThings3D (p_s) and Sintel (p_u), since KITTI is a real-world dataset, while Things and Sintel are both three-dimensional rendered datasets. When the fixed teacher (Fixed) is used, we can observe more stable learning. Our method (FS), enabling the supervisor learning along with the student, shows superior semi-supervised performance on both datasets than the EMA and the fixed teacher. We further analyze our method in the following sections.

Comparison to SemiFlowGAN [20]. We compare our method with the existing semi-supervised optical flow method [20] in Table 2a. SemiFlowGAN uses a domain adaptation-like approach by matching distributions of the error maps from each domain. Compared to SemiFlowGAN, our approach gives more direct supervision to optical flow predictions from the supervisor model. Here, we evaluate how much a supervised-only baseline, i.e., trained w/o KITTI, is able to be improved by exploiting the unlabeled target dataset, i.e. traind w/ KITTI. We can clearly observe much larger performance improvement (−6.8% vs. −42.1%) when our method is used.

Comparison to AutoFlow [31]. In Table 2b, we compare ours with AutoFlow, where our method shows better EPEs on both Sintel and KITTI. AutoFlow is devised to train a better neural network on target datasets by learning to generate data, as opposed to ours using semi-supervised learning. For instance, the

AutoFlow dataset, whose generator is optimized on Sintel dataset shows superiority over a traditional synthetic dataset, e.g., FlyingThings, in generalization on unseen target domains. On the other hand, our strategy is to utilize a synthetic dataset and an unlabeled target domain dataset by the supervision of the flow supervisor; it boosts performance on the target domain without labels.

Ablation Study. In Table 3, we compare ours with several alternatives.

Parameter Separation. Self-supervision with the shared network (see Self in Fig. 3) is unsuitable for semi-supervised optical flow learning. On the other hand, having the separate parameters for the supervisor network effectively prevents the divergence. This separation can be viewed as the predictor strategy in the self-supervised learning context [6]. We also analyze the separate network as a meta-learner, which learns knowledge specifically for supervision. We have shortly discussed this aspect in Sect. 3.3.

Table 3. Ablation experiments. We underline the final settings

Experiment		Sintel		KITTI	
		Clean	Final	EPE	Fl-all
Parameter	<u>on</u>	**1.30**	**2.46**	**3.35**	**11.12**
Separation	off	diverged		diverged	
Passing	<u>full</u>	1.30	2.46	3.35	11.12
Student	w/o res	1.34	2.50	6.16	12.34
Output	off	1.30	2.46	6.68	13.36
Shared	<u>on</u>	1.30	2.46	3.35	11.12
Encoder	off	1.33	2.58	3.80	12.03
Teacher	<u>TS</u>	**1.30**	**2.46**	4.69	14.48
Loss type	+TU	1.55	2.80	**3.35**	**11.12**
Teacher	<u>clean</u>	1.30	2.46	3.35	11.12
Input	aug	1.33	2.56	4.17	11.55

Passing Student Outputs $(\hat{\mathbf{y}}_s, \mathbf{h}_s)$. Our architecture passes the student output flow and internal state to the supervisor network to enable the supervisor to learn the residual function, as described in Eq. 4. In row 5 in Table 3, we show the results when we do not pass student outputs $(\hat{\mathbf{y}}_s, \mathbf{h}_s)$ to the teacher. Interestingly, the Sintel results remain the same even without passing student outputs. while the KITTI results benefit from passing student outputs. We ablate the residual connection from the network, while still passing student outputs to the supervisor (w/o res). In this case (w/o res), we can observe the better KITTI results over the no connection case (off), but worse than our full design. These results indicate that conditioning supervisor with the student helps find residual function $\Delta f_\phi(\hat{\mathbf{y}}_s) \approx \mathbf{y} - \hat{\mathbf{y}}_s$, especially on distant domains, i.e., Things $\leftrightarrow$ KITTI. Overall, passing with residual connection (full) performs consistently better.

Shared Encoder. Shared encoder design results in a better flow accuracy, as shown in Table 3. Our method uses the shared encoder design (Fig. 2b). Separating the encoder results in worse EPEs for Sintel and KITTI. Not only the accuracy, but it also results in a less efficient training pipeline due to the increased number of parameters by the encoder.

Teacher Loss Type. We propose to train the supervisor network with labeled and unlabeled data. Supervised teacher (TS) loss utilizes the labeled dataset for supervisor learning. In both datasets, TS improves the baseline performance. We additionally apply the unsupervised teacher loss (+TU), which results in better EPE in KITTI but is ineffective for Sintel. This is related to the results of pure unsupervised learning [30], where the loss is shown to be more effective on KITTI than on Sintel.

Virtual KITTI. With our method, we can utilize a virtual driving dataset, VKITTI [5], for training a better model for the real KITTI dataset. In Table 4, we show results obtained by VKITTI. In the supervised case,

Table 4. KITTI results of models trained on VKITTI [5]

Metric	Supervised		Semi-supervised
	RAFT	SepFlow [38]	RAFT+FS (ours)
EPE	3.64	2.60	**2.39**
Fl-all (%)	8.78	7.74	**7.63**

our base network (RAFT) shows 3.64 EPE on KITTI, and SeperableFlow [38] shows 2.60 EPE. In the semi-supervised case, our method leverages the unlabeled KITTI multiview set additional to VKITTI, and we train the RAFT network for 50k steps; the resulting network performs better on KITTI.

Supervisor vs. Student. In Fig. 4, we show the performance of the student and the supervisor networks by training steps. We use clean inputs for both the student and the supervisor networks for evaluation. Interestingly, we observe that the student is better than the supervisor during fine tuning. In addition, we could observe EPEs of the student and the supervisor are correlated, and

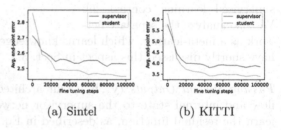

(a) Sintel   (b) KITTI

Fig. 4. Supervisor vs. student EPEs during semi-supervised fine tuning. EPEs measured on unseen portion of data

they are both improved by our semi-supervised training. In knowledge distillation, we can observe similar behavior [29], where a student model shows better validation accuracy than a teacher model.

4.3 Qualitative Results

We provide qualitative results on KITTI (Fig. 5, 6) and Sintel (Fig. 7). Since the KITTI dataset includes sparse ground truth flows, training by the ground truth supervision often results in incorrect results, especially in boundaries and deformable objects (e.g., person on a bike). Thus, in this case, we can expect better flows by exploiting semi-supervised methods. The Sintel Final dataset includes challenging blur, fog, and lighting conditions as shown in the examples.

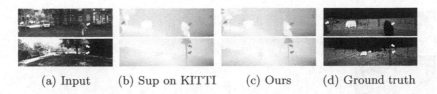

(a) Input   (b) Sup on KITTI   (c) Ours   (d) Ground truth

Fig. 5. Qualitative results on KITTI. We visualize optical flow predicted by **(b)** supervised on target dataset and **(c)** semi-supervised w/o target label. Note that sparse ground-truth **(d)** is not sufficient to make a clear boundary of objects (marked with arrows), while our method shows better results

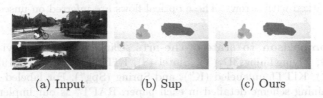

(a) Input   (b) Sup   (c) Ours

Fig. 6. Qualitative results on KITTI testing samples. We compare the supervised model (Sup) with the semi-supervised model (Ours). Both models exploit KITTI labels; ours utilizes additional unlabeled KITTI for fine tuning

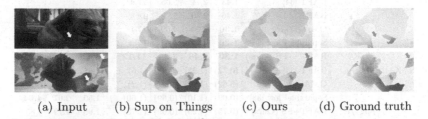

(a) Input   (b) Sup on Things   (c) Ours   (d) Ground truth

Fig. 7. Qualitative results on Sintel. We visualize optical flow predicted by **(b)** supervised on FlyingThings3D and **(c)** semi-supervised without target label. Though ours trained without target labels, it successfully adapts the pretrained model to the target domain. Improved areas are marked by arrows

Interestingly, the semi-supervision without a target dataset label helps improve the challenging regions, when our method is used.

In Fig. 8, we show results on DAVIS dataset [28] by the pretrained models and our fine tuned models; the dataset does not contain any optical flow ground truth. From the training set with 3,455 frames, we utilize 90% of frames for training and the rest for qualitative evaluation. Even though our fine tuning does not utilize ground truth, we can observe a clear positive effect in several challenging regions. Especially, our method improves blurry regions (e.g., moving hand of the dancer) and object boundaries.

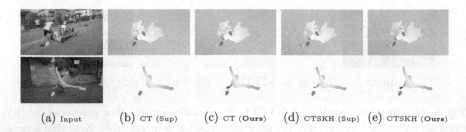

(a) Input   (b) CT (Sup)   (c) CT (Ours)   (d) CTSKH (Sup)   (e) CTSKH (Ours)

Fig. 8. Qualitative results on DAVIS dataset [28]. We fine tune each pretrained network (Sup) on Davis dataset by our semi-supervised method (Ours). Improved regions are marked with arrows. These optical flows are inferred on unseen portion of the dataset

Table 5. Comparison to state-of-the-arts. Data usage is abbreviated to FlyingChairs (C), FlyingThings3D (T), Sintel (S), KITTI (K), HD1K [19] (H), Sintel unlabeled (S^u), KITTI unlabeled (K^u), and Spring (Spg^u). For labeled datasets, we follow the training scheme detailed in each paper. $RAFT^{tf}$ is our implementation in TensorFlow

Labeled data	Unlabeled data	Method	Sintel (train)		KITTI (train)		Sintel (test)		KITTI (test)
			Clean	Final	EPE	Fl-all (%)	Clean	Final	Fl-all (%)
C+T	–	RAFT [34]	1.43	2.71	5.05	17.4	–	–	–
		$RAFT^{tf}$	1.46	2.80	5.79	18.8	–	–	–
		GMA [17]	**1.30**	2.74	4.69	17.1	–	–	–
		SeparableFlow [38]	**1.30**	2.59	4.60	15.9	–	–	–
	S^u/K^u	$RAFT^{tf}$+FS (Ours)	**1.30**	**2.46**	**3.35**	**11.12**	–	–	–
C+T+S+K+H	–	RAFT [34]	(0.77)	(1.27)	(0.63)	(1.5)	1.61	2.86	5.10
		GMA [17]	(0.62)	(1.06)	(0.57)	(1.2)	**1.39**	2.47	5.15
		SeparableFlow [38]	(0.69)	(1.10)	(0.69)	(1.60)	1.50	2.67	**4.64**
	Spg^u/K^u	RAFT+FS (Ours)	(0.75)	(1.29)	(0.69)	(1.75)	1.65	2.79	4.85
		GMA+FS (Ours)	(0.63)	(1.05)	(0.61)	(1.47)	1.43	**2.44**	4.95

4.4   Comparison to State-of-the-Arts

Experimental Settings. In this experiment we compare our method to the existing supervised methods. The biggest challenge in supervised optical flow is that we do not have ample ground truth flows for our target domains, e.g., 200 pairs labeled in KITTI. Thanks to our semi-supervised method, we can train with related videos for better performance on the target datasets. For GMA, we use $\alpha = 0.25$ (Sintel) and $\alpha = 0.05$ (KITTI).

Dataset Configuration. Results evaluated on the training sets of each dataset are experimented with the setting described in Sect. 4.1. On the other hand, the results on the test splits of the two benchmarks are obtained by justifiable external datasets for semi-supervised training. Though our method is able to utilize the unlabeled portion of Sintel, we bring another external set to avoid the relation to the testing samples, as follows. To assist Sintel performance, we use Spring (abbr. to Spg^u) [2], which is the 'open animated movie' by Blender Institute, similar to Sintel [3]. In Spring, we use the whole frames (frame no. 1-11,138) without any modification. Additionally, we use Sintel (train) with interval two as unlabeled. For KITTI, we additionally use KITTI multiview dataset, which does not contain ground truth optical flows; we use the training split of the dataset to avoid duplicated scenes with testing samples.

Results. In Table 5, we report the C+T result, which is a commonly used protocol to evaluate the generality of models. Since our method is designed to use unlabeled samples, our method exploits each target dataset – which is not overlapped with each evaluation sample – without ground truth. The results indicate we could achieve better accuracy than the supervised-only approaches. Interestingly, our approach performs better than the advanced architectures, i.e., GMA [17] and SeperableFlow [38], in the C+T category.

In 'C+T+S+K+H', we report the test results with the external datasets. In the KITTI test result where we have access to 200 labeled samples, using additional samples results in better Fl-all (5.10 → 4.85, 5.15 → 4.95). For Sintel, we test on two base networks: RAFT and GMA. In two networks, our method makes improvements on Sintel Final (test). However, our method does not improve accuracy on Sintel Clean set. That is because we use the external Spring dataset, which includes various challenging effects, e.g., blur, as Sintel Final, the student model becomes robust to those effects rather than clean videos. Note that, for Sintel test, our improvement is made by the video of a different domain which is encoded by a lossy compression, like most videos on the web.

4.5   Limitations

A limitation of our approach is that it depends on a supervised baseline, which is sometimes less preferable than an unsupervised approach. A handful of unsupervised optical flow researches have achieved amazing performance improvement. Especially, on KITTI (w/o target label), unsupervised methods have performed better than supervised methods, and the recent performance gap has been widened (EPE: 2.0 vs 5.0). Unfortunately, we observe that our method is not compatible with unsupervised baselines; the semi-supervised fine tuning of SMURF [30] with our method (T+K^u) results in a worse EPE (2.0 → 2.5) on KITTI. Thus, one of the future work lies upon developing a fine-tuning method to improve the unsupervised baselines.

Nonetheless, our work contributes to the research by ameliorating the limitation of a supervised method, suffering from worse generalization. A supervised method is often preferable than an unsupervised one for higher performance even without target labels; we show ours can be used in such cases. For example, on Sintel Final, ours shows better EPE (2.46) than the supervised one [34] (2.71) and the unsupervised method [30] (2.80).

5   Conclusion

We have presented a self-supervision strategy for semi-supervised optical flow, which is simple, yet effective. Our flow supervisor module supervises a student model, which is effective in the semi-supervised optical flow setting where we have no or few samples in a target domain. Our method outperforms various self-supervised baselines, shown by the empirical study. In addition, we show that our semi-supervised method can improve the state-of-the-art supervised models by exploiting additional unlabeled datasets.

Acknowledgments. This work was supported by the NRF (2019R1A2C3002833) and IITP (IITP-2015-0-00199, Proximity computing and its applications to autonomous vehicle, image search, and 3D printing) grants funded by the Korea government (MSIT). We thank the authors of RAFT, GMA, and SMURF for their public codes and dataset providers of Chairs, Things, Sintel, KITTI, VKITTI, and Spring for making the datasets available.

References

1. Bengio, Y., Bengio, S., Cloutier, J.: Learning a synaptic learning rule. Citeseer (1990)
2. Blender: Spring Open Movie. http://www.blender.org/press/spring-open-movie/
3. BlenderFoundation: Sintel, the durian open movie project. http://durian.blender.org/
4. Butler, D.J., Wulff, J., Stanley, G.B., Black, M.J.: A naturalistic open source movie for optical flow evaluation. In: Fitzgibbon, A., Lazebnik, S., Perona, P., Sato, Y., Schmid, C. (eds.) ECCV 2012. LNCS, vol. 7577, pp. 611–625. Springer, Heidelberg (2012). https://doi.org/10.1007/978-3-642-33783-3_44
5. Cabon, Y., Murray, N., Humenberger, M.: Virtual kitti 2 (2020)
6. Chen, X., He, K.: Exploring simple siamese representation learning. In: Proceedings of the IEEE/CVF Conference on Computer Vision and Pattern Recognition, pp. 15750–15758 (2021)
7. Dosovitskiy, A., et al.: Flownet: Learning optical flow with convolutional networks. In: Proceedings of the IEEE International Conference on Computer Vision, pp. 2758–2766 (2015)
8. Finn, C., Abbeel, P., Levine, S.: Model-agnostic meta-learning for fast adaptation of deep networks. In: International Conference on Machine Learning, pp. 1126–1135. PMLR (2017)
9. Ganin, Y., Lempitsky, V.: Unsupervised domain adaptation by backpropagation. In: International conference on machine learning, pp. 1180–1189. PMLR (2015)
10. Grill, J.B., et al.: Bootstrap your own latent: A new approach to self-supervised learning. arXiv preprint arXiv:2006.07733 (2020)
11. He, K., Zhang, X., Ren, S., Sun, J.: Deep residual learning for image recognition. In: Proceedings of the IEEE conference on computer vision and pattern recognition, pp. 770–778 (2016)
12. Hinton, G., Vinyals, O., Dean, J.: Distilling the knowledge in a neural network. arXiv preprint arXiv:1503.02531 (2015)

13. Hur, J., Roth, S.: Iterative residual refinement for joint optical flow and occlusion estimation. In: Proceedings of the IEEE Conference on Computer Vision and Pattern Recognition, pp. 5754–5763 (2019)
14. Ilg, E., Mayer, N., Saikia, T., Keuper, M., Dosovitskiy, A., Brox, T.: Flownet 2.0: Evolution of optical flow estimation with deep networks. In: Proceedings of the IEEE Conference on Computer Vision and Pattern Recognition, pp. 2462–2470 (2017)
15. Im, W., Kim, T.-K., Yoon, S.-E.: Unsupervised learning of optical flow with deep feature similarity. In: Vedaldi, A., Bischof, H., Brox, T., Frahm, J.-M. (eds.) ECCV 2020. LNCS, vol. 12369, pp. 172–188. Springer, Cham (2020). https://doi.org/10.1007/978-3-030-58586-0_11
16. Jaderberg, M., Simonyan, K., Zisserman, A., et al.: Spatial transformer networks. In: Advances in Neural Information Processing Systems, pp. 2017–2025 (2015)
17. Jiang, S., Campbell, D., Lu, Y., Li, H., Hartley, R.: Learning to estimate hidden motions with global motion aggregation. In: Proceedings of the IEEE/CVF International Conference on Computer Vision (ICCV), pp. 9772–9781 (October 2021)
18. Jonschkowski, R., Stone, A., Barron, J.T., Gordon, A., Konolige, K., Angelova, A.: What matters in unsupervised optical flow. arXiv preprint arXiv:2006.04902 (2020)
19. Kondermann, D., et al.: The hci benchmark suite: Stereo and flow ground truth with uncertainties for urban autonomous driving. In: Proceedings of the IEEE Conference on Computer Vision and Pattern Recognition Workshops, pp. 19–28 (2016)
20. Lai, W.S., Huang, J.B., Yang, M.H.: Semi-supervised learning for optical flow with generative adversarial networks. In: Advances in Neural Information Processing Systems, pp. 354–364 (2017)
21. Liu, P., Lyu, M., King, I., Xu, J.: Selflow: Self-supervised learning of optical flow. In: Proceedings of the IEEE Conference on Computer Vision and Pattern Recognition, pp. 4571–4580 (2019)
22. Liu, P., Lyu, M.R., King, I., Xu, J.: Learning by distillation: A self-supervised learning framework for optical flow estimation. IEEE Transactions on Pattern Analysis and Machine Intelligence (2021)
23. Long, M., Zhu, H., Wang, J., Jordan, M.I.: Unsupervised domain adaptation with residual transfer networks. arXiv preprint arXiv:1602.04433 (2016)
24. Mayer, N., et al.: What makes good synthetic training data for learning disparity and optical flow estimation? Int. J. Comput. Vision 126(9), 942–960 (2018)
25. Meister, S., Hur, J., Roth, S.: Unflow: Unsupervised learning of optical flow with a bidirectional census loss. In: Thirty-Second AAAI Conference on Artificial Intelligence (2018)
26. Menze, M., Geiger, A.: Object scene flow for autonomous vehicles. In: Proceedings of the IEEE Conference on Computer Vision and Pattern Recognition, pp. 3061–3070 (2015)
27. Novák, T., Šochman, J., Matas, J.: A new semi-supervised method improving optical flow on distant domains. In: Computer Vision Winter Workshop (2020)
28. Perazzi, F., Pont-Tuset, J., McWilliams, B., Van Gool, L., Gross, M., Sorkine-Hornung, A.: A benchmark dataset and evaluation methodology for video object segmentation. In: Computer Vision and Pattern Recognition (2016)
29. Stanton, S., Izmailov, P., Kirichenko, P., Alemi, A.A., Wilson, A.G.: Does knowledge distillation really work? arXiv preprint arXiv:2106.05945 (2021)

30. Stone, A., Maurer, D., Ayvaci, A., Angelova, A., Jonschkowski, R.: Smurf: Self-teaching multi-frame unsupervised raft with full-image warping. In: Proceedings of the IEEE/CVF Conference on Computer Vision and Pattern Recognition, pp. 3887–3896 (2021)
31. Sun, D., et al.: Autoflow: Learning a better training set for optical flow. In: Proceedings of the IEEE/CVF Conference on Computer Vision and Pattern Recognition, pp. 10093–10102 (2021)
32. Sun, D., Yang, X., Liu, M.Y., Kautz, J.: Pwc-net: Cnns for optical flow using pyramid, warping, and cost volume. In: Proceedings of the IEEE Conference on Computer Vision and Pattern Recognition, pp. 8934–8943 (2018)
33. Tarvainen, A., Valpola, H.: Mean teachers are better role models: Weight-averaged consistency targets improve semi-supervised deep learning results. arXiv preprint arXiv:1703.01780 (2017)
34. Teed, Z., Deng, J.: RAFT: recurrent all-pairs field transforms for optical flow. In: Vedaldi, A., Bischof, H., Brox, T., Frahm, J.-M. (eds.) ECCV 2020. LNCS, vol. 12347, pp. 402–419. Springer, Cham (2020). https://doi.org/10.1007/978-3-030-58536-5_24
35. Vapnik, V., Izmailov, R., et al.: Learning using privileged information: similarity control and knowledge transfer. J. Mach. Learn. Res. **16**(1), 2023–2049 (2015)
36. Yan, W., Sharma, A., Tan, R.T.: Optical flow in dense foggy scenes using semi-supervised learning. In: Proceedings of the IEEE/CVF Conference on Computer Vision and Pattern Recognition, pp. 13259–13268 (2020)
37. Yang, G., Ramanan, D.: Volumetric correspondence networks for optical flow. In: Advances in Neural Information Processing Systems, pp. 794–805 (2019)
38. Zhang, F., Woodford, O.J., Prisacariu, V.A., Torr, P.H.: Separable flow: Learning motion cost volumes for optical flow estimation. In: Proceedings of the IEEE/CVF International Conference on Computer Vision, pp. 10807–10817 (2021)
39. Zoph, B., et al.: Rethinking pre-training and self-training. arXiv preprint arXiv:2006.06882 (2020)

Flow Graph to Video Grounding for Weakly-Supervised Multi-step Localization

Nikita Dvornik[(✉)], Isma Hadji, Hai Pham, Dhaivat Bhatt, Brais Martinez, Afsaneh Fazly, and Allan D. Jepson

Samsung AI Center, New York, USA
n.dvornik@samsung.com

Abstract. In this work, we consider the problem of weakly-supervised multi-step localization in instructional videos. An established approach to this problem is to rely on a given list of steps. However, in reality, there is often more than one way to execute a procedure successfully, by following the set of steps in slightly varying orders. Thus, for successful localization in a given video, recent works require the actual order of procedure steps in the video, to be provided by human annotators at both training and test times. Instead, here, we only rely on generic procedural text that is not tied to a specific video. We represent the various ways to complete the procedure by transforming the list of instructions into a procedure flow graph which captures the partial order of steps. Using the flow graphs reduces both training and test time annotation requirements. To this end, we introduce the new problem of flow graph to video grounding. In this setup, we seek the optimal step ordering consistent with the procedure flow graph and a given video. To solve this problem, we propose a new algorithm - Graph2Vid - that infers the actual ordering of steps in the video and simultaneously localizes them. To show the advantage of our proposed formulation, we extend the CrossTask dataset with procedure flow graph information. Our experiments show that Graph2Vid is both more efficient than the baselines and yields strong step localization results, without the need for step order annotation.

Keywords: Procedures · Flow graphs · Instructional videos · Localization

1 Introduction

Understanding video content from procedural activities has recently seen a surge in interest with various applications including future anticipation [13,33], procedure planning [1,5], question answering [39] and multi-step localization [10,22,23,36,41]. In this work, we tackle multi-step localization, i.e., inferring

Supplementary Information The online version contains supplementary material available at https://doi.org/10.1007/978-3-031-19833-5_19.

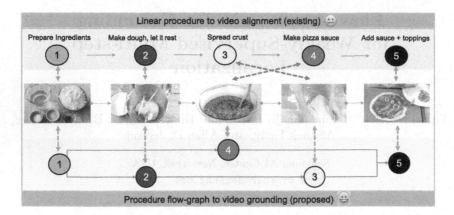

Fig. 1. Graph-to-Sequence Grounding. (top) instructional videos do not always strictly follow a prototypical procedure order (*e.g.*, recipe). (bottom) Therefore, we propose a new setup where procedural text is parsed into a flow graph that is consequently grounded to the video to temporally localize all steps using our novel algorithm.

the temporal location of procedure steps present in the video. Since fully-supervised approaches [12,21,36] entail expensive labeling efforts, several recent works perform step localization with weak supervision. The alignment-based approaches [4,10,29] are of particular interest here as for each video they only require the knowledge of step order to yield framewise step localization.

However, all such alignment-based approaches share a common issue. They all assume that a given procedure follows a strict order, which is often not the case. For example, in the task of making a pizza, one can either start with steps related to making dough, then steps involved in making the sauce, or vice-versa, before finally putting the two preparations together. Since the general procedure (*e.g.*, recipe) does not define a unique order of steps, the alignment-based approaches rely on human annotations to provide the exact steps order for each video. In other words, step localization via alignment requires using per-video step order annotations during inference, which limits the practical value of this setup.

To this end, we propose a new approach for step localization that does not rely on per-video step order annotation. Instead, it uses the general procedure description, common to all the videos of the same category (*e.g.*, the recipe of making pizza independent of the video sequence), to localize procedure steps present in any video. Figure 1 illustrates the proposed problem setup. We propose to represent a procedure using a flow graph [18,32], i.e., a graph-based procedure representation that encodes the partial order of instruction steps and captures all the feasible ways to execute a procedure. This leads us to the novel problem of multi-step localization from instructional videos under the graph-based setting, which we call flow graph to video grounding. To support the evaluation of our work we extend the widely used CrossTask dataset [41] with recipes and corresponding flow graphs. Importantly, in this work, the flow graphs are obtained by parsing procedural text (*e.g.*, a recipe) freely available online using an off-the-shelf parser, which makes the annotation step automatic and reduces the amount of human annotation even further.

To achieve our goal of step localization from flow graphs, we introduce a novel solution for graph-to-sequence grounding - Graph2Vid. Graph2Vid is an algorithm that, given a video and a procedure flow graph, infers the temporal location of every instruction step such that the resulting step sequence is consistent with the procedure flow graph. Our proposed solutions grounds each step in the video by: (i) expanding the original flow graph into a meta-graph, that concisely captures all topological sorts [37] of the original graph and (ii) applying a novel graph-to-sequence alignment algorithm to find the best alignment path in the metagraph with the given video. Importantly, our alignment algorithm has the ability to "drop" video frames from the alignment, in case there is not a good match among the graph nodes, which effectively models the no-action behavior. Moreover, our Graph2Vid algorithm naturally admits a differentiable approximation and can be used as a loss function for training video representation using flow graph supervision. As we show in Sect. 3, this can further improve step localization performance with flow graphs.

Contributions. In summary the main contributions of this work are fourfold.

1. We introduce flow graph to video grounding - a new task of multi-step localization in instructional videos given generic procedure flow graphs.
2. We extend the CrossTask dataset by associating procedure text with each category and parsing the instructions into a procedure flow graph.
3. We propose a new graph-to-sequence grounding algorithm (i.e., Graph2Vid) and show that Graph2Vid outperforms baseline approaches in step localization performance and efficiency.
4. We show Graph2Vid can be used as a loss function to supervise video representations with flow graphs.

The code will be made available at https://github.com/SamsungLabs/Graph2Vid.

2   Related Work

Sequence-to-Sequence Alignment. Sequence alignment has recently seen growing interest across various tasks [2–4,6,7,11,14,34], in particular, the methods seeking global alignment between sequences by relying on Dynamic Time Warping (DTW) [4,6,7,14,30]. Some of these methods propose differentiable approximations of the discrete operations (i.e., the min operator) to enable training with DTW [7,14]. Others, allow DTW to handle outliers in the sequences [3,24,25,27,31,35]. Of particular note, the recently proposed Drop-DTW algorithm [10] combines the benefits of all those methods as it allows dropping outliers occurring anywhere in the sequence, while still maintaining the ability of DTW to do one-to-many matching and enabling differentiable variations. However, as most other sequence alignment algorithms, Drop-DTW matches sequence elements with each other in a linear order, not consider possible element permutations within each sequence. In this work, we propose to extend Drop-DTW to work with partially ordered sequences. This is achieved by representing one of the sequences as a directed cyclic graph, thereby relaxing the strict order requirement.

Graph-to-Sequence Alignment. Aligning graphs to sequences is an important topic in computer science. One of the pioneering works in this area proposed a Dynamic Programming (DP) based solution for pattern matching where the target text is represented as a graph [26]. Many follow up works extend this original idea via enhancing the alignment procedure. Examples include, admitting additional dimensions in the DP tables for each alternative path [19], improving the efficiency of the alignment algorithm [16,28] or explicitly allowing gaps in the alignment, thereby achieving sub-sequence to graph matching [17]. A common limitation among all these methods is the assumption that only *one* of the paths in the graph aligns to the query sequence, while alternative paths and their corresponding nodes do not appear in the query sequence. Therefore, the goal in graph-to-sequence *alignment* is to find the specific path that best aligns with the query sequence. In contrast, we consider the novel problem of graph-to-sequence *grounding*. In particular, we consider the task where all nodes in the graph have a match in the query sequence and therefore our task is to ground each node in the sequence, while finding the optimal traversal in the graph that best aligns with the sequence. This problem is strictly harder than graph-to-sequence alignment and can not be readily tackled by the existing algorithms.

Video Multi-step Localization. The task of video multi-step localization has gained a lot of attention in the recent years [10,20,22] particularly thanks to instructional videos dataset availability that support this research area [36,40, 41]. The task consists of determining the start and end times of all steps present in the video, based on a description of the procedure depicted in the video. Some methods rely on full supervision using fine-grained labels indicating start and end times of each step (*e.g.,* [12,21,36]). However, these methods require extensive labeling efforts. Instead, other methods propose weakly supervised approaches where only steps order information is needed to yield framewise step localization [4,8,10,15,29,41]. However, these methods lack flexibility as they require *exact* order information to solve the step localization task. Here, we propose a more flexible approach where only partial order information, as given by a procedure flow graph, is required to localize each step. In particular, given a procedure flow graph, describing all possible step permutations that result in successful procedure execution, our method localizes the steps in a given video, by automatically grounding the steps of the graph in the video.

3   Our Approach

In this section, we describe our approach for flow graph to video grounding. We start with a motivation and formal definition of our proposed flow graph to sequence grounding problem. Next, we describe in detail our proposed solution to tackle the task of video multi-step localization using flow graphs.

3.1   Background

Ordered Steps to Video Alignment. If the true order of steps in a video (i.e., as they happen in a video) is given, the task of step grounding reduces to a well-defined problem of steps-to-video alignment, which can be solved with some existing sequence alignment method. In particular, the recent Drop-DTW [10] algorithm suits the task particularly well thanks to a unique set of desired properties: (i) it operates on sequences of continuous vectors (such as video and step embeddings) (ii) it permits one-to-many matching, allowing multiple video frames to match to a single step , and (iii) it allows for dropping elements from the sequence, which in turn allows for ignoring video frames that are unrelated to the sequence of steps. In Drop-DTW, the alignment is formulated as minimization of the total match cost between the video clips and instruction steps. It is solved using dynamic programming and can be made differentiable (see Alg. 1 in [10]). That is, given a video, $\mathbf{x}$, and a sequence of steps, $\mathbf{v}$, Drop-DTW returns the alignment cost, c^*, and alignment matrix, M^*, indicating the correspondences between steps and video segments.

Procedure Flow Graphs. In more realistic settings, procedure steps for many processes, such as cooking recipes, are often given as a set of steps in a partial order. Specifically, the partial ordering dictates that certain steps need to be completed before other steps are started, but that other subsets of steps can be done in any order. For example, when thinking of making a salad, one can cut tomatoes and cucumbers in one order or the other, however we are certain that both ingredients must be cut before mixing them into the salad. This is an example of a procedure with partially ordered steps; i.e., there are multiple valid ways to complete the procedure, all of which can be conveniently represented with a flow graph.

A procedure flow graph is a Directed Acyclic Graph (DAG) $\mathcal{G} = (V, E)$, where V is a set of nodes and E is a set of directed edges. Each node $v_i \in V$ represents a procedure step and an edge $e_j \in E$ connecting v_k and v_l declares that the procedure step v_k must be completed before v_l begins in any instruction execution. If a node v_k has multiple ancestors, all the corresponding steps must be completed before beginning instruction step v_k. In this work, we assume that $\mathcal{G}$ has a single root and sink nodes. For convenience, we automatically add them to the graph if they are not already present. From the definition of the flow graph, it follows that every topological sort [37] of the nodes in $\mathcal{G}$ (see Fig. 2, step 2) is a valid way to complete the procedure. This is an important property that forms the foundation of our Graph2Vid approach, described next.

Flow Graphs to Video Grounding. We define the task of grounding a flow graph $\mathcal{G}$ in a video $\mathbf{x} = [x_i]_{i=1}^{N}$, where N is the total number of frames, as the task of finding a disjoint set of corresponding video segments, $s_l = [x_i]_{i=start_l}^{end_l}$ for each node $v_l \in \mathcal{G}$ of the flow graph, such that the resulting segmentation conforms to the flow graph. Specifically, in a pair of resulting video segments, (s_i, s_j), segment s_i can only occur before s_j in the video if the corresponding node n_i is a predecessor of n_j in the flow graph $\mathcal{G}$. In this work, we assume that every procedure step v_l appears in the video exactly once.

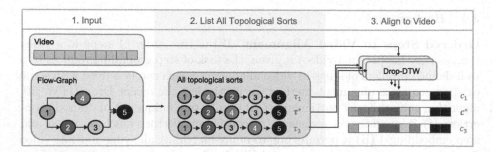

Fig. 2. Brute-force approach for flow-graph to video grounding. Given the flow-graph, the brute-force approach explicitly considers every topological sort and aligns it to the video with Drop-DTW independently, making the inference inefficient.

3.2   Graph to Video Grounding - A Brute-Force Approach

Before introducing our method, we first discuss a naive solution to the problem. As previously mentioned, we know that the procedure execution in the video follows some topological sort of the flow graph, $\mathcal{G}$. Thus, one can derive an algorithm for flow graph to video grounding by explicitly considering all the topological sorts of $\mathcal{G}$ as depicted in Fig. 2. More specifically, one can generate all topological sorts of the flow graph, try aligning each of them to the video, and select the best alignment as step grounding. This essentially reduces the problem of flow graph grounding to sequence-to-sequence alignment which can be solved using Drop-DTW. The procedure would iterate over all topological sorts $\tau \in \mathcal{T}$ of the flow graph $\mathcal{G}$ and align a sequence of nodes (re-ordered according to the topological sort) $\mathbf{v}^{\tau} = [v_{\tau_i}]_{i=1}^{|V|}$ to the video sequence, and pick the alignment M^* with the topological sort τ^* that has the minimum alignment cost c^*:

$$c^* = \text{Drop-DTW}(\mathbf{v}^{\tau^*}, \mathbf{x}); \quad \tau^* = \arg\min_{\tau \in \mathcal{T}} \text{Drop-DTW}(\mathbf{v}^{\tau}, \mathbf{x}) \qquad (1)$$

While simple, this approach has one crucial downside - its efficiency. As we show in Sect. 3.5, this algorithm has exponential complexity and becomes infeasible even for small flow graphs. Thus, we need a more scalable solution to the problem.

3.3   Graph2Vid - Our Approach

In this section we present a new, more efficient approach for flow graph to video grounding, that we term Graph2Vid (see the overview in Fig. 3). Graph2Vid operates in two stages: **(i)** given the flow graph, $\mathcal{G}$, we pack all the topological sorts of $\mathcal{G}$ into a novel compact graph-based representation $\mathcal{S}$ (that we call the tSort graph); **(ii)** we align the obtained tSort graph, $\mathcal{S}$, to the video, $\mathbf{x}$, using a proposed graph-to-video alignment algorithm, which we dub Graph-Drop-DTW. To compute the alignment we embed the procedure text in each node of the graph, v_{τ}, and the clips of the video sequence, x_i, using a model pre-trained on the large HowTo100M dataset [22]. The key to superior efficiency of Graph2Vid is the interplay between the tSort graph structure and the graph-to-video alignment algorithm, which allows for polynomial complexity of flow graph to video grounding[1]. Moreover, Graph2Vid allows for a differentiable approximation that can be used for training neural networks. In the following, we explain how to construct the tSort graph, $\mathcal{S}$, from the original flow graph, $\mathcal{G}$, how to extend Drop-DTW to perform graph-to-sequence alignment, and finally, how to use Graph2Vid as a differentiable loss function.

Creating the tSort Graph. As we have shown previously, grounding a flow-graph, $\mathcal{G}$, to a video requires considering all the topological sorts of $\mathcal{G}$, yet their explicit consideration is infeasible due to the exponential number of topological sorts. We note that the cause of such inefficiency is the redundancy and high overlaps between the topological sorts. This motivates us to encode all topological sorts into a tSort graph, $\mathcal{S}$, that effectively shares the common parts of different topological sorts and provides a more compact representation. Figure 3 illustration how for a simple flow graph input we construct the tSort graph encoding all the topological sorts (Fig. 2). Each path from root to sink in the tSort graph, $\mathcal{S}$, spells out a topological sort of $\mathcal{G}$. Thus, listing all root to sink paths in $\mathcal{S}$ is equivalent to listing all topological sorts of the original flow graph, $\mathcal{G}$.

Algorithm 1 gives a procedure for constructing the tSort graph $\mathcal{S}$. The first step to constructing the tSort graph is to connect all the nodes on separate threads in the original flow-graph $\mathcal{G}$ (i.e., like nodes $\{4\}$ and $\{2,3\}$ in Fig. 3) with undirected edges. Since the instruction steps on separate threads may follow one after another in an actual instruction execution, thus connection between them must exist. These connections yield an augmented graph, $\mathcal{G}_{aug}$. Then, in this augmented graph $\mathcal{G}_{aug}$, we run Breat First Search (BFS) traversal to find all the paths that lead from the root to the sink node of $\mathcal{G}_{aug}$ and conform to the original flow-graph $\mathcal{G}$. During the BFS traversals, the paths that have visited the same set of nodes so far are merged together and mapped into a single node in the tSort graph $\mathcal{S}$. Merging the traversals with the same set of visited nodes enables the tSort graph to represent all topological sorts efficiently. For more details on the tSort graph construction and a more efficient implementation description, we refer the reader to supplemental material.

Graph to Sequence Alignment Using Graph-Drop-DTW. Having access to the tSort graph, $\mathcal{S}$, (whose every path from root to sink is a valid topological sort of the flow graph, $\mathcal{G}$), we can cast flow graph to video grounding as graph-to-video alignment problem [26]. In this case, the graph-to-video alignment finds a traversal of the graph $\mathcal{S}$ that best aligns with the given video $\mathbf{x}$. Importantly, directly aligning the tSort graph to a video discovers the optimal path in the graph and the best alignment of this path to the video *simultaneously* (see Fig. 3, step 3). This is in contrast to the naive solution in Sect. 3.2, which uses sequence alignment as a subroutine to find the optimal topological sort.

---

[1] The tSort graph is polynomial for an assumed subset of flow graphs with a fixed maximum number of threads.

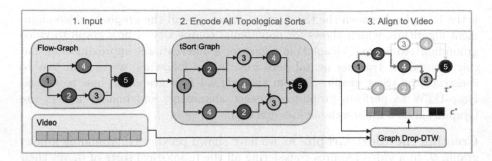

Fig. 3. Flow-graph to video grounding with Graph2Vid. Given the the procedure flow-graph and a video as input our method packs all topological sorts into a tSort Graph and then uses Graph-Drop-DTW to align it to the given video, producing video segmentation and the optimal topological sort τ^*.

Algorithm 1. tSort-graph Construction

1: **Inputs:** $\mathcal{G}$ - flow graph, s - root node in $\mathcal{G}$
2: $\mathcal{G}_{aug} = \text{aug}(\mathcal{G})$ ▷ *connect the nodes on parallel threads*
3: $E_{tSort} = []$ ▷ *init edge set of the tSort-graph*
4: $q = \text{queue}((s, \oslash))$ ▷ *init BFS queue*
5: **while** q **do**
6: 　　$v, P = q.\text{pop}()$ ▷ *active node v, set of visited nodes P*
7: 　　**for** v_d in get_descendants$(v, \mathcal{G}_{aug})$ **do**
8: 　　　　$P_d = P.\text{add}(v_d)$ ▷ *extend the visited nodes set*
9: 　　　　**if** get_predecessors$(v_d, \mathcal{G})$ in P **then** ▷ *the path P_d conforms to $\mathcal{G}$*
10: 　　　　　　$q.\text{append}((v_d, P_d))$
11: 　　　　　　$E_{tSort}.\text{add}(((v, P), (v_d, P_d)))$ ▷ *add edge to tSort graph*
12: $\mathcal{S} = \text{build\_graph\_from\_edges}(E_{tSort})$ ▷ *build the tSort graph*
13: **Output:** $\mathcal{S}$

In order to solve graph to video grounding, the graph-to-sequence alignment algorithm must have the following properties: **(i)** operate on continuous vectors, **(ii)** permit one-to-many matching and **(iii)** allow for unmatched sequence elements. To the best of our knowledge, a graph-to-sequence alignment algorithm with such properties does not exist. However, Drop-DTW [10] for sequence alignment satisfies all 3 criteria (see Sect. 3.1) Thus, we propose a new algorithm - Graph-Drop-DTW - which is an extension of Drop-DTW for graph-to-sequence alignment. We base Graph-Drop-DTW on Alg.1 in [10] and modify the dynamic programming recursion to take into account the graph structure as follows:

$$D_{i,j}^+ = C_{i,j} + \min\{\min_{k \in A(i)}\{D_{k,j-1}\}, D_{i,j-1}\} \tag{2}$$

$$D_{i,j}^- = d_j^x + D_{i,j-1}$$
$$D_{i,j} = \min\{D_{i,j}^+, D_{i,j}^-\},$$

where $C_{i,j}$ is the cost of matching the i-th node of the graph to the j-th video clip, and d_j^x is the cost of dropping the j-th video clip and not matching it to any node in the graph. We follow [10] and define $C_{i,j}$ as negative log-likelihood of the video clip j belonging to step i, and compute the drop cost d_j^x as a 30-th bottom percentile of $C_{i,j}$. Different from Drop-DTW, when computing $D_{i,j}^+$, Graph-Drop-DTW takes into consideration all the predecessors of the node i, (i.e., $k \in A(i)$) and selects the one minimizing the alignment cost. Intuitively, the minimum operation over the predecessors, $\min_{k \in A(i)}$, in Eq. (2), dynamically finds the traversal of the graph that aligns with the video best. Similar to Drop-DTW, Graph-Drop-DTW outputs the alignment cost c^* and the alignment path M^*, representing the optimal matching between the nodes of the input graph S and the video clips of $x_i \in \mathbf{x}$. It is important to note that Graph-Drop-DTW can only drop elements from the sequence (as a direct extension of Alg.1 in [10]) and does not support dropping nodes from the graph.

Graph2Vid for Flow Graph Grounding. Finally, Graph2Vid can be defined as the complete pipeline that chains tSort graph creation and its alignment to the video. Precisely, given the procedure flow graph, $\mathcal{G}$, and the video sequence, $\mathbf{x}$, Graph2Vid first transforms $\mathcal{G}$ into the tSort graph, $\mathcal{S}$, then aligns the graph, $\mathcal{S}$, to the video, $\mathbf{x}$, using Graph-Drop-DTW. This effectively provides the desired correspondence between every node, $v_i \in \mathcal{G}$, and a video segment in $\mathbf{x}$, that conforms to the flow graph, $\mathcal{G}$.

3.4   Graph2Vid for Representation Learning

We now describe a differentiable approximation of Graph2Vid to learn video representations using flow graphs as the source of supervision. To use Graph2Vid as a loss function, we must be able to backpropagate gradients with respect to the video input. That is, Graph-Drop-DTW must be differentiable. A differentiable version of Graph-Drop-DTW can be obtained by simply using a soft approximation of the min operator (*e.g.*, [7,14]) in Eq. (2). Here, we substitute the min in Eq. 2 with the smooth-min operator [14] defined as

$$\mathrm{smoothMin}(\boldsymbol{x}; \gamma) = \boldsymbol{x} \cdot \mathrm{softmax}(\boldsymbol{x}/\gamma) = \frac{\boldsymbol{x} \cdot e^{\boldsymbol{x}/\gamma}}{\sum_j e^{x_j/\gamma}}, \tag{3}$$

where $\gamma > 0$ is a hyper-parameter controlling the trade-off between smoothness and the error of the approximation.

With this differentiable version of Graph2Vid, we can use the matching cost between a video and it's corresponding flow graph as a training signal. Intuitively, the lower the cost of matching of a video to its corresponding procedure flow graph, the better are the learned representations. Specifically, we define the Graph-Drop-DTW loss as the cost of grounding the flow graph, $\mathcal{G}$, to video, $\mathbf{x}$:

$$\mathcal{L}_G(Z, \mathbf{x}) = c^* = \text{Graph-Drop-DTW}(\mathcal{G}, \mathbf{x}). \tag{4}$$

As we show in Sect. 4, using $\mathcal{L}_G$ for weakly-supervised learning (with flow-graph supervision) improves step localization performance.

3.5   On the Algorithm's Complexity

To develop some intuition on both the size of the generated tSort-graphs, and on the speed-up over the naive approach, we consider simple model problems where the flow graph, $\mathcal{G}$, consists of T separate, linearly-ordered threads, with $n_1, n_2, \ldots, n_T \geq 1$ nodes in each thread, for a total of $\sum_{t=1}^{T} n_t = n$ steps. As we show in supplemental, in this case, the number of topological sorts of $\mathcal{G}$, $N_{ts}(\mathcal{G})$ grows exponentially with n and has the complexity $O(T^n)$. On the other hand, the number of nodes in the tSort graph $\mathcal{S}$, $|V_S|$, is polynomial in the number of nodes n, i.e., $|V_S| = O(Tn^T)$ which is better than exponential growth in $N_{ts}(\mathcal{G})$, provided that T is not too large. As shown in the supplemental, the asymptotic speedup of Graph2Vid over the brute-force approach can be roughly described by the ratio $N_{ts}(\mathcal{G})/|V_s|$ which is still exponential in n, giving a large advantage to Graph2Vid. This is further confirmed in Sect. 4.5, where Graph2Vid is orders of magnitude faster than the brute-force approach on real procedure flow-graphs.

3.6   Creating Flow Graph from Procedural Text

To construct flow graphs from procedural text,we considered two automated alternatives; namely, a rule-based and a learning-based approach. In addition, we considered a manual approach, where we explicitly define nodes and edges.

Rule-Based Graph Parsing. Starting from regular procedural instructions, we first extract relevant text entities from each step description, including action verbs, direct and prepositional objects as suggested in [32]. Next, we define a set of rich semantic rules for the graph constructor to connect the text entities. Once edges are defined using those entities, flow graphs are collapsed into coarse sentence-level graphs to be used in our experiments.

Learning-Based Graph Parsing. Using the same procedural instructions, we consider a learning based approach, which relies on two steps. First, we identify 10 named entities using the the tagger of [38]. Second, we used the parser proposed recently in [9] to automatically find edges between the named entities defined in the first step. Once again, we finally collapse the fine-grained flow graphs into coarse sentence-level graphs as done with the rule-based parser.

   A detailed description of both approaches is in the supplemental material.

4   Experiments

To demonstrate the strengths of the proposed Graph2Vid algorithm, we first present our dataset construction in Sect. 4.1. Then we describe the metrics used to evaluate the task of multi-step localization from graphs as well as the adopted baselines in Sect. 4.2. Finally, we summarize our results in Sects. 4.3 through 4.5.

4.1   Dataset Construction

To evaluate our new formulation of graph-to-video grounding using the proposed Graph2Vid approach, we need a dataset with procedure steps captured in flow graphs and corresponding Ground Truth (GT) start and end times for each node in these graphs. To this end, we extend the widely used CrossTask datast [41] following three main steps: (i) For each procedure class (*e.g.*, *Build floating shelves* or *Making pancakes*), we grab the procedure text from the web[2] (ii) We extract flow graphs from the procedural text following the methods described in Sect. 3.6, such that each node in the flow graph corresponds to a step from the procedure text. (iii) Finally, we manually find correspondence between nodes in the graph and step instructions provided with the original datasets. These correspondences are used to associate the original GT temporal annotations of each step with nodes in our flow graph. These GT temporal annotations, now associated with our graph nodes, are used to evaluate our model on the task of multi-step localization. Importantly, these annotations are only necessary for evaluation, and not for training or inference.

4.2   Metrics and Baselines

We evaluate the performance of our Graph2Vid approach on multi-step localization using two different metrics: (i) **Framewise accuracy (Acc.)** [36], which is defined as the ratio between the number of frames assigned the correct step label (not including background) and the total number of frames, and (ii) **Intersection over Union (IoU)** [40], which is defined as the sum of the intersections between the predicted and ground truth time intervals for each step label divided by the sum of their unions.

As we are the first to tackle multi-step localization under this new paradigm of flow graph to video grounding, we consider three increasingly strong baselines for comparisons. (i) **Bag of steps.** In this baseline, we consider every steps as being a node in a separate thread in a graph (i.e., no graph structure or order is imposed). (ii) **Linear Procedure.** Here, we read the instructions extracted from the procedure text linearly and assume this order as the default ordering of steps. (iii) **GT Step Sequence.** This is the *upper bound* on our Graph2Vid; it uses the ground truth step order (i.e., as they happen in each video) provided with the dataset. For baseline (i) we use the proposed Graph-Drop-DTW to obtain a segmentation as we treat the bag of steps as a disconnected graph. On the other hand, in baselines (ii) and (iii), we use the Drop-DTW algorithm [10] to obtain the segmentations, which we chose for two main reasons. First, this algorithm directly relates to the proposed Graph-Drop-DTW. Second, Drop-DTW is currently state-of-the-art on CrossTask for step localization [10].

4.3   Graph2Vid for Step Localization

We begin by evaluating the proposed Graph2Vid technique as an inference time method for step localization in instructional videos. For this purpose, we follow

---

[2] We find the procedure text of CrossTask in www.wikihow.com.

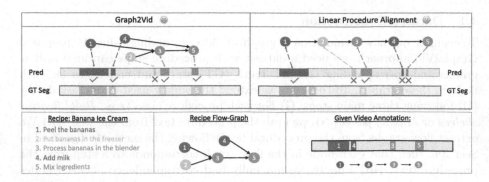

Fig. 4. Graph2Vid vs Linear Procedure Alignment for step localization on CrossTask. Given a video of making Banana Ice Cream (bottom), we compare video segmentation (into steps) produced by both methods. Graph2Vid (top-left) localizes all the present recipe steps by grounding the flow-graph into the video, while aligning linear recipe sequence to the video (top-right) fails in 2 out of 4 steps. This is because the order of instruction in the video (bottom-right) is different from the linear recipe, however it conforms to the flow-graph and thus can be grounded by Graph2Vid. Both methods incorrectly predict the step "2", that is actually not present in the video.

previous work [10,22] and rely on video and text features extracted from a model pre-trained on the HowTo100M dataset [23]. First, the results in Table 1 show better performance of the "Linear Procedure" baseline compared to the "Bag of Steps". This indicates that treating the recipe as a linear sequence of steps (i.e., having some prior on the order of steps) allows for better step localization than treating the recipe as unordered set of steps. However, treating the recipe as a flow graph (automatically extracted using the learning-based parser of Sect. 3.6) and grounding it in the video with Graph2Vid yields superior localization performance. This confirms the advantage of using the more flexible graph structure of the recipe for step localization. See Fig. 4 for an illustration of how Graph2Vid takes advantage of the nonlinear flow-graph structure in an example from the dataset. Unfortunately, there is still a large gap in performance between Graph2Vid and our upper bound, which relies on ground-truth ordered steps provided by human annotators. Closer examination of these results revealed that this gap is largely attributed to the fact that the GT of CrossTask does not conform to the assumed recipe flow graph structure, which we use in our Graph2Vid formulation. Specifically, while the flow graphs assume that each step happens once across the video, the GT of CrossTask allows for repeated steps (*e.g.,* [cut tomato, cut cucumber, cut tomato, mix ingredients]), where these repetitions are often a consequence of video post-production.

4.4   Graph2Vid for Representation Learning

Here, we show the benefits of using the differentiable approximation of Graph2Vid for weakly-supervised representation learning. We start from the

Table 1. Graph2Vid as an inference time procedure.

Inference method	Acc.↑	IoU ↑
Graph2Vid (ours)	**24.8**	**16.8**
Linear Procedure [10]	22.3	15.1
Bag of Steps	20.5	13.7
GT Step Sequence [10]	32.4	21.2

Table 2. Graph2Vid as a training loss.

Training method	Acc. ↑	IoU ↑
Graph2Vid (ours)	**26.3**	**19.1**
Linear Procedure + Drop-DTW	25.0	16.6
Bag of Steps + Soft Clustering	25.4	17.3
Pre-trained Features [22]	25.3	17.1
GT Step Seq. + Drop-DTW	35.7	25.3

same video and text features used in Sect. 4.3 and train a two-layer multi-layer perceptron (i.e., MLP) on top of the video representation. During training, we assume no access to ground-truth ordered step sequences, but only to the task label (*e.g.*, making pizza) and its corresponding flow graph. The flow graph is obtained automatically from the procedure text description of the task using the Table 1learning-based graph parser descibed in Sect. 3.6. Here, we compare Graph2Vid for representation learning with two other methods: **(i)** procedure to video alignment with Drop-DTW [10] (i.e., "Linear Procedure + Drop-DTW"), and **(ii)** aligning video to a set of instruction steps using soft clustering (i.e., "Bag of Steps + Soft Clustering"). We elaborate on these baselines in the supplementary material.

Once again, the results in Table 2 speak in favor of the proposed Graph2Vid approach, which better benefits from training compared to the considered baselines. Interestingly, training with "Linear Procdure" does slightly worse than no training at all, indicating that aligning the video to a potentially out-of-order sequences, which is often the case for a fixed instruction list, results in a poor training signal. In contrast, allowing Graph2Vid to infer the optimal topological sort of the flow-graph for aligning with the video results in a better training signal and improves video representations. Finally, using the GT ordered steps for training - a much richer source of supervision - yields best overall performance, however at the price of extra labeling effort.

4.5 Ablation Study

Here we evaluate the role of the flow graph parser and study the inference speed of our proposed Graph2Vid.

Role of the Flow Graph Parser. To better understand the connection between the flow graph construction method and Graph2Vid localization performance, we compare the two different parsers described in Sect. 3.6 as well as graphs obtained from manual annotation. As expected, the results summarized in Table 3, show that graphs from the rule-based parser yield performance slightly inferior to the manually generated graphs. Surprisingly, the flow-graphs from the learning-based parser do better than the manually annotated flow-graphs on CrossTask. After visually comparing the flow graphs produced by learning-based parser to the manual annotations, we realize that the former sometimes "misses" the edges present in the manual graph. This essentially allows for more flexible step ordering when aligning to a video, which benefits step localization on the CrossTask dataset.

This is because many CrossTask videos depict procedures that do not conform to the manually labeled flow graph, due to the post-editing of the videos. We provide more detailed analysis of this matter in Supplemental.

Table 3. Graph2Vid using different flow graph parsers.

Method	Acc.↑	IoU ↑
Manual Annotation	24.8	16.8
Rule-based Parser	24.3	16.3
Learning-based Parser	**25.3**	**17.1**

Evaluation of Execution Time. Here, we evaluate the speed of Graph2Vid for inference on CrossTask and compare it to running the brute force solution for flow graph grounding that considers all topological sorts explicitly (see Sect. 3.2). The flow graphs in CrossTask (obtained using the learning-based parser) have an average of 8.6 nodes and 2.7 separate threads. Such graphs, on average, produce 1,700 topological sorts and generate tSort graphs, $\mathcal{S}$, with about 60 nodes. With such compact tSort graphs, Graph2Vid takes ≈ 57 ms to ground a flow graph to a video. In contrast, the brute-force procedure requires $\approx 3.2 * 10^4$ ms, which is almost 3 order of magnitudes slower than Graph2Vid. This result speaks decisively in favor of our Graph2Vid approach for flow-graph to video grounding and confirms our theoretical derivations in Sect. 3.5.

5   Conclusion

In summary, we introduced a new formulation for step localization in instructional videos using procedure flow graphs. In particular, we proposed the novel task of flow graph to video grounding, which relies on task level procedure description to yield a step-wise segmentation of instructional videos. To this end, we rely on automatically generated *task-level* procedure flow graphs for step localization instead of relying on manually annotated, *per-video* step sequences. This effectively makes the proposed solution more scalable and practical. To solve the task of flow graph to video alignment, we developed a new graph-alignment-based algorithm - Graph2Vid - that demonstrates superior localization performance and efficiency compared to baselines. In addition, we could improve video representations by training with flow graphs as supervisory signal and using Graph2Vid as a loss function.

We believe that flow graphs are a more natural and informative representation of procedural activities, compared to linear instructions. Moreover, procedure flow graphs are only needed at the task level, rather than on a per video bases. As such, we believe the proposed formulation to hold a great promise in minimizing labeling efforts and defines new avenues for further research.

Acknowledgements. We thank Ran Zhang for the help with flow graph creation and processing.

References

1. Bi, J., Luo, J., Xu, C.: Procedure planning in instructional videos via contextual modeling and model-based policy learning. In: Proceedings of the International Conference on Computer Vision (ICCV) (2021)
2. Cai, X., Xu, T., Yi, J., Huang, J., Rajasekaran, S.: DTWNet: A dynamic time warping network. In: Advances in Neural Information Processing Systems (NeurIPS) (2019)
3. Cao, K., Ji, J., Cao, Z., Chang, C., Niebles, J.C.: Few-shot video classification via temporal alignment. In: Proceedings of the IEEE Conference on Computer Vision and Pattern Recognition (CVPR) (2020)
4. Chang, C., Huang, D., Sui, Y., Fei-Fei, L., Niebles, J.C.: D3TW: Discriminative differentiable dynamic time warping for weakly supervised action alignment and segmentation. In: Proceedings of the IEEE Conference on Computer Vision and Pattern Recognition (CVPR) (2019)
5. Chang, C.Y., Huang, D.A., Xu, D., Adeli, E., Fei-Fei, L., Niebles, J.C.: Procedure planning in instructional videos. In: Proceedings of the European Conference on Computer Vision (ECCV) (2020)
6. Chang, X., Tung, F., Mori, G.: Learning discriminative prototypes with dynamic time warping. In: Proceedings of the IEEE Conference on Computer Vision and Pattern Recognition (CVPR) (2021)
7. Cuturi, M., Blondel, M.: Soft-DTW: A differentiable loss function for time-series. In: International Conference on Machine Learning (ICML) (2017)
8. Ding, L., Xu, C.: Weakly-supervised action segmentation with iterative soft boundary assignment. In: Proceedings of the IEEE Conference on Computer Vision and Pattern Recognition (CVPR) (2018)
9. Donatelli, L., Schmidt, T., Biswas, D., Köhn, A., Zhai, F., Koller, A.: Aligning actions across recipe graphs. In: Proceedings of the 2021 Conference on Empirical Methods in Natural Language Processing (2021)
10. Dvornik, N., Hadji, I., Derpanis, K.G., Garg, A., Jepson, A.: Drop-DTW: Aligning common signal between sequences while dropping outliers. In: Advances in Neural Information Processing Systems (NeurIPS) (2021)
11. Dwibedi, D., Aytar, Y., Tompson, J., Sermanet, P., Zisserman, A.: Temporal cycle-consistency learning. In: Proceedings of the IEEE Conference on Computer Vision and Pattern Recognition (CVPR) (2019)
12. Caba Heilbron, F., Victor Escorcia, B.G., Niebles, J.C.: ActivityNet: A large-scale video benchmark for human activity understanding. In: Proceedings of the IEEE Conference on Computer Vision and Pattern Recognition (CVPR) (2015)
13. Girdhar, R., Grauman, K.: Anticipative Video Transformer. In: Proceedings of the International Conference on Computer Vision (ICCV) (2021)
14. Hadji, I., Derpanis, K.G., Jepson, A.D.: Representation learning via global temporal alignment and cycle-consistency. In: Proceedings of the IEEE Conference on Computer Vision and Pattern Recognition (CVPR) (2021)
15. Huang, D., Fei-Fei, L., Niebles, J.C.: Connectionist temporal modeling for weakly supervised action labeling. In: Proceedings of the European Conference on Computer Vision (ECCV) (2016)
16. Jain, C., Zhang, H., Gao, Y., Aluru, S.: On the complexity of sequence to graph alignment. J. Comput. Biol. 27(4), 640–654 (2020)
17. Kavya, V.N.S., Tayal, K., Srinivasan, R., Sivadasan, N.: Sequence alignment on directed graphs. J. Comput. Biol.?: J. Comput. Mol. Cell Biol. 261, 53–67 (2019)

18. Kiddon, C., Ponnuraj, G.T., Zettlemoyer, L., Choi, Y.: Mise en place: Unsupervised interpretation of instructional recipes. In: Proceedings of the Conference on Empirical Methods in Natural Language Processing (EMNLP) (2015)
19. Lee, C., Grasso, C., Sharlow, M.F.: Multiple sequence alignment using partial order graphs. Bioinformatics 18(3), 452–464 (2002)
20. Luo, H., et al.: UniVL: A unified video and language pre-training model for multimodal understanding and generation. arXiv preprint arXiv:2002.06353 (2020)
21. Ma, M., Fan, H., Kitani, K.M.: Going deeper into first-person activity recognition. In: Proceedings of the IEEE Conference on Computer Vision and Pattern Recognition (CVPR) (2016)
22. Miech, A., Alayrac, J.B., Smaira, L., Laptev, I., Sivic, J., Zisserman, A.: End-to-End Learning of Visual Representations from Uncurated Instructional Videos. In: Proceedings of the IEEE Conference on Computer Vision and Pattern Recognition (CVPR) (2020)
23. Miech, A., Zhukov, D., Alayrac, J.B., Tapaswi, M., Laptev, I., Sivic, J.: HowTo100M: Learning a Text-Video Embedding by Watching Hundred Million Narrated Video Clips. In: Proceedings of the International Conference on Computer Vision (ICCV) (2019)
24. Müller, M.: Information Retrieval for Music and Motion. Springer-Verlag, Berlin, Heidelberg (2007). https://doi.org/10.1007/978-3-540-74048-3
25. Nakatsu, N., Kambayashi, Y., Yajima, S.: A longest common subsequence algorithm suitable for similar text strings. Acta Inf. 18(2), 17–19 (1982)
26. Navarro, G.: Improved approximate pattern matching on hypertext. Theoret. Comput. Sci. 237(1), 455–463 (2000)
27. Needleman, S.B., Wunsch, C.D.: A general method applicable to the search for similarities in the amino acid sequence of two proteins. J. Mol. Biol. 48(3), 443–453 (1970)
28. Rautiainen, M., Mäkinen, V., Marschall, T.: Bit-parallel sequence-to-graph alignment. Bioinformatics 35(19), 3599–3607 (2019)
29. Richard, A., Kuehne, H., Iqbal, A., Gall, J.: NeuralNetwork-Viterbi: A framework for weakly supervised video learning. In: Proceedings of the IEEE Conference on Computer Vision and Pattern Recognition (CVPR) (2018)
30. Sakoe, H., Chiba, S.: Dynamic programming algorithm optimization for spoken processing recognition. In: IEEE International Conference on Acoustics, Speech and Signal Processing (ICASSP), vol.26, pp. 43–49 (1978)
31. Sakurai, Y., Faloutsos, C., Yamamuro, M.: Stream monitoring under the time warping distance. In: International Conference on Data Engineering (ICDE) (2007)
32. Schumacher, P., Minor, M., Walter, K., Bergmann, R.: Extraction of procedural knowledge from the web: A comparison of two workflow extraction approaches. In: Proceedings of the 21st International Conference on World Wide Web (2012)
33. Senner, F., Yao, A.: Zero-shot anticipation for instructional activities (2019)
34. Sermanet, P., et al.: Time-contrastive networks: Self-supervised learning from video. In: IEEE International Conference on Robotics and Automation (ICRA) (2018)
35. Smith, T.F., Waterman, M.S.: Identification of common molecular subsequences. J. Mol. Biol. 147(1), 195–197 (1981)
36. Tang, Y., et al.: COIN: A large-scale dataset for comprehensive instructional video analysis. In: Proceedings of the IEEE Conference on Computer Vision and Pattern Recognition (CVPR) (2019)

37. Wikipedia: Topological sorting – Wikipedia, the free encyclopedia. https://en.wikipedia.org/w/index.php?title=Topological%20sorting&oldid=1062117596. Accessed 07 Mar 2022
38. Yamakata, Y., Mori, S., Carroll, J.: English recipe flow graph corpus. In: Proceedings of the 12th Language Resources and Evaluation Conference (2020)
39. Yang, A., Miech, A., Sivic, J., Laptev, I., Schmid, C.: Just Ask: Learning to Answer Questions from Millions of Narrated Videos. In: Proceedings of the International Conference on Computer Vision (ICCV), (2021)
40. Zhou, L., Xu, C., Corso, J.J.: Towards automatic learning of procedures from web instructional videos. In: AAAI Conference on Artificial Intelligence (2018)
41. Zhukov, D., Alayrac, J.B., Cinbis, R.G., Fouhey, D., Laptev, I., Sivic, J.: Cross-task weakly supervised learning from instructional videos. In: Proceedings of the IEEE Conference on Computer Vision and Pattern Recognition (CVPR) (2019)

Deep 360° Optical Flow Estimation Based on Multi-projection Fusion

Yiheng Li[1], Connelly Barnes[2], Kun Huang[1], and Fang-Lue Zhang[1(✉)] [iD]

[1] School of Engineering and Computer Science, Victoria University of Wellington,
Wellington, New Zealand
{Yiheng.Li,Kun.Huang,Fanglue.Zhang}@vuw.ac.nz
[2] Adobe Research, Seattle, USA

Abstract. Optical flow computation is essential in the early stages of the video processing pipeline. This paper focuses on a less explored problem in this area, the 360° optical flow estimation using deep neural networks to support increasingly popular VR applications. To address the distortions of panoramic representations when applying convolutional neural networks, we propose a novel multi-projection fusion framework that fuses the optical flow predicted by the models trained using different projection methods. It learns to combine the complementary information in the optical flow results under different projections. We also build the first large-scale panoramic optical flow dataset to support the training of neural networks and the evaluation of panoramic optical flow estimation methods. The experimental results on our dataset demonstrate that our method outperforms the existing methods and other alternative deep networks that were developed for processing 360° content.

Keywords: Optical flow · 360° video · Spherical image projection

1 Introduction

If we take a sphere representing all viewing directions for 360° images and remove one point from it, then there is no projection of the resulting surface to a 2D plane that is both an equal area map and angle-preserving (conformal). This is because the sphere is not developable [10], as is well-known from cartography. This mathematical fact led to classical research into mesh parameterizations such as [28,30] that trade off between competing goals like area and angle-preservation when mapping textures on spherical surfaces. In this research, we were initially motivated to discover good projections for optical flow learning for 360° videos, which remains an interesting and open question in this field. We investigated three different projections from the sphere to the plane: cylindrical and cube-map, which are conformal within each chart, and equirectangular,

Supplementary Information The online version contains supplementary material available at https://doi.org/10.1007/978-3-031-19833-5_20.

which is neither area- nor angle-preserving. However, to our surprise, our experiments did *not* seem to indicate that any of our projections is always better than the others, but rather that these projections make *complex tradeoffs* in optical flow accuracy that appear to depend jointly on the input image and the mathematical properties of each projection.

Since empirically no single projection appears to always be best, we therefore propose to learn optical flow using multiple projections: we learn to fuse the complementary information into a single final optical flow on the sphere. We find that such learned fusion of multi-projection optical flows consistently outperforms the single-projection optical flows that were fused. We thus propose that multi-projection optical flow with fusion can be an important principle for 360-degree optical flow, even though more remains to be discovered in future work about e.g. the desired mathematical properties of good projections. Since there are no existing large-scale datasets with ground truth panoramic optical flow to learn the full field-of-view (FOV) features, we also build the first 360° optical flow dataset that contains various scenes and dynamic objects, including around 6000 panoramic frames for training our deep models.

Besides the above issue due to the mathematical properties of projections for 360° optical flow, there are common challenges with narrow FoV videos such as robustness to outliers, illumination changes, and possible large displacements, which have been well addressed in existing non-360° deep optical flow deep models [7,14,31,37,40]. Although such motion models are formulated on 2D regular grids with convolutions that do not inherently deform according to distortion or area changes in the projection, we can still utilize them as strong backbone models to generate accurate complementary regions for different projections. To make the maximum use of their pre-trained models that can handle complex dynamic objects, we did not use spherical kernels [6] to modify their convolutional layers, as we found the modified receptive field of such kernels led to worse results when finetuning the backbone models using our datasets.

In summary, this paper makes the following contributions: 1. We introduce a fusion framework for learning 360° optical flow, which learns to fuse the complementary optical flow prediction results generated using different projections; 2. We apply common map projection techniques to make two spherical image projection methods, namely tri-cylinder projection and cube padding projection that are complementary to equirectangular projection in terms of distorted regions and performance under fusion; 3. We build a novel 360° optical flow dataset with ground truth optical flow data with various camera paths and dynamic objects.

2   Related Work

This section reviews prior work in the relevant domains of optical flow estimation, datasets for training deep models, and 360° image and video processing.

Optical Flow Estimation. Optical flow shows the motion of objects in a video by a dense vector map pointing to the corresponding pixels between frames. The traditional methods mostly rely on feature constancy and local spatial coherence to solve the problem in an optimization framework [11,20–22,36]. In the era of end-to-end deep learning, the advances in optical flow estimation are driven by deep models [38]. The work of FlowNet [7] built a solid foundation for optical flow prediction using deep networks. They use FlowNetSimple to learn optical flow directly from adjacent frame pairs and use FlowNetCorrelation to learn the correlation between the patch-level features of the pair of input frames. FlowNet2 [14] presents some improvements based on FlowNet by proposing a stacked architecture and training schemes that benefit the convergence of the training process. PWC-Net [37] proposed to use Pyramid, Warping, and Cost volume to simplify the network structure and achieve high performance in optical flow estimation. RAFT [40] uses Recurrent All-Pairs Field Transforms that apply all-pairs correlation information into the neural network. In contrast, the above models only use nearby patches for correlation information for saving memory. Some other works focus on unsupervised learning schemes [18,19,24,42], fusing flows from multiple frames [32], and joint learning of optical flow and occlusions [13], aiming to train networks with the objective from view synthesis [45]. Despite promising results, generalizing these methods beyond narrow FOV videos remains challenging.

Optical Flow Dataset. Current optical flow prediction methods treat optical flow estimation as a supervised learning task that requires a considerable amount of data for training. As the real-world optical flow data is hard to access, most datasets are synthetic and rendered by Blender, while few of them are collected by camera and LIDAR. Sintel [3] is derived from a 3D movie to provide thousands of image pairs with dense ground truth optical flow. Wulff et al. [43] further extend it to two versions, Clean and Final, which contains RGB albedo and visual effects such as motion blur and fog, respectively. FlyingChairs [7] is generated by a set of 3D chairs models and applies the random 2D affine transformation to the scene. The idea was then expanded to generate FlyingThings3D [23] from the assets published in Stanford's ShapeNet, where random motions were applied on the dynamic objects. KITTI [8] [25] dataset was collected from real-world by cameras and LIDAR installed on a car. However, due to the device limitation, their optical flow is sparse, especially for the natural background where the LIDAR could not provide valid depth information. To address the sparsity issue of the KITTI dataset, Mayer et al. released a dataset called Driving [23], which renders a naturalistic city from the perspective of a driving car to generate dense optical flow maps. Moreover, for the convenience of nonrigid and softly articulated motion analysis, Monkaa [23] is designed to resemble Sintel using cartoon animations. A small scale dataset of 360° optical flow was proposed recently by Yuan and Richardt [46], which can only be used for evaluation due to its limited size. To support the training of 360° optical flow estimation networks, a new dataset is needed in this domain.

360° Image and Video Processing 360° images and videos have been attracting increasing attention from computer vision and graphics researchers. Due to the special representation of 360° images, dedicated methods were developed for the analysis and processing tasks, such as depth estimation [41], saliency detection [27,48], edit propagation [47], and video stabilization [16,39]. With the recent development of immersive technologies, researchers have been working on the specific problems of panoramic video-based applications, such as automatic 360° navigation/piloting [12,15], 360° video assessment [17], and immersive video editing [29]. The lack of reliable temporal correspondences that are globally consistent hinders many potential applications of 360° video generation. Our method is proposed to fill that gap.

The majority of current convolutional networks were developed for coping with perspective projection onto a planar camera sensor. Researchers proposed several solutions to adopt convolutions on spherical images to facilitate the feature extraction and interpretation by the deep networks. A representative method, namely SphereNet [6,44], changes the perceptual field of their convolutional kernels according to the latitude on the equirectangular domain. However, changing the kernels of 2D optical flow networks to spherical kernels may degrade the effect of the pre-trained models, as shown in our experiments. The kernel transform technique [35] was also considered in this field to let the convolutional layers learn how to transform the spherical kernels to the pre-trained weights on regular kernels that were initially trained by perspective images. However, the current optical flow networks all have a large number of layers, causing an impractical computation and memory cost to learn to transform all the layers. Projecting the spherical images to cube maps can avoid the distortion issues when utilizing deep neural networks, as in 360° saliency detection [5]. However, after testing with cubemap-based projection, we found the inconsistency of the predicted results along the cube face boundaries can not be trivially addressed, which also inspires us that using any single projections would meet more or fewer issues in certain regions. We thus propose to fuse optical flow results predicted using different projections to utilize their complementary information.

3   Dataset Generation

Due to the lack of ground truth data [1] of 360° optical flow, existing optical flow estimation networks could not be appropriately trained for 360° videos. We thus build a dataset with ground truth panoramic optical flow maps by rendering synthetic 360° videos of dynamic 3D scenes.

3.1   Optical Flow Generation

Two assumptions are made when generating panoramic optical flows when rendering a 3D scene, which are commonly followed by other optical flow datasets [23]. Firstly, all the visible points that appear on a frame can ideally be seen on the next frame. Secondly, the geometry of rendered objects is not deformed. Denote a pixel position as p, its position on the corresponding 3D object O [34] can be calculated using its model transformation matrix M that represents the object motion and the camera projection matrix P by $O = M^{-1}P^{-1}I$. For the successive frame, assume M' and P' represent its model matrix and camera matrix, respectively, the corresponding image pixel positions for the point O on the 3D object can be obtained by $I' = P'M'O$. In equirectangular projection, optical flow needs to be transformed into spherical coordinates from a 3D point $(x, y, z)^T$ on the unit sphere in the camera space by:

$$\theta' = \text{atan}\left(\frac{z'}{x'}\right), \quad \phi' = \text{atan}\left(\frac{y'}{\sqrt{(x')^2(z')^2}}\right) \tag{1}$$

From this, we can obtain the optical flow vectors $(\triangle\theta, \triangle\phi)$ in spherical coordinates. We can easily convert and store these in an equirectangular projection-based representation. More details are included in the supplementary materials.

3.2 3D Scenes

We built our panoramic RGB and optical flow frames using two types of scenes:

City Scene. We designed the City scene to resemble the data with similar properties as KITTI [8] and Driving [23]. The city's layout is automatically procedurally generated, and over 300 vehicles are randomly moving in the city. We enable collision detection for all the objects in the scene to ensure that it can avoid the situations of object-object and object-camera interpenetration. For the pre-training and preliminary experiments, we built two subsets named City1000UR and City100UR, which contain 1011 and 102 up-right frames for fine-tuning and testing. We divide the whole 3D city into two parts, where half is used for generating training data and the other half for the validation and testing data. We then generated City2000, City200, and City100 datasets, where the camera is rotated within 45° , containing 2000, 217, and 138 frames, respectively.

Equirectangular FlyingThings Scene. We designed the EquirectFlyingThings scene to resemble FlyingChairs [7] and FlyingThings3D [23]. In this scene, objects are randomly distributed around the camera. In our implementation, we choose car models from Stanford's ShapeNet dataset [4], which contains complex mesh shapes and textures. Compared to FlyingThings3D, the Equirect-FlyingThings dataset contains more objects in the scene because the camera takes panoramic photos. We rendered 300 objects to fill in the content and scale them to a suitable size. We also apply random translation and rotation to those objects. Furthermore, we change the camera rotation direction every 20 frames to keep randomness without camera shake. We built EFT2000, EFT200, and EFT100 datasets, and each of them contains 2211, 199, and 99 image pairs.

For our final models, we take the City2000 and EFT2000 as training datasets, while the City200 and EFT200 are used for validation. The final testing is performed on the City100 and EFT100 datasets.

4 Multi-Projection Fusion

To maximally leverage existing narrow FOV pre-trained models while minimizing the impact of various distortions that occur in spherical projections, we propose

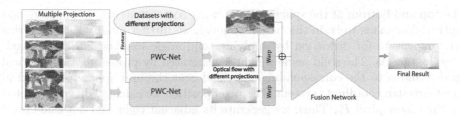

Fig. 1. Our multi-projection fusion method for estimating 360° optical flow

to use different methods to project the spherical images to planar images and feed them to finetune the models. A fusion layer is finally built to combine the transformed optical flow results for the final 360° optical flow.

We first perform preliminary experiments to select the best baseline model to finetune and predict the optical flow with equirectangular projections. We adopt the widely used models FlowNet2 [14] and PWC [37], and the most recent state-of-the-art method RAFT [40] to finetune on our 360° dataset using equirectangular projection. We found that PWC achieved the highest performance and the equirectangular representation is the best single projection for optical flow estimation. Because our experiments indicate that fused models always perform no worse (and in fact, better) than single projections, we choose PWC as our baseline model and use it to finetune the optical flow prediction model for each projection. In addition, we also modified all the PWC-Net's convolutional layers to Spherical convolutional kernels as in [6]. However, the experimental results show that the finetuning with spherical convolutions cannot achieve a good performance due to kernel shape changes from the original pre-trained PWC model. More results are demonstrated in later sections.

4.1 Projections for Spherical Images

Here, we investigate the performance of the deep models when feeding 2D images projected from the spherical domain using different kinds of projections. To utilize the pre-trained 2D deep models, ideally we would wish for the panoramic view to be an isometry to the original spherical surface, after making at least one cut. This ideal projection does not exist as the sphere is not developable, so distortion is necessary. In our experiments, we thus explore different mapping methods. It is also worth noting that we take the optical flow C^0 and C^1 continuity as another important consideration because we want the neural network to keep the integrity of moving objects. Some violations of these e.g. C^0 everywhere and C^1 almost everywhere may be acceptable given the tolerance of convolutional networks to various local transformations.

Equirectangular Projection. For 360° video, equirectangular projection is the most popular way to map a spherical surface to a 2D rectilinear plane. It can keep both C^0 and C^1 continuity in the optical flow map except for the boundary areas, which can be addressed by the circular padding scheme of CNNs. However, it is not conformal and introduces large distortions due to excessively sampling the top and bottom of the sphere. When using equirectangular frame pairs and optical flow maps to train the baseline model, we further modify the loss terms to compensate for distortion by applying solid angle weights onto their pixel-wise loss terms. The solid angle weight is generated by projecting the spherical grid θ and ϕ to the corresponding x, y, and z at the unit sphere presented in the Cartesian coordinate system. The pixel position we calculated is represented as the center pixel P_c. Then, we generate its adjacent right and downside pixel position P_r and P_d. Next, we calculate the area covered by each pixel S by:

$$P = (P_r - P_c) \times (P_d - P_c), \ S = \sqrt{P_x^2 + P_y^2 + P_z^2} \tag{2}$$

The covered area is used as the pixel-wise weight term in the loss function to reduce the effect caused by oversampling in training and testing.

Tri-cylindrical Projection. Unlike equirectangular projection, cylindrical projections preserve angle but are not equal-area. We use the Mercator projection to transform our equirectangular images to cylindrical images by converting the coordinate (θ_e, ϕ_e) to cylindrical coordinate (θ_c, h_c) by:

$$\theta_e = \theta_c, \quad \phi_e = 2\tan^{-1}(e^l) - \frac{\pi}{2} \tag{3}$$

Here, l is a value related to latitude in cylindrical coordinate. The inverse conversion between the two coordinates can be done using the following formula:

$$\theta_c = \theta_e, \quad h_c = \ln(\tan(\phi_c) + \sec(\phi_c)) \tag{4}$$

For a given cylindrical coordinate (θ_c, h_c), we use its corresponding equirectangular pixel to find the target pixel using its flow vector and convert the target pixel to cylindrical coordinates by Eq. 4 for obtaining the cylindrical optical flow. Since the Mercator projection generates a much larger area for the regions of high latitude, causing an even more serious distortion and oversampling problem, we just convert a limited vertical field of view to cylinders where the area change is less extreme (90° in our experiment). To ensure that every part of the spherical surface has an equal contribution, we propose to stack three cylindrical projection images together, where each cylinder to project is aligned with one of the X, Y, and Z-axis, as shown in Fig. 2.

To ensure a fair comparison, the solid angle weights for all the pixels are again generated using the same approach as in the equirectangular image. However, as we stack some pixels three times in the same image, we have to ensure every pixel is calculated only once. We use the distances between the spherical pixels and the equator of each cylinder to decide which view to use for that point. Intuitively, if a pixel is closer to one equator of a cylinder, the distortion should be less, leading to a more accurate result. After applying such a mask, the normalized weight map for our tri-cylindrical projection is shown in Fig. 2.

Cube-Padding Projection. Cube maps are another common representation of 360° images, with the advantages of using perspective images to represent a

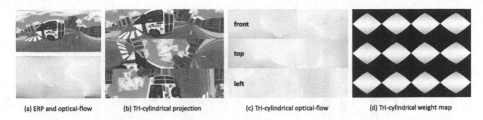

(a) ERP and optical-flow   (b) Tri-cylindrical projection   (c) Tri-cylindrical optical-flow   (d) Tri-cylindrical weight map

Fig. 2. A tri-cylindrical projection example. Note that different projections provide similar appearance with perspective images for different regions. The weight map is masked after applying solid angle weights to ensure every pixel is just calculated once.

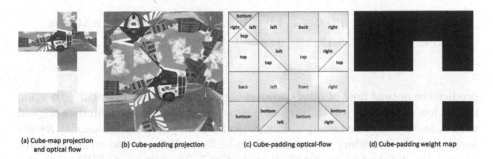

(a) Cube-map projection
and optical flow   (b) Cube-padding projection   (c) Cube-padding optical-flow   (d) Cube-padding weight map

Fig. 3. The 360° image and its optical flow projected by our cube-padding approach and the weight map applied on the loss functions.

panoramic image. Within each face of the cube, the projection is angle-preserving but not area preserving, and is suitable for the pre-trained model to be further finetuned. A drawback of the original cube map is that adjacency information is lost if the zero values fill the space out of the cross formed by the six connected cube faces. To ensure global C^0 continuity of the optical flow, i.e., connecting the outer boundary of the six faces to their neighboring faces in the cube, we repeatedly pad the faces to stitch the six faces into one picture, keeping the spatial continuity based on the original cross layout.

The layout of the faces is shown in Fig. 3, where some faces are rotated and trimmed to ensure the C^0 continuity along the boundaries. The drawback of this projection is that the optical flow can not keep C^1 continuity because the optical flow is projected onto image planes of different cameras, leading to the direction changes along the face boundaries. Thus, although using this kind of projection to finetune the baseline model can give a certain level of improvement, it does not outperform the equirectangular-based model in our later experiments. We use perspective projections to convert the spherical pixels to cube map faces for producing cube-padding projection results.

4.2 Fusion from Multiple Projections

We observe that the models trained by different projections provide complementary results in different regions. The equirectangular projection model can better

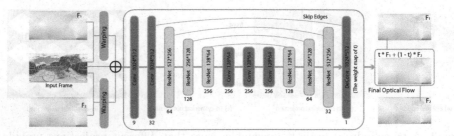

Fig. 4. Fusion network structure.

Table 1. Performance on City100UR using the finetuned models.

Model	FlowNet2	PWC-Net	PWC-Sph	RAFT-12	RAFT-24	RAFT-48
EPE	4.15	**3.17**	3.80	5.12	4.93	4.72

predict the optical flow of pixels around the equator. The cylindrical projection model has advantages at the top and bottom regions using the cylinders aligned with X and Z axis. The cube-padding projection can produce high-quality results besides all the boundary regions of the cube faces. Here we use error heatmaps to visualize different error distributions in Fig. 5. The minimum EPE value presented here shows that the prediction can be improved if appropriately blended with these estimations.

To utilize the advantages of different projections, we develop a fusion network to blend the result. The fusion network is a U-Net [33] with ResNet layers [9] to learn a confidence parameter t. The model structure is shown in the following table. The ResEncoder and ResDecoder are based on the ResNet structure shown is the Fig. 4. In addition, we take the Mish [26] as our activation function. The learnt confidence parameter is used to blend two models' predictions by: $P_{final} = t * P_a + (1-t) * P_b$, where a and b represent the predictions using different projection methods. More specifically, the prediction results are converted to equirectangular frame representations before fed to the network. Then the input frame will be concatenated with the warped frames by the two predicted optical flow maps before entering the convolutional layers. From the experiment results, fusing any two of the three models based on different projections can generate significantly better results than using an individual projection, showing the effectiveness of our fusion scheme for 360° optical flow estimation.

5 Experiments

We implement our method by utilizing state-of-the-art optical flow estimating models. In the preliminary experiments, we fine-tuned three state-of-the-art neural network structures: FlowNet2 [14], PWC [37], and RAFT [40] using our datasets. Our experiment found that the PWC structure with only supervising

Fig. 5. EPE maps for different projections: (E)-Equirectangular (C)-Cylindrical, and (P)-Cube-Padding. Here, the EPE values are normalized for visualization.

the final output layer can give us the best performance on our test datasets. Thus, we take the PWC structure for our backbone model. Our experiment result for different models is shown in Table 1. We trained PWC-Net using different loss terms and tried applying the normally used solid-angle weights [49] to find out the best loss function as our backbone model. Finally, we chose the top-layer loss without solid-angle weights as the best approach (see our supplementary materials). We also tried modifying the PWC-Net architecture by changing their convolutional kernels to spherical kernels [6] to adapt to the equirectangular distortion. However, as the pre-trained weights are achieved using the regular convolutional kernel shape, the perceptual field changes led to unsatisfactory finetuning results as shown in Table 1.

5.1 Implementation

For the data pre-processing and the projection conversion, we implement OpenCL programs to convert the equirectangular image into cylindrical projection and the planar padding format, respectively. Our model utilizes the PWC structure as the backbone, while the correlation layer is from the FlowNet2's implementation. Our model size is 9.4 MB, and the parameter number is 2.46 M. All the components have an O(N) complexity. The running time of each component on an RTX3090 is reported in Table 2. Note that our implementations of the projection operations can satisfy real-time requirements.

Data Scheduling. Panoramic videos contain irregular movements of objects and cameras, making the scene too complex to analyze. The experiment presented in FlowNet2 shows that training the network with simple features can help the learning process [14]. Thus, we fine-tune models with City1000UR where the camera does not rotate about the x and z axis during data generation.

Table 2. Running time of each component and projection.

Component	PWC-Net	Fusion Model	Projection-E2C	Projection-E2P
Time (ms)	25.6	25.9	8.8	6.8

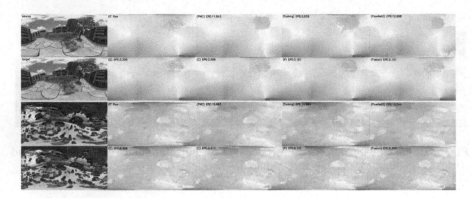

Fig. 6. Optical flow estimation results using PWC, tangent image-based method (Tan-Img), FlowNet2, single projections, and our final fusion model.

Table 3. Spherical Distance (SD)/End point errors (EPE) using equirectangular (Equi), cube-padding (Pad), cylindrical (Cyl) projections and their fusion models.

SD/EPE	Equi (E)	Pad (P)	Cyl (C)	C+P	E+P	E+C
City100	0.90/2.41	0.92/3.32	1.34/2.64	0.82/2.15	**0.75**/1.95	0.83/**1.79**
EFT100	2.98/6.65	2.98/6.25	2.82/5.2	2.77/5.06	2.95/5.84	**2.64/5.01**
Average	1.94/4.91	1.95/5.68	2.08/5.06	1.80/3.60	1.85/3.89	**1.74/3.40**

Fusion Network with Extra Parameters. We tested two versions of fusion layers. The first design takes the predictions P_e, P_c and the source images I_s. The other version also utilizes two channels of the latitude and longitude θ and ϕ of each pixel to enrich the information the network takes. Due to the possible overfitting to the spatial position, the second model has a higher EPE (2.65 v.s. 2.61). Thus, we discard the spatial position channels in our final network.

5.2 Fusion from Different Projections

The fusion module takes two branches of different projection results. For convenience when training the networks, we firstly trained models for equirectangular, cylindrical, and planar cube-padding, respectively. Thus, we can utilize these models to generate their estimation results and then warp all the flow estimations into the equirectangular projection for training the fusion network. The visualized optical flow results are shown in Fig. 6 and our supplementary materials. To quantitatively measure the quality of 360° optical flows, EPE may not be the best metric, especially for those high-altitude points. We added another metric spherical distance (SD) that is the geodesic distance on a sphere (also known as great-circle or orthodromic distance) between a point's ground truth and predicted optical flow. In Table 3, we report the SDs and EPEs of all the projection methods and their fusion models. Optical flow results of the models trained by

Table 4. Error bounds and the errors of our fused results (SD/EPE).

SD/EPE	E+C		E+P		C+P	
	CITY100	EFT100	CITY100	EFT100	CITY100	EFT100
Lower Bound	0.62/1.31	1.83/3.16	0.58/1.44	1.88/3.50	0.68/1.68	1.88/3.34
Upper Bound	1.62/3.74	3.96/8.69	1.23/4.29	4.08/9.40	1.58/4.27	3.91/8.10
Fusion Error	0.83/1.79	2.64/5.01	0.75/1.95	2.95/5.84	0.82/2.15	2.77/5.06

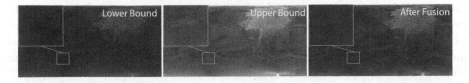

Fig. 7. Error maps. Green boxes show some fixed errors. (Color figure online)

the data with individual projections are all lower than the fusion model where they are involved. Note that equirectangular projection is the best single projection method, given its global continuity and subtle distortions for regions close to the equator. The EPE is 13.7% lower than the tri-cylindrical projection and 3.1% lower than the cube-padding projection. The best model is the fusion model from equirectangular and tri-cylindrical projections, with a 5.7% lower EPE than the second-best model (E+P). The reason is that the cylindrical projection on the cylinders aligned with the z and x-axis can provide more complementary information to the equirectangular projection to improve the prediction quality further. We can also see that even without the best single equirectangular projection, the model trained by fusing tri-cylindrical and cube-padding projection can also get a significantly better result than equirectangular with a 26.6% lower EPE, demonstrating that our fusion strategy is effective. Note that *fused models always outperform* the associated single projection models, which indicates the importance of our fusion principle. To further validate the effectiveness of our fusion model, we calculate the lower/upper bound for fusion using an oracle to choose the worst/best flow rather than learning fusion for all our test data. We show in Table 4 and Fig. 7 the lower/upper bound for fusion and ours is closer to the lower bound, so fusion performs well, but further improvements are possible.

In our multi-projection process, equirectangular projection contains the entire scene and provides contextual information that can be learned by our PWC-based network. Although the other two projections change the layout of the scene, we maintain useful local contexts for objects by duplicating some content. From our results, we can see that for any given object, PWC's context network can still gather useful contextual information for that object since most pixels in the surrounding region are not crossing atlas chart boundaries. Also, the coarse-to-fine scheme of PWC works as long as there is relevant information in the local contextual area in the receptive field of the pyramid. Equirectangular

Table 5. Comparison with other methods using Spherical Distance (SD)/EPE.

SD/EPE	PWC-Net	RAFT	TanImg	FlowNet2	Ours
City100	3.86/9.84	12.10/21.57	1.27/3.69	2.72/10.85	**0.82/1.79**
EFT100	6.26/15.64	20.21/29.64	4.61/8.06	4.91/14.88	**2.64/5.01**
Average	5.06/12.74	16.15/25.61	2.94/5.88	3.81/12.87	**1.73/3.40**

projection always incorporates a full context in a coarse-to-fine scheme due to cyclic convolution operations. For the other two projections, PWC's context network with six levels of pyramids has a receptive field that is still relatively local and does not consider the entire image compared to our resolution of 1000 pixels wide, and is thus applicable to incorporating contextual information.

5.3 Comparisons

Compare with 2D Optical Flow Estimation Methods. We compare our method with the state-of-the-art optical flow estimation methods, FlowNet2, PWC-Net, RAFT, and the method delicately designed for 360° optical flow estimation [46]. We feed equirectangular frames to all the compared methods. The results are shown in Table 5 and Fig. 6. Here, the FlowNet2, PWC, and RAFT methods are all using their original method and model to demonstrate the benefits from both of our dataset and multi-projection fusion approach. The SD/EPE of our method is **65.8%/73.3%**, **89.3%/86.7%**, and **54.6%/73.5%** lower than PWC, RAFT, FlowNet2 respectively.

Comparison with Tangent Image-Based Approach. [46] Although the tangent image-based method (TanImg) achieved a large margin of improvement on the panoramic optical flow quality in their own dataset of static objects with moving cameras, our SD and EPE are **41.1%** and **42.1%** lower than TanImg, respectively, as in Table 5. This shows that their method cannot adapt to the scenes with dynamic objects because they do not use a deep model to learn the useful cues for matching local textures of complex moving objects. We also choose the "circle" set of data in [46] to finetune our model since it is the only set with more than 600 frames (the other two sets both have only 180 frames). We use a 2:1 training and testing split. On the test set, we have an EPE of 4.73 if we directly use the original frames for training and an EPE of 3.8 if we use data augmentation using RGBShift and ChannelShuffle from Albumentations [2] to create a larger diversity. The result from our data-augmented model is slightly worse than their method (EPE: 3.5) when training by such a small scale dataset. But the significant improvement with only color-based data augmentation indicates that the amount of data is *not sufficient* for training a deep model, and it has a great potential to improve given more data.

Fig. 8. Our video editing application on real-world 360° videos. The results are generated using optical flow results of our method, PWC, and TanImg respectively.

5.4 Application for Video Editing

An accurate optical flow estimation is important for many tasks such as object tracking and video segmentation on 360° videos. To demonstrate the accuracy and the practical value of our method for real-world panoramic videos, we develop an application that utilizes the predicted optical flow to propagate edits across frames to evaluate our method visually. In our example shown in Fig. 8, we put a piece of graffiti at one frame and applied optical flow estimation to find the corresponding affected pixels on the rest of the video frames. More specifically, we use the backward optical-flow to find whether a pixel in the following frames is affected, so that the edits can be propagated densely. We use different optical flow predictions from the PWC model, tangent image-based method, and our method for comparisons. The optical flow estimated by PWC fails to match the distorted corresponding pixels in the upper region. TanImg method is better, but it accumulates errors when the frame number is increasing, leading to obvious artifacts after 30 frames. In contrast, our method well adapts to the distortions of panoramic video representation, generating much more consistent editing results across all the frames. See our supplementary for the full video.

Limitation and Future Work. Our dataset does not contain the real-world optical flow data. In the future, the 360° Lidar can be used for ground truth optical flow generation. We also consider adding modules to cope with occlusion regions and extending the work to 360° scene flow estimation for VR applications.

6 Conclusion

This paper presented a novel multi-projection fusion framework for 360° optical flow estimation. Besides the commonly used equirectangular projection, we proposed tri-cylindrical projection and circular cube-padding projection to provide complementary less distorted 2D panoramic representations to train the deep model. A fusion network is then applied to combine the warped frames based on the predicted panoramic optical flow using different projections for the final optical flow estimation. A novel dataset was also generated to enable the training of neural networks for 360° optical flow estimation. The experimental results demonstrate that our method has the best performance and is sufficiently practical to be applied to real-world use cases.

Acknowledgements. This work is supported by Marsden Fund Council managed by Royal Society of New Zealand (No. MFP-20-VUW-180).

References

1. Bhandari, K., Zong, Z., Yan, Y.: Revisiting optical flow estimation in 360 videos. In: 2020 25th International Conference on Pattern Recognition (ICPR), pp. 8196–8203. IEEE (2021)
2. Buslaev, A., Iglovikov, V.I., Khvedchenya, E., Parinov, A., Druzhinin, M., Kalinin, A.A.: Albumentations: Fast and flexible image augmentations. Information **11**(2) (2020). https://doi.org/10.3390/info11020125
3. Butler, D.J., Wulff, J., Stanley, G.B., Black, M.J.: A naturalistic open source movie for optical flow evaluation. In: Fitzgibbon, A., Lazebnik, S., Perona, P., Sato, Y., Schmid, C. (eds.) ECCV 2012. LNCS, vol. 7577, pp. 611–625. Springer, Heidelberg (2012). https://doi.org/10.1007/978-3-642-33783-3_44
4. Chang, A.X., et al.: ShapeNet: An Information-Rich 3D Model Repository. Tech. Rep. arXiv:1512.03012 [cs.GR], Stanford University – Princeton University – Toyota Technological Institute at Chicago (2015)
5. Cheng, H.T., Chao, C.H., Dong, J.D., Wen, H.K., Liu, T.L., Sun, M.: Cube padding for weakly-supervised saliency prediction in 360 videos. In: Proceedings of the IEEE Conference on Computer Vision and Pattern Recognition, pp. 1420–1429 (2018)
6. Coors, B., Condurache, A.P., Geiger, A.: Spherenet: Learning spherical representations for detection and classification in omnidirectional images. In: Proceedings of the European Conference on Computer Vision (ECCV), pp. 518–533 (2018)
7. Dosovitskiy, A., et al.: Flownet: Learning optical flow with convolutional networks. In: IEEE International Conference on Computer Vision (ICCV) (2015). http://lmb.informatik.uni-freiburg.de/Publications/2015/DFIB15
8. Geiger, A., Lenz, P., Urtasun, R.: Are we ready for autonomous driving? the kitti vision benchmark suite. In: Conference on Computer Vision and Pattern Recognition (CVPR) (2012)
9. He, K., Zhang, X., Ren, S., Sun, J.: Deep residual learning for image recognition. In: Proceedings of the IEEE conference on computer vision and pattern recognition, pp. 770–778 (2016)
10. Hilbert, D., Cohn-Vossen, S.: Geometry and the Imagination (2nd ed.). Chelsea (1952)
11. Horn, B.K., Schunck, B.G.: Determining optical flow. Artif. Intell. **17**(1–3), 185–203 (1981)
12. Hu, H.N., Lin, Y.C., Liu, M.Y., Cheng, H.T., Chang, Y.J., Sun, M.: Deep 360 pilot: Learning a deep agent for piloting through 360 sports videos. In: 2017 IEEE Conference on Computer Vision and Pattern Recognition (CVPR), pp. 1396–1405. IEEE (2017)

13. Hur, J., Roth, S.: Iterative residual refinement for joint optical flow and occlusion estimation. In: Proceedings of the IEEE/CVF Conference on Computer Vision and Pattern Recognition, pp. 5754–5763 (2019)
14. Ilg, E., Mayer, N., Saikia, T., Keuper, M., Dosovitskiy, A., Brox, T.: Flownet 2.0: Evolution of optical flow estimation with deep networks. In: IEEE Conference on Computer Vision and Pattern Recognition (CVPR) (Jul 2017). http://lmb.informatik.uni-freiburg.de//Publications/2017/IMKDB17
15. Kang, K., Cho, S.: Interactive and automatic navigation for 360° video playback. ACM Trans. Graph. **38**(4), 1–11 (2019)
16. Kopf, J.: 360 video stabilization. ACM Trans. Graph. (TOG) **35**(6), 1–9 (2016)
17. Li, C., Xu, M., Jiang, L., Zhang, S., Tao, X.: Viewport proposal cnn for 360° video quality assessment. In: 2019 IEEE/CVF Conference on Computer Vision and Pattern Recognition (CVPR), pp. 10169–10178. IEEE (2019)
18. Liu, L., et al.: Learning by analogy: Reliable supervision from transformations for unsupervised optical flow estimation. In: Proceedings of the IEEE/CVF Conference on Computer Vision and Pattern Recognition, pp. 6489–6498 (2020)
19. Liu, P., Lyu, M., King, I., Xu, J.: Selflow: Self-supervised learning of optical flow. In: Proceedings of the IEEE/CVF Conference on Computer Vision and Pattern Recognition, pp. 4571–4580 (2019)
20. Liu, S., Tan, P., Yuan, L., Sun, J., Zeng, B.: MeshFlow: minimum latency online video stabilization. In: Leibe, B., Matas, J., Sebe, N., Welling, M. (eds.) ECCV 2016. LNCS, vol. 9910, pp. 800–815. Springer, Cham (2016). https://doi.org/10.1007/978-3-319-46466-4_48
21. Liu, S., Yuan, L., Tan, P., Sun, J.: Steadyflow: Spatially smooth optical flow for video stabilization. In: Proceedings of the IEEE Conference on Computer Vision and Pattern Recognition (CVPR) (June 2014)
22. Lucas, B.D., Kanade, T.: An iterative image registration technique with an application to stereo vision. In: Proceedings of the 7th International Joint Conference on Artificial Intelligence - vol. 2, pp. 674–679. IJCAI'81, Morgan Kaufmann Publishers Inc., San Francisco, CA, USA (1981)
23. Mayer, N., et al.: A large dataset to train convolutional networks for disparity, optical flow, and scene flow estimation. CoRR abs/1512.02134 (2015). arxiv.org/abs/1512.02134
24. Meister, S., Hur, J., Roth, S.: Unflow: Unsupervised learning of optical flow with a bidirectional census loss. In: Thirty-Second AAAI Conference on Artificial Intelligence (2018)
25. Menze, M., Geiger, A.: Object scene flow for autonomous vehicles. In: Conference on Computer Vision and Pattern Recognition (CVPR) (2015)
26. Misra, D.: Mish: A self regularized non-monotonic activation function. arXiv preprint arXiv:1908.08681 (2019)
27. Monroy, R., Lutz, S., Chalasani, T., Smolic, A.: Salnet360: saliency maps for omnidirectional images with cnn. Signal Process. Image Commun. **69**, 26–34 (2018)
28. Nadeem, S., Su, Z., Zeng, W., Kaufman, A., Gu, X.: Spherical parameterization balancing angle and area distortions. IEEE Trans. Visualization Comput. Graph. **23**(6), 1663–1676 (2016)
29. Nguyen, C., DiVerdi, S., Hertzmann, A., Liu, F.: Vremiere: In-headset virtual reality video editing. In: Proceedings of the 2017 CHI Conference on Human Factors in Computing Systems, pp. 5428–5438 (2017)
30. Poranne, R., Tarini, M., Huber, S., Panozzo, D., Sorkine-Hornung, O.: Autocuts: simultaneous distortion and cut optimization for uv mapping. ACM Trans. Graph. (TOG) **36**(6), 1–11 (2017)

31. Ren, Z., Yan, J., Ni, B., Liu, B., Yang, X., Zha, H.: Unsupervised deep learning for optical flow estimation. In: Thirty-First AAAI Conference on Artificial Intelligence (2017)
32. Ren, Z., Gallo, O., Sun, D., Yang, M.H., Sudderth, E.B., Kautz, J.: A fusion approach for multi-frame optical flow estimation. In: 2019 IEEE Winter Conference on Applications of Computer Vision (WACV), pp. 2077–2086. IEEE (2019)
33. Ronneberger, O., Fischer, P., Brox, T.: U-Net: convolutional networks for biomedical image segmentation. In: Navab, N., Hornegger, J., Wells, W.M., Frangi, A.F. (eds.) MICCAI 2015. LNCS, vol. 9351, pp. 234–241. Springer, Cham (2015). https://doi.org/10.1007/978-3-319-24574-4_28
34. Sterzentsenko, V., et al.: Self-supervised deep depth denoising. In: ICCV (2019)
35. Su, Y., Grauman, K.: Kernel transformer networks for compact spherical convolution. CoRR abs/1812.03115 (2018). arxiv.org/abs/1812.03115
36. Sun, D., Roth, S., Black, M.J.: Secrets of optical flow estimation and their principles. In: 2010 IEEE Computer Society Conference on Computer Vision and Pattern Recognition, pp. 2432–2439. IEEE (2010)
37. Sun, D., Yang, X., Liu, M.Y., Kautz, J.: PWC-Net: CNNs for optical flow using pyramid, warping, and cost volume (2018)
38. Sun, D., Yang, X., Liu, M.Y., Kautz, J.: Models matter, so does training: An empirical study of cnns for optical flow estimation. IEEE Trans. Pattern Analysis Mach. Intell. **42**(6), 1408–1423 (2019)
39. Tang, C., Wang, O., Liu, F., Tan, P.: Joint stabilization and direction of 360° videos. ACM Trans. Graph. (TOG) **38**(2), 1–13 (2019)
40. Teed, Z., Deng, J.: RAFT: recurrent all-pairs field transforms for optical flow. CoRR abs/2003.12039 (2020), arxiv.org/abs/2003.12039
41. Wang, N.H., Solarte, B., Tsai, Y.H., Chiu, W.C., Sun, M.: 360sd-net: 360 stereo depth estimation with learnable cost volume. In: 2020 IEEE International Conference on Robotics and Automation (ICRA). pp. 582–588. IEEE (2020)
42. Wang, Y., Yang, Y., Yang, Z., Zhao, L., Wang, P., Xu, W.: Occlusion aware unsupervised learning of optical flow. In: Proceedings of the IEEE Conference on Computer Vision and Pattern Recognition, pp. 4884–4893 (2018)
43. Wulff, J., Butler, D.J., Stanley, G.B., Black, M.J.: Lessons and insights from creating a synthetic optical flow benchmark. In: Fusiello, A., Murino, V., Cucchiara, R. (eds.) ECCV 2012. LNCS, vol. 7584, pp. 168–177. Springer, Heidelberg (2012). https://doi.org/10.1007/978-3-642-33868-7_17
44. Yang, J., Liu, T., Jiang, B., Lu, W., Meng, Q.: Panoramic video quality assessment based on non-local spherical cnn. IEEE Trans. Multimedia **23**, 797–809 (2021). https://doi.org/10.1109/TMM.2020.2990075
45. Yin, Z., Shi, J.: Geonet: Unsupervised learning of dense depth, optical flow and camera pose. In: Proceedings of the IEEE Conference on Computer Vision and Pattern Recognition, pp. 1983–1992 (2018)
46. Yuan, M., Richardt, C.: 360-degree optical flow using tangent images. arXiv preprint arXiv:2112.14331 (2021)
47. Zhang, Y., Zhang, F.L., Lai, Y.K., Zhu, Z.: Efficient propagation of sparse edits on 360 panoramas. Comput. Graph. **96**, 61–70 (2021)
48. Zhang, Z., Xu, Y., Yu, J., Gao, S.: Saliency detection in 360 videos. In: Proceedings of the European Conference on Computer Vision (ECCV), pp. 488–503 (2018)
49. Zhao, J., Chalmers, A., Rhee, T.: Adaptive light estimation using dynamic filtering for diverse lighting conditions. IEEE Trans. Visual. Comput. Graph. **27**(11), 4097–4106 (2021)

MaCLR: Motion-Aware Contrastive Learning of Representations for Videos

Fanyi Xiao⬛, Joseph Tighe⬛, and Davide Modolo[✉]⬛

AWS AI Labs, Cambridge, USA
fyxiao@ucdavis.edu, {tighej,dmodolo}@amazon.com

Abstract. We present MaCLR, a novel method to explicitly perform cross-modal self-supervised video representations learning from visual and motion modalities. Compared to previous video representation learning methods that mostly focus on learning motion cues implicitly from RGB inputs, MaCLR enriches standard contrastive learning objectives for RGB video clips with a cross-modal learning objective between a Motion pathway and a Visual pathway. We show that the representation learned with our MaCLR method focuses more on foreground motion regions and thus generalizes better to downstream tasks. To demonstrate this, we evaluate MaCLR on five datasets for both action recognition and action detection, and demonstrate state-of-the-art self-supervised performance on all datasets. Furthermore, we show that MaCLR representation can be as effective as representations learned with full supervision on UCF101 and HMDB51 action recognition, and even outperform the supervised representation for action recognition on VidSitu and SSv2, and action detection on AVA.

1 Introduction

Supervised learning has enjoyed great successes in many computer vision tasks in the past decade. One of the most important fuel in this successful journey is the availability of large amount of high-quality labeled data. Notably, the ImageNet [17] dataset for image classification was the spark that ignited the deep learning revolution in vision. In the video domain, the Kinetics dataset [41] has long been regarded as the "ImageNet for videos" and has enabled the "pretrain-then-finetune" paradigm for many video tasks. Interestingly, though years old, ImageNet and Kinetics are still the to-go datasets for pretraining that are publicly available. This shows how much effort is needed to create these large-scale labeled datasets.

To mitigate the reliance on large-scale labeled datasets, *self-supervised learning* came with the promise to learn useful representations from large amount of *unlabeled* data. Following the recent success in NLP (e.g., BERT, GPT-3 [7,18]), some works have attempted to find its counterpart in vision. Among them, pioneering research has been conducted in the image domain to produce successful

---

F. Xiao—*Work done while at Amazon, now at Meta AI.*

© The Author(s), under exclusive license to Springer Nature Switzerland AG 2022
S. Avidan et al. (Eds.): ECCV 2022, LNCS 13695, pp. 353–370, 2022.
https://doi.org/10.1007/978-3-031-19833-5_21

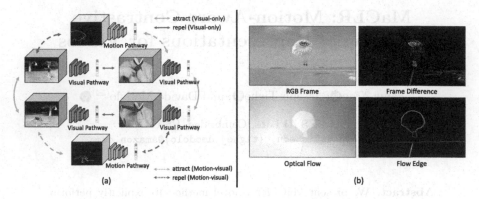

Fig. 1. (a) Cross-modal motion-visual learning. We propose Motion-aware Contrastive Learning of Representations (MaCLR) as an explicit method to learn motion-aware video representations without labels – Our visual pathway features are pushed to learn a representation aligns with our motion pathway and in doing so learn features that more robustly capture motion in the video. **(b) Motion inputs.** Given the RGB input (top-left), we compare three options for motion inputs. Best viewed on screen.

methods like MoCo [36] and SimCLR [12]. Compared to images, large-scale video datasets induce even higher annotation costs, making it even more important to develop effective self-supervised methods to learn generalizable representations for videos. Some recent video works attempted to learn such representations by training their models to solve pretext tasks, like predicting the correct temporal order of clips [6,9,28,49,78], predict future frames [19] and predict whether a video is played at its intrinsic speed [4]. Though successful to a certain extent, these methods do not explicitly make use of motion information derived from the temporal sequence, which has been shown to be important for supervised action recognition tasks [26,63,74].

In this paper, we propose MaCLR, a novel self-supervised video representation learning method that *explicitly* models motion cues during training. MaCLR (Motion-aware Contrastive Learning of Representations) consists of two pathways: Visual and Motion. It uses both pathways during self-supervised pretraining, but only transfers the Visual to downstream tasks. When trained alone, the Visual pathway learns from RGB inputs using the contrastive InfoNCE objective, which mostly focuses on visual semantic information. To help enriching the representation of Visual and make it motion-aware, we introduce a Motion pathway trained on motion inputs. We then connect Motion to Visual using a novel cross-modal contrastive objective that enables the Motion pathway to guide the learning of Visual towards relevant motion cues. As our experiments show, this formulation leads to rich video representations that capture both visual semantics and motion patterns.

To evaluate MaCLR, we perform self-supervised pretraining on Kinetics-400 and transfer its representation to 5 video datasets for both action recognition (UCF101 [65], HMDB51 [43], Something-Something [1], VidSitu [59]) and action detection (AVA [32]). Without bells and whistle, MaCLR outperforms all previous video self-supervised methods on all datasets, under all evaluation settings. For example, MaCLR improves top-1 accuracy by 17% and 16.9% on UCF101 and HMD51, over previous SOTA trained on Kinetics-400. Furthermore, on Something-Something, VidSitu and AVA, MaCLR even outperforms its fully-supervised counterparts, demonstrating the strength of our approach.

2 Related Work

Self-supervised Image Representation Learning. The goal of self-supervised image representation learning is to learn useful representations from large collections of unlabeled images. Early work focused on designing different pretext tasks with the intent of inducing generalizable semantic representations [20,50,51,84]. Though producing promising results, these methods could not match the performance of fully-supervised trained representations [42], as it is hard to prevent the network from utilizing shortcuts to solve pretext tasks (e.g., "chromatic aberration" in context prediction [20]). This changed when researchers re-visited the decade-old technique of contrastive learning [33,80]. Some of these recent work started to successfully produce results that were comparable to those of supervised learning on images [10,12–14,31,36,48]. Though related, these work were designed to learn from static images and thus cannot utilize the rich temporal information contained in videos.

Self-supervised Video Representation Learning. Videos present unique opportunities to extract self-supervision and the literature offers different directions. The first line of research focuses on designing video-specific *pretext tasks*. Besides the work mentioned earlier [4,19,28,49,78], others attempt to learn video representations by either tracking across frames patches [76], pixels [77], colors [70], predicting temporal context for videos [58,73], or by enforcing consistency along videos semantics and play speeds [38]. A more recent line of work overcomes the need for pretext tasks by leveraging the *contrastive learning* paradigm [24,57]. Though successful to a certain extent, none of above methods *explicitly* make use of the important motion cues derived from the video temporal sequence. To better exploit such important information, [72] applies a pretext task of regressing motion statistics, [30,35] mine and cluster RGB images with similar motion cues, while [39,46,60] exploit the correspondences between RGB and motion *pixels*. MaCLR belongs to this recent class of works that aim at improving video representation using motion cues. However, it differs from previous works in the way it utilizes visual-motion correspondence in a cross-modal contrastive framework at a higher level than pixels, which yields a method that is simpler, more robust and achieves considerably better results.

Motion in Video Tasks. Motion information has been heavily studied for many video tasks. As a prominent motion representation, optical flow has been utilized in many video action classification methods, either in the form of classical hand-crafted spatiotemporal features [16,44,71], or serve as input to deep CNN systems trained with supervised learning [25,26,74]. In contrast, our method focuses on exploiting motion information in the context of self-supervised learning. Beyond video classification, motion has also been exploited in many other tasks like video object detection [27,40,81,85], video frame prediction [45,61], video segmentation [3,15,68], object tracking [5,37,54], and 3D reconstruction [69].

3 MaCLR

We design MaCLR as a two-branch network consisting of a Visual pathway and a Motion pathway (Fig. 1a). The Visual pathway takes as input visual[1] clips and produces their visual embeddings. Similarly, the Motion pathway operates on motion clips (we will study different motion inputs in Sect. 3.2) and generates motion embeddings. MaCLR is trained using three contrastive learning objectives (Sect. 3.1): (i) a visual-only loss that pulls together visual clip embeddings that are sampled from the same video (solid green arrow in Fig. 1a) and pushes away that of different videos (solid red arrow); (ii) a motion-only loss that operates like (i), but on motion clips (omitted in Fig. 1a to avoid clutter) and (iii) a motion-visual loss to enforce alignment between embeddings of the visual and motion inputs (dashed arrows). As shown in Fig. 1a, we generate positive pairs from clips extracted from the same video (green arrows) and negative pairs from clips extracted from different videos (red arrows). After pretraining with MaCLR, *we then remove the Motion pathway and transfer the Visual pathway to target datasets for task-specific finetuning.*

3.1 Training MaCLR

Visual-Only Learning. We model this using a contrastive learning objective. Similar to [57], our model takes as input random clips with spatiotemporal jittering. As shown in Fig. 1a, given a random clip we produce its embedding v^q (query), and sample a second positive clip from the same video and produce its embedding v^k (key), as well as N negative embeddings v_i^n, $i \in \{1, ..., N\}$ from other videos. Then, we train the Visual pathway with the InfoNCE objective $\mathcal{L}_v = \text{IN}(v^q, v^k, v^n)$ [36,52]:

$$\mathcal{L}_v = -\log \frac{\exp(v^q \cdot v^k / \tau)}{\exp(v^q \cdot v^k / \tau) + \sum_{i=1}^{N} \exp(v^q \cdot v_i^n / \tau)}, \qquad (1)$$

where τ is a temperature parameter. This objective ensures that our Visual pathway pulls together embeddings v^q and v^k, while pushing away those of all the negative clips v_i^n.

---

[1] *Sometimes also referred to as "RGB" in the literature.*

Motion-Only Learning. To improve the discriminativeness of the Motion pathway, we add another InfoNCE objective $\mathcal{L}_m = \text{IN}(m^q, m^k, m^n)$, which is trained in a similar way to $\mathcal{L}_v$ but this time on motion embeddings m^q, m^k (both are sampled from the same video as v_q) and m^n (which denotes a set of negative motion embeddings). This ensures that the Motion pathway is able to embed similar motion patterns close to each other.

Motion-Visual Learning. We model this also with a contrastive learning objective, but with a different purpose compared to the previous two. Here, we aim at enriching the Visual pathway to be motion-aware with the help of the Motion pathway. Specifically, we train the model using the following InfoNCE objectives:

$$\mathcal{L}_{mv} = \text{IN}(v^q, m^k, v^n) + \text{IN}(m^q, v^k, m^n). \tag{2}$$

Note that v^q is *not necessarily in temporal synchronization* with m^k, but rather just a motion clip sampled from the same video (same for v^k and m^q). In our ablation, we show that allowing for this misalignment encourages the embedding to better learn semantic abstraction of visual and motion patterns, which leads to better performance.

One key difference to visual-only contrastive learning is on how we sample motion clips for both motion-only and motion-visual learning. Instead of sampling randomly, we constrain to only sample in temporal regions with strong motion cues. Specifically, we compute the sum of pixels P_i on the motion input and only sample frames with $\sum_{i=1}^{K} P_i / K > \gamma$, where K is the total number of pixels in a frame and γ is the threshold. This process helps avoid sampling irrelevant regions with no motion and thus leads to better representations.

Final Training Objective. The final training objective for MaCLR is the sum of all aforementioned loss functions:

$$\mathcal{L} = \mathcal{L}_v + \mathcal{L}_m + \mathcal{L}_{mv}. \tag{3}$$

Training MaCLR end-to-end is non-trivial, as video representation are expensive to compute and to maintain (as contrastive learning requires large batch sizes [12]). Inspired by [36,80], we solve this problem by adopting the idea of memory bank for negative samples. Specifically, we construct two memory banks of negative samples for visual and motion inputs, and maintain a momentum version of the Motion and Visual pathways updated as a moving average of their online counterparts with momentum coefficient λ: $\theta' \leftarrow \lambda\theta' + (1 - \lambda)\theta$, where θ and θ' are weights for the online and momentum version of the model respectively. One caveat is that when pushing negatives into the pool, we push the video index, along with the embedding, so that we can avoid sampling visual or motion clips that are from the same video as positive clips, which would otherwise confuse the network and hurt the representations. Similar to [36], we forward queries through the online model and keys through the momentum model to produce embeddings.

3.2   Design of Motion Inputs

There are many ways to represent a motion input. A straightforward way is to directly compute the difference of pixel values between two consecutive frames. While capturing motion to a certain extent, it also captures undesired signals like pixel value shifts caused by background motion (e.g., sea-wave in Fig. 1b top-right). A more appropriate representation might be optical flow [8,21,67,79]. However, a disadvantage of feeding in raw optical flow (or flow vector magnitude, as used in [29]) is that it is heavily influenced by factors like illumination change (Fig. 1b bottom-left) and it also captures absolute flow magnitude, which is not very useful for learning general motion patterns. To overcome these limitations, in MaCLR, we propose to use flow edge maps as inputs to the Motion pathway network. Specifically, we apply a Sobel filter [64] onto the flow magnitude map to produce the flow edges (Fig. 1b bottom-right). In our experiments, this simple operation turns out to produce significantly better motion representations that focus on foreground motion regions.

3.3   Visual and Motion Pathway Architectures

Our *Visual pathway* is a 3D ResNet50 (R3D-50) with a structure similar to that of "Slow-only" in [23,57], which features 2D convs in res_2, res_3 and non-degenerate 3D convs in res_4, res_5. It takes as input a tensor of size $3 \times 8 \times 224^2$, capturing 8 frames of size 224×224. The sampling stride is 8, which means that the visual input clip spans 8×8 frames, corresponding to ~2 s for videos at 30 FPS. To have larger temporal receptive field, we set the temporal kernel size of $conv_1$ to 5 following [57].

Our *Motion pathway* is a 2D ResNet50. and it takes as input a tensor of size $3 \times 16 \times 224^2$, stacking 16 motion frames. We use a sampling stride of 4, so that it spans for the same time as the visual input (i.e., ~2 s). Following the design philosophy of SlowFast Networks [23], we design our Motion pathway to be much more lightweight compared to our Visual pathway (1/8 channel sizes across the network), as motion inputs have intrinsically less variability (i.e., no variations on colors, illumination, etc.).

4   Experiments

4.1   Implementation Details

MaCLR Training Details. We train MaCLR on the Kinetics-400 (K400) dataset (CC-BY-4.0) [41]. The dataset consists of ~240k video clips that span at most 10 s. These were originally annotated with 400 different action classes, but we *do not* use any of these labels. We train MaCLR for 600 epochs on the whole 240k videos when we compare against the literature. For our ablation study, instead, we compare different variants of MaCLR trained for 100 epochs on a subset of 60k videos ("K400-mini"). We use a pool size (N in Eq. 1) of

Table 1. Ablating MaCLR. We present top-1 classification accuracy using the Linear Layer Training evaluation protocol (Sect. 4.2). In (a), V-only and M-only refers to the visual and motion only pretraining. In (b), Diff, Flow and Edge refer to motion inputs in the form of Frame Difference, Optical Flow and Flow Edges, respectively. Experiments in (b) and (c) are conducted on K400-mini. We use 8×8 R3D-50 model for finetuning.

Method	Data	UCF	HMDB
V-only	K400-mini	63.6	33.7
M-only	K400-mini	66.4	45.1
MaCLR	K400-mini	**78.1**	**47.2**
V-only	K400	74.6	46.3
MaCLR	K400	**85.5**	**57.7**

(a) **Motion-visual learning**

Inputs	UCF	HMDB
Diff	71.6	40.1
Flow	74.1	44.2
Edge	**78.1**	**47.2**

(b) **Motion inputs**

Components	UCF	HMDB
MaCLR	**78.1**	**47.2**
−t. jitter	77.4	47.1
−m. thresh	77.3	46.4
$-\mathcal{L}_m$	77.8	46.6

(c) **Dissect components**

65536 negative samples for both visual and motion inputs. We set the momentum update coefficient $\lambda = 0.999$ and temperature τ to 0.1. The embedding dimension is set to 128 for both Visual and Motion pathways. For the visual inputs, we apply random spatial cropping, temporal jittering, $p = 0.2$ probability grayscale conversion, $p = 0.5$ horizontal flip, $p = 0.5$ Gaussian blur, and $p = 0.8$ color perturbation on brightness, contrast and saturation, all with 0.4 jittering ratio. For motion inputs, we randomly sample flow edge clips in high motion regions (with motion threshold γ set to 0.02) and skip other augmentations. Our codebase is based on PySlowFast [22].

Flow Edge Maps. To compute flow edge map for frame t, we first compute optical flow from frame t to $t-5$, using RAFT-things [67] model trained entirely on synthetic data without human annotations. We hypothesize it would also work with flow computed from closer pairs, as long as the motion threshold γ is adjusted accordingly. Then, we apply a Sobel filter onto the magnitude map of optical flow and clamp the resulting edge map in [0, 10] as the final flow edge map. We note that this is an offline pre-processing that only needs to be done once and reused throughout training (and never during inference).

Baselines. We compare against two baselines: (i) *Self-Supervised Visual-only* is a strong self-supervised representation trained from RGB inputs using only the contrastive learning objective of Eq. 1 (i.e., without our motion learning objectives $\mathcal{L}_{mv}$ and $\mathcal{L}_m$); and (ii) *Supervised* is a fully supervised model trained for action classification on K400. Both baselines use a R3D-50 backbone.

4.2 Action Recognition on UCF101 and HMDB51

Datasets and Evaluation Protocol. We first evaluate MaCLR for action recognition on the two most popular datasets in the literature: UCF101 [65] and HMDB51 [43] (CC-BY-3.0). We follow the standard settings to perform self-supervised training on K400 and then transfer the learned weights to target datasets for evaluation. Two evaluation protocols are employed in the literature to evaluate the quality of the self-supervised representation: (i) *Linear Layer Training* freezes the trained backbone and simply trains a linear classifier on the target dataset, while (ii) *Full Network Training* finetunes the entire network end-to-end on the target dataset. For completeness, we evaluate using both protocols and report action classification top-1 accuracy. For all experiments on UCF101 and HMDB51, we report results using split1 for train/test split. In total, there are 9.5k/3.7k train/test videos with 101 action classes in UCF101, and 3.5k/1.5k train/test videos with 51 actions in HMDB51. We use the standard 10 (temporal) ×3 (spatial) crop sampling during test [23, 75]. We use these two datasets to compare against the state-of-the-art (SOTA). Additionally, we use K400-mini to conduct an extensive ablation study on the components of MaCLR. For the comparison with SOTA, we pretrain MaCLR with 8 × 8 inputs for 600 epochs on K400, and finetune with 32 × 8 inputs on downstream tasks, as these leads to the best performance. In our ablation study instead we simplify these settings for efficiency and pretrain for only 100 epochs and use 8 × 8 inputs for finetuning.

Ablation: Motion-Visual Learning (Table 1a). First and foremost, we study the importance of enriching visual embeddings with motion cues using the proposed motion-visual learning objective of Eq. 2. Results show that MaCLR improves substantially over Visual-only on both UCF and HMDB, when pretrained with either K400 or K400-mini. To understand if the benefit comes purely from the new motion objective $\mathcal{L}_m$, we also trained a Motion-only model on K400-mini. Interestingly, this model performs slightly better than Visual-only, but much worse than MaCLR, showing the importance of training a video representation that can capture *both* semantic and motion features. Finally, note how MaCLR trained on K400-mini also outperforms the Visual-only baseline pretrained on the full K400 (4× more data): +3.5/+0.9 on UCF/HMDB.

Ablation: Motion Representations (Table 1b). In Sect. 3 we discussed some conceptual advantages of using flow edge maps and here we evaluate it against two popular motion alternatives: Frame Difference and Optical Flow. As shown in Table 1b, Flow Edges is indeed the best way to represent motion for self-supervised training, thanks to its ability to prune background motion noise and absolute motion magnitude. That being said, even the much weaker Frame Difference representation outperforms the Visual-only baseline (Table 1a) by +8.0 top-1 accuracy on UCF and +6.4 on HMDB. This further confirms the importance of enriching video representations with motion cues.

Ablation: MaCLR Components (Table 1c). We now dissect MaCLR to study the importance of its components.

Temporal Jittering. Unlike previous work that learn self-supervised representation by exploiting pixel-level correspondences between RGB and optical flow inputs [46,60], we demonstrate that it's more effective to learn self-supervised representations by introducing temporal "misalignment" between them. Specifically, we compare MaCLR, which trains on RGB and motion clips that are temporally jittered, against a variant that is trained on synchronized RGB and motion clips (i.e., sync pairs $[v^q, m^k]$ and $[m^q, v^k]$ in Eq. 2). Our results show that the misaligned inputs lead to better representations (+0.7 on UCF), as it prevents the model from exploiting the shortcut of finding pixel correspondences using low-level visual cues.

Motion Thresholding. Next, we study the motion input sampling strategy discussed in Sect. 3.1. We compare MaCLR to a variant which randomly samples motion input clips, without removing those with little motion (i.e., setting threshold $\gamma = 0$, Sect. 4.1). Without this threshold, top-1 accuracy degrades by -0.8 on both datasets, due to the noise introduced by clips with too little motion.

Motion Loss $\mathcal{L}_m$. Finally, we study whether it's necessary to have the extra contrastive objective $\mathcal{L}_m$ between motion inputs (Eq. 3), which is included to help training more discriminative motion embeddings. Results show that this motion discrimination objective is indeed useful as it improves top-1 acc by +0.3 and +0.6 on UCF101 and HMDB51.

Comparison to State-of-the-Art (Table 2). We now compare MaCLR against previous self-supervised video representation learning methods in the literature using both the evaluation protocols introduced at the beginning of Sect. 4.2: Linear (✓ for column "Frozen") and Full (✗).

By only training a linear layer on top of our self-supervised learned representation, our method is able to achieve significantly better top-1 classification accuracy compared to the previous state-of-the-art trained on K400: +16.7 and +16.9 over CoCLR on UCF101 and HMDB51, respectively. Only the recent CVRL method comes close to our results on UCF, but still lacks on HMDB (−4.7). Moreover, MaCLR outperforms all previous methods, including those trained on 100×more data than K400 (e.g., IG65M and Youtube8M), and those that use extra modalities like audio and text (e.g., XDC, MIL-NCE).

Results using the end-to-end full training evaluation protocol show similar observations to the linear evaluation protocol: MaCLR again achieves competitive results among the methods trained on K400. When compared to previous approaches, only ρBYOL, XDC and GDT produce results comparable to MaCLR. Among them, ρBYOL is conceptually similar to our visual-only method, but augmented with the idea of sampling multiple clips ($\rho = 4$) per video for training, which is complementary to our main contribution. On the other hand, both XDC and GDT are trained on 270×more data (IG65M contains 21 years of video content vs.K400 only 28 days) and use extra audio modality as inputs. Furthermore, towards making the best effort in enabling fair comparison against the literature, we also present the results of a weaker MaCLR model trained with a smaller backbone (R18) and a smaller input size (128 × 128). Under this setting, our model again convincingly outperforms models with similar backbone and input resolutions (e.g., 3D-RotNet, CBT, GDT, CoCLR).

We also tried to keep the Motion pathway during inference and ensemble its prediction with those of the Visual pathway ("V+F"). This produces results that are nearly identical to those obtained using only our motion-aware Visual pathway ("V"), which suggests that our novel training paradigm is indeed able

Table 2. Comparison with state-of-the-art approaches. We report top-1 accuracy. In parenthesis, we show the total video duration in time (**d** for day, **y** for year). The top half of the table contains results for the Linear protocol (Frozen ✓), whereas the bottom half shows results for the Full end-to-end finetuning protocol (Frozen ✗). For Modality, V: visual only, A: audio, T: text narration.

Method	Date	Data (duration)	Arch.	Size	Modality	Frozen	UCF	HMDB
MemDPC [34]	2020	K400 (28d)	R-2D3D-34	224^2	V	✓	54.1	30.5
MIL-NCE [47]	2020	HTM (15y)	S3D	224^2	V+T	✓	82.7	53.1
MIL-NCE [47]	2020	HTM (15y)	I3D	224^2	V+T	✓	83.4	54.8
XDC [2]	2020	IG65M (21y)	R(2+1)D	224^2	V+A	✓	85.3	56.0
ELO [55]	2020	YT-8M (8y)	R(2+1)D	224^2	V+A	✓	–	64.5
AVSlowFast [82]	2020	K400 (28d)	AVSlowFast-50	224^2	V+A	✓	77.4	42.2
CoCLR [35]	2020	K400 (28d)	S3D	128^2	V	✓	74.5	46.1
CVRL [57]	2021	K400 (28d)	R3D-50	224^2	V	✓	89.8	58.3
MLFO [56]	2021	K400 (28d)	R3D-18	112^2	V	✓	63.2	33.4
BraVe [58]	2021	K600 (36d)	R3D-50	224^2	V	✓	88.8	61.8
MaCLR		K400 (28d)	R3D-18	128^2	V	✓	**90.4**	**57.5**
MaCLR		K400 (28d)	R3D-50	224^2	V	✓	**91.5**	**63.0**
w/o Pretrain	-		R3D-50	224^2	V	✗	69.0	22.7
CBT [66]	2019	K600+ (273d)	S3D	112^2	V	✗	79.5	44.6
DynamoNet [19]	2019	YT-8M-1 (58d)	STCNet	112^2	V	✗	88.1	59.9
XDC [2]	2020	IG65M (21y)	R(2+1)D	224^2	V+A	✗	94.2	67.4
AVSlowFast [82]	2020	K400 (28d)	AVSlowFast-50	224^2	V+A	✗	87.0	54.6
SpeedNet [4]	2020	K400 (28d)	S3D-G	224^2	V	✗	81.1	48.8
MemDPC [34]	2020	K400 (28d)	R-2D3D-34	224^2	V	✗	86.1	54.5
CoCLR [35]	2020	K400 (28d)	S3D	128^2	V	✗	87.9	54.6
GDT [53]	2020	K400 (28d)	R(2+1)D	112^2	V+A	✗	89.3	60.0
GDT [53]	2020	IG65M (21y)	R(2+1)D	112^2	V+A	✗	95.2	72.8
MIL-NCE [47]	2020	HTM (15y)	S3D	224^2	V+T	✗	91.3	61.0
ELO [55]	2020	YT-8M-2 (13y)	R(2+1)D	224^2	V+A	✗	93.8	67.4
CVRL [57]	2021	K400 (28d)	R3D-50	224^2	V	✗	92.9	67.9
MLFO [56]	2021	K400 (28d)	R3D-18	112^2	V	✗	79.1	47.6
ρBYOL [24]	2021	K400 (28d)	R3D-50	224^2	V	✗	**94.2**	**72.1**
MotionFit [30]	2021	K400 (28d)	S3D-G	224^2	V	✗	90.1	50.6
ASCNet [38]	2021	K400 (28d)	S3D-G	224^2	V	✗	90.8	60.5
BraVe [58]	2021	K600 (36d)	R3D-50	224^2	V	✗	92.6	69.2
MaCLR		K400 (28d)	R3D-18	128^2	V	✗	91.3	62.1
MaCLR		K400 (28d)	R3D-50	224^2	V	✗	94.0	67.4
MaCLR		K400 (28d)	R3D-50	224^2	V+F	✗	**94.2**	67.3
Fully-Supervised [83]		K400 (28d)	S3D	224^2	V	✗	96.8	75.9

to successfully "distill" motion information into the Visual pathway during pre-training. Finally, we also performed k-nearest-neighbor video retrieval to compare to the recent ASCNet work [38] in Table 3a. Despite similar accuracy when

Table 3. Video retrieval and low-shot learning on UCF101. (a) reports kNN video retrieval results on split1 of UCF101. A video is considered to be correctly predicted if its ground-truth label is among the labels of its k nearest neighbors retrieved from the training set. (b) Rows indicate different pretrainings on K400, while columns vary the % of UCF training data used for finetuning. All results are top-1 accuracy.

Method	1-NN	10-NN
ASCNet R18	58.9	82.2
MaCLR R18	**61.7**	**82.2**
MaCLR R50	73.4	88.2

(a) **kNN video retrieval**

Method	1%	5%	20%	40%	60%	80%	100%
Supervised	69.3	85.1	93.0	94.5	94.7	95.8	95.4
Visual-only	32.9	62.8	82.2	86.5	87.8	89.5	89.0
MaCLR	42.8	71.9	89.1	91.3	92.9	93.4	94.0
Δ	+9.9	+9.1	+6.9	+4.8	+5.1	+3.9	+5.0

(b) **Low-shot learning on UCF101**

$k = 10$, we largely outperform under the strictest 1-NN setting (+2.8%), which shows the higher precision of our representations.

Low-Shot Finetuning. We further investigate how the performance of MaCLR varies with respect to the amount of data available for finetuning on the target task. We evaluate using the Full Training protocol on the UCF101 dataset starting from just 1% of its training data (1 video per class) and gradually increase that to 100% (9.5k videos). We compare results against our two baselines: Visual-only and Supervised (Table 3b). MaCLR outperforms Visual-only across all training set sizes and it only requires 20% of the training videos to match the performance of Visual-only with 100% (89.1 vs 89.0). Another interesting observation is that the gap Δ between MaCLR and Visual-only reaches its maximum with the smallest training set (1%), suggesting that motion-visual learning is particularly helpful for generalization in low-shot scenarios.

4.3 Action Recognition on Something-Something

Next we evaluate MaCLR on Something-Something-v2 (SSv2) [1], a challenging action classification dataset that is heavily focused on motion. Different from UCF101 and HMDB51 which contain action classes similar to K400, SSv2 contains a very different set of actions featuring complex human object interactions, like "Moving something up" and "Pushing something from left to right". The dataset consists of 168k training, 24k validation and 24k test videos, all annotated with 174 action classes. We finetune on SSv2 with a recipe that mostly follows the official implementation of [23]: we use a clip size of 16×8 and a batchsize of 16 (over 8 GPUs); we train for 22 epochs with an initial learning rate of 0.03 and decay it by 10× twice at 14 and 18 epochs; and a learning rate warm-up is scheduled for 0.19 epochs starting from a learning rate of 0.0001.

We evaluate using both the Linear and Full finetune protocol. We compare methods that are pretrained in different ways: MaCLR and the Visual-only baseline are pretrained self-supervisedly on K400, whereas R3D-50 [23] is pretrained with full supervision on K400. Rand Init is a randomly initialized network without pretraining (Table 4a).

Table 4. Results on SSv2 and VidSitu. (a) reports top-1 accuracy. For finetuning, we use 16 × 8 clip as input following [23]. (b) reports top-1, top-5 accuracy and macro-averaged recall with five predictions on val set following [59]. All models use a R3D-50 backbone with 16 × 4 inputs.

Method	Pretrain	Sup.	acc@1	acc@5	rec@5	Method	Pretrain	Sup.	Full	Linear
Slow+NL	K400	✓	29.1	58.7	19.2	R3D-50	K400	✓	55.5	16.3
R3D-50	K400	✓	38.3	69.3	18.7	Rand Init	-	✗	45.4	-
Visual-only	K400	✗	32.8	61.6	13.6	Visual-only	K400	✗	54.9	16.6
MaCLR	K400	✗	**43.0**	**73.2**	17.5	**MaCLR**	K400	✗	**57.4**	**27.1**
(a) **Action classification on SSv2**						(b) **Verb prediction on VidSitu**				

For the Full protocol evaluation, it's clear that pretraining on K400 is beneficial and improves by almost +10 top-1 accuracy. Next, MaCLR outperforms the Visual-only baseline, showing once more the importance of learning from the added Motion pathway. Finally, when comparing to R3D-50 pretrained with full supervision, MaCLR not only closes the gap between self-supervised and fully-supervised methods, but even outperforms the supervised pretraining (+1.9).

Furthermore, we test with the Linear protocol, which is much more challenging due to the large difference between the label spaces of K400 and SSv2. As expected, Table 4a shows that the accuracy of all methods is much lower compared to their Full finetune results. However, it's notable that the gap between MaCLR and Visual-only significantly increases (+10.5 vs +2.5) compared to the Full protocol, which further demonstrates our method's generalization strength. Moreover, it's interesting to see the supervised baseline underperform both self-supervised methods, as it's harder to overcome taxonomy bias under Linear protocol compared to the Full protocol for a representation pretrained with a fixed label taxonomy. We believe this is a promising example showing how self-supervised training can remove the label taxonomy bias that is inevitable under supervised settings, and lead to more general video representations that can be better transferred to new domains.

In this section we evaluate how MaCLR pretrained on YouTube-style short clips (K400) generalizes to a very different video domain: movie clips. For this, we evaluate our video representation on the recent VidSitu benchmark [59] which features 30k movie clips from 3k different movies. Specifically, we benchmark on the *verb prediction* task of VidSitu, which contains 1560 action classes (e.g., speak, walk, run, climb). We compare different pretraining strategies, using the same R3D-50 backbone with 16 × 4 inputs, and we evaluate verb prediction results with top-1/top-5 accuracy and the macro-averaged recall metric with five predictions, as in [59]. The results are shown in Table 4b. For the supervised "R3D-50" baseline, we pretrained its backbone using the K400 labels and then fine-tuned it on VidSitu. As for self-supervised pretraining, we evaluate both the Visual-only baseline and our MaCLR. Similar to our observations on SSv2, MaCLR outperforms all methods on both acc@1 and acc@5 metrics. The improvement over the Visual-only baseline is also particularly substantial,

Table 5. Action detection on AVA. We use 8×8 clip as input for finetuning [23]. CVRL numbers are taken from [57].

Method	Pretrain Dataset	Sup.	mAP
Faster-RCNN [23]	ImageNet	✓	15.3
Faster-RCNN [23]	K400	✓	21.9
Rand Init	-	✗	6.6
CVRL [57]	K400	✗	16.3
Visual-only	K400	✗	18.6
MaCLR	K400	✗	**22.1**

which suggests that motion information is particularly important to help self-supervised representation generalize to different video domains.

4.4 Action Detection on AVA

In the previous section we showed that MaCLR can generalize to new video domains within the same downstream task (i.e., action recognition). However, we believe that our self-supervised representation can go beyond that and also generalize to novel downstream tasks, since it is not optimized for any task specific objective. To test this, we transfer MaCLR representation to the new task of action detection, which requires not only to recognize the action class, but also localize the person performing the action.

We evaluate action detection on the AVA dataset (CC-BY-4.0) [32] which contains 211k training and 57k validation videos. Spatiotemporal labels (i.e., action classes and bounding boxes) are provided at 1 FPS rate. We follow the standard evaluation protocol and compute mean Average Precision over 60 classes, using an IOU threshold of 0.5. We follow the Faster-RCNN detector design of [23] and use the Visual pathway architecture of Sect. 3.3 as the detector backbone. We fix the training schedule to 20 epochs with an initial learning rate of 0.1 and a batch size of 64 [23].

Results are shown in Table 5. Clearly, video pretraining plays a critical role in action detection, as demonstrated by the low mAP of 6.6 when training from scratch and the substantially lower AP achieved by supervised pretraining on ImageNet (pretrained 2D convs are inflated into 3D for fine-tuning [11]) compared to supervised pretraining on K400. As for self-supervised pretraining, both the Visual-only baseline and MaCLR outperform ImageNet supervised pretraining, again demonstrating the importance of pretraining on videos. Moreover, MaCLR again outperforms both the Visual-only baseline and the recent CVRL approach, which also only uses RGB inputs for pretraining.

Finally, note how MaCLR even outperforms the supervised Faster-RCNN pretrained on K400. To the best of our knowledge, we are the first to demonstrate that self-supervised video learning can transfer to action detection and match the performance of fully-supervised pretraining.

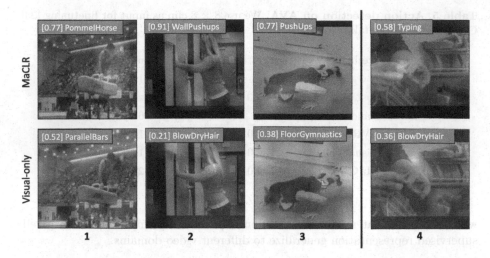

Fig. 2. Grad-CAM visualization for MaCLR (top) and Visual-only (bottom) **representations**. Predictions are overlaid on each frame.

4.5   Visualizing MaCLR Representations

To gain deeper insights on what MaCLR has learned in its representations, we adopt Grad-CAM [62] to visualize the spatiotemporal regions that contribute the most to the classification decisions on UCF101. As shown in Fig. 2, we observe that the representation learned by MaCLR focuses more on the "motion-sensitive" regions (i.e., regions where object motion likely occur). For example, in col-1, MaCLR makes the correct prediction of "PommelHorse" by focusing its attention on the person carrying out the motion. The Visual-only model, on the other hand, incorrectly predicted "ParallelBars" as it finds "bar-like" straight lines in the background. This pattern can also be observed in col-2 (Visual-only model predicts "BlowDryHair" after finding hair textures). Furthermore, we can observe another type of behavior in col-3. In both examples, the background scenes (gym) are associated with many fine-grained action classes (different gym activities), our model is able to distinguish them by focusing on the actual motion pattern. The baseline, instead, gets confused as it focuses too much on the background. Finally, we present a failure case in the last column where MaCLR correctly focuses on the right motion region (fingers), but confuses the finger motion of "Knitting" with "Typing".

Conclusion

We presented MaCLR to learn self-supervised video representations with explicit cross-modal motion-visual contrastive learning. We demonstrated SOTA self-supervised performance with MaCLR across various datasets and tasks. Moreover, we showed that MaCLR representations can be as effective as representations learned with full supervision for SSv2 action recognition, VidSitu verb prediction and AVA action detection. Given the simplicity of our method, we hope it will serve as a strong baseline for future research in self-supervised video representation learning.

References

1. 20BN-Something-Something Dataset V2
2. Alwassel, H., Mahajan, D., Korbar, B., Torresani, L., Ghanem, B., Tran, D.: Self-supervised learning by cross-modal audio-video clustering. In: NeurIPS (2020)
3. Bao, L., Wu, B., Liu, W.: CNN in MRF: video object segmentation via inference in a CNN-based higher-order spatio-temporal MRF. In: CVPR (2018)
4. Benaim, S., et al.: SpeedNet: learning the speediness in videos. In: CVPR (2020)
5. Bertinetto, L., Valmadre, J., Henriques, J.F., Vedaldi, A., Torr, P.H.: Fully-convolutional siamese networks for object tracking. In: ECCV (2016)
6. Brattoli, B., Buchler, U., Wahl, A.S., Schwab, M.E., Ommer, B.: LSTM self-supervision for detailed behavior analysis. In: CVPR (2017)
7. Brown, T.B., et al.: Language models are few-shot learners. In: NeurIPS (2020)
8. Brox, T., Malik, J.: Large displacement optical flow: descriptor matching in variational motion estimation. T-PAMI (2011)
9. Buchler, U., Brattoli, B., Ommer, B.: Improving spatiotemporal self-supervision by deep reinforcement learning. In: ECCV (2018)
10. Caron, M., Misra, I., Mairal, J., Goyal, P., Bojanowski, P., Joulin, A.: Unsupervised learning of visual features by contrasting cluster assignments. In: NeurIPS (2020)
11. Carreira, J., Zisserman, A.: Quo vadis, action recognition? a new model and the kinetics dataset. In: CVPR (2017)
12. Chen, T., Kornblith, S., Norouzi, M., Hinton, G.: A simple framework for contrastive learning of visual representations. In: ICML (2020)
13. Chen, X., Fan, H., Girshick, R., He, K.: Improved baselines with momentum contrastive learning. arXiv preprint arXiv:2003.04297 (2020)
14. Chen, X., He, K.: Exploring simple siamese representation learning. In: CVPR (2021)
15. Cheng, J., Tsai, Y.H., Hung, W.C., Wang, S., Yang, M.H.: Fast and accurate online video object segmentation via tracking parts. In: CVPR (2018)
16. Dalal, N., Triggs, B., Schmid, C.: Human detection using oriented histograms of flow and appearance. In: ECCV (2006)
17. Deng, J., Dong, W., Socher, R., Li, L.J., Li, K., Fei-Fei, L.: Imagenet: a large-scale hierarchical image database. In: CVPR (2009)
18. Devlin, J., Chang, M.W., Lee, K., Toutanova, K.: BERT: pre-training of deep bidirectional transformers for language understanding. In: NAACL (2019)
19. Diba, A., Sharma, V., Gool, L.V., Stiefelhagen, R.: DynamoNet: dynamic action and motion network. In: ICCV (2019)
20. Doersch, C., Gupta, A., Efros, A.A.: Unsupervised visual representation learning by context prediction. In: ICCV (2015)
21. Dosovitskiy, A., et al.: Flownet: learning optical flow with convolutional networks. In: ICCV (2015)
22. Fan, H., Li, Y., Xiong, B., Lo, W.Y., Feichtenhofer, C.: Pyslowfast. https://github.com/facebookresearch/slowfast (2020)
23. Feichtenhofer, C., Fan, H., Malik, J., He, K.: SlowFast networks for video recognition. In: ICCV (2019)

24. Feichtenhofer, C., Fan, H., Xiong, B., Girshick, R., He, K.: A large-scale study on unsupervised spatiotemporal representation learning. In: CVPR (2021)

25. Feichtenhofer, C., Pinz, A., Wildes, R.: Spatiotemporal residual networks for video action recognition. In: NeurIPS (2016)

26. Feichtenhofer, C., Pinz, A., Zisserman, A.: Convolutional two-stream network fusion for video action recognition. In: CVPR (2016)

27. Feichtenhofer, C., Pinz, A., Zisserman, A.: Detect to track and track to detect. In: ICCV (2017)

28. Fernando, B., Bilen, H., Gavves, E., Gould, S.: Self-supervised video representation learning with odd-one-out networks. In: CVPR (2017)

29. Fragkiadaki, K., Arbelaez, P., Felsen, P., Malik, J.: Learning to segment moving objects in videos. In: CVPR (2015)

30. Gavrilyuk, K., Jain, M., Karmanov, I., Snoek, C.G.: Motion-augmented self-training for video recognition at smaller scale. In: Proceedings of the IEEE/CVF International Conference on Computer Vision (2021)

31. Grill, J.B., et al.: Bootstrap your own latent: a new approach to self-supervised learning. In: NeurIPS (2020)

32. Gu, C., et al.: AVA: A video dataset of spatio-temporally localized atomic visual actions. In: CVPR (2018)

33. Hadsell, R., Chopra, S., LeCun, Y.: Dimensionality reduction by learning an invariant mapping. In: CVPR (2006)

34. Han, T., Xie, W., Zisserman, A.: Memory-augmented dense predictive coding for video representation learning. In: ECCV (2020)

35. Han, T., Xie, W., Zisserman, A.: Self-supervised co-training for video representation learning. In: NeurIPS (2020)

36. He, K., Fan, H., Wu, Y., Xie, S., Girshick, R.: Momentum contrast for unsupervised visual representation learning. In: CVPR (2020)

37. Henriques, J.F., Caseiro, R., Martins, P., Batista, J.: High-speed tracking with kernelized correlation filters. T-PAMI (2014)

38. Huang, D., et al.: ASCNet: self-supervised video representation learning with appearance-speed consistency. In: ICCV (2021)

39. Huang, L., Liu, Y., Wang, B., Pan, P., Xu, Y., Jin, R.: Self-supervised video representation learning by context and motion decoupling. In: CVPR (2021)

40. Kang, K., et al.: Object detection in videos with tubelet proposal networks. In: CVPR (2017)

41. Kay, W., et al.: The kinetics human action video dataset. arXiv preprint arXiv:1705.06950 (2017)

42. Kolesnikov, A., Zhai, X., Beyer, L.: Revisiting self-supervised visual representation learning. In: CVPR (2019)

43. Kuehne, H., Jhuang, H., Garrote, E., Poggio, T., Serre, T.: HMDB: a large video database for human motion recognition. In: ICCV (2011)

44. Laptev, I., Marszalek, M., Schmid, C., Rozenfeld, B.: Learning realistic human actions from movies. In: CVPR (2008)

45. Li, Y., Fang, C., Yang, J., Wang, Z., Lu, X., Yang, M.H.: Flow-grounded spatial-temporal video prediction from still images. In: ECCV (2018)

46. Mahendran, A., Thewlis, J., Vedaldi, A.: Cross pixel optical-flow similarity for self-supervised learning. In: ACCV (2018)

47. Miech, A., Alayrac, J.B., Smaira, L., Laptev, I., Sivic, J., Zisserman, A.: End-to-end learning of visual representations from uncurated instructional videos. In: CVPR (2020)

48. Misra, I., Maaten, L.V.D.: Self-supervised learning of pretext-invariant representations. In: CVPR (2020)
49. Misra, I., Zitnick, C.L., Hebert, M.: Shuffle and learn: unsupervised learning using temporal order verification. In: ECCV (2016)
50. Noroozi, M., Favaro, P.: Unsupervised learning of visual representations by solving jigsaw puzzles. In: ECCV (2016)
51. Noroozi, M., Pirsiavash, H., Favaro, P.: Representation learning by learning to count. In: ICCV (2017)
52. Oord, A.V.D., Li, Y., Vinyals, O.: Representation learning with contrastive predictive coding. arXiv preprint arXiv:1807.03748 (2018)
53. Patrick, M., et al.: Multi-modal self-supervision from generalized data transformations. In: ICCV (2021)
54. Perazzi, F., Khoreva, A., Benenson, R., Schiele, B., Sorkine-Hornung, A.: Learning video object segmentation from static images. In: CVPR (2017)
55. Piergiovanni, A., Angelova, A., Ryoo, M.S.: Evolving losses for unsupervised video representation learning. In: CVPR (2020)
56. Qian, R., et al.: Enhancing self-supervised video representation learning via multi-level feature optimization. In: ICCV (2021)
57. Qian, R., et al.: Spatiotemporal contrastive video representation learning. In: CVPR (2021)
58. Recasens, A., et al.: Broaden your views for self-supervised video learning. In: ICCV (2021)
59. Sadhu, A., Gupta, T., Yatskar, M., Nevatia, R., Kembhavi, A.: Visual semantic role labeling for video understanding. In: CVPR (2021)
60. Sayed, N., Brattoli, B., Ommer, B.: Cross and learn: cross-modal self-supervision. In: German Conference on Pattern Recognition (2018)
61. Sedaghat, N., Zolfaghari, M., Brox, T.: Hybrid learning of optical flow and next frame prediction to boost optical flow in the wild. arXiv preprint arXiv:1612.03777 (2016)
62. Selvaraju, R.R., Cogswell, M., Das, A., Vedantam, R., Parikh, D., Batra, D.: Grad-CAM: visual explanations from deep networks via gradient-based localization. In: ICCV (2017)
63. Simonyan, K., Zisserman, A.: Very deep convolutional networks for large-scale image recognition. In: ICLR (2015)
64. Sobel, I.: History and definition of the sobel operator (2014)
65. Soomro, K., Zamir, A.R., Shah, M.: A dataset of 101 human action classes from videos in the wild. In: ICCV Workshops (2013)
66. Sun, C., Baradel, F., Murphy, K., Schmid, C.: Contrastive bidirectional transformer for temporal representation learning. arXiv preprint arXiv:1906.05743 (2019)
67. Teed, Z., Deng, J.: Raft: Recurrent all-pairs field transforms for optical flow. In: ECCV (2020)
68. Tsai, Y.H., Yang, M.H., Black, M.J.: Video segmentation via object flow. In: CVPR (2016)
69. Ummenhofer, B., et al.: Demon: depth and motion network for learning monocular stereo. In: CVPR (2017)
70. Vondrick, C., Shrivastava, A., Fathi, A., Guadarrama, S., Murphy, K.: Tracking emerges by colorizing videos. In: ECCV (2018)
71. Wang, H., Schmid, C.: Action recognition with improved trajectories. In: ICCV (2013)

72. Wang, J., Jiao, J., Bao, L., He, S., Liu, Y., Liu, W.: Self-supervised spatio-temporal representation learning for videos by predicting motion and appearance statistics. In: CVPR (2019)

73. Wang, J., Bertasius, G., Tran, D., Torresani, L.: Long-short temporal contrastive learning of video transformers. arXiv preprint arXiv:2106.09212 (2021)

74. Wang, L., et al.: Temporal segment networks: towards good practices for deep action recognition. In: ECCV (2016)

75. Wang, X., Girshick, R., Gupta, A., He, K.: Non-local neural networks. In: CVPR (2018)

76. Wang, X., Gupta, A.: Unsupervised Learning of Visual Representations using Videos. In: ICCV (2015)

77. Wang, X., Jabri, A., Efros, A.A.: Learning correspondence from the cycle-consistency of time. In: CVPR (2019)

78. Wei, D., Lim, J.J., Zisserman, A., Freeman, W.T.: Learning and using the arrow of time. In: CVPR (2018)

79. Weinzaepfel, P., Revaud, J., Harchaoui, Z., Schmid, C.: Deepflow: large displacement optical flow with deep matching. In: ICCV (2013)

80. Wu, Z., Xiong, Y., Yu, S.X., Lin, D.: Unsupervised feature learning via non-parametric instance discrimination. In: CVPR (2018)

81. Xiao, F., Lee, Y.J.: Video object detection with an aligned spatial-temporal memory. In: ECCV (2018)

82. Xiao, F., Lee, Y.J., Grauman, K., Malik, J., Feichtenhofer, C.: Audiovisual slowfast networks for video recognition. arXiv preprint arXiv:2001.08740 (2019)

83. Xie, S., Sun, C., Huang, J., Tu, Z., Murphy, K.: Rethinking spatiotemporal feature learning: speed-accuracy trade-offs in video classification. In: ECCV (2018)

84. Zhang, R., Isola, P., Efros, A.A.: Colorful image colorization. In: ECCV (2016)

85. Zhu, X., Wang, Y., Dai, J., Yuan, L., Wei, Y.: Flow-guided feature aggregation for video object detection. ICCV (2017)

Learning Long-Term Spatial-Temporal Graphs for Active Speaker Detection

Kyle Min[1], Sourya Roy[2], Subarna Tripathi[1(✉)], Tanaya Guha[3],
and Somdeb Majumdar[1]

[1] Intel Labs, Santa Clara, USA
{kyle.min,subarna.tripathi,somdeb.majumdar}@intel.com
[2] UC Riverside, Riverside, USA
[3] University of Glasgow, Glasgow, Scotland

Abstract. Active speaker detection (ASD) in videos with multiple speakers is a challenging task as it requires learning effective audiovisual features and spatial-temporal correlations over long temporal windows. In this paper, we present SPELL, a novel spatial-temporal graph learning framework that can solve complex tasks such as ASD. To this end, each person in a video frame is first encoded in a unique node for that frame. Nodes corresponding to a single person across frames are connected to encode their temporal dynamics. Nodes within a frame are also connected to encode inter-person relationships. Thus, SPELL reduces ASD to a node classification task. Importantly, SPELL is able to reason over long temporal contexts for all nodes without relying on computationally expensive fully connected graph neural networks. Through extensive experiments on the AVA-ActiveSpeaker dataset, we demonstrate that learning graph-based representations can significantly improve the active speaker detection performance owing to its explicit spatial and temporal structure. SPELL outperforms all previous state-of-the-art approaches while requiring significantly lower memory and computational resources. Our code is publicly available: https://github.com/SRA2/SPELL.

1 Introduction

Holistic scene understanding in the wild is still a challenge in computer vision despite recent breakthroughs in several other areas. A *scene* represents real-life events spanning complex visual and auditory information, which are often intertwined. Active speaker detection (ASD) is a key component in scene understanding and is an inherently multimodal (audio-visual) task. The objective here is, given a video input, to identify which persons are speaking in each frame.

K. Min and S. Roy—Authors contributed equally.
S. Roy—Work partially done during an internship at Intel Labs.

Supplementary Information The online version contains supplementary material available at https://doi.org/10.1007/978-3-031-19833-5_22.

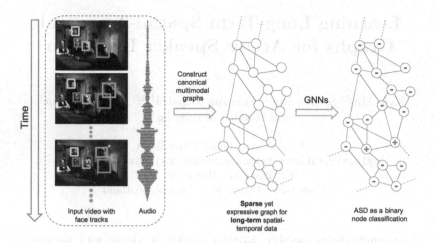

Fig. 1. SPELL converts a video into a canonical graph from the audio-visual input data, where each node corresponds to a person in a frame, and an edge represents a spatial or temporal interaction between the nodes. The constructed graph is dense enough for modeling long-term dependencies through message passing across the temporally-distant but relevant nodes, yet sparse enough to be processed within low memory and computation budget. The Active Speaker Detection (ASD) task is posed as a binary node classification in this long-range spatial-temporal graph.

This has numerous practical applications ranging from speech enhancement systems [1] to human-robot interaction [30,31].

Earlier efforts on ASD had limited success due to the unavailability of large datasets, powerful learning models, or computing resources [7–9]. With the release of AVA-ActiveSpeaker [26], a large and diverse ASD dataset, a number of promising approaches have been developed including both visual-only and audio-visual methods. As visual-only methods [8] are unable to distinguish between verbal and non-verbal lip movements, more recent approaches have focused on joint modeling of the audio-visual information. Audio-visual approaches [2,17,18,33,37] address the task by first encoding visual (primarily facial) and audio features from videos, and then by classifying the fused multi-modal features. Such models generally have multi-stage frameworks [2,17,18,37] and show good detection performance. However, state-of-the-art methods have relied on complex architectures for processing the audio-visual features with high computation and memory overheads. For example, TalkNet [33] suggests using a transformer-style architecture [34] to model the cross-modal information from the audio-visual input. ASDNet [17], which is the leading state-of-the-art method, uses a complex 3D convolutional neural network (CNN) to extract more powerful features. These approaches are not scalable and may not be suitable for real-world situations with limited memory and computation budgets.

In this paper, we propose an efficient graph-based framework, which we call SPELL (**Sp**atial-T**e**mporal Graph **L**earning). Figure 1 illustrates an overview of our framework. We construct a multimodal graph from the audio-visual data and cast the active speaker detection as a graph node classification task. First, we create a graph where each node corresponds to each person at each frame and the edges represent spatial or temporal relationships among them. The initial node features are constructed using simple and lightweight 2D CNNs instead of a complex 3D CNN or a transformer. Next, we perform binary node classification – active or inactive speaker – on this graph by learning a three-layer graph neural network (GNN) model each with a small number of parameters. In our framework, graphs are constructed specifically for encoding the spatial and temporal dependencies among the different facial identities. Therefore, the GNN can leverage this graph structure and model the temporal continuity in speech as well as the long-term spatial-temporal context, while requiring low memory and computation.

Although the proposed graph structure can model the long-term spatial-temporal information from the audio-visual features, it is likely that some of the short-term information may be lost in the process of feature encoding. This is because we use 2D CNNs that are not well-suited for processing the spatial-temporal information when compared to the transformer or the 3D CNNs. To encode the short-term information, we adopt TSM [19] - a generic module for 2D CNNs that is capable of modeling temporal information without introducing any additional parameters or computation. We empirically verify that SPELL can benefit both from the supplementary short-term information provided by TSM and the long-term information modeled by our graph structure.

We show the effectiveness of SPELL by performing extensive experiments on the AVA-ActiveSpeaker dataset [26]. Using our spatial-temporal graph framework on top of the TSM-inspired feature encoders, SPELL outperforms all previous state-of-the-art approaches. Critically, SPELL requires significantly less hardware resources for the visual feature encoding (0.7 GFLOPs, 11.2M #Params) compared to ASDNet [17] (13.2 GFLOPs, 48.6M params), which is the leading state-of-the-art method. In addition, SPELL achieved 2nd place in the AVA-ActiveSpeaker challenge at ActivityNet 2022[1], which also demonstrates the effectiveness of our method (please refer to the technical report [22]).

There are three main contributions in this paper:

- We present a graph-based approach for solving the task of active speaker detection over long time supports by casting it as a node classification problem.
- Our model, SPELL, learns from videos to model the short-term and long-term spatial-temporal information. Specifically, we propose to construct graphs on the TSM-inspired audio-visual features. The graphs are dense enough for message passing across temporally-distant nodes, yet sparse enough to model their interactions within tight memory and compute constraints.
- SPELL notably outperforms existing methods with lower memory and computation complexity on the active speaker detection benchmark dataset, AVA-ActiveSpeaker.

---

[1] https://research.google.com/ava/challenge.html.

2 Related Work

We discuss related works in two relevant areas: application of GNNs in video scene understanding and active speaker detection.

GNNs for Scene Understanding. CNNs, Long Short Term Memory (LSTM), and their variants have long dominated the field of video understanding. In recent times, two new types of models are gaining traction in many areas of visual information processing: Transformers [34] and GNNs. They are not necessarily in competition with the former models, but it has been shown that they can augment the performance of CNN/LSTM based models. Applications of specialized GNN models in video understanding include visual relationship forecasting [21], dialog modeling [11], video retrieval [32], emotion recognition [28], and action detection [38]. GNN-based generalized video representation frameworks have also been proposed [3,23,24] that can be used for multiple downstream tasks. For example, in Arnab et al. [3], a fully connected graph is constructed over the foreground nodes from video frames in a sliding window fashion, and a foreground node is connected to other context nodes from its neighboring frames. The message passing over the fully connected spatial-temporal graph is expensive in terms of the computational time and memory. Thus in practice such models end up using a small sliding window, making them unable to process longer-term sequences. SPELL also operates on foreground nodes - particularly, faces. However, the graph structure is not fully connected. We construct the graph such that it enables interactions only between relevant nodes over space and time. The graph remains sparse enough such that the longer-term context can be accommodated within a comparatively smaller memory and compute budget.

Active Speaker Detection (ASD). Earlier work on active speaker detection by Cutler et al. [7] detects correlated audio-visual signals using a time-delayed neural network. Subsequent works depend only on visual information and considers a simpler set-up focusing on lip and facial gestures [8]. More recently, high-performing ASD models rely on large networks - developed for capturing the spatial-temporal variations in audio-visual signals, often relying on ensemble networks or complex 3D CNN features [2,33]. Sharma et al. [27] and Zhang et al. [36] both used large 3D CNN architectures for audio-visual learning. The Active Speaker in Context (ASC) model [2] uses non-local attention modules with an LSTM to model the temporal interactions between audio and visual features encoded by two-stream ResNet-18 networks [13]. TalkNet [33] achieves superior performance through the use of a 3D CNN and a couple of Transformers [34] resulting in an effectively large model. Another recent work, the ASDNet [17], uses 3D-ResNet101 for encoding visual data and SincNet [25] for audio. The Unified Context Network (UniCon) [37] proposes relational context modules to capture visual (spatial) and audio-visual context based on convolutional layers. Much of these advances are due to the availability of the AVA-ActiveSpeaker dataset [26]. Previously available multimodal datasets (e.g. [4]) were either smaller or constrained or lacked variability in data. The work by Roth et al. [26] also introduced a competitive baseline along with the large dataset.

Their baseline involves jointly learning an audio-visual model that is end-to-end trainable. The audio and visual branches in this model are CNN-based which uses a depth-wise separable technique.

MAAS [18] presents a different multimodal graph approach. Our work differs from MAAS in several ways, where the main difference is in the handling of temporal context. While MAAS focuses on short-term temporal windows to construct their graphs, we focus on constructing longer-term audio-visual graphs. More specifically, in MAAS, different faces are connected only between consecutive frames. In contrast, SPELL directly connects faces in a longer-term neighborhood controlled by the time threshold hyperparameter, τ (defined in Sect. 3.2). In addition, SPELL exploits the temporal ordering patterns of the face tracks by using all the forward/backward/undirected edges in the time domain. In SPELL, each graph can span from 13 to 55 s (refer to Sect. 4.2) of a video depending on the number of nodes. This is significantly larger than MAAS where the time window size is fixed at 1.59 s. During inference, SPELL performs single forward pass, whereas MAAS performs multiple forward passes.

3 Method

In this section, we describe our approach in detail. Figure 2 illustrates how SPELL constructs a graph from an input video where each node corresponds to a face within a temporal window of the video. SPELL is unique in terms of its canonical way of constructing the graph from a video. The graph is able to reason over long temporal contexts for all nodes without being fully-connected. This is an important design choice to reduce memory and computation overheads. The edges in the graph are only between *relevant* nodes needed for message passing, leading to a sparse graph that can be accommodated within a small memory and computation budget. After converting the video into a graph, we train a lightweight GNN to perform binary node classification on this graph. The model architecture is illustrated in Figure 3. The model utilizes three separate GNN modules for the forward, backward, and undirected graph, respectively. Each module has three layers where the weight of the second layer is shared across all the above three modules. More details and the intuition behind the design choice are described in Sect. 3.4.

3.1 Notations

Let $G = (V, E)$ be a graph with the node set V and edge set E. For any $v \in V$, we define N_v to be the set of neighbors of v in G. We will assume the graph has self-loops, i.e., $v \in N_v$. In addition, let X denote the set of given node features $\{\mathbf{x}_v\}_{v \in V}$ where $\mathbf{x}_v \in \mathbb{R}^d$ is the feature vector associated with the node v. Given this setup, we can define a k-layer GNN as a set of functions $\mathcal{F} = \{f_i\}_{i \in [k]}$ for $i \geq 1$ where each $f_i : V \rightarrow \mathbb{R}^m$ (m will depend on layer index i). All f_i is parameterized by a set of learnable parameters. Furthermore, $X_V^i = \{\mathbf{x}_v\}_{v \in V}$ is the set of features at layer i where $\mathbf{x}_v = f_i(v)$. Here, we assume that f_i has access to the graph G and the feature set from the last layer X_V^{i-1}.

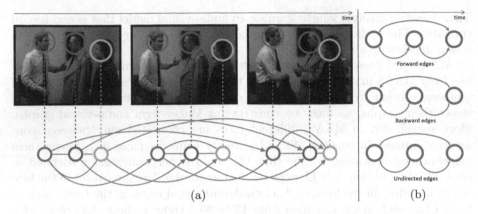

(a)   (b)

Fig. 2. (a): An illustration of our graph construction process. The frames above are temporally ordered from left to right. The three colors of blue, red, and yellow denote three identities that are present in the frames. Each node in the graph corresponds to each face in the frames. SPELL connects all the inter-identity faces from the same frame with the undirected edges. SPELL also connects the same identities by the forward/backward/undirected edges across the frames. In this example, the same identities are connected across the frames by the forward edges, which are directed and only go in the temporally forward direction. (b): The process for creating the backward and undirected graph is identical, except in the former case the edges for the same identities go in the opposite direction and the latter has no directed edge. Each node also contains the audio information which is not shown here. (Color figure online)

- SAGE-CONV aggregation: This aggregation was proposed by [12] and has a computationally efficient form. Given a d-dimensional feature set X_V^{i-1} , the function $f_i : V \to \mathbb{R}^m$ is defined for $i \geq 1$ as follows:

$$f(v) = \sigma \Big(\sum_{w \in N_v} \mathsf{M}_i \mathbf{x}_w \Big)$$

where $\mathbf{x}_w \in X_V^{i-1}$, $\mathsf{M}_i \in \mathbb{R}^{m \times d}$ is a learnable linear transformation, and $\sigma : \mathbb{R} \to \mathbb{R}$ is a non-linear activation function applied point-wise.

- EDGE-CONV aggregation: EDGE-CONV [35] models global and local-structures by applying channel-wise symmetric aggregation operation on the edge features associated with all the edges emanating from each node. The aggregation function $f_i : V \to \mathbb{R}^m$ can be defined as:

$$f_i(v) = \sigma \Big(\sum_{w \in N_v} \mathbf{g}_i \big(\mathbf{x}_v \circ \mathbf{x}_w \big) \Big)$$

where $\circ$ denotes concatenation and $\mathbf{g}_i : \mathbb{R}^{2d} \to \mathbb{R}^m$ is a learnable transformation. Often $\mathbf{g}_i$ is implemented by MLPs. The number of parameters for EDGE-CONV is larger than SAGE-CONV. This gives the EDGE-CONV layer more expressive power at a cost of higher complexity and possible risk of overfitting. For our model, we set $\mathbf{g}_i$ to be an MLP with two layers of linear transformation and a non-linearity. We describe the details in Sect. 4.

3.2   Video as a Multimodal Graph

We represent a video as a multimodal graph that is suitable for the task of active speaker detection. We assume that the bounding-box information of every face region in each frame is given as per the problem set up. For simplicity, we assume that the entire video is represented by a single graph - if the video has n faces in it, the graph will have n nodes. In our actual implementation, we temporally order the set of all faces in a video, divide them in contiguous sets, and then construct one graph for each such set.

Let B be the set of all face images cropped from an input video (i.e. face-crops). Then, each element $b \in B$ can be represented by a tuple (Box, Time, Id), where Box is the normalized bounding-box coordinates of a face-crop in its frame, Time is the time-stamp of its frame, and Id is a unique string that is common to all the face-crops that shares the same identity.

In other words, B can be represented by a set of nodes $[n]$ where $n = |B|$ is the total number of faces that appear in the video. Box is treated as a map such that $Box(i)$ is defined by the bounding-box coordinates of the i-th face for any $i \in [n]$. Similarly, $Time(i)$ and $Id(i)$ correspond to the time and identity of the i-th face, respectively. With this setup, the node set of $G = (V, E)$ is $V = [n] \cong B$, and for any $(i, j) \in [n] \times [n]$, we have $(i, j) \in E$ if either of the following two conditions are satisfied:

- $Id(i) = Id(j)$ and $|Time(i)\text{-}Time(j)| \leq \tau$
- $Time(i) = Time(j)$

where τ is a hyperparameter for the maximum time difference between the nodes having the same identities. In essence, we connect two nodes (faces) if they share the same identity and are temporally close or if they belong to the same frame. Thus, the interactions between different speakers and the temporal variations of the same speaker can jointly be modeled.

To pose the active speaker detection task as a node classification problem, we also need to specify the feature vectors for each node $v \in V$. We use a two-stream 2D ResNet [13] architecture as in [2,26] for extracting the visual features of each face-crop and the audio features of each frame. Then, a feature vector of node v is defined to be $x_v = [v_{visual} \circ v_{audio}]$ where v_{visual} is the visual feature of face-crop v and v_{audio} is the audio feature of v's frame where $\circ$ denotes the concatenation. Finally, we can write $G = (V, E, X)$ where X is the set of the node features.

3.3   ASD as a Node Classification Task

In the previous section, we described our graph construction procedure that converts a video into a graph $G = (V, E, X)$ where each node has its own audio-visual feature vector. During the training process, we have access to the ground-truth labels of all face-crops indicating if each of the face-crop is active speaker or not. Therefore, the task of active speaker detection can be naturally posed as a binary node classification problem in the constructed graph G, whether a

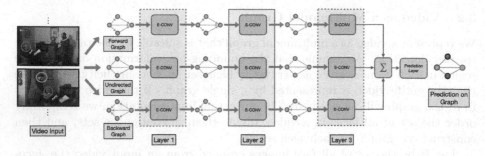

Fig. 3. An illustration of our proposed *Bi-directional* (a.k.a. *Bi-dir*) GNN model for active speaker detection. Here, we have three separate GNN modules for the forward, backward, and undirected graph, respectively. Each module has three layers where the weight of the second layer is shared by all three graph modules. The second layer is placed inside a solid-lined box to indicate the weight sharing while for the first and the third layer we use dotted-lines. E-CONV and S-CONV are shorthand for **EDGE-CONV** and **SAGE-CONV**, respectively. We use the color coding: blue and red to denote different identities in input frames. The output of the third layers are added together and then passed to the prediction layer. It applies the sigmoid function to the summed features of every node and produces node classification probabilities. (Color figure online)

node is speaking or not speaking. Specifically, we train a three-layer GNN for this classification task. The first layer in the network uses **EDGE-CONV** aggregation to learn pair-wise interactions between the nodes. For the last two layers, we observe that using **SAGE-CONV** aggregation provides better performance than **EDGE-CONV**, possibly due to **EDGE-CONV**'s tendency to overfit.

3.4 SPELL

We now describe how our graph construction and embedding strategy takes temporal ordering into consideration. Specifically, as we use the criterion: $|\text{Time}(i) - \text{Time}(j)| \leq \tau$ for connecting the nodes having the same identities across the frames, the resultant graph becomes undirected. In this process, we lose the information of the temporal ordering of the nodes. To address this issue, we explicitly incorporate temporal direction as shown in Fig. 2(b). The undirected GNN is augmented with two other parallel networks; one for going forward in time and another for going backward in time.

More precisely, in addition to the undirected graph, we create a forward graph where we connect (i, j) if and only if $0 \geq \text{Time}(i) - \text{Time}(j) \geq -\tau$. Similarly, (i, j) is connected in a backward graph if and only if $0 \leq \text{Time}(i) - \text{Time}(j) \leq \tau$. This gives us three separate graphs where each of the graphs can model different spatial-temporal relationships between the nodes. Furthermore, the weights of the second layer of each graph is shared across the three graphs. This weight sharing technique can enforce the temporal consistencies among the different information modeled by the three graphs as well as reduce the number of parameters. For the remaining parts of this paper, we will refer to this network that is augmented with the forward/backward graphs as *Bi-directional* or *Bi-dir* for short.

The proposed three-layer *Bi-dir* is illustrated in Fig. 3. We note that right before the *Bi-dir* is applied, the audio and the visual features are further encoded by two learnable MLP layers (linear transformation with ReLU activation) separately and then added to form the fused features for the graph nodes. After the fused features are processed by the first and the second layers, the third layer aggregates all the information and reduce the feature dimension to 1. These 1D features coming from the three separate graphs are added and applied to the sigmoid function to get the final prediction score for each node.

3.5   Feature Learning

Similar to ASC [2], we use a two-stream 2D ResNet [13] architecture for the audio-visual feature encoding. The networks take as visual input k consecutive face-crops and take as audio input the Mel-spectrogram of the audio wave sliced along the time duration of the face-crops for the visual stream. Although the 2D ResNet requires significantly lower hardware resources than 3D CNN counterparts or a transformer-style architecture [34], it is not specifically designed for processing spatial-temporal information that is crucial in understanding video contents. To better encode the spatial-temporal information, we augment the visual feature encoder with TSM [19], which provides 2D CNNs with a capability to model the short-term temporal information without introducing any additional parameters or computation. This additional use of TSM can greatly improve the quality of the visual features, and we empirically establish that SPELL benefits from the supplementary short-term information. The audio-visual features from the two stream are concatenated to be node features $\{\mathbf{x}_v\}$.

Data Augmentation. Reliable ASD models should be able to detect speaking signals even if there is a noise in the audio. To make our method robust to noise, we make use of data augmentation methods while training the feature extractor. Inspired by TalkNet [33], we augment the audio data by negative sampling. For each audio signal in a batch, we randomly select another audio sample from the whole training dataset and add it after decreasing its volume by a random factor. This technique can effectively increase the amount of training samples for the feature extractor by selecting negative samples from the whole training dataset.

Spatial Feature. The visual features encoded by the 2D ResNet do not have any information about where each face is spatially located in each frame because we only use the cropped face regions in the visual feature encoding. Here, we argue that the spatial locations of speakers can be another type of inductive bias. In order to exploit the spatial information of each face-crop, we incorporate the spatial features corresponding to each face as additional input to the node feature as follows: We project the 4-D spatial feature of each face region parameterized by the normalized center location, height and width (x, y, h, w) to a 64-D feature vector using a single fully-connected layer. The resulting spatial feature vector is then concatenated to the visual feature at each node.

Table 1. Performance comparisons with other state-of-the-art methods on the validation set of AVA-ActiveSpeaker dataset [26]. We report mAP (mean average precision). SPELL outperforms all the previous approaches. 3D Conv denotes an additional use of one or more 3D convolutional layers. Note that TSM [19] does not increase memory usage nor the computation cost.

Method	Feature encoding network	mAP (%)
Roth *et al.* [26]	MobileNet [14]	79.2
Zhang *et al.* [36]	3D ResNet-18 [29] + VGG-M [5]	84.0
MAAS-LAN [18]	2D ResNet-18 [13]	85.1
Chung *et al.* [6]	VGG-M [5] + 3D Conv	85.5
ASC [2]	2D ResNet-18 [13]	87.1
MAAS-TAN [18]	2D ResNet-18 [13]	88.8
UniCon [37]	2D ResNet-18 [13]	92.0
TalkNet [33]	2D ResNet-18/34 [13] + 3D Conv	92.3
ASDNet [17]	3D ResNeXt-18 [16] + SincDSNet [25]	93.5
SPELL (Ours)	2D ResNet-18-TSM [13,19]	**94.2**
SPELL+ (Ours)	2D ResNet-50-TSM [13,19]	**94.9**

4   Experiments

We perform experiments on the large-scale AVA-ActiveSpeaker dataset [26]. Derived from Hollywood movies, this dataset comes with a number of face tracks for active and inactive speakers and their audio signals. Its extensive annotations of the face tracks is a key feature that was missing in its predecessors.

Implementation Details. Following ASC [26], we utilize a two-stream network with a ResNet [13] backbone for the audio-visual feature encoder. In the training process, we perform visual augmentation including horizontal flipping, color jittering, and scaling and audio augmentation as described in Sect. 3.5. We extract the encoded audio, visual, and spatial features for each face-crop to make the node feature. For the visual features, we use a stack of 11 consecutive face-crops (resolution: 144×144). We implement SPELL using PyTorch Geometric library [10]. Our model consists of three GCN layers, each with 64 dimensional filters. The first layer is implemented by an EDGE-CONV layer that uses a two-layer MLP for feature projection. The second and third GCN layers are of type SAGE-CONV and each of them uses a single MLP layer. We set the number of nodes n to 2000 and τ parameter to 0.9, which ensures that each graph fully spans each of the face tracks. We train SPELL with a batch size of 16 using the Adam optimizer [15]. The learning rate starts at 5×10^{-3} and decays following the cosine annealing schedule [20]. The whole training process of 70 epochs takes less than an hour using a single GPU (TITAN V).

Table 2. Performance comparison of context-reasoning with state-of-the-art methods. SPELL without TSM [19] demonstrates the higher context-reasoning capacity of our method when compared to the other 2D CNN-based approaches.

Method	Stage-1 mAP	Final mAP	ΔmAP
MAAS-LAN [18]	79.5	85.1	5.6
ASC [2]	79.5	87.1	7.6
MAAS-TAN [18]	80.2	88.8	8.6
Unicon [37]	84.0	92.0	8.0
ASDNet [17]	**88.9**	93.5	4.6
SPELL (Ours)	88.0	**94.2**	6.2
SPELL (Ours) w/o TSM	82.6	92.0	**9.4**

4.1   Comparison with the State-of-the-Art

We summarize the performance comparisons of SPELL with other state-of-the-art approaches on the validation set of the AVA-ActiveSpeaker dataset [26] in Table 1. We want to point out that SPELL significantly outperforms all the previous approaches using the two-stream 2D ResNet-18 [13]. Critically, SPELL's visual feature encoding has significantly lower computational and memory overhead (0.7 GFLOPs and 11.2M parameters) compared to ASDNet [17] (13.2 GFLOPs, 48.6M #Params), the leading state-of-the-art method. A concurrent and closely related work MAAS [18] also uses a GNN-based framework. MAAS-LAN uses a graph that is generated on a short video clip. To improve the detection performance, MAAS-TAN extends MAAS-LAN by connecting the graphs over time, which makes 13 temporally-linked graph spanning about 1.59 s. This time span is relatively shorter than SPELL since the SPELL graph spans around 13–55 s, as explained in the next subsection. In addition, SPELL requires a single forward pass when MAAS performs multiple forward passes for each inference process.

4.2   Context-Reasoning Capacity

Most of the previous approaches have multi-stage frameworks, which includes a feature-encoding stage for audio-visual feature extraction that is followed by one or more context-reasoning stages for modeling long-term interactions and the context information. For example, SPELL has a single context-reasoning stage that uses a three-layer *Bi-dir* GNN for modeling long-term spatial-temporal information. In Table 2, we compare the performance of context-reasoning stages with previous methods. Specifically, we analyze the detection performance when using only the feature-encoding stage (Stage-1 mAP) and the final performance. The difference between the two scores can provide a good insight on the capacity of the context-reasoning modules. Because ASDNet [17] uses 3D CNNs, it is likely that some degree of the temporal context is already incorporated in the

Table 3. Complexity comparisons of the context-reasoning stage. SPELL achieves the best performance while requiring the lowest memory and computation consumption.

Method	#Params (M)	Size (MB)	mAP (%)
ASC [2]	1.13	4.32	87.1
MAAS-TAN [18]	0.16	0.63	88.8
ASDNet [17]	2.56	9.77	93.5
SPELL (Ours)	0.11	0.45	94.2

feature-encoding stage, which leads to a low context-reasoning performance. Similarly, using TSM [19] provides the short-term context information in the feature-encoding stage, which leads to a smaller score difference between the Stage-1 and Final mAP and thus underestimates the context-reasoning capacity. Therefore, we also estimate the performance of SPELL without TSM. In this case, the context-reasoning performance of SPELL outperforms all the other methods, which shows the higher context-reasoning capacity of our method, thanks to the longer-term context modeling. Note that although ASC [2], MAAS [18], Unicon [37], and SPELL use the same 2D ResNet-18 [13], their Stage-1 mAP can be different due to the inconsistency of input resolution, number of face-crops, and training scheme.

Long-Term Temporal Context. Note that τ ($= 0.9$ s in our experiments) in SPELL imposes *additional* constraint on direct connectivity across temporally distant nodes. The face identities across consecutive time-stamps are always connected. Below is the estimate of the effective temporal context size of SPELL. AVA-ActiveSpeaker dataset contains 3.65 million frames and 5.3 million annotated faces, resulting into 1.45 faces per frame. With an average of 1.45 faces per frame, a graph with 500 to 2000 faces in sorted temporal order spans over 345 to 1379 frames which correspond to 13 to 55 s for a 25-fps video. In other words, the nodes in the graph might have a time-difference of about 1 minute, and SPELL is able to reason over that long-term temporal window within a limited memory and compute budget, thanks to the effectiveness of the proposed graph structure. It is note worthy that the temporal window size in MAAS [18] is 1.9 s and TalkNet [33] uses up to 4 s as long-term sequence-level temporal context.

4.3   Efficiency of the Context-Reasoning Stage

In Table 3, we compare the complexity of the context-reasoning stage of SPELL with ASC [2], MAAS-TAN [18], and ASDNet [17]. These methods release the source code for their models, so we use the official code to compute the number of parameters and the model size of the context-reasoning stage. ASC has about 10 times more parameters and model size than ours. Nevertheless, SPELL achieves 7.1% higher mAP than ASC. SPELL has fewer number of parameters than MAAS-TAN even while achieving 5.4% higher mAP. When compared to the leading state-of-the-art method, ASDNet, SPELL is one order of magnitude more computationally efficient.

Table 4. Performance comparisons of different ablative settings: TSM [19], Cx-reason (context-reasoning only with an undirected graph), *Bi-dir* (augmenting with forward/backward graphs), Audio-aug (audio data augmentation), Sp-feat (spatial features).

TSM	Cx-reason	*Bi-dir*	Audio-aug	Sp-feat	mAP (%)
–	–	–	–	–	80.2
–	–	–	✓	–	82.6
✓	–	–	✓	–	88.0
✓	✓	–	✓	–	92.4
✓	✓	✓	✓	–	93.9
✓	✓	✓	✓	✓	94.2

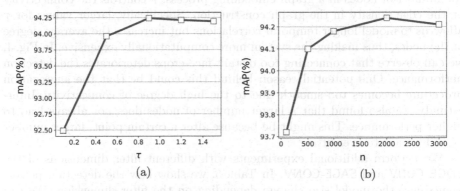

(a)   (b)

Fig. 4. Study on the impact of two hyperparameters, which are τ (when n is set to 2000) and n (when τ is fixed at 0.9).

4.4 Ablation Study

We perform an ablative study to validate the contributions of individual components, namely TSM, Cx-reason (context-reasoning only with an undirected graph), *Bi-dir* (augmenting context-reasoning with the forward/backward graphs), Audio-aug (audio data augmentation), and Sp-feat (spatial features). We summarize the main contributions in Table 4. We can observe that TSM, *Bi-dir* graph structure, and audio data augmentation play significant roles in boosting the detection performance. This implies that 1) retaining short-term information in the feature-encoding stage is important, 2) processing the spatial-temporal information using our graph structure is effective, and 3) the negatively sampled audio makes our model more robust to the noise. Additionally, the spatial features also bring meaningful performance gain.

Table 5. Comparisons of the detection performance and the model size with different filter dimensions.

Filter Dim	#Params (M)	Size (MB)	mAP (%)
16	0.02	0.10	93.5
32	0.05	0.21	93.9
64	0.11	0.45	94.2
128	0.29	1.14	94.1
256	0.88	3.38	94.1

In addition, we analyze the impact of two hyperparameters: τ (Sect. 3.2) and the number of nodes in a graph embedding process. τ controls the connectivity or the edge density in the graph construction. Specifically, larger values for τ allow us to model longer temporal correlations but increases the average degree of the nodes, thus making the system more computationally expensive. In Fig. 4, we can observe that connecting too distant face-crops deteriorates the detection performance. One potential reason behind this could be that the aggregation procedure becomes too smooth due to the high degree of connectivity. Interestingly, we also found that a larger number of nodes does not always lead to higher performance. This might be because after a certain point, larger number of nodes leads to over-fitting.

We perform additional experiments with different filter dimensions of the EDGE-CONV and SAGE-CONV. In Table 5, we show how the detection performance and the model size change depending on the filter dimension. We can observe that increasing the filter dimension above 64 does not bring any performance gain when the model size increases significantly.

We also perform an ablation study of the input modalities. When using only the visual features, the detection performance drops significantly from 94.2% to 84.9% mAP (when using only the audio: 55.6%), which shows that both the audio and video modalities are important for this application.

4.5   Qualitative Analysis

In the supplementary material, we show several detection examples to provide a qualitative analysis. The selected frames have multiple faces and have a long time-span about 5–10 s. In all of the provided examples in the supplementary material, SPELL correctly classifies all the speakers when the counterpart fails to do. The qualitative analysis demonstrates that SPELL is effective and that it is good at modeling spatial-temporal long-term information.

5   Conclusion

We proposed SPELL - an effective graph-based approach to active speaker detection in videos. The main idea is to capture the long-term spatial and temporal relationships among the cropped faces through a graph structure that is aware of the temporal order of the faces. SPELL outperforms all the previous approaches and requires significantly less hardware resources when compared to the leading state-of-the-art method. The model we propose is also generic - it can be used to address other video understanding tasks such as action localization and audio source localization.

References

1. Afouras, T., Chung, J.S., Zisserman, A.: The conversation: deep audio-visual speech enhancement. arXiv preprint arXiv:1804.04121 (2018)
2. Alcazar, J.L., et al.: Active speakers in context. In: IEEE Conference on Computer Vision and Pattern Recognition, pp. 12465–12474 (2020)
3. Arnab, A., Sun, C., Schmid, C.: Unified graph structured models for video understanding. arXiv preprint arXiv:2103.15662 (2021)
4. Chakravarty, P., Tuytelaars, T.: Cross-modal supervision for learning active speaker detection in video. ArXiv abs/1603.08907 (2016)
5. Chatfield, K., Simonyan, K., Vedaldi, A., Zisserman, A.: Return of the devil in the details: Delving deep into convolutional nets. In: Proceedings of the British Machine Vision Conference. BMVA Press (2014)
6. Chung, J.S.: Naver at activitynet challenge 2019 - task B active speaker detection (AVA). CoRR abs/1906.10555 (2019). http://arxiv.org/abs/1906.10555
7. Cutler, R., Davis, L.: Look who's talking: speaker detection using video and audio correlation. In: 2000 IEEE International Conference on Multimedia and Expo. ICME2000. Proceedings. Latest Advances in the Fast Changing World of Multimedia (Cat. No. 00TH8532), vol. 3, pp. 1589–1592. IEEE (2000)
8. Everingham, M., Sivic, J., Zisserman, A.: Hello! my name is... buffy"-automatic naming of characters in tv video. In: BMVC, vol. 2, p. 6 (2006)
9. Everingham, M., Sivic, J., Zisserman, A.: Taking the bite out of automated naming of characters in tv video. Image Vis. Comput. 27, 545–559 (2009)
10. Fey, M., Lenssen, J.E.: Fast graph representation learning with pytorch geometric. In: ICLR Workshop on Representation Learning on Graphs and Manifolds (2019). http://arxiv.org/abs/1903.02428
11. Geng, S., Gao, P., Hori, C., Le Roux, J., Cherian, A.: Spatio-temporal scene graphs for video dialog. arXiv e-prints pp. arXiv-2007 (2020)
12. Hamilton, W., Ying, Z., Leskovec, J.: Inductive representation learning on large graphs. Adv. Neural Inf. Process. Syst. 30 (2017)
13. He, K., Zhang, X., Ren, S., Sun, J.: Deep residual learning for image recognition. In: Proceedings of the IEEE Conference on Computer Vision and Pattern Recognition, pp. 770–778 (2016)
14. Howard, A.G., et al.: Mobilenets: efficient convolutional neural networks for mobile vision applications. arXiv preprint arXiv:1704.04861 (2017)
15. Kingma, D.P., Ba, J.: Adam: a method for stochastic optimization. arXiv preprint arXiv:1412.6980 (2014)

16. Kopuklu, O., Kose, N., Gunduz, A., Rigoll, G.: Resource efficient 3d convolutional neural networks. In: Proceedings of the IEEE/CVF International Conference on Computer Vision Workshops (2019)
17. Köpüklü, O., Taseska, M., Rigoll, G.: How to design a three-stage architecture for audio-visual active speaker detection in the wild. In: Proceedings of the Internal Conference on Computer Vision (2021)
18. León-Alcázar, J., Heilbron, F.C., Thabet, A., Ghanem, B.: MAAS: multi-modal assignation for active speaker detection. In: Internal Conference on Computer Vision (2021)
19. Lin, J., Gan, C., Han, S.: TSM: temporal shift module for efficient video understanding. In: Proceedings of the IEEE/CVF International Conference on Computer Vision, pp. 7083–7093 (2019)
20. Loshchilov, I., Hutter, F.: Sgdr: Stochastic gradient descent with warm restarts. In: International Conference on Learning Representations (ICLR) (2017)
21. Mi, L., Ou, Y., Chen, Z.: Visual relationship forecasting in videos. arXiv preprint arXiv:2107.01181 (2021)
22. Min, K., Roy, S., Tripathi, S., Guha, T., Majumdar, S.: Intel labs at activitynet challenge 2022: spell for long-term active speaker detection (2022)
23. Nagarajan, T., Li, Y., Feichtenhofer, C., Grauman, K.: Ego-topo: environment affordances from egocentric video. In: Proceedings of the IEEE/CVF Conference on Computer Vision and Pattern Recognition, pp. 163–172 (2020)
24. Patrick, M., et al.: Space-time crop & attend: improving cross-modal video representation learning. arXiv preprint arXiv:2103.10211 (2021)
25. Ravanelli, M., Bengio, Y.: Speaker recognition from raw waveform with sincnet. In: 2018 IEEE Spoken Language Technology Workshop (SLT), pp. 1021–1028. IEEE (2018)
26. Roth, J., et al.: Ava active speaker: an audio-visual dataset for active speaker detection. In: ICASSP 2020–2020 IEEE International Conference on Acoustics, Speech and Signal Processing (ICASSP), pp. 4492–4496. IEEE (2020)
27. Sharma, R., Somandepalli, K., Narayanan, S.: Crossmodal learning for audio-visual speech event localization. arXiv preprint arXiv:2003.04358 (2020)
28. Shirian, A., Tripathi, S., Guha, T.: Learnable graph inception network for emotion recognition. IEEE Trans. Multimedia 24 (2020)
29. Stafylakis, T., Tzimiropoulos, G.: Combining residual networks with lSTMS for lipreading. arXiv preprint arXiv:1703.04105 (2017)
30. Stefanov, K., Beskow, J., Salvi, G.: Vision-based active speaker detection in multiparty interaction. In: Grounding Language Understanding GLU2017 August 25, 2017, KTH Royal Institute of Technology, Stockholm, Sweden (2017)
31. Stefanov, K., Sugimoto, A., Beskow, J.: Look who's talking: visual identification of the active speaker in multi-party human-robot interaction. In: Proceedings of the 2nd Workshop on Advancements in Social Signal Processing for Multimodal Interaction, pp. 22–27 (2016)
32. Tan, R., Xu, H., Saenko, K., Plummer, B.A.: Logan: latent graph co-attention network for weakly-supervised video moment retrieval. In: Proceedings of the IEEE/CVF Winter Conference on Applications of Computer Vision, pp. 2083–2092 (2021)
33. Tao, R., Pan, Z., Das, R.K., Qian, X., Shou, M.Z., Li, H.: Is someone speaking? exploring long-term temporal features for audio-visual active speaker detection. In: Proceedings of the 29th ACM International Conference on Multimedia, pp. 3927–3935 (2021)

34. Vaswani, A., et al.: Attention is all you need. Adv. Neural Inf. Process. Syst. **30** (2017)
35. Wang, Y., Sun, Y., Liu, Z., Sarma, S.E., Bronstein, M.M., Solomon, J.M.: Dynamic graph CNN for learning on point clouds. ACM Trans. Graph. **38**(5), 1–12 (2019)
36. Zhang, Y.H., Xiao, J., Yang, S., Shan, S.: Multi-task learning for audio-visual active speaker detection. The ActivityNet Large-Scale Activity Recognition Challenge, pp. 1–4 (2019)
37. Zhang, Y., et al.: UniCon: Unified Context Network for Robust Active Speaker Detection, pp. 3964–3972. Association for Computing Machinery, New York, NY, USA (2021). https://doi.org/10.1145/3474085.3475275
38. Zhang, Y., Tokmakov, P., Hebert, M., Schmid, C.: A structured model for action detection. In: Proceedings of the IEEE/CVF Conference on Computer Vision and Pattern Recognition, pp. 9975–9984 (2019)

Frozen CLIP Models are Efficient Video Learners

Ziyi Lin[1], Shijie Geng[3], Renrui Zhang[2], Peng Gao[2(✉)], Gerard de Melo[4], Xiaogang Wang[1], Jifeng Dai[5], Yu Qiao[2], and Hongsheng Li[1,6]

[1] Multimedia Laboratory, The Chinese University of Hong Kong, Hong Kong, China
zylin@link.cuhk.edu.hk, hsli@ee.cuhk.edu.hk
[2] Shanghai AI Laboratory, Hong Kong, China
gaopeng@pjlab.org.cn
[3] Rutgers University, New Brunswick, USA
[4] Hasso Plattner Institute, Potsdam, Germany
[5] SenseTime Research, Hong Kong, China
[6] Centre for Perceptual and Interactive Intelligence Limited, Hong Kong, China

Abstract. Video recognition has been dominated by the end-to-end learning paradigm – first initializing a video recognition model with weights of a pretrained image model and then conducting end-to-end training on videos. This enables the video network to benefit from the pretrained image model. However, this requires substantial computation and memory resources for finetuning on videos and the alternative of directly using pretrained image features without finetuning the image backbone leads to subpar results. Fortunately, recent advances in Contrastive Vision-Language Pre-training (CLIP) pave the way for a new route for visual recognition tasks. Pretrained on large open-vocabulary image–text pair data, these models learn powerful visual representations with rich semantics. In this paper, we present **E**fficient **V**ideo **L**earning (EVL) – an efficient framework for directly training high-quality video recognition models with frozen CLIP features. Specifically, we employ a lightweight Transformer decoder and learn a query token to dynamically collect frame-level spatial features from the CLIP image encoder. Furthermore, we adopt a local temporal module in each decoder layer to discover temporal clues from adjacent frames and their attention maps. We show that despite being efficient to train with a frozen backbone, our models learn high quality video representations on a variety of video recognition datasets. Code is available at https://github.com/OpenGVLab/efficient-video-recognition.

Keywords: Video recognition · Efficient learning · Vision-language model · Spatiotemporal fusion

---

Supplementary Information The online version contains supplementary material available at https://doi.org/10.1007/978-3-031-19833-5_23.

S. Avidan et al. (Eds.): ECCV 2022, LNCS 13695, pp. 388–404, 2022.
https://doi.org/10.1007/978-3-031-19833-5_23

1   Introduction

As a fundamental component of video understanding, learning spatiotemporal representations remains an active research area in recent years. Since the beginning of the deep learning era, numerous architectures have been proposed to learn spatiotemporal semantics, such as traditional two-stream networks [35,40,53], 3D convolutional neural networks [5,10,11,17,30,36,38,42,44], and spatiotemporal Transformers [1,3,8,24,27,28,46]. As videos are high-dimensional and exhibit substantial spatiotemporal redundancy, training video recognition models from scratch is highly inefficient and may lead to inferior performance. Intuitively, the semantic meaning of a video snippet is highly correlated with each of its individual frames. Previous studies [1,3,5,46] have shown that the datasets and methodologies for image recognition can benefit video recognition as well. Owing to the close relationship between image and video recognition, as a routine practice, most existing video recognition models take advantage of pretrained image models by using them for initialization and then re-training all parameters for video understanding in an end-to-end manner.

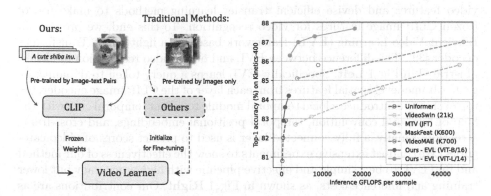

Fig. 1. Left: illustration of the difference between our **EVL** training pipeline and other video recognition methods. **Right:** despite that **EVL** targets efficient training, our models set new accuracy vs. *inference FLOPS* Pareto frontiers. On Kinetics-400, the 8-frame ViT-B/16 model achieves 82.9% top-1 accuracy with only 60 V100 GPU-hours of training.

However, the end-to-end finetuning regime has two major drawbacks. The first is *efficiency*. Video recognition models are required to process multiple frames simultaneously and are several times larger than their image counterparts in terms of model size. Finetuning the entire image backbone inevitably incurs an enormous computation and memory consumption cost. As a result, this issue limits the adoption and scalability of some of the largest image architectures for video recognition under restricted computational resources. The second issue is known as *catastrophic forgetting* [29] in the context of transfer learning. When conducting end-to-end finetuning on downstream video tasks, we risk destroying the powerful visual features learned from image pretraining and obtaining subpar results if the downstream videos are insufficiently informative. Both concerns suggest that end-to-end finetuning from pre-trained image models is not always an ideal choice, which calls for a more efficient learning strategy to transfer knowledge from images to videos.

Considerable efforts have been made on learning high-quality and general visual representations through contrastive learning [21,31], masked vision modeling [2,18,45], and traditional supervised learning [32,48]. Masked vision modeling approaches such as MAE [18] train an encoder–decoder architecture to reconstruct the original image from the latent representation and mask tokens. Supervised learning-based methods train image backbones with a fixed set of predefined category labels. Since they are usually trained uni-modally, they both lack the ability to represent rich semantics. In contrast, contrastive vision–language models such as CLIP [31] are pretrained with large-scale open-vocabulary image–text pairs. They can learn more powerful visual representations aligned with much richer language semantics. Another advantage of CLIP is its promising feature transferability, which forms a strong foundation for a series of transfer learning methods on various downstream tasks [13,22,34,51,52,54].

The above reasons inspire us to rethink the relationship between image and video features and devise efficient transfer learning methods to make use of frozen CLIP image features for video recognition. To this end, we propose an Efficient Video Learning (**EVL**) framework based on a lightweight Transformer decoder [39]. The difference between EVL and other video recognition models is illustrated in Fig. 1 **Left**. Specifically, EVL learns a query token to dynamically gather frame-level spatial features from each layer of the CLIP image encoder. On top of that, we introduce a local temporal module to collect temporal cues with the help of temporal convolution, temporal positional embeddings, and cross-frame attention. Finally, a fully-connected layer is used to predict scores of video categories. We conduct extensive experiments to show the effectiveness of our method and find EVL to be a simple and effective pipeline with higher accuracy but lower training and inference costs, as shown in Fig. 1 **Right**. Our contributions are as follows:

- We point out the shortcomings of the current end-to-end learning paradigm for video understanding and propose to leverage frozen CLIP image features to facilitate video recognition tasks.
- We develop EVL – an efficient transfer learning pipeline from image to video recognition, in which we train a lightweight Transformer decoder module on top of *fixed* transferable image features to perform spatiotemporal fusion.
- Extensive experiments demonstrate the effectiveness and efficiency of EVL. It incurs much shorter training time than end-to-end finetuning, yet achieves competitive performance. This makes video recognition accessible to a broader community with average computation resources.

2   Related Work

Video Recognition. Recent advances in video recognition can be divided into two major directions – improving model architectures and proposing new

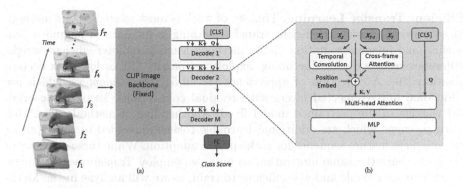

Fig. 2. Model architecture overview. (a) Top-level architecture: multiple intermediate feature maps from a massively pretrained image backbone are fed into a Transformer decoder to gather information from them. **(b)** Motion-enhanced Transformer
decoder block: temporal modeling is added on top of raw frame features X_i to retain
structural information of the spatiotemporal features.

training strategies. Following the success of Transformers in image recognition, video recognition has as well seen a transition from 3D-CNN [5,10,11]
to Transformer-based architectures [3,8,26,27]. Uniformer [24] is a custom fused
CNN-Transformer architecture achieving good speed–accuracy trade-off. Yan et
al. [46] propose a multi-stream Transformer operating on different resolutions
with lateral connections. Prior work [3,5,46] has shown the benefit of image pre-
training for video recognition tasks. However, the end-to-end finetuning remains
expensive, especially due to the large memory footprint. In terms of new training
strategies, pretext task design for self-supervised learning [12,43] and multi-task
co-training [15,47,50] are two mainstream directions. However, both are even
more expensive than regular supervised training. Unlike previous efforts, we
leverage fixed CLIP image features and directly learn an efficient video recognition model with an additional Transformer encoder.

Large-scale Image Representation Learning. With the availability of web-
scale weakly labeled data, we have witnessed a surge of new models for general
visual representation learning. Image models built with regular supervised learning have grown dramatically in size. For example, Zhai et al. [48] train a ViT-G
model on the large JFT-3B dataset. Riquelme et al. [32] create a Mixture-of-
Experts vision model that scales to over 10 billion parameters. To further boost
the visual representation power, efforts began to focus on large-scale contrastive
learning and self-supervised learning. The success of BERT [7] sparked an emerging direction of building large-scale vision models with masked vision modeling
[2,18,45]. Meanwhile, CLIP [31] and ALIGN [21] pretrain vision–language models with a contrastive loss on large-scale datasets consisting of open-vocabulary
image–text pairs. The multimodal pretraining environment makes them suitable
for downstream tasks requiring rich semantics.

Efficient Transfer Learning. This set of work is most related to our method. Most previous works on efficient transfer learning is for natural language processing and image recognition. Some methods learn parameter-efficient weight difference vectors during finetuning, exploiting sparsity [16] or low rank decomposition [20]. A collection of approaches [13,19,51] train *adapters*, which are additional fully-connected layers with residual connections, keeping the original weights in the pretrained model fixed. Another line of methods [23,25,54] learn *prompts*, which are additional learnable tokens appended to the input or intermediate feature sequence for task-specific adaption. While these category of methods share the same motivation as ours, we employ Transformer decoders, which is more flexible and also efficient to train, as we will analyze in the Methods section. In terms of video recognition, the exploration in efficient transfer learning is still limited. Ju at el. [22] transfer CLIP models to video recognition by learning prompts and temporal modeling. Wang et al. [41] utilize CLIP models for video recognition by traditional end-to-end finetuning. We will compare with them in the Experiments section. There are also several works utilizing transferable image features for video-text tasks [6,9,14], but these works focus more on cross-modality modeling. In contrast, our work aims to improve the single-modal video representations, which should be complementary to most of the video-text learning methods.

3   Our Method

The three primary goals of our image to video transfer learning pipeline are (1) capability to summarize multi-frame features and infer video-level predictions; (2) capability to capture motion information across multiple frames; and (3) efficiency. We thus propose the Efficient Video Learning (**EVL**) framework, which we detail in the following.

3.1   Overall Structure

The overall structure of EVL, as illustrated in Fig. 2, is a multi-layer spatiotemporal Transformer decoder on top of a fixed CLIP backbone. The CLIP backbone extracts features from each frame independently. The frame features are then stacked to form a spatiotemporal feature volume, modulated with temporal information, and fed into the Transformer decoder. The Transformer decoder performs global aggregation of multi-layer features: a video-level classification token [CLS] is learned to act as query, and multiple feature volumes from different backbone blocks are fed to the decoder blocks as key and value. A linear layer projects the output of the last decoder block to class predictions. Formally, the operations of the Transformer decoder can be expressed as follows:

$$\mathbf{Y}_i = \mathrm{Temp}_i\left([\mathbf{X}_{N-M+i,1}, \mathbf{X}_{N-M+i,2}, \ldots, \mathbf{X}_{N-M+i,T}]\right), \tag{1}$$

$$\tilde{\mathbf{q}}_i = \mathbf{q}_{i-1} + \mathrm{MHA}_i\left(\mathbf{q}_{i-1}, \mathbf{Y}_i, \mathbf{Y}_i\right), \tag{2}$$

$$\mathbf{q}_i = \tilde{\mathbf{q}}_i + \mathrm{MLP}_i\left(\tilde{\mathbf{q}}_i\right), \tag{3}$$

$$\mathbf{p} = \mathrm{FC}\left(\mathbf{q}_M\right), \tag{4}$$

where $\mathbf{X}_{n,t}$ denotes the frame features of the t-th frame extracted from the n-th layer of the CLIP backbone, $\mathbf{Y}_i$ denotes the temporal modulated feature volume fed into the i-th layer of the Transformer decoder, $\mathbf{q}_i$ is the progressively refined query token with $\mathbf{q}_0$ as learnable parameters and $\mathbf{p}$ is the final prediction. N, M denote the number of blocks in the backbone image encoder and the spatiotemporal decoder, respectively. MHA stands for multi-head attention, and the three arguments are the query, key, and value, respectively. Temp is the temporal modelling, which produces feature tokens modulated by more fine-grained temporal information, as is elaborated in the next section.

The network is optimized as a standard classification model by cross-entropy loss with ground-truth labels, except that the back-propagation stops at image features $\mathbf{X}$ and no weight in the image encoder is updated.

3.2   Learning Temporal Cues from Spatial Features

While CLIP models generate powerful spatial features, they entirely lack temporal information. Despite the Transformer decoder being capable of weighted feature aggregation, which is a form of global temporal information, fine-grained and local temporal signals may also be valuable for video recognition. Hence, we introduce the following temporal modules to encode such information before features are fed into the Transformer decoder.

Temporal Convolution. Temporal depthwise convolutions are capable of capturing local feature variations along the temporal dimension, and in known to be efficient and effective [10,37]. Formally the feature encoded by this convolution is written as $\mathbf{Y}_{\text{conv}}$, and

$$\mathbf{Y}_{\text{conv}}\left(t, h, w, c\right) = \sum_{\Delta t \in \{-1,0,1\}} \mathbf{W}_{\text{conv}}\left(\Delta t, c\right) \mathbf{X}\left(t + \Delta t, h, w, c\right) + \mathbf{b}_{\text{conv}}\left(c\right). \quad (5)$$

Temporal Positional Embeddings. We learn a set of T vectors of dimension C, denoted as $\mathbf{P} \in \mathbb{R}^{T \times C}$, to serve as temporal positional embedding. Image features are added with one of the vectors according to their temporal position t, or formally

$$\mathbf{Y}_{\text{pos}}\left(t, h, w, c\right) = \mathbf{P}\left(t, c\right). \quad (6)$$

While temporal convolutions may also capture temporal position information implicitly, positional embeddings are more explicit by making similar features at different time distinguishable. Positional embeddings are also more powerful for long-range temporal modelling, for which multiple convolutional blocks have to be stacked to achieve a large receptive field.

Temporal Cross Attention. Another interesting but often overlooked source of temporal information lies in the attention maps. As attention maps reflect feature correspondence, calculating attention maps between two frames naturally reveals object movement information. More specifically, we first construct attention maps between adjacent frames using the original query and key projections in CLIP:

$$\mathbf{A}_{\text{prev}}(t) = \text{Softmax}\left((\mathbf{QX}(t))^T(\mathbf{KX}(t-1))\right),$$
$$\mathbf{A}_{\text{next}}(t) = \text{Softmax}\left((\mathbf{QX}(t))^T(\mathbf{KX}(t+1))\right). \tag{7}$$

We omitted the attention heads for simplicity, and average across all heads in our implementation. Then we linearly project it into the feature dimension:

$$\mathbf{Y}_{\text{attn}}(t,h,w,c) = \sum_{h'=1}^{H}\sum_{w'=1}^{W}\mathbf{W}_{\text{prev}}(h-h',w-w',c)\,\mathbf{A}_{\text{prev}}(t,h',w')$$
$$+\mathbf{W}_{\text{next}}(h-h',w-w',c)\,\mathbf{A}_{\text{next}}(t,h',w'). \tag{8}$$

Experiments have shown that, despite the query, key, and input features all being learned from pure 2D image data, such attention maps still provide useful signals.

The final modulated features are obtained by blending the temporal features with the original spatial features in a residual manner, *i.e.* $\mathbf{Y} = \mathbf{X} + \mathbf{Y}_{\text{conv}} + \mathbf{Y}_{\text{pos}} + \mathbf{Y}_{\text{attn}}$.

3.3 Complexity Analysis

Inference. The additional Transformer decoder introduces only a negligible amount of computational overhead given that only one query token is used. To show this, we consider ViT-B/16 as our image backbone, and write out the FLOPS for a Transformer block as follows:

$$\text{FLOPS} = 2qC^2 + 2kC^2 + 2qkC + 2\alpha qC^2 \tag{9}$$

Here, q, k, C, α stand for the number of query tokens, number of key (value) tokens, number of embedding dimensions, and MLP expansion factor. With this formula, we can roughly compare the FLOPS of an encoder block and decoder block (h, w, t is the feature size along the height, width, temporal dimensions, and we adopt a common choices $\alpha = 4$, $h = w = 14$, $C = 768$ for estimation):

$$\frac{\text{FLOPS}_{\text{dec}}}{\text{FLOPS}_{\text{enc}}} \approx \frac{2hwtC^2}{t(12hwC^2 + 2h^2w^2C)} \approx \frac{1}{6} \tag{10}$$

From this, we can see that a decoder block is much more lightweight compared to an encoder block. Even with a full configuration (one decoder block on every encoder output, no channel reduction and all temporal modules enabled), the FLOPS increase is within 20% of the backbone.

Training. As we use a fixed backbone and a non-intrusive Transformer decoder head (i.e., our inserted module does not change the *input* of any backbone layer), we can completely avoid back-propagation through the backbone. This vastly reduces both the memory consumption and the time per training iteration.

4 Experiments

We benchmark our method on 2 datasets: Kinetics-400 and Something-Something-v2. Extra implementation details are provided in the appendix.

4.1 Main Results

In this section we provide a comparison with important baselines from recent work.

Table 1. Comparison with state-of-the-arts on Kinetics-400. We cite a series of models within similar range of accuracy as ours and compare the FLOPS. Frame counts are reported as frames per view × number of views.

Method	Pretraining	Acc. (%)	#Frames	GFLOPS
Uniformer-B [24]	ImageNet-1k	82.9	32 × 4	1,036
Swin-B [27]	ImageNet-21k	82.7	32 × 12	3,384
irCSN-152 [37]	IG-65M	82.6	32 × 30	2,901
MViT-S [43]	ImageNet-21k	82.6	16 × 10	710
Omnivore-B [15]	IN1k + SUN	83.3	32 × 12	3,384
ViViT-L FE [1]	JFT	83.5	32 × 3	11,940
TokenLearner 8at18 (L/16) [33]	JFT	83.2	32 × 6	6,630
MViT-L [43]	MaskFeat, K600	85.1	16 × 10	3,770
MTV-L [46]	JFT	84.3	32 × 12	18,050
EVL ViT-B/16 (Ours)	CLIP	82.9	8 × 3	444
		83.6	16 × 3	888
		84.2	32 × 3	1,777
EVL ViT-L/14 (Ours)	CLIP	86.3	8 × 3	2,022
		87.0	16 × 3	4,044
		87.3	32 × 3	8,088
EVL ViT-L/14 (336px, ours)		**87.7**	32 × 3	18,196

Comparison with State-of-the-Art. Comparisons with recent state-of-the-art video recognition models are provided in Table 1. While we aim to build a fast transfer learning pipeline, we find our models achieve competitive accuracy among regular video recognition methods. The models listed in Table 1 achieve similar accuracy as ours but require substantially more computation than our method.

Comparison with CLIP-Based Methods. To the best of our knowledge, there are two previous studies that utilize CLIP models for video recognition. As shown in Table 2, we achieve higher accuracy with fewer frames and a smaller number of new parameters, showing a more efficient use of CLIP.

Training Time and Reduced Memory. One of the major advantages of our efficient transfer pipeline is the vastly reduced training time. We cite the training time reported in several previous studies in Table 4 for comparison.[1] In this case, powerful pretraining leads to a roughly 10× training time reduction, and our efficient transfer learning scheme leads to a further reduction of about 8×. We also compare training times in an idealized setting in Table 5: We report single step time (forward + backward + update) using fake data on a single GPU. This bypasses the data loading and distributed communication overhead, which are confounding factors that may be unoptimized and difficult to control.

Table 2. Comparison with CLIP-based methods on Kinetics-400. All models use ViT-B/16 as backbone. As the paper [22] is vague about the details, we estimate their new parameters to be 3 Transformer blocks with feature size 512 and MLP expansion factor 4. For ActionCLIP [41], we do not count parameters in the text branch.

Method	New Params (M)	#Frames×#Views	Acc. (%)
Efficient-Prompting [22] (A5)	9.43*	16 × 5	76.9
ActionCLIP [41]	105.15	8 × 1	81.1
		16 × 1	81.7
		32 × 1	82.3
		16 × 3	82.6
		32 × 3	83.8
EVL ViT-B/16 (Ours, 1 Layer)	7.41	8 × 3	81.1
EVL ViT-B/16 (Ours, 4 Layers)	28.70	8 × 3	82.9
EVL ViT-B/16 (Ours, 4 Layers)	28.78	32 × 3	**84.2**

Table 3. Inference latency and throughput measured on actual hardware. Both models achieve 82.9% accuracy on Kinetics-400. Results are obtained using V100-32G with PyTorch-builtin mixed precision. Latency is measured using a batch size of 1 and throughput is measured using the largest possible batch size before running out of memory.

Model (# frames)	Acc. (%)	GFLOPS	Latency (ms)	Throughput (V/s)
Uniformer-B (32) [24]	**82.9**	1036 (1.00×)	314.58 (1.00×)	3.42 (1.00×)
EVL ViT-B/16 (Ours, 8)	**82.9**	**454** (0.44×)	**102.88** (0.33×)	**25.53** (7.47×)

Inference Latency and Throughput. Despite our method not being specially optimized for inference speed, we show an important advantage of utilizing large-scale pretrained models. Training on small datasets requires injecting

---

[1] Training time of Uniformer-B is estimated by halving the value for Kinetics-600 provided in their GitHub repo. Training time of TimeSformer is from our own reproduction, which we find to be a few times smaller than the reported number in their paper (reported value is around 400 h). Training time of ActionCLIP is estimated by doubling the value for 8-frame variant reported in their paper.

Table 4. Training time comparison.

Method (#Frames per View)	Acc. (#Views)	Pretraining	Training GPU hours
Uniformer-B [24] (32)	**82.9** (4)	ImageNet-1k	5000 × V100
TimeSformer [3] (8)	82.0 (3)	CLIP	100 × V100
ActionCLIP [41] (16)	82.6 (3)	CLIP	480 × RTX3090
EVL ViT-B/16 (8)	**82.9** (3)	CLIP	**60 × V100**

Table 5. Idealized training step time. 4 decoder layers are used. All data are measured on a single V100-16G GPU. The step time is measured with 64 training samples.

Backbone	Head	Max batch size	Step time (s)
CLIP (**Frozen**)	Global average pool	inf.	0.57
CLIP (Open)	Global average pool	8	3.39
CLIP (**Frozen**)	**EVL**	64	1.03
CLIP (Open)	**EVL**	8	4.41

hand-crafted inductive biases, which are not necessarily friendly to modern accelerators. On the contrary, ViT models consist almost entirely of standard linear algebra operations. The simplicity of ViT typically enables a higher utilization of hardware resources. As shown in Table 3, the latency and throughput are even better than the theoretical FLOPS improvement.

4.2 Ablation Studies

We provide detailed ablation studies to clarify the effects of each part of our design. Unless otherwise specified, results are obtained using ViT-B/16 backbone, 8 input frames and 3 testing views on Kinetics-400.

Intermediate Features. We vary the number of features and Transformer decoder layers and present the results in Table 6a and Table 6b. Utilizing multiple decoder blocks improves the accuracy by 1.0%. Feeding each decoder block with multi-layer intermediate features further improves by 0.8%. Another observation is that features in deeper layers provide more effective features for video recognition.

Spatiotemporal Features. We find a crucial design to achieve high transfer performance is to use high-resolution, unpooled feature maps. The results are shown in Table 6c, from which we can see that summarizing along either the temporal or spatial dimension leads to a significant drop in accuracy. We conjecture that this shows the importance of task-specific re-attention, e.g., for human action recognition datasets like Kinetics-400, features relating to the human body are very important, which could be different in the pretraining stage.

Pretraining Quality. One major factor driving the paradigm shift from fine-tuned to frozen backbone is the improvement in quality of pretrained models. We show that our method outperforms previous methods that fully finetune the backbone weights given the high quality CLIP backbones in Table 7. All models in the table use the same backbone architecture. While on ImageNet-21k pretrained backbones our method lags behind full-finetuning, on CLIP backbones our method outperforms the competitive full-finetuning baselines.

Table 6. Effects of multi-layer high-resolution feature maps. (a) Varying number of Transformer decoder blocks. (b) Varying number of feature maps. (c) Varying feature resolution.

<table>
<tr><td colspan="2" align="center">(a)</td><td colspan="2" align="center">(b)</td><td colspan="3" align="center">(c)</td></tr>
<tr><td>Depth</td><td>Acc. (%)</td><td>Feature Layers</td><td>Acc. (%)</td><td>Feature Shape</td><td>Reduction</td><td>Acc. (%)</td></tr>
<tr><td>1</td><td>81.1</td><td>$[-4,-3,-2,-1]$</td><td>**82.9**</td><td>Temporal only</td><td>Token</td><td>79.8</td></tr>
<tr><td>2</td><td>82.1</td><td>$[-2,-2,-1,-1]$</td><td>82.7</td><td>Temporal only</td><td>Avg</td><td>75.8</td></tr>
<tr><td>3</td><td>82.6</td><td>$[-1,-1,-1,-1]$</td><td>82.1</td><td>Spatial only</td><td>Avg</td><td>80.1</td></tr>
<tr><td>4</td><td>82.9</td><td>$[-2,-1,-2,-1]$</td><td>82.4</td><td>Spatiotemporal</td><td>-</td><td>**82.9**</td></tr>
<tr><td>5</td><td>**83.0**</td><td>$[-7,-5,-3,-1]$</td><td>82.0</td><td></td><td></td><td></td></tr>
</table>

We also find that, despite being designed for a frozen backbone, our model architecture with a finetuned backbone turns out to be a strong full-finetuning baseline. However, the tendency of higher training efficiency of frozen backbones given high-quality pretrained models remains the same, as shown in Fig. 3. Full-finetuning with our model architecture yields similar efficiency curve on ViT-B/16, but with the larger ViT-L/14, the gap of the training time to reach the same accuracy becomes clear. We point out that even ViT-L/14 is a relatively small pretrained model by modern standards, with about 300M parameters (for comparison, GPT-3 [4] for

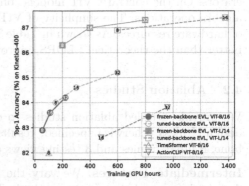

Fig. 3. Training time vs. accuracy with frozen or finetuned backbone. Numbers in the marker are numbers of frames per view. Frozen backbone is more efficient when pretraining quality is higher.

natural language processing has 175B parameters, and ViT-G [49] for computer vision has 1.8B parameters). We believe freezing the backbone may potentially bring further benefits if even larger pretrained models are released in the future.

4.3   Analysis of Temporal Information

An interesting property of our method is to provide a decomposed approach for video recognition: the spatial information is encoded almost entirely in the fixed, high quality CLIP backbone, while the temporal information is encoded only in the Transformer decoder head. As shown in Table 8, temporal modelling exhibits vastly different behaviors on the two datasets: On Kinetics-400, temporal modules bring accuracy gains of less than 0.5%, while on Something-Something-v2, adding the temporal module yields a dramatic +13.8% accuracy gain. This shows a clear difference between temporal information required for the two benchmarks. For Kinetics-400, temporal information is primarily captured in the form of global weighted feature aggregation, as shown in Table 6. For Something-Something-v2, local temporal features (e.g., object motion, feature variations) are also an important source of signals to achieve strong results.

Table 7. Results of different pretrained image features. A ViT-B/16 backbone and 8 frames are used unless otherwise specified. We compare with TimeSformer [3] and ActionCLIP [41]. Both of them conduct extensive experiments to determine competitive settings for end-to-end training on video datasets.

Model	Pretraining	Frozen backbone?	K-400 Acc. (%)
TimeSformer [3] - SOnly	ImageNet-21k	✗	76.9
TimeSformer [3] - JointST	ImageNet-21k	✗	77.4
TimeSformer [3] - DividedST	ImageNet-21k	✗	**78.0**
EVL (ours)	ImageNet-21k	✓	75.4
TimeSformer [3] - DividedST	CLIP	✗	82.0
EVL (ours)	CLIP	✓	**82.9**
ActionCLIP [41] (16 frames)	CLIP	✗	82.6
EVL (ours, 16 frames)	CLIP	✓	**83.3**
ActionCLIP [41] (32 frames)	CLIP	✗	83.8
EVL (ours, 32 frames)	CLIP	✓	**84.2**

Something-Something-v2 also tend to benefit from deep decoders more than Kinetics-400. As shown in Table 8b, Something-Something-v2 benefit from using all 12 decoder blocks, while for Kinetics-400 only around 4 blocks are required (see Table 6a).

Finally we provide our main results on Something-Something-v2 dataset in Table 9. While Something-Something-v2 is a motion-heavy dataset, our lightweight temporal learning module still learns meaningful motion information and reaches mainstream performance (for comparison, a linear probe of CLIP ViT-B/16 achieves only around 20% accuracy). We are also the first CLIP-based method to report results on Something-Something-v2, and we hope this is useful for future reference.

4.4 CLIP-Based Models Learn Complementary Knowledge

Another finding is that knowledge learned by our CLIP-based model is highly complementary to that of regular supervised learning. To show this, we consider an ensemble of our model with supervised models and observe the performance gain. Ensemble is done by weighted averaging the video-level prediction scores and the average weight $\alpha \in [0, 1]$ is searched with a coarse granularity of 0.1 on the validation set. As shown in Table 10 and Table 11, On both Kinetics-400 and Something-Something-v2, we consistently observe more performance gain if CLIP-based models are in the ensemble.

Table 8. Effects of temporal information for video recognition. (a) Local temporal information for both datasets. *T-Conv*: temporal convolution. *T-PE*: temporal positional embedding. *T-CA*: temporal cross attention. (b) Something-Something-v2 needs deeper decoder blocks.

<table>
<tr><td colspan="6" align="center">(a)</td><td colspan="2" align="center">(b)</td></tr>
<tr><th>T-Conv</th><th>T-PE</th><th>T-CA</th><th>K-400 Acc. (%)</th><th>SSv2 Acc. (%)</th><th>Depth</th><th>SSv2 Acc. (%)</th></tr>
<tr><td>✗</td><td>✗</td><td>✗</td><td>82.5</td><td>47.2</td><td>4</td><td>58.6</td></tr>
<tr><td>✓</td><td>✗</td><td>✗</td><td>**82.9**</td><td>57.1</td><td>6</td><td>60.1</td></tr>
<tr><td>✗</td><td>✓</td><td>✗</td><td>82.5</td><td>58.5</td><td>8</td><td>60.2</td></tr>
<tr><td>✗</td><td>✗</td><td>✓</td><td>82.6</td><td>59.5</td><td>10</td><td>60.5</td></tr>
<tr><td>✓</td><td>✓</td><td>✗</td><td>**82.9**</td><td>59.4</td><td>12</td><td>**61.0**</td></tr>
<tr><td>✓</td><td>✗</td><td>✓</td><td>82.7</td><td>60.0</td><td></td><td></td></tr>
<tr><td>✗</td><td>✓</td><td>✓</td><td>82.7</td><td>60.7</td><td></td><td></td></tr>
<tr><td>✓</td><td>✓</td><td>✓</td><td>**82.9**</td><td>**61.0**</td><td></td><td></td></tr>
</table>

Table 9. Main results on Something-Something-v2. *Ens* experiments combine *EVL* with *Uniformer-B (32)* pretrained on Kinetics-600.

Method	SSv2 Acc. (%)	#Frames	GFLOPS
EVL ViT-B/16	61.0	8×3	512
EVL ViT-B/16	61.7	16×3	1,023
EVL ViT-B/16	62.4	32×3	2,047
EVL ViT-L/14	65.1	8×3	2,411
EVL ViT-L/14	66.7	32×3	9,641
EVL ViT-L/14 (336px)	68.0	32×3	24,259
EVL ViT-B/16 Ens	72.1	$32 \times 3 + 32 \times 3$	2,824

The implications of these ensemble experiments are two-fold. First, they show that, practically, our CLIP-based models can be used in a two-stream fashion [35]. Compared to the optical-flow-based second stream in [35], a CLIP-based second stream avoids the expensive optical-flow calculation and is much faster to train. Second, the results suggest that there remains knowledge in the dataset that is not captured by our CLIP-based learning paradigm. This shows the potential of CLIP-based models to further improve once more knowledge from the datasets can be utilized.

Table 10. Ensemble results of different combinations. We combine different models with similar accuracy with the same model and measure the accuracy gain.

Model 1	Acc. 1	Model 2	Acc. 2	Model 1 + 2 Acc. (Δ)
Uniformer-B [24] (16)	82.0	Uniformer-B [24] (32)	82.9	83.6 (+1.6)
		Swin-B [27]	82.7	83.7 (+1.7)
		EVL ViT-B/16 (8)	82.9	**84.5 (+2.5)**
Swin-B [27]	82.7	Uniformer-B [24] (32)	82.9	84.7 (+2.0)
		EVL ViT-B/16 (8)	82.9	**85.0 (+2.3)**
Uniformer-B [24] (32)	82.9	Swin-B [27]	82.7	84.7 (+1.8)
		EVL ViT-B/16 (8)	82.9	**85.2 (+2.3)**

Table 11. Ensemble results on Something-Something-v2. Although *EVL (32)* has much lower accuracy, it still boosts the performance of a *Uniformer-B* model. In contrast, a TimeSformer model with slightly higher accuracy brings negligible gains.

Model 1	Acc. 1	Model 2	Acc. 2	Model 1 + 2 Acc. (Δ)
Uniformer-B [24] (32)	71.2	TimeSformer-L [3]	62.4	71.4 (+0.2)
		EVL ViT-B (32)	62.4	**72.1 (+0.9)**

5   Conclusion

We present a new form of pipeline for video action recognition: learning an efficient transfer learning head on top of fixed transferable image features. By freezing the image backbone, the training time is vastly reduced. Moreover, the accuracy loss due to the frozen backbone can be largely compensated by leveraging multi-layer high-resolution intermediate feature maps from the backbone. Thus, our method effectively leverage powerful image features for video recognition, while avoiding the heavy or prohibitive full-finetuning of very large image models. We further show that transferable image features learned in an open-world setting harbor knowledge that is highly complementary to that of labeled datasets, which may inspire more efficient ways to build state-of-the-art video models. We believe our observations have the potential to make video recognition accessible to a broader community, and push video models to a new state-of-the-art in a more efficient manner.

Acknowledgements. This work is supported in part by Centre for Perceptual and Interactive Intelligence Limited, in part by the General Research Fund through the Research Grants Council of Hong Kong under Grants (Nos. 14204021, 14207319), in part by CUHK Strategic Fund. This work is partially supported by the Shanghai Committee of Science and Technology (Grant No. 21DZ1100100).

References

1. Arnab, A., Dehghani, M., Heigold, G., Sun, C., Lučić, M., Schmid, C.: Vivit: a video vision transformer. In: Proceedings of the IEEE/CVF International Conference on Computer Vision, pp. 6836–6846 (2021)
2. Bao, H., Dong, L., Wei, F.: Beit: bert pre-training of image transformers. arXiv preprint arXiv:2106.08254 (2021)
3. Bertasius, G., Wang, H., Torresani, L.: Is space-time attention all you need for video understanding? In: Proceedings of the International Conference on Machine Learning (ICML) (2021)
4. Brown, T., et al.: Language models are few-shot learners. Adv. Neural. Inf. Process. Syst. **33**, 1877–1901 (2020)
5. Carreira, J., Zisserman, A.: Quo vadis, action recognition? a new model and the kinetics dataset. In: proceedings of the IEEE Conference on Computer Vision and Pattern Recognition, pp. 6299–6308 (2017)
6. Cheng, X., Lin, H., Wu, X., Yang, F., Shen, D.: Improving video-text retrieval by multi-stream corpus alignment and dual softmax loss. arXiv preprint arXiv:2109.04290 (2021)
7. Devlin, J., Chang, M.W., Lee, K., Toutanova, K.: Bert: pre-training of deep bidirectional transformers for language understanding. In: NAACL-HLT (2019)
8. Fan, H., et al.: Multiscale vision transformers. In: Proceedings of the IEEE/CVF International Conference on Computer Vision, pp. 6824–6835 (2021)
9. Fang, H., Xiong, P., Xu, L., Chen, Y.: Clip2video: mastering video-text retrieval via image clip. arXiv preprint arXiv:2106.11097 (2021)
10. Feichtenhofer, C.: X3d: expanding architectures for efficient video recognition. In: Proceedings of the IEEE/CVF Conference on Computer Vision and Pattern Recognition, pp. 203–213 (2020)
11. Feichtenhofer, C., Fan, H., Malik, J., He, K.: Slowfast networks for video recognition. In: Proceedings of the IEEE/CVF International Conference on Computer Vision, pp. 6202–6211 (2019)
12. Feichtenhofer, C., Fan, H., Xiong, B., Girshick, R., He, K.: A large-scale study on unsupervised spatiotemporal representation learning. In: Proceedings of the IEEE/CVF Conference on Computer Vision and Pattern Recognition, pp. 3299–3309 (2021)
13. Gao, P., et al.: Clip-adapter: better vision-language models with feature adapters. arXiv preprint arXiv:2110.04544 (2021)
14. Gao, Z., Liu, J., Chen, S., Chang, D., Zhang, H., Yuan, J.: Clip2tv: an empirical study on transformer-based methods for video-text retrieval. arXiv preprint arXiv:2111.05610 (2021)
15. Girdhar, R., Singh, M., Ravi, N., van der Maaten, L., Joulin, A., Misra, I.: Omnivore: A Single Model for Many Visual Modalities. arXiv preprint arXiv:2201.08377 (2022)
16. Guo, D., Rush, A.M., Kim, Y.: Parameter-efficient transfer learning with diff pruning. arXiv preprint arXiv:2012.07463 (2020)

17. Hara, K., Kataoka, H., Satoh, Y.: Learning spatio-temporal features with 3d residual networks for action recognition. In: Proceedings of the IEEE International Conference on Computer Vision Workshops, pp. 3154–3160 (2017)
18. He, K., Chen, X., Xie, S., Li, Y., Dollár, P., Girshick, R.: Masked autoencoders are scalable vision learners. arXiv preprint arXiv:2111.06377 (2021)
19. Houlsby, N., et al.: Parameter-efficient transfer learning for NLP. In: International Conference on Machine Learning, pp. 2790–2799. PMLR (2019)
20. Hu, E.J., et al.: Lora: low-rank adaptation of large language models. arXiv preprint arXiv:2106.09685 (2021)
21. Jia, C., et al.: Scaling up visual and vision-language representation learning with noisy text supervision. arXiv preprint arXiv:2102.05918 (2021)
22. Ju, C., Han, T., Zheng, K., Zhang, Y., Xie, W.: Prompting visual-language models for efficient video understanding. arXiv preprint arXiv:2112.04478 (2021)
23. Lester, B., Al-Rfou, R., Constant, N.: The power of scale for parameter-efficient prompt tuning. arXiv preprint arXiv:2104.08691 (2021)
24. Li, K., et al.: Uniformer: unified transformer for efficient spatiotemporal representation learning. In: ICLR (2022)
25. Li, X.L., Liang, P.: Prefix-tuning: optimizing continuous prompts for generation. arXiv preprint arXiv:2101.00190 (2021)
26. Li, Y., et al.: Improved multiscale vision transformers for classification and detection. arXiv preprint arXiv:2112.01526 (2021)
27. Liu, Z., et al.: Video swin transformer. arXiv preprint arXiv:2106.13230 (2021)
28. Patrick, M., et al.: Keeping your eye on the ball: Trajectory attention in video transformers. In: Advances in Neural Information Processing Systems (NeurIPS) (2021)
29. Pfeiffer, J., Kamath, A., Rücklé, A., Cho, K., Gurevych, I.: Adapterfusion: nondestructive task composition for transfer learning. arXiv preprint arXiv:2005.00247 (2020)
30. Qiu, Z., Yao, T., Mei, T.: Learning spatio-temporal representation with pseudo-3d residual networks. In: Proceedings of the IEEE International Conference on Computer Vision, pp. 5533–5541 (2017)
31. Radford, A., et al.: Learning transferable visual models from natural language supervision. arXiv preprint arXiv:2103.00020 (2021)
32. Riquelme, C., et al.: Scaling vision with sparse mixture of experts. arXiv preprint arXiv:2106.05974 (2021)
33. Ryoo, M.S., Piergiovanni, A., Arnab, A., Dehghani, M., Angelova, A.: Tokenlearner: what can 8 learned tokens do for images and videos? arXiv preprint arXiv:2106.11297 (2021)
34. Shridhar, M., Manuelli, L., Fox, D.: Cliport: what and where pathways for robotic manipulation. In: Proceedings of the 5th Conference on Robot Learning (CoRL) (2021)
35. Simonyan, K., Zisserman, A.: Two-stream convolutional networks for action recognition in videos. arXiv preprint arXiv:1406.2199 (2014)
36. Tran, D., Bourdev, L., Fergus, R., Torresani, L., Paluri, M.: Learning spatiotemporal features with 3d convolutional networks. In: Proceedings of the IEEE International Conference on Computer Vision, pp. 4489–4497 (2015)
37. Tran, D., Wang, H., Torresani, L., Feiszli, M.: Video classification with channel-separated convolutional networks. In: Proceedings of the IEEE/CVF International Conference on Computer Vision, pp. 5552–5561 (2019)

38. Tran, D., Wang, H., Torresani, L., Ray, J., LeCun, Y., Paluri, M.: A closer look at spatiotemporal convolutions for action recognition. In: Proceedings of the IEEE Conference on Computer Vision and Pattern Recognition, pp. 6450–6459 (2018)
39. Vaswani, A., et al.: Attention is all you need. In: Advances in Neural Information Processing Systems, pp. 5998–6008 (2017)
40. Wang, L., et al.: Temporal segment networks: towards good practices for deep action recognition. In: Leibe, B., Matas, J., Sebe, N., Welling, M. (eds.) ECCV 2016. LNCS, vol. 9912, pp. 20–36. Springer, Cham (2016). https://doi.org/10.1007/978-3-319-46484-8_2
41. Wang, M., Xing, J., Liu, Y.: Actionclip: a new paradigm for video action recognition. arXiv preprint arXiv:2109.08472 (2021)
42. Wang, X., Girshick, R., Gupta, A., He, K.: Non-local neural networks. In: Proceedings of the IEEE Conference on Computer Vision and Pattern Recognition, pp. 7794–7803 (2018)
43. Wei, C., Fan, H., Xie, S., Wu, C.Y., Yuille, A., Feichtenhofer, C.: Masked feature prediction for self-supervised visual pre-training. arXiv preprint arXiv:2112.09133 (2021)
44. Xie, S., Sun, C., Huang, J., Tu, Z., Murphy, K.: Rethinking spatiotemporal feature learning: speed-accuracy trade-offs in video classification. In: Proceedings of the European conference on computer vision (ECCV), pp. 305–321 (2018)
45. Xie, Z., et al.: Simmim: a simple framework for masked image modeling. arXiv preprint arXiv:2111.09886 (2021)
46. Yan, S., et al.: Multiview transformers for video recognition. arXiv preprint arXiv:2201.04288 (2022)
47. Yuan, L., et al.: Florence: a new foundation model for computer vision. arXiv preprint arXiv:2111.11432 (2021)
48. Zhai, X., Kolesnikov, A., Houlsby, N., Beyer, L.: Scaling vision transformers. arXiv preprint arXiv:2106.04560 (2021)
49. Zhai, X., Kolesnikov, A., Houlsby, N., Beyer, L.: Scaling vision transformers. In: Proceedings of the IEEE/CVF Conference on Computer Vision and Pattern Recognition, pp. 12104–12113 (2022)
50. Zhang, B., et al.: Co-training transformer with videos and images improves action recognition. arXiv preprint arXiv:2112.07175 (2021)
51. Zhang, R., et al.: Tip-adapter: training-free clip-adapter for better vision-language modeling. arXiv preprint arXiv:2111.03930 (2021)
52. Zhang, R., et al.: Pointclip: point cloud understanding by clip. arXiv preprint arXiv:2112.02413 (2021)
53. Zhou, B., Andonian, A., Oliva, A., Torralba, A.: Temporal relational reasoning in videos. In: Proceedings of the European Conference on Computer Vision (ECCV), pp. 803–818 (2018)
54. Zhou, K., Yang, J., Loy, C.C., Liu, Z.: Learning to prompt for vision-language models. arXiv preprint arXiv:2109.01134 (2021)

PIP: Physical Interaction Prediction via Mental Simulation with Span Selection

Jiafei Duan[1,2](✉)⬤, Samson Yu[3,4,6]⬤, Soujanya Poria[3]⬤, Bihan Wen[5]⬤, and Cheston Tan[1,6]⬤

[1] Institute for Infocomm Research, A*STAR, Singapore, Singapore
`duanj1@cs.washington.edu`
[2] University of Washington, Seattle, USA
[3] Singapore University of Technology and Design, Singapore, Singapore
[4] National University of Singapore, Singapore, Singapore
[5] Nanyang Technological University of Singapore, Singapore, Singapore
[6] Centre for Frontier AI Research, A*STAR, Singapore, Singapore

Abstract. Accurate prediction of physical interaction outcomes is a crucial component of human intelligence and is important for safe and efficient deployments of robots in the real world. While there are existing vision-based intuitive physics models that learn to predict physical interaction outcomes, they mostly focus on generating short sequences of future frames based on physical properties (e.g. mass, friction and velocity) extracted from visual inputs or a latent space. However, there is a lack of intuitive physics models that are tested on long physical interaction sequences with multiple interactions among different objects. We hypothesize that selective temporal attention during approximate mental simulations helps humans in physical interaction outcome prediction. With these motivations, we propose a novel scheme: **P**hysical **I**nteraction **P**rediction via Mental Simulation with Span Selection (PIP). It utilizes a deep generative model to model approximate mental simulations by generating future frames of physical interactions before employing selective temporal attention in the form of span selection for predicting physical interaction outcomes. To the best of our knowledge, attention has not been used with deep learning to tackle intuitive physics. For model evaluation, we further propose the large-scale SPACE+ dataset of synthetic videos with long sequences of three prime physical interactions in a 3D environment. Our experiments show that PIP outperforms human, baseline, and related intuitive physics models that utilize mental simulation. Furthermore, PIP's span selection module effectively identifies the frames indicating key physical interactions among objects, allowing for added interpretability, and does not require labor-intensive frame annotations. PIP is available on https://sites.google.com/view/piphysics.

J. Duan and S. Yu—Equal Contribution.

Supplementary Information The online version contains supplementary material available at https://doi.org/10.1007/978-3-031-19833-5_24.

Keywords: Computer vision · Scene understanding · Physical reasoning

1   Introduction

The ability to predict the outcomes of physical interactions among objects is a vital part of human intelligence [29,39]. Yet, it is very challenging for AI systems to acquire this ability. The key to tackling this challenge lies in understanding commonplace physical events. AI systems need to possess this ability before they can be safely and efficiently deployed in the physical world [13,33,57].

With the rapid advancements in computer vision, deep learning and embodied AI [4,12,18], there is an increase in intuitive physics models that aim to predict physical interaction outcomes. Many of these physical reasoning models [2,22,31,50,55] are inspired by *intuitive physics* in humans, which are found in cognitive science and neuroscience research [1,10,16,30,36,46]. One of the hypothesis from intuitive physics research postulates that humans predict physical interactions via the process of mental simulation. With only a few initial visual inputs of physical interaction, we can mentally reconstruct the scene with some initial approximations of the physical proprieties and dynamics of the objects. We can then predict the outcomes of physical interactions using this estimated information and the generated future visual states of objects during mental simulation. However, existing intuitive physics models are tested on short video sequences from datasets with mostly one continuous physical interaction among objects. Furthermore, it is uncertain whether humans can estimate physical properties accurately from visual inputs, and whether accurate physical property prediction is always useful for predicting physical interaction outcomes. In some cases, despite biases in estimations of physical properties [17,38,42], humans have been found to have adequately precise physical interaction outcome predictions [37]. This suggests that we might have other cognitive abilities on top of the physical property estimation that enable good physical interaction outcome prediction.

Past research has shown that humans make rational probabilistic inferences about physical interaction outcomes in a "noisy Newtonian" framework, assuming Newton's laws plus noisy observations [1]. We use noisy and approximate physical simulations to account for property, perceptual, dynamic and even collision uncertainties [1,5,21,24,35,43]. We posit that one of the beneficial cognitive abilities in humans for effective physical interaction outcome prediction is the ability to perform mental simulation with selective temporal attention to focus on physically relevant moments [15]. This might be because noisy observations and simulations are counterproductive except in moments when crucial physical interactions (e.g. collision events [21,35,46]) are present. We then posit that the selected moments in the mental simulation are used to predict the outcome.

Inspired by our hypothesis that humans use selective temporal attention in noisy mental simulations to reduce the negative effects of noise, we propose PIP, an intuitive physics model with future frame generation and span selection for predicting physical interaction outcomes. The span selection module serves as the temporal attention mechanism to focus on key physical interaction moments in the generated frames. Since state-of-the-art generative models in video generation still have artifacts and prediction errors in their generations [47,53], we simply use the well-established convolutional LSTM (ConvLSTM) [23,52] for future frame generation to approximate noisy mental simulations as a start.

Our contributions include: (a) PIP, a novel model for effective predictions of physical interaction outcomes among objects in long sequences disjointed interactions, (b) the SPACE+ dataset, the largest synthetic video dataset with long sequences of multiple disjointed object interactions for three fundamental physical interactions (*stability, contact* and *containment*) in a 3D environment, and (c) our experiments shown that PIP outperforms intuitive physics-inspired baselines and human performance while identifying the salient moment in frames of physical interactions, which makes PIP more interpretable.

2   Related Work

Several synthetic video datasets based on fundamental physical interactions among objects in 3D environments have been developed [3,8,11,22,55] with the growing importance of physical reasoning in AI research [10]. As a result, a diverse range of intuitive physics models [6,11,14,19,31,32] were also proposed for performing physical reasoning of object interactions. However, we find Physics 101 [50], Interpretable Intuitive Physics Model [55], and PhyDNet [23] to be the most relevant to our work as their intuitive physics models were also trained on video datasets of physical interactions.

Physics 101 [50] introduced a video dataset containing over 101 real-world physical interactions of objects in four different physical scenarios. It further proposed an unsupervised representation learning model to tackle the Physics 101 dataset. The model learns directly from unlabeled videos to output the estimates of physical properties of objects, and the generative component of the model can then be used for predicting the outcomes of physical interactions.

Interpretable Intuitive Physics Model [55] proposed an encoder-decoder framework for predicting future frames of collision events. The encoder layers will extrapolate the physical properties such as mass and friction from the input frames. The decoder then disentangles latent physics vectors by outputting optical flow. For a collision event, a bilinear grid sampling layer takes the optical flow and the input frames to produce a prediction of its outcome in the form of a future frame. The dataset used for training the model is a synthetic video dataset of collision events with 11 different object combinations of 5 unique basic objects generated using the Unreal Engine 4 (UE4) game engine.

PhyDNet [23] leverages the physical knowledge extracted from partial differential equations (PDE) to improve unsupervised video prediction on videos with physical interactions and dynamics. PhyDNet does so in a two-branch approach. PhyDNet's architecture separates the PDE dynamics from unknown complementary information. PhyCell, a deep recurrent physical model, performs PDE-constrained predictions for PDE dynamics, while a ConvLSTM [52] is used to model the complementary information. PhyDNet outperforms state-of-art methods in unsupervised video prediction of physical interaction outcomes.

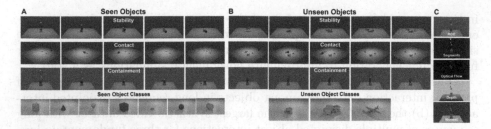

Fig. 1. Examples from SPACE+ dataset: (A) Frames of the three physical interaction tasks from the SPACE+ dataset for the seen object scenario. (B) Frames of the same tasks with new object classes for the unseen object scenario. (C) Visual information for one frame: RGB, object segmentation, optical flow, depth and surface normal vector.

The related works focus primarily on extracting physical properties of objects and dynamics from visual inputs for generating future frames, which are later used for predicting the outcome of physical interactions. In this work, we propose a new direction for mental simulation in predicting physical interaction outcomes by incorporating selective temporal attention. Our method first generates the future frames to model approximate mental simulation, then uses span selection to focus on key moments in the simulation.

3   SPACE+ Dataset

The proposed SPACE+ dataset, an improved extension of the SPACE dataset [11]. The original SPACE dataset comprises three novel video datasets synthesized by the SPACE simulator from 3D scenarios based on three fundamental physical interactions: stability, contact and containment. The SPACE dataset allows for the configuration of several parameters such as object shapes, the number of objects, object spawn locations and container types (only applicable to the containment task) during the generation.

The SPACE dataset has 15,000 unique scenarios with 5,000 scenarios for each of the three tasks. From there, 15,000 videos are generated lasting 3 s each at a frame rate of 50 frames per second (FPS), adding up to 2 million frames. However, there is an exception for the stability task, which is inherently unbalanced. During the stability task, for scenarios where two or three objects are spawned and land on top of each other, the objects that spawn above other objects will have higher chances of being unstable.

Our SPACE+ dataset expands and improves upon the existing SPACE dataset. Without altering the adjustable parameters, we further generate 42,057 unique scenarios on top of the original 15,000 scenarios created using the SPACE simulator. These scenarios follows the data distribution of the original SPACE dataset. We collect up to 57,057 videos with over 8 million frames in total. The overall data distribution ratio for SPACE+ is balanced with a ratio of 47:53 (positive:negative) for physical interaction outcomes, as shown in Fig. 2. Beyond

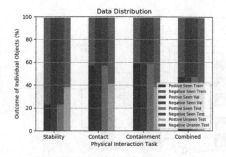

Fig. 2. Data distribution of the SPACE+ dataset used for training and testing.

scaling up the size of the dataset, we also add new object classes for all three fundamental physical interactions in the SPACE+ dataset, as shown in Fig. 1B. These new object classes will be used in an unseen object scenario that will help us evaluate the generalizability of our models and human performance, since unexpected physical interactions might arise due to the new and complex shapes of the new objects. The original object classes $O = \{cylinder, cone, inverted\ cone, cube, torus, sphere, flipped\ cylinder\}$ in the SPACE dataset are shown in Fig. 1A, and will be used in the seen object scenario, i.e. our models and humans will be able to train on or familiarize themselves with these object classes in the various physical interaction tasks before predicting their physical interaction outcomes in the tasks. For the SPACE+ dataset, besides the RGB frames, we also follow the SPACE paper in providing the object mask, segmentation map, optical flow map, depth map and surface normal vector map, as shown in Fig. 1C. Therefore, SPACE+ is the largest dataset of its kind as we have scaled up the SPACE dataset [11] by three folds and, further, added in unseen object classes, which aims to evaluate the generalizability of the trained model for unseen object shapes.

4   PIP

As shown in Fig. 3, PIP utilizes a ConvLSTM for future frame prediction to mimic noisy mental simulations and span selection to incorporate selective temporal attention. To the best of our knowledge, attention has not been used with deep learning to tackle intuitive physics tasks [10]. 2D/3D residual networks (ResNets) [25–27] and a pretrained BERT [9] are used to encode the necessary visual and task information for span selection [45]. PIP enables interpretability through span selection without the costly and subjective frame-based annotations needed for typical key frame selection approaches [54].

4.1   Mental Simulation

We use a ConvLSTM for future frame prediction to mimic noisy mental simulation as it is well-established and forms the backbone of recent video prediction

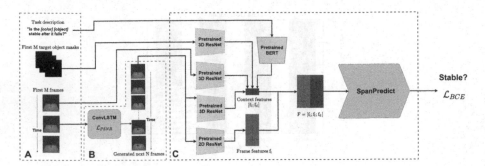

Fig. 3. PIP model architecture. (A) **Data inputs**: the original data inputs for our physical interaction prediction task comprise of the first M frames, the first M target object masks and the task description. (B) **Mental simulation**: the first M frames are fed into the mental simulation module that consists of a ConvLSTM to generate the next N frames. (C) **Span selection**: the original data inputs and the generated N frames are fed into the span selection module, where pretrained models will encode them into features before classification. All models are trained.

approaches [7,56]. The input frames are individually encoded into features with convolutional and transposed convolutional layers modelled after deep convolutional generative adversarial networks (DCGAN) [23,41] and individually fed as inputs into the ConvLSTM in sequence. We make use of teacher forcing [48] where we provide ground-truth frames to the model instead of generated frames to improve model learning. Starting from a specified frame, we train the ConvLSTM for future frame prediction.

A peak signal-to-noise ratio (PSNR) loss is used to train the convolutional layers and the ConvLSTM. The weights from each of them are shared across all three tasks in the combined training scenario.

4.2 Span Selection

PIP includes a span selection module to focus on salient frames while learning to predict physical interaction outcomes. It further allows for added interpretability by identifying the frames that are important for physical interaction prediction. Furthermore, this is done without labor-intensive frame-based annotations.

We use SpanPredict [45], a model used in natural language processing for document classification with only classification labels in the absence of ground-truth spans. Likewise, we focus on physical interaction outcome prediction in videos with only classification labels in the absence of ground-truth spans.

We modify SpanPredict to take in features for each generated frame. We obtain image features for each frame $f_{i,t} \in \mathbb{R}^i$ by passing them down a pretrained 2D ResNet50. To facilitate multi-task learning in the combined task and standardize inputs for all four tasks, we encode different language features for each of the three fundamental tasks. This helps to prevent model size from increasing with the number of tasks. For the stability, contact and containment tasks, we create the queries *"Does the [color] [object] get contacted by the red ball?"*, *"Is the [color] [object] contained within the containment holder?"* and *"Is the [color] [object] stable after it falls?"* respectively for each object in a scene. We obtain subword tokens for a query $Q = \{q_1, q_2, ..., q_n\}$ using the WordPiece tokenizer [51] and process the sequence as $[CLS]\ Q\ [SEP]$, as per the standard format for single sentence inputs into BERT models. We then feed the processed sequence into a pretrained BERT model (specifically bert-base-uncased). The language features $f_l \in \mathbb{R}^l$ are derived from the embeddings corresponding to the $[CLS]$ token, and are concatenated to each generated frame's feature.

In addition, for each generated frame's feature, we concatenate features $f_d \in \mathbb{R}^{d \times 3}$ from the first 3 frames, the first 3 segmentation masks for the target object and all generated frames. We pass each of them through a different pretrained 3D ResNet34 to get their features. Intuitively, these 3 sources of information provide the model with prior knowledge, object tracking and global contextual information respectively. The combined features for each generated frame $f_t = [f_{i,t}; f_l; f_d]$ are stacked to form a sequence of features $F = [f_1, f_2, ..., f_T]$.

In the following paragraph, we will briefly explain SpanPredict [45]. We set the number of spans, and for each span we provide a pair of trainable attention weights, $w_p, w_q \in \mathbb{R}^{i+l+d \times 3}$. This allows for flexibility for physical interactions that might require two or more disjointed segments in a video to determine their occurrence. Using these attention weights, we get vectors $\tilde{p} = \text{softmax}(F^T w_p)$ and $\tilde{q} = \text{softmax}(F^T w_q)$, which represent the probabilities of each frame being the start and end of a salient span respectively. We then produce a span representation r for each span using the cumulative sum function. Firstly, we sum up the set of probabilities for each span cumulatively such that $p = \text{cumsum}(\tilde{p})$ and $q = \text{cumsum}(\tilde{q}_{::-1})$, where $\tilde{q}_{::-1}$ is $\tilde{q}$ with its elements reversed. Intuitively, each element in p and q represents the probability that the start of a span has occurred by that element when coming from the left of the sequence and the probability that the end of a span has occurred by that element when coming from the right of the sequence respectively. We then combine both start and end positional information as $\tilde{r} = p \odot q$ to assign larger weights to frames that have high mass under both p and q, i.e. frames that are between the start and end points. Finally, we normalize $\tilde{r}$ such that its elements sum to 1: $r = \frac{p \odot q}{\Sigma_t (p \odot q)_t + \epsilon}$, where ϵ is a small constant. r gives us the final score of each frame's contribution to the span. We weigh the combined features F by r, then average its values across its temporal dimension to get $m = \text{average}(Fr) \in \mathbb{R}^{i+l+d \times 3}$. To get each span's contribution to the final classification, we use a third attention weight w_z to get $z = m w_z$, and we repeat this process for every span with the same w_z. Finally, the contribution scores for all spans are summed up and passed through a sigmoid layer to predict $\hat{y} \in \{0, 1\}$. An additional explicit penalty is also included in the form of the generalized Jensen-Shannon divergence [34] to make the spans more concise and distinct (i.e. minimize overlapping frames for multiple span selections) [45].

5 Experiments

5.1 Experimental Setup

The SPACE+ dataset is divided into stability, contact and containment tasks, and we further create a new combined task that contains an equal number of samples from each of the three fundamental tasks.

For each of the three fundamental tasks and the combined task, we use 1,000 scenes from the SPACE+ dataset that is representative of the full dataset and split it into 60% for the training set, and 20% for the validation and test set each. For the combined task, each of the splits has equal numbers of each of the three fundamental tasks to ensure that the dataset is balanced. For each scene, the physical interaction prediction is done for individual objects, i.e. the inputs are the same across objects in the same scene except for the object masks, and the labels are different across objects. To ensure a fair comparison of the models' performance with human performance, we used the same number of samples in the test set for both and did not use the full SPACE+ dataset for training.

For the unseen object scenario introduced with SPACE+, we also take 200 scenes for each of the three fundamental tasks and the combined task. The combined task contains equal numbers of each of the three fundamental tasks.

For each scene, there is a 3-s video with a FPS of 50 to make up 150 total frames. To limit the size of the dataset so as to improve computational runtime, we use a frame interval of 2 where we skip 1 frame every 2 frames, resulting in 75 frames in total. Of these 75 frames, we take the first 3 frames as initial frames to be shown to both human subjects and PIP, since there are no physical interactions among objects in these first 3 frames (i.e. first 6 frames in the original frame sequence with a frame interval of 1) in all scenes. For the ConvLSTM, we provide 37 subsequent frames from the 75 frames in addition to 3 initial frames to train it to learn future frame prediction. This is because 40 frames with a frame interval of 2 (i.e. 80 frames in the original frame sequence with a frame interval of 1) allow all outcomes of physical interactions among objects to be known. For each object in a scene, there are also 150 segmentation masks indicating its location in the 150 frames.

5.2 Evaluation Metric

To evaluate the performance of our selected methods, we use classification accuracy of physical interaction outcome predictions on the test sets of both seen and unseen object scenarios: score $= \mathbb{1}_{\hat{y}=y}$, where $y \in \{0, 1\}$ is the ground-truth label.

5.3 Human Baseline

We conduct a simple human experiment to obtain a benchmark for human performance in predicting physical interaction outcomes. Similar to other related works [22,31,32], we recruited ten participants anonymously from the internet for the

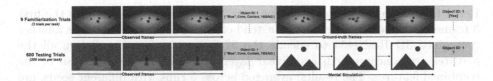

Fig. 4. Human trial setup on physical interaction prediction tasks. Trial structure for familiarization trials (*top*) and test trials (*bottom*) with the observed frames, task queries and ground-truth frames.

experiments. The participants first undergo a familiarization trial with nine questions (three questions for each of the three physical interaction tasks) for only the seen objects. In each familiarization trial, the participants are first shown a video with three continuous observed frames containing the initial moments of a physical interaction scenario. The participants are then asked to predict the outcome of the physical interaction by indicating either "YES" or "NO" for the specified objects. After the participants have completed indicating their prediction, they are shown the remaining parts of the video and are thus able to evaluate their predictions, as shown in Fig. 4. After completing the familiarization trials, they proceed to the actual test trials beginning with the scenarios with seen objects and then with unseen objects. The test trials are similar to the familiarization trials, but the full videos are not revealed to the participants at the end of each submission. Upon completion, their results are computed, and they are informed of their task-specific accuracy and the standard deviation of their performance for both the seen and unseen object scenarios.

5.4 Baseline

We establish baseline performance by building a model similar to PIP without the mental simulation and span selection modules. This baseline model takes in the first 3 frames, the first 3 segmentation masks and the BERT language features, and encodes the frames and the segmentation masks with separate pretrained 3D ResNet34s. It then uses linear layers for classification of the concatenated features. The results, averaged across 5 runs with different seeds, are shown in Table 1 as "Baseline". We use 3D ResNets as past intuitive physics models used well-established convolutional neural networks with great success.

5.5 PhyDNet

We modify PhyDNet [23] for a performance comparison between our approach and the incorporation of physical dynamics in mental simulations. PhyDNet is a state-of-the-art generative model for predicting physical dynamics and interactions in videos. Like PIP, this modified PhyDNet model takes in the first 3 frames, the first 3 segmentation masks and the BERT language features, and encodes the frames and the segmentation masks with separate pretrained 3D

ResNet34s. However, this model generates 37 subsequent frames using the first 3 frames with the PhyDNet model instead of a ConvLSTM. It then uses another pretrained 3D ResNet34 to encode the 37 frames as features, before all the features are concatenated, and linear layers are used for classification of the combined features. The results, averaged across 5 runs with different seeds, are shown in Table 1 as "PhyDNet".

5.6   PIP

Implementation Details. Models are implemented using PyTorch [40] and BERT is implemented using Hugging Face's Transformers [49]. We train using the Adam optimizer [28] for 20 epochs with a fixed learning rate of 1e-3 and a batch size of 2. We set a teacher forcing [48] rate of 0.1 for the ConvLSTM. Our ConvLSTM module consists of 3 ConvLSTM layers, 6 convolutional layers and 6 transposed convolution layers. We fine-tune the pretrained 2D ResNet50, 3D ResNet34s and BERT. We use PSNR loss to train the ConvLSTM and binary cross-entropy loss to train the entire model. To decide when to stop training, we monitor the validation classification accuracy for physical interaction outcome prediction. Our best model is selected based on its classification accuracy on the validation set of the seen object scenario. We train and test PIP over 5 runs with different random seeds and average the results. The number of spans extracted is set to 3. Experiments were run across NVIDIA GPU servers (RTX A6000, V100 and GeForce RTX 2080 Ti) and the total time for each epoch is about 2–3 h for a total of about 40–60 h for the entire process of 20 epochs.

Ablation Study. We conduct an ablation study to examine the effect of the span selection module. Like PIP, this ablation model takes in the first 3 frames, the first 3 segmentation masks and the BERT language features, and encodes the frames and the segmentation masks with separate pretrained 3D ResNet34s. Using the first 3 frames, this ablation model also generates 37 subsequent frames with a ConvLSTM. However, it uses another pretrained 3D ResNet34 to encode the 37 frames as features, before all the features are concatenated, and linear layers are used for classification of the combined features. We use the same hyperparameters and seed runs to train and test this model as those for PIP. The results, averaged across 5 runs with different see, are shown in Table 1 as "PIP w/o SS".

6   Results And Analysis

6.1   Human Performance

Based on the results obtained from the human experiments, as shown in Table 1 and Fig. 5A, we observe that human performance is consistent with an average standard deviation of 4.33 across all tasks in the seen object scenario. Hence, the performance of ten participants is representative of the general human performance, despite the smaller sample size. Human performance is also affected

Table 1. Accuracy results for seen (*left*) and unseen (*right*) object scenarios for all four physical interaction outcome prediction tasks.

Methods	Seen objects (%)				Unseen objects (%)			
	Stability	Contact	Containment	Combined	Stability	Contact	Containment	Combined
Human	80.24	59.54	76.19	69.54	65.88	56.07	**75.40**	61.95
Baseline	92.35	65.63	78.70	60.78	63.17	54.06	55.47	54.98
PhyDNet	**92.36**	61.23	79.47	62.03	63.78	55.41	59.10	55.61
PIP w/o SS	92.18	61.84	80.39	58.70	**67.07**	52.14	60.27	54.59
PIP (Ours)	92.33	**87.50**	**86.45**	**77.71**	66.41	**56.33**	55.99	**62.23**

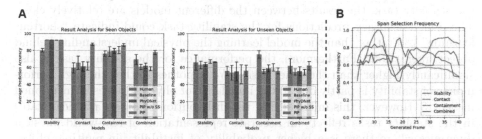

Fig. 5. (A) Average test prediction accuracy and standard deviation for seen (*left*) and unseen object (*right*) scenarios across all models and seeds. (B) PIP's frame selection frequencies on the test set for seen object scenarios across all seed runs.

by the complexity of the object shapes. Human performance has an average decrease of 6.54% from the seen object scenario to unseen object scenario across all tasks and a higher average standard deviation of 6.82, suggesting lower consistency. However, it has the lowest decrease when compared to the other models, suggesting the generalizability of human performance. Furthermore, human performance for the containment task in the unseen object scenario has the lowest decrease of 0.79% and is significantly higher than that of the other model methods by a difference of at least 15.13%. We believe this anomaly is due to the fact that humans can employ heuristics based on the estimation of physical properties (e.g. the width of the unseen object in comparison to the width of the container's entrance determines containment success) to improve predictions in the containment task. This ability is a known complement to the human mental simulation process [46].

6.2 PIP Test Performance

Based on our test results from Table 1, PIP achieve accuracies of 92.33% for *stability*, 87.50% for *contact*, 86.45% for *containment* and 77.71% for *combined* in the seen object scenario. PIP surpasses human performance by an average of 14.62% across all tasks with seen objects, the baseline model by 11.63% and the ablation model by 12.71%. PIP also surpasses the modified PhyDNet by 16.31% excluding for the stability task, where PIP performs slightly worse. Furthermore, the average standard deviation of PIP is only 1.36, which is the lowest compared to other models and human performance. Lastly, PIP is the only model that outperforms human performance in all four tasks in the seen object scenario and three tasks in the unseen object scenario.

The results suggests that PIP is effective in predicting the outcomes of physical interactions, as it outperforms most of the models significantly in seen object scenarios with a double-digit margin for some tasks. PIP is also highly consistent in its prediction accuracy for all tasks. Moreover, through comparison of PIP with the ablation results, it can be seen that the span selection mechanism improves the prediction performance. The only anomaly is in stability performance. For the stability task, the results between the different models are relatively close. These high accuracy predictions for the stability task could indicate "shortcut learning" [20] rather than the model learning the physical understanding behind object interactions. Furthermore, the performance for the stability task is also significantly higher than the other tasks. We hypothesize that the high performance of stability is partly due to the imbalance of physical states as mentioned in Sect. 3. However, this imbalance in the distribution of object physical states in the stability tasks reflects an accurate representation of real-world physical dynamics where there is a higher probability of instability in multiple object scenarios. This is further supported by our analysis of the SPACE+ dataset in the supplementary material. We also evaluate the generalizability of the models by testing them on unseen object scenarios. We show in Table 1 that all the methods perform more closely in relation to one another in unseen object scenarios with an maximum difference of 7.64% except for human performance in the containment task.

6.3   Span Selection

Based on our results, we show that PIP outperforms our ablation model by a huge average margin of 12.71%. This supports our premise that span selection as a form of selective temporal attention helps mental simulations to improve predictions of physical interaction outcomes. PIP also outperforms the modified PhyDNet model by 16.31%, suggesting that PIP contributes more to mental simulations than the incorporation of learned physical dynamics. Furthermore, PIP's span selection allows us to understand how important each frame is in its contribution to physical interaction outcome predictions, providing added interpretability. This added interpretability is a significant advantage as it gives us greater insights on how to improve model performance and build trust in applications where safety is a priority.

In our experiments, it is difficult for the model to follow a strict threshold of 0 for r during salient frame selection. It is also difficult to use a static threshold, even if it is normalized by generated frame sequence length N (i.e. $\frac{1}{N}$), due to the way r is calculated. Hence, we propose a new way to calculate the threshold for r as such:

$$\mathbf{p\_threshold} = \mathrm{cumsum}([\frac{1}{N}, \frac{1}{N}, ..., \frac{1}{N}]) \in \mathbb{R}^N$$

$$\mathbf{q\_threshold} = \mathbf{p\_threshold}_{::-1}$$

$$\mathbf{r\_threshold} = \frac{\mathbf{p\_threshold} \odot \mathbf{q\_threshold}}{\Sigma_t(\mathbf{p\_threshold} \odot \mathbf{q\_threshold})_t},$$

where N is the generated frame sequence length. Intuitively, this sets a uniform distribution normalized by sequence length as the threshold for $\mathbf{p}$ and $\mathbf{q}$ and calculates the threshold for $\mathbf{r}$ in the same way $\mathbf{r}$ is obtained from $\mathbf{p}$ and $\mathbf{q}$. We show in Fig. 6 an example of PIP's effective selection of salient frames using this threshold calculation.

In Fig. 5B, we show the frequencies of each generated frame being selected across all four tasks and all five seed runs, from frame 4 to frame 40, for the seen object scenario. Furthermore, upon inspection of the generated frames, we found that peaks in Fig. 5B indicate moments of key physical interactions among objects. For example, in Fig. 6, we illustrate for the stability task that frames 8–13, which corresponds to the first peak in the stability task's span selection frequencies, capture the first physical interactions among the ground and the falling object(s).

The span selection frequencies also highlight the complexity of each task. For example, the stability task's selected frames are mainly distributed into two distinct windows of frames 8–13 and 30–40 with high frequencies. This suggests that the stability task has two consistent and distinct moments of key physical interactions, which might allow for overfitting from generative models if they focus on these moments. On the other hand, for the contact task with a balanced distribution of selected frames, overfitting is more difficult. This highlights PIP's significance, since it outperforms all other models significantly for the contact task in the seen object scenario.

Finally, for the combined task, the span selection frequencies generally follow the trends of the three fundamental tasks in the first part before frame 15 with a small peak. The frequencies after frame 15 generally follow those of the contact task. More importantly, at frames 18 and 19, the frequencies decrease significantly in stark contrast to the containment task. Furthermore, the frequencies show a decreasing trend after a peak at frame 25, in contrast to the stability and containment tasks. This suggests that the combined task helps PIP to learn novel features that allow for generalizability across the three fundamental tasks. These features improve PIP's robustness, as seen in Table 1 where PIP has lowest accuracy decrease of 15.48% from the seen object scenario to the unseen scenario for the combined task, whereas there is a decrease of at least 25.92% for the other tasks.

7   Future Work

PIP currently performs worse on each of the three fundamental tasks when it is trained on the combined task than when it is both trained and tested on

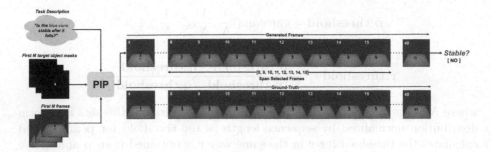

Fig. 6. An example of PIP's generation and span selection corresponding to the first window of peak span selection frequencies in the stability task. For visualizations of key physical interaction moments in the other tasks, refer to our supplementary material.

each of the three tasks. This is a common problem in multi-task learning [44]. Since PIP is only trained on a small number of samples for each of the three tasks in the combined task scenario, future work can be done with more data to improve PIP's robustness in multi-task settings. Furthermore, we assume that the generation artifacts and errors in the ConvLSTM's generations accurately model "noisy Newtonian" dynamics in human mental simulations. Future work can be done to better model "noisy Newtonian" dynamics in our model's mental simulations by investigating how the type of noise (e.g. disappearing objects, wrong trajectories), the variation in different physical properties (e.g. size and shape) and more constrained setups (e.g. attention on objects before generation) affect deep learning performance for the different physical interaction tasks.

8   Conclusion

Our ability to effectively predict the outcomes of physical interactions among objects in the real world is vital to ensure safety and success in performing complex tasks. This intuitive understanding of commonplace physical interactions is critical for complex real-world tasks such as human-robot collaboration and self-driving cars, which require reacting to ever-changing physical dynamics. In this work, we propose a new direction for intuitive physics models by proposing PIP, an intuitive physics model with selective temporal attention via span selection to improve physical interaction outcome prediction in noisy mental simulations. We evaluate PIP on the SPACE+ dataset, and show that PIP outperforms baseline and related intuitive physics models and human performance, while identifying key physical interaction moments and providing added interpretability.

Acknowledgements. This project is supported by funding allocation to C.T. by the Agency for Science, Technology and Research (A*STAR) under its SERC Central Research Fund (CRF) and its Centre for Frontier AI Research (CFAR), A*STAR's funding allocation to S.P. under its RIE 2020 AME programmatic grant RGAST2003 and project T2MOE2008 awarded by Singapore's MoE under its Tier-2 grant scheme.

References

1. Battaglia, P.W., Hamrick, J.B., Tenenbaum, J.B.: Simulation as an engine of physical scene understanding. Proc. Natl. Acad. Sci. **110**(45), 18327–18332 (2013)
2. Battaglia, P.W., Pascanu, R., Lai, M., Rezende, D., Kavukcuoglu, K.: Interaction networks for learning about objects, relations and physics. arXiv preprint arXiv:1612.00222 (2016)
3. Bear, D.M., et al.: Physion: Evaluating physical prediction from vision in humans and machines. arXiv preprint arXiv:2106.08261 (2021)
4. Bengio, Y., Lecun, Y., Hinton, G.: Deep learning for AI. Commun. ACM **64**(7), 58–65 (2021)
5. Bramley, N.R., Gerstenberg, T., Tenenbaum, J.B., Gureckis, T.M.: Intuitive experimentation in the physical world. Cogn. Psychol. **105**, 9–38 (2018)
6. Brubaker, M.A., Sigal, L., Fleet, D.J.: Estimating contact dynamics. In: 2009 IEEE 12th International Conference on Computer Vision, pp. 2389–2396. IEEE (2009)
7. Chai, Z., Yuan, C., Lin, Z., Bai, Y.: CMS-LSTM: context-embedding and multi-scale spatiotemporal-expression LSTM for video prediction. arXiv preprint arXiv:2102.03586 (2021)
8. Dasgupta, A., Duan, J., Ang Jr, M.H., Tan, C.: Avoe: a synthetic 3d dataset on understanding violation of expectation for artificial cognition. arXiv preprint arXiv:2110.05836 (2021)
9. Devlin, J., Chang, M.W., Lee, K., Toutanova, K.: Bert: pre-training of deep bidirectional transformers for language understanding. arXiv preprint arXiv:1810.04805 (2018)
10. Duan, J., Dasgupta, A., Fischer, J., Tan, C.: A survey on machine learning approaches for modelling intuitive physics. arXiv preprint arXiv:2202.06481 (2022)
11. Duan, J., Yu, S., Tan, C.: Space: a simulator for physical interactions and causal learning in 3d environments. In: Proceedings of the IEEE/CVF International Conference on Computer Vision, pp. 2058–2063 (2021)
12. Duan, J., Yu, S., Tan, H.L., Zhu, H., Tan, C.: A survey of embodied AI: from simulators to research tasks. arXiv preprint arXiv:2103.04918 (2021)
13. Duchaine, V., Gosselin, C.: Safe, stable and intuitive control for physical human-robot interaction. In: 2009 IEEE International Conference on Robotics and Automation, pp. 3383–3388. IEEE (2009)
14. Finn, C., Goodfellow, I., Levine, S.: Unsupervised learning for physical interaction through video prediction. Adv. Neural. Inf. Process. Syst. **29**, 64–72 (2016)
15. Firestone, C., Scholl, B.: Seeing stability: intuitive physics automatically guides selective attention. J. Vis. **16**(12), 689–689 (2016)
16. Fischer, J., Mikhael, J.G., Tenenbaum, J.B., Kanwisher, N.: Functional neuroanatomy of intuitive physical inference. Proc. Natl. Acad. Sci. **113**(34), E5072–E5081 (2016)
17. Fleming, R.W.: Visual perception of materials and their properties. Vision. Res. **94**, 62–75 (2014)
18. Forsyth, D., Ponce, J.: Computer Vision: A Modern Approach. Prentice hall (2011)
19. Fragkiadaki, K., Agrawal, P., Levine, S., Malik, J.: Learning visual predictive models of physics for playing billiards. arXiv preprint arXiv:1511.07404 (2015)
20. Geirhos, R., Jacobsen, J.H., Michaelis, C., Zemel, R., Brendel, W., Bethge, M., Wichmann, F.A.: Shortcut learning in deep neural networks. Nat. Mach. Intell. **2**(11), 665–673 (2020)

21. Gerstenberg, T., Tenenbaum, J.B.: Intuitive Theories. Oxford handbook of causal reasoning, pp. 515–548 (2017)
22. Groth, O., Fuchs, F.B., Posner, I., Vedaldi, A.: Shapestacks: learning vision-based physical intuition for generalised object stacking. In: Proceedings of the European Conference on Computer Vision (ECCV), pp. 702–717 (2018)
23. Guen, V.L., Thome, N.: Disentangling physical dynamics from unknown factors for unsupervised video prediction. In: Proceedings of the IEEE/CVF Conference on Computer Vision and Pattern Recognition, pp. 11474–11484 (2020)
24. Hamrick, J.B., Smith, K.A., Griffiths, T.L., Vul, E.: Think again? the amount of mental simulation tracks uncertainty in the outcome. Cognitive Science (2015)
25. Hara, K., Kataoka, H., Satoh, Y.: Can spatiotemporal 3d CNNS retrace the history of 2d cnns and imagenet? In: Proceedings of the IEEE Conference on Computer Vision and Pattern Recognition, pp. 6546–6555 (2018)
26. He, K., Zhang, X., Ren, S., Sun, J.: Deep residual learning for image recognition. In: Proceedings of the IEEE Conference on Computer Vision and Pattern Recognition (CVPR) (2016)
27. Kataoka, H., Wakamiya, T., Hara, K., Satoh, Y.: Would mega-scale datasets further enhance spatiotemporal 3d CNNS? arXiv preprint arXiv:2004.04968 (2020)
28. Kingma, D.P., Ba, J.: Adam: a method for stochastic optimization. arXiv preprint arXiv:1412.6980 (2014)
29. Kubricht, J.R., Holyoak, K.J., Lu, H.: Intuitive physics: current research and controversies. Trends Cogn. Sci. **21**(10), 749–759 (2017)
30. Kubricht, J.R., Holyoak, K.J., Lu, H.: Intuitive physics: current research and controversies. Trends Cogn. Sci. **21**(10), 749–759 (2017)
31. Lerer, A., Gross, S., Fergus, R.: Learning physical intuition of block towers by example. In: International Conference on Machine Learning, pp. 430–438. PMLR (2016)
32. Li, W., Azimi, S., Leonardis, A., Fritz, M.: To fall or not to fall: a visual approach to physical stability prediction. arXiv preprint arXiv:1604.00066 (2016)
33. Li, W., Leonardis, A., Fritz, M.: Visual stability prediction for robotic manipulation. In: 2017 IEEE International Conference on Robotics and Automation (ICRA), pp. 2606–2613. IEEE (2017)
34. Lin, J.: Divergence measures based on the shannon entropy. IEEE Trans. Inf. Theory **37**(1), 145–151 (1991). https://doi.org/10.1109/18.61115
35. Ludwin-Peery, E., Bramley, N.R., Davis, E., Gureckis, T.M.: Limits on simulation approaches in intuitive physics. Cogn. Psychol. **127**, 101396 (2021). https://doi.org/10.1016/j.cogpsych.2021.101396, https://www.sciencedirect.com/science/article/pii/S0010028521000190
36. McCloskey, M.: Intuitive physics. Sci. Am. **248**(4), 122–131 (1983)
37. Mitko, A., Fischer, J.: When it all falls down: the relationship between intuitive physics and spatial cognition. Cogn. Res. Princip. Impl. **5**(1), 1–13 (2020). https://doi.org/10.1186/s41235-020-00224-7
38. Mitko, A., Fischer, J.: A striking take on mass inferences from collisions. J. Vis. **21**(9), 2812–2812 (2021)
39. Moore, D.S., Johnson, S.P.: Mental rotation in human infants: a sex difference. Psychol. Sci. **19**(11), 1063–1066 (2008)
40. Paszke, A., et al.: Pytorch: an imperative style, high-performance deep learning library. In: Wallach, H., Larochelle, H., Beygelzimer, A., d' Alché-Buc, F., Fox, E., Garnett, R. (eds.) Advances in Neural Information Processing Systems, vol. 32, pp. 8024–8035. Curran Associates, Inc. (2019), http://papers.neurips.cc/paper/9015-pytorch-an-imperative-style-high-performance-deep-learning-library.pdf

41. Radford, A., Metz, L., Chintala, S.: Unsupervised representation learning with deep convolutional generative adversarial networks. arXiv preprint arXiv:1511.06434 (2015)
42. Rossi, F., Montanaro, E., de'Sperati, C.: Speed biases with real-life video clips. Front. Integr. Neurosci. **12**, 11 (2018)
43. Smith, K.A., Vul, E.: Sources of uncertainty in intuitive physics. Top. Cogn. Sci. **5**(1), 185–199 (2013)
44. Standley, T., Zamir, A., Chen, D., Guibas, L., Malik, J., Savarese, S.: Which tasks should be learned together in multi-task learning? In: International Conference on Machine Learning, pp. 9120–9132. PMLR (2020)
45. Subramanian, V., Engelhard, M., Berchuck, S., Chen, L., Henao, R., Carin, L.: Spanpredict: extraction of predictive document spans with neural attention. In: Proceedings of the 2021 Conference of the North American Chapter of the Association for Computational Linguistics: Human Language Technologies, pp. 5234–5258 (2021)
46. Ullman, T.D., Spelke, E., Battaglia, P., Tenenbaum, J.B.: Mind games: Game engines as an architecture for intuitive physics. Trends Cogn. Sci. **21**(9), 649–665 (2017)
47. Weissenborn, D., Täckström, O., Uszkoreit, J.: Scaling autoregressive video models. arXiv preprint arXiv:1906.02634 (2019)
48. Williams, R.J., Zipser, D.: A learning algorithm for continually running fully recurrent neural networks. Neural Comput. **1**(2), 270–280 (1989). https://doi.org/10.1162/neco.1989.1.2.270
49. Wolf, T., et al.: Huggingface's transformers: state-of-the-art natural language processing. arXiv preprint arXiv:1910.03771 (2019)
50. Wu, J., Lim, J.J., Zhang, H., Tenenbaum, J.B., Freeman, W.T.: Physics 101: learning physical object properties from unlabeled videos. In: BMVC. vol. 2, p. 7 (2016)
51. Wu, Y., et al.: Google's neural machine translation system: Bridging the gap between human and machine translation. arXiv preprint arXiv:1609.08144 (2016)
52. Xingjian, S., Chen, Z., Wang, H., Yeung, D.Y., Wong, W.K., Woo, W.c.: Convolutional lSTM network: a machine learning approach for precipitation nowcasting. In: Advances in Neural Information Processing Systems, pp. 802–810 (2015)
53. Yan, W., Zhang, Y., Abbeel, P., Srinivas, A.: Videogpt: video generation using VQ-VAE and transformers. arXiv preprint arXiv:2104.10157 (2021)
54. Yan, X., Gilani, S.Z., Feng, M., Zhang, L., Qin, H., Mian, A.: Self-supervised learning to detect key frames in videos. Sensors **20**(23) (2020). https://doi.org/10.3390/s20236941, https://www.mdpi.com/1424-8220/20/23/6941
55. Ye, T., Wang, X., Davidson, J., Gupta, A.: Interpretable intuitive physics model. In: Proceedings of the European Conference on Computer Vision (ECCV), pp. 87–102 (2018)
56. Zhang, L., et al.: Spatio-temporal convolutional lSTMS for tumor growth prediction by learning 4d longitudinal patient data. IEEE Trans. Med. Imaging **39**(4), 1114–1126 (2019)
57. Zheng, B., Zhao, Y., Yu, J., Ikeuchi, K., Zhu, S.C.: Scene understanding by reasoning stability and safety. Int. J. Comput. Vision **112**(2), 221–238 (2015)

Panoramic Vision Transformer
for Saliency Detection in 360° Videos

Heeseung Yun, Sehun Lee, and Gunhee Kim[✉]

Seoul National University, Seoul, Korea
{heeseung.yun,shlee}@vision.snu.ac.kr, gunhee@snu.ac.kr
https://github.com/hs-yn/PAVER

Abstract. 360° video saliency detection is one of the challenging benchmarks for 360° video understanding since non-negligible distortion and discontinuity occur in the projection of any format of 360° videos, and capture-worthy viewpoint in the omnidirectional sphere is ambiguous by nature. We present a new framework named **P**anoramic **V**ision Transformer (PAVER). We design the encoder using Vision Transformer with deformable convolution, which enables us not only to plug pretrained models from normal videos into our architecture without additional modules or finetuning but also to perform geometric approximation only once, unlike previous deep CNN-based approaches. Thanks to its powerful encoder, PAVER can learn the saliency from three simple relative relations among local patch features, outperforming state-of-the-art models for the Wild360 benchmark by large margins without supervision or auxiliary information like class activation. We demonstrate the utility of our saliency prediction model with the omnidirectional video quality assessment task in VQA-ODV, where we consistently improve performance without any form of supervision, including head movement.

Keywords: 360° videos · Saliency detection · Vision transformer

1 Introduction

360° video understanding is critical for providing intelligent systems with omnidirectional perception. Simultaneous view in every direction helps agents better react in challenging environments for indoor navigation [1], autonomous driving [9,52], and drone navigation [7], to name a few. Also, virtual reality and 360° action cameras have pervaded entertainment applications.

Visual saliency prediction is one of the representative benchmarks for 360° video understanding. It can filter irrelevant or redundant information in panoramic views, and thus promote summarization of 360° videos or dynamic rendering of virtual reality panorama. Unlike saliency detection in normal field-of-view (NFoV) imagery that often aims to distinguish salient foreground from

---

Supplementary Information The online version contains supplementary material available at https://doi.org/10.1007/978-3-031-19833-5_25.

background, saliency prediction in 360° videos stems from a simple yet nontrivial question: which direction to watch if you were in the scene? Foreground objects may not always be of interest, and salient direction is subjective and depends on context. Hence, 360° saliency prediction has often been interpreted as automated cinematography [12,39], highlight detection [28,54], and attention tracking [24].

There are a few challenges in predicting visual saliency in 360° videos. First, in any format of 360° videos (e.g., equirectangular, cubemap [22]), a non-negligible proportion of distortion and discontinuity hinders the accurate processing of omnidirectional view. Thus, it is nearly impossible to directly leverage models learned from normal videos at no cost. Some previous works [12,28,66] explicitly project a number of NFoV images from a panorama frame to estimate salient viewpoints. However, this may not be scalable in terms of both space and time since an order of magnitude larger number of NFoV images (e.g., 81 for [28]) should be processed per single panorama frame. In another line of works, transferrable architectures are proposed to utilize pretrained knowledge from the NFoV domain [18,37,38]. They can process 360° input without modification but at the cost of geometric error or additional modules for finetuning.

Second, ambiguity is another vital issue for saliency prediction in 360° videos. While previous works define saliency as intensity and orientation [25], self-information [4], and anomaly [45], there is no definitive answer for which constitutes capture-worthiness or saliency in 360° videos. A widely accepted tool to interpret saliency is class activation maps (CAM) [65] in both NFoV domain [32,51,58,59] and 360° domain [11]. Although CAM can readily capture objects in the scene, it depends on the class labels of the reference dataset and is challenging to integrate with self-supervised pretraining that has no labels. As 360° saliency detection has been usually addressed under minimal or zero supervision, some other works resolve ambiguity by leveraging additional information like the coordinates of target objects [24] or reference NFoV videos of the same topic [28,39,54].

To address these issues, we propose a novel framework for 360° video saliency prediction named **Pa**noramic **V**ision Transform**er** (PAVER). It is equipped with two components: a deformation-aware omnidirectional encoder and a consistency-oriented saliency map decoder. First, our encoder adopts deformable convolution [14] to represent a 360° video as a set of small patches with local tangent projection for minimal geometric error. It can replace the NFoV projection that previous works often use with 60× less geometric error at negligible computation overhead. Then, we use the Vision Transformer [17] to remove the need for additional finetuning to transfer pretrained weights from the NFoV domain. As a result, the geometric approximation happens *only once* in our framework, unlike previous deep CNN-based approaches that perform at every layer, relieving the model of layerwise geometric error accumulation [38]. Our work is the first attempt to exploit the vision transformer to process 360° imagery.

Second, for our decoder to determine capture-worthy context on panoramic videos without supervision or additional information, we decompose the saliency into three relative relationships of the local patch features from its surrounding contexts. If the context of a local patch diverges from the overall representation of the video (*local saliency*), the patch can be deemed anomalous and is usually worth noticing. Moreover, if the spatial and temporal neighbors of a patch are capture-worthy (*spatial & temporal saliency*), the patch should also be capture-worthy. By enforcing this simple yet straightforward objective in the feature dimension, we outperform the previous state-of-the-art model by 23% in the Wild360 dataset [11]. Also, we leverage this saliency prediction for omnidirectional video quality assessment for virtual reality (VR) in VQA-ODV [30], which is crucial for user experience in VR.

In conclusion, we summarize our main contribution as follows.

1. Our PAVER framework is the first attempt to adopt the Vision Transformer [17] to encode the omnidirectional imagery. Along with deformable convolution [14], our encoder alleviates geometric projection errors with no additional module and trivially processes panoramic videos in various formats by transferring the weights learned from the normal video datasets.
2. Thanks to our powerful encoder, we demonstrate that it is sufficient for 360° video saliency prediction to simply learn from relative relations among local patch features, outperforming state-of-the-art models for the Wild360 benchmark [11] by large margins with no additional annotations.
3. For the applicability of PAVER, we show that PAVER can consistently improve the performance of omnidirectional video quality assessment in the VQA-ODV [30] benchmark with no human supervision like head movement.

2 Related Work

Panoramic Video Processing. Efficient and accurate processing of 360° images or videos has been studied much. One of the most popular approaches is to project panorama into a set of normal field-of-view (NFoV) videos. Despite its simplicity, it has been effective in various tasks like vision-and-language navigation [66], language-guided view grounding [12], and 360° video summarization [28]. However, it requires explicit projection of up to 81 NFoV images per panoramic frame, which is less scalable in both space and time.

For the processing of spherical inputs, some prior works suggest designated architectures with spherical correlation [13], spherical convolution with spectral smoothness [19], or operations on unstructured grids [26]. Although they ensure favorable mathematical properties like rotational equivariance, they cannot be transferred from model weights trained with large sets of normal images or videos. Another compelling direction is to use transferrable architectures combined with geometric adaptation modules with finetuning [37,38], polyhedral approximation [29], or both [18,60]. However, additional modules for geometric alignment may be detrimental to latency, either in the training or inference step.

We use a transformer architecture where geometric approximation happens only once at the beginning, unlike previous approaches that perform in every layer. Pretrained weights from the NFoV domain are transferrable to our approach without pretraining for geometric adaptation. In addition, our approach is format-independent; not only the equirectangular format, but our model can also compute the cubemap or other formats without explicit conversion.

Visual Saliency Detection. Saliency detection has been a longstanding problem in computer vision research. In order to identify visual saliency, previous approaches utilize intensity and orientation with respect to stimulus [25], self-information maximization [4], intrinsic and extrinsic anomaly [45], and self-resemblance [35]. More recent work focuses on class activation maps [65], where high activation value of a certain class implies saliency. CAM-based methods are widely accepted for multi-source saliency detection [59], weakly supervised semantic segmentation [58], and object localization [32,51]. We point our readers to a survey of visual saliency detection [43] for further details.

On the other hand, saliency prediction in 360° videos needs to identify capture-worthy viewpoints within the omnidirectional surroundings. Given a number of possible candidate viewpoints, it aims at providing plausible viewpoints or a heatmap as if someone is watching the scene. Thus, the saliency in 360° videos is often ambiguous and depends on subjective context. To resolve this, some works exploit NFoV videos as exemplars of capture-worthiness [28,39,54]. Other works leverage human supervision of saliency maps [62] or object tracking information [24] for training. Some recent works also utilize learned class activation maps [11] or natural language narratives [12]. Our approach is also in line with [11,12] in that we do not require explicit supervision for training. One key difference is that we do not rely on additional information like CAM or narratives for training. Instead, we enforce local saliency and spatiotemporal saliency in the feature map of the local patch context.

Vision Transformers. Vision Transformers [17] have been drawing much attention for large-scale visual understanding since they reported impressive performance in image classification [42,55], object detection and semantic segmentation [31,50]. Recently, vision transformers have been adapted to broader domains, including point cloud [63] and video understanding [2,61]. Another line of works focuses on transferring pretrained knowledge of vision transformers in an unsupervised or semi-supervised manner by leveraging self-distillation [8], semantics reallocation [21], seed propagation [36], and normalized cut [47].

Our work is the first to adopt the vision transformer to process omnidirectional inputs. Closest to our approach is Yun *et al.* [57], which utilizes the transformer for indoor semantic segmentation with monocular 360° images. However, Yun *et al.* do not take into account 360° format when processing images but instead discard the near-polar region where the spherical distortion is severe. On the other hand, our approach can process the whole panorama in a format-aware manner without discarding any parts, while being applicable to both 360° images and videos with only trivial overhead.

3   Approach

We present a model named **Pan**oramic **V**ision Transform**er** (PAVER) for saliency detection in 360° videos, as illustrated in Fig. 1. Given a 360° input video in equirectangular format $V = \{v^t\}_{t=1}^T \in \mathbb{R}^{T \times 3 \times H \times W}$ with T frames, our objective is to compute their saliency maps, *i.e.*, $\{\hat{y}^t\}_{t=1}^T \in \mathbb{R}^{T \times H \times W}$. In Sect. 3.1, we

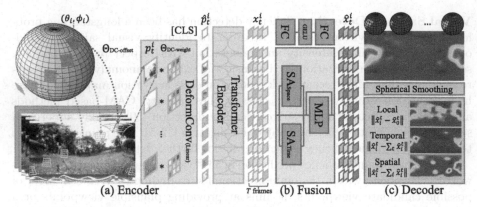

(a) Encoder T frames (b) Fusion   (c) Decoder

Fig. 1. Model architecture of **PAVER** (Panoramic Vision Transformer).

explain the Transformer encoder for encoding local patches with minimal geometric error (Fig. 1-(a)). Then, we deal with the spatiotemporal fusion module for learning consistent local and global features in Sect. 3.2 (Fig. 1-(b)). Finally, we account for the saliency map decoder with spherical smoothing and learning objectives in Sects. 3.3 and 3.4. Commonly used variables are described as follows:

S	Length of a tangential patch
W, H	Resolution of 360° video input (*e.g.*, $W = 448, H = 224$)
w, h	Number of patches along width and height, *i.e.*, $w = \frac{W}{S}, h = \frac{H}{S}$
N	Number of flattened patches, *i.e.*, $N = w \times h$
C	Number of channels per feature (*e.g.*, 768 for ViT-B/16 [17])

3.1 The Encoder for 360° Videos

Local Patch Projection. Naïve projection of local patches in vision transformers [17] cannot handle distortion and discontinuity in 360 domains. Hence, we leverage deformable convolution [14], which can process freeform deformation of convolution kernels with marginal computation overhead. For each 360° frame $v^t \in \mathbb{R}^{3 \times H \times W}$, we first compute tangential patches with a size of $S \times S$, namely $\{p_i^t\}_{i=1}^N$ where $N = wh = \frac{W}{S} \times \frac{H}{S}$. Then, we linearly project patches to obtain $\{\hat{p}_i^t\}_{i=1}^N$ where $\hat{p}_i^t \in \mathbb{R}^C$, using deformable convolution with fixed offsets:

$$\hat{p}^t = \text{Conv}(p^t) = \text{DeformConv}(v^t; \Theta_{\text{DC-weight}}, \Theta_{\text{DC-offset}}), \quad (1)$$

$$\Theta_{\text{DC-offset}}(\theta_i, \phi_i) = f_{\text{Sph}\to\text{ER}}(f_{\text{3D}\to\text{Sph}}(\mathcal{P} \times R(\theta_i, \phi_i)/\|\mathcal{P} \times R(\theta_i, \phi_i)\|_2)), \quad (2)$$

$$R(\theta_i, \phi_i) = \begin{pmatrix} \cos\phi_i \cos\theta_i & -\cos\phi_i \sin\theta_i & \sin\theta_i \\ \sin\theta_i & \cos\theta_i & 0 \\ \sin\phi_i \cos\theta_i & -\sin\phi_i \sin\theta_i & \cos\phi_i \end{pmatrix}, \quad (3)$$

where $(\theta_i, \phi_i) \in (0, 2\pi) \times (-\pi/2, \pi/2)$ is the longitude and latitude of the center of the i-th patch, and $\mathcal{P} \in \mathbb{R}^{S \times S \times 3}$ indicates sampled 3D points from an $S \times S$ patch on $z = 1$ plane. $f_{3D \rightarrow Sph}$ is the conversion from the 3D cartesian coordinates to the spherical coordinates, while $f_{Sph \rightarrow ER}$ is that from the spherical to the 2D equirectangular coordinates. In a nutshell, we compute the offset for DeformConv by rotating the reference patch $\mathcal{P}$ by θ_i and ϕ_i and projecting it onto an equirectangular plane. Please refer to the Appendix for more details.

In Eq. 1, the weights for linear projection $\Theta_{DC\text{-weight}}$ can be transferred from pretrained Vision Transformers [8,10,17,42] without additional tuning, as $\Theta_{DC\text{-offset}}$ locally projects curved surfaces to flat NFoV images. Unlike deformable convolutional networks [14], the offset $\Theta_{DC\text{-offset}}$ is computed only once and fixed throughout the training. That is, throughout our architecture, we apply geometric approximation only here for local tangential patches. Another benefit is that we can adapt any format other than equirectangular (e.g., cubemap) without an explicit conversion process as long as the offset $\Theta_{DC\text{-offset}}$ is computed from the conversion formula between different formats. Considering that recently more videos are using the equiangular cubemap format for better resolution, our approach can represent the video as-is, regardless of the formats.

Transformer Encoder. We prefix N patches $\{\hat{p}_i^t\}_{i=1}^N$ with a learnable vector $\hat{p}_0^t$ (i.e., [CLS] token) and feed them to the transformer encoder:

$$\{x_i^t\}_{i=0}^N = \text{Transformer}(\{\hat{p}_i^t\}_{i=0}^N; \Theta_{ViT}), \tag{4}$$

where $\{x_i^t\}_{i=0}^N$ is the output features of the patches. As in the local patch projection of Eq. 1, pretrained weights on the NFoV domain (e.g., ViT [17] trained with ImageNet-21k [15]) can be reused for Θ_{ViT} without finetuning or even additional modules. Unless mentioned otherwise, we use vanilla vision transformers with the ViT-B/16 weights [17]. Refer to Table 2-(b) later for the experiments with other transformer variants. More details are deferred to Appendix.

3.2 Spatiotemporal Fusion

Since the encoded features $\{x_i^t\}_{i=0}^N$ are obtained from each patch separately, we now train a spatiotemporal fusion module so that the local features are smoothly aligned with respect to space and time. We decouple global context x_0^t from the local patch context $\{x_i^t\}_{i=1}^N$ and model them separately. We observe that training both global and local context with identical weight is detrimental to performance, which is further discussed in Sect. 4.2.

Global Context. [CLS] tokens in Transformers are generally used as an input to a classification head to predict the output. Thus, we regard $x_0^t \in \mathbb{R}^C$, the output of transformer for the [CLS] input token, as encapsulating the global context of scenery in a sense. Finally, we encode global context $\hat{x}_0^t \in \mathbb{R}^C$ via a simple multilayer perceptron (MLP):

$$\hat{x}_0^t = \text{MLP}_G(x_0^t; \Theta_G), \tag{5}$$

where MLP refers to two fully-connected layers with GELU activation [23].

Local Context. To encode temporal information in the local patch context, we use features from all T frames $i.e.$, $X = \{\{x_i^t\}_{i=1}^N\}_{t=1}^T \in \mathbb{R}^{T \times N \times C}$. We extend the vanilla transformer encoder with multi-head self-attention [44] temporally:

$$\hat{X} = X' + \text{MLP}_{\text{L}}(X'; \Theta_{\text{L}}), \text{ where } X' = X + \frac{\text{SA}(X; \Theta_{\text{S}}) + \text{SA}(X^T; \Theta_{\text{T}})^T}{2}. \quad (6)$$

MLP_{L} indicates an MLP with residual connection, and SA respectively denotes multi-head self-attention along the temporal axis (T) and spatial axis (N). X^T is a transpose between the temporal and spatial axis, $i.e.$, $X^T \in \mathbb{R}^{N \times T \times C}$. By averaging two multi-head self-attentions, local patches have similar feature representation with their spatial and temporal neighbors altogether.

3.3   The Decoder for Saliency Map

Using both global and local contexts ($\{\hat{x}_0^t\}_{t=1}^T$ and $\{\{\hat{x}_i^t\}_{i=1}^N\}_{t=1}^T$), we first compute the saliency score of each local patch. We decompose the saliency into three terms: local, temporal, and spatial saliency. Instead of directly optimizing saliency scores, we measure relative relations between each local context feature and its neighbors and optimize them on the feature level.

First, the local saliency measures how much a local patch deviates from the global context. If the distance between the local patch and global context is large, it can be deemed as an anomalous patch, which may be worth viewing. Likewise, temporal and spatial saliency reflects how much a local patch deviates from the temporal or spatial mean of its neighbors. With more distance between, the context of the patch would more differ from those of its neighborhoods. Finally, our saliency score is computed as follows, where $\alpha = \beta = \gamma = 1$ for simplicity:

$$y_i^t = \alpha \left\| \hat{x}_i^t - \hat{x}_0^t \right\|_2^2 + \beta \left\| \hat{x}_i^t - \frac{1}{T} \sum_{t=1}^T \hat{x}_i^t \right\|_2^2 + \gamma \left\| \hat{x}_i^t - \frac{1}{N} \sum_{i=1}^N \hat{x}_i^t \right\|_2^2. \quad (7)$$

Spherical Gaussian Smoothing. To upsample from $\mathbb{R}^{h \times w}$ to $\mathbb{R}^{H \times W}$ while observing the spherical structure, we apply spherical Gaussian smoothing [16]. The scalar saliency score $\hat{y}^t$ is obtained as

$$\hat{y}_{ij}^t(\theta_i, \phi_i, \psi_j) = y_i^t \times \cos \phi_i \times \frac{a}{\sinh a} e^{a \cos \psi_j}, \text{ where } a = \frac{W^2}{4\pi^2 \sigma^2}. \quad (8)$$

ψ_j denotes how much the j-th pixel deviates from (θ_i, ϕ_i), and σ is the standard deviation of Gaussian smoothing. Note that spherical Gaussian smoothing is only applied for evaluation purposes.

3.4   Learning Objectives

Without any ground truth label or additional information, we train the model by ensuring spatiotemporal consistency while maintaining the global context.

Temporal Consistency Loss. It is natural for two adjacent frames to display similar saliency values and feature distributions. We take into account two neighboring frames, $i.e.$, $t+1$ and $t-1$ for the t-th frame:

$$\mathcal{L}_T = \frac{1}{NT} \sum_{t=1}^{T} \sum_{i=1}^{N} \left\| \hat{x}_i^t - \frac{\hat{x}_i^{t+1} + \hat{x}_i^{t-1}}{2} \right\|_2^2. \tag{9}$$

Spatial Consistency Loss. Adjacent patches should retain similar saliency scores and feature distributions. We use the geodesic distance between patches to reflect the spherical structure.

$$\mathcal{L}_S = \frac{1}{NT} \sum_{t=1}^{T} \sum_{i=1}^{N} \left\| \hat{x}_i^t - \sum_{j=1}^{N} \frac{\gamma_i \delta_{ij} \hat{x}_j^t}{g_{ij}} \right\|_2^2, \tag{10}$$

where $g_{ij} = \|(\theta_i, \phi_i) - (\theta_j, \phi_j)\|_g$ is the geodesic distance between the i-th and j-th patch, and $\delta_{ij} = 1$ when $0 < g_{ij} < \epsilon$ for some ϵ. γ_i is a scaling factor such that $\sum_{j=1}^{N} \frac{\gamma_i \delta_{ij}}{g_{ij}} = 1$. The idea of Eq. 10 is that the similarity of patches within a certain threshold of ϵ should be inversely proportional to their geodesic distance.

Global Context Loss. To train the $\mathrm{MLP_G}$ for global context, we encourage all T frames in a video to have a similar global context:

$$\mathcal{L}_G = \frac{1}{T} \sum_{t=1}^{T} \left\| \hat{x}_0^t - \frac{1}{T} \sum_{s=1}^{T} \hat{x}_0^s \right\|_2^2. \tag{11}$$

To sum up, our loss function is defined as follows:

$$\mathcal{L}_{\text{total}} = \lambda_T \mathcal{L}_T + \lambda_S \mathcal{L}_S + \lambda_G \mathcal{L}_G. \tag{12}$$

Training. We end-to-end train our model with a batch size of 1 and $T = 5$ frames per input. We fix the encoder weight with the pretrained weight of the Vision Transformer (ViT-B/16) [17]. We optimize with Adam optimizer [27] with a learning rate of 2e−7 for five epochs. For hyperparameter, we use $\lambda_T = 20, \lambda_S = 0.5, \lambda_G = 0.1$. Please refer to the Appendix for more details.

4   Experiments

For evaluation, we perform experiments on two benchmark tasks with Wild360 [11] and VQA-ODV [30] datasets. First, we evaluate our target task, saliency prediction on 360° videos, on Wild360 [11] as one of the most popular datasets. Second, we apply our approach to visual quality assessment on 360° videos on VQA-ODV [30]. The quality assessment of capture-worthy viewports is important in omnidirectional videos, and the models for this task usually require annotations from headgears or eye-trackers as well as human supervision of subjective assessment. If we can replace such expensive annotations with visual saliency maps, omnidirectional video quality assessment can become scalable without human supervision. We thus evaluate how much PAVER can improve the omnidirectional video quality assessment with no such annotations.

4.1   Experiment Setting

Datasets. Wild360 [11] is composed of 85 video clips about natural scenery, and split into 60 clips for training and 25 for test. Human annotated ground-truth saliency heatmaps are provided only for test split. VQA-ODV [30] consists of 540 impaired videos from 60 lossless reference videos. Nine types of impairment are applied to each reference video with varying degrees of compression levels and projection types (ERP, RCMP, TSP). The quality of each impaired video is scored by 20 subjects wearing a head-mounted display, and annotated with the head movement (HM) and eye movement (EM) of a subject.

Evaluation Metrics. We use the standard measures of the two benchmarks. For Wild360, we report three metrics for saliency detection: AUC-Judd [34], AUC-Borji [3], and Linear Correlation Coefficient (CC). AUC-Judd computes the true positive and false positive rate of the saliency map. AUC-Borji randomly samples pixels to calculate false positive rates of these pixels. CC measures the linear relationship between the proposed saliency map and ground truth. We regard CC as the most important metric as recommended by [6]. Please refer to [5] for more details.

For VQA-ODV, differential mean opinion score (DMOS) quantifies the quality of omnidirectional videos perceived by the viewers. Common objective metrics for visual quality assessment like structural similarity (SSIM) [48] and peak signal-to-noise ratio (PSNR) are not necessarily proportional to actual human perception. Hence, Pearson correlation coefficient (PCC), Spearman rank correlation coefficient (SRCC), root mean squared error (RMSE) and mean absolute error (MAE) between the DMOS and target metrics are utilized as the quantitative metrics, which we report.

Baselines. First, we compare our PAVER model against competitive baselines for predicting 360° video saliency based on optical flow [49], gradient flow [46], generative adversarial networks [33], and class activation map with optical flow [11]. We also report the performance of unsupervised saliency detection and unsupervised object discovery models based on vision transformers, including TS-CAM [21], DINO [8], LOST [36] and TokenCut [47]. For a fair comparison with our approach, we use the identical local patch projection module in Sect. 3.1 and the spherical Gaussian smoothing module in Sect. 3.3.

For the ablation study, we also report five variants of our approach. PAVER (Cartesian) replaces all 360° aware components in our model with normal field-of-view (NFoV) equivalents. PAVER (NoGlobal) is the model without the MLP_G projection of global context. PAVER (NoLocal) replaces the local context spatiotemporal fusion module with a simple MLP. PAVER (NoDecoupled) encodes both global and local contexts together in a single transformer encoder. PAVER (ScoreLoss) is trained with the spatiotemporal score consistency (*i.e.*, the sparse saliency map Y) instead of the feature map consistency.

For VQA-ODV, we report the performance of PSNR, WS-PSNR [40], and S-PSNR [53] with different weight conditions: uniform, random, our saliency map, and reversed saliency map. Here the primary comparison is PSNR variants between our saliency map and the ones with human head movement supervision since PSNR metrics weighted with human head and eye movement supervision are considerably better in quality assessment [30]. More details of baseline models' configuration can be found in Appendix.

Table 1. Comparison of saliency prediction accuracy on the Wild360 dataset [11].

	CC	AUC-J	AUC-B
Motion Magnitude [49]	0.288	0.687	0.642
ConsistentVideoSal [46]	0.085	0.547	0.532
SalGAN [33]	0.312	0.717	0.692
Equirectangular [11]	0.337	0.839	0.783
CubePad (Static) [11]	0.448	0.881	0.852
CubePad (CLSTM) [11]	0.420	0.898	0.859
TS-CAM [21]	0.414	0.831	0.802
DINO [8]	0.406	0.850	0.831
LOST [36]	0.444	0.809	0.786
TokenCut [47]	0.500	0.841	0.815
PAVER (NoGlobal)	0.376	0.814	0.797
PAVER (NoDecoupled)	0.492	0.881	0.860
PAVER (Cartesian)	0.549	0.898	0.875
PAVER (NoLocal)	0.561	0.895	0.873
PAVER (ScoreLoss)	0.575	0.906	0.883
PAVER	**0.616**	**0.923**	**0.899**

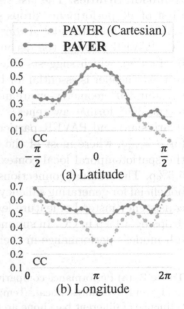

Fig. 2. Influence of distortion on Wild360 test split.

4.2 Results on Saliency Detection

Comparison with the Prior Arts. Table 1 compares the performance with prior arts on the Wild360 dataset. PAVER outperforms previous state-of-the-art models by large margins: +11.6%p (*i.e.*, 23%) in CC, +2.5%p in AUC-J, and +4.0%p in AUC-B. We achieve notable improvement especially in correlation coefficient (CC). That is, evaluating the relative relations among local patches is sufficient to achieve competent performance in the Wild360 dataset. Our approach is also time-efficient in that we do not require time-consuming computation for additional information like optical flow; for example, CubePad [11] requires 19 s per frame pair for flow computation [49].

Moreover, PAVER consistently achieves better performance compared to the baselines that use the vision transformer as the encoder backbone (*i.e.*, TS-CAM, DINO, LOST, and TokenCut). It is worth noticing that merely applying pretrained weights of the vision transformers does not guarantee superior performance. For instance, TS-CAM or DINO show slightly worse performance than the best performing non-ViT model. Although they are competent in detecting larger foreground objects, 360° videos usually contain multiple small objects of potential interest. As in Fig. 3-(a), the baselines with transformer encoders relatively fall short when multiple salient objects are worth viewing in the scene.

Ablation Studies. The last six rows in Table 1 compare the PAVER variants. First of all, performance drops significantly when the global context is poor, as PAVER without the global context encoder (*i.e.*, MLP_G) plummets by 24%p in CC. PAVER without the decoupled global-local context encoder decreases CC by 12.4%p, which suggests that independent parameter update for the global context encoder is essential for better performance. The performance of PAVER without 360° geometry-aware modules drops by 6.7%p, implying the importance of the 360° format awareness. Also, as in Fig. 2-(a), the gap between PAVER (Cartesian) and PAVER particularly widens in the near-polar region (*e.g.*, ×4 for $\theta = \frac{\pi}{2}$), where most of the distortion in 360° videos takes part. Replacing the spatiotemporal local context encoder with a simple MLP decreases CC by 5.5%p. The residual connections of both spatial and temporal self-attention are beneficial for generating saliency maps with high fidelity. If we enforce score-level consistency instead of feature-level consistency during training, the performance drops by 4.1%p in CC. In summary, all components in PAVER contribute to the full model's performance in their own ways.

Table 2. (a) Performance comparison with different saliency score compositions, where L, T, and S denotes Local, Temporal, and Spatial saliency score, respectively. (b) Influence of different backbone architectures, pretrained weights, and resolution in our encoder on the Wild360 Dataset [11].

<table>
<tr><td colspan="6" align="center">(a)</td></tr>
<tr><td>L</td><td>T</td><td>S</td><td>CC</td><td>AUC-J</td><td>AUC-B</td></tr>
<tr><td></td><td>✓</td><td></td><td>0.276</td><td>0.760</td><td>0.731</td></tr>
<tr><td>✓</td><td></td><td></td><td>0.548</td><td>0.897</td><td>0.875</td></tr>
<tr><td></td><td></td><td>✓</td><td>0.552</td><td>0.894</td><td>0.872</td></tr>
<tr><td>✓</td><td>✓</td><td></td><td>0.557</td><td>0.899</td><td>0.876</td></tr>
<tr><td>✓</td><td></td><td>✓</td><td>0.585</td><td>0.907</td><td>0.884</td></tr>
<tr><td>✓</td><td>✓</td><td>✓</td><td>**0.616**</td><td>**0.923**</td><td>**0.899**</td></tr>
</table>

<table>
<tr><td colspan="5" align="center">(b)</td></tr>
<tr><td>Backbone</td><td>Res.</td><td>CC</td><td>AUC-J</td><td>AUC-B</td></tr>
<tr><td>TimeSformer (T=16) [2]</td><td>224</td><td>0.465</td><td>0.863</td><td>0.843</td></tr>
<tr><td>DINO (B/16) [8]</td><td>224</td><td>0.524</td><td>0.893</td><td>0.871</td></tr>
<tr><td>DINO (B/8) [8]</td><td>224</td><td>0.563</td><td>0.905</td><td>0.881</td></tr>
<tr><td>ViT-Ti/16 [41]</td><td>224</td><td>0.540</td><td>0.904</td><td>0.881</td></tr>
<tr><td>ViT-B/16 [17]</td><td>384</td><td>0.567</td><td>0.893</td><td>0.871</td></tr>
<tr><td>ViT-B/16 [17]</td><td>224</td><td>**0.616**</td><td>**0.923**</td><td>**0.899**</td></tr>
</table>

Analysis on Saliency Score Composition. Table 2-(a) summarizes the influence of different saliency score components in Eq. 7. Computing saliency maps only with temporal saliency does not show acceptable performance. On the other hand, when the temporal saliency score is added to other sets of scores (*i.e.*, $S \rightarrow T + S$, $L + S \rightarrow L + T + S$), the performance consistently improves in all three metrics. Since the deviation of a local patch along the timeline is relatively small in magnitude, temporal saliency helps our saliency prediction update smoothly in time. Using only local or spatial saliency displays similar performance, but both of them fall short by 6–7%p when compared to the full model. These two saliency scores are complementary in that combining local and spatial saliency boosts performance by 3–4%p in CC.

Influence of Encoder Backbones. Table 2-(b) compares the performance of our model with different architectures, pretrained weights, and resolutions. First, we replace the video transformer in PAVER with TimeSformer [2]. It shows inferior performance mainly because the model is trained with a larger temporal hop size, as capturing subtle movement in scenery is essential for better saliency maps in the Wild360 dataset. When we use DINO [8], which requires even no labels as the backbone of our model, it shows better performance compared to the SOTA models. The model with a smaller patch size reports better CC by 4%p, which is presumably due to higher fidelity of the saliency map. Using ViT-Ti/16 [41], the performance drops by 6.6%p in exchange for 15× fewer model parameters. This is still better than existing SOTA models for all three metrics.

Table 3. Results of omnidirectional video quality assessment on VQA-ODV [30]. The better is higher PCC and SRCC or lower RMSE and MAE.

Weight	PSNR				WS-PSNR [40]				S-PSNR [53]			
	PCC	SRCC	RMSE	MAE	PCC	SRCC	RMSE	MAE	PCC	SRCC	RMSE	MAE
None	0.650	0.664	9.004	7.027	0.672	0.684	8.771	6.909	0.693	0.698	8.541	6.681
Random	0.650	0.663	9.004	7.027	0.672	0.684	8.771	6.909	0.693	0.698	8.540	6.680
Reverse	0.646	0.654	9.041	6.883	0.646	0.660	9.044	7.033	0.683	0.693	8.652	6.711
DINO [8]	0.657	0.677	8.934	7.105	0.674	0.690	8.747	7.033	0.699	0.710	8.468	6.665
PAVER	0.657	0.664	8.931	7.133	0.692	0.704	8.551	6.794	0.702	0.707	8.438	6.659
HM(Supervised)	0.733	0.726	8.054	6.479	0.731	0.722	8.086	6.565	0.736	0.741	8.022	6.305

4.3 Omnidirectional Video Quality Assessment

Table 3 reports performance metrics between PSNR variants and DMOS. When using random weights for PSNR computation, the results are nearly identical to the ones with no weight assignment. That is, providing weights that are irrelevant to saliency does not improve the performance. If we use saliency maps from the PAVER as PSNR weights, the performance consistently improves, *e.g.*, 0.7%p in PSNR, 2.0%p in WS-PSNR, and 0.9%p in S-PSNR, respectively for the PCC metric. On the other hand, if we use reverse saliency maps as weights, the performance worsens compared to the PSNR variants without weight assignment. For instance, using correct saliency maps and reversed saliency maps displays a 4.6%p gap for the PCC metric in WS-PSNR. This implies that proper assignment of saliency maps helps solve the omnidirectional quality assessment.

Comparison with Head Movement Supervision. The last row of Table 3 reports the performance of PSNR variants with actual human head movement as weights. Compared to S-PSNR with head movement supervision, S-PSNR with our saliency maps shows 3.4%p lower performance in PCC. Unlike ground truth labels that require trackable headgears for annotation, our saliency map can be automatically computed using a couple of videos.

4.4   Qualitative Results

Saliency Detection. Figure 3-(a) compares some examples of saliency prediction by different methods. In general, our PAVER better captures contexts that are worth viewing. For example, our model places the highest score on the penguin moving towards the camera (a-1) or the polar bear instead of a jeep or a flag nearby (a-2). Also, compared to PAVER(Cartesian), our model can propose more sphere-aware saliency maps as in the second and third rows of Fig. 3-(a).

Figure 3-(b–c) compares the PAVER results according to the score decompositions. Local-only and space-only saliency maps look alike in that they both assign higher scores on anomalous patches. However, unlike space-only saliency maps, local-only saliency maps tend to favor object-like patches for both supervised [17] and self-supervised pretraining [8]. Time-only saliency focuses on subtle movement in the scene, which helps generate smooth transitions of saliency maps. We present more qualitative examples in Appendix.

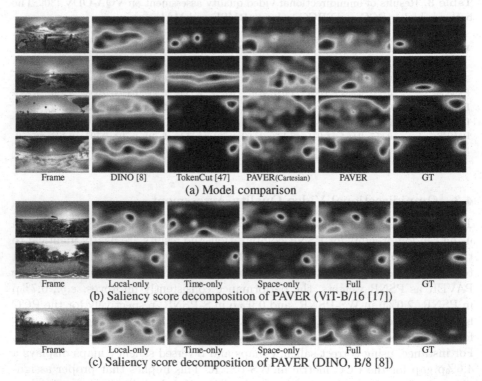

(a) Model comparison

(b) Saliency score decomposition of PAVER (ViT-B/16 [17])

(c) Saliency score decomposition of PAVER (DINO, B/8 [8])

Fig. 3. Qualitative comparison of saliency prediction on Wild360 [11].

Quality Assessment. Figure 4 illustrates our saliency prediction on the VQA-ODV dataset. Compared to head movement, our saliency maps are in line with what people think is worth viewing. Still, as in Fig. 4-(4), our model struggles in cases where the camera drastically moves.

360° Videos with Different Formats. Figure 5 displays our saliency prediction on varying 360° video projection formats, including equirectangular (ERP), cubemap (RCMP), and truncated square pyramid projection (TSP). Using randomly sampled videos from the test split of Wild360, we convert them from ERP to RCMP or TSP using 360tools[1]. We replace $\Theta_{DC\text{-offset}}$ for ER with the offsets for each video format. Computation of $\Theta_{DC\text{-offset}}$ for different video formats can be found in Appendix. Our model can process different 360° formats without explicitly converting from one to another while returning highly consistent saliency maps regardless of the formats, especially for the ones with severe regional sampling discrepancy like TSP.

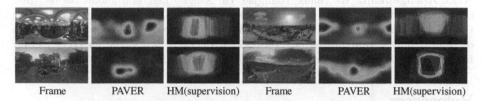

Frame   PAVER   HM(supervision)   Frame   PAVER   HM(supervision)

Fig. 4. Comparison of saliency and video quality prediction on VQA-ODV [30].

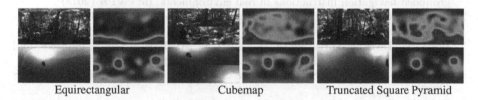

Equirectangular   Cubemap   Truncated Square Pyramid

Fig. 5. Prediction comparison of different projection formats for 360° videos.

5   Conclusion

We proposed a new model for 360° video saliency prediction named PAVER. We regarded 360° videos as a set of patches using deformable convolution, which alleviates the need for layerwise geometric approximation unlike other CNN-based approaches. We adopted the vision transformer to encode omnidirectional imagery by reusing pretrained knowledge from normal videos with no need for complex adaptation. Even with three simple feature-wise consistency objectives, PAVER outperformed prior arts that use additional annotations or vision transformers in Wild360. We also achieved consistent improvement in omnidirectional video quality assessment in VQA-ODV. Last but not least, all computations in PAVER can be adapted for various 360° formats without explicit conversion.

---

[1] https://github.com/Samsung/360tools.

There are multiple interesting future directions beyond this work. First, we can extend PAVER to be adaptable with multi-scale vision transformers such as Swin transformer [31], MViT [20], SegFormer [50], and SeTR [64]. Since they can be effective for fine-grained prediction, geometry-aware multi-scale encoding can be beneficial for a better understanding of omnidirectional imagery. Second, our work could be used as a generic omnidirectional encoder for various tasks like language-guided view grounding [12], embodied navigation [66], and 360° video question answering [56]. Another direction is to combine both 360° and NFoV inputs to train a unified architecture to leverage the complementary nature of the two formats.

Acknowledgement. We thank Youngjae Yu, Sangho Lee, and Joonil Na for their constructive comments. This work was supported by AIRS Company in Hyundai Motor Company & Kia Corporation through HKMC-SNU AI Consortium Fund and Institute of Information & communications Technology Planning & Evaluation (IITP) grant funded by the Korea government (MSIT) (No. 2019-0-01309, No. 2019-0-01082).

References

1. Anderson, P., et al.: Vision-and-language navigation: interpreting visually-grounded navigation instructions in real environments. In: CVPR (2018)
2. Bertasius, G., Wang, H., Torresani, L.: Is space-time attention all you need for video understanding? In: ICML (2021)
3. Borji, A., Tavakoli, H.R., Sihite, D.N., Itti, L.: Analysis of scores, datasets, and models in visual saliency prediction. In: ICCV (2013)
4. Bruce, N., Tsotsos, J.: Saliency based on information maximization. In: NIPS (2005)
5. Bylinskii, Z., et al.: MIT saliency benchmark (2015)
6. Bylinskii, Z., Judd, T., Oliva, A., Torralba, A., Durand, F.: What do different evaluation metrics tell us about saliency models? IEEE TPAMI **41**, 740–757 (2018)
7. Caron, G., Morbidi, F.: Spherical visual gyroscope for autonomous robots using the mixture of photometric potentials. In: ICRA (2018)
8. Caron, M., et al.: Emerging properties in self-supervised vision transformers. In: ICCV (2021)
9. Caruso, D., Engel, J., Cremers, D.: Large-scale direct SLAM for omnidirectional cameras. In: IROS (2015)
10. Chen, X., Xie, S., He, K.: An empirical study of training self-supervised vision transformers. In: ICCV (2021)
11. Cheng, H.T., Chao, C.H., Dong, J.D., Wen, H.K., Liu, T.L., Sun, M.: Cube padding for weakly-supervised saliency prediction in 360 videos. In: CVPR (2018)
12. Chou, S.H., Chen, Y.C., Zeng, K.H., Hu, H.N., Fu, J., Sun, M.: Self-view grounding given a narrated 360 video. In: AAAI (2018)
13. Cohen, T.S., Geiger, M., Köhler, J., Welling, M.: Spherical CNNs. In: ICLR (2018)
14. Dai, J., et al.: Deformable convolutional networks. In: ICCV (2017)
15. Deng, J., Dong, W., Socher, R., Li, L.J., Li, K., Fei-Fei, L.: ImageNet: a large-scale hierarchical image database. In: CVPR (2009)
16. Devaraju, B.: Understanding filtering on the sphere: experiences from filtering GRACE data. Ph.D. dissertation, Inst. Geodesy, Univ. Stuttgart (2015)

17. Dosovitskiy, A., et al.: An image is worth 16×16 words: transformers for image recognition at scale. arXiv:2010.11929 (2020)
18. Eder, M., Shvets, M., Lim, J., Frahm, J.M.: Tangent images for mitigating spherical distortion. In: CVPR (2020)
19. Esteves, C., Allen-Blanchette, C., Makadia, A., Daniilidis, K.: Learning SO(3) equivariant representations with spherical CNNs. In: Ferrari, V., Hebert, M., Sminchisescu, C., Weiss, Y. (eds.) ECCV 2018. LNCS, vol. 11217, pp. 54–70. Springer, Cham (2018). https://doi.org/10.1007/978-3-030-01261-8_4
20. Fan, H., et al.: Multiscale vision transformers. In: ICCV (2021)
21. Gao, W., et al.: Token semantic coupled attention map for weakly supervised object localization. In: ICCV (2021)
22. Greene, N.: Environment mapping and other applications of world projections. IEEE CGA **6**, 21–29 (1986)
23. Hendrycks, D., Gimpel, K.: Gaussian error linear units (GELUs). arXiv:1606.08415 (2016)
24. Hu, H.N., Lin, Y.C., Liu, M.Y., Cheng, H.T., Chang, Y.J., Sun, M.: Deep 360 pilot: learning a deep agent for piloting through 360 sports videos. In: CVPR (2017)
25. Itti, L., Koch, C., Niebur, E.: A model of saliency-based visual attention for rapid scene analysis. IEEE TPAMI **20**, 1254–1259 (1998)
26. Jiang, C.M., Huang, J., Kashinath, K., Marcus, P., Niessner, M., et al.: Spherical CNNs on unstructured grids. In: ICLR (2018)
27. Kingma, D.P., Ba, J.: Adam: a method for stochastic optimization. In: ICLR (2015)
28. Lee, S., Sung, J., Yu, Y., Kim, G.: A memory network approach for story-based temporal summarization of 360 videos. In: CVPR (2018)
29. Lee, Y., Jeong, J., Yun, J., Cho, W., Yoon, K.J.: SpherePHD: applying CNNs on a spherical PolyHeDron representation of 360deg images. In: CVPR (2019)
30. Li, C., Xu, M., Du, X., Wang, Z.: Bridge the gap between VQA and human behavior on omnidirectional video: a large-scale dataset and a deep learning model. In: ACMMM (2018)
31. Liu, Z., et al.: Swin transformer: hierarchical vision transformer using shifted windows. In: ICCV (2021)
32. Meng, M., Zhang, T., Tian, Q., Zhang, Y., Wu, F.: Foreground activation maps for weakly supervised object localization. In: ICCV (2021)
33. Pan, J., et al.: SalGAN: visual saliency prediction with generative adversarial networks. arXiv:1701.01081 (2017)
34. Riche, N., Duvinage, M., Mancas, M., Gosselin, B., Dutoit, T.: Saliency and human fixations: state-of-the-art and study of comparison metrics. In: ICCV (2013)
35. Seo, H.J., Milanfar, P.: Nonparametric bottom-up saliency detection by self-resemblance. In: CVPRw (2009)
36. Siméoni, O., et al.: Localizing objects with self-supervised transformers and no labels. In: BMVC (2021)
37. Su, Y.C., Grauman, K.: Learning spherical convolution for fast features from 360 imagery. In: NIPS (2017)
38. Su, Y.C., Grauman, K.: Kernel transformer networks for compact spherical convolution. In: CVPR (2019)
39. Su, Y.-C., Jayaraman, D., Grauman, K.: Pano2Vid: automatic cinematography for watching 360° videos. In: Lai, S.-H., Lepetit, V., Nishino, K., Sato, Y. (eds.) ACCV 2016. LNCS, vol. 10114, pp. 154–171. Springer, Cham (2017). https://doi.org/10.1007/978-3-319-54190-7_10
40. Sun, Y., Lu, A., Yu, L.: Weighted-to-spherically-uniform quality evaluation for omnidirectional video. SPL (2017)

41. Touvron, H., Cord, M., Douze, M., Massa, F., Sablayrolles, A., Jégou, H.: Training data-efficient image transformers & distillation through attention. In: ICML (2021)
42. Touvron, H., Cord, M., Sablayrolles, A., Synnaeve, G., Jégou, H.: Going deeper with image transformers. In: ICCV (2021)
43. Ullah, I., et al.: A brief survey of visual saliency detection. MTA (2020)
44. Vaswani, A., et al.: Attention is all you need. In: NIPS (2017)
45. Wang, M., Konrad, J., Ishwar, P., Jing, K., Rowley, H.: Image saliency: from intrinsic to extrinsic context. In: CVPR (2011)
46. Wang, W., Shen, J., Shao, L.: Consistent video saliency using local gradient flow optimization and global refinement. TIP **24**, 4185–4196 (2015)
47. Wang, Y., Shen, X., Hu, S., Yuan, Y., Crowley, J., Vaufreydaz, D.: Self-supervised transformers for unsupervised object discovery using normalized cut. In: CVPR (2022)
48. Wang, Z., Bovik, A.C., Sheikh, H.R., Simoncelli, E.P.: Image quality assessment: from error visibility to structural similarity. TIP **13**, 600–612 (2004)
49. Weinzaepfel, P., Revaud, J., Harchaoui, Z., Schmid, C.: DeepFlow: large displacement optical flow with deep matching. In: ICCV (2013)
50. Xie, E., Wang, W., Yu, Z., Anandkumar, A., Alvarez, J.M., Luo, P.: SegFormer: simple and efficient design for semantic segmentation with transformers. In: NeurIPS (2021)
51. Xie, J., Luo, C., Zhu, X., Jin, Z., Lu, W., Shen, L.: Online refinement of low-level feature based activation map for weakly supervised object localization. In: ICCV (2021)
52. Yogamani, S., et al.: WoodScape: a multi-task, multi-camera fisheye dataset for autonomous driving. In: ICCV (2019)
53. Yu, M., Lakshman, H., Girod, B.: A framework to evaluate omnidirectional video coding schemes. In: ISMAR (2015)
54. Yu, Y., Lee, S., Na, J., Kang, J., Kim, G.: A deep ranking model for spatio-temporal highlight detection from a 360° video. In: AAAI (2018)
55. Yuan, L., et al.: Tokens-to-token ViT: training vision transformers from scratch on ImageNet. In: ICCV (2021)
56. Yun, H., Yu, Y., Yang, W., Lee, K., Kim, G.: Pano-AVQA: grounded audio-visual question answering on 360deg videos. In: ICCV (2021)
57. Yun, I., Lee, H.J., Rhee, C.E.: Improving 360 monocular depth estimation via non-local dense prediction transformer and joint supervised and self-supervised learning. In: AAAI (2022)
58. Zeng, Y., Zhuge, Y., Lu, H., Zhang, L.: Joint learning of saliency detection and weakly supervised semantic segmentation. In: ICCV (2019)
59. Zeng, Y., Zhuge, Y., Lu, H., Zhang, L., Qian, M., Yu, Y.: Multi-source weak supervision for saliency detection. In: CVPR (2019)
60. Zhang, C., Liwicki, S., Smith, W., Cipolla, R.: Orientation-aware semantic segmentation on icosahedron spheres. In: ICCV (2019)
61. Zhang, Y., et al.: VidTr: video transformer without convolutions. In: ICCV (2021)
62. Zhang, Z., Xu, Y., Yu, J., Gao, S.: Saliency detection in 360° videos. In: Ferrari, V., Hebert, M., Sminchisescu, C., Weiss, Y. (eds.) ECCV 2018. LNCS, vol. 11211, pp. 504–520. Springer, Cham (2018). https://doi.org/10.1007/978-3-030-01234-2_30
63. Zhao, H., Jiang, L., Jia, J., Torr, P.H., Koltun, V.: Point transformer. In: ICCV (2021)
64. Zheng, S., et al.: Rethinking semantic segmentation from a sequence-to-sequence perspective with transformers. In: CVPR (2021)

65. Zhou, B., Khosla, A., Lapedriza, A., Oliva, A., Torralba, A.: Learning deep features for discriminative localization. In: CVPR (2016)
66. Zhu, F., Zhu, Y., Chang, X., Liang, X.: Vision-language navigation with self-supervised auxiliary reasoning tasks. In: CVPR (2020)

Bayesian Tracking of Video Graphs Using Joint Kalman Smoothing and Registration

Aditi Basu Bal[1]([⊠])[iD], Ramy Mounir[2][iD], Sathyanarayanan Aakur[3][iD], Sudeep Sarkar[2][iD], and Anuj Srivastava[1][iD]

[1] Florida State University, Tallahassee, FL 32309, USA
ab18z@fsu.edu, anuj@stat.fsu.edu
[2] University of South Florida, Tampa, FL 33620, USA
{ramy,sarkar}@usf.edu
[3] Oklahoma State University, Stillwater, OK 74078, USA
saakurn@okstate.edu

Abstract. Graph-based representations are becoming increasingly popular for representing and analyzing video data, especially in object tracking and scene understanding applications. Accordingly, an essential tool in this approach is to generate statistical inferences for graphical time series associated with videos. This paper develops a Kalman-smoothing method for estimating graphs from noisy, cluttered, and incomplete data. The main challenge here is to find and preserve the registration of nodes (salient detected objects) across time frames when the data has noise and clutter due to false and missing nodes. First, we introduce a quotient-space representation of graphs that incorporates temporal registration of nodes, and we use that metric structure to impose a dynamical model on graph evolution. Then, we derive a Kalman smoother, adapted to the quotient space geometry, to estimate dense, smooth trajectories of graphs. We demonstrate this framework using simulated data and actual video graphs extracted from the Multiview Extended Video with Activities (MEVA) dataset. This framework successfully estimates graphs despite the noise, clutter, and missed detections.

Keywords: Motion tracking · Graph-representations · Video graphs · Quotient metrics · Kalman smoothing · Nonlinear manifolds

1 Introduction

Graph-based representations in videos provide a convenient setting to represent and analyze higher-level structures of scenes. Graphs help focus us on information of interest while discarding irrelevant items for the given task. Graphs are also helpful in capturing spatiotemporal interactions between nodes (humans,

Supplementary Information The online version contains supplementary material available at https://doi.org/10.1007/978-3-031-19833-5_26.

objects, etc.) in video sequences while reducing the effects of noise, clutter and (appearance/scene) variability. This representation facilitates the modeling and testing of statistical variability across multiple observations within and across observation classes. The promise of graphical representations, especially in performing statistical analysis, is fueling interest in developing novel mathematical and statistical techniques for handling graph data [5, 6, 15, 16, 21, 22].

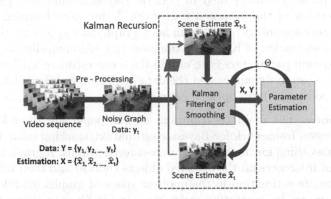

Fig. 1. An overview of time-series analysis for estimating graphs in video frames.

This paper advances the use of graphical methods for handling video streams in computer vision and artificial intelligence. It represents the detections at any time – **objects as nodes** and **their interactions as edges** in a graph. As the objects and interactions change over time, one obtains a time series of graphs representing an evolving scene. We focus on the problem of analyzing these *dynamical graphs or time-series of graphs*, where each time point represents a graph extracted from a frame (or a small set of consecutive frames). In this setup, the attributes associated with nodes and edges are typically real-valued vectors obtained by embedding concepts, and their co-occurrences in some large Euclidean space (as observed in Visual Genome [26], Action Genome [23], and ConceptNet [28, 37], to name a few). The nodes' attributes are often descriptive of the objects and their spatiotemporal locations in the scenes. The edge attributes are designed to capture pairwise relational properties of objects. The sequence of graphs as extracted video data forms our observed time series.

Time-series analysis of graphs, especially when dealing with noisy and cluttered data, requires novel tools. In the current context, corrupted data results from limitations in the pre-processing steps. These steps result in random perturbations in edge-node attributes, false detection of spurious concepts, and missed nodes when concepts go undetected. The goal is to use this data to estimate the underlying time series of true graphs. We aim to use model-based estimation, equipped with dynamical models and likelihood functions, to help overcome these data limitations and generate robust inferences. The classical toolsets in (Euclidean) time-series analysis are filtering, smoothing, prediction, and estimation. Can we directly apply them to the graph data? The answer is no. The main issue with graphs is that ordering nodes (or objects) in a graph is arbitrary. In other words, one can randomly re-order the nodes in a graph and still preserve the scene description, although it may change its mathematical representation. This motivates a representation space that is naturally a quotient space under re-ordering of nodes. Consequently, the graph space $\mathcal{G}$ is a non-Euclidean space where the past Euclidean filtering techniques do not apply directly.

This paper develops a Kalman filtering and smoothing approach adapted to the non-Euclidean geometry of $\mathcal{G}$ to perform Bayesian inference. Figure 1 provides an overview of the proposed framework. Using deep learning techniques (detailed in Supplementary), we obtain noisy graph data $\mathbf{y}_t$ at each time t. Then we apply a combination of Kalman estimation and maximum-likelihood estimation of the system parameters Θ to obtain the scene estimate $\hat{\mathbf{x}}_t$. This Bayesian estimate uses system dynamics and the data likelihood (while registering nodes across time points) to form optimal estimates.

Contributions. The main contributions of this paper are three-fold: (i) We introduce a novel framework for Bayesian estimation/tracking using Kalman filtering and smoothing for time-series of unregistered graphs. A graph-formulation provides joint inferences on the detected objects (nodes) and their relationships; (ii) We formulate estimation in the quotient space of graphs modulo the node-registration group. Incorporating registration inside filtering allows for optimal matching and tracking of nodes over time and handles the problem of missed and false nodes in noisy and cluttered data; and (iii) We demonstrate the effectiveness of the proposed approach through extensive experimental results on both simulated and real datasets. This is the first paper of its kind that formulates a time-series estimation on the quotient space of graphs.

2 Related Work

Graph-based representations are commonly used in the modeling and prediction of human trajectory [3,19,20,25,31,34,44]. In many cases, graphs are used to model the human-human and human-objects interactions in the context of trajectory and behavior prediction. Another common application of graph-based representations is Multiple Object Tracking (MOT), where the goal is to match detected objects across frames [4,27,47,48] and assign a registration for this graph matching problem. Graphs have also been used for modeling human activity [1,2] in videos by constructing graphs that exploit semantic and commonsense knowledge [37]. In such approaches, the graph representations are constrained by context and physical laws. Some other tasks, *e.g.*, video object segmentation [29,45], utilize graph representations to extract relevant information from neighboring frames in a video by employing an attentive mechanism.

Time series prediction over graphs has not been explored to a great extent in prior literature. The most common use of graphs in time series prediction [7,11,36,43,49] has been for modeling the relationships between the variables in multivariate time series data such as traffic forecasting [51] and action and gesture recognition [41,50]. There have been few works that address the prediction of actual graph structures over time using Gaussian process regression [32], manifolds-based prediction [33], Kalman and other filtering methods applied to graph or network data [10,24,35]. However, these methods typically assume graphs with fully registered nodes and do not account for clutter.

3 Background: Graph Representation and Quotient Metric

This section describes the necessary background for understanding the proposed approach. Specifically, we lay out the mathematical framework needed for analyzing unregistered graphs as elements of a quotient space [16,21,22].

Representing Graphs. We represent a graph G of n nodes by two sets of variables: an *adjacency matrix* and a *node attribute vector*. First, we define an adjacency matrix $A \in \mathbb{R}^{n \times n \times p}$ to capture the edge attributes, where an element $A_{ij} \in \mathbb{R}^p$ represents the interaction between node i and j. We assume that $\{A_{ij}\}$ is a symmetric matrix with diagonal elements being zero and has only $k_n = n(n-1)/2$ degrees of freedom in $\mathbb{R}^p$. (In case the interactions are directional, one will need to keep the full matrix A with $k_n = n^2$.) Hence, we can represent A by a long vector of its upper triangular sub-matrix: $\mathbf{w} \in \mathbb{R}^{k_n \times p}$. Note that there is a one-to-one relationship between the adjacency matrix A and the vector $\mathbf{w}$. Let $\phi(A) = \mathbf{w}$ denote the mapping of the adjacency matrix into a vector form; then $\phi^{-1}(\mathbf{w}) = A$ maps the vector back to the adjacency matrix. Second, we define a node attribute vector $\mathbf{v} \in \mathbb{R}^{n \times m}$ such that each element $\mathbf{v}_i \in \mathbb{R}^m$ denotes the attributes of the i-th node.

Metric Structure. We define a joint edge-node representation $X = (\mathbf{w}, \mathbf{v}) \in \mathcal{X}$, with the representation space given by $\mathcal{X}_n \doteq (\mathbb{R}^{k_n \times p} \times \mathbb{R}^{n \times m})$. $\mathcal{X}_n$ is a Euclidean space with the standard Euclidean metric. The distance on $\mathcal{X}$ is given by: for any $X^{(1)} \equiv (\mathbf{w}^{(1)}, \mathbf{v}^{(1)}), X^{(2)} \equiv (\mathbf{w}^{(2)}, \mathbf{v}^{(2)})$, define:

$$d_x(X^{(1)}, X^{(2)}) = \sum_{k=1}^{k_n} \|\mathbf{w}_k^{(1)} - \mathbf{w}_k^{(2)}\|^2 + \lambda \sum_{i=1}^{n} \|\mathbf{v}_i^{(1)} - \mathbf{v}_i^{(2)}\|^2, \quad (1)$$

where $\lambda > 0$ is the relative weight of the second term and d_x is a weighted combination of the corresponding metrics on both the edge and node attributes. The set of all graphs with different number of nodes is given by the union $\mathcal{X} = \cup_{n=1}^{\infty} \mathcal{X}_n$.

Graph Matching and Comparison. A critical issue in comparing graphs is that the size and ordering of nodes can be arbitrary in given data. Consequently, matching nodes across graphs becomes an intermediate problem when comparing different video frames. The computation of metric d_x requires registration of nodes between $X^{(1)}$ and $X^{(2)}$, which may not be known beforehand. Furthermore, the two graphs may have a different number of nodes (due to missing or false nodes), making node matching more difficult. To handle this *registration problem*, we introduce the action of the permutation group on $\mathcal{X}$ as follows. Let $\mathcal{P}_n$ denote the set of all $n \times n$ permutation matrices: each $P \in \mathcal{P}_n$ is an $n \times n$

Algorithm 1: Kalman Filtering for Graph Time Series Prediction

---

    Input : Observed Graph Sequence: $\mathbf{Y} = \{\mathbf{y}_t : t = 1, 2, \ldots, T\}$
    Output: Estimated Graph Sequence: $\hat{\mathbf{X}} = \{\hat{\mathbf{x}}_t : t = 1, 2, \ldots, T\}$

 1 **for** $t = 2$ *to* T **do**

      /* Registration Step (Performed only once for a dataset.)   */

 2      $P^* = \underset{P \in \mathcal{P}_n}{\operatorname{argmin}} \;\; d_x((\mathbf{y}_{t-1}^{(e)}, \mathbf{y}_{t-1}^{(n)}), (P \star \mathbf{y}_t^{(e)}, P\mathbf{y}_t^{(n)}))$

 3      $(\mathbf{y}_t^{(e)}, \mathbf{y}_t^{(n)}) \overset{\text{set}}{=} (P^* \star \mathbf{y}_t^{(e)}, P\mathbf{y}_t^{(n)})$

 4 **end**

 5 Initialize $\hat{\mathbf{x}}_{1|1} = \mathbf{y}_1$, $K_{1|1} = I$

 6 **for** $t = 1$ *to* T **do**

      /* Prediction Step   */

 7      $\hat{\mathbf{x}}_{t+1|t} = B^{(l)}\hat{\mathbf{x}}_{t|t}$

 8      $K_{t+1|t} = B^{(l)}K_{t|t}B^{(l)\prime} + Q^{(l)} \quad Q^{(l)} = C^{(l)}C^{(l)\prime}$

      /* Update Step   */

 9      $S_t = W_t E^{(l)} K_{t+1|t} E^{(l)\prime} W_t' + W_t \Lambda^{(l)} W_t'$

10      $G_t = K_{t+1|t} E^{(l)\prime} W_t' S_t^{-1}$

11      $\hat{\mathbf{x}}_{t+1|t+1} = \hat{\mathbf{x}}_{t+1|t} + G_t(W_t\mathbf{y}_{t+1} - W_t E^{(l)}\hat{\mathbf{x}}_{t+1|t})$

12      $K_{t+1|t+1} = K_{t+1|t} - G_t W_t E^{(l)} K_{t+1|t} \quad \Lambda^{(l)} = F^{(l)}F^{(l)\prime}$

13 **end**

---

matrix with only one 1 in each column and row and all other entries are 0. The mapping $\mathbf{v} \mapsto P\mathbf{v}$ permutes the elements of $\mathbf{v}$ according to the elements of P, changing the ordering of nodes in the graph. (Note that the ordering within the node attributes remains unchanged.) The corresponding adjacency matrix changes according to $A \mapsto PAP^T$, and the representation $\mathbf{w}$ becomes $\phi(P(\phi^{-1}(\mathbf{w})P^T)$. We will use $P \star \mathbf{w}$ to denote this transformed $\mathbf{w}$. Together, the action of $\mathcal{P}_n$ on $\mathcal{X}_n$ is given by: $(P, X) = (P, (\mathbf{w}, \mathbf{v})) = (P \star \mathbf{w}, P\mathbf{v}) \in \mathcal{X}$. The graph space is then defined as the quotient space $\mathcal{G}_n \doteq \mathcal{X}_n/\mathcal{P}_n$. Elements of this quotient space are the permutation orbits of a graph: $[X] = \{(P\star\mathbf{w}, P\mathbf{v}|P \in \mathcal{P}_n\}$. The distance between any two graphs of size n is given by:

$$d_g([X^{(1)}], [X^{(2)}]) = \min_{P \in \mathcal{P}_n} d_x((\mathbf{w}^{(1)}, \mathbf{v}^{(1)}), (P \star \mathbf{w}^{(2)}, P\mathbf{v}^{(2)})) . \qquad (2)$$

The optimization over $P \in \mathcal{P}_n$ is precisely the graph matching problem that has received a lot of attention in the literature [13,30,42]. We presently use the *Umeyama* approach laid out in [16] for this optimization and graph matching since it allows us to handle graphs of varying sizes seamlessly. The full graph space is given by the union: $\mathcal{G} = \cup_{n=1}^{\infty}\mathcal{G}_n$.

When comparing graphs of two different sizes, say n_1 and n_2, we introduce null nodes to make them size $n_1 + n_2$ each and then apply the above setup. Null nodes are used only for matching purposes and are assigned attributes carefully to reach a desired result (see [16] for details). A matching of a real node in one graph to a null node in the other graph implies a birth or a removal of a node from the representation.

Algorithm 2: Kalman Smoothing for Handling Missing or Noisy Input

    Input : Estimated Graphs Sequence: $\hat{\mathbf{X}} = \{\hat{\mathbf{x}}_t : t = 1, 2, \ldots, T\}$
    Output: Smoothed Graph Sequence: $\tilde{\mathbf{X}} = \{\tilde{\mathbf{x}}_t : t = 1, 2, \ldots, T\}$

1   **for** $t = T - 1$ *to* 1 **do**
2      $H_t = K_{t|t} B^{(l)} K_{t+1|t}^{-1}$
3      $\tilde{\mathbf{x}}_{t|T} = \hat{\mathbf{x}}_{t|t} + H_t(\tilde{\mathbf{x}}_{t+1|T} - \hat{\mathbf{x}}_{t+1|t})$
4      $\tilde{K}_{t|T} = K_{t|t} + H_t(\tilde{K}_{t+1|T} - K_{t+1|t})H_t'$
5   **end**

---

4   Bayesian Time-Series Analysis of Graphs

Problem Statement: In this work, we aim to model the evolution of graph structures using a time-series model and then estimate the true time-series from noisy data using Kalman smoothing [17]. Specifically, our goal is to estimate $\mathbf{X} = \{\mathbf{x}_t \in \mathcal{X} : t = 1, 2, \ldots, T\}$, given a possibly corrupted or noisy observations $\mathbf{Y} = \{\mathbf{y}_t : t = 1, 2, \ldots, T\}$. This also involves estimating model parameters $\Theta = \{B^{(l)}, C^{(l)}, E^{(l)}, F^{(l)} : l = e, n\}$ from the observed data. Here $l = e$ indexes the edges and $l = n$ indexes the nodes. To this end, we specify two models – one for capturing dynamics underlying the process generating graphs (S) and the other for the observations (O). Formally, we define these models as

$$S : \begin{cases} \mathbf{w}_{t+1} = & B^{(e)}\mathbf{w}_t + C^{(e)}\mathbf{u}_t^{(e)} & \in \mathbb{R}^{k_n \times p}, \\ \mathbf{v}_{t+1} = & B^{(n)}\mathbf{v}_t + C^{(n)}\mathbf{u}_t^{(n)} & \in \mathbb{R}^{n \times m} \end{cases} \tag{3}$$

$$O : \begin{cases} \mathbf{y}_{t+1}^{(e)} = & P_{t+1} \star (W_{t+1}E^{(e)}\mathbf{w}_{t+1}) + F^{(e)}\epsilon_{t+1}^{(e)} & \in \mathbb{R}^{k_n \times p}, \\ \mathbf{y}_{t+1}^{(n)} = & P_{t+1}W_{t+1}E^{(n)}\mathbf{v}_{t+1} + F^{(n)}\epsilon_{t+1}^{(n)} & \in \mathbb{R}^{n \times m} \end{cases} \tag{4}$$

where the superscripts (e) and (n) denote the models for edges and nodes respectively; $P_{t+1} \in \mathcal{P}_n$ is a random permutation matrix; B, C, E, F are unknown coefficient matrices that are estimated from the data. The quantities $\mathbf{u}_t^{(e)}, \mathbf{u}_t^{(n)}$ denote random perturbations in the system dynamics and are modeled with independent standard normal components. We assume the measurement noise $\epsilon_t^{(e)}, \epsilon_t^{(n)}$ to be multivariate normal with mean zero and identity covariances. Also, W_{t+1} is a matrix that encodes the dropping of actual nodes or adding false nodes; W_{t+1} is arbitrary but known for use in estimation and tracking. For brevity, we will use $\mathbf{x}_t = \{\mathbf{w}_t, \mathbf{v}_t\}$ to denote the underlying graph at time t and $\mathbf{y}_t = \{\mathbf{y}_t^{(e)}, \mathbf{y}_t^{(n)}\}$ as its noisy observation.

Since the dynamical model is a linear system with Gaussian distributions, the estimates are readily available in close form. The problem of estimating $\mathbf{X}$, given $\mathbf{Y}$ and Θ, can be solved using either the Kalman filter (forward pass) or smoother (forward and backward pass). The problem of finding Θ, given $\mathbf{Y}$ and $\mathbf{X}$, is relatively straightforward using maximum-likelihood estimation (MLE). Applying these two solutions iteratively, we apply a well-known EM-type algorithm for estimating $\mathbf{X}$ from $\mathbf{Y}$.

Algorithm 3: Parameter Estimation for the Kalman Smoother

Input   : Observed and Estimated Graph Sequences: $\{\mathbf{Y}, \hat{\mathbf{X}}\}$
Output: Estimated Parameters: $\Theta = \{\hat{E}, \hat{\Lambda}, \hat{B}, \hat{Q}\}$

1 $\hat{E}^{(l)} = (\sum_{t=1}^{T} \mathbf{y}_t \mathbf{x}_t')(\sum_{t=1}^{T} \mathbf{x}_t \mathbf{x}_t')^{-1}$

2 $\hat{\Lambda}^{(l)} = \frac{1}{T-1} \sum_{t=1}^{T} (\mathbf{y}_t - \hat{E}^{(l)} \mathbf{x}_t)(\mathbf{y}_t - \hat{E}^{(l)} \mathbf{x}_t)'$

3 $\hat{B}^{(l)} = (\sum_{t=1}^{T} \mathbf{x}_t \mathbf{x}_{t-1}')(\sum_{t=1}^{T} \mathbf{x}_{t-1} \mathbf{x}_{t-1}')^{-1}$

4 $\hat{Q}^{(l)} = \frac{1}{T-1} \sum_{t=1}^{T} (\mathbf{x}_t - \hat{B}^{(l)} \mathbf{x}_{t-1})(\mathbf{x}_t - \hat{B}^{(l)} \mathbf{x}_{t-1})'$

Focusing on estimating the unknown state variable $\mathbf{X}$ using the data $\mathbf{Y}$ (and a current estimate of Θ) we seek the posterior distribution – $f(\mathbf{x}_{t+1} | \mathbf{y}_1, \mathbf{y}_2, \ldots, \mathbf{y}_t, \mathbf{y}_{t+1})$. Given the linear-Gaussian nature of Eqs. 3 and 4, the posterior distribution at each time is a multivariate normal distribution. To characterize this posterior, one needs only to evaluate the associated mean $\hat{\mathbf{x}}_{t+1|t+1}$ and covariance $\hat{K}_{t+1|t+1}$. Kalman filter provides a recursive formula to compute these quantities at time $t + 1$, as a function of estimates at time t and the new data $\mathbf{y}_{t+1}$. We adopt and apply these expressions for the representation spaces of graphs and obtain filtering results. Algorithm 1 outlines this recursion. An important distinction from classical filtering is that not all nodes are visible in the data at all times. Sometimes some nodes are undetected, while other times, some extraneous nodes are added. To deal with this issue, we follow two steps. Firstly, we introduce a known matrix W_t whose rows are a subset of the rows of identity I depending on the elements that are missing in the observation $\mathbf{y}_t$. If no elements are missing in $\mathbf{y}_t$, then W_t is identity. Secondly, we utilize an optimization over $\mathcal{P}_n$, i.e., graph matching, which registers the observed graphs at successive times. While Kalman Filter provides a forward pass through the temporal graph data, the results can be further improved by performing an additional backward pass. In this process, one uses the full data (over the full interval) to improve estimates. Algorithm 2 outlines steps for implementing this smoother.

Parameter Estimation. So far, we have discussed estimation of $\mathbf{X}$ given $\mathbf{Y}$ (the extracted graphs) and Θ (the system parameters). However, in the real data, Θ is unknown and needs to be estimated itself. Given $\mathbf{X}$ (or rather its estimate) and $\mathbf{Y}$, one can estimate Θ using a maximum-likelihood criterion that results in closed-form expressions. These expressions are given in Algorithm 3. To put these pieces together, one initializes $\hat{\Theta}$ and iterates between the estimation of $\mathbf{X}$ and Θ using Algorithms 1, 2 and 3. This results in the estimated values of the graph sequence and the system parameters, as well as the registration of nodes between successive graphs.

5   Experimental Evaluation

5.1   Data, Metrics and Baselines

Data. For evaluating the proposed approach, we devise three experimental settings with two kinds of data - synthetic and real-world video data. Since there are no existing comparable benchmarks, we develop a synthetic dataset for simulating the problem of predicting the future states of a visual-semantic sequence such as graphs [26] or spatial-temporal graphs [46]. We consider two scenarios - without and with observation noise/clutter. The former refers to a setting where each frame in a long video is devoid of any degradation, such as object detection failures. All objects are correctly detected at all times, and no new object enters the scene. The latter refers to a more realistic scenario, where objects may enter and/or exit the scene, and some may even go undetected in certain frames. We also demonstrate that our approach can work well with real-world scenarios by evaluating on a complex activity detection dataset with multiple actors from surveillance videos. Due to space constraints, we briefly describe the data in detail below. More details are presented in the supplementary.

Synthetic Data 1 - Data with Registered Nodes: For evaluating in the *ideal* observation setting, we generate an ordered sequence of fully connected graphs with $n = 10$ nodes observed over $t = 5000$ time points. The node attributes $\mathbf{v}_t$ denote the position coordinates of objects in the scene ($m = 2$) while the edge attributes $\mathbf{w}_t$ are scalar ($p = 1$) and signify relationships between connecting nodes. To simulate a graph time series, we initialize $\mathbf{v}_0$ randomly on a unit circle and $\mathbf{w}_0$ using a uniform distribution. We set the model parameters in the system dynamics (S) to: $B^{(e)} = 0.95 I_{k_n}, Q^{(e)} = I_{k_n}, \Lambda^{(e)} = 0.01 I_{k_n}, E^{(e)} = 0.001 M + I_{k_n}, M \in \mathbb{R}^{k_n \times k_n}$ whose elements are i.i.d. standard normal, $B^{(n)} = I_{2n}, Q^{(n)} = 100 I_{2n} \; \Lambda^{(n)} = 10 I_{2n} \; E^{(n)} = 3M + I_{2n}, M \in \mathbb{R}^{2n \times 2n}$ whose elements are i.i.d, $\mathcal{N}(0, 0.01)$. Recall $k_n = n(n-1)/2$.

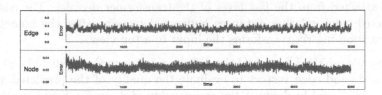

Fig. 2. Evolution of $\|\mathbf{w}_t - \mathbf{w}_{t+1}\|$ (top) and $\|\mathbf{v}_t - \mathbf{v}_{t+1}\|$ (bottom) versus t in a sample simulation.

Figure 2 shows the $\mathbb{L}^2$ norm between successive edge weights $\|\mathbf{w}_t - \mathbf{w}_{t+1}\|$ (top) and the node attributes $\|\mathbf{v}_t - \mathbf{v}_{t+1}\|$ (bottom). The large values indicate a significant changes in graphs over times. Similarly, Fig. 3 shows $\|\mathbf{w}_t - \mathbf{y}_t^{e)}\|$ (top) and $\|\mathbf{v}_t - \mathbf{y}_t^{n)}\|$ (bottom) over time. Once again, large values indicate a large level of noise in the observations. All baselines are trained with the first 4500 graphs and evaluated on the last 500 graphs.

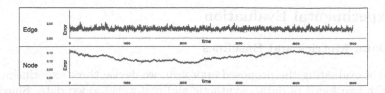

Fig. 3. Evolution of $\|\mathbf{w}_t - \mathbf{y}_t^{e)}\|$ (top) and $\|\mathbf{v}_t - \mathbf{y}_t^{n)}\|$ (bottom) in a sample run.

Synthetic Data 2 - Data with Missed and False Nodes: For creating second synthetic data with missing or false nodes, we start as above with graphs with $n = 10$ that are fully connected for t up to 5000. Then we randomly select some time points and randomly remove $2-3$ of the nodes in the graphs at each of the selected instants. This modification simulates missed detections and/or the exit and entry of objects as time progresses. To aid the registration process and simulate feature embeddings for objects in a video clip, we define the node attributes here to be the position coordinates concatenated with a simulated feature vector that is distinct for each node.

Real-World Video Data. For evaluation with real-world video data, we use a subset of the Multiview Extended Video with Activities (MEVA) [12] dataset, a large-scale human activity detection benchmark. It consists of over 9300 h hours of scripted scenarios and spontaneous background activities from indoor and outdoor viewpoints. For our experiments, we use a scene from an indoor bus station where the actors are continuously moving in and out of the camera field of view while performing different activities. The bus station scene is 5 min long (9000 frames). Each frame is represented by a graph, where each node is a person detection, and their node embeddings represent visual features. Specifically, we apply a pretrained object detector (DeTR [8]) on each frame and characterize the interactions and activities in the scene as an undirected graph. Each node $v_i \in V$ denotes a unique detection, where the node embeddings are the features vector extracted from the last layer of the transformer decoder. The edges are constructed using relative distances between detections after the homography transformation matrix transforms the input to a top view.

Metrics. We use the $\mathbb{L}^2$ norm of the difference between the predicted and actual system node and edge vectors to evaluate the quality of the predicted graphs. This metric is used in defining the components of d_x in Eq. 1 and is a natural choice of quantifying estimation performance.

Baselines. For a fair comparison with prior work on time series prediction, we devise three types of models: (i) multi-epoch training models, (ii) online training models, and (iii) static or reactive prediction models. For multi-epoch training models, we use the following baselines as SOTA techniques: 1-step feed-forward network (FFN) [14], recurrent neural networks [18,39], gated recurrent units (GRU) [9], transformers [40], seq2seq [38] with RNNs and GRUs. For online training models, we train an RNN and LSTM model in online fashion, *i.e.*, one graph at a time for 1-step prediction trained for 1 epoch continually. For

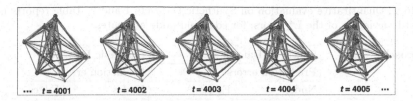

Fig. 4. For each t, we show $\mathbf{x}_t$ (blue), $\mathbf{y}_t$ (coral), and $\hat{\mathbf{x}}_t$ (green). The thickness of the edges are proportional to the edge values. (Color figure online)

static predictors, we predict either (i) the previous observation, (ii) the first observation, or (iii) the median of three successive graphs (current, previous, and the next). (For median filtering, we perform node registration using the well-known Hungarian algorithm.) Hyperparameters were chosen using a grid search and optimized using the Adam optimizer.

5.2 Evaluation on Synthetic Data 1

We apply Algorithm 1, 2 and 3 to the simulated data and obtain estimates $\hat{\mathbf{X}}$ from the given data $\mathbf{Y}$. Figure 4 shows an illustrative example of the estimation results. It shows five timeframes of system dynamics (blue) and its noisy observations (coral). The observed graphs are slightly distorted versions of the original ones with respect to both edge weights and node positions. Next, we run several iterations of Kalman smoother, and the estimated graph sequence is shown in green color.

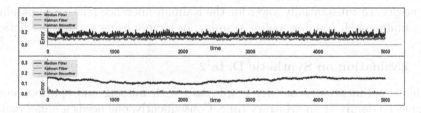

Fig. 5. Plots of $\|\mathbf{x}_t - \hat{\mathbf{x}}_t\|$ versus t for the edges (top) and nodes (bottom) for Synthetic Dataset 1. (Color figure online)

To visualize estimation error over the full interval, we present error plots in Fig. 5. Here, the y-axis represent $\|\mathbf{w}_t - \hat{\mathbf{w}}_t\|$ and $\|\mathbf{v}_t - \hat{\mathbf{v}}_t\|$ for (a) Edges and (b) Nodes respectively while the x-axis represents time t. For comparison, we observe that the Kalman smoother (red) estimation performs slightly better than that obtained from Kalman filter (only forward pass) (blue) and much better than the median filter (black).

Finally, we compute the performance summary over multiple simulated time series and compare our method with alternative ideas described earlier (under

Table 1. Quantitative evaluation on Synthetic Datasets 1 and 2. Table reports mean and std. deviation of the $\mathbb{L}^2$ errors, for edge and node estimates.

Approach	Synthetic Dataset 1		Synthetic Dataset 2	
	Prediction errors		Prediction errors	
	Nodes	Edges	Nodes	Edges
Multi-epoch training				
1-Step FFN	0.623 ± 0.0555	1.107 ± 0.084	0.198 ± 0.014	0.766 ± 0.090
RNN	0.303 ± 0.0239	0.496 ± 0.061	0.165 ± 0.019	0.472 ± 0.067
GRU	0.402 ± 0.0264	0.575 ± 0.062	0.164 ± 0.010	0.493 ± 0.076
Seq2Seq-RNN	0.470 ± 0.0274	0.747 ± 0.069	0.199 ± 0.025	0.771 ± 0.091
Seq2Seq-GRU	0.521 ± 0.0343	0.690 ± 0.074	0.165 ± 0.015	0.518 ± 0.064
Transformer	0.769 ± 0.0145	1.003 ± 0.015	0.284 ± 0.016	1.032 ± 0.030
Online training				
RNN	0.465 ± 0.089	0.932 ± 0.103	0.215 ± 0.031	0.876 ± 0.082
GRU	0.460 ± 0.065	0.877 ± 0.097	0.225 ± 0.033	0.847 ± 0.090
Kalman Filter	$\mathbf{0.009 \pm 0.003}$	$\mathbf{0.091 \pm 0.007}$	$\mathbf{0.008 \pm 0.004}$	$\mathbf{0.084 \pm 0.026}$
Kalman Smoother	$\mathbf{0.008 \pm 0.002}$	$\mathbf{0.091 \pm 0.007}$	$\mathbf{0.006 \pm 0.003}$	$\mathbf{0.085 \pm 0.020}$
Static prediction				
Median Filter	0.146 ± 0.009	0.153 ± 0.025	0.123 ± 0.002	0.156 ± 0.032
Previous observation	0.998 ± 0.000	0.713 ± 0.015	0.999 ± 0.000	0.712 ± 0.022
First observation	0.998 ± 0.000	1.017 ± 0.056	0.999 ± 0.000	1.038 ± 0.056

Baselines). These results are presented in Table 1. As the table shows, the estimation errors are substantially lower for the Kalman inference relative to baselines using multi-epoch training, online training, or simply using a static prediction.

5.3   Evaluation on Synthetic Data 2

In this experiment, we consider graph data with missing and spurious nodes inserted randomly at an arbitrary time. Consequently, one needs a *graph matching* step to match and track nodes across times. Every observed graph $\mathbf{y}_t$ is registered to the one before it, as stated in Algorithm 1. We use the *Umeyama* algorithm involving both edge and node attributes described in [16] for this purpose. The simulated graph time series after registration is shown in Fig. 6 at five consecutive time points. At $t = 239$, $\mathbf{x}_t$ has 10 nodes whereas $\mathbf{y}_t$ has 7 connected nodes and 3 more that are not connected to the rest of the graph. The latter three are *null nodes* which were added to $\mathbf{y}_{239}$ to facilitate the registration process and have degree 0. The graphs at $t = 239$ represent a situation where three objects went undetected. The *null nodes* are assigned the position coordinates of the corresponding nodes they were matched to in the previous time point.

Figure 6 shows the estimated graphs in green. The *null nodes* that appear isolated in $\mathbf{y}_{239}$ are connected in $\hat{\mathbf{x}}_{239}$ by weighted edges estimated by the Kalman

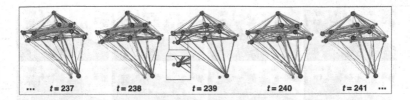

Fig. 6. Illustration of handling missed object detection. (Same color scheme as earlier.)
(Color figure online)

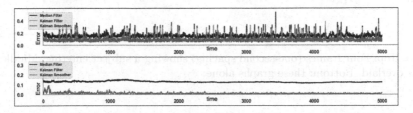

Fig. 7. Plots of the error $\|\mathbf{x}_t - \hat{\mathbf{x}}_t\|$ versus t for edges (top) and nodes (bottom) for
Synthetic Dataset 2. (Color figure online)

smoother. The error plots in Fig. 7 show high accuracy for the Kalman smoother.
The spikes here correspond to errors at time points with missed or false nodes.
In spite of these spikes, the Kalman smoother (red) performs better than the
Kalman filter (only forward pass) (blue) and the median filter (black). This result
emphasizes that the graph Kalman filter-smoother framework can detect-track
objects even when missing in some frames. Table 1 presents a more comprehensive study of estimation error for a number of alternative methods. Once again,
we see a clear superiority of Kalman smoother over other methods.

5.4 Real-World Evaluation

Next, we apply this framework to tracking human subjects in a bus station scene
introduced earlier. To focus on evaluation, we consider three short segments of
the full video sequence. Figure 8 shows 4 frames from an event where a subject
enters the bus station and eventually exits it. To compare estimation errors for
different methods, we have manually generated the *ground truth* **X**. It represents
each manually detected subjects in each frame of the sequence. This manual
annotation results in bounding boxes of true subjects using the Davinci Resolve
video editor. This software allows for manually annotating some keyframes and
linearly interpolating the bounding boxes (in positions and aspect ratios) to fill
in between. We treat the resulting sequence as the ground truth **X**.

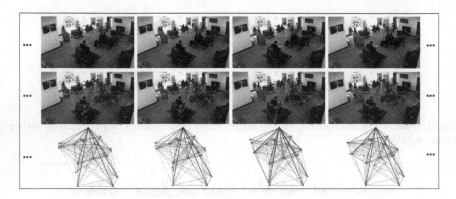

Fig. 8. Top: Four frames (one-second spacing) showing a subject entering. Middle: $\mathbf{x}_t$, $\mathbf{y}_t$, $\hat{\mathbf{x}}_t$ overlaid. Bottom: these graphs alone.

To aid the registration of the observed series $\{\mathbf{y}_t\}$, we combine several types of node attributes: (a) top-view node position coordinates obtained from homography transformation of the input camera view, (b) eight principal components of the 256 length node embeddings explaining 85.3% of the variation, and (c) four coordinates of the bounding box of the detected object, resulting in a $m = 14$-length attribute vector for each node. The edge weights in this setup come from Euclidean distances between the nodes.

With this setup, we apply Algorithms 1, 2 and 3 to get estimates of the underlying system graphs $\hat{\mathbf{X}}$ as well as the model parameters $\hat{\Theta}$. Note that results are sensitive to initialization of the system parameters. For each video clip, we measure the estimation error using three items: (a) $\|\mathbf{x}_t - \hat{\mathbf{x}}_t\|$, (b) the average count of noisy or spurious detections (present in only $\mathbf{y}_t$) and (c) the average

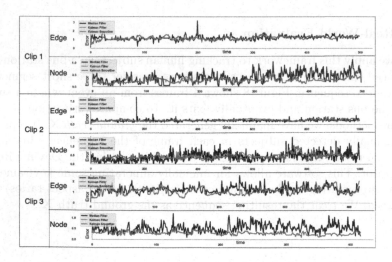

Fig. 9. Plots of the error $\|\mathbf{x}_t - \hat{\mathbf{x}}_t\|$ for edges and nodes in three video clips from *real-world* observations (MEVA dataset).

count of missed detections (present in only x_t). The $\mathbb{L}^2$ norm estimation errors in Fig. 9 indicate consistently high prediction accuracy for Kalman smoother. The average count of false and missed detections in Table 2 shows that the Kalman filter-smoother framework performs better at eliminating noise and retrieving missed detections. Figure 10 highlights some key features of the results obtained.

Table 2. Average count of nodes present in $\hat{x}_t$ but not in x_t (left) and average count of nodes present in x_t but not in $\hat{x}_t$ (right) for 3 video clips using Kalman smoother (KS), Kalman filter (KF) and median filter (MF)

Video clips	Rate of false detections			Rate of missed detections		
	KS	KF	MF	KS	KF	MF
Clip 1 ($t = 0$ to 500)	0.762	0.721	4.118	2.427	2.387	5.914
Clip 2 ($t = 0$ to 1000)	0.956	0.997	4.498	3.024	3.065	6.738
Clip 3 ($t = 782$ to 1200)	0.885	0.909	4.690	3.556	3.580	7.599

Fig. 10. Examples of successful (top) and failed (bottom) node placements given incorrect data: node 2 (top left), node 9 (top right), node 8 (bottom left) and node 17 (bottom right).

6   Discussion

This paper develops a Kalman smoother approach, adapted to the quotient space geometry of graph representations, to track objects of interest in video data. Specifically, it incorporates a node-registration step at each time to maintain tracks despite having noise and clutter in the scene. Utilizing the dynamics of system evolution, along with a likelihood model, this Bayesian framework helps overcome the issues raised by missed and false detections in the pre-processing step. This framework understandably outperforms several learning-based and some basic online ideas. To the best of our knowledge, this is the first paper to formulate and apply classical filtering techniques to quotient spaces of graphs.

While this approach can handle a small number of missed or false detections, it fails when this number grows large. The system dynamics, or temporal smoothing, of estimated states, can't make up for this large data corruption. One needs additional information to help track such objects.

Acknowledgements. This research was supported in part by the US National Science Foundation grants 1955154, IIS 2143150, IIS 1955230, CNS 1513126, and IIS 1956050.

References

1. Aakur, S., de Souza, F.D., Sarkar, S.: Going deeper with semantics: video activity interpretation using semantic contextualization. In: 2019 IEEE Winter Conference on Applications of Computer Vision (WACV), pp. 190–199. IEEE (2019)
2. Aakur, S.N., de Souza, F.D.M., Sarkar, S.: Generating open world descriptions of video using common sense knowledge in a pattern theory framework. Q. Appl. Math. **77**, 323–356 (2019)
3. Adeli, V., et al.: TRiPOD: human trajectory and pose dynamics forecasting in the wild. CoRR abs/2104.04029 (2021). https://arxiv.org/abs/2104.04029
4. Brasó, G., Leal-Taixé, L.: Learning a neural solver for multiple object tracking. CoRR abs/1912.07515 (2019). http://arxiv.org/abs/1912.07515
5. Bronstein, M.M., Bruna, J., LeCun, Y., Szlam, A., Vandergheynst, P.: Geometric deep learning: going beyond Euclidean data. IEEE Signal Process. Mag. **34**(4), 18–42 (2017)
6. Calissano, A., Feragen, A., Vantini, S.: Populations of unlabeled networks: graph space geometry and geodesic principal components (2020)
7. Cao, D., et al.: Spectral temporal graph neural network for multivariate time-series forecasting. In: Advances in Neural Information Processing Systems 33, pp. 17766–17778 (2020)
8. Carion, N., Massa, F., Synnaeve, G., Usunier, N., Kirillov, A., Zagoruyko, S.: End-to-end object detection with transformers. In: Vedaldi, A., Bischof, H., Brox, T., Frahm, J.-M. (eds.) ECCV 2020. LNCS, vol. 12346, pp. 213–229. Springer, Cham (2020). https://doi.org/10.1007/978-3-030-58452-8_13
9. Che, Z., Purushotham, S., Cho, K., Sontag, D., Liu, Y.: Recurrent neural networks for multivariate time series with missing values. Sci. Rep. **8**, 6085 (2018)
10. Chen, F., Chen, Z., Biswas, S., Lei, S., Ramakrishnan, N., Lu, C.T.: Graph convolutional networks with kalman filtering for traffic prediction. In: 28th International Conference on Advances in Geographic Information Systems (SIGSPATIAL 2020) (2020)
11. Cheng, D., Yang, F., Xiang, S., Liu, J.: Financial time series forecasting with multi-modality graph neural network. Pattern Recogn. **121**, 108218 (2022)
12. Corona, K., Osterdahl, K., Collins, R., Hoogs, A.: MEVA: a large-scale multiview, multimodal video dataset for activity detection. In: Proceedings of the IEEE/CVF Winter Conference on Applications of Computer Vision (WACV), pp. 1060–1068, January 2021
13. Gold, S., Rangarajan, A.: A graduated assignment algorithm for graph matching. IEEE Trans. Pattern Anal. Mach. Intell. **18**(4), 377–388 (1996)
14. Goodfellow, I., Bengio, Y., Courville, A.: Deep Learning. MIT Press (2016). http://www.deeplearningbook.org

15. Guo, X., Bal, A.B., Needham, T., Srivastava, A.: Statistical shape analysis of brain arterial networks (BAN). Ann. Appl. Stat. **16**(2), 1130–1150 (2022)
16. Guo, X., Srivastava, A., Sarkar, S.: A quotient space formulation for statistical analysis of graphical data. J. Math. Imaging Vis. **63**, 735–752 (2021)
17. Haykin, S.: Kalman Filtering and Neural Networks, vol. 47. Wiley, Hoboken (2004)
18. Hewamalage, H., Bergmeir, C., Bandara, K.: Recurrent neural networks for time series forecasting: current status and future directions. Int. J. Forecast. **37**(1), 388–427 (2021)
19. Huang, Y., Bi, H., Li, Z., Mao, T., Wang, Z.: STGAT: modeling spatial-temporal interactions for human trajectory prediction. In: Proceedings of the IEEE/CVF International Conference on Computer Vision, pp. 6272–6281 (2019)
20. Ivanovic, B., Pavone, M.: The trajectron: probabilistic multi-agent trajectory modeling with dynamic spatiotemporal graphs. In: Proceedings of the IEEE/CVF International Conference on Computer Vision, pp. 2375–2384 (2019)
21. Jain, B.J.: On the geometry of graph spaces. Discrete App. Math. **214**, 126–144 (2016)
22. Jain, B.J.: Statistical graph space analysis. Pattern Recogn. **60**, 802–812 (2016)
23. Ji, J., Krishna, R., Fei-Fei, L., Niebles, J.C.: Action genome: actions as compositions of spatio-temporal scene graphs. In: Proceedings of the IEEE/CVF Conference on Computer Vision and Pattern Recognition, pp. 10236–10247 (2020)
24. Knyazev, A., Malyshev, A.: Accelerated graph-based nonlinear denoising filters. Procedia Comput. Sci. **80**, 607–616 (2016)
25. Kosaraju, V., Sadeghian, A., Martín-Martín, R., Reid, I., Rezatofighi, S.H., Savarese, S.: Social-BiGAT: multimodal trajectory forecasting using bicycle-GAN and graph attention networks. arXiv preprint arXiv:1907.03395 (2019)
26. Krishna, R., et al.: Visual genome: connecting language and vision using crowd-sourced dense image annotations. Int. J. Comput. Vis. **123**(1), 32–73 (2017)
27. Li, J., Gao, X., Jiang, T.: Graph networks for multiple object tracking. In: Proceedings of the IEEE/CVF Winter Conference on Applications of Computer Vision (WACV), March 2020
28. Liu, H., Singh, P.: ConceptNet-a practical commonsense reasoning tool-kit. BT Technol. J. **22**(4), 211–226 (2004)
29. Lu, X., Wang, W., Danelljan, M., Zhou, T., Shen, J., Gool, L.V.: Video object segmentation with episodic graph memory networks. CoRR abs/2007.07020 (2020). https://arxiv.org/abs/2007.07020
30. Lyzinski, V., Fishkind, D.E., Fiori, M., Vogelstein, J.T., Priebe, C.E., Sapiro, G.: Graph matching: relax at your own risk. IEEE Trans. Pattern Anal. Mach. Intell. **38**(1), 60–73 (2016)
31. Mohamed, A., Qian, K., Elhoseiny, M., Claudel, C.: Social-STGCNN: a social spatio-temporal graph convolutional neural network for human trajectory prediction. In: Proceedings of the IEEE/CVF Conference on Computer Vision and Pattern Recognition, pp. 14424–14432 (2020)
32. Paaßen, B., Göpfert, C., Hammer, B.: Time series prediction for graphs in kernel and dissimilarity spaces. Neural Process. Lett. **48**(2), 669–689 (2018)
33. Rudi, A., Ciliberto, C., Marconi, G., Rosasco, L.: Manifold structured prediction. In: Advances in Neural Information Processing Systems 31 (2018)
34. Salzmann, T., Ivanovic, B., Chakravarty, P., Pavone, M.: Trajectron++: dynamically-feasible trajectory forecasting with heterogeneous data. In: Vedaldi, A., Bischof, H., Brox, T., Frahm, J.-M. (eds.) ECCV 2020, Part XVIII. LNCS, vol. 12363, pp. 683–700. Springer, Cham (2020). https://doi.org/10.1007/978-3-030-58523-5_40

35. Shi, L.: Kalman filtering over graphs: theory and applications. IEEE Trans. Autom. Control **54**(9), 2230–2234 (2009)
36. Song, C., Lin, Y., Guo, S., Wan, H.: Spatial-temporal synchronous graph convolutional networks: a new framework for spatial-temporal network data forecasting. In: Proceedings of the AAAI Conference on Artificial Intelligence, vol. 34, pp. 914–921 (2020)
37. Speer, R., Chin, J., Havasi, C.: ConceptNet 5.5: an open multilingual graph of general knowledge. In: Thirty-First AAAI conference on artificial intelligence (2017)
38. Sutskever, I., Vinyals, O., Le, Q.V.: Sequence to sequence learning with neural networks. CoRR arXiv:1409.3215 (2014)
39. Tealab, A.: Time series forecasting using artificial neural networks methodologies: a systematic review. Future Comput. Inform. J. **3**(2), 334–340 (2018)
40. Vaswani, A., et al.: Attention is all you need. arXiv:1706.03762 (2017)
41. Vázquez-Enríquez, M., Alba-Castro, J.L., Docío-Fernández, L., Rodríguez-Banga, E.: Isolated sign language recognition with multi-scale spatial-temporal graph convolutional networks. In: Proceedings of the IEEE/CVF Conference on Computer Vision and Pattern Recognition, pp. 3462–3471 (2021)
42. Vogelstein, J.T., et al.: Fast approximate quadratic programming for graph matching. PLOS One **10**(4), e0121002 (2015)
43. Wang, C., Gao, D., Qiu, Y., Scherer, S.: Lifelong graph learning. In: 2022 Conference on Computer Vision and Pattern Recognition (CVPR) (2022)
44. Wang, C., Cai, S., Tan, G.: GraphTCN: spatio-temporal interaction modeling for human trajectory prediction. In: Proceedings of the IEEE/CVF Winter Conference on Applications of Computer Vision, pp. 3450–3459 (2021)
45. Wang, W., Lu, X., Shen, J., Crandall, D.J., Shao, L.: Zero-shot video object segmentation via attentive graph neural networks. CoRR abs/2001.06807 (2020). https://arxiv.org/abs/2001.06807
46. Wang, X., Gupta, A.: Videos as space-time region graphs. In: Ferrari, V., Hebert, M., Sminchisescu, C., Weiss, Y. (eds.) ECCV 2018. LNCS, vol. 11209, pp. 413–431. Springer, Cham (2018). https://doi.org/10.1007/978-3-030-01228-1_25
47. Wang, Y., Kitani, K., Weng, X.: Joint object detection and multi-object tracking with graph neural networks. In: 2021 IEEE International Conference on Robotics and Automation (ICRA), pp. 13708–13715. IEEE (2021)
48. Weng, X., Wang, Y., Man, Y., Kitani, K.M.: GNN3DMOT: graph neural network for 3D multi-object tracking with 2D–3D multi-feature learning. In: Proceedings of the IEEE/CVF Conference on Computer Vision and Pattern Recognition, pp. 6499–6508 (2020)
49. Wu, Z., Pan, S., Long, G., Jiang, J., Chang, X., Zhang, C.: Connecting the dots: multivariate time series forecasting with graph neural networks. In: Proceedings of the 26th ACM SIGKDD International Conference on Knowledge Discovery and Data Mining, pp. 753–763 (2020)
50. Yan, S., Xiong, Y., Lin, D.: Spatial temporal graph convolutional networks for skeleton-based action recognition. In: Thirty-Second AAAI Conference on Artificial Intelligence (2018)
51. Yu, B., Yin, H., Zhu, Z.: Spatio-temporal graph convolutional networks: a deep learning framework for traffic forecasting. In: IJCAI (2018)

Motion Sensitive Contrastive Learning for Self-supervised Video Representation

Jingcheng Ni[1,2], Nan Zhou[1,2], Jie Qin[3(✉)], Qian Wu[4], Junqi Liu[4],
Boxun Li[4], and Di Huang[1,2(✉)]

[1] State Key Laboratory of Software Development Environment, Beihang University,
Beijing, China
dhuang@buaa.edu.cn
[2] School of Computer Science and Engineering, Beihang University, Beijing, China
[3] College of Computer Science and Technology, Nanjing University of Aeronautics
and Astronautics, Nanjing, China
[4] MEGVII Technology, Beijing, China

Abstract. Contrastive learning has shown great potential in video representation learning. However, existing approaches fail to sufficiently exploit short-term motion dynamics, which are crucial to various downstream video understanding tasks. In this paper, we propose Motion Sensitive Contrastive Learning (MSCL) that injects the motion information captured by optical flows into RGB frames to strengthen feature learning. To achieve this, in addition to clip-level global contrastive learning, we develop Local Motion Contrastive Learning (LMCL) with frame-level contrastive objectives across the two modalities. Moreover, we introduce Flow Rotation Augmentation (FRA) to generate extra motion-shuffled negative samples and Motion Differential Sampling (MDS) to accurately screen training samples. Extensive experiments on standard benchmarks validate the effectiveness of the proposed method. With the commonly-used 3D ResNet-18 as the backbone, we achieve the top-1 accuracies of 91.5% on UCF101 and 50.3% on Something-Something v2 for video classification, and a 65.6% Top-1 Recall on UCF101 for video retrieval, notably improving the state of the art.

Keywords: Video representation learning · Self-supervised learning · Local motion contrastive learning · Motion differential sampling

1 Introduction

Video understanding has become a necessity in the past decade due to the rapid and massive growth of data. In this challenging task, video representation is the most fundamental and important issue and has received consistently increasing attention. In the literature, many efforts have been made along with the release

Supplementary Information The online version contains supplementary material available at https://doi.org/10.1007/978-3-031-19833-5_27.

of several large-scale benchmarks, such as Kinetics [25] and YouTube-8M [1], where representations are learned in a supervised manner from manually annotated samples. Unfortunately, building such databases inevitably incurs enormous human and time cost.

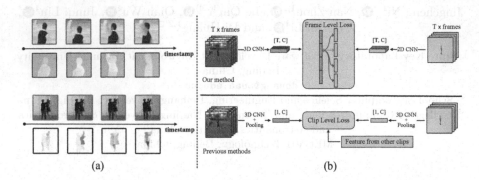

Fig. 1. (a) The RGB frames are not sensitive enough to short-term motion changes, while the optical flows are able to capture subtle motion dynamics between frames, where the changes of motion vectors (in different colors) are clearly observed from the flow maps. (b) Comparison between our method and previous ones using optical flows. Existing works generate clip-level features with temporal pooling, while we focus on more fine-grained frame-level features. (Color figure online)

Self-supervised learning has recently emerged as a promising alternative in visual representation. Different from the case on images that only considers spatial variations, that on videos puts more emphasis in temporal characteristics. A number of studies on videos have shown huge potential to learn general features by making use of a tremendous amount of unlabeled data available on the Internet, facilitating diverse downstream applications, including action recognition, action detection, video retrieval, *etc.*

Among current self-supervised video representation learning methods, contrastive learning based ones [12,36] have delivered a great success. They treat the clips from the same video as positive pairs while the ones from different videos as negative pairs and apply the InfoNCE loss [31] to train the model, which is expected to distinguish the clips of a given video from the ones of others. However, clip-level contrastive learning is relatively coarse and primarily benefits global (*a.k.a.* long-term) features [49] without meticulously capturing local (*a.k.a.* short-term) dynamics, thus limiting the performance, in particular in fine-grained scenarios.

More recently, some attempts have compensated this by designing and conducting contrastive learning across video clips with additional views, *e.g.* global *vs.* local [10] and long *vs.* short [4]. Although local temporal modeling is enhanced to some extent with decent improvements reported, they still suffer from two major downsides. On the one hand, for the continuity and redundancy of video data, it is really difficult to handle the discrepancy between the frames within a small time slot, *e.g.* at adjacent timestamps, without high-level supervision, making their representations not sufficiently powerful. On the other hand, existing global-local or long-short contrastive learning requires repetitive temporal interval sampling, leading to multiple forward processes, for a single video, which is both time- and memory-consuming.

In this paper, we propose a novel self-supervised contrastive based approach for video representation learning, namely Motion Sensitive Contrast Learning (MSCL). To overcome the shortcomings aforementioned, besides encoding the global motion from RGB frames, it also fully exploits local temporal clues by introducing optical flows since they prove sensitive to very short-term dynamics, as illustrated in Fig. 1 (a). To fulfill this, we propose Local Motion Contrastive Learning (LMCL) that directly leverages optical flows as the supervisory signal for frame-level local dynamics learning. Specifically, LMCL matches cross-modality (RGB *vs.* optical flows) features at the same timestamp so that subtle motions are modeled. Meanwhile, to restrict the temporal receptive field of flow features in frame-level contrast, different from previous works [16,37,51] on clip-level contrast, we adopt a lightweight 2D CNN as the encoder without temporal message passing, as illustrated in Fig. 1 (b) and elaborated in Sect. 2.2. In this way, those features capturing local dynamics can be efficiently obtained from the 2D flow encoder, bypassing the cumbersome phase of extra local interval sampling required in [4,10]. In addition, we present two practical strategies to further facilitate LMCL. First, as LMCL introduces frame-level contrast, clips with limited motions tend to bring negative effects to the learning process. To solve this problem, we design Motion Differential Sampling (MDS) to enhance the sampling probability of clips with large motion differential. Second, Flow Rotation Augmentation (FRA) takes rotated flows with different motion vectors as extra negative samples, thereby highlighting motion information on local features.

We summarize our main contributions as follows:

– We propose LMCL, taking advantage of optical flows to underline subtle motions for frame-level contrastive learning, which substantially strengthens self-supervised video representations.
– We present MDS and FRA to optimize temporal interval sampling and optical flow augmentation respectively, both of which further facilitate LMCL.
– We achieve competitive results on several standard benchmarks, *i.e.*, UCF101, HMDB51, and Something-Something v2, in video classification and retrieval.

2   Related Work

2.1   Self-supervised Video Representation Learning

Various self-supervised video representation learning methods have been devised to take advantage of unlabeled video data on the Internet. These methods learn to accomplish various human-designed pre-tasks, including frame sorting [27], pace prediction [45], speed prediction [5,19], and spatio-temporal jigsaw solving

[2,20]. More recent works have been inspired by the success of contrastive learning in the image domain such as [6,8,14,17], which can be viewed as instance discrimination tasks [50]. Since videos contain extra attributes that contribute to distinguishing instances, [12,36] take time-shift as the invariant attribute and [7,18] regard speed as the variant attribute. More generally, multiple attributes are explored jointly by the combination of temporal transforms in [22,33]. In [34], transforms are performed in the feature space to reduce memory consumption.

2.2 Optical Flows in Video Understanding

Temporal information is of high importance in video understanding. Optical flows, corresponding to motion vectors across frames, have shown potential in modeling dynamics in the two-stream structure [39]. However, [23,38] indicate that motion information does not work as expected. For example, in supervised action recognition, the shuffling operation at input stage has much more impact on RGB sequences than flow ones. The motivation behind is on the property of appearance-invariance [38], where the motion foreground is described with a low variety. Some self-supervised learning methods can also be seen as taking advantage of this property. COCLR [16] highlights the prior that videos belonging to the same class have similar flow patterns but significant variations in the RGB space, and MoDist [51] distills the flow information to make RGB features focus more on motion foreground. Unlike these methods, we make use of the motion information itself as guidance to improve the ability of modeling local dynamics in RGB features.

2.3 Fine-Grained Temporal Features

Learning local dynamics is an important topic for video understanding. Some works attempt to improve modeling through dedicatedly designed structures [24,47] or explicit constraints [48]. But in the self-supervised learning domain, existing methods do not pay enough attention to fine-grained temporal features. For instance, [12,36] can be viewed as learning slow features [49], which are more relevant to scene information. To encode more temporal clues in self-supervised video representation learning, LSFD [4] introduces feature contrast between long-term and grouped short-term features, and TCLR [10] directly compares features with different time-spans. Although these works do make improvements, they require extra sampled clips in the forward process for short views and cannot take advantage of local motion information in flows.

3 Method

In this section, we introduce the proposed self-supervised framework for video representation learning in detail. We begin by introducing the global and local feature extraction pipelines for the two modalities (*i.e.*, RGB and optical flow), respectively. Subsequently, we present the commonly-used global contrastive losses and the proposed Local Motion Contrastive Learning (LMCL), including sample pair construction and augmentation. Finally, we introduce the motion differential sampling policy, which provides meaningful samples for learning more effective local temporal features. An overview of our proposed framework is illustrated in Fig. 2.

3.1 Global and Local Feature Extraction

Given a sequence of video frames, we first extract optical flow images from pairs of frames with stride s. We learn both clip-level global and frame-level local features in terms of both RGB and optical flow modalities. Specifically, we adopt the spirit of contrastive learning to build self-supervised features, and randomly sample video clips $\{V^q, V^k\}$ with the corresponding optical flows $\{M^q, M^k\}$ as the queries and keys. As we follow the symmetric structure of MoCo [17] where queries and keys are encoded in a similar way, we only elaborate how to extract features for queries for brevity.

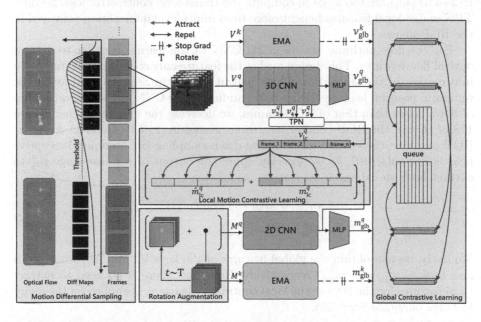

Fig. 2. Overview of the proposed Motion Sensitive Contrast Learning (MSCL) framework. Clips with large motion differentials are sampled from the video and random augmentations are employed for generating queries $\{V^q, M^q\}$ and keys $\{V^k, M^k\}$ w.r.t. the RGB and flow modalities. Then, global features $\{v_{\mathrm{glb}}^q, v_{\mathrm{glb}}^k, m_{\mathrm{glb}}^q, m_{\mathrm{glb}}^k\}$ are extracted for global contrastive learning, where EMA indicates the momentum key encoder in [17]. In order to inject motion dynamics from flow to RGB features, Local Motion Contrastive Learning (LMCL) is conducted based on local features $\{v_{\mathrm{lc}}^q, m_{\mathrm{lc}}^q\}$. To further enforce the model to focus on the motion information, rotation augmentation is applied on the flow inputs and the corresponding local features $\hat{m}_{\mathrm{lc}}^q$ are used to enhance negative samples in LMCL.

In the RGB pathway, a 3D CNN is employed as the feature encoder, where the output features of different stages (*i.e.*, conv3, conv4 and conv5 layers) are denoted as $\{\nu_3^q, \nu_4^q, \nu_5^q\}$, respectively. We extract video-level global features based on the output of the last stage (*i.e.*, ν_5^q). More concretely, we apply spatio-temporal pooling on ν_5^q, followed by a 2-layer MLP as the projection head. For frame-level local features, we use a 3-layer Temporal Pyramid Network (TPN) [54] to merge multi-level features. Specifically, we compute the global features ν_{glb}^q and the local features ν_{lc}^q in the RGB pathway as follows:

$$
\begin{aligned}
\nu_{glb}^q &= \mathrm{MLP}(\mathrm{STPool}(\nu_5^q)), \\
\nu_{lc}^q &= \mathrm{SPool}(\hat{\nu}_3^q), \quad \hat{\nu}_3^q, \hat{\nu}_4^q, \hat{\nu}_5^q = \mathrm{TPN}(\nu_3^q, \nu_4^q, \nu_5^q),
\end{aligned}
\tag{1}
$$

where STPool($\cdot$) and SPool($\cdot$) indicate spatio-temporal pooling and spatial pooling, respectively. In practice, we only use the first-stage output $\hat{\nu}_3^q$ from TPN, due to two reasons. First, the receptive fields of temporal features in later stages of 3D CNNs (especially those with temporal down-sampling, *e.g.*, S3D [52] and R(2+1)D [43]) are too large to compute the frame-level contrastive loss. Second, TPN makes local features benefit more from multi-level information conveyed in the RGB image.

For the flow pathway, we use a 2D CNN as the feature encoder to extract optical flow features. This design pushes the feature only containing the temporal information in the single flow which benefit LMCL in Sect. 3.3, and avoid the temporal position leakage [21] by zero padding in 3D CNN. Since the variability of flows is less than that of RGB frames, we decrease the number of channels to 1/8 of that of the RGB counterpart, as suggested in [11,51]. Different from the RGB pathway, there exists no temporal down-sampling (*i.e.*, temporal receptive field is not enlarged), so we directly apply the output of the last stage m_5^q to extract both global and local features as follows:

$$
\begin{aligned}
m_{glb}^q &= \mathrm{MLP}(\mathrm{STPool}(m_5^q)), \\
m_{lc}^q &= \mathrm{SPool}(m_5^q).
\end{aligned}
\tag{2}
$$

Similarly, we can obtain the global features of the keys V^k and M^k w.r.t. RGB and flow as ν_{glb}^k and m_{glb}^k, respectively. Note that there is no need to extract local features for the keys as the local contrastive learning is applied on the query features only (see Sect. 3.3).

3.2   Global Contrastive Learning

In this section, we introduce the global contrastive learning based on clip-level features. We follow the basic pipeline of MoCo [17] for both pathways, where the momentum encoder is employed for key inputs, and the memory bank is used for saving negative clips. There are two types of global contrastive losses in our method. The first intra-modality loss is applied on the features from either the RGB or the flow modality to make them discriminative in their own domains.

Specifically, we adopt the widely-used InfoNCE [31] loss for global contrastive learning, which is defined as:

$$L_{\text{RGB}} = -log\frac{h(\nu_{\text{glb}}^q, \nu_{\text{glb}}^k)}{h(\nu_{\text{glb}}^q, \nu_{\text{glb}}^k) + \sum_{i=1}^N h(\nu_{\text{glb}}^q, \bar{\nu}_{i,\text{glb}}^k)},$$
$$L_{\text{Flow}} = -log\frac{h(m_{\text{glb}}^q, m_{\text{glb}}^k)}{h(m_{\text{glb}}^q, m_{\text{glb}}^k) + \sum_{i=1}^N h(m_{\text{glb}}^q, \bar{m}_{i,\text{glb}}^k)},$$

(3)

where $h(x, y) = \exp(x^T y/\|x\|\|y\|\tau)$ is the distance between two feature vectors x and y; $\bar{\nu}_{i,\text{glb}}^k$ and $\bar{m}_{i,\text{glb}}^k$ represent the i-th global features of the two modalities in the memory bank with size N, respectively; τ is the temperature parameter. The second inter-modality loss is applied across the two modalities, with the aim of making the RGB features focus more on motion foreground areas [51], which contribute to the subsequent local contrastive learning. Concretely, the loss term is formulated as follows:

$$L_{\text{RF}} = - (log\frac{h(\nu_{\text{glb}}^q, m_{\text{glb}}^k)}{h(\nu_{\text{glb}}^q, m_{\text{glb}}^k) + \sum_{i=1}^N h(\nu_{\text{glb}}^q, \bar{m}_{i,\text{glb}}^k)} +$$
$$log\frac{h(m_{\text{glb}}^q, \nu_{\text{glb}}^k)}{h(m_{\text{glb}}^q, \nu_{\text{glb}}^k) + \sum_{i=1}^N h(m_{\text{glb}}^q, \bar{\nu}_{i,\text{glb}}^k)}),$$

(4)

and different from [51], the positive and negative keys come from the same modality, which we find in our experiments is more stable in early training. With the intra- and inter-modality losses, we can obtain discriminative global features for both modalities, and at the same time focus on motion foreground areas, which are essential for the subsequent local motion contrastive learning phase.

3.3   Local Motion Contrastive Learning

The features learned based on the global contrastive losses have difficulty in modeling local dynamics. To address this, we use optical flows to capture local motion information, and introduce frame-level contrastive losses for learning time-variant features. For the local features ν_{lc}^q and m_{lc}^q, we only take frame-level features at the same timestamp as positive pairs. Thus, the local motion contrastive loss can be formulated as:

$$L_{\text{LMC}} = - \sum_{i=1}^T log\frac{h(\nu_{\text{lc}}^q(i), m_{\text{lc}}^q(i))}{h(\nu_{\text{lc}}^q(i), m_{\text{lc}}^q(i)) + \sum_{j=1, j\neq i}^T h(\nu_{\text{lc}}^q(i), m_{\text{lc}}^q(j))},$$

(5)

where $\nu_{\text{lc}}^q(i)$ represents the frame-level features at timestamp i, and T is the total number of sampled video frames.

Flow Rotation Augmentation. To make this loss focus more on local motion information, we augment the optical flow with extra negative samples. Specifically, the flow is rotated with a specific angle that is randomly sampled from

$[\alpha, 2\pi - \alpha]$ and the corresponding local features after rotation are treated as negative samples. In this manner, the local motion contrastive loss turns into:

$$A(i) = \sum_{j=1, j\neq i}^{T} h(\nu_{\mathrm{lc}}^{q}(i), m_{\mathrm{lc}}^{q}(j)) + \sum_{j=1}^{T} h(\nu_{\mathrm{lc}}^{q}(i), \hat{m}_{\mathrm{lc}}^{q}(j)),$$

$$L'_{\mathrm{LMC}} = -\sum_{i=1}^{T} \log \frac{h(\nu_{\mathrm{lc}}^{q}(i), m_{\mathrm{lc}}^{q}(i))}{h(\nu_{\mathrm{lc}}^{q}(i), m_{\mathrm{lc}}^{q}(i)) + A(i)}, \tag{6}$$

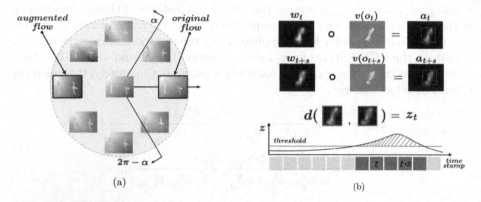

Fig. 3. (a) Illustration of Flow Rotation Augmentation (FRA). We randomly sample one angle from $[\alpha, 2\pi - \alpha]$ and rotate the motion vector. (b) Illustration of Motion Differential Sampling (MDS). The notations are consistent with those in Eq. (9). The foreground regions are highlighted for better viewing. (Color figure online)

where $\hat{m}_{\mathrm{lc}}^{q}$ is the local query feature of the augmented flow. As shown in Fig. 3 (a), the augmented flow shares the same outline but different motion vectors (reflected in different colors) with the original one. The augmentation strategy improves the ability of distinguishing local flows by motion vectors, which is in line with the goal of learning local dynamics.

The final learning objective is a linear combination of the global and local contrastive losses, simply weighted by a hyperparameter λ:

$$L = L_{\mathrm{RGB}} + L_{\mathrm{Flow}} + L_{\mathrm{RF}} + \lambda L'_{\mathrm{LMC}}. \tag{7}$$

3.4   Motion Differential Sampling

Temporal distinct features are expected to be learned after optimizing the above LMC loss. However, if the motion is similar across different timestamps, it is still difficult for the model to distinguish the corresponding local features. To address this issue, Motion Differential Sampling (MDS) is proposed to enhance the training procedure by choosing samples with larger motion differentials in the foreground. More concretely, suppose $o_t = \{x_t, y_t\}$ and $o_{t+s} = \{x_{t+s}, y_{t+s}\}$

are two adjacent flow maps, we calculate the weighted map w_t that coarsely locates the motion foreground at timestamp t as:

$$w_t = \text{softmax}(\text{up\_down}(\text{Sobel}(o_t))), \tag{8}$$

where Sobel$(\cdot)$ is the Sobel operator [40] for motion boundary detection and up_down$(\cdot)$ is a coarsening operator implemented by downsampling and upsampling with stride r, which is set to 28 in practice. Then, the motion differentials in the foreground area can be defined as:

$$\begin{aligned} a_t &= v(o_t) \circ w_t, \ a_{t+s} = v(o_{t+s}) \circ w_{t+s}, \\ z_t &= \text{sum}(d(a_t, a_{t+s})), \end{aligned} \tag{9}$$

where $v(\cdot)$ follows [3] to convert flows into RGB images, $d(\cdot)$ calculates the Euclidean distance along the channel dimension, s is the stride between frames, $\circ$ is the Hadamard product, and sum$(\cdot)$ is the summation operation in the spatial domain. More concretely, at timestamp t, we first calculate the pixel-level distance map between two masked flow maps in the RGB space, and then the differential value z_t is the summation of the distance map. As the samples with larger motion differentials in the foreground contribute more to LMCL, we use the differential value as measurement. For one clip, we take the averaged frame-level differential values as the clip-level score. Finally, MDS is performed by choosing those clips, whose differential values are above the threshold, which is simply the median of the values of all candidate clips in the same video.

4   Experiments

4.1   Datasets

The UCF101 [41] and Kinetics400 (K400) [25] datasets are used for pre-training. To evaluate the action classification task, we conduct experiments on UCF101, HMDB51 [26], as well as Something-Something v2 (SSv2) [13]. As for the video retrieval task, we employ the UCF101 and HMDB51 datasets.

4.2   Experimental Settings

Backbones. For the RGB pathway, we follow the common practice in [4,10] and choose ResNet3D-18 (R3D-18) as the general backbone. We also use S3D [52] as the auxiliary backbone for apple-to-apple comparison with more counterparts. For the flow modality, thanks to its simple appearances, we always use ResNet-18 with 1/8 channels as the backbone.

Pre-training Details. The input clip contains 8 frames with the stride of 16 for K400 and 8 for UCF101, as the latter does not have sufficient frames for large strides. We use a 2-layer MLP like [9] for both pathways. For the RGB inputs, we follow the augmentation in [9] including random grayscale, color jitter, Gaussian blur and horizontal flip. For the motion inputs, we extract flows by

Table 1. Ablation study on different designs of MSCL.

Contrastive losses		LMCL policies		3D	Finetune		Retrival R@1	
L_{RF}	L_{LMC}	FA	MDS		UCF101	SSV2	UCF101	HMDB51
					65.1	39.1	22.0	13.7
✓					71.4	41.0	36.5	22.1
✓				✓	71.2	41.3	35.6	23.6
	✓				70.5	40.3	31.2	19.6
✓	✓				75.6	42.2	45.7	26.7
✓	✓	✓			76.8	42.5	47.3	27.9
✓	✓		✓		76.4	42.6	46.5	27.2
✓	✓	✓	✓		77.3	42.9	48.0	28.1

RAFT [42] and visualize them to 3-channel images. For the consistency in motion information, we copy the flip transforms in RGB inputs to the corresponding motion ones and ignore other augmentations. During training, α is set to $\pi/3$ and the rotation angle keeps consistent in one clip. We set the memory size N to 65,536 and the temperature τ is 0.07. The model is pre-trained with 200 epochs on the K400 training set and 600 epochs on the UCF101 training set (split-1), with a batch size of 128. The initial learning rate is 0.01 and decreased by the cosine schedule [30]. The optimizer is SGD with a momentum of 0.9 and a weight decay of $1e-4$. After pre-training, the RGB backbone is used as initialization parameters for other video tasks. In ablation study, we conduct all experiments on the subset of K400 with 80k videos like [53] and reduce the epochs to 100.

Downstream Tasks. We follow the evaluation protocol in [16], including two types of downstream tasks. (1) Action classification: we add a single layer for classification and then train the full model with both the linear probe and fine-tune policy. We evaluate the top-1 accuracy. (2) Action retrieval: the backbone is directly used for feature extraction and no further training is required. We take the representations of videos from the test set to query the k-nearest neighbours (k-NNs) in the training set and report Recall at k (R@k) for comparison.

4.3 Ablation Study

Motion Sensitive Contrastive Learning. We analyze how different designs contribute to MSCL, including the contrastive losses L_{RF} and L_{LMC} as well as the MDS and FRA strategies. When only L_{RF} is used, we add the experiment with the 3D backbone in the flow pathway, as there is no need to keep the flow features corresponding to very short-term motions without LMCL. The results are summarized in Table 1. The cross-modality contrastive loss L_{RF} and local motion contrastive loss L_{LMC} are complementary. As shown in [51], L_{RF} forces the model to focus on motion areas, which improves the appearance-invariant property (features are activated on motion areas regardless of appearances). Then, L_{LMC} enhances modeling local dynamics, which exhibits consistent performance gains. The comparison also demonstrates the potential of motion information in optical flows, which is not fully explored in recent self-supervised works. MDS and FRA boost the results independently and their combination leads to further improvement. Their contributions lie in different perspectives: MDS provides better training samples for LMCL and FRA aims at motion-related features.

Feature Extractor. Here, we first study the effect of the 2D backbone in the flow pathway. To achieve this, we exchange 2D ResNet-18 with 3D ResNet-18, whose temporal receptive field is enlarged by pooling and convolution. From the results shown in Table 2, we can see that the 3D network delivers the worst performance, due to that zero padding incurs the leakage of the position information as [21] shows, which degrades LMCL. The result of a 3D network without reflect padding is also inferior, which verifies that detailed dynamics in the flow features encoded by 2D CNNs are more crucial to LMCL. We also present the effect of TPN in the RGB pathway. The model without TPN directly uses the conv3 output and adds one more fully-connected layer for consistency in depth. As Table 2 shows, TPN boosts the performance in terms of all the metrics. This can be attributed to the fact that multi-level local features improve the collaboration with global features (from conv5).

Table 2. Ablation study on the feature extractor.

Flow backbone		TPN	Finetune		Retrieval R@1	
Arch	T-pad		UCF101	SSV2	UCF101	HMDB51
R3D-18	Zero		71.3	41.3	35.6	23.6
R3D-18	Reflect		70.7	40.8	33.9	22.1
ResNet-18	Zero		72.3	40.8	38.6	23.9
ResNet-18	Zero	✓	75.6	42.2	45.7	26.7

Interval Sampling. We study the effect of the proposed MDS by ablating the score function. In Table 3, we observe that when combining both the weight and differential maps, the result is significantly improved, much better than either of the single ones. This phenomenon shows that large motion differentials on foreground areas are beneficial for LMCL.

Flow Rotation. Table 4 shows how different rotation ranges influence video representation learning. From the table, we can see that larger ranges usually lead to better results, which is probably due to that augmented flows increase the difficulty of LMCL, making the features focus more on motion dynamics. It is also noteworthy that the performance decreases a bit when the rotation angle is very small. In this case, the augmented flow is similar to the original one, which confuses the contrastive learning procedure.

How LMCL Works? The model can learn to optimize L_{LMC} from two aspects: the motion vector itself and the deformation of the object. We show that LMCL

Table 3. Ablation on sampling methods.   **Table 4.** Ablation on rotation ranges.

Score function	Finetune	
	UCF101	SSV2
–	75.6	42.2
sum(w_t)	75.7	42.2
sum(α_t)	76.1	42.3
sum($\alpha_t \circ w_t$)	76.8	42.5

Rotation range	Finetune	
	UCF101	SSV2
–	75.6	42.2
$[\pi/2, 3\pi/2]$	76.0	42.3
$[\pi/3, 5\pi/3]$	76.8	42.5
$[\pi/6, 11\pi/6]$	76.5	42.4

Table 5. Ablation study on different paradigms for learning motion information.

Flow input	L_{LMC}	Aug.	Finetune		Retrival R@1	
			UCF101	SSV2	UCF101	HMDB51
Flow	Eq. (5)	–	70.5	40.3	31.2	19.6
Boundary	Eq. (5)	–	68.2	39.3	30.2	17.7
–	–	–	65.1	39.1	22.0	13.7
Flow	Eq. (10)	shift	66.9	39.2	27.3	15.7
Flow	Eq. (10)	rotate	66.7	39.4	27.2	14.8
Flow	Eq. (10)	shift+rotate	66.9	39.5	27.2	15.7

indeed takes advantage of both factors. To verify this, we remove L_{RF} and conduct two kinds of experiments. First, we employ the original L_{LMC} without augmentation in Eq. (5), and take the motion boundary (extracted by the Sobel operator [40]) as input. In this manner, motion vectors are removed from the flow map. From Table 5, we can see the motion boundary obtains inferior results compared with the flow input, indicating both vector information and deformation are considered in LMCL. Second, we study the superiority of LMCL in learning motion information. To this end, we conduct experiments which directly learn to recognize these transforms. More concretely, we only use the augmented flows as negative samples, i.e., $A(i)$ in Eq. (6) becomes:

$$A(i) = \sum_{j=1}^{N} h(\nu_{\text{lc}}^q(i), \hat{m}_{j,\text{lc}}^q(i)), \tag{10}$$

where $\hat{m}_{j,\text{lc}}^q(i)$ indicates the local feature of the j-th augmented flow at timestamp i, and N is the number of augmentations, which is set to 3. Note that, different from Eq. (6), the augmented negative sample at each timestamp is independent. To take the deformation into consideration, we use shift with the same padding as the extra augmentation. Table 5 depicts the results, which, interestingly, show negligible improvement. This, once again, verifies the necessity and effectiveness of the proposed LMCL.

4.4   Comparison to State-of-the-Art Methods

Action Classification. We first evaluate our method on the action classification task. The results including the linear probe and fine-tune policy are shown in Table 6. In terms of the K400 pre-training setting, MSCL outperforms previous methods with the same R3D-18 backbone. For the major counterpart, MoDist [51], MSCL can achieve better top-1 accuracies on both datasets with only half of the epochs. We also notice that the results are still lower than those of the methods like CVRL or ρMoCo and the reason lies in that they use the more advanced R3D-50 backbone and more training epochs. When pre-training is applied on UCF101 only, MSCL can achieve better results. We also perform evaluation on the SSv2 dataset in Table 7 and reproduce MoDist [51] under the same training setting, where the results show MSCL outperforms others with a 50.3% top-1 accuracy.

Table 6. Action classification results on UCF101 and HMDB51. 'U+I' denotes the combination of UCF101 and ImageNet. Note that 'Sizes' refer to the test setting.

Method	Network	Year	Dataset	Sizes	Epochs	UCF101	HMDB51
Playback [56]	R18	2020	UCF101	16×112	300	69.0/–	33.7/–
CoCLR [16]	S3D	2020	UCF101	32 × 224	–	81.4/70.2	52.1/39.1
MFO [35]	R18	2021	UCF101	16 × 112	300	76.2/–	44.1/–
TCLR [10]	R18	2021	UCF101	16 × 112	400	82.4/–	52.9/–
SeCo [55]	R50	2021	U+I	–	–	88.2/–	55.5/–
MCL [28]	S3D	2021	U+I	16 × 224	–	90.5/79.8	63.5/–
Ours	R18	–	UCF101	8 × 112	400	82.1/72.5	53.7/39.9
Ours	R18	–	UCF101	16 × 112	400	86.7/77.1	58.9/45.3
TCLR [10]	R18	2021	K400	16 × 112	100	84.1/–	53.6/–
VideoMoCo [32]	R18	2021	K400	32 × 112	200	74.1/–	43.6/–
MFO [35]	R18	2021	K400	16 × 112	100	79.1/63.2	47.6/33.4
LSFD [4]	R18	2021	K400	16 × 112	500	77.2/–	53.7/–
ASCNet [18]	R18	2021	K400	16 × 112	200	80.5/–	52.3/–
MCN [29]	R18	2021	K400	32 × 128	500	89.7/73.1	59.3/42.9
TE [22]	R18	2021	K400	16 × 128	200	87.1/–	63.6/–
MoDist [51]	R18	2021	K400	32 × 112	800	91.3/90.4	62.1/57.5
CVRL [36]	R50	2021	K400	32 × 256	800	92.2/89.2	66.7/57.3
ρMoCo [12]	R50	2021	K400	8 × 256	200	91.0/–	–/–
Ours	R18	–	K400	16 × 112	200	90.7/86.1	62.3/55.6
Ours	R18	–	K400	16 × 112	400	91.5/88.7	62.8/56.5

Table 7. Action classification results on SSv2. [†] denotes our reproduced result.

Method	Network	Year	Dataset	Size	Epochs	Top-1
RSPNet [7]	R18	2021	K400	16×112	50	44.0
MoDist [51][†]	R18	2021	K400	16×112	200	49.1
Ours	R18	–	K400	16×112	200	50.3

Video Retrieval. Similar to the action classification task above, we validate our method with two pre-training datasets and the results are shown in Table 8. On the K400 dataset, our method outperforms the recent state-of-the-art ones with R@1 of 63.7 and 32.6, respectively. On the UCF101 dataset, our method performs better on UCF101 but slightly worse on HMDB51 when compared with the advanced counterpart TE [22]. It is worth noting that MCL [28] applies extra MoCo [17] pre-training on ImageNet, which takes advantage of more training data. These results also demonstrate the effectiveness of MSCL on the retrieval task.

Table 8. Video retrieval performance on UCF101 and HMDB51. [†] indicates additional pretraining on ImageNet is applied.

Method	Network	Year	Dataset	UCF101			HMDB51		
				R@1	R@5	R@10	R@1	R@5	R@10
MemDPC [15]	R18	2020	UCF101	20.2	40.4	52.4	7.7	25.7	40.6
CoCLR [16]	S3D	2020	UCF101	53.3	69.4	82.0	23.2	43.2	53.5
BE [46]	R18	2021	UCF101	11.9	31.3	44.5	–	–	–
TCLR [10]	R18	2021	UCF101	56.2	72.2	79.0	22.8	45.4	57.8
MFO [35]	R18	2021	UCF101	39.6	57.6	69.2	18.8	39.2	51.0
MCN [29]	R18	2021	UCF101	53.8	70.2	78.3	24.1	46.8	59.7
TE [22]	R18	2021	UCF101	63.6	79.0	84.8	32.2	61.3	71.6
MCL [28][†]	S3D	2021	UCF101	67.0	80.8	86.3	26.7	52.5	67.0
Ours	S3D	–	UCF101	63.2	78.7	83.9	25.8	52.1	66.5
Ours	R18	–	UCF101	65.6	80.3	86.1	28.9	56.2	68.3
SpeedNet [5]	S3D	2020	K400	13.0	28.1	37.5	–	–	–
STS [44]	R18	2021	K400	38.3	59.9	68.9	18.0	37.2	50.7
MFO [35]	R18	2021	K400	41.5	60.6	71.2	20.7	40.8	55.2
LSFD [4]	R18	2021	K400	44.9	64.0	73.2	26.7	54.7	66.4
Ours	R18	–	K400	63.7	79.1	84.0	32.6	58.5	70.5

5   Conclusion

In this work, we propose a self-supervised learning framework, namely MSCL, to build motion sensitive video representations. We perform clip-level contrastive learning with intra-modality and inter-modality losses as well as frame-level contrastive learning LMCL to inject motion dynamics from optical flows into RGB frames. Moreover, FRA and MDS are developed to further enhance the contrastive learning procedure by providing better motion-related features and training samples, respectively. Extensive experiments on standard benchmarks show that our MSCL leads to significant performance gains over state-of-the-art methods in terms of two downstream tasks.

Acknowledgment. This work is partly supported by the National Natural Science Foundation of China (62022011), the Research Program of State Key Laboratory of Software Development Environment (SKLSDE-2021ZX-04), and the Fundamental Research Funds for the Central Universities.

References

1. Abu-El-Haija, S., et al.: YouTube-8M: a large-scale video classification benchmark. arXiv preprint arXiv:1609.08675 (2016)
2. Ahsan, U., Madhok, R., Essa, I.: Video jigsaw: unsupervised learning of spatiotemporal context for video action recognition. In: WACV, pp. 179–189. IEEE (2019)
3. Baker, S., Scharstein, D., Lewis, J., Roth, S., Black, M.J., Szeliski, R.: A database and evaluation methodology for optical flow. IJCV **92**(1), 1–31 (2011)
4. Behrmann, N., Fayyaz, M., Gall, J., Noroozi, M.: Long short view feature decomposition via contrastive video representation learning. In: ICCV, pp. 9244–9253 (2021)
5. Benaim, S., et al.: SpeedNet: learning the speediness in videos. In: CVPR, pp. 9922–9931 (2020)
6. Caron, M., Misra, I., Mairal, J., Goyal, P., Bojanowski, P., Joulin, A.: Unsupervised learning of visual features by contrasting cluster assignments. In: NeurIPS 33, pp. 9912–9924 (2020)
7. Chen, P., et al.: RSPNet: relative speed perception for unsupervised video representation learning. In: AAAI, vol. 1, p. 5 (2021)
8. Chen, T., Kornblith, S., Norouzi, M., Hinton, G.: A simple framework for contrastive learning of visual representations. In: ICML, pp. 1597–1607. PMLR (2020)
9. Chen, X., Fan, H., Girshick, R., He, K.: Improved baselines with momentum contrastive learning. arXiv preprint arXiv:2003.04297 (2020)
10. Dave, I., Gupta, R., Rizve, M.N., Shah, M.: TCLR: temporal contrastive learning for video representation. arXiv preprint arXiv:2101.07974 (2021)
11. Feichtenhofer, C., Fan, H., Malik, J., He, K.: SlowFast networks for video recognition. In: ICCV, pp. 6202–6211 (2019)
12. Feichtenhofer, C., Fan, H., Xiong, B., Girshick, R., He, K.: A large-scale study on unsupervised spatiotemporal representation learning. In: CVPR, pp. 3299–3309 (2021)

13. Goyal, R., et al.: The "something something" video database for learning and evaluating visual common sense. In: ICCV, pp. 5842–5850 (2017)

14. Grill, J.B., et al.: Bootstrap your own latent-a new approach to self-supervised learning. In: NeurIPS 33, pp. 21271–21284 (2020)

15. Han, T., Xie, W., Zisserman, A.: Memory-augmented dense predictive coding for video representation learning. In: Vedaldi, A., Bischof, H., Brox, T., Frahm, J.-M. (eds.) ECCV 2020. LNCS, vol. 12348, pp. 312–329. Springer, Cham (2020). https://doi.org/10.1007/978-3-030-58580-8_19

16. Han, T., Xie, W., Zisserman, A.: Self-supervised co-training for video representation learning. In: NeurIPS 33, pp. 5679–5690 (2020)

17. He, K., Fan, H., Wu, Y., Xie, S., Girshick, R.: Momentum contrast for unsupervised visual representation learning. In: CVPR, pp. 9729–9738 (2020)

18. Huang, D., et al.: ASCNet: self-supervised video representation learning with appearance-speed consistency. In: ICCV, pp. 8096–8105 (2021)

19. Huang, Z., Zhang, S., Jiang, J., Tang, M., Jin, R., Ang, M.H.: Self-supervised motion learning from static images. In: CVPR, pp. 1276–1285 (2021)

20. Huo, Y., et al.: Self-supervised video representation learning with constrained spatiotemporal jigsaw. In: IJCAI, pp. 751–757, August 2021. https://doi.org/10.24963/ijcai.2021/104

21. Islam, M.A., Jia, S., Bruce, N.D.: How much position information do convolutional neural networks encode? arXiv preprint arXiv:2001.08248 (2020)

22. Jenni, S., Jin, H.: Time-equivariant contrastive video representation learning. In: ICCV, pp. 9970–9980 (2021)

23. Jhuang, H., Gall, J., Zuffi, S., Schmid, C., Black, M.J.: Towards understanding action recognition. In: ICCV, pp. 3192–3199 (2013)

24. Jiang, B., Wang, M., Gan, W., Wu, W., Yan, J.: STM: spatiotemporal and motion encoding for action recognition. In: ICCV, pp. 2000–2009 (2019)

25. Kay, W., et al.: The kinetics human action video dataset. arXiv preprint arXiv:1705.06950 (2017)

26. Kuehne, H., Jhuang, H., Garrote, E., Poggio, T., Serre, T.: HMDB: a large video database for human motion recognition. In: ICCV, pp. 2556–2563. IEEE (2011)

27. Lee, H.Y., Huang, J.B., Singh, M., Yang, M.H.: Unsupervised representation learning by sorting sequences. In: ICCV, pp. 667–676 (2017)

28. Li, R., Zhang, Y., Qiu, Z., Yao, T., Liu, D., Mei, T.: Motion-focused contrastive learning of video representations. In: ICCV, pp. 2105–2114 (2021)

29. Lin, Y., Guo, X., Lu, Y.: Self-supervised video representation learning with meta-contrastive network. In: ICCV, pp. 8239–8249 (2021)

30. Loshchilov, I., Hutter, F.: SGDR: stochastic gradient descent with warm restarts. arXiv preprint arXiv:1608.03983 (2016)

31. Van den Oord, A., Li, Y., Vinyals, O.: Representation learning with contrastive predictive coding. arXiv e-prints pp. arXiv-1807 (2018)

32. Pan, T., Song, Y., Yang, T., Jiang, W., Liu, W.: VideoMoCo: contrastive video representation learning with temporally adversarial examples. In: CVPR, pp. 11205–11214 (2021)

33. Patrick, M., et al.: On compositions of transformations in contrastive self-supervised learning. In: ICCV, pp. 9577–9587 (2021)

34. Patrick, M., et al.: Space-time crop & attend: improving cross-modal video representation learning. In: ICCV, pp. 10560–10572 (2021)

35. Qian, R., et al.: Enhancing self-supervised video representation learning via multi-level feature optimization. In: ICCV, pp. 7990–8001 (2021)

36. Qian, R., et al.: Spatiotemporal contrastive video representation learning. In: CVPR, pp. 6964–6974 (2021)
37. Recasens, A., et al.: Broaden your views for self-supervised video learning. In: ICCV, pp. 1255–1265 (2021)
38. Sevilla-Lara, L., Liao, Y., Güney, F., Jampani, V., Geiger, A., Black, M.J.: On the integration of optical flow and action recognition. In: Brox, T., Bruhn, A., Fritz, M. (eds.) GCPR 2018. LNCS, vol. 11269, pp. 281–297. Springer, Cham (2019). https://doi.org/10.1007/978-3-030-12939-2_20
39. Simonyan, K., Zisserman, A.: Two-stream convolutional networks for action recognition in videos. In: NeurIPS 27 (2014)
40. Sobel, I.: History and definition of the Sobel operator. Retrieved from the World Wide Web 1505 (2014)
41. Soomro, K., Zamir, A.R., Shah, M.: UCF101: a dataset of 101 human actions classes from videos in the wild. arXiv preprint arXiv:1212.0402 (2012)
42. Teed, Z., Deng, J.: RAFT: recurrent all-pairs field transforms for optical flow. In: Vedaldi, A., Bischof, H., Brox, T., Frahm, J.-M. (eds.) ECCV 2020. LNCS, vol. 12347, pp. 402–419. Springer, Cham (2020). https://doi.org/10.1007/978-3-030-58536-5_24
43. Tran, D., Wang, H., Torresani, L., Ray, J., LeCun, Y., Paluri, M.: A closer look at spatiotemporal convolutions for action recognition. In: CVPR, pp. 6450–6459 (2018)
44. Wang, J., Jiao, J., Bao, L., He, S., Liu, W., Liu, Y.H.: Self-supervised video representation learning by uncovering spatio-temporal statistics. IEEE TPAMI **44**, 3791–3806 (2021)
45. Wang, J., Jiao, J., Liu, Y.-H.: Self-supervised video representation learning by pace prediction. In: Vedaldi, A., Bischof, H., Brox, T., Frahm, J.-M. (eds.) ECCV 2020. LNCS, vol. 12362, pp. 504–521. Springer, Cham (2020). https://doi.org/10.1007/978-3-030-58520-4_30
46. Wang, J., et al.: Removing the background by adding the background: towards background robust self-supervised video representation learning. In: CVPR, pp. 11804–11813 (2021)
47. Wang, L., Tong, Z., Ji, B., Wu, G.: TDN: temporal difference networks for efficient action recognition. In: CVPR, pp. 1895–1904 (2021)
48. Weng, J., et al.: Temporal distinct representation learning for action recognition. In: Vedaldi, A., Bischof, H., Brox, T., Frahm, J.-M. (eds.) ECCV 2020. LNCS, vol. 12352, pp. 363–378. Springer, Cham (2020). https://doi.org/10.1007/978-3-030-58571-6_22
49. Wiskott, L., Sejnowski, T.J.: Slow feature analysis: unsupervised learning of invariances. Neural Comput. **14**(4), 715–770 (2002)
50. Wu, Z., Xiong, Y., Yu, S.X., Lin, D.: Unsupervised feature learning via nonparametric instance discrimination. In: CVPR, pp. 3733–3742 (2018)
51. Xiao, F., Tighe, J., Modolo, D.: MoDist: motion distillation for self-supervised video representation learning. arXiv preprint arXiv:2106.09703 (2021)
52. Xie, S., Sun, C., Huang, J., Tu, Z., Murphy, K.: Rethinking spatiotemporal feature learning for video understanding. arXiv preprint arXiv:1712.04851 1(2), 5 (2017)
53. Xie, S., Sun, C., Huang, J., Tu, Z., Murphy, K.: Rethinking spatiotemporal feature learning: speed-accuracy trade-offs in video classification. In: Ferrari, V., Hebert, M., Sminchisescu, C., Weiss, Y. (eds.) ECCV 2018. LNCS, vol. 11219, pp. 318–335. Springer, Cham (2018). https://doi.org/10.1007/978-3-030-01267-0_19
54. Yang, C., Xu, Y., Shi, J., Dai, B., Zhou, B.: Temporal pyramid network for action recognition. In: CVPR, pp. 591–600 (2020)

55. Yao, T., Zhang, Y., Qiu, Z., Pan, Y., Mei, T.: SeCo: exploring sequence supervision for unsupervised representation learning. In: AAAI, vol. 2, p. 7 (2021)

56. Yao, Y., Liu, C., Luo, D., Zhou, Y., Ye, Q.: Video playback rate perception for self-supervised spatio-temporal representation learning. In: CVPR, pp. 6548–6557 (2020)

Dynamic Temporal Filtering in Video Models

Fuchen Long[1], Zhaofan Qiu[1], Yingwei Pan[1(✉)], Ting Yao[1], Chong-Wah Ngo[2], and Tao Mei[1]

[1] JD Explore Academy, Beijing, China
longfc.ustc@gmail.com, zhaofanqiu@gmail.com, panyw.ustc@gmail.com,
tingyao.ustc@gmail.com, tmei@jd.com
[2] Singapore Management University, Singapore, Singapore
cwngo@smu.edu.sg

Abstract. Video temporal dynamics is conventionally modeled with 3D spatial-temporal kernel or its factorized version comprised of 2D spatial kernel and 1D temporal kernel. The modeling power, nevertheless, is limited by the fixed window size and static weights of a kernel along the temporal dimension. The pre-determined kernel size severely limits the temporal receptive fields and the fixed weights treat each spatial location across frames equally, resulting in sub-optimal solution for long-range temporal modeling in natural scenes. In this paper, we present a new recipe of temporal feature learning, namely Dynamic Temporal Filter (DTF), that novelly performs spatial-aware temporal modeling in frequency domain with large temporal receptive field. Specifically, DTF dynamically learns a specialized frequency filter for every spatial location to model its long-range temporal dynamics. Meanwhile, the temporal feature of each spatial location is also transformed into frequency feature spectrum via 1D Fast Fourier Transform (FFT). The spectrum is modulated by the learnt frequency filter, and then transformed back to temporal domain with inverse FFT. In addition, to facilitate the learning of frequency filter in DTF, we perform frame-wise aggregation to enhance the primary temporal feature with its temporal neighbors by inter-frame correlation. It is feasible to plug DTF block into ConvNets and Transformer, yielding DTF-Net and DTF-Transformer. Extensive experiments conducted on three datasets demonstrate the superiority of our proposals. More remarkably, DTF-Transformer achieves an accuracy of 83.5% on Kinetics-400 dataset. Source code is available at https://github.com/FuchenUSTC/DTF.

1 Introduction

Video is an electronic carrier that records the evolution of moving persons or objects. Modeling such evolution with time is essential to the understanding

---

F. Long and Z. Qiu—Contributed equally to this work.

© The Author(s), under exclusive license to Springer Nature Switzerland AG 2022
S. Avidan et al. (Eds.): ECCV 2022, LNCS 13695, pp. 475–492, 2022.
https://doi.org/10.1007/978-3-031-19833-5_28

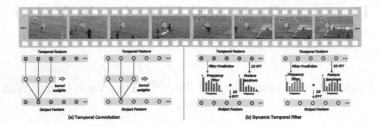

Fig. 1. Modeling the temporal evolution of two spatial regions (marked in pink and orange on the filmstrip) via (a) temporal convolution and (b) our DTF. (Color figure online)

of motion patterns in videos. The recent advances generally hinge on temporal convolution for temporal modeling in video models. Furthermore, the common recipe is to integrate temporal convolution into space-time 3D convolution [16,50] or explicitly utilize temporal convolution to co-work with spatial convolution. Figure 1(a) conceptually depicts the temporal modeling processes with 1D temporal convolution for two different spatial locations within the input video. The temporal convolution locally aggregates the features of the same spatial location in adjacent frames. The temporal receptive field is thus fixed and the corresponding kernel weights are the same across different spatial locations. This setting inevitably limits the temporal receptive field and ignores the inherent differences of spatial contexts at varied locations during temporal modeling. Figure 1 illustrates two spatial locations exhibiting different spatial contents: the pink dot refers to the track in the static background, while the orange dot shows a person moving rapidly across a constantly changing background. As the evolutions of spatial locations correspond to motion patterns specific to different movements, an optimal way of modeling is by having different kernels with varying size and weights that characterize their respective spatial context with sufficient temporal receptive field. Having the same kernel filters over different spatial locations will hurt the mining of long-range temporal dependency.

In this paper, we propose to mitigate these issues by formulating the temporal feature learning in the frequency domain, pursuing a dynamic spatial-aware temporal modeling with an enlarged temporal receptive field. Specifically, we design a dynamic temporal filter (see Fig. 1(b)) to characterize temporal evolution by learning frequency filter to adaptively modulate the spectrum of temporal features at different spatial locations. According to the convolution theorem [39], the point-wise multiplication of spectrums in frequency domain of two signals is equivalent to the temporal convolution between them. As such, considering that the learnt specialized frequency filter operates over all the frequencies, this frequency filter can be interpreted as a temporal convolution with a larger kernel size. The design nicely enhances the mining of long-term temporal dependency in the frequency domain, without increasing computational/memory overhead. Meanwhile, in an effort to deal with different contexts of spatial locations, we dynamically learn a specialized frequency filter for each spatial location based on its temporal features across time. Furthermore, frame-wise aggregation is uniquely exploited to strengthen the primary temporal feature of each location by accumulating its temporal neighbors with inter-frame attention, thereby facilitating the learning of frequency filter.

By the frequency domain temporal modeling conditioned on the dynamic change of spatial contexts, we present a novel Dynamic Temporal Filter (DTF) block in video models. Technically, we regard the features sliced across frames at a fixed spatial location as the temporal feature. In order to enhance the primary temporal feature, we measure the temporal correlation between adjacent frames to estimate the motion clues, which are further utilized for aggregating temporal neighbors with inter-frame correlation. With this enhanced temporal feature, the specialized frequency filter can be more effectively learnt to capture context surrounding a spatial location. At the same time, DTF converts the enhanced temporal feature of each spatial location into frequency feature spectrum via Fast Fourier Transform (FFT), which is further multiplied with the learnt frequency filter. Finally, inverse FFT is employed to reconstruct the temporal features from the modulated feature spectrum in frequency domain.

The DTF block can be viewed as a principled temporal modeling module, and is an alternative to standard 1D temporal convolution in the existing video backbones, such as CNN-based model or Transformer-based model, with favorable computation overhead. By directly inserting DTF block into the conventional 2D ResNet [15] and Swin Transformer [28], we construct two kinds of new video backbones, i.e., DTF-Net and DTF-Transformer. Through extensive experiments over a series of action recognition benchmarks, we show that our DTF-Net and DTF-Transformer outperform the state-of-the-art video backbones.

2 Related Work

We group the recent temporal modeling techniques into two directions: hand-crafted based methods and deep model based methods, where the latter group can be further categorized into CNN-based and Transformer-based approaches.

Hand-Crafted Video Modeling. The early works [19,21,22,44] construct hand-crafted video feature in two steps: detecting spatial-temporal interest points and formulating it by local descriptors. Trajectory is then adopted to convey motion cues. One is dense trajectory [54] that samples local patch-wise features at various scales and tracks them through optical flow. Nevertheless, such features are not optimized, thereby hardly to be generalized across different tasks.

CNN-Based Video Modeling. Early attempts for video CNN commonly apply 2D CNN for video input. Karpathy et al. [18] leverage spatial CNN to learn video representation by temporally stacking frame-level features. Two stream model [46] is adopted to employ 2D CNN over the inputs of visual frames and optical flow separately. Many variants [6,12,57,62] extend it in different aspects. To address the long-range modeling issue ignored by two stream models, LSTM-based networks [38,47] are proposed to capture temporal dynamics in videos. The above approaches only treat video as a sequence of frames, but leaving the pixel-level temporal evolution across consecutive frames unexploited. The pioneering work of 3D CNN (C3D [50]) is thus proposed to alleviate this issue. Furthermore, most subsequent research works [3,10,34,40,42,52,61,64] found that disentangling spatial and temporal convolution leads to better performances against original 3D convolution and presents good generalization ability on localization tasks [32,33,35]. However, CNN-based methods still face the challenge of long-range modeling and fail to handle the inherent differences of spatial contexts.

Transformer-Based Video Modeling. Inspired by the success of Vision Transformer (ViT) [7] in image recognition, a series of Transformer-based backbones start to emerge. Various variants [14,25,28,43,49,63] validated the power of self-attention for image feature learning. Similarly, the popularity of image Transformer leads to the investigation of the video Transformer architectures [1,2,8,29, 31]. TimeSformer [2] explores five different structures of space-time attention and suggests a factorized version for speed-accuracy tradeoff. MViT [8] further provides an alternative that formulates the video Transformer in a multi-scale manner. The pyramid features of MViT capture low-level visual information and high-level complex information. Our DTF block is a temporal modeling primitive and can be readily pluggable to the 2D Transformer for video learning.

In short, our work belongs to the deep model based video modeling. Unlike the traditional temporal convolution with a fixed kernel size that treats each spatial location equally, DTF performs convolution by dynamic spectrum filtering of each location in frequency domain with an enlarged receptive field. Moreover, DTF block enhances the primary temporal features through frame-wise feature aggregation and provides additional motion clues for frequency filter prediction.

3   Approach

We introduce a new Dynamic Temporal Filter (DTF) for temporal modeling. Motivated by convolution theorem, DTF aims to convert temporal convolution to spectrum filtering in frequency domain. Concretely, a novel temporal feature learning block, i.e., DTF block, is designed to perform such spectrum filtering for every spatial location in a video. The frequency filter is location-dependent for exploiting over-time contexts. By plugging DTF block into CNN and Transformer, we derive two video backbones, i.e., DTF-Net and DTF-Transformer.

3.1   Preliminaries: Convolution Theorem

To better understand the spirit of our DTF design, we first revisit the convolution theorem [39] in digital signal processing field. Formally, given a sequence of T points feature signals ($f[t], 0 \le t \le T-1$), its discrete spectrum $S[k]$ is calculated by Discrete Fourier Transform (DFT) as follows:

$$S[k] = \sum_{t=0}^{T-1} f[t]e^{-j(2\pi/T)kt}, \ 0 \le k \le T - 1, \tag{1}$$

where j is the imaginary unit. Here DFT is a kind of one-to-one orthogonality decomposition. Furthermore, based on the DFT outputs, inverse DFT (IDFT) is able to reconstruct the input signals:

$$f[t] = \frac{1}{T} \sum_{k=0}^{T-1} S[k] e^{j(2\pi/T)kt}, \ 0 \le t \le T - 1. \tag{2}$$

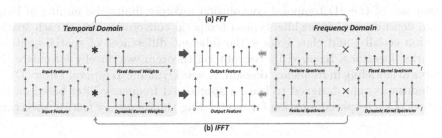

Fig. 2. Illustration of (a) transformation from 1D convolution learning with a fixed kernel to the equivalent spectrum filtering in frequency domain via FFT (upper), and (b) transformation from spectrum filtering in frequency domain to the equivalent 1D convolution learning with a dynamic kernel via IFFT (lower). The temporal feature signals (and its' spectrum) and 1D convolution kernel (and its' spectrum) are represented as blue and red points, respectively. (Color figure online)

Similarly, we achieve the spectrum $S_c[k]$ of the convolution kernel signal $f_c[t]$ via Fourier Transform. The convolution theorem states that the Fourier Transform of a convolution of two signals is equivalent to the product of their Fourier Transformers. As shown in Fig. 2, the output feature of convolution learning between the input feature and 1D kernel in temporal domain can be also learnt by the multiplication between their transformed spectrum through IDFT:

$$f[t] * f_c[t] = IDFT(S[k] \times S_c[k]), \tag{3}$$

where $*$ and $\times$ denotes convolution and element-wise multiplication, respectively.

Given a real convolution kernel with fixed size, the corresponding kernel spectrum is conjugate symmetric (see the top-right part in Fig. 2). This implies that only half of the spectrum points $(M = \lfloor T/2 \rfloor + 1)$ are capable of covering all information of frequency property. In other words, there exists information redundancy in kernel spectrum. To address this issue, we propose to learn a dynamic filter in frequency domain to modulate the feature spectrum. Specifically, as depicted in Fig. 2 (lower part), when multiplying the frequency feature spectrum with a frequency filter (i.e., kernel spectrum with varied contents in all frequencies), this process is equivalent to the convolution learning between input feature and dynamic kernel with an enlarged temporal receptive field.

For implementation of DFT, the Fast Fourier Transform (FFT) is commonly employed for engineering. The corresponding inverse DFT is thus implemented as inverse Fast Fourier Transform (IFFT). Thus, we choose FFT and IFFT as the basic transformation in the architecture of our Dynamic Temporal Filter.

3.2   Dynamic Temporal Filter (DTF)

Most existing temporal modeling approaches employ 1D temporal convolution to perform pixel-level aggregation across frames. Nevertheless, the pre-determined kernel size of the 1D temporal convolution severely limits the mining of long-range dependency. Meanwhile, typical temporal convolution treats each spatial position equally, and thus ignores the inherent differences of spatial contexts at varied locations. Inspired by convolution theorem, we novelly formulate the temporal modeling in frequency domain. A new Dynamic Temporal Filter (DTF) mechanism is thus designed to learn a specialized frequency filter based on the context of each spatial location for modulating the frequency feature spectrum.

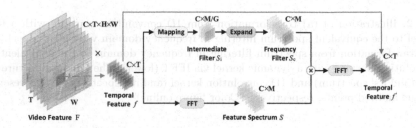

Fig. 3. Illustration of Dynamic Temporal Filter (DTF) mechanism.

Here we introduce the detailed formulation of DTF mechanism (see Fig. 3). Let F be the input 3D feature map with the size of $C \times T \times H \times W$, where C, $H \times W$, and T denotes the channels size, spatial size and temporal length, respectively. For each spatial location, we take the feature cube across time at that location in F as the temporal feature $f \in \mathbb{R}^{C \times T}$. For each channel in f, we apply Fast Fourier Transform (FFT) along the temporal dimension to obtain the whole feature spectrum $S \in \mathbb{C}^{C \times M}$. Please note that the point number of the spectrum of a real signal is $M = \lfloor T/2 \rfloor + 1$ and it is in the field of the complex numbers. Meanwhile, a specialized frequency filter $S_c \in \mathbb{C}^{C \times M}$ is learnt conditioned on the temporal feature f. It is natural to implement the estimator of frequency filter as a fully connected layer. However, directly predicting the frequency filter through linear mapping requires heavy memory overhead ($C^2 \times T \times M$ parameters). Hence we take the inspiration from group convolution, and significantly reduce the parameters of estimator by sharing some temporal filters across channels. Most specifically, we first project f into the intermediate filter $S_i \in \mathbb{C}^{C \times M/G}$, where the number of channels is decreased by a factor of G. After that, S_i is expanded along the channel dimension to achieve the complete frequency filter S_c. Next, we modulate the frequency feature spectrum S by multiplying it with the learnt frequency filter S_c, leading to the modulated feature spectrum S':

$$S' = S \times S_c. \tag{4}$$

Then, we adopt the inverse FFT to transform the modulated spectrum S' into the video feature f' in the temporal domain:

$$f' = IFFT(S').$$ (5)

Finally, the output temporal feature f_o of DTF is achieved by fusing the original temporal feature f and the modulated temporal feature f' as $f_o = f + f'$.

Accordingly, DTF mechanism triggers temporal modeling in the frequency domain by modulating the spectrum of temporal features with the learnt frequency filters. Compared to traditional 1D temporal convolution with fixed kernel size, the enlarged temporal receptive field derived from a learnt frequency filter in DTF strengthens the long-range dependency modeling. Moreover, unlike using the same kernel weights in 1D temporal convolution for all spatial locations, our DTF learns specialized frequency filter based on the different context of each spatial location, pursuing a dynamic spatial-aware temporal modeling.

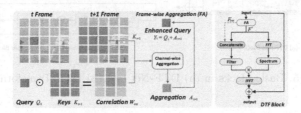

Fig. 4. The architectures of Frame-wise Aggregation (FA) and our DTF block.

3.3   DTF Block

Recall that our DTF mechanism characterizes the temporal evolution of each same spatial location across time in frequency domain by learning spatial-aware frequency filter. However, this way inevitably ignores the rich contextual information between each spatial location and its temporal neighbors in adjacent frames for temporal modeling. To alleviate this issue, we devise a DTF Block that capitalizes on a self-attention based frame-wise aggregation (FA) approach before DTF mechanism to enhance temporal features, which also provides additional motion clues to boost the learning of frequency filters.

Technically, inspired by self-attention learning [53,58], we first strengthen primary temporal feature of each spatial location by exploring inter-frame interaction and aggregating its temporal neighbors in adjacent frames. Figure 4 (left) details the process of the frame-wise aggregation in DTF block. Specifically, given the input 3D feature map $F \in \mathbb{R}^{C \times T \times H \times W}$, we take the feature at spatial location (x, y) of t-th frame as the query $Q_t \in \mathbb{R}^C$. For Q_t, all its temporal neighbors in $(t+1)$-th frame within the local region ($k \times k$ grid) centered at (x, y) are set as keys $K_{t+1} \in \mathbb{R}^{C \times \{k \times k\}}$. After that, we achieve the inter-frame correlation matrix $\mathbf{W}_{cor} \in \mathbb{R}^{1 \times \{k \times k\}}$ via self-attention:

$$\mathbf{W}_{cor} = Q_t \odot K_{t+1},$$ (6)

where $\odot$ is the matrix multiplication that measures the similarity between query Q_t and its' temporal neighbors K_{t+1} within the region of $k \times k$ grid. We further utilize the inter-frame correlation matrix as the attention weights to aggregate temporal neighbors K_{t+1} within the $(t+1)$-th frames as follows:

$$A_{t+1} = \mathbf{W}_{cor} \odot [K_{t+1}]^{Tr}, \tag{7}$$

where A_{t+1} is the aggregated temporal feature and $[\cdot]^{Tr}$ denotes the operation of matrix transposition. The aggregated feature is further employed to strengthen the query feature, and the enhanced query feature Y_t is thus measured as:

$$Y_t = Q_t + A_{t+1}. \tag{8}$$

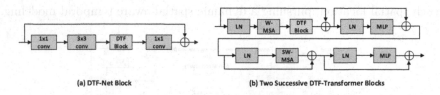

(a) DTF-Net Block   (b) Two Successive DTF-Transformer Blocks

Fig. 5. Basic blocks in (a) DTF-Net and (b) DTF-Transformer.

We operate frame-wise aggregation between every pair of consecutive frames, yielding the enhanced video representation $F' \in \mathbb{R}^{C \times T \times H \times W}$. Next, DTF mechanism takes the enhanced temporal feature F' as inputs, and transforms it into feature spectrum via FFT for frequency modulation. Considering that the inter-frame correlation $\mathbf{W}_{cor}$ reflects the pixel-level displacement information, we exploit it as additional guidance to strengthen the learning of frequency filter. In particular, as shown in Fig. 4 (right), DTF block directly squeezes the learnt correlation weights $\mathbf{W}_{cor}$ of all the temporal neighbors in FA as the correlation feature $F_{cor} \in \mathbb{R}^{k^2 \times T \times H \times W}$. Then, the enhanced temporal feature F' is concatenated with the correlation feature F_{cor} for learning the specialized temporal filter of each spatial location. In this way, DTF block additionally mines the motion clues from the correlation feature in FA to facilitate frequency filter prediction.

3.4   Video Backbones with DTF Block

Our DTF block is readily pluggable to existing 2D CNN or Vision Transformer to upgrade the vision backbones for video temporal modeling. Here we present how to insert DTF block into ResNet [15] and Swin Transformer [28]. Figure 5 depicts two different constructions of DTF block in building block in ResNet/Swin Transformer, namely DTF-Net and DTF-Transformer, respectively.

DTF-Net. Most of video architecture advances [3,41,52,61] typically factorize the conventional 3D convolution into 2D spatial convolution and 1D temporal convolution, and the 1D temporal convolution is commonly integrated after the spatial convolutional layers of 2D CNN for temporal modeling across frames. We follow this recipe and construct the DTF-Net by inserting DTF-Block after the 3×3 convolution within each basic residual building block in ResNet [15]. Based on the output feature of the final residual building block, the global pooling is employed to achieve the clip-level feature for video representation learning.

DTF-Transformer. Recently, the Transformer-style architectures with self-attention [7,28] have emerged as powerful backbones in compute vision field. Inspired by this, we further integrate DTF block into the Swin-Transformer [28] to build the Transformer-style video backbone, named as DTF-Transformer. Specifically, for every two successive Swin Transformer blocks in Swin Transformer, we directly plug the DTF block after the multi-head self-attention module with regular window (W-MSA), leading to the two successive DTF-Transformer building block. Here we reshape the output patch sequence of W-MSA module into the sequence of frame feature map with the normal size $(C \times T \times H \times W)$, and then feed it into the DTF block. Global pooling is utilized to obtain clip-level feature.

4 Experiments

4.1 Datasets and Implementation Details

Datasets. We empirically evaluate the effectiveness of our proposed video backbones (DTF-Net and DTF-Transformer) on three datasets, i.e., **Kinetics-400** [3], **Something-Something V1 and V2** [13]. The Kinetics-400 dataset is composed of 300K videos derived from 400 action categories. Each video is 10-seconds short clip cropped from the raw YouTube video. We split all the 300K videos into 240K, 20K, 40K for training, validation and testing, respectively. Something-Something V1 and V2 datasets include about 108K and 221K videos over 174 action categories. For Something-Something V1 and V2, there are 86K/11.5K/11K and 169K/25K/27K videos in the training/validation/testing set, respectively.

Network Training. We implement our proposal on PyTorch framework. The mini-batch Stochastic Gradient Descent (SGD) algorithm with cosine learning rate [36] is utilized for network optimization. The resolution of each frame is fixed as 224×224, which is randomly cropped from the video clip resized with the short size in [256, 340]. We set the input clip length within the range from 16 to 64. Each clip is randomly flipped along horizontal direction for data augmentation, except for Something-Something V1 and V2 in view of the direction-related classes. We set the size of the local region k and the factor G in DTF block as 3 and 16. The base learning rate is 0.04 for DTF-Net and 0.01 for DTF-Transformer, respectively. The dropout ratio is fixed as 0.5. The maximum training epoch number is 128/64 for Kinetics-40/Something-Something datasets. The mini-batch size and the weight decay parameter is 256 and 0.0001.

Network Inference. Two kinds of inference strategies are adopted to evaluate DTF-Net and DTF-Transformer. For DTF-Net, we follow the 3-crop strategy [11] to crop three 256×256 regions from each clip at inference. The video-level prediction is calculated by averaging all scores from 10 uniform sampled clips. For DTF-Transformer, we directly measure the video-level score based on the 4 uniform sampled clips. The 3-crop strategy is also adopted for score fusion.

4.2   Ablation Study on DTF Block

Here we perform ablation studies to examine each technical choice in DTF block of DTF-Net. Note that DTF-Net is constructed based on the ResNet-50, and we report the top-1 and top-5 accuracy on the validation set of Kinetics-400.

Dynamic Temporal Filter. We first evaluate how each design in our DTF block influences the overall performance of DTF-Net. Table 1a details the performance comparisons among different variants of DTF block. Note that all runs here are implemented by inserting DTF variants into the basic residual blocks at res_5 stage of ResNet-50. The run of **2D-ResNet** is regarded as a basic 2D bottleneck residual block and there is no temporal modeling. By integrating the basic block with the conventional temporal 1D convolution [52], $\mathbf{DTF}_{1d}$ obtains better performances, which demonstrate the advantage of temporally pixel-wise feature aggregation for motion modeling. Nevertheless, such operation employs the fixed weights over the feature cube of each spatial location. Instead, $\mathbf{DTF}_{1d+}$ learns

Table 1. Ablation study on DTF block in DTF-Net with 16-frame inputs on Kinetics-400 dataset. Top-1 and Top-5 accuracy (%), and the computational cost (estimated by GFLOPs) for forwarding one clip at inference are reported.

(a) **Dynamic Temporal Filter.** Comparisons among different variants of DTF. All runs are built by plugging each block into res_5 stage of ResNet-50.

Model	GFLOPs	Top-1	Top-5
2D-ResNet	23	72.0	90.3
DTF_{1d}	25	73.2	90.7
DTF_{1d+}	28	74.2	91.6
DTF_F	23	75.0	92.2
DTF	24	75.7	92.9

(b) **Frame-wise Aggregation.** Effect investigation of frame-wise aggregation and the correlation feature in DTF block. All runs are constructed by plugging each block into res_5 stage of ResNet-50.

Model		GFLOPs	Top-1	Top-5
Aggregation	Correlation			
DTF-baseline		23	74.9	92.3
✓		24	75.4	92.6
	✓	24	75.2	92.5
✓	✓	24	75.7	92.9

(c) **Location of DTF in DTF-Net.** Effect of plugging DTF blocks into different stages of ResNet-50.

Stage				GFLOPs	Top-1	Top-5
res_2	res_3	res_4	res_5			
2D-ResNet				23	72.0	90.3
			✓	24	75.7	92.9
		✓	✓	24	76.5	93.0
	✓	✓	✓	25	77.1	93.1
✓	✓	✓	✓	25	**77.7**	**93.2**

(d) **Temporal Modeling.** Comparisons among different temporal modeling methods based on ResNet-50 backbone.

Temporal Modeling	GFLOPs	Top-1	Top-5
2D-ResNet	23	72.0	90.3
Temporal Conv [52]	33	74.6	91.5
Temporal Shift [26]	23	74.8	91.5
Correlation [55]	23	75.1	91.6
Temporal Difference [56]	36	76.6	92.8
DTF	25	**77.7**	**93.2**

1D dynamic convolution for each location (i.e., the 1D variant of dynamic convolution [4]), and outperforms $\mathbf{DTF}_{1d}$. The results basically indicate the merit of dynamic kernel learning, but this block brings a clear overhead in computation cost. Instead of temporal modeling in temporal domain, $\mathbf{DTF}_F$ performs temporal modeling in frequency domain by modulating feature spectrum with a fixed frequency filter for each location. Benefiting from the equivalent enlarged temporal receptive field, $\mathbf{DTF}_F$ further boosts up the performances. $\mathbf{DTF}$ additionally triggers the dynamic spatial-aware temporal modeling of each spatial location with specialized frequency filter, thereby leading to a performance gain by 0.7% in top-1 accuracy with a slight computation overhead.

Frame-Wise Aggregation. Next, we investigate the effectiveness of the frame-wise aggregation and correlation feature in DTF block. Table 1b summarizes the performances across different variants of DTF block. DTF-baseline is the degraded version of DTF block without using frame-wise aggregation before FFT, which has already achieved 74.9% top-1 accuracy on Kinetics-400. Next, by equipping DTF-baseline with frame-wise aggregation, the performance is further improved to 75.4%. When solely exploring the correlation weights as the additional motion cues for frequency filter learning, the performance improvements against DTF-baseline are also attained. Furthermore, by simultaneously enhancing temporal feature via frame-wise aggregation and boosting filter learning with correlation weights, DTF block achieves the highest performances.

Location of DTF Block in DTF-Net. To examine the relationship between performance and the location of our DTF block in DTF-Net, we gradually plug DTF blocks into the stages in ResNet-50 backbone, and compare the performances. The performance trend shown in Table 1c indicates that the 2D-ResNet benefits more by inserting DTF blocks into more stages and the increase of the computation cost is very slight. Taking a closer look at the top-1 accuracy of different locations of DTF block, the injection of DTF blocks into the only one stage (res_5) already leads to a large improvement of 3.7% against 2D-ResNet, which clearly validates the temporal modeling ability of DTF. By further integrating all the four stages in ResNet-50 with DTF blocks, DTF-Net achieves the best performances, without requiring heavy computation overhead.

Temporal Modeling. We next make the comparison between DTF and other existing temporal modeling techniques. The performances of integrating the ResNet-50 backbone with different temporal modeling approaches are listed in Table 1d. Overall, our DTF leads to higher top-1 accuracy against other temporal modeling models with similar or even less computation cost. The results basically demonstrate the advantage of exploring dynamic spatial-aware temporal modeling in frequency domain. Specifically, by additionally modeling temporal dynamics via temporal convolution, Temporal Conv [52] is superior to 2D-ResNet. Correlation [55] explicitly captures motion displacement across frames, and outperforms Temporal Conv. By capturing long-range motion patterns through RGB/feature differences, Temporal Difference [55] shows better performances than Correlation. However, the performances of Temporal Differ-

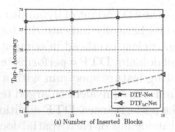
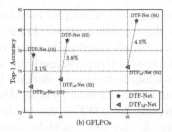

(a) Number of Inserted Blocks   (b) GFLPOs

Fig. 6. Performance comparisons between DTF-Net and DTF$_{1d}$-Net by using (a) different number of inserted blocks (with 16-frame input) and (b) different input clip length on Kinetics-400 (backbone: ResNet-50).

Table 2. Performance comparisons with state-of-the-art video backbones on Kinetics-400. The input clip length of DTF-Net is shown inside the bracket.

Approach	Backbone	GFLOPs × views	Top-1	Top-5
Convolutional Networks				
I3D [3]	Inception	108 × N/A	72.1	90.3
TSN [57]	Inception	80 × 10	72.5	90.2
MF-Net [5]	R34	11 × 50	72.8	90.4
R(2+1)D [52]	R34	152 × 10	74.3	91.4
S3D [61]	Inception	71 × 30	74.7	93.4
TSM [26]	R50	33 × 30	74.1	91.2
TEINet [30]	R50	33 × 30	74.9	91.8
TEA [24]	R50	33 × 30	75.0	91.8
SlowFast [11]	R50+R50	36 × 30	75.6	92.1
NL I3D [58]	R50	282 × 30	76.5	92.6
SmallBig [23]	R50	57 × 30	76.3	92.5
CorrNet [55]	R50	115 × 10	77.2	–
TDN [56]	R50	72 × 30	77.5	93.2
DTF-Net (16)	R50	25 × 30	77.7	93.2
DTF-Net (32)	R50	51 × 30	78.9	93.8
DTF-Net (64)	R50	111 × 30	**80.9**	**94.6**

Approach	Backbone	GFLOPs × views	Top-1	Top-5
Convolutional Networks				
ip-CSN [51]	R101	83 × 30	76.7	92.3
SmallBig [23]	R101	418 × 12	77.4	93.3
NL I3D [58]	R101	359 × 30	77.7	93.3
TDN [56]	R101	132 × 30	78.5	93.9
CorrNet [55]	R101	224 × 30	79.2	–
SlowFast [11]	R101+R101	234 × 30	79.8	93.9
DTF-Net (16)	R101	38 × 30	78.9	94.1
DTF-Net (32)	R101	76 × 30	80.1	94.3
DTF-Net (64)	R101	152 × 30	**81.8**	**94.9**
Vision Transformer				
TimeSformer [2]	ViT-B	2,380 × 3	80.7	94.7
ViViT [1]	ViT-L	3,992 × 12	81.3	94.7
MViT [8]	MViT-B	455 × 9	81.2	95.1
Video-Swin [29]	Swin-B	282 × 12	82.7	95.5
DTF-Transformer	Swin-B	266 × 12	**83.5**	**95.9**

ence are still below that of DTF block which dynamically modulates frequency feature spectrum with learnt frequency filter for temporal modeling.

4.3   Evaluation on Long-Range Temporal Modeling

The commonly adopted temporal convolution in existing video backbones is characterized with the fixed kernel size and limited temporal receptive field. They often stack multiple temporal modeling blocks to expand the temporal receptive field for long-range temporal modeling. Instead, our DTF novelly formulates temporal modeling in frequency domain with enlarged temporal receptive field. Therefore, even with a small number of inserted DTF blocks, DTF-Net should be still capable of capturing long-range dependencies. Moreover, DTF should benefit more from the longer input clip length through the dynamic temporal modeling. To validate these claims, we empirically compare the performances between DTF$_{1d}$-Net and DTF-Net on Kinetics-400 when capitalizing on different number of inserted blocks and input clip length in Fig. 6. Note that DTF$_{1d}$-Net is a degradation of DTF-Net by employing conventional temporal 1D convolution in each basic residual block for temporal modeling. As shown in this figure,

DTF-Net consistently outperforms DTF_{1d}-Net across different number of blocks and different number of input frames. More specifically, in Fig. 6(a), the accuracy of DTF_{1d}-Net decreases more sharply than that of DTF-Net when reducing the number of inserted blocks. Meanwhile, in Fig. 6(b), the performance gap between DTF_{1d}-Net and DTF-Net is increased when feeding into more frames. Both of the results confirm the merit of exploring temporal modeling in frequency domain to capture long-range dependency.

4.4 Comparisons with State-of-the-Art Methods

We compare our DTF-Net and DTF-Transformer with various state-of-the-art video backbones on Kinetics-400, Something-Something V1 (SSv1) and V2 (SSv2). All video backbones are grouped into two categories: Convolutional Networks and Vision Transformer. Here we implement our DTF-Net in two different CNN backbones, i.e., ResNet-50 (R50) and ResNet-101 (R101), and vary the input clip length within the range of {16, 32, 64}. DTF-Transformer is constructed based on the backbone of Swin Transformer (Swin-B) and we fix the input clip length as 64 frames. We measure the computational cost of each run by GFLOPs × views (views: the number of clips sampled from the full video at inference).

Table 3. Performance comparisons with state-of-the-art video backbones on Something-Something V1 and V2. The input clip length is shown in bracket.

Approach	Backbone	GFLOPs ×views	SSv1 Top-1	Top-5	SSv2 Top-1	Top-5
Convolutional Networks						
NL I3D+GCN [59]	R50	606	46.1	76.8	-	-
CPNet [27]	R34	N/A	-	-	57.7	84.0
TSM [26]	R50	98	47.2	77.1	63.4	88.5
TAM [9]	R50	48	48.4	78.8	61.7	88.1
GST [37]	R50	59	48.6	77.9	62.6	87.9
SmallBig [23]	R50	105	49.3	79.5	62.3	88.5
CorrNet [55]	R50	115 × 10	49.3	-	-	-
ACTION-Net [60]	R50	69	-	-	64.0	89.3
STM [17]	R50	67 × 30	50.7	80.4	64.2	89.8
MSNet [20]	R50	67	52.1	82.3	64.7	89.4
TEINet [30]	R50	99	52.5	-	65.5	89.8
MG-TEA [65]	R50	N/A	53.2	-	63.8	-
TDN [56]	R50	72	53.9	82.1	65.3	89.5
DTF-Net (16)	R50	25 × 3	54.2	82.3	65.5	89.6
DTF-Net (32)	R50	51 × 3	55.1	83.0	66.2	90.3
DTF-Net (64)	R50	111 × 3	56.2	83.9	67.1	90.9

Approach	Backbone	GFLOPs ×views	SSv1 Top-1	Top-5	SSv2 Top-1	Top-5
Convolutional Networks						
GSM [48]	Inception	268	55.2	-	-	-
CorrNet [55]	R101	224 × 30	53.3	-	-	-
MG-TEA [65]	R101	N/A	53.3	-	64.8	-
TDN [56]	R101	132	55.3	83.3	66.9	90.9
DTF-Net (16)	R101	38 × 3	55.4	83.4	67.1	91.5
DTF-Net (32)	R101	76 × 3	56.4	83.8	68.2	92.3
DTF-Net (64)	R101	152 × 3	57.1	84.1	68.9	92.6
Vision Transformer						
TimeSformer [2]	ViT-B	1,703 × 3	-	-	62.5	-
ViViT [1]	ViT-L	903	-	-	65.4	89.8
MViT [8]	ViT-B	455 × 3	-	-	67.7	90.9
Video-Swin [29]	Swin-B	321 × 3	-	-	69.6	92.7
DTF-Transformer	Swin-B	266 × 3	57.9	85.7	70.1	93.2

Table 2 summarizes the performance comparisons on Kinetics-400. In Convolutional Networks group, our DTF-Net achieves better performances than other baselines. In particular, DTF-Net (32) in R50 obtains 78.9% top-1 accuracy, surpassing the best competitor TDN by 1.4% and relatively reducing 30% computation cost in GFLOPs. Note that although TDN emphasizes the long-term temporal structure by cross-segment feature enhancement, its temporal receptive field is still restricted by the traditional block design. In contrast, our DTF is benefited from the mechanism of dynamic temporal modeling in frequency domain with enlarged temporal receptive field. DTF-Net (64) further improves the top-1 accuracy from 78.9% to 80.9% by exploiting more frames in each clip. When inserting DTF block into the advanced 2D Vision Transformer (Swin Transformer), DTF-Transformer achieves the best performance (83.5%) in top-1 accuracy. In comparison to the superior 3D Vision Transformer (Video-Swin), DTF-Transformer leads to 0.8% performance gain and with less computation cost. This basically verifies the better temporal modeling of spatial-aware feature spectrum filtering than the self-attention along temporal dimension.

Table 3 shows the performances on SSv1 and SSv2 datasets, where the common one-clip and 3-crops settings [2,8,29] are adopted for evaluation. Similar performance trends are observed on the two datasets, and DTF-Net (64) in R101 backbones outperforms the best competitor TDN by 1.8% and 2.0% top-1 accuracy on SSv1 and SSv2, respectively. By further plugging DTF block into the Swin-B backbone, DTF-Transformer obtains the best performances on both datasets, confirming the superiority of our DTF block in video modeling.

4.5   Visualization Analysis of Dynamic Temporal Filter Block

To better qualitatively analyze the temporal modeling of DTF block, we further visualize the class activation map with Grad-CAM [45], two selected spatial positions, the learnt frequency filter and the corresponding 1D convolution kernel for each selected spatial position in DTF-Net (backbone: R50) in Fig. 7. Note that Grad-CAM naturally reflects the meaningful motion cues that benefit action recognition, where the region with larger class activation response commonly refers to spatial position with larger movements tailored to the target action. Therefore we sample two spatial positions according to the class activation of Grad-CAM: one with large movement (in red box) and the other with small movement (in blue box). Next, for each spatial position, we visualize its frequency filter in res_5 stage of DTF-Net (resolution: 8×8), and the corresponding 1D convolution kernel is calculated by IFFT over frequency filter. Specifically, for

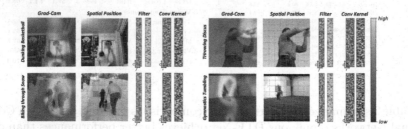

Fig. 7. Visualization of the Grad-CAM [45], two selected spatial positions, the learnt frequency filter and the corresponding 1D convolution kernel of DTF-Net in each position for four Kinetics-400 videos. We select two positions of each video based on Grad-CAM, where the blue and red box represents the position with small and large movements, respectively. The 1D convolution kernel is obtained by applying IFFT over the learnt filter. The visualization of frequency filter or 1D kernel is marked with box in the same color with the corresponding position. (Color figure online)

each video, the learnt frequency filter/1D convolution kernel of spatial position with large movement is clearly more active than that of location with small movement. The results validate that DTF block effectively captures differences of spatial contexts at varied locations, and learns a specialized frequency filter for each spatial location, leading to a dynamic spatial-aware temporal modeling.

5   Conclusions

In this work, we present a new Dynamic Temporal Filter (DTF) block that formulates dynamic temporal modeling in the frequency domain with an enlarged temporal receptive field. Particularly, DTF mechanism first takes all features across time in the same spatial location as temporal feature, and further learns specialized frequency filter based on the temporal feature. Next, the primary temporal feature is transformed into frequency feature spectrum via FFT, which are modulated by the learnt frequency filter. The modulated frequency spectrum is finally transformed back to temporal domain via IFFT. Going beyond DTF mechanism, DTF block additionally employs frame-wise aggregation module to not only contextualize temporal feature but also enable more effective learning of frequency filter. By plugging DTF block into ResNet and Swin-Transformer, we construct two new video backbones, i.e., DTF-Net and DTF-Transformer. Experiments conducted on three action recognition datasets demonstrate the superiority of both DTF-Net and DTF-Transformer.

Acknowledgment. This work was supported by the National Key R&D Program of China under Grant No. 2020AAA0108600.

References

1. Arnab, A., Dehghani, M., Heigold, G., Sun, C., Lucic, M., Schmid, C.: ViViT: a video vision transformer. In: ICCV (2021)
2. Bertasius, G., Wang, H., Torresani, L.: Is space-time attention all you need for video understanding? In: ICML (2021)
3. Carreira, J., Zisserman, A.: Quo Vadis, action recognition? A new model and the kinetics dataset. In: CVPR (2017)
4. Chen, Y., Dai, X., Liu, M., Chen, D., Yuan, L., Liu, Z.: Dynamic convolution: attention over convolution kernels. In: CVPR (2020)
5. Chen, Y., Kalantidis, Y., Li, J., Yan, S., Feng, J.: Multi-fiber networks for video recognition. In: Ferrari, V., Hebert, M., Sminchisescu, C., Weiss, Y. (eds.) ECCV 2018. LNCS, vol. 11205, pp. 364–380. Springer, Cham (2018). https://doi.org/10.1007/978-3-030-01246-5_22
6. Diba, A., Sharma, V., Gool, L.V.: Deep temporal linear encoding networks. In: CVPR (2017)
7. Dosovitskiy, A., et al.: An image is worth 16 × 16 words: transformers for image recognition at scale. In: ICLR (2021)
8. Fan, H., et al.: Multiscale vision transformers. arXiv preprint arXiv:2104.11227 (2021)

9. Fan, Q., Chen, C.F., Kuehne, H., Pistoia, M., Cox, D.: More is less: learning efficient video representations by big-little network and depthwise temporal aggregation. In: NeurIPS (2019)

10. Feichtenhofer, C.: X3D: expanding architectures for efficient video recognition. In: CVPR (2020)

11. Feichtenhofer, C., Fan, H., Malik, J., He, K.: SlowFast networks for video recognition. In: ICCV (2019)

12. Feichtenhofer, C., Pinz, A., Zisserman, A.: Convolutional two-stream network fusion for video action recognition. In: CVPR (2016)

13. Goyal, R., et al.: The "something something" video database for learning and evaluating visual common sense. In: ICCV (2017)

14. Han, K., Xiao, A., Wu, E., Guo, J., Xu, C., Wang, Y.: Transformer in transformer. In: NeurIPS (2021)

15. He, K., Zhang, X., Ren, S., Sun, J.: Deep residual learning for image recognition. In: CVPR (2016)

16. Ji, S., Xu, W., Yang, M., Yu, K.: 3D convolutional neural networks for human action recognition. IEEE Trans. PAMI **35**, 221–231 (2013)

17. Jiang, B., Wang, M., Gan, W., Wu, W., Yan, J.: STM: SpatioTemporal and motion encoding for action recognition. In: ICCV (2019)

18. Karpathy, A., Toderici, G., Shetty, S., Leung, T., Sukthankar, R., Fei-Fei, L.: Large-scale video classification with convolutional neural networks. In: CVPR (2014)

19. Klaser, A., Marszalek, M., Schmid, C.: A spatio-temporal descriptor based on 3D-gradients. In: BMVC (2008)

20. Kwon, H., Kim, M., Kwak, S., Cho, M.: MotionSqueeze: neural motion feature learning for video understanding. In: Vedaldi, A., Bischof, H., Brox, T., Frahm, J.-M. (eds.) ECCV 2020. LNCS, vol. 12361, pp. 345–362. Springer, Cham (2020). https://doi.org/10.1007/978-3-030-58517-4_21

21. Laptev, I.: On space-time interest points. Int. J. Comput. Vis. **64**(2–3), 107–123 (2005)

22. Laptev, I., Marszalek, M., Schmid, C., Rozenfeld, B.: Learning realistic human actions from movies. In: CVPR (2008)

23. Li, X., Wang, Y., Zhou, Z., Qiao, Y.: SmallBigNet: integrating core and contextual views for video classification. In: CVPR (2020)

24. Li, Y., Ji, B., Shi, X., Zhang, J., Kang, B., Wang, L.: TEA: temporal excitation and aggregation for action recognition. In: CVPR (2020)

25. Li, Y., Yao, T., Pan, Y., Mei, T.: Contextual transformer networks for visual recognition. IEEE Trans. PAMI (2022)

26. Lin, J., Gan, C., Han, S.: TSM: temporal shift module for efficient video understanding. In: ICCV (2019)

27. Liu, X., Lee, J.Y., Jin, H.: Learning video representations from correspondence proposals. In: CVPR (2019)

28. Liu, Z., et al.: Swin transformer: hierarchical vision transformer using shifted windows. In: ICCV (2021)

29. Liu, Z., et al.: Video Swin transformer. arXiv preprint arXiv:2106.13230 (2021)

30. Liu, Z., et al.: TEINet: towards an efficient architecture for video recognition. In: AAAI (2020)

31. Long, F., Qiu, Z., Pan, Y., Yao, T., Luo, J., Mei, T.: Stand-alone inter-frame attention in video models. In: CVPR (2022)

32. Long, F., Yao, T., Qiu, Z., Tian, X., Luo, J., Mei, T.: Gaussian temporal awareness networks for action localization. In: CVPR (2019)

33. Long, F., Yao, T., Qiu, Z., Tian, X., Luo, J., Mei, T.: Learning to localize actions from moments. In: Vedaldi, A., Bischof, H., Brox, T., Frahm, J.-M. (eds.) ECCV 2020. LNCS, vol. 12348, pp. 137–154. Springer, Cham (2020). https://doi.org/10.1007/978-3-030-58580-8_9

34. Long, F., Yao, T., Qiu, Z., Tian, X., Luo, J., Mei, T.: Bi-calibration networks for weakly-supervised video representation learning. arXiv preprint arXiv:2206.10491 (2022)

35. Long, F., Yao, T., Qiu, Z., Tian, X., Mei, T., Luo, J.: Coarse-to-fine localization of temporal action proposals. IEEE Trans. Multimedia **22**(6), 1577–1590 (2020)

36. Loshchilov, I., Hutter, F.: SGDR: stochastic gradient descent with warm restarts. In: ICLR (2017)

37. Luo, C., Yuille, A.: Grouped spatial-temporal aggregation for efficient action recognition. In: ICCV (2019)

38. Ng, J.Y.H., Hausknecht, M., Vijayanarasimhan, S., Vinyals, O., Monga, R., Toderici, G.: Beyond short snippets: deep networks for video classification. In: CVPR (2015)

39. Oppenheim, A.V., Willsky, A.S., Newab, S.H.: Signals and Systems. Prentice Hall, Englewood Cliffs (1998)

40. Qiu, Z., Yao, T., Mei, T.: Learning spatio-temporal representation with pseudo-3D residual networks. In: ICCV (2017)

41. Qiu, Z., Yao, T., Ngo, C.W., Mei, T.: Optimization planning for 3D ConvNets. In: ICML (2021)

42. Qiu, Z., Yao, T., Ngo, C.W., Tian, X., Mei, T.: Learning spatio-temporal representation with local and global diffusion. In: CVPR (2019)

43. Rao, Y., Zhao, W., Zhu, Z., Lu, J., Zhou, J.: Global filter networks for image classification. In: NeurIPS (2021)

44. Scovanner, P., Ali, S., Shah, M.: A 3-dimensional SIFT descriptor and its application to action recognition. In: ACM MM (2007)

45. Selvaraju, R.R., Cogswell, M., Das, A., Vedantam, R., Parikh, D., Batra, D.: Grad-CAM: visual explanations from deep networks via gradient-based localization. In: ICCV (2017)

46. Simonyan, K., Zisserman, A.: Two-stream convolutional networks for action recognition in videos. In: NIPS (2014)

47. Srivastava, N., Mansimov, E., Salakhutdinov, R.: Unsupervised learning of video representations using LSTMs. In: ICML (2015)

48. Sudhakaran, S., Escalera, S., Lanz, O.: Gate-shift networks for video action recognition. In: CVPR (2020)

49. Touvron, H., Cord, M., Douze, M., Massa, F., Sablayrolles, A., Jegou, H.: Training data-efficient image transformers and distillation through attention. arXiv preprint arXiv:2012.12877 (2020)

50. Tran, D., Bourdev, L., Fergus, R., Torresani, L., Paluri, M.: Learning spatiotemporal features with 3D convolutional networks. In: ICCV (2015)

51. Tran, D., Wang, H., Torresani, L., Feiszli, M.: Video classification with channel-separated convolutional networks. In: ICCV (2019)

52. Tran, D., Wang, H., Torresani, L., Ray, J., LeCun, Y., Paluri, M.: A closer look at spatiotemporal convolutions for action recognition. In: CVPR (2018)

53. Vaswani, A., et al.: Attention is all you need. In: NIPS (2017)

54. Wang, H., Klaser, A., Schmid, C., Liu, C.L.: Action recognition by dense trajectories. In: CVPR (2011)

55. Wang, H., Tran, D., Torresani, L., Feiszli, M.: Video modeling with correlation networks. In: CVPR (2020)

56. Wang, L., Tong, Z., Ji, B., Wu, G.: TDN: temporal difference networks for efficient action recognition. In: CVPR (2021)
57. Wang, L., et al.: Temporal segment networks: towards good practices for deep action recognition. In: ECCV (2016)
58. Wang, X., Girshick, R., Gupta, A., He, K.: Non-local neural networks. In: CVPR (2018)
59. Wang, X., Gupta, A.: Videos as space-time region graphs. In: Ferrari, V., Hebert, M., Sminchisescu, C., Weiss, Y. (eds.) ECCV 2018. LNCS, vol. 11209, pp. 413–431. Springer, Cham (2018). https://doi.org/10.1007/978-3-030-01228-1_25
60. Wang, Z., She, Q., Smolic, A.: ACTION-Net: multipath excitation for action recognition. In: CVPR (2021)
61. Xie, S., Sun, C., Huang, J., Tu, Z., Murphy, K.: Rethinking spatiotemporal feature learning: speed-accuracy trade-offs in video classification. In: Ferrari, V., Hebert, M., Sminchisescu, C., Weiss, Y. (eds.) ECCV 2018. LNCS, vol. 11219, pp. 318–335. Springer, Cham (2018). https://doi.org/10.1007/978-3-030-01267-0_19
62. Yao, T., Zhang, Y., Qiu, Z., Pan, Y., Mei, T.: SeCo: exploring sequence supervision for unsupervised representation learning. In: AAAI (2021)
63. Yuan, L., et al.: Tokens-to-token ViT: training vision transformers from scratch on ImageNet. In: ICCV (2021)
64. Zhao, Y., Xiong, Y., Lin, D.: Trajectory convolution for action recognition. In: NeurIPS (2018)
65. Zhi, Y., Tong, Z., Wang, L., Wu, G.: MGSampler: an explainable sampling strategy for video action recognition. In: ICCV (2021)

Tip-Adapter: Training-Free Adaption of CLIP for Few-Shot Classification

Renrui Zhang[1,2], Wei Zhang[1], Rongyao Fang[2], Peng Gao[1(✉)], Kunchang Li[1], Jifeng Dai[3], Yu Qiao[1], and Hongsheng Li[2,4]

[1] Shanghai AI Laboratory, Shanghai, China
{zhangrenrui,gaopeng,qiaoyu}@pjlab.org.cn
[2] The Chinese University of Hong Kong, Shatin, Hong Kong
hsli@ee.cuhk.edu.hk
[3] SenseTime Research, Shanghai, China
[4] Centre for Perceptual and Interactive Intelligence (CPII), Shatin, Hong Kong

Abstract. Contrastive Vision-Language Pre-training, known as CLIP, has provided a new paradigm for learning visual representations using large-scale image-text pairs. It shows impressive performance on downstream tasks by zero-shot knowledge transfer. To further enhance CLIP's adaption capability, existing methods proposed to fine-tune additional learnable modules, which significantly improves the few-shot performance but introduces extra training time and computational resources. In this paper, we propose a **T**raining-free adaption method for CL**IP** to conduct few-shot classification, termed as **Tip-Adapter**, which not only inherits the training-free advantage of zero-shot CLIP but also performs comparably to those training-required approaches. Tip-Adapter constructs the adapter via a key-value cache model from the few-shot training set, and updates the prior knowledge encoded in CLIP by feature retrieval. On top of that, the performance of Tip-Adapter can be further boosted to be state-of-the-art on ImageNet by fine-tuning the cache model for 10× fewer epochs than existing methods, which is both effective and efficient. We conduct extensive experiments of few-shot classification on 11 datasets to demonstrate the superiority of our proposed methods. Code is released at https://github.com/gaopengcuhk/Tip-Adapter.

Keywords: Vision-language learning · Few-shot classification · Cache model

1 Introduction

Vision and language are two modalities for humans to perceive the surrounding world and perform diverse interactions with the environment. The accuracy of

---

R. Zhang and W. Zhang—Indicates equal contributions.

Supplementary Information The online version contains supplementary material available at https://doi.org/10.1007/978-3-031-19833-5_29.

Table 1. Comparison of classification accuracy (%) and time efficiency for different methods on 16-shot ImageNet [10], where our proposed Tip-Adapter and Tip-Adapter-F achieve superior accuracy-efficiency trade-off. All experiments are tested with batch size 32 on a single NVIDIA GeForce RTX 3090 GPU. The column in blue records the performance gain relative to Zero-shot CLIP.

Models	Training	Epochs	Time	Accuracy	Gain	Infer. speed	GPU mem.
Zero-shot CLIP [48]	Free	0	0	60.33	0	10.22 ms	2227 MiB
Linear-probe CLIP [48]	Required	–	13 min	56.13	−4.20	–	–
CoOp [73]	Required	200	14 h 40 min	62.95	+2.62	299.64 ms	7193 MiB
CLIP-Adapter [16]	Required	200	50 min	63.59	+3.26	10.59 ms	2227 MiB
Tip-Adapter	**Free**	0	0	62.03	+1.70	10.42 ms	2227MiB
Tip-Adapter-F	Required	20	5 min	**65.51**	+5.18	10.53 ms	2227 MiB

vision tasks, such as classification [13,17,22,26,35,42,70], detection [5,9,51,64,69, 72] and 3D understanding [47,63,67,68] has been boosted significantly thanks to better neural architecture designs [22,58] and delicately designed frameworks [5, 37,51,71]. Language tasks concerning generation and understanding have also been largely improved due to large-scale self-supervised methods, including pre-training by mask prediction [11] and collected web-scale data [49]. As vision and language normally contain complementary information, joint learning of multi-modality representations has been proven to be quite effective on various tasks, such as visual question answering [1,2,31], image captioning [27,65], and referring expression [66]. Different from previous methods that independently learn vision and language representations on separate datasets [1,40,56], CLIP [48] proposed to learn transferable visual features from paired natural language supervisions and exerted amazing zero-shot image classification ability. Due to the interplay between language and vision, the encoded visual representations can be used in open-vocabulary recognition without further re-training.

Many follow-up works have proposed to utilize few-shot data to improve CLIP's adaption capability on downstream tasks. Following the direction of prompt design [4,38], CoOp [73] fine-tuned the pre-trained CLIP via learnable textual tokens and achieved strong performance on few-shot image classification. Recently, CLIP-Adapter [16] introduced to equip CLIP with a parametric feature adapter, which generates adapted features and combines them with the original CLIP-encoded features via a residual connection. It demonstrated promising performance for few-shot classification without utilizing prompt designs. Although CoOp [73] and CLIP-Adapter [16] have shown powerful capabilities on few-shot classification benchmarks, in comparison with Zero-shot CLIP [48] and Linear-probe CLIP [48], they require more computational resources to fine-tune the newly introduced learnable parameters. Thus, we ask the following question: can we achieve the best of both worlds, which not only takes the advantage of CLIP's training-free property for zero-shot classification but also enjoys the strong performance of training-required methods for few-shot classification?

To achieve the goal, we propose a **T**raining-free adaption method for **CLIP**, named **Tip-Adapter**, which appends the weight-frozen CLIP model with a novel non-parametric adapter. Different from existing methods, ours does not require extra training, but designs the adapter as a query-key cache model [18,30, 45] from the few-shot dataset. Specifically, Tip-Adapter extracts visual features of few-shot images by CLIP's visual encoder and transforms their corresponding labels into one-hot encodings. Then, a cache model containing few-shot visual features and one-hot labels is created, which are viewed as paired keys and values.

By the cache model, the training-free construction of Tip-Adapter exhibits great efficiency compared to traditional fine-tuning via Stochastic Gradient Descent (SGD) [32,39]. During inference, the test image first calculates its feature similarities with cached keys, and then aggregates cached values to form the adapter's prediction, which can be regarded as retrieving the few-shot knowledge from the cache model. After that, the adapter's prediction is combined with the original CLIP's prediction by a residual connection [22]. In this way, Tip-Adapter simultaneously exploits knowledge from both pre-trained CLIP and the few-shot training dataset. Surprisingly, Tip-Adapter without training could perform comparably to the fine-tuned CoOp and CLIP-Adapter. Furthermore, if we unfreeze the cached keys as learnable parameters and further fine-tune them, Tip-Adapter's performance could be significantly boosted with just a few training epochs. We term this fine-tuned version as **Tip-Adapter-F**, which only requires 20 epochs on ImageNet [10] to be state-of-the-art compared with 200 epochs adopted by CoOp and CLIP-Adapter. In Table 1, we list the comparison between all existing methods of their performance, training time and inference speed for 16-shot classification on ImageNet, which indicates great accuracy-efficiency trade-off of our methods.

The contributions of our paper are summarised below:

1. We propose Tip-Adapter, a training-free adaption method for CLIP, which discards the conventional SGD-based training by directly setting the adapter with a cache model.
2. Unfreezing the keys of cache model as learnable parameters, the fine-tuned Tip-Adapter, named Tip-Adapter-F, achieves state-of-the-art performance with super-fast convergence on ImageNet.
3. We evaluate Tip-Adapter and Tip-Adapter-F on 11 widely-adopted datasets for few-shot classification and conduct extensive ablation studies to demonstrate their characteristics.

2   Related Work

Data-Efficient Transfer Learning. The capability of deep neural networks is revealed with the assistance of large-scale and high-quality datasets [35]. However, collecting such data is challenging and expensive due to long-tail distributions, noisy annotations and the increasing labeling cost. Thus, transfer learning is proposed to alleviate this issue, which has become a popular research field. Supervised pre-training on image classification [10] have been widely adopted as a default basis for fine-tuning on downstream tasks (e.g. detection [51] and segmentation [21]). Self-supervised learning, such as MoCo [20] and BYOL [19], further discards the need of supervised signals and builds a contrastive pretext task for robust feature learning. Recently, CLIP [48], DeCLIP [36] and ALIGN [28] demonstrate that learning from simple contrastive vision-language pairs obtains promising transferable features for zero-shot recognition over diverse datasets. On top of that, CoOp [73], CLIP-Adapter [16] and WiSE-FT [60] significantly improve the CLIP with limited training data by freezing the pre-trained weights and training additive learnable modules. In contrast, our proposed Tip-Adapter aims at directly infusing few-shot supervisions into the pre-trained CLIP model in a training-free manner. By this, the construction of Tip-Adapter is much more efficient for both time and memory, which only requires calculating the features of few-shot training set once and then caches them.

Cache Model. A cache model stores features of training images and their labels as a key-value database. During inference, the feature encoded from a test sample is treated as query to aggregate information from the cache model by similarity-based retrieval [58]. The whole process is non-parametric [33] and involves no parameter update. The cache model has been equipped on various models to boost the performance for vision or language models, including kNN-LMs [30], Unbounded Cache [18], Matching Network [59] and others [43,53]. Although simple cache model [45] has shown promising results, the huge storage budget for training data is unaffordable to many applications. To reduce such cost, approximate kNN with highly-optimized similarity search system [29] is proposed, which however is slow and error-prone. Different from previous setup with pure vision or language caches, we construct a blended vision-language cache model by CLIP's contrastive multi-modality pre-training. Importantly, thanks to our few-shot setting with limited training samples, the total cache size is small and the retrieval can be efficiently calculated by two cascaded matrix multiplications. Moreover, the cache model in Tip-Adapter can be learnable and dynamically updated by Stochastic Gradient Descent (SGD), which further improves its performance.

3   Method

In Sect. 3.1, we first introduce our proposed training-free Tip-Adapter and its fine-tuned variant, Tip-Adapter-F. Then in Sect. 3.2, we discuss the relations between our approach and previous methods, such as CLIP-Adapter and cache-based networks.

3.1   Training-Free Adaption of CLIP

We propose Tip-Adapter, a training-free adaption method to enhance the few-shot classification performance of CLIP. We construct a key-value cache model from the few-shot training set in a non-parametric manner. Surprisingly, with this well-designed cache model, Tip-Adapter without fine-tuning can achieve comparable performance compared to those training-required approaches, including CoOp [73] and CLIP-Adapter [16]. In addition, if training is allowed, Tip-Adapter-F further surpasses state-of-the-art performance by fine-tuning the cached keys with super-fast convergence (Fig. 1).

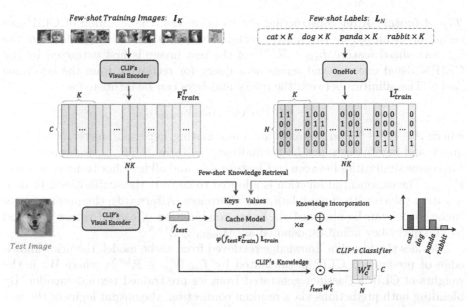

Fig. 1. The Pipeline of Tip-Adapter. Given a K-shot N-class training set, we construct a cache model to adapt CLIP on downstream tasks. It contains few-shot visual features $\mathbf{F}_{\text{train}}^T$ encoded by CLIP and their ground-truth labels $\mathbf{L}_{\text{train}}^T$ under one-hot encodings. After retrieval from the cache model, the few-shot knowledge is incorporated with CLIP's pre-trained knowledge, achieving the training-free adaption.

Cache Model Construction. Given the pre-trained CLIP [48] model and a new dataset with K-shot N-class training samples for few-shot classification, there are K annotated images in each of the N categories, denoted as I_K with their labels L_N. We aim at creating a key-value cache model as the feature adapter, which contains few-shot knowledge within N classes. For each training image, we utilize the CLIP's pre-trained visual encoder to extract its C-dimensional L2 normalized feature, and convert its ground-truth label into an N-dimensional one-hot vector. For all NK training samples, we denote their visual features and corresponding label vectors as $\mathbf{F}_{\text{train}} \in \mathbb{R}^{NK \times C}$ and $\mathbf{L}_{\text{train}} \in \mathbb{R}^{NK \times N}$,

$$\mathbf{F}_{\text{train}} = \text{VisualEncoder}(I_K), \tag{1}$$
$$\mathbf{L}_{\text{train}} = \text{OneHot}(L_N). \tag{2}$$

For the key-value cache, the CLIP-encoded representations $\mathbf{F}_{\text{train}}$ are treated as keys, while the one-hot ground-truth vectors $\mathbf{L}_{\text{train}}$ are used as their values. In this way, the key-value cache memorizes all the new knowledge extracted from the few-shot training set, which is for updating the prior knowledge encoded in the pre-trained CLIP.

Tip-Adapter. After constructing the cache model, the adaption of CLIP can be simply achieved by two matrix-vector multiplications. During inference, the L2 normalized feature $f_{\text{test}} \in \mathbb{R}^{1 \times C}$ of the test image is first extracted by the CLIP's visual encoder and serves as a query for retrieving from the key-value cache. The affinities between the query and keys can be estimated as

$$A = \exp\left(-\beta(1 - f_{\text{test}}\mathbf{F}_{\text{train}}^T)\right), \tag{3}$$

where $A \in \mathbb{R}^{1 \times NK}$ and β stands for a modulating hyper-parameter. Since both query and key features are L2 normalized, the term $f_{\text{test}}\mathbf{F}_{\text{train}}^T$ is equivalent to the cosine similarities between test feature f_{test} and all few-shot training features $\mathbf{F}_{\text{train}}^T$. The exponential function is adopted to convert the similarities into non-negative values with β modulating its sharpness. Afterwards, the prediction for cache model can be obtained via linear combination of cached values weighted by the query-key affinities, denoted as $A\mathbf{L}_{\text{train}} \in \mathbb{R}^{1 \times N}$.

Besides the few-shot knowledge retrieved from cache model, the prior knowledge of pre-trained CLIP is calculated by $f_{\text{test}}W_c^T \in \mathbb{R}^{1 \times N}$, where W_c is the weights of CLIP's classifier generated from its pre-trained textual encoder. By blending both predictions via a residual connection, the output logits of the test image by Tip-Adapter are then calculated as

$$\begin{aligned} \text{logits} &= \alpha A\mathbf{L}_{\text{train}} + f_{\text{test}}W_c^T \\ &= \alpha\varphi(f_{\text{test}}\mathbf{F}_{\text{train}}^T)\mathbf{L}_{\text{train}} + f_{\text{test}}W_c^T, \end{aligned} \tag{4}$$

where α denotes the residual ratio, and we define $\varphi(x) = \exp(-\beta(1 - x))$. Tip-Adapter's prediction therefore contains two terms, the former term adaptively summarizes information from the few-shot training dataset, and the latter term preserves the prior knowledge from the CLIP's classifier W_c^T. The two terms are balanced by the weight α. Empirically, α is set to be large if the domain gap between pre-trained and downstream few-shot tasks is large, since more knowledge from the few-shot set is required, and small otherwise.

Tip-Adapter with Fine-Tuning. Tip-Adapter can greatly boost CLIP by incorporating new knowledge in the few-shot training set. However, given more shots, Tip-Adapter without training gradually lags behind the training-required CoOp and CLIP-Adapter. To mitigate the gap while preserve the efficiency, we propose Tip-Adapter-F, which treats the keys in the cache model as a good initialization for learnable parameters, and fine-tunes them via SGD. Thanks to the advantageous starting point of cache model, Tip-Adapter-F achieves state-of-the-art performance with only 20-epoch fine-tuning on ImageNet [10], compared with CoOp and CLIP-Adapter's 200-epoch training.

More specifically, we unfreeze the cached keys $\mathbf{F}_{\text{train}}$, but still freeze the values $\mathbf{L}_{\text{train}}$ and the two encoders of pre-trained CLIP. The intuition is that updating the keys in the cache model can boost the estimation of affinities, which is able to calculate the cosine similarities between the test and training images more accurately. In contrast, values in the cache model are one-hot encodings representing ground-truth annotations and shall be kept frozen to well memorize the category information.

3.2 Relations with Previous Models

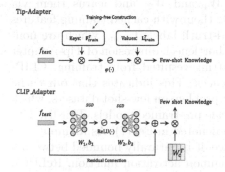

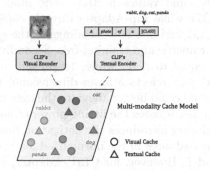

Fig. 2. Comparison of Tip-Adapter and CLIP-Adapter [16] to acquire few-shot knowledge. Tip-Adapter retrieves from the constructed cache model, but CLIP-Adapter encodes the knowledge by the learnbale adapter and obtains it aided by CLIP's classifier W_c.

Fig. 3. The multi-modality cache model of Tip-Adapter. Different from previous networks only with visual cache, Tip-Adapter caches both visual and textual knowledge by CLIP's encoders.

Relations with CLIP-Adapter. Following the adapter [25] in neural language processing, CLIP-Adapter [16] appends a lightweight two-layer Multi-Layer Perceptron (MLP) to the pre-trained weight-fixed CLIP model and optimizes its parameters via SGD. Specifically, for an input test image, its visual feature f_{test} is first obtained by CLIP's pre-trained visual encoder. Then, the MLP-based adapter with randomly initialized parameters W_1, b_1, W_2, b_2, is appended to output the adapted feature,

$$f_{\text{test}}^a = \varphi(f_{\text{test}}W_1^T + b_1)W_2^T + b_2, \tag{5}$$

where φ denotes the activation function in the MLP. Afterwards, the adapted feature f_{test}^a is linearly combined with the pre-trained CLIP's feature f_{test}, and output the final classification logits with a hyper-parameter $\alpha \in [0, 1]$,

$$\text{logits} = \alpha f_{\text{test}}^a W_c^T + f_{\text{test}}W_c^T, \tag{6}$$

where W_c^T is the weights of CLIP's classifier. The first terms in both Eqs. (4) and (6) represent the ways of Tip-Adapter and CLIP-Adapter to obtain the few-shot knowledge, respectively. As shown in Fig. 2, Tip-Adapter acquires the knowledge by retrieval from the cache model, but CLIP-Adapter first utilizes the learnable adapter to predict the adapted feature and then multiplies it with CLIP's W_c^T to form the final knowledge output.

With further analysis for Eqs. (4) and (6), CLIP-Adapter can be seen as a special form of our proposed Tip-Adapter,

$$W_1 = \mathbf{F}_{\text{train}}, \quad W_2 = \mathbf{L}_{\text{train}}^T W_c^{-1}, \quad b_1 = 0, \quad b_2 = 0, \tag{7}$$

$$\varphi(x) = \exp(-\beta(1 - x)), \quad \text{where} \quad x \in [0, 1]. \tag{8}$$

They have two key differences. Firstly, CLIP-Adapter randomly initializes both keys and values in the cache model as W_1 and W_2, and learns them via SGD, while Tip-Adapter directly constructs them with cached training features $\mathbf{F}_{\text{train}}$ and one-hot encodings of the ground-truth labels $\mathbf{L}_{\text{train}}$, which are non-parametric and training-free. Secondly, the bottleneck dimension of Tip-Adapter is equal to NK, while, to prevent over-fitting resulted from training, CLIP-Adapter selects a lower-dimensional bottleneck. This indicates that our cache model could better alleviate the over-fitting problem on few-shot datasets, which further releases the fitting power of large-scale pre-trained models. Thirdly, Tip-Adapter introduces the activation function denoted in Eq. (7). As its inputs are the distances in the normalized feature space, it is naturally bounded between 0 and 1. However, for CLIP-Adapter, the common activation function, ReLU($\cdot$), is chosen to handle unbounded inputs. In short, Tip-Adapter obtains a well-performing adapter without training, which is more efficient on few-shot classification.

Relations with Cache-Based Networks. Acquiring a cache model from few-shot training data has been explored by many previous methods, including Matching Network [59], Prototypical Networks [53], MAML [15], Relation Network [55] and others [6,7,12,57]. Our models differ from them in two points for both specific methods and experimental settings.

Firstly, previous works only constructs the cache of visual features, but Tip-Adapter adopts a multi-modality heterogeneous cache model with both visual and textual cached features extracted by CLIP, as shown in Fig. 3. In detail, the aforementioned cache model with keys $\mathbf{F}_{\text{train}}$ and values $\mathbf{L}_{\text{train}}$ serves as the visual cache, denoted as $\mathbf{F}_{\text{vis}}$ and $\mathbf{L}_{\text{vis}}$ here. As CLIP's classifier W_c is calculated from category texts by the textual encoder, $W_c \in \mathbb{R}^{N \times C}$ can be viewed as language features serving as keys $\mathbf{F}_{\text{tex}}$ for textual cache. The values of textual cache is then denoted by an identity matrix $\mathbf{L}_{\text{tex}} \in \mathbb{R}^{N \times N}$, since W_c respectively encodes N category knowledge and each of its row vector corresponds to a certain category. From this perspective, Eq. (4) is reformulated as

$$\text{logits} = \alpha \varphi(f_{\text{test}} \mathbf{F}_{\text{vis}}^T) \mathbf{L}_{\text{vis}} + (f_{\text{test}} \mathbf{F}_{\text{tex}}^T) \mathbf{L}_{\text{tex}}, \tag{9}$$

where the two terms represent knowledge retrieval from both visual and textual cached knowledge.

Secondly, prior works split the same dataset into three sub-sets of different categories, which respectively serve as training, support, and query sets. Although they test on query sets with a new set of categories, it is still within the same semantic domain. In contrast, Tip-Adapter adapts the pre-trained CLIP into a totally new dataset for evaluation, which generalizes to a new domain and thus more challenging. Importantly, we test our models on full test sets, the same as conventional methods [13,22] trained by the full training set. Compared to existing works [53,59] on the small query sets, our effectiveness is verified by much more test images of new categories.

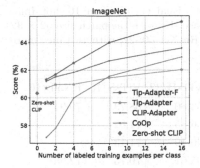

Fig. 4. Few-shot classification accuracy of different models on ImageNet [10].

Table 2. Classification accuracy (%) on ImageNet [10] of different models with quantitative values. The last row in blue records the performance gain of Tip-Adapter-F brought by further fine-tuning over Tip-Adapter.

Few-shot Setup	1	2	4	8	16
Zero-shot CLIP [48]: 60.33					
Linear-probe CLIP [48]	22.17	31.90	41.20	49.52	56.13
CoOp [73]	57.15	57.81	59.99	61.56	62.95
CLIP-Adapter [16]	61.20	61.52	61.84	62.68	63.59
Tip-Adapter	60.70	60.96	60.98	61.45	62.03
Tip-Adapter-F	**61.32**	**61.69**	**62.52**	**64.00**	**65.51**
	+0.62	+0.73	+1.54	+2.55	+3.48

4 Experiments

4.1 Training Settings

We conduct experiments for Tip-Adapter and Tip-Adapter-F on 11 widely-used image classification datasets: ImageNet [10], StandfordCars [34], UCF101 [54], Caltech101 [14], Flowers102 [44], SUN397 [62], DTD [8], EuroSAT [23], FGV-CAircraft [41], OxfordPets [46], and Food101 [3]. For few-shot learning, we compare the performance of 1, 2, 4, 8, 16 few-shot training sets, and test on the full test sets. For the CLIP backbone, we utilize ResNet-50 [22] as the visual encoder and a transformer [13] as the textual encoder. We obtain the pre-trained weights of both encoders from [48] and freeze them during training. We follow the data preprocessing protocol in CLIP [48], which is composed of random cropping, resizing, and random horizontal flip. Other than the learnable prompts in CoOp, we follow CLIP to adopt prompt ensembling especially on ImageNet and use single handcrafted prompt on other 10 datasets. The Tip-Adapter-F is fine-tuned using batch size 256, learning rate 0.001, and the AdamW [32] optimizer with a cosine scheduler. We set 100-epoch training for EuroSAT dataset and only 20-epoch training for other 10 datasets.

Performance comparison is conducted between Zero-shot CLIP [48], Linear-probe CLIP [48], CoOp [73] and CLIP-Adapter [16]. Therein, Zero-shot CLIP uses no extra training sample and conducts classification purely by pre-trained knowledge. Linear-probe CLIP trains an additional linear classifier after the weight-frozen CLIP on the few-shot training set. CoOp adopts learnable prompts for training, and we select its best-performing variant for comparison, that is, placing the class token at the end of the 16-token prompts without class-specific contexts. CLIP-Adapter appends a feature adapter [25] to narrow the domain gap between the pre-trained features and downstream tasks. We also report the best-performing variant of CLIP-Adapter with only the learnable visual adapter. We report their official scores in the papers for fair comparison.

Table 3. Classification accuracy (%) of different visual encoders on 16-shot ImageNet [10]. ViT-B/32 and ViT-B/16 denote ViT-Base [13] with the patch size 32 × 32 and 16 × 16, respectively, and RN50×16 denotes ResNet-50 [22] with 16 times more computation [48].

Models	ResNet-50	ResNet-101	ViT-B/32	ViT-B/16	RN50×16
Zero-shot CLIP [48]	60.33	62.53	63.80	68.73	70.94
CoOp [73]	62.95	66.60	66.85	71.92	–
CLIP-Adapter [16]	63.59	65.39	66.19	71.13	–
Tip-Adapter	62.03	64.78	65.61	70.75	72.95
Tip-Adapter-F	**65.51**	**68.56**	**68.65**	**73.69**	**75.81**

4.2   Comparison on ImageNet

Performance Analysis. As shown in Fig. 4 and Table 2, both Tip-Adapter and Tip-Adapter-F show outstanding performance over other methods. Compared to Zero-shot CLIP, Tip-Adapter consistently surpasses it without any training. When the numbers of training samples are limited, Tip-Adapter greatly exceeds the Linear-probe CLIP by +38.53%, +29.06% in 1-shot and 2-shot settings. With further fine-tuning, Tip-Adapter-F updates the keys in the cache model and achieves the best performance over all methods in all few-shot settings. The performance gain over Tip-Adapter becomes larger as the number of training samples increases, from 1-shot's +0.62% to 16-shot's +3.44%. This indicates that the fine-tuning with more training samples enables the network to build a more powerful cache model. In Table 3, we also implement different models with various visual encoders over ResNet [22] and ViT [13] backbones, where our Tip-Adapter-F still performs the best.

Efficiency Comparison. In Table 1, we show the comparison of training time and inference speed for different models. CLIP-Adapter, Tip-Adapter and Tip-Adapter-F are able to cache the textual features from CLIP in the beginning and load them during training or inference, but CoOp adopts learnable prompts, which requires to calculate through the whole textual encoder online for every iteration. Linear-probe CLIP utilizes logistic regression [61], so it cannot measure the training time by epochs and the inference speed on GPU. From the comparison, we observe that CoOp takes the most training time for learning prompts and has a +2.26% performance gain over Zero-shot CLIP. CLIP-Adapter significantly reduces the training time with better performance improvement of +3.26%, but still needs 200-epoch training. Aided by the cache model, Tip-Adapter gains +1.70% improvement but requires no extra training time, which makes it a good trade-off between performance and efficiency. Tip-Adapter-F further reaches state-of-the-art accuracy with only 1/10 of CLIP-Adapter and CoOp's training epochs, achieving the best of both worlds. As for inference speed and GPU memory consumption [52], our Tip-Adapter and Tip-adapter-F only produce marginal extra latency over Zero-shot CLIP and save much GPU memory compared to CoOp, which are quite efficient for applications.

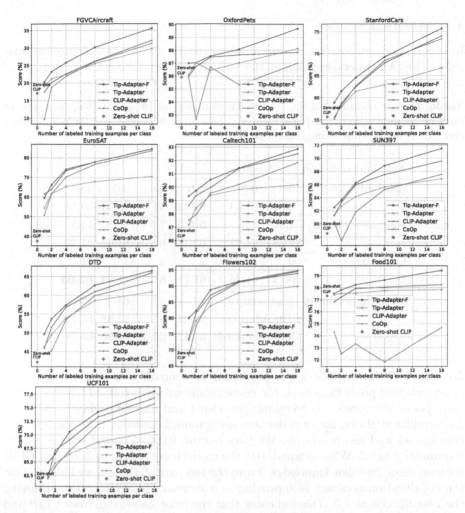

Fig. 5. Few-shot classification accuracy of different models on 10 datasets. Tip-Adapter largely improves Zero-shot CLIP without any training. Tip-Adapter-F consistently surpasses all compared methods by efficiently fine-tuning the cache model.

4.3   Performance on Other Datasets

Figure 5 shows the performance comparison on other 10 datasets listed in Sect. 4.1. Our triaining-free Tip-Adapter significantly boosts the classification accuracy over Zero-shot CLIP and surpasses CoOp trained by 1 or 2 shots on most datasets. Although Tip-Adapter underperforms CoOp and CLIP-Adapter trained by more shots, Tip-Adapter-F with a fewer-epoch fine-tuning can eliminate the gap and further surpass all other models, achieving comprehensively leading performance. The consistent superiority of Tip-Adapter-F over 10 datasets fully demonstrates the effectiveness and generality of our proposed cache model.

4.4   Ablation Studies

In this section, we conduct several ablation studies about Tip-Adapter on ImageNet [10]. All experiments adopt the 16-shot setting without training.

Table 4. Four ablation studies (%) of Tip-Adapter on ImageNet [10], from top to bottom: residual ratio α, sharpness ratio β, the size of cache model, and the performance given more shots while fixing cache size 16.

Ablation studies on Tip-Adapter						
Residual ratio α	0.0	0.5	**1.0**	2.0	3.0	4.0
	60.33	61.44	**62.03**	61.41	60.36	59.14
Sharpness ratio β	1.5	3.5	**5.5**	7.5	9.5	11.5
	61.82	61.91	**62.03**	61.76	61.62	61.40
Cache size	0	1	2	4	8	**16**
	60.33	61.45	61.71	61.79	61.83	**62.03**

More shots than 16	Shot setup	16	32	64	128
	Tip-Adapter	62.03	62.51	62.88	63.15
	Tip-Adapter-F	65.47	66.58	67.96	69.74

Residual Ratio α. The hyper-parameter α controls how much to combine newly adapted predictions from the cache model with pre-trained CLIP's, which can also be interpreted as weighing the visual and textual caches as in Eq. 9. As formulated above, larger α denotes using more knowledge from the few-shot training set and less otherwise. We vary α from 0.0 to 5.0, and set the hyper-parameter β as 5.5. When α equals 0.0, the model is equivalent to Zero-shot CLIP without using few-shot knowledge. From the top part of Table 4, we observe that the classification accuracy is improving as α increases from 0.0 to 1.0, achieving the best 62.03% at 1.0. This indicates that the prior knowledge from CLIP and the few-shot knowledge from cache model are equally important.

Sharpness Ratio β. In Eq. (3), β in the activation function φ controls the sharpness of the affinities. When β is large, only the most similar training samples to the test image in the embedding space have the large influences to the prediction and vice versa. In the second part of Table 4 with the α as 1.0, we observe that the variation of β has a limited impact and a moderate 5.5 for β leads to the best-performing Tip-Adapter.

Size of the Cache Model. We explore the influence of the size for cache model in Tip-Adapter. Given 16-shot training set, rather than caching all 16 samples per category, we construct the cache whose size is more than 0 but less than 16. Taking 8 as an example, we randomly divide 16 samples into 8 uniform groups and obtain 8 prototypes by averaging features of the 2 samples in each group. Considering such random division of samples might influence the performance, we experiment 5 times and report the average scores. The results from the third part of Table 4 illustrate that, the more samples we cache to preserve more few-shot knowledge, the higher accuracy Tip-Adapter can achieve.

Scaling Up to More Shots. Given more than 16 shots, we explore a way to still constrain the cache size as 16 and avoid the potential burden for both memory and computation. Taking 64 shots as an example, following the division strategy in the above paragraph, we obtain 16 prototypes from 4 groups to construct the cache model. The final part of Table 4 indicates that even if the cache size is restrained to 16, Tip-Adapter can well capture the knowledge from 32, 64, and 128 training samples per category. Also, the performance boost gradually slows down when more samples are provided, which implies a possible limit of cache size 16 without training. However, Tip-Adapter-F can break such limit by fine-tuning the keys and achieve better performance by more shots for training.

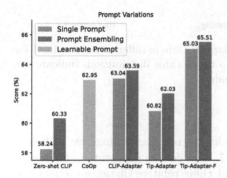

Fig. 6. Classification performance with different prompt designs: single prompt (Cyan), prompt ensembling (Orange) and learnable prompt (Purple). (Color figure online)

Table 5. The robustness (%) to distribution shift of different methods. The last row in blue records the performance gain of Tip-Adapter-F brought by further fine-tuning over Tip-Adapter.

Datasets	Source	Target	
	ImageNet [10]	-V2 [50]	-Sketch [24]
Zero-Shot CLIP [48]	60.33	53.27	35.44
Linear Probe CLIP [48]	56.13	45.61	19.13
CoOp [73]	62.95	54.58	31.04
CLIP-Adapter [16]	63.59	55.69	35.68
Tip-Adapter	62.03	54.60	35.90
Tip-Adapter-F	**65.51**	**57.11**	**36.00**
	+3.48	+2.51	+0.10

Prompt Design. We utilize prompt ensembling of 7 templates from [48] for Zero-shot CLIP, CLIP-Adapter, and Tip-Adapter as default. In Fig. 6, we test them only using a single prompt, "a photo of a [CLASS].", and observe slightly worse performance. The accuracy drops are smaller for Tip-Adapter-F and CLIP-Adapter, but larger for Tip-Adapter and Zero-shot CLIP, which indicates the better-performing models are less affected by the prompt variations.

4.5   Distribution Shift

We evaluate the out-of-distribution ability of our proposed Tip-Adapter and Tip-Adapter-F by learning from one dataset but testing on another. We set ImageNet [10] as the source dataset providing 16-shot training set, and adopt two target datasets for testing: ImageNetV2 [50] and ImageNet-Sketch [24], which contain compatible categories to ImageNet but with semantic gaps. As shown in

Table 5, Tip-Adapter without training exerts superior robustness to distribution shift, which surpasses CoOp [73] on ImageNet-V2 and CLIP-Adapter [16] on ImageNet-Sketch. This indicates the cache model is more advantageous to out-of-distribution evaluation, whose training-free construction alleviates the risk of over-fitting on the source dataset. Further, Tip-Adapter-F achieves the best of both worlds: the strong out-of-distribution performance brought by cache model and the leading in-distribution ability by fine-tuning.

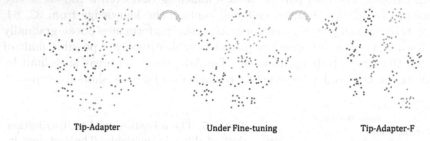

Tip-Adapter   Under Fine-tuning   Tip-Adapter-F

Fig. 7. t-SNE visualization of F_{train} in Tip-Adapter. Dots in different colors stand for embeddings of different categories. From left to right, three distributions indicate the variation of keys in cache model during fine-tuning.

5   Visualization

To better show the variation of cache model during fine-tuning, we utilize t-SNE [48] to visualize the keys F_{train} in Fig. 7. The dots in different colors denote 10 categories of 16-shot ImageNet [10], and their relative distances reflect the high-dimensional distributions of category embeddings. From left to right, the three sub-figures represent the training-free Tip-Adapter, Tip-Adapter during fine-tuning and the final Tip-Adapter-F, respectively. It could be observed that before training, the distribution has shown good discrimination thanks to the properly designed cache model construction. During fine-tuning, embeddings of the same category gradually converges together and different clusters become more contrastive and separate, contributing to stronger classification capability.

6   Conclusions

We propose Tip-Adapter, a non-parametric adaption method of CLIP, which acquires the adapter by a cache model constructed from the few-shot training set. In this way, the few-shot knowledge is retrieved from the cache model and incorporated with CLIP's pre-trained knowledge in a training-free manner. On top of that, Tip-Adapter can be further enhanced by fine-tuning the cached keys for just a few epochs, named Tip-Adapter-F, which achieves state-of-the-art performance among existing methods. Considering limitations, although it is marginal, Tip-Adapter-F still requires 20-epoch fine-tuning on ImageNet to learn the best-performing cache model. Our future work will focus on exploring new training-free methods for CLIP to fully unleash its power for visual representation.

Acknowledgment. This work is supported in part by Centre for Perceptual and Interactive Intelligence Limited, in part by the General Research Fund through the Research Grants Council of Hong Kong under Grants (Nos. 14204021, 14207319), in part by CUHK Strategic Fund, and in part by the Shanghai Committee of Science and Technology (Grant No. 21DZ1100100).

References

1. Anderson, P., et al.: Bottom-up and top-down attention for image captioning and visual question answering. In: Proceedings of the IEEE Conference on Computer Vision and Pattern Recognition, pp. 6077–6086 (2018)
2. Antol, S., et al.: VQA: visual question answering. In: Proceedings of the IEEE International Conference on Computer Vision, pp. 2425–2433 (2015)
3. Bossard, L., Guillaumin, M., Van Gool, L.: Food-101 – mining discriminative components with random forests. In: Fleet, D., Pajdla, T., Schiele, B., Tuytelaars, T. (eds.) ECCV 2014. LNCS, vol. 8694, pp. 446–461. Springer, Cham (2014). https://doi.org/10.1007/978-3-319-10599-4_29
4. Brown, T.B., et al.: Language models are few-shot learners. arXiv preprint arXiv:2005.14165 (2020)
5. Carion, N., Massa, F., Synnaeve, G., Usunier, N., Kirillov, A., Zagoruyko, S.: End-to-end object detection with transformers. In: Vedaldi, A., Bischof, H., Brox, T., Frahm, J.-M. (eds.) ECCV 2020. LNCS, vol. 12346, pp. 213–229. Springer, Cham (2020). https://doi.org/10.1007/978-3-030-58452-8_13
6. Chen, W.Y., Liu, Y.C., Kira, Z., Wang, Y.C.F., Huang, J.B.: A closer look at few-shot classification. arXiv preprint arXiv:1904.04232 (2019)
7. Chen, Y., Wang, X., Liu, Z., Xu, H., Darrell, T.: A new meta-baseline for few-shot learning. arXiv preprint arXiv:2003.04390 (2020)
8. Cimpoi, M., Maji, S., Kokkinos, I., Mohamed, S., Vedaldi, A.: Describing textures in the wild. In: Proceedings of the IEEE Conference on Computer Vision and Pattern Recognition, pp. 3606–3613 (2014)
9. Cui, Z., Qi, G.J., Gu, L., You, S., Zhang, Z., Harada, T.: Multitask AET with orthogonal tangent regularity for dark object detection. In: Proceedings of the IEEE/CVF International Conference on Computer Vision (ICCV), pp. 2553–2562, October 2021
10. Deng, J., Dong, W., Socher, R., Li, L.J., Li, K., Fei-Fei, L.: ImageNet: a large-scale hierarchical image database. In: 2009 IEEE Conference on Computer Vision and Pattern Recognition, pp. 248–255. Ieee (2009)
11. Devlin, J., Chang, M.W., Lee, K., Toutanova, K.: BERT: pre-training of deep bidirectional transformers for language understanding. arXiv preprint arXiv:1810.04805 (2018)
12. Dhillon, G.S., Chaudhari, P., Ravichandran, A., Soatto, S.: A baseline for few-shot image classification. arXiv preprint arXiv:1909.02729 (2019)
13. Dosovitskiy, A., et al.: An image is worth 16 × 16 words: transformers for image recognition at scale. In: ICLR (2021)
14. Fei-Fei, L., Fergus, R., Perona, P.: Learning generative visual models from few training examples: an incremental Bayesian approach tested on 101 object categories. In: 2004 Conference on Computer Vision and Pattern Recognition Workshop, p. 178. IEEE (2004)

15. Finn, C., Abbeel, P., Levine, S.: Model-agnostic meta-learning for fast adaptation of deep networks. In: International Conference on Machine Learning, pp. 1126–1135. PMLR (2017)
16. Gao, P., et al.: CLIP-Adapter: better vision-language models with feature adapters. arXiv preprint arXiv:2110.04544 (2021)
17. Gao, P., Ma, T., Li, H., Dai, J., Qiao, Y.: ConvMAE: masked convolution meets masked autoencoders. arXiv preprint arXiv:2205.03892 (2022)
18. Grave, E., Cissé, M., Joulin, A.: Unbounded cache model for online language modeling with open vocabulary. arXiv preprint arXiv:1711.02604 (2017)
19. Grill, J.B., et al.: Bootstrap your own latent: a new approach to self-supervised learning. arXiv preprint arXiv:2006.07733 (2020)
20. He, K., Fan, H., Wu, Y., Xie, S., Girshick, R.: Momentum contrast for unsupervised visual representation learning. In: Proceedings of the IEEE/CVF Conference on Computer Vision and Pattern Recognition, pp. 9729–9738 (2020)
21. He, K., Gkioxari, G., Dollár, P., Girshick, R.: Mask R-CNN. In: Proceedings of the IEEE International Conference on Computer Vision, pp. 2961–2969 (2017)
22. He, K., Zhang, X., Ren, S., Sun, J.: Deep residual learning for image recognition. In: Proceedings of the IEEE Conference on Computer Vision and Pattern Recognition, pp. 770–778 (2016)
23. Helber, P., Bischke, B., Dengel, A., Borth, D.: EuroSAT: a novel dataset and deep learning benchmark for land use and land cover classification. IEEE J. Sel. Top. Appl. Earth Observ. Remote Sens. 12(7), 2217–2226 (2019)
24. Hendrycks, D., Zhao, K., Basart, S., Steinhardt, J., Song, D.: Natural adversarial examples. In: Proceedings of the IEEE/CVF Conference on Computer Vision and Pattern Recognition, pp. 15262–15271 (2021)
25. Houlsby, N., et al.: Parameter-efficient transfer learning for NLP. In: ICML (2019)
26. Howard, A.G., et al.: MobileNets: efficient convolutional neural networks for mobile vision applications. arXiv preprint arXiv:1704.04861 (2017)
27. Huang, L., Wang, W., Chen, J., Wei, X.Y.: Attention on attention for image captioning. In: Proceedings of the IEEE/CVF International Conference on Computer Vision, pp. 4634–4643 (2019)
28. Jia, C., et al.: Scaling up visual and vision-language representation learning with noisy text supervision. In: ICML (2021)
29. Johnson, J., Douze, M., Jégou, H.: Billion-scale similarity search with GPUs. IEEE Trans. Big Data 7, 535–547 (2019)
30. Khandelwal, U., Levy, O., Jurafsky, D., Zettlemoyer, L., Lewis, M.: Generalization through memorization: Nearest neighbor language models. arXiv preprint arXiv:1911.00172 (2019)
31. Kim, J.H., Jun, J., Zhang, B.T.: Bilinear attention networks. arXiv preprint arXiv:1805.07932 (2018)
32. Kingma, D.P., Ba, J.: Adam: a method for stochastic optimization. arXiv preprint arXiv:1412.6980 (2014)
33. Kossen, J., Band, N., Lyle, C., Gomez, A.N., Rainforth, T., Gal, Y.: Self-attention between datapoints: going beyond individual input-output pairs in deep learning. arXiv preprint arXiv:2106.02584 (2021)
34. Krause, J., Stark, M., Deng, J., Fei-Fei, L.: 3D object representations for fine-grained categorization. In: Proceedings of the IEEE International Conference on Computer Vision Workshops, pp. 554–561 (2013)
35. Krizhevsky, A., Sutskever, I., Hinton, G.E.: ImageNet classification with deep convolutional neural networks. In: NIPS (2012)

36. Li, Y., et al.: Supervision exists everywhere: a data efficient contrastive language-image pre-training paradigm. arXiv preprint arXiv:2110.05208 (2021)
37. Lin, T.Y., Goyal, P., Girshick, R., He, K., Dollár, P.: Focal loss for dense object detection. In: Proceedings of the IEEE International Conference on Computer Vision, pp. 2980–2988 (2017)
38. Liu, P., Yuan, W., Fu, J., Jiang, Z., Hayashi, H., Neubig, G.: Pre-train, prompt, and predict: a systematic survey of prompting methods in natural language processing. arXiv preprint arXiv:2107.13586 (2021)
39. Loshchilov, I., Hutter, F.: Decoupled weight decay regularization. In: 7th International Conference on Learning Representations, ICLR 2019, New Orleans, LA, USA, 6–9 May 2019. OpenReview.net (2019). http://openreview.net/forum?id=Bkg6RiCqY7
40. Lu, J., Batra, D., Parikh, D., Lee, S.: ViLBERT: pretraining task-agnostic visiolinguistic representations for vision-and-language tasks. arXiv preprint arXiv:1908.02265 (2019)
41. Maji, S., Rahtu, E., Kannala, J., Blaschko, M., Vedaldi, A.: Fine-grained visual classification of aircraft. arXiv preprint arXiv:1306.5151 (2013)
42. Mao, M., et al.: Dual-stream network for visual recognition. arXiv preprint arXiv:2105.14734 (2021)
43. Merity, S., Xiong, C., Bradbury, J., Socher, R.: Pointer sentinel mixture models. arXiv preprint arXiv:1609.07843 (2016)
44. Nilsback, M.E., Zisserman, A.: Automated flower classification over a large number of classes. In: 2008 Sixth Indian Conference on Computer Vision, Graphics and Image Processing, pp. 722–729. IEEE (2008)
45. Orhan, A.E.: A simple cache model for image recognition. arXiv preprint arXiv:1805.08709 (2018)
46. Parkhi, O.M., Vedaldi, A., Zisserman, A., Jawahar, C.: Cats and dogs. In: 2012 IEEE Conference on Computer Vision and Pattern Recognition, pp. 3498–3505. IEEE (2012)
47. Qi, C.R., Su, H., Mo, K., Guibas, L.J.: PointNet: Deep learning on point sets for 3D classification and segmentation. In: Proceedings of the IEEE Conference on Computer Vision and Pattern Recognition, pp. 652–660 (2017)
48. Radford, A., et al.: Learning transferable visual models from natural language supervision. arXiv preprint arXiv:2103.00020 (2021)
49. Radford, A., Narasimhan, K., Salimans, T., Sutskever, I.: Improving language understanding by generative pre-training (2018)
50. Recht, B., Roelofs, R., Schmidt, L., Shankar, V.: Do ImageNet classifiers generalize to ImageNet? In: International Conference on Machine Learning, pp. 5389–5400. PMLR (2019)
51. Ren, S., He, K., Girshick, R., Sun, J.: Faster R-CNN: towards real-time object detection with region proposal networks. In: Advances in Neural Information Processing Systems 28, pp. 91–99 (2015)
52. Rumelhart, D.E., Hinton, G.E., Williams, R.J.: Learning Internal Representations by Error Propagation, pp. 318–362. MIT Press, Cambridge (1986)
53. Snell, J., Swersky, K., Zemel, R.S.: Prototypical networks for few-shot learning. arXiv preprint arXiv:1703.05175 (2017)
54. Soomro, K., Zamir, A.R., Shah, M.: UCF101: a dataset of 101 human actions classes from videos in the wild. arXiv preprint arXiv:1212.0402 (2012)
55. Sung, F., Yang, Y., Zhang, L., Xiang, T., Torr, P.H., Hospedales, T.M.: Learning to compare: Relation network for few-shot learning. In: Proceedings of the IEEE Conference on Computer Vision and Pattern Recognition, pp. 1199–1208 (2018)

56. Tan, H., Bansal, M.: LXMERT: learning cross-modality encoder representations from transformers. arXiv preprint arXiv:1908.07490 (2019)
57. Tian, Y., Wang, Y., Krishnan, D., Tenenbaum, J.B., Isola, P.: Rethinking few-shot image classification: a good embedding is all you need? In: Vedaldi, A., Bischof, H., Brox, T., Frahm, J.-M. (eds.) ECCV 2020. LNCS, vol. 12359, pp. 266–282. Springer, Cham (2020). https://doi.org/10.1007/978-3-030-58568-6_16
58. Vaswani, A., et al.: Attention is all you need. In: Advances in Neural Information Processing Systems, pp. 5998–6008 (2017)
59. Vinyals, O., Blundell, C., Lillicrap, T., Wierstra, D., et al.: Matching networks for one shot learning. In: Advances in Neural Information Processing Systems 29, pp. 3630–3638 (2016)
60. Wortsman, M., et al.: Robust fine-tuning of zero-shot models. arXiv preprint arXiv:2109.01903 (2021)
61. Wright, R.E.: Logistic regression (1995)
62. Xiao, J., Hays, J., Ehinger, K.A., Oliva, A., Torralba, A.: SUN database: large-scale scene recognition from abbey to zoo. In: 2010 IEEE Computer Society Conference on Computer Vision and Pattern Recognition, pp. 3485–3492. IEEE (2010)
63. Xu, S., Li, Y., Zhao, J., Zhang, B., Guo, G.: POEM: 1-bit point-wise operations based on expectation-maximization for efficient point cloud processing. arXiv preprint arXiv:2111.13386 (2021)
64. Xu, S., Zhao, J., Lu, J., Zhang, B., Han, S., Doermann, D.: Layer-wise searching for 1-bit detectors. In: Proceedings of the IEEE/CVF Conference on Computer Vision and Pattern Recognition, pp. 5682–5691 (2021)
65. You, Q., Jin, H., Wang, Z., Fang, C., Luo, J.: Image captioning with semantic attention. In: Proceedings of the IEEE Conference on Computer Vision and Pattern Recognition, pp. 4651–4659 (2016)
66. Yu, L., et al.: MAttNet: modular attention network for referring expression comprehension. In: Proceedings of the IEEE Conference on Computer Vision and Pattern Recognition, pp. 1307–1315 (2018)
67. Zhang, R., et al.: Point-M2AE: multi-scale masked autoencoders for hierarchical point cloud pre-training. arXiv preprint arXiv:2205.14401 (2022)
68. Zhang, R., et al.: PointCLIP: point cloud understanding by clip. In: Proceedings of the IEEE/CVF Conference on Computer Vision and Pattern Recognition, pp. 8552–8562 (2022)
69. Zhang, R., et al.: MonoDETR: depth-aware transformer for monocular 3D object detection. arXiv preprint arXiv:2203.13310 (2022)
70. Zhao, J., Xu, S., Zhang, B., Gu, J., Doermann, D., Guo, G.: Towards compact 1-bit CNNs via Bayesian learning. Int. J. Comput. Vis. **130**(2), 201–225 (2022)
71. Zhao, Z., Wu, Z., Zhang, Y., Li, B., Jia, J.: Tracking objects as pixel-wise distributions (2022)
72. Zheng, M., et al.: End-to-end object detection with adaptive clustering transformer. arXiv preprint arXiv:2011.09315 (2020)
73. Zhou, K., Yang, J., Loy, C.C., Liu, Z.: Learning to prompt for vision-language models. arXiv preprint arXiv:2109.01134 (2021)

Temporal Lift Pooling for Continuous Sign Language Recognition

Lianyu Hu(iD), Liqing Gao(iD), Zekang Liu(iD), and Wei Feng$^{(\boxtimes)}$(iD)

Tianjin University, Tianjin 300350, China
{hly2021,lqgao,lzk100953}@tju.edu.cn, wfeng@ieee.org

Abstract. Pooling methods are necessities for modern neural networks for increasing receptive fields and lowering down computational costs. However, commonly used hand-crafted pooling approaches, e.g., max pooling and average pooling, may not well preserve discriminative features. While many researchers have elaborately designed various pooling variants in spatial domain to handle these limitations with much progress, the temporal aspect is rarely visited where directly applying hand-crafted methods or these specialized spatial variants may not be optimal. In this paper, we derive temporal lift pooling (TLP) from the Lifting Scheme in signal processing to intelligently downsample features of different temporal hierarchies. The Lifting Scheme factorizes input signals into various sub-bands with different frequency, which can be viewed as different temporal movement patterns. Our TLP is a three-stage procedure, which performs signal decomposition, component weighting and information fusion to generate a refined downsized feature map. We select a typical temporal task with long sequences, i.e. continuous sign language recognition (CSLR), as our testbed to verify the effectiveness of TLP. Experiments on two large-scale datasets show TLP outperforms hand-crafted methods and specialized spatial variants by a large margin (1.5%) with similar computational overhead. As a robust feature extractor, TLP exhibits great generalizability upon multiple backbones on various datasets and achieves new state-of-the-art results on two large-scale CSLR datasets. Visualizations further demonstrate the mechanism of TLP in correcting gloss borders. Code is released (https://github.com/hulianyuyy/Temporal-Lift-Pooling).

Keywords: Lifting scheme · Continuous sign language recognition · Temporal lift pooling

1 Introduction

Sign language is one of the most commonly used communication tools for the deaf people. However, mastering this language is difficult for the hearing people,

Supplementary Information The online version contains supplementary material available at https://doi.org/10.1007/978-3-031-19833-5_30.

which forms an obstacle for communication between two groups. To handle this problem, continuous sign language recognition (CSLR) aims to translate sign videos into corresponding gloss sentences, which is feasible to bridge this gap.

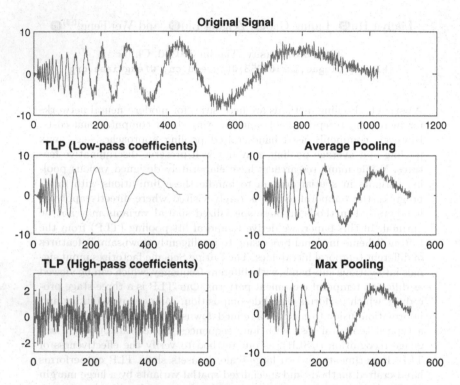

Fig. 1. Effects of temporal lift pooling (TLP) and hand-crafted pooling methods. TLP clearly decomposes input signal into various temporal patterns while hand-crafted pooling methods can't well distinguish noise from body movements.

Pooling methods are necessities for modern neural networks (NNs) for increasing receptive fields and generating discriminative representations. Several simple pooling methods, like max pooling and average pooling, are broadly employed in various domains [1,24,38] for their remarkable generalizability. While effective and efficient, simply using these hand-crafted methods may not fully consider local structures and optimally preserve features of different hierarchies. For the spatial domain, many researchers [11,13,31,32,38–40] have realized the limitations of hand-crafted pooling and elaborately designed many downsampling approaches for better preserving details. However, the temporal aspect is rarely explored where directly applying hand-crafted methods or these spatially specialized variants may not fit the temporal pattern well.

Our method is inspired by the Lifting Scheme [33] from signal processing, which is commonly used in information compression [27], reconstruction [7] and denoising [37]. The Lifting Scheme decomposes an input signal into various sub-bands with downscaled sizes of different frequencies, which is ideal for joint time-frequency analysis. Applying the idea of Lifting Scheme, we present temporal lift pooling (TLP) to factorize inputs into major and adjunctive movements and integrate them into a downsized refined representation. As shown in Fig. 1, the low-pass coefficients generated by TLP smoothly restore original low-frequency signals, which can be viewed as body movement patterns. The high-pass coefficients extract high-frequency components from inputs that represent detailed dynamics. In contrast, hand-crafted max pooling and average pooling fail to deal with mixed inputs and even amplify extremes or lose details sometimes.

TLP is consisted of three stages: lifting process, component weighting and fusion, which step by step decomposes input signal and reweights its components for a unified output. As a plug-and-play tool, TLP is implemented with tiny convolutional neural networks with only additional 0.4% computational costs. As an effective downsampling unit, it exhibits excellent generalizability upon multiple backbones on various datasets. By only replacing two pooling locations with TLP, a significant 1.5% performance boost is witnessed, which largely surpasses the hand-crafted methods and spatial pooling variants on CSLR. Besides, TLP achieves new state-of-the-art results on two large-scale CSLR datasets. Visualizations present the effects of TLP to correct gloss borders on accurate recognition.

2   Related Work

2.1   Continuous Sign Language Recognition

Earlier methods [8,10,14,21] in CSLR always employ hand-crafted features or HMM-based systems [22,23] to perform temporal modeling and translate sentences step by step. HMM-hybrid methods [22,23] typically first employ a feature extractor for representative features and then adopt an HMM for long-term temporal modeling. The success of convolutional neural networks (CNNs) and recurrent neural networks (RNNs) bring huge progress for CSLR. CTC loss [12] provides a new perspective to align target sentences with input frames which is broadly used by recent CSLR approaches [3,6,25,26,28,29]. They first rely on a feature extractor, i.e. 3D or 2D&1D CNN hybrids, to extract frame-wise features, and then adopt a LSTM module for capturing long-term temporal dependencies. However, several methods [6,29] found in such conditions the feature extractor is not well trained. Some recent approaches present the iterative training strategy to relieve this problem, but consume much more computations and multiple training stages. More recent studies [3,25,28] try to directly enhance the feature extractor by adding alignment losses [25] or adopt pseudo labels for supervision to tackle this issue [3].

2.2   Pooling Methods

Pooling has been commonly used in modern NNs for discriminative representations and reducing computational costs since Neocognitron [9]. Previous studies mainly focus on pooling in the spatial domain but rarely explore the temporal side. Max pooling and average pooling are two commonly used flexible hand-crafted methods in various tasks which could be dated back to LeNet [24] periods. Boureau et al. [1] prove max pooling can preserve more discriminative features than average pooling in terms of probability. Apart from these simple hand-crafted methods, various pooling variants have been proposed to better preserve details while maintaining efficiency. L_p pooling [13] introduces L_p norm to activate and normalize outputs, which can be viewed as a continuum between max and average pooling. Mixed pooling [38] tries to integrate the characteristics of max pooling and average pooling by a learned coefficient for better performance. Stochastic pooling [39] presents a multinomial sampling algorithm to select output values in the sampling window. S3Pool [40] attempts to introduce regulation in rows and columns, which can be viewed as some kind of data augmentation. Detail-preserving pooling (DPP) [31] aims to preserve details in 2D grids by selecting discriminative responses. LIP [11] formulates existing pooling methods under a general framework and designs a tiny convolutional network to generate local importance for values in a sampling window. Softpool [32] employs the softmax function to measure the contribution of values and adopts the normalized outputs as downscaled contents. LiftPool [41] introduces Lifting Scheme to design both downsampling and upsampling variants. However, it mainly tackles spatial tasks and doesn't consider temporal patterns. Besides, it fails to further measure the contribution of different components in sub-bands and doesn't deal with hierarchical features. Especially, all these approaches focus on the spatial aspect but don't explore the temporal side, while not all of them (e.g., DPP [31] and S3Pool [40]) are directly applicable for temporal tasks. Besides, directly applying hand-crafted pooling methods or these specialized spatial variants may not be optimal for temporal modeling. As shown in the experiments, our TLP surpasses all these counterparts by a large margin.

3   Methods

3.1   Overview

As shown in Fig. 2, recent CSLR methods [3,6,25,26,28,29] usually first employ a common 2D CNN to extract frame-wise features, and then deploy a 1D CNN consisted of a sequence of 1D Conv and pooling methods to model short-term temporal dependencies, followed by a two-layer BiLSTM and classifier for sentence prediction. Especially, two pooling layers are adopted in the 1D CNN to squeeze input length for downsampled discriminative representations to predict sentences. Practically, max pooling with kernel size of 2 and stride of 2 is used as default. As the downsampling process is intrinsically lossy, it's necessary to consider which information to be kept for subsequent sentence prediction. Inappropriate downsampling may lead to beneficial information loss and movement pattern deformation, thus affecting recognition performance. In this paper, we refer to Lifting Scheme [33] originated from signal processing to handle this issue and derive an efficient and effective pooling method.

3.2   Temporal Lift Pooling

Pooling methods are necessities for reducing computational costs and obtaining discriminative representations for temporal tasks with long input sequences, e.g., CSLR. Commonly used hand-crafted pooling methods may not well consider local patterns and don't optimally preserve critical representations. We derive temporal lift pooing (TLP) from the Lifting Scheme to exploit temporal correlations in signals to build a downsized approximation.

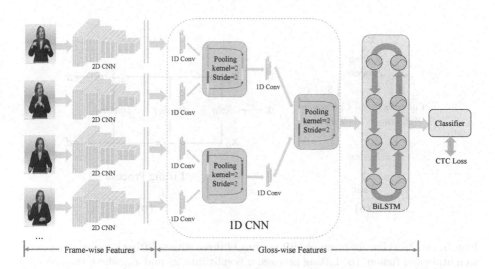

Fig. 2. Overview of recent CSLR methods. They first employ a common 2D CNN to extract frame-wise features, and then adopt a 1D CNN to perform short-term temporal modeling. A two-layer BiLSTM is used to capture long-term temporal dependencies, followed by a classifier to predict sentences. Especially, two pooling layers are adopted in 1D CNN for shortened discriminative representation. Practically, max pooling with kernel size of 2 and stride of 2 is used as default. We replace them with TLP to intelligently preserve discriminative features.

As shown in Fig. 3(a), our TLP is composed of three stages, i.e., lifting process, component weighting and fusion. We will detail them one by one.

Lifting Process. Given a 1D temporal signal $x = [x_1, x_2, x_3, \ldots, x_t]$ ($x \in \mathcal{R}^{C \times T}, t \in \mathcal{N}+$) where C denotes channel and T represents the sequence length, lifting process decomposes x into a downsized approximation s and a difference signal d as :

$$s, d = \mathcal{F}(x). \tag{1}$$

Here, $\mathcal{F}(\cdot) = f_{update} \circ f_{predict} \circ f_{split}$ is consisted of three functions: split, predict and update as shown in Fig. 3, where $\circ$ is the function composition operator.

Split f_{split}: $x \mapsto (x_e, x_o)$. It partitions input signal x into two disjoint sets x_e, x_o for downsized signal generation. Practically, x_e and x_o are generated with even and odd indices, respectively, where $x_e = [x_2, x_4, \ldots, x_{2k}]$ and $x_o = [x_1, x_3, \ldots, x_{2k-1}]$ ($k \in \mathcal{N}+$) are temporally closely correlated.

Predict $f_{predict}$: $(x_e, x_o) \mapsto d$. Given a selected set, e.g., x_e, $f_{predict}$ predicts another set x_o by a predictor $\mathcal{P}(\cdot)$. As only one basis x_e is given, the prediction is not required to be precise, which is expected to be collaborated with following f_{update}. So the difference signal d with high-pass coefficients is obtained as:

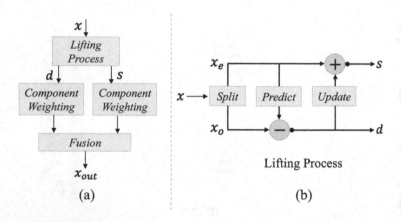

(a)   (b)

Fig. 3. (a) Overview for temporal lift pooling of three stages: lifting process, component weighting and fusion. (b) Lifting process. x is split into x_e and x_o, where the predictor and updater generate an approximation s and a difference signal d.

$$d = x_o - \mathcal{P}(x_e). \tag{2}$$

Update f_{update}: $(x_e, d) \mapsto s$. As the prediction process is undoubtedly aliasing and simply taking alternately sampled x_e as the approximation of x will cause inevitably information loss, an update function $\mathcal{U}(\cdot)$ takes the difference d as input for compensation and generates the smoothed downsized representations s as :

$$s = x_e + \mathcal{U}(d). \tag{3}$$

This update procedure can be viewed as applying a low-pass filter for x and thus s is the downsized approximation of original signal with low-pass coefficients. It's worth noting that the prediction and update procedure are intrinsically adversarial. If $f_{predict}$ precisely predicts x_o based on x_e, the difference signal d will be minor and thus the approximation s will be extremely biased towards x_e, resulting in aliasing downsampling. If $f_{predict}$ can't well perform prediction, the difference signal d will be huge and make the approximation s deformed from original signal x. Thus, $f_{predict}$ and $f_{predict}$ works in an antagonistic way, expecting to generate discriminative and detailed signals, s and d, respectively.

The classic Lifting Scheme methods apply predefined low-pass filters and high-pass filters to decompose x into different sub-bands. However, manually designing filters for $\mathcal{P}(\cdot)$ and $\mathcal{U}(\cdot)$ is difficult [42] and can't fit various conditions. Previously, [42] proposed to optimize filters in $\mathcal{P}(\cdot)$ and $\mathcal{U}(\cdot)$ by backward propagated gradients for signal processing. We design $\mathcal{P}(\cdot)$ and $\mathcal{U}(\cdot)$ with tiny fully convolutional networks which are optimized in an end-to-end manner as:

$$\mathcal{P}(\cdot) = \text{Tanh}() \circ \text{Conv}(k = 1) \circ \text{ReLU}() \circ \text{Conv}(k = K, g = C_{in}), \qquad (4)$$

$$\mathcal{U}(\cdot) = \text{Tanh}() \circ \text{Conv}(k = 1) \circ \text{ReLU}() \circ \text{Conv}(k = K, g = C_{in}). \qquad (5)$$

Here k denotes the kernel size and g represent the group number for convolution. We prefer to first deploy a 1D depth-wise convolution with kernel size K to aggregate local temporal patterns, followed by a ReLU activation. And then we use a normal 1×1 convolution to enable channel-wise aggregation, followed by a Tanh activation for feature prediction.

For generating discriminative representations, two loss constraints are employed apart from original task loss. Recall that the downsized approximation s is originated from x_e by Eq. 3, it's essentially close to x_e. We employ loss C_u to encourage x_e to approximate x_o as well, by minimizing the L2-Norm distance between s and x_o as:

$$C_u = \|s - x_o\|^2 = \|\mathcal{U}(d) + x_e - x_o\|^2. \qquad (6)$$

Another loss C_p is used to minimizing the L2-Norm of difference signal d as:

$$C_p = \|d\|^2 = \|x_o - \mathcal{P}(x_e)\|^2. \qquad (7)$$

Thus, for a certain task, the final loss functions can be written as:

$$\mathcal{L}_{total} = \mathcal{L}_{task} + \alpha_u C_u + \alpha_p C_p \qquad (8)$$

where $\mathcal{L}_{task}$ is the loss for a certain temporal task, e.g., CSLR in this paper, and α_u and α_p are coefficients for C_u and C_p, respectively.

Component Weighting. The approximation s and difference signal d represent low-pass coefficients and high-pass coefficients for original signal x, respectively, which can be viewed as dominating movement patterns and adhering action details for input sequences. As not all frequency components in s or d play an important role in depicting human dynamics, we design a component weighting module f_{weight} to dynamically emphasize or suppress certain components in s or d for robust temporal representations.

Specially, for each timestamp t, f_{weight} aims to generate a specific coefficient for each channel, resulting in a total weight matrix $W \in \mathcal{R}^{C \times T}$. We instantiate f_{weight} with a tiny fully convolutional network followed by a Sigmoid function at the end, which is optimized in an end-to-end manner to dynamically decide the weights. Each value ranging from $(0, 1)$ in W represents the importance of a certain component generated by the lifting process. Instead of directly multiplying

W with inputs for weighting, which we found badly hurts original representations, we perform component weighting in a residual way as:

$$X^{out} = (W - \frac{1}{2}\mathbb{1}) \times X_{in} + X_{in} \tag{9}$$

where $\mathbb{1} \in \mathcal{R}^{C \times T}$ is a full-one matrix. We first change values in W from $(0, 1)$ into $(-\frac{1}{2}, \frac{1}{2})$ and multiple W with X_{in} for obtaining biased components. Adding the biased components with X_{in} can effectively strengthen or weaken X_{in}, without hurting its original expressions.

Fusion. Given the low-pass and high-pass coefficients s^* and d^* after component weighting, we devise three simple strategies to fuse them into a single and robust representation as the temporal downsized output.

Sum. s^* and d^* are simply summed to combine their components as:

$$y = s^* + d^* \tag{10}$$

Concatenation. s^* and d^* are concatenated along channel dimension as:

$$y = \text{Concat}(s^*, d^*), \tag{11}$$

resulting in $y \in \mathcal{R}^{2C \times T}$ with double capacity.

Convolutional Bottleneck. We employ a tiny convolutional network consisted of sequences of convolution with kernel size 1, BatchNorm and ReLU to combine s^* and d^* as:

$$y = \text{ReLU}(\text{BN}(\text{Conv}(\text{Concat}(s^*, d^*)))). \tag{12}$$

Discussion. Max pooling and average pooling are two widely used pool methods in various tasks. However, they follow predefined mechanisms to select values, which may not be optimal. For example, max pooling typically puts all attention on the element with the largest activation. However, the assumption that the maximum activation stands for the most discriminative element, may not always be true. Besides, the max operator hinders gradient-based optimization where only the largest activation in a sampling region is assigned back-propagated gradients, which may slow down convergence. Although average pooling ensures all elements can contribute to outputs, it treats them equally which usually results in smoothed outputs and hurts small but discriminative responses. In this paper, we refer to Lifting Scheme from signal processing to decompose signals into different sub-bands with major movements or discriminative details, which naturally fit the problem. Our method dynamically generates the downsized output for each sample, which jumps out of the hand-crafted scope like max or average pooling. Besides, our method can smoothly behave like max or average pooling, which falls between them but keeps more representative features than both due to hierarchical signal decomposition.

4 Experiments

4.1 Datasets

We evaluate our method on two commonly used large-scale datasets: RWTH-PHOENIX-Weather-2014 (PHOENIX14) and RWTH-PHOENIX-2014-Weather-T (PHOENIX14-T).

PHOENIX14 [21] is recorded from the German TV weather by nine signers wearing dark clothes in front of a clean background. It contains 6841 sentences with a vocabulary of 1295 signs, divided into 5672 training instances, 540 development (Dev) instances and 629 testing (Test) instances. All videos are shot by 25 fps with resolution 210×260.

PHOENIX14-T [2] is available for both CSLR and Sign Language Translation (SLT) tasks which can be viewed as an extension of PHOENIX14. It contains 8247 sentences with a vocabulary of 1085 signs, split into 7096 training samples, 519 development (Dev) samples and 642 testing (Test) samples.

4.2 Training Details

ResNet18 [15] is adopted as the 2D CNN backbone for fair comparison with recent methods. The 1D CNN is consisted of a sequence of {K5, P2, K5, P2} layers where $K\sigma$ and $P\sigma$ denotes a 1D convolutional layer and a pooling layer with kernel size of σ, respectively. A two-layer BiLSTM with hidden size 1024 is adopted for long-term temporal modeling, followed by a fully connected layer for sentence prediction. We train our models for 80 epochs with initial learning rate 0.001 which is divided by 5 at epoch 40 and 60. Adam [19] optimizer is adopted as default with weight decay 0.001 and batch size 2. All input frames are first resized to 256×256, and then randomly cropped to 224×224 with 50% horizontal flipping and 20% temporal rescaling during training. During inference, a 224×224 center crop is simply adopted. Following VAC [25], we employ the visual enhancement loss and visual alignment loss for additional visual supervision, with weights of 1.0 and 25.0, respectively. We only substitute two pooling layers in the 1D CNN with our TLP, as shown in Fig. 2. The coefficients α_u and α_p for loss C_u and C_p are set as 0.001.

Word Error Rate (WER) is used as the metric of measuring similarity between predicted sentence and reference sentence. It's defined as the minimal number of substitution, insertion and deletion operations to convert the predicted sentence to the reference sentence as:

$$\text{WER} = \frac{\#\text{substitutions} + \#\text{insertions} + \#\text{deletions}}{\#\text{reference}}. \tag{13}$$

Note that the lower WER, the better.

4.3 Ablation Study

Configurations for $\mathcal{P}(\cdot)$ & $\mathcal{U}(\cdot)$. Table 1a ablates the performance when varying the kernel size K for $\mathcal{P}(\cdot)$ & $\mathcal{U}(\cdot)$. Notably, a larger kernel with more local aggregation ability consistently brings better performance. When K reaches 7, it brings no more performance gain. We thus set K as 5 by default. We then test other instantiations for $\mathcal{P}(\cdot)$ & $\mathcal{U}(\cdot)$, e.g., a simple combination of Conv and Tanh, and found it obtains lower performance than current design.

Configurations for Component Weighting. In the upper part of Table 1b, we first test different implementations for f_{weight} to dynamically strengthen or weaken various components. Compared to the two-Conv counterpart in the top, we observe a simpler design, i.e. $Sigmoid \circ IN \circ Conv$, achieves better performance which we employ as default. When varying the kernel size for f_{weight}, $k = 5$ performs best among all candidates. We further compare the effect of normalization methods in f_{weight} which are typically employed to accelerate convergence and promote performance. InstanceNorm (IN) [36] and commonly used BatchNorm (BN) [18] are compared. We find that IN achieves more stable and superior performance than BN, which results from cross-batch normalization

Table 1. Ablation study for different modules of TLP on PHOENIX14 dataset.

Configurations for $\mathcal{P}(\cdot)$ & $\mathcal{U}(\cdot)$	Dev(%)	Test(%)
$K=3$	20.0	21.1
$K=4$	19.9	21.1
$K=5$	**19.7**	**20.8**
$K=7$	19.9	21.0
$Tanh \circ Conv(k = 5)$	20.2	21.3

(a) Effects of different configurations for $\mathcal{P}(\cdot)$ & $\mathcal{U}(\cdot)$

Component weighting	Dev(%)	Test(%)
$Sigmoid \circ IN \circ Conv(k = 1) \circ Conv(k = 5, g = C_{in})$	20.1	21.2
$Sigmoid \circ IN \circ Conv(k = 3)$	20.0	21.2
$Sigmoid \circ IN \circ Conv(k = 5)$	**19.7**	**20.8**
$Sigmoid \circ IN \circ Conv(k = 7)$	19.9	20.9
$Sigmoid \circ BN \circ Conv(k = 5)$	21.1	22.3
$X^{out} = W \times X_{in}$	20.9	21.9
$X^{out} = (W - \frac{1}{2}\mathbf{1}) \times X_{in} + X_{in}$	**19.7**	**20.8**
-	20.2	21.4
Shared for s & d	19.9	20.9
Independent for s & d	**19.7**	**20.8**

(b) Effects of different configurations for component weighting.

Fusion	Dev(%)	Test(%)	Locations for TLP	Dev(%)	Test(%)
Only s^*	20.2	21.2	-	21.2	22.3
Sum	**19.7**	**20.8**	First location	20.1	21.3
Concatenation	19.9	21.1	Second location	20.3	21.1
Convolutional bottleneck	20.1	21.4	Two locations	**19.7**	**20.8**

(c) Effects of different fusion methods.   (d) Effects of locations for TLP hurting the feature distribution for each sample. We then compare the choice of directly weighting with our residual architecture for component weighting. Seen from the middle in Table 1b, the residual architecture outperforms directly weighting by a large margin, where the latter inevitably hurts the original representation and leads to unstable expressions. We finally test the effects of component weighting under different configurations. Compared to w/o component weighting, deploying component weighting in an either shared or independent way for s & d achieves better performance. Furthermore, independent weighting for s & d brings more performance boost by considering the specific characteristics of two pathways.

Fusion Methods. Table 1c ablates different configurations for fusion of s^* and d^*. s^* and d^* generated by lifting process correspond to different hierarchical features, while our TLP allows to flexibly choose which sub-band to be kept as downsized outputs. We note that only preserving s^* obtains lower performance than other variants, which demonstrates the effectiveness of combining low-pass coefficients s^* and high-pass coefficients d^* for effective recognition. Table 1c shows that simply summing s^* and d^* gives the best performance among all candidates, which we employ as default in the following experiments.

Locations for TLP. We incrementally add one or more TLPs in different locations to verify its effectiveness in Table 1d. Compared to our baseline w/o TLP, adding one TLP in either the first or second location brings considerable 1.1% and 0.9% performance boost, respectively. Replacing total two pooling instances with TLP gives notable 1.5% promotion without any other architecture change, demonstrating the key role of temporal pooling and the effect of TLP for robust discriminative representations.

Table 2. Computational efficiency of TLP against commonly used max pooling and average pooling on PHOENIX14 dataset.

Methods	GFLOPs	Throughout(Vids/s)	Memory(M)	Dev(%)	Test(%)
Max pooling	3.671	12.22	8827	21.2	22.3
Average pooling	3.671	12.40	8827	21.1	22.1
TLP (Ours)	3.686	12.12	8846	19.7 (+1.5)	20.8 (+1.5)

4.4 Computational Efficiency

Our TLP is an efficient plug-and-play tool with little computational overhead. Under the formula of Eq. 4, Eq. 5 and Eq. 9, two TLPs totally consumes 7.5M × 2 = 15.0M FLOPs[1], which is negligible (0.4%) compared to our 2D backbone ResNet18 (3.64G FLOPs). Considering our TLP is composed of highly

---

[1] FLOPs denote floating point operations, which measure the computational costs of models.

specialized operators like convolution and activation functions, it enjoys high computational efficiency on GPUs with little delay. As shown in Table 2, compared to commonly used max pooling and average pooling, our TLP exhibits similar GFLOPs, throughout and memory usage with significantly higher performance, which is a both effective and efficient plug-and-play tool for temporal tasks.

Table 3. Comparison of our TSP with other pooling variants on the Dev and Test set of PHOENIX14 and PHOENIX14-T dataset.

Pooling methods	PHOENIX14		PHOENIX14-T	
	Dev (%)	Test (%)	Dev (%)	Test (%)
Max pooling (**Baseline**)	21.2	22.3	21.1	22.8
Stochastic pooling	22.2 (−1.0)	23.4 (−1.1)	22.3 (−1.2)	23.7 (−0.9)
Mixed pooling	21.5 (−0.3)	22.6 (−0.3)	21.3 (−0.2)	23.0 (−0.2)
L_p pooling ($p = 3$)	21.5 (−0.3)	22.5 (−0.2)	21.3 (−0.2)	23.1 (−0.3)
SoftPool	21.3 (−0.1)	22.5 (−0.2)	21.1 (+0.0)	22.9 (−0.1)
L_p pooling ($p = 2$)	21.1 (+0.1)	22.3 (+0.0)	21.2 (−0.1)	22.7 (+0.1)
Average pooling	21.1 (+0.1)	22.1 (+0.2)	20.9 (+0.2)	22.6 (+0.2)
TLP (Ours)	19.7 (**+1.5**)	20.8 (**+1.5**)	19.4 (**+1.7**)	21.2 (**+1.6**)

4.5 Comparison with Other Pooling Methods

We compare our TSP with other pooling variants to demonstrate its effectiveness in Table 3. Most of these counterpart pooling methods are elaborately designed for preserving critical spatial features. As shown in Table 3, except L_p pooling ($p = 2$) and average pooling, most pooling methods cause performance decline on both PHOENIX14 dataset and PHOENIX14-T dataset. L_p pooling ($p = 2$) and average pooling bring marginal performance boost ($\leq 0.2\%$). Although most of these variants are elaborately designed for spatial tasks with superior performance, they don't exhibit much superiority on temporal tasks, e.g., CSLR. In contrast, some of them even lead to lower performance. Hand-crafted pooling methods, like max pooling and average pooling, show robust performance on both datasets, demonstrating their excellent generalization ability. Compared to these pooling variants, our TLP consistently exhibits superior performance ($\geq 1.5\%$) upon both datasets and largely surpasses all of them by a large margin. These results verify the effectiveness of our TLP by combining different sub-bands for discriminative hierarchical representations.

Table 4. Generalizability of TLP upon various backbones on both PHOENIX14 dataset and PHOENIX14-T dataset.

Methods	PHOENIX14		PHOENIX14-T	
	Dev (%)	Test (%)	Dev (%)	Test (%)
ResNet18 [15]	21.2	22.3	21.1	22.8
ResNet18 w/ TLP	19.7 (+1.5)	20.8 (+1.5)	19.4 (+1.7)	21.2 (+1.6)
SqueezeNet [17]	23.2	23.5	21.7	23.1
SqueezeNet w/ TLP	22.2 (+1.0)	22.3 (+1.2)	20.6 (+1.1)	22.0 (+1.1)
RegNetX-800Mf [30]	21.4	22.5	21.0	22.3
RegNetX-800Mf w/ TLP	20.0 (+1.4)	21.1 (+1.4)	19.5 (+1.5)	20.9 (+1.4)
RegNetY-800Mf [30]	21.3	22.2	20.7	21.8
RegNetY-800Mf w/ TLP	19.7 (+1.6)	20.5 (+1.7)	19.1 (+1.6)	20.1 (+1.7)

Table 5. Comparison with other state-of-the-art methods on the PHOENIX14 and PHOENIX14-T datasets. * indicate extra clues such as face or hand features are included. 'C+L+H' denotes the abbreviation of 'CNN+HMM+LSTM [20]'

Methods	Backbone	PHOENIX14				PHOENIX14-T	
		del/ins	WER	del/ins	WER	Dev (%)	Test (%)
		Dev (%)		Test (%)			
SubUNet [4]	CaffeNet	14.6/4.0	40.8	4.3/4.0	40.7	–	–
Staged-Opt [5]	VGG-S	13.7/7.3	39.4	12.2/7.5	38.7	–	–
Align-iOpt [29]	3D-ResNet	12.6/2	37.1	13.0/2.5	36.7	–	–
Re-Sign [23]	GoogLeNet	–	27.1	–	26.8	–	–
SFL [26]	ResNet18	7.9/6.5	26.2	7.5/6.3	26.8	25.1	26.1
STMC [43]	VGG11	–	25.0	–	–	–	–
DNF [6]	GoogLeNet	7.8/3.5	23.8	7.8/3.4	24.4	–	–
FCN [3]	Custom	–	23.7	–	23.9	23.3	25.1
CMA [28]	GoogLeNet	7.3/2.7	**21.3**	7.3/2.4	**21.9**	–	–
VAC [25]	ResNet18	7.9/2.5	**21.2**	8.4/2.6	**22.3**	–	–
SLT* [2]	GoogLeNet	–	–	–	–	24.5	24.6
C+L+H* [20]	GoogLeNet	–	26.0	–	26.0	22.1	24.1
DNF* [6]	GoogLeNet	7.3/3.3	23.1	6.7/3.3	22.9	–	–
STMC* [43]	VGG11	7.7/3.4	**21.1**	7.4/2.6	**20.7**	19.6	**21.0**
Baseline	ResNet18	7.9/2.5	21.2	8.4/2.6	22.3	21.1	22.8
TLP (Ours)	ResNet18	6.3/2.8	**19.7**	6.1/2.9	**20.8**	19.4	**21.2**

4.6   Generalizability

We apply TLP to several backbones including ResNet18 [15], SqueezeNet [17], RegNetX-800Mf [30] and RegNetY-800Mf [30] on both datasets to demonstrate its generalizability. As shown in Table 4, TLP consistently brings significant performance boost ($\geq$1.0%) across different backbones. We observe an interesting phenomenon where the effect of TLP seems to be proportional to the strength of backbones. For example, the boost by TLP is relatively smaller (1.0%) for less powerful SqueezeNet [17] (23.2%). In contrast, TLP brings much more performance boost ($\geq$1.7%) for more powerful backbones, e.g., RegNetY-800Mf [30] (21.3%). Other backbones like MobileNet-V2 [16], EfficientNet-B0 [35] and MNASNet [34] are found out of memory upon current devices.

4.7   Comparison with the State-of-the-Art

We compare our model against other state-of-the-art methods on the PHOENIX14 and PHOENIX14-T dataset in Table 5. The entries notated with * indicate these methods such as SLT [2], CNN+LSTM+HMM [20], DNF [6] and STMC [43] utilize additional factors like face or hand features for better performance. We observe that our method outperforms all previous approaches with video information only. We also notice that our method even surpasses those approaches equipped with additional factors when only using video information, which demonstrates the effectiveness of our TLP.

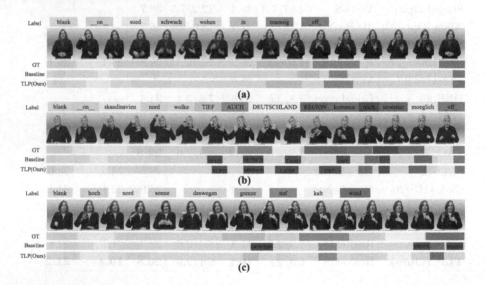

Fig. 4. Predictions of our baseline and TLP for several example videos. (a) All glosses are correctly recognized by both our baseline and TLP. (b) The same four glosses are wrongly recognized by both our baseline and TLP. (c) Our baseline wrongly recognizes several glosses while TLP makes correct predictions. Wrong recognized glosses (except del) are marked in red. (Color figure online)

5   Visualizations

To better understand the effects of TLP, we visualize several videos with their predictions of our baseline and TLP from the Dev set of PHOENIX14 dataset in Fig. 4. Wrong recognized glosses (except del) are marked in red. We show three different cases to help demonstrate the effect of TLP in various conditions. All glosses in Fig. 4(a) are correctly recognized by both our baseline and TLP. The same four glosses in Fig. 4(b) are wrongly recognized by both our baseline and TLP. Our baseline wrongly recognizes several glosses in Fig. 4(c) while TLP makes correct predictions. We notice in all cases, TLP predicts more centralized gloss borders than our baseline which helps accurate recognition.

6   Conclusion

In this paper, we derive temporal lift pooling (TLP) from the Lifting Scheme in signal processing to decompose input signals into various sub-bands, each corresponding to a specific movement pattern. Combining different components of TLP results in a refined downsized feature map, well preserving discriminative representations. TLP exhibits excellent generalizability upon multiple backbones upon two large-scale CSLR datasets with significant performance boost. Visualizations verify the effects of TLP for correcting gloss borders.

Acknowledgment. This work is supported by NSFC 62072334 Project.

References

1. Boureau, Y.L., Ponce, J., LeCun, Y.: A theoretical analysis of feature pooling in visual recognition. In: Proceedings of the 27th International Conference on Machine Learning (ICML-10), pp. 111–118 (2010)
2. Camgoz, N.C., Hadfield, S., Koller, O., Ney, H., Bowden, R.: Neural sign language translation. In: Proceedings of the IEEE Conference on Computer Vision and Pattern Recognition, pp. 7784–7793 (2018)
3. Cheng, K.L., Yang, Z., Chen, Q., Tai, Y.-W.: Fully convolutional networks for continuous sign language recognition. In: Vedaldi, A., Bischof, H., Brox, T., Frahm, J.-M. (eds.) ECCV 2020. LNCS, vol. 12369, pp. 697–714. Springer, Cham (2020). https://doi.org/10.1007/978-3-030-58586-0_41
4. Cihan Camgoz, N., Hadfield, S., Koller, O., Bowden, R.: SubUNets: end-to-end hand shape and continuous sign language recognition. In: ICCV (2017)
5. Cui, R., Liu, H., Zhang, C.: Recurrent convolutional neural networks for continuous sign language recognition by staged optimization. In: CVPR (2017)
6. Cui, R., Liu, H., Zhang, C.: A deep neural framework for continuous sign language recognition by iterative training. TMM **21**(7), 1880–1891 (2019)
7. Dogiwal, S.R., Shishodia, Y.S., Upadhyaya, A.: Efficient lifting scheme based super resolution image reconstruction using low resolution images. In: Kumar Kundu, M., Mohapatra, D.P., Konar, A., Chakraborty, A. (eds.) Advanced Computing, Networking and Informatics- Volume 1. SIST, vol. 27, pp. 259–266. Springer, Cham (2014). https://doi.org/10.1007/978-3-319-07353-8_31

8. Freeman, W.T., Roth, M.: Orientation histograms for hand gesture recognition. In: International Workshop on Automatic Face and Gesture Recognition, vol. 12, pp. 296–301. IEEE Computer Society, Washington, DC (1995)

9. Fukushima, K., Miyake, S.: Neocognitron: a self-organizing neural network model for a mechanism of visual pattern recognition. In: Amari, Si., Arbib, M.A. (eds.) Competition and Cooperation in Neural Nets. LNB, vol. 45, pp. 267–285. Springer, Heidelberg (1982). https://doi.org/10.1007/978-3-642-46466-9_18

10. Gao, W., Fang, G., Zhao, D., Chen, Y.: A Chinese sign language recognition system based on SOFM/SRN/HMM. Pattern Recognit. **37**(12), 2389–2402 (2004)

11. Gao, Z., Wang, L., Wu, G.: Lip: local importance-based pooling. In: Proceedings of the IEEE/CVF International Conference on Computer Vision, pp. 3355–3364 (2019)

12. Graves, A., Fernández, S., Gomez, F., Schmidhuber, J.: Connectionist temporal classification: labelling unsegmented sequence data with recurrent neural networks. In: Proceedings of the 23rd International Conference on Machine Learning, pp. 369–376 (2006)

13. Gulcehre, C., Cho, K., Pascanu, R., Bengio, Y.: Learned-norm pooling for deep feedforward and recurrent neural networks. In: Calders, T., Esposito, F., Hüllermeier, E., Meo, R. (eds.) ECML PKDD 2014. LNCS (LNAI), vol. 8724, pp. 530–546. Springer, Heidelberg (2014). https://doi.org/10.1007/978-3-662-44848-9_34

14. Han, J., Awad, G., Sutherland, A.: Modelling and segmenting subunits for sign language recognition based on hand motion analysis. Pattern Recognit. Lett. **30**(6), 623–633 (2009)

15. He, K., Zhang, X., Ren, S., Sun, J.: Deep residual learning for image recognition. In: Proceedings of the IEEE Conference on Computer Vision and Pattern Recognition, pp. 770–778 (2016)

16. Howard, A., Zhmoginov, A., Chen, L.C., Sandler, M., Zhu, M.: Inverted residuals and linear bottlenecks: mobile networks for classification, detection and segmentation (2018)

17. Iandola, F.N., et bal.: Squeezenet: AlexNet-level accuracy with 50x fewer parameters and 0.5 mb model size. arXiv preprint arXiv:1602.07360 (2016)

18. Ioffe, S., Szegedy, C.: Batch normalization: accelerating deep network training by reducing internal covariate shift. In: International Conference on Machine Learning, pp. 448–456. PMLR (2015)

19. Kingma, D.P., Ba, J.: Adam: a method for stochastic optimization. arXiv preprint arXiv:1412.6980 (2014)

20. Koller, O., Camgoz, N.C., Ney, H., Bowden, R.: Weakly supervised learning with multi-stream CNN-LSTM-HMMs to discover sequential parallelism in sign language videos. PAMI **42**(9), 2306–2320 (2019)

21. Koller, O., Forster, J., Ney, H.: Continuous sign language recognition: towards large vocabulary statistical recognition systems handling multiple signers. Comput. Vis. Image Underst. **141**, 108–125 (2015)

22. Koller, O., Zargaran, O., Ney, H., Bowden, R.: Deep sign: hybrid CNN-HMM for continuous sign language recognition. In: Proceedings of the British Machine Vision Conference 2016 (2016)

23. Koller, O., Zargaran, S., Ney, H.: Re-sign: re-aligned end-to-end sequence modelling with deep recurrent CNN-HMMs. In: CVPR (2017)

24. LeCun, Y., et al.: Handwritten digit recognition with a back-propagation network. In: Advances in Neural Information Processing Systems 2 (1989)

25. Min, Y., Hao, A., Chai, X., Chen, X.: Visual alignment constraint for continuous sign language recognition. In: ICCV (2021)
26. Niu, Z., Mak, B.: Stochastic fine-grained labeling of multi-state sign glosses for continuous sign language recognition. In: Vedaldi, A., Bischof, H., Brox, T., Frahm, J.-M. (eds.) ECCV 2020. LNCS, vol. 12361, pp. 172–186. Springer, Cham (2020). https://doi.org/10.1007/978-3-030-58517-4_11
27. Pesquet-Popescu, B., Bottreau, V.: Three-dimensional lifting schemes for motion compensated video compression. In: 2001 IEEE International Conference on Acoustics, Speech, and Signal Processing. Proceedings (Cat. No. 01CH37221), vol. 3, pp. 1793–1796. IEEE (2001)
28. Pu, J., Zhou, W., Hu, H., Li, H.: Boosting continuous sign language recognition via cross modality augmentation. In: ACM MM (2020)
29. Pu, J., Zhou, W., Li, H.: Iterative alignment network for continuous sign language recognition. In: CVPR (2019)
30. Radosavovic, I., Kosaraju, R.P., Girshick, R., He, K., Dollár, P.: Designing network design spaces. In: Proceedings of the IEEE/CVF Conference on Computer Vision and Pattern Recognition, pp. 10428–10436 (2020)
31. Saeedan, F., Weber, N., Goesele, M., Roth, S.: Detail-preserving pooling in deep networks. In: Proceedings of the IEEE Conference on Computer Vision and Pattern Recognition, pp. 9108–9116 (2018)
32. Stergiou, A., Poppe, R., Kalliatakis, G.: Refining activation downsampling with softpool. arXiv preprint arXiv:2101.00440 (2021)
33. Sweldens, W.: The lifting scheme: a construction of second generation wavelets. SIAM J. Math. Anal. 29(2), 511–546 (1998)
34. Tan, M., et al.: MnasNet: platform-aware neural architecture search for mobile. In: Proceedings of the IEEE/CVF Conference on Computer Vision and Pattern Recognition, pp. 2820–2828 (2019)
35. Tan, M., Le, Q.: EfficientNet: rethinking model scaling for convolutional neural networks. In: International Conference on Machine Learning, pp. 6105–6114. PMLR (2019)
36. Ulyanov, D., Vedaldi, A., Lempitsky, V.: Instance normalization: the missing ingredient for fast stylization. arXiv preprint arXiv:1607.08022 (2016)
37. Wu, Y., Pan, Q., Zhang, H., Zhang, S.: Adaptive denoising based on lifting scheme. In: Proceedings 7th International Conference on Signal Processing, 2004. Proceedings, ICSP 2004, vol. 1, pp. 352–355. IEEE (2004)
38. Yu, D., Wang, H., Chen, P., Wei, Z.: Mixed pooling for convolutional neural networks. In: Miao, D., Pedrycz, W., Ślęzak, D., Peters, G., Hu, Q., Wang, R. (eds.) RSKT 2014. LNCS (LNAI), vol. 8818, pp. 364–375. Springer, Cham (2014). https://doi.org/10.1007/978-3-319-11740-9_34
39. Zeiler, M.D., Fergus, R.: Stochastic pooling for regularization of deep convolutional neural networks. arXiv preprint arXiv:1301.3557 (2013)
40. Zhai, S., et al.: S3pool: pooling with stochastic spatial sampling. In: Proceedings of the IEEE Conference on Computer Vision and Pattern Recognition, pp. 4970–4978 (2017)
41. Zhao, J., Snoek, C.G.: Liftpool: bidirectional convnet pooling. arXiv preprint arXiv:2104.00996 (2021)
42. Zheng, Y., Wang, R., Li, J.: Nonlinear wavelets and BP neural networks adaptive lifting scheme. In: The 2010 International Conference on Apperceiving Computing and Intelligence Analysis Proceeding, pp. 316–319. IEEE (2010)
43. Zhou, H., Zhou, W., Zhou, Y., Li, H.: Spatial-temporal multi-cue network for continuous sign language recognition. In: AAAI (2020)

MORE: Multi-Order RElation Mining for Dense Captioning in 3D Scenes

Yang Jiao[1,2], Shaoxiang Chen[3], Zequn Jie[3], Jingjing Chen[1,2(✉)], Lin Ma[3(✉)], and Yu-Gang Jiang[1,2]

[1] Shanghai Key Lab of Intell. Info. Processing, School of CS, Fudan University, Shanghai, China
chenjingjing@fudan.edu.cn
[2] Shanghai Collaborative Innovation Center on Intelligent Visual Computing, Shanghai, China
[3] Meituan Inc., Beijing, China

Abstract. 3D dense captioning is a recently-proposed novel task, where point clouds contain more geometric information than the 2D counterpart. However, it is also more challenging due to the higher complexity and wider variety of inter-object relations contained in point clouds. Existing methods only treat such relations as by-products of object feature learning in graphs without specifically encoding them, which leads to sub-optimal results. In this paper, aiming at improving 3D dense captioning via capturing and utilizing the complex relations in the 3D scene, we propose MORE, a Multi-Order RElation mining model, to support generating more descriptive and comprehensive captions. Technically, our MORE encodes object relations in a progressive manner since complex relations can be deduced from a limited number of basic ones. We first devise a novel Spatial Layout Graph Convolution (SLGC), which semantically encodes several first-order relations as edges of a graph constructed over 3D object proposals. Next, from the resulting graph, we further extract multiple triplets which encapsulate basic first-order relations as the basic unit, and construct several Object-centric Triplet Attention Graphs (OTAG) to infer multi-order relations for every target object. The updated node features from OTAG are aggregated and fed into the caption decoder to provide abundant relational cues, so that captions including diverse relations with context objects can be generated. Extensive experiments on the Scan2Cap dataset prove the effectiveness of our proposed MORE and its components, and we also outperform the current state-of-the-art method. Our code is available at https://github.com/SxJyJay/MORE.

Keywords: Point cloud · Graph · Caption generation

Y. Jiao and S. Chen—Equal contribution.

Supplementary Information The online version contains supplementary material available at https://doi.org/10.1007/978-3-031-19833-5_31.

1   Introduction

Dense captioning, which aims at comprehending the visual scene through jointly localizing and describing multiple objects, has been extensively studied in the 2D computer vision community [9,10,13,20,39]. However, 2D data such as images and videos inherently lack the ability of accurately capturing the physical extent of objects and their locations in the scene. Recently, the 3D dense captioning task has been proposed by Chen et al. [11], where pure point clouds are adopted as the visual representation to perform object localization and captioning on. By connecting 3D scenes with natural language, 3D dense captioning has widespread application prospects in the field of human-machine interaction in augmented reality [21,43], autonomous agents [32,42], etc.

The abundant geometric information contained in 3D point clouds can support describing object relations and the holistic scene (scene layouts) in a diversified manner, since the 3D point clouds are less limited by the occlusion and better capture object size and relative position. For example, as shown in Fig. 1, the circled chair can be described with diversiform relations like *"on the right side"* and *"second ... from ..."*. So in 3D dense captioning, mining the complex inter-object relations is of vital importance for generating comprehensive captions. But directly adapting relation modeling techniques in 2D images [8,17–19,26,27,33,38] to 3D point clouds can lead to poor performances as discussed in the previous work [11]. Scan2Cap, as the first 3D dense captioning work, develops a graph-based encoder to provide relation feature for the caption decoder and achieves promising results. However, it treats inter-object relations as by-products derived from node recognition in a graph, overlooking the gap between the visual world (represented by point clouds) and semantic concepts. Hence, complex relations, such as *"between"*, *"surrounded by"*, *"rightmost"*, etc., can not be properly mapped into the semantic space, which leads to unitary descriptions being generated. As illustrated in Fig. 1, Scan2Cap tends to describe the target object by capturing simple relations (*"on the left"*).

To address the above problem, we propose MORE, a Multi-Order RElation mining model which can support generating more descriptive captions for objects in 3D point clouds. The core motivation behind MORE lies in the confidence that the multi-order relations can be deduced from a limited number of basic first-order relations. For example, given a scene where there are three objects in a row, dubbed A, B, and C, and *the relations between AB and BC are both "on the left of"*, then the conclusion that *C is the rightmost one* can be made. Hence, the main goal of our MORE is to first explicitly extract and encode basic first-order spatial relations among objects and then try to further infer multi-order relations for generating comprehensive captions.

Concretely, as shown in the Fig. 1 (green background part), MORE consists of two components: Spatial Layout Graph Convolution (SLGC) and Object-centric Triplet Attention Graphs (OTAG). First, to capture the concepts of basic first-order relation, SLGC adaptively introduces spatial semantics into the edges of an object graph. Afterward, inside the OTAG, triplets in the form of $<node_1, edge, node_2>$ are extracted from the previous graph as the basic

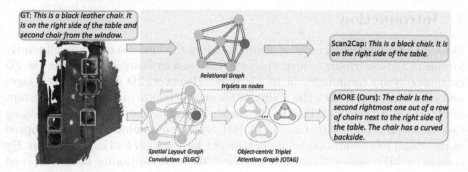

Fig. 1. The comparison of our proposed Multi-Order RElation mining model (MORE) with the previous method (i.e., Scan2Cap [11]). The core components of our MORE and the Scan2Cap are distinguished with green and blue background, respectively. Scan2Cap treats the inter-object relations as by-products derived from node feature learning in the relational graph, thus the diverse spatial relations are under-explored. While in our MORE, we model such relations via a Spatial Layout Graph Convolution (SLGC) and Object-centric Triplet Attention Graphs (OTAG) to progressively encode more complex spatial relations. For simplicity, we only show the caption of one specific object (in the dashed circle) from different models. It is clear that our method can describe more complex relations. (Color figure online)

descriptors of first-order inter-object relations, then several such object-centric triplet graphs are constructed where the triplets targeting the same object serve as nodes within the same triplet graph. On top of these graphs, the attention-based multi-order relation reasoning is performed within each of them. The advantage of using such triplets is that the basic relations are more explicitly preserved, and we can also flexibly extend a triplet to cover larger contexts. Finally, our caption decoder receives the target object feature and performs node aggregation on OTAG as the context for sentence generation. As illustrated by our captioning results in Fig. 1, the captions generated by MORE are more descriptive and comprehensive compared with the baseline method.

In summary, our contributions are threefold: (1) We propose a Multi-Order RElation mining model (MORE) for 3D dense captioning, which can generate more descriptive and comprehensive captions for each object. (2) Within the MORE, a Spatial Layout Convolution (SLGC) and Object-centric Triplet Attention Graphs (OTAG) are proposed and coupled together, where the former semantically encodes basic first-order spatial relations among objects in a 3D scene, and the latter infers the multi-order relations via attention-based graph reasoning. (3) Extensive experimental results prove that our MORE achieves superior performances than existing 3D dense captioning methods on prevalent benchmarks.

2 Related Work

Image and Video Captioning. Generating captions for 2D visual data (i.e., images and videos) has recently attracted significant research interest [9,10,13,20,23,37,39,45,47]. It is acknowledged that exploring the inter-object relationship benefits the caption generation, and such an idea has been widely investigated [20,23,37,44,45,47]. Yang et al. [44] directly adopt the global image feature as context. To further introduce extra linguistic prior upon various object relations, scene graph detectors are utilized by some image captioning methods [45,47] to parse the give image and assign textual tags to the relations. However, such detectors require expensive annotations to train. As an alternative, the part-of-speech tags are utilized as the prior to explicitly encode relations between objects in [20]. Although they are effective in 2D image and video caption generation, the spatial structures are much more complicated in the 3D scene, hence they can not be directly transferred to 3D dense captioning task.

3D Dense Captioning and Visual Grounding. Recently, investigating the 3D point cloud data and natural language has become a trending research topic [1,5,11,14,16,48]. Among the pioneer works, Chen et al. [5] and Achloptas et al. [1] first proposed two datasets, referred to as ScanRefer and ReferIt3D, respectively, which both contain descriptions for real-world 3D objects in Scan-Net [12]. On top of them, 3D visual grounding [1,5,14,16,48] and 3D dense captioning [11], as two dual tasks, are concurrently investigated, where the former focuses on localizing 3D objects described by natural language queries and the latter aims at generating descriptions for 3D objects in RGB-D scans. Exploring object relations is essential for both tasks, and many relevant attempts have been made in recent works [11,14–16,46,48,50].

In the 3D visual grounding task, earlier works, namely TGNN [16] and InstanceRefer [48], construct a directed instance graph with instance features as vertices and relative instance coordinates as edges. Later, in order to capture the object-object and object-scene co-occurrence, FFD [14] develops a multi-level proposal relation graph module with a geometric structure feature of each bounding box encoded in each graph node. Aiming at a unified intra- and inter-modalities modeling scheme, Transfer3D [15], 3DVG [50], and SAT [46] adopt a standard Transformer architecture [34] for promoting inter-object relations. However, these methods overlooked the importance of encoding the multi-order visual object relations, which might be because that the key to improve grounding performance is learning the explicit correspondence between vision and language. And existing methods still struggle at establishing such correspondence due to the lack of semantics in the point clouds data [46].

In the 3D dense captioning task, Scan2Cap [11] first proposes a relational graph implemented with a static version of EdgeConv [40] to enhance object relation representation. However, the inter-object relations are only treated as by-products of graph node recognition, thus leads to sub-optimal results. Theoretically, 3D visual relation detectors [3,36,41] can mitigate such the problem, however, the current results delivered by them are unsatisfactory when faced with highly unrestricted scene compositions [25,49]. Therefore, in this paper, we aim to develop a relation mining method which can properly encode both the basic first-order and complex multi-order relations contained in the 3D scene, so as to benefit more comprehensive caption generation.

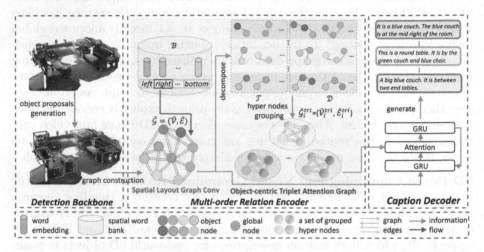

Fig. 2. The overall framework of our proposed method, which consists of three parts: the detection backbone, the multi-order relation encoder, and the caption decoder. Given a 3D scene represented by point clouds, the detection backbone extracts a set of object proposals. Then, based on the objects, first-order and multi-order spatial relations are progressively encoded through a novel Spatial Layout Graph Convolution (SLGC) and several Object-centric Triplet Attention Graphs (OTAG), respectively. Finally, the OTAG's output, which encapsulates rich spatial relational cues, are served as the context to aid comprehensive caption generation. To keep the figure concise, we omit part of the object nodes and their corresponding captions, as well as the attention calculation of each triplet graph.

3   Multi-Order Relation Mining Network

The overall framework of our Multi-Order RElation mining (MORE) network consists of three main components: an object detection backbone, a multi-order relation encoder, and a caption decoder. As shown in Fig. 2, given a point cloud as input, the detection backbone extracts several 3D object proposals with bounding boxes (Sect. 3.1). Then, as the core component of our framework, the multi-order relation encoder first takes object proposals as input and explicitly encodes the first-order spatial relations via our proposed Spatial Layout Graph Convolution (SLGC). During this process, SLGC maintains a bank of spatial words and dynamically selects word embeddings from it as graph edges, so as to narrow the gap between point cloud and relational concepts. The resulting graph is decomposed into triplets and recomposed as several Triplet Object-centric Attention

Graphs (OTAG) for multi-order spatial relation reasoning (Sect. 3.2). Finally, the decoder takes updated node features from OTAG as inputs to incorporate contextual cues with an attention module and generates language descriptions for the corresponding objects (Sect. 3.3).

3.1 Detection Backbone

Given a 3D scene input represented by a point cloud $\mathcal{P} = \{(p_i, f_i)\}_{i=1}^{N_P}$ (N_P is the number of points), where $p_i \in \mathbb{R}^3$ and $f_i \in \mathbb{R}^3$ are the coordinates (x-y-z) and the color (r-g-b) of the i-th point, respectively, we adopt the PointNet++ [31] backbone and the voting module in VoteNet [30] to extract a set of object proposals. We denote these object proposals as $\mathcal{O} = \{(x_i, c_i)\}_{i=1}^{N_O}$ (N_O is the number of valid object proposals), where $x_i \in \mathbb{R}^{128}$ is the i-th object proposal's visual feature and $c_i = (b^x, b^y, b^z, b^h, b^w, b^l)$ is the location indicator of the corresponding bounding box. b^x, b^y, b^z are the coordinates of the box center and b^h, b^w, b^l are height, width, length of the box, respectively.

3.2 Multi-order Relation Encoding

The key to generating accurate and diverse captions for 3D real world is to capture or infer the complicated spatial relations, however, this is overlooked by the previous method [11]. As the core component of our method, the multi-order relation encoder takes object proposals $\mathcal{O}$ as input, and is responsible for explicitly encoding the basic first-order spatial relations by Spatial Layout Graph Convolution (SLGC) and further inferring possible multi-order relations via Object-centric Triplet Attention Graphs (OTAG). In the rest of this section, we will elaborate on each of them.

Spatial Layout Graph Convolution. Following [11], we wish to connect each object with its K nearest neighboring instances, and thereby construct an object graph to represent the spatial layout of the whole scene, denoted as $\mathcal{G} = (\mathcal{V}, \mathcal{E})$. Note that in addition to the object proposals, we also add a global node into $\mathcal{V}$ to model the interaction between each object and the whole scene. Formally, $\mathcal{V} = \{v_i\}_{i=1}^{N_O+1}$, where $v_j = x_j$ ($j = 1, \ldots, N_O$) and $v_{N_O+1} = g$. g is the feature of global node calculated by averaging all object proposals' features.

As for the edges, conventional methods [11,14] treat the graph edges $\mathcal{E}$ as the by-products derived from node representation learning, thus the edges do not have clear semantics. So we construct our spatial layout graph by delicately encoding basic first-order spatial relational concepts that are transferred from the linguistic embedding space.

First, we maintain a spatial word bank $\mathcal{B}$ to provide semantic concepts of basic first-order spatial relations:

$$\mathcal{B} = \{ \text{"left", "right", "front", "behind", "besides", "top", "bottom"} \}. \tag{1}$$

For illustration purpose, we list the spatial words in $\mathcal{B}$, while we use their corresponding GloVE [29] word embeddings in our model. These relations can be divided into horizontal and vertical subsets, $\mathcal{B}_h$ and $\mathcal{B}_v$, respectively[1].

Next, we need to select a corresponding item from the word bank as the edge to describe the spatial relationship of the two connected nodes, however, this is nontrivial in the 3D world, as the varying viewpoints may bring ambiguity to the horizontal spatial relations. To this end, we select the horizontal spatial word in an adaptive manner, and the less ambiguous vertical spatial word based on rules. To compute the horizontal spatial relation between objects i and j, we first calculate the relative coordinates $c_{j,i}$ and object feature $v_{j,i}$, and combine them to predict a distribution $\alpha_{j,i} \in \mathbb{R}^{N_h}$ of the horizontal relational words:

$$v_{j,i} = W_v[v_i; v_j - v_i], \quad c_{j,i} = W_c[b_j^x - b_i^x; b_j^y - b_i^y],$$
$$\alpha_{j,i} = \text{softmax}(W_\alpha \tanh(v_{j,i} + c_{j,i})), \tag{2}$$

where $[;]$ represents the concatenation operation, and $W_v \in \mathbb{R}^{256 \times 128}$, $W_c \in \mathbb{R}^{2 \times 128}$, and $W_\alpha \in \mathbb{R}^{128 \times N_h}$ are weight matrices. Afterward, the horizontal spatial relational feature $r^h \in \mathbb{R}^{300}$ can be calculated by a weighted combination of the corresponding items of the spatial word bank:

$$r^h = \alpha_{j,i} \cdot \mathcal{B}_h, \tag{3}$$

where $\cdot$ is the dot product operation. In this way,

As for the vertical spatial relations, namely "top" and "bottom", we design a metric to directly infer vertical relation between a given pair of objects i and j. We first generate the box corner coordinates $b_i^c, b_j^c \in \mathbb{R}^8$ according to their initial box coordinates c_i and c_j. Then, we calculate the relative vertical distance between each pair of corner points between objects i and j, and obtain the pairwise distances $d_{j,i}^v \in \mathbb{R}^{64}$. The vertical spatial relations can then be inferred by taking the sign of the maximum or the minimum element of $d_{j,i}^v$. And we can formulate the process of obtaining vertical spatial relational feature r^v as:

$$r^v = \mathbb{I}(\min(d_{j,i}^v) > 0) \times \mathcal{B}_v^{top} + \mathbb{I}(\max(d_{j,i}^v) < 0) \times \mathcal{B}_v^{bottom} \tag{4}$$

where $\mathbb{I}(\cdot)$ is the indicator function, which equals 1 when the condition inside the bracket is satisfied, otherwise 0, and $\mathcal{B}_v^{top}$ and $\mathcal{B}_v^{bottom}$ are the corresponding items in the word bank, respectively. Finally, the first-order spatial relation between object i and j, also known as the directed graph edge $e_{j,i}$, can be obtained through combining two relational features r^h and r^v:

$$e_{j,i} = W_e[r^v; r^h], \tag{5}$$

where $W_e \in \mathbb{R}^{600 \times 128}$ is the projection matrix. As for the global node g, we manually assign its center coordinates as the location of the scene's center for the horizontal relational feature calculation. And the vertical relational feature is an all-zero vector due to that no bounding box is available for the whole scene.

---

[1] "Top" and "bottom" are the vertical relations we focus on.

At this point, we have constructed the initial spatial layout graph $\mathcal{G}$ and the basic first-order spatial relations between objects have been incorporated into the graph edges via the semantically rich word embeddings. Then, we perform message passing upon the spatial layout graph to enhance the node features by letting them aggregate information from neighboring nodes:

$$\beta_{j,i} = (W_1 v_i)^{\mathrm{T}} (W_2 v_j + W_3 e_{j,i}), \quad \hat{\beta}_{j,i} = \frac{\exp(\beta_{j,i})}{\sum_{k \in \mathcal{N}(i)} \exp(\beta_{k,i})},$$

$$v_i' = W_4 v_i + \sum_{j \in \mathcal{N}(i)} \hat{\beta}_{j,i} \odot (W_5 v_j + W_6 e_{j,i}), \tag{6}$$

where the $\odot$ represents the element-wise multiplication with broadcast operation. Note that when computing aggregation weights, we also take the semantic edges into consideration. The above Spatial Layout Graph Convolution (SLGC) can be stacked multiple times and we denote the final resulting graph as $\widetilde{\mathcal{G}} = (\widetilde{\mathcal{V}}, \widetilde{\mathcal{E}})$, whose node and edge features can be denoted as $\widetilde{\mathcal{V}} = \{\widetilde{v}_i\}_{i=1}^{N_O+1}$ and $\widetilde{\mathcal{E}} = \{\widetilde{e}_{i,j}\}_{i,j=1}^{N_O+1}$.

Object-Centric Triplet Attention Graph. Theoretically, by conducting multiple rounds of message passing with stacked SLGC, the model can become aware of the multi-order relations, however, we find in our experiments (Table 4) that this can not achieve the expected effects since the captioning performance does not improve with more layers. We postulate such a phenomenon might be caused by the over-smoothing problem [7,51], and the experimental results (will be analyzed in detail) in Table 4 support our assumption to some extent. Thus we decide to not solely rely on the SLGC, but further specifically design an object-centric graph that preserves more information of the target objects and the relations.

Concretely, based on the first-order spatial relation aware graph $\widetilde{\mathcal{G}}$ that we obtained from SLGC, we directly extract a set of $<node_1, edge, node_2>$ triplets from it, and the $node_2$ is the target object that we wish to generate caption for. Formally, these triplets can be represented as $\mathcal{T} = \{< \widetilde{v}_j, \widetilde{e}_{j,i}, \widetilde{v}_i >\}_{j \in \mathcal{N}(i), i=1:N_O}$. Note that we do not extract triplets targeting the global node, since currently we are focusing on generating captions for the objects but not the whole scene. Such triplets are a combined representation of a target object and its surrounding contexts, as well as their relations, and the target object is emphasized in each triplet graph so that its information will not be overwhelmed in the following operations. To enlarge the context, we can further extend these triplets via constructing a new set of quintuplets which can be represented as $\mathcal{Q} = \{(\widetilde{v}_k, \widetilde{e}_{k,j}, \widetilde{v}_j, \widetilde{e}_{j,i}, \widetilde{v}_i)\}_{k \in \mathcal{N}(j), j \in \mathcal{N}(i), i=1:N_O}$. In practice, we find these extended quintuplets to be helpful.

We then take the triplets/quintuplet $(\mathcal{T}/\mathcal{Q})$ as hyper-nodes, and construct object-centric graphs upon them. The triplets/quintuplets targeting the same object node are regarded as related hyper-nodes and we will further model their relations as a object-centric triplet attention graph. We denote the recomposed triplet graph that is centered at object i as $\mathcal{G}_i^{tri} = (\mathcal{V}_i^{tri}, \mathcal{E}_i^{tri})$ $(i = 1, \ldots, N_O)$.

Since the hyper-nodes from $\mathcal{T}$ and $\mathcal{Q}$ have different formats, we first unify their channel dimensions by mapping them into the same lower-dimensional space:

$$v_{j,i} = W_t[\tilde{v}_j; \tilde{e}_{j,i}; \tilde{v}_i], \quad v_{k,j,i} = W_q[\tilde{v}_k; \tilde{e}_{k,j}; \tilde{v}_j; \tilde{e}_{j,i}; \tilde{v}_i], \tag{7}$$

where $W_t \in \mathbb{R}^{384 \times 128}$ and $W_q \in \mathbb{R}^{640 \times 128}$ are projection matrices. Then, the hyper-nodes can be represented as $\mathcal{V}_i^{tri} = \{v_{j,i}\}_{j \in \mathcal{N}(i)} \cup \{v_{k,j,i}\}_{k \in \mathcal{N}(j), j \in \mathcal{N}(i)}$. As for the edges $\mathcal{E}_i^{tri}$, we connect each pair of nodes in $\mathcal{V}_i^{tri}$ by computing the edge weights via attention:

$$e_{\{j,i\},\{k,i\}} = \frac{\exp(\sigma(W_7 v_{j,i})\sigma(W_8 v_{k,i}))}{\mathcal{Z}_{j,i}}, \tag{8}$$

where $\{j,i\}$ and $\{k,i\}$ represents two hyper-nodes of triplets (or quintuplets), W_7, W_8 are projection matrices, and σ is an activation function (e.g., ReLU). We denote the normalization denominator as $\mathcal{Z}_{j,i}$ to avoid clutter. We then aggregate neighbor information through

$$v'_{j,i} = \sum_{k \in \mathcal{N}(i)} e_{\{j,i\},\{k,i\}} W_9 v_{k,i}. \tag{9}$$

Here we only include triplet-based hyper-nodes for clarity, and quintuplets can be similarly incorporated. By performing the above message passing among hyper-nodes, the model can infer multi-order relations while significantly preserving the target object's information. The final object-centric triplet graph after pair-wise node attention calculation (i.e., Eq. (10) and Eq. (11)) is denoted as $\tilde{\mathcal{G}}_i^{tri} = (\tilde{\mathcal{V}}_i^{tri}, \tilde{\mathcal{E}}_i^{tri})$ $(i = 1, \ldots, N_O)$.

3.3 Caption Generation

It is a common practice to make the caption decoder responsible for incorporating contextual cues generated by the encoder [2,11]. We design our decoder based on a two-layer GRU network, and equip it with an attention module in between the two layers to aggregate OTAG's object-centric nodes that are aware of multi-order spatial relations.

In particular, the caption is iteratively generated in a word-by-word manner. At the t-th time step, the first GRU takes the concatenation of the GloVE embedding of the word $w^{(t-1)}$, the previous hidden state $h_2^{(t-1)}$ of the second GRU, as well as the initial visual feature x_i of the target object proposal as inputs, and update the its hidden state $h_1^{(t)}$ as:

$$h_1^{(t)} = \text{GRU}_1([w^{(t-1)}; h_2^{(t-1)}; x_i]; h_1^{(t-1)}), \tag{10}$$

Next, depending on the updated hidden state $h_1^{(t)}$ of the first GRU, we adaptively compute aggregation weights for $\tilde{\mathcal{G}}_i^{tri}$'s node features, which contains spatial relation cues between the target object and its neighbors, and these node features are then aggregated by a weighted sum:

$$\gamma_i = W_\gamma(\tanh(W_{10}h_1^{(t)} + W_{11}\tilde{v}_i^{tri})), \quad \hat{\gamma}_i = \frac{\exp(\gamma_i)}{\sum_{j \in \mathcal{N}(i)} \exp(\gamma_j)},$$

$$\hat{v}^{(t)} = \sum_{i=1}^{N_O} \hat{\gamma}_i \odot \tilde{v}_i^{tri}, \tag{11}$$

where $\hat{v}^{(t)}$ is the resulting contextual feature vector with spatial relations embedded in it. Afterward, the contextual vector $\hat{v}^{(t)}$, together with the hidden state $h_1^{(t)}$ of the first GRU, are fed into the second GRU to obtain its updated hidden state $h_2^{(t)}$:

$$h_2^{(t)} = \text{GRU}_2([\hat{v}^{(t)}; h_1^{(t)}]; h_2^{(t-1)}), \tag{12}$$

Finally, $h_2^{(t)}$ is leveraged to predict the current word $w^{(t)}$ through a linear classifier. The details about the captioning loss and model training process can be found in the supplementary materials.

4 Experiments

4.1 Experimental Setup

Dataset. Following previous work [6,11], we use the ScanRefer [5] dataset, which consists of 51,583 descriptions for 11,046 objects in 800 ScanNet [12] scenes. The descriptions include the appearance of the objects (e.g. "this is a black tv"), and the spatial relations between the target object and surrounding objects (e.g. "the cabinet is next to the desk"). The dataset is split into train/val sets with 36,665 and 9,508 samples respectively following the ScanRefer [5] benchmark. Scenes in the train and val sets are disjoint with each other. Since the test set has not been officially released, all experimental results and analysis in the following sections are conducted on top of the val set.

Evaluation Metrics. To jointly evaluate the quality of detected bounding boxes and generated captions, a combined metric $m@kIoU = \frac{1}{N}\sum_{i=1}^{N} m_i u_i$ defined in [11] is adopted, where u_i is set to 1 if the IoU score for the ith box is greater than k, otherwise 0, and m can be one of the caption metrics, such as CiDEr [35], BLEU-4 [28], METEOR [4], and ROUGE [24], abbreviated as C, B-4, M, R in the following part, respectively. Meanwhile, mean average precision (mAP) at specified IoU threshold is utilized to evaluate the object detection performance.

Implementation Details. In our experiment, we randomly sample 40,000 points from every ScanNet scenes. The maximum number of object proposals K is set as 256. Unless otherwise specified, we utilize the color $(r\text{-}g\text{-}b)$ of each point as the input visual feature to conduct experiments. The number of stacked SLGC layers are set as 1 and 2 when the point color and multi-view feature are adopted, respectively. We train our model with the Adam optimizer [22], and set the learning rate to $1e^{-4}$, weight decay to $1e^{-5}$, and batch size to 12. Following [11], we adopt the same data augmentation strategy and truncate the descriptions longer than 30.

4.2 Comparison with State-of-the-Art

We compare our method with the state-of-the-art approach Scan2Cap [11] on the ScanRefer [5] benchmark as shown in Table 1, where the VoteNet [30] is adopted as the detector and the entire network is trained end-to-end. Note that the results that we reproduced with the officially released code of Scan2Cap [11] have discrepancy with the results reported in the paper, and we report our reproduced results in Table 1, denoted as "Scan2Cap*". The methods in the first three rows are simple baselines provided in the previous work [11]. The results demonstrate that our method achieves consistent improvements across most of the evaluation metrics, especially on CiDEr. When using "r-g-b" color and multiview features as additional point features, compared with Scan2Cap, our method obtains 5.16% and 6.09% improvements on C@0.25IoU, as well as 3.78% and 1.86% improvements on C@0.5IoU in respectively. We emphasize the CIDEr metric because compared with other evaluation metrics, CiDEr shows higher agreement with consensus as assessed by humans [35]. Overall, the significant improvements on C@0.25IoU and C@0.5IoU can prove the superiority of our method.

Table 1. Comparison with state-of-the-art methods on the ScanRefer dataset with VoteNet [30] as the detector of all methods. "Scan2Cap*" represents the results we reproduced with the officially released code. We use subscript "rgb" and "mul" to denote using "r-g-b" color and multi-view feature as additional point features.

Method	C@0.25IoU	B-4@0.25IoU	M@0.25IoU	R@0.25IoU	C@0.5IoU	B-4@0.5IoU	M@0.5IoU	R@0.5IoU	mAP@0.5
2D-3D Proj. [11]	18.29	10.27	16.67	33.63	8.31	2.31	12.54	25.93	10.50
3D-2D Proj. [11]	19.73	17.86	19.83	40.68	11.47	8.56	15.73	31.65	31.83
VoteNetRetr [30]	15.12	18.09	19.93	38.99	10.18	13.38	17.14	33.22	31.83
Scan2Cap$_{mul}$ [11]	56.82	34.18	26.29	55.27	39.08	*23.32*	*21.97*	*44.78*	32.21
Scan2Cap*$_{mul}$ [11]	53.88	32.71	25.64	53.87	38.11	22.63	21.60	44.06	31.47
MORE$_{mul}$	*62.91*	*36.25*	*26.75*	*56.33*	*40.94*	22.93	21.66	44.42	*33.75*
Scan2Cap$_{rgb}$ [11]	53.73	34.25	26.14	54.95	35.20	22.36	21.44	43.57	29.13
Scan2Cap*$_{rgb}$ [11]	51.05	32.99	25.59	53.82	35.11	22.26	21.44	43.70	28.86
MORE$_{rgb}$	**58.89**	**35.41**	**26.36**	**55.41**	**38.98**	**23.01**	**21.65**	**44.33**	**31.93**

Meanwhile, considering that the overall performances of the dense captioning can be affected by the detector, we adopt ground-truth bounding boxes as input to specifically compare the captioning performance as shown in Table 2. Methods in the first three lines are simple baselines provided in [11]. Since now the performance is no longer affected by the detection results, we omit the mAP and captioning results with the 0.25 IoU threshold. We observe from the table that our method surpasses the baseline with a large margin across all evaluation metrics. Besides, the improvements over Scan2Cap are more evident than in Table 1 where VoteNet is used as the detector. This indicates that when the context objects are more reliable, our method can benefit more and perform relation encoding with a higher quality, thereby promoting the captioning performances.

4.3 Comprehensive Analysis

Ablation Studies. We conduct ablation studies to verify the effectiveness of our proposed SLGC and OTAG designs, and the results are shown in Table 3. In the baseline method (the first row), we remove OTAG and the edge feature $e_{j,i}$ in Eq. (6) when performing message passing and keep other settings of SLGC the same. As shown in the second[2] row, including SLGC improves C@0.5IoU by 1.79% comparing to the baseline, and other metrics are also improved.

This demonstrates that explicitly encoding the basic first-order spatial relational concepts when updating node features is helpful to improving the captioning accuracy. In the third row, OTAG alone brings 4.28% C@0.5IoU improvement over the baseline, which indicates that these recomposed object-centric graphs could effectively enhance our model's ability to capture multi-order relations,

Table 2. Comparison with state-of-the-art methods on the ScanRefer dataset using ground-truth bounding boxes for all methods. Since the experimental results using ground-truth bounding boxes with "r-g-b" as additional point features are not reported by Scan2Cap, we only report our reproduced results with their officially released code.

	C@0.5IoU	B-4@0.5IoU	M@0.5IoU	R@0.5IoU
OracleRetr2D [11]	20.51	20.17	23.76	50.98
Oracle2Cap2D [11]	58.44	37.05	28.59	61.35
OracleRetr3D [11]	33.03	23.36	25.80	52.99
Scan2Cap$_{mul}$ [11]	67.95	41.49	29.23	63.66
Scan2Cap*$_{mul}$ [11]	65.51	39.62	29.23	62.87
MORE$_{mul}$	**70.39**	**42.34**	**29.55**	**64.31**
Scan2Cap*$_{rgb}$ [11]	64.19	38.90	28.96	62.38
MORE$_{rgb}$	**67.15**	**43.52**	**29.55**	**65.09**

Table 3. Ablation studies of the individual components, including the SLGC for first-order relation encoding, and the OTAG for multi-order relation modeling.

SLGC	OTAG	C@0.5IoU	B-4@0.5IoU	M@0.5IoU	R@0.5IoU	mAP@0.5
		33.67	20.92	20.87	42.60	29.14
✓		35.46	21.31	21.01	43.10	29.18
	✓	37.95	21.55	21.17	43.49	29.53
✓	✓	**38.98**	**23.01**	**21.65**	**44.33**	**31.93**

---

[2] Results of this setting can be found in the supplementary materials of [11].

thus significantly boosting the performance. Combining the SLGC and OTAG, as shown in the last row, can achieve the highest performance, especially for the C@0.5IoU (38.98%), which outperforms the baseline with a large margin of 5.31%. These experiments demonstrate that the key components of our model (SLGC and OTAG) are both beneficial to generating high quality dense captions, and that our multi-order encoding of the inter-object relations is effective.

Why Not Stacking SLGC for Multi-order Relation Modeling? Theoretically, multi-order relations can be modeled by message passing on a graph for several rounds so that one node can reach out to further neighbors, but as our studies in Table 4 demonstrate, such an approach cannot attain ideal outcomes. In the first four rows, we stacked SLGC of 1, 2, 3, and 4 layers, respectively, and then feed the output nodes directly to the caption generation decoder as in Scan2Cap [11]. We can see that although stacking two layers of SLGC can bring clear improvements over using only one SLGC layer However, adding more layers of SLGC hurts the model's performance. When the number of the SLGC layers increase to 3 and 4, the model's performance gradually degrades. Since stacking SLGC only changes the node features we fed to the caption decoder, we conjecture that the performance degradation might be due to the over-smoothing issue as described in [7,51]. We will further analyze this issue and provide evidence in the subsequent paragraph. Next, instead of stacking multiple layers of SLGC, we stack our OTAG on top of 1-layer SLGC. The results are shown in the last row of Table 4, and by comparing it with the SLGC-only results, we can observe that SLGC×1+OTAG outperforms the best results of stacking SLGC (SLGC×2). This proves that constructing OTAG is a more suitable approach of modeling multi-order relations under our scenario.

Why is OTAG More Suitable? As shown in Eq. (10), (11), (12), the caption generation is conditioned on the target object feature x_i and its context feature $\hat{v}^{(t)}$, and the context feature is adaptively computed based on the decoding state and the encoder's graph nodes. Hence, obtaining distinctive node feature representation $\hat{v}^{(t)}$ from the multi-order relation encoder is the key to generate diverse captions. However, if the multi-order relation encoder is simply composed of multiple graph convolution layers, the node representation might suffer from the over-smoothing issue [7,51] (i.e., features of the graph nodes from different classes would become indistinguishable when stacking multiple graph layers [7]),

Table 4. Comparison of different configurations of message passing for multi-order relation modeling in the graph structure.

	C@0.5IoU	B-4@0.5IoU	M@0.5IoU	R@0.5IoU	mAP@0.5	MADGap
SLGC×1	35.46	21.31	21.01	43.10	29.18	17.46
SLGC×2	38.06	22.26	21.35	43.64	29.98	14.49
SLGC×3	38.27	21.99	21.16	43.43	30.43	13.17
SLGC×4	36.58	21.46	21.05	42.93	29.94	12.28
SLGC×1+OTAG	**38.98**	**23.01**	**21.65**	**44.33**	**31.93**	**21.70**

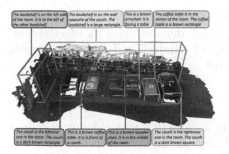
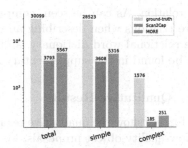

Fig. 3. The illustration of dense captions for objects within a whole scene predicted by our method. We distinguish the captions for each object with different colors.

Fig. 4. Statistics of relational words in captions generated by different methods. "simple" and "complex" roughly represents first- and multi-order relations, respectively, and "total" is the sum of all relational words.

which hurts obtaining distinctive context features. Hence we conduct experiments to verify our OTAG is a more suitable graph layer that can learn more distinguishable node features to benefit the caption decoder.

In order to quantitatively evaluate the distinctiveness of graph nodes, we calculate the MADGap, a metric introduced in [7] to evaluate over-smoothness of graph nodes. The results are shown in the last column of Table 4. As can be observed, when the number of stacked graph layers increases from 1 to 4, the corresponding MADGap value decreases, which indicates that the node features gradually become more similar. Although 1-layer SLGC can achieve higher MADGap value, its overall performances of caption generation are inferior to the 2-layer SLGC, which is mainly due to that the spatial relations are not sufficiently encoded into the nodes with only one graph layer. When stacking more than 2 layers of SLGC, the MADGap and the overall captioning performances both decrease, demonstrating the over-smoothing is correlated with captioning quality degradation to some extent. Finally, combining 1-layer SLGC with our proposed OTAG, our method achieves much higher MADGap value than stacking any number of layers of SLGC, while also performs the best on caption generation. This indicates that the object-centric graph construction in OTAG can preserve distinctive information of the node features, make the aggregated context of in the caption decoder more diverse, and finally boost the captioning performances.

Relational Words Statistics. To give a more intuitive analysis on the advantages of our method, we inspect the performance improvement gained by our method in terms of relation capturing. Figure 4 compares the relational words in the sentences generated by Scan2Cap and our MORE, as well as in ground-truth annotations. Specifically, we maintain a dictionary of all the relational words in the corpus. Then we classify these words into "simple" and "complex" according to whether multiple objects should be jointly considered to support predicting the relation. As can be seen, comparing to Scan2Cap, our MORE can capture more relations when describing an object, which demonstrates its effectiveness. The relational word dictionary, and the split of "simple" and "complex" words can be found in the supplementary materials.

4.4   Qualitative Results

We further show the qualitative result in Fig. 3. Note that to avoid clutter caused by low-quality object proposals, we directly use the ground-truth bounding box of each object. We can observe that our method is able to capture diverse spatial relations among objects. For example, relations like "on the left side of", "in front of" and "opposite of" are all properly leveraged to describe objects. Besides, our method can also accurately describe multi-order relations, such as "leftmost" and "rightmost", which are used to describe the two couches at both ends of the scene. The results demonstrate that our MORE is effective in capturing and describing diverse spatial relations for multiple objects in 3D world.

5   Conclusions

In this paper, we improved 3D dense captioning by proposing a novel relation modeling method, named Multi-order RElation Mining Network (MORE). We progressively modeled spatial relations by encoding first-order and multi-order ones with our proposed Spatial Layout Graph Convolution (SLGC) and Object-centric Triplet Attention Graphs (OTAG), respectively. Extensive experimental results demonstrated the effectiveness and the advantage of MORE over the current state-of-the-art method.

Acknowledgements. This work was supported in part by Shanghai Pujiang Program (No. 20PJ1401900) and Shanghai Science and Technology Program (No. 21JC1400600).

References

1. Achlioptas, P., Abdelreheem, A., Xia, F., Elhoseiny, M., Guibas, L.: ReferIt3D: neural listeners for fine-grained 3D object identification in real-world scenes. In: Vedaldi, A., Bischof, H., Brox, T., Frahm, J.-M. (eds.) ECCV 2020. LNCS, vol. 12346, pp. 422–440. Springer, Cham (2020). https://doi.org/10.1007/978-3-030-58452-8_25
2. Anderson, P., et al.: Bottom-up and top-down attention for image captioning and visual question answering. In: Proceedings of the IEEE Conference on Computer Vision and Pattern Recognition, pp. 6077–6086 (2018)
3. Armeni, I., et al.: 3D scene graph: a structure for unified semantics, 3D space, and camera. In: Proceedings of the IEEE/CVF International Conference on Computer Vision, pp. 5664–5673 (2019)
4. Banerjee, S., Lavie, A.: Meteor: an automatic metric for MT evaluation with improved correlation with human judgments. In: Proceedings of the ACL Workshop on Intrinsic and Extrinsic Evaluation Measures for Machine Translation and/or Summarization, pp. 65–72 (2005)

5. Chen, D.Z., Chang, A.X., Nießner, M.: ScanRefer: 3D object localization in RGB-D scans using natural language. In: Vedaldi, A., Bischof, H., Brox, T., Frahm, J.-M. (eds.) ECCV 2020. LNCS, vol. 12365, pp. 202–221. Springer, Cham (2020). https://doi.org/10.1007/978-3-030-58565-5_13

6. Chen, D.Z., Wu, Q., Nießner, M., Chang, A.X.: D3Net: a speaker-listener architecture for semi-supervised dense captioning and visual grounding in RGB-D scans. arXiv preprint arXiv:2112.01551 (2021)

7. Chen, D., Lin, Y., Li, W., Li, P., Zhou, J., Sun, X.: Measuring and relieving the over-smoothing problem for graph neural networks from the topological view. In: Proceedings of the AAAI Conference on Artificial Intelligence, vol. 34, pp. 3438–3445 (2020)

8. Chen, J., et al.: Zero-shot ingredient recognition by multi-relational graph convolutional network. In: Proceedings of the AAAI Conference on Artificial Intelligence, vol. 34, pp. 10542–10550 (2020)

9. Chen, S., Jiang, W., Liu, W., Jiang, Y.-G.: Learning modality interaction for temporal sentence localization and event captioning in videos. In: Vedaldi, A., Bischof, H., Brox, T., Frahm, J.-M. (eds.) ECCV 2020. LNCS, vol. 12349, pp. 333–351. Springer, Cham (2020). https://doi.org/10.1007/978-3-030-58548-8_20

10. Chen, S., Jiang, Y.G.: Towards bridging event captioner and sentence localizer for weakly supervised dense event captioning. In: Proceedings of the IEEE/CVF Conference on Computer Vision and Pattern Recognition (CVPR), pp. 8425–8435, June 2021

11. Chen, Z., Gholami, A., Nießner, M., Chang, A.X.: Scan2cap: context-aware dense captioning in RGB-D scans. In: Proceedings of the IEEE/CVF Conference on Computer Vision and Pattern Recognition, pp. 3193–3203 (2021)

12. Dai, A., Chang, A.X., Savva, M., Halber, M., Funkhouser, T., Nießner, M.: ScanNet: richly-annotated 3D reconstructions of indoor scenes. In: Proceedings of the IEEE Conference on Computer Vision and Pattern Recognition, pp. 5828–5839 (2017)

13. Deng, C., Chen, S., Chen, D., He, Y., Wu, Q.: Sketch, ground, and refine: top-down dense video captioning. In: Proceedings of the IEEE/CVF Conference on Computer Vision and Pattern Recognition, pp. 234–243 (2021)

14. Feng, M., et al.: Free-form description guided 3D visual graph network for object grounding in point cloud. arXiv preprint arXiv:2103.16381 (2021)

15. He, D., et al.: Transrefer3D: entity-and-relation aware transformer for fine-grained 3D visual grounding. In: Proceedings of the 29th ACM International Conference on Multimedia, pp. 2344–2352 (2021)

16. Huang, P.H., Lee, H.H., Chen, H.T., Liu, T.L.: Text-guided graph neural networks for referring 3D instance segmentation. In: Proceedings of the AAAI Conference on Artificial Intelligence, vol. 35, pp. 1610–1618 (2021)

17. Ji, Z., Chen, K., Wang, H.: Step-wise hierarchical alignment network for image-text matching. In: IJCAI, pp. 765–771 (2021)

18. Jiao, Y., Jie, Z., Chen, J., Ma, L., Jiang, Y.G.: Suspected object matters: rethinking model's prediction for one-stage visual grounding. arXiv preprint arXiv:2203.05186 (2022)

19. Jiao, Y., et al.: Two-stage visual cues enhancement network for referring image segmentation. In: Proceedings of the 29th ACM International Conference on Multimedia, pp. 1331–1340 (2021)

20. Kim, D.J., Choi, J., Oh, T.H., Kweon, I.S.: Dense relational captioning: triple-stream networks for relationship-based captioning. In: Proceedings of the

IEEE/CVF Conference on Computer Vision and Pattern Recognition, pp. 6271–6280 (2019)

21. Kim, K., Billinghurst, M., Bruder, G., Duh, H.B.L., Welch, G.F.: Revisiting trends in augmented reality research: a review of the 2nd decade of ISMAR (2008–2017). IEEE Trans. Vis. Comput. Graph. **24**(11), 2947–2962 (2018)

22. Kingma, D.P., Ba, J.: Adam: a method for stochastic optimization. arXiv preprint arXiv:1412.6980 (2014)

23. Li, X., Jiang, S.: Know more say less: image captioning based on scene graphs. IEEE Trans. Multimedia **21**(8), 2117–2130 (2019)

24. Lin, C.Y.: ROUGE: a package for automatic evaluation of summaries. In: Text Summarization Branches Out, pp. 74–81 (2004)

25. Milewski, V., Moens, M.F., Calixto, I.: Are scene graphs good enough to improve image captioning? arXiv preprint arXiv:2009.12313 (2020)

26. Pan, Y., Mei, T., Yao, T., Li, H., Rui, Y.: Jointly modeling embedding and translation to bridge video and language. In: Proceedings of the IEEE Conference on Computer Vision and Pattern Recognition, pp. 4594–4602 (2016)

27. Pan, Y., Yao, T., Li, Y., Mei, T.: X-linear attention networks for image captioning. In: Proceedings of the IEEE/CVF Conference on Computer Vision and Pattern Recognition, pp. 10971–10980 (2020)

28. Papineni, K., Roukos, S., Ward, T., Zhu, W.J.: BLEU: a method for automatic evaluation of machine translation. In: Proceedings of the 40th annual meeting of the Association for Computational Linguistics, pp. 311–318 (2002)

29. Pennington, J., Socher, R., Manning, C.D.: Glove: global vectors for word representation. In: Proceedings of the 2014 Conference on Empirical Methods in Natural Language Processing (EMNLP), pp. 1532–1543 (2014)

30. Qi, C.R., Litany, O., He, K., Guibas, L.J.: Deep hough voting for 3D object detection in point clouds. In: Proceedings of the IEEE/CVF International Conference on Computer Vision, pp. 9277–9286 (2019)

31. Qi, C.R., Yi, L., Su, H., Guibas, L.J.: PointNet++: deep hierarchical feature learning on point sets in a metric space. arXiv preprint arXiv:1706.02413 (2017)

32. Savva, M., et al.: Habitat: a platform for embodied AI research. In: Proceedings of the IEEE/CVF International Conference on Computer Vision, pp. 9339–9347 (2019)

33. Song, X., Chen, J., Wu, Z., Jiang, Y.G.: Spatial-temporal graphs for cross-modal text2video retrieval. IEEE Trans. Multimedia (2021)

34. Vaswani, A., et al.: Attention is all you need. In: Advances in Neural Information Processing Systems 30 (2017)

35. Vedantam, R., Lawrence Zitnick, C., Parikh, D.: CIDEr: consensus-based image description evaluation. In: Proceedings of the IEEE Conference on Computer Vision and Pattern Recognition, pp. 4566–4575 (2015)

36. Wald, J., Dhamo, H., Navab, N., Tombari, F.: Learning 3D semantic scene graphs from 3D indoor reconstructions. In: Proceedings of the IEEE/CVF Conference on Computer Vision and Pattern Recognition, pp. 3961–3970 (2020)

37. Wang, D., Beck, D., Cohn, T.: On the role of scene graphs in image captioning. In: Proceedings of the Beyond Vision and Language: Integrating Real-world Knowledge (LANTERN), pp. 29–34 (2019)

38. Wang, H., Zhang, Y., Ji, Z., Pang, Y., Ma, L.: Consensus-aware visual-semantic embedding for image-text matching. In: Vedaldi, A., Bischof, H., Brox, T., Frahm, J.-M. (eds.) ECCV 2020. LNCS, vol. 12369, pp. 18–34. Springer, Cham (2020). https://doi.org/10.1007/978-3-030-58586-0_2

39. Wang, J., Jiang, W., Ma, L., Liu, W., Xu, Y.: Bidirectional attentive fusion with context gating for dense video captioning. In: Proceedings of the IEEE Conference on Computer Vision and Pattern Recognition, pp. 7190–7198 (2018)
40. Wang, Y., Sun, Y., Liu, Z., Sarma, S.E., Bronstein, M.M., Solomon, J.M.: Dynamic graph CNN for learning on point clouds. ACM Trans. Graph. (TOG) **38**(5), 1–12 (2019)
41. Wu, S.C., Wald, J., Tateno, K., Navab, N., Tombari, F.: SceneGraphFusion: incremental 3D scene graph prediction from RGB-D sequences. In: Proceedings of the IEEE/CVF Conference on Computer Vision and Pattern Recognition, pp. 7515–7525 (2021)
42. Xia, F., Zamir, A.R., He, Z., Sax, A., Malik, J., Savarese, S.: Gibson Env: real-world perception for embodied agents. In: Proceedings of the IEEE Conference on Computer Vision and Pattern Recognition, pp. 9068–9079 (2018)
43. Xiong, J., Hsiang, E.L., He, Z., Zhan, T., Wu, S.T.: Augmented reality and virtual reality displays: emerging technologies and future perspectives. Light Sci. Appl. **10**(1), 1–30 (2021)
44. Yang, L., Tang, K., Yang, J., Li, L.J.: Dense captioning with joint inference and visual context. In: Proceedings of the IEEE Conference on Computer Vision and Pattern Recognition, pp. 2193–2202 (2017)
45. Yang, X., Tang, K., Zhang, H., Cai, J.: Auto-encoding scene graphs for image captioning. In: Proceedings of the IEEE/CVF Conference on Computer Vision and Pattern Recognition, pp. 10685–10694 (2019)
46. Yang, Z., Zhang, S., Wang, L., Luo, J.: SAT: 2D semantics assisted training for 3D visual grounding. arXiv preprint arXiv:2105.11450 (2021)
47. Yao, T., Pan, Y., Li, Y., Mei, T.: Exploring visual relationship for image captioning. In: Ferrari, V., Hebert, M., Sminchisescu, C., Weiss, Y. (eds.) Computer Vision – ECCV 2018. LNCS, vol. 11218, pp. 711–727. Springer, Cham (2018). https://doi.org/10.1007/978-3-030-01264-9_42
48. Yuan, Z., et al.: InstanceRefer: cooperative holistic understanding for visual grounding on point clouds through instance multi-level contextual referring. In: Proceedings of the IEEE/CVF International Conference on Computer Vision, pp. 1791–1800 (2021)
49. Zhang, H., Niu, Y., Chang, S.F.: Grounding referring expressions in images by variational context. In: Proceedings of the IEEE Conference on Computer Vision and Pattern Recognition, pp. 4158–4166 (2018)
50. Zhao, L., Cai, D., Sheng, L., Xu, D.: 3DVG-transformer: relation modeling for visual grounding on point clouds. In: Proceedings of the IEEE/CVF International Conference on Computer Vision, pp. 2928–2937 (2021)
51. Zhou, K., Huang, X., Li, Y., Zha, D., Chen, R., Hu, X.: Towards deeper graph neural networks with differentiable group normalization. In: Advances in Neural Information Processing Systems, vol. 33, 4917–4928 (2020)

SiRi: A Simple Selective Retraining Mechanism for Transformer-Based Visual Grounding

Mengxue Qu[1,2], Yu Wu[3], Wu Liu[4], Qiqi Gong[1,2], Xiaodan Liang[5],
Olga Russakovsky[3], Yao Zhao[1,2], and Yunchao Wei[1,2(✉)]

[1] Institute of Information Science, Beijing Jiaotong University, Beijing, China
qumengxue@bjtu.edu.cn, wychao1987@gmail.com
[2] Beijing Key Laboratory of Advanced Information Science and Network Technology,
Beijing, China
[3] Princeton University, Princeton, USA
yuwu@princeton.edu
[4] JD Explore Academy, Beijing, China
[5] Sun Yat-sen University, Guangzhou, China

Abstract. In this paper, we investigate how to achieve better visual grounding with modern vision-language transformers, and propose a simple yet powerful **S**elective **R**etraining (SiRi) mechanism for this challenging task. Particularly, SiRi conveys a significant principle to the research of visual grounding, *i.e.*, a better initialized vision-language encoder would help the model converge to a better local minimum, advancing the performance accordingly. In specific, we continually update the parameters of the encoder as the training goes on, while periodically re-initialize rest of the parameters to compel the model to be better optimized based on an enhanced encoder. SiRi can significantly outperform previous approaches on three popular benchmarks. Specifically, our method achieves 83.04% Top1 accuracy on RefCOCO+ *testA*, outperforming the state-of-the-art approaches (training from scratch) by more than 10.21%. Additionally, we reveal that SiRi performs surprisingly superior even with limited training data. We also extend it to transformer-based visual grounding models and other vision-language tasks to verify the validity. Code is available at https://github.com/qumengxue/siri-vg.git.

Keywords: Visual grounding · Transformer · Generalization

1 Introduction

Visual grounding [32,51], also known as Referring Expression Comprehension (REC), aims to predict the location of a region referred to by the language

M. Qu—Work done during an internship at JD Explore Academy.

Supplementary Information The online version contains supplementary material available at https://doi.org/10.1007/978-3-031-19833-5_32.

expression in an image. Previous solutions can be roughly divided into two-stage methods [16,17,27,41,42,44,50,52,55] and one-stage methods [3,26,34,46,48]. The two-stage methods start with the process of generating region proposals via object detectors [9] and then learning to identify the expected object from hundreds of candidates. On the other hand, the one-stage methods perform the grounding in an end-to-end manner, and often with inferior performances. However, the performance of these models is significantly limited due to the huge semantic gap between diverse referring descriptions and various visual appearances. The reason is that visual grounding needs to consider many open or fine-grained (e.g., girl, boy, child) categories, which is significantly different from the common vision tasks (e.g., classification, detection, and segmentation) where each image or individual object has a clear class label. Therefore, due to the diversity of descriptions in the human world, the model may easily overfit the descriptions in *train* while hard to correctly understand the referring expressions in *val* and *test* when the training data is insufficient.

Recently, many researchers focus on using the attention mechanism in Transformer for Vision-Language (V-L) modeling [6,21,30,38]. With both visual and linguistic elements as the inputs, the Transformer encoder can perceive multi-modal data and thoroughly model the visual-linguistic relationship. Although these Transformer-based methods have achieved great success in vision-language modeling, they heavily rely on pre-training with extra large-scale vision-language data pairs to improve the generalization ability of the encoder and relieve the over-fitting issue, accordingly.

However, without large-scale data pre-training, the model shows significant performance degradation on visual grounding tasks. We observe that the relationship between the given expression and the image perceived by the Transformer encoder leaves much to be desired based on the poor V-L interaction attention map in Fig. 1. The reason may be that the Transformer encoder, started with randomly initialized parameters, may easily over-fit a small number of training pairs and make the model

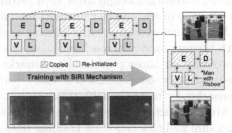

Fig. 1. The sketch of our SiRi mechanism of three retraining periods. "V": Visual Backbone, "L": Language Backbone, "E": Visual-Language Transformer Encoder, "D": Transformer Decoder. The right part shows that we only take the last retrained model for the final test. Best viewed in color. (Color figure online)

be trapped into a poor local minimum. With such an observation, we raise the question of *whether the V-L model will converge to a better local minimum by equipping the Transformer encoder with better-initialized parameters?*

To answer the above question, in this paper, we investigate a new training mechanism to improve the Transformer encoder, named **Selective Retraining** (SiRi), which repeatedly reactivates the learning of the encoder in the pro-

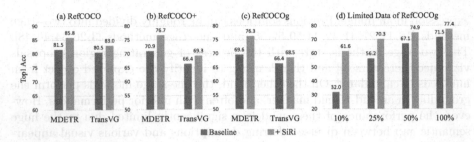

Fig. 2. (a)–(c) illustrates the performance enhancement of SiRi on MDETR [21] and TransVG [6]. We test on three popular visual grounding datasets RefCOCO, Ref-COCO+, RefCOCOg. (d) shows that when training with 10%, 25%, 50%, 100% *training* data, the top1 accuracy improvement of SiRi on the RefCOCOg *validation* set.

cess of continuous retraining and progressively provide better-initialized parameters for the encoder in the next stage. Specifically, while we *continually update* parameters of the encoder as the training goes on, we *periodically re-initialize* all the other modules (*e.g.*, vision/language backbones and the Transformer decoder). In this way, the SiRi promotes the encoder to continually learn better vision-language relationships by periodically getting out of the sub-optimal saddle point. Figure 1 shows the sketch of SiRi and the visualization of the encoder's attention weight after each retraining period, where we can clearly see the progress of the encoder in multi-modal modeling.

We conduct extensive experiments to validate the effectiveness of our method. With the proposed SiRi mechanism, our model remarkably outperforms previous approaches on three popular benchmarks. Particularly, we achieve 83.04% at top-1 accuracy on RefCOCO+ *testA* [51], outperforming the state-of-the-art approaches by more than 10.21%.

More importantly, we further observe that the SiRi mechanism helps model generalize well to small-scale training data as shown in Fig. 2 (d). To be specific, our model with a quarter of training data outperforms previous state-of-the-art methods (with full training data) by 1.65% on the RefCOCOg *val* set. With even less training data (*e.g.*, only 10%), we almost double the accuracy (61.58% *versus* 32.00%) compared to the baseline. Additionally, we complement more extensibility studies in other visual grounding model and other V-L tasks related to visual grounding. We found SiRi can further improve the top-1 accuracy by an average of 2% in TransVG [6], which is also a Transformer-based visual grounding model. We visualize the improvement of different model with SiRi on three datasets in Fig. 2 (a)–(c). In other V-L tasks, including referring expression segmentation, phrase grounding, and visual question answering tasks, we can also improve the baseline using the SiRi mechanism.

2   Related Work

2.1   Visual Grounding

Existing methods for Visual Grounding based on CNN can be roughly divided into two categories, namely two-stage methods and one-stage methods.

Two-Stage Methods. [16,17,24,25,27,41–44,50,52,55] typically utilize an object detector to generate region proposals in the first stage, and then find the best matched region-text pair. The object-text pair matching is commonly used in visual grounding task and other V-L tasks, *e.g.*, retrieval tasks [54]. MattNet [50] takes a modular approach to progressively understand and unify visual and linguistic semantic information in terms of attributes, relationships, and location. Additionally, some approaches further enhance the modeling ability of multi-modal relations using graph structures [42,44,45], multi-modal tree structures [27].

One-Stage Methods. [3,26,34,46,48] avoid being constrained by the quality of the proposal by directly fusing visual and linguistic features. FAOA [48] represents the text input with a language vector and leverages it into the YOLOv3 detector [33] to align the referred instance. RCCF [26] regards the visual grounding problem as a correlation filtering process [1,14], and the peak value in the correlation heatmap is selected as the center of target objects. In ReSC [46], the limitation of FAOA [48] on grounding complex queries is broken through with a recursive sub-query construction module.

In the previous CNN-based visual grounding model, the V-L fusion is performed throughout the decoding process, which is weak interpretability and performance compared to the V-L fusion module in Transformer-based model. Therefore, we adopt Transformer-based model for better V-L interaction.

2.2   Transformer-Based Methods in REC

Recently, Transformer [40] has been widely used to address the multi-modal semantic alignment problem. However, Transformer is data-hungry and thus usually needs additional large-scale pretraining. Motivated by the excellent performance of BERT [7], some researchers [4,8,22,30,38,39,49] construct similar structures and propose multi-modal pre-training for Visual-Language Pretraining (VLP) tasks. These approaches introduce pretext tasks for better interaction of vision and language, *e.g.*, masked language modeling [30,38], image-text matching [22]. However, these VLP methods usually require pre-training with large-scale data and fine-tuning on downstream tasks to achieve good results. Recently, TransVG [6] study the Transformer-based framework without pretraining. Without extracting region proposals in advance, TransVG directly regresses bounding box coordinates and predicts the referring objects.

These works have validated the effectiveness of Transformer for multi-modal modeling. However, most of them require large-scale data to pretrain a Transformer-based model. Differently, in this work, we focus on exploring a way to train better encoders *without* large-scale pretraining.

2.3   Re-training

Some early works avoid getting trapped in a local minimum by introducing randomness. For example, ensemble learning [12,23] introduces randomness by retraining the model with different random initialized parameters to converge to different local minimums. Due to these studies requiring an overwhelming cost, a number of retraining methods, *e.g.*, Dropout [37], Distillation [15], are proposed to reduce the cost of retraining in ensemble learning. More recently, Snapshot Ensemble [18] proposes to retrain the same model to access multiple local minimums by the cyclic learning rate. Similarly, the cyclic learning rate is used in the retraining process to detect noisy labels in O2U-Net [19]. However, Transformer [40] is very sensitive to the learning rate and sometimes requires a warm-up or inverse square root learning rate, which makes the cyclic learning rate [36] inapplicable. The proposed weight initialization scheme T-Fixup in [20] enables Transformer training without warmup or layer normalization. Han *et al.* [11] proposes DSD retraining mechanism with reference to the model pruning, which avoids over-fitting caused by over-capturing of noisy data.

The SiRi mechanism proposed in this paper is somehow similar to the above methods but SiRi is designed for the V-L fusion module in V-L tasks. The main motivation of re-training in this paper is to provide the V-L fusion Transformer with better-initialized parameters.

3   Method

In this section, we first briefly review the basic visual grounding architecture adopted by this work in Sect. 3.1. Then we elaborate on our proposed SiRi mechanism in Sect. 3.2 and the Multi-task SiRi in Sect. 3.3.

3.1   Base Architecture

We follow the state-of-the-art model MDETR [21] as our base architecture, which consists of four main modules: (1) Visual Backbone; (2) Language Backbone; (3) Visual-Language Transformer Encoder; (4) Transformer Decoder Module.

Visual Backbone $\mathcal{V}$ & **Language Backbone** $\mathcal{L}$. We adopt the convolutional backbone ResNet-101 [13] to obtain the visual representation for an input image **I**. In previous work MDETR [21], they only take the output of the last CNN stage as visual features. Differently, we believe the features of shallow stages (*e.g.*, the third stage in ResNet-101) benefit localizing objects if the sentence contains a detailed low-level description such as color. Therefore, we take the output of the third stage of ResNet-101 and transform it with two dilated convolution layers. Then we add the adjusted dimensionality low-level feature together using the final-stage output of ResNet-101 as the final visual representations. Then we encode referring expressions with the pretrained language model RoBERTa [28].

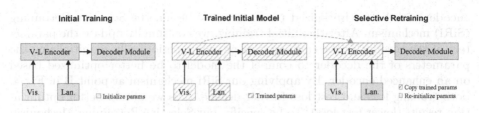

Fig. 3. The training process of our SiRi mechanism. The parameters of the module with solid color background are initialized as the original rules, while those with slash background are trained. The base architecture contains four main modules: (1) "Vis.": Visual Backbone; (2) "Lan.": Language Backbone; (3) "V-L Encoder": Visual-Language Transformer Encoder; (4) "Decoder Module": Transformer Decoder Module.

Visual-Language Transformer Encoder $\mathcal{E}$. We use a Transformer [40] as the encoder for vision-language interaction, where the model performs the cross-modal fusion and association. To do so, we flatten the visual features and add 2-D positional embeddings to conserve spatial information. After that, we project both the flattened visual features and text features into a shared embedding space and then concatenate them into a single sequence of image and text features. The sequence is then input to the cross encoder Transformer for further visual-language interaction.

Transformer Decoder $\mathcal{D}$. Following DETR [2], we use a Transformer decoder to predict the target bounding boxes. The decoder takes as input a set of learnable object queries, cross-attends to the encoder output and predicts embeddings for each query. After that, we decode the embeddings into box coordinates and class labels by the regression and classification heads. Considering that the number of relevant referred targets is fewer than the total number of objects of an image, we limit the decoder to have 16 query inputs only. Considering there is only sentence-level correspondence in visual grounding, we remove box-token contrastive alignment loss [21]. Accordingly, we also reduce the length of the soft tokens to 2, standing for whether the object box belongs to the expression.

3.2 SiRi: Selective Retraining Mechanism

The transformer model may easily get over-fitted without large-scaled pretraining. As shown in Fig. 4, the test loss increases even though the training loss still declines after point A of the initial training stage. Simply having more training iterations would not further improve the test performance.

Motivated by our hypothesis that a V-L model may converge to a better local minimum by equipping the Transformer

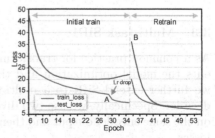

Fig. 4. The train and test loss curves in *Initial train* stage and *Retrain* stage.

encoder with better initialized parameters, we design the Selective Retraining (SiRi) mechanism. After the initial training, we continually update the parameters of the encoder as the training goes on, while periodically re-initializing the parameters of the decoder to compel the model to be better optimized based on an enhanced encoder. By applying our SiRi mechanism at point B in Fig. 4, both training loss and test loss further decline, thus we obtain better optimization results (lower test loss). To be specific, our Selective Retraining Mechanism is set up as follows.

Initial Training. We initialize the visual Backbone $\mathcal{V}$ and the language Backbone $\mathcal{L}$ using the ResNet-101 [13] model pre-trained from ImageNet [5] and the RoBERTa model pre-trained from language corpus datasets, respectively.

The rest of our model (*e.g.*, Transformer encoder and decoder) are randomly initialized using the Xavier initialization [10]. We denote the initialized parameters of the Visual Backbone together with the visual linear projection layer as $\mathcal{V}_0$, and Language Backbone together with the corresponding linear projection layer as $\mathcal{L}_0$. Similarly, the model weights of Transformer Encoder and Transformer Decoder are denoted as $\mathcal{E}_0$ and $\mathcal{D}_0$, respectively. We then train the model using a combination of the object coordinates regression losses (L1 & GIoU) and soft-token prediction loss (cross-entropy loss) while keeping the learning rate unchanged. The model training stops when the validation performance stays stable. We denote the trained model weights to be $\mathcal{V}_0', \mathcal{L}_0', \mathcal{E}_0', \mathcal{D}_0'$ after the initial training.

Selective Retraining. To further improve the encoder with better vision-language understanding, we continually train the encoder after the initial training, while *re-initialize* the other modules to avoid getting stuck in local minimums. We show the pipeline of SiRi in Fig. 3. Specifically, for the t-th round of the selective retraining, we only keep the encoder $\mathcal{E}_t$ to be up-to-date, *i.e.*, $\mathcal{E}_t \leftarrow \mathcal{E}_{t-1}'$, where $\mathcal{E}_{t-1}'$ is the previous trained encoder from $t-1$ round. As for other modules including the decoder $\mathcal{D}_t$, the visual backbone $\mathcal{V}_t$, and the language backbone $\mathcal{L}$, we drop the trained weights and re-initialize them using their original initialization at the initial training stage, *i.e.*, either initializing from the pre-trained weights (*e.g.*, $\mathcal{V}_0$ and $\mathcal{L}_0$), or random initialization (*e.g.*, the decoder D). We then re-train the whole model using the same learning rate until it converges.

3.3   Multi-task SiRi

As a common practice for transformer models, multi-task learning usually benefits the model optimization and thus alleviates over-fitting issues. Therefore, we further extend SiRi to a multi-task version by incorporating an auxiliary decoder. Specifically, we use two diverse decoders to generate predictions based on the same encoder output and then optimize the encoder using the two decoder losses.

To ensure the two decoders are different from each other, we design two different object queries (positional embeddings) for decoders. Previous DETR [2] uses *learnable* positional embeddings as the object query to attend to the encoder output. Differently, we adopt a *constant* positional encoding sequence, *i.e.*, the sine-cosine position encoding function, to generate the object queries for the other decoder. The two decoders take different queries to attend to the same encoder output, which would urge the encoder to be more robust in vision-language interaction. The details are shown in the supplementary materials.

4   Experiments

4.1   Datasets

RefCOCO/RefCOCO+ are proposed in [51]. There are 19,994 images in RefCOCO with 142,209 refer expressions for 50,000 objects. Similarly, 19,992 images are included in RefCOCO+ which contains 141,564 expressions for 49,856 objects. In these datasets, each image contains two or more objects from the same category. In RefCOCO+ dataset, positional words are not allowed in the referring expression, which is a pure dataset with appearance-based referring expression, whereas RefCOCO imposes no restriction on the phrase. In addition to the training set and validation set, the test set for RefCOCO/RefCOCO+ is divided into a *testA* set (containing several people in an image) and a *testB* set (containing multiple instances of other objects in an image).

RefCOCOg [32] contains 26,711 images with 85,474 referring expressions for 54,822 objects, and each image usually contains 2–4 objects of the same category. The length of referring expressions in this dataset is almost twice as long as those in RefCOCO and RefCOCO+.

4.2   Experimental Settings

Implementation Details. Following MDETR [21], all parameters in the network are optimized using AdamW [29] with the learning rate warm-up strategy. The model is trained using 4 GPUs with a batch size of 72. We set the learning rate of the language backbone RoBERTa [28] to be 1×10^{-5}, and all the rest parameters to be 5×10^{-5}. In initial training, the model with a single decoder is trained for 55 epochs, and the model with a dual decoder (multi-task SiRi) is trained for 35 epochs since it converges quickly. Each retraining stage takes another 30 training epochs. We set the maximum side length of the input image as 640 while keeping the original aspect ratio. Images in the same batch are padded with zeros until acquiring the largest size of that batch. Similarly, sentences in one batch will be adjusted to the same length as well. We continually retrain the model until the validation performance converges (usually 5 to 8 rounds).

Evaluation Metrics. Following the proposal setting in the previous work, we use the metric Prec@0.5 to evaluate our method, where a predicted region will be regarded as a positive sample if its intersection over union (IoU) with the ground-truth bounding box is greater than 0.5.

4.3   Comparison with State-of-the-Art Methods

We compare our method with other state-of-the-art methods on three common benchmarks of Referring Expression Comprehension, *i.e.*, RefCOCO, Ref-COCO+, and RefCOCOg. Results are reported in Table 1. Our method displays significant improvement over previous methods on all three datasets. Compared to models without large-scale pretraining, which is a fair comparison, we outperform them by more than 6.39% on RefCOCO@testA, 10.21% on Ref-COCO+@testA, and 9.07% on RefCOCOg@test. Even compared to those large-scaled pretrained models, *e.g.*, MDETR pretrained using more than one million aligned image-text pairs, our method still achieves comparable results on Ref-COCO without those extra data.

Table 1. Comparisons with state-of-the-art methods on RefCOCO [51], Ref-COCO+ [51], and RefCOCOg [32] in terms of top-1 accuracy. We also report official MDETR implementation [21] without pretraining (denoted as MDETR w/o pretrain) and our improved MDETR implementation (see Sect. 3.1) (denoted as MDETR*). "MT SiRi" means "Multi-task SiRi".

Method	Venue	Visual backbone	RefCOCO			RefCOCO+			RefCOCOg	
			val	testA	testB	val	testA	testB	val	test
CNN-based:										
CMN [17]	CVPR'17	VGG16 [35]	–	71.03	65.77	-	54.32	47.76	–	–
MAttNet [50]	CVPR'18	ResNet-101 [13]	76.65	81.14	69.99	65.33	71.62	56.02	66.58	67.27
RvG-Tree [16]	TPAMI'19	ResNet-101	75.06	78.61	69.85	63.51	67.45	56.66	66.95	66.51
NMTree [27]	ICCV'19	ResNet-101	76.41	81.21	70.09	66.46	76.02	57.52	65.87	66.44
FAOA [48]	ICCV'19	DarkNet-53 [33]	72.54	74.35	68.50	56.81	60.23	49.60	61.33	60.36
RCCF [26]	CVPR'20	DLA-34 [53]	–	81.06	71.85	–	70.35	56.32	–	65.73
MCN [31]	CVPR'20	DarkNet-53	80.08	82.29	74.98	67.16	72.86	57.31	66.46	66.01
ReSC-Large [46]	ECCV'20	DarkNet-53	77.63	80.45	72.30	63.59	68.36	56.81	67.30	67.20
Transformer-based Pretrained:										
ViLBERT [30]	NeurIPS'19	ResNet-101	–	–	–	72.34	78.52	62.61	–	–
ERNIE-ViL [49]	AAAI'20	ResNet-101	–	–	–	75.95	82.07	66.88	–	–
UNTIER [4]	ECCV'20	ResNet-101	81.41	87.04	74.17	75.90	81.45	66.70	74.86	75.77
VILLA [8]	NeurIPS'20	ResNet-101	82.39	87.48	74.84	76.17	81.54	66.84	76.18	76.71
MDETR [21]	ICCV'21	ResNet-101	86.75	89.58	81.41	79.52	84.09	70.62	81.64	80.89
Transformer-based without Pretrained:										
TransVG [6]	ICCV'21	ResNet-101	81.02	82.72	78.35	64.82	70.70	56.94	68.67	67.73
MDETR (w/o pretrain)	ICCV'21	ResNet-101	78.01	82.18	72.56	68.01	72.83	55.57	65.54	65.99
MDETR*	–	ResNet-101	81.49	84.67	76.58	70.93	75.65	59.27	69.59	70.22
MDETR* + SiRi	–	ResNet-101	**85.83**	88.56	**81.27**	76.68	82.01	66.33	76.63	76.46
MDETR* + MT SiRi	–	ResNet-101	85.82	**89.11**	81.08	**77.47**	**83.04**	**67.11**	**77.39**	**76.80**

4.4   Ablation Studies

Different Retraining Module. Besides continually updating the encoder while periodically re-initializing all the other parts, we also evaluate different re-initializing modules.

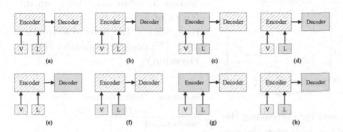

Fig. 5. Schematic of the eight retraining variants with different combinations of selective modules. The solid color background means re-initializing parameters, while the slash background means continually updated parameters from previous periods. Best viewed in color. (Color figure online)

Table 2. Performance comparison of different selective modules. The eight mode are shown in Fig. 5.

Mode	RefCOCO+ @val
Initial	71.45
(a) V, L, E, D	71.98
(b) V, L, E	72.12
(c) V, D	72.14
(d) V, E	73.25
(e) L, E	73.44
(f) E, D	73.80
(g) D	72.76
(h) E	**74.14**

We show eight variants of our SiRi Mechanism in Fig. 5, For a fair comparison, we keep all hyperparameters the same and retrain these variants from the same initial trained model. We show their correspondence results after the first retraining in Table 2. The encoder with better initialized parameters is the critical factor for the whole model converging to a better local minimum.

Comparing mode (d) with mode (h), we find that re-initializing the *visual* backbone has great impact on performance boosting, which verifies our motivation that re-initializing the input of encoder helps to get out of local minimums while keeping the essential cross-modeling ability of previous models. Similar results can be found for *language* backbone by comparing mode (e) with mode (h). Interestingly, we find that the performance is competitive to Mode (h) when we use Mode (f), where we keep the parameters of both encoder and decoder. For simplicity, we only keep the encoder updated continually in all the other experiments.

Retraining Periods. In Fig. 6, we show the validation performance curves during selective retraining. Zero indicates the initial trained model in the figure. We can see the model performance increases a lot in the first three retraining periods and then tends to converge after several retraining periods. The highest performances are achieved in the fifth retraining period, where SiRi outperforms the initial trained model by 5.18% (72.29% versus 77.47%) and 5.86% (71.53% versus 77.39%) on RefCOCO+ and RefCOCOg, respectively.

Different Object Queries in Multi-task SiRi. We can also see the consistent performance gap between the single SiRi and the multi-task SiRi in Fig. 6. The multi-task SiRi always performs better than single SiRi during all the retraining periods. We further study the impact of different object queries (*e.g.*, learnable queries and constant queries) used in Multi task SiRi. The results of the initial trained models using different quires in multi-task learning are shown in Table 3.

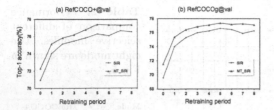

Fig. 6. Performance achieved by increasing the training periods. The blue line indicates the single SiRi model and the red line indicates the multi-task SiRi model. "MT" indicates multi-task. (Color figure online)

Table 3. Ablation studies on different object query types in multi-task SiRi. ("L": learnable queries, and "C": constant queries, "Dec.": Decoder.)

Structure	Object Queries		RefCOCO+
	1st Dec.	*2nd* Dec.	
Single-task	L	–	70.93
	C	–	70.72
Multi-task	L	L	70.27
	C	C	71.24
	L	C	**72.29**

Although learnable and constant object queries achieve similar results for single task training, the combination of them in multi-task learning achieves higher performance (72.29% *versus* 70.93% on RefCOCO+). Note that multi-task structure with two identical object query types (*e.g.*, both learnable or both constant) does not outperform single task learning. It indicates that taking different queries to attend the same encoder output may help the encoder to be more robust on vision-language interaction.

4.5 Qualitative Results

We visualize the attention weight of encoders along with the retraining progress in Fig. 7. To be specific, we calculate the cross-modal attention weights (vision output tokens based on language input tokens) from the last layer of the Transformer encoder, and then visualize them in the original image size. We believe the values of cross-modal attention weights indicate the encoder's ability of vision-language understanding.

We show two test samples in the figure with the corresponding input sentences. From left to right, we show the bounding box predictions together with the attention maps generated by the initial trained, 1st, 3rd, 5th, and 7th retrained encoders, respectively. It can be intuitively seen that the encode learns to better perceive the relationship between expressions and images as the continuous SiRi training goes. Taking the upper sample as an example, the predicted bounding box is incorrect from the initial trained model, where we can see the attention map of the first encoder does not highlight the referred object, either.

After selective retraining, the encoder gets better and better, which can be seen from the more accurate attention maps. Therefore, the predicted boxes are also better than the initial ones. It validates our motivation that the better encoder initialization helps the model converge to a better local minimum. Continually updating the encoder while periodically re-initializing other modules can strengthen the visual-linguistic modeling.

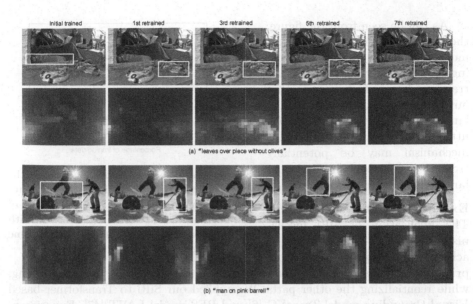

Fig. 7. Visualization of the predicted box and the encoder's cross-modal attention weights in inference. The columns represent initial trained, 1st retrained, 3rd retrained, 5th retrained, 7th retrained model, respectively, from left to right. As we can see, the model prediction gets better as the encoder attention map gets clear.

4.6   Extensibility Studies

To better show the generality, we further extend SiRi to more visual grounding settings, models, and tasks.

Extend to Small Data Size. First, we study how SiRi performs with fewer training data, where the over-fitting issue is more severe. To do so, we randomly sample 10%, 25%, and 50% of training data from the RefCOCOg training set as the new training splits, respectively. Then we train the model following the SiRi mechanism[1] and then evaluate the performance on the full validation set of RefCOCOg (the same validation set for all). The results are shown in Fig. 8.

Compared with the initial trained model, our SiRi model shows very impressive performance gains, e.g., almost doubling the performance at 10% sampling rate.

---

[1] We train more epochs until converging in small-scale experiments.

As can be seen from the figure, the performance is improved much more significantly when employing the SiRi mechanism on fewer training data, which verifies that our SiRi can generalize the vision-language encoder and avoid overfitting. It suggests that our SiRi mechanism may be potentially treated as a strong alternative to large-scale pre-training models.

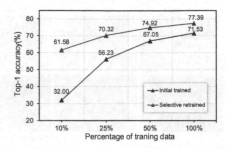

Fig. 8. Performance improvement of the model with SiRi with limited training samples. We randomly sample 10%, 25%, 50% of training data from RefCOCOg and train with SiRi. All models are evaluated on the same RefCOCOg *val* set.

Extend to other V-L models. The application of SiRi mechanism on other V-L models can be achieved by simply following the principle: keeping the parameters of V-L fusion module continuously training, while reinitializing the other parts. We applied our SiRi to Transformer-based Visual Grounding model TransVG [6] and RES model LAVT [47]. Experimental details are presented in the supplementary materials. For TransVG [6], we report REC and Phrase Grounding results in Table 4. We found that SiRi could further improve the performance of TransVG by an average of 2% at top-1 accuracy on all four REC datasets, and the performance has also been effectively improved on Phrase Grounding dataset Flickr30k dataset. For LAVT [47], We report the results of SiRi in RES dataset RefCOCO+ three splits *val*, *testA*, *testB* in Table 5.

Extend to Other V-L Tasks. We also test our SiRi in more vision-language tasks, including referring expression segmentation, phrase grounding, and visual question answering. For these experiments, we took the transformer-based MDETR model (without pre-training) as our baseline. The specific settings of how to apply SiRi on these tasks are stated as follows.

-Referring Expression Segmentation (RES). RES is to segment the objects according to the given language description. We further perform the segmentation task on the trained visual grounding model. We keep the original MDETR model architecture the same but modify the hyperparameters according to the settings used in training visual grounding in this paper. We test the SiRi model on three RES datasets, *i.e.*, RefCOCO, RefCOCO+, RefCOCOg. In

Table 4. REC and phrase grounding results of TransVG [6] with SiRi mechanism.

Model	Backbone	Referring expression comprehension									PhraseGround	
		RefCOCO			RefCOCO+			RefCOCOg	ReferIt		Flickr30k	
		val	testA	testB	val	testA	testB	g-val	val	test	val	test
TransVG	ResNet-50	80.49	83.28	75.24	66.39	70.55	57.66	66.35	71.60	69.76	77.19	78.47
+SiRi	ResNet-50	82.97	84.42	79.04	69.30	73.27	59.93	68.54	74.28	71.36	77.99	79.17

Table 5. Referring expression segmentation results of LAVT [47] with SiRi.

RefCOCO+	Model	P@0.5	P@0.6	P@0.7	P@0.8	P@0.9	oIoU	mIoU
val	LAVT	74.44	70.91	65.58	56.34	30.23	62.14	65.81
	+SiRi	**75.56**	**72.39**	**67.88**	**58.33**	**30.79**	**62.86**	**66.78**
testA	LAVT	80.68	77.96	72.90	62.21	32.36	68.38	70.97
	+SiRi	**82.20**	**79.18**	**74.54**	**63.99**	**32.62**	**68.87**	**71.93**
testB	LAVT	65.66	61.85	55.94	47.56	27.24	**55.10**	59.23
	+SiRi	**66.41**	**62.86**	**57.37**	**49.23**	**27.90**	55.03	**59.70**

Table 6. Experiment results on RES. We report precision Pr@0.5, 0.7, 0.9 and overall IoU on the *val* set of RefCOCO, RefCOCO+, RefCOCO.

Stage	RefCOCO				RefCOCO+				RefCOCOg			
	Pr@0.5	Pr@0.7	Pr@0.9	oIoU	Pr@0.5	Pr@0.7	Pr@0.9	oIoU	Pr@0.5	Pr@0.7	Pr@0.9	oIoU
Initial-train	77.76	68.89	28.58	62.12	68.36	61.11	25.89	52.48	64.34	54.84	20.42	51.39
3rd-retrain	82.58	74.33	32.57	68.02	75.27	67.76	28.21	60.11	72.20	61.46	25.12	58.33
5th-retrain	**83.56**	**75.37**	**32.79**	**69.34**	**76.46**	**68.47**	**28.26**	**61.15**	**73.24**	**63.25**	25.08	**59.69**

Table 6, we report the RES performance of the SiRi model after *Initial-train*, *3rd-train*, and *5th-train* stages. It can be seen that SiRi can steadily improve RES models during the retraining process.

-Phrase Grounding. The task is to locate objects in an image based on the phrases which may be inter-related. We evaluate the SiRi mechanism on the Flickr30k entities dataset. For the input image, we set the maximum size to 800. We show the model performance of different SiRi stages in Table 7. We can see SiRi further improves the initial trained model by 1%–2% on Recall@1, Recall@5, Recall@10 (denoted as R@1, R@5, R@10, respectively).

-Visual Question Answering. Given an image and a question in natural language, this task is to infer the correct answer. We use the scene graph provided in GQA to align question words and the boxes as in MDETR. We verify the validity of SiRi on the visual question answering task in GQA *balanced* split

Table 7. Experiment results of Phrase Grounding on the validation set of Flickr30k and the VQA performance on the GQA *balance test* set.

Stage	Phrase Grounding@Flickr30k			GQA
	R@1	R@5	R@10	Accuracy
Initial-train	76.22	87.19	90.26	55.75
1st-retrain	78.41	88.42	91.31	56.38
2nd-retrain	**78.63**	**88.62**	**91.62**	**57.25**

dataset. The results of SiRi model from different training stages are reported in Table 7. The accuracy is improved from 55.75 to 57.45.

5   Conclusion

In this paper, we present a novel training mechanism namely Selective Retraining (SiRi) for visual grounding, where we keep updating the Transformer encoder while re-initialize the other modules to get out of local minimums. We further propose multi-task SiRi to train a better encoder by incorporating an auxiliary decoder with constant input queries. Extensive experiments prove our method helps the Transformer encoder better perceive the relationship between the visual and the corresponding expression, outperforming state-of-the-art methods on the three visual grounding datasets. Interestingly, we find SiRi also performs superior even with very limited training data. Even with a quarter of training data, we outperform state-of-the-art methods (with full training data) by 1.65% on the RefCOCOg validation set. We also extend SiRi to other Transformer-based visual grounding models and other V-L tasks. We hope our work will help motivate more researchers in the V-L research community in the future.

Acknowledgements. This work was supported in part by the National Key R&D Program of China (No.2021ZD0112100), the National NSF of China (No. U1936212, No. 62120106009), the Fundamental Research Funds for the Central Universities (No. K22RC00010). We thank Princeton Visual AI Lab members (Dora Zhao, Jihoon Chung, and others) for their helpful suggestions.

References

1. Bolme, D.S., Beveridge, J.R., Draper, B.A., Lui, Y.M.: Visual object tracking using adaptive correlation filters. In: CVPR (2010)
2. Carion, N., Massa, F., Synnaeve, G., Usunier, N., Kirillov, A., Zagoruyko, S.: End-to-end object detection with transformers. In: Vedaldi, A., Bischof, H., Brox, T., Frahm, J.-M. (eds.) ECCV 2020. LNCS, vol. 12346, pp. 213–229. Springer, Cham (2020). https://doi.org/10.1007/978-3-030-58452-8_13
3. Chen, X., Ma, L., Chen, J., Jie, Z., Liu, W., Luo, J.: Real-time referring expression comprehension by single-stage grounding network. arXiv preprint arXiv:1812.03426 (2018)
4. Chen, Y.-C., et al.: UNITER: learning universal image-text representations (2019)
5. Deng, J., Dong, W., Socher, R., Li, L.-J., Li, K., Fei-Fei, L.: ImageNet: a large-scale hierarchical image database. In: CVPR (2009)
6. Deng, J., Yang, Z., Chen, T., Zhou, W., Li, H.: TransVG: end-to-end visual grounding with transformers. In: ICCV (2021)
7. Devlin, J., Chang, M.-W., Lee, K., Toutanova, K.: BERT: pre-training of deep bidirectional transformers for language understanding. arXiv preprint arXiv:1810.04805 (2018)
8. Gan, Z., Chen, Y.-C., Li, L., Zhu, C., Cheng, Y., Liu, J.: Large-scale adversarial training for vision-and-language representation learning. In: NeruIPS (2020)
9. Girshick, R.: Fast R-CNN. In: ICCV (2015)

10. Glorot, X., Bengio, Y.: Understanding the difficulty of training deep feedforward neural networks. In: AISTATS (2010)
11. Han, S., et al.: DSD: dense-sparse-sense training for deep neural networks. In: ICLR (2017)
12. Hansen, L.K., Salamon, P.: Neural network ensembles. IEEE Trans. Pattern Anal. Mach. Intell. **12**, 993–1001 (1990)
13. He, K., Zhang, X., Ren, S., Sun, J.: Deep residual learning for image recognition. In: CVPR (2016)
14. Henriques, J.F., Caseiro, R., Martins, P., Batista, J.: High-speed tracking with kernelized correlation filters. IEEE Trans. Pattern Anal. Mach. Intell. **37**, 583–596 (2014)
15. Hinton, G., Vinyals, O., Dean, J.: Distilling the knowledge in a neural network. arXiv preprint arXiv:1503.02531 (2015)
16. Hong, R., Liu, D., Mo, X., He, X., Zhang, H.: Learning to compose and reason with language tree structures for visual grounding. IEEE Trans. Pattern Anal. Mach. Intell. (2019)
17. Hu, R., Rohrbach, M., Andreas, J., Darrell, T., Saenko, K.: Modeling relationships in referential expressions with compositional modular networks. In: CVPR (2017)
18. Huang, G., Li, Y., Pleiss, G., Liu, Z., Hopcroft, J.E., Weinberger, K.Q.: Snapshot ensembles: train 1, get m for free. In: ICLR (2017)
19. Huang, J., Qu, L., Jia, R., Zhao, B.: O2U-Net: a simple noisy label detection approach for deep neural networks. In: ICCV (2019)
20. Huang, X.S., et al.: Improving transformer optimization through better initialization. In: ICML (2020)
21. Kamath, A., Singh, M., LeCun, Y., Synnaeve, G., Misra, I., Carion, N.: MDETR-modulated detection for end-to-end multi-modal understanding. In: ICCV (2021)
22. Kim, W., Son, B., Kim, I.: ViLT: vision-and-language transformer without convolution or region supervision. In: ICML (2021)
23. Krogh, A., Vedelsby, J., et al.: Neural network ensembles, cross validation, and active learning. In: NeruIPS (1995)
24. Liang, C., Wu, Y., Luo, Y., Yang, Y.: ClawCraneNet: leveraging object-level relation for text-based video segmentation. arXiv preprint arXiv:2103.10702 (2021)
25. Liang, C., et al.: Rethinking cross-modal interaction from a top-down perspective for referring video object segmentation. arXiv preprint arXiv:2106.01061 (2021)
26. Liao, Y., et al.: A real-time cross-modality correlation filtering method for referring expression comprehension. In: CVPR (2020)
27. Liu, D., Zhang, H., Wu, F., Zha, Z.-J.: Learning to assemble neural module tree networks for visual grounding. In: ICCV (2019)
28. Liu, Y., et al.: RoBERTa: a robustly optimized BERT pretraining approach. arXiv preprint arXiv:1907.11692 (2019)
29. Loshchilov, I., Hutter, F.: Fixing weight decay regularization in adam (2018)
30. Jiasen, L., Batra, D., Parikh, D., Lee, S.: ViLBERT: pretraining task-agnostic visiolinguistic representations for vision-and-language tasks. In: NeruIPS (2019)
31. Luo, G., et al.: Multi-task collaborative network for joint referring expression comprehension and segmentation. In: CVPR (2020)
32. Mao, J., Huang, J., Toshev, A., Camburu, O., Yuille, A.L., Murphy, K.: Generation and comprehension of unambiguous object descriptions. In: CVPR (2016)
33. Redmon, J., Farhadi, A.: YOLOv3: an incremental improvement. arXiv preprint arXiv:1804.02767 (2018)
34. Sadhu, A., Chen, K., Nevatia, R.: Zero-shot grounding of objects from natural language queries. In: ICCV (2019)

35. Simonyan, K., Zisserman, A.: Very deep convolutional networks for large-scale image recognition. In: ICLR (2015)
36. Smith, L.N.: Cyclical learning rates for training neural networks. In: WACV, pp. 464–472. IEEE Computer Society (2017)
37. Srivastava, N., Hinton, G., Krizhevsky, A., Sutskever, I., Salakhutdinov, R.: Dropout: a simple way to prevent neural networks from overfitting. J. Mach. Learn. Res. **15**, 1929–1958 (2014)
38. Weijie, S., et al.: VL-BERT: pre-training of generic visual-linguistic representations. In: ICLR (2020)
39. Tan, H., Bansal, M.: LXMERT: learning cross-modality encoder representations from transformers. In: EMNLP (2019)
40. Vaswani, A., et al.: Attention is all you need. In: NeuruIPS (2017)
41. Wang, L., Li, Y., Huang, J., Lazebnik, S.: Learning two-branch neural networks for image-text matching tasks. IEEE Trans. Pattern Anal. Mach. Intell. **41**, 394–407 (2018)
42. Wang, P., Qi, W., Cao, J., Shen, C., Gao, L., van den Hengel, A.: Neighbourhood watch: referring expression comprehension via language-guided graph attention networks. In: CVPR (2019)
43. Wu, Y., Jiang, L., Yang, Y.: Switchable novel object captioner. IEEE Trans. Pattern Anal. Mach. Intell., 1 (2022)
44. Yang, S., Li, G., Yu, Y.: Dynamic graph attention for referring expression comprehension. In: ICCV (2019)
45. Yang, S., Li, G., Yu, Y.: Graph-structured referring expression reasoning in the wild. In: CVPR (2020)
46. Yang, Z., Chen, T., Wang, L., Luo, J.: Improving one-stage visual grounding by recursive sub-query construction. In: Vedaldi, A., Bischof, H., Brox, T., Frahm, J.-M. (eds.) ECCV 2020. LNCS, vol. 12359, pp. 387–404. Springer, Cham (2020). https://doi.org/10.1007/978-3-030-58568-6_23
47. Yang, Z., et al.: LAVT: language-aware vision transformer for referring image segmentation. In: CVPR (2022)
48. Yang, Z., Gong, B., Wang, L., Huang, W., Yu, D., Luo, J.: A fast and accurate one-stage approach to visual grounding. In: ICCV (2019)
49. Yu, F., et al.: ERNRE-ViL knowledge enhanced vision-language representations through scene graph (2020)
50. Yu, L., et al.: MAttNet: modular attention network for referring expression comprehension. In: CVPR (2018)
51. Yu, L., Poirson, P., Yang, S., Berg, A.C., Berg, T.L.: Modeling context in referring expressions. In: Leibe, B., Matas, J., Sebe, N., Welling, M. (eds.) ECCV 2016. LNCS, vol. 9906, pp. 69–85. Springer, Cham (2016). https://doi.org/10.1007/978-3-319-46475-6_5
52. Zhang, H., Niu, Y., Chang, S.-F.: Grounding referring expressions in images by variational context. In: CVPR (2018)
53. Zhang, Y., Wang, C., Wang, X., Zeng, W., Liu, W.: FairMOT: on the fairness of detection and re-identification in multiple object tracking. Int. J. Comput. Vis. **129**, 3069–3087 (2021)
54. Zheng, K., Liu, W., Liu, J., Zha, Z.-J., Mei, T.: Hierarchical Gumbel attention network for text-based person search. In: ACM Multimedia, pp. 3441–3449. ACM (2020)
55. Zhuang, B., Wu, Q., Shen, C., Reid, I., Van Den Hengel, A.: Parallel attention: a unified framework for visual object discovery through dialogs and queries. In CVPR (2018)

Cross-Modal Prototype Driven Network for Radiology Report Generation

Jun Wang[(✉)], Abhir Bhalerao, and Yulan He

Department of Computer Science, University of Warwick, Coventry, UK
{jun.wang.3,abhir.bhalerao,yulan.he}@warwick.ac.uk

Abstract. Radiology report generation (RRG) aims to describe automatically a radiology image with human-like language and could potentially support the work of radiologists, reducing the burden of manual reporting. Previous approaches often adopt an encoder-decoder architecture and focus on single-modal feature learning, while few studies explore cross-modal feature interaction. Here we propose a Cross-modal PROtotype driven NETwork (XPRONET) to promote cross-modal pattern learning and exploit it to improve the task of radiology report generation. This is achieved by three well-designed, fully differentiable and complementary modules: a shared cross-modal prototype matrix to record the cross-modal prototypes; a cross-modal prototype network to learn the cross-modal prototypes and embed the cross-modal information into the visual and textual features; and an improved multi-label contrastive loss to enable and enhance multi-label prototype learning. XPRONET obtains substantial improvements on the IU-Xray and MIMIC-CXR benchmarks, where its performance exceeds recent state-of-the-art approaches by a large margin on IU-Xray and comparable performance on MIMIC-CXR (The code is publicly available at https://github.com/Markin-Wang/XProNet.).

Keywords: Radiology report generation · Cross-modal pattern learning · Prototype learning · Transformers

1 Introduction

Radiology images, e.g., X-Ray and MRI, are widely used in medicine to support disease diagnosis. Nonetheless, traditional clinical practice is laborious since it requires the medical expert, such as a radiologist, to carefully analyze an image and then produce a medical report, which often takes more than five minutes [13]. This process could also be error-prone due to subjective factors, such as fatigue and distraction. Automatic radiology report generation, as an alternative to expert diagnosis, has therefore gained increasing attention from

Supplementary Information The online version contains supplementary material available at https://doi.org/10.1007/978-3-031-19833-5_33.

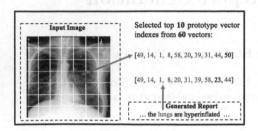 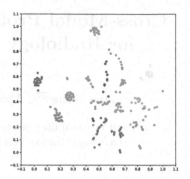

Fig. 1. An example generated report and the selected cross-modal prototype indices using XPRONET. The selected word "lungs" is marked as red and the associated image patch is highlighted in the red rectangle. The prototype indices selected both from the image patch and from the text instance are marked as red. (Color figure online)

Fig. 2. A visualization of the cross-modal prototype matrix on the MIMIC-CXR dataset using T-SNE [25]. Points with the same colour come from the same prototype category.

researchers. Automatic medical report generation has the potential to rapidly produce a report and assist a radiologist to make the final diagnosis significantly reducing the workload of radiologists and saving medical resources, especially in developing countries where well-trained radiologists can be in short supply.

Owing to developments in computer vision models for image captioning and availability of large-scale datasets, recently there have been significant advancements in automated radiology report generation [13,22,44]. Nevertheless, radiology report generation still remains a challenging task and is far from being solved. The reasons are three-fold. Firstly, unlike the traditional image captioning task which often produces only a single sentence, a medical report consists of several sentences and its length might be four-times longer than an image caption. Secondly, medical reports often exhibit more sophisticated linguistic and semantic patterns. Lastly, commonly used datasets suffer from notable data biases: the majority of the training samples are of normal cases, any abnormal regions often only exist in a small parts of an image, and even in pathological cases, most statements may be associated with a description of normal findings, e.g. see Fig. 4. Overall, these problems present a substantial challenge to the modelling of cross-modal pattern interactions and learning informative features for accurate report generation.

Existing methods often focus on learning discriminative, *single*-modal features and ignore the importance of cross-modal interaction, essential for dealing with complex image and text semantic interrelationships. Thus, cross-modal interaction is of great importance as the model is required to generate a meaningful report only given the radiology image. Previous studies normally model cross-modal interaction by a self-attention mechanism on the extracted visual and textual features in an encoder-decoder architecture, which cannot adequately capture complex cross-modal patterns. Motivated by this, we propose a novel framework called *Cross-modal PROtotype driven NETwork* (XPRONET) which learns the cross-modal prototypes on the fly and utilizes them to embed cross-modal information into the single-model features. XPRONET regards the cross-modal prototypes as intermediate representations and explicitly establishes a cross-modal information flow to enrich single-modal features. Figure 1 shows an example of the cross-modal information flow where the visual and textual features select almost the same (9 of top 10) cross-modal prototypes to perform interaction. These enriched features are more likely to capture the sophisticated patterns required for accurate report generation. Additionally, the imbalance problem is addressed by forcing single-model features to interact with their cross-modal prototypes via a class-related, cross-modal prototype querying and responding module. Our work makes three principal contributions:

1. We propose a novel end-to-end cross-modal prototype driven network where we utilize the cross-modal prototypes to enhance image and text pattern interactions. Leveraging cross-modal prototypes in this way for RRG has not been explicitly explored.
2. We employ a memory matrix to learn and record the cross-modal prototypes which are regarded as intermediate representations between the visual and textual features. A cross-modal prototype network is designed to embed cross-modal information into the single-modal features.
3. We propose an improved multi-label contrastive loss to learn cross-modal prototypes while simultaneously accommodating label differences via an adaptive controller term.

After a discussion of related work, our methods and implementation are described in detail in Sect. 3. Experimental results presented in Sect. 4 demonstrate that our approach outperforms a number of state-of-the-art methods over two widely-used benchmarks. We also undertake ablation studies to verify the effectiveness of individual components of our method. Discussion and proposals are given to inspire future work.

2   Related Work

Image Captioning. Image captioning aims to generate human-like sentences to describe a given image. This task is considered as a high-level visual understanding problem which combines the research of computer vision and natural language processing. Recent state-of-the-art approaches [20,24,32,33,38,42] follow an encoder-decoder architecture and have demonstrated a great improvement in some traditional image captioning benchmarks. In particular, the most successful models [5,8,11,30] usually adopt the Transformer [36] as their backbone due to its self-attention mechanism and its impressive capability of extracting meaningful features for the task. However, these methods are designed for short textual description generation and are less capable for generating long reports. Though several works [16,26] have been proposed to deal with long text generation, they often cannot capture the specific medical observations and tend to produce reports ignoring abnormal regions in images, resulting in unsatisfactory performance.

Radiology Report Generation. Inspired by the great success of encoder-decoder based frameworks in image captioning, recent radiology report generation methods have also employed similar architectures. Specifically, Jing et al. [13] developed a hierarchical LSTM model to produce long reports and proposed a co-attention mechanism to detect abnormal patches. Liu et al. [22] proposed to firstly determine the topics of each report, which are then conditioned upon for report generation. Similarly, Zhang et al. [44] also ascertained the disease topics and utilized prior knowledge to assist report generation via a pre-constructed knowledge graph. Liu et al. [21] extended this work by presenting a PPKED model which distills both the prior and posterior knowledge into report generation. A few works [27,29] have investigated reinforcement learning for improving the consistency of the generated reports. These encoder-decoder approaches often focus on extracting discriminative single-modal features (visual *or* textual), while few study explores the importance of the cross-modal pattern interactions.

The most similar work to ours is R2GenCMN [3] which utilizes an extra memory to learn the cross-modal patterns. Nonetheless, there are three main differences. First, we design a shared cross-modal prototype matrix to learn the class-related cross-modal patterns and propose an improved multi-label contrastive loss, while Chen et al. [3] randomly initialize a memory matrix and use a cross entropy loss. Additionally, our querying and responding process is class-related, that is, cross-modal pattern learning is only performed over the cross-modal prototypes sharing the *same* labels rather than on all cross-modal prototypes. Moreover, we adopt a more effective approach to distill the cross-modal information into the single-modal representations rather than the simple averaging function used in R2GenCMN. XPRONET is driven by the cross-modal *prototypes* which, to the best of our knowledge, has not been explored before in radiology report generation.

3   Methods

Our aim is to learn important informative cross-modal patterns and utilize them to explicitly model cross-modal feature interactions for radiology report generation, Fig. 3 shows the overall architecture of XPRONET. The details of the main three modules, i.e., the image feature extractor, the cross-modal prototype network, and the encoder-decoder are described in the following subsections.

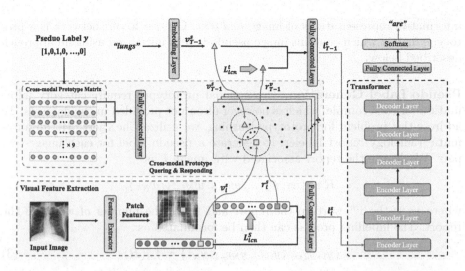

Fig. 3. The architecture of XPRONET: An image is fed into the Visual Feature Extractor to obtain patch features. A word at time step T (e.g. "lungs") is mapped onto a word embedding via an embedding layer. The visual and textual representations are then sent to the cross-modal prototype querying and responding module to perform cross-modal interaction on the selected cross-modal prototypes based on the associated pseudo label. Then the single-model feature are enriched by the generated responses through a linear layer and taken as the source inputs of the Transformer encoder-decoder to generate the report (Color figure online).

3.1 Image Feature Extractor

Given an input radiology image I, a ResNet-101 [9] is utilized to extract the image features $v \in \mathbb{R}^{H \times W \times C}$, shown in the blue-dashed rectangle in Fig. 3. In particular, image features v are extracted from the last convolution layer, before the final average pooling operation. Here H, W and C are the height, width and the number of channels of an image, respectively. Once extracted, we linearize the image features v by concatenating the rows of the image features and regard each region (position) feature as a visual word token. The final feature representation sequence $v_s \in \mathbb{R}^{HW \times C}$ is taken as the input for the subsequent modules and is expressed as:

$$\{v_1^s, v_2^s, ..., v_i^s, ..., v_{N^s-1}^s, v_{N^s}^s\} = f_{ife}(I), \tag{1}$$

where v_i denotes the region features in the ith position of v_s, $N^s = H \times W$, and $f_{ife}(\cdot)$ is the image feature extractor.

3.2 Cross-Modal Prototype Network

Learning complex related patterns between image features and related textual descriptions is challenging. But cross-modal learning enables jointly learn informative representations of image *and* text. Central to our network is a prototype matrix which contains image pseudo-labels, initialized using an approach described below.

Pseudo Label Generation. Cross-modal prototypes require category information for each sample, which is however often not provided in the datasets. To address this problem for prototype learning, we utilize CheXbert [34], an automatic radiology report labeler, to generate a pseudo label for each image-text pair. We denote the report associated with image I as:

$$R = \{w_1, w_2, ..., w_i, ..., w_{N^r-1}, w_{N^r}\}, \tag{2}$$

where w_i is the ith word in the report and N^r is the number of words in the report. The labelling process can then be formulated as:

$$\{y_1, y_2, ..., y_i, ..., y_{N^l-1}, y_{N^l}\} = f_{al}(R), \tag{3}$$

where the result is an one-hot vector and $y_i \in \{0, 1\}$ is the prediction result for i^{th} category. Note that the value of one indicates the existence of that category, N^l is the number of categories, and $f_{al}(\cdot)$ denotes the automatic radiology report labeler.

Prototype Matrix Initialization. Existing methods often directly model the cross-modal information interactions using the encoded features and learn implicitly cross-modal patterns. The length of the report, the imbalanced distribution of text descriptions of normal and abnormal cases, and complex cross modal patterns, make it hard to capture cross-modal patterns effectively. For better cross-modal pattern learning, we design a shared cross-modal prototype matrix $PM \in \mathbb{R}^{N^l \times N^p \times D}$ to learn and store the cross-modal patterns, which can be considered as intermediate representations. Here N^p and D are the number of learned cross-modal prototypes for each category and the dimension for each prototype, respectively. PM is updated and learned during training, and then utilized by the class-related prototype querying and responding modules to explicitly embed the cross-modal information to the single-modal features.

The initialization of the prototype matrix is critical. One way is to randomly initialize the matrix [3], but this does not capture any meaningful semantic information and hampers the subsequent prototype learning. Therefore, we propose to utilize prior information to initialize a semantic cross-modal prototype matrix. Specifically, for an image-text pair $<I, R>$ with the associated pseudo class labels y, we employ a pretrained ResNet-101 and BERT [34] to extract the global visual and textual representations, $o^i \in \mathbb{R}^{1 \times C_1}$ and $o^t \in \mathbb{R}^{1 \times C_2}$, where C_1 and C_2 are the number of channels extracted of the visual and textual representations, respectively. To improve robustness, we also extract the flipped image features $o^{if} \in \mathbb{R}^{1 \times C_1}$. By repeating this process on all the training samples, we can obtain a group of feature sets for each class, formulated as:

$$R_k^I = \{o_u^{i(f)} | y_{u,k} = 1\}, \quad R_k^T = \{o_u^t | y_{u,k} = 1\}. \tag{4}$$

Here $\boldsymbol{R}_k^I$ and $\boldsymbol{R}_k^T$ are the visual and textual feature sets for category k, $i(f)$ means either the original image i or the flipped image if, and $y_{u,k}$ denotes the label of category k for sample u. After that, we concatenate the visual and textual representations to form the cross-modal features, $r \in \mathbb{R}^{1 \times D}$. Note that $D = C_1 + C_2$. Finally, K-Means [23] is employed to cluster each feature set into N_p clusters and the average of features in each cluster is used as an initial cross-modal prototype for $\boldsymbol{PM}$. This process can be summarised as:

$$o_u = Concat(o_u^{i(f)}, o_u^t), \tag{5}$$

$$\{\boldsymbol{g}_1^k, ..., \boldsymbol{g}_{N^p-1}^k, \boldsymbol{g}_{N^p}^k\} = f_{km}(\boldsymbol{R}_k), \qquad \boldsymbol{g}_i^k = \{o_1^{k,i}, ..., o_{N_{k,i}^d}^{k,i}\}, \tag{6}$$

$$\boldsymbol{PM}(k,i) = \frac{1}{N_{k,i}^s}\sum_{j=0}^{N} r_j^{k,i}, \tag{7}$$

where o_u and $\boldsymbol{R}_k$ are the concatenated cross-modal representation for sample u and the cross-modal feature set for category k, $\boldsymbol{g}_i^k$ is the ith grouped cluster for k^{th} category returned by the K-Mean algorithm f_{km}. $N_{k,i}^d$ is the number of samples in the ith cluster for k^{th} category. $\boldsymbol{PM}(k,i)$ then represents the ith vector in the cross-modal prototype set for the kth category.

Cross-Modal Prototype Querying. After obtaining the prototype matrix, similar to [3], we adopt a querying and responding process to explicitly embed the cross-modal information into the single-modal features. Different from [3], given an image, our cross-modal prototype querying measures the similarity between its single-modal representation and the cross-modal prototype vectors under the same label as the image, and selects the top γ vectors having the highest similarity to interact with the single-model representations. This process is illustrated in the yellow-dashed rectangle in Fig. 3.

Given the image-text training pair $<\boldsymbol{I}, \boldsymbol{R}>$ and the associated pseudo label $\boldsymbol{y}$, the queried cross-modal prototype vectors for the sample are then generated. The queried cross-modal prototype vectors $\boldsymbol{pv} = \{\boldsymbol{PM}(k)|\ y_k = 1\}$, where $\boldsymbol{PM}(k)$ is the cross-modal prototype set for the kth category generated by Eqs. (5)–(8). To filter out possible noise, a linear projection is applied to $\boldsymbol{pv}$ to map it to C_P dimensions before sending it into the querying process, as follows:

$$\boldsymbol{p} = \boldsymbol{pv} \cdot \boldsymbol{W}_{pv}, \tag{8}$$

where $W_{pv} \in \mathbb{R}^{D \times C_P}$ is a learnable weight matrix.

We denote the report representation output by the embedding layer as $\boldsymbol{v}_t = \{v_1^t, v_2^t, ..., v_i^t, ..., v_{N^t-1}^t, v_{N^t}^t\}$ and a cross-modal prototype vector as p_i, where $v_i^t \in \mathbb{R}^{1 \times C}$ is the ith word embedding of the report. Before performing the querying, we linearly project the visual feature sequence $\boldsymbol{v}_s$, textual report embeddings $\boldsymbol{v}_t$ and the cross-modal prototype vector p_i into the same dimension d since they may have different dimensions:

$$v_i^{s*} = v_i^s \cdot \boldsymbol{W}_v, \quad v_i^{t*} = v_i^t \cdot \boldsymbol{W}_v, \quad p_i^* = p_i \cdot \boldsymbol{W}_p, \tag{9}$$

where $\boldsymbol{W}_v \in \mathbb{R}^{C \times d}$ and $\boldsymbol{W}_p \in \mathbb{R}^{C_P \times d}$ are two learnable weights. A similarity between each single-modal feature and cross-modal prototype vector pair is computed by:

$$D^s_{(i,u)} = \frac{v^{s*}_j \cdot p^*_u}{d}, \quad D^t_{(j,u)} = \frac{v^{t*}_j \cdot p^*_u}{d}. \tag{10}$$

Since the majority of the cross-modal prototypes might be irrelevant to the queried vectors, which may introduce noisy cross-modal patterns, we only select γ most similar vectors to respond to the query vectors. After that, we calculate the weights among these selected prototype vectors based on the similarities. This process between a cross-modal prototype p^*_u, a visual region representation v^{s*}_i and a textual word embedding v^{t*}_i is captured by:

$$w^s_{(i,u)} = \frac{D^s_{(i,u)}}{\sum_{j=1}^{\gamma} D^s_{(i,j)}}, \quad w^t_{(i,u)} = \frac{D^t_{(i,u)}}{\sum_{j=1}^{\gamma} D^t_{(i,j)}} \tag{11}$$

Cross-Modal Prototype Responding. After obtaining the top γ similar cross-modal prototype vectors and their weights, the next step is to generate the responses for the visual and textual features. In particular, we firstly transform the queried prototype vectors to the same representation space of the query vectors via a fully connected layer. The responses for the visual and textual features are created by taking the weighted sum over these transformed cross-modal prototype vectors:

$$e^s_{(i,j)} = p^{s*}_{(i,j)} \cdot \boldsymbol{W}_e, \qquad e^t_{(i,j)} = p^{t*}_{(i,j)} \cdot \boldsymbol{W}_e, \tag{12}$$

$$r^s_i = \sum_{j=1}^{\gamma} w^s_{(i,j)} \cdot e^s_{(i,j)}, \qquad r^t_i = \sum_{j=1}^{\gamma} w^t_{(i,j)} \cdot e^t_{(i,j)}, \tag{13}$$

where $p^{s*}_{(i,j)}$ and $p^{t*}_{(i,j)}$ are the jth prototype vectors in the most similar cross-modal prototype sets for the ith image patch and word, respectively. Similarly, the jth transformed prototype vectors for i^{th} image patch and word are denoted as $e^s_{(i,j)}$ and $e^t_{(i,j)}$. We represent the responses for i^{th} image patch and word as r^s_i and r^t_i. The $w^s_{(i,j)}$ and $w^t_{(i,j)}$ are the weights obtained by Eqs. (11) to (12).

Feature Interaction Module. The selected cross-modal prototype vectors contain class-related and cross-modal patterns. The last step is to introduce these informative patterns into the single-modal features via feature interaction. In [3], this is achieved by directly adding the single-model features and their associated responses, which pays the same attention to the responses and the single-modal features. However, this simple approach might be suboptimal given possibly noisy responses or non-discriminative single-model features. To mitigate this problem, we propose to automatically learn the importance difference and filter out noisy signals.

Specifically, we firstly concatenate the single-modal features with their associated responses. A linear layer is then applied to fuse the single-modal features and the cross-modal prototype vectors. Remember that the fused representations contain rich class-related features and cross-modal patterns. The process is:

$$l^s = FCN(Concat(v^s, r^s)), \quad l^t = FCN(Concat(v^t, r^t)), \quad (14)$$

where FCN denotes the fully connected layer and $Concat$ is the concatenating function. The outputs of the Feature Interaction Module are taken as the source inputs for the following Transformer module to generate the reports.

3.3 Reports Generation with Transformer

Transformers have been shown to be quite potent for NLP tasks, e.g., sentiment analysis [4,40,41], machine translation [2,39,43] and question answering [15,28,45]. Consequently, we adopt a transformer to generate the final reports. Generally, the Transformer consists of the Encoder and Decoder. At the first step, the responded visual features l^s are fed into the Encoder to obtain the intermediate representations. Combined with the current fused textual representation sequence $l^t = \{l_1^t, l_2^t, ..., l_i^t, ..., l_{T-1}^s\}$, these intermediate representations are then taken as the source inputs for the Decoder to predict the current output. In general, the encoding and decoding processes can be expressed as:

$$\{m_1, m_2, ..., m_{N^s}\} = Encoder(l_1^s, l_2^s, ..., l_{N^s}^s), \quad (15)$$

$$p_T = Decoder(m_1, m_2, ..., m_{N^s}; l_1^t, l_2^t, ..., l_{T-1}^t), \quad (16)$$

where p_T denotes the word prediction for time step T. The complete report is obtained by repeating the above process.

3.4 Improved Multi-label Contrastive Loss

Though the cross-modal prototype matrix is determistically initialized, further learning is required to learn class-related and informative cross-modal patterns, since the cross-modal patterns are actually far more sophisticated than the simple concatenation of the visual and textual representations in the Prototype Initialization module. Moreover, the cross-modal prototype features extractor (pretrained ResNet-101 and BERT) are not trained on our target benchmarks, leading to potentially noisy signals. Therefore, online cross-modal prototype learning becomes of greater significance.

A simple way is to utilize the widely used contrastive loss to supervise the learning of the cross-modal prototypes. Nonetheless, the vanilla contrastive loss is designed for the single-label prototype learning, while each training sample can belong to multiple categories in our task. Therefore, we modify the contrastive loss into a multi-label scenario by regarding the samples having at least one common label (excluding label 0) as positive pairs. If two samples do not share any common label, they form a negative pair. Instead of employing the contrastive loss on the responded features, we propose applying the loss on the responses since the fused features are used for medical report generation rather than for classification.

Given the visual responses $r^s = \{r_1^s, r_2^s, ..., r_i^s, ..., r_{N^s-1}^s, r_{N^s}^s\}$ and textual responses $r^t = \{r_1^t, r_2^t, ..., r_i^t, ..., r_{N^t-1}^t, r_{N^t}^t\}$, our modified multi-label contrastive loss is formulated as:

$$L_{icn}^s = \frac{1}{B^2} \sum_{i=1}^{B} \sum_{j:y_i \otimes y_j \neq 0}^{B} (\theta^{-\frac{h_d}{h_t}} - Sim(\sigma(r_i^s, r_j^s)))$$
$$+ \sum_{j:y_i \otimes y_j = 0}^{B} \max(Sim(\sigma(r_i^s, r_j^s)) - \alpha, 0) \tag{17}$$

Here B denotes the number of training samples in one batch and $\otimes$ is the dot product operation. $y_i \otimes y_j \neq 0$ ensures that the responses r_i^s and r_j^s have at least one common label (excluding 0). $\sigma(\cdot)$ and $Sim(\cdot)$ are the average function over all the image patch responses followed by the L_2 normalization and the cosine similarity function, respectively. Only negative pairs with similarity larger than a constant margin α can make a contribution to L_{cn}^s.

Note that different from a standard contrastive loss, the maximum positive similarity (or one) is replaced with a label difference term, $\theta^{(\cdot)}$. In this way, the model can tolerate some dissimilarity between the positive pairs in terms of the label difference, instead of forcing them to be the same which is unreasonable under a multi-label setting:

$$h_d = \epsilon(abs(y_i - y_j)), \quad h_t = \epsilon(y_i + y_j), \tag{18}$$

where abs and ϵ are the absolute value and the summary functions, respectively. h_d calculates the number of different labels and h_t denotes the number of total labels of two training samples (excluding zero). Thus θ controls the relative tolerance where a smaller value represents less tolerance given the same label difference. An improved contrastive loss for textual responses L_{icn}^t is obtained in a similar way.

Objective Function. Given the entire predicted report sequence $\{p_i\}$ and the associated ground truth report $\{w_i\}$, XPRONET is jointly optimized with a cross-entropy loss and our improved multi-label contrastive loss by:

$$L_{ce} = -\frac{1}{N^r} \sum_{i=1}^{N^r} w_i \cdot log(p_i), \tag{19}$$

$$L_{fnl} = L_{ce} + \lambda L_{icn}^s + \delta L_{icn}^t, \tag{20}$$

Here λ an δ are two hyper-parameters which balance the loss contributions.

4   Experiments

We verify the effectiveness of XPRONET on two widely used medical report generation benchmarks, i.e., IU-Xray and MIMIC-CXR. Four common natural language processing evaluation metrics: BLEU{1-4} [31], ROUGE-L [19],

Table 1. Comparative results of XPRONET with previous studies. The best values are highlighted in bold and the second best are underlined. BL, RG and MTOR are the abbreviations of BLEU, ROUGE and METEOR. The symbol * denotes our replicated results with the official codes.

Dataset	Method	BL-1	BL-2	BL-3	BL-4	RG-L	MTOR	CIDEr
IU-Xray	ST [35]	0.216	0.124	0.087	0.066	0.306	–	–
	$ADAATT$ [24]	0.220	0.127	0.089	0.068	0.308	–	0.295
	$ATT2IN$ [33]	0.224	0.129	0.089	0.068	0.308	–	0.220
	$SentSAT + KG$ [44]	0.441	0.291	0.203	0.147	0.304	–	0.304
	$HRGR$ [18]	0.438	0.298	0.208	0.151	0.322	–	0.343
	$CoAT$ [13]	0.455	0.288	0.205	0.154	0.369	–	0.277
	$CMAS - RL$ [12]	0.464	0.301	0.210	0.154	0.362	–	0.275
	$KERP$ [17]	0.482	0.325	0.226	0.162	0.339	–	0.280
	$R2GenCMN^*$ [3]	0.474	0.302	0.220	0.168	0.370	0.198	–
	$XPRONET(Ours)$	**0.525**	**0.357**	**0.262**	**0.199**	**0.411**	**0.220**	**0.359**
MIMIC-CXR	$RATCHET$ [10]	0.232	–	–	–	0.240	0.101	–
	ST [35]	0.299	0.184	0.121	0.084	0.263	0.124	–
	$ADAATT$ [24]	0.299	0.185	0.124	0.088	0.266	0.118	–
	$ATT2IN$ [33]	0.325	0.203	0.136	0.096	0.276	0.134	–
	$TopDown$ [1]	0.317	0.195	0.130	0.092	0.267	0.128	–
	$R2GenCMN^*$ [3]	**0.354**	0.212	0.139	0.097	0.271	0.137	–
	$XPRONET(Ours)$	0.344	**0.215**	**0.146**	**0.105**	**0.279**	**0.138**	–

METEOR [7] and CIDEr [37], are utilized to gauge performance. The implementation details are given in Appendix A.1.

Datasets. IU-Xray [6] is a widely used benchmark which contains 7,470 X-ray images and 3,955 corresponding reports established by Indiana University. The majority of patients provided both the frontal and lateral radiology images. MIMIC-CXR [14] is a recently released large chest X-ray dataset with 473,057 X-ray images and 206,563 reports provided by the Beth Israel Deaconess Medical Center. Both of these two datasets are publicly available[1] We follow the same data splits proportions as [18] to divide the IU-Xray dataset into train (70%), validation (10%) and test (20%) sets, while the official data split is adopted for the MIMIC-CXR dataset.

Comparisons with Previous Studies. Here, we compare the experimental results with previous studies on the IU-Xray and MIMIC-CXR datasets. As shown in Table 1, ours (XPRONET) outperforms the previous best SOTA method of R2GenCMN by a noteable margin on the IU-Xray dataset. In particular, XPRONET surpasses the second best-performing method by 4.3%, 3.1% and 4.1% on BLEU-1, BLEU-4 and RG-L scores respectively. A similar pattern can be seen on the MIMIC-CXR benchmark where XPRONET achieves the best performance on all the evaluation metrics except BLEU-1 in which it is slightly inferior to R2GenCMN. We mainly attribute the improved performance to the enriched single-modal feature representation via the cross-modal proto-

---

[1] https://openi.nlm.nih.gov/
https://physionet.org/content/MIMIC-cxr-jpg/2.0.0/.

Table 2. The experimental results of ablation studies on the IU-Xray and MIMIC-CXR datasets. The best values are highlighted in bold. BL and RG are the abbreviations of BLEU and ROUGE.

IU-Xray	BL-1	BL-2	BL-3	BL-4	RG-L	METEOR
XPRONET	**0.525**	**0.357**	**0.262**	**0.199**	**0.411**	**0.220**
w/o PI	0.476	0.307	0.218	0.160	0.371	0.196
w/o IMLCS	0.471	0.307	0.215	0.159	0.377	0.196
w/o CMPNet	0.467	0.303	0.210	0.155	0.367	0.197
MIMIC-CXR	BL-1	BL-2	BL-3	BL-4	RG-L	METEOR
XPRONET	**0.344**	**0.215**	**0.146**	**0.105**	**0.279**	**0.138**
w/o PI	0.329	0.205	0.139	0.100	0.275	0.133
w/o IMLCS	0.336	0.204	0.137	0.098	0.269	0.135
w/o CMPNet	0.321	0.198	0.133	0.095	0.273	0.131

type learning. The superiority of XPRONET on IU-Xray is more obvious than MIMIC-CXR. This could be partly explained by the data size differences as the number of samples in MIMIC-CXR is almost 50 times larger than IU-Xray, hence it is more difficult to learn informative and class-related cross-modal prototypes. We present a visual example in Fig. 4 and give a further analysis below.

Ablation Analysis. Ablation studies were conducted to further explore the impact of each component of XPRONET on report generation performance. We investigated the following variants:

- **XPRONET w/o CMPNet**: the base model which only consists of the visual extractor (ResNet-101) and the encoder-decoder (Transformer) without other extensions.
- **XPRONET w/o PI**: XPRONET without the cross-modal Prototype Initialization (PI), i.e., the cross-modal prototype matrix is randomly initialized.
- **XPRONET w/o IMLCS**: XPRONET without the improved multi-label contrastive loss (IMLCS). We replace the adaptable maximum similarity $\theta^{-\frac{h_d}{h_t}}$ in Eq. (17) with one to switch it back to the standard multi-label contrastive loss.

The main results of the ablation studies of XPRONET are shown in Table 2. First, all the three components, i.e., prototype initialization, improved multi-label contrastive loss and the whole cross-modal prototype network architecture, significantly boost the performance as a notable drop can be seen when any of them is removed. For instance, the BLEU-4 score decreases from 0.199 to 0.160 and 0.105 to 0.100 on the IU-Xray and MIMIC-CXR datasets when the prototype initialization is removed. Similarly, removing the improved multi-label contrastive loss lead to lower scores on BLEU-2 and ROUGE-L. These results verify the importance of informatively initializing the cross-modal prototype and

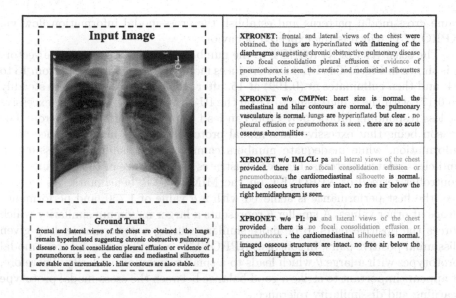

Fig. 4. An example of the report generated by different models. The ground truth report is shown in the blue dashed rectangle. Words that occurred in the ground truth are marked as red (Color figure online).

allowing some dissimilarity between positive pairs under the multi-label, cross-modal prototype learning settings.

Moreover, the biggest performance drop can be seen on the model without the whole cross-modal prototype network on all the evaluation metrics, e.g., 0.525 to 0.467 and 0.344 to 0.321 of BL-1 on IU-Xray and MIMIC-CXR dataset respectively. An example visualization is shown in Fig. 4 to illustrate the strength of XPRONET. More example visualizations are given in Appendix A.2. As we can see, XPRONET can capture the abnormal information and generate a better report, while the reaming models tend to produce sentences ignoring the abnormal patterns observed in images. This could be attributed to the well-learned cross-modal prototypes and the class-related querying and responding module which better capture the cross-modal flow and embed the prototype information into the feature learning procedure. We illustrate the cross-modal prototype matrix extracted from the linear projection (Eq. (8)) in Fig. 2. It can be seen that there is an obvious clustering pattern shown in the cross-modal prototype matrix. It should be mentioned that XPRONET can tolerate some dissimilarities between positive pairs, hence a category always occurring with other categories may lead to the associated prototypes being scattered with others (e.g., the orange), which is an expected outcome. To further explore the effectiveness of the XPRONET, we show an example of the generated report and the selected cross-modal prototype indices in Fig. 1. For the word "lungs" and its corresponding image patch, the majority (nine of ten) of their selected responding cross-modal prototypes are the same, indicating that they learn the same cross-modal patterns and establish the cross-modal information flow via XPRONET, which is the expected behavior.

The sensitivity of XPRONET to the number of responding prototype vectors γ is shown in Fig. 5. The BL-4 score reduces modestly when γ increases from 13 to 14, and then culminates at (0.199) at 15, after which the score decreases steadily to 0.171 with the γ increasing to 17 on the IU-Xray dataset. Generally, excessive or less responding prototype vectors can lead to notable performance drop. The reason being that excessive cross-modal prototype vectors may introduce noisy information, while inadequate numbers cannot provide sufficient cross-modal and class-related patterns. Figure 6 illustrates the influence of the tolerance rate controller term θ of XPRONET on the MIMIC-CXR benchmark. As we can see, the best performance is achieved with a θ value of 1.750, and performance drops at other values. A smaller θ represents a larger maximum similarity which forces the positive pairs to be more similar, causing a performance drop given dissimilar positive pairs. In contrast, XPRONET cannot learn useful cross-modal prototypes with a large θ which leads to a small maximum similarity. Therefore, it appears important to strike a good balance between the cross-modal prototype learning and dissimilarity tolerance.

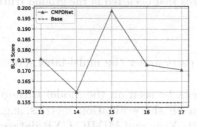 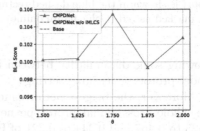

Fig. 5. Effect of varying γ, number of responding prototype vectors on (BLEU-4 score).

Fig. 6. Effect of varying θ, tolerance rate control on (BLEU-4 score).

5   Conclusions

We propose a novel cross-modal prototype driven framework for medical report generation, XPRONET, which aims to explicitly model cross-modal pattern learning via a cross-modal prototype network. The class-related cross-modal prototype querying and responding module distills the cross-modal information into the single-model features and addresses the data bias problem. An improved multi-label contrastive loss is designed to better learn the cross-moadal prototypes and can be easily incorporated into existing works. Experimental results on two publicly available benchmark datasets verify the superiority of XPRONET. We also provide ablation studies to demonstrate the effectiveness of the proposed component parts. A potential way to improve XPRONET is to increase the number of cross-modal prototypes, especially for larger datasets. In addition, we speculate that a more effective clustering approach in cross-modal prototype matrix initialization could bring further improvements.

References

1. Anderson, P., et al.: Bottom-up and top-down attention for image captioning and visual question answering. In: Proceedings of the IEEE Conference on Computer Vision and Pattern Recognition, pp. 6077–6086 (2018)
2. Bao, G., Zhang, Y., Teng, Z., Chen, B., Luo, W.: G-transformer for document-level machine translation. In: Proceedings of the 59th Annual Meeting of the Association for Computational Linguistics and the 11th International Joint Conference on Natural Language Processing (Volume 1: Long Papers), pp. 3442–3455 (2021)
3. Chen, Z., Shen, Y., Song, Y., Wan, X.: Cross-modal memory networks for radiology report generation. In: Proceedings of the 59th Annual Meeting of the Association for Computational Linguistics and the 11th International Joint Conference on Natural Language Processing (Volume 1: Long Papers), pp. 5904–5914 (2021)
4. Cheng, J., Fostiropoulos, I., Boehm, B., Soleymani, M.: Multimodal phased transformer for sentiment analysis. In: Proceedings of the 2021 Conference on Empirical Methods in Natural Language Processing, pp. 2447–2458 (2021)
5. Cornia, M., Stefanini, M., Baraldi, L., Cucchiara, R.: Meshed-memory transformer for image captioning. In: Proceedings of the IEEE Conference on Computer Vision and Pattern Recognition, pp. 10578–10587 (2020)
6. Demner-Fushman, D., et al.: Preparing a collection of radiology examinations for distribution and retrieval. J. Am. Med. Inform. Assoc. **23**(2), 304–310 (2016)
7. Denkowski, M., Lavie, A.: Meteor 1.3: automatic metric for reliable optimization and evaluation of machine translation systems. In: Proceedings of the Sixth Workshop on Statistical Machine Translation, pp. 85–91 (2011)
8. Guo, L., Liu, J., Zhu, X., Yao, P., Lu, S., Lu, H.: Normalized and geometry-aware self-attention network for image captioning. In: Proceedings of the IEEE/CVF Conference on Computer Vision and Pattern Recognition, pp. 10327–10336 (2020)
9. He, K., Zhang, X., Ren, S., Sun, J.: Deep residual learning for image recognition. In: Proceedings of the IEEE Conference on Computer Vision and Pattern Recognition, pp. 770–778 (2016)
10. Hou, B., Kaissis, G., Summers, R.M., Kainz, B.: RATCHET: medical transformer for chest X-ray diagnosis and reporting. In: de Bruijne, M. (ed.) MICCAI 2021. LNCS, vol. 12907, pp. 293–303. Springer, Cham (2021). https://doi.org/10.1007/978-3-030-87234-2_28
11. Ji, J., et al.: Improving image captioning by leveraging intra-and inter-layer global representation in transformer network. In: Proceedings of the AAAI Conference on Artificial Intelligence, vol. 35, pp. 1655–1663 (2021)
12. Jing, B., Wang, Z., Xing, E.: Show, describe and conclude: on exploiting the structure information of chest x-ray reports. In: Proceedings of the 57th Annual Meeting of the Association for Computational Linguistics, pp. 6570–6580 (2019)
13. Jing, B., Xie, P., Xing, E.: On the automatic generation of medical imaging reports. In: Proceedings of the 56th Annual Meeting of the Association for Computational Linguistics (Volume 1: Long Papers), pp. 2577–2586 (2018)
14. Johnson, A.E., et al.: MIMIC-CXR-JPG, a large publicly available database of labeled chest radiographs. arXiv preprint arXiv:1901.07042 (2019)

15. Kacupaj, E., Plepi, J., Singh, K., Thakkar, H., Lehmann, J., Maleshkova, M.: Conversational question answering over knowledge graphs with transformer and graph attention networks. In: Proceedings of the 16th Conference of the European Chapter of the Association for Computational Linguistics: Main Volume, pp. 850–862 (2021)
16. Krause, J., Johnson, J., Krishna, R., Fei-Fei, L.: A hierarchical approach for generating descriptive image paragraphs. In: Proceedings of the IEEE Conference on Computer Vision and Pattern Recognition, pp. 317–325 (2017)
17. Li, C.Y., Liang, X., Hu, Z., Xing, E.P.: Knowledge-driven encode, retrieve, paraphrase for medical image report generation. In: Proceedings of the AAAI Conference on Artificial Intelligence, vol. 33, pp. 6666–6673 (2019)
18. Li, Y., Liang, X., Hu, Z., Xing, E.P.: Hybrid retrieval-generation reinforced agent for medical image report generation. In: Advances in Neural Information Processing Systems 31 (2018)
19. Lin, C.Y.: ROUGE: a package for automatic evaluation of summaries. In: Text Summarization Branches Out, pp. 74–81 (2004)
20. Liu, F., Ren, X., Liu, Y., Wang, H., Sun, X.: simNet: stepwise image-topic merging network for generating detailed and comprehensive image captions. In: Proceedings of the 2018 Conference on Empirical Methods in Natural Language Processing, pp. 137–149 (2018)
21. Liu, F., Wu, X., Ge, S., Fan, W., Zou, Y.: Exploring and distilling posterior and prior knowledge for radiology report generation. In: Proceedings of the IEEE Conference on Computer Vision and Pattern Recognition, pp. 13753–13762 (2021)
22. Liu, G., et al.: Clinically accurate chest X-ray report generation. In: Machine Learning for Healthcare Conference, pp. 249–269. PMLR (2019)
23. Lloyd, S.: Least squares quantization in PCM. IEEE Trans. Inf. Theory **28**(2), 129–137 (1982)
24. Lu, J., Xiong, C., Parikh, D., Socher, R.: Knowing when to look: adaptive attention via a visual sentinel for image captioning. In: Proceedings of the IEEE Conference on Computer Vision and Pattern Recognition, pp. 375–383 (2017)
25. van der Maaten, L., Hinton, G.: Visualizing data using t-SNE. J. Mach. Learn. Res. **9**, 2579–2605 (2008)
26. Melas-Kyriazi, L., Rush, A.M., Han, G.: Training for diversity in image paragraph captioning. In: Proceedings of the 2018 Conference on Empirical Methods in Natural Language Processing, pp. 757–761 (2018)
27. Miura, Y., Zhang, Y., Tsai, E., Langlotz, C., Jurafsky, D.: Improving factual completeness and consistency of image-to-text radiology report generation. In: Proceedings of the 2021 Conference of the North American Chapter of the Association for Computational Linguistics: Human Language Technologies, pp. 5288–5304 (2021)
28. Naseem, T., et al.: A semantics-aware transformer model of relation linking for knowledge base question answering. In: Proceedings of the 59th Annual Meeting of the Association for Computational Linguistics and the 11th International Joint Conference on Natural Language Processing (Volume 2: Short Papers), pp. 256–262 (2021)
29. Nishino, T., et al.: Reinforcement learning with imbalanced dataset for data-to-text medical report generation. In: Findings of the Association for Computational Linguistics: EMNLP 2020, pp. 2223–2236 (2020)
30. Pan, Y., Yao, T., Li, Y., Mei, T.: X-linear attention networks for image captioning. In: Proceedings of the IEEE Conference on Computer Vision and Pattern Recognition, pp. 10971–10980 (2020)

31. Papineni, K., Roukos, S., Ward, T., Zhu, W.J.: BLEU: a method for automatic evaluation of machine translation. In: Proceedings of the 40th Annual Meeting of the Association for Computational Linguistics, pp. 311–318 (2002)

32. Pei, W., Zhang, J., Wang, X., Ke, L., Shen, X., Tai, Y.W.: Memory-attended recurrent network for video captioning. In: Proceedings of the IEEE/CVF Conference on Computer Vision and Pattern Recognition, pp. 8347–8356 (2019)

33. Rennie, S.J., Marcheret, E., Mroueh, Y., Ross, J., Goel, V.: Self-critical sequence training for image captioning. In: Proceedings of the IEEE Conference on Computer Vision and Pattern Recognition, pp. 7008–7024 (2017)

34. Smit, A., Jain, S., Rajpurkar, P., Pareek, A., Ng, A.Y., Lungren, M.: Combining automatic labelers and expert annotations for accurate radiology report labeling using BERT. In: Proceedings of the 2020 Conference on Empirical Methods in Natural Language Processing (EMNLP), pp. 1500–1519 (2020)

35. Sukhbaatar, S., Weston, J., Fergus, R., et al.: End-to-end memory networks. In: Advances in Neural Information Processing Systems, vol. 28 (2015)

36. Vaswani, A., et al.: Attention is all you need. In: Advances in Neural Information Processing Systems 30 (2017)

37. Vedantam, R., Lawrence Zitnick, C., Parikh, D.: CIDEr: consensus-based image description evaluation. In: Proceedings of the IEEE Conference on Computer Vision and Pattern Recognition, pp. 4566–4575 (2015)

38. Wang, J., Tang, J., Luo, J.: Multimodal attention with image text spatial relationship for OCR-based image captioning. In: Proceedings of the 28th ACM International Conference on Multimedia, pp. 4337–4345 (2020)

39. Wang, Q., et al.: Learning deep transformer models for machine translation. In: Proceedings of the 57th Annual Meeting of the Association for Computational Linguistics, pp. 1810–1822 (2019)

40. Wang, Z., Wan, Z., Wan, X.: TransModality: an End2End fusion method with transformer for multimodal sentiment analysis. In: Proceedings of The Web Conference 2020, pp. 2514–2520 (2020)

41. Yang, K., Xu, H., Gao, K.: CM-BERT: cross-modal BERT for text-audio sentiment analysis. In: Proceedings of the 28th ACM International Conference on Multimedia, pp. 521–528 (2020)

42. You, Q., Jin, H., Wang, Z., Fang, C., Luo, J.: Image captioning with semantic attention. In: Proceedings of the IEEE Conference on Computer Vision and Pattern Recognition, pp. 4651–4659 (2016)

43. Zhang, J., et al.: Improving the transformer translation model with document-level context. In: Proceedings of the 2018 Conference on Empirical Methods in Natural Language Processing, pp. 533–542 (2018)

44. Zhang, Y., Wang, X., Xu, Z., Yu, Q., Yuille, A., Xu, D.: When radiology report generation meets knowledge graph. In: Proceedings of the AAAI Conference on Artificial Intelligence, vol. 34, pp. 12910–12917 (2020)

45. Zhao, X., Xiao, F., Zhong, H., Yao, J., Chen, H.: Condition aware and revise transformer for question answering. In: Proceedings of The Web Conference 2020, pp. 2377–2387 (2020)

TM2T: Stochastic and Tokenized Modeling for the Reciprocal Generation of 3D Human Motions and Texts

Chuan Guo[ID], Xinxin Zuo, Sen Wang, and Li Cheng[✉]

University of Alberta, Edmonton, Canada
{cguo2,xzuo,sen9,lcheng5}@ualberta.ca

Abstract. Inspired by the strong ties between vision and language, the two intimate human sensing and communication modalities, our paper aims to explore the generation of 3D human full-body motions from texts, as well as its reciprocal task, shorthanded for text2motion and motion2text, respectively. To tackle the existing challenges, especially to enable the generation of multiple distinct motions from the same text, and to avoid the undesirable production of trivial motionless pose sequences, we propose the use of motion token, a discrete and compact motion representation. This provides one level playing ground when considering both motions and text signals, as the motion and text tokens, respectively. Moreover, our motion2text module is integrated into the inverse alignment process of our text2motion training pipeline, where a significant deviation of synthesized text from the input text would be penalized by a large training loss; empirically this is shown to effectively improve performance. Finally, the mappings in-between the two modalities of motions and texts are facilitated by adapting the neural model for machine translation (NMT) to our context. This autoregressive modeling of the distribution over discrete motion tokens further enables non-deterministic production of pose sequences, of variable lengths, from an input text. Our approach is flexible, could be used for both text2motion and motion2text tasks. Empirical evaluations on two benchmark datasets demonstrate the superior performance of our approach on both tasks over a variety of state-of-the-art methods. Project page: https://ericguo5513.github.io/TM2T/

Keywords: Motion captioning · Text-to-motion generation

1 Introduction

The interplay of vision and language is important in our daily life and social functions. It has motivated considerable research progresses in related topics

Supplementary Information The online version contains supplementary material available at https://doi.org/10.1007/978-3-031-19833-5_34.

Fig. 1. An illustration of our bidirectional TM2T approach that captures the interplay between text (left) and 3D human motion (right) through the text2motion and motion2text modules. Note the stochastic nature of our text2motion module allows the generation of different 3D motions from the same textural description.

such as image or video captioning [47,52], and language grounded generation of images or videos [24,53,57]. On the other hand, when coming to human motion analysis, the connections between visual and textural aspects of human motions are much less studied. Existing efforts primarily focus on unidirectional mapping of either motion captioning (motion2text) [13,41] or language grounded motion generation (text2motion) [2,11,25], with only two [35,54] exploring the integration of visual 3D motions and their textural descriptions. However, both studies tend to produce static pose sequences when motion lengths are longer than 3–4 s. Both requires as input the initial pose & target motion length. They are also deterministic methods. That is, each of them always generates the same motions from a given text script. The first phenomenon of lifeless motions could be largely attributed to the direct use of raw 3D poses as their motion representation, which is unnecessarily redundant and yet fails to capture the local contexts of the underlying motion dynamics. The second issue is rooted in their deterministic motion generation processes, that are in contrary to our daily experiences, where multiple distinct motion styles often exist for a character to perform under a same textural script. The conditioning on initial state and target length further imposes strict constraint toward being practically feasible.

The aim of this paper is to investigate the bi-directional ties between 3D human full-body motions and their language descriptions, as illustrated in Fig. 1. Given the asymmetric nature of the two underlying tasks, where text2motion is typically a much harder problem than the reciprocal task, motion2text, our primary focus is text2motion, with a secondary emphasis on motion2text. It is worth noting that in our approach, the module (also called motion2text for simplicity) developed for motion2text task, is also utilized as an integral part of our text2motion training process, referred to as inverse alignment in Fig. 2(c). Empirical evidences suggest the benefit of this strategy in improving our performance for the text2motion problem. To address the lifeless motion issue, we introduce motion token, a compact and semantically rich representation for 3D motions. This is achieved by adapting the deep vector quantization [43] in our context to learn a spatial-temporal codebook from the 3D pose sequences in the training set, with each entry in the codebook describing a particular kind of motion segments. 3D motions are then reconstructed by decoding the compositions of a list of codebook entries. This way, a 3D human motion is represented as a list of motion tokens (i.e. discrete indices to the codebook entries), each encoding its local spatial-temporal context. This discrete representation also facilitates the follow-up neural machine translators (NMTs) [4,44] to construct mappings between the stream of motion tokens from the motion side, and the stream of text tokens from the language side. Furthermore, our proposed approach is able to explicitly model the underlying distribution of 3D motions conditioned on texts, instead of regressing the mean motions as in previous works [2,11,25,35,54], thus allows non-deterministic text2motion generation.

Our main contributions can be summarized as follows: (i) a motion token representation that compactly encodes 3D human motions. Together with the other key ingredients, including NMT mappings in-between the motion-token and text-token sequences, the motion2text-based inverse alignment, as well as the distribution sampling for non-deterministic predictions, our approach is capable of generating 3D motions (i.e. pose sequences) that are distinct in their lengths and styles, visually pleasing, and importantly, semantically faithful to the same input script. Our approach is also flexible, in that it can be use for both text2motion and motion2text tasks. (ii) Extensive empirical evaluations over two motion-language benchmark datasets demonstrate the superior performance of our approach over a variety of state-of-the-art methods when examined on each of the two tasks.

2   Related Work

Image/Video Captioning and Motion2text. Vision grounded text generation has a long history with extended literature. Here we only focus on the closely related topic of image and video captioning. Early methods [21,22] commonly approach this problem by tagging parts of sentences such as nouns and verbs from visual contents, followed by filling in pre-defined sentence templates. With the advent of deep neural networks, the tools used for visual captioning have been significantly changed. Take [47] for example, it starts by extracting high-level image features from pre-trained GoogleNet, which are then fed into a LSTM decoder to produce captions. In [46], an RNN-based video captioning model is considered, that extracts individual frame features from pre-trained CNN, and translates them to sentences through sequence-to-sequence learning. Further extensions are made through e.g. incorporating attention mechanism for better vision-language alignment [49,52]. More recent methods consider the use of various deep learning apparatus such as GANs [17,30], deep reinforcement learning [10,36], and transformers [8,12].

In contrast, research efforts on captioning 3D human motions are considerably more limited. [41] learns the mapping from human motions to language relying on two statistical models: one associates motions with words; the other assembles words back to form sentences. Recurrent networks are utilized by

[35,54] to address this task. In [54], motion and text features are extracted by two autoencoders respectively; this is followed by generating texts and motions from each other through shared latent vectors. Sequence-to-sequence RNNs are adopted in [35] to translate motions to scripts. Recently, the work of [13] proposes SeqGAN that extends NMT model with a discriminator. Some common issues with existing motion2text results are typically short in length, often incomplete in content, and sometimes lack in details.

Human Motion Modeling and Text2motion. The importance of human motion modeling has been manifested through the extensive research efforts in recent years, where motions are produced based on various forms of inputs, such as partial pose sequences, control signals, action category, and text. Future motion prediction aims to generate short [51] and long [27,31] future pose sequences based on partial pose sequences. This has been traditionally modeled in one-to-one mapping fashion until recent works [3,28,56] that take account the stochastic nature of human motion dynamics. The efforts of [1,6,7,48] proceed to predict multi-person or scene-aware 3D motions. Meanwhile, [18,19,40] attempts to model human motions according to instant control signals such as velocity and directional readouts. In [19], feet contact information is fed into a phase function to produce blending weights of four expert MLP networks. The blended MLP network then predicts next pose state given current state and goal control signals. This is extended in [18,43] where the phase function is replaced by a learnable gating network. Action category based human motion generation also draws considerable interests by resorting to a diverse range of learning strategies, including GANs [50], VAEs [15,16], Transformers [33] and GCNs [55].

In terms of text based human motion modeling (text2motion), the sequence-to-sequence RNN models have been considered by [25,35]; in [2], a latent embedding space is proposed, which is shared by both text and pose sequences and is trained via curriculum learning. The work of [11] considers the topology of human skeleton, and proposes a hierarchical two-stream pose generator. Note existing techniques developed in text2motion are predominantly deterministic. This is in contrast to our proposed stochastic motion generation process.

Discrete Vector Quantization. [43] advocates the quantization of continuous features into discrete latent representation by training a variational autoencoder. This is followed up by several more recent efforts to improve the representation quality and reconstruction accuracy, including hierarchical feature representation [39], gumbel-softmax relaxation [38] and adversarial training [9]. In [32], hierarchical vector quantization is carried out in encoding and generating diverse image patches for inpainting; the work of [37] leverages quantized video frame representation to synthesize future frames. These prior arts inspire the motion token scheme considered in our approach.

3   Our Approach

In what follows, we first detail how discrete motion tokens are obtained from raw 3D motions via vector quantization in Sect. 3.1. Based on this new motion

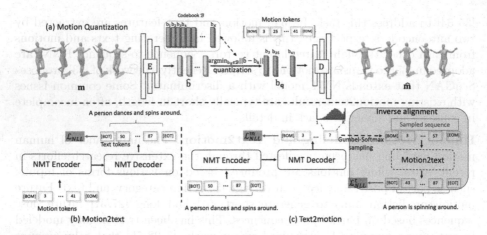

Fig. 2. Approach overview. (a) A 1D CNN based latent quantization model is firstly learned to reconstruct training motions. After training, a motion can be subsequently converted to a tuple of discrete motion tokens (i.e., codebook-indices). [BOM] and [EOM] are indicators of start and end added in a motion token sequence. (b–c) Mappings between motion and text tokens are modeled by autoregressive NMT networks and optimized by maximizing the log-likelihood of the targets ($\mathcal{L}_{NLL}$ and $\mathcal{L}^m_{NLL}$). (c) While training text2motion, motion tokens sampled from the resulting discrete distributions are inversely mapped to the text space via the learned motion2text model. Loss $\mathcal{L}^t_{NLL}$ penalizes the inverse alignment error. Finally, the 3D pose sequence is obtained by decoding motion tokens via the decoder D in (a).

representation, autoregressive NMT networks are used for modeling the bi-modal mappings of motion2text (Sect. 3.2) and text2motion (Sect. 3.3), with inverse alignment elaborated in Sect. 3.3.

3.1   Motion Tokens

We pre-train a latent quantization model on 3D human motions as presented in Fig. 2 (a). Given the pose sequence $\mathbf{m} \in \mathbb{R}^{T \times D_p}$, where T denotes the number of poses and D_p pose dimension, a series of 1D convolutions are applied along the time (i.e. 1st) dimension that yields latent vectors $\hat{\mathbf{b}} \in \mathbb{R}^{t \times d}(t < T)$ with d being number of convolution kernels. This process could be written as $\hat{\mathbf{b}} = E(\mathbf{m})$.

Then, $\hat{\mathbf{b}}$ is transformed to a collection of codebook entries $\mathbf{b_q} \in \mathbb{R}^{t \times d}$ through discrete quantization. Specifically, the learnable codebook $\mathcal{B} = \{\mathbf{b}\}^K_{k=1} \subset \mathbb{R}^d$ consists of K latent embedding vectors with each a d-dimensional vector. The process of quantization $Q(\cdot)$ is operated by replacing each row vector $\hat{\mathbf{b}}_i \in \mathbb{R}^d$ in $\hat{\mathbf{b}}$ with its nearest codebook entry $\mathbf{b}_k$ in $\mathcal{B}$, defined as

$$\mathbf{b_q} = Q(\hat{\mathbf{b}}) := \left(\text{argmin}_{\mathbf{b}_k \in \mathcal{B}} \|\hat{\mathbf{b}}_i - \mathbf{b}_k\| \right) \in \mathbb{R}^{t \times d}. \tag{1}$$

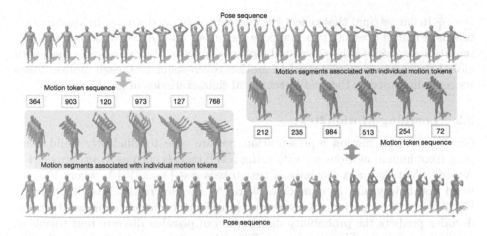

Fig. 3. Exemplar results of motion tokens (middle) and their corresponding pose sequences (top and bottom). Here two 24-frame pose sequence examples are presented; each is reconstructed from a motion token sequences of size 6. Each motion token is associated with a specific local spatial-temporal context, visualized in 4-frame motions.

A following de-convolutional decoder D projects $\mathbf{b_q}$ back to the 3D motion space as a pose sequence, $\hat{\mathbf{m}}$. Now, the entire process can be formulated as

$$\hat{\mathbf{m}} = D(\mathbf{b_q}) = D(Q(E(\mathbf{m}))). \tag{2}$$

This is trained via a reconstruction loss combined with embedding commitment loss terms that encourage latent alignment and stabilize training process:

$$\mathcal{L}_{vq} = \|\hat{\mathbf{m}} - \mathbf{m}\|_1 + \|sg[E(\mathbf{m})] - \mathbf{b_q}\|_2^2 + \beta\|E(\mathbf{m}) - sg[\mathbf{b_q}]\|_2^2, \tag{3}$$

where $sg[\cdot]$ denotes the stop-gradient operation, and β a weighting factor. Straight-through gradient estimator [43] is employed to allow gradient back-propagation through the non-differentiable quantization operation in Eq.(1) that simply copies the gradients from the decoder D to the encoder E.

During inference, a pose sequence $\mathbf{m} \in \mathbb{R}^{T \times D_p}$ can be represented as a sequence of discrete codebook-indices $s \in \{1, ..., |\mathcal{B}|\}^t$ (namely *motion tokens*) of quantized embedding vectors $\mathbf{b_q}$, where $s_i = k$ such that $(\mathbf{b_q})_i = \mathbf{b_k}$. By mapping motion tokens back to their corresponding codebook entries $\mathbf{b_q} = (\mathbf{b}_{s_i})$, human poses are then readily recovered using decoder $\hat{\mathbf{m}} = D(\mathbf{b_q})$. [BOM] and [EOM] are respectively added to the start and end of a motion token sequence as boundary indicators.

Motion Token Contexts. With vector quantization, each motion token is associated with a particular type of motion contexts, thus a 3D motion can be regarded as a meaningful composition of motion tokens. We decode each entry in the learned codebook $\mathcal{B}$ using decoder D and get 4-frame motion segments

($t = \frac{T}{4}$ in our setting) that reflect the contexts associated with individual motion tokens. Figure 3 presents two raw pose sequences and their motion token representations, as well as the associated motion segments. We can observe that, with global dependencies maintained in motion token sequences, each motion token successfully captures the spatial-temporal characteristics in local contexts.

3.2   Learning Motion2text

Given tokenized motion representation, we are able to efficiently build mapping from human motions to texts using NMT models such as Transformer [44]. Assume the target is a sequence of text tokens $x \in \{1, ..., |\mathcal{V}|\}^N$, where $\mathcal{V}$ is the word vocabulary and N number of words in the description. As described in Fig. 2 (b), source motion tokens are fed into Transformer encoder and then the decoder predicts the probability distribution of possible discrete text tokens at each step $p_\theta(x|s) = \prod_i p_\theta(x_i|x_{<i}, s)$. Thus the training goal is to maximize the log-likelihood of the target sequence,

$$\mathcal{L}_{NLL} = - \sum_{i=0}^{N-1} \log p_\theta(x_i|x_{<i}, s). \tag{4}$$

3.3   Learning Text2motion

Similarly, generating motions from language description can be modeled as autoregressive next-token predictions conditioned on textual inputs. Here we investigate two NMT models as our backbone: attentive GRU and Transformer, and examine our idea of *inverse alignment* on GRU-based model. Since Transformer is typically trained with full teacher force, optimizing the Transformer-based text2motion with inverse alignment is extremely complicated. In other words, every time when generating the density function of next motion token, we need to input the whole history to the Transformer decoder and feed forward. As a result, to sample a complete motion token sequence, the computational (or optimization) graph will be extremely high. Therefore, we specifically introduce the procedure of using GRU based model as an example.

As is shown in Fig. 2 (c), firstly, a bi-directional GRU (i.e., NMT Encoder) models the temporal dependencies in language $x \in \{1, ..., |\mathcal{V}|\}^N$, and produces sentence feature vector $s \in \mathbb{R}^{d_l}$ as well as word feature vectors $w \in \mathbb{R}^{N \times d_l}$, with d_l denoting the dimensionality of hidden vectors. The NMT decoder, modeled as attention-based GRU, processes s and w and predicts the probability distribution over discrete motion tokens $\{1, ..., |\mathcal{B}|\}$ autoregressively. In particular, GRU decoder is initialized by sentence vector s, and then takes the attention vector w_{att} together with motion token as input at each time step. The attention vector w_{att}^t at time t is obtained via

$$\mathbf{Q} = \mathbf{h}_{t-1}\mathbf{W}^Q, \mathbf{K} = \mathbf{w}\mathbf{W}^K, \mathbf{V} = \mathbf{w}\mathbf{W}^V, \tag{5}$$

$$\mathbf{w}_{att}^t = \text{softmax}\left(\frac{\mathbf{Q}\mathbf{K}^T}{\sqrt{d_{att}}}\right)\mathbf{V}, \tag{6}$$

where $\mathbf{h}_{t-1} \in \mathbb{R}^{d_h}$ is previous hidden state in decoder, $\mathbf{W}^K, \mathbf{W}^V \in \mathbb{R}^{d_l \times d_{att}}$ and $\mathbf{W}^Q \in \mathbb{R}^{d_h \times d_{att}}$ are trainable weights with d_h and d_{att} denoting the dimension of hidden unit and attention vector respectively. During generation, motion tokens are sampled from predicted distribution $p_\phi(s_i|s_{<i}, x)$ recursively until the end token (i.e., [EOM]) comes with maximum probability.

Inverse Alignment. Here we re-utilize the motion2text model in Sect. 3.2 to further align the semantics between texts and generated motions. In detail, motion token sequence $\hat{s}$ is sampled from the approximated distribution $p_\phi(s|x)$, which is taken as input to the learned motion2text model and mapped to language tokens x with probability $p_\theta(x|\hat{s})$. Note motion2text model is no longer updated here. However, sampling from discrete distribution is non-differentiable that does not allow the gradients back-propagating to the text2motion encoder and decoder. We instead resort to *Gumbel-Softmax* reparameterization trick [20] to approximate the discrete sampling process. As the temperature τ of Gumbel-Softmax approaches 0, the resulting Gumbel-Softmax distribution becomes identical to the discrete distribution $p_\phi(s_i|s_{<i}, x)$ and the sampled vectors become one-hot.

In summary, the final training objective turns to be

$$\mathcal{L} = -\left(\sum_{i=0}^{K-1} \log p_\phi(s_i|s_{<i}, x) + \sum_{i=0}^{N-1} \log p_\theta(x_i|x_{<i}, \hat{s}) \right). \tag{7}$$

3D pose sequences can finally be obtained by decoding sampled motion tokens $\hat{s}$ using quantization decoder D as described in Sect. 3.1. With discrete motion tokens and autoregressive modeling, variable motion lengths are implicitly modeled by text2motion, that the NMT model particularly learns to predict the end token i.e. [EOM] with maximum probability as signal of termination. Moreover, our proposed approach is easy to train, and does not suffer from the known shortcomings in GAN and VAE such as "mode collapse".

4 Experiments

Extensive experiments are conducted to evaluate our learned motion2text (Sect. 4.3) and text2motion mapping models (Sect. 4.4).

4.1 Datasets

Two 3D human motion-language datasets are considered for evaluation:

- *HumanML3D* [14] is a large 3D human motion dataset that covers a broad range of human actions such as locomotion, sports, and dancing. It consists of 14,616 motions and 44,970 text descriptions. Each motion clip comes with at least 3 descriptions. Motions are re-scaled to 20 frames per second (FPS), resulting in duration ranges from 2 to 10 s.

- *KIT Motion-Language* [34] contains 3,911 3D human motion clips and 6,278 text descriptions. For each motion, the corresponding number of text descriptions ranges from one to four. Following [2,11], these pose sequences are all sub-sampled to 12.5 FPS.

Both datasets are split into training, testing and validation sets with ratio of 0.8:0.15:0.05, which are further augmented by mirroring motions and replacing corresponding words in their text descriptions (e.g., 'left' → 'right').

4.2   Metrics

Besides traditional measurements, we also manage to evaluate the correspondences between motion and language using deep multimodal features. In particular, we train a simple framework that engages a motion feature extractor and a text feature extractor under contrastive assumption, that learn to produce geometrically closed feature vectors for matched text-motion pairs, and vice versa. Further details are relegated to supplementary file due to limited space.

R-Precision and Multimodal Distance are proposed to gauge how well a text and a motion are semantically aligned. Take the evaluation of motion2text mapping for an example. For each generated description, we take its corresponding motion as well as 31 randomly selected mismatched motions from the test set as a motion pool. With text and motion feature extractors available, Euclidean distances between the description feature and each motion feature in the pool are calculated and ranked. The ground truth entry falling into the top-k (k = 1, 2, 3) candidates is regarded as a successful retrieval. Then we count the average accuracy at top-k places, known as *top-k R-precision*. Meanwhile, *multimodal distance* is computed as the average Euclidean distance between text feature of each generated description and motion feature of its corresponding motion in the test set. Computing R-precision and multimodal distance for text2motion mapping is analogically carried out except generated motions and ground truth description are accordingly used.

Overall, an extensive set of metrics including Bleu [29], Rouge [26], Cider [45], BertScore [58], R Precision and multimodal distance are adopted to quantitatively measure the performance of our motion2text mapping. For evaluation of non-deterministic text2motion mapping, we primarily follow [15] which uses Frechet Inception Distance (FID), diversity and multimodality, and our complementary metrics, R precision and multimodal distance. Details of metrics are deferred to be presented in supplementary file.

4.3   Evaluation of Motion-to-Text Translation

We adopt RAEs [54] and SeqGAN [13] as our baseline methods; RAEs [54] learns a shared embedding space for language and human motions via two recurrent autoencoders, while SeqGAN [13] combines recurrent sequence-to-sequence model with a discriminator that judges whether a sentence is real or not. We further equip the vanilla RNN model in Seq2Seq [35] with late attention as another

Table 1. Quantitative evaluation results for motion-to-text translation on HumanML3D and KIT-ML test sets. For each metric, the best score is highlighted in **bold**, with the second best highlighted using underscore.

Datasets	Methods	R Precision↑			MM Dist↓	Bleu@1↑	Bleu@4↑	Rouge↑	Cider↑	BertScore↑
		Top 1	Top 2	Top 3						
Human ML3D	**Real Desc**	0.523	0.725	0.828	2.901	–	–	–	–	–
	RAEs [54]	0.100	0.188	0.261	6.337	33.3	10.2	37.5	22.1	10.7
	Seq2Seq(Att)	0.436	0.611	0.706	3.447	51.8	17.9	46.4	58.4	29.1
	SeqGAN [13]	0.332	0.457	0.532	4.895	47.8	13.5	39.2	50.2	23.4
	Ours w/o MT	<u>0.483</u>	<u>0.678</u>	<u>0.783</u>	<u>3.124</u>	<u>59.5</u>	<u>21.2</u>	<u>47.8</u>	<u>68.3</u>	<u>34.9</u>
	Ours	**0.516**	**0.720**	**0.823**	**2.935**	**61.7**	**22.3**	**49.2**	**72.5**	**37.8**
KIT-ML	**Real Desc**	0.399	0.618	0.793	2.772	–	–	–	–	–
	RAEs [54]	0.034	0.063	0.106	9.364	30.6	0.10	25.7	8.00	0.40
	Seq2Seq(Att)	<u>0.293</u>	0.450	0.555	4.455	34.3	9.30	36.3	37.3	5.30
	SeqGAN [13]	0.109	0.345	0.425	6.283	3.12	5.20	32.4	29.5	2.20
	Ours w/o MT	0.284	<u>0.466</u>	<u>0.595</u>	<u>3.979</u>	<u>42.8</u>	<u>14.7</u>	<u>39.9</u>	<u>60.1</u>	<u>18.9</u>
	Ours	**0.359**	**0.561**	**0.668**	3.298	**46.7**	**18.4**	**44.2**	**79.5**	**23.0**

strong baseline (termed as Seq2Seq(Att)). A variant of our method not using motion tokens (ours w/o MT) is also engaged to analyze the role of motion token. Note that grammatical tense and plural of words are neglected in our setting in order to ease the learning process. Descriptions are produced using beam search strategy with size of 2 throughout all experiments.

Quantitative Analysis. Table 1 presents the quantitative evaluation results of motion to language mapping on HumanMl3D and KIT-ML test sets. The R precision and multimodal distance of **real** descriptions are provided for reference.

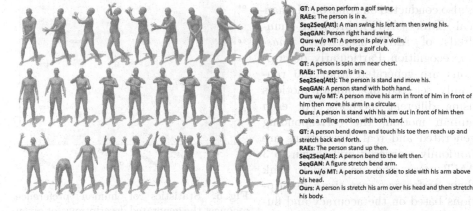

GT: A person perform a golf swing.
RAEs: The person is in a.
Seq2Seq(Att): A man swing his left arm then swing his.
SeqGAN: Person right hand swing.
Ours w/o MT: A person is play a violin.
Ours: A person swing a golf club.

GT: A person is spin arm near chest.
RAEs: The person is in a.
Seq2Seq(Att): The person is stand and move his.
SeqGAN: A person stand with both hand.
Ours w/o MT: A person move his arm in front of him in front of him then move his arm in a circular.
Ours: A person is stand with his arm out in front of him then make a rolling motion with both hand.

GT: A person bend down and touch his toe then reach up and stretch back and forth.
RAEs: The person stand up then.
Seq2Seq(Att): A person bend to the left then.
SeqGAN: A figure stretch bend arm.
Ours w/o MT: A person stretch side to side with his arm above his head.
Ours: A person is stretch his arm over his head and then stretch his body.

Fig. 4. Examples of motion-to-text translation results from different approaches. Grammatical tense and plural of words are not considered for simplifying learning process. More results are provided in supplementary files.

The high R precision of real descriptions also evidences the effectiveness of learned motion & text feature extractors and R precision metric. Overall, our method clearly outperforms all baseline methods over a large margin on all datasets and metrics. RAEs [50] suffers from limited capability on modeling long-term dependencies between 3D motion and language, thus resulting in low R precision and linguistic evaluation scores. This is mitigated by introducing attention mechanism in Seq2Seq(Att) or adversarial learning in SeqGAN, which effectively lifts the top-1 R precision up by more than 20% on HumanML3D and 10% on KIT-ML test sets. By utilizing motion token in our framework (ours), we can observe a obvious jump on both linguistic quality (i.e., Bleu, BertScore) and motion-retrieval precision (i.e., R precision) of generated language descriptions, which is surprisingly approaching the scores of real descriptions.

Qualitative Comparisons. Figure 4 qualitatively compares the generated descriptions from different methods grounded on the same 3D human motions. RAEs [35] consistently produces descriptions with simple patterns like "is in a", resulting in meaningless linguistic combinations; descriptions from Seq2Seq(Att) and SeqGAN are relatively more complex which however are usually incomplete and lack of details. Our approach without motion tokens starts to generate long and complex descriptions. Nonetheless, these descriptions sometimes fail to capture the characteristics of the input 3D motions (e.g., "play a violin"). In contrast, our approach is able to provide fluent and descriptive sentences that accurately depict various aspects of 3D motions, such as body part ("both hand"), action category ("swing", "stretch"), spatial relations ("over head").

User Study. Beside the aforementioned objective evaluations, a crowd-sourced subjective assessment is also conducted on Amazon Mechanical Turk (AMT) involving hundreds of AMT users with *master* recognition. Particularly, descriptions are generated from 100 randomly selected 3D human motions using different methods. For each human motion, the corresponding generated and real descriptions are randomly reordered and shown to 3 AMT users, who are asked to rank their preference over these descriptions based on the accuracy and fluency (Fig. 5).

As shown in Fig. 3, our method earns the most appreciation from users over all baselines. In detail,

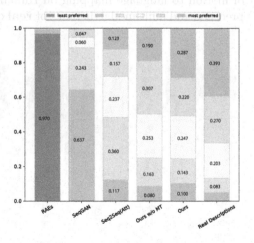

Fig. 5. Statistics of human preference amongst the generated descriptions for given human motions. For each method, a color bar (from blue to red) indicated the percentage of its preference level (from least to most preferred).

Table 2. Quantitative evaluation results for text-to-motion mapping on HumanML3D and KIT-ML test sets. All baselines requires fixed motion lengths, and initial poses are further in demand for deterministic methods (first 4 baselines), which are all unnecessary in our approach. ± indicates 95% confidence interval, and → means the closer to the real motion the better. For each metric, the best score is highlighted in **bold**, while the second best is hightlighted using underscore.

Datasets	Methods	R Precision↑			FID↓	MM Dist↓	Diversity→	MModality↑
		Top 1	Top 2	Top 3				
Human ML3D	**Real motions**	$0.511^{\pm.003}$	$0.703^{\pm.003}$	$0.797^{\pm.002}$	$0.002^{\pm.000}$	$2.974^{\pm.008}$	$9.503^{\pm.065}$	–
	Seq2Seq [25]	$0.180^{\pm.002}$	$0.300^{\pm.002}$	$0.396^{\pm.002}$	$11.75^{\pm.035}$	$5.529^{\pm.007}$	$6.223^{\pm.061}$	–
	Language2Pose [2]	$0.246^{\pm.002}$	$0.387^{\pm.002}$	$0.486^{\pm.002}$	$11.02^{\pm.046}$	$5.296^{\pm.008}$	$7.676^{\pm.058}$	–
	Text2Gesture [5]	$0.165^{\pm.001}$	$0.267^{\pm.002}$	$0.345^{\pm.002}$	$5.012^{\pm.030}$	$6.030^{\pm.008}$	$6.409^{\pm.071}$	–
	Hier [11]	$0.301^{\pm.002}$	$0.425^{\pm.002}$	$0.552^{\pm.004}$	$6.532^{\pm.024}$	$5.012^{\pm.018}$	$8.332^{\pm.042}$	–
	MoCoGAN [42]	$0.037^{\pm.000}$	$0.072^{\pm.001}$	$0.106^{\pm.001}$	$94.41^{\pm.021}$	$9.643^{\pm.006}$	$0.462^{\pm.008}$	$0.019^{\pm.000}$
	Dance2Music [23]	$0.033^{\pm.000}$	$0.065^{\pm.001}$	$0.097^{\pm.001}$	$66.98^{\pm.016}$	$8.116^{\pm.006}$	$0.725^{\pm.011}$	$0.043^{\pm.001}$
	Ours baseline (T)	$\underline{0.351}^{\pm.003}$	$0.521^{\pm.003}$	$0.627^{\pm.003}$	$\underline{1.669}^{\pm.025}$	$4.046^{\pm.018}$	$\mathbf{9.632}^{\pm.072}$	$\mathbf{4.352}^{\pm.149}$
	Ours baseline	$\underline{0.351}^{\pm.002}$	$\underline{0.526}^{\pm.002}$	$\underline{0.635}^{\pm.002}$	$1.739^{\pm.022}$	$\underline{3.965}^{\pm.010}$	$\underline{8.651}^{\pm.083}$	$\underline{3.139}^{\pm.083}$
	Ours	$\mathbf{0.424}^{\pm.003}$	$\mathbf{0.618}^{\pm.003}$	$\mathbf{0.729}^{\pm.002}$	$\mathbf{1.501}^{\pm.017}$	$\mathbf{3.467}^{\pm.011}$	$8.589^{\pm.076}$	$2.424^{\pm.093}$
KIT-ML	**Real motions**	$0.424^{\pm.005}$	$0.649^{\pm.006}$	$0.779^{\pm.006}$	$0.031^{\pm.004}$	$2.788^{\pm.012}$	$11.08^{\pm.097}$	–
	Seq2Seq [25]	$0.103^{\pm.003}$	$0.178^{\pm.005}$	$0.241^{\pm.006}$	$24.86^{\pm.348}$	$7.960^{\pm.031}$	$6.744^{\pm.106}$	–
	Language2Pose [2]	$0.221^{\pm.005}$	$0.373^{\pm.004}$	$0.483^{\pm.005}$	$6.545^{\pm.072}$	$5.147^{\pm.030}$	$9.073^{\pm.100}$	–
	Text2Gesture [5]	$0.156^{\pm.004}$	$0.255^{\pm.004}$	$0.338^{\pm.005}$	$12.12^{\pm.183}$	$6.964^{\pm.029}$	$9.334^{\pm.079}$	–
	Hier [11]	$0.255^{\pm.006}$	$\underline{0.432}^{\pm.007}$	$0.531^{\pm.007}$	$5.203^{\pm.107}$	$4.986^{\pm.027}$	$9.563^{\pm.072}$	–
	MoCoGAN [42]	$0.022^{\pm.002}$	$0.042^{\pm.003}$	$0.063^{\pm.003}$	$82.69^{\pm.242}$	$10.47^{\pm.012}$	$3.091^{\pm.043}$	$0.250^{\pm.009}$
	Dance2Music [23]	$0.031^{\pm.002}$	$0.058^{\pm.002}$	$0.086^{\pm.003}$	$115.4^{\pm.240}$	$10.40^{\pm.016}$	$0.241^{\pm.004}$	$0.062^{\pm.002}$
	Ours baseline (T)	$\underline{0.260}^{\pm.005}$	$0.426^{\pm.007}$	$\underline{0.538}^{\pm.008}$	$\underline{4.628}^{\pm.126}$	$4.835^{\pm.076}$	$\underline{12.16}^{\pm.120}$	$\underline{4.436}^{\pm.106}$
	Ours baseline	$0.251^{\pm.007}$	$0.418^{\pm.008}$	$0.535^{\pm.007}$	$4.814^{\pm.145}$	$\underline{4.682}^{\pm.048}$	$\mathbf{10.13}^{\pm.117}$	$\mathbf{4.486}^{\pm.117}$
	Ours	$\mathbf{0.280}^{\pm.005}$	$\mathbf{0.463}^{\pm.006}$	$\mathbf{0.587}^{\pm.005}$	$\mathbf{3.599}^{\pm.153}$	$\mathbf{4.591}^{\pm.026}$	$9.473^{\pm.117}$	$3.292^{\pm.081}$

RAEs [54] is the least preferred method, from which 97% descriptions are ranked at the last place; Seq2Seq(Att) and SeqGAN [13] gain comparably more positive feedback from users; while our method without motion tokens comes to the second to the best. This objective study solidly substantiates the capability of our approach toward generating natural as well as motion-aligned language descriptions.

4.4 Evaluation of Text-to-Motion Generation

Mapping language to 3D human motions in a non-deterministic fashion is relatively new. Here we compare our method to four state-of-the-art methods: Seq2Seq [25], Language2Pose [2], Text2Gesture [5] and Hier [11]. As with all existing methods, they are unfortunately deterministic methods. Therefore, two stochastic methods in other related fields are adopted here for more fair and in-depth evaluations: MoCoGAN [42] and Dance2Music [23]. MoCoGAN is widely used for conditioned video sequence synthesis, and Dance2Music learns to map sequential audio signals to 2D human dance motions. Proper changes are made to these methods for language-grounded 3D human motion generation. Ours baseline and ours basclinc (T) ablates inverse alignment module during training Text2motion and map texts to motions using GRU and Transformer respec-

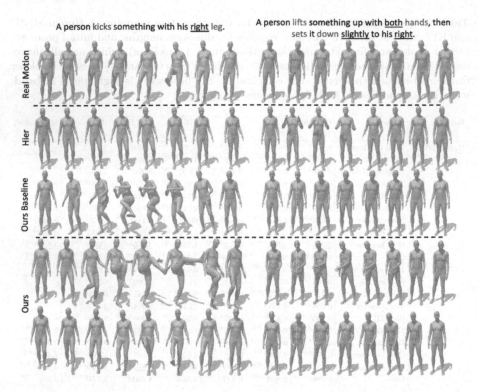

Fig. 6. Visual comparisons of generated motions from the same language descriptions. For each description, we show its corresponding real motion, one motion from Hier [11] (since it's determinstic) and ours method without inverse alignment, as well as two motions from our method. Key frames of variable-length motion clips are shown. Refer to supplementary files for complete motions and more results.

tively. We repeat each experiment 20 times and report the mean value with 95% statistical confidence interval.

Quantitative Analysis. Table 2 shows the quantitative evaluation results of language grounded 3D human motion generation. We can observe that the motions from non-determinstic baselines, MoCoGAN [42] and Dance2Music [23], suffers from severely low quality and diversity, as reflected by their low R precision and mutimodality score. Deterministic baselines such as Seq2Seq [25] and Text2Gesture [5] autoregressively regress human poses from textual input via vanilla sequence-to-sequence RNN and transformer respectively. However, such straightforward approaches find difficulty in maintaining textual semantics during generating human dynamics, which results in low motion-based text retrieval precision and high multimodal distance. Language2Pose [2] and Hier [11] propose to learn a co-embedding space between language and human motions, while Hier [11] go one step forward by incorporating the hierarchical topology of human skeleton. These have effectively boosted the performance on both datasets. Nevertheless, there still remain a significant gap between the synthetic results and real motions. Our framework of incorporating motion token and NMT model (*ours, ours baseline/baseline (T)*) in general achieve better performance, while the inverse alignment strategy greatly benefits this framework (*ours*) with the top-1 and top-3 precision increased by nearly 7% and 10% on HumanML3D.

Visual Comparisons. In Fig. 6, we visually compares the generated motions from our method (ours), our method not using inverse alignment (ours baseline), and the best performing state of the art, Hier [11]. The corresponding real motions are also provided for reference. Hier [11] could somewhat capture partial concept (e.g., "kick") in descriptions, while the produced motions are unfaithfully in low-mobility. Our method without inverse alignment is capable of generating natural and plausible human motions. It sometimes however still fail to present fine details (e.g., "right leg") from texts. On the contrary, our approach consistently produce visually appealing motions which precisely convey the language concepts in descriptions.

4.5 Limitations and Discussions

Although our proposed TM2T achieves superior performance on both tasks, some limitations and potential remedies can be taken into accounts in future studies. First, the approximation in motion quantization is unfortunately not lossless, which sometimes lead to blurriness and artifacts in local body (e.g., foot sliding). Second, dealing with long and complex descriptions for text2motion is somewhat beyond our capability. This could be possibly solved by using more advanced NMT models. Third, our motion2text model is trained independently with text2motion. Learning these two mapping functions jointly and reciprocally could be another interesting topic.

5   Conclusion

This paper presents TM2T, a general framework that works on the bi-modal mutual mappings between 3D human motions and texts, where motion2text is further reciprocally integrated as a part of text2motion learning through inverse alignment. A new motion representation, motion token, is proposed that compress 3D motions into short sequence of discrete variables. With motion token, neural machine translation networks efficiently build mappings in-between two modalities, that is able to produces accurate descriptions as well as sharp and diverse 3D human motions. Our proposed framework is shown to produce state-of-the-art results on two motion-language dataset in both tasks.

Acknowledgement. This work was partly supported by the NSERC Discovery, UAHJIC, and CFI-JELF grants. I also appreciate that the university of Alberta fund me with the Alberta Graduate Excellence Scholarship.

References

1. Adeli, V., Adeli, E., Reid, I., Niebles, J.C., Rezatofighi, H.: Socially and contextually aware human motion and pose forecasting. IEEE Robot. Autom. Lett. **5**(4), 6033–6040 (2020)
2. Ahuja, C., Morency, L.P.: Language2pose: natural language grounded pose forecasting. In: 2019 International Conference on 3D Vision (3DV), pp. 719–728. IEEE (2019)
3. Aliakbarian, S., Saleh, F., Petersson, L., Gould, S., Salzmann, M.: Contextually plausible and diverse 3D human motion prediction. In: Proceedings of the IEEE/CVF International Conference on Computer Vision, pp. 11333–11342 (2021)
4. Bahdanau, D., Cho, K., Bengio, Y.: Neural machine translation by jointly learning to align and translate. arXiv preprint arXiv:1409.0473 (2014)
5. Bhattacharya, U., Rewkowski, N., Banerjee, A., Guhan, P., Bera, A., Manocha, D.: Text2gestures: a transformer-based network for generating emotive body gestures for virtual agents. In: IEEE Virtual Reality and 3D User Interfaces (VR), pp. 1–10. IEEE (2021)
6. Cao, Z., Gao, H., Mangalam, K., Cai, Q.-Z., Vo, M., Malik, J.: Long-term human motion prediction with scene context. In: Vedaldi, A., Bischof, H., Brox, T., Frahm, J.-M. (eds.) ECCV 2020. LNCS, vol. 12346, pp. 387–404. Springer, Cham (2020). https://doi.org/10.1007/978-3-030-58452-8_23
7. Corona, E., Pumarola, A., Alenya, G., Moreno-Noguer, F.: Context-aware human motion prediction. In: Proceedings of the IEEE/CVF Conference on Computer Vision and Pattern Recognition, pp. 6992–7001 (2020)
8. Dubey, S., Olimov, F., Rafique, M.A., Kim, J., Jeon, M.: Label-attention transformer with geometrically coherent objects for image captioning. arXiv preprint arXiv:2109.07799 (2021)
9. Esser, P., Rombach, R., Ommer, B.: Taming transformers for high-resolution image synthesis. In: Proceedings of the IEEE/CVF Conference on Computer Vision and Pattern Recognition, pp. 12873–12883 (2021)
10. Gao, J., Wang, S., Wang, S., Ma, S., Gao, W.: Self-critical n-step training for image captioning. In: Proceedings of the IEEE/CVF Conference on Computer Vision and Pattern Recognition, pp. 6300–6308 (2019)
11. Ghosh, A., Cheema, N., Oguz, C., Theobalt, C., Slusallek, P.: Synthesis of compositional animations from textual descriptions. In: Proceedings of the IEEE/CVF International Conference on Computer Vision, pp. 1396–1406 (2021)
12. Ging, S., Zolfaghari, M., Pirsiavash, H., Brox, T.: COOT: cooperative hierarchical transformer for video-text representation learning. In: Advances in Neural Information Processing Systems, vol. 33, pp. 22605–22618 (2020)
13. Goutsu, Y., Inamura, T.: Linguistic descriptions of human motion with generative adversarial Seq2Seq learning. In: 2021 IEEE International Conference on Robotics and Automation (ICRA), pp. 4281–4287. IEEE (2021)
14. Guo, C., et al.: Generating diverse and natural 3D human motions from text. In: Proceedings of the IEEE/CVF Conference on Computer Vision and Pattern Recognition, pp. 5152–5161 (2022)
15. Guo, C., et al.: Action2video: generating videos of human 3D actions. Int. J. Comput. Vis., 1–31 (2022)
16. Guo, C., et al.: Action2motion: conditioned generation of 3D human motions. In: Proceedings of the 28th ACM International Conference on Multimedia, pp. 2021–2029 (2020)

17. Guo, L., Liu, J., Yao, P., Li, J., Lu, H.: MSCap: multi-style image captioning with unpaired stylized text. In: Proceedings of the IEEE/CVF Conference on Computer Vision and Pattern Recognition, pp. 4204–4213 (2019)
18. Holden, D., Kanoun, O., Perepichka, M., Popa, T.: Learned motion matching. ACM Trans. Graph. (TOG) **39**(4), 53–1 (2020)
19. Holden, D., Komura, T., Saito, J.: Phase-functioned neural networks for character control. ACM Trans. Graph. (TOG) **36**(4), 1–13 (2017)
20. Jang, E., Gu, S., Poole, B.: Categorical reparameterization with Gumbel-softmax. arXiv preprint arXiv:1611.01144 (2016)
21. Kojima, A., Tamura, T., Fukunaga, K.: Natural language description of human activities from video images based on concept hierarchy of actions. Int. J. Comput. Vis. **50**(2), 171–184 (2002)
22. Kulkarni, G., et al.: Babytalk: understanding and generating simple image descriptions. IEEE Trans. Pattern Anal. Mach. Intell. **35**(12), 2891–2903 (2013)
23. Lee, H.Y., et al.: Dancing to music. In: Advances in Neural Information Processing Systems 32 (2019)
24. Li, Y., Min, M., Shen, D., Carlson, D., Carin, L.: Video generation from text. In: Proceedings of the AAAI Conference on Artificial Intelligence, vol. 32 (2018)
25. Lin, A.S., Wu, L., Corona, R., Tai, K., Huang, Q., Mooney, R.J.: Generating animated videos of human activities from natural language descriptions. Learning **2018**, 1 (2018)
26. Lin, C.Y.: ROUGE: a package for automatic evaluation of summaries. In: Text Summarization Branches Out, pp. 74–81 (2004)
27. Liu, Z., et al.: Towards natural and accurate future motion prediction of humans and animals. In: Proceedings of the IEEE/CVF Conference on Computer Vision and Pattern Recognition, pp. 10004–10012 (2019)
28. Mao, W., Liu, M., Salzmann, M.: Generating smooth pose sequences for diverse human motion prediction. In: Proceedings of the IEEE/CVF International Conference on Computer Vision, pp. 13309–13318 (2021)
29. Papineni, K., Roukos, S., Ward, T., Zhu, W.J.: BLEU: a method for automatic evaluation of machine translation. In: Proceedings of the 40th Annual Meeting of the Association for Computational Linguistics, pp. 311–318 (2002)
30. Park, J.S., Rohrbach, M., Darrell, T., Rohrbach, A.: Adversarial inference for multi-sentence video description. In: Proceedings of the IEEE/CVF Conference on Computer Vision and Pattern Recognition, pp. 6598–6608 (2019)
31. Pavllo, D., Feichtenhofer, C., Auli, M., Grangier, D.: Modeling human motion with quaternion-based neural networks. Int. J. Comput. Vis. **128**(4), 855–872 (2020)
32. Peng, J., Liu, D., Xu, S., Li, H.: Generating diverse structure for image inpainting with hierarchical VQ-VAE. In: Proceedings of the IEEE/CVF Conference on Computer Vision and Pattern Recognition, pp. 10775–10784 (2021)
33. Petrovich, M., Black, M.J., Varol, G.: Action-conditioned 3D human motion synthesis with transformer VAE. In: Proceedings of the IEEE/CVF International Conference on Computer Vision, pp. 10985–10995 (2021)
34. Plappert, M., Mandery, C., Asfour, T.: The kit motion-language dataset. Big Data **4**(4), 236–252 (2016)
35. Plappert, M., Mandery, C., Asfour, T.: Learning a bidirectional mapping between human whole-body motion and natural language using deep recurrent neural networks. Robot. Auton. Syst. **109**, 13–26 (2018)
36. Qin, Y., Du, J., Zhang, Y., Lu, H.: Look back and predict forward in image captioning. In: Proceedings of the IEEE/CVF Conference on Computer Vision and Pattern Recognition, pp. 8367–8375 (2019)

37. Rakhimov, R., Volkhonskiy, D., Artemov, A., Zorin, D., Burnaev, E.: Latent video transformer. arXiv preprint arXiv:2006.10704 (2020)
38. Ramesh, A., et al.: Zero-shot text-to-image generation. In: International Conference on Machine Learning, pp. 8821–8831. PMLR (2021)
39. Razavi, A., Van den Oord, A., Vinyals, O.: Generating diverse high-fidelity images with VQ-VAE-2. In: Advances in Neural Information Processing Systems, vol. 32 (2019)
40. Starke, S., Zhang, H., Komura, T., Saito, J.: Neural state machine for character-scene interactions. ACM Trans. Graph. **38**(6), 209–1 (2019)
41. Takano, W., Nakamura, Y.: Statistical mutual conversion between whole body motion primitives and linguistic sentences for human motions. Int. J. Robot. Res. **34**(10), 1314–1328 (2015)
42. Tulyakov, S., Liu, M.Y., Yang, X., Kautz, J.: MoCoGAN: decomposing motion and content for video generation. In: Proceedings of the IEEE Conference on Computer Vision and Pattern Recognition, pp. 1526–1535 (2018)
43. Van Den Oord, A., Vinyals, O., et al.: Neural discrete representation learning. In: Advances in Neural Information Processing Systems 30 (2017)
44. Vaswani, A., et al.: Attention is all you need. In: Advances in Neural Information Processing Systems, vol. 30 (2017)
45. Vedantam, R., Lawrence Zitnick, C., Parikh, D.: CIDEr: consensus-based image description evaluation. In: Proceedings of the IEEE Conference on Computer Vision and Pattern Recognition, pp. 4566–4575 (2015)
46. Venugopalan, S., et al.: Sequence to sequence-video to text. In: Proceedings of the IEEE International Conference on Computer Vision, pp. 4534–4542 (2015)
47. Vinyals, O., Toshev, A., Bengio, S., Erhan, D.: Show and tell: a neural image caption generator. In: Proceedings of the IEEE Conference on Computer Vision and Pattern Recognition, pp. 3156–3164 (2015)
48. Wang, J., Xu, H., Narasimhan, M., Wang, X.: Multi-person 3D motion prediction with multi-range transformers. In: Advances in Neural Information Processing Systems, vol. 34 (2021)
49. Wang, L., et al.: Temporal segment networks: towards good practices for deep action recognition. In: Leibe, B., Matas, J., Sebe, N., Welling, M. (eds.) ECCV 2016. LNCS, vol. 9912, pp. 20–36. Springer, Cham (2016). https://doi.org/10.1007/978-3-319-46484-8_2
50. Wang, Z., et al.: Learning diverse stochastic human-action generators by learning smooth latent transitions. In: Proceedings of the AAAI Conference on Artificial Intelligence, vol. 34, pp. 12281–12288 (2020)
51. Xu, C., Govindarajan, L.N., Zhang, Y., Cheng, L.: Lie-x: depth image based articulated object pose estimation, tracking, and action recognition on lie groups. Int. J. Comput. Vis. **123**(3), 454–478 (2017)
52. Xu, K., et al.: Show, attend and tell: neural image caption generation with visual attention. In: International Conference on Machine Learning, pp. 2048–2057. PMLR (2015)
53. Xu, T., et al.: AttnGAN: fine-grained text to image generation with attentional generative adversarial networks. In: Proceedings of the IEEE Conference on Computer Vision and Pattern Recognition, pp. 1316–1324 (2018)
54. Yamada, T., Matsunaga, H., Ogata, T.: Paired recurrent autoencoders for bidirectional translation between robot actions and linguistic descriptions. IEEE Robot. Autom. Lett. **3**(4), 3441–3448 (2018)

55. Yu, P., Zhao, Y., Li, C., Yuan, J., Chen, C.: Structure-aware human-action genera-
    tion. In: Vedaldi, A., Bischof, H., Brox, T., Frahm, J.-M. (eds.) ECCV 2020. LNCS,
    vol. 12375, pp. 18–34. Springer, Cham (2020). https://doi.org/10.1007/978-3-030-
    58577-8_2
56. Yuan, Y., Kitani, K.: DLow: diversifying latent flows for diverse human motion
    prediction. In: Vedaldi, A., Bischof, H., Brox, T., Frahm, J.-M. (eds.) ECCV 2020.
    LNCS, vol. 12354, pp. 346–364. Springer, Cham (2020). https://doi.org/10.1007/
    978-3-030-58545-7_20
57. Zhang, H., et al.: StackGAN: text to photo-realistic image synthesis with stacked
    generative adversarial networks. In: Proceedings of the IEEE International Con-
    ference on Computer Vision, pp. 5907–5915 (2017)
58. Zhang, T., Kishore, V., Wu, F., Weinberger, K.Q., Artzi, Y.: Bertscore: evaluating
    text generation with BERT. arXiv preprint arXiv:1904.09675 (2019)

SeqTR: A Simple Yet Universal Network for Visual Grounding

Chaoyang Zhu[1], Yiyi Zhou[1], Yunhang Shen[3], Gen Luo[1], Xingjia Pan[3], Mingbao Lin[3], Chao Chen[3], Liujuan Cao[1(✉)], Xiaoshuai Sun[1,4], and Rongrong Ji[1,2,4]

[1] MAC Lab, Department of Artificial Intelligence, School of Informatics, Xiamen University, Xiamen, China
{cyzhu,luogen}@stu.xmu.edu.cn,
{zhouyiyi,caoliujuan,xssun,rrji}@xmu.edu.cn
[2] Institute of Energy Research, Jiangxi Academy of Sciences, Jiangxi, China
[3] Tencent Youtu Lab., Shanghai, China
shenyunhang01@gmail.com, xjia.pan@gmail.com, linmb001@outlook.com,
aaronccchen@tencent.com
[4] Institute of Artificial Intelligence, Xiamen University, Xiamen, China

Abstract. In this paper, we propose a simple yet universal network termed *SeqTR* for visual grounding tasks, *e.g.*, phrase localization, referring expression comprehension (REC) and segmentation (RES). The canonical paradigms for visual grounding often require substantial expertise in designing network architectures and loss functions, making them hard to generalize across tasks. To simplify and unify the modeling, we cast visual grounding as a point prediction problem conditioned on image and text inputs, where either the bounding box or binary mask is represented as a sequence of discrete coordinate tokens. Under this paradigm, visual grounding tasks are unified in our SeqTR network without task-specific branches or heads, *e.g.*, the convolutional mask decoder for RES, which greatly reduces the complexity of multi-task modeling. In addition, SeqTR also shares the same optimization objective for all tasks with a simple *cross-entropy* loss, further reducing the complexity of deploying hand-crafted loss functions. Experiments on five benchmark datasets demonstrate that the proposed SeqTR outperforms (or is on par with) the existing state-of-the-arts, proving that a simple yet universal approach for visual grounding is indeed feasible. Source code is available at https://github.com/sean-zhuh/SeqTR.

Keywords: Visual grounding · Transformer

1 Introduction

Visual grounding [21,34,36,52,55] has emerged as a core problem in vision-language research, as both comprehensive intra-modality understanding and accurate one-to-one inter-modality correspondence establishment are required.

S. Avidan et al. (Eds.): ECCV 2022, LNCS 13695, pp. 598–615, 2022.
https://doi.org/10.1007/978-3-031-19833-5_35

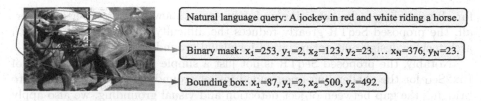

Fig. 1. Illustration of the serialization of grounding information. Our model directly generates the sequence of points representing the bounding box or binary mask.

According to the manner of grounding, it can be divided into two groups, *i.e.*, *phrase localization* or *referring expression comprehension* (REC) at bounding box level [6,16,24,25,27,29,32,44,49,50,54,58,59], and *referring expression segmentation* (RES) at pixel level [2,8,10,15,18,19,24,28,31,32,48,51,54].

To accomplish the accurate vision-language alignment, existing approaches often require substantial prior knowledge and expertise in designing network architectures and loss functions. For instance, MAttNet [54] decomposes language expressions into *subject, location,* and *relationship* phrases, and designs three corresponding attention modules to compute matching score individually. Despite being faster, one-stage models also require the complex language-guided multi-modal fusion and reasoning modules [16,25,32,33,49], or sophisticated cross-modal alignment via various attention mechanisms [8,10,15,28,31,32,51]. Loss functions in existing methods are also complex and tailored to each individual grounding task, such as GIoU loss [41], set-based matching loss [1], focal loss [26], dice loss [35], and contrastive alignment loss [20]. Under a multi-task setting, coefficients among different losses also need to be carefully tuned to accommodate different tasks [24,32]. Despite great progress, these highly customized approaches still suffer from the limited generalization ability.

Recent endeavors [6,8,20,24] in visual grounding shift to simplifying network architectures via Transformers [45]. Concretely, the multi-modal fusion and reasoning modules are replaced by a simple stack of transformer encoder layers [6,8,20]. However, the loss function used in these transformer-based methods is still highly customized for each individual task [1,20,26,35,41]. Moreover, these approaches still require task-specific branches or heads [24,32], *i.e.*, the bounding box regressor and convolutional mask decoder.

In this paper, we take a step forward in simplifying the modeling of visual grounding tasks via a simple yet universal network termed *SeqTR*. Specifically, inspired by the recently proposed Pix2Seq [3], we first reformulate visual grounding as a point prediction problem conditioned on image and text inputs, where the grounding information, *e.g.*, the bounding box, is serialized into a sequence of discrete coordinate tokens. Under this paradigm, different grounding tasks can be universally accomplished in the proposed SeqTR with a standard transformer encoder-decoder architecture [45]. In SeqTR, the encoder serves to update the multi-modal feature representations, while the decoder directly predicts the discrete coordinate tokens of the grounding information in an auto-regressive manner. In terms of optimization, SeqTR only uses a simple *cross-entropy* loss for all grounding tasks, requiring no further prior knowledge or expertise. Overall, the proposed SeqTR greatly reduces the difficulty and complexity of both architecture design and optimization for visual grounding.

Notably, the proposed SeqTR is not just a simple multi-modal extension of Pix2Seq for the challenging open-ended visual grounding tasks. In addition to bridging the gap between object detection and visual grounding, we also apply the sequential modeling to RES via an innovative *mask contour sampling* scheme. As shown in Fig. 1, SeqTR transforms the pixel-wise binary mask into a sequence of N points by performing clockwise sampling on the mask contour. In this case, RES, as a language-guided segmentation task, can be seamlessly integrated into the proposed SeqTR network without the additional convolutional mask decoder, demonstrating the high generalization ability of SeqTR across grounding tasks.

The proposed SeqTR achieves or is on par with the state-of-the-art performance on five benchmark datasets, *i.e.*, RefCOCO [55], RefCOCO+ [55], RefCOCOg [34,36], ReferItGame [21], and Flickr30K Entities [37]. SeqTR also outperforms a set of large-scale BERT-style models [4,20,30,43] with much less pre-training expenditure. Main contributions are summarized as follows:

- We reformulate visual grounding tasks as a point prediction problem, and present a novel and general network, termed SeqTR, which unifies different grounding tasks in one model with the same *cross-entropy* loss.
- The proposed SeqTR is simple yet universal, and can be seamlessly extended to the referring expression segmentation task via an innovative *mask contour sampling* scheme without network architecture modifications.
- We achieve or maintain on par with the state-of-the-art performance on five visual grounding benchmark datasets, and also outperform a set of large-scale pre-trained models with much less expenditure.

2   Related Work

2.1   Referring Expression Comprehension

Early practitioners [13,14,27,29,47,54,57,60] tackle referring expression comprehension (REC) following a two-stage pipeline, where region proposals [40] are first extracted then ranked according to their similarity scores with the language query. Another line of work [6,16,25,32,44,49,50,58,59], being simpler and faster, advocates one-stage pipeline based on dense anchors [40]. RealGIN [58] proposes adaptive feature selection and global attentive reasoning unit to handle the diversity and complexity of language expressions. ReSC [49] recursively constructs sub-queries to predict the parameters of the normalization layers in the visual encoder, which is used to scale and shift visual features. LBYL [16] designs landmark feature convolution to encode the contextual information. Recent works [6,8,20,24,59] resort to Transformer-like structure [45] to perform multi-modal fusion. MDETR [20] further demonstrates that Transformer is efficient when pre-trained on a large corpus of data. Compared with existing approaches, our work is simple in both the architecture and loss function, which has little requirement of task priors and expert engineering.

2.2 Referring Expression Segmentation

Compared to REC, referring expression segmentation (RES) grounds language query at a fine-granularity *i.e.*, the precise pixel-wise binary mask. Typical solutions are to design various attention mechanisms to perform cross-modal alignment [2,8,10,15,17,18,28,31,32,51]. EFN [10] transforms the visual encoder into a multi-modal feature extractor with asymmetric co-attention, which fuses multi-modal information at the feature learning stage. CGAN [31] performs cascaded attention reasoning with instance-level attention loss to supervise attention modeling at each stage. LTS [19] first performs relavance filtering to locate the referent, and uses this visual object prior to perform dilated convolution for the final segmentation mask. VLT [8] produces a set of queries representing different understandings of the language expression and proposes a query balance module to focus on the most reasonable and suitable query, which is then used to decode the mask via a mask decoder. In this work, we are the first to regard RES as a point prediction problem, thus the proposed SeqTR can be seamlessly extended to RES without any network architecture modifications.

2.3 Multi-task Visual Grounding

Multi-task visual grounding aims to jointly address REC and RES. Prior art MCN [32] constrains the REC and RES branches to attend to the same region by applying consistent energy maximization. In this way, REC can help RES better localize the referent, and RES can help REC achieve superior cross-modal alignment. RefTR [24] tackles multi-task visual grounding by sharing the same transformer architecture, but it requires an additional convolutional mask decoder for RES. In contrast, the proposed SeqTR is universal across different grounding tasks without additional branch or head. Under the point prediction paradigm, SeqTR can segment the referent without the aid from REC branch.

3 Method

In this section, we introduce our simple yet universal SeqTR network for visual grounding, of which structure is depicted in Fig. 2. The objective function is detailed in Sect. 3.1. Sequence construction from grounding information is elaborated in Sect. 3.2. The architecture and inference are presented in Sect. 3.3.

3.1 Problem Definition

Unlike existing visual grounding models [6,8,10,19,32], SeqTR aims to predict the discrete coordinate tokens of the grounding information, *e.g.*, the bounding box or binary mask. To this end, we define the optimization objective under the point prediction paradigm as:

$$\mathcal{L} = -\sum_{i=1}^{2N} w_i \log P(T_i | F_m, S_{1:i-1}), \tag{1}$$

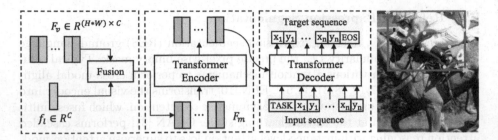

Fig. 2. Overview of the proposed SeqTR network, of which all components, *i.e.*, multi-modal fusion, cross-modal interaction, and loss function, are standard operations and shared across grounding tasks.

where S and T are the input and target sequences for decoder as shown in Fig. 2. $F_m \in R^{(H*W) \times C}$ is the multi-modal features detailed in Sect. 3.3. A per-token weight w_i is used to scale the loss. Note that the input sequence $S_{1:i-1}$ only contains the preceding coordinate tokens when predicting the i-th one. It can be implemented by putting a causal mask [38] on attention weights to only attend to previous coordinate tokens.

We construct the input sequence by prepending a [TASK] token before the sequence of points $\{x_i, y_i\}_{i=1}^N$, and the target sequence is the one appended with an [EOS] token. These two special tokens indicate the start or end of the sequence, which are learnable embeddings. [TASK] token also indicates which grounding task the model performs on. To achieve multi-task visual grounding, we can equip each task with the corresponding [TASK] token randomly initialized with different parameters, showing great simplicity and generalization ability.

Under our point prediction reformulation, the simple *cross-entropy* loss conditioned on multi-modal features and preceding discrete coordinate tokens can be directly shared across tasks, avoiding the complex deployment of hand-crafted loss functions and loss coefficient tuning [1,20,26,35,41].

3.2 Sequence Construction From Grounding Information

A key design in SeqTR is to serialize and quantize the grounding information, *e.g.*, the bounding box or binary mask, into a sequence of discrete coordinate tokens, which enables different grounding tasks to be universally addressed in one network architecture with the same objective.

We first review the serialization and quantization of the bounding box introduced in Pix2Seq [3]. Given a sequence of floating points $\{\tilde{x}_i, \tilde{y}_i\}_{i=1}^N$ representing the top-left and bottom-right corner points of the bounding box (N is 2), these floating coordinates are quantized into integer bins by

$$x_i = \text{round}(\frac{\tilde{x}_i}{w} * M), \qquad y_i = \text{round}(\frac{\tilde{y}_i}{h} * M), \qquad (2)$$

where each coordinate is normalized by image width w and height h, and M is the number of quantization bins. We refer readers to Pix2Seq [3] for more

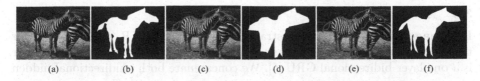

(a)   (b)   (c)   (d)   (e)   (f)

Fig. 3. Visualization of different sampling strategies. (a-b) are the original image and ground-truth. (c-d) are the sampled points and reassembled mask of center-based sampling, respectively, while (e-f) are the ones of uniform sampling.

discretization details. In practice, we construct a shared embedding vocabulary $E \in R^{M \times C}$ for both x-axis and y-axis.

While bounding boxes can be naturally determined by two of its corner points and serialized into a sequence as in Eq. 2, binary masks can not. A binary mask consists of infinite points, of which both quantities and positions impact the details of the mask significantly, thus the above serialization and quantization for bounding boxes is not directly applicable to binary masks.

To address this issue, we propose an innovative *mask contour sampling* scheme for the sequence construction from binary masks. As shown in Fig. 3, we sample N points clockwise from the consecutive mask contour of the referred object, then, the sequence of sampled points can be quantized via Eq. 2. Following sampling strategies are experimented:

- **Center-based sampling.** Starting from the mass center of the binary mask, N rays are emitted with the same angle interval. The intersection points between these rays and the mask contour are clockwise sampled.
- **Uniform sampling.** We uniformly sample N points clockwise on top of the mask contour, which is much simpler compared to the first strategy.

Compared to the center-based sampling, uniform sampling distributes the sampled points along the mask contour more evenly, and can better represent the irregular mask especially when the outline between two adjacent sampled points is tortuous. As shown in Fig. 3, center-based sampling loses the fine details of the zebra legs, while uniform sampling preserves the mask contour more precisely.

In practice, the proposed sampling scheme slightly restricts the performance upper-bound of RES, *e.g.*, uniformly sampling 36 points from ground-truth masks will achieve 95.63 mIoU on RefCOCO *validation* set. Considering current state-of-the-art performance, such a defect is still acceptable. Besides, even if we take as ground-truth the precise binary mask, the upper-bound still will not reach 100 mIoU since down-sampling operations are often necessary.

Both center-based and uniform sampling use deterministic (clockwise) ordering in the sequence of points for the binary mask, however, a binary mask is only determined by points' positions instead of the ordering. Hence we randomly shuffle points' order, which enables the model to learn which point to predict next. In Sect. 4.5, we thoroughly study the proposed sampling scheme.

3.3   Architecture

Language Encoder. To demonstrate the efficacy of SeqTR, we do not opt for the pre-trained language encoders such as BERT [7], hereby the language encoder is a one layer bidirectional GRU [5]. We concatenate both unidirectional hidden states $h_t = [\overrightarrow{h_t}; \overleftarrow{h_t}]$ at each step t to form word features $\{h_t\}_{t=1}^T$.

Visual Encoder. The multi-scale features of the visual encoder are unidirectionally down-sampled from the finest to coarsest spatial resolution, and flattened to generate visual features $F_v \in R^{(H*W) \times C}$ as input to the fusion module. H and W are 32 times smaller of the original image size. In contrast to previous work, we only use the coarsest scale visual features instead of the finest ones for RES task [10,19,31,32], as we do not predict the binary mask pixel-wisely, which reduces the memory footprint during training.

Fusion. Different from Pix2Seq [3], which only perceives the pixel inputs, we devise a simple yet efficient fusion module to align vision and language modalities. Given visual features F_v and word features $\{h_t\}_{t=1}^T$, we first construct language feature $f_l \in R^C$ by *max* pooling word features along the channel dimension. We use Hadamard product between F_v and f_l without the linear projection to produce the multi-modal features $F_m \in R^{(H*W) \times C}$ to transformer encoder:

$$F_{m,i} = \sigma(F_{v,i}) \odot \sigma(f_l), \tag{3}$$

where σ is tanh function. Note that we do not concatenate word features and visual features then use the transformer encoder to perform fusion as in [6,8,20], because that the complexity will quadratically increase.

Transformer and Predictor. The standard transformer encoder updates the feature representations of multi-modal features F_m, while the decoder predicts the target sequence in an auto-regressive manner. The hidden dimension of transformer is set to 256, the expansion rate in feed forward network (FFN) is 4, and the number of encoder and decoder layers are 6 and 3, respectively. This results in the transformer being extremely compact. Since the transformer is permutation-invariant, the F_m and the input sequence are added with *sine* and *learned* positional encoding [45], respectively. To predict the coordinate tokens, an MLP with a final softmax function is used.

Inference. During inference, coordinates are generated in an auto-regressive manner, each coordinate is the *argmax*-ed index of the probabilities over the vocabulary E, and mapped back to the original image scale via the inversion of Eq. 2. We predict exactly 4 discrete coordinate tokens for REC, while leaving the decision of when to prediction to [EOS] token for RES. The predicted sequence is assembled to form the bounding box or binary mask for evaluation.

4   Experiments

4.1   Datasets

RefCOCO/RefCOCO+/RefCOCOg. RefCOCO [55] contains 142,210 referring expressions, 50,000 referred objects, and 19,994 images. Referring expressions in testA set mostly describe people, while the ones in testB set mainly describe objects except people. Similarly, RefCOCO+ [55] contains 141,564 expressions, 49,856 referred objects, and 19,992 images. Compared to RefCOCO, referring expressions of RefCOCO+ describe more about attributes of the referent, *e.g.*, color, shape, digits, and avoid using words of absolute spatial location. RefCOCOg [34,36] has two types of partition strategy, *i.e.*, the *google* split [34] and *umd* split [36]. Both splits have 95,010 referring expressions, 49,822 referred objects, and 25,799 images. We use the validation set as the test set following [10,16,48,49] for *umd* split. The language length of RefCOCOg is 8.4 words on average while that of RefCOCO and RefCOCO+ are only 3.6 and 3.5 words.

ReferItGame [21] contains 120,072 referring expressions and 99,220 referents for 19,997 images collected from the SAIAPR-12 [9] dataset. We use the cleaned berkeley split to partition the dataset, which consists of 54,127, 5,842, and 60,103 referring expressions in train, validation, and test set, respectively.

Flickr30K. Language queries in Flickr30K Entities [37] are short region phrases instead of sentences which may contain multiple objects. It contains 31,783 images with 427K referred entities in train, validation, and test set.

Pre-training Dataset. Following [20], we merge region descriptions from Visual Genome (VG) [23] dataset, annotations from RefCOCO [55], RefCOCO+ [55], RefCOCOg [34,36], and ReferItGame [21] datasets, and Flickr entities [37]. This results in approximately 6.1M distinct language expressions and 174k images in train set, which are less than 200k images as in [20].

4.2 Evaluation Metrics

For REC and phrase localization, we evaluate the performance using Precision@0.5. The prediction is deemed correct if its intersection over union (IoU) with ground-truth box is larger than 0.5. For RES, we use $mIoU$ as the evaluation metric. Precision at 0.5, 0.7, and 0.9 thresholds are also used for ablation.

4.3 Implementation Details

We train SeqTR 60 epochs for REC and phrase localization, and 90 epochs for RES with batch size 128. The Adam [22] optimizer with an initial learning rate 5e-4 is used, which decays the learning rate 10 times after 50 epochs and 75 epochs for the detection and segmentation grounding tasks, respectively. Following standard practices [6,8,19,32], image size is resized to 640×640, and the length of language expression is trimmed at 15 for RefCOCO/+ and 20 for RefCOCOg. For ablation, we train SeqTR 30 epochs unless otherwise stated. During pre-training, SeqTR is trained 15 epochs and fine-tuned another 5 epochs. The number of quantization bins is set to 1000. We use DarkNet-53 [39] as the visual encoder. More details are provided in the appendix.

4.4 Comparisons with State-of-the-Arts

In this section, we compare the proposed SeqTR with the state-of-the-art methods on five benchmark datasets, *i.e.*, RefCOCO, RefCOCO+, RefCOCOg, ReferItGame, and Flickr30K Entities. Table 1 and Table 3 show the performance on

Table 1. Comparison with the state-of-the-arts on the REC task. Visual encoders of models with † is trained without excluding val/test images of the three datasets. RN101 refers to ResNet101 [12] and DN53 denotes DarkNet53 [39].

Models	Visual encoder	RefCOCO			RefCOCO+			RefCOCOg			Time
		val	testA	testB	val	testA	testB	val-g	val-u	test-u	(ms)
Two-stage											
CMN [14]	VGG16	–	71.03	65.77	–	54.32	47.76	57.47	–	–	–
VC [57]	VGG16	–	73.33	67.44	–	58.40	53.18	62.30	–	–	–
ParalAttn [60]	VGG16	–	75.31	65.52	–	61.34	50.86	58.03	–	–	–
MAttNet [54]	RN101	76.40	80.43	69.28	64.93	70.26	56.00	–	66.58	67.27	320
CM-Att-Erase [29]	RN101	78.35	83.14	71.32	68.09	73.65	58.03	–	67.99	68.67	–
DGA [47]	VGG16	–	78.42	65.53	–	69.07	51.99	–	–	63.28	341
RvG-Tree [13]	RN101	75.06	78.61	69.85	63.51	67.45	56.66	-	66.95	66.51	–
NMTree [27]	RN101	76.41	81.21	70.09	66.46	72.02	57.52	64.62	65.87	66.44	–
One-stage											
RealGIN [58]	DN53	77.25	78.70	72.10	62.78	67.17	54.21	–	62.75	62.33	35
FAOA† [50]	DN53	71.15	74.88	66.32	56.86	61.89	49.46	–	59.44	58.90	39
RCCF [25]	DLA34	–	81.06	71.85	–	70.35	56.32	–	–	65.73	**25**
MCN [32]	DN53	80.08	82.29	74.98	67.16	72.86	57.31	–	66.46	66.01	56
ReSC$_L^†$ [49]	DN53	77.63	80.45	72.30	63.59	68.36	56.81	63.12	67.30	67.20	36
Iter-Shrinking [44]	RN101	-	74.27	68.10	–	71.05	58.25	–	–	70.05	–
LBYL† [16]	DN53	79.67	82.91	74.15	68.64	73.38	59.49	62.70	–	–	30
TransVG [6]	RN101	81.02	82.72	78.35	64.82	70.70	56.94	<u>67.02</u>	68.67	67.73	62
TRAR† [59]	DN53	–	81.40	<u>78.60</u>	–	69.10	56.10	–	68.90	68.30	–
SeqTR (ours)	DN53	<u>81.23</u>	<u>85.00</u>	76.08	<u>68.82</u>	<u>75.37</u>	<u>58.78</u>	–	<u>71.35</u>	<u>71.58</u>	50
SeqTR† (ours)	DN53	**83.72**	**86.51**	**81.24**	**71.45**	**76.26**	**64.88**	**71.50**	**74.86**	**74.21**	50

REC and RES tasks. Table 4 reports the result of SeqTR pre-trained on the large corpus of data. The performance on ReferItGame and Flickr30K Entities datasets are given in Table 2.

The performance of SeqTR on REC and phrase localization tasks is illustrated in Table 1 and Table 2. From Table 1, our model performs better than two-stage models, especially MAttNet [54] while being 6 times faster. We also surpass one-stage models that exploit prior and expert knowledge, with +2–7% absolute improvement over LBYL [16] and ReSC [49]. Despite we predict discrete coordinate tokens in an auto-regressive manner, the inference speed* of SeqTR is only 50 ms, which is real-time and comparable with one-stage models. For transformer-based models, SeqTR surpasses TransVG [6] and TRAR [59] with up to 6.27% absolute performance improvement. Our SeqTR achieves new state-of-the-art performance with a simple architecture and loss function on the RefCOCO [55], RefCOCO+ [55], and RefCOCOg [34,36] datasets. On the ReferItGame and Flickr30K Entities datasets which mostly contain short noun phrases, the performance boosts to 69.66 and 81.23 with a large margin over previous one-stage methods [25,42,49,50] and is comparable with current state-of-the-art methods [6,24].

---

*Tested on GTX 1080 Ti GPU, batch size is 1.

Table 2. Comparison with the state-of-the-art models on the test set of Flickr30K Entities [37] and ReferItGame [21] datasets.

Models	Visual encoder	ReferItGame test	Flickr30k test	Time (ms)
Two-stage				
MAttNet [54]	RN101	29.04	–	320
SimilarityNet [46]	RN101	34.54	60.89	184
DDPN [56]	RN101	63.00	73.30	–
One-stage				
FAOA [50]	DN53	60.67	68.71	**23**
ZSGNet [42]	RN50	58.63	63.39	–
RCCF [25]	DLA34	63.79	–	25
ReSC$_L$ [49]	DN53	64.60	69.28	36
TransVG [6]	RN101	70.73	79.10	62
RefTR [24]	RN101	**71.42**	78.66	40
SeqTR (ours)	DN53	69.66	**81.23**	50

SeqTR can be seamlessly extended to RES without any network architecture modifications since we reformulate the task as a point prediction problem. As shown in Table 3, we outperform various models with sophisticated cross-modal alignment and reasoning mechanisms [10, 17, 19, 28, 31, 32, 51]. SeqTR is on par with current state-of-the-art VLT [8] which selectively aggregates responses from the diversified queries, whereas we directly produce the corresponding segmentation mask and establish one-to-one correspondence. When initialized with the pre-trained parameters using the large corpus of data, the performance boosts up to 10.78% absolute improvement, proving that a simple yet universal approach for visual grounding is indeed feasible.

From Table 4, when pre-trained on the large corpus of text-image pairs, SeqTR is more data-efficient than the current state-of-the-art [20]. Our transformer architecture only contains 7.9 M parameters which is twice as few as MDETR [20], while the performance is superior especially on the RefCOCOg dataset with up to 2.48% improvement.

4.5 Ablation Studies

To give a comprehensive understanding of SeqTR, we discuss ablative studies on the validation set of the RefCOCO [55], RefCOCO+ [55], and RefCOCOg [36] datasets in this section.

Construction of Language Feature. Language feature in Sect. 3.3 can be constructed by either *max/mean* pooling of word features or directly using the final hidden state of bi-GRU. As shown in the upper part of Table 5, *max* pooling performs best, and is the default construction throughout this paper.

Table 3. Comparison with the state-of-the-arts on the RES task. Model with ∗ is pre-trained on the large corpus of data.

Models	Visual encoder	RefCOCO			RefCOCO+			RefCOCOg		
		val	testA	testB	val	testA	testB	val-g	val-u	test-u
MAttNet [54]	RN101	56.51	62.37	51.70	46.67	52.39	40.08	–	47.64	48.61
CMSA [51]	RN101	58.32	60.61	55.09	43.76	47.60	37.89	39.98	–	–
STEP [2]	RN101	60.04	63.46	57.97	48.19	52.33	40.41	46.40	–	–
BRINet [15]	RN101	60.98	62.99	59.21	48.17	52.32	42.11	48.04	–	–
CMPC [17]	RN101	61.36	64.53	59.64	49.56	53.44	43.23	49.05	–	–
LSCM [18]	RN101	61.47	64.99	59.55	49.34	53.12	43.50	48.05	–	–
CMPC+ [28]	RN101	62.47	65.08	60.82	50.25	54.04	43.47	49.89	–	–
MCN [32]	DN53	62.44	64.20	59.71	50.62	54.99	44.69	–	49.22	49.40
EFN [10]	WRN101	62.76	65.69	59.67	51.50	55.24	43.01	**51.93**	–	–
BUSNet [48]	RN101	63.27	66.41	61.39	51.76	56.87	44.13	50.56	–	–
CGAN [31]	DN53	64.86	68.04	62.07	51.03	55.51	44.06	46.54	51.01	51.69
LTS [19]	DN53	65.43	67.76	63.08	54.21	58.32	48.02	–	54.40	54.25
VLT [8]	DN56	65.65	68.29	62.73	55.50	59.20	49.36	49.76	52.99	56.65
SeqTR (ours)	DN53	67.26	69.79	64.12	54.14	58.93	48.19	–	55.67	55.64
SeqTR∗ (ours)	DN53	**71.70**	**73.31**	**69.82**	**63.04**	**66.73**	**58.97**	–	**64.69**	**65.74**

Table 4. Comparison with pre-trained models on RefCOCO [55], RefCOCO+ [55], and RefCOCOg [36] datasets. We only count the parameters of transformer architecture.

Models	Visual encoder	Params (M)	Pre-train images	RefCOCO			RefCOCO+			RefCOCOg	
				val	testA	testB	val	testA	testB	val-u	test-u
ViLBERT [30]	RN101	–	3.3M	–	–	–	72.34	78.52	62.61	–	–
VL-BERT$_L$ [43]	RN101	–	3.3 M	–	–	–	72.59	78.57	62.30	–	–
UNITER$_L$ [4]	RN101	–	4.6 M	81.41	87.04	74.17	75.90	81.45	66.70	74.86	75.77
VILLA$_L$ [11]	RN101	–	4.6 M	82.39	87.48	74.84	76.17	81.54	66.84	76.18	76.71
ERNIE-ViL$_L$ [53]	RN101	–	4.3 M	–	–	–	75.95	82.07	66.88	–	–
MDETR [20]	RN101	17.36	200K	86.75	89.58	81.41	**79.52**	84.09	70.62	81.64	80.89
RefTR [24]	RN101	17.86	**100K**	85.65	88.73	81.16	77.55	82.26	68.99	79.25	80.01
SeqTR (ours)	DN53	**7.90**	174K	**87.00**	**90.15**	**83.59**	78.69	**84.51**	**71.87**	**82.69**	**83.37**

Token Weight. If previously predicted points are inaccurate, model can not recover from the wrong predictions since the inference is sequential. Hence we increase a few former token weights to penalize more on the first several predicted discrete coordinate tokens. As shown in the lower part of Table 5, increasing the weight of first token is better than increasing the latter tokens, and setting the 1st token weight to 1.5 and subsequent tokens to 1 gives the best performance. We set $w_i = 1, \forall i$ for RES task.

Sampling Scheme. We verify the upper bound as the mIoU of the assembled mask from the sampled points and original ground-truth. From Fig. 4 (a), we can see that the mIoU approaches nearly 100 when the number of sampled points increases, *i.e.*, 95.57 for uniform sampling, and 91.58 for center-based sampling. Therefore, though the upper bound is limited theoretically, in practice,

Table 5. Ablation experiments on the construction of language feature and token weight. The first token is the [TASK] token, while subsequent tokens are discrete coordinate tokens, *i.e.*, (x_1, y_1, x_2, y_2).

Language feature	Token weight					RefCOCO	RefCOCO+	RefCOCOg
	1st	2nd	3rd	4th	5th	val	val	val-u
Mean pooling	1	1	1	1	1	79.73	67.12	68.97
Max pooling						**80.07**	**68.31**	**69.95**
Final hidden state						79.85	67.46	69.93
Max pooling	1	1	1	1	1	80.07	68.31	69.95
	1.5	1	1	1	1	80.10	**68.63**	**70.05**
	2	1	1	1	1	**80.19**	68.33	70.01
	3	1	1	1	1	80.08	67.81	69.45
	1	2	2	1	1	79.70	67.22	69.51
	2	2	2	1	1	80.16	67.83	69.45

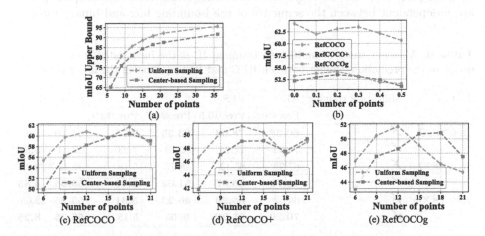

Fig. 4. Ablative experiments on RES task. (a) The upper bound is averaged over validation sets (the fluctuation is within 0.2). (b) Shuffling percentage refers to the fraction of shuffled sequences within a batch, uniform sampling strategy is used. (c-e) depict the impact of sampling strategies and the number of sampled points.

the research effort might be better spent on improving the real-world performance. In terms of sampling strategies, from Fig. 4 (a) and Fig. 4 (c-e), uniform sampling is consistently better than center-based sampling in terms of both the upper bound and the performance, which preserves more details of the mask illustrated in Fig. 3. The number of sampled points controls the trade-off between the inference speed and performance, from Fig. 4 (c-e), we can see that 18 and 12 points are the best for RefCOCO and RefCOCO+/RefCOCOg datasets.

Shuffling Percentage. We train SeqTR 60 epochs instead of 30 as we empirically found that point shuffling takes a longer time to converge, since the ground-truth is different for each coordinate token at each forward pass. Fig. 4 (b) shows that no shuffle and 0.2 are best for RefCOCO and RefCOCO+/RefCOCOg. As the number of shuffled sequences increases, the performance drops slightly, and we observe that SeqTR is under-fitting since the mIoU during training is lower than the one without shuffling.

Multi-task Training. Previous multi-task visual grounding approaches require REC to help RES locate the referent. In contrast, *SeqTR is capable to locate the referent at pixel level without the aid from REC*. We train SeqTR 60 epochs and test whether multi-task supervision can bring further improvement. For the input sequence construction of multi-task grounding, please see the supplementary material. From Table 6, we can see that multi-task supervision even slightly degenerates the performance compared to the single-task variant. Though the inconsistency error significantly decreases, the location ability of RES measured by Prec@0.5, 0.7, and 0.9 stays the same, suggesting that the sampled points are independent between the sequence of the bounding box and binary mask.

Table 6. Ablation study of multi-task training. IE is the inconsistency error [32] to measure the prediction conflict between REC and RES, ↓ denotes the lower is better.

Dataset	Multi-task training	REC	RES			mIoU	IE↓
		Prec@0.5	Prec@0.5	Prec@0.7	Prec@0.9		
RefCOCO	✗	**80.38**	**78.03**	**63.35**	**9.75**	**64.20**	13.93
	✔	79.65	77.24	60.29	7.23	62.93	**5.86**
RefCOCO+	✗	67.98	65.11	48.27	5.19	52.22	22.22
	✔	**68.79**	**66.67**	**51.02**	**5.46**	**53.65**	**4.85**
RefCOCOg	✗	69.63	**65.20**	**46.23**	**5.31**	**53.25**	22.65
	✔	**70.29**	**65.20**	46.05	5.15	**53.25**	**8.25**

4.6   Qualitative Results

We visualize the cross attention map averaged over decoder layers and attention heads in Fig. 5. At each prediction step, SeqTR generates a coordinate token given previous output tokens. Under this setting, a clear pattern emerges, *i.e.*, attends to the left side of the referent when predicting x_1, the top side of the referent when predicting y_1, and so on. This axial attention is sensitive to the boundary of the referent, thus can more precisely ground the referred object. The predicted masks are visualized in Fig. 6. SeqTR can well comprehends attributive words and absolute or relative spatial relations, and the predicted mask aligns with the irregular outlines of the referred object such as *"left cow"*. More qualitative results are given in the appendix.

Fig. 5. Visualization of normalized cross attention map in transformer decoder. From left to right column, we generate (x_1, y_1, x_2, y_2) in sequential order.

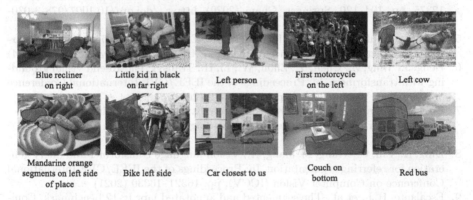

Fig. 6. Example mask predictions by SeqTR on the validation set of RefCOCO dataset, best viewed in color.

5 Conclusions

In this paper we reformulate visual grounding tasks as a point prediction problem and present an innovative and general network termed SeqTR. Based on the standard transformer encoder-decoder architecture and *cross-entropy* loss, SeqTR unifies different visual grounding tasks under the same point prediction paradigm without any modifications. Experimental results demonstrate that SeqTR can well ground language query onto the corresponding region, suggesting that a simple yet universal approach for visual grounding is indeed feasible.

Acknowledgements. This work was supported by the National Science Fund for Distinguished Young Scholars (No. 62025603), the National Natural Science Foundation of China (No. U21B2037, No. 62176222, No. 62176223, No. 62176226, No. 62072386,

No. 62072387, No. 62072389, and No. 62002305), Guangdong Basic and Applied Basic Research Foundation (No. 2019B1515120049), and the Natural Science Foundation of Fujian Province of China (No. 2021J01002).

References

1. Carion, N., Massa, F., Synnaeve, G., Usunier, N., Kirillov, A., Zagoruyko, S.: End-to-end object detection with transformers. In: Vedaldi, A., Bischof, H., Brox, T., Frahm, J.-M. (eds.) ECCV 2020. LNCS, vol. 12346, pp. 213–229. Springer, Cham (2020). https://doi.org/10.1007/978-3-030-58452-8_13
2. Chen, D.J., Jia, S., Lo, Y.C., Chen, H.T., Liu, T.L.: See-through-text grouping for referring image segmentation. In: Proceedings of the IEEE/CVF International Conference on Computer Vision (ICCV), pp. 7454–7463 (2019)
3. Chen, T., Saxena, S., Li, L., Fleet, D.J., Hinton, G.: Pix2seq: a language modeling framework for object detection. In: International Conference on Learning Representations (ICLR) (2022)
4. Chen, Y.C., et al.: UNITER: uNiversal image-TExt representation learning. In: Vedaldi, A., Bischof, H., Brox, T., Frahm, J.-M. (eds.) ECCV 2020. LNCS, vol. 12375, pp. 104–120. Springer, Cham (2020). https://doi.org/10.1007/978-3-030-58577-8_7
5. Chung, J., Gulcehre, C., Cho, K., Bengio, Y.: Empirical evaluation of gated recurrent neural networks on sequence modeling. arXiv preprint arXiv:1412.3555 (2014)
6. Deng, J., Yang, Z., Chen, T., Zhou, W., Li, H.: Transvg: end-to-end visual grounding with transformers. In: Proceedings of the IEEE/CVF International Conference on Computer Vision (ICCV), pp. 1769–1779 (2021)
7. Devlin, J., Chang, M.W., Lee, K., Toutanova, K.: Bert: Pre-training of deep bidirectional transformers for language understanding. arXiv preprint arXiv:1810.04805 (2018)
8. Ding, H., Liu, C., Wang, S., Jiang, X.: Vision-language transformer and query generation for referring segmentation. In: Proceedings of the IEEE/CVF International Conference on Computer Vision (ICCV), pp. 16321–16330 (2021)
9. Escalante, H.J., et al.: The segmented and annotated iapr tc-12 benchmark. Comput. Vis. Image Understand. (CVIU) **114**(4), 419–428 (2010)
10. Feng, G., Hu, Z., Zhang, L., Lu, H.: Encoder fusion network with co-attention embedding for referring image segmentation. In: Proceedings of the IEEE/CVF Conference on Computer Vision and Pattern Recognition (CVPR), pp. 15506–15515 (2021)
11. Gan, Z., Chen, Y.C., Li, L., Zhu, C., Cheng, Y., Liu, J.: Large-scale adversarial training for vision-and-language representation learning. Adv. Neural Inf. Process. Syst. (NeurIPS) **33**, 6616–6628 (2020)
12. He, K., Zhang, X., Ren, S., Sun, J.: Deep residual learning for image recognition. In: Proceedings of the IEEE Conference on Computer Vision and Pattern Recognition (CVPR), pp. 770–778 (2016)
13. Hong, R., Liu, D., Mo, X., He, X., Zhang, H.: Learning to compose and reason with language tree structures for visual grounding. IEEE Trans. Pattern Anal. Mach. Intell. (TPAMI) (2019)
14. Hu, R., Rohrbach, M., Andreas, J., Darrell, T., Saenko, K.: Modeling relationships in referential expressions with compositional modular networks. In: Proceedings of the IEEE Conference on Computer Vision and Pattern Recognition (CVPR), pp. 1115–1124 (2017)

15. Hu, Z., Feng, G., Sun, J., Zhang, L., Lu, H.: Bi-directional relationship inferring network for referring image segmentation. In: Proceedings of the IEEE/CVF Conference on Computer Vision and Pattern Recognition (CVPR), pp. 4424–4433 (2020)
16. Huang, B., Lian, D., Luo, W., Gao, S.: Look before you leap: learning landmark features for one-stage visual grounding. In: Proceedings of the IEEE/CVF Conference on Computer Vision and Pattern Recognition (CVPR), pp. 16888–16897 (2021)
17. Huang, S., et al.: Referring image segmentation via cross-modal progressive comprehension. In: Proceedings of the IEEE/CVF Conference on Computer Vision and Pattern Recognition (CVPR), pp. 10488–10497 (2020)
18. Hui, T., Liu, S., Huang, S., Li, G., Yu, S., Zhang, F., Han, J.: Linguistic structure guided context modeling for referring image segmentation. In: Vedaldi, A., Bischof, H., Brox, T., Frahm, J.-M. (eds.) ECCV 2020. LNCS, vol. 12355, pp. 59–75. Springer, Cham (2020). https://doi.org/10.1007/978-3-030-58607-2_4
19. Jing, Y., Kong, T., Wang, W., Wang, L., Li, L., Tan, T.: Locate then segment: a strong pipeline for referring image segmentation. In: Proceedings of the IEEE/CVF Conference on Computer Vision and Pattern Recognition (CVPR), pp. 9858–9867 (2021)
20. Kamath, A., Singh, M., LeCun, Y., Synnaeve, G., Misra, I., Carion, N.: Mdetr-modulated detection for end-to-end multi-modal understanding. In: Proceedings of the IEEE/CVF International Conference on Computer Vision (ICCV), pp. 1780–1790 (2021)
21. Kazemzadeh, S., Ordonez, V., Matten, M., Berg, T.: Referitgame: referring to objects in photographs of natural scenes. In: Proceedings of the Conference on Empirical Methods in Natural Language Processing (EMNLP), pp. 787–798 (2014)
22. Kingma, D.P., Ba, J.: Adam: A method for stochastic optimization. arXiv preprint arXiv:1412.6980 (2014)
23. Krishna, R., et al.: Visual genome: connecting language and vision using crowd-sourced dense image annotations. Int. J. Comput. Vis. (IJCV) **123**(1), 32–73 (2017)
24. Li, M., Sigal, L.: Referring transformer: a one-step approach to multi-task visual grounding. Adv. Neural Inf. Process. Syst. (NeurIPS) **34**, 19652–19664 (2021)
25. Liao, Y., et al.: A real-time cross-modality correlation filtering method for referring expression comprehension. In: Proceedings of the IEEE/CVF Conference on Computer Vision and Pattern Recognition (CVPR), pp. 10880–10889 (2020)
26. Lin, T.Y., Goyal, P., Girshick, R., He, K., Dollár, P.: Focal loss for dense object detection. In: Proceedings of the IEEE International Conference on Computer Vision (ICCV), pp. 2980–2988 (2017)
27. Liu, D., Zhang, H., Wu, F., Zha, Z.J.: Learning to assemble neural module tree networks for visual grounding. In: Proceedings of the IEEE/CVF International Conference on Computer Vision (ICCV), pp. 4673–4682 (2019)
28. Liu, S., Hui, T., Huang, S., Wei, Y., Li, B., Li, G.: Cross-modal progressive comprehension for referring segmentation. IEEE Trans. Pattern Anal. Mach. Intell. (TPAMI) (2021)
29. Liu, X., Wang, Z., Shao, J., Wang, X., Li, H.: Improving referring expression grounding with cross-modal attention-guided erasing. In: Proceedings of the IEEE/CVF Conference on Computer Vision and Pattern Recognition (CVPR), pp. 1950–1959 (2019)
30. Lu, J., Batra, D., Parikh, D., Lee, S.: Vilbert: pretraining task-agnostic visiolinguistic representations for vision-and-language tasks. Adv. Neural Inf. Process. Syst. (NeurIPS) **32** (2019)

31. Luo, G., Zhou, Y., Ji, R., Sun, X., Su, J., Lin, C.W., Tian, Q.: Cascade grouped attention network for referring expression segmentation. In: Proceedings of the 28th ACM International Conference on Multimedia (MM), pp. 1274–1282 (2020)

32. Luo, G., et al.: Multi-task collaborative network for joint referring expression comprehension and segmentation. In: Proceedings of the IEEE/CVF Conference on Computer Vision and Pattern Recognition (CVPR), pp. 10034–10043 (2020)

33. Luo, G., et al.: Towards language-guided visual recognition via dynamic convolutions. arXiv preprint arXiv:2110.08797 (2021)

34. Mao, J., Huang, J., Toshev, A., Camburu, O., Yuille, A.L., Murphy, K.: Generation and comprehension of unambiguous object descriptions. In: Proceedings of the IEEE Conference on Computer Vision and Pattern Recognition (CVPR), pp. 11–20 (2016)

35. Milletari, F., Navab, N., Ahmadi, S.A.: V-net: fully convolutional neural networks for volumetric medical image segmentation. In: Proceedings of the Fourth International Conference on 3D Vision (3DV), pp. 565–571. IEEE (2016)

36. Nagaraja, V.K., Morariu, V.I., Davis, L.S.: Modeling context between objects for referring expression understanding. In: Leibe, B., Matas, J., Sebe, N., Welling, M. (eds.) ECCV 2016. LNCS, vol. 9908, pp. 792–807. Springer, Cham (2016). https://doi.org/10.1007/978-3-319-46493-0_48

37. Plummer, B.A., et al.: Flickr30k entities: collecting region-to-phrase correspondences for richer image-to-sentence models. Int. J. Comput. Vis. (IJCV) **123**(1), 74–93 (2017)

38. Radford, A., Wu, J., Child, R., Luan, D., Amodei, D., Sutskever, I., et al.: Language models are unsupervised multitask learners. OpenAI blog **1**(8), 9 (2019)

39. Redmon, J., Farhadi, A.: Yolov3: an incremental improvement. arXiv preprint arXiv:1804.02767 (2018)

40. Ren, S., He, K., Girshick, R., Sun, J.: Faster r-cnn: towards real-time object detection with region proposal networks. Adv. Neural Inf. Process. Syst. (NeurIPS) **28**(2015)

41. Rezatofighi, H., Tsoi, N., Gwak, J., Sadeghian, A., Reid, I., Savarese, S.: Generalized intersection over union: a metric and a loss for bounding box regression. In: Proceedings of the IEEE/CVF Conference on Computer Vision and Pattern Recognition (CVPR), pp. 658–666 (2019)

42. Sadhu, A., Chen, K., Nevatia, R.: Zero-shot grounding of objects from natural language queries. In: Proceedings of the IEEE/CVF International Conference on Computer Vision (ICCV), pp. 4694–4703 (2019)

43. Su, W., et al.: Vl-bert: pre-training of generic visual-linguistic representations. arXiv preprint arXiv:1908.08530 (2019)

44. Sun, M., Xiao, J., Lim, E.G.: Iterative shrinking for referring expression grounding using deep reinforcement learning. In: Proceedings of the IEEE/CVF Conference on Computer Vision and Pattern Recognition (CVPR). pp. 14060–14069 (2021)

45. Vaswani, A., et al.: Attention is all you need. Adv. Neural Inf. Process. Syst. (NeurIPS) **30** (2017)

46. Wang, L., Li, Y., Huang, J., Lazebnik, S.: Learning two-branch neural networks for image-text matching tasks. IEEE Trans. Pattern Anal. Mach. Intell. (TPAMI) **41**(2), 394–407 (2018)

47. Yang, S., Li, G., Yu, Y.: Dynamic graph attention for referring expression comprehension. In: Proceedings of the IEEE/CVF International Conference on Computer Vision (ICCV), pp. 4644–4653 (2019)

48. Yang, S., Xia, M., Li, G., Zhou, H.Y., Yu, Y.: Bottom-up shift and reasoning for referring image segmentation. In: Proceedings of the IEEE/CVF Conference on Computer Vision and Pattern Recognition (CVPR), pp. 11266–11275 (2021)
49. Yang, Z., Chen, T., Wang, L., Luo, J.: Improving one-stage visual grounding by recursive sub-query construction. In: Vedaldi, A., Bischof, H., Brox, T., Frahm, J.-M. (eds.) ECCV 2020. LNCS, vol. 12359, pp. 387–404. Springer, Cham (2020). https://doi.org/10.1007/978-3-030-58568-6_23
50. Yang, Z., Gong, B., Wang, L., Huang, W., Yu, D., Luo, J.: A fast and accurate one-stage approach to visual grounding. In: Proceedings of the IEEE/CVF International Conference on Computer Vision (ICCV), pp. 4683–4693 (2019)
51. Ye, L., Rochan, M., Liu, Z., Wang, Y.: Cross-modal self-attention network for referring image segmentation. In: Proceedings of the IEEE/CVF Conference on Computer Vision and Pattern Recognition (CVPR), pp. 10502–10511 (2019)
52. Young, P., Lai, A., Hodosh, M., Hockenmaier, J.: From image descriptions to visual denotations: new similarity metrics for semantic inference over event descriptions. Trans. Assoc. Comput. Linguist. (TACL) **2**, 67–78 (2014)
53. Yu, F., et al.: Ernie-vil: knowledge enhanced vision-language representations through scene graph. arXiv preprint arXiv:2006.16934 (2020)
54. Yu, L., et al.: Mattnet: modular attention network for referring expression comprehension. In: Proceedings of the IEEE Conference on Computer Vision and Pattern Recognition (CVPR) (2018)
55. Yu, L., Poirson, P., Yang, S., Berg, A.C., Berg, T.L.: Modeling context in referring expressions. In: Leibe, B., Matas, J., Sebe, N., Welling, M. (eds.) ECCV 2016. LNCS, vol. 9906, pp. 69–85. Springer, Cham (2016). https://doi.org/10.1007/978-3-319-46475-6_5
56. Yu, Z., Yu, J., Xiang, C., Zhao, Z., Tian, Q., Tao, D.: Rethinking diversified and discriminative proposal generation for visual grounding. arXiv preprint arXiv:1805.03508 (2018)
57. Zhang, H., Niu, Y., Chang, S.F.: Grounding referring expressions in images by variational context. In: Proceedings of the IEEE Conference on Computer Vision and Pattern Recognition (CVPR), pp. 4158–4166 (2018)
58. Zhou, Y., et al.: A real-time global inference network for one-stage referring expression comprehension. IEEE Trans. Neural Netw. Learn. Syst. (TNNLS) (2021)
59. Zhou, Y., et al.: Trar: routing the attention spans in transformer for visual question answering. In: Proceedings of the IEEE/CVF International Conference on Computer Vision (ICCV), pp. 2074–2084 (2021)
60. Zhuang, B., Wu, Q., Shen, C., Reid, I., Van Den Hengel, A.: Parallel attention: a unified framework for visual object discovery through dialogs and queries. In: Proceedings of the IEEE Conference on Computer Vision and Pattern Recognition (CVPR), pp. 4252–4261 (2018)

VTC: Improving Video-Text Retrieval with User Comments

Laura Hanu[1] , James Thewlis[1(✉)] , Yuki M. Asano[2] ,
and Christian Rupprecht[3]

[1] Unitary Ltd., London, UK
james@unitary.ai
[2] University of Amsterdam, Amsterdam, Netherlands
[3] University of Oxford, Oxford, England

Abstract. Multi-modal retrieval is an important problem for many applications, such as recommendation and search. Current benchmarks and even datasets are often manually constructed and consist of mostly clean samples where all modalities are well-correlated with the content. Thus, current video-text retrieval literature largely focuses on video titles or audio transcripts, while ignoring user comments, since users often tend to discuss topics only vaguely related to the video. Despite the ubiquity of user comments online, there is currently no multi-modal representation learning datasets that includes comments. In this paper, we a) introduce a new dataset of videos, titles and comments; b) present an attention-based mechanism that allows the model to learn from sometimes irrelevant data such as comments; c) show that by using comments, our method is able to learn better, more contextualised, representations for image, video and audio representations. Project page: https://unitaryai. github.io/vtc-paper.

1 Introduction

Training large scale multi-modal models from paired visual/text data from the web has seen great success in video understanding and retrieval. However, typically only the caption (i.e. title or "alt text") is used, ignoring potentially relevant text present on the web page such as user comments.

We explore how to leverage comments for the task of video-text retrieval. We consider how comments can be seen as an extra modality, yet with the peculiar characteristics that they are neither inherently derived from the video (as text from speech or OCR would be), nor are they merely extra captions which can be used in place of the title. This results in two different, yet equally interesting research questions: "Can we use comments to augment and adapt

---

Supplementary Information The online version contains supplementary material available at https://doi.org/10.1007/978-3-031-19833-5_36.

The original version of this chapter was revised: Place and country of the first affiliation have been corrected. The correction to this chapter is available at https://doi.org/10.1007/978-3-031-19833-5_43

S. Avidan et al. (Eds.): ECCV 2022, LNCS 13695, pp. 616–633, 2022.
https://doi.org/10.1007/978-3-031-19833-5_36

our title representations?" and "Can we use them to adapt our video features?" We address both of these in this paper.

A challenge is that comments may often be only tangentially related to the contents of the video (e.g. "cool video!"), or may be relevant but non-distinctive ("cute cat!" applies to many videos). Yet, since comments often discuss contextual details lacking from the title or video themselves, we hypothesize that correctly leveraging this signal can improve retrieval, endowing either the query or target features with extra context.

Other modalities can also exhibit this behavior, for example, many current works that learn from audio-visual correspondence [1,2,41] leverage clean datasets such as Kinetics [7] or VGGSound [8] to learn meaningful correspondence between videos and sound, whereas online videos tend to have for example background music that replaces the actual sounds happening in the video, or images overlaid with sounds.

In this paper, we propose a method that can take advantage of this auxiliary context provided by comments while simultaneously filtering it for meaningful information. Most current models enforce a strict correlation between the different input modalities under the assumption that all are informative of the content. The main intuition of our work is that when training a model on partially unrelated data, we need to introduce a mechanism that allows the model to discount auxiliary data when it is not helpful for the task.

To this end, we build a model with a hierarchical attention structure. Current representation learning models that are based on transformer architectures already exploit the idea of an attention mechanism to model the correlation between different *parts* of an input signal. For example in text understanding, the attention mechanism is applied per word, allowing the model to understand the structure of natural language. Even though in principle one could use the same scheme to model the importance of different text inputs on a per-word basis, we find that this makes it difficult to learn the individual importance of inputs. Moreover, due to the computational complexity of current transformers (squared with sequence length) this approach would only work for a small number of comments. We thus add a second layer of attention *per processed input* that allows the model to assess the amount of information at a higher level of features. With quantitative and qualitative experiments, we find that this mechanism aligns well with the intuition that some inputs are very relevant to the problem and others can be disregarded.

To the best of our knowledge, there is no large scale dataset that contains videos, titles, and user comments. Thus, to advance the field of representation learning, we introduce "VTC" (Videos, Titles and Comments), a new dataset of 339k videos and titles with an average of 14 comments per video with which we train and evaluate our representations. A more detailed summary of the dataset statistics can be found in the Appendix. In our experiments we show that we can indeed learn meaningful information from user comments for three different modalities: audio, images, and video and that representations learned can generalize to other datasets. Additionally, we show that the model can correctly identify whether auxiliary information is informative of the content of a video or not.

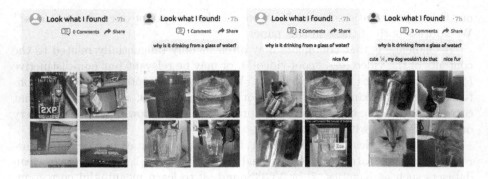

Fig. 1. Video retrieval from title and comments. We show the top 4 videos retrieved for the ambiguous title *"Look what I found!"*. From left to right, we progressively add more comments which our model uses to refine the results.

The ability to incorporate auxiliary contextual information also opens up possibilities for useful applications. In the video retrieval setting, our method can be used to iteratively refine a text descriptor with new inputs as shown in Fig. 1, allowing incremental searching. In the zero-shot video classification setting (*i.e.*, "retrieving" the correct class description prompt), the prediction for an ambiguous video can be steered towards the correct class using surrounding text from a webpage or user hints.

Overall this paper has three main contributions: 1) We quantify the value of the *comments* modality for video-text learning. 2) For this, we propose, train, and evaluate on a new dataset VTC of videos, titles, and comments. And 3) we introduce a new hierarchical attention method that learns how to identify relevant auxiliary information, and that can learn representations that even generalize to other datasets.

2   Related Work

In this work, we focus on multi-modal learning with a particular focus on learning video-text encoders for retrieval by proposing a novel, multi-modal adaptation module.

Video-text Pretraining. Originating from the NLP domain, where the transformer architectures has been a key ingredient and subject to optimization in a multitude of ways [11,14,15,27–30,33,46,47,50,58], it has recently found applications in the vision-language domain. For example, recent works have leveraged transformers to learn generalizeable image [9,12,51], multi-modal image-text [10,31,34,36,53,56] or video-multilingual text [21] representations. A few works [37,54,55,63] combine visual and text modalities as inputs to a BERT model to simultaneously learn semantic video and text representations. For representation learning, the availability of large-scale datasets such as HowTo100M [40] has enabled more effective pretraining of video-text representations for multiple downstream tasks. More recently, [44] show that adding a generative objective to contrastive pretraining can yield gains in video-text downstream tasks. Based on the CLIP model [45], which works well even without finetuning for some retrieval tasks [38], [4] train video-text CLIP-initialized models by gradually scaling up video training from image training and a custom dataset. While we also start with a CLIP initialization as in [38], the focus of our paper lies in developing a novel method for leveraging user comments, a modality that has previously been overlooked as a valuable source of information in the text-video retrieval literature. We also note that there has been a surge in recent vision-text pretrained models inspired by CLIP [4,32,42,62]. As we show in the experiments section, our method is agnostic to the pretraining method employed and generalizes beyond CLIP. There are many existing video-text datasets [20,25,49,59,61] but these do not include comments.

Multi-modal domain adaptation. While residual adapters for1 domain adaptation have been explored for uni-modal models such as CNNs, e.g. in [48], there are no works that translate this concept to the multi-modal domain, where cross-modal learning dominates [1,2,41].

Vision-text Pretraining. While there is a wealth of image-text datasets that provide images with captions, such as OpenImages [26], ConceptualCaptions [52], or COCO [35], the recent state of the art methods train on large-scale weakly-supervised datasets that are obtained from image descriptions from for example Reddit (RedCaps [13]) or YFCC [57].

Comment Datasets. To the best of our knowledge, there is only one vision dataset which does include user-comments, the LiveBot dataset [39]. However this dataset, which contains under 3000 videos, is constructed for artificial comment generation and uses the less common "video barrage" (*i.e.* time-synchronous) type of comments. Despite this, we evaluate our method on this dataset and also find performance gains for video-text representation learning when using comments. In the context of learning from comments, there is little prior work. While the work of [17] is somewhat related, as it uses comments and reactions to posts to refine harm predictions on a social media site, we are the first to demonstrate that user comments can be used as a complementary modality when learning video-text representations.

3   VTC Dataset

We collect a dataset "VTC" of videos along with their titles and comment threads from social news site reddit.com, using their provided API. The videos are collected and used in a manner compatible with national regulations on usage of data for research. Unlike most curated video datasets, this data is more representative of the types of videos shared "in the wild", containing a large proportion of videogames, screenshots and memes.

Using a classifier trained on a small amount of labelled data, we estimate that videogame footage makes up 25% of examples, other screenshots, memes and comics make up 24%, live action footage is 49% and artistic styled content (such as drawn animation) is 2%. The average video length is 33 s.

From 1 million raw videos collected, we perform deduplication and filtering, ending up with a training set of 461k videos. For the experiment in Table 8 on training without faces we do further filtering to remove faces, finding that about 65% of videos contain a face. To compensate for the decrease in quantity of training data we gather extra non-face-containing videos, ending up with 339k videos. For the evaluation results we use a test set consisting of 5000 videos with at least three comments each.

For each example in the dataset we obtain: The `title` of the post, a high quality `preview image`, which is generated automatically by Reddit, typically 640 pixels wide and corresponding to the middle frame of the video, the `video` itself, downloaded in low quality and resized to have height 320 pixels for storage reasons, and up to 500 randomly selected `comments` per post.

For all the image-based experiments, we use the high quality preview image, whereas for the video experiments in Table 7 we use the extracted video frames. To fairly compare video and image models given the lower video resolution and quality, in Table 7 the "1 frame" case corresponds to the first frame from the video rather than the high quality preview image.

Deduplication. We use the GPU implementation of the FAISS similarity search toolkit [22] to efficiently deduplicate the dataset by indexing the video thumbnail embeddings obtained from a ImageNet pretrained ResNet18 [19]. These indices are then used to discard video entries with a high similarity to other posts.

Safety and Privacy. Additionally, we remove toxic text content (such as slurs and hate speech) from titles and comments using the detoxify library [18]. Table 1 show the prevalence of content that has been removed this way.

Table 1. Prevalence of toxic text before filtering. We report the proportion of posts, titles, and comments that are flagged as having potentially offensive content by the open-source library Detoxify. We use a threshold of 0.9

Detoxify label	% titles	% comments
Toxicity	2.32	5.62
Severe toxicity	0.00	0.00
Obscenity	1.23	3.73
Identity attack	0.00	0.00
Insult	0.82	1.95
Threat	0.05	0.07
Sexually explicit	0.09	0.22

It is crucial that a dataset is well-conceived and potential risks are thought-out before release. We take two steps to ensure safety and usefulness of our proposed dataset. First, for the releasing the dataset we further filter the dataset to exclude videos that contain faces using the automatic face-detection filtering process from PASS [3]. In our experiments we show that this does not lead to a significant change in performance. Second, we provide a *Datasheet* [16] for the proposed dataset which can be found in the supplementary material. This dataset will be released for research use together with the paper.

4   Methods

In this section we will first recap the mechanism behind current contrastive, multi-modal representation learning methods that rely on clean data. We will then introduce our Context Adapter Module that allows learning from the auxiliary modality through an attention mechanism. Finally, we will describe how we can extend an existing backbone for images to videos and audio, to be able to leverage large, pretrained models.

4.1   Background

In multi-modal representation learning we are given a dataset $\mathcal{X}$ of N samples $x_i \in \mathcal{X}, i \in \{1, \ldots N\}$ that individually consists of different signals. Most previous work focuses on two modalities and we will—for now—also adhere to this standard to simplify the notation. This means that each input sample $x_i = (v_i, t_i)$ is a pair of—in our case—a visual input $v_i \in \mathcal{V}$ and its associated text, often the title, $t_i \in \mathcal{T}, 1 \leq i \leq N$.

The goal is now to learn mappings $f_v : \mathcal{V} \mapsto \mathcal{Y}, f_v(v_i) = \phi_{v,i}$ and $f_t : \mathcal{T} \mapsto \mathcal{Y}, f_t(t_i) = \phi_{t,i}$ from each of the modalities to a d-dimensional, joint embedding space $\mathcal{Y} = \mathbb{R}^d$. Recent methods, such as [45], learn the mapping (in their case from images and their captions) to the embedding space with a double contrastive loss over a mini-batch $\mathcal{B} \subset \mathcal{X}$ using an affinity matrix A computed between all pairs of samples in the batch:

$$A_{ij} = \left\langle \frac{\phi_{v,i}}{\sqrt{\tau}\|\phi_{v,i}\|}, \frac{\phi_{t,j}}{\sqrt{\tau}\|\phi_{t,j}\|} \right\rangle \tag{1}$$

An entry A_{ij} measures the similarity between the embeddings $\phi_v(v_i)$ and $\phi_t(t_i)$ via cosine similarity that is scaled by a temperature parameter τ. The idea is now to maximize the similarity between the embeddings from the *same* sample, *i.e.* the diagonal of A and minimize all non-diagonal entries. This can be achieved efficiently using a double-contrastive formulation that operates across columns and rows of A,

$$\mathcal{L}(A) = \frac{1}{2} \sum_{i=1}^{|\mathcal{B}|} \frac{A_{ii}}{\log \sum_{j=1}^{|\mathcal{B}|} \exp A_{ij}} + \frac{A_{ii}}{\log \sum_{j=1}^{|\mathcal{B}|} \exp A_{ji}}. \tag{2}$$

This formulation has the neat effect that it accomplishes maximizing the diagonal entries and minimizing all other entries of A in one self-balancing formulation. However, it makes the critical assumption that both modalities are equally informative of each other. In the case of sometimes irrelevant data, or when one modality has much less information content than the other (*e.g.* *"nice video!"*), this assumption does not hold and training with this objective will result in a very volatile learning objective and thus a sub-optimal joint embedding.

In the next section we will introduce our Context Adapter Module that is able to deal with this type of inputs by allowing it to discount information when it is not relevant for the context.

4.2   Context Adapter Module

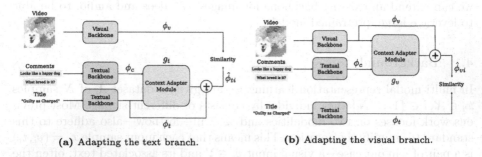

(a) Adapting the text branch.   (b) Adapting the visual branch.

Fig. 2. Method Overview. We introduce a context adapter module that uses inputs of the auxiliary modality to adapt the embedding of another branch. With this module the model is able to accept or discount information.

In order to capture and filter the relevant information from the comments, we propose a transformer-based Context Adapter Module (CAM) which operates in a residual fashion, additively adapting either the visual or text branch of CLIP with contextual information obtained from the comments (see Fig. 2). Formally, we are now adding another modality—the comments—to the input which extends it to $x_i = (v_i, t_i, c_{i,1}, \ldots, c_{i,M})$ with $c_{i,k} \in \mathcal{T}$. To reduce clutter in the notation, we have defined a fixed number of comments M for each sample. Since both title and comments share the same modality (*i.e.* text), we can leverage the same encoder to transform comments to embeddings $f_t(c_{ik}) = \phi_{c,ik}$.

As we expect the comments to be sometimes unrelated, our Context Adapter Module needs a mechanism to discount off-topic comments and update the primary modality $\phi_v(v_i)$ or $\phi_t(t_i)$, steering it in the most informative direction.

We introduce this mechanism as a function of both the primary modality and the comment embeddings $\phi_{c,ik}$, as we want to compare the informativeness of all these inputs at a high level. To this end, we design adapter modules g_v and g_t that extract information from the comments in the form of a residual:

$$\hat{\phi}_{oi} = \phi_{oi} + g_o(\phi_{oi}, \phi_{c,i,1}, \ldots, \phi_{c,i,M}), o \in \{v,t\} \tag{3}$$

With the adapted embeddings $\hat{\phi}_{vi}$ and $\hat{\phi}_{ti}$ we recompute the affinity matrix (now $\hat{A}$) (Eq. 1) and use it for the loss $\mathcal{L}(\hat{A})$. This design has several advantages.

On one hand, extracting "only" a residual from the auxiliary inputs c_{ik} means that the model is easily able to ignore them by predicting $g(\cdot) = 0$. On the other hand, this effectively allows us to skip the adapter module when we evaluate without comments, while still learning the joint embedding from richer data.

In practice, we implement g as a small transformer architecture. Rather than operating on tokenised words, this transformer operates on embeddings (ϕ_{vi} and ϕ_{ti}) themselves, taking as input the encoded feature from the branch to be adapted, along with comment features $\phi_{c,ik}$. By treating embeddings as tokens in their own right, we allow the embeddings to attend to each other and learn what combinations of the inputs should be used to update the original feature through the residual connection.

Additionally, to avoid bleeding information between the two modalities through the Context Adapter Module, during training, we only adapt either the video embedding with g_v or the text embedding with g_t. If we would use both adapters simultaneously, there is a trivial solution that minimizes the loss $\mathcal{L}$: when the adapters learn to remove the original embedding through the residual, $e.g.$ $g_o(\phi_{oi}, \{\phi_{c,i,k},\}) = -\phi_{oi} + \phi_{c,i,1}$ both adapted embeddings become the same $\hat{\phi}_{vi} = \hat{\phi}_{ti}$ which trivially maximizes their similarity, thus preventing the model to learn a meaningful modality alignment. To prevent the model from learning a transformation of the embedding space through the residual, we train only one adapter at a time. We also randomly skip the adapter entirely with probability 0.5, which ensures that the un-adapted features are still meaningful in isolation, and the adapter can be bypassed at evaluation time if comments are not available.

4.3   Video

To leverage the capacity of large pre-trained computer vision models, we adopt the architecture by [45] as our backbone models f_v and f_t. While this transformer was trained on a huge volume of image-text data, it cannot be applied directly to videos since it is built for images and has no temporal extent. To take advantage of the temporal information present in video data, we use the Divided Space-Time attention mechanism recently introduced in the TimeSformer architecture [5]. We modify the image transformer architecture by adding patchwise self-attention across 8 frames in time to each of the 12 residual attention blocks, followed in each case by a zero-initialised linear layer. We also add a learned temporal position embedding which is summed to the input and again zero-initialised. The initialisation is transparent, such that when loading pretrained weights trained from images, at initialization time, the modifications do not affect the inference of the model. During training, the model can then gradually activate the additional temporal components to learn from the temporal information of a video. Full details on the architecture are provided in the Appendix.

4.4   Audio

To further compare the effect of the newly proposed comments modality with another common modality besides text, we also conduct experiments using audio. For this we utilize the audio-encoder from GDT [43] that was pretrained on a large video-audio dataset. The audio-encoder works on 2s audio segments converted into a spectrogram, please see the Appendix for further details.

5   Experiments

This section has two main objectives. The first is to show how the additional modality of user comments can be used to improve multi-modal representation learning. Second, the experiments show how our new dataset VTC can be used to learn video, audio, image and text representations.

Implementation details. We use CLIP [45] (ViT-B/32 checkpoint unless otherwise mentioned) as the initialisation for the backbone. Our concrete implementation of the CAM g is a 2-layer transformer, consisting of two residual multihead self-attention blocks. The input consists of $M + 1$ input embeddings (for the M comments and title/video embedding ϕ_{oi}) having 512 dimensions each. Each block performs 8-head self-attention on the inputs, followed by two linear layers with output size 2048 and 512 respectively. LayerNorm normalisation is used, along with GELU activation following the first linear layer. From the $M + 1$ outputs of the transformer, we then normalize, take the mean and renormalize. We use the Adam [24] optimizer with a learning rate of 1×10^{-6} when training the entire model on its own or with the adapter. All implementation and architecture details can be found in the Appendix.

We report the standard Recall@N metrics as a percentage (often abbreviated R@N), giving the proportion of results where the ground truth is ranked in the top N. We show both Text-Video-Retrieval (TVR) and Video-Text-Retrieval (TVR). Unless otherwise mentioned we use 5 comments for evaluation.

5.1   Additional Datasets

LiveBot Dataset. Prior work on building a dataset with videos and comments is LiveBot [39], which consists of 2361 videos and 895,929 comments, obtained from Chinese social network Bilibili. This differs a lot from our setting, since the comments in question are made while the video is being streamed live and associated with certain timecodes, and comments and titles are in Chinese rather than English. Nevertheless, in order to evaluate how well our method works for this sort of data, we use automatic translation to translate the titles and five comments for the 100 videos in the LiveBot test set, which we call LiveBotEN and show in Table 7. Due to duplicate video and missing split metadata in the original LiveBot release, we follow the split used in [60].

KineticsComments. As an additional video dataset with comments, we construct a dataset based on Kinetics-700 [6,23], for which we download the videos along with associated YouTube metadata including title, description and comments. We translate non-English titles and descriptions into English using a commercial translation API. We use the title as the primary text modality, and for auxiliary context we use comments. We construct a test set, consisting of videos from the Kinetics test set for which we have at least 3 comments, giving a set of 6292 videos which we use to evaluate our method in Table 7.

5.2 Evaluating the Context Adapter Module

In this section we evaluate our Context Adapter Module on the above described datasets with comments.

Table 2. Adaption Mechanisms. Comparing different ways in incorporate auxiliary information: adapting the title with 5 comments

Method	TVR R@1	TVR R@10	VTR R@1	VTR R@10
No comments (zero-shot)	11.1	26.0	11.1	25.3
No comments (fine-tuned)	15.5	34.9	14.4	33.4
Averaging (zero-shot)	7.3	22.7	6.9	20.0
Averaging (fine-tuned)	16.6	42.3	18.1	43.3
Ours	**18.4**	**43.2**	**18.6**	**44.0**

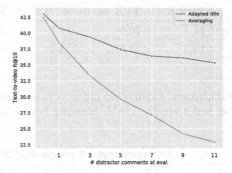

Fig. 3. Influence of Distractor Comments. We gradually add irrelevant distractor comments during evaluation. The context adapter module is able to deal with irrelevant information much better than baseline, showing that it has learned to down-weigh uninformative content

Context Adapter Module. To verify that the Context Adapter Module is indeed able to learn better representations from the comment modality, we compare it to several baselines in Table 2. The most trivial baseline is to ignore any comments and to train simply with image-title pairs. This results in the lowest performance, showing that there is valuable information in the comment data. Another baseline consists of averaging the features from the titles with the features of the comments, which is a direct way to incorporate the comments. We make these baselines stronger by fine-tuning the backbone during training which does result in a performance improvement. Finally, a baseline where all text is concatenated would be interesting to evaluate, however due to memory/text-length limitations concatenating more than 2–3 comments is intractable with current encoder architectures.

Finally, our context adapter module is able to improve over all baselines. We hypothesize that this comes from the ability of the adapter module to ignore irrelevant comments. To test this, we perform an experiment where we add random irrelevant distractor comments (during evaluation only) and measure the impact of distractors on the performance.

The results of this experiment can be seen in Fig. 3, where we gradually increase the number of distractors and evaluate retrieval performance. The averaging baseline is strongly affected by this "misinformation" whereas the context adapter module has implicitly learned to ignore irrelevant information during training. Note that there is no explicit supervision for this during training and the model has to learn this behavior directly form the data. As the backbone is trained also for the averaging baseline, both methods can learn to ignore generally uninformative content ("look what I found") but the context adapter module can learn to exploit the context of the title with relation to the comments through the attention mechanism.

Table 3. Backend Fine-tuning. Effect of fine-tuning the encoders

Method	TVR R@1	TVR R@10	VTR R@1	VTR R@10
No fine-tuning	11.1	26.0	11.1	25.3
Fine-tuning	15.5	34.9	14.4	33.4

Table 4. Encoder Backbones. Comparing different pre-trained encoders. We keep the encoders frozen and just train the CAM. Showing Recall @ 10, retrieving image from text+comments

Backbone	No comments	5 comments	20 comments
FiT [4]	8.8	12.0	12.8
SLIP (ViT-B) [42]	9.3	10.2	11.6
CLIP (ResNet50) [45]	22.7	27.4	27.9
CLIP (ViT-B/32) [45]	25.3	32.3	34.1
CLIP (ViT-L/14) [45]	32.9	42.0	44.1

Comparing Encoders. As in all current multi-modal approaches, the architecture and pre-training of the visual/text/audio encoder is important. In Table 3 we show that fine-tuning the (in this case CLIP [45]) encoder does improve the performance by a significant margin. This shows that even though the encoder was trained on an extremely large image/text dataset, there is a domain gap with VTC (videos and comments) that can be bridged by fine-tuning.

In Table 4 we compare different model types of CLIP [45] with other current models: SLIP [42] and FiT [4]. Naturally, larger architectures perform better, in line with ResNet50 falling behind ViT based encoders for CLIP. Comparing to CLIP, FiT and SLIP have been trained on roughly two orders of magnitude smaller datasets (400M image-text pairs for CLIP) resulting in decreased image and text understand capabilities.

Additionally, we find that adding comments improves the performance of *all* encoders. Adding more comments consistently improves the performance again, however with diminishing returns. We further investigate this behavior in Fig. 4, where we vary the number of comments during training and evaluation time. All models benefit from using comments compared to not using comments. Interestingly, training with one comment seems to be insufficient to learn how to extract additional information when there is more than one available.

Different Modalities. The intuition behind the context adapter module is that it allows to adapt information in a feature with potentially unreliable auxiliary data. As described earlier, the comments can be used to either adapt the information in the image or in the title. In Table 5 we compare these two options and find that adapting the image results in a larger performance improvement than

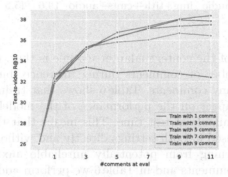

Fig. 4. Varying Number of Comments. We show the influence of varying the number of comments during training and testing time. All variants benefit from using comments. Training with a single comment is not enough to learn a stable filtering behavior

Table 5. Adaption Modality. Comparing different ways to incorporate auxiliary information: adapting the title or image with comments

Method	TVR R@1	TVR R@10	VTR R@1	VTR R@10
None	15.5	34.9	14.4	33.4
Title	18.0	43.2	18.7	43.9
Image	28.2	51.2	25.1	49.9

adapting the title. This can be explained by the modality gap between visual and textual information. When adapting the image information with the text from the comments, the context adapter module can learn to close the information gap between text and image much more effectively than when adapting the tile with the text from the comments. However, we find that in the context of retrieval and multi-modal representation learning a more realistic (and challenging) scenario is posed when the title is adapted (as for example seen in Fig. 1).

Table 6. Combining Modalities. We show that our method is robust to different combinations of modalities, both at train and at test time

Training	Inference	Text→ Video		Video→ Text	
		R@1	R@10	R@1	R@10
CLIP	img+title	11.1	26.0	11.1	25.3
img+title	img+title	15.5	34.9	14.4	33.4
img+title+cmts	img+title	15.5	34.5	14.4	33.3
img+title+cmts	img+title+cmts	18.0	43.2	18.7	43.9
img+title+cmts+audio	img+title	15.4	34.0	14.3	32.9
img+title+cmts+audio	img+title+audio	15.8	36.9	12.2	30.4
img+title+cmts+audio	img+title+cmts+audio	19.6	45.6	20.6	47.2

Another benefit of the context adapter module is that, not only can it deal with a variable number of comments during inference, but it also allows for evaluation without any comments. Table 6 shows that training with comments does not have an impact on the performance of the model in a setting where no comments are available at test time. This means that the learned model is flexible and can be used in both settings directly and without any changes.

The idea of learning from potentially unreliable auxiliary data extends beyond the use of comments and in Table 6 we perform additional experiments using the audio information in the videos. In many current video datasets the quality of the audio varies drastically. For example, some videos replace the natural audio with music, removing any aural clues about the content of the video. Similar to comments, including audio in the context adapter module during training allows the model to identify irrelevant audio information. This results in a virtually unchanged performance when no audio is available during test time, but further improves the final performance when considering all four modalities.

Video Data. In this section we evaluate the impact of using videos instead of single frames in combination with also adding comments. For video evaluation we take the 8 initial frames with a stride of 16. In Table 7 we find that on all datasets adding comments boosts the retrieval performance for both video-to-text (VTR) and text-to-video (TVR) significantly, confirming the value of the modality. It is important to note, that all models were trained only on VTC and the improvements translate directly to KineticsComments and LiveBotEN. In most cases, the improvement gained from adding comments is considerably larger than the information gained by incorporating temporal information. This is an additional data point for the importance of the comment modality. While VTC test set does not benefit largely from video training itself, using videos during training still improves the performance on the other datasets.

Table 7. Video results. Experiments using video frames. Trained adapting the video branch with comments, with either one or eight frames from the video. Showing Recall@10

		VTC		KineticsComms		LiveBotEN	
Inference	#frames	VTR	TVR	VTR	TVR	VTR	TVR
Video	1	28.9	28.3	48.8	46.9	48.0	49.0
Video+comments	1	40.8	41.0	61.1	59.2	64.0	64.0
Mean-pooling	8	19.3	24.2	54.1	49.8	69.0	66.0
Video	8	28.9	27.6	56.9	55.8	70.0	72.0
Video+comments	8	41.5	41.9	68.0	66.1	69.0	80.0

Privacy. Finally, we perform an experiment on the effect of removing all videos from the dataset that contain a face. Table 8 shows that even though this reduces the size of the training set, the performance is not negatively affected. The evaluation is performed on the same test set. We can even see a small increase in performance, that could potentially be attributed to a more balanced training set, as videos of humans tend to dominate the dataset before the face removal.

Table 8. Privacy – Removing Faces. Effect of removing all videos that contain a face from the dataset. The evaluation is performed on the same test set (that contains faces). The difference in performance is marginal

Method	TVR R@1	TVR R@10	VTR R@1	VTR R@10
With faces	18.0	43.2	18.7	43.9
Without faces	18.2	44.0	18.1	45.0

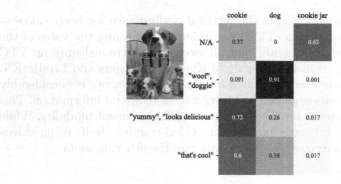

Fig. 5. Failure Case. A heatmap showing the similarities between the image adapted with different comments (rows), and captions (columns). The adapter can steer away the embedding from the right association "cookie jar" depending on the comment input. This means that adversarial comments could affect the performance of the model

6   Discussion and Conclusions

Limitations. We find that the context adapter can be led to override the information in a title if we adversarially craft comments that all point to different content. Qualitative examples of this can be seen in Fig. 5. The model without comments, correctly associates the image with a cookie (jar), however when adding a comment about a "dog" the model prefers the dog label over cookie.

Conclusion. We have presented VTC, a new dataset with videos, titles, and comments and a context adapter module, which is able to extract information from auxiliary input sources for learning a joint, multi-modal embedding. The dataset fills a gap in current vision-text datasets as it includes comments that potentially provide additional information about the content. In our experiments, we are able to show that learning from comments improves video-text retrieval when adapting the representation with user comments. Moreover, the context adapter module is able to identify whether an auxiliary input is relevant to the content in the other modalities or not. This mechanism could, for example, be used to filter datasets for meaningful auxiliary content.

Acknowledgement. This project is supported by Innovate UK (project 71653) on behalf of UK Research and Innovation (UKRI). Y.M.A. and C.R. were also supported by an AWS Machine Learning Research Award (MLRA). We also thank Sasha Haco from Unitary for her support for this project.

References

1. Alwassel, H., Korbar, B., Mahajan, D., Torresani, L., Ghanem, B., Tran, D.: Self-supervised learning by cross-modal audio-video clustering. In: NeurIPS (2020)
2. Asano, Y.M., Patrick, M., Rupprecht, C., Vedaldi, A.: Labelling unlabelled videos from scratch with multi-modal self-supervision. In: NeurIPS (2020)

3. Asano, Y.M., Rupprecht, C., Zisserman, A., Vedaldi, A.: Pass: an imagenet replacement for self-supervised pretraining without humans. In: Thirty-fifth Conference on Neural Information Processing Systems Datasets and Benchmarks Track (Round 1) (2021)
4. Bain, M., Nagrani, A., Varol, G., Zisserman, A.: Frozen in time: a joint video and image encoder for end-to-end retrieval. arXiv preprint arXiv:2104.00650 (2021)
5. Bertasius, G., Wang, H., Torresani, L.: Is space-time attention all you need for video understanding? arXiv preprint arXiv:2102.05095 (2021)
6. Carreira, J., Noland, E., Hillier, C., Zisserman, A.: A short note on the kinetics-700 human action dataset. arXiv preprint arXiv:1907.06987 (2019)
7. Carreira, J., Zisserman, A.: Quo vadis, action recognition? a new model and the kinetics dataset. In: Proceedings of the IEEE Conference on Computer Vision and Pattern Recognition, pp. 6299–6308 (2017)
8. Chen, H., Xie, W., Vedaldi, A., Zisserman, A.: VGGsound: a large-scale audio-visual dataset. In: ICASSP 2020–2020 IEEE International Conference on Acoustics, Speech and Signal Processing (ICASSP), pp. 721–725. IEEE (2020)
9. Chen, M., Radford, A., Child, R., Wu, J., Jun, H.: Generative pretraining from pixels. In: ICML (2020)
10. Chen, Y.C., et al.: Uniter: learning universal image-text representations. arXiv preprint arXiv:1909.11740 (2019)
11. Clark, K., Luong, M.T., Le, Q.V., Manning, C.D.: ELECTRA: pre-training text encoders as discriminators rather than generators. In: ICLR (2020)
12. Desai, K., Johnson, J.: Virtex: learning visual representations from textual annotations. arXiv preprint arXiv:2006.06666 (2020)
13. Desai, K., Kaul, G., Aysola, Z., Johnson, J.: Redcaps: Web-curated image-text data created by the people, for the people. arXiv preprint arXiv:2111.11431 (2021)
14. Devlin, J., Chang, M.W., Lee, K., Toutanova, K.: Bert: pre-training of deep bidirectional transformers for language understanding. In: ACL (2019)
15. Fang, H., Xiong, P., Xu, L., Chen, Y.: Clip2video: mastering video-text retrieval via image clip. arXiv preprint arXiv:2106.11097 (2021)
16. Gebru, T., et al.: Datasheets for datasets. Commun. ACM **64**(12), 86–92 (2021)
17. Halevy, A., et al.: Preserving integrity in online social networks. arXiv preprint arXiv:2009.10311 (2020)
18. Hanu, L., Unitary team: detoxify. Github. https://github.com/unitaryai/detoxify (2020)
19. He, K., Zhang, X., Ren, S., Sun, J.: Deep residual learning for image recognition. In: Proceedings of the IEEE Conference on Computer Vision and Pattern Recognition, pp. 770–778 (2016)
20. Hendricks, L.A., Wang, O., Shechtman, E., Sivic, J., Darrell, T., Russell, B.: Localizing moments in video with temporal language. In: Empirical Methods in Natural Language Processing (EMNLP) (2018)
21. Huang, P.Y., Patrick, M., Hu, J., Neubig, G., Metze, F., Hauptmann, A.: Multilingual multimodal pre-training for zero-shot cross-lingual transfer of vision-language models. In: Meeting of the North American Chapter of the Association for Computational Linguistics (NAACL) (2021)
22. Johnson, J., Douze, M., Jégou, H.: Billion-scale similarity search with GPUS. arXiv preprint arXiv:1702.08734 (2017)
23. Kay, W., et al.: The kinetics human action video dataset. arXiv preprint arXiv:1705.06950 (2017)
24. Kingma, D.P., Ba, J.: Adam: a method for stochastic optimization. In: ICLR (2015)

25. Krishna, R., Hata, K., Ren, F., Fei-Fei, L., Carlos Niebles, J.: Dense-captioning events in videos. In: CVPR (2017)
26. Kuznetsova, A., et al.: The open images dataset v4. Int. J. Comput. Vis. **128**(7), 1956–1981 (2020)
27. Lei, C., et al.: Understanding chinese video and language via contrastive multi-modal pre-training. In: Proceedings of the 29th ACM International Conference on Multimedia, pp. 2567–2576 (2021)
28. Lei, J., et al.: Less is more: ClipBERT for video-and-language learning via sparse sampling. CVPR (2021)
29. Lewis, M., Ghazvininejad, M., Ghosh, G., Aghajanyan, A., Wang, S., Zettlemoyer, L.: Pre-training via paraphrasing. arXiv preprint arXiv:2006.15020 (2020)
30. Lewis, M., et al.: Bart: denoising sequence-to-sequence pre-training for natural language generation, translation, and comprehension. In: ACL (2020)
31. Li, G., Duan, N., Fang, Y., Gong, M., Jiang, D., Zhou, M.: Unicoder-vl: a universal encoder for vision and language by cross-modal pre-training. In: AAAI (2020)
32. Li, J., Li, D., Xiong, C., Hoi, S.: Blip: bootstrapping language-image pre-training for unified vision-language understanding and generation (2022)
33. Li, L., Chen, Y.C., Cheng, Y., Gan, Z., Yu, L., Liu, J.: Hero: Hierarchical encoder for video+ language omni-representation pre-training. EMNLP (2020)
34. Li, L.H., Yatskar, M., Yin, D., Hsieh, C.J., Chang, K.W.: Visualbert: a simple and performant baseline for vision and language. arXiv preprint arXiv:1908.03557 (2019)
35. Lin, T.-Y., et al.: Microsoft COCO: common objects in context. In: Fleet, D., Pajdla, T., Schiele, B., Tuytelaars, T. (eds.) ECCV 2014. LNCS, vol. 8693, pp. 740–755. Springer, Cham (2014). https://doi.org/10.1007/978-3-319-10602-1_48
36. Lu, J., Batra, D., Parikh, D., Lee, S.: Vilbert: pretraining task-agnostic visiolinguistic representations for vision-and-language tasks. In: NeurIps (2019)
37. Luo, H., et al.: UniVL: a unified video and language pre-training model for multi-modal understanding and generation. arXiv preprint arXiv:2002.06353 (2020)
38. Luo, H., et al.: Clip4clip: an empirical study of clip for end to end video clip retrieval. arXiv preprint arXiv:2104.08860 (2021)
39. Ma, S., Cui, L., Dai, D., Wei, F., Sun, X.: Livebot: generating live video comments based on visual and textual contexts. In: AAAI 2019 (2019)
40. Miech, A., Zhukov, D., Alayrac, J.B., Tapaswi, M., Laptev, I., Sivic, J.: Howto100m: learning a text-video embedding by watching hundred million narrated video clips. In: ICCV (2019)
41. Morgado, P., Vasconcelos, N., Misra, I.: Audio-visual instance discrimination with cross-modal agreement. arXiv preprint arXiv:2004.12943 (2020)
42. Mu, N., Kirillov, A., Wagner, D., Xie, S.: Slip: Self-supervision meets language-image pre-training. arXiv preprint arXiv:2112.12750 (2021)
43. Patrick, M., et al.: Multi-modal self-supervision from generalized data transformations (2021)
44. Patrick, M., et al.: Support-set bottlenecks for video-text representation learning. arXiv preprint arXiv:2010.02824 (2020)
45. Radford, A., et al.: Learning transferable visual models from natural language supervision. arXiv preprint arXiv:2103.00020 (2021)
46. Radford, A., Wu, J., Child, R., Luan, D., Amodei, D., Sutskever, I.: Language models are unsupervised multitask learners. OpenAI Blog **1**(8), 9 (2019)
47. Raffel, C., et al.: Exploring the limits of transfer learning with a unified text-to-text transformer. arXiv preprint arXiv:1910.10683 (2019)

48. Rebuffi, S.A., Bilen, H., Vedaldi, A.: Learning multiple visual domains with residual adapters. In: NeurIPS (2017)
49. Rohrbach, A., et al.: Movie description. Int. J. Comput. Vis. **123** (2017)
50. Ruan, L., Jin, Q.: Survey: transformer based video-language pre-training. AI Open (2022)
51. Sariyildiz, M.B., Perez, J., Larlus, D.: Learning visual representations with caption annotations. In: ECCV. pp. 153–170, Springer (2020)
52. Sharma, P., Ding, N., Goodman, S., Soricut, R.: Conceptual captions: a cleaned, hypernymed, image alt-text dataset for automatic image captioning. In: Proceedings of the 56th Annual Meeting of the Association for Computational Linguistics (Volume 1: Long Papers), pp. 2556–2565 (2018)
53. Su, W., et al.: VL-BERT: pre-training of generic visual-linguistic representations. arXiv preprint arXiv:1908.08530 (2019)
54. Sun, C., Baradel, F., Murphy, K., Schmid, C.: Learning video representations using contrastive bidirectional transformer. arXiv preprint arXiv:1906.05743 (2019)
55. Sun, C., Myers, A., Vondrick, C., Murphy, K., Schmid, C.: Videobert: a joint model for video and language representation learning. In: ICCV (2019)
56. Tan, H., Bansal, M.: Lxmert: learning cross-modality encoder representations from transformers. In: EMNLP (2019)
57. Thomee, B., et al.: Yfcc100m: the new data in multimedia research. Commun. ACM **59**(2), 64–73 (2016)
58. Vaswani, A., et al.: Attention is all you need. In: NeurIPS (2017)
59. Venugopalan, S., Rohrbach, M., Donahue, J., Mooney, R., Darrell, T., Saenko, K.: Sequence to sequence - video to text. In: Proceedings of the IEEE International Conference on Computer Vision (ICCV) (2015)
60. Wu, H., Jones, G.J., Pitie, F.: Response to livebot: generating live video comments based on visual and textual contexts. arXiv preprint arXiv:2006.03022 (2020)
61. Xu, J., Mei, T., Yao, T., Rui, Y.: MSR-VTT: a large video description dataset for bridging video and language. In: CVPR (2016)
62. Yao, L., et al.: FILIP: fine-grained interactive language-image pre-training. In: International Conference on Learning Representations (2022)
63. l Zhu, L., Yang, Y.: Actbert: learning global-local video-text representations. In: CVPR (2020)

FashionViL: Fashion-Focused Vision-and-Language Representation Learning

Xiao Han[1,2](✉), Licheng Yu[3], Xiatian Zhu[1,4], Li Zhang[5], Yi-Zhe Song[1,2], and Tao Xiang[1,2]

[1] Centre for Vision, Speech and Signal Processing (CVSSP), University of Surrey, Guildford, England
{xiao.han,xiatian.zhu,y.song,t.xiang}@surrey.ac.uk
[2] iFlyTek-Surrey Joint Research Centre on Artificial Intelligence, Guildford, Surrey, England
[3] Meta AI, 1 Hacker Way, Menlo Park, CA 94025, USA
lichengyu@fb.com
[4] Surrey Institute for People-Centred Artificial Intelligence, University of Surrey, Guildford, England
[5] School of Data Science, Fudan University, Shanghai, China
lizhangfd@fudan.edu.cn

Abstract. Large-scale Vision-and-Language (V+L) pre-training for representation learning has proven to be effective in boosting various downstream V+L tasks. However, when it comes to the fashion domain, existing V+L methods are inadequate as they overlook the unique characteristics of both fashion V+L data and downstream tasks. In this work, we propose a novel *fashion-focused* V+L representation learning framework, dubbed as **FashionViL**. It contains two novel fashion-specific pre-training tasks designed particularly to exploit two intrinsic attributes with fashion V+L data. First, in contrast to other domains where a V+L datum contains only a single image-text pair, there could be multiple images in the fashion domain. We thus propose a Multi-View Contrastive Learning task for pulling closer the visual representation of one image to the compositional multimodal representation of another image+text. Second, fashion text (*e.g.*, product description) often contains rich fine-grained concepts (attributes/noun phrases). To capitalize this, a Pseudo-Attributes Classification task is introduced to encourage the learned unimodal (visual/textual) representations of the same concept to be adjacent. Further, fashion V+L tasks uniquely include ones that do not conform to the common one-stream or two-stream architectures (*e.g.*, text-guided image retrieval). We thus propose a flexible, versatile V+L model architecture consisting of a modality-agnostic Transformer so that it can be flexibly adapted to any downstream tasks. Extensive experiments show that our FashionViL achieves new state of the art

Supplementary Information The online version contains supplementary material available at https://doi.org/10.1007/978-3-031-19833-5_37.

S. Avidan et al. (Eds.): ECCV 2022, LNCS 13695, pp. 634–651, 2022.
https://doi.org/10.1007/978-3-031-19833-5_37

across five downstream tasks. Code is available at https://github.com/ BrandonHanx/mmf.

Keywords: Vision and Language · Representation learning · Fashion

1   Introduction

Recently, Vision-and-Language (V+L) pre-training has received increasing attention [8,29,31,32,35,41,48,53,55,64]. The objective is to learn multimodal representations from large-scale image-text pairs, in order to improve various downstream unimodal or multimodal tasks. These models have proven to be highly effective thanks to two main factors: (*i*) There are a plenty of image-text pairs on the Web providing abundant training data for free (no additional annotation required), and (*ii*) Transformer-based model architectures have been widely used to learn the contextualized representation of multimodal inputs.

Title: Strappy floral tiered maxi dress

Style: Ivory sunrise

Description: Sun baked flower fall around the tiered skirt of a romantic maxi dress fashioned with ruffled trim at the neckline and an adjustable tie belt at the waist.

Caption: A man is standing in front of a brick storefront wearing a black jacket.

Fig. 1. Examples from (*left*) fashion dataset FACAD [68] and (*right*) Flickr30k [46]. Often, fashion data present multiple images in different angles, associated with structured titles and descriptions with multiple fine-grained attributes (highlighted in color)

In this work, we consider the fashion domain with focus on V+L model pre-training. This is inspired by the following reasons. *First*, fashion V+L data are not just copious in volume but also high in quality. This is because online fashion shopping is increasingly ubiquitous. On an e-commerce website, each product detail page (PDP) contains product images and text, both are of very high quality (*i.e.*, often generated by domain experts). *Second*, driven by such strong commercial forces, a larger number of downstream tasks are naturally resulted in real-world applications, ranging from multimodal product understanding [36,42], cross-modal retrieval [18], to text-guided image retrieval [65]. When applied to the fashion domain, however, we observe that existing V+L pre-training methods [18,77] are less effective compared to other domains (see Sect. 4). We believe that this is because they are not designed to exploit unique characteristics of both fashion V+L data and downstream tasks.

In particular, in most existing generic domain V+L datasets (*e.g.*, COCO [37] and Flickr30k [46]), each datum is a single image-text pair with brief text (*e.g.*, an image caption as shown in Fig. 1). In contrast, fashion datasets are collected mostly from PDPs on e-commerce sites with two specialties: (*i*) There are typically more than one images associated with a given text, as shown in Fig. 1. The garment "maxi dress" is presented from three different views for offering online shoppers with rich product information. (*ii*) There are many more fine-grained concepts in the text description due to the product description nature. As shown in Fig. 1, the fashion text is more focused on the garment itself with very detailed adjectives and nouns, describing its appearance in the title, style, and description. In a statistical perspective, we calculate the ratio on four combined fashion datasets [22,50,58,68] and two combined generic datasets [37,46]. It is found that 82% of the words in the fashion captions are adjectives or nouns, *versus* only 59% with the generic captions. None of the existing V+L models are capable of exploiting these specialties of fashion data.

Fashion downstream tasks are also more diverse, posing a challenge to the V+L pre-training model architecture design. Specifically, in the generic V+L domain, existing models are of single-stream or two-stream, depending on the intended downstream tasks. For example, operating on concatenated image and text tokens, a single-stream model [8,27,29,32,53] is suitable for multimodal fusion tasks such as VQA [2], VCR [71] and RefCOCO [70]. Instead, a two-stream model [28,41,48,54,55] is typically designed for efficient cross-modal retrieval tasks[1]. In the fashion domain, apart from image-text fusion and cross-modal retrieval, we also need to tackle other downstream tasks for which neither single-stream nor two-stream architectures are suitable. For instance, the text-guided image retrieval task [21,60,65] not only requires a strong fusion of a reference image and a modifying text, but also an efficient matching between the fused multimodal representation and any candidate image. Given such diverse downstream tasks in fashion, the existing one-stream and two-stream methods are limited in both flexibility and versatility.

To overcome the aforementioned limitations of existing methods, we introduce a novel fashion-focused V+L representation learning framework termed **FashionViL**. Two fashion-focused pre-training tasks are proposed to fully exploit the specialties of fashion data. *(I) Multi-View Contrastive Learning (MVC)*: Given a fashion datum with multiple images/views and one text description, we require that each individual modality (unimodal or multimodal representation) should be semantically discriminative *w.r.t* the same product. To that end, other than the common image-text matching, we further minimize the distance between (*i*) the multimodal representation of one view and text and (*ii*) the other views. *(II) Pseudo-Attributes Classification (PAC)* is designed to exploit the rich fine-grained fashion concepts in the description: We first extract those common attributes/noun phrases from the fashion datasets and construct a pseudo attribute set. The model then learns to predict those attributes explicitly during pre-training. Our intuition is that, the fashion items with the same attribute(s) should be clustered together, *i.e.*, semantically discriminating in

---

[1] A single-stream model can also be applied at a cost of traversing *every query-gallery pair*, resulting in unacceptable retrieval speed in large-scale applications.

the attribute space. As shown in Sect. 4.3, MVC and PAC both are effective and complementary to conventional V+L pre-training tasks such as Image-Text Contrastive Learning (ITC) and Masked Language modeling (MLM).

Moreover, we formulate a flexible and versatile model architecture capable of adapting a pre-trained model easily to a diverse set of downstream tasks. Specifically, our model consists of an image encoder and a modality-agnostic Transformer module, which can be used as either a text encoder or a multimodal fusion encoder. This supports fine-tuning for different downstream modes as: (i) Early-fusion single-stream mode for multimodal joint representation learning, e.g., multimodal classification; (ii) Late-fusion two-stream mode for unimodal representation learning, e.g., cross-modal retrieval; (iii) Early-fusion two-stream mode for multimodal compositional representation learning, e.g., text-guided image retrieval. As a result, our design fuses synergistically the strength of single-stream model in modality fusion and two-stream model in scalability. Crucially, it also caters for fashion-unique tasks, e.g., text-guided image retrieval and outfit complementary item retrieval.

Our **contributions** are summarized as follows: (1) A novel fashion-focused V+L pre-training framework is proposed to exploit the specialties of fashion data through two new V+L pre-training tasks. (2) A versatile and flexible architecture consisting of a modality-agnostic Transformer is introduced to accommodate a set of diverse downstream tasks in the fashion domain. (3) For extensive evaluation, we consider *five* fashion V+L tasks together: image-to-text retrieval, text-to-image retrieval [50], text-guided image retrieval [65], (sub)category recognition [50] and outfit complementary item retrieval [58]. Our experiments show that FashionViL achieves new state of the art with a consistent and significant performance boost per task. To the best of our knowledge, this is the first work capable of addressing 5 diverse fashion tasks together.

2   Related Work

With the advent of Transformer [59] and its success in NLP [10] and CV [13], there has been great success in applying large-scale V+L pre-training to generic domain [8,31,32,48]. Some recent studies started to focus on e-commerce domains including fashion [11,18,74,76,77]. Existing works differ in two main aspects: architecture design and pre-training tasks.

Model Architecture. All V+L pre-training methods use image and text embedding sequences as input for modeling inter-modal and optionally intra-modal interactions through a CNN or Transformer architecture, and output a contextualized feature sequence [6]. There are many options on architecture designs on different aspects, including singe-stream early fusion [8,32,35,53] vs. two stream late fusion [17,28,41,48,55], or different visual features (e.g., detector-based regions [73] vs. ConvNet patches [27] vs. linear projections [29,67]). In many case, the design is driven by the intended downstream tasks (e.g., VQA requires earlier fusion to enhance joint representation whereas cross-modal retrieval requires later fusion to speed up inference). There are also efforts for alleviating the gap between different architectures through retrieve-and-rerank strategy [19,54] or knowledge distillation [39,63]. Unlike them, inspired by the recent advances in modality-agnostic models [1,33,61,62,69], we introduce a unified architecture that can be easily switched between the single-stream or two-stream mode, so there is no need to modify the architecture for different downstream tasks.

Pre-training Tasks. Various tasks have been proposed for V+L pre-training. Masked Language Modeling (MLM) and Image-Text Matching (ITM) are the direct counterparts of the BERT objectives [10,32]. Masked Image Modeling (MIM) is the extension of MLM on the visual modality, including several variants like masked region classification [41,53] and masked region feature regression [8]. Some other tasks are also proved to be effective, such as predicting object tags [26,35], sequential caption generation [64,75] and image-text contrastive learning [31,34,48]. However, none of these tasks are able to take advantage of the two specialities of fashion data as discussed earlier. We therefore propose two fashion-focused pre-training tasks in this work.

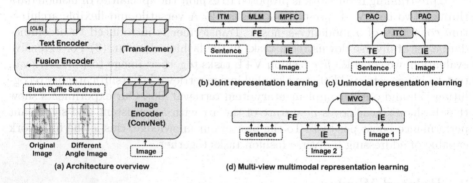

Fig. 2. Overview of the proposed FashionViL model architecture, consisting of an image encoder, a text encoder and a fusion encoder. Text encoder and fusion encoder *share the same parameters*. We adopt six pre-training tasks for richer representation learning

3   Methodology

3.1   Model Overview

The model architecture of FashionViL is illustrated in Fig. 2(a), which is composed of an image encoder (IE) and a Transformer module that can be used for both text encoder (TE) and fusion encoder (FE). Specifically, our image encoder uses ConvNet as its backbone to convert the raw pixels into a sequence of visual embeddings by rasterizing the grid features of the final feature map. For the text encoder, we follow BERT [10] to tokenize the input sentence into WordPieces [66]. Each sub-word token's embedding is obtained by summing up its word embedding and learnable position embedding, followed by Layer Normalization (LN) [3].

One novelty of the model design lies in the shared Transformer for TE and FE, which allows us to flexibly build various multimodal model architectures, each of which is suited for different types of downstream tasks. For example, Fig. 2(b) shows an early-fusion model architecture, where the raw sentence and the computed image embeddings are jointly fed into the multimodal fusion encoder. Note that when we use the Transformer as the fusion encoder, we will further add the modality embeddings to the visual embeddings and word embeddings, helping the model distinguish the modality type. This architecture is exactly the same as the well-known single-stream models in many previous pre-training works [8,18,32]. Then in Fig. 2(c) we show a late-fusion two-stream model architecture, where we apply the shareable Transformer as the text encoder. The outputs from image encoder and text encoder are interacted with a simple dot product to compute the similarity between two modalities. This architecture has been widely adopted for efficient large-scale cross-modal retrieval [19,54]. Furthermore, we can fine-tune this shared Transformer to a more complicated two-stream architecture variant, shown in Fig. 2(d). Here, one stream operates in an early-fusion manner while the other stream is an image encoder. This architecture is needed for some fashion-focused retrieval tasks with multimodal query, $e.g.$, text-guided image retrieval [60,65]. Note that all FE and TE in the above three architectures are actually the same Transformer, and the mere difference lies in its input.

Given an image-text pair, we denote its raw visual inputs as $\mathbf{v}_i = \{\mathbf{v}_i^1, \ldots, \mathbf{v}_i^K\}$, and its input words as $\mathbf{w}_i = \{\mathbf{w}_i^{\text{cls}}, \mathbf{w}_i^1, \ldots, \mathbf{w}_i^T\}$, where the subscript i indicates the i-th pair in the dataset. An additional special [CLS] token is inserted at the beginning of the text sequence, as well as the multimodal sequence when modalities are concatenated. We follow the common pre-training + fine-tuning pipeline when applying the model to downstream tasks.

3.2 Pre-training Tasks

We first introduce two new pre-training tasks. This is followed by the other conventional pre-training tasks adopted in our framework.

Multi-view Contrastive Learning (MVC). As can be seen in Fig. 1, each fashion item is often associated with multiple views to provide a comprehensive overview of the product. To take advantage of the reciprocal information between different views, we propose to build a correlation between (i) the visual representation of the original view $\mathbf{v}$, and (ii) the compositional representation of another view $\mathbf{d}$ and the text $\mathbf{w}$. In cases where there is only one view of the product, we augment another view by randomly cropping or horizontally flipping the given view. As shown in Fig. 2(d), the visual representation of the original view is extracted by the image encoder while the compositional representation is calculated in an early fusion way. Therefore, the similarity between the multimodal input $[\mathbf{w}; \mathbf{d}]^2$ and $\mathbf{v}$ can be computed as:

---

[2] We randomly dropout some words in $\mathbf{w}$ and patches in $\mathbf{d}$ with the probability of 15% to make the learning process more robust.

$$s\left(\left[\mathbf{w}_i; \mathbf{d}_i\right], \mathbf{v}_j\right) = g_\theta\left(\mathbf{d}_i^{\mathrm{avg}}|\mathbf{w}_i\right)^T g_\theta\left(\mathbf{v}_j^{\mathrm{avg}}\right), \tag{1}$$

where g represents a linear transformation that projects the average pooled features into the normalized low-dimensional latent space. Next, we apply two symmetrical InfoNCE losses [44] to pull closer the matched compositional representations and visual representations in the shared latent space:

$$\mathcal{L}_{\mathrm{InfoNCE}}(x, y) = -\mathbb{E}_{(x,y)\sim B} \log \frac{\exp(s(x,y)/\tau)}{\sum_{\hat{y}\in\hat{B}} \exp(s(x,\hat{y})/\tau)}, \tag{2}$$

$$\mathcal{L}_{\mathrm{MVC}} = \frac{1}{2}\left[\mathcal{L}_{\mathrm{InfoNCE}}([\mathbf{w}; \mathbf{d}], \mathbf{v}) + \mathcal{L}_{\mathrm{InfoNCE}}(\mathbf{v}, [\mathbf{w}; \mathbf{d}])\right], \tag{3}$$

where τ is a learnable temperature and $\hat{B}$ contains the positive sample y and $|\hat{B}| - 1$ negative samples drawn from a mini-batch B.

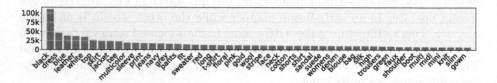

Fig. 3. Histogram of the top-50 pseudo attributes

Pseudo-Attribute Classification (PAC). As mentioned in Sect. 1, we found that there are a large number of fine-grained attributes in the fashion description. We propose to mine the pseudo-attribute concepts from all the available textual information, including title, description and meta-info. Specifically, we extract all nouns and adjectives via NLTK tagger [5] and only keep those that appear more than 100 times, resulting in a list of 2,232 attributes. We show the histogram of the top-50 pseudo attributes in Fig. 3. It is observed that all of them are truly highly-related to the fashion domain.

Then we explore how to utilize such mined concepts. We aim to let our model learn to explicitly recognize those pseudo attributes during the pre-training stage. We model this task as a multi-label classification problem, called Pseudo-Attribute Classification (PAC). As shown in Fig. 2(c), we apply the PAC to both visual and textual modalities so that both encoders can learn to capture the fine-grained concepts. As this is a weakly-supervised learning setting, we leverage label smoothing to generate the labels [24] considering that the mined labels can be noisy. We use A to denote the whole 2,232 pseudo-attribute set and a as the smoothed soft-target for each class. For example, if one sample has two ground truth labels at position 0 and 1, then $a_0 = a_1 = 0.5$ while $a_i = 0$ $(i \neq 0, 1)$. Our objective is as follows:

$$\mathcal{L}_{\mathrm{PAC}} = -\mathbb{E}_{(\mathbf{w},\mathbf{v})\sim D}\mathbb{E}_{a\sim A}\left[a \log P_\theta\left(a|\mathbf{w}\right) + a \log P_\theta\left(a|\mathbf{v}\right)\right], \tag{4}$$

where θ is the learnable parameters and each pair $(\mathbf{w}, \mathbf{v})$ is sampled from the whole training set D.

Masked Patch Feature Classification (MPFC). While the naive masked feature regression has been shown not helpful in V+L pre-training [14,29], we found empirically our version of masked patch modeling being effective in the fashion domain. Specifically, we disregard the feature reconstruction of each masked patch, but instead predict the patch label given by an offline image tokenizer. To this end, we first train a discrete VAE [15,49,57] as the image tokenizer on our collected fashion images with the perceputal loss [12]. We also adopt exponential moving average (EMA) to update the codebook, which is proved to be useful for increasing the utilization of codewords [12,57]. We randomly replace 25% patch features with zeros through block-wise masking strategy [4][3]. Since now we have discrete labels for each patch, the model can be trained to predict the label of each masked patches $\mathbf{v_m}$ given the remaining patches $\mathbf{v_{\backslash m}}$ by optimizing:

$$\mathcal{L}_{\text{MPFC}} = -\mathbb{E}_{(\mathbf{w},\mathbf{v}) \sim D} \log P_\theta \left(\mathbf{v}_\mathbf{m}^\mathbf{t} | \mathbf{v}_{\backslash \mathbf{m}}, \mathbf{w} \right), \tag{5}$$

where $\mathbf{v}_\mathbf{m}^\mathbf{t}$ is the estimated target label for the masked patch.

Image-Text Contrastive Learning (ITC). We also use ITC to encourage the two unimodal representations to be close in the latent space. As shown in Fig. 2(c), the similarity of $\mathbf{w}$ and $\mathbf{v}$ is measured by the dot product of their average pooled features after being projected to the latent space with two linear transformations f and g: $s(\mathbf{w}_i, \mathbf{v}_j) = f_\theta \left(\mathbf{w}_i^{\text{avg}} \right)^T g_\theta \left(\mathbf{v}_j^{\text{avg}} \right)$. The ITC loss is:

$$\mathcal{L}_{\text{ITC}} = \frac{1}{2} \left[\mathcal{L}_{\text{InfoNCE}}(\mathbf{w}, \mathbf{v}) + \mathcal{L}_{\text{InfoNCE}}(\mathbf{v}, \mathbf{w}) \right]. \tag{6}$$

Masked Language Modeling (MLM). In MLM, we randomly mask out the input words with a probability of 15%, and replace all subwords belonging to the masked words $\mathbf{w_m}$ with special token [MASK][4]. The goal of MLM is to predict these masked sub-words based on the observation of their surrounding words $\mathbf{w_{\backslash m}}$ and all image patches $\mathbf{v}$, by minimizing the negative log-likelihood:

$$\mathcal{L}_{\text{MLM}} = -\mathbb{E}_{(\mathbf{w},\mathbf{v}) \sim D} \log P_\theta \left(\mathbf{w_m} | \mathbf{w_{\backslash m}}, \mathbf{v} \right). \tag{7}$$

Image-Text Matching (ITM). In ITM, the input is an image-text pair and the target is a binary label $z \in \{0, 1\}$, indicating if each input pair is a match. Following [31], we sample the hard negative pairs from the similarity matrix $s(\mathbf{w}_i, \mathbf{v}_j)$ computed by ITC and then make a mini-batch H containing 50% negative pairs. We extract the hidden output of [CLS] at the last layer to represent the joint representation of both modalities, then feed it into a FC layer to do a two-class classification. We apply cross-entropy loss for ITM:

$$\mathcal{L}_{\text{ITM}} = -\mathbb{E}_{(\mathbf{w},\mathbf{v}) \sim H} \log P_\theta \left(z | \mathbf{w}, \mathbf{v} \right). \tag{8}$$

---

[3] Following UNITER, we use conditional masking for MLM/MPFC, i.e., only masking one modality while keeping the other one intact at each time.

[4] Following BERT and UNITER, we decompose this 15% into 10% random words, 10% unchanged, and 80% [MASK].

4   Experiments

In this section, we introduce our pre-training dataset and 5 practical downstream tasks. We use MMF [52] and PyTorch [45] for the implementation. For the image encoder, we use an off-the-shelf ResNet50 [23] to fairly compare with previous methods, most of which also used ResNet50. For the text encoder and multimodal fusion encoder (using the shared Transformer), we use the BERT-base-uncased [53] as the initialization. We use 4 RTX 3090 GPUs for pre-training. The details of the hyper-parameters are listed in the supplementary file.

Table 1. Statistics of the datasets used for pre-training

Datasets	FashionGen [50]		FACAD [68]		Fashion200k [22]		PolyvoreOutfits [58]		Total	
	#products	#pairs	#products	#pairs	#products	#pairs	#products	#pairs	#products	#pairs
Train	60k	260k	164.5k	847k	77k	172k	72k	72k	373.5k	1.35M
Val	7.5k	32.5k	18k	94k	13k	30k	14.5k	14.5k	53k	171k

4.1   Pre-training Dataset and Downstream Tasks

Pre-training Dataset. Our pre-training dataset consists of 4 public fashion-related datasets, namely, FashionGen [50], FACAD [68], Fashion200K [22] and PolyvoreOutfits [58]. In total, these datasets provide us with 373.5K fashion products for pre-training. Because each product may contain multiple images from different angles, we have about 1.35 million image-text pairs on hand. The detailed statistics are provided in Table 1.

Cross-modal Retrieval. Image-to-Text Retrieval (ITR) is a cross-modal retrieval task. Given an image query, our model finds the most aligned text from a large candidate pool. Previous fashion-domain pre-training works [18,77] use the joint representation over the [CLS] token to predict the matching score, which results in an impractical time complexity due to the exhaustive matching between each query item and all gallery items in the early-fusion model [19,39,54,63,72]. While one of our model architectures can do the same (as Fig. 2b), we opt to use the two-stream late-fusion model in Fig. 2(c) to compute the cosine similarity for a far more efficient retrieval as [28,48]. Text-to-Image Retrieval (TIR) is an inverse problem of ITR, where the query modality and gallery modality are swapped. The architecture for TIR is the same as ITR.

Text-Guided Image Retrieval (TGIR). TGIR is a special type of image retrieval problem, whose query is a multimodal composition [20,21,60,65]. Specifically, given a query image and a modified sentence, the model is required to retrieve another image which has the similar outlook as the query image but with some appearance changes according to the query text. It has many practical applications in fashion, such as retrieving another garment according to a user's reference garment and his/her feedback. To handle the uniqueness of the multimodal query, several interesting fusion approaches have been proposed in the past, such as the gating mechanism [51,60], hierarchical attention [7], and style-content modification [30]. In this work, we follow [40] to simply apply an early fusion model to encode the compositional representation of the query image and modified text, which is shown in Fig. 2(d).

Category/Subcategory Recognition (CR/SCR). The (sub)category is a vital attribute for describing a product. (S)CR requires the model to produce a reliable joint representation. Following previous works [18,77], we directly append a linear layer on top of [CLS] to predict the label for these tasks.

Outfit Complementary Item Retrieval (OCIR). OCIR aims at finding visually compatible item(s) of several given items to complete an outfit. This is a very practical task as people often buy garments that match previously selected or purchased ones. OCIR can be a helpful recommendation feature for online retailers [25,38]. To address this task, we replace the backbone of CSA-Net [38] with the pre-trained image encoder of FashionViL. Note that unlike all multimodal/cross-modal tasks above, only the pre-trained image encoder is used in this downstream task. We leverage this task to evaluate the performance of our image encoder under the proposed multimodal pre-training.

Table 2. Results of cross-modal retrieval on FashionGen [50] with the protocol same as KalcidoBERT [77]. *-e2e*: Without end-to-end training, *i.e.*, the image encoder is fixed. *-pt*: Directly fine-tuning without multimodal pre-training

Mean		VSE++ [16]	ViLBERT [41]	VLBERT [53]	Image-BERT [47]	Fashion-BERT [18]	OSCAR [35]	Kaleido-BERT [77]	Ours *-e2e*	*-pt*	*-pt*
ITR	R@1	4.59	20.97	19.26	22.76	23.96	23.39	27.99	21.13	58.84	**65.54**
	R@5	14.99	40.49	39.90	41.89	46.31	44.67	60.09	46.82	89.46	**91.34**
	R@10	24.10	48.21	46.05	50.77	52.12	52.55	68.37	58.71	95.84	**96.30**
TIR	R@1	4.60	21.12	22.63	24.78	26.75	25.10	33.88	25.83	57.16	**61.88**
	R@5	16.89	37.23	36.48	45.20	46.48	49.14	60.60	51.54	84.34	**87.32**
	R@10	28.99	50.11	48.52	55.90	55.74	56.68	68.59	63.53	91.90	**93.22**
Mean		15.69	36.36	35.47	40.22	41.89	41.92	53.25	44.59	79.59	**82.60**

4.2   Comparative Results

Cross-modal Retrieval. We evaluate the cross-modal retrieval on the FashionGen [50] test split (not included in pre-training), including both ITR and TIR. Table 2 compares the performance of the previous V+L pre-training methods with our FashaionViL. Because previous works [18,77] are designed with a single-stream architecture, they can only be evaluated on a small retrieval set. For example, for TIR, the models are required to pick the best-matched image from only 101 images given a text query[5]. Recall (over 1K retrievals) is reported

---

[5] In the 101 images, 1 is positively paired with the text and the other 100 are randomly paired but sharing the same sub-category as the positive, increasing the difficulty.

as the metric. The same setting is used for ITR. For a fair comparison, we strictly follow the same evaluation protocol, reporting the recall for 1K retrievals[6].

In Table 2, we compare our FashionViL and its two variants with existing methods. In particular, -e2e and -pt denotes our model without end-to-end training (image encoder is fixed) and multimodal pre-training respectively. We have the following observations: (1) Even with the fixed image encoder and without pre-training, FashionViL already achieves comparable results with the existing methods. This suggests that the performance of late fusion can be as effective as early-fusion for such fine-grained cross-modal retrieval. (2) When we unfreeze the image encoder for end-to-end training, we observe that $R@1$ jumps from 21.13 to 58.84, suggesting that end-to-end training is very efficient and redundant pre-processing may be unnecessary. (3) When we further utilize our proposed multimodal pre-training, our model achieves SOTA performance as in the last column of Table 2, whose $R@1$ is more than twice of the previous SOTA.

Note that our model architecture for this task is two-stream. This means that it can be applied to large-scale retrieval, unlike the compared baselines. Therefore, we additionally report the evaluation results on the full test set (of 32K image-text pairs), i.e., each query item is compared with every gallery item in the full test set. The results can be found in Table 3. We encourage the future works to also follow such a full evaluation protocol to measure the performance.

Table 3. Results of cross-modal retrieval on FashionGen [50] with full evaluation

ITR			TIR			Mean
R@1	R@5	R@10	R@1	R@5	R@10	
42.88	71.57	80.55	51.34	75.42	84.75	67.75

Table 4. Results of text-guided image retrieval on FashionIQ [65]

Image encoder		Fixed ResNet 152				ResNet 50					
Fusion module		CIRR-pt	CIRR [40]	Ours-pt	Ours	TIRG [60]	VAL [7]	CoSMo [30]	TIRG [60]	Ours-pt	Ours
Text encoder						GRU [9]	GRU [9]	GRU [9]	BERT [53]		
		(1)	(2)	(3)	(4)	(5)	(6)	(7)	(8)	(9)	(10)
Dress	R@10	14.38	17.45	20.97	**22.66**	23.65	26.28	24.49	27.17	28.46	**33.47**
	R@50	34.66	40.41	42.64	**46.60**	49.93	50.25	51.01	53.25	54.24	**59.94**
Shirt	R@10	13.64	17.53	17.62	**18.74**	21.98	21.69	18.99	22.28	22.33	**25.17**
	R@50	33.56	38.31	41.32	**41.56**	46.61	45.53	43.57	45.58	46.07	**50.39**
Toptee	R@10	16.44	21.64	21.67	**25.29**	27.84	27.43	25.19	27.84	29.02	**34.98**
	R@50	38.34	45.38	46.46	**50.28**	55.07	56.25	54.00	57.11	57.93	**60.79**
Mean		25.17	30.20	31.78	**34.19**	37.51	37.91	36.21	38.87	39.67	**44.12**

---

[6] Because the authors did not release their 1K retrieval set, we report the average recall of 5 experiments with 5 randomly selected 1K retrieval sets.

Text-Guided Image Retrieval. For TGIR, we compare our FashionViL with the previous V+L pre-training methods and the task-specific methods on FashionIQ [65][7]. The results are shown in Table 4. For more comprehensive comparisons, we use two different implementations adopted by previous methods, *i.e.*, training with fixed image encoder [40] or end-to-end training [7,30,60].

We first report the results with the fixed ResNet 152 from Column 1 to Column 4 (C1–C4). CIRR adopts OSCAR [35] as the fusion module and uses the global image features as the input. We find FashionViL consistently outperforms CIRR with a relative 10%–20% gain with or without the multimodal pre-training (C1 *vs.* C3, C2 *vs.* C4). This improvement demonstrates that the patch-level features are superior to the global features for the compositional multimodal fusion. With our proposed pre-training, the performance further improves from 31.78 to 34.19 (C3 *vs.* C4), showing our pre-training also works well on the off-the-shelf fixed image encoder.

We then report the results under the end-to-end training paradigm (C5-C10). We find that simply replacing GRU with BERT (C5 *vs.* C8) already leads to a 4% relative gain (from 23.65 to 27.17), indicating the importance of having a higher-quality text encoder. Additionally, all previous works apply a late interaction between the image embeddings and modified text embeddings with an elaborately designed fusion module, *e.g.*, TIRG [60]. We argue that an earlier fusion of the two modalities should result in an even better compositional embedding for the query purpose. Comparing C9 and C8, our FashionViL without pre-training already outperforms TIRG+BERT, indicating better query multi-

Table 5. Results of category/subcategory recognition on FashionGen [50]

Methods		FashionBERT [18]	ImageBERT [47]	OSCAR [35]	KaleidoBERT [77]	Ours *-pt*	
CR	Acc	91.25	90.77	91.79	95.07	97.07	**97.48**
	Macro$\mathcal{F}$	70.50	69.90	72.70	71.40	84.72	**88.60**
SCR	Acc	85.27	80.11	84.23	88.07	91.45	**92.23**
	Macro$\mathcal{F}$	62.00	57.50	59.10	63.60	78.13	**83.02**
Mean		77.76	74.57	76.96	79.54	87.84	**90.33**

Table 6. Results of outfit complementary item retrieval on PolyvoreOutfits [58]

Methods		Type-aware [58]	SCE-Net [56]	CSA-Net [38]	ADDE-O [25]	CSA-Net *reproduced*	Ours *-pt*	
OCIR	R@10	3.66	4.41	5.93	6.18	2.69	4.38	**5.83**
	R@30	8.26	9.85	12.31	13.79	6.29	10.54	**12.61**
	R@50	11.98	13.87	17.85	18.60	9.14	14.77	17.49
Mean		7.97	9.38	12.03	12.86	6.04	9.90	**11.98**

---

[7] Details for the reproduction of previous methods are in the supplementary file.

modal embeddings are learned in our model. Note that our text encoder and fusion encoder are shared, so FashionViL also saves more training parameters than TIRG+BERT. With the help of pre-training, our FashionViL achieves the new SOTA result with another significant 11.2% relative gain (C9 *vs.* C10).

Category/Subcategory Recognition. Following KaleidoBERT [77], we evaluate CR and SCR on the FashionGen dataset [50]. The joint representation of the model architecture in Fig. 2(b) is used to predict the classification score. The results are shown in Table 5. Once again, the end-to-end learning and the well-designed fashion-specific pre-training tasks help our FashionViL outperform the two previous works by significant margins (10.4% and 3.2%, respectively). Furthermore, we also simulate a new task – multi-image subcategory recognition (M-SCR) to evaluate the performance of FashionViL with multiple input images. See more results in the supplementary file.

Outfit Complementary Item Retrieval. In addition to the aforementioned multimodal and instance-level downstream tasks, we also examine FashionViL on the unimodal outfit-level task, *i.e.*, OCIR. We compare our model with the previous task-specific methods [25,38] on the Disjoint split of Polyvore Outfits [58][8]. As shown in Table 6, our multimodal pre-training benefits the performance with a 21.0% improvement, even when only the image encoder is tuned.

4.3 Ablation Study

We analyze the effectiveness of different pre-training tasks and the sharing TE/FE strategy through ablation studies over the aforementioned five down-

Table 7. Evaluation on pre-training tasks using ITR, TIR, TGIR, SCR and OCIR as downstream tasks. Each number is the mean value of all metrics for one specific downstream task. Meta-sum stands for the summation of all numbers in each row. The three shades of grey represent the top three results when sharing TE and FE

	Pre-training Tasks	ITR	TIR	TGIR	SCR	OCIR	Meta-sum
(0)	None	62.50	68.09	39.67	84.79	9.90	265.04
(1)	MVC (use augmented image only)	62.85	68.58	40.50	84.86	9.53	266.32
(2)	MPFC	62.10	68.12	40.22	86.39	10.05	266.88
(3)	MLM (mask attribute words only)	62.32	67.93	40.46	85.83	10.38	266.92
(4)	MLM	62.15	67.43	40.29	86.72	10.38	266.97
(5)	PAC	63.15	69.30	40.68	86.36	9.58	269.07
(6)	MVC	63.30	68.32	40.94	85.99	10.83	269.38
(7)	ITC	64.63	70.61	43.13	86.25	10.69	275.31
(8)	ITC + MLM + MPFC	64.28	70.02	43.31	87.21	11.12	275.94
(9)	ITC + MLM + MPFC + ITM	64.37	70.44	43.56	87.17	11.08	276.62
(10)	ITC + MLM + MPFC + ITM + MVC	64.88	70.34	43.94	87.12	11.56	277.84
(11)	ITC + MLM + MPFC + ITM + MVC + PAC	65.00	70.63	44.12	87.63	11.98	279.36
(12)	ITC + MLM + MPFC + ITM + MVC + PAC (w/o sharing TE and FE)	64.16	69.15	42.87	86.22	11.31	273.71

---

[8]   We have no access to the data splits of CSA-Net, so constructed the Polyvore Outfits [58] and reproduced CSA-Net by ourselves according to the original paper [25,38].

stream tasks. The complete results are listed in Table 7. In addition to the standard metrics for each benchmark, we use the Meta-sum (sum of all scores across all the benchmarks) as a global metric.

First, we establish a baseline without any multimodal pre-training in Line 0 (L0), *i.e.*, the image/text encoder is initialized with the off-the-shelf ResNet50 or BERT, which is pre-trained in vision-only or language-only domain.

Second, we validate the effectiveness of each pre-training task by their standalone performance, *i.e.*, each time we pick only one task for pre-training. We show the results of MPFC, MLM, PAC, MVC, ITC in L2, L4, L5, L6 and L7. It is clear from Table 7 that all of these pre-training tasks can benefit the downstream tasks. However, we found that a pre-training task tends to be relatively more helpful to downstream tasks of its similar type. For example, both MPFC (L2) and MLM (L4) are focusing on modeling the cross-modal interaction, thus they bring more gain to SCR but contribute relatively less to ITR and TIR. In contrast, since ITC (L7) has the same objective with ITR and TIR, it significantly boosts the cross-modal performance. As for TGIR, it requires not only high-quality compositional representation but also high-quality unimodal representations, thus each of the 5 pre-training tasks have a positive impact.

Third, we validate the effectiveness of the proposed PAC (L5) and MVC (L6). For PAC, we implement a comparative experiment: MLM only on those pre-defined pseudo-attribute words (L3). The main difference between L3 and L5 is whether the multi-label supervision is performed on each masked text token or the global representation. L3 leads to much lower performance than L5, indicating that the supervision of pseudo attributes on the global representation is a better choice. Interestingly, L3 achieves a comparable result to L4, where each word (including those other than the pseudo attributes) can also be masked. This means merely masking the fine-grained words is as effective as masking all the words uniformly, which indicates the most important text cues lie in those fine-grained concept words. We then verify the superiority of MVC. To this end, we add an ablation study that does not utilize multi-angle images (L1), *i.e.*, replacing the sampled different angle image with an augmented version of the original image. Comparing L1 and L6, we confirm that the improvement of MVC mainly comes from the contrastive learning on the images from different angles.

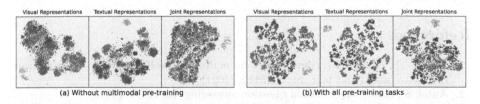

<table>
<tr><td>Visual Representations</td><td>Textual Representations</td><td>Joint Representations</td><td>Visual Representations</td><td>Textual Representations</td><td>Joint Representations</td></tr>
</table>

(a) Without multimodal pre-training   (b) With all pre-training tasks

Fig. 4. T-sne of the learned visual/textual/joint representations from FashionViL

Next, we study the effect of different combinations of those tasks. When we add MLM and MPFC to ITC (L8), we observe a gain on Meta-sum, while the performance of ITR and TIR slightly drops. This is expected as different tasks may provide different update directions for the same parameters, which causes some tasks to overshadow the effects of others. However, minor conflicts between different tasks can be largely alleviated by employing more tasks. As shown in L9, the overall performance can be further boosted by adding ITM. The same happens when we add MVC into them (L10). When all six tasks are jointly trained (L11), we observe a significant performance gain across all benchmarks. Notably, the two new fashion-specific tasks of MVC and PAC play the most important roles to achieve the SOTA performance.

Finally, we demonstrate the superiority of sharing TE and FE. We implement a comparative model (L12) with the same pre-training tasks as L11 but using separate TE and FE. We observe a clear performance drop when breaking the parameter sharing. This indicates our modality-agnostic sharing strategy not only reduces the number of parameters but also performs far better.

4.4   Visualization

We visualize the representations from the image encoder, text encoder, and fusion encoder via t-SNE [43] in Fig. 4. Specifically, we feed all image-text pairs from FashionGen's test split into our model. We visualize the most popular 10 categories using different colors. We compare the t-SNE of the model without multimodal pre-training (initialized with ResNet+BERT) and the model with the full 6 pre-training tasks. We found the clusters become more discriminative when more pre-training tasks are added, indicating that FashionViL learns to acquire more fine-grained concepts. See more in the supplementary file.

5   Conclusions

We have introduced FashionViL, a novel end-to-end large-scale pre-training framework for V+L representation learning in the fashion domain. We proposed two effective fashion-specific pre-training tasks and introduced a novel modality-agnostic text/fusion encoder for a flexible and versatile multimodal architecture. Our FashionViL achieves new SOTA performance with superior efficiency on 5 popular fashion-related tasks.

References

1. Akbari, H., et al.: Vatt: transformers for multimodal self-supervised learning from raw video, audio and text. In: NeurIPS (2021)
2. Antol, S., et al.: VQA: Visual question answering. In: ICCV (2015)
3. Ba, J.L., Kiros, J.R., Hinton, G.E.: Layer normalization. arXiv preprint arXiv:1607.06450 (2016)
4. Bao, H., Dong, L., Piao, S., Wei, F.: Beit: bert pre-training of image transformers. In: ICLR (2022)
5. Bird, S., Klein, E., Loper, E.: Natural language processing with python: analyzing text with the natural language toolkit (2009). https://www.nltk.org

6. Bugliarello, E., Cotterell, R., Okazaki, N., Elliott, D.: Multimodal pretraining unmasked: a meta-analysis and a unified framework of vision-and-language berts. TACL (2021)
7. Chen, Y., Gong, S., Bazzani, L.: Image search with text feedback by visiolinguistic attention learning. In: CVPR (2020)
8. Chen, Y.C., et al.: Uniter: universal image-text representation learning. In: ECCV (2020)
9. Cho, K., et al.: Learning phrase representations using RNN encoder-decoder for statistical machine translation. In: EMNLP (2014)
10. Devlin, J., Chang, M.W., Lee, K., Toutanova, K.: BERT: pre-training of deep bidirectional transformers for language understanding. In: NAACL-HLT (2019)
11. Dong, X., et al.: M5product: a multi-modal pretraining benchmark for e-commercial product downstream tasks. arXiv preprint arXiv:2109.04275 (2021)
12. Dong, X., et al.: Peco: perceptual codebook for bert pre-training of vision transformers. arXiv preprint arXiv:2111.12710 (2021)
13. Dosovitskiy, A., et al.: An image is worth 16 x 16 words: transformers for image recognition at scale. In: ICLR (2020)
14. Dou, Z.Y., et al.: An empirical study of training end-to-end vision-and-language transformers. arXiv preprint arXiv:2111.02387 (2021)
15. Esser, P., Rombach, R., Ommer, B.: Taming transformers for high-resolution image synthesis. In: CVPR (2021)
16. Faghri, F., Fleet, D.J., Kiros, J.R., Fidler, S.: Vse++: improving visual-semantic embeddings with hard negatives. In: BMVC (2018)
17. Fei, N., et al.: Wenlan 2.0: make AI imagine via a multimodal foundation model. arXiv preprint arXiv:2110.14378 (2021)
18. Gao, D., et al.: Fashionbert: text and image matching with adaptive loss for cross-modal retrieval. In: SIGIR (2020)
19. Geigle, G., Pfeiffer, J., Reimers, N., Vulić, I., Gurevych, I.: Retrieve fast, rerank smart: cooperative and joint approaches for improved cross-modal retrieval. arXiv preprint arXiv:2103.11920 (2021)
20. Guo, X., Wu, H., Cheng, Y., Rennie, S., Tesauro, G., Feris, R.S.: Dialog-based interactive image retrieval. In: NeurIPS (2018)
21. Han, X., He, S., Zhang, L., Song, Y.Z., Xiang, T.: UIGR: unified interactive garment retrieval. In: CVPR workshops (2022)
22. Han, X., et al.: Automatic spatially-aware fashion concept discovery. In: ICCV (2017)
23. He, K., Zhang, X., Ren, S., Sun, J.: Deep residual learning for image recognition. In: CVPR (2016)
24. Hoe, J.T., Ng, K.W., Zhang, T., Chan, C.S., Song, Y.Z., Xiang, T.: One loss for all: deep hashing with a single cosine similarity based learning objective. In: NeurIPS (2021)
25. Hou, Y., Vig, E., Donoser, M., Bazzani, L.: Learning attribute-driven disentangled representations for interactive fashion retrieval. In: ICCV (2021)
26. Hu, X., et al.: Vivo: visual vocabulary pre-training for novel object captioning. In: AAAI (2021)
27. Huang, Z., Zeng, Z., Liu, B., Fu, D., Fu, J.: Pixel-bert: aligning image pixels with text by deep multi-modal transformers. arXiv preprint arXiv:2004.00849 (2020)
28. Jia, C., et al.: Scaling up visual and vision-language representation learning with noisy text supervision. In: ICML (2021)
29. Kim, W., Son, B., Kim, I.: VILT: Vision-and-language transformer without convolution or region supervision. In: ICML (2021)

30. Lee, S., Kim, D., Han, B.: Cosmo: Content-style modulation for image retrieval with text feedback. In: CVPR (2021)
31. Li, J., Selvaraju, R., Gotmare, A., Joty, S., Xiong, C., Hoi, S.C.H.: Align before fuse: vision and language representation learning with momentum distillation. In: NeurIPS (2021)
32. Li, L.H., Yatskar, M., Yin, D., Hsieh, C.J., Chang, K.W.: Visualbert: a simple and performant baseline for vision and language. arXiv preprint arXiv:1908.03557 (2019)
33. Li, L.H., You, H., Wang, Z., Zareian, A., Chang, S.F., Chang, K.W.: Unsupervised vision-and-language pre-training without parallel images and captions. In: NAACL-HLT (2021)
34. Li, W., et al.: Unimo: towards unified-modal understanding and generation via cross-modal contrastive learning. In: ACL-IJCNLP (2021)
35. Li, X., et al.: Oscar: object-semantics aligned pre-training for vision-language tasks. In: ECCV (2020)
36. Liao, L., He, X., Zhao, B., Ngo, C.W., Chua, T.S.: Interpretable multimodal retrieval for fashion products. In: ACM MM (2018)
37. Lin, T.Y., et al.: Microsoft coco: common objects in context. In: ECCV (2014)
38. Lin, Y.L., Tran, S., Davis, L.S.: Fashion outfit complementary item retrieval. In: CVPR (2020)
39. Liu, H., Yu, T., Li, P.: Inflate and shrink: enriching and reducing interactions for fast text-image retrieval. In: EMNLP (2021)
40. Liu, Z., Rodriguez-Opazo, C., Teney, D., Gould, S.: Image retrieval on real-life images with pre-trained vision-and-language models. In: ICCV (2021)
41. Lu, J., Batra, D., Parikh, D., Lee, S.: Vilbert: pretraining task-agnostic visiolinguistic representations for vision-and-language tasks. In: NeurIPS (2019)
42. Ma, Y., Jia, J., Zhou, S., Fu, J., Liu, Y., Tong, Z.: Towards better understanding the clothing fashion styles: a multimodal deep learning approach. In: AAAI (2017)
43. Van der Maaten, L., Hinton, G.: Visualizing data using T-SNE. JMLR (2008)
44. Oord, A.V.D., Li, Y., Vinyals, O.: Representation learning with contrastive predictive coding. arXiv preprint arXiv:1807.03748 (2018)
45. Paszke, A., et al.: Pytorch: an imperative style, high-performance deep learning library. In: NeurIPS (2019)
46. Plummer, B.A., Wang, L., Cervantes, C.M., Caicedo, J.C., Hockenmaier, J., Lazebnik, S.: Flickr30k entities: collecting region-to-phrase correspondences for richer image-to-sentence models. In: ICCV (2015)
47. Qi, D., Su, L., Song, J., Cui, E., Bharti, T., Sacheti, A.: Imagebert: cross-modal pre-training with large-scale weak-supervised image-text data. arXiv preprint arXiv:2001.07966 (2020)
48. Radford, A., et al.: Learning transferable visual models from natural language supervision. In: ICML (2021)
49. Ramesh, A., et al.: Zero-shot text-to-image generation. In: ICML (2021)
50. Rostamzadeh, N., et al.: Fashion-gen: the generative fashion dataset and challenge. arXiv preprint arXiv:1806.08317 (2018)
51. Shin, M., Cho, Y., Ko, B., Gu, G.: Rtic: Residual learning for text and image composition using graph convolutional network. arXiv preprint arXiv:2104.03015 (2021)
52. Singh, A., et al.: MMF: a multimodal framework for vision and language research (2020). https://github.com/facebookresearch/mmf
53. Su, W., et al.: VL-BERT: pre-training of generic visual-linguistic representations. In: ICLR (2020)

54. Sun, S., Chen, Y.C., Li, L., Wang, S., Fang, Y., Liu, J.: Lightningdot: pre-training visual-semantic embeddings for real-time image-text retrieval. In: NAACL-HLT (2021)
55. Tan, H., Bansal, M.: LXMERT: learning cross-modality encoder representations from transformers. In: EMNLP-IJCNLP (2019)
56. Tan, R., Vasileva, M.I., Saenko, K., Plummer, B.A.: Learning similarity conditions without explicit supervision. In: ICCV (2019)
57. Van Den Oord, A., Vinyals, O., et al.: Neural discrete representation learning. In: NeurIPS (2017)
58. Vasileva, M.I., Plummer, B.A., Dusad, K., Rajpal, S., Kumar, R., Forsyth, D.: Learning type-aware embeddings for fashion compatibility. In: ECCV (2018)
59. Vaswani, A., et al.: Attention is all you need. In: NeurIPS (2017)
60. Vo, N., Jiang, L., Sun, C., Murphy, K., Li, L.J., Fei-Fei, L., Hays, J.: Composing text and image for image retrieval - an empirical odyssey. In: CVPR (2019)
61. Wang, J., et al.: UFO: a unified transformer for vision-language representation learning. arXiv preprint arXiv:2111.10023 (2021)
62. Wang, W., Bao, H., Dong, L., Wei, F.: VLMO: unified vision-language pre-training with mixture-of-modality-experts. arXiv preprint arXiv:2111.02358 (2021)
63. Wang, Z., Wang, W., Zhu, H., Liu, M., Qin, B., Wei, F.: Distilled dual-encoder model for vision-language understanding. arXiv preprint arXiv:2112.08723 (2021)
64. Wang, Z., Yu, J., Yu, A.W., Dai, Z., Tsvetkov, Y., Cao, Y.: Simvlm: simple visual language model pretraining with weak supervision. In: ICLR (2021)
65. Wu, Het al.: Fashion IQ: a new dataset towards retrieving images by natural language feedback. In: CVPR (2021)
66. Wu, Y., et al.: Google's neural machine translation system: bridging the gap between human and machine translation. arXiv preprint arXiv:1609.08144 (2016)
67. Xu, H., et al.: E2E-VLP: End-to-end vision-language pre-training enhanced by visual learning. In: ACL-IJCNLP (2021)
68. Yang, X., et al.: Fashion captioning: towards generating accurate descriptions with semantic rewards. In: ECCV (2020)
69. You, H., et al.: Ma-clip: towards modality-agnostic contrastive language-image pre-training. OpenReview (2021)
70. Yu, L., Poirson, P., Yang, S., Berg, A.C., Berg, T.L.: Modeling context in referring expressions. In: ECCV (2016)
71. Zellers, R., Bisk, Y., Farhadi, A., Choi, Y.: From recognition to cognition: Visual commonsense reasoning. In: CVPR (2019)
72. Zhang, L., et al.: Vldeformer: learning visual-semantic embeddings by vision-language transformer decomposing. arXiv preprint arXiv:2110.11338 (2021)
73. Zhang, P., et al.: VINVL: revisiting visual representations in vision-language models. In: CVPR (2021)
74. Zhang, Z., et al: UFC-bert: unifying multi-modal controls for conditional image synthesis. In: NeurIPS (2021)
75. Zhou, L., Palangi, H., Zhang, L., Hu, H., Corso, J., Gao, J.: Unified vision-language pre-training for image captioning and VQA. In: AAAI (2020)
76. Zhu, Y., et al.: Knowledge perceived multi-modal pretraining in e-commerce. In: ACM MM (2021)
77. Zhuge, M., et al.: Kaleido-bert: vision-language pre-training on fashion domain. In: CVPR (2021)

Weakly Supervised Grounding for VQA in Vision-Language Transformers

Aisha Urooj Khan[1]([✉]) , Hilde Kuehne[2,3] , Chuang Gan[3] ,
Niels Da Vitoria Lobo[1] , and Mubarak Shah[1]

[1] University of Central Florida, Orlando, FL, USA
aishaurooj@gmail.com
[2] Goethe University Frankfurt, Frankfurt, Hesse, Germany
[3] MIT-IBM Watson AI Lab, Cambridge, MA, USA

Abstract. Transformers for visual-language representation learning have been getting a lot of interest and shown tremendous performance on visual question answering (VQA) and grounding. However, most systems that show good performance of those tasks still rely on pre-trained object detectors during training, which limits their applicability to the object classes available for those detectors. To mitigate this limitation, this paper focuses on the problem of weakly supervised grounding in the context of visual question answering in transformers. Our approach leverages capsules by transforming each visual token into a capsule representation in the visual encoder; it then uses activations from language self-attention layers as a text-guided selection module to mask those capsules before they are forwarded to the next layer. We evaluate our approach on the challenging GQA as well as VQA-HAT dataset for VQA grounding. Our experiments show that: while removing the information of masked objects from standard transformer architectures leads to a significant drop in performance, the integration of capsules significantly improves the grounding ability of such systems and provides new state-of-the-art results compared to other approaches in the field. (Code is available at https://github.com/aurooj/WSG-VQA-VLTransformers)

Keywords: Multimodal understanding · Visual grounding · Visual question answering · Vision and language

1 Introduction

Empowering VQA systems to be explainable is important for a variety of applications such as assisting visually-impaired people to navigate [16,63] or helping radiologists in early diagnosis of fatal diseases [1,64]. A system that only produces a good answering accuracy will not be sufficient in these applications. Instead, VQA

Supplementary Information The online version contains supplementary material available at https://doi.org/10.1007/978-3-031-19833-5_38.

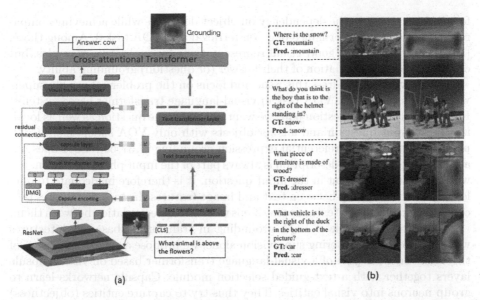

Fig. 1. (a) **Proposed architecture**: Given the question-image pair, grid features are used to obtain visual capsules using a Capsule encoding layer. Output embedding for [CLS] token from text transformer layer is then used to do capsule features selection. Selected capsules encodings with position information is then input to the visual encoder. We use sentence embedding from each textual transformer layer to select capsules for each visual transformer layer. The selected capsules are then input to the next visual transformer layer along with the output of the previous layer in the visual encoder. Finally, a cross-attentional block allows for a fine-grained interaction between both modalities to predict the answer. (b) **Attention from the proposed vision-language transformer with VQA supervision.** We look at the self-attention of the [IMG] token on the heads of the last layer. These maps show that the model automatically learns to ground relevant objects with VQA-only supervision leading to weakly-supervised grounded VQA (GVQA). *blue box: ground truth, orange: predicted box.* (Color figure online)

systems for such uses should ideally also provide an answer verification mechanism and grounding is a convincing way to obtain this direct verification.

On the heels of success in natural language processing and multi-modal understanding, a variety of transformer-based methods have been introduced for joint representation learning of vision and language and respective downstream tasks, including VQA. Such approaches, e.g., [33,39,56] are usually trained based on region masks of detected objects generated by a pre-trained object detector [26]. The assumption that object masks are provided at input time limits detection to pretrained objects only and comes at the risk of image context information being unused.

Detector-free methods avoid this bias toward pre-trained object classes while being simpler and faster because they do not need to extract region-based features from a pre-trained object detector. Other works [10,22,27,48] have therefore focused on removing the dependency on object detectors while achieving comparable if not better performance (e.g., on retrieval and VQA tasks). Among those, [10] and [48] also show good visual representations by qualitative examples, but do not provide an evaluation of their answer (or question) grounding ability.

In this work, we address this issue and focus on the problem of weakly supervised grounding for the VQA task in visual-language transformer based systems. For the input image-question pair, we want to answer the question as well as localize the relevant question and answer objects with only VQA supervision. Compared to detector-free referential expression grounding [7,37,60], VQA does not assume that the region description is always part of the input phrase as the answer word may not be present in the input question. It is therefore inadequate to only learn a direct mapping between text and image features. Instead, it requires processing multiple image-text mapping steps with the correct relation between them.

To address the task of VQA grounding in transformer-based architectures with the question-answering supervision alone, we propose a generic extension of the visual encoder part of a visual-language transformer based on visual capsule layers together with a text-guided selection module. Capsule networks learn to group neurons into visual entities. They thus try to capture entities (objectness) and relationships among them with promising results on various visual detection and segmentation tasks [12,13,30]. To make use of this ability in the context of transformers, we transfer inputs as well as intermediate layers' feature tokens to capsule encodings, from which the most relevant ones will be selected by the textual tokens of a parallel language encoder. This text-guided selection facilitates choosing features at entity-level, similar to attending object features, instead of an independent feature selection. We interleave transformer layers with such masked residual capsule encodings. This extension provides a combination of visual input routing and text-based masking which significantly improves the visual grounding ability of such systems.

We evaluate existing methods as well as the proposed approach on the challenging GQA and VQA-HAT datasets. To this end, we consider the attention output obtained from these methods and evaluate it on various metrics, namely overlap, intersection over union, and pointing game accuracy. Our results on the original architectures show a significant gap between task accuracy and grounding of existing methods indicating that existing vision-language systems are far from learning an actually grounded representation. The proposed method bridges the gap and outperforms the best contenders in terms of overlap, intersection over union, and pointing game accuracy achieving SOTA performance on the GQA dataset. It also achieves best mean-rank correlation score on VQA-HAT [8] dataset among methods which do not use attention supervision.

We summarize the contributions of our architecture as follows: a) we propose a capsule encoding layer to generate capsule-based visual tokens for transformers; b) we propose a text-guided capsule selection with residual connections to guide the visual features at each encoding step; and c) the proposed generic interleaved processing of capsules and self-attention layers can be integrated in various vision language architectures.

2   Related Work

Visual-language Representation Learning. Learning a robust visual-language representation is currently an active area of research [26] with impressive progress on downstream tasks including VQA [6,31,33,34,38,39,42,55,56]. A majority of these methods rely on object detections making the downstream task simpler. Some works have attempted to avoid this dependency on object detections and show comparable performance using spatial features or image patches [21,22,27,32]. Our work falls into the later category and uses grid features as input.

Weakly-Supervised Grounding and VQA. Weakly-supervised visual grounding is well studied for phrase-grounding in images [3,5,7,9,37,57,60]. Some works also focused on phrase grounding in videos [20,54,61]. However, less attention has been paid to grounding in VQA despite having significance for many critical applications. There is much research on making questions visually grounded [44,49,53,58,66,67], but only a handful of works focus on evaluating their grounding abilities [8,24,25,47,51,53]. GQA leverages scene graphs from Visual Genome dataset providing visual grounding labels for question and answer making it feasible to evaluate VQA logic grounding. Recently, xGQA [45] has been introduced as a multilingual version of the GQA benchmark. GQA [24] and [25] discuss the evaluation of VQA systems for grounding ability. VQA-HAT [8] on the other hand, provides human attention maps used for answering the question in a game-inspired attention-annotation setup. A handful of methods [40,47,62] evaluate their systems for correlation between machine-generated attention and human attention maps on VQA-HAT. With the emergence of transformers as the current SOTA, the focus moves towards grounding abilities of those systems for the VQA task. Unfortunately, none of these transformer-based methods have yet focused on the evaluation of weakly supervised grounding. Additionally, the fact that only few real-world datasets provide grounding labels makes this task challenging. We therefore finetune three existing detector-free transformer methods on GQA and evaluate them for the weak grounding task.

Transformers with Capsules. Some research has focused on the idea of combining transformers and capsules [11,15,36,41,43,46,59]. For instance, [59] studies text-summarization, image-processing, and 3D vision tasks; [43,46] uses capsule-transformer architecture for image-classification, and [36] uses capsules-transformers for predicting stock movements. To the best of our knowledge, the combination of capsules with transformers for VQA grounding has not been studied.

3   Proposed Approach

Given an input image-question pair with image I and question Q, we want to localize the relevant question and answer objects with only VQA supervision. We start from a two stream visual-language model (Fig. 1) where the language encoder L_e guides input and intermediate respresentations of the visual encoder

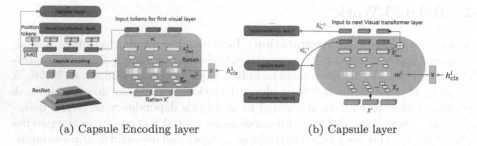

(a) Capsule Encoding layer   (b) Capsule layer

Fig. 2. (a) Capsule encoding layer: grid features $X' \in \mathbb{R}^{h \times w \times d}$ are transformed into capsules X_c for each spatial position. Output embedding h_{cls}^1 for $[CLS]$ token from the first text encoder layer generates a mask m^1 for capsule selection. The selected capsules X_{mc}^1 are flattened along capsule dimension to get a set of visual tokens (of length $h * w$) where each token is denoted by $x_{j_{mc}}^1, j = \{1, 2, ..., hw\}$; $x_{j_{mc}}^1 \in \mathbb{R}^{d_c}$ where d_c=capsule dimension, is then upsampled to model dimension d using a fully connected layer. A position embedding is added to visual tokens with the special token [IMG] at position 0. The output capsule encodings are then input to the visual transformer for future steps. **(b) Capsule layer** prepares the input for the next visual transformer layer i by combining previous layer's output (layer $i - 1$) with selected capsules using output for [CLS] token h_{cls}^i from the ith text encoder layer. Similar to the Capsule encoding, input tokens X' are first transformed into capsules X_c. The aggregated output feature h_{cls}^i from the ith text encoder layer generates a mask m^i to select certain capsules for input to the ith visual encoder layer. The resulting capsules are then flattened and upsampled (denoted by $\hat{x}_{j_{mc}}^i$) and added to the output $h_{v_j}^{i-1}$ of the previous visual transformer layer $i - 1$ to obtain input features $\hat{h}_{v_j}^i$ for visual transformer layer i.

V_e. The input text to language encoder L_e is a sequence of word tokens from a vocabulary V appended with special tokens $[CLS]$ and $[SEP]$ at the start and end of the word tokens. As input to the visual encoder, our model takes convolutional features as image embeddings. The convolutional features $X \in \mathbb{R}^{h \times w \times d1}$ are extracted from a pre-trained ResNet model, h, w are the feature height and width, and $d1$ is the extracted features dimension. A 2D convolutional layer then yields an embedding X' of size $\mathbb{R}^{h \times w \times d}$, where d is the model dimension size. These input embeddings produce capsule encodings X_c as explained in Sect. 3.2.

In the following, we first explain the motivation to use capsules in Sect. 3.1 followed by details about the capsule encoding in Sect. 3.2, the text-guided selection of the capsules in Sect. 3.3, as well as the text-based residual connection in Sect. 3.4. We close the section with an overview of the pretraining procedure in Sect. 3.5 and describe the details of the VQA downstream task in Sect. 4.1.

3.1   Capsule Networks

Standard neural networks lack the ability to dynamically represent a distinct part-whole hierarchy tree structure for each image [17]. This inability motivated the introduction of a type of model called Capsule Networks [18] which was later formalized in [52]. A Capsule Network is a neural network that is designed to model part-whole hierarchical relationships more explicitly than Convolutional Neural Networks (CNNs), by using groups of neurons to encode entities and learning the relationships between these entities. The promising performance of capsules can be attributed to their ability to learn part-whole relationships for object entities via routing-by-agreement [52] between different capsule layers. A capsule is represented by a group of neurons; each capsule layer is comprised of multiple capsules and multiple capsule layers can be stacked together. Capsule routing is a non-linear, iterative and clustering-like process that occurs between adjacent capsule layers, dynamically assigning *part* capsules i in layer ℓ to *object* capsules j in layer $\ell+1$, by iteratively calibrating the routing coefficients γ [50]. Unlike most previous works which use a loss over object classes to learn a set of capsule classes, we do not have any object level supervision available for capsules, but instead combine the power of transformers and capsules by interleaving capsules as intermediate layers within the transformer and use VQA supervision to model visual entities as capsules.

3.2   Capsule Encodings

We use matrix capsules [19] as follows: given an image embedding $X' \in \mathbb{R}^{h \times w \times d}$, matrix capsules $X_c \in \mathbb{R}^{h \times w \times d_c}$, as shown in Fig. 2(a), are obtained as follows: The image embedding X' is input to a convolutional layer producing primary capsules X_p where each capsule has a pose matrix of size $K \times K$ and an activation weight. The primary capsule layer outputs C_p number of capsules for each spatial location. The output dimensions for poses is $\mathbb{R}^{h \times w \times C_p \times K \times K}$ and for activation is $\mathbb{R}^{h \times w \times C_p \times 1}$. To treat each capsule as a separate entity, the pose matrix and activation are grouped together for each capsule. Hence, the primary capsules X_p have the dimensions $\mathbb{R}^{h \times w \times d_p}$ where $d_p = C_p \times (K \times K+1)$. The primary capsules are then passed through an EM-Routing layer to vote for capsules in the next layer. Assuming we have C_v number of capsules in the next layer, the routing yields capsule encodings X_c where $X_c \in \mathbb{R}^{h \times w \times d_c}$, $d_c = C_v \times (K \times K + 1)$. We use an equal number of capsules in both layers, i.e., $C = C_p = C_v$. Our system employs the capsule representation X_c as visual embeddings.

Since transformers take a sequence of tokens as input, we flatten the capsule embeddings across spatial dimension to get a sequence of visual tokens of length $h*w$, where each visual token is denoted by $x_j \in \mathbb{R}^{d_c}$ for $j \in 1, 2, ..., hw$. A special trainable token $[IMG]$ is then concatenated to these tokens to form the final set of visual tokens $\{[IMG], x_1, x_2, ..., x_{hw}\}$. A learnable position embedding is added to these visual tokens to keep the notion of spatial position in the sequence. Each of the visual tokens except $[IMG]$ is represented by C capsules.

3.3   Text-Guided Capsule Selection

As the language encoder is attending different words at each layer, we select visual capsules based on the text representation at each visual encoder layer. Let h_{cls}^i be the feature output corresponding to $[CLS]$ token from the ith text encoder layer; we take the feature output h^1_{cls} corresponding to $[CLS]$ token from the first text encoder layer and input it to a fully connected layer ϕ. The output is C logits followed by a softmax function to learn presence probability $m^1 \in \mathbb{R}^C$ of attended words at layer 1. This mask is applied to X_c to select the respective capsules and mask out the rest resulting in the masked capsule representation X^1_{mc}.

$$m^1 = softmax(\phi(h^1_{cls})). \tag{1}$$

$$X^1_{mc} = m^1 \odot X_c \tag{2}$$

The masking is only applied to the visual tokens x_j without affecting $[IMG]$ token.

3.4   Text-Based Residual Connection

To keep the capsule representation between intermediate layers, we add capsules via a residual connection to the inputs of each intermediate visual encoder layer. The input capsules to the intermediate layer are also selected based on the intermediate features output from the text encoder. Let m^i be the probability mask for attended words in the text feature output h^i_{cls} from the ith layer:

$$m^i = softmax(\phi(h^i_{cls})), \forall i \in \{1, 2, ..., L\}, \tag{3}$$

and $x^i_{j_{mc}}$ denotes the jth token with visual capsules selected using mask m^i.

$$x^i_{j_{mc}} = m^i \odot X_c, \tag{4}$$

The ith visual encoder layer takes features from the $(i-1)^{th}$ layer to produce features $h^i_{v_j}$ for the jth position. Let f^i_v be the ith layer in the visual encoder. The output and input follow the notation below:

$$h^i_{v_j} = f^i_v(h^{i-1}_{v_j}). \tag{5}$$

To keep information flowing from text to image, we propose to add the residual connection from visual capsules for the jth token by adding $x^i_{j_{mc}}$ to the input of the ith encoder layer. However, there is a dimension mismatch between $x^i_{j_{mc}} \in \mathbb{R}^{d_c}$ and $h^{i-1}_{v_j} \in \mathbb{R}^d$. We upsample $x^i_{j_{mc}}$ to dimension size d using a fully connected layer σ and get the upsampled capsule-based features $\hat{x}^i_{j_{mc}} \in \mathbb{R}^d$. The input to the visual encoder layer will be as follows:

$$\hat{h}^{i-1}_{v_j} = f^i_v(h^{i-1}_{v_j} + \hat{x}^i_{j_{mc}}). \tag{6}$$

The output feature sequences from both encoders are then input to our cross attentional module which allows token-level attention between the two modalities. The aggregated feature outputs corresponding to $[CLS]$ and $[IMG]$ tokens after cross attention are input to a feature pooling layer followed by respective classifiers for pretraining and downstream tasks. We discuss the implementation about modality-specific encoders, feature pooling, and cross attention in detail in the supplementary material.

3.5 Training

To perform well, transformers require pretraining on large-scale datasets before finetuning for the downstream tasks, i.e., GQA and VQA-HAT in our case. Therefore, we first pretrain our capsules-transformer backbone on three pre-training tasks: image-text matching (ITM), masked language modeling (MLM), and visual question answering (VQA). The system is pre-trained in two stages: first, we do joint training of modality-specific encoders only to learn text-guided capsules representation; the representation learned in encoders is kept fixed during the second stage of pre-training where we add cross-attentional blocks on top of the modality encoders allowing token-level interaction between text features and visual features. While the first stage of pretraining uses pooled features from text and from visual encoders, the second stage pools features after cross attention: therefore, the second stage pre-training tasks uses cross-modal inputs as language and image features. For details about pretraining tasks in context of our method, refer to Sect. 1.2 in supplementary. We finally finetune the pretrained capsules-transformer backbone to solve VQA as our downstream task.

4 Experiments and Results

4.1 Datasets

Pre-training. We use image-caption pairs from MSCOCO [35] and Visual Genome [29] for pretraining our backbone. Specifically, we use the same data as [56] which also include MSCOCO-based VQA datasets: Visual7W, VQAv2.0, and Visual Genome based GQA. However, we exclude the GQA validation set from pretraining and finetuning as we evaluate grounding on this set because scene graphs for GQA test and testdev are not publicly available. We use train sets of MSCOCO and VG with ∼7.5M sentence-image pairs for pretraining. MSCOCO val set is used for validating pretraining tasks.

Downstream. We consider two datasets for the downstream task, GQA [24] and VQA-HAT [8].

GQA poses visual reasoning in the form of compositional question answering. It requires multihop reasoning to answer the question, so GQA is a special case of VQA. GQA is more diverse than VQA2.0 [14] in terms of coverage of relational, spatial, and multihop reasoning questions. It has 22M QA pairs with 113K images. GQA provides ground truth boxes for question and answer objects making it a suitable test bed for our task.

VQA-HAT dataset provides human attention maps for VQA task. This dataset is based on VQA v1.0 [2] dataset and provides 1374 QA pairs with 488 images in the validation set. To evaluate on this dataset, we train our system on VQA v1.0. The answer vocabulary of VQA train set has a long tail distribution. We follow previous works [2,8] and use 1000 most frequent answers. We first combine training (248,349 QA pairs) and validation data (121,512 QA pairs) to get a total of 368,487 QA pairs. We then filter out the questions with out-of-vocabulary answers resulting in 318,827 QA pairs.

4.2   Evaluation Metrics

For GQA, VQA accuracy is reported for task accuracy. For grounding task on transformers, we take attention scores from [IMG] token to visual tokens from the last cross-attentional layer for all heads. Answer (or question) grounding performance is evaluated in terms of the following: **Overlap**– overlap between the ground truth bounding box for answer object and the detected attention region is reported in terms of precision (P), recall (R), and F1-score (F1); **IOU**– intersection over union (IOU) between the ground truth object and detected region is reported in terms of P, R, and F1-score. **Pointing Game**– proposed by [65] is a metric for weakly-supervised visual grounding methods. For pointing game, we consider the point detected from each head as a part of distribution, and perform k-means clustering (k = 1) on those points. The cluster center is considered as the detected point from the system and used for evaluating accuracy. For VQA-HAT, we report **mean rank correlation** between system generated attention and human attention maps to compare with previous methods. Mean rank correlation is an order-based metric for finding the degree of association between two variables based on their ranks and thus is invariant to absolute spatial probability values [8].

4.3   Implementation Details

We use $L = 5$ layers in both text and image encoders, and 2 layers in cross-attention module. The transformer encoder layers have the same configuration as BERT with 12 heads and feature dimension $d = 768$. A batch size of 1024 with learning rate $lr = 1e-4$ is used for pretraining. First stage pretraining is done for 20 epochs and further trained for 10–15 epochs during the second stage. We use Imagenet pre-trained ResNet model to extract features of dimensions $7 \times 7 \times 2048$. For finetuning on GQA, we use batch size = 32 with $lr = 1e-5$ and 5–10 training epochs. For VQA-HAT, we use batch size = 64 with $lr = 4e-5$ trained for 20 epochs. To evaluate the grounding results, we follow [4] and consider the last cross-attentional layer's output for the attention map. To compute overlap and IOU for GQA, we threshold over the attention map with an attention threshold of 0.5 to get high attention regions. Each connected region is considered a detection. For pointing game, we find the single cluster center over maximum attention points from all heads and use it for evaluation. We ignore the test samples with empty ground truth maps for pointing game since there is no ground truth bounding box to check for a hit or a miss. For the VQA-HAT evaluation, we follow [8] and use mean rank correlation between the generated attention maps and the ground truth.

4.4   Comparison to State-of-the-Art

We compare the performance of our method to other best-performing methods in the field of weakly supervised VQA grounding and VQA in general, namely MAC [23] and MAC-Caps [25] as representation of visual reasoning architectures,

Table 1. Pointing game accuracy for GQA. For MAC and MAC-Caps, mean attention maps over reasoning steps are used. For transformer-based methods, maximum attention points from all heads are used for clustering. The cluster center is then used for the pointing game evaluation. For ALBEF, GC = GradCAM output, ATN = attention output. Ours-no-init is the full model trained from scratch (no initialization from BERT or ViT), Ours-nogqa uses no GQA samples at pretraining stage. Numbers are in percentages.

Method	Layer	Pointing game acc.
Random	–	18.80
Center	–	33.30
MAC [23]	Mean	8.90
MAC-Caps [25]	Mean	28.46
LXMERT [56]	Last	29.00
ALBEF [32]-GC	Last	32.13
ALBEF [32]-ATN	Last	32.11
ViLT [27]	Last	11.99
Ours-no-init ($C = 16$)	Last	**34.59**
Ours-no-init ($C = 32$)	Last	**34.43**
Ours-nogqa ($C = 32$)	Last	**37.04**

and LXMERT [56], ViLT [27], and ALBEF [32] as state-of-the-art transformer architectures without object features.

For LXMERT, we take the provided backbone pre-trained on object features and finetune it using image patches of size $32 \times 32 \times 3$ on GQA. In case of ViLT, we use the provided pre-trained backbone and finetune it on GQA. Following ViLT, we generate a heat map using the cosine similarity between image and word tokens evaluating the similarity scores as well as raw attention for grounding performance for all three metrics. For ALBEF we report results on the last layer as well as on layer 8 which is specialized for grounding [32] using the visualizations from gradcam as well as raw attention maps.

GQA. We first look at the results of our evaluation on GQA, considering pointing game accuracy in Table 1 and for overlap and IOU in Table 2. Our method outperforms both MAC and MAC-Caps for answer grounding on the last attention map. We achieve an absolute gain of 16.47% (overlap F1-score) and 2.67% increase in IOU F1-score, and an improvement of 25.69% in pointing game accuracy for MAC. When compared with MAC-Caps, our best method ($C = 16$, no-init) improves overlap F1-score by 15.71% ↑, IOU F1-score by 2.32% ↑, and pointing game accuracy by 6.13% ↑. Similar performance gain is observed for question grounding with an improvement of 38.2% ↑ for overlap F1-score and 3.67% ↑ gain for IOU F1-score.

To evaluate LXMERT finetuned on image patches (LXMERT-patches), we take the attention score maps from the last cross modality layer. We improve

Table 2. Results on GQA validation set (for last layer). All methods are evaluated for weak VQA grounding task. For transformer-based models, attention was averaged over all heads. Results are based on grounding of objects referenced in the answer (A) and the question (Q). C = no. of capsules, we report results from our best model with C = 16. Refer to Table 4 for more variants. For ViLT, we obtain results using cosine similarity (cos.) between text and image features as proposed by the authors as well as from raw attention scores (ATN). For ALBEF, GC is the gradcam output used for evaluation, ATN is the attention output. ALBEF uses layer 8 as grounding layer, we also report grounding performance on this layer. Our method outperforms all baselines for overlap F1-score and IOU F1-score. See Sect. 4.4 for more details. Numbers are in percentages.

Method	Obj.	Backbone	Pre-training	Layer	Acc.	Overlap			IOU		
						P	R	F1	P	R	F1
MAC [23]	A	ResNet	–	Last	57.09	5.05	24.44	8.37	0.76	3.70	1.27
MAC-Caps [25]	A	ResNet	–	Last	55.13	5.46	27.9	9.13	0.97	4.94	1.62
LXMERT-patches	A	Faster RCNN	MSCO,VG	Last	48.65	7.13	64.21	12.83	0.95	8.66	1.71
ALBEF [32]-GC	A	ViT+BERT		Last	64.16	6.94	99.92	12.98	0.89	13.43	1.67
ALBEF [32]-ATN	A	ViT+BERT	MSCO,VG,	Last	64.20	5.13	99.92	9.75	0.64	12.98	1.21
ALBEF [32]-GC	A	ViT+BERT	SBU,GCC	8	64.20	4.41	99.92	8.44	0.54	12.85	1.04
ALBEF [32]-ATN	A	ViT+BERT		8	64.20	4.82	99.92	9.19	0.60	12.88	1.14
ViLT [28]	A	ViT	MSCO,VG,	Last-cos	66.33	0.34	6.13	0.65	0.04	0.63	0.07
ViLT [28]	A	ViT	SBU,GCC	Last-ATN	66.33	0.28	4.10	0.53	0.08	1.20	0.15
Ours (C = 16)	A	ResNet	MSCO,VG	Last	57.21	**14.53**	85.47	**24.84**	**2.30**	13.61	**3.94**
MAC [23]	Q	ResNet	–	Last	57.09	10.79	16.38	13.01	1.39	2.09	1.67
MAC-Caps [25]	Q	ResNet	–	Last	55.13	17.39	28.10	21.49	1.87	2.96	2.29
LXMERT-patches	Q	Faster RCNN	MSCO,VG	Last	48.65	32.46	64.02	43.08	3.48	6.87	4.62
ALBEF [32]-GC	Q	ViT+BERT		Last	64.20	22.15	99.90	36.26	1.96	9.22	3.24
ALBEF [32]-ATN	Q	ViT+BERT	MSCO,VG,	Last	64.20	16.50	99.90	28.33	1.40	8.90	2.43
ALBEF [32]-GC	Q	ViT+BERT	SBU,GCC	8	64.20	14.21	99.90	24.88	1.19	8.71	2.09
ALBEF [32]-ATN	Q	ViT+BERT		8	64.20	15.51	99.90	26.85	1.31	8.77	2.27
ViLT [28]	Q	ViT	MSCO,VG,	Last-cos	66.33	1.02	5.64	1.73	0.10	0.54	0.17
ViLT [28]	Q	ViT	SBU,GCC	Last-ATN	66.33	0.34	1.56	0.56	0.08	0.38	0.14
Ours (C=16)	Q	ResNet	MSCO,VG	Last	57.21	**47.03**	81.67	**59.69**	**4.72**	8.08	**5.96**

over LXMERT by 12.01% ↑ absolute points w.r.t overlap F1-score, 2.23% ↑ w.r.t. IOU F1-score and 5.43% ↑ gain in pointing game accuracy. For question grounding, LXMERT achieves an overlap F1-score: 43.08% (vs. ours 59.69%) and IOU F1-score of 4.62% (vs. ours 5.96%).

ViLT outperforms all methods in terms of VQA accuracy of 66.33%. However, on the grounding task, it demonstrates the lowest performance for all metrics (Table 1: row 7, Table 2: rows 8–9). Similar behavior is observed for the question grounding task.

ALBEF produces visualization using GradCAM. We compare with ALBEF using both GradCAM output and attention maps. ALBEF has a very high recall (R) both in terms of overlap and IOU. However, it lacks in precision (P) leading to lower F1-scores for both metrics. Our best model outperforms ALBEF-VQA by a significant margin on both answer grounding and question grounding.

Table 3. Results on VQA-HAT val dataset. *Unsupervised*: no attention supervision, *Supervised*: use attention refinement.

Method	Mean rank-correlation
Random	0.000 ± 0.001
Human	0.623 ± 0.003
Unsupervised	
SAN [62]	0.249 ± 0.004
HieCoAtt [40]	0.264 ± 0.004
Ours (C = 16)	**0.479 ± 0.0001**
Supervised	
HAN [47]	0.668 ± 0.001

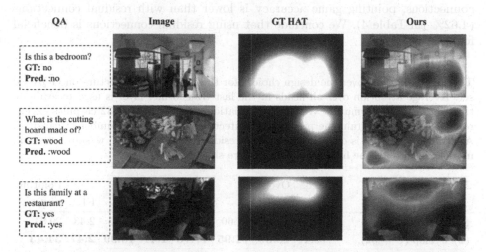

Fig. 3. Success cases for VQA-HAT dataset. VQA-HAT provides 3 human attention maps for each image. Here, we show the best matched ground truth map (GT HAT).

VQA-HAT. We further evaluate our system on the VQA-HAT dataset. To this end, we follow the protocol of VQA-HAT and resize the human attention maps and the output attention maps from our system to the common resolution of 14 × 14. We then rank both of them. VQA-HAT val set provides three human attention maps for each question. We compute the rank correlation of generated attention map with each human attention map and take the average score. Mean rank correlation score over all QA pairs is reported.

We compare our approach on VQA-HAT with three different baselines: SAN [62] and HieCoAtt [40] as unsupervised bounding box free systems, and HAN [47] which uses attention supervision during training. The evaluation is shown in Table 3. It shows that the proposed system is able to significantly outperform both methods using VQA-only supervision.

Without any attention supervision during training, we are able to narrow the gap between unsupervised methods and methods such as HAN, which use human ground truth attention maps during training. Figure 3 shows success cases on VQA-HAT, comparing our generated attention result to the closest human attention map.

4.5   Ablations and Analyses

Impact of Residual Connections. We compare our full system with an ablated variant without residual connections. We observe a drop in performance in terms of overlap, but a slight increase in terms of IOU. Without residual connections, pointing game accuracy is lower than with residual connections (4.62% ↓in Table 4). We conclude that using residual connections is beneficial for pointing game.

Table 4. Ablations over the design choices for the proposed architecture on GQA val set. Average attention over all heads in the last transformer layer is used to evaluate the grounding performance. We perform ablation study with $C = 32$ caspules except rows 3–6 where we train the proposed architecture with varying number of capsules. Ablation (1) no skip is our system without residual connections, (2) w/skip is the full model. Results for the final design choices are shown in bold.

Method	Acc.	Overlap			IOU			Pointing
		P	R	F1	P	R	F1	game
(1) no skip($C = 32$)	56.83	11.06	77.60	19.37	1.39	9.85	2.43	29.81
(2) w/skip ($C = 32$)	55.41	**10.09**	**71.95**	**17.70**	**1.41**	**10.09**	**2.47**	**34.43**
(3) w/skip ($C = 16$)	57.21	**14.53**	**85.47**	**24.84**	**2.30**	**13.61**	**3.94**	**34.59**
(4) w/skip ($C = 24$)	56.26	10.90	74.03	19.00	1.54	10.56	2.69	31.08
(5) w/skip ($C = 32$)	55.41	10.09	71.95	17.70	1.41	10.09	2.47	34.43
(6) w/skip ($C = 48$)	53.65	10.28	68.94	17.89	1.59	10.73	2.78	29.70
(7) no-init ($C = 32$)	55.41	**10.09**	**71.95**	**17.70**	**1.41**	**10.09**	**2.47**	**34.43**
(8) vit-bert init ($C = 32$)	58.86	11.11	74.67	19.34	1.55	10.44	2.69	27.06

Number of Capsules. We ablate our system with varying number of capsules. We train the proposed system with $C = 16, 24, 32,$ and 48 capsules. We observe that increase in number of capsules not only decreases VQA accuracy, but also hurts the overlap and IOU in terms of precision, recall and F1-score. Our best method uses 16 capsules with residual connections and pre-trained from scratch.

ViT + BERT + Ours. ViLT and ALBEF initialize their image and text encoders from ViT and/or BERT weights. Although our model is shallower than both models (5 layers in modality specific encoders compared to 12 layers in ViLT and ALBEF), we experimented to initialize our text encoder with BERT weights and image encoder with ViT weights from last 5 layers. We find a gain in VQA accuracy (58.86% vs. 57.21%) but it get less grounding performance.

4.6   Qualitative Analysis

In Fig. 4, for all examples including the ones where our system mispredicted the answer, the grounding attention was correct (row 1, 4 and 5). Also, the answers are plausible. For instance, in row 3, the correct answer is 'aircraft', and

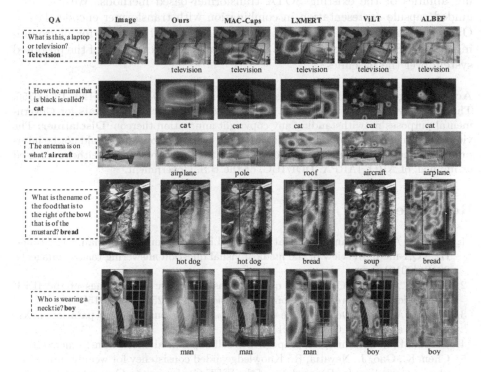

Fig. 4. Qualitative comparison: each row shows the input example, and the last layer's attention visualizations (averaged over all heads) with the predicted answer from all methods. Column 1 shows the question and ground truth answer, column 2 is the input image, column 3 shows the attention (grounding) output from our method, column 4–7 are results from the baselines. Blue box is the ground truth bounding box for the answer object, orange boxes are the detected regions from each system. We can see that ours is attending relevant answer object with the plausible predicted answer even when the prediction mismatches with the ground truth answer (row 3–5). In row 4, the question is vague; therefore we can say, except LXMERT, all methods choose the correct answer. ALBEF has attention spread over all image which explains the high recall it achieves for overlap and IOU. Refer to Sect. 4.6 for more details and discussion. Best viewed in color. (Color figure online)

our method predicted it as 'airplane' with the correct localization. Overall, we notice that compared to our method, the baselines were either attending most of the image (ALBEF in rows 1,3, and 5 which explains the high recall in Table 2), or generate small attention maps (MAC-Caps, ViLT) or look at the wrong part of the image (LXMERT). More examples and analysis are in the supplementary material.

5   Conclusion

In this work, we show the trade-off between VQA accuracy and the grounding abilities of the existing SOTA transformer-based methods. We use text-guided capsule representation in combination with transformer encoder layers. Our results demonstrate significant improvement over all baselines for all grounding metrics. Extensive experiments demonstrate the effectiveness of the proposed system over the baselines.

Acknowledgement. Aisha Urooj is supported by the ARO grant W911NF-19-1-0356. The U.S. Government is authorized to reproduce and distribute reprints for Governmental purposes notwithstanding any copyright annotation thereon. **Disclaimer:** The views and conclusions contained herein are those of the authors and should not be interpreted as necessarily representing the official policies or endorsements, either expressed or implied, of ARO, IARPA, DOI/IBC, or the U.S. Government.

References

1. Abacha, A.B., Hasan, S.A., Datla, V.V., Liu, J., Demner-Fushman, D., Müller, H.: VQA-med: overview of the medical visual question answering task at imageclef 2019. (2019)
2. Antol, S., et al.: VQA: visual question answering. In: Proceedings of the IEEE International Conference on Computer Vision, pp. 2425–2433 (2015)
3. Arbelle, A., et al.: Detector-free weakly supervised grounding by separation. arXiv preprint arXiv:2104.09829 (2021)
4. Caron, M., et al.: Emerging properties in self-supervised vision transformers (2021)
5. Chen, K., Gao, J., Nevatia, R.: Knowledge aided consistency for weakly supervised phrase grounding. In: Proceedings of the IEEE Conference on Computer Vision and Pattern Recognition, pp. 4042–4050 (2018)
6. Chen, Y.C., et al.: Uniter: learning universal image-text representations (2019)
7. Chen, Z., Ma, L., Luo, W., Wong, K.Y.K.: Weakly-supervised spatio-temporally grounding natural sentence in video. arXiv preprint arXiv:1906.02549 (2019)
8. Das, A., Agrawal, H., Zitnick, C.L., Parikh, D., Batra, D.: Human Attention in Visual Question Answering: Do Humans and Deep Networks Look at the Same Regions? In: Conference on Empirical Methods in Natural Language Processing (EMNLP) (2016)
9. Datta, S., Sikka, K., Roy, A., Ahuja, K., Parikh, D., Divakaran, A.: Align2ground: weakly supervised phrase grounding guided by image-caption alignment. In: Proceedings of the IEEE/CVF International Conference on Computer Vision, pp. 2601–2610 (2019)

10. Desai, K., Johnson, J.: VirTex: learning visual representations from textual annotations. In: CVPR (2021)

11. Duan, S., Cao, J., Zhao, H.: Capsule-transformer for neural machine translation. arXiv preprint arXiv:2004.14649 (2020)

12. Duarte, K., Rawat, Y., Shah, M.: Videocapsulenet: a simplified network for action detection. In: Advances in Neural Information Processing Systems, pp. 7610–7619 (2018)

13. Duarte, K., Rawat, Y.S., Shah, M.: Capsulevos: semi-supervised video object segmentation using capsule routing. In: Proceedings of the IEEE International Conference on Computer Vision, pp. 8480–8489 (2019)

14. Goyal, Y., Khot, T., Summers-Stay, D., Batra, D., Parikh, D.: Making the V in VQA matter: elevating the role of image understanding in visual question answering. In: Proceedings of the IEEE Conference on Computer Vision and Pattern Recognition, pp. 6904–6913 (2017)

15. Gu, S., Feng, Y.: Improving multi-head attention with capsule networks. In: Tang, J., Kan, MY., Zhao, D., Li, S., Zan, H. (eds.) NLPCC 2019. LNCS (LNAI), vol. 11838, pp. 314–326. Springer, Cham (2019). https://doi.org/10.1007/978-3-030-32233-5_25

16. Gurari, D., et al.: Vizwiz grand challenge: answering visual questions from blind people. In: Proceedings of the IEEE Conference on Computer Vision and Pattern Recognition, pp. 3608–3617 (2018)

17. Hinton, G.: How to represent part-whole hierarchies in a neural network. arXiv preprint arXiv:2102.12627 (2021)

18. Hinton, G.E., Krizhevsky, A., Wang, S.D.: Transforming auto-encoders. In: Honkela, T., Duch, W., Girolami, M., Kaski, S. (eds.) ICANN 2011. LNCS, vol. 6791, pp. 44–51. Springer, Heidelberg (2011). https://doi.org/10.1007/978-3-642-21735-7_6

19. Hinton, G.E., Sabour, S., Frosst, N.: Matrix capsules with EM routing. In: International Conference on Learning Representations (2018)

20. Huang, D.A., Buch, S., Dery, L., Garg, A., Fei-Fei, L., Niebles, J.C.: Finding" it": weakly-supervised reference-aware visual grounding in instructional videos. In: Proceedings of the IEEE Conference on Computer Vision and Pattern Recognition, pp. 5948–5957 (2018)

21. Huang, Z., Zeng, Z., Huang, Y., Liu, B., Fu, D., Fu, J.: Seeing out of the box: End-to-end pre-training for vision-language representation learning. In: The IEEE Conference on Computer Vision and Pattern Recognition (CVPR) (2021)

22. Huang, Z., Zeng, Z., Liu, B., Fu, D., Fu, J.: Pixel-bert: aligning image pixels with text by deep multi-modal transformers. CoRR abs/2004.00849 (2020). https://arxiv.org/abs/2004.00849

23. Hudson, D.A., Manning, C.D.: Compositional attention networks for machine reasoning. In: International Conference on Learning Representations (ICLR) (2018)

24. Hudson, D.A., Manning, C.D.: GQA: a new dataset for real-world visual reasoning and compositional question answering. Conference on Computer Vision and Pattern Recognition (CVPR) (2019)

25. Khan, A.U., Kuehne, H., Duarte, K., Gan, C., Lobo, N., Shah, M.: Found a reason for me? weakly-supervised grounded visual question answering using capsules (2021)

26. Khan, S., Naseer, M., Hayat, M., Zamir, S.W., Khan, F.S., Shah, M.: Transformers in vision: a survey. arXiv preprint arXiv:2101.01169 (2021)

27. Kim, W., Son, B., Kim, I.: VILT: vision-and-language transformer without convolution or region supervision. In: Meila, M., Zhang, T. (eds.) Proceedings of the 38th International Conference on Machine Learning. Proceedings of Machine Learning Research, vol. 139, pp. 5583–5594. PMLR (2021). https://proceedings.mlr.press/v139/kim21k.html

28. Kim, W., Son, B., Kim, I.: VILT: vision-and-language transformer without convolution or region supervision. In: Meila, M., Zhang, T. (eds.) Proceedings of the 38th International Conference on Machine Learning. Proceedings of Machine Learning Research, vol. 139, pp. 5583–5594. PMLR (2021). https://proceedings.mlr.press/v139/kim21k.html

29. Krishna, R., et al.: Visual genome: connecting language and vision using crowd-sourced dense image annotations. Int. J. Comput. Vision **123**(1), 32–73 (2017)

30. LaLonde, R., Bagci, U.: Capsules for object segmentation. arXiv preprint arXiv:1804.04241 (2018)

31. Li, G., Duan, N., Fang, Y., Gong, M., Jiang, D.: Unicoder-vl: a universal encoder for vision and language by cross-modal pre-training. In: Proceedings of the AAAI Conference on Artificial Intelligence, vol. 34, pp. 11336–11344 (2020)

32. Li, J., Selvaraju, R.R., Gotmare, A.D., Joty, S., Xiong, C., Hoi, S.: Align before fuse: vision and language representation learning with momentum distillation. In: NeurIPS (2021)

33. Li, L.H., Yatskar, M., Yin, D., Hsieh, C.J., Chang, K.W.: Visualbert: a simple and performant baseline for vision and language. arXiv preprint arXiv:1908.03557 (2019)

34. Li, X., et al.: OSCAR: Object-semantics aligned pre-training for vision-language tasks. In: Vedaldi, A., Bischof, H., Brox, T., Frahm, J.-M. (eds.) ECCV 2020. LNCS, vol. 12375, pp. 121–137. Springer, Cham (2020). https://doi.org/10.1007/978-3-030-58577-8_8

35. Lin, T.-Y., et al.: Microsoft COCO: common objects in context. In: Fleet, D., Pajdla, T., Schiele, B., Tuytelaars, T. (eds.) ECCV 2014. LNCS, vol. 8693, pp. 740–755. Springer, Cham (2014). https://doi.org/10.1007/978-3-319-10602-1_48

36. Liu, J., et al.: Transformer-based capsule network for stock movement prediction. In: Proceedings of the First Workshop on Financial Technology and Natural Language Processing, pp. 66–73 (2019)

37. Liu, Y., Wan, B., Ma, L., He, X.: Relation-aware instance refinement for weakly supervised visual grounding. In: Proceedings of the IEEE/CVF Conference on Computer Vision and Pattern Recognition, pp. 5612–5621 (2021)

38. Lu, J., Batra, D., Parikh, D., Lee, S.: Vilbert: pretraining task-agnostic visiolinguistic representations for vision-and-language tasks. arXiv preprint arXiv:1908.02265 (2019)

39. Lu, J., Goswami, V., Rohrbach, M., Parikh, D., Lee, S.: 12-in-1: multi-task vision and language representation learning. In: Proceedings of the IEEE/CVF Conference on Computer Vision and Pattern Recognition, pp. 10437–10446 (2020)

40. Lu, J., Yang, J., Batra, D., Parikh, D.: Hierarchical question-image co-attention for visual question answering. Adv. Neural Inf. Process. Syst. **29** (2016)

41. Mazzia, V., Salvetti, F., Chiaberge, M.: Efficient-capsnet: capsule network with self-attention routing. arXiv preprint arXiv:2101.12491 (2021)

42. Miech, A., Alayrac, J.B., Laptev, I., Sivic, J., Zisserman, A.: Thinking fast and slow: efficient text-to-visual retrieval with transformers. In: Proceedings of the IEEE/CVF Conference on Computer Vision and Pattern Recognition, pp. 9826–9836 (2021)

43. Mobiny, A., Cicalese, P.A., Nguyen, H.V.: Trans-caps: transformer capsule networks with self-attention routing (2021). https://openreview.net/forum?id=BUPIRa1D2J

44. Niu, Y., Tang, K., Zhang, H., Lu, Z., Hua, X.S., Wen, J.R.: Counterfactual VQA: a cause-effect look at language bias. In: Proceedings of the IEEE/CVF Conference on Computer Vision and Pattern Recognition, pp. 12700–12710 (2021)

45. Pfeiffer, J., et al.: XGQA: cross-lingual visual question answering. arXiv preprint arXiv:2109.06082 (2021)

46. Pucci, R., Micheloni, C., Martinel, N.: Self-attention agreement among capsules. In: Proceedings of the IEEE/CVF International Conference on Computer Vision, pp. 272–280 (2021)

47. Qiao, T., Dong, J., Xu, D.: Exploring human-like attention supervision in visual question answering. In: Proceedings of the AAAI Conference on Artificial Intelligence, vol. 32 (2018)

48. Radford, A., et al.: Learning transferable visual models from natural language supervision (2021)

49. Ramakrishnan, S., Agrawal, A., Lee, S.: Overcoming language priors in visual question answering with adversarial regularization. arXiv preprint arXiv:1810.03649 (2018)

50. Ribeiro, F.D.S., Duarte, K., Everett, M., Leontidis, G., Shah, M.: Learning with capsules: a survey. arXiv preprint arXiv:2206.02664 (2022)

51. Riquelme, F., De Goyeneche, A., Zhang, Y., Niebles, J.C., Soto, A.: Explaining VQA predictions using visual grounding and a knowledge base. Image Vision Comput. **101**, 103968 (2020)

52. Sabour, S., Frosst, N., Hinton, G.E.: Dynamic routing between capsules. In: NIPS (2017)

53. Selvaraju, R.R., et al.: Taking a hint: leveraging explanations to make vision and language models more grounded. In: Proceedings of the IEEE/CVF International Conference on Computer Vision, pp. 2591–2600 (2019)

54. Shi, J., Xu, J., Gong, B., Xu, C.: Not all frames are equal: weakly-supervised video grounding with contextual similarity and visual clustering losses. In: Proceedings of the IEEE/CVF Conference on Computer Vision and Pattern Recognition, pp. 10444–10452 (2019)

55. Su, W., et al.: Vl-bert: pre-training of generic visual-linguistic representations. arXiv preprint arXiv:1908.08530 (2019)

56. Tan, H., Bansal, M.: Lxmert: learning cross-modality encoder representations from transformers. In: Proceedings of the 2019 Conference on Empirical Methods in Natural Language Processing (2019)

57. Wang, L., Huang, J., Li, Y., Xu, K., Yang, Z., Yu, D.: Improving weakly supervised visual grounding by contrastive knowledge distillation. In: Proceedings of the IEEE/CVF Conference on Computer Vision and Pattern Recognition, pp. 14090–14100 (2021)

58. Whitehead, S., Wu, H., Ji, H., Feris, R., Saenko, K.: Separating skills and concepts for novel visual question answering. In: Proceedings of the IEEE/CVF Conference on Computer Vision and Pattern Recognition (CVPR), pp. 5632–5641 (2021)

59. Wu, L., Liu, X., Liu, Q.: Centroid transformers: learning to abstract with attention. arXiv preprint arXiv:2102.08606 (2021)

60. Xiao, F., Sigal, L., Jae Lee, Y.: Weakly-supervised visual grounding of phrases with linguistic structures. In: Proceedings of the IEEE Conference on Computer Vision and Pattern Recognition, pp. 5945–5954 (2017)

61. Yang, X., Liu, X., Jian, M., Gao, X., Wang, M.: Weakly-supervised video object grounding by exploring spatio-temporal contexts. In: Proceedings of the 28th ACM International Conference on Multimedia, pp. 1939–1947 (2020)
62. Yang, Z., He, X., Gao, J., Deng, L., Smola, A.: Stacked attention networks for image question answering. In: Proceedings of the IEEE Conference on Computer Vision and Pattern Recognition, pp. 21–29 (2016)
63. Zeng, X., Wang, Y., Chiu, T.Y., Bhattacharya, N., Gurari, D.: Vision skills needed to answer visual questions. Proc. ACM Hum. Comput. Interact. **4**(CSCW2), 1–31 (2020)
64. Zhan, L.M., Liu, B., Fan, L., Chen, J., Wu, X.M.: Medical visual question answering via conditional reasoning. In: Proceedings of the 28th ACM International Conference on Multimedia, pp. 2345–2354 (2020)
65. Zhang, J., Bargal, S.A., Lin, Z., Brandt, J., Shen, X., Sclaroff, S.: Top-down neural attention by excitation backprop. Int. J. Comput. Vision **126**(10), 1084–1102 (2018)
66. Zhang, S., Qu, L., You, S., Yang, Z., Zhang, J.: Automatic generation of grounded visual questions. arXiv preprint arXiv:1612.06530 (2016)
67. Zhang, Y., Niebles, J.C., Soto, A.: Interpretable visual question answering by visual grounding from attention supervision mining. In: 2019 IEEE Winter Conference on Applications of Computer Vision (WACV), pp. 349–357 (2019). https://doi.org/10.1109/WACV.2019.00043

Automatic Dense Annotation of Large-Vocabulary Sign Language Videos

Liliane Momeni[1]($\boxtimes$), Hannah Bull[2], K. R. Prajwal[1], Samuel Albanie[3], Gül Varol[4], and Andrew Zisserman[1]

[1] Visual Geometry Group, University of Oxford, Oxford, UK
{liliane,prajwal,az}@robots.ox.ac.uk
[2] LISN, Univ Paris-Saclay, CNRS, Orsay, France
hannah.bull@lisn.upsaclay.fr
[3] Department of Engineering, University of Cambridge, Cambridge, UK
albanie@robots.ox.ac.uk
[4] LIGM, École des Ponts, Univ Gustave Eiffel, CNRS, Villeurbanne, France
gul@robots.ox.ac.uk
https://www.robots.ox.ac.uk/~vgg/research/bsldensify/

Abstract. Recently, sign language researchers have turned to sign language interpreted TV broadcasts, comprising (i) a video of continuous signing and (ii) subtitles corresponding to the audio content, as a readily available and large-scale source of training data. One key challenge in the usability of such data is the lack of sign annotations. Previous work exploiting such weakly-aligned data only found *sparse* correspondences between keywords in the subtitle and individual signs. In this work, we propose a simple, scalable framework to *vastly* increase the *density* of automatic annotations. Our contributions are the following: (1) we significantly improve previous annotation methods by making use of synonyms and subtitle-signing alignment; (2) we show the value of pseudo-labelling from a sign recognition model as a way of sign spotting; (3) we propose a novel approach for increasing our annotations of *known* and *unknown* classes based on *in-domain exemplars*; (4) on the BOBSL BSL sign language corpus, we increase the number of confident automatic annotations from 670K to 5M. We make these annotations publicly available to support the sign language research community.

Keywords: Sign language recognition · Automatic dataset construction · Novel class discovery

1 Introduction

Sign languages are visual-spatial languages that have evolved among deaf communities. They possess rich grammar structures and lexicons that differ

---

L. Momeni, H. Bull and K. R. Prajwal—Equal contribution.

Supplementary Information The online version contains supplementary material available at https://doi.org/10.1007/978-3-031-19833-5_39.

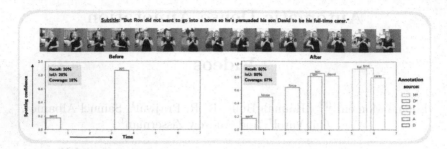

Fig. 1. Densification: For continuous sign language, we show automatic sign annotation timelines, along with their confidence and annotation source, *before* and *after* our framework is applied. M, D, A refer to automatic annotations from previous methods from mouthings [2], dictionaries [44] and the Transformer attention [61]. M*, D*, P, E, N refer to new and improved automatic annotations we collect in this work. Annotation methods are compared in the appendix.

considerably from those found among spoken languages [58]. An important factor impeding progress in automatic sign language recognition – in contrast to automatic speech recognition – has been the lack of large-scale training data. To address this issue, researchers have recently made use of sign language interpreted TV broadcasts, comprising (i) a video of continuous signing, and (ii) subtitles corresponding to the audio content, to build datasets such as Content4All [9] (190 h) and BOBSL [1] (1460 h).

Although such datasets are orders of magnitude larger than the long-standing RWTH-PHOENIX [10] benchmark (9 h) and cover a much wider domain of discourse (not restricted to only weather news), the supervision they provide on the signed content is limited in that it is *weak* and *noisy*. It is weak because the subtitles are temporally aligned with the audio content and not necessarily with the signing. The supervision is also noisy because the presence of a word in the subtitle does not necessarily imply that the word is signed; and subtitles can be signed in different ways. Recent works have shown that training automatic sign language translation models on such *weak* and *noisy* supervision leads to low performance [1,9,61].

In an attempt to increase the value of such interpreted datasets, multiple works [2,44,61] have leveraged the subtitles to perform lexical *sign spotting* in an approximately aligned continuous signing segment – where the aim is to determine *whether* and *when* a subtitle word is signed. Methods include using visual keyword spotting to identify signer mouthings [2], learning a joint embedding with sign language dictionary video clips [44], and exploiting the attention mechanism of a transformer translation model trained on weak, noisy subtitle-signing pairs [61]. These works leverage the approximate subtitle timings and subtitle content to significantly reduce the correspondence search space between temporal windows of signs and spoken language words. Although such methods are effective at automatically annotating signs, they only find *sparse* correspondences between keywords in the subtitle and individual signs.

Our goal in this work is to produce *dense* sign annotations, as shown in Fig. 1. We define densification in two ways: (i) reducing gaps in the timeline so that we have a densely spotted signing sequence; and also (ii) increasing the number of words we recall in the corresponding subtitle. This process can be seen as automatic annotation of lexical signs. Automatic dense annotation of large-vocabulary sign language videos has a large range of applications including: (i) *substantially* improving recall for retrieval or intelligent fast forwards of online sign language videos; (ii) enabling *large-scale* linguistic analysis between spoken and signed languages; (iii) providing *supervision* and *improved alignment* for continuous sign language recognition and translation systems.

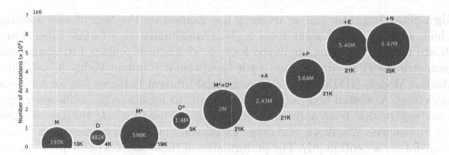

Fig. 2. Yield of automatic annotations and vocabulary size: We highlight the increase in the number of automatic annotations and vocabulary size at each stage in our proposed framework. M, D, A refer to annotations from previous methods. M*, D*, P, E, N refer to new and improved annotations collected in this work. The number of annotations is shown within each circle. The vocabulary size is reported below each circle and also represented by the circle diameter.

In this paper, we ask the following questions: (1) Can we improve current methods to improve the yield of automatic sign annotations whilst maintaining precision? (2) Can we increase the vocabulary of annotated signs over previous methods? (3) Can we 'fill in the gaps' that current spotting methods miss? The answer is yes, to all three questions, and we demonstrate this on the recently released BOBSL dataset of British Sign Language (BSL) signer interpreted video.

We make the following four contributions: (1) we significantly improve previous methods by making use of synonyms and subtitle-signing alignment; (2) we show the value of pseudo-labelling from a sign recognition model as a way of sign spotting; (3) we propose a novel approach for increasing our annotations of *known* and *unknown* sign classes based on in-domain exemplars; (4) we will make all 5 million automatic annotations publicly available to support the sign language research community. Our increased yield and vocabulary size is shown in Fig. 2. Our final vocabulary of 24.8K represents the vocabulary of English words (including named entities) from the subtitles which have been automatically associated to a sign instance; different words may have the same sign.

We note that this work is focused on *interpreted* data, which can differ from *conversational* signing in terms of style, vocabulary and speed [6]. Although our long-term aim is to move to conversational signing, learning good representations of signs from interpreted data can be a 'stepping stone' in this direction. Moreover, non-lexical signs, such as a pointing sign and spatially located signs, are essential elements of sign language, but our method is limited to the annotation of lexical signs associated to words in the text.

2   Related Work

Our work relates to several themes which we give a brief overview of below.

Sign Spotting. One line of research has focused on the task of *sign spotting*, which seeks to detect signs from a given vocabulary in a target video. Early efforts for sign spotting employed lower-level features (colour histograms and geometric cues) in combination with Conditional Random Fields [67], Hidden Markov Models (HMMs) [62] and Sequential Interval Patterns [48] for temporal modelling. A related body of work has sought to localise signs while leveraging weak supervision from audio-aligned subtitles. These include the use of external dictionaries [26,42,44] and other localisation cues such as mouthing [2] and Transformer attention [61]. The performance of these approaches depends on the quality of the visual features, keywords, and the search window. In this work, we show improved yield of existing sign spotting techniques by employing automatic subtitle alignment techniques to adjust the time window and incorporating synonyms when forming the keywords. Going further beyond the spotting task explored in prior work, we use the automatic spottings to initiate additional algorithms for sign discovery based on *in-domain* exemplar matching (Sect. 3.1). This is similar to dictionary-based sign spotting techniques [26,44] except we do not source the exemplars from external dictionaries, avoiding the domain gap issue. Besides in-domain *sign* exemplars as in [26], we explore the weak *subtitle* exemplars with unknown sign locations.

A recent progress in mouthing-based keyword spotting was presented by *Transpotter* [51]. This architecture comprises a transformer joint encoder of visual features and phoneme features that is trained to regress both the presence and location of the target keyword in a sequence from mouthing patterns. Preliminary small-scale experimental results reported by Prajwal et al. [51] demonstrated that Transpotter can perform visual keyword spotting in signing footage. Here, we showcase its suitability for the large-scale annotation regime, and further train it on sign language data to obtain a greater density of sign annotations.

In this work, we demonstrate the additional value of *pseudo-labelling* [38,68] with a sign classifier as an effective mechanism for sign spotting. While pseudo-labelling has been explored previously for category-agnostic sign segmentation [52] and temporal alignment of glosses [14,37] to the best of our knowledge, this is the first use of pseudo-labelling for sign spotting by directly leveraging the predictions of a sign classifier in combination with a pseudo-label filter constructed from the subtitles themselves.

Sign Language Recognition. Efforts to develop visual systems for sign recognition stretch back to work in 1988 from Tamaura and Kawasaki [59], who sought to classify signs from hand location and motion features. There were later efforts to design hand-crafted features for sign recognition [13,47,57,64,65]. Deep convolutional neural networks then came to dominate sign representation [36], particularly via 3D convolutional architectures [2,31,39,42] with extensions to focus model capacity around human skeletons [25] and non-manual features [24].

In the domain of continuous sign language recognition, in which the objective is to infer a sequence of sign glosses, prior work has explored HMMs [3,35] in combination with Dynamic Time Warping (DTW) [70], RNNs [17] and architectures capable of learning effectively from CTC losses [14,72]. Recently, sign representation learning methods inspired by BERT [19] have shown the potential to learn effective representations for both isolated [23] and continuous [73] recognition. Koller [34] provides an extensive survey of the sign recognition literature, highlighting the extremely limited supply of datasets with large-scale vocabularies suitable for continuous sign language recognition. In our work, we aim to take a step towards addressing this gap by developing "densification" techniques for constructing such datasets automatically.

Sign Language Translation. The task of translating sign language video to spoken language sentences was first tackled with neural machine translation by Camgöz et al. [10], who also introduced the PHOENIX-Weather-2014T dataset to facilitate research on this topic. Several frameworks have been proposed to employ transformers for this task [12,69], with extensions to improve temporal modelling [41], multi-channel cues [11] and signer independence [27]. Related work has also sought to contribute to progress on this task by exploiting monolingual data [71] and gloss sequence synthesis [40,45]. To date, various works have shown promise on the PHOENIX-Weather 2014T [10] and CSL Daily [71] benchmarks. However, sign language translation has not yet been demonstrated for a large vocabulary across multiple domains of discourse. Differently from the works above, this paper focuses on developing methods that are applicable to large/open vocabulary regimes.

Weakly-Supervised Object Discovery and Localisation. Our approach is also related to the rich body of literature on object cosegmentation [29,33,53,54], weakly supervised object localisation [18,22,46,55,66], object colocalisation [30, 60] and unsupervised object discovery and localisation [15,63]. Here, we propose an algorithm for discovering and localising novel signs (i.e. for which we have no labelled examples), but instead have weak supervision in the form of subtitles containing keywords of interest. Moving beyond initial work that sought to learn from subtitles in an aligned setting [20], classical approaches for sign discovery using subtitles have included Multiple Instance Learning where the subtitles are considered as positive and negative bags for a particular keyword [7,32,50] and a priori mining [16]. Differently from these works, we first bootstrap our sign discovery process with sign spotting to both obtain initial candidates and learn robust sign representations, then propagate these examples across video data by leveraging the similarities between the resulting representations together with noisy constraints imposed by the subtitle content.

3   Densification

Our goal is to leverage several ways of sign spotting to achieve dense annotation on continuous signing data. To this end, we introduce both new sources of automatic annotations, and also improve the existing sign spotting techniques. We start by presenting two new spotting methods using in-domain exemplars: to mine more sign instances with individual *exemplar signs* (Sect. 3.1) and to discover novel signs with weak *exemplar subtitles* (Sect. 3.2). We also show the value of pseudo-labelling from a sign recognition model for sign spotting (Sect. 3.3). We then describe key improvements to previous work which substantially increase the yield of automatic annotations (Sect. 3.4). Finally, we present our evaluation framework to measure the quality of our sign spottings in a large-vocabulary setting (Sect. 3.5). The contributions of each source of annotation are assessed in the experimental results.

3.1   Mining More Spottings Through In-domain Exemplars (E)

The key idea is: given a continuous signing video clip and a set of exemplar clips of a particular sign, we can use the exemplars to search for that sign within the video clip. In our case, the exemplars are obtained from other *automatic* spotting methods (M*, D*, A, P), described in Sect. 3.3 and Sect. 3.4, and come from the same *domain* of sign language interpreted data, i.e. the same training set. We hypothesise that signs from the same domain are more likely to be signed in a similar way and in turn help recognition; in contrast, for example, to signs from a different domain such as dictionaries.

Formally, suppose we have a reference video V_0 in which we wish to localise a particular sign w, whose corresponding word occurs in the subtitle. We also have N video exemplars $V_1, \ldots, V_N$ of the sign w. For each video, V_i, let C_i denote the set of possible temporal locations of the sign w and let $c = (f, p) \in C_i$ denote a candidate with features f at temporal location p. We compute a score map between our reference video V_0 and each exemplar $V_1, \ldots, V_N$ by computing the cosine similarity between each feature at each position in $c_0 \in C_0$ and $(c_1, c_2, \ldots c_n) \in C_1 \times \cdots \times C_N$. This results in N score maps of dimension $|C_0| \times |C_i|$ for $i = 1 \ldots N$. We then apply a max operation over the temporal dimension of the exemplars, giving us N vectors of length $|C_0|$, which we call $M_1, \ldots, M_N$.

We subsequently apply a voting scheme to find the location of the common sign w in V_0. Specifically, we let $L = \frac{1}{N} \sum_{i=1}^{N} \mathbb{1}_{(M_i > h)}$ for a threshold h, where the vector $\mathbb{1}_{(M_i > h)}$ takes the value 1 for entries of M_i which are greater than h and 0 otherwise. The candidate location of w in V_0 is then $c = (f, p) \in C_0$ where p corresponds to the position of the maximum non-zero entry in the vector L (see Fig. 3 for a visual illustration). If there are multiple maxima, we assign p to be the midpoint of the largest connected component. If all entries in L are zero, we conclude w is not present. We perform two variants of this approach using mean and max pooling of the score maps (instead of voting); these are described in the appendix. We note that for a given signing sequence, we only focus on finding signs for words in the subtitle that have *not* been annotated by other methods.

3.2 Discovering Novel Sign Classes (N)

One limitation of our proposed method in Sect. 3.1 is that we are only able to collect more sign instances from a *closed* vocabulary, determined by sign exemplars obtained from other methods (described in Sect. 3.3 and Sect. 3.4). Here, we extend our approach to localise *novel* signs, for which we have no exemplar signs but whose corresponding word appears in the subtitle text. We follow our approach described in Sect. 3.1, computing score maps between our reference video and exemplar subtitles (instead of exemplar signs, see Fig. 3). We note that by 'exemplar subtitle', we are referring to the video frames corresponding to the subtitle timestamps. Non-lexical signs, such as pointing signs or pause gestures, are very common in sign language. To avoid annotating such non-lexical signs as the common sign across V_0 and $V_1, \ldots, V_N$, we also choose N^- negative subtitle exemplars $U_1 \ldots U_{N^-}$ presumed to not contain w (due to the absence of w in the subtitle). We compute L^+ and L^- using the score maps from positive exemplars $V_1, \ldots, V_N$ and negative exemplars $U_1, \ldots, U_{N^-}$ respectively. We then let $L = L^+ - L^-$. Implementation details on the number of positive and negative exemplars used can be found in the appendix.

3.3 Pseudo-labelling as a Form of Sign Spotting (P)

We propose to re-purpose a pretrained large-vocabulary sign classification model (see vocabulary expansion in Sect. 3.5) for the task of sign spotting. Specifically, we predict a sign class from a fixed vocabulary for each time step in a continuous signing video clip. We subsequently filter the predicted signs to words which

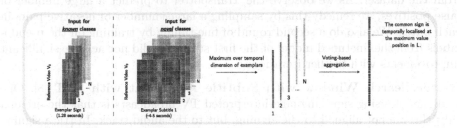

Fig. 3. Sign spotting through exemplars to find instances of known classes (E) and novel classes (N): By comparing a reference video V_0 to a set of exemplars (either sign exemplars for known sign class instances or weak subtitle exemplars for novel sign class instances), we can find the common lexical sign in the collection. We (1) form a set of score maps by calculating the cosine similarities between reference and exemplar representations; (2) we perform a maximum operation over the temporal dimension of exemplars; (3) we apply a voting-based aggregation to find the temporal location of the common sign in V_0. The duration of exemplar signs is fixed.

occur in the corresponding English subtitle. Similarly to [61], here the task is to recognise the sign from scratch, without a query keyword. The subtitle is only used as a post-processing step to filter out signs which are less likely performed (due to absence in the subtitle).

3.4   Improving the Old (M*, D*)

Here, we briefly describe our improvements over the existing sign spotting techniques, additional details are provided in the appendix.

Better Mouthings with an Upgraded KWS from Transpotter [51]. In previous work [1], an improved BiLSTM-based visual-only keyword spotting model of Stafylakis et al. [56] from [43] (named "P2G [56] baseline") is used to automatically annotate signs via mouthings. In this work, we make use of the recently proposed transformer-based *Transpotter* architecture [51], provided by the authors, that achieves state-of-the-art results in visual keyword spotting on lipreading datasets. We follow the procedure described in [1,2] to query words in the subtitle in continuous signing video clips.

Finetuning KWS on Sign Language Data through Bootstrapping. The visual keyword spotting Transpotter architecture in [51] is trained on silent speech segments, which differ considerably from signer mouthings. In fact, signers do not mouth continuously and sometimes only partly mouth words [5]. In order to reduce this severe domain gap, we propose a dual-stage finetuning strategy. First, we extract high-confidence mouthing annotations using the pre-trained Transpotter from [51] on the BOBSL training data. We query for the words in the subtitle and obtain the temporal localization of the word in the video. We finetune on this pseudo-labeled data using the same training pipeline of [51], where the spotted mouthings (word-video pairs) act as positive samples. For the negative samples, we pair a given word with a randomly sampled video segment from the dataset. As we observe the Transpotter to predict a large number of false positives, we remedy this by sampling a larger number of negative pairs in each batch. We also do a second round of fine-tuning by training on the pseudo-labels from the finetuned model of the first stage. We did not achieve significant improvements with further iterations.

Better Search Window with Subtitle Alignment with SAT [8]. One challenge in using sign language interpreted TV broadcasts is that the original subtitles are not aligned to the signing, but to the audio track. In [1], a signing query window is defined as the audio-aligned subtitle timings together with padding on both sides to account for the misalignment. We automatically align spoken language text subtitles to the signing video by using the SAT model introduced in [8], trained on manually aligned and pseudo-labelled subtitles as described in [1]. By using subtitles which are better aligned to the signing, we reduce the probability of missing spottings.

Better Keywords with Synonyms and Similar Words. To determine whether a keyword belongs to a subtitle, previous works [1] check whether the raw form, the lemmatised form, or the text normalised form (e.g. *two* instead of *2*) appears in the subtitle text. We notice that this is sub-optimal as multiple words may correspond to the same sign, often due to (i) English synonyms, (ii) identical signs for similar words, or (iii) ambiguities in spoken language. For example, *dad* and *father* or *today* and *now* can be the same signs in BSL. In this work, we investigate whether the automatic annotation yield could be improved by querying words beyond the subtitle, by querying synonyms and similar words to the words in the subtitle. We collect the additional words to query through (i) English synonyms from WordNet [21], (ii) the metadata present in online sign language dictionaries such as SignBSL[1] [44] and BSL Sign-Bank[2] which provide a set of 'related words' for each sign video entry; (iii) words with GloVe [49] cosine similarity above 0.9 to account for ambiguities in spoken language.

3.5   Evaluation Framework

Our framework consists of three stages: (a) a costly end-to-end classification training to learn sign category aware video features given an initial set of sign-clip annotation pairs; (b) a lightweight classification training given pre-extracted video features for a large number of annotations; (c) a sliding window evaluation of the trained lightweight model by comparing dense sign predictions against the subtitles (see Sect. 4.1). These stages are illustrated in Fig. 4. Note that the *annotations* we refer to are always *automatically* localised sign spottings from continuous videos using subtitle information. The motivation for the video backbone and lightweight classifier is purely related to computational costs. Unlike traditional video recognition datasets, we work with untrimmed video data of 1400 h, where the set of sign-clip pairs is not fixed. Instead, our goal is to increase the number of sign-clip pairs within the continuous stream, and assess the quality of the expanded annotation yield on the proxy task of continuous sign language recognition. Next, we describe the training stages for the video backbone and the lightweight classifier.

Improving the I3D Feature Extractor through Vocabulary Expansion. Following previous works [1,2,31,39], we use the I3D spatio-temporal convolutional architecture to train an end-to-end sign recognition model. We input 16 consecutive RGB frames and output class probabilities. The details about optimisation are provided in the appendix. As explained above, this model forms the basis of sign video representation which corresponds to the spatio-temporally pooled latent embedding before the classification layer. The prior work of [1] trains this classifier on the BOBSL dataset (see Sect. 4.1) with 2K categories obtained through the vocabulary of mouthing spottings. As a first step, we perform a vocabulary expansion and construct a significantly increased vocabulary of 8K categories. This is achieved by including each sign that has at least 5 training spottings above 0.7 confidence from both mouthing (M) and dictionary (D) annotations. The confidence for the mouthing annotation corresponds to

---

[1] www.signbsl.com.

[2] https://bslsignbank.ucl.ac.uk.

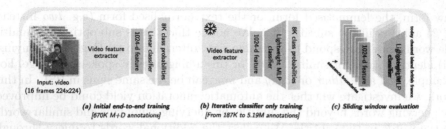

Fig. 4. Evaluation framework: (a) Video features are obtained by training an I3D architecture end-to-end given M + D annotations from [1]. The I3D ingests 16-frames of video and has a linear classifier for 8K sign categories. The end-to-end training is a costly procedure which is not affordable to repeat for each set of our new sign spottings that are on the order of several million training samples. (b) As new sets of spottings are generated, a light weight MLP classifier is trained on the pre-extracted I3D features. This relatively inexpensive training procedure means that we benefit from new annotations without the expense of end-to-end training. (c) The MLP is applied in a sliding window fashion to the signing sequence to generate sign predictions.

the probability that a text keyword (corresponding to the sign) is mouthed at a certain time frame, as computed in [2]. The confidence for the dictionary annotation corresponds to the cosine similarity (normalised between 0–1) between the representations of a dictionary clip of the sign and the continuous signing at each time frame, as in [44]. The resulting M+D training set comprises 670K annotations, with a long-tailed distribution. Furthermore, we note that the categories are noisy where multiple categories may correspond to the same sign, and vice versa. Despite this noise, we empirically show that this model provides better performance than its 2K-vocabulary counterpart. We use our improved I3D model for two purposes: as the frozen feature extractor and as the source of pseudo-labelling for sign spotting (see Sect. 3.3).

Lightweight Sign Recognition Model. Following [61], we opt for a 4-layer MLP module (with one residual connection) to assess the quality of different sets of annotations. Given pre-extracted features, this model is trained for sign recognition into 8K categories. We note that we do not train on a larger vocabulary to avoid the presence of many singletons in the training set. The efficiency of the MLP allows faster experimentation to analyse the value of each of our sign spotting sets. The input is one randomly sampled feature around the sign spotting location (the receptive field of one feature 16 frames). The MLP weights are randomly initialised. Additional training and implementation details are given in the appendix Sect. B.5 and B.6.

4   Experiments

We start by describing our dataset and evaluation metrics (Sect. 4.1). We then present experimental results on the contribution of each source of annotation and show qualitative examples (Sect. 4.2).

4.1   Data and Evaluation Protocol

BOBSL [1] is a public dataset consisting of British Sign Language interpreted BBC broadcast footage, along with English subtitles corresponding to the audio content. The data contains 1,962 episodes, which have a total duration of 1,467 h spanning 426 different TV shows. BOBSL has a total 1,193K subtitles covering a total vocabulary of 78K words. We note that in this work we use the word *subtitle* to refer to the processed BOBSL sentences from [1] as opposed to the raw subtitles. There are a total of 39 signers in the dataset. Further dataset statistics can be found in [1]. For a subset of 36 episodes in BOBSL, referred to as SENT-TEST in [1], the English subtitles have been manually aligned *temporally* to the continuous signing video. We make use of this test set to evaluate the quality of our predicted automatic annotations. SENT-TEST covers a total duration of 31 h and contains 20,870 English subtitles. The total vocabulary of English words is 13,641, of which 5,604 are singletons. The 3 signers in SENT-TEST are different to the signers in the training set, this enables signer-independent BSL recognition to be evaluated.

Evaluation Protocol. Given an English subtitle and the *temporally* aligned continuous signing video clip, we evaluate our predicted signs for the clip using (i) *intersection over union* (IoU); (ii) *recall* between signs and the English word sequence; and (iii) *temporal coverage*: this is defined as the proportion of frames in the clip assigned to signs that occur in the word sequence, where a sign is given a fixed duration of 16 frames (25 Hz video). Note that none of these metrics depend on the word order of the English subtitle, only the words it contains. All metrics are rescaled from the range 0–1 to 0–100% for readability.

For this evaluation, stop words are filtered out since often they are not signed. This reduces the number of test subtitles from 20,870 to 20,547: subtitles such as "is it?", "Oh!", "but no" are removed. The sign and word sequences are also lemmatised. We also remove repetitions from the predicted sign sequence and allow the prediction of synonyms of words in the English subtitle. This processing is highlighted in Fig. 5, where the IoU and recall are computed for a pair of predicted signs and English text. While this evaluation is suboptimal due to the simplified word-sign correspondence assumption, it tests the capacity of the sign recognition model in a large-vocabulary scenario, necessary for open-vocabulary sign language technologies.

Note, the predicted signs for a clip can be produced in two ways. In the first way, the signs are obtained from the automatic annotations using knowledge of the content of the English subtitle – we refer to these as *Spottings*. In the second, signs are predicted directly from the clip using the MLP sign predictions, without access to the corresponding English subtitle. These are referred to as *MLP predictions*. Spottings are evaluated using all the words; this metric is important to monitor how dense we can automatically annotate the data. The MLP evaluation is limited to the fixed classification vocabulary (of size 8K in our experiments). We note that when different annotations are combined, the sign spotting methods are applied independently.

Subtitle: Lemmatise, no stopwords (L+NS):	I hope they taste really good! hope taste really good	**Recall** = 0.75 (MLP predicts 3 out of 4 words in subtitle)
MLP predictions: L+NS+combine *synonym* classes:	do hope miss mouth taste delicious delicious good do do do hope miss mouth taste good	**IoU** = 0.5 (Intersection=3, union=6)
Subtitle: Lemmatise, no stopwords (L+NS):	So one of the first indicators of spring? one first indicator spring	**Recall** = 0.75 (MLP predicts 3 out of 4 words in subtitle)
MLP predictions: L+NS+combine synonym classes:	receive green year grow sell true start start start spring spring spring spring one one fast charles receive green year spring sell true first one fast charles	**IoU** = 0.27 (Intersection=3, union=11)

Fig. 5. Evaluation illustration on sample prediction: We illustrate the processing applied to the predicted sign sequence from the MLP predictions and corresponding English subtitle for calculating our metrics. As the MLP model predicts one sign per time-step, some predictions are repeated and irrelevant words appear at transition periods between signs, decreasing the IoU. Some signs are not predicted as they are not signed, showing the limitations of using the subtitle to measure performance.

Table 1. Comparison of I3D video features: We highlight the improved performance of I3D on the test set (SENT-TEST) when trained on a larger vocabulary (8K instead of 2K) with more samples (670K instead of 426K).

Annot. source	Num. I3D train annot.	Vocab. size	I3D predictions (subtitle independent)		
			Recall	IoU	Coverage
M [2]+D [44]	426K	2K	25.5	6.4	15.5
M [2]+D [44]	670K	8K	**26.3**	**7.9**	**16.3**

4.2 Results

Comparison of Video Features. By finetuning our Kinetics pretrained I3D model on BOBSL M+D annotations from [1] using an 8K vocabulary instead of a 2K vocabulary, we improve predictions on the test set, as shown in Table 1. We increase the recall from 25.5 to 26.3 and the coverage from 15.5 to 16.3. We therefore use the 8K M+D model for the rest our experiments as the frozen feature extractor. We note that we restrict the M+D annotations to the high-confidence ones (over 0.8 threshold) used for the I3D baseline in [1], as these present an appropriate signal-to-noise ratio. We use the same threshold for subsequent automatic annotations unless stated otherwise.

Oracle. As the MLPs are trained on a restricted 8K vocabulary, it is not possible to predict the full vocabulary of 13,641 words present in the test set subtitles. Furthermore, not all words in the subtitle are signed and vice versa. This means a recall, IoU and coverage of 100% is not achievable between predicted signs and English subtitle words. However, we propose an oracle in Table 2 whereby we measure the recall and IoU assuming each word in the subtitle, which either falls within the 8K vocabulary or corresponds to a synonym of a word in the 8K vocabulary, is signed and correctly predicted. The oracle achieves a recall of 86.7 and IoU of 86.3. For the coverage metric, we assume each correctly predicted sign has a duration of 16 frames and no signs overlap. The resulting oracle coverage is 55.2. This low coverage is partly due to the signer pausing within subtitles

Table 2. Improved mouthing and dictionary spottings: We evaluate different sets of spottings and their respective MLP predictions. M [51] shows our finetuned version for all the rows in the last block. We quantify the effects of subtitle alignment and querying synonyms. We also show the oracle performance and a translation baseline.

Annotation source	Subtitle Alignment	Synonyms	Training set			Spottings [full] (subtitle dependent)			MLAP predictions [8K] (subtitle independent)		
			full Vocab	#ann [full]	#ann. [8K]	Recall	IoU	Coverage	Recall	IoU	Coverage
Oracle			–	–	–	–	–	–	86.7	86.3	55.2
Translation baseline [1]			–	–	–	–	–	–	11.7	8.3	7.6
M [2]			13.6K	197K	187K	2.5	2.2	1.3	15.1	3.2	8.7
M [51] (no finetuning)			21.5K	725K	661K	9.4	8.3	4.9	20.4	4.8	11.9
M [51]			18.6K	445K	412K	7.1	6.5	3.9	23.6	4.8	13.8
M [51] (M*)	✓		19.6K	598K	552K	8.9	8.2	4.9	27.4	6.3	16.7
M [51]	✓	✓	19.6K	1.38M	1.25M	11.8	10.4	6.1	25.3	6.2	16.3
D [44]			4.4K	482K	482K	6.5	6.3	3.7	24.0	7.2	15.1
D [44]	✓		4.5K	535K	535K	7.0	6.9	4.0	24.2	7.3	15.3
D [44] (D*)	✓	✓	5.0K	1.40M	1.39M	12.5	11.6	7.0	26.0	7.3	16.9
M*+ D*	✓	✓(D-only)	20.9K	2.00M	1.94M	19.0	17.6	10.5	29.0	7.9	18.4
M*+ D*+ A [61]	✓	✓(D-only)	20.9K	2.43M	2.37M	**21.9**	**20.1**	**11.8**	**29.6**	**9.1**	**19.0**

and also due to the presence of non-lexical signs. In fact, the percentage of fully lexical signs in three other sign language corpora (Auslan [28], ASL [28] and LSF [4]) is estimated to be only 70–85% of total signing.

Translation Baseline. Although the goal in this work is not translation, but achieving dense annotations, we can nevertheless compare our MLP predictions to the translation baseline in [1]. Using the test set translation predictions from this model, we perform the same processing as highlighted in Fig. 5 to calculate our metrics. As shown in Table 2, all our simple MLP models clearly outperform the transformer-based translation model used in [1], demonstrating that we are able to recognise more signs in the English subtitle.

Improving Mouthing and Dictionary Spottings. As shown in Table 2, by using the Transpotter [51] for spotting mouthings M, our yield of total annotations triples from 197K to 725K. The quality of these new annotations is reflected in the increased performance of the MLP: the recall increases from 15.1 to 20.4 and the coverage from 8.7 to 11.9. Finetuning the keyword spotter on sign language data through pseudo-labelling also helps considerably despite the drop in the number of training annotations since there are less false positives; recall increases from 20.4 to 23.6 and coverage from 11.9 to 13.8. Subtitle alignment improves the yield of both mouthing and dictionary annotations, as shown in Table 2. This translates to a significant boost for mouthings on the MLP performance; the recall increases from 23.6 to 27.4 and the coverage from 13.8 to 16.7. For dictionary annotations, the improvement by using aligned subtitles is less striking. By querying synonyms when searching for mouthings, the yield more than doubles. However, these additional annotations seem to be quite noisy as they decrease the performance of our MLP. Due to the nature of sign language interpretation, it is possible that signers are far more likely to mouth a word

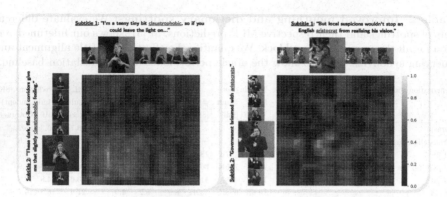

Fig. 6. Discovering novel sign classes (N): For two pairs of continuous signing sentences, we plot the score maps (as described in Sect. 3.1) between their feature sequences. We highlight the ability of our approach to spot novel sign classes.

Table 3. Ablation on mining exemplar-based spottings for known signs E: We perform different ablations for mining known signs which have been unannotated by previous methods (M*, D*, A, P). We experiment with the source of exemplar data (same episode, same signer, all data), the confidence of exemplar signs (0,0.5,0.8), the number of samples of exemplar data (5,10,20) and the pooling mechanism (average, max, vote). We evaluate on the test set (SENT-TEST).

Ann src.	ex. data	ex. thres	ex. #	ex. pooling	Training set full vocab	#ann [full]	#ann [8K]	Spottings [full] (subtitle dependent) Recall	IoU	Coverage	MLP predictions [8K] (subtitle independent) Recall	IoU	Coverage
E	Same ep	0	Var	Avg	11.6K	869K	833K	10.4	9.6	5.8	25.1	6.9	15.3
E	Same signer	0	20	Avg	15.9K	505K	421K	7.8	7.5	4.4	23.1	5.6	14.2
E	All	0	20	Avg	16.7K	351K	252K	5.7	5.7	3.3	21.5	5.1	13.4
E	All	0.5	20	Avg	16.6K	370K	261K	5.9	5.8	3.4	21.9	5.2	13.5
E	All	0.8	20	Avg	16.6K	458K	358K	7.4	7.3	4.3	25.2	6.2	15.7
E	All	0.8	20	Max	15.4K	1.48M	1.38M	20.2	18.6	10.8	27.6	8.4	17.7
E	All	0.8	10	Max	15.4K	1.07M	982K	15.2	14.0	8.3	27.9	8.0	17.7
E	All	0.8	5	Max	15.3K	740K	664K	10.7	10.0	6.0	27.6	7.6	17.4
E	All	0.8	20	Vote	15.9K	1.76M	1.63M	**25.8**	**23.3**	**13.5**	**28.4**	**8.5**	**18.1**
E	All	0.8	10	Vote	15.8K	1.32M	1.21M	20.0	18.1	10.7	28.4	8.3	18.1

which is actually in the written subtitle than a synonym of that word. We therefore do not query synonyms for mouthing spottings. For dictionary spottings, we observe the opposite effect. By incorporating synonyms, the yield of dictionary spottings more than doubles and the recall of the MLP predictions also increases from 24.2 to 26.0. We denote our best performing mouthing and dictionary spottings with M* and D*, respectively. Adding attention spottings from [1] (with a threshold of 0) adds around 400K additional annotations and boosts the MLP performance; increasing recall from 29.0 to 29.6 and coverage from 18.4 to 19.0, compared to the oracle recall of 86.7 and coverage of 55.2.

Sign Recognition as a Form of Pseudo-labelling. Pseudo-labels P are a source of over 1M new annotations (when using a threshold of 0.5) on top of our best M*, D*, A spottings. As shown in Table 4, they greatly increase the spottings recall from 21.9 to 25.4 and coverage from 11.8 to 13.9, while only marginally increasing the recall and coverage for MLP predictions. As the pseudo-labels come from our 8K I3D model in Table 1 whose frozen features are also used for training the MLP, P may not be providing additional information for our downstream evaluation. Nevertheless, they provide a great source of additional spottings (not found by previous methods) for our goal of dense annotation.

Mining more Examples of Known and Novel Sign Classes with In-domain Exemplars. By explicitly querying words in the subtitle text which are not present in our annotations, we can obtain significantly more annotations. Table 3 shows multiple methods to use exemplar signs to find additional annotations for these signs. The best performing method takes spotting exemplars from across the whole training set, irrespective of signer or episode, and uses the voting scheme described in Sect. 3.1 to localise signs. By using 20 spotting exemplars, we acquire 1.63M additional annotations. An MLP model trained *only* on these additional annotations achieves a recall of 28.4 and coverage of 18.1. Table 4 illustrates the impact of combining these additional annotations from spotting exemplars to M*, D*, A and P annotations. With the additional exemplar-based annotations E, recall increases from 29.8 to 30.7 and coverage increases from 19.2 to 19.8, where the oracle recall and coverage are 86.7 and 55.2. Furthermore, by mining instances of novel sign classes N (see Fig. 6), we increase our total vocabulary to 24.8K and total number of annotations to 5.47M.

Table 4. Pseudo-label spottings P & Exemplar-based sign spottings for known E and novel classes N: We highlight the boost in annotations by adding our pseudo-label annotations (P) as well as exemplar-based spottings of known (E) and novel (N) classes. We evaluate Spottings and MLP predictions on the test set (SENT-TEST). For the novel classes, we only show the evaluation of spottings since these are beyond the 8K training vocabulary of the MLP.

Annotation source	Training set			Spottings [full]			MLP predictions [8K]		
	full	#ann.	#ann.	(subtitle dependent)			(subtitle independent)		
	vocab	[full]	[8K]	Recall	IoU	Coverage	Recall	IoU	Coverage
M* + D* + A [61] + P	20.9K	3.64M	3.56M	25.4	23.5	13.9	29.8	8.9	19.2
M* + D* + A [61] + P + E	20.9K	5.40M	5.19M	45.3	40.7	23.3	**30.7**	**9.5**	**19.8**
M* + D* + A [61] + P + E + N	24.8K	5.47M	–	**45.6**	**40.9**	**23.4**	–	–	–

5 Conclusion

Progress in sign language research has been accelerated in recent years due to the availability of large-scale datasets, in particular sourced from interpreted TV broadcasts. However, a major obstacle for the use of such data is the lack of available sign level annotations. Previous methods [2,44,61] only found *sparse* correspondences between keywords in the subtitle and individual signs. In our work, we propose a framework which scales the number of confident automatic annotations from 670K to 5.47M (which we make publicly available). Potential future directions for research include: (1) increasing our number of annotations by incorporating context from *surrounding* signing to resolve ambiguities; (2) investigating *linguistic* differences between spoken English and British Sign Language such as the different word/sign ordering; (3) leveraging our automatic annotations for sign language translation.

Acknowledgements. This work was supported by EPSRC grant ExTol, a Royal Society Research Professorship and the ANR project CorVis ANR-21-CE23-0003-01. LM would like to thank Sagar Vaze for helpful discussions. HB would like to thank Annelies Braffort and Michéle Gouiffés for the support.

References

1. Albanie, S., et al.: BOBSL: BBC-Oxford British Sign Language Dataset. arXiv preprint arXiv:2111.03635 (2021)
2. Albanie, S., et al.: BSL-1K: scaling up co-articulated sign language recognition using mouthing cues. In: Vedaldi, A., Bischof, H., Brox, T., Frahm, J.-M. (eds.) ECCV 2020. LNCS, vol. 12356, pp. 35–53. Springer, Cham (2020). https://doi.org/10.1007/978-3-030-58621-8_3
3. Bauer, B., Hienz, H.: Relevant features for video-based continuous sign language recognition. In: Proceedings Fourth IEEE International Conference on Automatic Face and Gesture Recognition (Cat. No. PR00580), pp. 440–445. IEEE (2000)
4. Belissen, V., Braffort, A., Gouiffés, M.: Experimenting the automatic recognition of non-conventionalized units in sign language. Algorithms **13**(12), 310 (2020)
5. Boyes Braem, P., Sutton-Spence, R.: The Hands are the Head of the Mouth. The Mouth as Articulator in Sign Languages. Signum Press, Hamburg (2001)
6. Bragg, D., et al.: Sign language recognition, generation, and translation: an interdisciplinary perspective. In: ACM SIGACCESS (2019)
7. Buehler, P., Zisserman, A., Everingham, M.: Learning sign language by watching tv (using weakly aligned subtitles). In: 2009 IEEE Conference on Computer Vision and Pattern Recognition, pp. 2961–2968. IEEE (2009)
8. Bull, H., Afouras, T., Varol, G., Albanie, S., Momeni, L., Zisserman, A.: Aligning subtitles in sign language videos. In: ICCV (2021)
9. Camgoz, N., et al.: Content4all open research sign language translation datasets. arXiv:abs/2105.02351 (2021)
10. Camgoz, N.C., Hadfield, S., Koller, O., Ney, H., Bowden, R.: Neural sign language translation. In: Proceedings of the IEEE Conference on Computer Vision and Pattern Recognition, pp. 7784–7793 (2018)
11. Camgoz, N.C., Koller, O., Hadfield, S., Bowden, R.: Multi-channel transformers for multi-articulatory sign language translation. In: Bartoli, A., Fusiello, A. (eds.) ECCV 2020. LNCS, vol. 12538, pp. 301–319. Springer, Cham (2020). https://doi.org/10.1007/978-3-030-66823-5_18
12. Camgoz, N.C., Koller, O., Hadfield, S., Bowden, R.: Sign language transformers: joint end-to-end sign language recognition and translation. In: IEEE Conference on Computer Vision and Pattern Recognition (CVPR) (2020)

13. Charayaphan, C., Marble, A.: Image processing system for interpreting motion in American sign language. J. Biomed. Eng. **14**(5), 419–425 (1992)
14. Cheng, K.L., Yang, Z., Chen, Q., Tai, Y.-W.: Fully convolutional networks for continuous sign language recognition. In: Vedaldi, A., Bischof, H., Brox, T., Frahm, J.-M. (eds.) ECCV 2020. LNCS, vol. 12369, pp. 697–714. Springer, Cham (2020). https://doi.org/10.1007/978-3-030-58586-0_41
15. Cho, M., Kwak, S., Schmid, C., Ponce, J.: Unsupervised object discovery and localization in the wild: Part-based matching with bottom-up region proposals. In: Proceedings of the IEEE Conference on Computer Vision and Pattern Recognition, pp. 1201–1210 (2015)
16. Cooper, H., Bowden, R.: Learning signs from subtitles: a weakly supervised approach to sign language recognition. In: 2009 IEEE Conference on Computer Vision and Pattern Recognition, pp. 2568–2574. IEEE (2009)
17. Cui, R., Liu, H., Zhang, C.: Recurrent convolutional neural networks for continuous sign language recognition by staged optimization. In: Proceedings of the IEEE Conference on Computer Vision and Pattern Recognition, pp. 7361–7369 (2017)
18. Deselaers, T., Alexe, B., Ferrari, V.: Localizing objects while learning their appearance. In: Daniilidis, K., Maragos, P., Paragios, N. (eds.) ECCV 2010. LNCS, vol. 6314, pp. 452–466. Springer, Heidelberg (2010). https://doi.org/10.1007/978-3-642-15561-1_33
19. Devlin, J., Chang, M.W., Lee, K., Toutanova, K.: Bert: pre-training of deep bidirectional transformers for language understanding. arXiv preprint arXiv:1810.04805 (2018)
20. Farhadi, A., Forsyth, D.: Aligning ASL for statistical translation using a discriminative word model. In: CVPR (2006)
21. Feinerer, I., Hornik, K.: wordnet: WordNet Interface (2020). https://CRAN.R-project.org/package=wordnet, r package version 0.1-15
22. Gokberk Cinbis, R., Verbeek, J., Schmid, C.: Multi-fold mil training for weakly supervised object localization. In: Proceedings of the IEEE Conference on Computer Vision and Pattern Recognition, pp. 2409–2416 (2014)
23. Hu, H., Zhao, W., Zhou, W., Wang, Y., Li, H.: Signbert: pre-training of hand-model-aware representation for sign language recognition. In: Proceedings of the IEEE/CVF International Conference on Computer Vision, pp. 11087–11096 (2021)
24. Hu, H., Zhou, W., Pu, J., Li, H.: Global-local enhancement network for NMF-aware sign language recognition. ACM Trans. Multimedia Comput. Commun. Appl. TOMM **17**(3), 1–19 (2021)
25. Huang, J., Zhou, W., Li, H., Li, W.: Attention-based 3D-CNNs for large-vocabulary sign language recognition. IEEE Trans. Circuits Syst. Video Technol. **29**(9), 2822–2832 (2018)
26. Jiang, T., Camgoz, N.C., Bowden, R.: Looking for the signs: identifying isolated sign instances in continuous video footage. In: IEEE International Conference on Automatic Face and Gesture Recognition (2021)
27. Jin, T., Zhao, Z.: Contrastive disentangled meta-learning for signer-independent sign language translation. In: Proceedings of the 29th ACM International Conference on Multimedia (2021)
28. Johnston, T.: Lexical frequency in sign languages. J. Deaf Stud. Deaf Educ. **17**(2), 163–193 (2012)
29. Joulin, A., Bach, F., Ponce, J.: Discriminative clustering for image co-segmentation. In: 2010 IEEE Computer Society Conference on Computer Vision and Pattern Recognition, pp. 1943–1950. IEEE (2010)

30. Joulin, A., Tang, K., Fei-Fei, L.: Efficient image and video co-localization with Frank-Wolfe algorithm. In: Fleet, D., Pajdla, T., Schiele, B., Tuytelaars, T. (eds.) ECCV 2014. LNCS, vol. 8694, pp. 253–268. Springer, Cham (2014). https://doi.org/10.1007/978-3-319-10599-4_17

31. Joze, H.R.V., Koller, O.: MS-ASL: a large-scale data set and benchmark for understanding American sign language. arXiv preprint arXiv:1812.01053 (2018)

32. Kelly, D., Mc Donald, J., Markham, C.: Weakly supervised training of a sign language recognition system using multiple instance learning density matrices. IEEE Trans. Syst. Man Cybern. Part B (Cybernetics) **41**(2), 526–541 (2010)

33. Kim, G., Xing, E.P., Fei-Fei, L., Kanade, T.: Distributed cosegmentation via submodular optimization on anisotropic diffusion. In: 2011 International Conference on Computer Vision, pp. 169–176. IEEE (2011)

34. Koller, O.: Quantitative survey of the state of the art in sign language recognition. arXiv:abs/2008.09918 (2020)

35. Koller, O., Forster, J., Ney, H.: Continuous sign language recognition: towards large vocabulary statistical recognition systems handling multiple signers. Comput. Vis. Image Underst. **141**, 108–125 (2015)

36. Koller, O., Ney, H., Bowden, R.: Deep hand: How to train a CNN on 1 million hand images when your data is continuous and weakly labelled. In: Proceedings of the IEEE Conference on Computer Vision and Pattern Recognition, pp. 3793–3802 (2016)

37. Koller, O., Zargaran, S., Ney, H.: Re-sign: re-aligned end-to-end sequence modelling with deep recurrent CNN-HMMs. In: Proceedings of the IEEE Conference on Computer Vision and Pattern Recognition, pp. 4297–4305 (2017)

38. Lee, D.H., et al.: Pseudo-label: the simple and efficient semi-supervised learning method for deep neural networks. In: Workshop on Challenges in Representation Learning, ICML, vol. 3, p. 896 (2013)

39. Li, D., Rodriguez, C., Yu, X., Li, H.: Word-level deep sign language recognition from video: a new large-scale dataset and methods comparison. In: Proceedings of the IEEE/CVF Winter Conference on Applications of Computer Vision, pp. 1459–1469 (2020)

40. Li, D., et al.: Transcribing natural languages for the deaf via neural editing programs. arXiv preprint arXiv:2112.09600 (2021)

41. Li, D., et al.: Tspnet: hierarchical feature learning via temporal semantic pyramid for sign language translation. arXiv preprint arXiv:2010.05468 (2020)

42. Li, D., Yu, X., Xu, C., Petersson, L., Li, H.: Transferring cross-domain knowledge for video sign language recognition. In: Proceedings of the IEEE/CVF Conference on Computer Vision and Pattern Recognition, pp. 6205–6214 (2020)

43. Momeni, L., Afouras, T., Stafylakis, T., Albanie, S., Zisserman, A.: Seeing wake words: audio-visual keyword spotting. BMVC (2020)

44. Momeni, L., Varol, G., Albanie, S., Afouras, T., Zisserman, A.: Watch, read and lookup: learning to spot signs from multiple supervisors. In: ACCV (2020)

45. Moryossef, A., Yin, K., Neubig, G., Goldberg, Y.: Data augmentation for sign language gloss translation. In: MTSUMMIT (2021)

46. Nguyen, M.H., Torresani, L., De La Torre, F., Rother, C.: Weakly supervised discriminative localization and classification: a joint learning process. In: 2009 IEEE 12th International Conference on Computer Vision, pp. 1925–1932. IEEE (2009)

47. Ong, E.J., Cooper, H., Pugeault, N., Bowden, R.: Sign language recognition using sequential pattern trees. In: 2012 IEEE Conference on Computer Vision and Pattern Recognition, pp. 2200–2207. IEEE (2012)

48. Ong, E.J., Koller, O., Pugeault, N., Bowden, R.: Sign spotting using hierarchical sequential patterns with temporal intervals. In: Proceedings of the IEEE Conference on Computer Vision and Pattern Recognition, pp. 1923–1930 (2014)

49. Pennington, J., Socher, R., Manning, C.: GloVe: global vectors for word representation. In: Proceedings of the 2014 Conference on Empirical Methods in Natural Language Processing (EMNLP) (2014)

50. Pfister, T., Charles, J., Zisserman, A.: Large-scale learning of sign language by watching tv (using co-occurrences). In: BMVC (2013)

51. Prajwal, K., Momeni, L., Afouras, T., Zisserman, A.: Visual keyword spotting with attention. In: BMVC (2021)

52. Renz, K., Stache, N.C., Fox, N., Varol, G., Albanie, S.: Sign segmentation with changepoint-modulated pseudo-labelling. In: Proceedings of the IEEE/CVF Conference on Computer Vision and Pattern Recognition, pp. 3403–3412 (2021)

53. Rother, C., Minka, T., Blake, A., Kolmogorov, V.: Cosegmentation of image pairs by histogram matching-incorporating a global constraint into MRFs. In: 2006 IEEE Computer Society Conference on Computer Vision and Pattern Recognition (CVPR 2006), vol. 1, pp. 993–1000. IEEE (2006)

54. Rubinstein, M., Joulin, A., Kopf, J., Liu, C.: Unsupervised joint object discovery and segmentation in internet images. In: Proceedings of the IEEE Conference on Computer Vision and Pattern Recognition, pp. 1939–1946 (2013)

55. Shi, Z., Hospedales, T.M., Xiang, T.: Bayesian joint topic modelling for weakly supervised object localisation. In: Proceedings of the IEEE International Conference on Computer Vision, pp. 2984–2991 (2013)

56. Stafylakis, T., Tzimiropoulos, G.: Zero-shot keyword spotting for visual speech recognition in-the-wild. In: Ferrari, V., Hebert, M., Sminchisescu, C., Weiss, Y. (eds.) ECCV 2018. LNCS, vol. 11208, pp. 536–552. Springer, Cham (2018). https://doi.org/10.1007/978-3-030-01225-0_32

57. Starner, T.E.: Visual recognition of American sign language using hidden Markov models. Technical report, Massachusetts Inst Of Tech Cambridge Dept Of Brain And Cognitive Sciences (1995)

58. Sutton-Spence, R., Woll, B.: The Linguistics of British Sign Language: An Introduction. Cambridge University Press, Cambridge (1999)

59. Tamura, S., Kawasaki, S.: Recognition of sign language motion images. Pattern Recogn. 21(4), 343–353 (1988)

60. Tang, K., Joulin, A., Li, L.J., Fei-Fei, L.: Co-localization in real-world images. In: Proceedings of the IEEE Conference on Computer Vision and Pattern Recognition, pp. 1464–1471 (2014)

61. Varol, G., Momeni, L., Albanie, S., Afouras, T., Zisserman, A.: Read and attend: temporal localisation in sign language videos. In: CVPR (2021)

62. Viitaniemi, V., Jantunen, T., Savolainen, L., Karppa, M., Laaksonen, J.: S-pot-a benchmark in spotting signs within continuous signing. In: Proceedings of the 9th International Conference on Language Resources and Evaluation (LREC 2014), ISBN 978-2-9517408-8-4. European Language Resources Association (LREC) (2014)

63. Vo, V.H., Sizikova, E., Schmid, C., Pérez, P., Ponce, J.: Large-scale unsupervised object discovery. In: Advances in Neural Information Processing Systems, vol. 34 (2021)

64. Vogler, C., Metaxas, D.: Adapting hidden Markov models for ASL recognition by using three-dimensional computer vision methods. In: 1997 IEEE International Conference on Systems, Man, and Cybernetics. Computational Cybernetics and Simulation, vol. 1, pp. 156–161. IEEE (1997)

65. Vogler, C., Metaxas, D.: ASL recognition based on a coupling between HMMS and 3D motion analysis. In: Sixth International Conference on Computer Vision (IEEE Cat. No. 98CH36271), pp. 363–369. IEEE (1998)
66. Wang, C., Ren, W., Huang, K., Tan, T.: Weakly supervised object localization with latent category learning. In: Fleet, D., Pajdla, T., Schiele, B., Tuytelaars, T. (eds.) ECCV 2014. LNCS, vol. 8694, pp. 431–445. Springer, Cham (2014). https://doi.org/10.1007/978-3-319-10599-4_28
67. Yang, H.D., Sclaroff, S., Lee, S.W.: Sign language spotting with a threshold model based on conditional random fields. IEEE Trans. Pattern Anal. Mach. Intell. **31**(7), 1264–1277 (2008)
68. Yarowsky, D.: Unsupervised word sense disambiguation rivaling supervised methods. In: 33rd Annual Meeting of the Association for Computational Linguistics, pp. 189–196 (1995)
69. Yin, K., Read, J.: Better sign language translation with STMC-transformer. In: COLING (2020)
70. Zhang, J., Zhou, W., Li, H.: A threshold-based HMM-DTW approach for continuous sign language recognition. In: Proceedings of International Conference on Internet Multimedia Computing and Service, pp. 237–240 (2014)
71. Zhou, H., Zhou, W., Qi, W., Pu, J., Li, H.: Improving sign language translation with monolingual data by sign back-translation. In: Proceedings of the IEEE/CVF Conference on Computer Vision and Pattern Recognition, pp. 1316–1325 (2021)
72. Zhou, H., Zhou, W., Zhou, Y., Li, H.: Spatial-temporal multi-cue network for continuous sign language recognition. In: Proceedings of the AAAI Conference on Artificial Intelligence (2020)
73. Zhou, Z., Tam, V.W., Lam, E.Y.: SIGNBERT: a Bert-based deep learning framework for continuous sign language recognition. IEEE Access **9**, 161669–161682 (2021)

MILES: Visual BERT Pre-training with Injected Language Semantics for Video-Text Retrieval

Yuying Ge[1], Yixiao Ge[2], Xihui Liu[4], Jinpeng Wang[5], Jianping Wu[6],
Ying Shan[2], Xiaohu Qie[3], and Ping Luo[1(✉)]

[1] The University of Hong Kong, Hong Kong, China
yuyingge@hku.hk, pluo@cs.hku.hk
[2] ARC Lab, Beijing, China
{yixiaoge,yingsshan}@tencent.com
[3] Tencent PCG, Shenzhen, China
tigerqie@tencent.com
[4] UC Berkeley, Berkeley, USA
xihui.liu@berkeley.edu
[5] National University of Singapore, Singapore, Singapore
jinpengwang@u.nus.edu
[6] Tsinghua University, Beijing, China
jianping@cernet.edu.cn

Abstract. Dominant pre-training work for video-text retrieval mainly adopt the "dual-encoder" architectures to enable efficient retrieval, where two separate encoders are used to contrast global video and text representations, but ignore detailed local semantics. The recent success of image BERT pre-training with masked visual modeling that promotes the learning of local visual context, motivates a possible solution to address the above limitation. In this work, we for the first time investigate masked visual modeling in video-text pre-training with the "dual-encoder" architecture. We perform Masked visual modeling with Injected LanguagE Semantics (MILES) by employing an extra snapshot video encoder as an evolving "tokenizer" to produce reconstruction targets for masked video patch prediction. Given the corrupted video, the video encoder is trained to recover text-aligned features of the masked patches via reasoning with the visible regions along the spatial and temporal dimensions, which enhances the discriminativeness of local visual features and the fine-grained cross-modality alignment. Our method outperforms state-of-the-art methods for text-to-video retrieval on four datasets with both zero-shot and fine-tune evaluation protocols. Our approach also surpasses the baseline models significantly on zero-shot action recognition, which can be cast as video-to-text retrieval.

Y. Ge—Work done during internship in ARC Lab, Tencent PCG.

Supplementary Information The online version contains supplementary material available at https://doi.org/10.1007/978-3-031-19833-5_40.

Keywords: Masked visual modeling · Video-text retrieval

1   Introduction

Pre-training visual-language models to learn transferable representations for downstream video-text retrieval has attracted increasing attention in recent years. The "dual-encoder" architectures [6,18,31,35,41,51,53], where two individual encoders are used to contrast global video and text representations, become the most popular practice to enable efficient retrieval. Despite the high efficiency, recent studies [30] have shed light on the limitations of such dual-encoder representation learning: the coarse-grained alignment constraint on global video-text features hinders the capture of detailed local semantics and the further improvements in video-text retrieval.

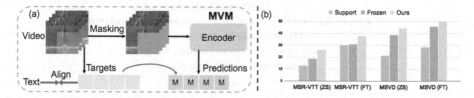

Fig. 1. (a) The diagram of Masked visual modeling with Injected LanguagE Semantics (MILES) in video-text pre-training, which aims to reconstruct the masked video content to the targets that are are aligned with the language semantics through reasoning with the spatial and temporal context of the visible video patches. (b) Comparison between recent "dual-encoder" methods for video-text pre-training in text-to-video retrieval on MSR-VTT and MSVD with both the zero-shot (ZS) and fine-tune (FT) evaluation protocols (R@1 as the metric).

Inspired by masked language modeling [12] in natural language processing, a pioneering work, BEIT [7], introduces the pretext task of masked visual modeling (MVM) to promote the learning of local visual context in image pre-training. A proportion of image patches are randomly masked, and the vision Transformer [14] is trained to recover the vision tokens that are obtained from a pre-learned image "tokenizer" [38] as the reconstruction targets. The great success of MVM in image pre-training provides a possible solution to encourage the learning of local visual semantics in video-text retrieval.

We would like to recall the key factor that makes MVM successful is the denoising training objective, where the design of the masked prediction targets turns out to be the most critical. The follow-up works [13,54] of BEIT confirm this by introducing better image tokenizers that are more aware of the high-level perceptions. So *what makes for good targets of masked visual prediction in video-text pre-training?* We argue that, towards the goal of accurate video-text retrieval, besides the spatial and temporal visual context understanding, the local alignment with language semantics serves as another important objective for the prediction of masked video patches as illustrated in Fig. 1(a).

To build masked video prediction targets with injected language semantics, we use a snapshot video encoder as an evolving "tokenizer" to produce regressed targets for masked video patches. The snapshot video encoder aggregates the knowledge of the in-training video encoder in prior epochs, whose predictions gradually approach the text domain under the global video-text contrastive constraint. By imposing MVM regularizations towards the targets from the snapshot encoder, the in-training video encoder can be iteratively improved to capture more detailed video semantics that are locally aligned with the languages, which, in turn, further enhances the evolving "tokenizer", *i.e.*, snapshot encoder. Our method successfully applies the idea of MVM in video-text pre-training without extra pre-training stages for obtaining a proper cross-modality "tokenizer".

Specifically, based on the "dual-encoder" architecture, we employ an extra snapshot video encoder to provide masked vision modeling regularization only for pre-training if not specified, that is, retaining the high efficiency of an ordinary dual-encoder structure in retrieval. In each iteration, we randomly mask a large proportion of patches in sparsely sampled videos along both the spatial and temporal dimensions to enforce a high-level understanding of local contents and temporal dynamics. The masked videos are fed into the video encoder for performing denoising auto-encoding, while the raw videos are fed into the snapshot video encoder for producing the reconstruction targets. Intuitively, given the highly corrupted video, the video encoder is trained to recover text-aligned features of the masked video content via reasoning among the visible regions along the spatial and temporal dimensions, enhancing not only the discriminativeness of local visual features but also the fine-grained cross-modality alignment.

Our contributions are three-fold. (1) We are the first to explore the potential of BERT-style pre-training in video-text retrieval with dual-encoder models. We study the pretext task of masked visual modeling in video-text pre-training and indicate its advantages in both fine-grained video context understanding and video-text local semantic alignment. (2) We introduce a flexible and effective method with a snapshot video encoder as the evolving "tokenizer" to produce learning targets for the masked video patch prediction. The video encoder gradually improved by the denoising regularizations can be used, in turn, to enhance the "tokenizer". (3) Extensive empirical results on text-to-video retrieval on four datasets with both zero-shot and fine-tune evaluation protocols fully demonstrate the superiority of our method (Fig. 1(b)). We further evaluate zero-shot action recognition on two datasets, which can be cast as a video-to-text retrieval task. Our method significantly surpasses its competitive counterparts by a large margin. As an additional benefit, we surprisingly find that our method achieves competitive performance on single-modality action recognition with much fewer video hours for pre-training.

2   Related Work

Pre-training for Video-Text Retrieval. Previous pre-training methods for video-text retrieval can be divided into two categories. Methods in the first category [6,15,16,18,29,31,35,41,48,51,53], adopt the "dual-encoder" architectures, where two individual encoders are used to contrast global video and text representations, and contrastive learning [24,33] is utilized to distinguish paired video-text data with unpaired data. Although these methods are efficient for video-text retrieval, they ignore local semantics and fine-grained alignment between modalities. Methods in the second category [27,28,30,46,50,55] adopt the "joint-encoder" architectures to interact cross-modality local features through concatenating videos and texts as inputs with a binary classifier to predict whether videos and texts are aligned or not. Despite they can build local associations between videos and texts, they sacrifice the retrieval efficiency since every text-video pair needs to be fed into the encoder during inference. In this work, we adopt the "dual-encoder" architecture for efficient retrieval and use the pretext task of masked visual modeling in video-text pre-training to enhance both fine-grained video context understanding and video-text local semantic alignment.

Image Pre-training with Masked Visual Modeling. Recent works introduce masked visual modeling (MVM) to image self-supervised pre-training, where MVM masks a proportion of the visual patches and optimizes the vision Transformers to reconstruct the missing content. The reconstruction targets are proven to be the most critical. For example, [21] reconstructs the masked image patches in the pixel space, which makes the model focus on short-range dependencies and high-frequency details. [7] predicts the discrete visual tokens from a pre-learned image "tokenizer" [38], which requires one more pre-training stage on extra data (250M images [38]). Our method uses a snapshot encoder as the evolving "tokenizer" without additional pre-training stages. A concurrent work, iBOT [54], uses a similar online tokenizer to guide MVM for image pre-training. However, we have different purposes. While iBOT encourages MVM to focus more on the high-level visual semantics rather than trivial low-level reconstruction, our method uses a self-training pipeline to progressively inject the text-aware semantics into the MVM targets, aligning the text and visual domains in both global and local representations.

Masked Region/Frame Modeling in Video-Text Pre-training. Similar techniques, masked region modeling (MRM) and masked frame modeling (MFM), were introduced in the "joint-encoder" methods for video-text pre-training. For example, [55] uses MRM, which masks the object regions of video frames with a pre-trained detection model [39] and predicts a distribution over fixed vocabulary for the masked-out frame region. [28,30,50] adopts MFM, which masks video frames and recovers the masked frames to the features encoded from an off-the-shelf video feature extraction network [49]. Both MRM and MFM rely on pre-trained models with extra data to obtain visual-only reconstruction targets, while our work evolves a snapshot video encoder to provide video-text aligned reconstruction targets without additional training stage on extra data.

3   Method

3.1   Revisiting Dual-Encoder for Video-Text Pre-training

As shown in Fig. 2, we adopt the "dual-encoder" structure to maintain high efficiency for video-text retrieval, which contains a text encoder to encode text representations from natural languages, and a video encoder to produce video representations from raw video frames. We first feed a video to the video encoder and the corresponding text description (*e.g.*, "A woman in a jumpsuit is walking along the edge of a pool") to the text encoder to embed their respective representations, which are projected to a common feature space as v^{cls} and t^{cls} via two separate linear layers. We calculate the similarity between the video and the text by performing the dot product between two projected embeddings v^{cls} and t^{cls}. We adopt a contrastive objective [24,33] to maximize the similarity between positive video-text pairs in the batch and minimize the similarity between all other negative combinations in the batch. The separate dual encoders ensure the high efficiency for retrieval since only the dot product between video and text representations is calculated during inference.

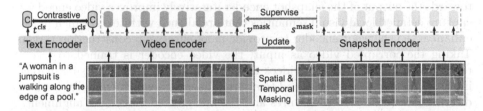

Fig. 2. The video-text pre-training pipeline of Masked visual modeling with Injected LanguagE Semantics (MILES). Based on the "dual-encoder" architecture, *i.e.* a text encoder and a video encoder, we use a snapshot video encoder to provide reconstruction targets with injected language semantics. We first mask a proportion of a video along the spatial and temporal dimension. The masked video is fed into the video encoder to predict features of the masked video patches as v^{mask}, while the raw video is fed into the snapshot encoder to produce the reconstruction targets as s^{mask}. The snapshot encoder is progressively updated from the in-training video encoder under the constraint of contrasting global video representations v^{cls} and text representations t^{cls}.

3.2   Masked Visual Modeling in Video-Text Pre-training

Overview. As illustrated in Fig. 2, we impose the regularization with injected language semantics for masked visual modeling (MVM) through using a snapshot video encoder to produce reconstruction targets for masked patches in the video, besides dual encoders for efficient retrieval. Specifically, we train the model using the pretext task of MVM with the following steps.

In the first step, a sparsely sampled video is divided and projected into a sequence of tokens following [6]. A proportion of video tokens are masked out along the spatial and temporal dimensions by being replaced with a [MASK] token, which is a learnable embedding to indicate masked patches. Positional embeddings are further added to the token sequence after [MASK] token replacement as the input token sequence. **In the second step**, the input token sequence is fed into the video encoder for performing denoising auto-encoding. The video encoder predicts the features of the masked video tokens as v^{mask} through resorting to visible video patches of spatial and temporal neighbors. **In the third step**, the raw video is fed into the snapshot video encoder to provide regularization for MVM. Features of those tokens that correspond to masked video patches for the video encoder are obtained as the reconstruction targets s^{mask}. **In the fourth step**, token-level supervision is imposed on the video encoder through minimizing the ℓ_2 distance between its predicted features v^{mask} and the reconstruction targets s^{mask} embedded from the snapshot encoder.

We progressively update the snapshot video encoder from the video encoder under the constraint of contrasting global video representations v^{cls} from the video encoder and text representations t^{cls} from the text encoder, which will be explained in the following section. Since the snapshot video encoder aggregates the knowledge of the in-training video encoder, its embedded visual features gradually align with language semantics. Imposing the regularization of MVM towards the output of the snapshot encoder iteratively improves video encoder to capture detailed local visual semantics that are aligned with texts, which in turn enhances the snapshot encoder to provide more effective reconstruction targets. Taking the corrupted video as input, the video encoder is trained to recover text-aligned local features of videos through reasoning with the visible patches in the video along the spatial and temporal dimension, which enhances both the discriminativeness of local features and the fine-grained video-text alignment.

Evolving Snapshot Video Encoder. We use a snapshot video encoder to embed text-aligned video features as reconstruction targets for MVM, which does not require pre-training with extra data. Inspired by previous work [9], we freeze the snapshot encoder over an epoch, and update its parameters in the k-th epoch denoted as $\{\theta_s\}_k$ with Exponentially Moving Averaged (EMA) [22] mechanism as $\{\theta_s\}_k = \lambda\{\theta_s\}_{k-1} + (1 - \lambda)\{\theta_v\}_{k-1}$, where $\{\theta_v\}_{k-1}$ denotes the parameters of the video encoder at the end of the $(k-1)$-th epoch. The updating mechanism makes the snapshot encoder evolve more smoothly and thus provide more consistent reconstruction targets for MVM. We also explore other update rules for the snapshot encoder in Sect. 4.5, which show inferior performances.

Masking Strategy. Videos usually exhibit similar visual patterns in adjacent patches within a frame or patches of neighboring frames (spatio-temporal neighbors), which makes the masked video patches easy to recover through interpolating between the spatio-temporal neighbors. To make masked visual modeling more challenging and improve model's spatial and temporal understanding, we adopt the "tube" masking strategy, which masks blocks of video patches along the spatial and temporal dimension instead of independently masking random patches for each frame. Specifically, we first sample a 2D mask through block-wise masking following [7], and then extend the 2D mask to 3D mask through repeating it in the temporal dimension, such that the spatially masked patches are the same for each frame. Our masking strategy refrains the video encoder from reconstructing the masked video content by extrapolation from adjacent visual patterns, and instead requires actual visual reasoning among visible patches along the spatial and temporal dimension. Other masking strategies are discussed in Sect. 4.5, which achieve worse results.

3.3   Pre-training Objectives

We combine two objectives to optimize the entire model in an end-to-end manner including a contrastive objective with Noise-Contrastive Estimation (NCE) [24, 33] and a regressive objective with ℓ_2 distance, formulated as below,

$$\mathcal{L} = \mathcal{L}_{\text{vanilla}} + \mathcal{L}_{\text{mvm}} \tag{1}$$

$$\mathcal{L}_{\text{vanilla}} = \sum_{i=1}^{B} NCE(v_i^{\text{cls}}, t_i^{\text{cls}}) + \sum_{i=1}^{B} NCE(t_i^{\text{cls}}, v_i^{\text{cls}}) \tag{2}$$

$$\text{NCE}(x_i, y_i) = -\log \frac{\exp(x_i^T y_i / \tau)}{\sum_{j=1}^{B} \exp(x_i^T y_j / \tau)} \tag{3}$$

$$\mathcal{L}_{\text{mvm}} = \sum_{i=1}^{B} ||s_i^{\text{mask}} - v_i^{\text{mask}}||_2 \tag{4}$$

where B is the batch size and τ is the temperature hyper-parameter.

3.4   Model Architecture

Video Encoder. Video encoder takes the video as input and produces final video representations and predicts features of the masked video content. A video $V \in R^{M \times 3 \times H \times W}$ sampling M frames is first divided into $M \times N$ patches, and are further fed into a linear projection head to get a sequence of $M \times N$ tokens. We follow BERT [12] to add a learnable [CLS] token to the beginning of the token sequence for global video representations. A proportion of video tokens are replaced with a [MASK] token, which is a learnable embedding. The token sequence after [MASK] token replacement are further added with learnable spatial and temporal positional embeddings. All tokens within the same frame are given the same temporal positional embedding, and all tokens in the same spatial location of different frames are given the same spatial positional embedding, so that the video encoder learns to ascertain the position of video patches. Following [6], the video encoder consists of a stack of space-time self-attention blocks, where each block sequentially performs temporal self-attention and then spatial self-attention on the output of previous block.

Text Encoder. Text encoder takes the nature language as input and outputs final text representations from the [CLS] token, which is concatenated to the beginning of the input text. We adopt a multi-layer bidirectional transformer structure [42] for the text encoder.

Snapshot Encoder. Snapshot encoder takes the original video as input and produces the reconstruction targets for MVM only in pre-training and is neglected for retrieval. It has exactly the same architecture as the video encoder.

4   Experiments

4.1   Pre-training Datasets

We follow [6] to jointly pre-train our model on an image dataset Google Conceptual Captions (CC3M) [43] and a video dataset WebVid-2M [6]. CC3M contains 3.3M image-text pairs with captions harvested from the web. WebVid-2M contains 2.5M video-text pairs with manually generated captions. We do not use the large-scale video-text dataset HowTo100M [32] with 136M video-text pairs. As [6] points out, the captions in HowTo100M are extracted from ASR transcription of continuous narration with incomplete sentences, thus are noisy.

4.2   Downstream Tasks

Text-to-Video Retrieval. (a). **MSR-VTT** [52] consists of 10K YouTube videos with 200K descriptions, which is divided into 9K and 1K videos for training and testing. (b). **MSVD** [11] contains 1,970 videos from YouTube with 80K descriptions. 1200, 100 and 670 videos are split out for training, validation and testing respectively. (c). **LSMDC** [40] consists of 118,081 video clips from 202 movies, where the validation set and the test set contain 7,408 and 1,000 videos. (d). **DiDeMo** [5] contains 10K Flickr videos with 40K sentences. 1K videos are split out for testing. We follow [6] to concatenate all sentences of a video as a single description. We perform evaluation with both the zero-shot and fine-tune setups, and adopt Recall and Median Rank as the evaluation metric.

Action Recognition. (a). **HMDB51** [26], which consists of 6,766 videos with 51 categories. (b). **UCF101** [44], which consists 13,320 videos with 101 action classes. Both datasets have three standard training/test splits. We explore three experimental settings for evaluation, including **linear**, where we fix the parameters of the video encoder and only optimize a linear classifier, **fully fine-tuning**, where we optimize the parameters of the video encoder and the linear classifier together, and **zero-shot**, where we preform video-to-text retrieval through describing a video with the name of its action class following [37]. Averaged results over three training/test splits are reported.

4.3   Implementation Details

For fair comparison, we follow the recent work [6] for implementation. We first resize a video to 224×224, and then divide a video into M equal segments. We randomly sample a single frame within each segment for training and uniformly sample a single frame within each segment for testing. We adopt the same model architecture as [6] with a video encoder and a text encoder. The video encoder consists of 12 space-time self-attention blocks [8] with patch size $P = 16$, and sequence dimension $D = 768$. We initialize the video encoder with ViT [14] weights trained on ImageNet-21k following [6, 34]. The text encoder is instantiated as DistilBERT [42] pre-trained on English Wikipedia and Toronto Book Corpus. The snapshot video encoder has the same architecture as the video encoder, and is updated over an epoch with the weights of the video encoder using $\{\theta_s\}_k = \lambda\{\theta_s\}_{k-1} + (1 - \lambda)\{\theta_v\}_{k-1}$, where θ is set as 0.996 in our experiments. We set the dimension of the common feature space as 256 and the temperature hyper-parameter of the contrastive objective as 0.05. For visual augmentation, we randomly crop and horizontally flip during training, and center crop the maximal square crop during testing. We adopt a temporal curriculum learning following [6], where we first pre-train our model on the

Table 1. Text-to-video retrieval results on MSR-VTT test set, where **higher** R@k and **lower** MedR (Median Rank) are better. Zero-shot evaluation results are shown on the top while fine-tuning on the bottom. "Video Input" lists the model to extract 3D features, where "Raw Videos" means training on raw video frame pixels without using pre-extracted features. "Pairs" lists the number of video-text pairs for pre-training.

Method	Year	Video input	Pre-train dataset	Pairs	R@1	R@5	R@10	MedR
ActBERT [55]	2020	ResNet-3D	HowTo100M	120M	8.6	23.4	33.1	36.0
MMV [2]	2020	Raw Videos	HowTo100M, AudioSet	138M	9.3	23.0	31.1	38.0
MIL-NCE [31]	2020	Raw Videos	HowTo100M	120M	9.9	24.0	32.4	29.6
VATT [1]	2021	Raw Videos	HowTo100M, AudioSet	138M	–	–	29.7	49.0
NoiseEst [4]	2021	ResNeXt-101	HowTo100M	110M	8.0	21.3	29.3	33.0
TACo [53]	2021	I3D, S3D	HowTo100M	120M	9.8	25.0	33.4	29.0
VideoCLIP [51]	2021	S3D	HowTo100M	110M	10.4	22.2	30.0	–
MCN [10]	2021	ResNeXt-101	HowTo100M	120M	10.5	25.2	33.8	–
SupportSet [35]	2021	R(2+1)D-34	HowTo100M	120M	12.7	27.5	36.2	24.0
Frozen [6]	2021	Raw Videos	CC3M, WebVid-2M	5.5M	18.7	39.5	51.6	10.0
AVLnet [41]	2021	ResNeXt-101	HowTo100M	120M	19.6	40.8	50.7	9.0
Ours	2022	Raw Videos	CC3M, WebVid-2M	5.5M	**26.1**	**47.2**	**56.9**	**7.0**
ActBERT [55]	2020	ResNet-3D	HowTo100M	120M	16.3	42.8	56.9	10.0
UniVL [30]	2020	S3D	HowTo100M	110M	21.2	49.6	63.1	6.0
MMT [15]	2020	S3D	HowTo100M	120M	26.6	57.1	69.6	4.0
HERO [28]	2021	SlowFast	TV and HowTo100M	120M	16.8	43.4	57.7	–
NoiseEst [4]	2021	ResNeXt-101	HowTo100M	110M	17.4	41.6	53.6	8.0
ClipBert [27]	2021	Raw Videos	COCO, VisGenome	5.6M	22.0	46.8	59.9	6.0
AVLnet [41]	2021	ResNeXt-101	HowTo100M	120M	27.1	55.6	66.6	4.0
VLM [50]	2021	S3D	HowTo100M	110M	28.1	55.5	67.4	4.0
TACo [53]	2021	I3D, S3D	HowTo100M	120M	28.4	57.8	71.2	4.0
SupportSet [35]	2021	R(2+1)D-34	HowTo100M	120M	30.1	58.5	69.3	3.0
VideoCLIP [51]	2021	S3D	HowTo100M	110M	30.9	55.4	66.8	-
Frozen [6]	2021	Raw Videos	CC3M, WebVid-2M	5.5M	31.0	59.5	70.5	3.0
Ours	2022	Raw Videos	CC3M, WebVid-2M	5.5M	**37.7**	**63.6**	**73.8**	**3.0**

image dataset CC3M and video dataset WebVid-2M sampling 1 frame, and then on the video dataset WebVid-2M sampling 4 frames. Pre-training with 1 frame takes 16 epochs with the batch size of 2048 and the learning rate of 1×10^{-4}, where the first epoch trains the model with only the contrastive objective as a warm-up. Pre-training with 4 frames takes 4 epochs with the batch size of 1024 and the learning rate of 3×10^{-5}. We adopt random mask sampling with the masking ratio of 75% for 1-frame pre-training and block-wise mask sampling with the masking ratio of 75% for 4-frame pre-training, where the spatial mask is repeated in the temporal dimension. For evaluating downstream tasks, we uniformly sample 4 frames for text-to-video retrieval and 16 frames for action recognition following the setting of [6,31]. We follow [6] to expand the temporal embeddings through filling zeros to enable the training of longer frames.

4.4   Main Results

Text-to-Video Retrieval. Results on MST-VTT [52] can be seen in Table 1. We have the following observations. First of all, our method outperforms all recent work by a large margin. The significant improvement of the performance under the zero-shot evaluation protocol indicates that our pre-trained model is more generalizable that can be used for out-of-domain text-to-video retrieval. Fine-tuning our pre-trained model on the training set of MSR-VTT also achieves better performance. Second, the majority of previous work pre-extract 3D features from "expert" models as the input of the video encoder (*e.g.* SupportSet [35] uses expert features from a 34-layer, R(2+1)-D model pre-trained on IG65M [17]). By contrast, our model takes raw video frame pixels as inputs without using any pre-extracted features and surpasses its counterparts. Third, previous work mainly pre-train their models on the large-scale HowTo100M [32], which is 20× lager in terms of video-text pairs than CC3M [43] and WebVid-2M [6], thus higher computation cost is required. Our pre-trained model achieves higher performance with lower computation cost. Finally, some work [27,28,30,50,55] adopts a joint encoder to concatenate videos and texts as inputs, thus every text-video pair needs to be fed into the encoder during inference, resulting in low efficiency for retrieval. By comparison, our model adopts the efficient "dual-encoder" architecture with only a video encoder and a text encoder for inference.

We further show text-to-video retrieval results on MSVD [11] in Table 2, LSMDC in Table 3, and DiDeMo [5] in Table 4. Under both the zero-shot (top) and the fine-tune (bottom) evaluation protocols, our model achieves the best performance on three datasets, demonstrating the effectiveness of our method in utilizing the pretext task of masked visual modeling in video-text pre-training to learn fine-grained cross-modality alignment between videos and texts.

Table 2. Text-to-video retrieval results on MSVD test set.

Method	R@1	R@5	R@10	MedR
NoiseEst [4]	13.7	35.7	47.7	12.0
SupportSet [35]	21.4	46.2	57.7	6.0
Frozen [6]	38.7	70.1	80.1	2.0
Ours	**44.4**	**76.2**	**87.0**	**2.0**
NoiseEst [4]	20.3	49.0	63.3	6.0
SupportSet [35]	28.4	60.0	72.9	4.0
Frozen [6]	45.6	79.8	88.2	2.0
Ours	**53.9**	**83.5**	**90.2**	**1.0**

Table 3. Text-to-video retrieval results on LSMDC test set.

Method	R@1	R@5	R@10	MedR
AVLnet [41]	1.4	5.9	9.4	273.5
NoiseEst [4]	4.2	11.6	17.1	119.0
Frozen [6]	9.3	22.0	30.1	51.0
Ours	**11.1**	**24.7**	**30.6**	**50.7**
NoiseEst [4]	6.4	19.8	28.4	39.0
MMT [15]	12.9	29.9	40.1	19.3
Frozen [6]	15.0	30.8	39.8	20.0
Ours	**17.8**	**35.6**	**44.1**	**15.5**

Action Recognition. We evaluate zero-shot action recognition on HMDB51 [26] and UCF101 [44], which is cast as video-to-text retrieval by using the name of a video's action class as its description following [37]. Table 5 lists the results, where our model outperforms the competitive baselines by a large margin. Our model improves the averaged top-1 accuracy over three splits by 16.9% and 10.5% on HMDB51, 24.9% and 6.8% on UCF101 compared with ClipBert [27] and Frozen [6]. Our method learns powerful cross-modality representations that enable effective zero-shot action recognition.

Fig. 3. The visualizations of the local cross-modality alignment between the text token and visual tokens. Compared with the model that is not trained with MVM, our pretrained model aligns words with corresponding visual regions accurately, indicating that MVM can effectively train the model to capture local video-text alignment.

Table 4. Text-to-video retrieval results on DiDeMo test set.

Method	R@1	R@5	R@10	MedR
VideoCLIP [51]	16.6	46.9	–	–
Frozen [6]	21.1	46.0	56.2	7.0
Ours	**27.2**	**50.3**	**63.6**	**5.0**
HERO [28]	2.1	–	11.4	–
CE [29]	16.1	41.1	82.7	8.3
ClipBert [27]	20.4	48.0	60.8	6.0
Frozen [6]	31.0	59.8	72.4	3.0
Ours	**36.6**	**63.9**	**74.0**	**3.0**

We further explore the single-modality video representations, where the features from the video encoder are extracted and are fed into a linear classifier. In Table 6, our model achieves higher accuracy than some competitive methods, which pre-train their models on datasets with considerably longer video duration. For example, XDC [3] pre-trains on IG-Kinetics that is 14× longer than our pre-training dataset, but gets worse results. Although MMV [2] surpasses our method when it pre-trains the model on HowTo100M and AudioSet (11× longer than ours) and utilizes extra modalities such as audio and text, its performance is far worse than ours with only text and video or audio and video as inputs.

Table 5. Zero-shot action recognition results on HMDB51 and UCF101, with top-1 accuracy as the evaluation metric. "S" denotes different testing splits and "Mean" reports the averaged results over three splits.

Method	HMDB51				UCF101			
	S1	S2	S3	Mean	S1	S2	S3	Mean
ClipBert [27]	20.0	22.0	22.3	21.4	27.5	27.0	28.8	27.8
Frozen [6]	27.5	28.3	27.7	27.8	45.4	44.7	47.7	45.9
Ours	**38.4**	**38.6**	**37.8**	**38.3**	**51.8**	**53.4**	**52.8**	**52.7**

Table 6. Action recognition results on HMDB51 and UCF101 under linear evaluation (Linear) and fully fine-tuning evaluation (Full), with top-1 accuracy as the evaluation metric. "Modality" denotes the extra modality used for pre-training besides videos, *i.e.*, audio (A), text (T), optical flow (OF), motion vector (MV). "Length" denotes the video length for pre-training in K hours.

Method	Modality	Length (K)	HMDB		UCF101	
			Linear	Full	Linear	Full
CCL [25]	–	1.8	29.5	37.8	54.0	69.4
CBT [45]	–	1.8	29.5	44.5	54.0	79.5
MemDPC [19]	OF	1.8	30.5	54.5	54.1	86.1
CoCLR [20]	OF	1.8	52.4	62.9	77.8	90.6
MVCGC [23]	MV	1.8	53.0	63.4	78.0	90.8
XDC_R [3]	A	188.3	49.9	61.2	80.7	88.8
XDC_K [3]	A	188.3	56.0	63.1	85.3	91.5
MIL-NCE [31]	T	134.5	54.8	59.2	83.4	89.1
Frozen [6]	T	13.0	61.3	66.3	87.8	89.8
VATT [1]	A, T	139.8	63.3	–	89.2	–
ELO [36]	A, OF	115.0	64.5	67.4	–	93.8
MMV [2]	A	134.5	53.6	–	77.1	–
MMV [2]	T	134.5	55.1	–	86.8	–
MMV [2]	A, T	139.8	67.1	75.0	91.8	95.2
Ours	T	13.0	65.4	70.5	89.5	92.2

Visualization. We visualize the cross-modality alignment between text tokens and visual tokens by calculating the similarity map between features embedded from the text encoder and video encoder. As shown in Fig. 3, compared with the model that is not pre-trained with MVM, our pre-trained model aligns words with corresponding visual regions accurately. For example, visual features of the football region above the man's head in the second row exhibits large similarity with the features of the word "football". Performing MVM with the video-text aligned features as the reconstruction targets effectively trains the model to enhance local video-text alignment with the "dual-encoder" architecture.

4.5   Ablation Study

Reconstruction Targets. We explore different reconstruction targets for MVM in video-text pre-training including raw frame pixels as in [21], discrete visual tokens from a learned image "tokenizer" [38] as in [7], and the text-aligned features in this work. As shown in Table 7, using masked visual modeling with different targets improves performance than the baseline model in the first row with only the contrastive objective. Imposing the regularization for MVM with text-aligned features achieves better results than with other visual-only reconstruction targets, which indicates that the local video-text alignment serves as an important objective for the prediction of masked video patches. Besides the "dual-encoder", we further adopt a joint encoder to interact videos with texts for performing denoising auto-encoding, which improves the performance over the "dual-encoder" structure with pixels and discrete tokens as the reconstruction targets. Using the joint encoder with the aligned features as the targets brings poorer results, since the learning of cross-modality alignment is mainly achieved by the joint encoder, which does not benefit dual encoders for retrieval. When the reconstruction targets contain video-text aligned semantics, it is more effective to impose MVM regularization on the output local video tokens.

Table 7. Ablation studies on different reconstruction targets, where "Joint" denotes the use of a joint encoder to concatenate videos and texts. Results of zero-shot text-to-video retrieval on MSR-VTT are reported.

Targets	Joint	R@1↑	R@5↑	R@10↑	MnR↓
–	×	21.9	43.5	53.5	52.8
Pixels	×	22.9	44.2	53.7	53.3
Pixels	√	24.4	45.2	55.3	53.1
Discrete tokens	×	24.1	46.6	56.0	51.9
Discrete tokens	√	25.0	47.1	56.6	51.8
Aligned features	√	25.2	47.1	55.6	48.3
Aligned features	×	**26.1**	**47.2**	**56.9**	**46.9**

Updating Mechanism of the Snapshot Encoder. We compare different strategies to update the snapshot video encode from the video encoder. In our method, we use the video encoder of the previous epoch with momentum update as the snapshot encoder and freeze the snapshot encoder over an epoch. As shown in Table 8, compared with our updating mechanism in the last row, using the video encoder of the current iteration, or of the previous iteration with or without momentum update all achieve less competitive performance. Since these mechanisms update the snapshot encoder in each iteration, the reconstruction targets are less consistent to impose effective regularization for MVM. Using the video encoder of previous epoch without momentum update also drops performances, since it masks the evolution of the snapshot encoder more sharp.

Table 8. Ablation studies on the updating mechanism of the snapshot video encoder. "Mom" indicates whether the momentum update is used. Results of zero-shot text-to-video retrieval on MSR-VTT are reported.

Mechanism	Mom	R@1↑	R@5↑	R@10↑	MnR↓
Current iter	–	25.0	47.1	55.7	48.8
Previous iter	×	24.7	46.4	54.6	48.9
Previous iter	√	24.5	46.2	55.3	48.8
Previous epoch	×	23.8	47.0	56.3	48.2
Previous epoch	√	**26.1**	**47.2**	**56.9**	**46.9**

Masking Strategy. We explore different strategies of masking the videos along the spatial and temporal dimension to perform MVM for multi-frame pre-training. We first propose a frame-wise masking, where a proportion of full frames are masked (*e.g.* 25% masking ratio means masking one random frame among four sampled frames), so that the model can only resort to neighboring visible frames to recover the masked frames. As shown in Table 9, frame-wise masking strategy degrades performance, which indicates that reasoning with visible patches along the spatial dimension is also essential. When "tube" masking [47] is not adopted and each frame is spatially masked individually, the model achieves the worst results because the model could temporally "interpolate" between frames with visible patches for reconstruction. We further compare different spatial masking strategies with "tube" temporal masking. Compared with block-wise masking, which tends to mask large blocks, masking with random sampling achieves less satisfactory performance because it makes the model easier to reconstruct the masked patches by resorting to visible patches within the frame. Finally, we study the effect of the masking ratio and find that our method with block-wise masking works reasonably well at a ratio of 75%, but degrades at 65% when the reconstruction task becomes easier and also degenerates at a ratio 85% when the reconstruction task is too difficult.

Table 9. Ablation studies on the masking strategy. "Tube" denotes whether the spatially masked patches are the same for each frame. Results of zero-shot text-to-video retrieval on MSR-VTT are reported.

Masking	Ratio	Tube	R@1↑	R@5↑	R@10↑	MnR↓
Frame	25%	–	25.3	46.2	55.8	47.9
Frame	50%	–	25.5	46.6	55.9	47.8
Random	65%	√	24.9	46.6	56.1	47.4
Random	75%	√	25.0	46.8	56.4	47.2
Random	85%	√	25.1	47.0	56.4	47.2
Block	75%	×	24.9	45.9	55.4	47.3
Block	65%	√	25.7	46.9	56.2	47.0
Block	85%	√	25.8	46.6	55.5	47.0
Block	75%	√	**26.1**	**47.2**	**56.9**	**46.9**

5   Conclusion

In this work, we explore masked visual modeling in video-text pre-training with the "dual-encoder" architecture for efficient video-text retrieval. We introduce an effective method with a snapshot video encoder to produce reconstruction targets with injected language semantics for the masked video patch prediction, which does not require extra pre-training stages. Training the video encode to recover the text-aligned features of masked video patches through reasoning with the visible regions along the spatial and temporal dimension strengthens both the awareness of local visual features and the fine-grained cross-modality alignment. Extensive evaluations on the text-to-video retrieval and action recognition clearly show the great advantage of our method.

Acknowledgement. Ping Luo is supported by the General Research Fund of HK No. 27208720, No. 17212120, and No. 17200622.

References

1. Akbari, H., et al.: VATT: transformers for multimodal self-supervised learning from raw video, audio and text. arXiv preprint arXiv:2104.11178 (2021)
2. Alayrac, J.-B., et al.: Self-supervised multimodal versatile networks. NeurIPS **2**(6), 7 (2020)
3. Alwassel, H., Mahajan, D., Korbar, B., Torresani, L., Ghanem, B., Tran, D.: Self-supervised learning by cross-modal audio-video clustering. In: NeurIPS 2020 (2020)
4. Amrani, E., Ben-Ari, R., Rotman, D., Bronstein, A.: Noise estimation using density estimation for self-supervised multimodal learning. In: AAAI, vol. 35, pp. 6644–6652 (2021)
5. Hendricks, L.A., Wang, O., Shechtman, E., Sivic, J., Darrell, T., Russell, B.: Localizing moments in video with natural language. In: ICCV, pp. 5803–5812 (2017)

6. Bain, M., Nagrani, A., Varol, G., Zisserman, A.: Frozen in time: a joint video and image encoder for end-to-end retrieval (2021)

7. Bao, H., Dong, L., Wei, F.: BEiT: BERT pre-training of image transformers. In: ICLR (2022)

8. Bertasius, G., Wang, H., Torresani, L.: Is space-time attention all you need for video understanding. arXiv preprint arXiv:2102.05095 (2021)

9. Caron, M., et al.: Emerging properties in self-supervised vision transformers. In: ICCV, pp. 9650–9660 (2021)

10. Chen, B., et al.: Multimodal clustering networks for self-supervised learning from unlabeled videos. arXiv preprint arXiv:2104.12671 (2021)

11. Chen, D., Dolan, W.B.: Collecting highly parallel data for paraphrase evaluation. In: ACL, pp. 190–200 (2011)

12. Devlin, J., Chang, M.-W., Lee, K., Toutanova, K.: BERT: pre-training of deep bidirectional transformers for language understanding. In: NAACL (2019)

13. Dong, X., et al.: PeCo: perceptual codebook for BERT pre-training of vision transformers. arXiv preprint arXiv:2111.12710 (2021)

14. Dosovitskiy, A., et al.: An image is worth 16x16 words: transformers for image recognition at scale. In: ICLR (2020)

15. Gabeur, V., Sun, C., Alahari, K., Schmid, C.: Multi-modal transformer for video retrieval. In: Vedaldi, A., Bischof, H., Brox, T., Frahm, J.-M. (eds.) ECCV 2020. LNCS, vol. 12349, pp. 214–229. Springer, Cham (2020). https://doi.org/10.1007/978-3-030-58548-8_13

16. Ge, Y., et al.: Bridging video-text retrieval with multiple choice questions. In: Proceedings of the IEEE/CVF Conference on Computer Vision and Pattern Recognition, pp. 16167–16176 (2022)

17. Ghadiyaram, D., Tran, D., Mahajan, D.: Large-scale weakly-supervised pre-training for video action recognition. In: CVPR, pp. 12046–12055 (2019)

18. Ging, S., Zolfaghari, M., Pirsiavash, H., Brox, T.: COOT: cooperative hierarchical transformer for video-text representation learning. In: NeurIPS (2020)

19. Han, T., Xie, W., Zisserman, A.: Memory-augmented dense predictive coding for video representation learning. In: Vedaldi, A., Bischof, H., Brox, T., Frahm, J.-M. (eds.) ECCV 2020. LNCS, vol. 12348, pp. 312–329. Springer, Cham (2020). https://doi.org/10.1007/978-3-030-58580-8_19

20. Han, T., Xie, W., Zisserman, A.: Self-supervised co-training for video representation learning. In: NeurIPS, vol. 33, pp. 5679–5690 (2020)

21. He, K., Chen, X., Xie, S., Li, Y., Dollár, P., Girshick, R.: Masked autoencoders are scalable vision learners. arXiv preprint arXiv:2111.06377 (2021)

22. He, K., Fan, H., Wu, Y., Xie, S., Girshick, R.: Momentum contrast for unsupervised visual representation learning. In: Proceedings of the IEEE/CVF Conference on Computer Vision and Pattern Recognition, pp. 9729–9738 (2020)

23. Huo, Y., et al.: Compressed video contrastive learning. In: NeurIPS, vol. 34 (2021)

24. Jozefowicz, R., Vinyals, O., Schuster, M., Shazeer, N., Wu, Y.: Exploring the limits of language modeling. arXiv preprint arXiv:1602.02410 (2016)

25. Kong, Q., Wei, W., Yoshinaga, T., Deng, Z., Murakami, T.: Cycle-contrast for self-supervised video representation learning (2020)

26. Kuehne, H., Jhuang, H., Garrote, E., Poggio, T., Serre, T.: HMDB: a large video database for human motion recognition. In: ICCV, pp. 2556–2563. IEEE (2011)

27. Lei, J., et al.: Less is more: ClipBERT for video-and-language learning via sparse sampling. In: CVPR, pp. 7331–7341 (2021)

28. Li, L., Chen, Y.-C., Cheng, Y., Gan, Z., Yu, L., Liu, J.: HERO: hierarchical encoder for video+ language omni-representation pre-training. In: EMNLP, pp. 2046–2065 (2020)

29. Liu, Y., Albanie, S., Nagrani, A., Zisserman, A.: Use what you have: video retrieval using representations from collaborative experts. arXiv preprint arXiv:1907.13487 (2019)

30. Luo, H., et al.: UniVL: a unified video and language pre-training model for multi-modal understanding and generation. arXiv preprint arXiv:2002.06353 (2020)

31. Miech, A., Alayrac, J.-B., Smaira, L., Laptev, I., Sivic, J., Zisserman, A.: End-to-end learning of visual representations from uncurated instructional videos. In: CVPR, pp. 9879–9889 (2020)

32. Miech, A., Zhukov, D., Alayrac, J.-B., Tapaswi, M., Laptev, I., Sivic, J.: Howto100m: learning a text-video embedding by watching hundred million narrated video clips. In: ICCV, pp. 2630–2640 (2019)

33. van den Oord, A., Li, Y., Vinyals, O.: Representation learning with contrastive predictive coding. arXiv preprint arXiv:1807.03748 (2018)

34. Pan, J., Lin, Z., Zhu, X., Shao, J., Li, H.: Parameter-efficient image-to-video transfer learning. arXiv preprint arXiv:2206.13559 (2022)

35. Patrick, M., et al.: Support-set bottlenecks for video-text representation learning. In: ICLR (2020)

36. Piergiovanni, A.J., Angelova, A., Ryoo, M.S.: Evolving losses for unsupervised video representation learning. In: CVPR, pp. 133–142 (2020)

37. Radford, A., et al.: Learning transferable visual models from natural language supervision. arXiv preprint arXiv:2103.00020 (2021)

38. Ramesh, A., et al.: Zero-shot text-to-image generation. In: ICML (2021)

39. Ren, S., He, K., Girshick, R., Sun, J.: Faster R-CNN: towards real-time object detection with region proposal networks. In: NeurIPS, vol. 28 (2015)

40. Rohrbach, A., Rohrbach, M., Tandon, N., Schiele, B.: A dataset for movie description. In: CVPR, pp. 3202–3212 (2015)

41. Rouditchenko, A., et al. AVLNet: learning audio-visual language representations from instructional videos. arXiv preprint arXiv:2006.09199 (2020)

42. Sanh, V., Debut, L., Chaumond, J., Wolf, T.: DistilBERT, a distilled version of BERT: smaller, faster, cheaper and lighter. arXiv preprint arXiv:1910.01108 (2019)

43. Sharma, P., Ding, N., Goodman, S., Soricut, R.: Conceptual captions: a cleaned, hypernymed, image alt-text dataset for automatic image captioning. In: ACL, pp. 2556–2565 (2018)

44. Soomro, K., Zamir, A.R., Shah, M.: UCF101: a dataset of 101 human actions classes from videos in the wild. arXiv preprint arXiv:1212.0402 (2012)

45. Sun, C., Baradel, F., Murphy, K., Schmid, C.: Learning video representations using contrastive bidirectional transformer. arXiv preprint arXiv:1906.05743 (2019)

46. Sun, C., Myers, A., Vondrick, C., Murphy, K., Schmid, C.: VideoBERT: a joint model for video and language representation learning. In: ICCV, pp. 7464–7473 (2019)

47. Tong, Z., Song, Y., Wang, J., Wang, L.: VideoMAE: masked autoencoders are data-efficient learners for self-supervised video pre-training. arXiv preprint arXiv:2203.12602 (2022)

48. Wang, J., et al.: Object-aware video-language pre-training for retrieval. In: Proceedings of the IEEE/CVF Conference on Computer Vision and Pattern Recognition, pp. 3313–3322 (2022)

49. Xie, S., Sun, C., Huang, J., Tu, Z., Murphy, K.: Rethinking spatiotemporal feature learning: speed-accuracy trade-offs in video classification. In: Ferrari, V., Hebert, M., Sminchisescu, C., Weiss, Y. (eds.) ECCV 2018. LNCS, vol. 11219, pp. 318–335. Springer, Cham (2018). https://doi.org/10.1007/978-3-030-01267-0_19

50. Xu, H., et al.: VLM: task-agnostic video-language model pre-training for video understanding. arXiv preprint arXiv:2105.09996 (2021)

51. Xu, H., et al.: VideoClip: contrastive pre-training for zero-shot video-text understanding. arXiv preprint arXiv:2109.14084 (2021)

52. Xu, J., Mei, T., Yao, T., Rui, Y.: MSR-VTT: a large video description dataset for bridging video and language. In: CVPR, pp. 5288–5296 (2016)

53. Yang, J., Bisk, Y., Gao, J.: TACO: token-aware cascade contrastive learning for video-text alignment. In: ICCV, pp. 11562–11572 (2021)

54. Zhou, J., et al.: iBOT: image BERT pre-training with online tokenizer. In: ICLR (2022)

55. Zhu, L., Yang, Y.: ActBERT: learning global-local video-text representations. In: CVPR, pp. 8746–8755 (2020)

GEB+: A Benchmark for Generic Event Boundary Captioning, Grounding and Retrieval

Yuxuan Wang[1], Difei Gao[1], Licheng Yu[2], Weixian Lei[1], Matt Feiszli[2], and Mike Zheng Shou[1(✉)]

[1] Show Lab, National University of Singapore, Singapore, Singapore
mike.zheng.shou@gamil.com
[2] Meta AI, Menlo Park, USA

Abstract. Cognitive science has shown that humans perceive videos in terms of events separated by the state changes of dominant subjects. State changes trigger new events and are one of the most useful among the large amount of redundant information perceived. However, previous research focuses on the overall understanding of segments without evaluating the fine-grained status changes inside. In this paper, we introduce a new dataset called **Kinetic-GEB+**. The dataset consists of over 170k boundaries associated with captions describing status changes in the generic events in 12K videos. Upon this new dataset, we propose three tasks supporting the development of a more fine-grained, robust, and human-like understanding of videos through status changes. We evaluate many representative baselines in our dataset, where we also design a new **TPD (Temporal-based Pairwise Difference) Modeling** method for visual difference and achieve significant performance improvements. Besides, the results show there are still formidable challenges for current methods in the utilization of different granularities, representation of visual difference, and the accurate localization of status changes. Further analysis shows that our dataset can drive developing more powerful methods to understand status changes and thus improve video level comprehension. The dataset is available at https://github.com/Yuxuan-W/GEB-Plus.

Keywords: Video captioning · Generic event understanding · Status changes · Difference modelling

1 Introduction

According to cognitive science [24], humans perceive videos in terms of different events, which are separated by the status changes of dominant subjects in the video. For example, in Fig. 1, humans perceive the process of "javelin

Supplementary Information The online version contains supplementary material available at https://doi.org/10.1007/978-3-031-19833-5_41.

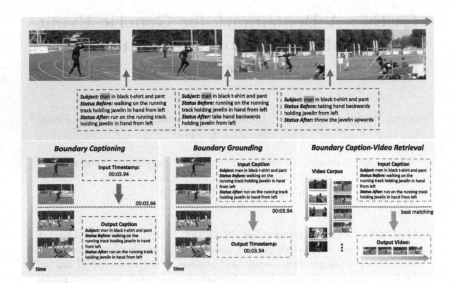

Fig. 1. An example of generic event boundaries with captions in Kinetic-GEB+, as well as three downstream tasks designed upon the boundaries

sport" by the action events such as "walking", "running" and "throwing". These events are triggered by the athletes status changes, like the instantaneous change from "walking" to "running". The moment that instantly triggers status changes of persons, objects, or scenes often conveys useful and interesting information among a large amount of repeated, static, or regular events. Therefore, developing the understanding of the salient, instantaneous status changes is another step towards a more fine-grained and robust video understanding. Previous works, like Dense Video Captioning [12,15,17,32,38] and Video Grounding [5,9,10,21,25,35,36] attempt to develop the understanding of events in video or video segments. However, these works only focus on developing an overall understanding of events rather than delving into the fine-grained status changes in the video. Other researches focusing on image level changes [13,22] employ the visual difference modeling to capture the status changes in image pairs. However, since the image contains only static information, the state changes exhibited by the two images involve only a few simple patterns, e.g., appear, move. These tasks are hard to evaluate the ability on understanding generic status changes.

More recently, *Shou et al.* [27] proposes Kinetic-GEBD dataset with annotated boundary timestamps for detection in Kinetic-400 videos [6], where a boundary is defined as the splitter between two status of the subject. Though the videos in Kinetic-400 [6] are categorized, the events selected inside are generic and mostly independent from the whole video's category. However, in addition to letting the model predict where is the boundary, it is more important to understand why this is the boundary, which associates the visual information of boundaries with natural human languages.

Motivated by this idea, we build a new dataset called **Kinetic-GEB+ (Generic Event Boundary Captioning, Grounding and Retrieval)** which

Table 1. Comparison with most relevant Video Captioning datasets. Our *Kinetic-GEB+* has comparable scale and is the only one targeting the generic boundaries, while conventional datasets focus on entire videos or video segments

	#Videos	Video domain	#Captions	Caption target	Target type	Annotation in segments
MSR-VTT	7,180	20 categories	200K	Video	Generic event	Caption
VATEX	41,250	in-the-wild	825K	Video	Action	Caption
Charades	67,000	household	20K	Segment	Action	Time range + caption
MSVD	2,089	in-the-wild	85K	Segment	Generic event	Time range + caption
YouCook2	2,000	kitchen	15K	Segment	Action	Time range + caption
ActivityNet Captions	20,000	in-the-wild	100K	Segment	Action	Time range + caption
Kinetics-GEB+	12,434	in-the-wild	177K	Boundary	Generic event	Timestamp/range + caption

includes the video boundaries indicating status changes happening in generic events. For every boundary, our Kinetic-GEB+ provides the temporal location and a natural language description, which consists of the dominant *Subject, Status Before* and *Status After* the boundary. In total, our dataset includes 176,681 boundaries in 12,434 videos selected from all categories in Kinetic-400 [6]. The detailed definition of our boundary is described in Sect. 3.1. For future applications like AI assistant robots, with the comprehension developed from the visual status changes and natural language captions, they could understand the real time, instantaneous occurrences without hints to assist the users.

In order to comprehensively evaluate the machines understanding of our boundaries, we further propose three downstream tasks shown in Fig. 1: *(1) Boundary Captioning.* Provided with the timestamp of a boundary, the machine is required to generate sentences describing the status change at the boundary. *(2) Boundary Grounding.* Provided with a description of a boundary, the machine is required to locate that boundary in the video. *(3) Boundary Caption-Video Retrieval.* Provided with the description of a boundary, the machine is required to retrieve the video containing that boundary from video corpus.

In the experiment, we compare several state-of-the-art methods [3,16,20,37, 39] along with many variants on our datasets to analyze the limitation of current methods and show the challenges of the proposed tasks. Due to the need of visual difference for understanding the status changes, we further propose a **Temporal-based Pairwise Difference (TPD) Modeling** method representing a fine-grained visual difference before and after the boundary. This method brings a significant performance improvement. On the other hand, the results show that there are still formidable challenges for current SOTA methods in developing the comprehension of status changes.

2   Related Work

Video Captioning is a conventional task with many benchmarks [7,15,33, 34,38] established which aim to caption trimmed videos with natural language descriptions. More recently, several works [12,15,17,32,38], e.g., Dense Video Captioning [15], focus on captioning the self-proposed event segments in videos.

All tasks above are evaluating the overall understanding of an event, whether the event is presented in the form of a trimmed video or a video segment. In contrast, our Boundary Captioning task is to develop the comprehension of instantaneous status changes happening at boundaries, i.e., describing the important moment that caused a dramatic change in the state of persons, objects or scenes. As a result, there is a more urgent need for models to understand the changes in various granularity of visual concepts, e.g., action, attributes, scene status, etc. In Table 1, we compare the most relevant video captioning datasets with ours.

Image Change Captioning is a task evaluating the ability on capturing and describing the difference between two images. There are many existing benchmarks targeting at this task. Early works [19,28] focus on changes in aerial imagery for monitoring disaster. Some other datasets [1,13] are about captioning the changes in street scenes, e.g., Spot-the-diff [13]. Recently, [22] proposes a more challenging change caption dataset, CLEVR-change, which utilizes the CLEVR engine to construct complicated synthetic scenes to evaluate models on finding more subtle change. One crucial limitation of previous works is that images can only present static information, thus status changes presented by two images can only involve a limited number of patterns, e.g., "appear", "disappear", "add" and "move". Towards a generic understanding of change, we extend the setting from images to videos which supports a open set of change pattern, including human action change, scene state change, etc.

Video Retrieval and Grounding are both language-to-vision tasks. Given a text description of a video or event, Video Retrieval requires models to select the target video from the corpus [3,8,23], and Video Grounding requires models to locate the target event segment (i.e. start and end boundaries) from an untrimmed video [5,10,21,35,36]. These tasks are based on the event level understanding to find the best matching video or time span. Compared with previous works, our Boundary Caption-Video Retrieval and Boundary Grounding tasks requires locating the two states of the subject, while traditional grounding only localizes one event. Besides, our captions are more fine-grained (describing detailed status changes) than those in traditional tasks (describing a general event).

Generic Understanding is a popular topic aiming to drive models from understanding predefined classes to open world vocabulary. Many pioneer works [4] propose open-set recognition tasks, which extend image classification tasks to generic understanding versions. Some works [15,38] introduce datasets for the generic event understanding requiring models to describe videos with natural language. More recently, a new dataset called Kinetic-GEBD (Generic Event Boundary Detection) [27] is proposed, which focuses on detecting the status changes between generic events. Our work is an extension to Kinetic-GEBD. We also study the boundary between events. However, we believe a sophisticated model should not only know where is the boundary but also understand why it is a boundary. Thus, this paper constructs a dataset with a large scale of boundary captions and introduces new boundary language-related tasks.

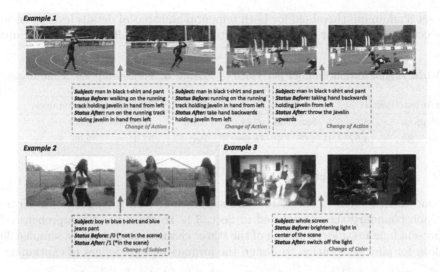

Fig. 2. Three samples from Kinetic-GEB+. Each boundary consists of a temporal position and an associated caption, with the boundary type noted at the bottom

3 Benchmark Construction: Kinetic-GEB+

To build the Kinetic-GEB+ dataset, we select 12,434 videos from the Kinetic-400 dataset [14] and annotate 176,681 boundaries following a designed guideline and format. In total, our selected videos cover all the 400 categories of the Kinetic-400. It is then split into 70% train, 15% val and 15% test non-overlapping sets. Several samples of boundaries are shown in Fig. 2.

3.1 Boundary Collection

When annotating Kinetic-GEB+, one simple way would be directly captioning the boundaries in Kinetic-GEBD [27]. However, our annotators did their jobs quicker when being asked to re-annotate the boundary positions than to interpret GEBD's boundaries. Yet, the boundaries from GEBD and GEB+ are highly consistent: when following Supp., nearly 90%/70% boundary positions in GEB+ reaching f1 scores higher than 0.5/0.7 with the boundaries in GEBD.

Format and Guideline. Following GEBD [27], a boundary is defined as the splitter between two status of the subject in the video. Generally, we categorized our boundaries into five types: Change of Action, Change of Subject, Change of Object, Change of Color and Multiple Changes. When annotating, we accept both single timestamps and time ranges as in [27], and each video is allocated to at least five annotators. Each annotator could independently decide whether to accept or reject the video following the criteria. The statistical results of annotation numbers and formats is shown in Table 2 and Table 3. Following [27], we set a minimum threshold for both temporal and spatial details level to ensure the consistency among different annotators. Further details are shown in Supp.

Table 2. Annotation number per video

#Annotations	1	2	3	4	5
#Videos	605	536	582	928	9783
Per. (%)	4.87	4.31	4.68	7.46	78.68

Table 3. Timestamp v.s. Time Range

Boundary	Timestamp	Time range
Num	172103	4578
Per. (%)	97.41	2.59

3.2 Caption Collection

In our Kinetic-GEB+, annotators are supposed to add a language description to each boundary they annotated in Sect. 3.1. To clearly and comprehensively represent humans understanding of the status changes, we randomly sampled 300 videos for pilot annotation to design the formats and guidelines of captioning.

Format. Our final format of caption consists of three compulsory items: *(1)* Dominant *Subject* that performs the status changes. *(2)* Subject's *Status Before* the boundary. *(3)* Subject's *Status After* the boundary. In the pilot stage, we compare different versions of annotation formats as shown in Fig. 3:

	Valid Percentage (%)	
Sentence: The man in black t-shirt and pant used to walk on the running track holding the javelin in hand from left, then at the boundary, he starts to running with the javelin in his hand.	Valid Percentage (%)	93.87
	Avg. Annotation Time (s)	74.3
	Avg. Evaluation Time (s)	20.3
Subject: man in black t-shirt and pant **Change:** first walked on the running track holding the javelin in hand from left, then at the boundary, starts to running with the javelin in his hand.	Valid Percentage (%)	97.60
	Avg. Annotation Time (s)	58.0
	Avg. Evaluation Time (s)	17.9
Subject: man in black t-shirt and pant **Status Before:** walking on the running track holding javelin in hand from left **Status After:** run on the running track holding javelin in hand from left	Valid Percentage (%)	99.53
	Avg. Annotation Time (s)	50.2
	Avg. Evaluation Time (s)	12.5

Fig. 3. Three candidate formats of Boundary Captions and their evaluation results, respectively *One-Sentence format, Two-Item format* and *Our Finalized format*

One-Sentence Format: Annotators use a single sentence to describe the status change happening at each boundary. In order to obtain an open-vocab description close to daily language, we do not restrict or request anything to the expression and annotators have full autonomy in narrating. Though this format enables fluent and natural descriptions, there are significant problems in the annotations: *(1) Ambiguity of subject*: Annotators tend to describe the subject shortly without further restriction, causing ambiguity, e.g., in a scene full of people, a short description like "a man" might indicate multiple persons. *(2) Dual changes*: Without restriction, annotators could wrongly combine two state changes of different subjects together in caption, like "Musician stops playing and an auditor starts clapping". *(3) Low efficiency*: Long sentences costs annotators more time to construct and takes our raters more time to understand.

Two-Items Format: To address the problems in the one-sentence format, we separate the sentence into a *Subject* item and its *Change* item as shown in Fig. 3. For *Subject*, annotators should fill in a noun phrase. We notice that this separation makes it easier for annotators to check the singularity and specification of *Subject*. Although we see that the efficiency of both annotation and evaluation are improved, this scheme still have some shortcomings: *(1) Incomplete status*: Annotators sometimes forgot to describe the status before the boundary. For example, when describing an athletes changing from walking to running, an annotator only filled "starts to run on the track" in *Change* and forgot to mention the "walking" status before the boundary. *(2) Low efficiency*: Even though this separation improves the efficiency, the *Change* item could still be too long for auditors to evaluate. Therefore, we further separate *Change* into *Status Before* and *Status After* to ensure the completeness of the status change description. Finally, we found this fully separated format the most efficient and robust for annotation, as shown in Fig. 3.

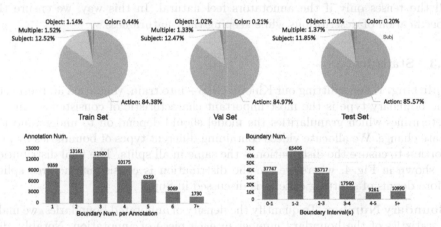

Fig. 4. *Top.* Distribution of boundary types in Train/Val/Test split. *Bottom Left.* Annotation numbers versus the numbers of boundary in the annotation. *Bottom Right.* Boundary numbers versus the duration of the interval before the boundary

Guideline. In our Kinetic-GEB+, the caption is defined as the reason why the annotator separates the preceding and succeeding segment of the boundary. Following the format of annotation, we brought up some specific guidance for annotating the items. Specifically, when annotating the *Subject* item, annotators are required to provide distinguishable attributes of the dominant subject. However, in complex cases where the subject is difficult to describe without ambiguity (e.g. many people dressing similarly in the scene), the annotator could just describe some attributes to avoid verbose descriptions.

When annotating *Status Before* and *Status After*, annotators are required to limit their attention to the time range between the proceeding boundary and succeeding boundary, thus to ensure all the status changes in the same video are

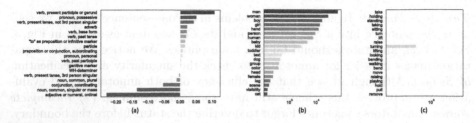

Fig. 5. *(a)* The parts of speech distribution of the *Status Before* and *Status After* compared with that of the Subject part. The two status parts contains more verbs and focus more on motions. *(b)* The 20 most frequent nouns in *Subject*. *(c)* The 20 most frequent verbs in *Status Before* and *Status After*

at the same temporal level. To further improve the consistency of expressions, we employ the symbol */1* and */0* to represent the appearance and disappearance of a subject in the scene, as shown in *Example 2* of Fig. 2. Finally, we embrace all the tenses only if the annotators feel natural. In this way, we ensure the specification of descriptions while keeping their naturalness.

3.3   Statistics

Splitting. When splitting our Kinetic-GEB+ into train, validation and test sets, the boundary type is the most important characteristic of consistency, since it determines which granularities the model should depend on to understand the state change. We allocate videos containing different types of boundaries by proportion to ensure the distribution is the same in all splits. The final distribution is shown in Fig. 4, where we see the distribution is consistent in three splits. More details of splitting criteria is discussed in Supp.

Boundary Number. To quantify the density of annotated boundaries, we make a statistics of the boundary number in each piece of annotation. Notably, due to the variant understanding of annotator, annotations of the same video could have different numbers of boundaries. The bottom left side of Fig. 4 shows the counts of annotations versus their boundary numbers, from which we could see that most of annotations have 1 to 4 boundaries.

Boundary Interval. Furthermore, to investigate the duration of events located between two boundaries, we conduct the statistics on the length of intervals. For the first boundary in the video, we take the distance to the start of the video as its interval duration. The result is shown in the bottom right side of Fig. 4 which is similar to the statistic of boundary numbers.

Part of Speech Comparison in Caption. For the captions in our dataset, we first analyze and compare the part of speech distributions in the subject and two status parts. In Fig. 5(a), the comparison result indicates that the status parts contain more verbs and focus more on actions than the subject part. On the other hand, the subject part includes more nouns and adjectives than the two status parts, suggesting it focuses more on appearance information.

Frequent Subjects and Actions in Caption. To further analyze the different aspects of information in the three parts. In Fig. 5(b)(c), we extract the first noun in every *Subject* as well as the first verb in all *Status Before* and *Status After*, and then illustrate the 20 most frequent words. Same with Kinetic-400, we see that both the nouns and verbs in our datasets are mainly correlated with the appearance and motions of humans. This conforms to the scenarios of practical application, since humans are also the dominant subject in most of the scenes.

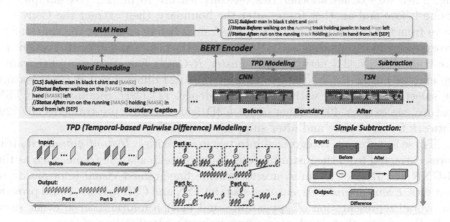

Fig. 6. *Top.* A general modification for BERT model showing on **ActBERT-revised**. *Bottom.* Our difference modeling methods designed for BERT model

3.4   Adjustment for Downstream Tasks

For downstream tasks, we select one annotator whose labeled boundaries are mostly consistent with others to reduce noise and duplication. Then, we use these boundaries timestamps as the anchors to merge other annotators captions, preserving the diversity of different opinions. Thus, one video corresponds to multiple boundaries, and each boundary could be with multiple captions. Finally, this selection includes 40k anchors from all videos. Furthermore, we find two different boundaries in the same video could be occasionally too similar in semantics for even humans to tell. For *Boundary Grounding*, we mark these pair of boundaries as equal in the ground truth. More details are discussed in Supp.

4   Experiments

Kinetic-GEB+ dataset enables us to benchmark how well current mainstream methods could comprehend the instantaneous status changes in videos. For each task, we implement and compare among SOTA models with our modifications, as well as further explorations on ablation and visual difference modeling methods.

4.1   Methods

Granularities of Input Features. We extract multiple granularities of features and utilize different combinations of them in experiments. Given each boundary, we sampled multiple frames before and after the timestamp and one frame at the timestamp for further extraction.

Our features include: *(1) ResNet*: Firstly, we extract a 1024 dimensional ResNet-roi feature using ResNet [11] followed by Region of Interest (RoI) pooling. Then we extract another ResNet-conv feature to fit [22]: We sample one frame before and another frame after the boundary, then extract the Conv features from the two frames. *(2) TSN*: For frames before and after the timestamp, we extract a 2048 dimensional TSN feature for the before and after snippets using pre-trained TSN [31] network. *(3) Faster R-CNN*: For every sampled frame, we employ Faster R-CNN [26] to extract the 1024 dimensional R-CNN feature by selecting 20 objects with highest confidence. *(4) C3D*: Similar to the TSN feature, we extract 4096 dimensional C3D features with pre-trained C3D [29] network for the before and after snippets to fit [37].

These features are categorized into two granularities: *Instant-granularity* features extracted from the instantaneous appearance in a single frame, such as the R-CNN and ResNet features, are to provide fine-grained visual information of instants. *Event-granularity* features, like the TSN and C3D feature, could provide an overall representation of appearance and motion information in event snippets. We assume that developing a fine-grained understanding of status changes requires both the granularities.

Backbones. We implement the following backbones with various adoption and modification according to the tasks: *(1) CNN+LSTM*: A rudimentary backbone that simply uses a vanilla LSTM which takes the CNNs extracted features as input. The output of LSTM is mapped to caption tokens in Boundary Captioning, or is max-pooled to be the matching score in other two tasks. *(2) Dual Dynamic Attention Model (DUDA)*: The baseline method in [22] which consists of a CNN-based Change Detector and a LSTM-based Dynamic Speaker. Besides, it utilizes a simple visual difference modeling by subtraction. *(3) ActionBERT-revised*: A one-stream BERT architecture using early fusion from [39]. We modify the structure by applying difference modeling after the embedding and employing different feature combinations. *(4) UniVL-revised*: A two-stream BERT architecture from [20], which includes a caption encoder, a context encoder and a cross-encoder for late fusion. We apply difference modeling to the context encoder with different feature combinations. *(5) FROZEN-revised*: A two-stream BERT architecture from [3], which includes a caption encoder and a context encoder with no fusion. The revision is the same as *UniVL-revised*. *(6) TVQA*: The baseline method in [16], where we remove all the "answer" substreams and process each visual granularity with one stream. *(7) 2D-TAN*: The baseline method in [37], where we only keep the diagonal elements in the 2D map.

Visual Difference Modeling. Developing a fine-grained understanding of status changes at the boundary requires visual difference information. Most

Table 4. Performance of Different Methods in Boundary Captioning. For *UniVL-revised* and *ActBERT-revised*, we apply the *TPD Modeling* and take the "ResNet-roi+TSN" combination as input feature

Method	CIDEr				SPICE				ROUGE_L			
	Avg.	Sub.	Bef.	Aft.	Avg.	Sub.	Bef.	Aft.	Avg.	Sub.	Bef.	Aft.
CNN+LSTM	49.73	80.11	34.39	34.69	13.62	18.84	9.92	12.10	26.46	39.77	20.77	18.83
DUDA	58.56	**104.41**	47.12	24.14	16.34	**21.72**	14.63	12.68	27.57	**42.76**	21.76	18.18
UniVL-revised (two-stream)	65.74	91.51	56.58	49.13	18.06	21.08	17.06	16.05	26.12	40.67	19.42	18.28
ActBERT-revised (one-stream)	**74.71**	85.33	**75.98**	**62.82**	**19.52**	20.10	**20.66**	**17.81**	**28.15**	39.16	**23.70**	**21.60**

existing methods are focused on image-pair differences [22], where the difference is obtained by simply subtracting the "before" image from the "after" image. A simple inference of this method on video tasks is by pooling the sampled frames then doing subtraction. However, this method only provides an event-granularity representation of the visual difference between the before and after snippets, and thus loses the instant-granularity visual differences.

To address this problem, we design a new method of **Temporal-based Pairwise Difference (TPD) Modeling** for BERT models. As shown in Fig. 6, we first compute the pairwise subtraction between the embedding of frames in "before" and "after" as *Part a*, where the embeddings of the frames are sampled in Sect. 4.1. This provides us a fine-grained and wide-viewing visual comparison between the status before and after. To represent the visual difference between the boundary and other sampled timestamps, we further compute *Part b* and *Part c*, which includes the pairwise subtraction between the frame embeddings at the boundary and that before or after the boundary. Finally, we concatenate all these differences together as the output of *TPD Modeling*.

The advantage of our *TPD Modeling* is that, compared with previous methods designed for image tasks, it provides multiple granularities of information and ensures the fine-grained representation of visual differences. In the ablation study of Boundary Captioning, we design an experiment to explore the difference modeling methods and verify our perceptions.

4.2 Boundary Captioning

For Boundary Captioning, we first implement and compare the performance of *CNN+LSTM, DUDA, UniVL-revised* and *ActBERT-revised*. To further explore how different input granularities support the understanding, we design a series of ablation studies using *ActBERT-revised* for all combinations of input features. In these two experiments, we apply our *TPD Modeling* as shown in Fig. 6.

To find the best schemes to represent visual difference, we further compare the performances of three schemes on *ActBERT-revised*: *(1)* Embedding with no difference modeling. *(2)* Max-pooling the frames before and after the boundary and simply subtracting one from another, which is inferred from the current method in [22]. *(3)* Using *TPD Modeling* to represent the visual differences. In Supp., we conduct an ablation study of different parts of *TPD Modeling* and explore on several other methods for visual difference representation.

Implementation. For *CNN+LSTM* and *DUDA*, we utilize the ResNet-conv feature following [22]. For *UniVL-revised* and *ActBERT-revised*, we utilize the ResNet-roi feature and TSN feature described in Sect. 4.1, where the sampling range is from the preceding boundary to the succeeding boundary. In evaluation, we separate the prediction into the three items, and then compute the similarity score of each item with the ground truth. After that, we employ CIDEr [30], SPICE [2] and ROUGE_L [18] as evaluation metrics, which are widely utilized in image and video captioning benchmarks. Further details are discussed in Supp.

Table 5. *Upper.* Ablation study results of the Boundary Captioning utilizing *ActBERT-revised* with *TPD Modeling* employed to all rows with "ResNet-roi". *Lower.* The performance comparison of visual difference modeling methods, where the *TPD Modeling* is employed to the last row

Input Granularity	CIDEr				SPICE				ROUGE_L			
	Avg.	Sub.	Bef.	Aft.	Avg.	Sub.	Bef.	Aft.	Avg.	Sub.	Bef.	Aft.
ResNet-roi	51.93	67.79	46.59	41.42	14.30	16.01	13.54	13.34	24.20	35.42	19.04	18.13
ResNet-conv	66.18	**96.86**	54.77	46.91	17.07	20.58	15.82	14.8	26.30	40.38	19.71	18.82
TSN	70.80	92.54	65.64	54.21	19.00	**20.97**	18.98	17.04	26.89	**40.53**	20.82	19.32
ResNet-roi + ResNet-conv	56.64	83.82	45.64	40.45	15.68	19.17	13.77	14.1	25.46	38.64	19.26	18.47
ResNet-conv + TSN	69.58	83.56	68.88	56.3	18.95	20.15	19.51	17.2	27.14	38.52	22.36	20.53
ResNet-roi + TSN	**74.71**	85.33	**75.98**	**62.82**	**19.52**	20.10	**20.66**	**17.81**	**28.15**	39.16	**23.70**	**21.60**
ResNet-roi + ResNet-conv + TSN	65.83	80.9	63.22	53.38	18.69	19.37	19.25	17.46	26.84	37.82	22.11	20.59
ResNet-roi + TSN (w/o Diff.)	67.38	**85.59**	63.06	53.49	18.47	19.84	18.69	16.87	24.23	31.65	21.14	19.90
ResNet-roi + TSN (simple)	67.75	85.31	64.28	53.65	18.96	**20.35**	19.13	17.39	26.78	39.14	21.20	20.00
ResNet-roi + TSN (TPD)	**74.71**	85.33	**75.98**	**62.82**	**19.52**	20.10	**20.66**	**17.81**	**28.15**	39.16	**23.70**	**21.60**

Result. From Table 4, we see that the *ActBERT-revised* backbone performs the best. However, the results in are still far from satisfactory, thus we further analyze the challenges of our task through the result in Table 5:

Accurate Captioning of the Status Changes Requires Both the Instant and Event Granularities. First, the event-granularity features perform as the base of the understanding. In Table 5, the "ResNet-roi+TSN" combination outperforms all the groups using only the instant-granularity features (e.g. the combinations of ResNet features). Second, a proper usage of the instant-granularity features could help to enrich the understanding. As in Table 5, the "ResNet-roi+TSN" combination outperforms the single TSN feature.

Our Task Requires Adaptive Usage of Different Granularities. Machines need to know when to look at which granularity. Simply assembling different features together could sometimes disturb the attention resulting in worse performance. In Table 5, when only utilizing the TSN feature, the performance is better than using either "ResNet-roi+TSN" or "ResNet-roi+ResNet-conv+TSN" combination.

Understanding the Status Changes Requires Effective Modeling of Visual Differences. In the comparison of difference modeling schemes in Table 5, the plain embedding without difference modeling performs the worst, while the utilization of simple-subtraction difference modeling brings little improvement to the performance. At the same time, the group with our *TPD Modeling* method significantly outperforms others. This gap in performance conforms to our perspective that learning a fine-grained understanding of status changes requires not only an overall but also a fine-grained representation of visual differences.

Table 6. Performance comparison among different methods in Boundary Grounding. For *UniVL-revised* and *ActBERT-revised*, we apply *TPD Modeling* and take the "ResNet-roi+TSN" combination as input feature

Method	Threshold (s)								
	0.1	0.2	0.5	1	1.5	2	2.5	3	Avg.
Random Guess	2.14	4.56	11.46	22.81	31.63	40.43	48.06	54.37	26.93
TVQA	2.60	5.30	12.90	23.73	32.94	41.33	48.56	55.17	27.82
2D-TAN	2.91	6.32	15.04	26.95	36.94	45.34	51.87	58.22	30.45
ActBERT-revised	3.12	6.14	14.79	26.78	36.61	45.45	52.99	59.41	30.66
FROZEN-revised	**4.28**	**8.54**	18.33	**31.04**	**40.48**	47.86	54.81	61.45	**33.35**
FROZEN-revised-GEBD	4.20	8.48	**18.49**	29.91	39.54	**48.37**	**55.29**	**61.55**	33.23

Table 7. Performance comparison of different methods in Boundary Caption-Video Retrieval. For *FROZEN-revised*, we add another group without difference modeling

Method	mAP	R@1	R@5	R@10	R@50
Random	0.39	0.05	0.23	0.44	2.52
CNN+LSTM	9.25	4.08	12.49	19.53	42.26
ActBERT-revised (one-stream)	19.14	9.52	28.89	40.14	64.50
FROZEN-revised (two-stream)	**23.39**	**12.80**	**34.81**	**45.66**	**68.10**
FROZEN-revised (two-stream) w/o diff	22.44	12.12	33.42	43.89	65.61

4.3 Boundary Grounding

In Boundary Grounding, we compare the performance of four backbones: *TVQA*, *2D-TAN*, *FROZEN-revised* and *ActionBERT-revised*. Given a video and a caption query, the model computes the matching scores of each candidate sampled from the video, followed with post-processing to finalize the prediction.

Implementation. In the training period, we use the ground truth boundaries processed in Sect. 3.4 and their timestamps. In testing, we employ two strategies to sample the timestamp candidates for groups as specified in their suffix. More details are discussed in Supp. For *2D-TAN*, we utilize the C3D feature as in [37]. For *TVQA*, we utilize the R-CNN and ResNet-roi features as context. Besides, we build the triplets consisting of one positive and two negative pairs, and then compute the cross-entropy loss for each triplet in training. In *ActBERT-revised* and *FROZEN-revised*, we apply the contrastive loss in [3] as objective and implemented a batch-randomed sequential sampler in training. The batch-randomed sampler allocates the boundaries in the same video to the same batch, encouraging the model to learn the visual differences within videos.

After the models generate the matching scores of all candidate timestamps, we apply the Laplace-of-Gaussian filter in [27] to derive local maximas of the scores. Then we select the top-k maximas as final prediction, where k is subject to the statistical number of ground truth timestamps marked in Sect. 3.4. To evaluate the accuracy of the prediction, we compute F1 scores based on the absolute distance between ground truth timestamps and predicted timestamps, with the threshold varying from 0.1s to 3s. Further details are discussed in Supp.

Result. We see that *FROZEN-revised* performs the best in the comparison of SOTA methods in Table 6. However, all the SOTA methods struggle when the threshold is less than 1s, indicating that *improving the temporal resolution of understanding is still a main challenge of our task*. Future improvements still need to focus on how to delve deeper into the temporal details and prevent the models from taking a glance and learning a rough impression of status changes.

4.4 Boundary Caption-Video Retrieval

We implement and compare the performance of the *CNN+LSTM*, *FROZEN-revised* and *ActionBERT-revised* backbones. Same as in Boundary Grounding, the backbones is to compute the matching score between the query and context.

Implementation. In order to find the target video from the corpus, each query is to be tried to match with every boundary candidate from all videos. Considering the corpus size, we only apply the baseline in [27] to generate the boundary candidates. When implementing *CNN+LSTM*, we take the R-CNN and ResNet-roi features as visual contexts. For *FROZEN-revised* and *ActBERT-revised*, we utilize the same configuration with Boundary Grounding. To evaluate the retrieval accuracy, for each query, we sort all the videos by the highest scores of their boundary candidates and then compute the mAP and recall metrics.

Result. In Table 7, *FROZEN-revised* with difference modeling performs the best, but the performance gap is significantly smaller than in Boundary Grounding, suggesting that this video-level retrieval task relies less on the fine-grained visual differences. It is natural since the overall video-level understanding is already enough to distinguish the target among different videos.

5   Conclusion

In this paper, we have introduced our new dataset *Kinetic-GEB+* with the methods of benchmark construction and proposed three tasks that aim to develop a more fine-grained, robust and human-like understanding of videos based on status changes. We further explore the challenges with designed experiments, where we design a new *Temporal-based Pairwise Difference (TPD)* modeling method to represent visual differences and obtain significant improvement in performance. Concluding the results from the experiments, we summarize the challenges of our benchmarks as three parts: *(1)* How to adaptively utilize multiple granularities of features and exclude the disturbance. *(2)* How to effectively represent the visual differences around the boundary. *(3)* How to improve the temporal resolution of understanding. We believe our work could be a stepping stone for the following works to develop more powerful methods to understand status changes and thus improve video-level comprehension.

Acknowledgments. This project is supported by the National Research Foundation, Singapore under its NRFF Award NRF-NRFF13-2021-0008, and Mike Zheng Shou's Start-Up Grant from NUS. The computational work for this article was partially performed on resources of the National Supercomputing Centre, Singapore.

References

1. Alcantarilla, P.F., Stent, S., Ros, G., Arroyo, R., Gherardi, R.: Street-view change detection with deconvolutional networks. Auton. Robot. **42**(7), 1301–1322 (2018). https://doi.org/10.1007/s10514-018-9734-5
2. Anderson, P., Fernando, B., Johnson, M., Gould, S.: SPICE: semantic propositional image caption evaluation. In: Leibe, B., Matas, J., Sebe, N., Welling, M. (eds.) ECCV 2016. LNCS, vol. 9909, pp. 382–398. Springer, Cham (2016). https://doi.org/10.1007/978-3-319-46454-1_24
3. Bain, M., Nagrani, A., Varol, G., Zisserman, A.: Frozen in time: a joint video and image encoder for end-to-end retrieval. In: ICCV, pp. 1728–1738 (2021)
4. Bendale, A., Boult, T.: Towards open world recognition. In: Proceedings of the IEEE Conference on Computer Vision and Pattern Recognition, pp. 1893–1902 (2015)
5. Cao, M., Chen, L., Shou, M.Z., Zhang, C., Zou, Y.: On pursuit of designing multi-modal transformer for video grounding. In: EMNLP, pp. 9810–9823 (2021)
6. Carreira, J., Zisserman, A.: Quo vadis, action recognition? a new model and the kinetics dataset. In: CVPR, pp. 6299–6308 (2017)
7. Chen, D., Dolan, W.: Collecting highly parallel data for paraphrase evaluation. In: ACL, pp. 190–200, June 2011. www.aclanthology.org/P11-1020
8. Cheng, X., Lin, H., Wu, X., Yang, F., Shen, D.: Improving video-text retrieval by multi-stream corpus alignment and dual softmax loss. arXiv preprint arXiv:2109.04290 (2021)
9. Gao, J., Sun, C., Yang, Z., Nevatia, R.: Tall: Temporal activity localization via language query. In: ICCV, pp. 5267–5275 (2017)
10. Ge, R., Gao, J., Chen, K., Nevatia, R.: MAC: mining activity concepts for language-based temporal localization. In: WACV, pp. 245–253. IEEE (2019)
11. He, K., Zhang, X., Ren, S., Sun, J.: Deep residual learning for image recognition. In: Proceedings of the IEEE Conference on Computer Vision and Pattern Recognition, pp. 770–778 (2016)
12. Iashin, V., Rahtu, E.: Multi-modal dense video captioning. In: CVPR, pp. 958–959 (2020)
13. Jhamtani, H., Berg-Kirkpatrick, T.: Learning to describe differences between pairs of similar images. In: EMNLP (2018)

14. Kay, W., et al.: The kinetics human action video dataset. arXiv preprint arXiv:1705.06950 (2017)
15. Krishna, R., Hata, K., Ren, F., Fei-Fei, L., Carlos Niebles, J.: Dense-captioning events in videos. In: ICCV, pp. 706–715 (2017)
16. Lei, J., Yu, L., Bansal, M., Berg, T.L.: TVQA: localized, compositional video question answering. In: EMNLP (2018)
17. Li, Y., Yao, T., Pan, Y., Chao, H., Mei, T.: Jointly localizing and describing events for dense video captioning. In: CVPR, pp. 7492–7500. IEEE Computer Society (2018)
18. Lin, C.Y.: Rouge: A package for automatic evaluation of summaries. In: Text Summarization Branches Out, pp. 74–81 (2004)
19. Liu, Z., Li, G., Mercier, G., He, Y., Pan, Q.: Change detection in heterogenous remote sensing images via homogeneous pixel transformation. IEEE Trans. Image Process. 27(4), 1822–1834 (2017)
20. Luo, H., et al.: Univl: a unified video and language pre-training model for multimodal understanding and generation. arXiv preprint arXiv:2002.06353 (2020)
21. Mun, J., Cho, M., Han, B.: Local-global video-text interactions for temporal grounding. In: CVPR, pp. 10810–10819 (2020)
22. Park, D.H., Darrell, T., Rohrbach, A.: Robust change captioning. In: ICCV, pp. 4624–4633 (2019)
23. Portillo-Quintero, J.A., Ortiz-Bayliss, J.C., Terashima-Marín, H.: A straightforward framework for video retrieval using CLIP. In: Roman-Rangel, E., Kuri-Morales, Á.F., Martínez-Trinidad, J.F., Carrasco-Ochoa, J.A., Olvera-López, J.A. (eds.) MCPR 2021. LNCS, vol. 12725, pp. 3–12. Springer, Cham (2021). https://doi.org/10.1007/978-3-030-77004-4_1
24. Radvansky, G.A., Zacks, J.M.: Event perception. Wiley Interdisc. Rev. Cogn. Sci. 2(6), 608–620 (2011)
25. Regneri, M., Rohrbach, M., Wetzel, D., Thater, S., Schiele, B., Pinkal, M.: Grounding action descriptions in videos. TACL 1, 25–36 (2013)
26. Ren, S., He, K., Girshick, R., Sun, J.: Faster R-CNN: towards real-time object detection with region proposal networks. In: NIPS, vol. 28 (2015)
27. Shou, M.Z., Lei, S.W., Wang, W., Ghadiyaram, D., Feiszli, M.: Generic event boundary detection: a benchmark for event segmentation. In: ICCV, pp. 8075–8084 (2021)
28. Tian, J., Cui, S., Reinartz, P.: Building change detection based on satellite stereo imagery and digital surface models. IEEE Trans. Geosci. Remote Sens. 52(1), 406–417 (2013)
29. Tran, D., Bourdev, L., Fergus, R., Torresani, L., Paluri, M.: Learning spatiotemporal features with 3d convolutional networks. In: ICCV, pp. 4489–4497 (2015)
30. Vedantam, R., Lawrence Zitnick, C., Parikh, D.: Cider: consensus-based image description evaluation. In: Proceedings of the IEEE Conference on Computer Vision and Pattern Recognition, pp. 4566–4575 (2015)
31. Wang, L., et al.: Temporal segment networks for action recognition in videos. PAMI 41(11), 2740–2755 (2018)
32. Wang, T., Zhang, R., Lu, Z., Zheng, F., Cheng, R., Luo, P.: End-to-end dense video captioning with parallel decoding. In: ICCV, pp. 6847–6857 (2021)
33. Wang, X., Wu, J., Chen, J., Li, L., Wang, Y.F., Wang, W.Y.: Vatex: a large-scale, high-quality multilingual dataset for video-and-language research. In: ICCV, pp. 4581–4591 (2019)
34. Xu, J., Mei, T., Yao, T., Rui, Y.: Msr-vtt: A large video description dataset for bridging video and language. In: CVPR, pp. 5288–5296 (2016)

35. Yuan, Y., Mei, T., Zhu, W.: To find where you talk: Temporal sentence localization in video with attention based location regression. In: AAAI, vol. 33, pp. 9159–9166 (2019)
36. Zeng, R., Xu, H., Huang, W., Chen, P., Tan, M., Gan, C.: Dense regression network for video grounding. In: CVPR, pp. 10287–10296 (2020)
37. Zhang, S., Peng, H., Fu, J., Luo, J.: Learning 2d temporal adjacent networks formoment localization with natural language. In: AAAI (2020)
38. Zhou, L., Xu, C., Corso, J.J.: Towards automatic learning of procedures from web instructional videos. In: AAAI (2018)
39. Zhu, L., Yang, Y.: Actbert: learning global-local video-text representations. In: CVPR, pp. 8746–8755 (2020)

A Simple and Robust Correlation Filtering Method for Text-Based Person Search

Wei Suo[1,4], Mengyang Sun[2,4], Kai Niu[1,4], Yiqi Gao[1,4], Peng Wang[1,4(✉)], Yanning Zhang[1,4(✉)], and Qi Wu[3]

[1] School of Computer Science and Ningbo Institute, Northwestern Polytechnical University, Xi'an, China
{suowei1994,gyqiz}@mail.nwpu.edu.cn,
{kai.niu,peng.wang,ynzhang}@nwpu.edu.cn
[2] School of Cybersecurity, Northwestern Polytechnical University, Xi'an, China
sunmenmian@mail.nwpu.edu.cn
[3] University of Adelaide, Adelaide, Australia
qi.wu01@adelaide.edu.au
[4] National Engineering Laboratory for Integrated Aero-Space-Ground-Ocean Big Data Application Technology, Xi'an, China

Abstract. Text-based person search aims to associate pedestrian images with natural language descriptions. In this task, extracting differentiated representations and aligning them among identities and descriptions is an essential yet challenging problem. Most of the previous methods depend on additional language parsers or vision techniques to select the relevant regions or words from noise inputs. But there exists heavy computation cost and inevitable error accumulation. Meanwhile, simply using horizontal segmentation images to obtain local-level features would harm the reliability of models as well. In this paper, we present a novel end-to-end Simple and Robust Correlation Filtering (SRCF) method which can effectively extract key clues and adaptively align the discriminative features. Different from previous works, our framework focuses on computing the similarity between templates and inputs. In particular, we design two different types of filtering modules (*i.e.,* denoising filters and dictionary filters) to extract crucial features and establish multi-modal mappings. Extensive experiments have shown that our method improves the robustness of the model and achieves better performance on the two text-based person search datasets. Source code is available at https://github.com/Suo-Wei/SRCF.

Keywords: Text-based person search · Correlation filtering · Vision and language

1 Introduction

Text-based person search [6,16,17] aims to retrieve the corresponding pedestrian in an image database by given language descriptions, which provides various

S. Avidan et al. (Eds.): ECCV 2022, LNCS 13695, pp. 726–742, 2022.
https://doi.org/10.1007/978-3-031-19833-5_42

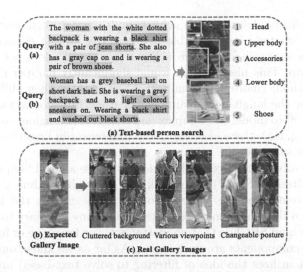

Fig. 1. (a) The illustration of the text-based person search. The left texts represent the language-based queries, and the right image indicates the corresponding pedestrian. Models are required to extract differentiated clues from noisy queries and images. Then aligning the body parts and corresponding descriptions in a common space. (b) The monitoring gallery we expect has clean backgrounds and the body parts of pedestrians are evenly distributed in each stripe to help the model achieve local alignments. (c) The actual gallery is with a cluttered background, and it is difficult to ensure that the body parts are fixed due to the changes in the viewpoints and pedestrian postures.

potential applications such as missing person searching and suspects tracking. As shown in Fig. 1(a), to retrieve the pedestrian "the woman with the white dotted backpack ... a pair of brown shoes.", models must have the ability to collect the differentiated clues (*e.g.* "black shirt, jean shorts") and relevant regions from noisy inputs. Then aligning these features in a common space (*e.g.* "white dotted backpack" and corresponding regions). Hence, the main challenges of text-based person search are how to accurately localize the discriminative regions (or key words) and how to align these multi-modal representations.

To refine crucial visual and textual contents from the background noise, previous methods usually depend on additional tools (*e.g.* the NLTK [1,23,39] and image parsing [14,30]) or attention mechanism [5,8,22,37] to localize key words and regions of interest (ROIs). However, on the one hand, these frameworks are capped by the tools with an inevitable error accumulation (if the discriminative noun phrases or significant body parts can not be captured, the retrieval capability of models would be weakened). Besides, these auxiliary operations could bring a huge amount of computational expenses, it would destroy the real-time requirement in video surveillance. On the other hand, the attention mechanism would ignore some relatively important regions due to the sum of attention weights being 1 among all image or text features.

For the second issue, since the parts of the human body are evenly arranged in the images as shown in Fig. 1 (b), existing methods mostly use sliced images as supervision to guide models to achieve multi-modal alignment [4,5,7,8,22]. However, this strategy is vulnerable and sensitive to the changes of viewing conditions. For example, as shown in Fig. 1 (c), "head" does not always occur in the first strip. This phenomenon would significantly hamper the robustness of existing methods (more details in Sect. 4.3) and make them difficult to apply in practice. For the language domain, simply using fully-connected layers [5] or adding tokens [8] to model the complex and changeable language is also difficult. As we see in Fig. 1(a), there exist enormous differences in linguistic descriptions, even facing the same person.

In order to solve the above challenges, we propose a novel Simple and Robust Correlation Filtering (SRCF) framework that through building a group of general semantic-templates (*i.e.,* filters) to effectively extract the key clues and adaptively align the multi-modal features without any auxiliary tools. The critical intuition behind SRCF is that no matter how the language or image changes, distinguishing components are unchanging. As far as we know, our paper is the first work that utilizes the idea of filtering to solve text-based image retrieval. Compared with the previous attention-based methods [5,22,37] which aim to learn a group of sparse wights by derived from inputs, our framework focuses on computing the similarity between templates and inputs. Specially, we design two different types of filtering modules (*i.e.,* denoising filters and dictionary filters) to achieve foreground separation and multi-modal alignment. Based on this conclusion that the similarity between the foreground is greater than the similarity with the background [34], we design two lightweight but effective denoising filters to help model separate pedestrian regions as well as meaningful words. Based on this insights that all pedestrians have the same body parts (such as heads, upper body, legs) and corresponding descriptions, we propose a novel matching search method with dictionary filters. It can be dynamically updated by moving-averaged strategy in the forward propagation. Moreover, the response maps from each dictionary filter would be used to local the specific semantic features with global search. As for flexible and diverse language, similar dictionary filters are also adopted to find out the words that correspond to body parts. To summarize, the main contributions of our paper are as follows:

1) We propose a novel simple and robust end-to-end method SRCF which can effectively extract key clues and adaptively align local features without any helps from external tools. 2) We design two lightweight denoising filters to refine the regions of interest (or meaningful words) from noisy inputs. Meanwhile, we build the dictionary filters to align body parts and corresponding texts by matching search. 3) The proposed SRCF not only achieves new state-of-the-art performance on CUHK-PEDES [17] and ICFG-PEDES [5] benchmark datasets, but also has better robustness and reliability compared with previous methods.

2   Related Work

Text-Based Person Search. Text-based person search is the task of finding the best matched pedestrian with a ranking strategy based on a given expression. This task needs to separate the distinguished regions from cluttered inputs and align these features in a common space. Previous methods usually depend on extra tools to extract useful information [1,14,22,23,30,38]. Specially, [22] focuses on multi-granularity alignment, they use extra alignment between the global image and noun phrases, as well as horizontal image stripes and the whole sentence to build the cross-granularity mapping. To localize the ROIs in images, [30] builds an additional attribute segmentation strategy to guide the alignment. [14] introduce a multi-granularities attention structure to align vision-and-language local information with human pose estimation.

Due to the above approaches being sensitive to the reliability of the external tools, several text-based person search methods are proposed to avoid the pre-processing and reduce additional computation such as [5,8,9,26]. [26] attempts to learn modality-invariant representations in a shared space by adversarial learning. [8] utilizes joint alignments over multi-scaled representations with a novel structure and a locality-constrained BERT. [5] uses an attention mechanism to select words in sentences and achieve joint alignments over full-scale representations. [33] constructs a representation learning approach, which depends on color-reasoning sub-tasks to align the cross-modal representations.

Different from the above methods, SRCF can effectively extract the key regions and discriminative words with an end-to-end training. Moreover, based on dictionary filters and expanded search space, our method also improves the robustness and reliability of the model.

Correlation Filtering. The correlation filtering is a popular technology that is used in many different fields. [2] introduces the correlation filter into the Fourier domain and achieves fast and accurate tracking. Classification network [15,27] can be translated into a correlation filtering task, where the output of global pooling is a filter kernel and weight matrix is search space. [21] propose vector correlation filter (VCF), which can adapt remarkable within-class variations while being discriminative against background. [18] reformulates the referring expression comprehension as a correlation filtering process. The text is converted as a filter and performs correlation filtering on the image.

Inspired by previous works, we introduce two different types of filters to achieve the text-based person search. For global-level alignment, the learnable filters are used to help model separate the discriminative foreground and the parameters are learnable by normal Back Propagation (BP) [11]. While the dictionary filters would be updated only in the forward propagation and it would be utilized to alleviate the difficulties of alignments due to the changes of viewpoints and the order of the words.

3 Our Approach

In this section, we introduce our SRCF framework. Our aim is to find the best matched pedestrian by the queries expression without any pre-processing. The SRCF is composed of a "global-level alignment" module and a "local-level alignment" module, as shown in Fig. 2.

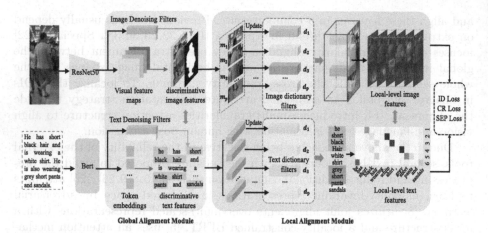

Fig. 2. The architecture for our framework. It consists of three main modules: (a) Encoder module: CNN and BERT models are used for image and language features extraction, respectively. (b) Global Alignment module: this module utilizes denoising filters to separate the discriminative regions and words. (c) Local Alignment module: this module utilizes dictionary filters to model local alignments by correlation matching in the global scope.

Different from previous methods, our model focus on extracting the key clues and adaptively aligning image-text inputs. Specially, representations of queries and images are first extracted by the language and visual encoders respectively. Image features would be further divided into "foreground" and "background" parts based on denoising filters. Then we feed the foreground features to the local-level alignment module, where several dictionary filters are built to learn the correlation between the body parts of different persons. Similar calculations also are executed in the language domain. Next, we describe the components of our model in details.

3.1 Encoder

Visual Encoder. For each given pedestrian image $I \in R^{W \times H \times 3}$, where $W \times H \times 3$ denotes the size of the image, we follow [5,8] that adopt the ResNet-50 [10] model as the backbone to extract visual features. Specially, we first resize the given image I to the size of $3 \times 384 \times 128$. Then it is fed into the encoder network to obtain the feature maps $G = \{g_i\}_{i=1}^{w \times h}, g_i \in R^d$, where the feature maps spatial resolution is $w \times h$, and each g_i represents a grid feature for the output feature map G.

Language Encoder. Following [8,33,37], we use the uncased BERT [29] as our language encoder. For a given query $Q = \{q_t\}_{t=1}^T$, where q_t represents the t-th word in this sentence, each word in this description is first mapped to the corresponding word embedding. Then, each q_t and its index t (q_t's absolute position in the sentence) is fed into language encoder. Before entering subsequent modules, we remove special tokens such as [CLS], [SEP] and [PAD] due to semantic fuzziness. Finally, we obtain text feature $E = \{e_t\}_{t=1}^T, e_t \in R^d$, note that here we add a 1×1 convolution layer with batch normalization and RELU to map them all to the same dimension as images d.

3.2 Global-Level Alignment Module

Inspired by [34, 39], from a global-level point of view, each pedestrian image can be simply divided into two parts ("foreground" and "background"). We expand this idea to language domain and achieve tool-free separation. For simplicity, the "differentiated words" and the "undifferentiated words" in the sentences are also called "foreground" and "background", respectively. Intuitively, foregrounds are beneficial to retrieval, instead, the background noise would be harmful to the models. To filter out these noises, we introduce the lightweight denoising filters which contain foreground filters and background filters to learn the global-level correlation of foregrounds and background respectively.

Taking images for an example, the input of global-level alignment module is image features $G = \{g_i\}_{i=1}^{w \times h}$. As shown in Fig. 2, we set image denoising filters as two learnable filters that are named "foreground filter" $v_f \in R^d$ and "background filter" $v_b \in R^d$, respectively. We first use v_f and v_b to compute the similarity with the visual feature map G, which can be formulated as:

$$s_i^f = \frac{v_f^T g_i}{\|v_f\| \|g_i\|},$$
$$s_i^b = \frac{v_b^T g_i}{\|v_b\| \|g_i\|}, \tag{1}$$

where $\|\cdot\|$ represents the L_2-normalization, the s_i^f and s_i^b are response maps which are utilized to estimate if the g_i should be accepted. We would divide images into two classes rely on s_i^f and s_i^b. However, because the foreground annotations are unavailable and simply using the strategy of heuristic tuning (such as setting threshold) would introduce additional hyper-parameters as well [37]. Therefore, we add a mutual-exclusion-loss [35] to ensure the s^f and s^b are orthogonal to each other (more details in Sect. 3.4). Then, the foreground $G^f = \{g_i^f\}_{i=1}^{w \times h}$ can be obtained by

$$a_i^f, a_i^b = \text{softmax}([s_i^f; s_i^b]), \tag{2}$$
$$g_i^f = a_i^f g_i, \tag{3}$$

where [;] indicates to concatenate these two response maps s_i^f and s_i^b, we compute the softmax over the response maps to obtain foreground and background response scores a_i^f and a_i^b, and then all a_i^f and a_i^b are jointed spatially to get a^f and a^b respectively. Moreover, we also perform a similar calculation in the domain of language and obtain the differentiated words $E^f = \{e_t^f\}_{t=1}^T$. To align images and language, we utilize Global MAX Pooling (GMP) on G^f and E^f to obtain the global-level image feature $g_g \in R^d$ and text feature $e_g \in R^d$. The similarity matrix between global-level features of one image-text pair is denoted as follow:

$$S_g = \frac{g_g^T e_g}{\|g_g\| \|e_g\|} \tag{4}$$

3.3 Local-Level Alignment Module

As discussed in the previous section, most of previous methods adopt horizontal segmentation images and multi-branch fully-connected layers [5,8,22,23] to offer local-level features. But they are vulnerable and sensitive to various viewpoints and the order of the words. To achieve the local-level alignments, we build the dictionary filters which can learn the correlation of body parts between different pedestrians and improve the robustness of model.

Dictionary Filters. As shown in Fig. 2, we introduce the dictionary filters and a strategy of momentum update to learn the body parts correlation between different persons. Taking images for example, following [5,22,23], the output of global-level alignment module G^f is first segmented into P horizontal stripes, which are denoted as $\{G_1^f, G_2^f, \cdots, G_P^f\}$, $G_p^f \in R^{\frac{h}{P} \times w \times d}$. For each strip G_p^f, the GMP is used to obtain body parts feature vector $m_p \in R^d$. Then, we define visual dictionary filters as $D_g \in R^{P \times d}$, which is randomly initialized and further updated by a moving average operation [13] in one mini-batch. It can be formulated as:

$$\hat{d}_p = \alpha * d_p + (1 - \alpha) * \frac{1}{n} \sum_{i=1}^{n} m_{pi}, \tag{5}$$

$$m_p = \mathrm{GMP}(G_p^f), \tag{6}$$

where $\hat{d}_p$ indicates that the p-th filter in the D_g is updated, the α and n are momentum coefficient and batch size.

Expanded Search Space. Different from previous methods that simply use striped images to extract local-level features, we expand the search space to global scope. Specially, each filter $\hat{d}_p$ in the dictionary would compute one response map with G^f, then the softmax is utilized to obtain response scores. The local-level image features g_{lp} are obtained by summarizing g_i^f based on corresponding scores. The above computations can be formulated as:

$$s_i^p = \frac{\hat{d}_p^T g_i^f}{\|\hat{d}_p\| \|g_i^f\|}, \tag{7}$$

$$a_1^p, a_2^p, \cdots, a_{w \times h}^p = \mathrm{softmax}(s_1^p, s_2^p, \cdots, s_{w \times h}^p), \tag{8}$$

$$g_{lp} = \sum_{i=1}^{w \times h} (a_i^p \cdot g_i^f). \tag{9}$$

Note that our dictionary filters are updated only in the forward propagation and use "straight-through" trick [24] to avoid the gradient stop. As for language, we use multi-branch fully connected layers to obtain P language features followed by [5,8]. Then the similar dictionary filters and updating mechanism are implemented to learn the correlation for body parts' descriptions. Finally, we can obtain the similarity matrices $S_l = \{S_{lp}\}_{p=1}^{P}$. To align the local-level images and language, the S_{lp} is denoted as follow:

$$S_{lp} = \frac{g_{lp}^T e_l}{\|g_{lp}\| \|e_l\|}, \tag{10}$$

where e_l denotes local-level language features. During testing, we would directly obtain the local-level features based on updated dictionary filters and the strategy of horizontal partitioning is discarded. Following the previous work [5], we also use a transformer-style non-local module to establish the connection between local-level features. The outputs are used to obtain non-local similarity matrices S_n.

3.4 Optimization

Compound Ranking (CR) loss L_{cr} is utilized to optimize the S_g, S_l and S_n respectively. In particular, L_{cr} applies a constraint that the intra-class similarity score must be larger than the inter-class similarity by a margin. Meanwhile, L_{cr} also exploits more diversely textual descriptions as complementary sentences for each image. More information on L_{cr} can be found in the [5].

Besides, following [5,8,14,39], we also add ID loss L_{id} to achieve identity-level matching. More importantly, it is also used as labels for our foreground and differentiated words in this paper. For g_g and e_g, the identification loss is defined as follows:

$$L_{id} = - (y_{id}\log(\text{softmax}(W_{id}g_g)) + y_{id}\log(\text{softmax}(W_{id}e_g))), \tag{11}$$

where W_{id} is a shared transformation matrix to classify the different persons and y_{id} is the ground true identity. In addition, a mutual-exclusion-loss is used to separate the response maps:

$$L_{sep} = \left\| A^T A \odot (1 - K) \right\|_F^2, \tag{12}$$

where matrix A is the a^f and a^b in Eq. 2 by concatenated in the last dimension. 1 is the matrix of ones and K is an identity matrix. The total loss in SRCF is defined as:

$$Loss = L_{cr} + \lambda_1 L_{id} + \lambda_2 L_{sep}, \tag{13}$$

following [5] and [35], where λ_1 and λ_2 is set to 1.

At inference time, the similarity score between a text-image pair is the sum of S_g, S_l and S_n. Note that our model completely avoided the traditional horizontal partitioning during testing and local-level features are straightforward obtained by dictionary filters.

4   Experiments

4.1   Experimental Setting

Datasets. We evaluate the proposed SRCF on the CUHK-PEDES [17] dataset and ICFG-PEDES [5] dataset. The CUHK-PEDES is the first large-scale dataset for text-to-image person search. It contains totally 80,412 textual descriptions for 13,003 different persons in 40,206 pedestrian images. This dataset is split into 34,054 images for 11,003 identities with 68,108 descriptions in the training set, 3,078 images for 1,000 identities in validation set and the test set contains 3,074 images for 1,000 persons.

Recently, a new dataset ICFG-PEDES [5] is conducted, this dataset has more identities and textual descriptions. It contains 54,522 pedestrian images from MSMT17 [31] of 4,102 different persons. The ICFG-PEDES is divided into 34,674 image-text pairs of 3,102 identities in the training set, and the test set contains 19,848 image-text pairs for 1,000 persons.

Implementation Details. Following previous methods [8,33], we also use ResNet-50 pretrained on ImageNet [25] as our visual backbone and adopt the BETR-Base-Uncase [29] for textual encoder. We follow [5] to resize an input image to 384×128 and use random horizontal flipping for data augmentation [30]. The size of the feature map is $24 \times 8 \times 2048$. The text length and the number of body part dictionary is set to 64 and 6, respectively. We follow [13] to set the momentum coefficient α to 0.99.

During training, we use Adam as our optimizer and the batch size is set to 32. The initial learning rate of our overall model is $5e-5$ and decreased by 0.1 per 10 epochs after 20 epochs. Following [8], the BERT encoder is frozen and we fine-tune the visual backbone with the learning rate to $1/10$ of the whole model. Our dictionary filters are only updated to 25 epochs. We train our model on one 2080Ti GPU for 60 epochs.

Evaluation. Following the standard evaluation setting, we adopt top-K accuracy (K=1, 5, 10) as our evaluation metric. Specially, given a person description, the search is considered as correct if top-K images contain at least one corresponding person to the given description.

4.2   Quantitative Results

We compare our proposed SRCF with the state-of-the-art methods on the CUHK-PEDES dataset and ICFG-PEDES dataset, as shown in Table 1. For a fair comparison, all methods use the ResNet-50 as the backbone to extract visual representations. Depending on which query embedding is adopted, we divide these approaches into two types: LSTM-based methods and BERT-based methods. In the "Language or Image Parsing" column, we list whether the approach uses additional language parsing tools or image pre-processing methods.

In Table 1, it can be observed that although these networks based on pre-processing methods [1,14,22,23,30,37,39] also achieve good performance, they

Table 1. Comparisons with the state-of-the-art methods on the CUHK-PEDES and ICFG-PEDES datasets. We report Top-1, Top-5 and Top-10 accuracies.

Methods	Language embedding	Language or Image Parsing	CUHK-PEDES			ICFG-PEDES		
			Top-1	Top-5	Top-10	Top-1	Top-5	Top-10
Dual Path [38]	Word2vec	–	44.40	66.26	75.07	38.99	59.44	68.41
CMPM/C [36]	LSTM	–	49.37	–	79.27	43.51	65.44	74.26
MIA [22]	LSTM	NLTK [19]	53.10	75.00	82.90	46.49	67.14	75.18
CMPM/C+TC&IC [33]	LSTM	–	53.33	–	83.20	–	–	–
PMA [14]	LSTM	NLTK [19]+Pose [3]	53.81	73.54	81.23	–	–	–
ViTAA [30]	LSTM	CoreNLP [20]+Seg [28]	55.97	75.84	83.52	50.98	68.79	75.78
CMAAM [1]	LSTM	NLTK [19]	56.68	77.18	84.86	–	–	–
DSSL [39]	LSTM	NLTK [19]	59.98	80.41	87.56	–	–	–
SSAN [5]	LSTM	-	61.37	80.15	86.73	54.23	72.63	79.53
TIMAM [26]	BERT	–	54.51	77.56	84.78	–	–	–
TDE [23]	BERT	SpaCy [12]	55.25	77.46	84.56	–	–	–
CMP_adv [33]	BERT	–	55.05	-	85.09	–	–	-
CMP_adv+TC&IC [33]	BERT	–	57.00	–	85.62	–	–	–
HGAN [37]	BERT	NLTK [19]	59.00	79.49	86.62	-	-	-
NAFS [8]	BERT	-	59.94	79.86	86.70	–	–	–
SRCF-LSTM (ours)	LSTM	-	**62.87**	**81.81**	**87.85**	**55.69**	**73.07**	**80.84**
SRCF-BERT (ours)	BERT	-	**64.04**	**82.99**	**88.81**	**57.18**	**75.01**	**81.49**

have to depend on additional language parsing [12,19,20] or vision models [3,28] to extract useful information. Instead, our proposed SRCF can adaptively extract key clues by end-to-end training with higher accuracy.

In addition, we compare the performance of our method with the methods without any tools [5,8,26,33,36,38]. We observe that our SRCF uses the denoising filters and the dictionary filters to achieve better performance than the previous methods. Specially, in CUHK-PEDS dataset, we observe that our method outperforms the start-of-the-art method [5] and [8] 1.5% and 4.1% respectively on Top-1 accuracies. In ICFG-PEDES dataset, the performance of SRCF over [5] 1.46% with LSTM and 2.95% with BERT.

4.3 Robustness of Model

In this section, we further design experiments to verify the robustness and reliability of our SRCF by simulating real-world situations. As shown in the Fig. 3, the first row is the original gallery image examples from CUHK-PEDES dataset (short for "Raw"). In 2–5 rows of Fig. 3, we implement four different experimental settings on this dataset which include random horizontal translation, random vertical translation, random rotating and random cropping (they are short for "New").

We use the weights trained on the "Raw" dataset provided by the state-of-the-art methods [5,8] and test them on the "New" galleries. The Top-1 accuracy results between our proposed SRCF and the state-of-the-art methods [5,8] are shown in the three columns at the right side of Fig. 3. In order to compare the decline degree under these four different galleries, we use the red font to represent the largest decrease, the green font for the second, and the blue font for the lowest percentage decrease.

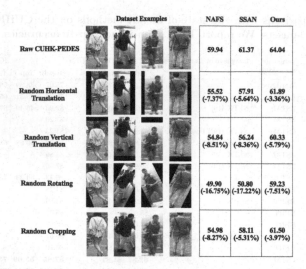

Fig. 3. Compare the performance between our method and the state-of-the-art methods under four different experimental settings, which include horizontal translation, vertical translation, rotating and cropping on the original CUHK-PEDES dataset. We use red font to represent the largest decrease, the green font for second, and the blue font for the lowest percentage decrease. (Color figure online)

As we mentioned in Sec. 1, the state-of-the-arts methods [5,8] are vulnerable and sensitive to changeable conditions. For example, with the upper and lower offset of the pedestrian position in the third row of the Fig. 3, both NAFS [8] and SSAN [5] methods have declined more than 8%. Furthermore, when we rotate the person images randomly, the retrieval accuracy of NAFS and SSAN methods even decreases by more than 15%. It is worth noting that our SRCF has the lowest percentage decline in all cases. These quantitative results effectively demonstrate the robustness and stability of our model under changeable conditions.

4.4 Ablation Studies

In this section, we conduct several ablation studies on the CUHK-PEDES to demonstrate the effectiveness.

Effectiveness of Main Modules. First, to systematically evaluate the contributions of different model components, we design various ablation experiments. As shown in Table 2, "Global" and "Local" are global-global and local-local alignment, respectively. Specially, "Global" indicates Max-pooling is performed on the output of CNN and BERT. Then we use ranking loss and identification loss to align them. "Local" indicates images are horizontally partitioned into 6 parts and six textual fully connected layers are used to align corresponding the stripes of images. We observe that the performance can increase by

Table 2. Ablation studies on the CUHK-PEDES dataset.

	Global	Local	Image denoising filters	Text denoising filters	Image dictionary filters	Text dictionary filters	Top-1	Top-5	Top-10
1	✓						59.76	79.82	86.45
2	✓	✓					61.27	80.43	87.07
3	✓	✓	✓				62.59	81.56	87.88
4	✓	✓		✓			62.69	81.40	87.93
5	✓	✓	✓	✓			63.16	81.82	88.14
6	✓	✓	✓	✓	✓		63.60	82.55	88.74
7	✓	✓	✓	✓		✓	63.71	82.86	88.61
8	✓	✓			✓	✓	63.19	81.34	88.16
Ours	✓	✓	✓	✓	✓	✓	**64.04**	**82.99**	**88.81**

Table 3. The effects of different model settings.

	Method	Top-1	Top-5	Top-10
1	SA + WA + Dictionary filtering	61.89	80.77	87.24
2	Denoising filtering + CNLA	60.85	80.15	87.31
3	Denoising filters moving-update	62.69	81.35	87.64
4	Dictionary filters BP-update	62.15	81.61	87.67
5	Share denoising filters	61.99	81.34	87.70
6	Share dictionary filters	61.45	80.70	87.62
7	Avg-pooling	63.97	82.31	88.40
8	Without mutual-exclusion-loss	62.44	81.61	87.43
9	Ours (Denoising filtering + Dictionary filtering)	**64.04**	**82.99**	**88.81**

multi-grained alignment and they would be used as our baselines. In Table 2, the "Image (Text) Denoising Filters" denotes denoising filters in image domain or language domain. The column of "Image (Text) Dictionary Filters" indicates image-based or language-based dictionary filters. As shown in 3–5 rows of Table 2, we follow the baseline and add the two learnable denoising filters to demonstrate the effectiveness of our method. The results show that denoising filters can effectively improve the performances and combining them in both domains would boost the baseline accuracy by 3.40% and 1.89% on Top-1. In addition, in 8 row of Table 2, we find employing "Dictionary Filters" in both domains can outperform the baseline by 3.43% and 1.92% on Top-1, respectively. Meanwhile, the language-based and image-based dictionary filters have similar contributions to the model (in 6–7 rows of Table 2). While, when we integrate the denoising filters and dictionary filters together, the performance improves to 64.04 on Top-1 over the baseline model by 4.28% and 2.77%.

Alternative Model Settings. In Table 3, we exploit some comparative experiments about the different model settings. We first compare the performance of our method with attention-based methods. In the first row of Table 3, we use popular Space Attention (SA) [32] and Word Attention (WA) [5] as global attention to replace our denoising filters. In row 2, we utilize Contextual Non-Local

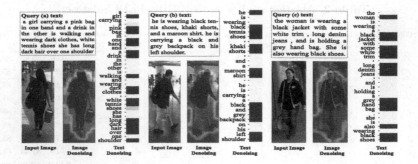

Fig. 4. Visualizations of response maps of images and texts from denoising filters.

Attention (CNLA) as local-level attention module from SOTA method [8] to take the place of our dictionary filters. The results prove that our correlation-based approach is significant better than previous attention-based methods.

In the third row of Table 3, the moving-averaged mechanism is used to replace the back propagation for our "Denoising filters". The results show this strategy of moving-average is not suitable for localizing the discriminative foreground. The main reason is that comparing with stabilized body parts and corresponding descriptions, the changes of background are more drastic. If the filters are updated in the forward propagation, a lot of irrelevant noises would be mixed into denoising filters and it is harmful to the correlation learning. Instead, in row 4 of Table 3, when we utilize Back Propagation to learn the parameters in dictionary filters, the overall performance would also be degraded. This result shows that learning the consistency of body parts between different pedestrians can bring greater gains.

As shown in rows 5–6 of Table 3, we share the denoising filters and dictionary filters in both domains. The results show that the shared filters would influence the performance. It can also prove that the inter-modal variations are larger than intra-modal variations.

The row 7 of Table 3 shows the impact of avg-pooling on the performance. We observe our method is insensitive to different the strategy of pooling. In the row 8 of Table 3, we remove the mutual-exclusion-loss. We find that this loss is important for separating useful information.

4.5 Qualitative Results

To better explore the aligning processes learned by our method, we visualise sample results along with the response distribution from the "foreground filter". We take Fig. 4 Query (a) for example, the red regions in the image and text represent higher response scores for foreground filter, while the blue regions in the image and light color in the text indicate the lower scores.

It can be observed that the background noises in the image (such as passers-by, tiles and plants) have lower response scores. On the other hand, our method

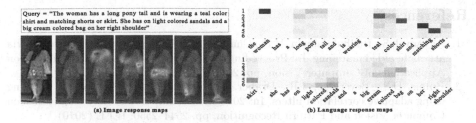

Fig. 5. Visualizations of response maps of image and text from dictionary filters.

is able to reserve gender, attributes ("long dark hair", "white tennis shoes"), and accessories ("pink bag", "black and grey backpack") from textual queries, which are key clues for subsequent local alignments of the model.

We further demonstrate response maps of our "dictionary filters" during the testing. Figure 5 (a) shows the response maps of six different body parts which are correspond with "dictionary filters". Meanwhile, the response distribution of our language-based dictionary filters are shown in Fig. 5 (b). It can be observed that "woman" and "long pony tail" have relatively higher response scores in the first row of the query text. Accordingly, the crucial regions (*i.e.*, head) have higher response scores in the first response map of the image. The important words that each language-based dictionary filter pays attention to can be found in the visual dictionary feature maps. It suggests that our method can adaptively localize the differentiated regions or words without any additional information (such as semantic annotations or language processing toolkits).

5 Conclusion

In this paper, we propose a novel end-to-end Simple and Robust Correlation Filtering (SRCF) framework which can effectively extract the key clues and adaptively align the local features without any auxiliary tools. Meanwhile, we introduce two different types of filters to achieve the global-level and local-level alignments. They can help model refine pedestrian regions as well as meaningful words. The experimental results show that SRCF achieves better performance on both accuracy and robustness.

Acknowledgement. This work was supported by National Key R&D Program of China (No. 2020AAA0106900), the National Natural Science Foundation of China (No. 62101451, No. U19B2037), Shaanxi Provincial Key R&D Program (No. 2021KWZ-03), Natural Science Basic Research Program of Shaanxi (No. 2021JCW-03), Open Projects Program of National Laboratory of Pattern Recognition (202100028), and Fundamental Research Funds for the Central Universities (D5000210733).

References

1. Aggarwal, S., Radhakrishnan, V.B., Chakraborty, A.: Text-based person search via attribute-aided matching. In: Proceedings of the IEEE/CVF Winter Conference on Applications of Computer Vision, pp. 2617–2625 (2020)
2. Bolme, D.S., Beveridge, J.R., Draper, B.A., Lui, Y.M.: Visual object tracking using adaptive correlation filters. In: 2010 IEEE Computer Society Conference on Computer Vision and Pattern Recognition, pp. 2544–2550. IEEE (2010)
3. Cao, Z., Simon, T., Wei, S.E., Sheikh, Y.: Realtime multi-person 2D pose estimation using part affinity fields. In: Proceedings of the IEEE Conference on Computer Vision and Pattern Recognition, pp. 7291–7299 (2017)
4. Chen, Y., Zhang, G., Lu, Y., Wang, Z., Zheng, Y.: TIPCB: a simple but effective part-based convolutional baseline for text-based person search. Neurocomputing **494**, 171–181 (2022)
5. Ding, Z., Ding, C., Shao, Z.: Semantically self-aligned network for text-to-image part-aware person re-identification. arXiv preprint arXiv:2107.12666 (2021)
6. Dong, Q., Gong, S., Zhu, X.: Person search by text attribute query as zero-shot learning. In: Proceedings of the IEEE/CVF International Conference on Computer Vision, pp. 3652–3661 (2019)
7. Farooq, A., Awais, M., Kittler, J., Khalid, S.S.: AXM-net: Implicit cross-modal feature alignment for person re-identification (2022)
8. Gao, C., et al.: Contextual non-local alignment over full-scale representation for text-based person search. arXiv preprint arXiv:2101.03036 (2021)
9. Han, X., He, S., Zhang, L., Xiang, T.: Text-based person search with limited data. arXiv preprint arXiv:2110.10807 (2021)
10. He, K., Zhang, X., Ren, S., Sun, J.: Deep residual learning for image recognition. In: Proceedings of the IEEE Conference on Computer Vision and Pattern Recognition, pp. 770–778 (2016)
11. Hecht-Nielsen, R.: Theory of the backpropagation neural network. In: Neural Networks for Perception, pp. 65–93. Elsevier (1992)
12. Honnibal, M., Johnson, M.: An improved non-monotonic transition system for dependency parsing. In: Proceedings of the 2015 Conference on Empirical Methods in Natural Language Processing, pp. 1373–1378 (2015)
13. Huang, Z., Zeng, Z., Huang, Y., Liu, B., Fu, D., Fu, J.: Seeing out of the box: end-to-end pre-training for vision-language representation learning. In: Proceedings of the IEEE/CVF Conference on Computer Vision and Pattern Recognition, pp. 12976–12985 (2021)
14. Jing, Y., Si, C., Wang, J., Wang, W., Wang, L., Tan, T.: Pose-guided multi-granularity attention network for text-based person search. In: AAAI, vol. 34, pp. 11189–11196 (2020)
15. Krizhevsky, A., Sutskever, I., Hinton, G.E.: Imagenet classification with deep convolutional neural networks. Adv. Neural. Inf. Process. Syst. **25**, 1097–1105 (2012)
16. Li, S., Xiao, T., Li, H., Yang, W., Wang, X.: Identity-aware textual-visual matching with latent co-attention. In: Proceedings of the IEEE International Conference on Computer Vision, pp. 1890–1899 (2017)
17. Li, S., Xiao, T., Li, H., Zhou, B., Yue, D., Wang, X.: Person search with natural language description. In: Proceedings of the IEEE Conference on Computer Vision and Pattern Recognition, pp. 1970–1979 (2017)
18. Liao, Y., et al.: A real-time cross-modality correlation filtering method for referring expression comprehension. In: Proceedings of the IEEE/CVF Conference on Computer Vision and Pattern Recognition, pp. 10880–10889 (2020)

19. Loper, E., Bird, S.: Nltk: The natural language toolkit. arXiv preprint cs/0205028 (2002)
20. Manning, C.D., Surdeanu, M., Bauer, J., Finkel, J.R., Bethard, S., McClosky, D.: The stanford corenlp natural language processing toolkit. In: Proceedings of 52nd Annual Meeting of the Association for Computational Linguistics: System Demonstrations, pp. 55–60 (2014)
21. Naresh Boddeti, V., Kanade, T., Vijaya Kumar, B.V.K.: Correlation filters for object alignment. In: Proceedings of the IEEE Conference on Computer Vision and Pattern Recognition, pp. 2291–2298 (2013)
22. Niu, K., Huang, Y., Ouyang, W., Wang, L.: Improving description-based person re-identification by multi-granularity image-text alignments. TIP **29**, 5542–5556 (2020)
23. Niu, K., Huang, Y., Wang, L.: Textual dependency embedding for person search by language. In: ACM MM, pp. 4032–4040 (2020)
24. Oord, A.V.D., Vinyals, O., Kavukcuoglu, K.: Neural discrete representation learning. arXiv preprint arXiv:1711.00937 (2017)
25. Russakovsky, O., et al.: Imagenet large scale visual recognition challenge. Int. J. Comput. Vision **115**(3), 211–252 (2015)
26. Sarafianos, N., Xu, X., Kakadiaris, I.A.: Adversarial representation learning for text-to-image matching. In: Proceedings of the IEEE/CVF International Conference on Computer Vision, pp. 5814–5824 (2019)
27. Simonyan, K., Zisserman, A.: Very deep convolutional networks for large-scale image recognition. arXiv preprint arXiv:1409.1556 (2014)
28. Sun, K., Xiao, B., Liu, D., Wang, J.: Deep high-resolution representation learning for human pose estimation. In: CVPR, pp. 5693–5703 (2019)
29. Vaswani, A., et al.: Attention is all you need. In: Advances in Neural Information Processing Systems, pp. 5998–6008 (2017)
30. Wang, Z., Fang, Z., Wang, J., Yang, Y.: ViTAA: visual-textual attributes alignment in person search by natural language. In: Vedaldi, A., Bischof, H., Brox, T., Frahm, J.-M. (eds.) ECCV 2020. LNCS, vol. 12357, pp. 402–420. Springer, Cham (2020). https://doi.org/10.1007/978-3-030-58610-2_24
31. Wei, L., Zhang, S., Gao, W., Tian, Q.: Person transfer GAN to bridge domain gap for person re-identification. In: Proceedings of the IEEE Conference on Computer Vision and Pattern Recognition, pp. 79–88 (2018)
32. Woo, S., Park, J., Lee, J.-Y., Kweon, I.S.: CBAM: convolutional block attention module. In: Ferrari, V., Hebert, M., Sminchisescu, C., Weiss, Y. (eds.) ECCV 2018. LNCS, vol. 11211, pp. 3–19. Springer, Cham (2018). https://doi.org/10.1007/978-3-030-01234-2_1
33. Wu, Y., Yan, Z., Han, X.: Lapscore: language-guided person search via color reasoning. In: ICCV, pp. 1624–1633 (2021)
34. Yang, C., Zhang, L., Lu, H., Ruan, X., Yang, M.H.: Saliency detection via graph-based manifold ranking. In: Proceedings of the IEEE Conference on Computer Vision and Pattern Recognition, pp. 3166–3173 (2013)
35. Yang, Z., Chen, T., Wang, L., Luo, J.: Improving one-stage visual grounding by recursive sub-query construction. In: Vedaldi, A., Bischof, H., Brox, T., Frahm, J.-M. (eds.) ECCV 2020. LNCS, vol. 12359, pp. 387–404. Springer, Cham (2020). https://doi.org/10.1007/978-3-030-58568-6_23
36. Zhang, Y., Lu, H.: Deep cross-modal projection learning for image-text matching. In: Ferrari, V., Hebert, M., Sminchisescu, C., Weiss, Y. (eds.) ECCV 2018. LNCS, vol. 11205, pp. 707–723. Springer, Cham (2018). https://doi.org/10.1007/978-3-030-01246-5_42

37. Zheng, K., Liu, W., Liu, J., Zha, Z.J., Mei, T.: Hierarchical Gumbel attention network for text-based person search. In: Proceedings of the 28th ACM International Conference on Multimedia, pp. 3441–3449 (2020)
38. Zheng, Z., Zheng, L., Garrett, M., Yang, Y., Xu, M., Shen, Y.D.: Dual-path convolutional image-text embeddings with instance loss. ACM Trans. Multimedia Comput. Commun. Appl. (TOMM) **16**(2), 1–23 (2020)
39. Zhu, A., Wang, Z., Li, Y.: DSSL: deep surroundings-person separation learning for text-based person retrieval. In: Proceedings of the 29th ACM International Conference on Multimedia, pp. 209–217 (2021)

Correction to: VTC: Improving Video-Text Retrieval with User Comments

Laura Hanu ⓘ, James Thewlisⓘ, Yuki M. Asano ⓘ,
and Christian Rupprechtⓘ

Correction to:
Chapter "VTC: Improving Video-Text Retrieval with User
Comments" in: S. Avidan et al. (Eds.): *Computer*
***Vision – ECCV 2022*, LNCS 13695,**
https://doi.org/10.1007/978-3-031-19833-5_36

In the originally published version of chapter 36, the place and country of the first affiliation, Unitary Ltd., erroneously showed "Moscow, Russia" instead of "London, UK". This has been corrected.

The updated original version of this chapter can be found at
https://doi.org/10.1007/978-3-031-19833-5_36

© The Author(s), under exclusive license to Springer Nature Switzerland AG 2023
S. Avidan et al. (Eds.): ECCV 2022, LNCS 13695, p. C1, 2023.
https://doi.org/10.1007/978-3-031-19833-5_43

Author Index

Printed in the United States
by Baker & Taylor Publisher Services